D0205744

ENCYCLOPEDIA OF AFRICAN AMERICAN BUSINESS HISTORY

ENCYCLOPEDIA OF AFRICAN AMERICAN BUSINESS HISTORY

Edited by
JULIET E. K. WALKER

GREENWOOD PRESS
Westport, Connecticut • London

Library of Congress Cataloging-in-Publication Data

Encyclopedia of African American business history / edited by Juliet
   E. K. Walker.
      p.   cm.
   Includes bibliographical references and index.
   ISBN 0–313–29549–2 (alk. paper)
   1. Afro-American business enterprises—History.   2. Afro-American
business enterprises—Encyclopedias.   3. Slavery—United States—
Chronology.   I. Walker, Juliet E. K., 1940–   .
HD2344.5.U6E53   1999
338.6'422'08996073—dc21   98–44218

British Library Cataloguing in Publication Data is available.

Library of Congress Catalog Card Number: 98–44218
ISBN: 0–313–29549–2

First published in 1999

Greenwood Press, 88 Post Road West, Westport, CT 06881
An imprint of Greenwood Publishing Group, Inc.
www.greenwood.com

Printed in the United States of America

The paper used in this book complies with the
Permanent Paper Standard issued by the National
Information Standards Organization (Z39.48–1984).

10 9 8 7 6 5 4 3 2 1

Every reasonable effort has been made to trace the owners of copyright materials in this book, but
in some instances this has proven impossible. The author and publisher will be glad to receive
information leading to more complete acknowledgments in subsequent printings of the book and in
the meantime extend their apologies for any omissions.

To Free Frank McWorter's (1777–1854) Descendants,
Great, Great, Great, Great, Grandchildren

Zachary Edward Walker (1991–   )
Brianna Janise Walker (1992–   )
Bryce Jansen Walker (1997–   )

Contents

Acknowledgments

First, I would like to thank John N. Ingham, who recommended to Greenwood that I be the editor of the *Encyclopedia of African American Business History*. Also, I owe a special debt of gratitude to Professor David Krugler. When work began on the *Encyclopedia* in the summer of 1994, David was my research assistant. His work in organizing files, xeroxing, setting up computer programs, handling correspondence, taking telephone inquiries, and locating and even persuading several potential contributors to submit entries was invaluable. Also, he suggested names of potential contributors. During the fall of 1994, when I was away as a Shelby Cullom Davis Fellow at Princeton, and in 1995, when I was on a Fulbright in South Africa, David was the liaison between contributors, Greenwood, and myself. Then when David left to pursue his dissertation research, Cheryl Pettus assumed his duties in filing entries and informing me of correspondence from contributors, and I am deeply thankful to her.

At the same time, the Internet enabled me to maintain communication with some contributors through e-mail. Consequently, I owe a debt of gratitude to the University of Witwatersrand in Johannesburg, South Africa, where I was teaching African American history, who provided me with Internet facilities. Since then Professor Bruce Murray, who was chair of the History Department at Wits, and who also provided support in my research on black business in South Africa, has continued his interest and support of my work in African American business history.

I returned to the United States in January 1996, and throughout that year my publication energies were focused on completing my book *The History of Black Business in America*, which I finished the following January 1997. At that time, only 30 contributors had responded to the *Encyclopedia*. By the end of the summer of 1997, however, there were 106 contributors. Foremost, then, I wish to thank the contributors, many of whom stopped work on their own projects to write their entry for the *Encyclopedia*. I also wish to thank the History Department at the University of Illinois for subsidizing the costs of several hundred long-distance calls, especially in the summer and fall of 1997, which enabled me to maintain personal communication with contributors, as well as postage. Also, the Minority Affairs Office, under the direction of Dr. William Trent, provided funds to pay for secretarial assistance to handle the increasing correspondence in the summer of 1997. Jacinth Thomas and Mukeni Tamu Mitchell enabled me to catch up on mailings and also did library research to secure sources that I needed to validate entries in the *Encyclopedia*.

Several University of Illinois students provided assistance: Oluwatoyin Caldwell and Tim Fields assisted in the continuing correspondence, typing, and organization of entries and biographies, whereas computer assistance was provided by Todd Larson. Editing of the entries, however, was a sole undertaking, which took me seven months to complete Also, Quincy T. Mills, a former student, prepared the "Chronology of Black Business History." The History Department secretarial staff—Aprel Orwich, Stanley Hicks, and Jan Langerdorrf—provided support in the laser printing of the *Encyclopedia* manuscript.

Throughout various stages of the project, friends, family, and colleagues have encouraged my work in African American business history. My sons James and Jeffrey Walker, my daughters-in-law Stephanie and Faye, my brothers Allen and David Kirkpatrick, my sisters-in-law Deloris and Lorraine, and my numerous nieces, nephews, cousins have been there for me from the beginning, as was my sister Marye Alberta Kirkpatrick Taylor, who died in 1995. My mother, Thelma Elise McWorter Kirkpatrick Wheaton, remains my strongest supporter.

The *Encyclopedia of African American Business History*, then, represents a collaborative project in many ways, with special thanks, again, to the contributors, without whom this project would not have been completed.

A Note on Using the Encyclopedia

The *Encyclopedia* provides information on the African American business experience from the 1600s to the 1990s in three types of entries: biographies of black businesspeople; topics in black business history; and, surveys of black business participation in selected industries. At the beginning of each biographical entry information is provided on the geographic location and name of or type of business activity that distinguishes the businessperson. The general format of a biography is to provide an overview of the individual's business activities followed by a broader discussion of the development and successes or failures of the enterprises. In some entries a chronological discussion of the early life of the individual precedes the information presented on the founding and development of his/her business activities.

The entries on business history topics focus on black enterprise activities distinctive to a specific historic period such as slave business activities, free black enterprises, and black business during the Great Migration. There are also entries on topics in black business history distinctive to the post–Civil Rights era. The several comprehensive survey entries review the history of black business participation in a particular industry, such as blacks in transportation.

The more than 200 entries included in the *Encyclopedia* are arranged alphabetically. Additional topics related to an entry are indicated by an asterisk (*). As an example, biographical entries of black businesspeople often detail specific examples of their philanthropy. The term philanthropy will have an asterisk to indicate that there is a specific entry on philanthropy. In the biographical entry on Harold Washington, black mayors will have an asterisk to indicate that there is a separate entry on that topic.

Each entry includes a selected bibliography that lists sources used by contributors as well as sources important to locating additional information on that topic. A detailed, comprehensive subject index provides further assistance in identifying complementary or supplementary information on a particular topic in black business history. A general bibliography is also provided. The books listed are grouped in six categories. The General Studies category include books on black business history, economics, biographies, and references. Post–civil rights era studies include titles of books on both black business and entrepreneurship and on black and white corporate America. There is also a listing of books on black women and business. Books listed under biographies and autobiographies are divided into two groups: books on individuals in the nineteen century under ''from slavery to freedom'' and books on individuals whose business activities took place in the twentieth century. Also books on minorities and women in business and on general studies in American and international business are listed.

Information in *The Encyclopedia of African American Business History*, then, not only provides an introduction to black business activities but also a comprehensive survey of topics that illuminates this much neglected topic in the historical study of black America. Also, a detailed chronology provides an overview of the black business historical experience in America from 1619 to 1999.

Introduction

The *Encyclopedia of African American Business History* has two purposes: to illuminate the historic continuity of black business in America from the colonial era to the post–civil rights era and to underscore the diversity of black business activities from slavery to freedom. Historically, business activities have provided African Americans with their greatest economic success. As George Fraser, a leading promoter of black business in the late twentieth century, has said: "Success Runs in Our Race." Yet while the names of multimillionaires John H. Johnson of *Ebony* and Berry Gordy, founder of Motown Records, are recognized by most black Americans, and many whites as well, other leading black entrepreneurs are less well known. Simply put, black business history has remained peripheral in the scholarly study of the African American experience. Rather, the oral black history tradition and the black press have contributed more to sustaining the collective memories of black business activities and leading black entrepreneurs than the published scholarly record. Indeed, recognition of the icon of black business history, the early twentieth-century millionaire hair care products manufacturer Madame C. J. Walker, in a U.S. postal stamp in 1997 reflects the sustaining power of the black written and oral history in the public record.

Incontrovertibly, slavery remains the defining experience for blacks in America. Even in the closing decade of the twentieth century, full freedom from racism and complete equality for the descendants of former slaves have yet to be obtained. Yet in their continuing search for freedom, the agency of blacks in forging their own economic liberation through business activities and entrepreneurship has had a long tradition. Even during slavery, leading black entrepreneurs accumulated wealth in the hundreds of thousands of dollars from their business activities. Indeed, the estate of the nation's first black millionaire, William Leidesdorff, was settled at $1.5 million, but it was only after his death in 1848 that San Francisco's first city treasurer, Leidesdorff, was found to be of African descent. Still, John Jacob Astor, reportedly the richest man in America at the time of his death, also in 1848, left an estate conservatively estimated at $20 million.

Before the Civil War, however, the largest number of the leading black entrepreneurs lived in Louisiana. By 1857, according to the R. G. Dun & Company mercantile credit rating records, the Soulie brothers in New Orleans were worth $500,000, whereas Francois LaCroix in 1860 was worth $300,000 and his brother, Julien, $250,000. Dun was specific in noting that they were "free men of color." In the North, Stephen Smith, known as "Black Steve," was the leading black entrepreneur. Based on Dun records, Smith was worth $100,000 in 1850, $250,000 in 1860, and $500,000 by 1865. The success of America's antebellum black entrepreneurs was a result of the propelling force of capitalism, specifically, the government protection of the private ownership of property, which, paradoxically, also provided the foundation for the institutionalization of blacks as slaves, chattel property, in this nation's history.

Interestingly, there was a greater diversity of black business activity, which paralleled mainstream American business, in the nation's preindustrial economy than in industrial America. With the end of the Civil War, the wealth of the Soulie and LaCroix brothers dwindled substantially, whereas Louisiana's leading black planters and slaveholders were virtually wiped out. Yet there were blacks who established successful enterprises during Reconstruction, who also lost out on their investments. The former slave Benjamin Montgomery acquired the cotton plantations once owned by the Jefferson Davis (president of the Confederacy) family. Montgomery's slave owner was the brother of Jefferson. Under Montgomery's ownership, (he had managed his owner's plantation both before and during the Civil War), the R. G. Dun & Company valued the plantations as worth over $400,000. Once restored to its productivity, the land and property, however, were reacquired by the Davis family.

Even by the early twentieth century, however, public knowledge of the business activities and wealth acquired by these nineteenth-century black entrepreneurs, both before and after the Civil War, was lost to the historical record. Even such an astute student of the black business experience, W.E.B. Du Bois, asserted that the black business class in the post–Civil War period emerged from the house servant class. The historic reality, however, is that there was a continuation of black business activity by both antebellum free black businesspeople as well as slave entrepreneurs in addition to the emergence of a new group of black businesspeople, who had not participated in business prior to the Civil War, including many former field slaves. Moreover, slave artisans were in a much better position to establish enterprises after 1865 than were former house slaves.

Moreover, in the late twentieth century, even the business successes of some of the leading early twentieth-century entrepreneur millionaires—such as Annie Turnbo-Malone, a black hair care products manufacturer, and Anthony Overton, who built a banking, insurance, and publishing conglomerate on his million-dollar black cosmetic manufacturing company—were relegated to virtual historic obscurity. Indeed, a 1924 issue of *Forbes*, in an article entitled "The Largest Negro Commercial Enterprise in the World," which provided a report on the conglomeration of enterprises of the Atlanta-based entrepreneur Herman Perry in banking, insurance, construction, and real estate development, emphasized: "For, let it be remembered, Herman Perry is the directing genius of a $30,000,000 enterprise . . . and is said to be worth $8,000,000."

Few, however, remember Herman Perry or the multimillion-dollar conglomerate established by Chicago's S. B. Fuller, the leading black entrepreneur in the mid-twentieth century. Consequently, even in the late twentieth century, only a few of the leading black entrepreneurs have gained recognition in the national black community, such as Arthur Gaston, who in 1992 was named by *Black Enterprise* as "BE's Entrepreneur of the Century." Born in 1892, Gaston's $140 million conglomeration of enterprises was established in several areas—insurance, banking, construction, real estate development, manufacturing, and communication. Moreover, even after he was 100 years old, Gaston went to his office every day to work. He died in 1996.

Increasingly, leading black entrepreneurs of the post–civil rights era, who have established multimillion-dollar enterprises, have gained national recognition—Herman Russell in construction, Edward Gardner and George Johnson in hair products manufacturing, and Joshua Smith in computers. Particularly, the 1987 leveraged buyout of Beatrice International by Reginald Lewis, the first African American to acquire majority interest in a billion-dollar enterprise, put Wall Street on notice that there was a significant entrepreneurial presence in the nation's business community. *Forbes* acknowledged their presence in a 1997 issue, which focused not only on leading black business owners but also on the increasing number of blacks both in executive management positions in white Corporate America and, especially, those who are carving out significant positions in investment banking, which provides the fuel of equity financing, which drives business in America.

Yet most black entrepreneurs and their business activities seldom cross the pages of history, unlike their white counterparts. Indeed, the names of the leading white entrepreneurs, from the Du Ponts, Morgans, Rockefellers, Andrew Carnegie, and Henry Ford to Ray Kroc, Sam Walton, Donald Trump, and William Gates, are, perhaps, more familiar to Americans, black and white, than those of some of the nation's past presidents. Simply put, entrepreneurs presented for study in American business and economic history have ranged from merchant and planter capitalists, who in the eighteenth century bankrolled both the transatlantic slave trade and the American Revolution, to the turn-of-the-century robber barons/captains of industry. In the twentieth century, the business leaders emphasized by scholars are the finance and managerial capitalists, primarily the heads of *Fortune* 500 corporations.

In American business and economic history, then, the topics emphasized have been limited to the industrial and transportation revolutions, the rise of big business in oil, iron, steel, and the automobile and electronic industries. In the late twentieth-century deindustrialization of America, the focus has been on the expansion of the nation's multinational corporations as they compete in a global economy. The expansion of service enterprises in the new information age, the franchise entrepreneurs in fast foods and discount retail stores, and the technocrat entrepreneurs in the expanding telecommunications and computer industries have also generated new areas of scholarly interest. Even in these studies, however, there is a notable absence of information on black business activities and black entrepreneurs.

In the broader stream of this nation's history, blacks are studied primarily as workers, and the institution of slavery continues to generate the most interest. By 1860 there were almost 4 million slaves. While some 10 percent were industrial slaves and 5 percent were urban slaves, the rest were agricultural workers, primarily plantation field hands who worked on the large cotton, sugar, and rice plantations. After the Civil War to the first decades of the twentieth century, the focus on the economic life of blacks in American history has been on their continued activities as agricultural workers, trapped in a life of debt peonage, as sharecroppers and tenant farmers. Indeed, until 1940, when more than 50 percent of the black population lived in urban areas, a substantial proportion of blacks were involved in agriculture as laborers. With the twentieth-century industrialization and urbanization of America, emphasis is placed on black workers in service occupations and as unskilled laborers or their activities in organized labor. Moreover, since the Great Depression, both the unemployment status and the underemployed status of blacks have been points of emphasis.

With the post–civil rights era entry of blacks into the nation's large corporations, a few even achieving senior management positions, American business and economic history has been contextualized in the controversy of affirmative action and preferential treatment. Rather than focusing on the continuing racial inequities that exist in the nation's labor force, the competency of blacks not only in Corporate America but also in local civil service employment areas has emerged as a major focus of research in the study of black economic life. Charges that black workers deprive qualified whites of ''their'' jobs and that ''scheming'' black businessmen are depriving white businessmen of contracts that are ''rightfully theirs'' have also generated new studies and debates in the scholarly literature on the equal protection clause in the Fourteenth Amendment.

Consequently, from a review of the recent scholarly literature, it appears that black business activity has been primarily a post–civil rights era phenomenon. Yet while historians have come late to the study of black business history, some of the pioneering research in black business was undertaken by black scholars in sociology and economics, beginning with the turn-of-the-century Atlanta Uni-

versity studies in black business by the sociologist/historian/premier public intellectual W.E.B. Du Bois. Several decades later, Du Bois's work was continued
by economists Abram Harris, in his study of black banks (1936), and Merah
Stuart, on black insurance companies (1940), and mathematician Joseph Pierce
in his 1946 study on black business.

In 1991, sociologist John Sibley Butler in *Entrepreneurship and Self-Help
among Black Americans: A Reconsideration of Race and Economics* utilized
their findings in his review of early twentieth-century black financial institutions
and black business districts as a basis for his conceptualization of the sociology
of black entrepreneurship and its contemporary policy implications. Beginning
with the civil rights era, white scholars began an intensive examination of black
business. Economist Timothy Bates has published extensively on black business
since the late 1960s. Ironically, despite their primary focus on the post–civil
rights era, economists and sociologists, even in the late twentieth century, continue to provide most of the scholarship on black business. The work of economist David Whitten in his 1971 study of the black sugar planter and slaveholder
Andrew Durnford still remains the most systematic study of the business activities of an antebellum black entrepreneur.

While historians have come late to the study of black business, a coherent
body of scholarly literature in black business history is developing. As with the
early black economists and sociologists, the initial focus of historians has been
on the study of black financial institutions, specifically insurance companies, as
seen in the works of Walter Weare (1973), Alexa Benson Henderson (1990),
and Robert Weems (1995). With few exceptions, that is, the papers of black
slaveholders and records from black financial institutions, there is a dearth of
business records for blacks prior to the twentieth century. Still, as an initial basis
for expanding the field of African American business history, black entrepreneurs, who have been lost to the historical record, must be identified. The most
significant contribution made in establishing the existence of the nation's leading
black entrepreneurs, while also delineating the numerous sources that provide
information on their business activities, is *African-American Business Leaders:
A Biographical Dictionary* (1994). In this study, historian John N. Ingham and
freelance researcher and editor Lynne Feldman detail the business activities of
123 black business leaders. Their concentration is on the period from 1880 to
the World War II, but biographies of black business leaders before and after
that time period, including those in the post–civil rights era, are also included.
With few full-length biographies published on America's black entrepreneurs,
the Ingham-Feldman study is invaluable as a source in black business history.
Also, the 1998 publication of Juliet E. K. Walker's *The History of Black Business in America: Capitalism, Race, Entrepreneurship*, the first comprehensive
history of African American business, provides information on black business
from its origin in the commercial culture of West Africa during the era of the
transatlantic slave trade to the business activities of both slave and free blacks
from the colonial era to the Civil War and, from then, to the 1990s.

The study of black business, then, is emerging as a new growth area in the field of African American history. The entries in the *Encyclopedia of African American Business History* reflect this expansion of scholarship in the study of black business. They underscore not only the history of the diversity of black business activities but also the increasingly interdisciplinary study of black business history. The 106 contributors include not only leading scholars in the study of black business but also those whose research interests in part have covered various aspects of black business. Their fields of scholarship range from history to economics, sociology, business, law, politics, journalism, psychology, literature, and theology. There are also entries from freelance writers, businesspeople, and business promoters. Several entries were written by doctoral students in history and university seniors, now in graduate or law school, who took independent study courses to research and write their entries.

The *Encyclopedia*, then, is unprecedented in its compilation of information on the history of black business and the multiplicity and diversity of these enterprises. The entries include biographies, black business history topics, and historic surveys of black business activities in selected industries. Even so, space limitation precludes a detailing of the full scope of the history of black business activities in America, as well as the inclusion of biographies of even all of the most prominent black business persons. A compilation of that magnitude, which would detail the almost 400 years of the business activities of African Americans, would be a monumental undertaking, requiring a 50-volume, state-by-state assessment of black business history. It would also require an expansion in scholarly research in the newly developing field of African American business history.

Yet, historically, self-employment has been important in the economic life of black Americans. In the face of limited income from low-paying jobs, as well as the difficulties faced in securing employment, a significant number of blacks since the colonial era have developed profit-making enterprises. Most were small-scale ventures, beginning with trade and marketing activities that had their origins in the African commercial culture. In America, blacks as slaves and also as free men and women were truck farmers, vendors, hawkers, hustlers, itinerant peddlers, and small shopkeepers who provided goods and services to both black and white consumers. These economic activities were undertaken for profit. While most were limited in net earnings, these were business activities. Indeed, most blacks in their oral family histories can identify at least one relative who pursued some kind of self-employed activity, even part-time, as a means to supplement the family income.

Moreover, from slavery to freedom, there were also blacks who made a profit from their enterprises, including those who operated businesses competitive to whites. Indeed, some were more than businessmen; they were entrepreneurs. Innovation, risk taking, the ability to sense the wants of consumers, even to create new markets—entrepreneurial expertise—distinguished their business activities. In most instances, however, reconstructing the life of just one black businessman requires extensive detailed research, first to identify that individual and then to document his or her business activities from a wide variety of primary sources, since few black businesspeople left records of their enterprises.

The research undertaken in my study *Free Frank: A Black Pioneer on the Antebellum Frontier* (1983) required identifying and then locating source materials in three states—South Carolina, Kentucky, and Illinois. The slave-born Free Frank McWorter (1777–1854), an entrepreneur, was also the nation's first black town founder. In 1836, he established New Philadelphia, Illinois, on land he purchased from the federal government. Also, through a diversity of enterprises, land speculation, commercial farming, and the sale of town lots, Free Frank purchased 16 family members from slavery, including himself. His entry in the business world was first as a slave entrepreneur, who established a saltpeter manufactory in Kentucky during the War of 1812, using the profits to buy his freedom, only after paying his owner to hire his own time. Primary sources were necessary to document his business activities. Unlike antebellum blacks whose lives are a matter of historical record, Free Frank, who was illiterate, left no personal papers.

That this antebellum black entrepreneur was rescued from historic obscurity can be attributed to his family's oral history tradition. In the new reconstruction of black business history, oral history will prove invaluable in identifying the countless numbers of blacks who established business enterprises, especially in providing the initial clues as to where to locate primary sources to document their business activities. The primary sources used to document Free Frank's various business activities included federal censuses, archival documents, and local and state records on his owner. Then, for Free Frank, county and state property deed record books, plat books, documents from manuscript collections in the archives of state and local historical societies, and federal manuscript censuses were the major sources used to document his life. In addition, there were family papers, generated from both public and private records, his manumission papers (blacks without free papers could be apprehended as fugitives), certificates of good character written by whites, and property tax receipts.

There is an entry on Free Frank in the *Encyclopedia*. Contrasted with the economic lives of antebellum free blacks and also those of plantation, urban, and industrial slaves, the several kinds of business activities developed by Free Frank on the nation's frontiers and in agricultural communities advance historical knowledge of the diversity of black economic activities before the Civil War. At the same time, there is an entry on the independent economic activities of plantation slaves and also one on slave plantation market activities. Also, Free Frank's mining of crude niter to produce saltpeter was not the only instance of black involvement in the extractive industries, and a comprehensive entry is provided on blacks as business owners in the extractive industries in the nineteenth and twentieth centuries. Free Frank's life also provides insight into slave entrepreneurship, and an entry on that topic is included as well as biographical entries on several slave entrepreneurs, such as Charles Ball and Anthony Weston.

There were also slave intrapreneurs (bondsmen who managed their owner's enterprises), including Simon Gray and Benjamin Montgomery. Some slave intrapreneurs and entrepreneurs who made enough money from their business activities purchased their freedom. Several emerged as leading free black businessmen, including Stephen Smith and William Ellison. There are entries on both men, whose lives show how antebellum black entrepreneurs used their profits. Whereas Smith, through his philanthropy, supported the institutional development of the black community and abolitionist activities, Ellison, a leading cotton gin manufacturer, purchased slaves and land for the building of his plantation enterprise. The *Encyclopedia* also includes entries on both the large black slaveholders and leading antebellum black entrepreneurs.

There is also a comprehensive entry on black craftsmen as manufacturers and in the construction industry. Black craftsmen—carpenters, furniture makers, carriage makers, blacksmiths, wheelwrights—established shops. An entry is included on Thomas Day, whose furniture in the late twentieth century has been collected as museum pieces. There is also an entry on black architects, some who established construction firms.

In 1619, Jamestown, Virginia, was the site of the entry of the first Africans in English America and until the Civil War had the largest slave population. That state, consequently, has special historical significance in the African American experience. The entry on blacks and agribusiness in Virginia, however, details the commercial life of black farm owners and their declining numbers in agribusiness from the early to the late twentieth century. Also, since the majority of the African American population, until the mid-twentieth century, lived in the South, several entries provide information on black business activities in that region from 1790 to 1930. There is an entry on black business in Georgia from 1890 to 1915, and the Black Wall Street entry examines black entrepreneurial enclaves as well as the black business districts in Tulsa, Oklahoma, and Durham, North Carolina. Also, there is an entry on black businesses in black towns, including Mound Bayou, Mississippi, founded by the son of Benjamin Montgomery.

By the twentieth century, although blacks had established businesses in virtually every town and city in which they lived, most were personal service enterprises. Barbershops, beauty shops, dressmaking, millinery, and tailoring shops, repair shops, groceries, restaurants, laundries, secondhand clothing and furniture stores, taverns, pool halls, and funeral parlors were all black enterprises ubiquitous to every town and city with a concentrated black population. Entries on the Great Migration and protected markets provide information on the twentieth-century development of these enterprises.

Yet, interestingly, notwithstanding that the funeral business is the only industry, nationally, in which blacks are proportionately represented, this area of black business has not been pursued systematically, much less enthusiastically, in any great detail in the scholarly literature. Consequently, there are three entries on the funeral business, one by a historian, another by a sociologist, and the other by a third-generation member of a funeral business family. Also, there is an entry on Arthur George Gaston, who built a multimillion-dollar conglomerate from profits initially earned from the Booker T. Washington Burial Society, which he founded in 1923. Yet while blacks in the funeral business have been assured, literally, of some success as businesspeople (after all, who gets through life without dying?), new developments in the funeral industry—international conglomerate takeovers—might erode this area of enterprise for blacks as business owners.

Although blacks in the funeral business have high rates of economic success (the average income for owners is $300,000), black retail merchants, on the other hand, have had high rates of failure. And, interestingly, the difficulties blacks encounter in attempts to succeed as retail merchants have provided the basis for analysis in much of the scholarly literature. Indeed, one could say that black business history, as presently written, provides more lessons on black business failures than on black business successes. Certainly, few scholarly studies are available that document the business activities of successful black retail merchants. The early twentieth-century Muskogee, Oklahoma, retail merchant T. J. Elliott established the largest black department store in the country. Even in the 1990s the Elliott department store is discussed with awe and a great deal of pride in the Oklahoma black oral history tradition. Yet in the absence of any scholarly study that documents the business activities of T. J. Elliott, no entry is included on this important black businessman.

Moreover, even in instances when a black businessperson has been identified, scholarly research, invariably, will focus on that individual's community, civic, or political activities. While Mifflin W. Gibbs (1823–1915) developed several businesses, as a retail merchant in both San Francisco, California, and Vancouver, British Columbia, where he was also a railroad builder and director of the Queen Charlotte Island Coal Company, the historic record emphasizes his distinguished political career. Gibbs was the first African American judge, appointed in 1873 in Arkansas (he studied law at Oberlin). In the 1860s, he even held an elective political office in the Victoria City Council. Also, in 1897 Gibbs was the U.S. consul to Madagascar. Still, in addition to his political activities, Gibbs not only was a businessman; he also promoted black business, which included financing a conference in 1885 to build an industrial school. However, other than his autobiography and information on his political career from the contemporary press, there are no scholarly studies to document Gibbs's entrepreneurial activities, which precluded inclusion of an entry on Gibbs.

Biographical information on several successful black retail merchants is provided in the *Encyclopedia* but primarily because these men succeeded in other businesses, including S. B. Fuller, whose conglomerate enterprises included a South Side Chicago department store. While Fuller was the most successful black entrepreneur in the United States from the 1940s to the early 1960s (he died in 1988), not one scholarly journal article, much less a full-scale biography, has been published to document his business activities, which could be written under the title "The Rise and Fall of the House of Fuller."

While few blacks have succeeded as retail store owners of general merchandise, in black business history, participation in food service industries has provided a basis for the development of several kinds of successful enterprises. In the nineteenth century, catering was a profitable enterprise for blacks, and a comprehensive entry is included on that topic. Also, blacks were important in the wholesale food distribution industry, an area of enterprise lost in the era of European immigration in the late nineteenth century. Participation of blacks in this industry is reviewed in a biographical entry on the founders of the West Virginia–based James Produce Company, a food processing and wholesale and retail distribution enterprise, established in 1883, and now the oldest black-owned business in the United States. In the late 1990s, the company is still owned and managed by members of the fourth generation and ranks as one of the leading 100 black businesses.

A biographical entry is also included on James Bruce Llewellyn, who ranks as one of the leading black entrepreneurs in the post–civil rights era. Venture capital for Llewellyn's subsequent entrepreneurial success and conglomerate holdings was built on his ownership of a chain of food stores, which he developed into a multimillion-dollar enterprise. Also, a biographical entry is included on the founder of the Famous Amos Chocolate Chip Cookie Company. Wallace Amos, whose ownership in his company lasted only 12 years, from 1973 to 1985, however, initiated the franchise cookie store ventures Mrs. Fields and Dave's, which developed in America in the late twentieth century. In addition, there is an entry on franchises.

The major purpose of the *Encyclopedia*, then, is to illuminate, historically, the diversity of black business activities, but in the selection of an entry, another important criterion used was the extent to which a business activity reflected a distinctive phase, unique development, or extraordinary aspect of black business history. In New York, the city's twentieth-century black business history, unlike in most large metropolitan centers, has been influenced substantially by a West Indian immigrant population. Their significant business presence is due in large part to access to venture capital, which they obtained through rotating credit associations. Consequently, while there is a specific entry on rotating credit associations and the Caribbean Chamber of Commerce in New York, the entry also informs the existence of rotating credit associations, established in other cities that have significant West Indian immigrant populations.

In Chicago, unlike New York, however, black business activity has been distinguished by a substantial migration of southern blacks. Of course, southern blacks also migrated to New York and other large urban industrial centers in the Northeast and Midwest, including Detroit, as well as to large cities and towns in the South. Yet it was primarily in reference to Chicago, as a destination point, that black southerners in their migration said they were "bound for the Promised Land." Moreover, it was only in reference to Chicago that a national black community leader said: "If a Negro can't make it in Chicago, he can't make it no [sic] where else."

From the early twentieth century, Chicago has been the major city where black businesses were established with national markets, particularly black hair care products manufacturing enterprises and publishing enterprises. Also, unlike other northern urban centers, from the early twentieth century on, several black financial institutions, banks, and insurance companies were established in that city. With Chicago as the national center of multimillion-dollar black businesses, its distinctiveness in African American business history in the twentieth century is that Chicago emerged as the quintessential city for black entrepreneurship. Consequently, there is a specific entry on Chicago's black business history. In New York, however, the distinctiveness of black business development in that city reflects to a large extent the entrepreneurship of black financial capitalists in the post–civil rights era.

Some of the distinctive historic entrepreneurial activities of blacks in that city are included in several biographical entries. The entries on realtors Philip Alan Payton, often called the "father of Harlem," and the Nails family, father and son, reflect black business activities in real estate in response to the ghettoization of urban America, whereas while entries on the post–civil rights era business activities of New Yorkers Percy Sutton, James Bruce Llewellyn, Earl Graves, and Reginald Lewis reflect a new phase in black business history, distinguished by finance capitalism in the building of black conglomerates. In the closing decades of the twentieth century, proximity to Wall Street has distinguished black business history in New York City, which doubtless also symbolizes the wave of the future in the expansion of big black business in the twenty-first century.

Consequently, the biographies selected for inclusion in the *Encyclopedia* are those that illuminate, historically, important areas of black business activities and development. At the same time, the process in determining whose biography should be included was based also on providing a balance between the historically most significant black businesspeople and those whose business activities have earned only local recognition. For example, there is an entry on Gilbert Faustina, whose prominence as a businessman was limited to the Mobile, Alabama, Gulf port community in which he lived. Also, selection of biographical entries was based on whether or not the activities of a black businessperson have been documented in the scholarly literature, particularly in sources readily available to the general public. Moreover, while black business history is expanding, the historical information available is still limited primarily to black business activity primarily in the Northeast, Midwest, and South.

Yet while there is a biographical entry on Durham's Charles Clinton Spaulding of North Carolina Mutual Life Insurance Company, the nation's largest black insurance company, information on his counterpart, insurance executive

Earl B. Dickerson, is provided in the entries on Chicago's Supreme Life Insurance Company and Chicago's black business history. There is, however, an entry on Harry Pace, also with Supreme, but his significance in black business history has been linked, especially, to establishing the first successful black record company in the early 1920s, the Black Swan Record Company. There is also a comprehensive entry on black insurance history. Selection of entries, then, was also based on limiting excessive duplication of information.

Moreover, there are biographical entries on blacks who promoted black business, such as John Wesley Dobbs, who in Atlanta is credited with promotion of that city's black business district, "Sweet Auburn Avenue." Historic recognition of Dobbs beyond local studies, however, has been only as that of the father of the internationally acclaimed opera singer Mattiwilda Dobbs. And few contemporary sources note that Dobbs, the business promoter, financial officer of the Masons, one of the founders of the black National Postal Alliance, was also the grandfather of Atlanta's first black mayor, Maynard Jackson. His activities in promoting black business are included in the entry on black mayors, as well as a separate entry on his investment banking activities.

Also, biographical entries on key black entrepreneurs who achieved historic recognition in the local or national oral black tradition but whose business activities have not been documented in the scholarly record have not been included. The Louisiana black philanthropist Thomy Lafon is mentioned in various black histories of the state, and John Hope Franklin in *From Slavery to Freedom* said of Lafon: "[T]he tycoon of New Orleans was worth $500,000 at the time of his death." Yet no scholarly studies have been undertaken that document Lafon's business activities in the late nineteenth century, primarily real estate speculation. Lafon's documented philanthropy supports the oral record that he was quite wealthy, as well as other incidents from the oral tradition. One account states that because Lafon was so wealthy, a white bank in New Orleans had a special chair reserved for his use.

Unlike Lafon, there is an entry on Stephen Smith, the leading antebellum black entrepreneur in the North, a shrewd black businessman in lumber, coal, real estate, and the currency exchange market who owned and ran his own railroad cars before the Civil War. While few of Smith's contemporaries knew the full monetary extent of his financial success, the R. G. Dun & Company mercantile credit records, with information obtained from banks and municipal and county property deed and tax records, have been used to document Smith's business activities and extensive wealth holding. Those same sources can also be used to document Lafon's activities.

Until my 1986 article "Racism, Slavery, Free Enterprise: Black Entrepreneurship in the United States before the Civil War," published in the Harvard *Business History Review*, historians, in the absence of records to document claims of Smith's extensive wealth holding and with their emphasis in antebellum black history on slavery and abolitionists, ignored Smith as an important figure in antebellum black history. Indeed, in reconstructing the antebellum black experience, it is ironic that the study of black survival under adversity and in impoverished circumstances merits historic study, as it should, but at the same time, paradoxically, evidence of the achievement of economic success by blacks in an era where they had to contend not only with societal racial constraints but also with the forces of slavery is generally ignored.

Yet while biographical entries reflect distinctive areas of black business activities, and while the post–civil rights era has seen a broad expansion of black business activities, with the *Encyclopedia*'s historic focus, there are few entries on leading black businesspeople in the 1990s, especially those whose ages range from the late twenties to the early forties. Consequently, the *Encyclopedia* does not include biographical information on young black businessmen, such as Chicago's John W. Rogers, Jr., formerly with Sloan's Calvert Fund, who established one of the first African American equity mutual fund companies, Ariel Capital Management, Inc. Ariel manages billions of dollars in investments.

Moreover, there is no biographical entry on Maceo K. Sloan, formerly chief investment officer for North Carolina Mutual (NCM). Until he established his own investment firm, Sloan represented the fourth generation of his family at that company. The Durham-based Sloan Financial Group and its subsidiaries, NCM Capital Management Group, established in 1985, and New Africa Advisers, established in 1991, with $4 billion in assets, is the largest minority-owned money management firm in the nation. Sloan has also moved into the personal communication services (PCS) industry in cellular and cordless phones, with his Sloan PCS Development. Also, information is not included on the extent to which black entrepreneurs in the development of conglomerates have provided experience and opportunities for young blacks in executive management positions in black Corporate America, such as Justin Beckett who not only heads the Johannesburg office of Sloan's New Africa Advisers but also has an investment partnership in Sloan PCS.

Significantly, with the Internet and other resource media, information on contemporary leading black businesspeople who have moved into broad new areas of enterprises since the 1980s is readily available. While Internet sources illuminate current black business activities, the most comprehensive coverage of black business activity since the 1970s has been provided by *Black Enterprise*, the magazine founded by publisher Earl Graves, an entrepreneur who has built a multimillion-dollar conglomerate. In the documenting of black business history in the late twentieth century, *Black Enterprise* is invaluable. The magazine, which has singularly chronicled all aspects of black business activity in the post–civil rights era, consequently, has made a distinctive contribution in African American business history.

The black publishing industry, particularly newspapers and magazines, then, is important not only as a business enterprise since the founding of *Freedom's Journal*, the first black newspaper in 1827, but also as a repository for information on black business history. Indeed, extant documentation for much of the information available on black business, even in the post–civil rights era, exists because of black publications. From the *Chicago Defender*, founded by Robert Abbott in 1905, historically significant as the first black newspaper to profit substantially as a business enterprise, to *Ebony*, founded in 1945, in addition to *Black Enterprise*, much of the information available on black business and black entrepreneurs in the twentieth century has been published in black newspapers and magazines. In addition to biographical entries on several black publishers, there are entries on black book publishers, bookstores, and black museums (as a non–profit-making enterprise) in their attempts to preserve and provide information on black history and culture.

Other entries in the *Encyclopedia* also provide comprehensive surveys on black business participation in several industries and areas of enterprise, including an entry that surveys the history of black-owned transportation enterprises. From the post–Revolutionary War era, free blacks developed enterprises in ocean, lake, and river shipping, shipbuilding, and repair. These enterprises are also discussed in the entries on Paul Cuffe, James Forten and the Chesapeake Marine Railway and Dry Dock Company, and Marcus Garvey. Also, from the mid-nineteenth century to the early twentieth century, blacks owned railroad lines, freight coaches, and railroad yards, in addition to urban busses and trolley car companies, also discussed in entries on Wiley Jones and Richard Boyd. There is also an entry on black taxicab companies, an important black enterprise in the twentieth century until the civil rights era.

Also, in the early twentieth century, there was even a black automaker, discussed in the entry on the Patterson-Greenville automobile. It was not until the post–civil rights era that black auto parts manufacturers achieved a significant entry in the auto parts industry. Both government and subsequent corporate affirmative action directives, in addition to the changes in auto manufacturing developed by the American auto industry to compete with foreign automakers, especially, the Japanese, were important in this area of black enterprise. There is also an entry on black auto dealers, whose business receipts comprise a substantial proportion of the total black business receipts of the nation's 200 leading black businesses. Blacks were even involved in the early aeronautical industry, continuing their participation to the post–civil rights era. There are several entries on pre–World War II black participation in aeronautics.

There are also comprehensive entries on blacks in the banking and insurance industries, in addition to separate entries on several major black insurance companies, which include information on their founders. And there are specific biographical entries on black founders of insurance companies who also founded banks, such as Jesse Binga and Anthony Overton, and other enterprises. Harry Pace founded Swan Records before he became an insurance executive for Supreme Liberty Life, whereas Overton was a leading manufacturer of black cosmetics, with Binga making substantial profits in real estate. There are also entries on black investment banking activities and on black corporations listed on the stock exchange, both primarily representing post–civil rights era phenomena. Yet both black banking and insurance activities had their historic origins beginning in the late eighteenth century in the black mutual aid societies and fraternal organizations, also discussed in the entries on the Free African Society, mutual aid/insurance enterprises, and fraternal organizations.

There is also an entry on Maggie Lena Walker, whose business activities in promoting the growth of black financial institutions in both insurance and banking provide insights on the historic importance of black fraternal organizations. Walker has historic distinction in American business and economic history as the first woman to found a bank in this country and also as the first American woman bank president. Indeed, black women in business have been involved in virtually the same kinds of enterprises as African American men. A comprehensive entry is included in the *Encyclopedia*, which surveys the history of black women in business, in addition to biographical entries on specific businesswomen, such as Mary Ellen Pleasant, Naomi Sims, and Oprah Winfrey. Biographical entries are included on several black scientists and inventors who established enterprises—Garrett Morgan, Percy Julian, and Theodore K. Lawless—as examples of some success in the field of science; on the other hand, the entry on Jan Matzeliger provides an example of a black whose inventions were important to his industry but who never secured the venture capital to establish a viable business enterprise.

In the entry on sports, there is information on black superstar athletes who are enterprises in themselves. Also, as businessmen, their salaries, especially from the late 1980s on, have provided them venture capital for the development of enterprises. This phenomenon contrasts sharply with the difficulties blacks have had, historically, in securing access to capital and credit to fund their business ventures. Even in the post–civil rights era, with federally funded programs in effect to encourage black business participation, such as minority set-asides, blacks continued to fund most of their business ventures. Indeed, since the 1970s, according to a 1991–1992 *Wall Street Journal* study, over 90 percent of the venture capital for black businesses was generated by blacks from their savings and loans from black family members and friends. In African American business history, then, the most distinctive theme is that, from the 1600s, start-up capital for black businesses has been generated primarily by blacks, even most of the multimillion-dollar enterprises established in the twentieth century.

The most lucrative business, as an enterprise for blacks, women as well as men, has been in the health and beauty aids industry, specifically in the manufacturing of black hair care products and also in cosmetics. There is a comprehensive entry on blacks in the hair care products industry as well as biographical entries on the leading entrepreneurs in the industry, including Annie Turnbo-Malone, Madame C. J. Walker, and Anthony Overton, who established their enterprises in the early twentieth century, and Sarah [Sara] Spencer Washington, who by the 1930s was the leader in this industry until the 1950s.

In the post–civil rights era, a new group of black entrepreneurs emerged who achieved success from the 1960s on, including George E. Johnson, Edward G. Gardner, and Fred Luster, Sr., whose enterprises have made Chicago the black hair care products manufacturing center in the nation. Since the 1980s, several black hair care products companies have been represented in the *Black Enterprise* listing of the top 100 black businesses. Fashion Fair, the leading black cosmetic company, is discussed in several entries.

In the post–civil rights era, the black health and beauty aids industry in its manufacturing of hair care products and cosmetics, and the record industry, have been two major areas of black business activity. A comprehensive entry on blacks in the recording industry is included, along with several biographical entries on leading businesspeople in this industry. Since the 1970s, these industries have encountered relentless competition from multibillion-dollar white American and other multinational corporations, and two of the giants, Johnson Products and Motown, sold out to competitors.

The entertainment industry has been highly competitive for blacks. There are comprehensive entries on blacks in radio, filmmaking, and television, in addition to biographies of leading blacks in those industries, including the early twentieth-century black filmmaker Oscar Micheaux and Robert L. Johnson, multimillionaire founder of BET (Black Entertainment Television). Also, for the telecommunications industry, an entry on blacks and the Internet is also included.

Federal government programs and affirmative action policies in investment banking, since the civil rights era, however, have been significant for some black business development in white Corporate America. The investment banking activities of Reginald Lewis provided him access to Wall Street and his subsequent purchases, first of McCall Patterns and then Beatrice International. Finance capitalism is becoming important in the development of black business, and there are entries on both the stock market and on investment banking. At the other extreme, there have been instances when successful black businesspeople acquired their initial venture capital through enterprises that were not considered conducive to encouraging community morality, such as saloons and gambling establishments and "policy," or the "numbers game." Entries are provided on early twentieth-century businessmen William Adams and Robert Church, Sr., who used profits from saloons and gambling to invest in legitimate enterprises, fund the building of black community institutions, and provide venture capital for black businesses. There is also an entry on illegal black businesses and organized criminal activities.

Also, entries are included on various black business organizations that, historically, have made efforts to promote black business participation, including the antebellum National Negro Convention, which met for the first time in 1830. While this organization has been studied primarily for its political agenda, opposition to the American Colonization Society, founded by whites to encourage free blacks to immigrate to Africa, specifically Liberia, and its antislavery activities, its economic agenda was clearly pronounced. Indeed, many of the delegates were businesspeople who called for boycotts against slave-produced goods, black consumer support of black business, the organization of a black national bank, and the promotion of international trade in the African diaspora.

An entry on the National Negro Business League (NNBL), which in the first half of the twentieth century was the most prominent organization to promote business participation, is included. The NNBL was founded in 1900 by Booker T. Washington, whose public stance, fundamentally, was that the pursuit of political freedom and civil rights should be subordinated to economic development. Yet it was W.E.B. Du Bois who emerged as one of the leading proponents of black political and civil rights and first proposed the formation of an organization to promote black business in 1898 at the Atlanta Conference on "the Negro in Business," which he convened. Information is provided on both Washington and Du Bois.

With the founding of the NNBL, there was an expansion in the number of black business organizations, which have proliferated in number since the 1960s, reflecting the increasing participation of blacks in a diversity of business enterprises. There are entries on several black business organizations, including the National Black MBA Association. With the opening of white Corporate America to blacks, a result of new federal laws in the 1960s passed to end race-based employment discrimination, the numbers of blacks in business schools increased. There are entries on financing the development of historically black colleges and universities from 1865 to 1930, in addition to three entries on blacks and business schools. Biographical entries are included on several early black scholars in business and economics—Abram Harris, Oliver Cox, Joseph A. Pierce, and Phyllis Wallace.

As with leading contemporary black businesspeople, information is available on the scholarship of contemporary black economists. Their publications inform many of the entries on black business history in the post–civil rights era, and many of their articles are listed in suggested bibliographies that are included with each entry. The insight provided on blacks in business from an interdisciplinary review of the scholarly literature is included in my forthcoming Greenwood publication *African American Business and Entrepreneurship: Critical Historiographical Assessments in the Economic and Cultural Life of Blacks and Capitalism*, whereas my manuscript-in-progress "Captive Capitalists: Race, Class and Black Entrepreneurship" explores black intellectual thought on business and the implications of race and class for blacks in an increasingly multicultural society.

The *Encyclopedia*'s emphasis is on the historical diversity and multiplicity of black business activities in the traditional periods in American history. And in black business history in the late twentieth century, the civil rights era had a profound effect on blacks and American business. That impact is discussed in several entries, including the civil rights movement and black business and economic boycotts in which information is provided on Dr. Martin Luther King. Also, there are biographical entries on black ministers Reverend Jesse Jackson and Leon Sullivan, known for his efforts in promoting black business both nationally and internationally. The Sullivan principles established guidelines for white Corporate America in using their financial strength to force an end to apartheid in South Africa.

Historically, the black church and its leaders have been strong supporters and promoters of black business. Indeed, the founders of the nation's first independent black churches were successful businessmen. In 1793, Absalom Jones founded the African Episcopal Church of St. Thomas, and Richard Allen founded the Methodist Mother Bethel Church, which in 1816 became the first autonomous black denomination, the African Methodist Episcopal (AME) Church. Also, both men purchased their freedom from money generated through business activities while they were slaves. As free blacks, even before establishing their churches, they were the founders of the Philadelphia Free African Society in 1787, one of the first black mutual aid societies. Also, in 1810, Jones founded the first black insurance company, the African Insurance Company in Philadelphia.

In addition to entries on antebellum mutual aid societies, a comprehensive entry is included on the black independent church and business from 1890 to 1997. In the twentieth century, increasingly, black religious institutions and organizations have been distinguished by establishing business enterprises. Several entries provide information on black religious leaders who established business enterprises in conjunction with the religious sects or organizations they founded, including Father Divine and his Peace Mission Movement in the 1930s and Elder Lightfoot Michaux in the 1940s and early 1950s, who founded the Church of God and used its finances to establish businesses. The business activities of Elijah Muhammad and Louis Abdul Farrakhan are discussed in the entry on the Nation of Islam, which developed enterprises valued at $140 million before Muhammad's death in 1975.

There are also entries that provide information on black businesses in the post–civil rights era, including entries on black business ownership since 1969, franchise units, traditional and emerging lines of black business, employment patterns in black business, joint venturing, enterprise zones, market structure barriers for black business, set-asides and minority businesses, the social capital of black business owners, and asian/black entrepreneurship, compared. There is also an entry on black mayors in the promotion of black business and one on Chicago Mayor Harold Washington. Several entries provide information on the recent history of blacks in white Corporate America, which illuminate a new development in black business activity in the late twentieth century, including entries on black managers and executives in white Corporate America, networking, and downsizing.

The impact on black business, as a result of the retrenchment of federal affirmative action policies, beginning in the 1980s and escalating in the 1990s, is found in several entries, including one on disparity studies. Despite a history of black business participation that dates to the colonial era in American history, in the final decade of the twentieth century, black American businesses comprised only 3.1 percent of all businesses in the United States. Blacks comprise almost 13 percent of the nation's population, whereas their percentage of all U.S. business receipts amount to only 1.0 percent of total American business receipts.

Indeed, in 1996, total sales of the leading 100 black businesses and the leading 100 auto dealers generated only $14.1 billion (including the $2.230 billion in sales by TLC Beatrice International). In the *Fortune* 500, a company with sales at $14.1 billion would rank 83rd in its listing. Consequently, there are two entries on ethics and entries on antitrust regulations and reparations and black business offer a remedy, whereas, the entries on joint venturing and business motivation and guidelines suggest the best 10 areas of business enterprise for blacks in the twenty-first century.

While the focus of the *Encyclopedia* is African American business history, there are several entries that illuminate business practices in West Africa after the transatlantic slave trade legally ended, for the United States in 1808—entries on Jaja of Opobo and Eyo Honesy Nsa II. Along with African American entrepreneurs, those two West African businessmen provide examples of preindustrial nineteenth-century black diaspora capitalism. Also, there is an entry on indigenous capitalism development in Africa from colonization through decolonization to neocolonization, providing a comparative historical international perspective of the limited African diaspora advances in capitalism made by black businesspeople in a global economy.

Given the increasingly high-tech–driven economy that will shape and dominate economic life in a global economy of the twenty-first century, it is time for a new lesson from the past for black Americans. Black business history broadens the chronicles of the black experience, offering examples of the possibilities of economic advancement, as opposed to an African American history, which contextualizes only a blueprint for the economic survival of blacks in American life as workers. African American history presently constructed offers blacks a past that has no future. A deconstructed history of the black experience is needed to ensure the future economic advancement of African Americans, a history inclusive of information on blacks who broke the chains of economic constraints through business participation.

ENCYCLOPEDIA OF
AFRICAN AMERICAN
BUSINESS HISTORY

A

ABBOTT, ROBERT S. (1868–1940), Chicago, newspaper publisher.

Since America's first black newspaper, *Freedom's Journal*, was started in 1827, many writers and historians have chronicled the role of newspapers, magazines, and other media communications forms as carriers and preservers of black life and culture. These media have become notable primarily for their crusading image—speaking for, defending, and promoting the interests of black people. For years, the publications, primarily weeklies, shined a bright spotlight on the ugly legacy of America's racially segregated past—lynchings, boycotts, mass demonstrations, Ku Klux Klan marches, discrimination in the workplace, and so forth. Of course, they also trumpeted black achievement in sports, education, science, government, entertainment, and other areas long before the majority press reported about successful African Americans.

Although financial problems choked out the lives of several thousand black publications over the years (primarily because they could not obtain advertising), several newspapers and magazines managed to survive, tributes to the individuals who founded, nurtured, and guided them over the years. These were media institutions that proved themselves to be successful, both as crusading advocates for black Americans and as financially well-run business enterprises. Among some of the "leaders" who helped to put the black press on a solid financial footing, nearly a dozen names are often mentioned as important in enabling this economic institution to survive and thrive.

By no means is this an exhaustive list; nonetheless, among the earlier leaders were Robert S. Abbott (*Chicago Defender*); John H. Murphy, Jr. (*Afro-American*); Christopher James Perry, Sr. (*Philadelphia Tribune*); Robert Lee

Vann (*Pittsburgh Courier*); William Alexander Scott II (*Atlanta Daily World*); Dr. Clilan B. Powell (*New York Amsterdam News*); Leon Washington, Jr. (*Los Angeles Sentinel*); and William O. Walker (*Cleveland Call and Post*). Of all the pioneers in black journalism, Abbott is often singled out because of his breakthrough success with the *Defender*.

Before Abbott founded the paper in 1905, there were no large-circulation black newspapers. Readership was limited to the educated—at that time a very small percentage of the black population. Focusing on stories that would appeal to a larger audience, the *Defender* had at least 230,000 readers by 1915. In his biography of Abbott, Roi Ottley pointed to the editor-publisher's "northern campaign" as being the turning point in the publication's success. In 1917, Abbott began using the pages of the *Defender* to encourage southern blacks to migrate North, where, he argued, they would find far greater opportunities for advancement. More than 100,000 southern blacks moved to Chicago in those years.

Nonetheless, Abbott was not without his critics. Some accused him of sensationalizing racial problems in both the North and the South to boost circulation. Others criticized the *Defender* for talking down to its audience and ignoring the black middle class in order to build a connection with less-well-educated masses. Unfazed, Abbott continued to beat the drum for racial equality, and by 1925, the *Defender*'s circulation had mushroomed to more than 250,000. Abbott is viewed as a significant force in black journalism not only because he achieved unimaginable success and prosperity with the *Defender* but also because his success demonstrated to the Scotts in Atlanta, the Powells in New York, the Murphys in Baltimore, and others the readership potential of their publications.

Eventually, editors and owners of newspapers in almost every large city in the United States observed their publications expand their reach. In 1944, when sociologist Gunnar Myrdal wrote "the Negro press . . . is rightly characterized as the greatest single power in the Negro race," there were 150 black newspapers with a total circulation of 1.6 million. The three largest papers at that time were the *Pittsburgh Courier* (257,000), the *Chicago Daily Defender* (202,000), and the *Baltimore Afro-American* (137,000). Almost 30 years later, the 1972 *Editor & Publisher Year Book* listed 203 black newspapers and their total circulation as 3,971,086.

Heading toward the twenty-first century, African American newspapers have found themselves on something like a roller-coaster ride. Their circulation, readership, and advertising revenues have been bittersweet. In more prosperous economic times, they fare well. During every economic downturn since 1971, they have encountered turbulence. In some respects, Abbott can claim credit for this predicament: He built the *Defender* on a footing that depended on circulation as its base—this, during a time when the rest of America's newspaper media were shifting to an advertising-oriented basis for support. In addition to the cost characteristics of publishing changing, the majority press now began to cover African Americans more routinely. Both of these factors—insufficient advertising revenues and losing the historic monopolylike grip on black audiences—have placed Abbott's *Defender* and other large city black newspapers on less predictable footing.

Of course, majority newspapers in large cities have faced comparable uncertainties, and many of them have been going out of business during this same period, largely because of competition from electronic media and the spiraling high costs of labor and newsprint. Just as it was Abbott's innovativeness that took the *Defender* from obscurity to prominence, the leaders of today's black press also will have to develop new, exciting, and different strategies to renew and resuscitate ties to their audience.

SELECTED BIBLIOGRAPHY: Fred Black and Gail Baker Woods, eds., *Milestones in Black Newspaper Research* (Washington, D.C.: National Newspaper Publishers Association, 1994); Mary Costello, "Blacks in the News Media," *Editorial Research Reports* 11, 7 (1972); Frederick G. Detweiler, *The Negro Press in the United States* (College Park, MD: McGrath Publishing Co., 1968); Gunnar Myrdal, *An American Dilemma; Negro Problem and Modern Democracy* (New York: Harper & Bros., 1944); Armistead S. Pride and Clint C. Wilson II, *A History of the Black Press* (Washington, DC: Howard University Press, 1997); Roland E. Woseley, *The Black Press, U.S.A.* (Ames: Iowa State University Press, 1971).

William E. Berry

ADAMS, WILLIAM LLOYD (c. 1914–), Maryland, entrepreneur, philanthropist, civil rights activist, political operative.

An accomplished businessman, soft-spoken William "Little Willie" Adams has loaned millions of start-up dollars to Baltimore-area African American entrepreneurs. A lifelong advocate of African American economic self-empowerment, Adams's passionate desire is to see black-owned firms become among the largest in the United States. Most of Adams's business loans were interest free and made on a handshake. In return for providing most of the seed capital, Adams typically asked for a 50 percent stake of a fledgling business. Failed businesses and broken promises abounded, but a noteworthy exception was the Parks Sausage Company, in Baltimore. Were it not for Adams's unflagging moral and financial support of Henry Parks, Parks Sausage would never have started operation in 1951.

Adams came to Baltimore from Zebulon, North Carolina, in 1929 with a seventh-grade education and expertise working in North Carolina cotton fields. He gravitated toward Baltimore's underground lottery [policy/numbers game], where his hustle and math ability made him a top numbers operator. He also earned his high school diploma and graduated from a two-year business school. Eager to diversify and leave the numbers business behind, Adams created a multimillion-dollar real estate concern, whose construction projects range from Florida to Rhode Island. He also opened a number of popular entertainment venues for African Americans during the Jim Crow era. One, Carr's Beach in Annapolis, Maryland, was refurbished for $150,000 in 1949 and had an open-air pavilion where entertainers such as Billy Eckstine performed. A fiercely competitive golfer, who often played with boxer Joe Louis, Adams was angered by the inferior condition of Baltimore's blacks-only public golf course. He and three other plaintiffs filed a federal lawsuit in the 1950s that helped desegregate public golf courses nationwide.

The state of Maryland, which now has a state-run lottery, tried several times to prosecute Adams on numbers charges. Maryland never succeeded in getting a lottery charge to stick against Adams, including one case overturned by the Supreme Court. A generous contributor to the National Association for the Advancement of Colored People (NAACP) and other civil rights organizations, Adams became heavily involved in Baltimore politics as an organizer and campaign backer in the 1950s, 1960s, and 1970s. A close friend and supporter of former Baltimore mayor and Maryland governor William Donald Schaefer, Adams was responsible for getting Maryland's first black state senator, Harry Cole, into office. Adams also helped his wife, Victorine Adams, and Henry Parks to become the second and third black politicians, respectively, to win seats on Baltimore's city council.

SELECTED BIBLIOGRAPHY: William Lloyd Adams, Personal Papers, Oral Interviews, Press Clippings in possession of Blair S. Walker, Adams Archives, Columbia, Maryland; Blair S. Walker "Getting Rich By the Numbers," unpub. ms.

Blair S. Walker

ADVERTISING. For the first half of the twentieth century, minority advertising agencies rarely existed. Talented, ambitious African Americans who sought careers in the advertising field were shut out of an industry, where images of blacks either were nonexistent or were the stereotypical ads of Aunt Jemima or the butler serving Hiram Walker whiskey. According to Jannette Dates in *Split Image: African Americans in the Mass Media*, the advertising industry ignored the black market until the 1960s, even though articles written in the 1930s through the 1950s documented a separate, distinct, and viable $28 billion black consumer market. Indeed, publishing pioneer John H. Johnson,* founder of Johnson Publications, recognized and addressed the need for targeted ethnic advertising in a film he produced in 1947.

About 10 years later, Vincent Cullers,* an art director turned entrepreneur, founded the country's first African American–owned full-service advertising agency. During the 1960s and 1970s a number of black-owned advertising companies began to color the advertising landscape and develop successful campaigns aimed at black consumers. Notable are Caroline Jones, Barbara Proctor, and the Mingo Group. By 1997 approximately 25 major black-owned agencies were in existence, and many have been the training ground for blacks who have moved into general market agencies.

In 1997 *Fortune* magazine estimated that the advertising industry was a $173 billion market. According to *Target Market News*, national marketers spent an estimated $865 million to reach black consumers last year, with $330 million, or one-third of the overall dollars, spent with black-owned agencies. In the 1990s a small but significant number of black-owned advertising agencies became successful at winning major general market accounts. Mars Inc. Three Musketeers account went to Uniworld in New York, and McDonald's to the Burrell Communications Group in Chicago. As diversity in the American marketplace increases, and ethnic-owned agencies continue to demonstrate their ability to effectively cross over into mainstream media, the line between the ethnic market and the main market may begin to blur. According to Thomas J. Burrell*, president of the Burrell Communications Group, "Black people know more about white consumers than white people know about black consumers. We live in a white society, and we have to learn to function in a white world. Also, the black market has become the leading edge for other segments, especially youth."

SELECTED BIBLIOGRAPHY: Jannette L. Dates, "Half a Loaf: The Advertising Industry," in Jannette L. Dates and William Barlow, eds., *Split Images: African Americans in the Mass Media* (Washington, D.C.: Howard University Press, 1990); *Fortune*, April 1997.

Teresa Savage

ADVERTISING, GENERAL MARKETING AGENCIES AND BLACKS.

A majority of the black-owned advertising agencies surfaced in the mid-1970s to early 1980s to penetrate the untapped African American market. These black agencies felt they understood what the black consumer wanted and could deliver their needs better than white agencies. General market agencies did not understand the culture, wants or needs, or the purchasing power to effectively segment the market. The first known black consumer research study was done in the 1930s by the National Negro Business League.* The results showed a spending power of $1.65 billion. This purchasing power increased 30 to 40 years later with a $30 billion black consumer market. Black-owned agencies have tried to vie for general market accounts for growth opportunities and to prove that they are not limited to targeting black consumers.

The quest for black-owned advertising agencies to penetrate the industry has fluctuated from very few in the 1970s to several in the 1980s and negated progress in the 1990s. Prior to the late 1960s, companies did not see a need in targeting the black consumer. Neither their purchasing power nor their differentiation was respected. Looking for growth opportunities, many companies began allocating budgets specifically for the black consumer market. Many black advertising professionals monitored the shift in the industry to segment the untapped black consumer market, a perfect opportunity for them to exercise their entrepreneurial keenness by opening an ad agency that specialized in this market. Black ad agencies argued that they could best target the black consumer because they understood the wants and needs of the market, which were different from the general market. Frank Mingo of The Mingo Group considered the black marketed agencies to be "the Right on School of Advertising." After all, a black agency should understand the black consumer.

Consequently, many black advertising professionals took their skills and experience from the general market to start their own enterprises. Vince Cullers Advertising, Inc. of Chicago, founded by Vincent Cullers* in 1956, was the first black-owned full-service advertising agency. Cullers's philosophy of the black consumer in the late 1960s was shaped by the politics of the period in the Black Power movement. In 1968, he produced a Newport cigarette ad featuring a "black revolutionary wearing a dashiki." Many of his clients wanted to portray racial pride in their ads. Cullers's view was to show black separatism in a positive light.

Barbara Gardner Proctor struggled for advancement in the advertising industry. After limited opportunities, as she became an entrepreneur, she proclaimed, "They loved my work when I worked for someone else. Let's see how much they love me now." In establishing Proctor and Gardner Advertising Inc. in 1970, Proctor became the first black woman to own an ad agency. Proctor was a sole proprietor, although the name of the business suggests otherwise. Her rationale was that clients would assume Proctor was a figurehead for a man named Gardner. She did not think the industry was quite ready to deal with a woman with power.

She financed her venture with an $80,000 loan, the first service loan provided to anyone by the Small Business Administration. Her philosophy in focusing on the black consumer market is exemplified through her statement, "I have the opportunity to show the strength, beauty, humor and family respect that is a very proud tradition in the Black experience." She refused to accept accounts that would portray negative stereotypes of blacks. Within three years, Proctor boasted billings at approximately $4.5 million. In 1978, billings increased to $6.8 million. Her success prompted President Ronald Reagan, in 1984, to cite her as an example of entrepreneurial spirit as he proclaimed, "[She] rose from a ghetto shack to build a multimillion-dollar advertising agency in Chicago."

There existed several other black ad agencies who made contributions to the industry. Uniworld Group Inc. was founded by Byron Lewis* in 1968 and would become a key player among black ad agencies. Burrell Advertising, founded by Thomas Burrell* in 1971, held the reign as the largest black-owned ad agency for years. Lockhart & Pettus, Inc., was founded in New York by Keith Lockhart and Theodore Pettus in 1977. The Mingo Group, Inc., was founded in 1977 in New York as well, by Frank Mingo. The company was previously named Mingo-Jones Advertising before Caroline Jones left to start her own ad agency, Caroline Jones Inc., in 1987.

Other known black ad agencies were: Anderson Communications (1972) in Atlanta; R. J. Dale Advertising (1979) in Chicago; Brainstorm Advertising (1981) in Chicago; The Wimbley Group (1988) in Rolling Meadows, Illinois; E. Morris, Communications (1987) in Chicago; Cognos Advertising (1989) in Detroit; Sharp Advertising (1990) in Atlanta; Great Ideas, Inc. (1992) in Washington, D.C.; Articy Advertising in Boston; Junius Edwards in New York; Marshall & Associates in Chicago; Howard Sanders Advertising in New York; and Vomack Advertising.

Black agencies were successful in landing big accounts with large companies. Mingo-Jones created the slogan "We Do Chicken Right" for Kentucky Fried Chicken. Burrell created the "I assume you drink Martell" phrase for the Martell alcohol. Burrell had many major accounts including McDonald's, Procter & Gamble, Coca-Cola, and Ford. Proctor and Gardner handled such accounts as Jewel Food Stores, Sears, Gillette, and Gallo Winery. Uniworld did business with AT&T, Kraft Foods, Quaker Oats, and many others. Caroline Jones had accounts with Anheuser-Busch, the United Negro College Fund, and others. According to the *Standard Directory of Advertising Agencies*, there were 14 agencies who specialized in the African American market, in 1996, with total billings of $371.8 million. Uniworld led the way with $125 million; Burrell was second with $90 million, and The Mingo Group was third with billings of $53 million. Uniworld ranked six among *Black Enterprise*'s (*BE*) Industrial/Service 100 in 1996 and 1997; billings in 1997 amounted to $157.9 million. Burrell ranked seven in 1996 and nine in 1997; billings in 1997 amounted to $134.7 million.

When the general marketing advertising agencies saw market potential in the black consumer as black agencies gained new accounts, they began to move into the once black-dominated market and compete with black agencies. Black agencies, on the other hand, were beginning to seek general market accounts. African Americans have been forced into acculturation with white America. While their understanding of American culture is by default or by internalization, black advertising agencies have demonstrated the capacity for diversification in dealing with any consumer, black or white. However, whites only ventured to understand the African American culture when profits were involved. In the advertising business, it is extremely important that the agency understands the values of the targeted consumer. The future success of black advertising agencies will be contingent on their long-term success in the general market and on maintaining their market share in the African American market.

SELECTED BIBLIOGRAPHY: "The Battle for Black Accounts," *Advertising Age*, February 5, 1996; Jannette L. Dates, "Half a Loaf: The Advertising Industry," in Jannette L. Dates and William Barlow, eds., *Split Images: African Americans in the Mass Media* (Washington, DC: Howard University Press, 1990); Ricki Franks, "Success Story Good News: Proctor Takes Gamble and Hits the Jackpot," *Working Woman*, August 1979; John N. Ingham and Lynne B. Feldman, *African-American Business Leaders: A Biographical Dictionary* (Westport, CT: Greenwood Press, 1994); National Register Publishing, *Standard Directory of Advertising Agencies* (New York: National Register Publishing Co., 1971 and 1996).

Quincy T. Mills

AFRICA, INDIGENOUS CAPITALISM DEVELOPMENT. The European African transatlantic slave trade and then colonialism had a significant impact on the development of indigenous capitalism in Africa in much the same way as local laws and institutions limited African American business participation in the United States. Given the nature of European colonialism, it was inevitable that European domination would conflict with the growth and development of indigenous African entrepreneurship. Under colonialism, the annexation of Africa was usually accompanied by efforts to exploit the resources of the new territories and make them available to the economies of the metropole.

As a result of the significant risks associated with investment in the colonies, private entrepreneurs in the metropolitan countries were quite reluctant to commit funds and human capital to economic activities in Africa. To attract private capital to the new colonies, the metropolitan governments instructed officers in the colonies to restructure property rights to make the territories more attractive for flows of capital from Europe. The solution adopted by the British government was to offer private firms exclusive rights to exploit and develop an area's resources. Monopolies were created and protected by the colonial government. Firms to whom these monopoly rights were assigned would then provide capital to exploit the resources of their respective concessions.

The creation of these concessions most often involved the confiscation of communal property rights that belonged to Africans and the subsequent establishment of private property rights that were then assigned to European colonists or settlers. This process effectively stunted the development of African entrepreneurial activities in the affected areas. In several instances, scholars have suggested that colonialism actually benefited the development of indigenous capitalism. According to this view, colonialism destroyed traditional African economic and political systems, which had constrained the emergence of indigenous capitalism, paving the way for the latter to come to reality. The benefit, as they argue, was that Europeans brought to the colonies institutions that enhanced the development of indigenous capital. One example given is that settlers introduced plantation agriculture, competition, and private property rights, providing a demonstration effect for indigenous farmers.

Proponents of this school of thought—which argues that indigenous capitalism in Africa is a product of colonial rule—also note that not all forms of colonial exploitation led to the emergence of an indigenous entrepreneurial class and subsequently to capitalist development. In South Africa, race-based legislation made it impossible for Africans, who interacted with settlers, to establish plantations of their own or develop other forms of capitalist participation. During the struggle for independence, African nationalists argued that high levels of poverty and deprivation among the indigenous peoples were the results of the monopolization of enterprise by the resident European commercial and entrepreneurial classes.

The latter were said to intentionally stunt the development of an African entrepreneurial class, which could later become effective competition to them in the colonial economy. In addition, many European plantation owners believed that the rise of indigenous capitalism could significantly reduce the labor pool they relied on for inexpensive workers for their farms and other economic activities. Thus, European entrepreneurs worked closely with the colonial government to stunt the development of African capitalism.

Throughout Africa, indigenous entrepreneurship, especially in the modern industrial sector, seems to be marginal. Most industrial activities, including those in the important mining subsector, are dominated by foreign capital. Domination and control of economic activities in the African economies date back to the colonial period when European entrepreneurs were granted monopoly rights by the colonial government to exploit the resources of the territories. In each concession, the Europeans enforced the new laws established to protect their property rights very vigorously. As a consequence, large numbers of African entrepreneurs were denied access to the resources of the concessions. For example, in the Niger territories and on the Cameroon River district, annexation involved the seizure of land and the confiscation of middle-man monopoly trading rights from African groups and their subsequent reassignment to Europeans. In the Niger concessions, Brass trader lost to the Royal Niger Company, and on the Cameroon River district, the Duala, who had controlled the trade between the coast and the interior for many years, lost to German plantation companies.

After losing their ancestral lands, many of these Africans became landless peasants and an important source of cheap labor for the European plantations. The dominant method of production of export crops in each colony determined the extent to which African property rights in land were abrogated. In colonies with large populations of settlers (e.g., Southern Rhodesia, South Africa, Algeria, Angola, Mozambique, Kenya, and Namibia), most export crops were produced by the latter. In these colonies, most of the fertile and cultivable land was seized and transferred to the colonists. Production on these farms required a lot of labor, and colonial policies were designed to force Africans to provide the labor that these planters needed. The attitude of Europeans toward the rights of Africans in land were appropriately expressed by French Governor of Algeria General Bugeaud when he remarked in 1841 that ''[w]herever the water supply is good and the land fertile, there we must place colonists without worrying about previous owners. We must distribute the lands [with] full title to the colonists.'' European planters, facing a serious labor shortage, devised many ways to force Africans to provide the needed labor services.

In the late 1800s, farmers in the Transvaal and the Orange Free State (OFS) introduced a kind of *corvée*, or labor tax, that was used effectively to secure African labor for white plantations. Many European settlers in South Africa did not believe in the concept of internal exit for black workers. In other words, white farmers did not want Africans to travel freely in search of opportunities to maximize returns to their labor services. In addition, they did not want Africans to become entrepreneurs; they wanted them to remain suppliers of labor services to white plantations and industrial activities. Thus, the colony's laws and institutions were designed to dispossess the African of his landholdings, prevent his mobility, and impose on him taxes that could only be paid with currency earned from working for a settler.

One of the most important issues to be determined shortly after independence in the African countries was a development model, one that could be used to effect significant improvements in the standard of living of the people. Many of the new African leaders argued that the market-oriented resource allocation systems inherited from the colonialists were actually constraints to rapid economic growth and development. They opted for statism, a development model that emphasized state control of economic activities and the minimization of the functions of the market system. Statism was expected to provide the state with the wherewithal to eliminate mass poverty and deprivation and provide for rapid industrialization in the country. These African leaders believed that statism would capture the enormous profits that had accrued to European middlemen during colonialism and make them part of the pool of resources to be used for spending on social services.

After independence, many African countries adopted statism as their development model. This approach to resource allocation emphasized government ownership and control. By deemphasizing the market, statism failed to promote the development of indigenous capitalism, while encouraging bureaucratic corruption and rent seeking. The laws and institutions adopted by the African countries at independence, like those during colonialism, became obstacles to the development of African capitalism. Moreover, after more than 40 years of the control of economic activities, the state has failed to rid Africa of high levels of poverty and deprivation. In addition, excessive government intervention in private exchange has enhanced and promoted nepotism, corruption, and rent seeking and discouraged the development of viable economic infrastructures; it has also stunted the development of indigenous capitalism.

Also, in many African countries, government regulations have created a large urban elite whose welfare is dependent primarily on the public sector and surplus extraction from the rural agricultural sector. As a result, the postindependence political economy in these countries has been characterized by intense conflict between urbanites, who benefit from government regulation of agriculture, and the rural sector, which must supply the surplus used to subsidize the urban sector. Such state activities have generally had negative effects on food production and prevented these countries from achieving self-sufficiency in food production.

Moreover, the modern industrial sectors of many African countries are dominated by either foreign firms or state-owned enterprises. In fact, in some countries, the state actively seeks and encourages foreign investment, while at the same time passing laws that discourage the development of indigenous capital. As a result of state intervention, firm profitability in the industrial sectors of many African countries is not determined by competition and managerial expertise but by state subsidies, discretionary tax relief, and other forms of regulation. Thus, in those few African countries with indigenous businesses, owners must spend a great deal of time and resources lobbying and bribing politicians and civil servants in an effort to minimize the burden of ruinous state regulations on their enterprises and improve profit levels.

The result has been the sustaining of firms that are efficient at rent seeking, but not necessarily at production and distribution of goods and services, and the stunting of the development of indigenous entrepreneurship. Changes in the global political economy during the period 1989–1991 have provided Africans opportunities to reexamine their laws and institutions and develop new ones to enhance their ability to participate more effectively in the new global economy. The collapse of socialism in eastern Europe and the subsequent disintegration of the Soviet Union resulted in the cessation of superpower rivalry and significantly reduced Africa's strategic importance to the cold war protagonists. As a consequence, Africans have a rare opportunity to design by themselves, and without interference from the West or the East, institutional arrangements that will enhance development of indigenous entrepreneurship and provide for sustainable development.

In 1994, apartheid was demolished in South Africa, significantly improving the climate for reform in the continent. In addition, since 1989, several longtime dictatorships have fallen and have been replaced by democratically elected leaders. Today, most economies in Africa are highly regulated and suffer from high levels of opportunism including corruption and rent seeking. It has been determined that while the extent and scope of rent seeking are minimized by competitive exchange, a monopolized exchange system actually enhances rent seeking. Government regulation, especially in the African economies, is often quite essential for effective monopolization of private markets.

Monopolization of markets, even if it is undertaken by domestic groups, will have a significantly negative impact on the development of indigenous capitalism. To minimize monopolization and provide the competitive environment that enhances capitalist development, it is necessary to elaborate in the constitution procedural rules that guarantee the protection of property rights and the rights of market participants to freely engage in exchange and contract. The laws so designed should protect private markets and prevent unnecessary intervention by the state in private exchange. Consequently, to make certain that the proper environment is provided for the development of indigenous entrepreneurship in Africa, constitutional provisions, which guarantee economic freedoms and thus enhance the ability of entrepreneurs to engage in wealth creation, must be provided. These freedoms should be elaborated in the constitution in order to prevent their abrogation by ordinary legislation to enhance entrepreneurship and the development of indigenous capitalism.

SELECTED BIBLIOGRAPHY: Sir A. C. Burns, *History of Nigeria* (London: George Allen, 1963); George M. Fredrickson, *White Supremacy: A Comparative Study in American and South African History* (Oxford: Oxford University Press, 1981); James D. Gwartney, Robert Lawson, and Walter Block, eds., *Economic Freedom of the World,*

1975–1995 (Vancouver, BC: Fraser Institute, 1996); John M. Mbaku, *Institutions and Reform in Africa: The Public Choice Perspective* (Westport, CT: Praeger, 1997); John M. Mbaku, "Markets and the Economic Origins of Apartheid in South Africa," *Indian Journal of Social Science* 6, 2 (1993): 139–158.

John Mukum Mbaku

AGRIBUSINESS, VIRGINIA'S BLACK FARMERS. After the Civil War, although large quantities of land were available, few black freedmen were in a position to pay even the most modest amounts of money to acquire independent holdings. Many looked to the Freedmen's Bureau to assist them. The phrase "40 acres and a mule" represented the hope of blacks, who believed their turn at land ownership had finally arrived. In fact, in Virginia, the Freedmen's Bureau never held more than 100,000 acres at any one time. With few jobs available and with the promise of paid agricultural labor, many blacks continued as agricultural farm laborers. The sharecropping system that emerged, however, continued to benefit the landowner. Thus, the new pattern of black-white relations in agriculture resembled its pre–Civil War societal racial structure—black mobility was limited, and economic stability tied to the production of staple crops was reinforced.

By the turn of the century, three-fourths of all blacks in agriculture were tenant farmers (696,000 in the South), and of this group of nonowners, over 40 percent were sharecroppers (293,000). Yet the late nineteenth century was marked by a sharp decline in Virginia's status as a plantation state, as evidenced by the decreasing average acres per farm (340 acres in 1850, 245 acres in 1870, 120 acres in 1900) and an increase in the number of farms. The census of 1890 recorded 13,715 black farm owners and 18,180 black tenant farmers in Virginia. For those tenants who passed into the status of owner-operator, it should be noted that the acres converted were generally the poorest, least desirable for profitable cultivation. Still, by 1900, the number of black farmers in Virginia had increased to 44,834, a little over one-fourth (27 percent) of all farmers reported for the state. In 1910, while the number of black farmers had increased to 48,114, the percentage dropped slightly to 26 percent.

The main crops produced on black farms were cotton, sweet potatoes, and tobacco. Prior to World War I, black farmers contributed 40 percent of the total cotton crop raised in the United States, 20 percent of the sweet potatoes, and 10 percent of the total tobacco harvest. At this time in Virginia, 60 percent of the black farms were producing cotton, amounting to one-half of the cotton produced by the state. Over one-third of the black farms in Virginia were growing sweet potatoes and tobacco, which comprised 30 percent of the total of each of these crops produced in the state. Yet events surrounding the first world war affected the pattern of participation of blacks in agriculture in Virginia and throughout the South. Specifically, blacks in farming, particularly property owners, lost their land or gave up farming in large numbers during this period.

Agriculture in Virginia in the 1920s, however, did not show the same changes that prevailed in states of the Deep South. While there were fewer black owners in 1920 than in 1910 (25,520 in 1920, 26,820 in 1910, −4.8 percent change), the decrease was not at the levels experienced in other southern states. The percentage change in black tenant farmers nearly equaled the loss in black farm owners from 1910 to 1920 (15,706 black tenants in 1910, 16,640 black tenants in 1920, +5.9 percent change). Unlike blacks, during this time period, the number of white farm owners showed an increase of nearly 4,000.

Then, from 1920 to 1930, after a 16 percent decrease in the black farm population in Virginia, a modest 4 percent increase occurred between 1930 and 1935. This increase, however, was short-lived, as statistics on black farm operators in Virginia for the decade 1930–1940 show a decrease from 39,673 in 1930 to 35,090 in 1940. This decrease of 12 percent for black operators can be compared with the increase of 7 percent for white operators during the same time. Changes by race and tenure of operator indicated a decrease in the proportion of black owners (−1.4 percent) and black tenants (−15.5 percent) with increases for white owners (+10.3 percent) and white tenants (+4.5 percent).

The state-level figures would seem to indicate a movement of blacks out of agriculture during the depression years, whereas the proportion of whites was increasing, especially white farm owners. Despite a decrease in the proportion of black tenant farmers in the South from 1930 to 1940, the percentage of tenant farmers who were sharecropping was at its highest in 1940 (57 percent). Although the factors contributing to the decreases in blacks in farming during this period were many, the lack of access to timely information and technical expertise could be included among them.

The county extension agent was paramount to the survival of many farmers. However, black representation among county agents declined from a high of 15 percent in 1925 to 13 percent in 1941. At a time when there were so many changes introduced that affected the structure of agriculture, information and expertise available to the black farmer decreased. Within the area of farm demonstration, for example, minority agents declined from a high of 14 percent in 1925 to a low of 12 percent in 1941. Even more dramatic, the decrease in black county agents responsible for youth club work went from 29 percent in 1925 down to 10 percent in 1941. The failure to educate and generate interest among this next generation clearly had an impact on the future viability of blacks in farming.

From World War I through World War II, then, blacks lost ground in farming. With the increasing use of mechanization and government programs to limit production of certain crops, most black farmers were unable to stay competitive, to make a living from agriculture. Indeed, among black tenant farmers, government programs frequently meant the displacement of the marginal black farmer. Lacking ownership of his land, the black tenant had no defense against mechanization. In addition, the curtailment of crop allotments (fewer acres being planted) often resulted in disproportionate losses for the black tenant compared with whites. For these reasons, black tenancy in the United States dropped 70 percent between 1945 and 1959; the proportion of black farm owners decreased 33 percent.

Other trends in post–World War II farming have included an increase in the size of farms and diversification. Among white southern farmers, diversification has been indicated by the increasing proportion of whites in livestock, dairy, and poultry farming and truck crops. Southern black farmers, however, continue to remain concentrated in cotton, tobacco, and peanut cultivation. In the closing decade of the twentieth century, understanding the possible causes of the structural changes occurring in U.S. agriculture and their effect on black participation in farming requires an assessment of the complete network comprising the food and fiber system. Unlike the stereotype of the autonomous farmer, individual farms today are generally part of an elaborate chain of agricultural production where changes in any one link may force changes throughout any of the sectors—input suppliers, farms, processors, wholesalers-supermarkets, and consumers.

The black family farmer, today, maintains private ownership of his land less in practice than in legal theory. In Virginia, for example, a survey of farmers indicated that, on the average, one-fourth of their farmland was rented or leased. Additionally, data reported on Virginia farm liabilities show significant increases in real estate debts and total farm debts over the last several decades. As the increasing cost of land prohibits outright purchase, the move toward rental and leasing arrangements and/or increasing mortgage debts further erodes the independence of the black farmer. In addition to constraints within the food and fiber network, dynamics outside the agricultural production process also affect the structure of the farm and the black farmer's autonomy. External factors that have been shown to have an impact upon farm structure include technology, capital requirements, and taxes.

Technology in the form of increased mechanization of agriculture affected the relationship of labor and capital to production. Specifically, the increased use of equipment such as tractors, planting, and harvesting machinery required an increase in capital investments and resulted in a decreased need for labor. The increased availability and adoption of new machinery frequently meant that smaller black farms became less competitive due to the lack of sufficient capital investments—that is, the optimal (least-cost) farm size necessarily increased. The larger farms with greater output had a lower per unit cost than smaller farms. With profit directly related to yield, black farms had to be able to use those technologies and cropping systems that maximize production in the smallest amount of time possible.

Particularly, the financial assets required to enter farming become more prohibitive with time. Land, particularly prime agricultural land, is a finite endowment—and one decreasing in amount all the time. The limited availability of agricultural land guarantees a premium price at the time of sale. Also, pressures from suburban development inflate the value of agricultural lands near metropolitan areas, making their purchase by new, young black farmers unlikely and inflating taxes for farmers currently owning the land. Testimony on the operations of corporate and nonfarm investors indicated a common practice was to offer a bonus of $100 per acre for large landholdings (hundreds/thousands of acres), thus making acquisition of smaller parcels of land by individual black farmers virtually impossible. The long-range effects of these trends may be more devastating to the structure of agriculture than the short-range inflationary competition. The increase in capital requirements also affects the tenure status of farmers. If fewer black farmers are able to purchase farmlands, those who choose to remain in farming may have to rent or lease additional land to farm.

One of the dynamics affecting the structure of agriculture is the inflationary tax rate imposed on farmers who own land with development potential. Rather than tax the farmer for the current productive value of his agricultural land, tax rates are assessed on the potential value of the land if it were developed for commercial or residential use. This policy not only acts as a barrier to entry in farming but, in many cases, forces the sale of agricultural land when profits from agricultural production fail to yield sufficient income to compensate for the inflated tax valuation—a self-fulfilling prophecy.

Another key aspect of taxes and their effect on agricultural structure is the idea of tax-loss farming. The two main facets of tax-loss farming are: (1) the postponement of taxes—unlike nonagricultural businesses, the farmer only pays taxes on products sold (not on inventory held at the end of the year); and (2) the reduction of the tax rate. Although in principle all farmers are equally eligible to use tax rules to their own advantage, those who benefit most from these deductions and concessions are farmers with large nonfarm incomes. For these farmers, losses in farming become deductions from their nonfarm income. Thus, these tax laws disproportionately favor the largest farming operations.

One more area of concern in current tax policies is the problem of estate taxes at the time of inheriting property. Frequently the debt level of the farm prohibits using it as collateral to secure additional loans to pay the inheritance tax. In this situation the family may be forced to sell some of the farm assets to pay the taxes levied or may have to relinquish the entire farm if its level of productivity is insufficient. Inheritance tax relief is repeatedly mentioned as necessary to slow the loss of black agricultural land to nonagricultural uses in rural communities. In 1930, census figures indicated that blacks operated less than 12 percent of all the farmland in Virginia. Their level of control over farmland in 1992 indicates that they had decreased the portion of natural resources they held to less than 3 percent. Also, the average size of black farms in Virginia, in the South, and in the United States in 1900 were comparable (49.7 acres in Virginia, 50.9 acres in the South, 51.2 acres in the United States). Figures for whites in farming suggest the smallest averages for white farms in Virginia (143.7 acres), followed by 172.1 acres as the average for white farms in the South and 160.3 acres as the average in the United States.

One of the key sources of funding for capitalization of farm operations and farm ownership has been the Farmers Home Administration (FmHA). Between

1979 and 1980 black representation on FmHA committees in Virginia decreased 40.8 percent (from 49 to 29 members). Nationally, in 1981, FmHA operating loans to minorities were only 10.3 percent of the loans granted and farm ownership loans to blacks constituted less than 2 percent of the total granted (of the $800,000 distributed in farm ownership loans, $10,000 went to blacks). Thus, the undercapitalization of black farms and complications resulting from the formalization and centralization of the marketing process were among the factors contributing to the loss of black farmland.

Although, nationally, the number of persons employed in farming has declined since the depression, the decrease in the number of blacks in Virginia agriculture is particularly dramatic. From the 45,000 black farmers in Virginia at the turn of the century, there were 10,000 fewer by 1940. In 1982, Virginia reported 2,771 black farmers, and in 1992, fewer than 1,400 blacks were engaged in agriculture in the state. A second factor to consider in the recent representation of blacks in Virginia agriculture is the position occupied by the farm operator within the tenure hierarchy. The farmer who owns all the land he operates—the full owner—has more control over the means of agricultural production than an operator who rents some land or one who is a manager, tenant, or sharecropper. In this respect, the status of the black farmers in Virginia has likewise followed the national trend of shifting from a more equal representation of owners and tenants to a tenure system dominated by owners. For 1982 and 1992 the proportion of black farmers who were tenants in Virginia agriculture was less than 10 percent. Among black owners, 60 percent were full owners in 1982, compared with 63 percent in 1992.

Finally, regarding the sustainability of the blacks remaining in farming in Virginia, one-fourth (699) of the farmers in 1982 had sales of agricultural products totaling $10,000 or more. The average size of these farms was 185 acres, and the average cropland harvested was 120 acres for black-owned farms. By 1992, one-third of the black farms reported sales of $10,000 or more, the average size of these more successful farms was 228 acres, and the average cropland harvested by black owners remained at 120 acres. Despite an overall market value of agricultural products from black farms in Virginia in 1992 of $24.9 million, this figure was actually less than the figure for black Virginia farms in 1930 ($27.1 million).

Since 1920, black farmers nationally have lost ground. According to the Department of Agriculture, there were 6,453,991 farms in the United States. In 1920 blacks owned 925,710 farms, 14 percent of the total, amounting to 50 million acres of the nation's farm land. In 1964 there were 3,157,857 farms, and blacks at that time owned 184,004 farms, 6 percent of the total. In 1992 there were 1,925,300 farms in the United States of which blacks owned only 18,816 farms, 1 percent of the total. Only 4,400 black farmers nationally had more than $10,000 in sales from farm produce.

SELECTED BIBLIOGRAPHY: "Black Farmers Say They've Been Cheated: Agriculture Dept. Accused of Bias in Providing Funds," *USA Today*, January 5, 1999, 9A; James Brovard, "Farm Loans: Only Bad Risks Need Apply," *Wall Street Journal*, May 21,

1996; William Henry Brown, *The Education and Economic Development of the Negro in Virginia* (Charlottesville, VA: Suber-Arundale Company, 1923); Jo Ann Hickey, "Agriculture in Virginia, 1930–1978: The Effect of Structural Change on Blacks" (master's thesis, George Mason University, 1983); Jessie Carney Smith and Carroll Peterson, eds., *Historical Statistics on Black America*, vol. I, *Agriculture* (New York: Gale Research Inc., 1995); U.S. Commission on Civil Rights, *Report of the Equal Opportunity in Farm Programs: An Appraisal of Services Rendered by the U.S.D.A.* (Washington, DC: Government Printing Office, 1965); Ed Wiley III, "Entrepreneurial Scholars Tackle Black Agricultural Decline," *Black Issues in Higher Education* (June 1989).

Jo Ann S. Hickey

ALEXANDER, SADIE TANNER MOSSELL (1898–1989), Philadelphia, economist, lawyer, civil rights activist.

In 1921, Sadie Tanner Mossell Alexander, the second black woman Ph.D., was the first black woman in the United States to receive a Ph.D. in economics. She was awarded the doctorate in economics from the University of Pennsylvania for her dissertation "The Standard of Living among One Hundred Negro Migrant Families in Philadelphia." In this study, Mossell analyzed the incomes and expenditures of a group of migrant families to measure standards of living and "judge the degree of adaptation." Despite the outstanding research done by Sadie Tanner Mossell, confronted as she was by race and gender discrimination, she was unable to find employment in the economics profession in Philadelphia or in the surrounding areas. Even in some black colleges in the 1920s, black women faced barriers to employment at some of those colleges.

Mossell, whose minor was in insurance and actuarial science, however, found employment as an assistant actuary at the black-owned North Carolina Mutual Life Insurance Company* from 1921 to 1923. In 1924, she entered the University of Pennsylvania Law School, becoming the first African American woman to graduate in 1927 and the first black woman admitted to the Pennsylvania bar in the same year. During her career, Alexander distinguished herself as a lawyer in both the public and private sectors, working as assistant city solicitor in the City of Philadelphia in 1928–1930 and 1930–1934 and serving as a Truman appointee to the Committee on Human Rights, a Kennedy appointee to the Lawyer's Committee on Civil Rights, and the Carter-appointed chair of the White House Conference on Aging. She was also active as the secretary of the National Urban League* for 25 years, a member of the National Advisory Council of the American Civil Liberties Union, and the first national president of Delta Sigma Theta Sorority (the largest black woman's public service organization) and its legal adviser for 35 years.

Alexander's doctoral dissertation on migration is her sole contribution to the economics literature. Sadie married Raymond Alexander in 1923, a lawyer, Philadelphia city councilman (1951–1959), and Philadelphia Court of Common Pleas jurist. They had two daughters, Sadie's grandfather was a bishop in the African Methodist Episcopal Church, an uncle was noted artist Henry O. Tanner, and her aunt Hallie Tanner Johnson was a physician and founder of the nurse's school and hospital at Tuskegee Institute.

SELECTED BIBLIOGRAPHY: Paula Giddings, *In Search of Sisterhood: Delta Sigma Theta and the Challenge of the Black Sorority Movement* (New York: William Morrow, 1988); Julianne Malveaux, "Missed Opportunity: Sadie Tanner Mossell Alexander and the Economics Profession," *American Economic Review* 81 (May 1991): 307–310; Sadie Tanner Mossell, "The Standard of Living among One Hundred Negro Migrant Families in Philadelphia," *Annals of the American Academy of Social and Political Science* (November 1921).

Julianne Malveaux

AMOS, WALLACE, JR. (1936–   ), Los Angeles, cookie manufacturer.

Known as the man who glamorized the chocolate chip cookie, "Famous" Amos exploded on the scene in the late 1970s and reigned as the supreme cookie king until the mid-1980s. Amos's "superstar" cookies achieved what no other cookie had ever done: They became an American status symbol. Also, in 1980, Amos's trademark Hawaiian shirt and Panama hat were put on exhibit in the Business Americana Collection at the Smithsonian. According to *African-American Business Leaders: A Biographical Dictionary*, not only was this the first time an American food company was included in this exhibit, but Amos was the "first black businessman to be represented in the collection." Amos achieved supremacy as a cookie manufacturer through skillful promotion of his product, regarded as a status symbol by the Hollywood elite.

Wallace (Famous) Amos, Jr., was born in Tallahassee, Florida, to Ruby and Wallace Amos, Sr. After their divorce, when he was 12, Amos was sent to Washington Heights in New York City to live with his Aunt Della. It was in the home of Aunt Della that young Amos was introduced to the chocolate chip cookie, which would eventually contribute to his success. While Amos attended the Food Trade Vocational High School, with the hope of becoming a chef, he left after two years. In 1953, at the age of 17, he joined the air force. After serving his tour, Wallace Amos returned to New York, eventually working at the William Morris Talent Agency, where he was promoted from secretary to talent scout after "discovering" Simon and Garfunkel, who signed with the agency.

Subsequently, William Morris set up a Rock and Roll department and made Amos an agent within the division. While at the agency, Amos helped manage several artists, including the Temptations and Dionne Warwick, before he left on his own to manage entertainers and musicians independently in 1967. He eventually left this business. One of Wallace's good friends, Leroy Robinson, a writer and director, stated that "Wally found lying and indirect answers so often in this industry that it might have driven him to try something else." Disillusioned, Amos began baking cookies based on his Aunt Della's recipe, and subsequently, his show business connections and background in promotion provided the foundation for his phenomenal success. Recording artist Marvin Gaye, United Artists Record president Artie Mogull, and Helen Reddy and her husband Jeff Wald invested $25,000 as venture capital for Amos to start his cookie business.

Amos opened up his first store on Sunset Boulevard in March 1975. After the grand opening, with some 1,500 in attendance, primarily entertainers and the media, Amos's cookies business took off with a bang. Believing that promotion was the key in obtaining a successful business, Amos planned everything out very carefully. He presented himself as carefree, labeling the cover of his Famous Amos cookie boxes with his smiling face and wearing a Hawaiian print shirt and Panama hat. The most important factor that contributed to the success of his cookies, however, was Amos's association with Hollywood stars. It became a status symbol of elitism for them to purchase Famous Amos Chocolate Chip cookies, which enabled Amos to corner the cookie market from the late 1970s through the mid-1980s.

During that period, Wallace Amos's cookie business grew at a phenomenal rate, from $300,000 gross income in its first year in 1975 to $4 million in 1979 and $5 million in 1980. In this five-year period Amos opened stores in Los Angeles, Santa Monica, and four in Hawaii. Amos also had wholesale bakeries in Nutley, New Jersey, and Van Nuys, California, and his cookies were exclusively sold in top-rated department stores like Marshall Fields in Chicago, Neiman-Marcus in Houston, Burdines in Florida, and Macy's in San Francisco. Yet even though by 1985 the company had net sales of more than $10 million annually, the company was suffering from losses of $300,000 annually. While confronted with competition from two new cookie manufacturers, Mrs. Fields and David's, most of Amos's losses were due to the inefficiency of the day-to-day workings of the company.

Amos's carefree management hurt his cookie business. His interest was in using his new celebrity status to promote his cookies. Moreover, after he moved to Hawaii, Amos was rarely seen at his Los Angeles corporate headquarters, where he left management of his company in the hands of others, whom he later realized were not qualified to run his business. Faced with bankruptcy, Amos looked for additional financing and in the end had to sell the majority of his personal stock to outside investors to save the company. The new investors instituted stiff financial rules on the undisciplined company, and Amos, who maintained an 8 percent stock interest in the company, was no longer a factor in the decision-making process. Initially, he continued to promote his former company but eventually sold his remaining interest in Famous Amos Cookies.

In 1991, Amos launched a new company to make cookies under the name "Wally Amos Presents: Chip and Cookie." His company, however, was forced to close after 18 months because the owners of the Famous Amos company enjoined Wallace from using his own name and likeness. After a year in litigation, Amos was told, by a federal court, that he could not use the name "Famous Amos" in conjunction with cookies, food, beverages, or any restaurant franchise. Amos's concession was that he retained publicity rights. In 1994 Amos launched another cookie company by the name of the Uncle Noname Cookie Company. Amos commented, "There's a lot of wisdom and spirituality in the cookies." Amos began promoting his cookies, which included five varieties, nationwide. He also hired a professional management firm to secure the financial manners of his business.

Wallace, however, continued to use his celebrity to promote community advancement. He is an active board member of the Cities in Schools Program, a dropout prevention program. He also participates in the literacy movement and has been the national spokesman for Literacy Volunteers of America, hosting two television series to promote literacy. Amos summed up his unselfish attitude despite his ups and downs by stating, "I believe that giving is receiving, and that if life hands you a lemon, you turn it into lemonade."

SELECTED BIBLIOGRAPHY: Wally Amos, with Leroy Robinson, *The Famous Amos Story: The Face That Launched a Thousand Chips* (Garden City, NY: Doubleday, 1983); J. Gregory Clemons, "The King of Cookie Mountain," *Black Enterprise*, January 1981, 34; Bill Eppridge, "The Hot New Rich," *Time*, June 13, 1977, 80; Ron Harris, "For Famous Amos the Cookie Crumbles Just Right," *Ebony*, September 1979; John N. Ingham and Lynne B. Feldman, *African-American Business Leaders: A Biographical Dictionary* (Westport, CT: Greenwood Press, 1994).

Charles Gibson

ANTEBELLUM BALTIMORE, BLACK BUSINESS. On the eve of the Civil War, Baltimore's African American population numbered 25,680 free persons, the largest in the nation, and 2,218 slaves. As a border city with economic ties to both the North and the South, Baltimore was the chief labor market in the state. By the 1850s the economic picture began to change as the influx of immigrants into Baltimore led to labor competition within the semiskilled and unskilled occupations (hod carriers, carters, draymen, and caulkers) that had formerly been dominated by free black laborers. Unlike many of the native-born whites, the immigrants from Ireland and Germany, specifically, had no qualms about working at certain menial types of jobs. Frederick Douglass observed that "every hour sees the black man elbowed out of employment by some newly arrived immigrant whose hunger and color are thought to give him a better title to the place."

Throughout the decade of the 1850s free African American workers felt the economic squeeze of immigrant workers and fought as best they could to hold on to their positions as caulkers, draymen, and carters. Riots broke out among black and white workers at two brickyards on Federal Hill in 1858, causing one of the brickyards to close. Black caulkers at Fells Point also found themselves under attack as white workers sought to break the monopoly that they felt the black caulkers had over the shipyards. To make themselves more attractive to the shipyard owners the white caulkers agreed to work for $.50 less per day. A year later two additional incidents occurred between black and white workers, one at Fells Point, again involving caulkers, and the other at Camden Railway Station.

On several occasions petitions were sent to the state legislature proposing economic limitations on free blacks. An 1840 bill was introduced but never passed to ''prevent the employment of Negroes in the state tobacco warehouses in Baltimore,'' and a few years later, white mechanics petitioned that free blacks be ''kept from pursuing the mechanical branch of trade.'' Each of these incidents spoke to the growing competition between white immigrant workers and free African Americans. Although some free African Americans were forced to retreat from these competitive occupations, most were determined to work even harder and to parlay their skills and connections with white employers into a better life. Despite efforts to the contrary, the large free African American community in Baltimore generally prospered and in turn provided a market for a variety of small businesses.

Unlike Charleston and New Orleans, each of which boasted an affluent free African American business community, Baltimore's was thriving but modest. By the 1850s the Baltimore City Directory listed more than 30 occupations and businesses in which African Americans were involved. Among these were caterers, owners of ice cream parlors and barbershops, a cigar maker, a cabinetmaker/undertaker, a clothing store owner, the owner of a livery stable, and a dressmaker. John Jordan's success as a cabinetmaker led him to become one of two antebellum undertakers. By 1850 his business was well established, and he had stock on hand that consisted of 200 coffins of poplar, walnut, and pine valued at $1,600 and other personal property totaling $9,000.

One of the earliest businesses owned by an African American was the Union Blacking Shop advertised by Don Carlos Hall in the *Baltimore American* in 1809. The advertisement indicated that he had discovered a ''blacking process . . . not to be surpassed in North America. It preserved the leather which retained an indescribable gloss. Additionally, Hall stated that he had a superior varnish for both black and white shoes, a composition for boot tops, and every other article necessary for the accommodation of gentlemen's boots or ladies' shoes.'' The ad concluded that he had also invented a powder for cleaning plate that exceeded any offered to the public and encouraged interested persons to inquire relative to his service at his shop, which was located at No. 8 North Calvert Street.

Don Carlos Hall's business was successful, and he provided well for his wife and children. In his 1823 will he specified that the sum of $6,000 be invested in public stock and securities and the interest paid to his wife as long as she remained unmarried. His will also provided that his servant boy be placed out to a trade of his choice for a period of three years and at the end of that time he was to be released from all servitude to the Hall family. In 1833, Garrison Draper was listed as a cigar maker in Charles Varle's *View of Baltimore*. Although this was a rather unusual business for an African American, by 1850 Draper had invested over $1,200 in capital and employed two workers at $44 a year each. When he died in 1864 he had accumulated over $4,600 in stock and $2,500 in the Savings Bank of Baltimore. Peter Dode, a tailor by profession, operated a three-story brick clothing store on Pratt Street, where he employed seven persons. By 1850 Dode's merchandise was valued at $4,000.

African American barbers numbered among their ranks some of the city's most affluent citizens. Henry Jakes was both a successful caterer and barber. He opened his first barbershop in October 1839 and by 1846 had been successful enough to open a second shop. Ten years later his personal property was assessed at over $15,000. Thomas Green immigrated to Baltimore from the West Indies and operated a barbershop on Light Street in downtown Baltimore. By the 1850s, tax records indicate that Green was Baltimore's most affluent African American with 10 lots valued at over $17,000 in addition to his home and furnishings (listed as a two-story brick dwelling) valued at over $4,000.

By 1860, Baltimore's 10 African American barbers had businesses valued in excess of $50,000. In Baltimore, as in other cities, African Americans had greater opportunities to acquire both real and personal property. Eleven out of 12 free African Americans in Maryland, worth more than $1,000, lived in Baltimore. Between 1830 and 1860 there were 500 persons with property holdings from $500 to $1,000; 116 with holdings from $1,000 to $3,000; 25 with property from $3,000 to $5,000; 20 with property valued at over $5,000; and 10 with property over $10,000.

Although Baltimore's free black community felt the sting of repressive legislation and discrimination in occupations and education, they refused to be defined by what happened to them, preferring instead to build a community that would endure. From the early decades of the nineteenth century onward, the more economically advantaged free blacks helped to build institutions and organizations that provided the infrastructure necessary for their survival. Because their children could not attend the public schools of Baltimore even though the taxes that they paid helped to support these schools, private schools were established and operated within the churches and in private homes. Nelson Wells, for example, provided in his will that the sum of $7,000 should be used for the education of black children in Baltimore. Thomas Green, the affluent black barber, allowed a small group of Presbyterians to hold prayer meetings at his home until a building could be located; later he paid $300 of the $1,200 cost of the property.

On the eve of the Civil War, African Americans had formed over 35 beneficial societies, all of which had money on deposit in the Bank of Baltimore. The major church denominations also represented substantial investments in land and buildings. The survival of these institutions and organizations was due in no small measure to the hard work and perseverance of the African American businessmen and property owners who maintained a small but significant position in Baltimore's antebellum economic structure.

SELECTED BIBLIOGRAPHY: Ira Berlin, *Slaves without Masters: The Free Negro in the Ante-Bellum South* (New York: Oxford University Press, 1981); Ray Della, "An Analysis of Baltimore's Population in the 1850s," *Maryland Historical Magazine* (Spring 1973); Bettye J. Gardner, "The Ante-Bellum Black Community of Baltimore, 1800–1860" (Ph.D. diss., George Washington University, 1974).

Bettye J. Gardner

ANTEBELLUM CHARLESTON, BLACK BUSINESS. Both free and enslaved African Americans engaged in business enterprise in Charleston, South Carolina, where, until 1860, the black population exceeded the number of whites. Moreover, with the possible exception of New Orleans, blacks in Charleston, where they dominated many skilled trades, enjoyed greater business opportunity than elsewhere in the United States before the Civil War. In 1850, 63 percent of all employed free black males in Charleston were artisans, a figure exceeded only by New Orleans. That same year, Charleston African Americans had the highest average value of real estate holdings ($4,268) among free blacks in the United States. Black artisans did not require much capital to start their own businesses. They usually began businesses in workshops at their homes and plied trades that did not require a specific location, such as carpentry, bricklaying, and painting.

Also, a small free African American elite did own businesses in Charleston that competed with whites: wood dealers (Richard Dereef and Robert Howard), stable keeper and harness shop (Richard Holloway), planters (Thomas Bonneau and Richmond Kincloch), and builders (primarily as carpenters and bricklayers). Still, African Americans, slave and free, were more likely to be involved in providing services for white clientele in the areas of clothing and food preparation. In occupational lists, African Americans, however, are conspicuously absent as clerks, dealers in various goods, printers, and professionals such as physicians, lawyers, druggists, dentists, engineers, brokers, and bankers.

In Charleston, as in Louisiana, many of the free African American business owners were descendants of white settlers or immigrants from the Caribbean who came to the United States with financial resources and business experience. A small but influential number of business owners settled in Charleston and to a larger extent in New Orleans after the Haitian Revolution. These free men of color often came from slaveholding backgrounds and continued the practice in the United States. In 1790, there were only 586 free African Americans in Charleston, a figure that grew to 3,785 by 1860. Mulattos constituted about 25 percent of Charleston's population but only 5 percent of South Carolina's population.

Many free African Americans owned slaves. In South Carolina, Thomas Bonneau owned a plantation outside Charleston that was worked by three of his slaves. Free black businessmen in Charleston also used slaves in their businesses and as household servants. Thomas Small, a carpenter, used several slaves in his business, whereas Jacob and Samuel Weston used five slaves in their tailor shop. Thomas Inglis, one of Charleston's wealthiest free men of color, had a barbershop on one of the city's main streets. He speculated in slaves, purchasing them when the prices were low and selling them when the prices were high. He owned 15 slaves in 1820. When he died in 1835, Inglis left property valued at $36,662 including 10 slaves and four houses, plus stocks and bonds.

Moreover, while many southern states frowned upon or actually prohibited white women from owning businesses, there were no such restrictions against black women, who were more likely to have businesses as mantua makers, seamstresses, laundresses, and pastry cooks. The 1848 Charleston City census lists 16 free black women pastry cooks and only one white woman. Sally Seymour owned a pastry shop in Charleston. Several black women owned businesses as caterers, confectioners, and cooks. Eliza Seymour Lee enjoyed a reputation as one of the best cooks in the South. She and her husband, John Lee, operated Lee's Boarding House and later the Mansion House, which offered some of the best meals in town. The English actress Frances Kemble praised Eliza Lee for having the best lodgings in Charleston. When her sons settled in the North and encountered financial problems, they sold to the J. H. Heinz Company the rights to some of her recipes for pickling and preserving, which became part of the Heinz "57 Varieties."

Jehu Jones, a tailor, owned the most famous hotel in Charleston, the only place where the governor of South Carolina would stay on visits to the city. In 1816, Jones purchased the Burrows–Hall House for $13,000. Built in 1774, it was a 10-room brick house with a kitchen, carriage house, and stable as outbuildings. In 1832, Thomas Hamilton, an English traveler, lodged at Jones Inn and observed that every Englishman who visits Charleston should have his baggage directed to Jones Inn, where everything was well managed and the rooms were good. Jones also owned a hotel on Sullivan's Island, a resort frequented by Charleston's upper crust. He left an estate valued at more than $40,000.

Enslaved African Americans also participated in business activities. Marketing in food provisions and handicraft goods provided a basis for small-scale slave economic activities. Some urban slaves sold both produce from small garden plots that they cultivated for themselves and handicrafts made during evening hours and on weekends, as did some plantation slaves who brought their goods to the city for sale in its markets. Charleston was surrounded primarily by rice plantations, where slaves worked under the task system. Generally, they had more discretion over their time, since under the task system they were given a specific assignment in the fields to accomplish each day. Once finished, they were allowed to pursue their own activities, unlike the gang system where slaves labored together in the fields from sunup to sundown. The state placed restrictions on both enslaved and free African American economic activities by limiting the types of property they could own. Also, the state prohibited slaves from engaging in commerce for fear that the goods they sold were stolen from slaveholders. Free African Americans had to have licenses to sell some goods and could not own boats except as fishermen.

Some South Carolina slaveholders allowed their slaves to hire their own time* in Charleston. Such slaves agreed to pay their masters an agreed-upon sum and to take care of their own food, shelter, and clothing. Whatever was left after they met their obligation to the master was their own. Many of these slaves managed small businesses and acted as nominal or virtually free slaves. Anthony Weston* was one of the most resourceful virtually free slaves in the South. Charleston planter Plowden Weston allowed Anthony to hire his own time six months of the year. Anthony Weston was a millwright who built rice mills and repaired threshing machines. He invested his savings in real estate and speculated in buying and selling other slaves. He made his purchases in the name of his wife Maria, a free African American. By 1860, he was one of the wealthiest black men in South Carolina with real estate valued at $40,075.

Although many African American entrepreneurs found a business niche for themselves in Charleston, they still experienced racial discrimination. Thomas Bonneau operated a school for free colored children until the law of 1834 forbade free African American schools. Bonneau's school was large enough to require two assistants. Bonneau was also a founder of the Minors' Moralist Society established in 1803 with Richard Holloway and several other African American men to maintain and to educate free colored orphans. The organization grew to 50 patrons who pledged $5 to join and paid $.25 a month. In Charleston, Daniel Alexander Payne, who later became a bishop in the African Methodist Episcopal Church, attended the Minor's Moralist Society school until age 18, when he opened his own school in Charleston. His school enrolled 60 pupils at one point, but he, too, had to close his school after the 1834 law prohibited any free person of color from teaching either slaves or free African Americans how to read and write.

The economic status of Charleston's free black business elite provided the basis for the many self-help organizations founded by this group. In the eighteenth century, many prominent free African Americans belonged to St. Philip's Episcopal Church, where they were married and their children baptized but could not be buried in the church cemetery. To provide for decent burials, five prominent African American men formed the Brown Fellowship Society on November 1, 1790. The initiation fee was set at $50, and members paid monthly dues. Some of the funds were used to provide benefits to the sick at $1.50 a week during the period of incapacitation in addition to funds for funerals for a member who did not leave sufficient money in his estate for that purpose. Children of deceased members who could not afford an education were to be educated by the society until age 14. Indigent widows could receive annuities up to $60.

Until 1824, members could borrow money from the organization at twice the value of their collateral. This provision helped some members to start or to expand businesses. The Brown Fellowship Society purchased a burial plot and offered internment to both members and nonmembers who paid the necessary fees and could prove that they had been baptized. Members and their immediate families could be interred free. Others had to be subscribers or pay a fee of $10. For $4, the society would supply a horse, hearse, and pall for the funeral.

Several scholars have suggested that a rival mutual aid organization, the Humane Brotherhood, was organized in Charleston because the Brown Fellowship Society limited its membership to mulattoes or free African Americans of light complexion. Although there certainly were color, caste, and class distinctions among African Americans in Charleston, those lines were not as rigidly drawn

as in New Orleans. Although the Brown Fellowship Society supposedly consisted of free brown men and the Humane Brotherhood was allegedly made up
of free dark men, there were dark complexion and light complexion men in both
groups. The Humane Brotherhood also maintained a burial ground next to that
of the Brown Fellowship Society but separated by a fence. Members of the
Brown Fellowship Society were men of financial substance. They were generally
older and were more likely to be shopkeepers and small businessmen, whereas
their counterparts were primarily skilled artisans. Brown Fellowship Society men
were also fairly substantial slaveowners.

After the Denmark Vesey conspiracy, the size of free African American slave-
holdings began to decline. Also, even before the conspiracy was uncovered in
1822, South Carolina had taken measures to limit the growth of its free black
population. In 1820, the legislature outlawed manumission except by act of the
legislature and prohibited the immigration of free blacks into the state. Denmark
Vesey was a carpenter who won a state lottery in 1800, purchased his freedom,
and opened a carpenter shop. He belonged to the African Methodist Episcopal
Church in Charleston. State officials, who were concerned about the presence
of an independent black church, claimed that the conspiracy was hatched there.
The church, established in 1818 in Charleston, was seen as a threat to slavery.
The congregation grew rapidly to some 1,848 members, making it the second
largest African Methodist Episcopal Church in the United States. Its members
had ties to the parent church in Philadelphia, a city white Charlestonians saw
as a seedbed of abolitionism.

African American church members attended annual conferences in Philadelphia and invited northern black ministers to preach in Charleston. After the
Vesey plot, however, the African Methodist Episcopal Church was destroyed,
and not more than three African Americans, slave or free, could meet together
without the presence of a white person.

Prosperous African Americans were affected by the aftermath of the Vesey
conspiracy. Jehu Jones, Jr., also a tailor and innkeeper, traveled to New York
to visit a daughter who had not been allowed to return to South Carolina and
found that he also was forbidden from reentering the state. He had to sell his
property and remain exiled from his home state. Moses Irvine, a Charleston
shoemaker, purchased his wife and children in 1828 and petitioned the state
legislature for permission to free them. The legislature denied his appeal, although he later won the right for his family to inherit his property. In 1830, 407
free African Americans in Charleston owned 2,195 slaves, a figure that declined
to 137 free African American owners of only 544 slaves by 1860.

Although free African Americans in Charleston experienced greater difficulty
in owning slaves by 1860, they continued to prosper in their businesses. The
value of their property holdings increased. Speculation in land became more of
an avenue to secure and to maintain wealth. Some black property owners in
Charleston invested not only in real estate but in cattle and livestock. They also

held shares in the Charleston Planters and Mechanics Bank. It was their investments in real estate that sustained them after the Civil War, as the number of black artisans and small business owners who depended on white clientele declined.

SELECTED BIBLIOGRAPHY: Robert L. Harris, Jr., "Charleston's Free Afro-American Elite: The Brown Fellowship Society and the Humane Brotherhood," *South Carolina Historical Magazine* 82, 4 (October 1981): 289–310; Larry Koger, *Black Slaveowners: Free Black Slave Masters in South Carolina 1790–1860* (Jefferson, NC: McFarland & Co., 1985); Loren Schweninger, *Black Property Owners in the South, 1790–1915* (Urbana: University of Illinois Press, 1990).

Robert L. Harris, Jr.

ANTEBELLUM NEW ORLEANS, BLACK BUSINESS. From the founding of New Orleans, blacks were an integral part of the economy. In some respects the business of New Orleans was black business—from the auction of slaves to the black-owned establishments, New Orleans had the largest community of free people of color in the United States. First appearing in 1722, they were active and vital during the French and Spanish eras before Louisiana was acquired by the United States in the Louisiana Purchase of 1803. The French and Spanish laws governing African Americans—*Le Code Noir*, or Black Codes, and *Partidas Siete*—were more liberal than the American laws. During the French era, free people of color, or *gens de couleur libres*, and other people of African descent were observed as "competent, desperately needed and far from powerless," according to Gwendolyn Midlo Hall's *Africans in Colonial Louisiana*.

During Spanish rule, 1763–1803, the free people of color population boomed. In 1769 out of a total count of 1,700 people in New Orleans, there were 99 free people of color, or about 17.2 percent of the total population. By the end of Spanish rule in 1803, their numbers had increased to 1,355. They were engaged in numerous types of jobs, ranging from unskilled to skilled, and industrial to professional, and many acquired property. Among the free Negro men, asserts Robert C. Reinders, "the ratio of skilled to unskilled was considerably higher than among Irish and German immigrants."

Even after Louisiana came under control of the United States in 1803, free people of color continued to dominate certain skilled trades. By 1850, according to the director of the 1850 census, J.B.D. DeBow, there were 355 carpenters, 325 masons, 156 cigar makers, 92 shoemakers, 61 clerks, 52 merchants, 43 coopers, 41 barbers ("the birthright of the free Negro"), 39 carmen, and 28 painters. Skilled free women of color worked as seamstresses, hairdressers, and dressmakers and even had their own professional organization, the Societé des Artisans. An earlier record, the 1841–1842 register of 1,873 free people of color, was more precise in listing the numbers of those in business, including 176 listed as proprietors and 22 listed as manufacturers. There were also 22 who were listed as professional men and women, including 5 midwives, 3 professors,

2 musicians, 1 schoolteacher, 6 music teachers, 4 "sick nurses," and 1 minister. In addition, prominent physicians included Oscar Gumbillotte, Alexandre Chaumette, and Louis Charles Roundanez.

Several businesses in which free persons of color participated were not listed, including those who were commission brokers, such as Thomy Lafon and Honore Pottier. Also, several were moneylenders. Pierre A. D. Casenave had a thriving commission business in 1853 and in 1857 was worth an estimated $30,000 to $40,000, with an excellent credit rating. Several years later he opened an undertaking shop with a hearse, four carriages, and a cab and reportedly was "the grandest undertaker of funeral splendor in New Orleans." With an almost exclusively white clientele, he had assets of around $100,000. As with other businessmen, Casenave had been a benefactor of aid through the instrumentality and assistance of unusual white clientele and merchants.

One of the most noted free black business owners was Madame Céceé McCarty, who inherited $12,000 and by her death in 1845 had built it up to a business worth $155,000. Anchored by an import business in New Orleans, she had a depot outside New Orleans in Plaquemine and further south in the Attakapas country. One authority concludes that she had "unlimited credit" and had a sideline in note discounting. Although mostly small affairs, free men of color owned retail sale of groceries and liquors. Most grocers were not as well capitalized as Francis Snaer, A. Blandin, and G. N. Ducroix, "who were worth over $10,000." P. Le Blanc had a "prosperous dry goods store." The clothier industry had such tailors as Joseph Dumas, LeGoasters brothers (Philipe Aime and Erasme), Louis Boise, and Adolphe Lacroix. The latter was worth $150,000 while serving his selective clientele. Joseph Colvis and Joseph Dumas of Colvis & Dumas at 124 Chartres Street were prosperous. These two young men spent time in Louisiana and Paris, where Dumas "is believed to have been related to the French novelist Alexandre Dumas." Colvis's son Joseph later married Joseph Dumas's daughter Marguerite Dumas during Reconstruction, joining two powerful estates.

The business arena was less restrictive than the professions, and numerous free persons of color who were artists, poets, teachers, and authors also participated in business. In New Orleans, sculptors Eugene and Daniel Warbourg had a private studio for marble cutting tombs and statuary on St. Peter Street. Born in the 1820s to Daniel Warbourg, a wealthy German-Jewish real estate speculator, and his slave Marie Rose Blondeau, who he later freed, Eugene studied sculpture with French teachers. The poet Nicol Riquet was also a prosperous cigar maker and, significantly, the sugar industry was revolutionized by the inventor Robert Norbert Rillieux (1806–1894), son of the Frenchman Vincent Rillieux and free woman of color Constance Vivant. While he first worked as a blacksmith and later became an expert machinist, Rillieux invented the pan method of processing sugar.

Real estate ownership provided avenues for much of the business activities and wealth of the antebellum free persons of color. Drauzin Barthelemely

McCarty had holdings valued at $35,000, Philipe Amie LeGoaster (or Leguasterd) "owned $51,000 worth of taxable property in the Dryades-Perdido-South Rampart street area and other property worth $150,000"; Aristide Mary owned an entire city block on Canal and Old Levee street. Others who owned city blocks of property included: Adele Pavageau, Simon Bahan, J. V. Foneal, and Etienne Vanette, whereas Francois Lacroix had over $240,000 worth of real estate. By 1850, the free people of color of Louisiana comprised only 7 percent of the South's free black population, but they controlled 59 percent of the region's free black real estate holdings. A decade later, with the same proportion of the population, they still controlled 43 percent of the real estate, nearly five times the total of the next highest state. "A large percentage of these real estate holdings—44%—were owned by women." Many of these wealthy persons also owned slaves. Total property owned by free people of color was over $2 million.

There were many small businesses and businesspersons among the free people of color of New Orleans. Rosine Allain, native of Santo Domingo, maintained a rooming house in the Fourth Ward. At the age of 40 in 1860 she owned real estate valued at $2,500 and personal property at $6,000. Sarah Cook had personal property worth $4,000 and had a similar rooming house and was able to send the youngest of her six children to school. Other free colored persons whose net worth amounted from $3,000 to $20,000 included: J. B. Lanoise, who owned a fruit stand; B. LeBlanc, a wood dealer; Francois Victor, a tailor; Joseph Green, a drayman; N. Larose, a clerk; and Elizabeth Reid, a lodginghouse keeper. B. Rey and Terrence Le Blanc were listed as "capitalists" in the 1850 census.

Despite their success, free people of color in business in New Orleans faced increasing obstacles in all areas of their life under the American government. Even their church property and church congregations could be required to disband. In addition, the newspapers were critical of their presence. According to Robert Reinders, there were migrations to France in the 1830s, and in later years, interest in immigration to Africa and especially Haiti was widespread. In 1856, the state and city had passed laws preventing free blacks from obtaining liquor licenses, and three years later the legislature made it illegal for them to own a billiard hall or coffeehouse or retail store where liquor was sold.

In spite of the hostile environment in New Orleans, the free people of color who participated in business represented the wealthiest group of blacks in the South and indeed in the nation. By 1860, free blacks in New Orleans numbered 10, 939. Estimates on the amount of property on which they paid taxes have ranged from $2.2 million in 1850 to around $22 million. Many of the largest free black landholders were not listed by race, resulting in the undervaluing of real estate, slaves, stocks and bonds, and business property. The extensive antebellum business activities of free people of color declined after the Civil War.

SELECTED BIBLIOGRAPHY: John W. Blassingame, *Black New Orleans, 1860–1880* (Chicago: University of Chicago Press, 1973); Donald Edward Everett, "Free Persons of Color in New Orleans, 1803–1865" (Ph.D. diss., Tulane University, 1952); Gwendolyn Midlo Hall, *Africans in Colonial Louisiana: The Development of Afro-Creole Culture in the Eighteenth Century* (Baton Rouge: Louisiana State University Press, 1992); Robert C. Reinders, "The Free Negro in the New Orleans Economy, 1850–1860," *Louisiana History* 6, 3 (Summer 1965); H. E. Sterkx, *Antebellum Free Negro in Louisiana* (Rutherford, NJ: Fairleigh Dickinson University Press, 1972).

Charles Vincent

ANTITRUST REGULATIONS AND AFRICAN AMERICAN BUSINESS.

Antitrust law and even antitrust concepts have scarcely been used to help solve the problems of black business development, but there is evidence that these tools are being looked to as sources of potential remedies to overcome discriminatory barriers. In 1971, an attempt was made by the National Association for the Advancement of Colored People (NAACP) and others to block an attempted bank acquisition in California on grounds that the resulting combined entity would be anticompetitive. Wells Fargo Bank had moved to acquire a smaller but significant multibranch bank. Opponents asked the courts and regulators to require Wells Fargo to divest itself of a number of branches and to see that they were acquired by black and other investors, as a condition of approval of the merger. The attempted intervention was denied. Some years later, the Community Reinvestment Act (CRA) allowed, and perhaps even encouraged, community groups and civil rights organizations to act to delay or block bank mergers if they believed the result would lead to any decline in customer access to credit and financial services. The CRA also allowed the possibility that divestiture could be required as a price of completion of the transactions.

Some observers believe that an antitrust-based philosophy offers further creative possibilities in manufacturing and service industries broadly and that a creative theory could be developed successfully from existing law. Meanwhile, new legislation could extend antitrust philosophy to address what can be called *racial overconcentration*. Racial overconcentration is defined as existing whenever any race, in the aggregate, controls more than 95 percent of an industry's aggregate sales or assets. The concept rests on the perception that the American economy is broadly characterized by exclusion of African American businesses from significant participation in most industrial sectors. There are, therefore, overconcentrated industries in which white businesses control vastly disproportionate market and asset shares.

According to an antitrust-based analysis, this racial concentration must be viewed as creating a persistent monopoly by race. The largest 2,000 corporations are owned and controlled almost entirely by one racial group. This is a market situation in which one racial group "jointly possesses undue market power." As in classical antitrust legal theory, this concentration presents an exclusionary high barrier to entry to African American investors and business operators. Moreover, their prior absence tends to discourage subsequent entry and development at significant scale. This exclusion is contrary to the broad public interest in a diverse society like the United States. Enhanced competition and participation are desirable. Antitrust policy, however, can be used to create and maintain equal opportunity in economic activity at larger scale and inhibit exaggerated levels of economic power by whites in the aggregate relative to blacks.

The lack of African American ownership suggests inherent racial exclusion in the structure of markets. This inherent bias restricts black entry and participation. So the concept of monopoly is modified beyond its usual narrow meaning to address this problem. Monopoly impedes innovation, distorts prices, and restricts production, and racial monopoly does, too. But it appears to be difficult to apply existing law to address this kind of inherent structural racial exclusion, since it is difficult to show intent and culpable conduct—the usual standards. If racial monopoly is to be addressed, a new tool is required. That means that market structure, rather than conduct, would become the focus. The racial over-concentration, in and of itself, and apart from any conduct of decision makers, results in acceptable concentrations of social, economic, and political power and unacceptable opportunities for abuse. Public policy should curb that undue market power both individually and jointly possessed.

An antitrust proposal would address exclusion by requiring divestiture to African Americans, wherever practicable, which would structurally realign markets, whenever feasible, and also reduce the dominance of one race relative to the other. This would lead to an increase in competition and efficiency. The total absence of African American investors and businesses from any industry would be considered, on its face, to be proof of unfair exclusion by structure. Even if no intentional efforts to exclude were found, it would be concluded that market structure per se is the problem. In examining market structure, the Justice Department and the Federal Trade Commission would apply a measure of racial concentration and would encourage increased racial diversity wherever feasible.

The remedy of divestiture, then, would be applied to increase the level of participation by African Americans, thus reducing exclusionary barriers to entry. Title 2 of the Sherman Act would be amended to achieve these results. Negotiated divestiture would be the major instrument, so that whenever a merger is proposed, in any industry, a condition would be a sale of some going concern, product line, facility, division, or other independent unit to African Americans; if necessary, divestiture could also be facilitated by grants, by loans, by loan guarantees, or, in other ways, by federal subsidy.

SELECTED BIBLIOGRAPHY: Richard F. America, *Paying the Social Debt: What White America Owes Black America* (New York: Praeger, 1993); Eleanor M. Fox, Robert Pitofsky, and Harry First, eds., *Revitalizing Antitrust in its Second Century: Essays on Legal, Economic, and Political Policy* (New York: Quorum Books, 1991).

Richard F. America

ARCHITECTS. There are four periods of African American participation in the design and construction of the African American architect/builder in the

United States. The first three are slavery, the Jim Crow period, and the civil rights era; the fourth era of today is shaped by the unfulfilled promises of the civil rights era. In a very perverse way, the most active period of African American involvement in the design and building was during the period of slavery. African craftsmen-slaves were the primary builders of the South, usually under the strict control of a "master," yet often in the role of "supervisor-designer-builder." Based on their superior skills, freed slaves also were involved in much building of the North during this period. Slave narratives tell us that slave builders were so prolific, efficient, and established that many of the plantation and slave owners did not know how to build and had to be taught after slavery ended.

The end of slavery marked the beginning of the political effort to establish the Jim Crow laws. The Jim Crow era marked the end of the great African American participation in the designing and building of the American environment. Constituting a major shift from the free and abundant labor of the slave economy to the paid labor of postslavery, the Jim Crow economy discriminated against and marginalized newly freed black builders/designers. Despite their skill and experience, in the new "open" labor market, white labor, despite its inexperience and limited availability, was preferred. The strict segregation of this period limited opportunities in architecture and development to black community institutions and towns, especially for the new generation of black professionals who could not gain design or building commissions elsewhere.

Black churches and educational institutions not only constituted support and opportunities for the African American architect; they also emerged as the centers of African American intellectual development and political thought and action for these architects. The black colleges were the birthplaces of the new professional class as well as the highly articulated and prolific debates about the direction and leadership of the black community. Several black colleges taught architecture and building design to large numbers of African American students. These schools included Hampton Institute in Virginia, Tuskegee Institute in Alabama, Howard University in Washington, D.C., and Morgan State University in Baltimore. Tuskegee, along with the other schools, became a center of teaching and learning for the black building industry.

Robert R. Taylor, the first African American to receive a degree in architecture (Massachusetts Institute of Technology, 1892), worked for years teaching in the Department of Mechanical Industries and founded the first architecture division in the country to educate black students at Tuskegee Institute. There he educated many of the next generation of African American professional architects such as John Lankford, Wallace Rayfield, and Vertner Tandy, who became prominent church architects in the African American communities of Atlanta and Savannah.

The black churches, universities, businesses, and other organizations were essentially the sole client base, seeking a limited scope of building types for the small but emerging group of professional African American architects during the period that lasted from the late nineteenth century to the mid-twentieth century. There were certainly no opportunities for African American women to practice architecture anywhere during this period and virtually no work for the black architects in the larger society. There were a few exceptions, however, including Julian Abel, a graduate from the University of Pennsylvania in 1902, who designed much of Duke University and the Philadelphia Public Library while working for Horace Trumbauer and Associates. Paul R. Williams, also a noted exception, educated at the University of Southern California in the late 1910s, designed many homes for Hollywood stars and received numerous government and private commissions.

For the most part, however, the segregated environment of the larger society was reflected in the form of delivery of architectural services. Architecture was practiced within the isolation of the black community with black clients and black users. The black architect and builder had the skills and access to these special skills through the black colleges and from the tradition of building during slavery. This isolation produced adjustments in business practices, design process, and in more subtle ways, different theoretical and aesthetic considerations. This isolation and denial of participation of African American architects in the larger field of building clearly fostered an architecture that served the particular needs and aspirations of the black community, while not requiring the racist physical separation built into the Jim Crow aesthetic. Yet the architecture of the black community would rarely bring acceptance from the mainstream market.

The civil rights era brought about another shift in the evolution of the African American architect/builder. This period started during the 1950s, manifested major activism during the 1960s, and realized policies in the 1970s and 1980s. Numerous black architects were educated and gained access to the architecture profession as a result of the civil rights movement. Norma Sklarek became the first African American female architect and director of the American Institute of Architects (AIA) in California during this period. Harvey Gantt fought and won admission to Clemson as the first African American to attend that university. Taylor Culver was elected president of the American Institute of Architects Student Chapter (AIAS) in 1968. Robert Nash of Washington, D.C., was elected vice president of the AIA in 1970, becoming the first black architect to hold this national office. Several other examples of significant achievements of African American architects resulted from the civil rights movement. Although legal barriers to the active involvement of the African American architect in all segments of the profession and with all clients were lifted as a result of civil rights law, discriminatory practices existed, and hidden discriminatory practices are still part of the profession today. Census and research conducted by the University of Cincinnati established that there are approximately 1,200 registered African American architects in the United States, which represents approximately 1 percent of all registered architects. The same research identifies approximately 90 African American women registered architects, approximately one-tenth of 1 percent of all architects.

The main client base and building type for today's African American architect has shifted to the government and quasi-government institutions. The primary client base today for African American architects is the government, made possible by the gains of affirmative action policies in support of minority-owned businesses, recognizing past discrimination. Also, one of the major professional organizations that grew out of the climate of the affirmative action policies is the National Organization of Minority Architects (NOMA). NOMA's main function is to keep its membership of nearly 3,000 African American and other "minority" design professionals and approximately 1,500 architecture students informed of, and active in, current mainstream architecture issues, while networking and advocating issues important to African American and "minority" architectural practice and education.

NOMA grew out of the AIA during the 1971 American Institute of Architects National Convention in Detroit, Michigan. Several African American AIA members had become increasingly dissatisfied with the AIA and its lack of direct focus on the important urban design issues of the inner cities as well as those issues related to African American professionals in their practice. A caucus of architects, which included Wendell Campbell of Gary, Indiana, Harry Overstreet of San Francisco, California, Robert Coles of Buffalo, New York, Charles McAfee of Wichita, Kansas, Harold Williams of Los Angeles, California, and seven others, met to organize NOMA as a national professional organization to specifically address the concerns of African American and other minority architects. The founders of NOMA announced the following as one of its purposes: Careful thought, good design, and fresh ideas, multiplied by the strength of numbers and reinforced by the minority experience in this country, can and will contribute to the solution of the problems confronting our environment. Our concern is that this contribution not be restricted by past and current barriers to equal participation in the mainstream of national life. NOMA's specific goals are modeled, somewhat, after AIA goals and directions with a particular eye to advance African American and other minority architects and to examine the environmental health of African American neighborhoods.

SELECTED BIBLIOGRAPHY: Richard K. Dozier, "The Black Architectural Experience in America," in Jack Travis, ed., *African American Architects in Current Practice* (New York: Princeton Architectural Press, 1991); Bradford Grant, "Accommodation and Resistance: The Built Environment and the African American Experience," in Thomas Dutton and Lian H. Mann, eds., *Reconstructing Architecture* (Minneapolis: University of Minnesota Press, 1996); Bradford Grant and Dennis Mann, *Directory of African American Architects* (Cincinnati: University of Cincinnati Press, 1991; Addendum 1995); *NOMA News* 21, 1 (1991); John Michael Vlach, "Afro-Americans," in Dell Upton, ed., *American's Architectural Roots: Ethnic Groups That Built America* (Washington, D.C.: Preservation Press, 1986).

Bradford C. Grant

ASIAN/BLACK ENTREPRENEURSHIP, COMPARISON. Disadvantaged minorities often have high rates of self-employment and small business ownership. Because they face barriers to employment in the economic mainstream—due to low education, language difficulty, or pure discrimination—their members must create their own enterprises. This is Ivan Light's "disadvantage theory" of ethnic entrepreneurship. It provides a rationale for the comparative study of business enterprise among African Americans and Asian Americans. While these two ethnic groups have different cultures and histories, and thus are not directly comparable, both have experienced conditions that, according to disadvantage theory, would lead to high levels of entrepreneurship. Both groups are ethnic minorities. Both have suffered from discrimination. Despite these similarities, African Americans have a low level of entrepreneurship, whereas Asian Americans have a high level.

This disparity can be summarized with a few statistics calculated by William P. O'Hare. In 1987, the rate of business ownership among African Americans was 15 firms per 1,000 African Americans. For Asian Americans, it was 57 firms per 1,000 Asian Americans. Moreover, some Asian American groups had rates of business ownership that approached or exceeded the rates of whites (67 firms per 1,000 whites). These groups, and their rates of business ownership per 1,000 group members, were: Koreans, 102; Asian Indians, 76; Japanese, 66; and Chinese, 63.

Why do African Americans and Asian Americans have different patterns of entrepreneurship? Foremost, Asian Americans have greater levels of *ethnic resources*. Ethnic resources are the special cultural features of an ethnic group that can be utilized by the group's members to start businesses. Among the most widely cited ethnic resources are (1) kinship- and ethnicity-based social networks that are used to obtain credit, advice, labor, and patronage and (2) cultural institutions, such as rotating credit associations, which enable members of an ethnic group to raise the financial capital needed for business starts.

According to Light, prewar immigrants from China and Japan used their ethnic resources to create business enclaves, which, in turn, helped them advance economically, despite hostility from the larger society. In contrast, African Americans have lacked similar ethnic resources. As a result, their entrepreneurial efforts have been insufficient to overcome discrimination. Light attributed this dearth of ethnic resources to two things: the practice of slavery in the United States, which discouraged self-reliance and enterprise among the enslaved, and the social class schisms of African American communities, which hampered collective efforts to raise capital for cooperative entrepreneurial ventures. Light recognized that there has been a very old tradition of successful African American entrepreneurs in the United States, but he added that this tradition is one of successful individuals, not one of collective experience.

An alternative view is proposed by John Sibley Butler. In taking issue with the assertion that entrepreneurship among African Americans has been individualistic, he documents numerous examples of collective efforts by African Americans to found banks, mutual aid societies, and other self-help organizations. Through these efforts, he argued, African Americans developed business enclaves in Tulsa, Oklahoma, and Durham, North Carolina. Moreover, Butler maintains, the entrepreneurial patterns of African Americans, unlike those of other minorities, have been shaped mainly by racial segregation and blocked opportunities to do business with whites. He suggests that African American entrepreneurs were forced by racism to take an "economic detour," because their establishments were restricted by racism to African American communities, which, according to Butler, has been the reason why African Americans have lower rates of self-employment and small business ownership than other groups.

While Butler emphasizes that African Americans and Asian Americans have had unequal opportunities to exploit consumer markets beyond their own respective ethnic communities, he notes that African American entrepreneurs were kept out of the economic mainstream by racism. In contrast, Asian American entrepreneurs did not face the same restriction. In fact, Butler noted that whites were the main clients of the prewar Japanese American entrepreneurs. Yet since whites have refused to provide African Americans with services requiring intimate contact, within their racially segregated communities African American entrepreneurs have gravitated into personal services, such as barbering, beauty cultures, and undertaking. In these fields, African Americans have had "protected markets."

As late as the 1960s, businesses owned by African Americans were concentrated in these fields. Conversely, relatively few African American entrepreneurs have gone into the more lucrative areas of retailing and wholesaling. Even within African American communities, these fields have been dominated by foreign-born merchants—in the past, Italians and Jews, but since the 1970s, Asians and Middle Easterners. These immigrants are called "middleman minorities," for they serve as economic intermediaries between African American consumers and the manufacturing and wholesaling firms of whites. This middleman minority niche gives the middleman ethnic group an important commercial relationship with the more affluent majority group. For this reason, this niche has been a key factor in the ability of Asian Americans to use small businesses to advance economically. Lacking a middleman minority niche, many African American entrepreneurs have been limited to protected markets, serving a lower-income African American clientele.

African American entrepreneurs, unlike Asian American entrepreneurs, therefore, depend heavily upon the patronage of coethnic customers and on protected markets. For this reason, the relatively large and concentrated African American population is an ethnic resource for African American entrepreneurs. In large metropolitan areas, Robert Boyd found that both the likelihood of self-employment for African Americans and the earnings of self-employed African Americans were positively associated with the relative size of the African American population. The earnings of self-employed African Americans, furthermore, were positively associated with the residential segregation of the black population, unlike Asian American entrepreneurs.

A salient issue in recent studies of ethnic entrepreneurship is the relative importance of ethnic resources versus *class resources*. Class resources are endowments of human capital, such as education and work experience, and financial capital. These resources facilitate the success of minorities in small business, according to economist Timothy Bates. Thus, a question arises: Are Asian Americans more successful entrepreneurs because they have more class resources than do African Americans? In recent studies, the answer is yes. Bates found that high levels of human capital and financial capital, not ethnic resources, are the major factors in the entrepreneurial success of Asian Americans. For instance, the enterprises of Korean Americans last longer and are more profitable than those owned by African Americans, Bates concluded, because Korean Americans start their businesses with larger inputs of education and investment capital.

Interestingly, Bates also found that while the financial investments of Korean American entrepreneurs were much greater, African American entrepreneurs had higher sales and profits per dollar invested. Moreover, Boyd found that the disparity in the earnings of self-employed African Americans and Asian Americans was due mainly to group differences in levels of human capital—education, labor force experience, and hours worked. The rates of return to these human capital attributes were not significantly different for self-employed workers from the two groups. It appears, then, that while African American entrepreneurs have fewer class resources (i.e., less education and financial capital), they make the most of what they do have. These findings suggest the ethnic resources explanation of group differences in entrepreneurship may be more relevant to the prewar era studied by Light than to the present.

Yet there is evidence that ethnic resources are important. Assistance from family members, in particular, plays a significant role in entrepreneurship. According to Bates, the family members of Korean American entrepreneurs positively contributed to the survival of their businesses. This finding, however, was not observed for African American entrepreneurs. Similarly, I discovered that Asian Americans who were married and had children were more successful entrepreneurs than were Asian Americans in other types of family arrangements. The former were more likely to be self-employed and also earned more from self-employment. In contrast, family structure did not affect the self-employment or self-employment earnings of African Americans. Boyd also found that Asian American entrepreneurs were more likely to be assisted by unpaid family workers than were African American entrepreneurs. These findings suggest that differences in the use of family members in business may partly explain the dissimilar patterns of entrepreneurship among African Americans and Asian Americans.

In sum, the early Asian American entrepreneurs used their ethnic resources to occupy middleman minority niches and thereby establish commercial relationships with whites. In contrast, African American entrepreneurs were, during most of the twentieth century, confined mainly to racially segregated protected markets, serving a low-income African American clientele in the less profitable field of personal services. More recently, high levels of human capital and financial capital have helped Asian American entrepreneurs enter the economic mainstream and start larger, more profitable enterprises than they did in the past. African American entrepreneurs, then, have been disadvantaged in both class resources and access to the economic mainstream.

It follows, then, that disparities in entrepreneurship between African American and Asian American entrepreneurs might be reduced by two things: (1) by increases in the class resources of African American entrepreneurs and (2) by improvements in the access of African American entrepreneurs to the larger business world. Yet researchers should not overlook the apparently significant role of ethnic resources in entrepreneurship. An important topic for future study is the extent to which differences in ethnic resources—in particular, the involvement of family members in the business enterprise—may cause differences in the patterns of entrepreneurship among African Americans and Asian Americans.

SELECTED BIBLIOGRAPHY: Timothy Bates, ''An Analysis of Korean-Immigrant-Owned Small-Business Start-ups with Comparisons to African American and Nonminority-Owned Firms,'' *Urban Affairs Quarterly* 30 (December 1994); Timothy Bates, ''Social Resources Generated by Group Support Networks May Not Be Beneficial to Asian Immigrant–Owned Small Businesses,'' *Social Forces* 72 (March 1994); Robert L. Boyd, ''Black and Asian Self-Employment in Large Metropolitan Areas: A Comparative Analysis,'' *Social Problems* 37 (May 1990); Robert L. Boyd, ''Inequality in the Earnings of Self-Employed African and Asian Americans,'' *Sociological Perspectives* 34 (Winter 1991); John Sibley Butler, *Entrepreneurship and Self-Help among African Americans: A Reconsideration of Race and Economics* (Albany: State University of New York Press, 1991); Robert W. Farlie, *Ethnic and Racial Entrepreneurship: A Study of Historical and Contemporary Differences* (New York: Garland Publishing, 1996); Ivan H. Light, *Ethnic Enterprise in America: Business and Welfare among Chinese, Japanese, and Blacks* (Berkeley: University of California Press, 1972); William P. O'Hare, ''America's Minorities—The Demographics of Diversity,'' *Population Bulletin* (Washington, DC: Population Reference Bureau, 1992).

Robert L. Boyd

ATLANTA LIFE INSURANCE COMPANY—ALONZO FRANKLIN HERNDON (1858–1927), Georgia, entrepreneur, insurance company founder, barber, philanthropist, **AND NORRIS BUMSTEAD HERNDON** (1897–1977), Georgia, insurance executive, philanthropist.

The second leading and largest proprietary black-owned insurance company, Atlanta Life was established in 1905 by Alonzo Franklin Herndon. This enterprise, created with a capital investment of $5,000, served as an example of the inspiring efforts of African Americans to build and sustain financial organizations at the turn of the century. From its beginning as a small mutual aid association, Atlanta Life endured many obstacles caused by economic hardships and the racial spirit of the time. It successfully weathered bouts with epidemics, migration, depression, and wars and triumphed in the face of business reversals and upheavals in the industry. In spurts of expansion, the company grew until its territory included over a dozen states in the South and Midwest. As one of the significant black financial institutions to emerge in the twentieth century, the company represented important aspects of the perennial quest of African Americans to achieve economic equality.

In the early years the assets of Atlanta Life were quite small and the business operated in the category of a mutual assessment organization. Its policyholders, barely exceeding 25,000 in 1910, provided the majority of the revenue of the enterprise through premium payments and periodic assessments. The company offered one contract, an industrial health and accident policy, sometimes called "sick benefit," which provided a small death payment. Anxious to achieve a position of greater viability, the company in 1916 increased capitalization to $25,000 and became a stockholder enterprise. In contrast to the frailties of a mutual assessment organization, the stock corporation generated capital and offered greater potential for advancement and security. It was controlled by stockholders, and resources were obtained through the sale of stock. Its financial basis was strengthened also by the requirement of a higher amount of reserve capital. Approximately 90 percent of the stock sold by Atlanta Life in 1916 was purchased by the president, Alonzo Herndon.

A well-respected barber and rising entrepreneur, Herndon was born on June 26, 1858, in Walton County, Georgia, near Social Circle. He moved to Atlanta a few years after emancipation, where he operated several profitable barbershops and acquired a good deal of real estate, including several valuable parcels of land. The largest and best equipped of the barbershops was the famed Herndon Barbershop located in downtown Atlanta. It was outfitted elaborately with chandeliers and gold mirrors and fittings and, by many accounts, was one of the finest shops in the country. Herndon was immensely successful and respected as a barber, and his all-white clients included some of Atlanta's leading businessmen, politicians, planters, and preachers. His real estate holdings eventually included more than 100 lots, a large block of commercial property on Atlanta's renowned Auburn Avenue, and a large tract in Tavares, Florida. The profits from barbering and property acquisitions boosted his fortune over the years, and in 1905, he was able to deposit $5,000 in bonds and other securities acquired with his personal funds with the state of Georgia to secure the original charter for Atlanta Life and, in 1916, to increase the reserve capital to $25,000. By his death in 1927, Herndon was considered the wealthiest African American in Atlanta.

In promoting Atlanta Life, Alonzo Herndon joined the ranks of men and women whose efforts helped advance the ideals of self-help and race independence. He belonged to the group of black capitalists whose activities transformed mutual aid societies, church and secret societies, and other benevolent endeavors into more efficient secular operations. Influenced by Booker T. Washington* and others in the movement to expand black business involvement among African Americans, Herndon joined other black entrepreneurs like John Merrick and Samuel Rutherford in solidifying the new link between mutual aid and capitalism. Like many other African Americans of his day, he believed that greater economic consciousness and involvement would combat barriers against black opportunity and achievement in all areas.

Herndon's wealth and involvement in business ventures placed him among a group of progressive blacks in Atlanta with influence and power. In addition to Atlanta Life, he was an associate in several business ventures, including the Southview Cemetery Association (1885), the Atlanta Loan and Trust Company (1891), and the Atlanta State Savings Bank (1909). He assumed a good deal of social responsibility and maintained a vigorous philanthropic posture in the local community. He gave financial support to local institutions and charities such as the YMCA, the Leonard Street, Carrie Steele, and Diana Pace orphanages, and Atlanta University. In 1905, Herndon and his first wife, Atlanta University professor Adrienne McNeil Herndon, joined with Mrs. John Hope and other progressive black women in organizing the Gate City Free Kindergarten Association. The Herndons took a deep interest in the association and supported its work for 30 years. He was also a steady supporter of the aims and causes of Atlanta's First Congregational Church, of which he was a leading trustee and treasurer. Herndon was close to the church's pastor, the Reverend Henry Hugh Proctor, a pioneer in the development of innovative church programs to uplift and advance the black community, and he frequently augmented support of one or another of the church's causes through his private benevolence. And while much of his charity was known and applauded, a good deal of what he did in the way of philanthropy remained unknown by the public.

On the national level, between 1900 and 1905, Herndon met on several occasions with different groups to set agendas for the advancement of African Americans. In 1900, he was among the Atlanta delegates attending the founding meeting of the National Negro Business League.* He believed firmly in the doctrines espoused by League proponents and, in his own speeches, stressed the need for patronage and business cooperation among blacks. Herndon also responded to the call by W.E.B. Du Bois to selected black leaders throughout the country to organize the Niagara Movement. Demonstrating his concern for progress among blacks in areas other than economics, Herndon joined with representatives of the black "talented tenth" to found an organization promoting their liberation in political and social areas. He also joined black Georgians in a petition movement to foil the disfranchisement efforts of the Georgia legislature in 1907. His protest against the disfranchisement measure along with Judson W. Lyons and Henry W. Rucker, two of Georgia's leading black politicians, indicated his stature and influence in the community as well as his progressive position on voting and disfranchisement.

As president of Atlanta Life, Herndon was at the helm for more than 20 years. More than any other individual, he set the company on the way toward becoming one of the most successful black insurance firms in the country. After failing in several efforts to propel the company forward into new territory and sales and experiencing other reversals caused by external and internal problems, Atlanta Life in 1922 increased capitalization to $100,000 and became a legal reserve company. As a legal reserve company, authorized to write all classes of life insurance, it joined a select group among insurance companies owned by African Americans, which in 1922 included Mississippi Life, Standard Life, North Carolina Mutual,* and National Benefit Life. Over the next few years, an emphasis on growth prevailed as the company moved vigorously to expand its operations into several states, including Florida, Alabama, Tennessee, Kentucky, Missouri, Kansas, and Texas. In 1925, concluding 20 years of operations, Atlanta Life was one of the more significant black enterprises in the South. With over $19 million in insurance in force, the enterprise's share was approximately 13 percent of the total $141 million of insurance held by the eight leading black insurance companies in 1925.

Over the next decade, Atlanta Life developed a reputation for rescuing failing black enterprises and preserving black jobs. In the wake of several alarming developments in the black insurance industry, including the downfalls of Standard Life, National Benefit Life, Mississippi Life, and Victory Life, Atlanta Life reinsured several weaker black companies that were on the brink of failing. Solvent and sound during the critical depression period and in the face of weakening confidence in black business generally, Atlanta Life made a noble effort to lessen the impact of black business failures by underwriting policies and reducing the aggregate loss to policyholders. For Alonzo Herndon and other Atlanta Life officials, the burden of black entrepreneurs was twofold: to save failing black businesses whenever possible and to pressure newspapers, especially the black press, to keep failures out of the public eye.

The founder-president of Atlanta Life died in Atlanta at age 69. His large financial interest in the company was bequeathed to his second wife, Jessie Gillespie Herndon, and his son, Norris Bumstead. Keenly aware of the pitfall of many black enterprises that failed at the death of the founder or major benefactor, Herndon not only had prepared his son to step into the presidency but also had groomed a cadre of capable and loyal associates to carry the enterprise forward. Herndon's only child Norris was a graduate of Atlanta and Harvard Universities with a master's degree in business administration. The younger Herndon had spent many summer vacations working either in the home office under his father's supervision or in the field as an agent's apprentice. As he grew to adulthood he gained experience in various aspects of the enterprise, and after graduation from Harvard in 1921, he returned to Atlanta and assumed full-time employment with Atlanta Life.

Norris Bumstead Herndon officially assumed the reins of Atlanta Life after being elected as the second president in 1928. Over the next few years, as the depression severely tested their mettle, Herndon and his associates proved capable of guiding the firm through perilous periods. Stretching over a period of 45 years, Norris Herndon's leadership adhered closely to a strategy for business survival that included prudent investments, skillful and sensible management, and careful economies that permitted few frills. The territory covered by Atlanta Life increased from 9 to 11 states, assets grew to $57 million by 1960, and insurance in force increased to $176 million. The company acquired $1 million in capital stock in 1943 and doubled that figure again in 1948. In 1955 another stock increase pushed the amount to $4 million. Committed to continuing growth in this area, the company took another major step forward in 1962, when the board authorized increasing the capital stock by stages up to a maximum of $20 million.

A distinctive humanitarian and philanthropic influence also emanated from Norris Herndon. A predilection for privacy and a desire to preserve anonymity prevented his active participation in most causes or movements. He chose instead to make his participation quiet and unobtrusive. He continued the Herndon custom of giving financial support to local and national organizations, benefiting groups such as the National Association for the Advancement of Colored People (NAACP), National Urban League,* United Negro College Fund (UNCF), YMCA, Atlanta University, Morris Brown College, and the First Congregational Church. Important, too, was the social consciousness exemplified by the firm through the active leadership of some of its officers and other personnel. With Herndon's backing, Atlanta Life and its leadership were in a position to undergird civil rights and protest activities economically by promising employment to a fired teacher or posting bail for jailed students or providing meeting space and printing and communications facilities to groups and organizations.

In 1973, having established the Alonzo F. and Norris B. Herndon Foundation as a nonprofit corporation to which the majority block of Atlanta Life stock that he owned would be bequeathed at his death, Norris Herndon retired. The financial record of the company at his retirement showed $84.5 million in admitted assets and more than $346 million in insurance in force. Jesse Hill, Jr., University of Michigan graduate and company actuary, was elected president and chief executive officer. Hill's appointment and the formation of a new executive team signaled the first major change in Atlanta Life's administration since the 1920s, although Herndon remained as chairman of the Board of Trustees. Following Herndon's death in 1977, ownership of Atlanta Life shifted to the Herndon Foundation, and for the first time in its 72-year history, the company was not controlled directly by a member of the Herndon family.

Atlanta Life made a smooth transition under the new arrangement. It remained firmly in black control as the company approached 75 years of corporate existence. Over the next years, the firm recorded gains in every category, including assets in 1979 of more than $107 million and insurance in force of $980.5 million. In the 1980s the company continued to demonstrate financial growth, remaining the largest shareholder life insurance company controlled by African Americans in the nation. A new six-story, rose-hued marble and glass structure costing $10 million to construct and located on Atlanta's historic Auburn Avenue was dedicated as the new corporate headquarters in 1980. The agenda for the new era stressed efficient methods, attractive portfolios, new acquisitions, and new markets.

In 1993, the last year of Hill's presidency, company assets reached $163 million, with $3.2 billion in insurance in force, and premium income of $25.6 million. Hill retired the next year, and Atlanta Life underwent another executive change after 20 years. His replacement, Don M. Royster, Sr., served a short stint as president and was followed by Charles H. Cornelius. The newest executives, charged with overseeing Atlanta Life as it approached the ninety-fifth anniversary and the new millennium, were faced with increasing competition from white companies, rising expenses associated with technological change, declining confidence in black firms following several high-profile insolvencies, and increased policy cancellations caused by a high unemployment rate among black patrons. In these difficult times, as in others, the challenge for this firm was to maintain its standing as one of the nation's outstanding examples of black financial achievement.

SELECTED BIBLIOGRAPHY: Alexa Benson Henderson, "Alonzo F. Herndon and Black Insurance in Atlanta," *Atlanta Historical Bulletin* 21 (Spring 1977): 34–47; Alexa Benson Henderson, *Atlanta Life Insurance Company: Guardian of Black Economic Dignity* (Tuscaloosa: University of Alabama Press, 1990); John N. Ingham and Lynne B. Feldman, *African-American Business Leaders: A Biographical Dictionary* (Westport, CT: Greenwood Press, 1994); Merah Stevens Stuart, *An Economic Detour: A History of Insurance in the Life of American Negroes* (New York: Wendell Malliett and Company, 1940), 117–125.

Alexa Benson Henderson

ATLANTIC SLAVE TRADE PROFITS. The Atlantic slave trade, which had its origins in the mid-1400s and lasted to the mid-1800s, was one of the largest movements of mankind in world history. Between 1501, when the first Africans were transported across the Atlantic for enslavement, and 1885, when slavery was abolished in Brazil, "at least" 10 to 15 million Africans were landed in the Americas and the Caribbean. While a minimum 2 million died on the voyages, untold millions died on the continent, as a result of the trade. African slavery in the Americas, however, provided the foundation of the multiangular Atlantic trading system, which encouraged the exploitation of resources and creation of new societies in the Americas. It contributed to the accumulation of wealth in Europe and the United States, which provided a foundation for the rise of capitalism and the industrial revolution in the West and the subsequent colonization and the "underdevelopment of Africa."

The commerce in slaves or captives, however, could never have reached the scale that it did without a complex system of procurement, transport, and sale on the continent of Africa controlled by Africans. In his autobiography, Olaudah Equiano, who lived in Eastern Nigeria before he was captured for enslavement in the mid-eighteenth century, noted that raiding specifically for captives to sell into slavery had emerged. The 1700s marked the peak period of the Atlantic slave trade. Between 70,000 and 100,000 captives a year were shipped to the Americas. Throughout the period of the trade, less than 5 percent of all the slaves sold in the new world ended up in the United States; some 600,000 Africans landed in the United States between 1700 and 1808.

This commerce configurated the early development of the American economy. Cool climate and rocky soils limited the New England and mid-Atlantic colonies to small-scale farming, lumbering, fur trading, and fishing until the late 1600s, when the Royal African Company lost its monopoly charter on slave trading. Puritan and Quaker merchants in these colonies, who had already developed a fishing and shipbuilding culture, moved quickly into the business of transporting slaves. Between 1700 and 1776 shipyards in Boston, Salem, Providence, New Port, New York, and Philadelphia built over 1,000 ships, many designed specially to carry slaves. Thousands of carpenters, blacksmiths, boatwrights, lumberjacks, caulkers, sailmakers, leathersmiths, and teamsters depended on this industry for a living.

Despite the average loss of 20 percent of the transported captives, net profits from slave trading investment averaged returns of 50 to 100 percent for the various investors in the several facets of the Atlantic slave trading enterprise. Moreover, as early as 1726 the slave trade had contributed fundamentally to the structuring of the American economy into the commercial North and the agrarian South, the two sectors that would dominate the American political economy for the next 200 years. Merchants took their profits and organized banks and insurance firms. Others organized joint slave trading companies that employed lawyers, accountants, and clerks. Small American farmers and rum distillers to tavern keepers and ladies of the night in seaport towns all earned some or a large part of their livelihoods from the slave trade.

The wealth of the slave trade and slavery produced some of the great families, philanthropists, and civil and political leaders of Colonial America, from the Belchers, Pepperells, and Browns of New England, to the Galloways of Philadelphia, to the Washingtons, Jeffersons, and Byrds of Virginia. Wealth from the slave trade also contributed to the endowments of Harvard, Yale, Princeton, the College of William and Mary, and the University of Virginia.

Then, too, during the Revolutionary War era, while much has been said on how the Stamp and Tea Acts contributed to American independence, the conflicts between the American colonies and England over the lucrative slave trade and its impact on the Colonial American economy are not usually emphasized. The Sugar Act of 1764 was designed to end the long-standing but illegal trade of sugar and slaves to the French West Indies. Both James Otis and the Massachusetts Trade and Fisheries Association noted that it would lead to massive unemployment not only among the seamen but also among those who worked in trades allied with the shipping industry, coopers, tanners, and ship carpenters. Even farmers would lose out when denied access to the Atlantic trade. England's efforts to enforce the Sugar Act and regulate the slave trade were as important as the Stamp and Tea Acts, among events that precipitated the American Revolution.

With independence from England achieved in 1783, there was a sharp but short rise in the slave trade to the United States, especially after the invention of the cotton gin in 1793. In 1807 Congress voted to end American participation in the transatlantic slave trade, although W.E.B. Du Bois in his classic study on the slave trade estimated that 200,000 slaves were smuggled into the United States from 1808 to 1865. Also, a very significant part of the profits accumulated in the eighteenth century from the Atlantic slave trade was invested in the emerging New England factory system that funded the industrial revolution. Eventually, it would be proponents of the industrial culture of the North in opposition to the attempts by the South to expand slavery into the western territories, contrary to the interest of free white labor, that ultimately led to the Civil War (1861–1865) and the end of slavery.

SELECTED BIBLIOGRAPHY: Ronald Bailey, " 'Out of Sight, Out of Mind': The Struggle of African American Intellectuals Against the Invisibility of the Slavery Trade in World Economic History," in Thomas D. Boston, ed., *A Different Vision: Race and Public Policy* (London: Routledge, 1997); Jay Coughtry, *The Notorious Triangle: Rhode Island and the Slave Trade, 1700–1807* (Philadelphia: Temple University Press, 1981); Philip Curtin, *The Atlantic Slave Trade* (Madison: University of Wisconsin Press, 1969); William Darity, Jr., "Mercantilism, Slavery, and the Industrial Revolution," *Research in Political Economy* 5 (1982); W.E.B. Du Bois, *Suppression of the African Slave Trade to the U.S.A. 1638–1870* (New York: Russell & Russell, 1965); Museum of Slavery in the Atlantic, available from: http://www.squash.la.psu.edu/smuseum/homepage.html; Kevin Shillington, *History of Africa* (New York: Macmillan, 1993); Eric Williams, *Capitalism and Slavery* (Chapel Hill: University of North Carolina Press, 1944).

Gary J. Hunter

AUTO DEALERS. The automobile industry, owing to U.S. domination in the first half of the twentieth century, had profound implications for the history of this century. Through mass production techniques, the industry spurred the technological advances of the twentieth century. The coincidental emergence of the large-scaled business organization made it possible for the automotive industry to afford the heavy investment into plants and tooling that mass production required. These two factors caused the virtual disappearance of the small independent producers. The mass production of the automotive industry was indicative of the mass consumption by Americans of automobiles. In 1940, there were 27 million passenger automobiles. By 1960, that number had increased by nearly 230 percent, to 62 million. Out of every consumer dollar spent for travel in 1968, $.93 went for the purchase and upkeep of automobiles.

In the United States, restricted franchise dealerships were awarded to selected applicants. In return for the award of the franchise and a guarantee of sales territory, the recipient dealer must sell only the cars specified by the manufacturer and must pay cash on delivery. The manufacturer may give the dealer some financial or advertising assistance. In the United States, this form of distribution by the automotive industry caused General Motors (GM), Ford, and Chrysler to be among the top 20 on the list of *Fortune* Global 500 Industrials. The advertising, as well as the awarding of franchising, was up to the discretion of the manufacturer. For example, in the 1950s, although African Americans were buying vehicles, John H. Johnson* of Johnson Publishing Company could not obtain an advertising account from Chrysler until 1954. During a 10-year period, he sent a salesman to the Chrysler headquarters in Detroit every week in an attempt to persuade the automaker to advertise in *Ebony*. Although Ed Davis was the first black-owned car dealership, granted a franchise by Chrysler, auto dealerships from the three auto manufacturers were still hard to come by for African Americans.

It was not until 1967 that General Motors granted a dealership to Albert W. Johnson, the first African American to be granted a dealership by that company. Johnson was born in 1923 in East St. Louis, Illinois and attended the University of Illinois at Urbana-Champaign, where he graduated in 1943 with a B.S. in business. After receiving a graduate degree in hospital administration from Northwestern University, he became regional director at United Public Works. Later, he took a position as an administrative assistant to the administrator at Homer Phillips Hospital in St. Louis, Missouri. Johnson started selling cars in 1953 on a commission of $25 for each paying customer he brought into the Buick dealership from which he had bought an automobile. He realized that he could make more money from moonlighting as an automobile salesman than he was making at his $12,000-a-year position with the hospital, of which his father, a prominent East St. Louis physician, was one of the founders.

Johnson sold cars through a dealer in Kirkwood, Illinois. Since African Americans were denied the right to work on showroom floors, he was forced to sell the automobiles from the Olds Fact Book. After earning enough money to leave the position at the hospital, Johnson pursued a dealership. With the civil rights movement, black civic leaders urged General Motors to grant dealerships to blacks. Johnson was eventually granted an Oldsmobile dealership. General Motors realized that it needed to show support for minority economic development. The best way to accomplish this task was to start an initiative of establishing black-owned dealerships. Johnson was granted a failing dealership in Chicago. His lack of knowledge on how to run a dealership became apparent. General Motors had loaned Johnson $355,000, while First National Bank loaned him $250,000 for the real estate. On October 1, 1967, the dealership opened, but by April 1, 1968, failure seemed imminent. The problem, Johnson stated, was "Negroes had never spent this kind of money with their own people before, and they were scared."

He sought assistance from another Oldsmobile dealer, John Watson, a nearby competitor. John Watson and four other dealers met with Johnson weekly for four months. By the third month, Al Johnson, Inc., was showing a marginal profit. Within three years his net profit before taxes was $142,405. In 1971, Johnson sold his Oldsmobile dealership to another black entrepreneur. He then purchased a Cadillac dealership, partially financed through General Motors, which he paid off in nine months. Hence, Johnson became the first African American to *own* a General Motors dealership.

Chiefly due to the efforts and experiences of Albert Johnson, General Motors developed an official training program for their new dealers who did not have prior experience in the business. In 1972, along with a sales training and management development firm, General Motors started the training program for its prospective dealers. After several months of research into the problem of failing minority dealerships, General Motors determined that the problem stemmed from mistakes in selection of dealers and the location of dealerships, as well as the insufficient amount of management assistance.

Moreover, from the mid- to late 1970s, many dealerships felt the effects of the energy crisis. In 1982 the recession claimed even more casualties in the automobile industry. It was during the early 1980s that Johnson decided to capitalize on the emerging market for the smaller, more fuel-efficient foreign cars. He was politely refused a franchise from Japanese automakers but was granted a dealership from the Swedish car company, Saab, in 1981, the first black dealership for this company. By 1987, his Cadillac dealership was suffering, but the combined sales of Johnson Cadillac-Saab was $21.4 million, making him the seventy-first highest in revenue on the *Black Enterprise* (*BE*) list of the top 100.

While the influx of foreign cars caused many auto dealerships to go out of business, Albert Johnson, however, saw it as an opportunity to make another step forward. The 1990s, unfortunately, brought an end to several companies who had been on the *BE* 100 list every year since its inception. Al Johnson Cadillac-Avanti-Saab, Inc., was one of them. He sold his company back to General Motors in 1994.

The encroachment of foreign cars on the automobile market in the 1980s caused the entire U.S. automobile industry to be concerned with its survival. General Motors, Ford, and Chrysler were much too concerned with their own survival to be of any real help to their dealerships. It was at this point in time that automobile dealers from across the nation went to Washington, D.C., to address Congress. They wanted Congress to evaluate the problem and develop solutions to the onslaught of foreign car imports. Congress, however, stated that individual ethnic groups seeking the same solution could not be handled separately.

Consequently, an organization, the National Association of Minority Automobile Dealers (NAMAD), was formed, with membership from all of the minority automobile dealerships. Its first mission was to develop a direct loan program with the U.S. Department of Commerce and the Small Business Administration. NAMAD's objectives were to increase the number of minority dealers, locate them in modern facilities within viable markets, and establish a network of communication to assist the ''Big Three'' in making available dealer development programs, which would increase the quality and quantity of minority dealerships. There are now substantially more such dealerships than there were in 1980 due to the advocacy of NAMAD.

During the same year that Albert Johnson was ranked seventy-first, there was another black-owned dealership who ranked fourteenth in the *BE* 100. Dick Gidron Cadillac and Ford, Inc., had gross sales of $46.5 million in 1986. By 1987, Richard D. Gidron was ranked fourth with gross sales of $57.5 million. Richard Gidron, born in 1938 in Chicago, was raised by his mother and grandmother, after the death of his father in 1952. He worked part-time as a car jockey for General Motors in 1958. He graduated in 1959 from Bryant Stratton College, with a degree in business. Gidron became the first black salesman for General Motors, when he started as a service salesman, a position he held for five years. In 1966 he became the first black new car salesman for Cadillac.

In 1967 Gidron was the top salesman for the country, having an income of $100,000. He held this honor for four consecutive years and in 1971 became assistant branch manager at this same Chicago dealership, whose clientele was approximately 75 percent white. He was soon promoted to general manager as a reward for his increasing sales, which was attributed to his ability to convert customer service accounts into new car buyers. In 1972 Gidron bought a dealership in the Bronx, which, owing to its central location, also served a racially and ethnically mixed clientele. It was purchased by Gidron for $650,000; he made a downpayment of $150,000. The remaining balance was financed by General Motors. By consolidating operations and emphasizing service, Gidron's dealership operated in the black from the beginning. He paid off his loan of more than $500,000 in 18 months.

As was true for other dealerships, Gidron's sales slumped in the late 1970s and early 1980s. He survived and in 1980 was ranked in the top 10 of the 1,600 Cadillac dealers in the United States. He had sales of $17 million in 1982. In 1983, Gidron paid $650,000 in cash for a Ford Motors dealership, which in 1982 sold only 395 cars and 166 trucks. In 1988, Ford sales numbers at that dealership had increased to 1,120 cars and 520 trucks. In 1989 Gidron, an employer of over 300 and the owner of four franchises, was named *BE*'s ''Auto Dealer of the Year.''

Yet Richard Gidron, after a 23-year term as a dealer of General Motor's automobiles, had his franchise abruptly taken away by General Motors. In 1996, GM, claiming that the franchise agreement was violated when the Internal Revenue Service placed a lien against the dealership, forcing its doors to close, notified Gidron that his dealership in the Bronx was turned over to another dealer. Gidron filed a lawsuit against General Motors, claiming that the automobile manufacturer did not offer him the same financing arrangements as that given to other dealerships.

The early 1990s proved not to be so prosperous for Richard Gidron, as the ''Big Three'' suffered from the depleted market for American-made cars. While Chrysler and Ford had shown a 25 percent increase in the percentage of automotive sales in relation to their gross sales in the period from 1989 through 1994, GM sales remained relatively the same. *BE*'s list for 1992 showed that many of the dealerships on its list had gross revenues at least 10 percent below the previous year's showing.

Out of the 13 auto dealerships on the original *BE* 100 list, there is only 1 that has appeared on every list since 1973, Conyers Riverside Ford. Nathan G. Conyers was the son of John Conyers, Sr., a man who worked on the assembly line of Chrysler. Nathan and his brother, John, Jr., were lawyers when Ford Motor Company started searching for potential dealerships to address the economic disenfranchisement of the predominantly black inner city of Detroit. The Conyers brothers were able and willing to put up the cash needed to start a dealership. The responsibility of the dealership was determined by a coin toss. Nathan Conyers assumed responsibility and by 1973 had a sales of $7.1 million, ranking them sixteenth on the *BE* 100. In 1997, his rank was lowered to thirty-fourth, but his sales had increased to $49.1 million.

Nathan Conyers, believing that one must give back to the community, has given back not only to the community that he serves but also to his employees. He has trained many of his former employees to become dealers, and this has culminated in the opening of 35 new dealerships by African Americans, many of them women. He has also trained his five children to take over the helm of his flourishing dealership. Conyers has stated that as black-owned businesses continue to grow and survive, the issue of succession is now of imminent concern. Nathan Conyers, who was named the "Dean of Auto Dealers" in the *Black Enterprise* June 1997 issue, admits that government support and promotion of minority businesses at the time he started were of great help to the establishment of his business.

Despite the limited and ever decreasing support now offered by government entities, Conyers feels that African Americans should continue to seek opportunities to become entrepreneurs. He states that there are four important components that will give any business a better chance of success. Location is primary in that it must be viable. Capitalization has always been important, even though getting competitive rates for black-owned businesses is as much a problem today as it was 25 years ago. This problem can be compounded if the location is not right for the chosen business. The third component is understanding the chosen business. Conyers emphasizes that too many dealers have gone into the business after leaving a training program but not understanding or knowing the community in which it is located. This influences the last component of commitment: Business owners must become committed to being a part of the community that they serve.

SELECTED BIBLIOGRAPHY: Derek T. Dingle, "Pursuing a Strategic Vision," *Black Enterprise* (June 1997); Joslyn DiPasalegne, "NAMAD: A History of Survival," available from http://www.usbol.com/ctjournal/NAMADcnfl.html; Alfred Edmond, Jr., "Milestones of the BE 100s," *Black Enterprise* (June 1997): 86–102; John N. Ingham and Lynne B. Feldman, *African-American Business Leaders: A Biographical Dictionary* (Westport, CT: Greenwood, 1994), 280–286, 351–356; Patrick J. Spain and James R.

Talbot, eds., *Hoover's Handbook of American Business: Profiles of Major U.S. Companies*, vol. 1, *Companies A–L* (Austin, TX: Reference Press, Inc., 1995); Margaret Whigham-Desir, "Marathon Men—Auto Dealer Who Made Every List of BE 100s," *Black Enterprise* (June 1997).

Alcarcilus Shelton-Boodram

AUTOMOBILE, PATTERSON-GREENFIELD. The Patterson-Greenfield, manufactured in 1916, was the first and only car made by a black automaker. Frederick Douglass Patterson (1871–1932), son of Charles Patterson (1833–1910), who founded the company, designed and manufactured the company's two models: a roadster and a four-door touring car, both priced at $850. The *Standard Catalog* states that Frederick "may have built his first car as early as 1902." The description provided in the company's sales bulletin indicated that the company manufactured two models, a roadster and a touring car. Its engine was a 30-horsepower from Continental with the following special features: "Full floating rear axel, Cantilever spring, Demountable rims, Left Hand Drive, Center Control, Electric Starting and Lighting System, One-man Top, Ventilating windshield."

The black-founded and -owned Greenfield, Ohio, Patterson, Sons and Company in Ohio was established in 1865 as the C. R. Patterson and Sons Carriage Company by slave-born Charles Patterson, a blacksmith by trade. By 1900 the company was manufacturing some 28 different buggy models, school wagons, surreys, and hearses. Its most popular model was the doctor's buggy. With almost 50 employees, the company was producing some 500 horse-drawn wagons and buggies annually, with earnings of $75,000 annually. When Charles died, his son Frederick took over the company as general manager.

By 1919 Patterson, however, had manufactured and sold only 30 cars, compared to the Detroit automakers' manufacturing facilities for mass production, where a car a minute was made, according to Henry Ford. After 1920, the company stopped making cars and began manufacturing truck bodies and also bus bodies for Ohio school buses and the Cincinnati municipal transportation system. It also had a contract with the Ford Motor Company. After Frederick's death, the company continued operations until it closed in 1938.

SELECTED BIBLIOGRAPHY: William Newton Hartshorn, *An Era of Progress and Promise* (Boston: Priscilla Publishing, 1910); Beverly Rae Kimes and Henry Austin Clark, Jr., *Standard Catalog of American Cars* (Iola, WI: Krause Publications, 1989); Reginald Larrie, "Forgotten Faces: Black Automaker among Early Trailblazers," *African Americans on Wheels* (Winter 1996): 1, 10, 11; George Reasons and Sam Patrick, *They Had a Dream*, vol. 3 (Los Angeles: Los Angeles Times Syndicate, 1971); Juliet E. K. Walker, *The History of Black Business in America: Capitalism, Race, Entrepreneurship* (New York: Macmillan/Prentice Hall International, 1998).

Juliet E. K. Walker

AUTO PARTS SUPPLY INDUSTRY, AFRICAN AMERICANS. The entry of African Americans into the auto parts supply industry can be attributed to the civil rights era and the activities of the 1960s. The events during that decade changed the climate of the country and created a public awareness in the eyes of the nation that minorities could no longer be ignored. In Detroit, the riots of 1967 and the subsequent Kerner Commission report brought to light the need to address the lack of economic opportunity in the African American community. During the riots, automotive executives at Ford, looking out over Detroit from the "glass house" office tower in the nearby suburb of Dearborn, could see the eastern horizon covered with smoke. A stark manifestation of the city's turmoil was the initial inspiration that moved the Big Three automakers to take a proactive role. So began the impetus to establish African American companies as parts suppliers to the industry. Qualified African Americans were sought and recruited to run the companies. Technical and management assistance was provided, and major automotive firms assisted in securing capital.

After the riots of the 1960s, many government officials and African American activists began to recognize that achieving true social equality and civil rights must be based on increasing economic power. In 1968, Ford Motor Company was unable to find any minority suppliers with which to do business. By 1972 Ford had contracts with 170 minority suppliers, resulting in $8.6 million in revenues. Although Ford's minority purchasing represented less than 1 percent of total purchases for that year ($9 billion with 25,000 different suppliers), this initial commitment to minority firms was a positive step in the right direction.

Renmuth, Inc., typifies the experience of many African American automobile parts suppliers during those early days. Started in 1969 by two African American Ford employees, Renmuth was one of the earliest African American stamping plants. The company, like many of the initial African American automobile parts suppliers, was established with a great deal of support from a *Fortune* 500 corporation. Renmuth was sponsored by Ford with loans from private lending institutions, the U.S. Small Business Administration, and several other financing programs. Such arrangements were routinely developed during those days to assist African Americans and other minorities in establishing their own businesses.

Like many of the other minority parts suppliers, Renmuth was given initial commitments by the Big Three for business orders and was sent equipment and machinery on consignment. The company was able to succeed for many years, despite discouraging odds. As Robert Renfroe, Renmuth's chairman in 1974, said: "There were problems. We did not have the expertise we now have. We did not have qualified people. We have now developed and trained qualified people and are in a better position to operate in a more professional manner." Despite a lack of formal business and manufacturing management training in their personnel ranks, African American automobile parts suppliers were still able to do well and post high earnings. Renmuth listed sales of over $3 million in 1973.

In the late 1970s and early 1980s, however, many African American automobile parts suppliers suffered badly owing to the economic downturns of the automotive industry. These minority firms, which were initially not well funded, were scarcely able to make the necessary adjustments for survival. Robert Renfroe elaborated during a 1974 crisis, "The problem that Renmuth has, like most small businesses, is lack of working capital, which means we have to pinch every penny. And if a good deal comes up—say in steel—we can't afford to go out and buy it for inventory." Despite the determination of the entrepreneurs and the programs established to provide them assistance, many post–civil rights era firms, including Renmuth, faded from existence, remembered as pioneers of the early days of African American involvement in the automobile supplier industry.

One of the more interesting developments of the past 20 years is that in the 1990s, the federal government began to attack and dismantle the assistance and set-aside programs it authored in the late 1960s and early 1970s. Federal courts have recently ruled against several prominority programs. One such initiative, the "Rule of Two" program, allowed federal contracts to be reserved for small disadvantaged businesses, when there were two or more such companies that were qualified and available. Also, there was a ruling pending from the Justice Department, requiring federal business programs to conform with the Adarand standards, which were established to eliminate race-oriented standards for purchasing programs. The new rule is likely to require a preponderance of evidence for a business entity to claim a socioeconomic disadvantage.

Despite the shift in policy, the African American automobile parts suppliers that survived have continued to do extremely well. Some 30 years after these programs began, the automakers are spending more with minority suppliers than ever. In 1992, General Motors purchased approximately $1.2 billion in goods and services from over 600 minority suppliers. In that same year, Ford Motor Company purchased over $1 billion, and Chrysler $500 million from minority suppliers. The future holds the potential for billions more dollars in revenue for African American firms poised to successfully compete. In 1996, General Motors awarded Chevis Products a $1 billion contract. This represented the largest purchase of goods from an African American–controlled automobile parts supplier in history. This award was made possible by Chevis's strategic minority/majority joint venture with Johnson Controls, a *Fortune* 500 company, in which Chevis retained control of the partnership.

In the past, automakers—particularly in the United States—sourced multiple suppliers for the same parts and forced them to compete on price. Recently, the increased importance of technology and quality in the automobile industry has forced automakers to change the way they relate to suppliers. In the future, automakers will work more closely with a few firms in the development of complete parts "modules" (such as a complete instrument panel) and smaller components parts. These new relationships, with their long-term orientation, will reward those supplier organizations that are flexible and reliable enough to meet the demands of the automakers.

In recent years, the Big Three have begun to rely less on the "old boy" networks of supplier relationships. This open door policy positions many African American–owned auto suppliers to reap economic success in the days ahead. Many of these companies have begun to diversify their product offerings and enter into partnerships with one another and majority-owned firms, such as the Chevis-Johnson Controls venture, to meet the automakers' needs. Another recent development in the industry has been with African American firms requesting that the federal government allow minority status for publicly traded companies that have at least 20 percent minority ownership. A favorable decision by the government would give minority firms greater access to capital through equity financing in addition to receiving the special benefits associated with minority status. The future also holds great promise for African American auto executives considering early retirement to take advantage of opportunities to purchase divisions that might be sold off or to acquire major automotive supplier companies already in existence.

The Big Three have begun to pressure their Tier One suppliers to use minority suppliers. In 1996 Chrysler made minority purchasing improvement part of its Pentastar supplier award program. Under the program, Tier One suppliers risk losing business with Chrysler by not scoring as well as their competitors in purchasing from minority suppliers. While the early years of African American–owned automotive parts suppliers were difficult and survival often tenuous, owing to the lack of technology, lack of capital, and lack of access to the total market, the new millennium offers new hope and opportunities for those companies well positioned in today's automotive supply base.

SELECTED BIBLIOGRAPHY: Richard J. Fosdick, "Minority Suppliers," *Automotive Industries*, July 1, 1974; Tim Keenan, "Minority Suppliers Are Rolling," *Wards Auto World* (July 1994): 38–40; April W. Kimley, "Minority Business Partnerships: A Successful Past and Promising Future," *Black Enterprise* (June 1997); Ralph Kisiel, "General Motors Seeks Revised Minority Ownership Rules," *Automotive News*, May 15, 1997.

William F. Pickard with the assistance of James A. Robinson, Ronald Rivers, and Marlo R. Jenkins

B

BALL, CHARLES (1780–?), South Carolina, slave.

Charles Ball was raised in Maryland and sold south to Georgia and South Carolina, where he participated in the informal economy developed by slaves. In South Carolina, Ball bartered goods, primarily fish and other food staples, with white traders. While a slave in South Carolina Ball worked in a fishery after each cotton season and became successful in illegally trading portions of his catch with riverboat captains. Ball's life reflects the hardships slaves endured and the initiative taken to improve their material well-being.

Ball spent his early adulthood in Maryland, where he farmed and worked in a Washington, D.C., shipyard. He was sold to a slave trader soon after marrying his first wife, Judah, and then sold again to a planter in South Carolina, where he successfully bartered goods. Sold again to an owner in Georgia, Ball escaped, perhaps in 1820, and made his way back to Maryland, where he married his second wife, Lucy, and farmed as a free black. Possibly in 1830 Ball was captured and returned to slavery, again in Georgia. He escaped and stowed away on a ship that took him to Philadelphia. Having lost track of his family who had been made slaves, Ball settled in Pennsylvania and recounted his life to a white lawyer named Isaac Fisher. Nothing is known about the end of his life, as he avoided attention for fear of being returned to slavery, where he was sold many times, removing him from his mother and, later, his two wives and children.

The economic activities of Ball are important for providing evidence of slave participation and activities in the South's informal economy, as well as the black market that also existed in which whites involved slaves in the trade of illegally obtained goods.

SELECTED BIBLIOGRAPHY: Charles Ball, *Fifty Years in Chains; or The Life of an American Slave* (New York: H. Dayton, 1859); John W. Blassingame, ed., *Slave Testimony: Two Centuries of Letters, Speeches, Interviews, and Autobiographies* (Baton Rouge: Louisiana State University Press, 1977).

David F. Herr

BANKING, CHICAGO COMMUNITY DEVELOPMENT BANKS AND COMMUNITY REINVESTMENT ACT (CRA). In 1908 Jesse Binga,* who became one of the wealthiest and most respected blacks in Chicago, established the Binga Bank, the first black commercial bank in Chicago. The Binga Bank, which emphasized real estate lending, became one of the most celebrated black business ventures in the nation and was considered a model for black banking success. Originally a private bank, it received a state charter in 1921. Then, in 1922, the Douglass National Bank, the first black national bank in Chicago, was opened by the wealthy entrepreneur and former slave Anthony Overton.* During the 1920s the Douglass Bank, which also specialized in real estate loans, provided healthy competition for the Binga Bank. In that decade, these two south-side institutions grew and prospered. The two banks accounted for over two-thirds of the nation's total deposits in black banks. They also provided the financial basis for Chicago blacks to become property holders.

During the Great Depression, one third of the nation's banks failed. In 1931 Binga Bank became the first Chicago bank to fail. After three major bank runs, the Douglass Bank stopped operations in 1932. After the depression there was little black banking activity in Chicago until the inception of Independence Bank, founded in 1964 by black millionaires Alvin Boutte, a chain drugstore owner, and George Johnson,* founder of Johnson Products, manufacturer of black hair care products. One year later, Seaway National Bank was founded by a black consortium of black businessmen, including real estate leader Dempsey Travis.* Subsequently, several black banks were created in the 1970s, Gateway National Bank, Guaranty Bank and Trust, Highland Community Bank, South Side Bank, Community Bank of Lawndale, and Washington National Bank.

Independence and Seaway competed for the position of the largest black bank in the nation. In 1979, Independence acquired the deposits of two insolvent black banks, Guaranty Bank and Trust and Gateway National. The following year Indecorp, a bank holding company, was formed to acquire Independence Bank. When Indecorp bought Drexel National Bank in 1988, it marked the first example of a black bank acquiring a financially healthy non–minority-owned bank, which established it as the largest black bank holding company in the nation. Seaway continued to expand. In 1993 it acquired another black bank, Highland

Community Bank, making it the nation's largest black commercial bank. In 1995, however, it was sold to the white Shorebank holding company, which had filed a merger application to acquire Indecorp Inc.

Indecorp had won praise for prospering by expanding into activities not normally pursued by black banks, such as foreign currency exchange, trust services, and underwriting municipal bonds. Nonetheless, it was also faulted for insufficient lending to its community. Highland Community Bank received similar criticisms before it was acquired by Seaway. While some are more optimistic about their potential contribution, few contend that black banks, by themselves, can accomplish sufficient community development. The contribution of black banks in developing black communities such as in Chicago has been subject to ongoing controversy.

Particularly, black banks, like majority-owned banks, have been criticized for inadequate commitment to community development. Specifically, both black and white commercial banks have failed to provide credit to low- and moderate-income communities, thereby contributing to neighborhood deterioration. The Community Reinvestment Act (CRA)* of 1977 was one response by the federal government to bank neglect of black communities. The CRA directs commercial banks and savings and loan institutions (thrifts) to meet the credit needs of the local communities in which they were chartered in a safe and responsible manner. Regulatory agencies are charged with monitoring and evaluating bank and thrift compliance with the CRA. Financial institutions having unsatisfactory CRA ratings risk losing the regulatory approval necessary to establish new branches or engage in new activities. For example, in 1989 Hyde Park Bank and Trust's application to buy a thrift was rejected by the Federal Deposit Insurance Corporation for inadequate compliance with the CRA.

The CRA, then, has been credited for spurring banks to increase their inner-city activities. In 1984 First Chicago initiated a $100 million loan program for low- and moderate-income borrowers, which some believe was partially motivated to remove any possible CRA objections to First's acquisition of American National Bank and Trust Company. In the 1980s and 1990s, several major Chicago banks such as First Chicago, Harris Bankcorp, and Cole Taylor located facilities in low- and moderate-income urban areas. Also, Bank of America/ Continental pledged $1 billion in 1994 and First Chicago pledged $2 billion in 1995 for loans designated to low- and moderate-income neighborhoods.

Still, the CRA has generated substantial controversy, and some have called for its elimination. While community activists criticize it for lax enforcement, approximately 90 percent of all banks receive satisfactory ratings. Yet banks complain that the act is vague, arbitrary, and costly and requires excessive paperwork. Moreover, while critics charge that profitable lending opportunities have gone unfunded, to justify the paucity of their inner-city lending, banks have cited high-risk and low-return considerations. In searching for a remedy for America's decaying urban communities, increasing attention has been devoted to community development banks that specialize in economic development of low- and moderate-income communities.

South Shore Bank, established in 1972, the nation's first community development bank, is included among only 8 percent of banks that the Federal Deposit Insurance Corporation has given an "outstanding" Community Reinvestment Act rating. Shorebank (known until 1986 as the Illinois Neighborhood Development Corporation) owns South Shore Bank and has achieved international fame as the prototype for community reinvestment. The white-owned Shorebank, which has over $275 million in assets, is located in South Shore, a community of over 75,000 inhabitants, some nine miles south of downtown Chicago. In the decade of the 1960s, the community changed from being basically all white to being 70 percent African American. In the late 1990s, about 95 percent of the residents were African American. About 20 percent are on public assistance.

In the 1970s residential housing deteriorated, some apartment buildings were abandoned, and many businesses and financial institutions moved on. In 1972, the last remaining bank, South Shore National Bank, requested approval to move downtown, but the Office of the Comptroller of the Currency, in the wake of community protests and opposition from a downtown bank fearing new competition, denied the request on December 5, 1972. Later in August 1973, South Shore Bank was purchased by Shorebank, the brainchild of Ronald Grzywinski, a banker who raised funds from churches, charities, and socially oriented investors. He assembled a four-person management team that previously worked together at Hyde Park Bank and Trust lending to minority small businesses.

Shorebank's primary goals were to transform the deteriorating South Shore area and to improve the declining profit performance of the bank. Inner-city banks are reputed to channel deposit funds from their low- and moderate-income neighborhoods into loans for more affluent communities. In contrast, South Shore Bank raises funds from relatively affluent outside sources and lends strictly to its community. Over half of the bank's deposits are development deposits that come from outside the community, from 50 states and 17 countries. Shorebank's equity shares are not tradable and do not pay dividends. Shareholders include 37 corporations, various foundations, churches, and wealthy individuals.

Although South Shore Bank finances more minority-owned business—primarily small, undercapitalized ventures—than any other bank in Chicago, commercial lending has not been as successful as expected. Instead, the bank's major success has come through mortgage lending to finance multifamily housing. Currently over half of its loan portfolio is comprised of real estate loans. Shorebank has invested almost $300 million in South Shore in the last 20 years and has spearheaded the community's resurgence by assisting in the rehabilitation of one third of its housing units. It has financed or assisted in the renovation of 12,000 housing units and more than 7,700 apartments. Also, Shorebank has encouraged the growth of housing entrepreneurs and has initiated and nurtured other development projects.

The bank's strategy for success incorporates several principles. First, although the bank is flexible in working with borrowers, it adheres to conservative banking practices such as rigorous underwriting standards and stringent collection procedures. It has experienced relatively few bad loans and has been profitable every year since 1975. Furthermore, to concentrate resources on a limited area, Shorebank confines its lending to five neighborhoods in South Shore. It found that rehabilitating key buildings encourages reclamation of nearby buildings. Finally, Shorebank emphasizes that revitalization requires not only increased bank lending but also the establishment of a bank holding company to coordinate banks and several development subsidiaries in its multipronged attack on a deteriorating community.

Among its current subsidiaries is City Lands Corporation, a real estate development company that develops and manages residential and commercial real estate for low- and moderate-income residents. An affiliate, the nonprofit Neighborhood Institute, seeks out government, foundation, and other development funds to operate economic and social development programs for low-income residents. The Neighborhood Institute has a for-profit subsidiary, the Development Corporation, that develops rental and cooperative housing for low-income residents. Because City Lands and the Neighborhood Institute are separately capitalized, they can enter a neighborhood and rehabilitate several strategic buildings. Surrounding smaller properties may then be purchased and rehabilitated by residents with bank financing. Shorebank also established The Neighborhood Fund, a Small Business Association–licensed investment corporation that finances small businesses, and Shorebank Advisory Services, a consulting firm for providing technical assistance on community development banking.

Shorebank believes that its model of development can be applied selectively to other inner-city communities having sufficient promise of economic viability. In February 1987, after extensive research, South Shore opened a loan production office on the west side of Chicago in the community of Austin. Also, it has opened sites in rural Arkansas, the Upper Peninsula of Michigan, and Cleveland and was invited to revitalize the troubled and minority-owned Douglass Bank of Kansas City. In addition, it is training lenders to administer a small business loan fund in Poland. Shorebank, acknowledged by some as one of the nation's inner-city success stories of the last 25 years, served as a model for President Bill Clinton, who signed a bill in 1994 providing $382 million to assist community development banks.

Within Chicago's black community, although some welcomed the expansion of Shorebank to new neighborhoods, at the same time, some black community leaders and organizations protested its 1995 acquisition of Indecorp, Inc., since Shorebank is not minority owned. Furthermore, compared to Shorebank, several black Chicago banks have received less-than-satisfactory CRA evaluations. Black banks have charged that the CRA has impeded their economic performance. In response, the CRA was amended on May 4, 1995, to rely more heavily on performance-based, rather than process-based, criteria.

Black banks had been established, at least in part, to fill the vacuum created by the neglect of majority-owned banks. Yet black banks are constrained by inadequate size, unstable deposits, high loan losses, low loan-to-deposit ratios, and inexperienced management, so their potential contribution to black community development, when compared to white-owned banks, is extremely limited. The solution: outside support to raise funds, more deposits from governmental agencies and large corporations, and black bank mergers.

SELECTED BIBLIOGRAPHY: Andrew Brimmer, "The Black Banks: An Assessment of Performance and Prospects," *Journal of Finance* 26 (May 1971): 379–405; John Cole, Alfred Edwards, Earl Hamilton, and Lucy Reuben, "Black Banks: A Survey and Analysis of the Literature," *Review of Black Political Economy* (Summer 1985): 29–49; Ronald Grzywinski, "The New Old-Fashioned Banking," *Harvard Business Review* (May–June 1991): 87–98; Richard Taub, *Community Capitalism* (Boston: Harvard Business School Press, 1994).

Nicholas A. Lash

BANKING, MINORITY, 1865–1996. The history of black and other minority banking in the United States has been fraught with unique challenges and controversies since its inception. Led by official public policy, augmented by private banking industry mores that sought to inhibit black Americans from exercising the right to enter the banking industry, black Americans have had to endure many obstacles and barriers to their efforts to successfully function in this industry. This history of minority banking in the United States covers the period from 1865, when the first bank was organized in behalf of former slaves, to the end of 1996, a period of 131 years. This era encompasses several periods characterized by different levels of growth and survival, driven by the environmental forces that affected the development of black and other minority banks, in the context of what was driving the total industry. Included in this analysis are the numerous minority banks that were chartered; those that failed; the assets, income, and expense management strategies and experience of these banks; and the challenges they face that differ from the rest of the banking industry.

Black banking originated immediately following the Civil War. Unclaimed funds in special military savings banks that were created to encourage thrift among black Union soldiers were used to create a savings bank for the newly freed slaves. This institution, named the Freedman's Savings and Trust Company (see Freedman's Bank*), was created by an act of the U.S. Congress, and the legislation was signed into law by President Abraham Lincoln on March 3, 1865. Headquartered initially in New York City, later, Washington, D.C., the Freedman's Bank functioned as a philanthropic, venture capital institution that clearly defied the wisdom of sound commercial banking. Given this operating philosophy, this bank was destined to—and did, in fact—fail in 1874. The short-term nature of the deposit structure of commercial banks precludes their being able to serve as primary social lenders without stressing the creditworthiness of the borrower, nor can a commercial bank invest venture capital into an unproved business without appropriate collateral.

Since there were no experienced black bank executives in 1865, predictably, the management of the bank was white. The bank failed despite a valiant last-minute attempt by the eminent Frederick Douglass to save it by assuming the presidency and investing $10,000 of his personal funds. Congressional investigations revealed that the failure of the bank was due to the congressional revision of the bank's investment policy in 1870, combined with mismanagement by dubious administrators.

Fourteen years, following the failure of the Freedman's Bank, the first black-owned bank was organized in 1888 in Richmond County, Virginia, by the United Order of True Reformers, a fraternal insurance company. After 20 years, the bank failed. Significantly, 134 black-controlled financial institutions termed *bank* were organized between 1888 and 1934, primarily by black fraternal organizations. The banks served as depositories for these organizations. Equally significant is that most of these banks failed. As will be shown later, however, this period of banking was considered precarious by any standard in American banking history, for numerous nonminority banks also failed.

For example, between 1921 and 1935, 318 banks were organized in Chicago alone. By the end of 1935, however, 263, or 83 percent, of these banks had failed. Similarly, Brunswick County, Virginia, exemplifying the rural situation, organized its first bank in 1890, and by 1921, there were 6, with 2 in towns with population under 400. Of the 9 banks established since 1890, 75 percent had failed by the end of 1933. Senator Carter Glass of Virginia, the most powerful congressional figure dealing with bank legislation, stated in congressional debate, "Little banks? Little corner grocery men who run banks, who get together $10,000 or $15,000 . . . and then invite the deposits of their community, and at the first gust of disaster, topple over and ruin their depositors!" He argued that "the lack of 'real bankers' had been an important factor in the wide spread failures of the banks." Testifying before Senator Glass's committee, the president of Chemical Bank of New York stated, "We had too many banks and too few bankers." For example, deposits had expanded by $18 billion between 1921 and 1930, only to decline by $19 billion in the next three years. Many bank failures resulted.

The number of banks reached approximately 30,000 during the decade of the 1920s, only to fall back to approximately half that number by the time of the Bank Moratorium that was declared by President Franklin Delano Roosevelt in 1933, a period during which banks were failing so fast that the president called a four-day closing of the banking industry while new bank regulations and the Federal Deposit Insurance Corporation (FDIC) were organized.

After the banking crisis ending 1933, there were only 9 black banks still in operation. There were no other minority group banks in existence at that time. Moreover, only two black state-chartered banks were organized during the 30 succeeding years, ending 1963—Memphis State Bank of Memphis, Tennessee, and Douglas State Bank of Kansas City, Kansas. Both opened for business in 1947. Significantly there were no nationally chartered black-controlled banks in existence in 1963, nor had there been any since 1922. At the end of 1962, there were only 10 black-controlled banks with an aggregate total of $77 million in assets.

Then came Riverside Bank. With $500,000 in capital and a 5,000-square-foot state-of-the-art facility, Riverside opened for business in 1964. At that time, Texas was one of nine Unit Bank states in the United States, which permitted only one site per bank, giving rise to pockets of opportunity in those states. Dr. Edward D. Irons was one of the founders of the Riverside Bank in Houston, Texas. Professor of Finance at Texas Southern University, Irons had recently received a doctorate from Harvard University in Finance and had moved to Houston for the purpose of organizing a bank. The opening of Riverside National Bank made national news when, generally, a bank opening is only local news. Businessmen and-women from 15 states attended. The senior black member of the U.S. House of Representatives from Michigan, Charles Diggs, made the keynote remarks, along with speeches by city leaders and bank regulators, including James Saxon, comptroller of the currency from Washington, D.C., the chief regulatory officer of national banks. His attendance was also unprecedented.

Moreover, before the end of 1964, 3 other black-controlled banks were opened. While only 4 black banks were founded from 1945 to 1962, 26 "black-controlled" banks were established from 1963 to 1972. Only 6 of those banks, including Riverside, were located in the South. At the time of the organization of Riverside National Bank, national bank regulations stipulated that before a bank could open for business, it must have experienced bank managers. Unfortunately, there were no black bank executives in major banks in the United States at that time, and the few black banks in existence lacked sufficient management depth to allow one of their numbers to accept a job with a new bank. Consequently, to open for business, Riverside Bank had to borrow an experienced bank executive from Douglas State Bank in Kansas City, Kansas. Mr. Edward Tillmon, president of Douglas State Bank, became the chief operating manager of the bank until a permanent manager could be recruited. In the interim, Edward Irons, who owned 4 percent of the stock, was elected the first chief executive officer (CEO) of Riverside.

At the same time, a significant milestone in the renaissance of black banking was made with the professionalization of the National Bankers Association (NBA), the trade association of the black banks of the country. In existence since 1927, with an initial membership of 14 banks, the association had been primarily an annual social gathering of a handful of bankers, with little or no programmatic activity at or between the annual meetings. In 1967, the NBA appointed Dr. Irons its executive director, who successfully sought a $230,000 grant from the Economic Development Administration of the U.S. Department of Commerce to develop a new program that would revitalize the NBA. It was composed of six components: (1) a research program to identify bank operational weaknesses and then to develop solutions; (2) a $100 million deposit development program from major corporations and all levels of government, local and federal; (3) an assistance program for organization of new banks; (4) a middle-management training program for minority banks, utilizing major banks as training institutions; (5) a top management and board member training program; and (6) a program to upgrade the quality of the programs at annual meetings.

This newly organized program of services, provided to both the existing and potential banks, together with the supportive regulatory environment and the concomitant social responsibility of Corporate America and the major banks of the nation, gave rise to the rapid growth and development of minority banks. Beginning in 1963, minority banks grew rapidly until about 1980. As the next two decades proved, the regulatory climate was supportive of minority banking. Also, the confidence of the minority community that they could organize and manage a bank had been established, once the renaissance of black banking had been set in motion.

By the end of 1970, there were 44 minority-controlled banks with total assets of $835 million. Of the 44 banks, 35 were black controlled, but at that time they held only 0.3 percent of the total assets of the banking industry of the United States. By 1979, minority banking assets had grown to $2.3 billion, of which $1.2 billion, or 52 percent was controlled by black banks; Hispanic Americans controlled 30 percent ($698 million), and Asian Americans controlled 11 percent ($265 million). For a period of about 15 years, since 1964, the climate for minority banks was supportive, both legislatively and attitudinally. After 1980, a number of minority banks began to fail. By the end of 1996, there were 105 banks with total assets of $21.4 billion. The number of minority banks reached a peak of 110 in 1995 and fell back to 105 by the end of 1996.

Several factors can account for their failure. Minority Americans were not permitted to get management experience in the industry until after the social upheavals of the 1960s; thus, there was a shortage of experienced bank managers within these ethnic groups. Couple this fact with the changes in regulatory climate, both legislatively and attitudinally, and the less-than-affluent markets that they served, it is not surprising that many of these banks failed. The establishment of the FDIC stabilized the banking industry from 1933 to 1980, when the Depository Institution Deregulation and Monetary Act of 1980, which abolished Regulation "Q," was passed.

Regulation Q placed a ceiling beyond which banks and other depositories could pay interest rates on savings accounts. Not coincidentally, when this ceiling was lifted, banks began to fail. For example, while bank failures averaged about 6 per year, during the 30-year period ending 1975, banks failed at the rate of 146 annually during the decade ending 1992, reaching a peak of 280 during 1988. Contrary to earlier periods, many of these banks were multibillion-dollar institutions. In fact, all of the major banks of Texas failed during this period, some of which had $20 billion or more in assets. The evidence cited above suggests that failure of minority banks was well within the experience of the industry generally.

Predictably, then, minority banks have been impacted by the same economic and regulatory forces that impact the industry generally. For example, they grew rather rapidly from 11 banks with $77 million in assets in 1963 (at the time, all black) to a high of 110 in 1995, dropping to 105 in 1996. Their assets had grown to $21.4 billion by the end of 1996, a 2,700 percent change during this 33-year period. Black banks increased in number from 11 in 1963 to 47 in 1980, dropping to 34 in 1990 and 33 in 1996. Their assets increased from $77 million in 1963 to $2.8 billion in 1996. Hispanic and Asian American banks, which were not in existence at the beginning of that period, increased to 24 and 34, respectively, in 1996. As the evidence shows, these banks grew larger than black-controlled banks, reaching total assets of $10.1 billion and $7.3 billion, respectively, by the end of 1996.

It is striking that while black banks increased their assets to $2.8 billion during this period, their percentage of minority bank assets fell to 13 percent at the end of 1996. The number of Hispanic banks decreased to 24 percent, whereas their share of assets increased to 47 percent. Asians, on the other hand, increased their share of the number of banks, whereas their share of assets decreased to 34 percent. Thus, Asian and Hispanic banks outgrew black-controlled banks during this period. Significantly, however, Puerto Rican banks based in Puerto Rico are designated minority banks, although they are billion-dollar banks in a sovereign country. Asian banks are primarily on the West Coast, where heavy Japanese investment is common.

The reduction of minority banks resulted from a combination of change in regulatory climate and inexperienced management. As set forth above, the advent of the deregulation of interest rates (Regulation Q) decreased the banking industry significantly, in number, since that time, dropping from 14,496 at the end of 1984 to 10,491 at the end of 1994, a 28 percent decrease, and the decrease is likely to continue in the foreseeable future.

As for asset management, most major financial institutions, black banks, in general, compare favorably with other minority groups. Also, minority banks over three years old compare favorably with nonminority banks of their size categories. For example, loans as a percentage of assets (asset management strategy) is almost identical among each of the several ethnic groups. Somewhat less comparable is their return on assets. They each earn between 0.38 percent and 0.55 percent on their assets, with Asian banks coming in highest, with black banks second at 0.47 percent. When minority banks reach $300 million in assets, however, the return on assets is comparable to nonminority peer banks, or 1.1 percent to 1.2 percent for nonminority banks.

The top banks in the industry earn approximately 1.0 percent on their assets. Bearing on this fact, however, is the fact that the industry, typically, has approximately $2 million in assets for each employee, whereas minority banks have $1.6 million in assets for each employee. It, thus, costs minority banks more to operate. A major part of this increased cost stems from the fact that minority banks, in general, have smaller accounts. Thus, minority banks have less assets per employee to invest than the industry generally.

The abolishment of Regulation Q in 1980 set in motion a competitive environment that can pit small banks against the giants. When interest rates go up above that which is common on consumer loans, housing, and small business loans, the loan market for small banks will dry up. When this happens, small and minority banks will be unable to compete for deposits in competition with the giants and will either fail or merge. In preparation for that possibility, minority banks, and small banks generally, would be wise to develop flexible liquidity management plans that will enable them to ride out such a period until interest rates fall to the market levels that accommodate their customer base.

SELECTED BIBLIOGRAPHY: Lila Ammons, "The Evolution of Black-Owned Banks between the 1880s and the 1990s, *Journal of Black Studies* 26 (March 1996): 467–489; Randall W. Bennett and Christine Loucks, "Politics and Length of Time to Bank Failure," *Contemporary Economic Policy* 14 (October 1996): 29; Federal Reserve Board, *Minority Bank Assets, by Ethnic Group* (Washington, DC: GPO, 1992, 1993, 1994, 1995, 1996); Charlotte Hall, "A History of the NBA: A Look into the Past" (NBA Convention Publication, October 1971, Chicago, IL); Abram Harris, *The Negro as Capitalist: A Study of Banking and Business among American Negroes* (College Park, MD: McGrath Publishing Company, 1936); Edward D. Irons, "Black Banking, Problems and Prospects," *Journal of Finance* 26 (1971): 407–425; Edward D. Irons, "Black Banks, Gray Skies and Green Hopes," in Rudy Winston, ed., *Minority Enterprise in the 90's: A Questionable Future* (Babson Park, MA: Babson College, 1991); Gregory N. Price, "Minority Owned Banks: History and Trends," Federal Reserve Bank of Cleveland, *Economic Commentary* (July 1990): 1–5.

Edward D. Irons with assistance of Patricia M. Tucker

BANKS, COMMERCIAL AND GOVERNMENT DEPOSITS. There are several sources of government deposits in black-owned commercial banks (BCBs). One generalization that could be made is that, relative to all commercial banks, BCBs on average have a higher ratio of U.S government deposits to total deposits. This generalization is partly a result of BCBs being the beneficiaries of explicit federal policy interventions, some of which are presumably designed to make BCBs more viable. For BCBs, two sources of U.S government deposits are available: (1) Treasury Tax and Loan (TTL) accounts and (2) deposits received through the Minority Bank Deposit Program (MBDP). While national banking law designates both as public money, there are important differences with regard to their purpose, eligibility criteria, collateral requirements, and interest cost.

The TTL accounts at commercial banks represent excess operating cash of the U.S. Treasury and payments by employers/corporations for federal taxes due.

The TTL account system was established in 1917 to mitigate the impact of the U.S. government's financial operations on the distribution and level of bank reserves and money supply. To promote this goal, the TTL system encourages businesses to make their payments of various federal taxes directly to eligible financial institutions. Eligibility criteria for participation in the TTL system require financial institutions to be designated as TTL depositories. Eligibility certification is obtained through district Federal Reserve Banks or Branches. Coordination and administration of the TTL system is a joint effort of the Treasury Department and the Federal Reserve System.

Potential U.S. government deposits available to TTL depositories include payments by employers/corporations for backup withholding, withheld income and social security taxes, corporate income taxes, railroad retirement, and excise taxes. As TTL accounts constitute public money, TTL depositories are required to pledge collateral to secure the accounts. Generally, collateral requirements on TTL accounts are relevant for that portion of the accounts that exceeds the Recognized Insurance Coverage (RIC). The RIC pertains to insurance provided by the Federal Deposit Insurance Corporation, the Federal Savings and Loan Insurance Corporation, the National Credit Union Share Insurance Fund, and other insurance organizations specifically qualified by the secretary of the treasury.

In October 1977, the secretary of the treasury was authorized to invest Treasury excess operating cash in obligations of depositories maintaining TTL accounts. The TTL investment program allowed TTL depositories to participate under two options: (1) remittance option and (2) note option. Under the remittance option, funds equivalent to the amount of deposits credited by a depository to its TTL account is withdrawn by the Federal Reserve Bank, upon receipt by the Federal Reserve Bank of the advice of credit supporting such deposits. Under the note option, the Treasury invests its excess operating cash in open-ended notes of the depositories. The depositories hold the accounts until they are needed by the Treasury and called in by the Federal Reserve Bank.

Deposits received under either option must be secured by acceptable collateral as mentioned above. Under the remittance option, TTL deposits are submitted immediately to the Treasury. Under the note option, participating financial institutions have use of the funds until called by the Treasury at a cost of the federal funds rate less 25 basis points. Financial institutions participating as TTL depositories are reimbursed for processing and maintaining TTL accounts. Prior to 1978, no interest payments were required on TTL accounts. After 1978, TTL depositories were required to pay an interest rate equal to the Federal Funds Rate less 25 basis points, for TTL deposits held more than one day. Minority-owned financial institutions were not subject to interest payments on TTL accounts until 1983.

The Minority Bank Deposit Program represents another source of government deposits in BCBs. The MBDP grew out of President Richard Nixon's Executive Order 11458 in 1969, which established an Advisory Council for minority enterprise. To coordinate and implement the objectives of Executive Order 11458, the Minority Business Development Agency (MBDA) was created shortly thereafter. While the provisions of Executive Order 11458 contained no explicit reference to minority financial institutions, in 1970 the Treasury Department announced the formation of the MBDP.

Within this context, the MBDP seems consistent with the vision then held by the Nixon administration of developing "Black Capitalism." In general, and as suggested by G. N. Price in 1993, it appears that the MBDP was one element of an overall policy paradigm that was favorable to the idea of fostering black business enterprise in the late 1960s. The intent of the MBDP was to promote the establishment and viability of minority financial institutions. To promote this goal, the MBDP encourages federal agencies, state and local governments, and the private sector to use qualified MBDP participants as depositories and financial agents.

Eligibility criteria for MBDP participation require financial institutions to be designated as a Depository and Financial Agent of the U.S. Government. Eligible financial institutions include minority-owned or-controlled commercial banks insured by the Federal Deposit Insurance Corporation or with deposits that are insured by a state, or agency thereof, or by a corporation chartered by a state for the sole purpose of insuring such deposits or accounts. Also, minority-owned or -controlled savings and loan associations, mutual savings and loan associations insured by the Federal Savings and Loan Insurance Corporation, or businesses that hold deposits insured by a state or agency are eligible, as are corporations chartered by a state for the sole purpose of insuring such deposits or accounts. Also eligible are credit unions insured by the administrator of the National Credit Union Administration or with deposits that are insured by a state, or agency, or by a corporation chartered by a state for the sole purpose of insuring such deposits or accounts. A majority of its members, however, must have an annual income below the minimum level standard of living established by the Bureau of Labor Statistics.

Executive Orders 11625 and 12138 deem minority status to include but not be limited to black Americans, Asian Americans, Hispanic Americans, Native Americans, Eskimos, Aleuts, and women. Minority ownership refers to commercial banks, and stock savings and loan associations, in which minority groups own more than 50 percent of the outstanding stock. Minority control is applicable to situations where minorities hold voting trusts or proxy agreements such that minorities control more than 50 percent of the outstanding stock. Eligibility certification is obtained from the Financial Management Service (FMS), Department of Treasury. The FMS is responsible for coordinating the MBDP within federal, state, and local government by maintaining a roster of eligible participants and distributing it periodically to federal agencies and state and local governments.

The MBDA is responsible for similar coordination within the private sector. Types of U.S. government deposits available to MBDP participants include both transaction and nontransaction accounts. Potential deposits available include public money such as TTL deposits, cash advances to federal contractors and grantees, Postal Service deposits, and certificates of deposit constituting non-appropriated federal agency funds. As public money, U.S. government deposits received through MBDP require collateral to secure the deposits. Acceptable collateral, unless otherwise specified by the secretary of the treasury, includes: obligations issued or fully insured or guaranteed by the United States or any U.S. government agency and obligations of government-sponsored corporations that under specific statute may be accepted as security for public funds, at face value. Other acceptable criteria include obligations issued or fully insured by the International Bank for Reconstruction and Development, the Inter-American Development Bank, or the Asian Development Bank, at face value.

In general, collateral requirements are relevant only for that portion of deposits in excess of the RIC. MBDP participants are not reimbursed for processing or maintaining non-TTL MBDP deposits. The interest cost of non-TTL MBDP deposits is determined by the market. In particular, the interest rate paid by MBDP participants on non-TTL U.S. government deposits is determined by what they are willing to pay, as governed by market conditions subject to any relevant regulatory restrictions on the payment of interest.

In reviewing the consequences of government deposits, it can be noted that with the exception of the analyses of Price, no research on commercial banks (CBs) has directly examined the consequences of U.S. government deposits on the balance sheet of CBs. Price reports that deposits received through the MBDP program may increase asset risk for CBs. This suggests that the MBDP as policy may conflict with bank regulatory objectives of a sound and viable banking system, since increased asset risk increases bank failure probabilities. In general, deposits received through the MBDP are expensive relative to other types of deposits on the balance sheet. This finding undermines the presumption noted by Scott, Gardner, and Mills that such deposits would be inexpensive and should therefore lower deposit costs for BCBs.

There also appear to be some adverse consequences associated with the collateral requirements of MBDP deposits. In particular, the collateral requirements may encourage CBs to make less loans available to the communities they serve. It appears that MBDP deposits induce CBs to make portfolio decisions that ultimately favor investments other than loans, due to MBDP deposits being below the RIC. Finally, the availability of deposits received through the MBDP may not be the best way to encourage the formation of new CBs. Relative to policy interventions that render banking markets more competitive, a policy that favors CBs as depositories for U.S government deposits appears to have less of an effect on BCB entry.

Any conclusive assessment of the merits of CBs having U.S. government deposits on their balance sheet is not possible, given the limited research that has been completed to date. Government deposits received through the MBDP are not race-specific programs per se, a realization particularly important for policy considerations in the 1990s, a time period characterized by a substantial amount of debate over programs that presumably have particular racial groups in mind as beneficiaries. Whether or not the MBDP is a viable and tenable policy instrument is indeed a good question. An answer requires further research.

SELECTED BIBLIOGRAPHY: G. N. Price, "The Cost of Government Deposits for Black-Owned Commercial Banks," *Review of Black Political Economy* 23, 1 (1994); G. N. Price, "The Determinants of Entry for Black-Owned Commercial Banks," *Quarterly Review of Economics and Finance* 35, 3 (1995); G. N. Price, "Three Essays on Black-Owned Commercial Banks" (Ph.D. diss., University of Wisconsin at Milwaukee, 1993); W. L. Scott, M. J. Gardner, and D. L. Mills, "Expense Preference and Minority Banking: A Note," *Financial Review* 23(1988): 103–114.

Gregory N. Price

BINGA, JESSE (1865–1950), Illinois, bank founder, realtor, business leader, and philanthropist.

The Binga Bank founded in 1908 was the first black-owned, -managed, -controlled, and -established bank in the North. Its founder, Jesse Binga, was born in Detroit, the youngest of 10 children of William W. Binga, a barber, and Adelphia (Powers) Binga, a real estate investor and manager. After two years of high school, and learning barbering and real estate investment and management from his parents, Binga traveled for eight years working as a barber, an entrepreneur, and a railroad porter. He arrived in Chicago in 1893 with about $10. By 1898, still with virtually no money, Binga started his meteoric climb to success by opening a real estate office in Chicago. His clientele was the rapidly growing African American community, including many who migrated to Chicago during and after World War I. Binga purchased dilapidated buildings, rehabilitated them with his own hands, and rented them out. Some charged that he prospered by overcharging his tenants. Yet Binga's increasing wealth was also the result of a fortunate marriage. In 1912, after launching both his successful real estate and banking career, Binga married Eudora Johnson, daughter of Chicago's wealthiest black underworld figure, who had inherited $200,000 from her father. Some accused the handsome Binga of marrying for social prominence and wealth.

In developing Chicago's South Side in the 1920s, Binga, however, had few peers. He acquired 1,200 apartment leaseholds, and by 1926, he reportedly owned more property on State Street south of Twelfth Street than any other person. He also established the Binga Safe Deposit Company and promoted a black insurance company, and in 1929, he constructed the impressive Arcade building to spearhead South Side development. Nonetheless, Binga had many critics who accused him of being arrogant, hard-driving, belligerent, and even ruthless. Yet by leasing apartments and funding mortgages in areas previously barred to blacks, Binga generated white hostility. His properties were vandalized, and his real estate office was bombed twice in 1919. His home was bombed between three to seven times in 1919 and 1920. Binga refused to run, instead, hiring private guards and carrying a gun. He also refused to succumb to racial hatred. Binga also promoted interracial business associations and was founder and secretary of the Associated Business Club, which was affiliated with the National Negro Business League.*

Binga's business philosophy was based on hard work, thrift, self-help, and honesty, espoused in his pamphlet *Certain Sayings of Jesse Binga*—although by the late 1920s, it appears that Binga had some difficulty adhering to that philosophy. After a change in Illinois laws abolished private banks, Binga reorganized his bank as a state bank in 1920 with capital of $100,000 and a surplus of $20,000, which virtually doubled by 1924. The Binga State Bank was perceived as assisting the African American community by providing a valuable new source of credit, where previously there were only inhospitable banks and loan sharks. Bank deposits grew rapidly from $300,083 in 1921 to $1,474,680 in 1928.

Yet Binga, the major stockholder and founder, fought for exclusive control over lending decisions. The board of directors, composed of leading African American businessmen, complained that he was dictatorial and arrogant. Binga removed some who challenged him, whereas others quit. But in its operations the bank did have some major weaknesses. A large amount of its capital was tied up in unsecured loans. There was also excessive investment in expensive, nonearning bank buildings and fixtures, but overreliance on real estate loans proved catastrophic when the real estate market plummeted in 1929. In addition, its major holding of securities, those of the Binga Safe Deposit Company, eventually proved worthless.

In 1929, realizing that his bank was in trouble, Binga solicited assistance. Anthony Overton,* African American head of Douglass National Bank, offered help, but Binga refused his terms, even though other black institutions and major white banks refused to help. Binga next attempted to organize a national bank to absorb the troubled loans of the Binga State Bank. Although he collected $29,000 from the sale of national bank stock, the bank was never started, and Binga kept the money for his own purposes, for which he was later indicted. The Binga State Bank, whose liabilities exceeded its assets by over half a million dollars, was closed on July 31, 1930. The collapse shattered a symbol of hope for the South Side, wiped out many small depositors, and destroyed both Binga's fortune and the rest of his life. Some blame the banking community for not providing more assistance, but others feel little could have been done in such perilous times—9,000 American banks failed from 1930 to 1933.

Subsequently, Binga was indicted for embezzlement that included overdrawing his own account by $7,000, booking bogus loans to companies from which he received thousands of dollars, and defrauding individuals by having them sign promissory notes or checks that went into his own account. The first trial ended in a hung jury in 1931. In the second trial in 1933, he was convicted on five counts for the issuance of fraudulent loans and sentenced to 10 years in prison. Following 2 years of futile appeals, Binga entered Joliet State Penitentiary in 1935. Petitions by leading African American citizens, religious leaders,

Clarence Darrow, and many others eventually succeeded in freeing Binga after 3 years' imprisonment. At the age of 73, he was released to spend the rest of his life as a custodian at St. Anselm's Catholic Church. Soon after, he was evicted from his home, moved in with his nephew, and died penniless in Chicago on June 13, 1950.

Still, during the height of his banking and real estate activities, Binga was a hero, a role model, a respected philanthropist, and a racial leader. The Bingas were social leaders, famous for their charity work for the Catholic Church, to which they belonged, for the Old Folks Home that Mrs. Binga helped found, and for their financial assistance to the YMCA. They also provided college scholarships and Christmas parties for the needy. Mrs. Binga died in March 1933 during her husband's trial. They never had children.

SELECTED BIBLIOGRAPHY: Abram Harris, *The Negro as Capitalist: A Study of Banking and Business among American Negroes* (College Park, MD: McGrath Publishing Company, 1936); John N. Ingham and Lynne B. Feldman, *African-American Business Leaders: A Biographical Dictionary* (Westport, CT: Greenwood Press, 1994); Carl R. Osthaus, "The Rise and Fall of Jesse Binga, Black Financier," *Journal of Negro History* (January 1973): 39–71.

Nicholas A. Lash

BLACK COLLEGES, FINANCING, 1860–1900. Immediately following the Civil War, various attempts were made throughout the South to offer some form of formal schooling to the nation's 4 million black freedmen. What emerged was a number of educational institutions specifically designated to educate the majority of southern blacks in the South. In most instances, these educational institutions opened as normal schools for blacks. Normal schools were considered to be the "equivalent" to the nation's elementary and secondary schools. Moreover, they were created as part of a dual educational system to accommodate the society's discriminative practices of segregating blacks and whites. Yet because of the ever-increasing demand to train more black teachers for the South's black normal schools, many of these postwar institutions became the first historically black colleges and universities in the nation.

Financing for the creation of these schools came primarily through private donation and governmental assistance. Philanthropic societies, private groups, and black churches assumed the burden of financing these schools in the early years. Charitable funds were among the first to respond to the educational needs of freedmen. Yet such funds were often given with a political agenda or for a specific purpose. In 1867, George Peabody pledged $1 million to be used for the education of the most needy in the South, regardless of race. However, among the many donations offered by the Peabody Fund, most went to creating primary and secondary schools for whites and toward supporting and maintaining a racially "separate but unequal" school system. Jabez L. M. Curry, a well-known southern white and the primary agent for the Slater Fund, solicited $1 million to be used at black schools and colleges emphasizing industrial and domestic education. Clearly, Curry's efforts, like those of the Peabody Fund, were politically motivated because funding was only allotted to schools willing to restrict their curriculum from promoting a traditional liberal or classical emphasis utilized at the majority of white universities at this time.

However, the monetary reward promoting industrial education and the sudden rise of industrial education in black schools during the 1880s should not lead one to presume that most black colleges abandoned a traditional liberal or classical curriculum. Under the leadership of various missionary societies, most black colleges relegated industrial education to a subordinate role in favor of the traditional or classical curriculum taught at white universities. Despite the financial restriction, these institutions never adopted the Hampton-Tuskegee model of black industrial education. Furthermore, they gave minimal priority to all forms of industrial training, because as Robert G. Sherer asserted, "Washington and the Hampton-Tuskegee Idea were outside the mainstream of black educational thought."

Additionally, there were individuals and groups that did not adopt the Peabody and Slater policy for fund allocation. During the 1870s, Reverend Barnes Sears preferred to appropriate money to Fisk University—a historically black college established in 1866—in Nashville, Tennessee, and other historically black colleges and universities, rather than traditionally white universities, because of the scarcity of fiscal resources available at these schools. Before Sears in 1866, General Clinton B. Fisk, assistant commissioner of the Freedmen's Bureau for Tennessee, personally donated $30,000 to officially open the doors of Fisk University. Such individuals were few, and the funds they donated—though beneficial—were minor when compared to philanthropic endowments that mandated a political agenda.

By the end of the nineteenth century, practically every philanthropic endowment was motivated by economic, social, and political implications. The staunch resistance and militia-type tactics used by southern whites to limit the education and enfranchisement of blacks in the South hindered funding for the progression of black colleges and universities. Few governmental agencies outside of the state-supported Freedmen's Bureau acted in favor of the development of black colleges and universities in the South. In 1862, the federal government created the Morrill Fund, but it was enacted to provide land-grant schools for whites, not blacks. The fund required that the states provide the resources for buildings and certain facilities. It was only after 1890, with segregation firmly established in the South, that Congress included blacks under this legislation. Consequently, this agreement aggressively maintained separate educational systems for blacks and whites.

The separate schools created for blacks can be best described as "secondary," when compared with the colleges and universities whites maintained. However, this position stemmed primarily from the limited financial resources available, not the educational effectiveness of the schools. For example, from its beginning to 1945, Fisk University, arguably considered one of the best black colleges during this time period, was near bankruptcy. In the early years of the school's establishment, the missionary associations offering endowments to Fisk had many other institutions to support, not just in higher education but in primary and secondary schooling as well. Consequently, balancing the budget at the school was a frantic struggle every year as administrators sought to pay its faculty comparable salaries to faculty at traditionally white institutions. During this era of Reconstruction and Jim Crow, most of the faculty at historically black colleges and universities were paid one-third of the salary whites were paid at other institutions of higher education. Subsequently, Fisk, and its struggling internal fiscal demands, characterized the majority of black colleges and universities that emerged during this time period.

What haphazardly restricted the financial well-being of schools like Fisk and others to the endowments of particular missionary associations was the minimal fiscal support that could be offered collectively by blacks. The overwhelming majority of blacks in the South were new freedmen. Additionally, funding by "well-to-do" blacks throughout the nation was limited. In 1889, a black Nashville woman, upon her death, left a legacy of $1,000 to establish the Lucian Bedford Scholarship at Fisk. Such acts of unwarranted generosity were few and far between for many blacks. For the most part, southern blacks could make only small contributions, since the majority worked within the labor-repressive and minuscule wage-paying domestic and agricultural systems utilized in the South. Most of the lucrative philanthropic foundations that aided black education were created after 1900, but as aforementioned, some support was received by the Peabody and John F. Slater Fund.

Nevertheless, a number of successful black colleges and universities arose between 1860 and 1900 in the South, despite minimal external funding. Private donations from the Rosenwald's, American Missionary Association (AMA), the Boston Education Society, the Friends Association for the Aid and Elevation of the Freedmen, the Freedmen's Aid Society of the Methodist Episcopal Church, the American Baptist Home Mission Society, the African Methodist Episcopal Church, the Colored Methodist Episcopal Church, the African Methodist Episcopal Zion Church, and others all provided external funding for southern institutions founded between 1860 and 1900.

SELECTED BIBLIOGRAPHY: James D. Anderson, *The Education of Blacks in the South, 1860–1935* (Chapel Hill: University of North Carolina Press, 1988); Ullin Whitney Leavell, *Philanthropy in Negro Education* (Westport, CT: Negro Universities Press, 1970); Gordon Lee, *The Struggle for Federal Aid* (New York: Columbia University Press, 1949); Harry Morgan, *Historical Perspectives on the Education of Black Children* (Westport, CT: Praeger, 1995); Office for Advancement of Public Negro Colleges, *Directory of Traditionally Black Colleges and Universities in the United States* (New York: U.S. Plywood-Champion Papers Inc., 1970); Joe Richardson, *Christian Reconstruction: The American Missionary Association and Southern Blacks, 1861–1890* (Athens: University of Georgia Press, 1986).

Christopher M. Span

BLACK COLLEGES, FINANCING, 1900–1930. Under slavery, blacks had long desired to be educated. Once they achieved freedom, blacks all over the South did all they could to ensure that they and/or their children would be educated. From 1900 to 1935 there was an important shift in the funding of black higher education institutions. According to James D. Anderson, the funding shifted from missionary or religious funding to primarily large industrial philanthropic funding. Along with a shift in funding came a shift in the type of education blacks would receive at the turn of the twentieth century. Black colleges and universities at the turn of the twentieth century were faced with much financial difficulty, not that different from what black schools face today. The federal and state governments only gave minimal support to these schools. The funding inequities of black schools, as compared to white colleges and universities, were extremely unequal. This inequity was legally sanctioned by the *Plessy v. Ferguson* decision of 1896. Although the Supreme Court decision called for "separate but equal," separate but unequal had been the southern way of life all throughout slavery and during and since the end of Reconstruction. So the government could not be called upon to financially assist schooling for African Americans.

Another financial difficulty faced by African American colleges was the financial collapse of missionary and black religious philanthropy. These religious entities included the American Missionary Association, which founded schools such as Fisk University and Straight University (Dillard); the Freedman's Aid Society of the Methodist Episcopal Church founded Meharry Medical College and Morgan College; and the American Baptist Home Mission Society sponsored Morehouse, Spelman, and Virginia Union. The African American religious organizations were the African Methodist Episcopal (AME) Church, which founded and supported Allen University, Morris Brown College, and Wilberforce College; the African Methodist Episcopal Zion Church, which supported Livingston College; and the Colored Methodist Episcopal Church, which owned Lane, Texas, Paine, and Miles Memorial. Black Baptists financed Arkansas Baptist College, Selma University, and Virginia College and Seminary. In all, African American religious institutions provided less than 15 percent of the total financial support awarded to black colleges and universities. As many of these religious entities, both black and white, began to lose money in their educational ventures, historically black colleges and universities were left in shambles.

While African American schools struggled financially, the opposition of many industrial philanthropic giants added frustration to the financial efforts of many black colleges. The wealthy industrialists created foundations to finance education. The Peabody Education Fund was established by George Peabody in 1867. Between 1867 and 1914, the Peabody Fund provided $3.5 million toward education in the South. The main goals of the Peabody Fund were "the promotion and encouragement of intellectual, moral, or industrial education among the young of the more destitute portions of the Southern and Southwestern States of our Union.'' John F. Slater created the John F. Slater Fund in 1882 primarily to aid 12 colleges that trained African American teachers.

John D. Rockefeller gave his financial support through the General Education Board, which had the education of black people as one of its special interests. The board's objective was ''the promotion of education within the United States of America, without distinction of race, sex, or creed.'' The board was to ''do and perform all things necessary or convenient for the promotion of the object of the corporation.'' Rockefeller gave over $53 million for the board to distribute. Anna T. Jeanes gave over $1 million to the General Education Board as well for the enlargement of the board in 1905. The board established a fund that appointed industrial teachers to rural schools. The Phelps-Stokes Fund was focused largely on the financing of black schools and educational development. In 1910, the Julius Rosenwald Fund was established to aid black colleges as well. Rosenwald even sat on the Tuskegee Institute Board of Trustees in 1912.

All of the money in these various funds was not earmarked for or allocated to African American schools. However, these philanthropic giants donated enough money to control the curriculum of the schools. Their educational policy was implemented through the Southern Education Board, which was established in 1901 to propagate southern whites' belief that universal education was beneficial for the South. The General Education Board acted as the financial arm for northern industrialists. The two boards joined together in 1914 under the General Education Board, since membership on both boards overlapped.

The educational policy of northern industrial philanthropists was to make a better worker out of black people. William H. Baldwin, president of the General Education Board, expressed the policy Donald Spivey called ''schooling for the new slavery.'' Baldwin stated that the South needed Negroes educated so that they could be directed to be the best possible laborers. With the right kind of education, the Negro will willingly work menial jobs, and that would open up an opportunity for southern whites to ''perform more expert labor.'' Baldwin's statements clearly express the position of the General Education Board on black education. The board did not have any intention of financing black education for the sake of black people's upliftment and achievement. Rather, the board wanted to train teachers at black colleges and normal schools to teach black youth that they were to accept their subjugation. In other words, black colleges were financed by northern industrial philanthropists to teach future black leaders to lead their people in acceptance of a degrading position in the southern social order.

Black colleges and universities at the onset of the twentieth century sought out financial aid from northern philanthropists because of their severe financial problems. But unlike the financial influence of black and white religious organizations, the northern philanthropist wanted to create a labor class that would reconstruct the southern economy.

SELECTED BIBLIOGRAPHY: James D. Anderson, *The Education of Blacks in the South, 1860–1935* (Chapel Hill: University of North Carolina Press, 1988), 238–278; John Hope Franklin, *From Slavery to Freedom: A History of Negro Americans* (New

York: McGraw-Hill, 1988), 239–244; Vincent P. Franklin and James D. Anderson, eds., *New Perspectives on Black Educational History* (Boston, MA: G. K. Hall & Co., 1978), 97–109; Ullin Whitney Leavell, *Philanthropy in Negro Education* (Westport, CT: Negro Universities Press, 1970), 57–80; Donald Spivey, *Schooling for the New Slavery, Black Industrial Education, 1868–1915* (Westport, CT: Greenwood Press, 1978).

Dionne Danns

BLACK POWER, BLACK BUSINESS, 1960s. The Black Power movement of the 1960s was a nationalist surge in the African American community that sought to ensure their full acceptance in all dimensions of life in the United States. During the Black Power era, the strategies, tactics, and visions of its advocates differed, but they shared several basic assumptions. First, they agreed that Black Power could not be achieved until African Americans had meaningful political and economic input in national decision making. Second, they insisted that their primary goal was not individual success but success for the African American community as a whole. Third, they maintained that African Americans had to perfect the politics of self-interest if they were to achieve their goals. Fourth, they urged that the African American community take the lead in charting its development. Fifth, all expressed confidence that strategies emphasizing blackness could succeed. Finally, all believed that African American empowerment would remain a slogan unless and until they achieved a stake in the American capitalist system commensurate with their 12 percent of the American population. Needless to say, even non–Black Powerites agreed with them in the latter assessment, and objective economic measures confirmed the minuscule role played in the economy by African Americans.

Black Powerites argued that the economy of the United States is a capitalist one, which means that it is guided by the individual profit motive and that the major means of production (i.e., banks, factories, farms, mines, etc.) are owned by corporations and individual capitalists or a combination of them. Business is the method used to satisfy wants and utilize resources in the system. They went on to insist that the most effective measure of the economic strength of any ethnic group in the United States is the extent of its ownership of means of production and participation in business; the status of African Americans by this measure is extremely low.

In 1969, there were 163,000 black-owned firms, with total receipts of $4,174 million. The majority were one-man or one-woman operations of self-employed artisans or merchants. Only 38,000 employed workers and therefore could be considered capitalist enterprises, if small ones, in the proper sense of the word. The total number of employees was 152,000. In both sales and employment, black firms accounted for only 0.25 percent (one-fourth of 0.1 percent) of all businesses in the country. Viewing stark statistics on African American economic powerlessness, it is not surprising that Talmadge Anderson, an advocate of African American economic empowerment, concluded: ''Black involvement and participation in the economic system is simply peripheral and subservient by the design and tactics of the white capitalist.''

In the late nineteenth and early twentieth centuries, two figures stand out as stalwarts in the attempt to promote capitalist values among blacks, Booker T. Washington* (1856–1915) and Marcus Garvey* (1887–1940). Washington, born enslaved, became the most well-known African American spokesperson at the turn-of-the-century height of Jim Crow. Lionized by white industrialists and philanthropists, Washington taught that African Americans would advance in the United States only when they deemphasized the struggle for political and civil rights, a mistake they had made during Reconstruction, and focused instead on achieving a powerful base in business and industry, while emphasizing: "No race that has anything to contribute to the markets of the world is long in any degree ostracized."

To facilitate the spread of his message in the African American community, in 1900 he founded the National Negro Business League* to "generate high character," "develop racial respect," and "lay the economic groundwork for future generations." Black Powerites of the 1960s disagreed violently with Washington's apoliticism but agreed with him that African American political power would be of minimal value unless it was based on economic power. Marcus Garvey, an immigrant from Jamaica, formed an organization there in 1914 called the Universal Negro Improvement Association (UNIA) to uplift black people politically and economically in all parts of the world where they were present. He came to the United States, where he established branches of the UNIA, headquartered in Harlem. In the 11 years that he was active in the United States (1916–1927), he transformed the organization into one of the most powerful black organizations, not only in the United States but all over the world.

In addition to calling for the liberation of Africa, the creation of a vibrant black nationalism, and respect for black culture, Garvey, like Washington, taught that political power without economic power will not be respected and blacks were deluding themselves, if thinking otherwise. Garvey urged branches of the UNIA to set up businesses, and he collected funds from African Americans and blacks worldwide to build a steamship line—the Black Star Line. The Black Star Line was created both to link the black world in commerce and to show the rest of the world that black-run enterprises could succeed. Unfortunately, the Black Star Line went bankrupt, and Garvey was convicted on fraud charges—some say that were trumped up—in connection with the selling of Black Star Line stocks. Garvey was deported to Jamaica in 1927, after which the UNIA declined, but his message of assertive black nationalism and black capitalist power resonated strongly in the Black Power movement.

In the 1960s, Black Powerite supporters of black capitalism agreed that it was needed but could not arrive at a consensus on how to achieve economic growth in the black community. A review of the literature on black capitalism during the era shows that three schools of thought developed. The first saw the acquisition of skills, job placement, and equal opportunity in employment as the starting points for the future creation of an African American economic base.

Supporters of this view campaigned strongly for affirmative action, a program that has had mixed results. The second called for the amassing of independent African American capital and using the accumulation to spur the industrialization of African American communities as a first step to black capitalist empowerment in the United States at large. In the decades of the 1960s and 1970s, the prime exemplar of this mode of thinking was Elijah Muhammad of the Nation of Islam.* The Black Power era brought thousands into the Nation of Islam, and its leadership used the resulting financial growth to expand into new and larger areas of business—the fishing industry, publishing, trucking, commercial farming, banking, and so on.

The third school, represented by activists like Roy Innis of the Congress of Racial Equality (CORE), did not feel that the African American community, which he compared to an underdeveloped country, had the means to pull itself up by its own bootstraps. In this view, black capitalism could succeed only if the federal government, business, and the American society at large made its achievement a national priority. The third orientation was the most popular one with black and white politicians and businessmen and the American public. Indeed, by 1969, President Richard Nixon had become a convert and launched a campaign for black capitalism to give blacks a greater stake in the American economy. However, neither the business establishment nor the federal government committed significant funding to the plan, and by 1975 it had fizzled out. In 1973 the federal government granted $26 billion in credits to white corporations but less than $1 billion to black businesses.

The drive for black capitalism during the Black Power era failed to achieve its goals. According to U.S. census data, the number of black businesses increased from 424,165 in 1987 (2.4 percent of total businesses in the United States) to 620,912 (3.5 percent). In the late 1990s, the goal of an African American stake in the American economic system commensurate with their numbers remains elusive.

SELECTED BIBLIOGRAPHY: Talmadge Anderson, "Black Economic Liberation under Capitalism," in Roland W. Bailey, ed., *Black Business Enterprise: Historical and Contemporary Perspectives* (New York: Basic Books, 1971), 339; John Sibley Butler, *Entrepreneurship and Self-Help among Black Americans* (Albany: State University of New York Press, 1994), 66; Flounroy A. Coles, Jr., *Black Economic Development* (Chicago: Nelson Hall, 1975), 72–89; John T. McCartney, *Black Power Ideologies: An Essay in African-American Political Thought* (Philadelphia: Temple University Press, 1992).

John T. McCartney

BLACK TOWN ENTERPRISES—MOUND BAYOU; ISAIAH T. MONTGOMERY (1847–1924), Mississippi, entrepreneur, merchant, town founder, land speculator, political activist; AND CHARLES BANKS (1873–1923), Mississippi, banker, merchant, planter, cotton broker, real estate dealer, National Negro Business League leader, political activist, Masonic Order member.

From the post–Reconstruction era to World War I, there were over 60 black towns founded in the United States. The first town established by an African American, however, was New Philadelphia, Illinois, founded in 1836 by the former slave Free Frank McWorter.* In the post–Civil War era, enterprising blacks who believed in black economic solidarity also established all-black towns. These black town founders envisioned the economic advancement of blacks and the tremendous business opportunities that could be developed. During this period Mound Bayou, Mississippi, founded in 1887, and Boley, Oklahoma, in 1904 were two of the most prominent and highly recognized towns because of their ties with Booker T. Washington.* Indeed, in Oklahoma, there were 25 black towns. There were also black towns established outside of the South, including: Brooklyn, Illinois (1874); Nicodemus, Kansas (1877); Allensworth, California (1908); Deerfield, Colorado (1911); and Robbins, Illinois (1917). Primarily, only blacks lived in these towns although in some towns, such as Buxton, Iowa, there were a few whites. The town of Brooklyn, founded by whites in the mid-1830s, became an all-black town (renamed Lovejoy) as blacks gained political power after the Civil War, as would its neighbor East St. Louis, Illinois, in the civil rights era.

The businesses established in black towns were enterprises that provided goods and services for both townspeople and blacks who lived in the agricultural hinterlands. Black farmers were important in providing the population threshold necessary to support black town businesses. Ironically, as the American economy was becoming industrialized in the late nineteenth century, most black towns, however, had an agrarian-based economy. Cotton was the cash crop of Mound Bayou, Langston, and Boley, since Mississippi and Oklahoma were major cotton-producing states. Nicodemus, located in the arid Great Plains, was dependent on black farmers who produced wheat as a cash crop.

Brooklyn, while located in a productive agriculture area in southeastern Illinois, was the only black town dependent on the industrial employment of its townspeople for its economic survival. Many Brooklynites worked in the industries of East St. Louis. Also, black town leaders hoped to capitalize on the coal mining operations in the region. The significance of Brooklyn was that it provides the first example of a black town that attempted to develop an economic base from the industrialization of America. At the turn of the century, however, the most economically successful towns were in the South. Mound Bayou, one of the few surviving black towns, however, also attempted to develop an industrial base from the processing of agricultural commodities.

The town of Mound Bayou was founded by the former slave Isaiah Montgomery, son of Benjamin Montgomery,* also a slave. Isaiah, at 12 years of age, was made secretary for Jefferson Davis. His literate slave parents had taught him how to read. In addition, they had hired a tutor to further his learning. With skills of reading, writing, and arithmetic, the young slave eventually handled the bookkeeping of the plantation. He became free after the Civil War, when he began to assist his father Ben in managing the business affairs of the Montgomery family. After the Civil War, Benjamin Montgomery had purchased the

Davis Bend plantations. Isaiah assisted in the management of the Davis Bend plantations. Also, by 1883, he had accumulated over $6,000 and had part ownership in a prosperous saw mill. Isaiah's most successful business venture was the founding of the all-black town of Mound Bayou, Mississippi, in 1887.

While the population growth of Mound Bayou was slow in its first decade, by 1901 the enterprising Mound Bayou residents had founded a number of business concerns in the town. There were at least 24 black businesses established, doing an aggregate business of $116,801. In 1904, there were at least 35 businesses doing an aggregate business of $139,854. By 1905, these figures continued to increase, with at least 44 businesses doing an aggregate business of $205,605. There were over 10 entrepreneurs who had an annual business income over $5,000.

In addition, the Mound Bayou black business community included general merchandising stores, meat markets, restaurants, saw mills, blacksmith shops, real estate companies, cotton gins, a newspaper (the *Demonstrator*), all of which assisted in the growth of the town. Through this five-year span, Montgomery was involved in real estate, he owned a land agency, and he was a cotton commission merchant, with an average annual income of $27,000. His wife, Mary, owned the most prosperous merchandising stores in the town and also held a controlling interest in the gin and saw mill—with average gross business receipts of $15,000 over five years.

In the surrounding agricultural area, black farmers owned 10,000 acres of land on which they raised and marketed 5,000 bales of cotton annually, the sale of which put more than $250,000 annually in circulation in the town. The Mound Bayou Oil Mill and Manufacturing Company symbolized the effort of this all-black town to establish an industrial basis for economic self-sufficiency. This company, founded in 1908, was capitalized at $100,000 and was the largest cotton oil mill in the state when it began operations in 1913. It was also considered to be among the largest black enterprises in the South, warranting the address by Booker T. Washington at its opening.

Ties with Washington helped the town's businesses flourish, although the mill subsequently failed. The economic success of black towns was dependent upon capital for business ventures and the extension of credit from wholesale merchants, invariably white. Consequently, black leaders attempted to target potential settlers who already had capital for business investments and who could also extend credit to fellow residents. Invariably, the prices of goods sold by black town merchants were high, because they could not afford to buy their merchandise in bulk. Therefore, many merchants traded goods for labor and in many cases extended credit.

Also, many blacks settled in black towns without much money and depended on credit from local retailers to get themselves started in planting their crop, but many black town businesses lacked adequate credit and looked to white merchants. Business leaders looked to organized banks to keep a constant circulation of money in the town to support regular business operations. The goal of bank founders was to free black merchants of credit ties with whites and to guide the economic destiny of black farmers. These banks often overextended themselves in providing loans to merchants and local farmers, which resulted in many of their failures.

The enterprises of Charles Banks of Mound Bayou, who founded a bank in that town, provide an example of how settlers with investment capital could contribute to the business success of a town. At age 18, Charles Banks began his business career in the mercantile trade in Clarksdale, Mississippi. Later he would become actively involved in the National Negro Business League (NNBL),* organized by Booker T. Washington in 1900. In 1901, Banks was elected third vice president at the convention held in Chicago.

In 1903, Banks divested his mercantile activities in Clarksdale and moved to Mound Bayou, Mississippi, where he organized the Bank of Mound Bayou in 1904, with a capital stock of $10,000. Between September of 1905 and January of 1906, total clearings were in excess of $300,000. Banks also organized the Mound Bayou Loan and Investment Company, capitalized at $50,000, in 1906, so farmers' mortgages would not be canceled by outside companies. In addition, Banks owned a saw mill, 1,000 acres of land in Bolivar County, 250 town lots valued at $7,000, stock in 11 banks, and interest in several small businesses in town. Booker T. Washington considered him the "most influential Negro Business man in the United States" and "the leading Negro banker in Mississippi."

Business leaders in black towns recognized the importance of having ties with Booker T. Washington and the NNBL. After its formation in 1900, business leaders in black towns rushed to join the organization, so they could market their respective towns to hundreds of black businessmen and -women with capital. At the convention in 1914 at Muskogee, Oklahoma, business leaders from these black towns either sat in the audience or spoke to the convention. Some of the black towns represented at the convention were Mound Bayou, Allensworth and in Oklahoma, Taft, Foreman, Rentiesville, Tullahassee, Wybark, Clearview, and Boley. Charles Banks of Mound Bayou was vice president of the NNBL and a very close friend to Washington. This relationship is certainly a factor in this town's success.

Yet few black towns survived. Black farmers who supported black town economies failed to diversify their crops or were hit by environmental factors before doing so. In 1896, Eatonville, Florida, was hit by the "Great Freeze" of Florida, which ruined the orange trees in the state. This hurt the town's economy, and they decided to diversify their farm products. In 1906, a wilt disease destroyed approximately two-thirds of Mound Bayou's cotton crop. In Clearview, Oklahoma, farmers were forced to turn to truck gardening after crop failure in 1910 and 1911. Boley and Mound Bayou also attempted to develop a new agricultural economic base but were not successful.

Black town business failures resulted from a lack of capital and credit. An elite group of businessmen often owned multiple businesses. Consequently, this oligopoly limited reinvestments in black town businesses, which also resulted in an unequal distribution of income. Black town merchants felt increasing pressure to advance credit, but they often had extensive credit obligations with local banks and carried a large accounts receivable balance from customers. In the case of crop failures or other economic failures, such as the pre–World War I depression, farmers could not pay the merchants, and the merchants could not pay the banks. Situations such as this resulted in several black business failures and overall black town failures.

SELECTED BIBLIOGRAPHY: Sundiata Cha-Jua, "Founded Chance, Sustained by Courage: Brooklyn, Illinois" (Ph.D. diss., University of Illinois at Urbana, 1993); Norman Crockett, *The Black Towns* (Lawrence: Regents Press of Kansas, 1979); Kenneth Hamilton, *Black Towns and Profit: Promotion and Development in the Trans-Appalachian West, 1877–1915* (Urbana: University of Illinois Press, 1991); Neil R. McMillen, *Dark Journey: Black Mississippians in the Age of Jim Crow* (Urbana: University of Illinois Press, 1989); Quincy Mills, "Contrasting Black Economic Nationalism in the Age of Booker T. Washington, a Tale of Two Cities: Mound Bayou and Jackson, Mississippi," *Journal of Negro History*, forthcoming); Records of the National Negro Business League, *Annual Conference Proceedings and Organizational Records* (Lanham, MD: University Publication of America, 1906); Harold Rose, "The All-Negro Town: Its Evolution and Function," *Geographic Review* 55 (1965):363–381.

Quincy T. Mills

BLACK WALL STREET. In the early twentieth century, *Black Wall Street* was a term used to describe two wealthy black business districts, one in Tulsa, Oklahoma, and the other in Durham, North Carolina. In Tulsa, Greenwood Avenue was the center of the black business community. Between 1907 and 1921, the total number of business establishments and professional offices increased dramatically. By 1921, within this district, there were over 600 flourishing businesses, a black bus line, schools, hospitals, libraries, parks, churches, real estate companies, wealthy oil men, construction companies, entrepreneurs, and many other successful business owners, who established their enterprises in the two- and three-story brick commercial buildings that lined Greenwood. There were 41 grocers and meat markets, 30 restaurants, and four hotels by 1921, in addition to six real estate companies.

Black lawyers and approximately 15 physicians and surgeons located their offices along this street as well. Black physician Dr. Berry owned the bus line, and his income averaged $500 a day. Among this elite class of black businesspeople and professionals, some were rumored to have assets over $100,000. Indeed, there were several black millionaires—six of whom owned private airplanes during this period, when the entire state of Oklahoma only had two airports. Their consumer base was primarily black. Many black domestic workers flocked to the business district on their days off. The service-centered businesses targeted the wage-earning population. From an economic perspective, Black Wall Street relied heavily on the wages paid to blacks by white employees. Therefore, whites had a bit of influence in the growth of this thriving business community. But unlike other black business districts, black oil money was an important factor in the financial success of the black businesses located in Tulsa's Greenwood district.

Black Wall Street also referred to an enterprising black business community in Durham, North Carolina. The south side of Parrish Street in downtown Durham was dominated by astute black businessmen, whereas the north side of the street was occupied by white businesses. Among the 5,000 or more blacks, their economic zeal proved prosperous and encouraging to fellow blacks. There were approximately 15 grocery stores, eight barbershops, seven meat and fish dealers, and two drugstores, with inventories averaging from $2,000 to $8,000 in value.

John Merrick, C. C. Spaulding,* and R. B. Fitzgerald were three pioneers who helped build Durham's black business community. In 1898, Merrick (a black entrepreneur who owned six barbershops), along with the help of Spaulding, founded the North Carolina Mutual and Provident Association, later named the North Carolina Mutual Insurance Company,* the largest black business in the world. Business income increased from less than $1,000 in 1899 to $125,000 in 1910. The company employed, on average, 550 men and women. In 1911, their gross income amounted to $53,313; a year later, in 1912, it had increased to $313,516. Their new office building on Parrish Street, the second tallest in the city, became the center of Durham's black business district. It was specifically constructed so it would not exceed in height the tallest white building in Durham.

With the North Carolina Mutual Insurance Company at the center of Black Wall Street in Durham, these enterprising blacks established several successful businesses. The office of the Mechanics and Farmers' Bank was located in the building of the insurance company. It had a paid-in capital of $11,000, with $17,000 in deposits by over 500 people. The R. B. Fitzgerald brickyard was integral in the black business district. Fitzgerald had the capacity to produce 30,000 bricks per day, and his yard had a volume of $17,000. He in turn invested his money—$1,500 in a lot resold for $6,000 five years later. Farmland purchased for $800 was sold for $3,000 some 10 years later. Some 30 years later, Fitzgerald had accumulated over $100,000 in assets. In addition, the Durham Textile Mill was the only hosiery mill in the world completely owned and operated by blacks but whose product was sold by black and white salesmen.

The thriving black business districts in both Durham and Tulsa greatly enhanced their reputations as the Black Wall Streets, which are described by sociologist John Sibley Butler as entrepreneurial enclaves* in his *Entrepreneurship and Self-Help among Black Americans*. In Durham, unlike Tulsa, where the black business district was destroyed in a riot in 1921, whites in the Jim Crow age of segregation and discrimination allowed black businessmen to prosper and excel without interference.

SELECTED BIBLIOGRAPHY: John Sibley Butler, *Entrepreneurship and Self-Help among Black Americans* (Albany: State University of New York Press, 1994); W.E.B. Du Bois, "The Upbuilding of Black Durham," *World's Work* 23 (January 1912); Scott

Ellsworth, *Death in a Promised Land* (New Orleans: Louisiana State University Press, 1982); Clement Richardson, "What Are Negroes Doing in Durham?" *Southern Workman* 42 (July 1913); Booker T. Washington, "Durham, North Carolina, a City of Negro Enterprises," *Independent* 70 (March 30, 1911); John Jay Wilson and Ron Wallace, *Black Wallstreet: A Lost Dream* (Tulsa, OK: Black Wallstreet Pub. Co., 1992).

Quincy T. Mills

BOOK PUBLISHERS, COMMERCIAL. There are three types of commercial book publishers in the African American–owned book publishing segment of the American book publishing industry. They are magazine publishers who engage in book publishing, newspaper publishers who also publish books, and trade book publishers. The earliest African American magazine publisher who published books was Thomas Hamilton, Sr., who began publishing the *Anglo-African Magazine* in New York City in 1859. Hamilton's firm issued its first book in 1861: Robert Campbell's *A Pilgrimage to My Motherland: An Account of a Journey among the Igbas and Yorubas of Central Africa, in 1859–60.*

In the twentieth century other African American magazine publishers occasionally issued books. For example, the Colored Cooperative Publishing Company, which published the *Colored American Magazine* in Boston from 1900 to 1904, issued Pauline Hopkins's novel *Contending Forces* in 1900. *Unsung Heroes*, a collective biography of famous blacks, by Elizabeth Haynes, was released in 1921 by the Du Bois and Dill Publishing Company in New York City, which published *The Brownies Book*, a magazine for children, from 1920 to 1921. In the 1990s, one of the most successful African American magazine publishing companies that is an active book publisher is the Book Division of Johnson Publishing Company. This Chicago-based publisher has released a host of titles since 1961, when the Book Division was started. Among some of its titles are *Before the Mayflower: A History of Black America*, by Lerone Bennett, Jr., 5th ed. (1982) and *In Words and Pictures: Bill Cosby*, by Robert E. Johnson (1989).

The first African American newspaper to participate in book publishing was the Afro-American Publishing Company of Baltimore, which publishes the *Afro-American* in several regional editions. In 1900 this firm released Harvey Elijah Johnson's *The White Man's Failure in Government*. The Guide Publishing Company, which publishes the weekly *Journal and Guide* in Norfolk, Virginia, entered book publishing with the 1937 publication of *A History of the Virginia State Teachers Association* by historian Luther Porter Jackson. But the company only occasionally published other books. Among the titles published by the St. Louis Argus Publishing Company, which issues the St. Louis *Argus*, was *Immediate Jewel of His Soul*, a novel by Herman Dreer, in 1919. Other African American newspaper publishers that issued books have been the Iowa State Bystander Publishing Company (publisher of the Iowa State *Bystander* in Des Moines from 1894 to 1974) and the Dabney Publishing Company in Cincinnati, Ohio, which published the weekly *Union* from 1907 to 1952.

One of the first African American commercial trade book publishing firms in the United States was the Orion Publishing Company, established in Nashville, Tennessee by the Reverend Sutton E. Griggs in 1900. Griggs started the firm to publish books that he authored. Notable among the titles published were his *Overshadowed* (1902) and *The Hindered Hand or Reign of the Repressionist* (1905). Other African American book publishing firms active between 1900 and 1960 were J. A. Rogers Publications (New York City), Associated Publishers (Washington, D.C.), and A. Wendell Malliet Company (New York City).

After 1960, when the Black Revolution ignited in the black community a thirst for more knowledge about black culture, a plethora of African American commercial trade book publishing firms were established. Poet/librarian Dudley Randall started Broadside Press in Detroit in 1966. In Chicago, Haki Madhabuti established the Third World Press in 1967. Joseph Okpaku organized the Third World Press in New York in 1970. At the century's end, Third World Press, Path Press (Chicago), Black Classics Press (Baltimore), and Winston-Derek Publishers (Nashville) are among the leading black commercial book publishers in the United States. Popular titles from these firms are *Claiming Earth: Race, Rage, Rape, Redemption*, Haki R. Madhubuti (Third World Press, 1994); *American Diary: A Personal History of the Black Press*, Enoch P. Waters (Path Press, 1987); NAACP, *Burning at the Stake in the United States* (1919; reprint, Baltimore, MD: Black Classics Press, 1986); and *Blacks Who Died for Jesus*, Mark Hyman (Winston-Derek Publishers, 1983).

African American commercial publishers have made a significant contribution to American book publishing. They have provided publishing opportunities for many African American writers. Additionally, many titles published by these firms explore subjects in black history and culture that are not found in the works of mainstream publishers.

SELECTED BIBLIOGRAPHY: John H. Johnson and Lerone Bennett, Jr., *Succeeding Against the Odds* (New York: Warner Books, 1989); Donald Franklin Joyce, *Black Book Publishers in the United States: A Historical Dictionary of the Presses, 1817–1990* (New York: Greenwood Press, 1991).

Donald Franklin Joyce

BOOK PUBLISHERS, INSTITUTIONAL AND RELIGIOUS. Since 1871 several black institutions have engaged in book publishing. These institutions have been colleges and universities, professional and civil rights organizations, and cultural organizations. In 1871, when books appeared with the "Hampton Institute Press," historically black colleges and universities entered the book publishing market. All of these institutions, which occasionally published books, had no publishing units with editorial offices but printed and bound books using their own printing departments or contracted the services of a local printer. Between 1871 and 1972 many notable titles appeared bearing the imprints of Atlanta University Press, The Tuskegee Institute Press, Fisk University Press, Xavier University Press, and Howard University Press.

In 1972 Howard University launched the first university press in a historically black university replete with editorial offices. Two years later, in 1974, Howard University Press made its debut to the publishing world with the publication of its first annual list of titles. Among some of these new titles were *Pillars in Ethiopian History: The William Leo Hansberry African History Notebook*, vol. 1, edited by Joseph E. Harris (1974); and *A Poetic Equation: Conversations between Nikki Giovanni and Margaret Walker* (1974).

Professional and civil rights organizations also published books. The American Negro Academy, which was founded in 1896, was the earliest black professional organization to develop a publishing program that included the publication of books. Before its demise in 1924, the American Negro Academy had published such titles as *Occasional Papers 18–19* (1915) and *The Negro in American History*, by John Wesley Cromwell (1916). The Association for the Study of Negro Life and History began in 1918 a very ambitious book publishing program that lasted until 1950 and included such titles as *The Rural Negro*, by Carter G. Woodson (1930), and *The Negro in Reconstruction Virginia*, by A. A. Taylor (1926). The National Association for the Advancement of Colored People (NAACP) started publishing books occasionally in 1913, with the publication of a children's book, *Hazel*, by Mary Ovington White. Marcus Garvey's* Universal Publishing House, based in New York, published two titles authored by Garvey before its demise in 1927. Beginning in 1927, the National Urban League* became a very active book publisher, releasing annually many sociological, political, and economic studies on black life.

There were also several cultural organizations that published books. In 1959, the Free Lance Press, the publishing arm of Cleveland's Free Lance Poetry and Prose Workshop, began publishing books with publication of poet Conrad Kent Rivers's *Perchance to Dream*. And in Chicago, the DuSable Museum of African American History began publishing books in 1965 with the release under its imprint of Eugene Feldman's *Figures in Negro History*.

In addition to institutional book publishers, there have been several important African American religious book publishers. Founded by the African Methodist Episcopal Church in 1817 in Philadelphia, the A.M.E. Book Concern was the first religious book publishing enterprise established by African Americans in the United States. The first title issued by this pioneer religious black book publisher was *The Book of Discipline* (1817). In 1952, after 135 years of extensive book publishing, the A.M.E. Book Concern was discontinued by the General Conference of the African Methodist Episcopal Church.

Before the end of the nineteenth century, four other African American religious book publishers came into existence. Each of these firms is active today. In 1841 the A.M.E.Z. Publishing House was opened in New York City by the African Methodist Episcopal Zion Church. This firm moved to Charlotte, North Carolina, in 1894, where the denomination constructed in 1911 "the first publishing house in the country built by Negroes." *Zion's Historical Catechism*, edited by Cicero Richardson Harris (1898), and *The African Methodist Episcopal*

Zion Church: Reality of the Black Church, by William J. Wall (1974), are examples of titles released by this publisher.

The Colored Methodist Episcopal Church, currently known as the Christian Methodist Episcopal Church, established the C.M.E. Publishing House in 1870 in Jackson, Tennesssee. This religious publishing house moved to Memphis in 1966. Among titles issued by the C.M.E. Publishing House are *The Religious Educational Opportunity of the Local Church*, by Julian Smith (1936), and *The C.M.E. Primer: Our Heritage*, by C. D. Holman (1970).

A second book publishing enterprise was founded by the African Methodist Episcopal Church in 1882: the A.M.E. Sunday School Union and Publishing House. Originally located in Bloomington, Indiana, in 1881, the A.M.E. Sunday School Union and Publishing House moved to Nashville in 1886, where it is an active publisher today. Among some of the titles released by this firm are *Reflections of Seventy Years*, by Daniel A. Payne (1888); *The Negro at Mount Bayou*, by Aurelius P. Hood (1910); and *Of Men and Arms*, by John Gregg (1945).

One of the most successful black religious publishing firms established in the nineteeth century was the National Baptist Publishing Board. It was organized in 1896 by Richard Henry Boyd* in Nashville under the auspices of the National Baptist Convention of America. By 1913, the National Baptist Publishing Board had a physical plant valued at $350,000. In 1914 the National Baptist Convention of America split over the ownership of the National Baptist Publishing Board. Today this firm is one of the largest black publishing firms in the United States, releasing such titles as *An Operative Faith for Oppressed People*, by Walter Malone, Jr. (1987), and *A Black Man's Dream: The First Hundred Years; Richard Henry Boyd and the National Baptist Publishing Board*, by Bobby L. Lovett (1993).

In the first two decades of the twentieth century, two black religious firms came into existence. Both publishers are located in Tennessee. The Church of God in Christ opened the Church of God in Christ Publishing House in Memphis in 1907. Today this thriving publisher is expanding its annual list with such titles as *Yes, Lord! The Church of God in Christ Hymnal* (1988) and C.H. Mason's *Story Book for Children* (1989). The National Baptist Convention, U.S.A., Inc., organized the Sunday School Publishing Board in 1916 in Nashville after the National Baptists split over the ownership of the National Baptist Publishing Board. Today the Sunday School Publishing Board of the National Baptist Convention, U.S.A., Inc., is a leading religious publisher. In 1956 the Nation of Islam* organized a publishing firm in Chicago: Muhammad's Temple No. 2, Publications Department. This publisher has issued such titles as *A First Grade Reader*, by Christine Johnson (1963), and *How to Eat to Live*, by Elijah Muhammad* (1974). Beginning in 1979, FCN Publishing Company in Chicago began publishing titles for the Nation of Islam, issuing such books as Louis Farrakhan's* *A Torchlight for America* (1993).

Within the African American–owned book publishing segment of the American book publishers industry, religious book publishers have experienced the greatest longevity. As business enterprises, they are the most stable publishers in the African American segment of the American book publishing industry.

SELECTED BIBLIOGRAPHY: Donald Franklin Joyce, ed., *Black Book Publishers in the United States: A Historical Dictionary of the Presses, 1817–1990* (Westport, CT: Greenwood Press, 1991); Donald Franklin Joyce, *Gatekeepers of Black Culture: Black-Owned Book Publishing in the United States, 1817–1981* (Westport, CT: Greenwood Press, 1983).

Donald Franklin Joyce

BOOKSTORES, COMMERCIAL. African American bookstores are significant institutions in the black community. Historically their proprietors have been motivated more by cultural commitment than by the desire for financial gain. The history of black bookstores, consequently, has been predominated by a struggle to achieve a balance between efforts to provide cultural enrichment and the need to be financially viable. A 1996 African American Booksellers Conference seminar revealed that independent book dealers typically have to use 60 percent of their income to purchase merchandise, leaving only 40 percent for operating expenses and profits. In 1995 the average independent bookseller had $800,000 in sales and managed only a 2 percent profit. Many African American bookstores have been even less profitable and often struggle just to keep the doors open. Several proprietors of black book shops are unable to pay themselves a regular salary. A number of stores are staffed by the owner's family or volunteers. Like other independent book dealers, black booksellers tend to have low profit margins, as they must compete for market share with bookstore chains.

More than 500 black book-vending enterprises exist in the United States. They range from mail and web site operations to full-service stores. Often located in the heart of the African American community, black bookstores provide resources, services, and programming that promote, disseminate, and preserve African American history and culture. In addition to selling books, journals, greeting cards, games, art, and other items, they provide a forum for classes, discussion groups, literacy projects, health seminars, films, music recitals, poetry readings, and political events. African American booksellers are often the only vendors who stock the publications of smaller black presses. The works of highly publicized black authors, published by the large publishing houses, can be found in any of the major bookstore chains. However, these mainstream book dealers are much less likely to carry works by smaller African American presses or out-of-print black publications.

For many decades, African American bookstores have played integral roles in black intellectual life. Among the most celebrated was the National Memorial Bookstore in Harlem, founded in the 1930s by Lewis H. Michaux, a cultural force in Harlem for half a century. Michaux's bookstore was a center of research and study for great numbers of people who utilized the store's holdings of over 200,000 books, periodicals, photographs, and other resources. In addition to selling books, Michaux made his resources available for reading, browsing, and researching, and his shop served as a center for frequent discussions and debates. A 1976 *Publishers Weekly* article called the store a Harlem landmark that "attracted customers from all over the world," including Kwame Nkrumah, Malcolm X, and W.E.B. Du Bois, who met his wife, Shirley Graham, there. Michaux sold books from a wagon before he opened a shop on Adam Clayton Powell Jr. Boulevard and 125th Street.

The black consciousness movement of the 1960s and early 1970s brought about an extraordinary increase in the quantity of publications on the African American experience both from the large publishing houses and the newer black independent presses, including Jihad, Broadside, Third World Press, Alkebu-lan, and Julian Richardson Associates. Alfred and Bernice Ligon's Aquarian Bookshop had been serving the Los Angeles black community for many years. During this period a number of new African American bookstores opened, including Liberation Bookstore in New York, Third World Books in Chicago, Shrine of the Black Madonna in Detroit, Kalamazoo, and Atlanta, and Marcus Books in the San Francisco Bay Area.

Marcus Books, which was established by Julian and Raye Richardson, has been an important cultural presence in the San Francisco Bay Area for several decades. Richardson started out in the Bay Area in printing, a trade he had learned at Tuskegee Institute. His initial idea was to publish a black weekly, but his interest in black books grew whereby he eventually found himself engaged in the book trade. "I began ordering so many black books for Raye and myself and for friends, that I had to hire a clerk. Before I knew it the front of the printshop had been transformed into the Success Bookstore."

In 1964 the bookstore became Marcus Books. Today the Richardsons operate bookstores in San Francisco and in Oakland. Marcus Books contains a wealth of black publications, particularly scarce, out-of print, or smaller press titles, but the most valuable resource is Julian Richardson himself. He is a repository of information on African American culture and social movements. Author Earl Conrad notes: "Rich runs more than a bookstore. . . . He's really a San Francisco institution, a one man reference center on Black culture." Also, Richardson established a publishing house, Julian Richardson Associates. It has published a number of books, including the popular *Stolen Legacy* by George James.

Black bookstore owners emphasize the importance of continuing to make available the classic and historic literature of the African diaspora, as well as contemporary best-sellers. At the same time, black bookstores are vulnerable to such problems as inadequate financing, difficulties with distributors and publishers, competition from megastores and discount chains, and obstacles to keeping their locations in the communities that they serve. In 1968 National Memorial Bookstore in Harlem was moved to a new location on 125th Street to make room for a new state office building. Six years later, Michaux faced another battle to keep it open. While hundreds of Harlem residents protested a state eviction order that would remove the bookshop from the community, Michaux was forced to close, and the African American community lost a historical and cultural landmark.

Over the years, many other African American bookstores have been forced to close their doors or change their focus. In the early 1970s, one midwestern bookshop had to change its stock from black titles to textbooks in order to survive financially. In 1977 Freedom Bookstore in New York closed one month after celebrating its seventh anniversary. In spite of valiant efforts, proprietor James Jones was eventually overcome by such problems as uninsured rain damage, inability to get a bank loan, and unsuccessful negotiations with the landlord. Another tragedy took place in 1992, when Bernice and Alfred Ligon's venerable Aquarian Bookshop was destroyed by fire during the rioting in South Central Los Angeles, following the Rodney King verdict.

Fortunately, many black booksellers have managed to thrive in the face of challenges. In 1995 the Richardsons were able to overcome structural building problems to keep their Oakland store open and remain committed to maintaining a branch of Marcus Books in that city. During the same year African Americans in New Orleans were relieved to discover that the Community Book Center, which had suddenly disappeared from its Ursulines Street location, had in fact been moved to a more spacious and structurally sound facility. In 1994 Clara Villarosa, proprietor of Hue-Man Experience Bookstore in Denver, was the Commerce Department's Minority Entrepreneur of the Year. The store opened in 1984 with 300 titles. That number has grown to over 4,700, and Hue-Man, which has a mail-order component, is now one of the largest black bookstores in the country.

Miss Villarosa has been on the cutting edge of enhancing the business capabilities of African American bookstores. At the 1996 American Booksellers Association annual meeting, she and other industry professionals organized the African American Booksellers Conference, which provides information on such issues as accounting, financial planning, marketing, public relations, competing with major chains, demographics of black book purchasers, and the roles that black bookstores play in the success of African American publishers and writers.

Significant factors in the improving financial position of black bookstores in the 1990s include a steady increase in the numbers of Afro-American book buyers and a growing number of blockbuster publications by African American authors. This phenomenon has been tracked by Blackboard African American Bestsellers List as well as such publications as *ABBWA Journal* (*American Black Book Writers Association*), *QBR: The Black Book Review*, and *Target Market News*. Foremost among the best-selling writers is Terri Macmillan. Her novels, most notably *Waiting to Exhale*, lured record numbers of buyers, especially African American women, into bookstores. While in these stores, many of them purchased additional books.

Another major political as well as publishing event was Colin Powell's *My*

American Journey. Sales of his book were fueled by speculation about the possibility of the popular and charismatic general's presidential candidacy and a brilliantly orchestrated book tour that drew record numbers of autograph seekers and fans from coast to coast. Several of the participating bookstores were African American, including Phoenix, a relatively new bookstore in San Bernardino, California. The proprietor of Phoenix, Joann Roberts, astounded numerous skeptics by pulling off this coup, which was accomplished by convincing the city government of the plan's feasibility, engaging community support, and meeting Random House's requirement to sell 2,000 copies of the book.

African Americans, especially parents, educators, writers, librarians, and publishers, have a compelling interest in supporting black bookstores. Without them, many Afro-American books and journals would be unavailable to the public. This is particularly true of publications of smaller presses and works by new writers. Quite a few authors have acknowledged the role of black booksellers in their success. Along with black-oriented museums, research collections, theater groups, and other cultural institutions, the bookstore is an essential component of the educational and intellectual fabric of African American life.

SELECTED BIBLIOGRAPHY: American Booksellers Association, *The Future of Black Book Selling* (Washington, DC: National Audio Video, 1996), audiocassette; Willard Dickerson, *Understanding and Using Financial Documents and Management Decisions*, African American Booksellers Conference, 1996 (Washington, DC: National Audio Video, 1996), audiocassette; Ernest Holsendolph, "Small Bookshops Turn the Page to Survival," *Emerge* (June 1995); David Philip, "Is the Black Bookstore an Endangered Species?" *Amsterdam News*, January 1977; D. W. Steele, "Black Book Sales in the 1990s: Will This Be the Decade for Black Books and Black Writers?" *ABBWA Journal* (Spring 1993).

Rosemary M. Stevenson

BOYCOTTS, ECONOMIC. The use of the boycott by blacks in the struggle against racial discrimination has a long history in the African American experience. In 1833, a resolution was passed at the National Negro Convention* that "black businesspeople would only sell, and black consumers would only buy those products that had not been produced from slave labor." Also, delegates were urged to return home and form free labor produce societies to support the boycott. While a few black merchants complied and a few consumers, such as black female reformer Francis Ellen Watkins Harper, most blacks did not have the discretionary income to support the boycott in purchasing the more expensive alternatives to slave-produced goods.

Then, from the late 1890s to the 1990s, there were four waves of black economic boycotts. The first wave occurred in the South at the turn of the century, the second during the depression of the 1930s, followed some 30 years later by the massive economic boycotts in the South during the civil rights movement of the 1950s and 1960s. In the post–civil rights era, economic boycotts by blacks were launched at both local and national levels.

The 1890s marked the beginning of the movements in southern states in response to the 1896 Supreme Court *Plessy v. Ferguson* decision, which declared separate but equal public accommodations constitutional. With solid legal support, southern states and cities rushed to enact legislation mandating segregated public facilities including theaters, parks, schools, rest rooms, and seating in courts, libraries, trains, and local streetcars and trolleys. Laws requiring segregated streetcars, however, had appeared in Tennessee (1881) and Georgia (1891). Initially, complaints from streetcar companies citing the expense and difficulty of enforcement, the fear of losing black customers, and the apathy of the white public resulted in erratic enforcement. The rise of radical racism in the wake of *Plessy* fundamentally changed the social environment of the South. While streetcar companies continued to oppose segregation, white public and white political leaders demanded Jim Crow transportation facilities. Louisiana passed the first statewide law requiring segregated public transportation in 1902, Mississippi in 1904, Tennessee and Florida in 1905, followed by Virginia, Oklahoma, the Carolinas, Alabama, Arkansas, and Texas.

Protest response to segregated municipal transportation facilities in the South, which were used on a daily basis by African Americans, provoked a widespread boycott movement across the South. In just about every major city, African American leaders urged blacks to stay off streetcars until Jim Crow laws were overturned. The response of the African American community was immediate. Boycott movements were launched in Atlanta, Georgia, 1900–1903; Rome, Georgia, 1900; Augusta, Georgia, 1900–1903; Montgomery, Alabama, 1900–1902; Jacksonville, Florida, 1901; Mobile, Alabama, 1902; New Orleans and Shreveport, Louisiana, 1902–1903; Little Rock Arkansas, and Columbia, South Carolina, 1903; Houston, Texas, 1903–1905; Vicksburg and Natchez, Mississippi, 1904; San Antonio, Texas, and Richmond, Virginia, 1904–1905; Memphis, Chattanooga, and Knoxville, Tennessee, and Pensacola and Jacksonville, Florida, 1905; Nashville, Tennessee, 1905–1906; Danville, Lynchburg, Portsmouth, and Norfolk, Virginia, and Savannah, Georgia, 1906–1907.

In Little Rock, Arkansas, black patronage of streetcars dropped from 60 percent to 5 percent. In Houston, Atlanta, Jacksonville, Mobile, and Nashville, reports show the boycotts were almost 100 percent effective. In many cities African Americans who dared to ride streetcars were snatched off by boycotters or publically denounced at mass meetings. Blacks who owned hacks (taxis) in many cities lowered their prices in support of the movements. While black businessmen in Savannah, Norfolk, and Nashville tried to organize their own trolley companies, threats of violence, economic intimidation, white intransigence, divisions in the black community, and most of all, the lack of black voting power doomed the movements. By 1910 Jim Crow public transportation was firmly established, symbolic of white supremacy in southern culture, and would not be challenged until Montgomery in 1955.

Competition from white merchants in urban black business districts in the post–World War I era and black unemployment during the depression led to the second wave in the organized black economic boycott movement. In an effort to discourage blacks from shopping at white groceries, the Colored Merchants Association (CMA) was founded in the late 1920s. In 1928 Albion Holsey of the National Negro Business League* assumed leadership of the CMA, a co-operative group of African American merchants. The CMA purchased goods at the cheaper wholesale level for their members so that they could compete with white chain store prices. The CMA promoted membership on an ideological foundation based on encouraging black consumers to "buy black." As Holsey noted, "The Negro purchasing power of over $300 million worth of consumers goods could be harnessed as a foundation for the development of African American business development." CMA stores were established in Washington, Richmond, New York, and Baltimore.

While the CMA "buy black" movement collapsed in the mid-1930s, at the same time during the depression, blacks launched boycotts against white-owned stores that were supported by black patronage but did not employ them. The first boycott movement, or "Jobs for Negroes Campaign," started in Chicago in 1929 and was led by ex-prize fighter Big Bill Tate and a local African American newspaper, the Chicago *Whip*, which launched a massive "Don't Buy Where You Can't Work" campaign. Unlike the previous southern bus boycott, the 1930s "Don't Buy Where You Can't Work" campaigns were often accompanied by picketing at the offending businesses and spread across the entire nation, although primarily in the large urban centers in the North, involving a wide variety of leadership and levels of success.

Some of the more well-publicized movements surfaced around the Colored Clerks Circle (1929) in St. Louis; the New Negro Alliance in Washington, D.C. (1933); the *Sentinel* effort (1934) in Los Angeles: and the "Don't Buy Where You Can't Work" campaign in Atlanta led by the Atlanta *World* in 1934. Similar campaigns emerged in Philadelphia led by the local Urban League and in Baltimore (1933) by the colorful Prophet Kiowa Costonie. The most turbulent "Don't Buy Where You Can't Work" campaigns appeared in Harlem, New York City, where there were competing movements led by Mystic Sufi Abdul Hamid; Episcopalian minister John Johnson of the Citizens League for Fair Play; the African Patriotic League; and the Harlem Labor Union—all while street corner orators harangued shoppers and led picketing against offending stores.

These "action boycotts" would play a role in the eruption of the 1935 Harlem Riot and led to the early career of the young Abyssinian Baptist Church minister Adam Clayton Powell, Jr. He organized the Citywide Coordinating Committee. It led a job campaign that placed blacks in Harlem stores as well as jobs with the Edison Electric Company, Bell Telephone Company, the New York bus system, and the 1939 New York World's Fair. Nationwide, however, not more than a few thousand African Americans secured jobs as a result of these economic boycotts. The "Don't Buy Where You Can't Work" movements ended with employment created by the demands of World War II, but black community organizations continued to address a wide variety of issues. Powell forged his "jobs for Negroes campaign" into a political organization, which helped in his election to the city council and, in 1944, to Congress.

The third wave of economic boycotts began with the Montgomery bus boycott of 1955 led by E. D. Nixon and Martin Luther King, Jr., which launched the modern civil rights movement. Like the bus boycott movement of the turn of the century, the Montgomery movement inspired similar efforts in Tallahassee, Florida, Savannah, Georgia, and New Orleans in the late 1950s. After 1960, the boycott became one of several "direct action" tactics utilized in the civil rights movement, sit-ins, freedom rides, mass marches, picketing, and voter registration campaigns. Boycotts against segregated business accompanied the sit-ins in Nashville, Atlanta, Albany, Georgia, and Greensboro, North Carolina. Boycotts also preceded Dr. King's demonstrations in Birmingham, Selma, and Chicago. Blacks also staged partial boycotts of businesses and schools during the voter registration campaigns in the freedom summer project in Mississippi in 1964.

In both the 1930s and the 1960s, the use of the economic boycott by blacks did not go unchallenged. In 1934 Kauffman Five and Dime and Sanitary Drugstore in Washington, D.C., secured a temporary injunction against the New Negro Alliance boycott, contending that pickets were "unlawful assemblies that restrained trade, endangered lives of pedestrians and could result in violent riots." The New Negro Alliance appealed the injunction. In 1938 the Supreme Court ruled that black organizations had the right to organize boycotts against discrimination. In 1966 the use of a "secondary boycott" was challenged in Claiborne County, Mississippi. The Claiborne Hardware Store sued the local National Association for the Advancement of Colored People (NAACP), for financial damages the hardware store incurred during a general boycott over county-wide racial issues. The state court upheld Claiborne Hardware's contention that the boycott was illegal, but after a long appeal, the Supreme Court in 1982 ruled that the boycott was a legal exercise of free speech.

When used in conjunction with other tactics, boycotts in the past have proven an effective tool. Since the civil rights era, economic boycotts have taken place sporadically. Operation PUSH (People United to Save Humanity), led by Reverend Jesse Jackson,* launched several campaigns from the 1970s through the 1990s to increase black employment in white-owned companies.

SELECTED BIBLIOGRAPHY: Gary Hunter, "Don't Buy Where You Can't Work: Black Economic Boycotts during The Depression" (Ph.D diss., University of Michigan, 1977); August Meier and Elliot Rudwick, *Along the Color Line: Explorations of the African American Experience* (Urbana: University of Illinois Press, 1962); *N.A.A.C.P. v. Claiborne Hardware Company*, 458. U.S. 886 (1982); Juliet E. K. Walker, *The History of Black Business in America: Capitalism, Race, Entrepreneurship* (New York: Macmillan/Prentice Hall International, 1998); Juliet E. K. Walker, "Promoting Black Entrepreneurship and Business Enterprise in Antebellum America: The National Negro Convention, 1830–1860," in Thomas D. Boston, ed., *A Different Vision: Race and Public Policy* (London: Routledge, 1997), 280–318.

Gary J. Hunter

BOYD, RICHARD HENRY (1843–1922), Tennessee, publisher, manufacturer, real estate investor, bank founder, municipal bus company founder, minister, civic leader, activist, college founder.

In 1896 Reverend Richard H. Boyd, representing the National Baptist Convention but with his own venture capital and business connections, financed the establishment of the National Baptist Publishing House at Nashville, building a printing plant that covered half a city block, which he purchased. By 1910, the annual company payroll was $200,000. In 1912, the printing plant, valued at $350,000, had published 128 million copies of religious literature. A 1915 audit and subsequent court order divested the National Baptist Convention from ownership of the plant. Boyd had chartered the publishing house as a private corporation, which, under his management since 1906, had earned $2.4 million.

The most successful black entrepreneurs at the turn of the century tapped a national black consumer market. By 1920, the National Baptist Publishing House was one of the largest black businesses in the nation. Boyd's expansive business empire also included the One Cent Savings and Bank Trust he founded in 1904, renamed the Citizens Savings Bank and Trust in 1920, noted for its conservative fiscal policies; the *Nashville Globe*, founded in 1905; the Globe Publishing Company; the National Negro Doll Company, 1909–1929; the National Baptist Church Supply Company, which manufactured church furniture; and in 1905, the Union Transportation Company, founded in response to transportation segregation laws.

The Union Transportation Company owned 5 steam-driven busses and 14 electric busses, powered by the electric dynamo of the National Baptist Publishing Company. The white-owned Railway and Light Company, which supplied electric power to Nashville, had reneged on its promise to supply power. The short-lived bus company failed in 1906. The company was initially undercapitalized, but a specially imposed municipal tax on the busses, the dispersed residential patterns of Nashville's black passengers, and a per bus limit of only 20 passengers also contributed to its profit losses.

Boyd was also an officer in the National Negro Business League* founded by Booker T. Washington* in 1900 and shared the latter's business philosophy that "business development was intimately connected with black social and economic independence and that this, in turn, was the key to true freedom for his race." Boyd, however, was also a strong proponent of Du Bois's ideology of organized militant protest against racism. Boyd's political activism and financial support secured the establishment of Tennessee State University, founded in 1912 as the Tennessee Agricultural and Industrial School in Nashville.

The Mississippi slave-born Boyd managed his owner's plantation during the Civil War, marketing the cotton in Mexico. After the Civil War he worked as a cowboy and cotton trader in Texas before his career in the ministry. Boyd did not learn to read until he was 30 and studied briefly at Bishop College. In 1869, he married Hattie Moore. They were the parents of nine children. Richard H. Boyd was 53 when he initiated his first business venture.

SELECTED BIBLIOGRAPHY: Richard H. Boyd, *A Story of the National Baptist Publishing Board: The Why, How, When, and By Whom It Was Established*, rev. ed. (Nashville: National Baptist Publishing Board, 1922); John N. Ingham and Lynne B. Feldman, *African-American Business Leaders: A Biographical Dictionary* (Westport, CT: Greenwood Press, 1994); Donald Franklin Joyce, *Gatekeepers of Black Culture: Black-Owned Book Publishing in the United States, 1817–1981* (Westport, CT: Greenwood Press, 1983); Lester C. Lamon, *Black Tennesseans, 1900–1930* (Knoxville: University of Tennessee Press, 1977); Bobby L. Lovett, *A Black Man's Dream, The First 100 Years: Henry Boyd and the National Baptist Publishing Board* (Jacksonville, FL: Mega Corp., 1993).

Juliet E. K. Walker

BRONNER, NATHANIEL H. (1914–1993), Georgia, founder of Bronner Bros. of Atlanta.

The Bronner Bros. enterprise includes not only a hair care products line but a renowned international beauty show, a contemporary African American magazine, and a hot springs spa and motel. In 1992, Bronner Bros. had $19.5 million in sales and ranked 72nd on the *Black Enterprise* list of the top 100 black-owned businesses. Bronner Bros. sells about 50 ethnic cosmetic and hair care products including the ''African Royale'' brand. Bronner was born in Jasper County about 60 miles south of Atlanta, Georgia, in a family of 11 children. At the age of 6, he was contributing to the family income by selling the *Grit* newspaper. At the age of 16, he left his rural Georgia home, moved to Atlanta to live with relatives, and landed a job delivering the *Atlanta Daily World*, a leading African American newspaper.

While one of his sisters was attending an Apex Beauty College, Bronner developed an interest in the cosmetology business. He observed that while newspaper subscribers sometimes lacked money to pay for the newspaper, they always managed to buy beauty products. When his sister opened her own beauty salon, Bronner set up a small sidewalk stand in front and sold beauty products, newspapers, and other items. He later became a salesman for Apex News and Hair Co. In 1940, Bronner graduated with a degree in business from Morehouse College. Beginning in 1941, he served in the military for four and a half years. Upon his return from duty, he worked with his sister's salon.

In 1947 Bronner formed a wholesale distributorship—Bronner Bros. Later his brother, Arthur E. Bronner, joined him, and they formed Bronner Bros., Incorporated. The motto of the business was ''Beauty: the depression proof business.'' Other family members were also brought into the business. In 1947, the first annual International Beauty and Trade Show was held, and 300 people attended. In 1996, more than 100,000 people attended, including delegates from Africa, Europe, and the Caribbean.

In 1978, Bronner shifted the company's gears to manufacturing products such as BB Double Strength Super Gro, the Cosmopolitan Curl Line, and African Royale. In 1991 the company acquired the Cottonwood Hot Springs Spa and Motel in Cottonwood, Alabama. Also, in the 1990s, *Upscale* magazine, which boasts 1 million–plus readers, was established by the Bronner company. Bronner established the "Black on Black Love Campaign," which provides clothing and shoes for poor children. The company also established a scholarship fund for underprivileged children who want to enter the cosmetic's industry. Bronner Bros. remains a family business, operated by the heirs of the founders.

SELECTED BIBLIOGRAPHY: Tom Bennett, "Nathaniel Bronner Sr.," *Atlanta Journal and Constitution*, July 20, 1997; "Bronner Remembered as a Pioneer: Hair-Care Show Gets Global Attention," *Atlanta Journal and Constitution*, July 21, 1993; William Gordon, "The Bronners of Atlanta," *The World & I* (April 1991); "Grooming the Kids to Take Over: Successful Black Family Firms Deal with Succession," *Atlanta Journal and Constitution*, January 28, 1991; Shelia M. Poole, "Hair-Care Patriarch Bronner Opens Alabama Spa," *Atlanta Journal and Constitution*, October 11, 1991.

Nancy J. Dawson

BROWN, RONALD HARMON (1941–1996), Washington, D.C., Secretary of Commerce, lawyer, lobbyist.

Ronald Harmon Brown was the most preeminent individual to ever hold the position of U.S. secretary of commerce and also the first African American appointed to this position. He served in that position for three years, from 1993 until 1996, when he was killed in a plane crash. As secretary of commerce, Brown's activities were important for the American business community, especially in bringing minority businesses, not only African American but also Asian and Hispanic American, into the global economy. On his death, President William Clinton said: "Ron Brown walked and ran and flew through life, and he was a magnificent life force."

The plane that took Brown's life collided into a mountainside, only two miles from his destination, the Croatian city of Dubrovnik. Brown was on a peace mission to determine postwar reconstruction plans for the two war-torn European countries Bosnia and Croatia. While secretary of commerce, Brown traveled the world and generated more international business deals for American business than any previous secretary of commerce. In three years, Brown made 15 trade missions to more than 25 countries, including Russia, Germany, India, Indonesia, People's Republic of China, Japan, Chile, Bolivia, Brazil, and South Africa. Brown's trade missions resulted in some $80 billion in contracts for American business. Indeed, in three years, he increased American exports by 26 percent.

Brown was born in Freedmen's Hospital in Washington, D.C., to Gloria Osborne and William Harmon Brown. His early life was spent in New York City, where he grew up in Harlem and lived in the famed Hotel Theresa, which his father managed. In 1962 Brown received his B.A. from Middlebury College in

Vermont. He also attained his ROTC commission as a second lieutenant and served his tour of duty in West Germany and Korea from 1962 to 1966, when he was honorably discharged with the rank of captain. He then attended St. John's University Law School for his J.D. degree.

Brown then worked for the National Urban League* from 1967 until 1979. In 1980 he worked on the Senator Edward Kennedy presidential campaign. In 1981, he became the first black partner at the Washington law firm of Patton, Boggs and Blow, where he worked as both a lawyer and lobbyist until his appointment as secretary of commerce in 1993. Also, in 1988, he was convention manager for the Reverend Jesse Jackson* when he ran for president of the United States.

Brown was survived by his wife of 33 years, Alma Brown, son Michael, daughter Tracey, and two grandchildren. On his death, Hugh B. Price, president of the National Urban League, said: "We believe that history will show that he was one of the most effective secretaries of commerce—a bridge builder who opened up global trade and created jobs in America while engineering the Information Super Highway so that it also includes the inner cities." Despite his accomplishments, Brown had been charged with financial irregularities in his private business life, with charges still continuing even after his death.

SELECTED BIBLIOGRAPHY: "America's Top Business Advocate," *Black Enterprise* (June 1993); George E. Curry, "Attacking Ron Brown, *Emerge* (September 1997); Michael K. Frisby, "The Unsinkable Ron Brown," *Black Enterprise* (December 1995); Joyce Jones, "The Best Commerce Secretary Ever," *Black Enterprise* (June 1996).

Jeffrey E. Walker

BROWN, TONY [WILLIAM ANTHONY] (1933–), New York City, Television producer, author, black business promoter.

The *Tony Brown's Journal* show is the oldest black public television show, aired to 250 stations across the nation. It has been on the air since 1976, initially as the *Black Journal* show until 1978. Brown uses the forum of his show to promote the philosophy of self-help in encouraging black business expansion. In 1985, he initiated the "Buy Freedom" campaign in which he urged African Americans to spend half of their consumer dollars with black businesses. He also publishes a magazine, *Tony Brown's Journal*, to advance his philosophy of black economic nationalism.

Brown, as a stanch economic nationalist, has generated support for his promotion of black business, but at the same time, his political affiliation is questioned. Brown is a Republican who believes that this party provides a more realistic agenda for the resolution of black economic limitations. In one commentary, Brown said "You can talk about the other problems of our community, but the real cause is that we have failed to get into business. We have to do something to shore up our economic institutions, to generate jobs within the community." While Brown's promotion of black business is accepted, at the same time, his indictment of blacks for not being more aggressive in establishing business has generated controversy.

Brown, the first dean of the Howard University School of Communications, appointed in 1972, was born in Charleston, West Virginia. He served in the military from 1953 to 1955, then attended Wayne State University in Detroit, graduating with a B.A. degree in 1959 and a M.S.W. in social work in 1961. He practiced as a psychiatric social worker while also writing a newspaper column. In 1980 Brown sponsored the first annual Black College Day in Washington, D.C., which was attended by 18,000 black students. He used this forum to emphasize the importance of preserving the historically black colleges and universities, indicating that only 3 out of 10 black students attending predominantly white colleges graduated. Brown is the author of several books that promote his philosophy of economic black nationalism, whereas he uses the communication media to promote technology to minorities.

SELECTED BIBLIOGRAPHY: Tony Brown, *Black Lives, White Lies: The Truth According to Tony Brown* (New York: William Morrow, 1995); Tony Brown, *Empower the People: A 7-Step Plan to Overthrow the Conspiracy That Is Stealing Your Money and Freedom* (New York: William Morrow, 1998); George C. Fraser, *Race for Success: The Ten Best Business Opportunities for Blacks in America* (New York: William Morrow, 1998); Randall L. Kennedy, "Black Conservatism's Would-Be Spokesmen," *QBR: The Black Book Review* 3 (November–December 1995).

Jeffrey E. Walker

BURRELL, THOMAS J. (1939–), Illinois, advertising executive, public relations promoter.

Thomas Burrell is chairman and chief executive officer of Burrell Communications Group (BCG), a Chicago-based African American advertising agency that provides public relations, consumer promotions, and direct marketing services. In 1996 Burrell Communications Group handled $135 million in annual sales, with 141 employees and offices in Chicago, New York, and Atlanta. Burrell Communications Group has received numerous advertising awards, including two Clio Awards, the advertising industry's highest honor of achievement.

Thomas Burrell was born in Chicago and grew up on the city's South Side. He described his early days in high school as unmotivated and troublesome until he changed high schools and found peers who aspired to go to college and become doctors and lawyers. Burrell thrived in this new environment and learned that he had a talent for writing and art. He went on to college, graduating from Roosevelt University in Chicago in 1961 with a degree in English, and a commitment to a field that offered no role models for people of color. Starting as a clerk in the mail room of Wade Advertising in 1960, he advanced to copy trainee and copywriter, a position he held when he worked for Leo Burnett, from 1964 to 1967, and Foot Cone & Belding London, from 1967 to 1968. From 1968 to 1971 he was employed as copy supervisor for Needham Harper

& Steers. His experiences at white agencies helped him better understand the cultural differences between white consumers and black consumers. He felt that black consumers tended to be more complex and wanted advertisements that played back the positive reality of succeeding, surviving, overcoming, achieving, and aspiring.

From 1971 to 1974 Burrell was the co-owner and chair of Burrell McBain Advertising, when he founded Burrell Communications Group. The business was started without bank loans. Within six months, Burrell won his first account. It was with Philip Morris. Other major companies followed. The BCG company has handled many prestigious accounts including Swanson Frozen Foods, Vic. Chem, Alka-Seltzer, Coca-Cola, Procter & Gamble, McDonald's, Ford Motor, K-Mart, and Pillsbury. Burrell's ads are known for being positive and upbeat.

Burrell won his first Clio Award in 1977 for a TV spot for Coke with five black kids sitting on a stoop in Manhattan singing "Coke adds life." In 1978 he won a second Clio for a McDonald's commercial, "A Family Is." A 1995 acquisition of DFA, a New York mainstream agency, helped topple his company over the $100 million mark. In 1985 Burrell was selected Person of the Year by the Chicago Advertising Club. In 1990 the University of Missouri honored him with the prestigious Missouri Honor Medal for Distinguished Service in Journalism. In 1995 Burrell was named one of the "50 Who Made a Difference" by *Advertising Age*. Thomas Burrell is married to Joli Burrell. They have three children.

SELECTED BIBLIOGRAPHY: *Advertising Age*, June 3, 1996; Edd Applegate, *The Ad Men and Women: A Biographical Dictionary of Advertising* (Westport, CT: Greenwood Press, 1994); *Black Enterprise* (March 1996); *Emerge* (March 1996).

Teresa Savage

BUSH, JOHN EDWARD (1856–1916), Arkansas, real estate speculator, founder of Mosaic Templars, federal officeholder, civil rights activist.

The slave-born John Edward Bush, like his close friend Booker T. Washington,* was an advocate of black self-help. Both believed that blacks could escape the sharp barbs of Jim Crow through the development of their own economic institutions. Subsequently, when Bush was approached by Washington, who was seeking support for the establishment of a National Negro Business League (NNBL),* he gave him enthusiastic support. Bush was also a charter member of the NNBL when it was officially founded by Washington in 1900. Bush's own efforts toward achieving economic independence began in 1875 when, at the age of 19, he purchased a Little Rock city lot for $150. He later sold the lot for enough profit to buy three other pieces of real estate in the city. By 1907 he had acquired property in and around Little Rock valued at $30,000. By 1910 he had built a massive Victorian home valued in excess of $10,000 and amassed a personal fortune of $100,000.

In 1882 Bush founded the Mosaic Templars, a black-owned and -operated fraternal and business organization. Officially chartered by the state of Arkansas in 1883, the Templars' charter empowered the fraternal organization to operate its own financial institutions. Subsequently, the Templars, under Bush's leadership, organized their own savings and loan association and insurance company. The founding of both represented Bush's desire to lay a sound financial foundation for the economic success and progress of his people. Following official incorporation, the Templars experienced rapid growth. By 1918, the organization had become international with chapters in Central America, Panama, and the West Indies and had a membership in excess of 80,000 and assets exceeding $300,000.

John E. Bush was born in Moscow, Tennessee, the son of a white planter and a slave woman. He and his mother were brought to Arkansas in 1862 by their owner in an effort to escape advancing Union troops in Tennessee. Shortly after their arrival in Little Rock, Bush's mother died, and he became an orphan and drifter. In 1869 he was forced to enter Little Rock's Capitol Hill public school for blacks, which had just opened. According to his teacher who remembered the "red-haired, fair complexion" youngster, he "quickly became one of the brightest, most studious, and seemed to eat up the work." Bush had to work to finance his education. It took him seven years to complete his high school education, but he graduated with honors in 1876 and was hired as one of the school's teachers, but Bush kept his night job as a postal clerk in the Railway Service of Arkansas.

Bush's appointment in 1875 as a postal clerk was a federal patronage appointment and represented the beginning of a long career in federal service until 1913. He was active in the Republican Party and participated in their state conventions, beginning in 1883, as an elected representative of the sixth ward of Pulaski County (Little Rock and North Little Rock). In 1884, he was named secretary to the convention and elected to one of five at-large positions on the Pulaski County Republican Central Committee. He was a delegate to the 1892 Republican National Convention. In 1898 President William McKinley appointed Bush Receiver of United States Lands (Monies) at Little Rock, which made him the highest-ranking federal officeholder in Arkansas. He held the post until 1913, when Democrat Woodrow Wilson became president.

Bush used his prestigious position to lobby the state and national party for more black appointments and to fight a growing tide of racial discrimination and Jim Crow legislation in Arkansas. In 1891 he led a vigorous effort by a group of prominent blacks in Little Rock to prevent the passage of a state law requiring segregation of the races in public transportation. In a petition against the proposed legislation known as the "Separate Coach Law," Bush said that the passage of the law would subject blacks "to the special insult, contumely and imposition of a certain well known class of white persons." The Separate Coach Law was passed, but Bush continued to fight racial discrimination. In 1905 he led a successful effort to prevent the state from passing a statute that would have funded the state's segregated public schools from taxes paid by each race. Black schools would have been funded only from taxes paid by blacks.

While a successful businessman, Bush's contributions to the black community in Arkansas during a time of escalating racism stand as a monument to a man dedicated to uplifting his race. The *American Guide* said that he was "an honest, active, dedicated politician and Race man, [who] must be included as one of the four as representatives of his people."

SELECTED BIBLIOGRAPHY: A. E. Bush and P. L. Dorman, *History of the Mosaic Templars of America, Its Founders and Officials* (Little Rock: Central Printing Co., 1924); Willard Gatewood, *Aristocrats of Color: The Black Elite, 1880–1920* (Bloomington: Indiana University Press, 1990), 92–93; C. Calvin Smith, "John E. Bush: The Politician and the Man, 1880–1916," *Arkansas Historical Quarterly* 54, 2 (Summer 1995): 115–133.

C. Calvin Smith

BUSINESS, TRADITIONAL AND EMERGING LINES. The African American business community is profoundly different in the 1990s than it was in the 1960s. As size and scope have expanded, industry diversity has flourished. The growing lines of black business are dominated today by larger-scale firms that are likely to serve a racially diverse clientele and are commonly run by college-educated entrepreneurs. Particularly rapid growth areas include skill-intensive service industries: finance, business services, and various professional services. Such growth industries are commonly called "emerging" lines of minority enterprise. They are emerging in the sense that the presence of African American ownership in these industries has historically been minimal.

As recently as the early 1960s, black entrepreneurship was not a major route to upward mobility in the United States. Business owners have most commonly struggled to make a living running marginal enterprises, particularly in small-scale retailing and personal services. Traditionally, the typical firm in the black business community has been the Mom-and-Pop food store, the beauty parlor, and the barbershop. These tiny firms were concentrated in black residential areas and served a local clientele. This type of enterprise has been in a state of decline for over 30 years.

Since the 1960s, the African American business community has started to diversify and expand in response to an influx of entrepreneurial talent and financial capital. Aggregate figures on black-owned business understate this progress because they fail to identify two divergent trends: absolute decline in many traditional lines of business and real progress in emerging fields. Why the decline in the traditional strongholds? The large traditional sector of the black business community developed under pervasive racial segregation. Partial desegregation in housing, the workplace, commercial establishments, and public accommodations contributed to the decline of these firms: Desegregation widened the range of retail and service markets accessible to black consumers.

Desegregation did not, however, lead to significant white patronization of black-owned businesses. Many of the traditional black firms—long excluded from the mainstream economy—were ill-equipped to exploit the new opportunities desegregation offered.

The constraints that shaped the traditional African American business community—limited capital access, barriers to education and training, and so forth—have changed substantially since the 1960s. The availability of government loan guarantees (against default risk) in conjunction with Community Reinvestment Act* (*see* Banking, Chicago Community Development Banks and Community Reinvestment Act) pressure from government induced many banks to extend business loans, thus eroding a tradition of minimal contact between blacks and commercial bank lending departments. College enrollments by black students increased dramatically in the 1960s and 1970s; enrollment growth in business-related fields was particularly rapid.

Gains in higher education typify how reductions in discriminatory barriers are translated into significant progress in the African American business community. Fewer than 300,000 African Americans were enrolled nationwide in colleges and universities in 1965. By 1980, enrollment figures for blacks had risen to 1,107,000. Whereas African Americans receiving bachelor's degrees in 1965 were concentrated very heavily in the education field, business and technical fields emerged as the most popular undergraduate majors by the late 1970s. In less than one generation, college enrollment nearly quadrupled, and the fields of concentration pursued by African American college students shifted dramatically.

The educational gains that took place a generation ago are particularly relevant to comprehending present-day trends in the black business community. Self-employment is rarely pursued full-time by recent college graduates. Entry into small business is most widespread among persons in their late thirties and forties, people who possess 15 to 20 years of work experience. Thus, the full impact of the educational gains of the late 1960s and 1970s is reflected in the number and the nature of the business formations undertaken by African Americans in the late 1980s and 1990s.

Growth in today's black business community derives from increasing penetration of nonminority markets, not from sales to residents of urban minority communities. In this milieu, industry diversification has flourished. Highly educated entrepreneurs are the norm in many lines of business; bank credit is more widely available. Black emerging businesses are progressing rapidly overall, but they must still contend with a range of problems that typify small business in general, as well as several additional ones that disproportionally affect black firms. A key factor that is responsible for black enterprise growth is the rising incidence of highly educated entrepreneurs in nontraditional lines of business. A key factor that continues to retard black business growth is the paucity of equity capital available for investment in small firms. Personal wealth holdings are traditionally a major source of capital for small business creation and expansion. Disparities in personal wealth holdings discourage entry into self-employment and handicap black business start-ups.

Data describing family-wealth holdings indicate that black households nationwide had a median net worth of $3,397 versus $39,135 for white households: For every $1 of wealth in the median white family, the median black family has $.09. While only 8.6 percent of the white households had zero or negative net worth, 31 percent of the black households held absolutely no wealth whatsoever. Wealth in the form of business equity was most commonly observed among black households whose income exceeded $24,000. Business equity was held by 3.5 percent of the black upper-middle-income ($24,000 to $48,000) households and by 14.0 percent of the black high-income households. In contrast, the fraction of white households with business equity ownership surpassed that of black households at every income level. At the upper-, middle-, and high-income levels, respectively, 11.0 percent and 21.5 percent of the white households held wealth in the form of small business equity.

The financial capital constraint facing black-owned business is unlikely to ease anytime soon. The low net-worth holdings that typify most black households will be alleviated, at best, only gradually over a period of many years. Low levels of personal wealth restrict business viability in several ways. Commercial banks lend most freely to those who possess significant amounts of equity capital to invest their businesses. Beyond banks, the second and third most important sources of debt capital for small business are family and friends, respectively. The low net-worth holdings of black households in general restrict the availability of debt capital that family and friends can invest in small business operations. Minimal intergenerational wealth lessens the ability of elderly African Americans to finance the business aspirations of their grown children.

As growth in the African American business community increasingly derives from participation in broader markets, inner-city black communities are increasingly being left out of the business development process. All of the basic elements of black business viability—talented entrepreneurs, financial capital, and markets—are threatened in the inner-city milieu: banks redline, better educated entrepreneurs are pulling out, and markets are weak. In light of the reorientation of emerging black enterprise toward racially diverse or largely nonminority clienteles, choice business locations are increasingly found outside of minority neighborhoods.

In the world of the 1990s, a new and different black business community has become dominant. Particularly in the public policy realm, however, there is a strong nostalgia for the world of black entrepreneurship under segregation. The three lines of black enterprise that rely least upon minority clients—business services, manufacturing, and construction—all grew very rapidly in the 1980s: Employment more than doubled; sales nearly quadrupled nationwide. The two traditional industry groups most heavily reliant upon minority clients—personal services and retailing—generated no growth. Opportunities for the younger, emerging generation clearly lie in the broader marketplace; public policy is determined to prop up the traditional black-owned firms that cater largely to minority clients.

SELECTED BIBLIOGRAPHY: Timothy Bates, *Banking on Black Enterprise* (Washington, DC: Joint Center for Political and Economic Studies, 1993); Timothy Bates, "Commercial Bank Lending to Black and White-Owned Businesses," *Quarterly Review of Economics and Business* 31(1991): 64–80; Timothy Bates, "Self-Employment Entry across Industry Groups," *Journal of Business Venturing* 10 (1995): 1–4; Timothy Bates, "Small Business Viability in the Urban Ghetto," *Journal of Regional Science* 29 (1989): 625–643; Gerald David Jaynes and Robin Williams, *A Common Destiny: Blacks and American Society* (Washington, DC: National Academy Press, 1989).

Timothy Bates

BUSINESS DEVELOPMENT, TWENTIETH CENTURY. The devastating aftermath of the Civil War and southern white resentment over Reconstruction resulted in white southerners establishing a de jure segregated society directed at maintaining tyrannical rule over former slaves by punishing and controlling black aspirations, respectively, in business and politics. In 1883, the U.S. Supreme Court reinforced this sectional course by declaring the Civil Rights Act of 1875 unconstitutional. This was followed by the 1896 Supreme Court decision of *Plessy v. Ferguson*, which upheld legal segregation under the "separate but equal" doctrine. Between 1890 and 1910, Mississippi, South Carolina, Louisiana, North Carolina, Alabama, Virginia, Georgia, and Oklahoma legally disfranchised blacks as part of their state constitutions. In response to these severe legal obstacles, a black urban elite advocated and actively promoted the development of all-black institutions.

Consequently, from the post–Civil War period through the turn of the century, many black businesses originated from the black church and black fraternal orders and lodges. These developments eroded the position of the older black entrepreneurial class whose businesses previously centered on serving a largely white clientele. As a result of the hardening of the two segregated societies and markets, this new class of black entrepreneurs found itself with little outside white business competition in serving, almost exclusively, a low-income but underserved black consumer market. It was also during this period that the first private black banks and insurance companies began to emerge, including the North Carolina Mutual Life Insurance Company,* founded in 1898 by John Merrick; the Capital Savings Bank of Washington, D.C., founded in 1888; and the True Reformers Bank of Richmond, founded in 1898.

With the advent of Booker T. Washington's* National Negro Business League (NNBL)* in 1900, a new class of black entrepreneurs had already begun to emerge, replacing much of the older black business class. The new black entrepreneurial class was protected by the legal barrier of segregation especially in the areas of retail and personal services, and they existed alongside a growing educated black middle class that served the black community, chiefly as teachers and church leaders. Albon Holsey's 1938 study claimed that between 1914 and

1938 three out of every four black college graduates were either teachers or preachers. The majority of the college-trained black middle class refrained from business ownership as a career.

While protected, segregated markets gave a distinct advantage to black-owned small retail and personal service firms, and to some extent black banking and insurance, lack of access to national markets and investment capital doomed many black manufacturing firms. By 1940, few black-owned manufacturing businesses were left. The few that survived the depression struggled, mostly unsuccessfully, against large majority firms that had greater access to markets and investment capital, which enabled them to employ more efficient technologies. Joseph Pierce's classic 1944 study of nearly 4,000 black-owned businesses across 12 cities documented that the distribution of black business had not changed appreciably since the antebellum period. Some 70 percent of all black businesses surveyed were in the personal service or small retail sector— beauty shops and barbershops, restaurants, grocery stores, cleaning and pressing shops, shoe shine and repair, and funeral homes. Whatever success that blacks in business enjoyed in the pre–civil rights era in restaurants, hotels, insurance, and banking was due, in part, to the fact that those areas were, in effect, protected markets. But with the dismantling of legal segregation, that protective barrier was effectively removed.

In the modern era, with the dismantling of legal segregation, black businesses that continued to restrict themselves to the black consumer market experienced little growth and high failure rates since that market increasingly became open to competition from the general business sector. Increasingly, well-educated, professionally trained black entrepreneurs began seeking self-employment opportunities in areas that serve the largest potential market in order to provide enough profitable opportunities to warrant applying their talent to entrepreneurship over salary employment in the general economy. This important trend in black business development is reflected in the dramatic increase in college enrollment among black students majoring in business-related fields. Bates reports that college-educated self-employed blacks increased 120 percent between 1970 and 1980.

Evidence from business programs at historically black colleges and universities concerning the number of business majors and graduation rates indicate that this trend accelerated between 1980 and 1990. A newer generation of black entrepreneurs has been entering more technically challenging lines of business with more lucrative opportunities. More than half of the black business owners in the nontraditional, higher-growth areas of finance, insurance and real estate, business service, wholesaling, and manufacturing are college graduates. Currently, two out of every three self-employed blacks in the emerging fields of finance and real estate attended college, compared to 28 percent among all black entrepreneurs generally.

The Asian American* business sector, which for years has sold to both their own ethnic group and to the larger general market, has experienced business participation rates far in excess of their population share. Evidence also indicates that the newer, larger, employment-generating black firms are able to compete successfully in the larger market. On reviewing 1,450 minority firms registered to do business with the City of Atlanta in 1994, Thomas Boston found that 80 percent were first-generation entrepreneurs with average gross revenues in excess of $600,000. In addition, two-thirds of the newly successful entrepreneurs were college graduates, with one-quarter having graduate degrees. Boston is finding a similar dynamic operating in many other cities in the country.

Over the years every survey of black business owners has cited limited access to capital as the major constraint to expanding the black-owned business sector. Studies conducted in this area cite the prevalence of undercapitalization of black-owned businesses compared to the level needed for success. These studies suggest that because of their limited access to capital, black entrepreneurs historically have had to concentrate in circumscribed, traditional, low-profit-making fields (restaurants, laundries, barbershops, and other predominantly small service and retail establishments serving the black community) precisely because they can be started with little capital. The restricted access to capital certainly limited earlier black entrepreneurs to operating small-scale enterprises in less promising product lines. Moreover, the paucity of investment capital has been so pronounced and endemic to black business development over so many decades that even in these less capital-intensive areas, traditional small businesses still found themselves undercapitalized relative to their real capital needs.

The level of business capitalization has repeatedly been found to be highly correlated with the business success of black firms. The consensus of research in the area has confirmed that successful black firms, in any given industry, have capitalization levels that are more than twice the capitalization of black firms that fail. The inference to be drawn is that the skewed distribution of types of businesses in black communities and their limited size and rate of growth are the result of the limited availability of outside capital and limited retained earnings due to the restricted markets of small black enterprises.

The importance of equity capital has been confirmed by several researchers, who found that family financial assets are strongly and positively correlated with the likelihood of individuals becoming entrepreneurs. The 1971 study by Henry Terrell found that black families have, on average, 20 percent of the average wealth accumulation of white families. A 1997 study by Melvin Oliver and Thomas Shapiro confirmed that middle-income black families have 33 percent of the median net worth and 3 percent of the median net financial assets of white middle-class families. Among high-income earners, black families have 52 percent of the median net worth and 23 percent of the net financial assets of high-income white families. Moreover, among minority groups in the United States, personal financial assets are lowest among African Americans, with Asian Americans highest. In fact, Asian Americans have family assets that are comparable to white businessmen in the small business sector. This may help to explain the relatively high business formation rates among Asians compared to blacks.

The importance of African American–owned firms in generating employment opportunities as a basis for economic development in the black community has also been receiving increased attention. Separate research by Timothy Bates, Thomas Boston, and Margaret Simms confirms the importance of minority-owned firms in the hiring of black employees. Simms found that 60 percent of all minority-owned firms actively hire in low-income neighborhoods, and the majority of minority-owned firms in the central city have a workforce that is more than 50 percent black. Boston found that the most successful African American firms in Atlanta are eight times more likely to employ African American workers than all firms generally.

Data also indicate that larger, more nontraditional lines of black businesses that hire significant numbers of black workers have benefited greatly from opportunities created by federal government contract programs, as well as from state and local set-aside programs.* One-third of the largest 100 employment-generating black-owned firms, for instance, participated early in their development as SBA-8(a) federal contracting firms. In 1996 over 6,000 firms employing more than 158,000 workers received over $5 billion in 8(a) federal contract awards. Challenges to the constitutionality of set-asides and economically disadvantaged business programs in the recent Supreme Court decisions of *Richmond v. Croson* (109 U.S. 706, 1989) and *Adarand v. Pena* (115 U.S. 2097, 1995) place a serious constraint on the potential growth and hiring capabilities of many emerging black-owned firms.

The Survey of Minority-Owned Business Enterprises (SMOBE), conducted by the U.S. Census Bureau, is the major data source for African American, Asian, and Hispanic businesses in the United States. SMOBE data include the number of firms and size of receipts by industry and location for sole proprietorships, partnerships, and subchapter S corporations, but they do not include data on subchapter C corporations. As a result of this omission, the largest, most successful employment-generating black-owned firms in every major metropolitan area are excluded from the survey. The most significant source of growth in the black-owned business sector is not covered at all by the SMOBE survey.

The underestimation of reported sales and employment of the black business sector due to the omission of subchapter C corporations in the SMOBE data is estimated to be more than 50 percent. One vital area not reported in SMOBE, for instance, includes the significant sales and employment growth of the largest 100 black-owned corporations over the last 25 years. The *Black Enterprise* (*BE*) 100 largest black businesses grew from a sales level of $473 million and 9,267 employees in 1973 to sales of $14.3 billion and employment in excess of 55,000 by 1997. By comparison, SMOBE data reported that total sales for all black-owned sole proprietorships, partnerships, and subchapter S corporations in the United States amounted to $32.2 billion in 1992. The total sales of all firms on the *BE* 100 would rank it 83rd on the *Fortune* 500.

SELECTED BIBLIOGRAPHY: Timothy Bates, *Banking on Black Enterprise* (Washington, DC: Joint Center for Political and Economic Studies, 1993); Thomas D. Boston, "Characteristics of Black-Owned Enterprises in Atlanta: With Comments on the SMOBE

Undercount,'' *Review of Black Political Economy* 23, 4 (Spring 1995); Roy Lee, *The Setting for Black Business Development* (New York: Cornell University, School of Industrial and Labor Relations, 1973); Melvin Oliver and Thomas Shapiro, *Black Wealth/ White Wealth: A New Perspective on Racial Inequality* (New York: Routledge, 1995); Joseph Pierce, *Negro Business and Business Education* (New York: Harper, 1947); Margaret Simms and Winston Allen, ''Is the Inner City Competitive?'' *Review of Black Political Economy* 24, 2–3 (Fall–Winter 1996).

John W. Handy

BUSINESS MOTIVATION, GUIDELINES FOR THE TWENTY-FIRST CENTURY. The time for black wealth creation has come. The next 100 years will be a century of tremendous progress. All the signs are evident. The needs are great, but the opportunities to serve, to invest, and to capitalize are even greater. The opportunities are so great that blacks are stumbling over and into them rather than taking full advantage of them. To bring future wealth to black America, blacks need to experience more than a shift of consciousness; they need a shift in conscious action. Guidance is all around them. Since the civil rights era, more and more black people have been speaking and writing about it—daily, weekly, monthly. There is a new vision, and blacks are in the process of changing the mantra of the 1950s and 1960s—which was ''Get a good education, then get a good job.'' Now ''Get a good education and create a job'' dominates their thinking. Doing well while doing good must always be a career objective. There must be nothing more important than the success of black people and black businesses, for this becomes the basis of black America's moral, spiritual, and financial freedom.

Balancing need and opportunity sometimes requires uncompromising sacrifice and a self-serving agenda. All great achievers understand this and find a way to reconcile it in their hearts and minds. In the field of education, for example, teachers must find a way to teach, even though many of their urban students come from homes and neighborhoods where parents must struggle to feed them and maintain a value system. There is a decline in the number of black teachers, especially males. Blacks will have to find a way to stop the decline and increase the number of black teachers guiding and nurturing their children. Teaching is an honorable and fulfilling profession. The need is great at all educational levels to share and market their knowledge for a greater good. For at the core of the problem of their ''image of incompetence'' lies the greatest opportunity to change that image. Each time a black person stands before an audience to teach, consult, or speak, that image changes. While most who enter this realm will not become rich, they will be enriched. Some will see a career in education as a sacrifice, others as a joy. Either way, as the need to improve education is critical, from providing after-school classes to teaching basic skills to those transitioning from welfare to reeducating all sectors of America's workers, the opportunities and budgets in education will continue to grow.

Thousands of blacks will also be needed in the areas of finance and banking.

The focus should be on economic development strategies. Blacks need training in capital market investment instruments, venture funds, and wealth creation. The manifestation of black power will be driven by the level of sophistication blacks use to leverage their enormous wealth, which is estimated to be over 1 trillion within 20 years. When blacks master the playing field of banking and finance, they will earn global respect and dominance in the world marketplace. Creating new jobs and financial institutions is a top economic priority. The corporate brain drain of the 1960s and 1970s will diminish, and many more will be focusing on small business development by starting new businesses, buying existing businesses, and marketing their skills through franchise opportunities, multilevel marketing, and home-based businesses.

Self-employment and blacks working for blacks should climb from the 1 million plus today to 3 to 4 million (20 to 25 percent of the black workforce) in the next 20 years. Black colleges are gearing up for this quantum leap. Cashing in on the technology revolution will play a major role in helping to create future wealth. The trendsetting power of urban young people and the creative prowess of black advertising* agencies will help make computers "cool." Just as sneakers, jeans, pagers, and portable radios were made stylish and cool, urban culture will help mainstream the computer and the accompanying software. With easy access to vast amounts of information via the Internet, productivity will skyrocket, leveling the economic and opportunity playing fields.

Expanding black America's output in the publishing world with more books and magazines and developing new venues such as a national black weekly newspaper will present a wealth of new information and opportunities and a point of view presently little known in America. Those who seize new opportunities in mainstream and niche publishing will tell the African American story in a more balanced and enlightened way.

Billions of dollars will be spent on rebuilding black neighborhoods. Opportunities in the construction trades and crafts, as well as in sales, marketing, loans, management, and development, are significant. Major urban centers like New York, Chicago, Detroit, and Philadelphia are planning to spend hundreds of millions over the next 10 years to build new homes, upgrade public housing, rehabilitate old housing stock, and also build new centers of commerce on some of the most valuable and strategically located land in America. Center-city locations and downtown living and entertainment are on the way back. This is where blacks live, and it's time for them to cash in.

Dr. Claud Anderson, author of *Black Labor, White Wealth*, suggests that blacks employ vertical integration business strategies to control industries in which they are disproportionately represented (entertainment and sports, for example) or consumer products that blacks disproportionately purchase (athletic wear, electronic equipment, movies, etc.). Vertical integration means to control the raw materials, production, distribution, and retailing of a product or service. Progress has been slow but incremental, and the money, management skills, and vision are now in place. Blacks have seen it with the recent financing of their own films (Spike Lee's profitable *Get on the Bus*), movie theaters (Magic Johnson/Sony Theaters), sports franchises (Isaiah Thomas's investment in the Toronto Raptors basketball team), and ownership of numerous television and radio stations, and in greater control in rap and gospel music. More opportunities will come, as blacks gain expertise in the variety of jobs now available in the entertainment and sports worlds.

But Geannine Amber, writing in *Essence*, warns that blacks "must never let violence become a marketable commodity, A Rite of Passage and a badge of authenticity for our young people. We don't need violence to create wealth at any level in Black America, and we must resist the corporations who tempt us with millions of dollars to act up, act out, and act crazy in the name of keeping it real."

As the health care industry is downsized and restructured, black physicians and dentists must protect their customer base by forming new alliances and venturing into smaller communities where black doctors are underrepresented and blacks are underserved. Black doctors are needed, and black nurses and technicians will be in demand in a society growing older and increasingly oriented toward wellness and home care. Small business opportunities are everywhere in this category, and many entrepreneurs will gradually become rich.

Just as other cultures moved to America from their homelands to start new businesses and set up pipelines of distribution for merchants back home, blacks must begin to do the same. Global commerce is the order of the day. Opportunities in the motherland are slowly evolving, with South Africa leading the way. The concept of vertical integration can start there, where raw materials and channels of distribution will be controlled by blacks. The Caribbean and sub-Saharan Africa are other places where their color can work to their advantage. South America and the Pacific Rim are also geographical regions where blacks heavily influence the music, entertainment, and sports products. Exporting and controlling commodities related to these industries must become part of a black strategy for financial freedom in America.

Succeeding in any one of these areas begins with personal decision making and coming to terms with oneself. Blacks have each been there—that crossroads where one is forced to look at their life and make a choice for the future. The previously mentioned categories expanding businesses offer opportunities to make a profit and make a difference.

SELECTED BIBLIOGRAPHY: Claud Anderson, *Black Labor, White Wealth: The Search for Power and Economic Justice* (Edgewood, MD: Duncan & Duncan, 1994); George C. Fraser, *Race for Success: The Ten Best Business Opportunities for Blacks in America* (New York: William Morrow, 1998); John Hagel III and Arthur G. Armstrong, *Net Gain: Expanding Markets through Virtual Communities* (Boston: Harvard Business School Press, 1997); Gloria Ladson-Billings, *The Dreamkeepers: Successful Teachers of African American Children* (San Francisco: Jossey-Bass, 1994); Kenneth L. Shropshire, *In Black and White: Race and Sports in America* (New York: New York University Press, 1996); Wilson Simmons III, *Inside Corporate America: A Guide for African Amer-*

icans (New York: Berkeley Publishing Group, 1996); Robert Wallace, *Black Wealth through Black Entrepreneurship* (Edgewood, MD: Duncan & Duncan, 1994).

George C. Fraser

BUSINESS OWNERSHIP, SINCE 1969. Black participation in the ownership of American businesses before 1969 has been assessed a number of times. The pioneer attempt in inventory taking and assessment was made by W.E.B. Du Bois at the beginning of the century in 1900. Subsequent studies have included Pierce in 1944, Drexel Institute in Philadelphia in 1964, and a third by the Indiana Business School in 1968. In 1971, reviewing black historical participation in the ownership of American businesses, Bailey wrote: "[T]he trend of black business activity over the last 60 years followed a general pattern: there were brief periods of 'expanding opportunities' and then sustained periods of depression. The most significant factor affecting these cycles of expansion and depression was the shifting tendencies toward segregation and integration in American society."

A new era in black business history began following the Civil Rights Act of 1964 and provided a new basis for the inventorying of black-owned businesses in the United States. In 1969 the Bureau of the Census began publication of its five-yearly Survey of Minority-Owned Business Enterprises (SMOBE). In 1973 Earl Graves* began publishing his annual June listing of the top 100 black-owned industrial/service enterprises, leading automobile dealerships, and ranking financial institutions in *Black Enterprise* (*BE*), a monthly periodical that he founded in 1970. Publication of these two periodical surveys generated a new level of interest and much needed scholarly attention to business ownership by black Americans.

Over 90 percent of all black-owned businesses operate as sole proprietorships—SMOBE counts all of them and counts, as well, partnerships and 1120 S corporations. Therefore, the SMOBE counts provide a consistently comprehensive, adequate basis on which to look at typical black business ownership patterns in the United States Yet Thomas Boston found that the SMOBE "does not include all corporations in its survey universe," which leads to the omission of "1120 C" corporations. Consequently, some 3 percent of the number of black-owned businesses are excluded from the SMOBE survey. The *BE* annual surveys, however, focus on just such 1120 C corporations. In this sense, the two different surveys are important in providing a complementary assessment of black businesses.

In its assessment of black-owned business from 1969 to 1992, the SMOBE data show that the number increased from 163,000 to 621,000—an average annual growth rate of approximately 7 percent. In computing comparative national rates, Sol Ahiarah indicates that black business growth was 2.5 times the U.S. national average annual growth rate (approximate 2.63) for number of businesses and more than quadruple the 1.55 average annual growth rate of the black population in the period. The number of black-owned businesses per 1,000 blacks grew from 7.27 to 19.62. The gross receipts (in constant 1992 dollars) went from $17.1 billion in 1969 to $32.2 billion in 1992. On a per capita basis (that is, dollars generated by black-owned businesses per black American), these translate to $762.58 in 1969 and $1,017.09 in 1992. Although these gross receipts did not grow with the same consistency as the number of businesses (given a nearly 10 percent decline between 1977 and 1982), the 3.21 percent average annual rate at which they grew in the period was better than the comparable 2.34 percent national average growth rate. These data suggest that progress is being made—that more and more blacks are recognizing their need for economic empowerment via business ownership.

Growth in black business participation or ownership in the United States is a function of the interaction or synergy of individual-specific, group-specific, and environment-consequent factors. Of the three, the environment-consequent factors can be viewed as the most pernicious in inhibiting black business ownership historically. Although the attention here is focused on the period since 1969 for the reasons given, three distinct periods in the twentieth century are really apparent, namely: pre–civil rights (before the 1960s), the civil rights (the 1960s and 1970s), and the post–civil rights (from 1980s to the present).

During the pre–civil rights period, the environment placed black Americans in a caste system characterized by legally tolerated racial discrimination; lack of access to capital, relevant education, manpower, and role models; and little or no access to the mainstream market. While blacks did develop a number of banks, insurance companies, funeral parlors, and ethnic-focused businesses in cosmetics and magazines, the black business ownership rate was minimal relative to the succeeding periods, a reflection of significant change in their environment, which occurred in the 1960s, although during the civil rights era, except for a few black church groups (for example, Reverend Leon Sullivan's*), which focused on real estate or agricultural businesses, black groups and leaders seemed to emphasize political power rather than economic empowerment through business formation. Their emphasis was not necessarily misplaced. Black elected officials were the ones who pushed through most of the set-aside* programs, which in turn have helped fuel the growth reflected in SMOBE's data. Affirmative action programs and set-asides allowed for more access to education, capital, and markets (at least, government-oriented ones). And in the private sector, some major companies, including AT&T, K-Mart, General Motors, Chrysler, and Digital Equipment Corporation, voluntarily started "affirmative buying" in this period.

At the same time, blacks gained equal legal access to elite and prestigious schools where they could receive the same education and training as the majority. More blacks entered the professions, which contributed to faster growth of the black middle class. As reported in Jaynes and Williams, *A Common Destiny: Blacks and American Society*: "In 1970, 15.7 percent of black families had incomes over $35,000; by 1986, this proportion had grown to 21.2 percent (in 1986 constant dollars). Similarly, the proportion of black families with incomes of more than $50,000 increased from 4.7 percent in 1970 to 8.8 percent in 1986.''

Also, a new class of black business owners emerged during the post–civil rights era. In 1992, according to one estimate, of the 25 largest black-owned firms, 6 were born in this period. The generation succeeding the civil rights era is better educated and does not view itself in terms of inferiority to the majority population, and many have had experience in Corporate America that they can now put to use. The businesses that this generation of black entrepreneurs are forming are not necessarily the Mom-and-Pop types. They have learned how to use strategic alliances with majority firms to do business with everyone instead of targeting black consumers alone. Also, they understand how the premier capital market in the world (Wall Street) works.

Moreover, this new generation does not lack mentors, as they continue to expand their networks for mutual business benefit through the formation of new organizations. A partial list of such groups includes: (1) Association of Minority Enterprises of New York, (2) Interracial Council for Business Opportunity, (3) National Minority Supplier Development Council, (4) Minority Business Enterprise Legal Defense and Education, (5) National Association of Minority Contractors, (6) National Bankers Association, (7) National Minority Business Council, and (8) National Small Business United. Also, the heightened group awareness of the importance of increasing black business ownership was reflected in the theme of the National Urban League's* 87th annual conference: ''Economic Power: The Next Civil Rights Frontier.''

The interaction of able and willing individuals, group activities, and a more conducive environment have contributed to encouraging growth in black business ownership reflected in SMOBE data. The mainstream press has also noticed these changes. For the first time *Fortune* magazine, in an August 1997 issue, featured a group of 13 blacks representative of this new generation of African American entrepreneurs. Still, SMOBE data reveal that the proportion of black business ownership is less than what should be expected—at least, equal to the black proportion of the U.S. population. In 1992 blacks constituted about 12.40 percent of the U.S. population, but their share of the number of U.S. businesses was approximately 3 percent. Also, the associated gross receipts still remained less than 1 percent of total U.S. businesses' gross receipts. The $1,017 black business gross receipts per capita was only about 2 percent of the estimated $49,148 national business gross receipts per capita.

The effect of decades of calculated subjugation and continuing subtle discrimination and oppression cannot be expected to wear off suddenly. But a new era is here, and a new class of black businesspeople is emerging. The fact that the number of black-owned businesses is growing on the average, at a rate that is faster than the national average, suggests that the business ownership proportion that should be expected could, in time, be achieved. The post–civil rights era, then, did lead to a change in the environment in a manner that has implications for black business ownership. This change, however, has had repercussions, manifested in legal and political attempts to roll back the affirmative action and set-aside programs of the civil rights era.

The Supreme Court's rulings in the *Bakke* and the *City of Richmond v. J. A. Croson Co.* cases and the state of California's Proposition 209 outlawing affirmative action programs are examples. The loss of affirmative action programs will, undoubtedly, affect the rate of growth of black participation in business ownership. Fortunately, however, gains made during the civil rights period cannot be easily wiped out. Attitudes are changing, even if slowly, and there is greater willingness by the majority to work with minorities, as many Americans are realizing that the minority population cannot be ignored if the country's future economic viability is to be assured.

SELECTED BIBLIOGRAPHY: Sol Ahiarah, "Black Americans' Business Ownership Factors: A Theoretical Perspective," *Review of Black Political Economy* 22, 2(Fall 1993); R. W. Bailey, "Introduction/Black Business Enterprise: Reflections on Its History and Future Development," in R. W. Bailey, ed., *Black Business Enterprise: Historical and Contemporary Perspectives* (New York: Basic Books, 1971); T. Boston, "Characteristics of Black Owned Corporations in Atlanta (with Comments on the SMOBE Undercount)," *Review of Black Political Economy* 23, 4 (Spring 1995); S. Green and P. Pryde, *Black Entrepreneurship in America* (New Brunswick, NJ: Transaction Publishers, 1990); Gerald David Jaynes and Robin Williams, *A Common Destiny: Blacks and American Society* (Washington, DC: National Academy Press, 1989); L. E. Wynter, "The Path to Power," *Wall Street Journal*, April 3, 1992.

Sol Ahiarah

BUSINESS SCHOOLS, HISTORICALLY BLACK COLLEGES AND UNIVERSITIES (HBCUs). A diverse group of master's, bachelor's, and associate degree programs in business administration and management are offered by 95 of America's 103 historically black colleges and universities (HBCUs). Twenty-one HBCUs award the M.B.A. or other master's degrees in business and management. Eighty-one HBCUs offer baccalaureate degree programs in business administration, whereas 25 offer associate degrees in business. Master's programs at public HBCUs outnumber those at private HBCUs 18 to 3. During the 1993–1994 academic year, all but 1 of the nation's 40 public four-year HBCUs produced blacks with bachelor's degrees in business, as did 42 of the 49 private four-year HBCUs. The 10 public and 3 of the 4 private two-year HBCUs conferred associate degrees in business.

In 1993–1994, slightly less than 16 percent of black college students were enrolled in historically black colleges and universities. However, HBCUs accounted for about 28 percent of blacks earning bachelor's degrees. In the same year, blacks received 20,366 (approximately 8 percent) of the 246,654 bachelor's degrees in business awarded in the United States. Business programs at HBCUs produced 6,165 (slightly more than 30 percent) of these black degree recipients. Among four-year institutions producing the largest numbers of black recipients of business degrees, 9 of the top 10 were HBCUs.

Florida A&M University and Howard University lead in the production of blacks with business bachelor's degrees, with 245 graduates each. Morehouse College produced the most black males with undergraduate business degrees (177), whereas Howard produced the largest number of black females (164). The oldest graduate business program at an HBCU—the Clark Atlanta University School of Business, which was founded by Atlanta University in 1946— was also the nation's leading producer of black M.B.A.s (88) in 1993–1994. Black master's degree recipients constituted less than 6 percent of the nation's total. HBCUs as a group accounted for 480 (roughly 9 percent) of the 5,213 black master's degree recipients. HBCUs accounted for an even smaller proportion of associate degrees awarded to blacks—less than 3 percent.

Sixteen HBCUs have achieved national accreditation of their business degree programs. Clark Atlanta University, Howard University, Jackson State University, Morgan State University, Norfolk State University, North Carolina A&T University, and Tennessee State University are accredited by the American Assembly of Collegiate Schools of Business (AACSB), the older and more widely recognized of the two bodies accrediting business programs. Alabama State University, Albany State University, Grambling State University, Kentucky State University, Langston University, Lawson State Community College, North Carolina Central University, Philander Smith College, and Virginia Union University are accredited by the Association of Collegiate Business Schools and Programs. Howard and North Carolina A&T also have separately accredited (by AACSB) accounting programs.

In addition, there are 11 HBCUs in candidacy for AACSB accreditation of their business programs: University of Arkansas at Pine Bluff, Grambling State University, University of Maryland Eastern Shore, Morehouse College, North Carolina Central University, Prairie View A&M University, South Carolina State University, Southern University, Southern University at New Orleans, Texas Southern University, and Virginia State University.

SELECTED BIBLIOGRAPHY: Cheryl D. Fields, "Taking Care of Business (Schools): HBCUs Attracting Cream of the Cream," *Black Issues in Higher Education* (December 1996); "Preparing Future Business Leaders Today," *Black Enterprise* (February 1997); U.S. Department of Education, National Center for Educational Statistics, *Historically Black Colleges and Universities* (Washington, DC: Government Printing Office, 1996).

Willis B. Sheftall, Jr.

BUSINESS SCHOOLS, NEW PROFESSIONAL PROGRAM, SCHOOL OF BUSINESS AND INDUSTRY (SBI), FLORIDA A&M UNIVERSITY.

Although Florida A&M University (FAMU) had offered business and business-related courses for many years, it was in 1945 that President William H. Gray recruited Professor John Vernon Anderson, the first chairman to have a graduate degree, from his position as business manager of Bishop College to establish the business program as a department in the College of Arts and Sciences.

Professor Anderson, a University of Pittsburgh M.B.A., brought the rich insights of his experiences in both accounting and management. He was charged to organize a faculty and curriculum that would become a force in the development of business professionals to penetrate the business sector. While expanding the popular existing programs such as Business Education, Secretarial Science, and Office Administration, Professor Anderson aggressively pursued the development of less popular programs (accounting, finance, and management), which would develop both entrepreneurs and officers for the mainstream of the business world. His vision was to prepare students to capitalize on the opportunities that existed, as well as preparing them to penetrate opportunities then denied.

Under Professor Anderson, the department gained respectability, as graduates were accepted by major graduate schools and landed increasingly high professional positions. Professor Anderson was succeeded in 1958 by Dr. Lucy Rose Adams, who was the first chair to hold the doctorate degree. During the period 1958–1970, Dr. Adams brought great growth in enrollment and faculty and grew the program at a faster pace than business opportunities emerged. After having joined the Business Department faculty as assistant professor of accounting in 1963, Dr. Sybil Mobley was promoted to department chair to succeed Dr. Adams in 1970. She quickly began to implement changes in the curriculum and methodology that, in 1974, resulted in the department becoming the School of Business and Industry (SBI), an autonomous School of Business.

From its inception over 20 years ago, the goal of SBI has been to build a business school that would fully prepare graduates for success in the competitive world marketplace. This program, which is of great appeal to the major corporations who recruit, hire, and provide internships to SBI students, was neither a simple nor an overnight success story. To achieve the desired professional thrust, Secretarial Science, Office Administration, and Business Education programs were transferred to the College of Education. This modification of SBI's course and program offerings enabled SBI to greatly elevate its admission requirements and its overall standards of performance. This was a first step taken to move SBI closer to its goal, to be able to compete with the Harvards and Whartons in recruitment and education but, most of all, in the preparation and placement of students in major firms throughout the world.

Since top students were recognized as a key to gaining credibility, SBI faced what appeared to be an insurmountable challenge. The top students were being courted by the top universities, and many had not heard of FAMU. However, SBI met this challenge by using the national lists of high school seniors who scored high on the Scholastic Aptitude Test (SAT) to identify the top performers and then applying a "one-on-one" personal approach to recruiting. Although success was limited, this approach permitted SBI to gain a much-needed base of scholars anxious to share their excitement about the quality of the program and the opportunities it afforded. Later, with significant corporate support, SBI was able to reach the nation's high schools by hosting banquets in various cities to honor National Achievement Scholars, where information was provided students, principals, and counselors. The strategy was successful.

Simultaneously, SBI sought scholarship funds to permit it to compete with the competition. SBI's corporate partners provided not only scholarships but also internships and curriculum support, including agreements by corporate executives to come to SBI to deliver class lectures and formal presentations. Corporate executives also sponsored many receptions and dinners to develop the students' ability to function at business social events. SBI's mission was to develop a comprehensive business culture and environment where students would develop the needed qualities and skills in a controlled, corporate learning environment.

Inspired to extend beyond technical competence, SBI instituted the Professional Development Program as a separate division, which in the 1990s became a major component of SBI's prestigious Five-Year Professional Program. The SBI Five-Year Professional M.B.A. has become the signature degree of SBI. It uniquely accommodates the new world realities in producing graduates who are both competent and seasoned in dealing with the urgencies of today's global business marketplace. It is SBI's contention that the "sea change," which revolutionized the rules of management in the corporate community, dictated that comparable changes be made in the educational community, if it is to be relevant. Moreover, technology has replaced many of the positions that were major employment attractions in the past but that as entry-level positions no longer exist on the rungs on the corporate ladder or have been reduced. Firms are no longer willing to finance the adjustment, orientation, training, and other steps required for an employee to become productive. SBI is anxious to and capable of providing the education and training necessary to deliver the employee at whatever stage demanded by the employers.

SBI's flagship program, the Five-Year Professional M.B.A., is significantly different from traditional M.B.A. programs. While many M.B.A. programs identify themselves as professional programs, most are actually very consistent with conventional academic models. Professional schools by definition and tradition are five-year programs; maintain close relationships with the practicing professionals; have in-house laboratories; require internships and externships; employ a significant proportion of their faculty who have professional experience; and produce graduates who are "ready to run."

Since its creation, SBI has had a very flat organization structure. Instead of the usual five or six departments, SBI has only two divisions—Academic Programs and Professional Development, supported by the Internship Office. The SBI process is cumulative. At each level, the focus is on the acquisition of specific behavioral competencies and a body of academic content that is applied at each subsequent level. The Professional M.B.A. combines a traditional emphasis on accounting, finance, marketing, etcetera, with a rigorous professional component that permits students to internalize those important qualities that require a long period of gestation. Students function in miniature corporations, progressing throughout their college years in positions from operating staff to supervisors, managers, and executives. Each is assigned to positions in in-house companies structured to develop their professional skills. Each student is also required to complete three internships in three different corporations and in three different regions of the world. The SBI Complex in expansion will include a World Cultures Plaza. Only rarely will English be spoken in the Plaza.

The unique and rigorous SBI curriculum extends far beyond the standard offerings of traditional programs. The expanded requirements were made possible by the elimination of the duplication (e.g., core courses) that exists in normal B.S. and M.B.A. programs and the SBI accelerated learning and internalization methodologies.

SELECTED BIBLIOGRAPHY: Florida Women's Hall of Fame at http://legal.firn.edu/units/fcs/hallmbr.html and, Women Business School Deans at http://www.aacsb.edu/women.html

Sybil Collins Mobley

BUSINESS SCHOOLS AND BLACKS. Historically black colleges and universities (HBCUs) are tailoring their business school curriculums to address the increasing needs of the changing global economy entering into the twenty-first century. Their primary focus is to prepare talented students for corporate, community, and entrepreneurial leadership. They are setting the stage for their students to become strategic thinkers, with an international mind-set, in a highly technological society. Despite the top-notch business professionals HBCU black business schools are producing, they are not receiving the recognition deserved due to competition from the "elite" status of major white institutions.

Historically, black business schools concentrated on equipping their students with the competencies needed to climb the corporate ladder. However with unfair hiring and promotion practices, the glass ceiling, and downsizing, blacks were not being allowed to progress up the ladder as envisioned. Therefore, the routine of receiving an education to work for someone began to become decreasingly important in the 1990s. Although most HBCUs do not offer entrepreneurship majors, as Jackson State University does, they offer entrepreneurial development programs to expose students to business initiative and leadership. Jackson State University makes "nontraditional loans" through their minority capital fund to student entrepreneurs. Business students at Tennessee State can take small business classes and are given the opportunity to provide consulting, particularly to the black business community. The Florida A&M School of Business has 28 student-run companies, of which 4 are for-profit, such as the School of Business and Industry (SBI) Fund and SBI Surety. Financing for these companies comes from corporate donations. Some freshmen business courses at Tuskegee require students to develop a product and business plan, who can then seek financing through the school's loan fund. Many of these programs are more often seen at the M.B.A. level. However, HBCU business schools are concentrating on the demand and supply of certain skills in the business world and are equipping their students with these skills early in their college career.

HBCU business schools are tailoring their curriculums to parallel the changing technological and global environment. The Internet* and other technological advances have become mainstays in the mid-1990s, going into the twenty-first century. Students are expected not only to be knowledgeable concerning its uses but also to know how to strategically integrate them into their own businesses or into the corporation for which they work to improve efficiency and create competitive advantages. Both black and white businesses are looking overseas for both expansion and market penetration. Therefore, HBCU business schools are providing education on international business and experience when possible. South Carolina State offers internships in Indonesia and is looking to add the Dominican Republic, Jamaica, South Africa, and Zimbabwe. Morehouse receives corporate support to take ''20–25 students abroad each spring.'' Increasingly, business students are receiving such experience on the undergraduate and graduate levels.

Black business students, as well as white, understand the increasing need to further their business education beyond a bachelor's degree. Many black students feel they can receive the same, if not better, graduate-level education at an HBCU. Clark Atlanta University has one of the oldest M.B.A. programs, among HBCUs, with approximately 2,500 black M.B.A.s. At one point, they were the largest producer of black M.B.A.s in the country in 1993–1994, with 88. At Florida A&M,* all freshmen entering the business school in 1995 or later were required to get an M.B.A. This is a five-year program with the first three years of undergraduate courses and the last two years of M.B.A. courses. They are one of a few, if not the only university, black or white, that has such a requirement. Howard University is ''exploring an executive MBA program with the medical and dental schools.''

Yet it is perceived that anyone can gain admission to an HBCU business program, but only the best and brightest can get into the top white business programs. Therefore, HBCU business schools do not receive the press that major white business schools receive. Corporate America will recruit only the top 20 percent at HBCU business schools and forget about the remaining 80 percent, leaving many aspiring black business students to seek admission in white business schools for more opportunities. A business degree from Harvard is considered a ticket to the *Fortune* 500. Blacks graduating from the top white business schools are considered, by Corporate America and society as a whole, to be the ''elite'' of the black professional class. Therefore, being a Harvard M.B.A. will present more options than being a Florida A&M M.B.A. Yet African American representation at these ''elite'' institutions has been sparse in both faculty and student.

Black faculty presence at the leading business schools is little to none. There are two reasons that can be attributed to this lack of representation: a low emphasis on faculty diversity and a low pool of black Ph.D. students in business. If business schools were concerned with maintaining the status quo, blacks were not even considered to join the faculty. According to a study done by Milton Moskowitz, *Business and Society Review* in 1994, the top business schools have an average black faculty of 2 percent. Dartmouth and the University of Pittsburgh had the highest percentage of black faculty, at 6 percent each. Harvard's percentage of black faculty was 3 percent, and Stanford had 1 percent. Among top schools with no black faculty members were University of Chicago, Carnegie-Mellon, and Cornell. As Corporate America cracked the door open to let a few blacks in, the higher salaries often pulled away those blacks considering entrance in doctoral programs in business. The KPMG Peat Marwick Foundation started the Ph.D. Project, in 1992, to help increase the pool of black Ph.D.s in business. According to the National Center for Educational Statistics, in 1988, of the 1,149 Ph.D.s awarded in business and management, only 19 were to African Americans. In 1993, of the 1,364 Ph.D.s awarded, only 38 were to African Americans. In 1993, the Ph.D. Project assisted 24 African Americans who enrolled in doctoral programs.

In the pre–civil rights era there was very little demand for African American managers and executives in white Corporate America. The attitude was that white workers would not be comfortable with taking orders from a black person, and white customers would be uneasy doing business with a black person. Therefore, African Americans steered away from business schools owing to this lack of inclusion. Some black pioneers did seek to create opportunities where none existed. For instance, H. Naylor Fitzhugh was the first black to graduate, with an M.B.A., from Harvard's Business School in 1933. Despite his Harvard M.B.A., the color of his skin seemed to be more important because his employment options were limited. In 1934, he became a faculty member of Howard University's business program, where he later founded their marketing department.

The first black woman to graduate from the Wharton School of Business at the University of Pennsylvania, in 1953, saw no jobs available for her as well. She decided to go into business because it was a different career from what other women, black or white, were undertaking. Lillian Lincoln was the first black woman to graduate from Harvard School of Business, with an M.B.A., in 1969. She paralleled her experience at Harvard with going to the dentist: "You hate going through the agony of the pain, but you're glad when it's over." These business school graduates had to fight their way through the system, in many cases alone. Being the only black, they had no one to study with, as they watched the white students study together with old exams. Also, they had to face the stigma that they did not belong there and were not really qualified to be there. Even after finishing these M.B.A. programs, blacks still did not have the job opportunities they expected.

With affirmative action, Corporate America began to hire African Americans in middle-management positions, which led white business schools to seek black students. The Consortium for Graduate Study in Management funded 193 black M.B.A. students of the total 322 minority recipients at member institutions. The Consortium was founded by Sterling Schoen, a white business professor. It partners with 10 graduate business schools, mainly in the Midwest, and over 200 corporate sponsors to increase the minority presence in graduate business schools. In the mid-1960s, less than 50 blacks were enrolled in M.B.A. programs.

By 1991, approximately 2,500 blacks received M.B.A.s, according to the National Black MBA Association,* a networking organization, founded in 1970, to assist black M.B.A.s in career development and advancement. According to *Business and Society Review*, the University of Michigan's M.B.A. program has averaged a 15 percent black enrollment in the early 1990s, more than any other white institution, and they also graduate the most black M.B.A.s each year. In 1991, Harvard had a 6 percent black enrollment in its business school of 810 students. With the move toward retrenchment in afffirmative action, undoubtedly black enrollments in white business schools will not increase; perhaps, they will even decline.

SELECTED BIBLIOGRAPHY: Cheryl Fields, "Taking Care of Business (Schools)," *Black Issues in Higher Education* (December 1996); "Harvard Business School Has a New Dean: What Now Is the Outlook for Blacks?" *Black Issues in Higher Education* (Winter 1995); Milton Moskowitz, "The Best Business Schools for Blacks," *Business and Society Review* (Winter 1994); "Preparing Future Business Leaders Today," *Black Enterprise* (February 1997); Cathy Raphael, "Business Schools That Beckon Blacks," *Business and Society Review* (Fall 1992); Vanessa Williams, "Filling the Teaching Void in Business Schools," *Black Enterprise* (August 1996).

Quincy T. Mills

BUSINESS TRENDS, POST-1960s. In the past few decades, a number of black-owned business firms have become successful to the point of attaining a degree of national recognition. These firms and their owners, written about in both black and general audience business magazines, have been included in lists of the largest minority businesses. Also, they are used as examples of black and minority business success. Yet with the exception of one unusual black-owned company, TLC Beatrice International Holdings, the conglomerate end product of a leveraged buyout by the late black financial whiz Reginald Lewis,* even the largest black-owned businesses are very small in comparison to the largest mainstream American *Fortune* 500 corporations. In 1993, TLC Beatrice had sales of $1.7 billion, whereas the other largest black-owned companies had sales of $400 million or less. Only 12 firms had more than $100 million in sales.

Considering the difficulties that black entrepreneurs have faced and continue to face, these sales figures are impressive. Almost all, even the largest black-owned companies, are privately owned, rather than publicly traded, corporations. Growth, then, must be financed via retained earnings or private investment rather than by public equity offerings. Also, black-owned companies fall into certain patterns and categories, rather than run the spectrum of business types and industries. Auto dealerships* comprise a large proportion of black businesses. Of the largest 100 black-owned firms, compiled annually by *Black Enterprise* magazine, the next largest number of companies were in the food and beverage wholesaling and/or retailing industry. Other industries regularly represented in the listings are construction/contracting, media/publications, oil/coal distribution, health care/cosmetics, entertainment, computer technology, miscellaneous manufacturing, and miscellaneous services.

Moreover, unlike the largest mainstream companies, the majority of America's largest black-owned firms, with the exception of health and beauty aids manufacturers and magazine publishers, are neither national nor regional in product distribution nor are they general, multiproduct companies. Rather, most are single-location operations, serving a particular local market with a specific product line or service. Also, the markets served by these companies are predominantly black or minority markets. Furthermore, this profile has not changed over the past two decades since such listings were first compiled; about 10 percent of the total tend to be national or regional rather than local.

A number of conclusions can be drawn. One is that automobile dealerships constitute the strongest segment of larger black businesses. Since the rise of "Black Capitalism" as a social goal in the 1960s, the various American (and more recently, foreign) automobile manufacturers have felt a need to assist black entrepreneurs in acquiring or starting car dealerships, usually in the inner cities. Thus, it is now quite common for urban areas having major minority populations to have one or more local, minority-owned auto dealerships. Yet this segment has also been highly volatile, with the number of firms rising and falling significantly with the national trends in automobile sales and production. If the retail automobile industry were not constrained by a system of manufacturers' geographic franchises, many of these large black-owned automobile dealers would find themselves under great competitive pressure from white-owned dealerships (with greater financial strength) currently limited by their franchises to other geographic markets.

Another trend over the past two decades includes the rise and fall in the number of oil/coal firms on the listings, as energy prices rose and fell, and the gradual increase in the number of computer technology firms in the listings, as the importance of this technology has grown throughout our economy. Moreover, since the 1960s, a major factor determining which types of black-owned firms are the largest is the existence of federal and local minority procurement set-aside* programs. Both the construction/contracting and the oil/coal distribution industries benefited from such programs, which generated significant sales volumes for some companies. With the future of these programs threatened, it can be expected that these two business categories will decline in prominence in future *Black Enterprise* listings. Survival rates for these firms tend to be dangerously low, especially for the lower-ranked firms in the top 100 listings.

While 10-year survival rates for the highest deciles tend to average about 50 percent, the survival rates in the bottom deciles are even lower. Companies that have truly national or regional markets are more likely to survive, as do firms supported by government purchasing programs and retail distributors supported by major manufacturers. Yet all large black-owned businesses are especially vulnerable in the economy and to other environmental factors, partly because black-owned firms tend to carry heavier burdens of debt in comparison to mainstream firms. Still, the future looks promising. Recent data indicate that new black entrepreneurs are younger, better financed, better educated, bigger risk takers and are more likely to have both mainstream corporate experience and political support than did earlier black entrepreneurs. They are more frequently aiming at white markets and more often in service industries. While blacks currently own only about 3 percent of all American businesses, such black ownership is growing strongly, up 38 percent from 1982 to 1987. The future of America's largest black-owned businesses has strong potential.

SELECTED BIBLIOGRAPHY: *Black Enterprise*, "B.E. 100" listings, June, annually; Jeanne Saddler, "Black Entrepreneurship: The Next Generation," *Wall Street Journal*, May 12, 1994; Matthew C. Sonfield, "An Exploratory Analysis of the Largest Black-Owned U.S. Companies," *Journal of Small Business Management* 24 (October 1986); Matthew C. Sonfield, "Progress and Success in the Development of Black-Owned Franchise Units," *Review of Black Political Economy* 22 (Fall 1993).

Matthew C. Sonfield

C

CARVER, GEORGE WASHINGTON (c. 1865–1943), Alabama, scientist, agricultural researcher, educator, businessman.

The Tuskegee Institute scientist George Washington Carver was an advocate of the commercial development of commodities using farm products and native clays, which led to the formation of the Carver Penol Company, the Carver Products Company, and the Carvoline Company. In addition, Carver was a noted lecturer in numerous forums, including tours of white college campuses sponsored by the Commission on Interracial Cooperation. Born a slave, Carver never knew his father and lost his mother during the Civil War. He was raised by his mother's former owners in southwest Missouri. Barred from the local school because of race, he left home early to seek an education. He encountered numerous obstacles but obtained a master's degree in agriculture from Iowa State College in 1896.

The faculty members at Iowa, which included two future secretaries of agriculture, were impressed by Carver's abilities—especially in plant hybridization and mycology, the study of fungi. Because of his talents, Carver took charge of the greenhouses and taught freshman botany while a postgraduate student. The first black instructor at Iowa, he was asked to become a permanent faculty member. Had Carver remained at Iowa State, he would probably have gotten his doctorate and engaged in hybridization or mycological research, but he believed he had a responsibility to help other African Americans. Consequently, Carver accepted an offer by Booker T. Washington* to head the agricultural department at Tuskegee Normal and Industrial Institute in Macon County, Alabama, in 1896.

Focusing on Washington's priorities, Carter soon established an agricultural experiment station—the only one entirely staffed by African Americans. Both its low funding ($1,500 annually) and Carver's desire to aid poor, landless share-croppers influenced his work. Most standard practices of scientific agriculture were too costly for impoverished small-scale farmers. The major problem for tenant farmers was debt. Without land they had to borrow against their future crops for provisions. State laws often required sharecroppers to work for a land-owner as long as they owed money. Landowners could make it difficult or even impossible for their croppers to get out from under the crushing burden of debt. The less tenant farmers purchased, the more likely they were to escape virtual peonage.

Recognizing these problems, Carver focused his research on procedures and products to replace purchased goods. To substitute for expensive fertilizers, he advocated green manuring by plowing under vegetable matter, use of animal manure where available, and composting. The need for crop rotation led Carver to experiment with new crops as alternatives to the soil-depleting cotton that dominated southern agriculture. Bulletins prepared by Carter on such crops as sweet potatoes, cow peas, and peanuts not only explained their cultivation but also suggested uses to replace goods bought from stores. Another bulletin told readers how to make paints from native clay deposits.

A myth later emerged that Carver was responsible for the invention of nu-merous commercial products. That myth not only distorts the truth but also contradicts the goals of Carver's original work. The development of commercial products offered no relief for landless farmers who had no money with which to manufacture them—or even to purchase them. What they needed were alter-natives to the purchased goods that they bought on credit for high prices. The roots of the claims that Carver invented hundreds of products are found in his many recipes that he published in his agricultural bulletins, leaflets, and articles. Two examples of such bulletins were *How to Make Sweet Potato Flour, Starch, Sugar, Bread and Mock Coconut* (1918) and *How to Grow the Cow Pea and Forty Ways of Preparing It as a Table Delicacy* (1925). His "cookstove chemistry," as he called this research, eventually provided substitutes for many nonfood items as well, but the bulk of his published work centered on food preparation.

Carver was a sensitive and proud man, who was often dismissed as a dreamer by the eminently practical Booker T. Washington. After a series of humiliating defeats in campus power struggles, Carver became increasingly tired of defend-ing his work to people who did not understand or respect his goals of leading poor sharecroppers to self-sufficiency. He smarted from comments such as those in a letter from Washington's brother, who criticized Carver's paint from native clays because it was not "something that can be put into commercial form and sold in competition with such material as is produced in other sections of the country." Carver first responded to that charge by explaining, "When I started this work, I had in mind primarily the rural school-teacher and farmer" to provide them with ways to beautify their surroundings "easily, effectively and inexpensively." Nevertheless, to prove that his ideas were "practical," Carver made several attempts to market various products. He also began to develop elaborate exhibits of his multiple products, which caught the eyes of some businessmen.

In 1911 Carver and Emmett J. Scott, Washington's secretary, planned a commercial venture to manufacture the paints Carver had developed from native clays. First, however, they agreed to begin with products less costly to produce and package. They decided upon talcum and face powders that Carver made from clay. They checked out packaging costs and applicable provisions of the Pure Food and Drug Act, before deciding that Carver's laboratory did not have the equipment needed to substantiate the purity standards of the Food and Drug Administration (FDA). They tried again in 1916 to found a company, but Carver became involved in finding substitutes for shortages that occurred as a result of World War 1. As a result, the Bureau of Plant Industry of the United States Department of Agriculture invited Carver to come to Washington for consultation in January 1918. His hosts were especially pleased with Carver's sweet potato flour and suggested that it had commercial possibilities.

For several years various people approached Carver with commercial proposals, and Ernest Thompson, a young white man from the town of Tuskegee, assumed the role of Carver's business manager. Thompson followed up numerous leads from both individuals and such companies as Ralston-Purina and Lister Brothers. Problems quickly emerged. Neither Carver nor Thompson wanted to pay the expenses of obtaining patents, and without patents, Carver was reluctant to give potential investors enough information to determine the commercial feasibility of his products.

Nothing advanced beyond the talking stage until 1923, when Carver applied for his first patent. At the same time, a number of prominent white businessmen from Atlanta, including former Georgia governor Hugh Dorsey, incorporated the Carver Products Company. Officers included Charles W. Wickersham, president of the Atlanta and West Point Railroad, as president; Scott W. Allen, vice president and general manager of a grocery store chain; and Ernest Thompson as secretary-treasurer. Headquartered in Atlanta, the company had no plans to manufacture anything but to serve as a kind of holding company to sell Carver's processes to manufacturers—either outright or on a royalty basis.

Carver refused to discuss his compensation, but one newspaper reported he would get 10 percent of the net income. The Carver Products Company issued a prospectus and began selling shares of stock at $1.00 a share. The directors planned to capitalize at $125,000 but apparently were unable to interest enough investors. To a large extent the company was selling Carver himself instead of any tangible product. His fame drew interest, not investors. Newspapers announced the incorporation, and in September 1923, the *Manufacturers' Record* proclaimed that the company would be in operation in a short time. Directors approached the leading businesspeople of Atlanta, including Robert Woodruff of the Coca-Cola Company, who agreed to test Carver's paint in barrel painting operations.

In the end the venture produced a lot of publicity but little else. One proposed paint company got as far as hiring an engineer to draw up the specifications for a plant, and Carver was granted three patents: two for making paint from clay and one for producing cosmetics from clay and peanuts. During the 1920s the only commodity actually manufactured was an emulsion of creosote and peanuts called Penol. Creosote was commonly used for treatment of respiratory problems, and Carver believed the peanuts added nutritional value and enhanced the taste.

The Carver Penol Company was founded by a number of white Tuskegee businessmen. Incorporated under the laws of Delaware, Penol printed a stock offering with 150,000 shares. Again investors were hard to find, and production began on a very small scale sometime in 1926. Sales were limited, and in 1932, a Danville, Virginia, firm that already distributed an "herbal extract" and a laxative took over production and sale of the product. The company's president, J. T. Hamlin, changed its name to Herb-Juice-Penol Company and arranged for Sharps and Dohme Pharmaceutical Laboratory to manufacture Penol. By that time Carver had given over all rights to Ernest Thompson, who had invested much of his inheritance in attempts to exploit Carver's products. Sales remained weak and tapered off to practically nothing by 1937.

Only two other products reached production stage during Carver's lifetime. One was a massage oil made from peanuts that Carver had used with some success on polio victims. Although his massage skills were probably the secret to his success, a United Press release made it sound as if the oil was a cure for polio, and demand for it soared. African American chemist Austin Curtis, who had been hired as Carver's assistant by Tuskegee Institute, began making both the massage oil and a hair preparation in 1939. That same year another group of white citizens in Tuskegee won Carver's approval to produce both products and to name their company the Carvoline Company. In return they were to pay royalties to the George Washington Carver Foundation, which Carver had founded to continue his legacy at Tuskegee. The company generated few profits and did not survive after Carver's death in 1943. Austin Curtis, however, left Tuskegee and founded a company in Detroit that did survive.

None of Carver's products became huge commercial successes. The most popular uses of peanuts—peanut butter, cooking oil, salted, and in candies—all predated Carver's work with peanuts. Nevertheless, Carver did advise a number of peanut manufacturers, such as the Tom Huston Company in Columbus, Georgia, but refused to accept compensation for his services and declined employment offers from such diverse white entities as Thomas Edison to the Libby Company. Carver willingly shared his expertise with all, black and white, individuals and corporations.

His income remained limited almost entirely to his salary of $1,200 a year. Never much concerned with money, Carver would even forget to deposit his paychecks. Nevertheless, he was able to leave about $60,000 to the Carver Foundation, because he also spent little money. Living in a boys' dorm and eating in the dining hall, Carver had few expenses. He preached that nature produced no waste and never threw much away. He wore clothes until they were practically rags and then made such items as rugs from them. Consequently, most of his money sat in banks, drawing interest.

Carver has been credited with developing numerous commercial products, but such claims miss the point of his original research. He was seeking replacements for purchased goods to free impoverished sharecroppers from the crushing burden of debt. The very point of his work was to develop processes practically anyone could reproduce from available resources. For a period of time, Carver became seduced by the lure of commercializing his products—not for money but for recognition by "practical" men. By the time of his death, however, Carver had returned to his original vision and recommended that cooking demonstrations take the place of his elaborate exhibits. Nevertheless, his legacy was considerable. His fame encouraged blacks to become scientists or businesspeople; his efforts improved the quality of life for countless poor farmers; and the George Washington Carver Foundation continues to provide funding for black scientists.

SELECTED BIBLIOGRAPHY: George Washington Carver Papers, Tuskegee University, Alabama; Gary R. Kremer, *George Washington Carver in His Own Words* (Columbia: University of Missouri Press, 1987); Harry Makintosh, "George Washington Carver: The Making of a Myth," *Journal of Southern History* 42 (November 1976); Linda O. McMurry, *George Washington Carver: Scientist and Symbol* (New York: Oxford University Press, 1981).

Linda O. McMurry

CATERING, INNS, HOTELS. From the colonial era, blacks, both slave and free, developed enterprises in food services. Most were hawkers and street vendors of prepared food, but some accumulated profits to rent property and, as did free black street vendors, open cook shops. With profits from these enterprises, some slaves were able to purchase their freedom. The more successful free blacks expanded their food service activities and opened restaurants, whereas some established catering enterprises or specialized in areas such as baking and pastry making. In both the North and South, a few free blacks established inns and hotels. Blacks in the food services industry, however, enjoyed their greatest success before the Civil War in catering.

The food services enterprises established by blacks first began to pay off in the eighteenth century. In 1736 the Baroons, Emanuel Manna and wife Mary, former slaves who purchased their freedom, opened a catering establishment in Providence, Rhode Island. During the late eighteenth century, several blacks made a successful living in pastry making, including the "Dutchess" Quamino of Newport and the Philadelphia baker Cyrus Bustill, born in 1732, who also established a bakery in that city. He also served in the Continental Army, as did the most successful African American in food services in the eighteenth century, Samuel "Black Sam" Fraunces, a West Indian, who immigrated to the American colonies in the 1750s.

He embarked in food services as a caterer in New York in 1755. Then in 1761, Fraunces purchased a mansion, where he established a tavern and inn that soon gained the reputation as "the finest hostlery in colonial America." He expanded his business and in 1765 opened a resort establishment, known as a vaux hall, on the outskirts of New York, where he provided musical entertainment and a wax-work exhibit. In 1773 the resort was sold, and Fraunces put all his emphasis on his New York enterprise, Fraunces Tavern and Restaurant. It quickly became the meeting place for the Revolutionary War leaders, the Second Continental Congress, and General George Washington and his staff. Fraunces also served in the Continental Army, as a private in Washington's own division until 1782, and with Washington's election, Fraunces was also the White House first chef. His tavern remained open until 1803, still retaining its reputation as a meeting place for the nation's leading politicians and businessmen. Blacks, however, were not allowed to eat there or stay over in the inn, which was the pattern for the leading black hotel keepers and restaurateurs during the age of slavery.

The black catering industry was at its height in the antebellum nineteenth century, and Philadelphia was the center of the most successful black caterers before the Civil War. While many of the early leading Philadelphia caterers were from the French West Indies, including the Haitian-born Peter Augustin, the American-born Robert Bogle (?–1837) was recognized as having professionalized the industry for blacks. According to Henry Minton, Bogle "conceived the idea that instead of those who desired to entertain being inconvenienced by having to temporarily enlarge the retinue of their kitchens to prepare the viands for a formal dinner, he would contract to furnish the entire meal with his own help." His success, the elegant dinners and banquets he served in the homes of the wealthy, was such that Nicholas Biddle, president of the Bank of the United States, wrote a poem in 1829 to honor him, "Ode to Bogle." Bogle first owned a coffeeshop before he became a caterer.

As black catering enterprises expanded in number, they remained family enterprises, some of which continued into the twentieth century, with catering families often intermarrying. The leading antebellum catering families were the Bogles, Augustins, Prossers, Dorseys, Jones, and Mintons. Haitian-born Peter Augustin established his catering business in 1818 and eventually had an international reputation. European travelers to America who attended dinners served by Augustin and his waiters on their return home placed orders for transatlantic delivery of his specialty terrapin soup to Paris and London. Augustin's son Theodore married Clara, the daughter of another leading Philadelphia caterer, Eugene Baptiste, who also established his catering enterprise in 1818. As the enterprise expanded, Augustin worked from three large kitchens, and he employed from 40 to 100 people in all areas of food preparation and service. The

Augustin-Baptiste firm also continued operations into the early twentieth century. In 1910 their business was worth $60,000. The catering enterprise established by Peter Dutrieuille in 1873 remained in the family until 1974.

A new group of black caterers emerged by the 1840s, including American-born Henry Jones from Virginia, who died in 1875 and was known for having left "a considerable estate"; Thomas Dorsey (1810–1875); and Henry Minton, who Martin Delany said in 1850 was "the proprietor of a fashionable restaurant and resort for business men and gentlemen of the city." Restaurant ownership, invariably, was the first step for many to a catering enterprise. Catering was a highly profitable enterprise, and it was reported that Philadelphia caterers sold their dinners or banquets by the plate, with prices as high as $50 per plate. That the catering business was recognized as part of the formal economy is seen in the credit reports of these enterprises. Their enterprises were even listed in the Dun Mercantile credit reports. When Minton's son went into business, Dun reported that he was the: "single son of Henry Minton who keeps a restaurant at 204 South 12th St. & who owns cons'd [considerable] city ppty [property], furnishes the capital & set his son up in the business here. . . . He is backed up by his father in that way is safe for all his bus wants."

Black caterers, who were also known as "public waiters," did more than cook and service. The New York jeweler Edward V. Clark, who established his business in 1849, was a caterer, but he also loaned silver and glassware to the "upper ten" for their dinners and parties. He was forced out of business as a result of the Panic of 1857. The leading New York black caterers was the Downing family, who established catering enterprises in both New York and Rhode Island. The New York business was started by the Virginia slave-born Thomas who moved to that city in 1812. In addition to his catering enterprise, he also established a restaurant and oyster house in the city's business district. His son George Downing* expanded the family's enterprise in 1844, when he established his own catering and restaurant business in Newport.

With financial backing from his father, George purchased a large building known as Sea Girt Hotel, a $30,000 property, which housed eight large stores on the first floor, with hotel accommodations provided on the upper floors. An 1848 advertisement illustrates the menu and the kinds of catering services he provided, including "a suite of Game and Oyster Supper Rooms," which could accommodate up to 30 people in addition to rooms, where women could be served in private, including a "Private Ice Cream Saloon for ladies." Also Downing provided delivery service to private resort cottages. The Sea Girt building was destroyed by fire at a complete loss of $30,000. Downing subsequently rebuilt on the site that became known as Downing's block, and a newspaper advertisement in 1850 stated: "George L. Downing is now building three handsome and commodious Stores, . . . which will be let as soon as completed, . . . apply immediately to the builder . . . or George L. Downing."

In the South, the leading blacks in food service enterprises were also those who established exclusive restaurants and first-class hotels. In South Carolina, the former tailor Jehu Jones purchased an inn for $13,000 in 1816, which he turned into an exclusive hotel, known first as the Jones Inn, then the Jones Hotel. An English traveler recommending the hotel noted its clean tablecloths, the silver, and claret and emphasized that the usual "salt pork and greasy corn cake were not served." The hotel changed hands several times after Jones's death in 1833. In 1847, it was purchased by John and Eliza Lee, whose brother William Seymour also owned a tavern and inn. Invariably the hotel staff, cooks, maids, and waiters were slaves owned by these black hotel and inn proprietors. On his death in 1833, Jones's total property holdings in his hotel and slaves had amounted to $40,000. Also, these leading black caterers made additional money by training the slaves of wealthy slaveowners, while some slaves were sent abroad by their owners to develop skills in European cooking, especially from the French.

In addition to the large restaurants and hotels that served only an elite white clientele, blacks also owned cook shops, groceries, and grog shops patronized by both free blacks and slaves. While it was illegal to serve liquor to slaves, grog shops remained in business. Usually, cook shops were used as a cover for these enterprises. In Richmond, Virginia, free black Clinton James ran a multipurpose enterprise, a grocery, bar room, snack room, and kitchen on the first floor of a building he owned, which was located behind one of Richmond's exclusive hotels. Another well-known grog shop was run by free black Richard Taylor, who ran the "Taylor House," which provided all the services of a hotel in addition to alcohol, gambling, and prostitution. Even so, with the profits earned from these enterprises, their owners had the respect of the black community and often emerged as their leaders.

Northern free blacks were not restricted in the selling of liquor. In Cincinnati the Dumas Hotel served liquor and also allowed gambling. On the Rocky Mountain frontier, the intrepid black explorer James P. Beckwourth (1797–1867), one of the founders of Denver, Colorado, established a hotel and trading post in 1852 in what is now Beckwourth Valley. Beckwourth, a fugitive slave from St. Louis, joined a Fur Expedition in 1815 as a scout, hunter, and Indian fighter. During the gold rush the trail he discovered, Beckwourth Pass, became the main route for settlers moving to California during the gold rush. On the California frontier in 1846, William Leidesdorff* opened the first luxury hotel in San Francisco. With the 1848 gold rush, free blacks and former slaves in California established food service enterprises.

Even after the Civil War, several of the leading antebellum Philadelphia black catering families continued running successful enterprises, including Thomas Dorsey, who died in 1876, and Henry Minton, who died in 1884. Also it was reported that the Philadelphia caterer Levi Cromwell and P. J. Augustine in 1879 were worth $50,000. While a few blacks in the catering business, such as wealthy Boston caterer Joseph Lee, who invented a bread-making machine, continued to serve the white elite, they were a decided minority. For the most part, after the Civil War, black caterers began to experience greater competition from whites. While the successful antebellum black caterer George Downing managed the Capitol Café in Washington, D.C., from 1866 to 1879, his Newport catering business went into a decline, especially in the face of increasing competition from whites. Even before the end of the nineteenth century, they controlled the resort catering industry in Rhode Island.

Even as early as 1865, black caterers in New York recognized that their hold on the catering industry was being challenged by whites. In 1869, 12 black caterers founded the Corporation of Caterers, which was incorporated, and also the Public Waiters Association. Their major purpose was to maintain professional standards. Also, they recognized the need to pool their resources, silver, china, and crystal, if they were to continue to meet the demands required in catering large parties and banquets. By 1870, there were 500 members, and as membership expanded to include employees in the catering industry, the group reorganized in 1872 as the Waiters' Beneficial Association, with emphasis on mutual aid insurance benefits, as opposed to protecting the interests of the self-employed caterers. The leading caterers in Philadelphia also organized in attempts to maintain their hold on the industry by founding two organizations. The Philadelphia's Caterers Association was founded in 1866, but despite their organization, black caterers declined both in numbers and in income. By the late nineteenth century, less than 10 black caterers had annual incomes that ranged from $3,000 to $5,000. In response, the Caterers Manufacturing and Supply Company was founded in 1894. It purchased catering items—tables, chairs, linens, glasses, silver, and chinaware—wholesale that were either sold at cost or rented to its membership.

Even while there was an overall decline of blacks in the industry, there were continued attempts made by them to maintain their hold on the industry. And, indeed, several black caterers who entered the field in the late nineteenth century did enjoy some success, primarily as a result of the innovations they brought to the catering industry. In Chicago, Charles H. Smiley (1851–?) in catering weddings provided not only the food and wedding cake but also floral arrangements, church decorations, and security guards who were placed discreetly to watch the gifts. Smiley was not only the largest employer of blacks in Chicago in the early twentieth century; he was also one of the few leading black businessmen who maintained a white clientele. Also, in Westchester County, New York, Francis J. Moultrie's (1842–?) catering enterprises by the 1890s were grossing $25,000 annually. In Germantown, Pennsylvania, John S. Trower (1849–?), who established a restaurant in 1870, tapped a new customer base in 1889, when he began providing catering services to the Cramps Ship Building Company. With his profits, Trower purchased a $75,000 three-story building, which enabled him to expand his catering business and tap a market in several cities in the South and West.

With changing food tastes and racial attitudes in post–Civil War America, elite black caterers were no longer a status symbol for the rich, a factor that contributed to the demise of the black caterer; in addition, new licensing laws enacted to regulate the industry also worked to their detriment. By the late 1880s, several states, including Pennsylvania, required caterers to post a $2,000 bond to secure a liquor license in addition to paying an annual license fee that ranged from $500 to $900. Yet even if black caterers could afford those costs, there were also laws that required that liquor could only be sold in a business that was permanently located. Black caterers just did not have the facilities, nor could they compete with the food services provided by European chefs in the new restaurants and luxurious hotels. There were, of course, always exceptions.

The Washington, D.C., black-owned Wormley's Hotel established by wealthy caterer James Wormley (1819–1884), which opened in 1871, was the leading hotel in the nation's capital for politicians and foreign dignitaries even into the 1890s, when it was sold by Wormley's son, James. Indeed, at the time it opened, the facilities and services were said to set standards for the new post–Civil War luxury hotels. The Wormley was a five-story elevator building, with telephone service provided in each room or apartments in addition to an elegant first-floor dining room. Also, the Athens, Ohio, Berry Hotel, also an elevator building, established by E. C. Berry in 1893, had a predominantly white clientele, since Berry did not allow blacks to stay at his hotel. He had owned a restaurant before establishing his 50-room hotel, with baths, and grossed $35,000 annually. In the early twentieth century, J. L. Thomas in Union Springs, Alabama, who owned both a restaurant and a grocery store, grossing $40,000 annually, established a hotel—but for whites only. He was quickly encouraged to sell out, which he did.

Yet, ironically, as the black caterering industry declined at the turn of the century, having relied primarily on whites, the black hotel industry expanded, with their all-black clientele. Many of the owners, incidentally, had been in the catering or restaurant business. Other blacks who opened hotels were in the real estate business. In Washington, D.C., in 1877, the Nail* brothers, John Bennett (1853–1942) and Edward (?–1899), established the Shakespeare House for blacks, and in the 1890s, they opened a New York hotel for blacks. Also, in Cincinnati several black hotels for blacks were established in the late 1890s. Consequently, while a few Philadelphia caterers, with their expertise in French cooking, continued to provide food services in the homes of the nouveau riche, most black caterers survived by providing catering services to small home dinner parties and other social occasions for the white middle class. In Cincinnati, Ed J. Berry, one of the city's leading black caterers, continued to serve whites at receptions of all kinds but expanded his business to provide food services for the large summer resorts in the area. Moreover, by 1905 membership in the New York Public Waiters Association had declined to only 33 members, and those black caterers still in business relied primarily on blacks as their clientele.

The Civil War, then, marked a turning point in the participation of African Americans in the food service and hotel industries. And by the turn of the century, most blacks in these industries had lost their wealthy white clientele, which had provided the basis for antebellum black caterers and hotel owners to earn substantial profits. Whereas before the Civil War, employing black caterers and staying in the black-owned inns, hotels, and resorts was a mark of status for wealthy whites, this was no longer the case after 1865, although there were a few black caterers and hotel owners who were able to maintain profitable enterprises to the turn of the century. By then, however, racial attitudes and mores discouraged white support of black businesses, which made it increasingly difficult for blacks in the personal services to compete in providing the kinds of luxurious services they had provided wealthy whites before the Civil War.

In the twentieth century, then, while whites would continue to hire blacks as cooks, their catering needs were increasingly provided by whites. On the other hand, the two worlds of race sanctioned by the 1896 *Plessy v. Ferguson* decision provided the basis for the growth of the black hotel industry that would expand until the 1954 *Brown* decision. Even by the late 1950s, as blacks increasingly took advantage of their access to public accommodations, the black hotel industry was in a rapid decline. On the other hand, since the 1970s and the increasing acceptability of African American food preferences, blacks in the food services now have an expanded market in mainstream American food services. Even so, black participation rates in this industry remain low. Of the 349,946 eating and drinking places in the United States, according to the 1992 Survey of Minority-Owned Business Enterprises (SMOBE), only 13,832 were black-owned enterprises. There were a total of 77,788 hotels and other lodging places, but only 1,657 were owned by African Americans.

SELECTED BIBLIOGRAPHY: Martin R. Delany, *The Condition, Elevation, Emigration and Destiny of the Colored People of the United States* (Philadelphia, 1852; reprint, New York: Arno Press, 1968); William E. B. Du Bois, *The Philadelphia Negro* (Philadelphia: University of Pennsylvania Press, 1899), 33–36; George Edmund Haynes, *The Negro at Work in New York City: A Study of Economic Progress* (New York: Columbia University Press, 1912), 97; Henry M. Minton, M.D., "Early History of Negroes in Business in Philadelphia" (paper read before the American Historical Society, Moorland-Spingarn Research Center, Howard University, Washington, D.C., March 1913); SMOBE web data, http://www.census.gov/agfs/smobe/view/b__1.txt and http://www.census.gov/agfs/smobe/view/u__1.txt; Tinsley L. Spraggins, "The History of the Negro Business Prior to 1860" (master's thesis, Howard University, 1935); Juliet E. K. Walker, *The History of Black Business in America: Capitalism, Race, Entrepreneurship* (New York: Macmillan/Prentice Hall International, 1998).

Juliet E. K. Walker

CHESAPEAKE MARINE RAILWAY AND DRY DOCK COMPANY

(1866–1884). The Chesapeake Marine Railway and Dry Dock Company (CMRDDC) was organized by black community leaders of Baltimore, Maryland, in 1866, a direct result of increasing racial tensions in the city's shipyards. Its primary purpose was to secure employment for black shipyard workers in the city. There was a record of black labor organization in the Baltimore area going back to at least 1838 in The Caulkers' Association, which was able to bargain collectively with shipyard owners. Subsequently, before the Civil War, many blacks received higher wages than their white counterparts. Blacks controlled the caulking market because it was considered a low-skilled occupation, which whites found undesirable.

However, during the 1850s, as a result of the Panic of 1857 and increased European immigration to the United States, white competition for this formerly black-only labor market increased significantly, which led to a series of strikes and riots. In 1858, whites rioted and attacked black caulkers and other shipyard workers. While some shipyard companies hired police to protect their black workers, others refused to hire blacks, even though they oftentimes had to recruit whites from other cities. The situation normalized through the Civil War, but in 1865 the most severe strike against blacks occurred. White caulkers and ship carpenters demanded that blacks no longer be allowed to work in the shipyards, and they had the support of the local government and police.

In 1865, a group of prominent members of the Baltimore black community, most of whom were also leaders in business and the African Methodist Episcopal (AME) and Methodist Episcopal Churches, organized and founded the CMRDDC. Isaac Myers (1835–1891), a well-known labor leader, president of the Colored Caulkers' Trades Union Society of Baltimore, president of the (Colored) National Labor Union, however, generally is given credit as the principal organizer of the corporation. He also served as one of the first elected directors of the CMRDDC, which was capitalized at $40,000, with 8,000 $5 shares, and was headed by a board of 12 directors.

The yard was subleased from William Applegarth, a white businessman, for a period of 18 years. Although formed in 1866, it did not become legally incorporated until 1868 and functioned until the original lease was recalled by Applegarth in 1888. The day-to-day function of the relatively successful CMRDDC was overseen by Applegarth and cofounder John H. Smith, and it grew into a shipyard that employed over 300 men, black and white. The CMRDDC functioned successfully until it became known to company's financiers that the property was not owned by the CRMDDC but rather leased. In 1879, a group of complainants filed suit against the company, charging that the initial investments had been misrepresented.

Debate over ownership led to the eventual decline, as investigations by the complainants also revealed problems within the company's management. Also, no dividends were paid during the 1870s, not for lack of profitability but rather from the inability to collect the company's outstanding balance due. Indebtedness also persisted because the shipbuilding industry soured this decade. Then, in 1884 the original leases were reclaimed from Applegarth by James N. Muller and the Susquehanna Steam Company. Yet the directors continued to meet until 1910 in order to work toward the collection and payment of unpaid bills. The CRMDCC, then, provides an example of a temporarily successful business venture in the post–Civil War era. It was born out of need to protect black jobs in a racially hostile southern city and the desire by blacks to earn greater incomes as entrepreneurs.

SELECTED BIBLIOGRAPHY: Philip S. Foner, *History of the Labor Movement in the United States* (New York: International Publishers, 1947); Leroy Graham, *Baltimore: The Nineteenth Century Black Capital* (Washington, DC: University Press of America, 1982); Bettye C. Thomas, "A Nineteenth Century Black Operated Shipyard, 1866–1884: Reflections upon Its Inception and Ownership," *Journal of Negro History* 59 (1974).

Scott C. Woods

CHICAGO, BLACK BUSINESS HISTORY. Black Chicago's history in business enterprise predates the very existence of the city that bears the Native American name "Eschecagou." As early as the 1770s Jean Baptiste Pointe DuSable, a Haytian of mixed West African and French heritage, settled at a point where the "river meets the lake," a favorite trading place for native peoples. DuSable arrived in the area determined to build a successful trading emporium, a well-documented venture in which he succeeded immensely. His profitable fur and other trading activities extended over several decades until he decided, for some unknown reason, to move his family southward from the region in 1800. Yet for Chicago's African Americans of the nineteenth century who followed, DuSable probably did not provide an easily recognizable model of business success; for those of the mid-twentieth century, who were much more aware of the origins of the city's traditions, he appeared as an incomparable business model and confirmed the basis of the successes they were attaining.

As a factor explaining the near meteoric twentieth-century rise of black business, popular knowledge of black Chicago's business triumphs in numerous business directories, beginning with Isaac C. Harris's *Colored Men's Professional and Business Directory* in 1885 and extending to today's "Black Pages," published annually. These written sources served two major functions. First, in and of themselves, they represented the potential for successful business operations in the city. These earliest, profitably printed guides paved the way for the more lucrative publications of the next century, such as Robert S. Abbott's* *Chicago Defender* newspaper, which made him a millionaire by the 1920s. Second, they chronicled and illuminated the extent of black business activities and development during any particular historical period, establishing a documented record of success that encouraged emulation.

Moreover, the organized efforts of businesspersons, remarkably evident early in this century with the Chicago chapter of the National Negro Business League,* the Colored Men's Physicians, Dentists and Pharmacists Club, and the Musician's Protective Union, marked an evolutionary stage in the formation of positive black attitudes toward group-oriented business ventures. In addition, the depression era generated popular, nonbusiness group interest in and support for black business expansion that persists until today. By 1930, the Chicago *Whip* newspaper began the popular, and nationally emulated, "Don't Spend Your Money Where You Can't Work" campaign aimed at increasing black employment in white businesses operating in the Black Metropolis. By extension, this action stimulated many organized attempts to guarantee black employment and economic advancement through the expansion of black businesses. Last, the continuous increase in the black population accompanied a heightened commitment to an ideology of racial support for community businesses, but not only businesspersons themselves promoted racial solidarity and self-help but also the clergy and civic leaders.

Historically, while the nineteenth century witnessed few black businesses because there was only a small population to support them, the belief that blacks did not patronize black businesses rang true. John Jones,* as an antebellum merchant-tailor, rose individually to respectable heights in Chicago's business community, catering to a white clientele. However, in Chicago, by the post-Reconstruction period, when the population reached 30,000, Harris's *Directory* reported on the beginning of black support for black services, but a white clientele in certain service areas such as barbering, saloon keeping, and restauranting also existed. This period represented an incipient stage of growth for both black businesspersons and an African American market. It further validated Abram Harris's* analysis that a spirit of business enterprise grew throughout the nation shortly after the Emancipation. In *The Negro as Capitalist*, the noted economist wrote: "From the [18]80s on, the Negro masses, urged by their leaders, were led to place increasing faith in business and property as a means of escaping poverty and achieving economic independence."

This confidence reached fruition in the twentieth century when the first, full-blown generation of black entrepreneurs and businesspersons appeared. D. A. Bethea's *The Colored People's Blue Book and Business Directory of Chicago* of 1905, and again in 1906, listed at least 100 self-employed movers and expressmen, 10 laundries, 21 grocers, 39 lawyers, three dozen music teachers, four bakers, one architect, and over 80 barbers among scores of business operations. In 1918, *Black's Blue Book* recounted a similar pattern. These data, of course, contradict Spear's contention (*Black Chicago*) that black business success before the 1920s was virtually nonexistent beyond the formation of Abbot's *Defender* in 1905, Jesse Binga's* bank in 1908, Rube Foster's American Giants professional baseball team, Sandy Trice's downtown clothing store, and the arrival of Anthony Overton* from Kansas City with his Overton Hygienic cosmetic manufacturing. Of the latter, Spear described the Overton company in 1915 as capitalized at $268,000, employing 32 workers, and offering the public 62 different products. So not only was there an extant business base; it appeared to thrive and provide the foundation for the unbridled success of black businesses in the following decade.

With national postwar prosperity, the decade of the 1920s heralded the debut of the Black Metropolis, the attempt by blacks to build a self-contained city within the city. Scoffed at by some, but endorsed by many more, the claim of maintaining a Black Metropolis grew to rest on the potential of a solid political and economic base. While some black businesses depended on a white clientele, the arrival of an additional 50,000 migrating workers, mainly adults, expanded the black consumer base. Drake and Cayton contended that it was their arrival that provided the consumer base for the black businesses. Yet the existing pro-business attitudes held by the black entrepreneur and businessperson as well as consumer greeted these new Chicagoans. The result was a melding of the forces that allowed business enterprises to take advantage of the prosperity of the decade.

These halcyon days of the 1920s saw the maturation of the Binga Bank, established in 1908, as a personal operation, into the Binga State Bank in 1921 and the emergence of Anthony Overton's Douglass National Bank in 1923. These two banks, according to Abram Harris, represented the largest black banks ever established, controlling one-third of all black bank resources nationally. Just as impressively, black Chicagoans organized insurance companies on the modern corporate model, bypassing the stage common in the South of evolution from mutual aid* and fraternal activities. Three major insurance companies joined the banks in the financial sphere: Supreme Liberty Life, Metropolitan Mutual, and Victory Life, a spin-off of Overton's bank and manufacturing firm. In transportation, one enterprising gentleman, Walter L. Lee, started Your Cab Company. Lee put a fleet of 70 vehicles on the streets daily, each driven by a uniformed chauffeur operating from his garage. In manufacturing, Parker House Sausage Company and Walter Johnson's Therapeutic Light Company joined the ranks of business enterprise. The Associated Business Club, led by Robert S. Abbott, Jesse Binga, Oscar De Priest,* and others, provided organizational support for economic development.

Documenting this expansion along with the explosion in newspapers' business coverage were two business directories. Simms's and Black's *Blue Books* contained pages illuminating the activities of scores of many smaller retail and service operations. The dream of a Black Metropolis foundered, however, on the rocks of the Great Depression. Both banking giants failed, and so did many smaller businesses. Supreme and Metropolitan did manage to survive the economic disaster. Financial bright spots appeared in 1935, with the organization of a new financial operation, Illinois Federal Savings and Loan, and a business group, the Cosmopolitan Chamber of Commerce. The former, while small for the day, assumed a larger role with its growing assets in the postwar economy. This pattern proved true for the Johnson Publishing Company, created in the middle of the war.

The post–World War II era heralded another opportunity for the nation to experience peace accompanied by prosperity. Not unexpectedly, black Chicago was as ready to expand in economic development as any other segment of the nation. New businesses developed with an expanded range of goods and services relevant for new tastes in a more sophisticated and expanded market. By the 1950s, Johnson Products, a hair care firm, emerged and for 30 years would be a national giant in hair care products. By 1965, two new banks were formed in the black community—Seaway National and Independence Bank. Within a decade, five other black-owned banks joined them in operating in the city and a neighboring suburb.

The ranks of the middle class were burgeoning as were those of organized and unorganized labor, and their support for black business was spurred on by the impetus of "Black Pride" accompanying the civil rights and black empowerment eras. With employment high, halcyon days had returned to the black communities with hundreds of small businesses operating throughout the black neighborhoods of Chicago. All tried to meet the needs in goods and services of a population that had reached 1 million. Further working to stimulate business growth were civil rights groups such as the Negro Labor Relations League, the Chicago Urban League, and the Southern Christian Leadership Conference's (SCLC) Operation Breadbasket (later PUSH [People United to Save Humanity]).

The years of the Nixon-Ford presidencies were plagued by national economic distress, and the pressures were evident in black Chicago with rising unemployment and inflation. Ominously, an easing of racist resistance to black shoppers meant that white competitors joined black businesses in the pursuit of black dollars. Still, counterbalancing these trends, these Republican administrations featured support for "Black Capitalism," seen in government support for small black businesses. The vitality of black banking was manifested in 1978 in a proposed merger between Seaway and Independence. It failed, but the latter purchased two other black banks the following year and, shortly after that, purchased a third. So the picture remained challenging and moderately bright. One major highlight of the decade was Johnson Products going public and selling shares on the American Stock Exchange.

The Chicago black business community courageously struggled in a depressed economy during the Reagan-Bush era of the 1980s. Unemployment increased as global pressures transformed the shape of the city's economy completely. The number of black banks now fell to three. Impressively, though, two black firms operated on prestigious South Michigan Avenue on the city's fabled lakefront, and in 1982, *Black Enterprise* listed Chicago as the home to 7 of the top 100 black businesses in the nation: Johnson Publishing, Johnson Products, Johnson Cadillac (all nonrelated), R. L. Dukes Olds, Inner City Foods, Parker House Sausage, and Thomas Distributors (beverages). The city's nearest competitor, the Greater New York City area, had a dozen.

Johnson Publishing rose the next year, in 1983, to become the nation's biggest black moneymaker, surpassing Motown, while Soft Sheen Products, a hair care firm, joined *Black Enterprise*'s (*BE*) 100. Black financial ventures in investments, brokerage, money management, and commercial banking continued to grow. Illinois Service Federal Savings and Loan (S&L), for example, expanded, becoming the second largest black S&L in the nation. Insurance companies made modest profits, as they faced competition from white firms eyeing the lucrative black-dominated market in insurance.

By the 1990s, a new reality dawned: Increased white corporate business penetration of traditional black markets coupled with a black professional talent drain alternated to deplete the ranks of small businesses and the potential pool of African American entrepreneurs and businesspersons from among the college-trained. The bright side to the decade, according to Daryl Grisham, president of the 64-year-old Parker House Sausage Company, occurred in the vertical, or selective, progress evidenced by new starts in truck distributorships, Chicago having the largest black-owned GMC and Ford operations, in finance, and in real estate development, both with comprehensive and "in-fill" housing construction.

However, previous horizontal, across-the-board, growth has been replaced with stagnation, as the black retail trade of past years has disappeared from major commercial thoroughfares, yielding its place to other ethnic groups or the lure of suburban shopping. Food previously cooked at small restaurants has been shunted aside by large franchises, offering innumerable fast-food selections. Even the funeral business* has come under the scrutiny of whites, who seek to purchase black-owned operations and manage them through black personnel. The 1990s also saw Johnson Products sold to a white conglomerate, Johnson Cadillac sold back to General Motors, and the Independence Bank purchased by a large white bank. Seaway National remains as the city's sole black-owned bank. Overall, business prospects for the new century appear as mixed and uncertain as those for the twentieth century appeared promising.

SELECTED BIBLIOGRAPHY: D. A. Bethea, *The Colored People's Blue-Book and Business Directory of Chicago*, (Chicago: Celebrity Print Company, n.d.); F. S. Black, *Black's Blue Book; Business and Professional Directory; A Compilation of Names, Addresses and Telephones of all Chicago's Colored Business and Professional People* (Chicago: F. S. Black, 1905, 1906); St. Clair Drake and Horace R. Cayton, *Black Metropolis: A Study of Negro Life in a Northern City*, 2 vols. (1945; reprint, New York: Harcourt, Brace & World, 1970); Abram Harris, *The Negro as Capitalist: A Study of Banking and Business among American Negroes* (College Park, MD: McGrath Publishing Company, 1936); I. C. Harris, *The Colored Men's Professional and Business Directory of Chicago* (Chicago: I. C. Harris, 1885); James N. Simms, *Simms' Blue Book and National Negro Business and Professional Directory* (Chicago: J. N. Simms, 1923); Allan H. Spear, *Black Chicago: The Making of a Negro Ghetto, 1890–1920* (Chicago: University of Chicago Press, 1967).

Christopher R. Reed

CHICAGO METROPOLITAN ASSURANCE COMPANY. Chicago Metropolitan commenced business in 1925 as the Metropolitan Funeral System Association (MFSA). It subsequently grew from a local burial insurance association into one of America's largest black insurance companies. The central figure during the company's formative years was Robert A. Cole, Sr., who served as its president from 1927 to 1956. Cole, a controversial figure who earned an outside fortune as a professional gambler, nonetheless gained widespread respect for the programs he and his company promoted. Besides providing for the insurance needs of working-class African Americans, Chicago Metropolitan, during Cole's presidency, instituted a myriad of noninsurance-related community improvement activities. Among these projects, many of which were partially funded by Cole's outside gambling income, were publication of the *Bronzeman* magazine (a precursor of *Ebony* and *Jet*); purchase of the Chicago American Giants (the Windy City's representative in the Negro Baseball Leagues); and the 1940 construction of the Parkway Ballroom, the most elegant black-owned facility of its type during the 1940s and 1950s.

In 1946, the MFSA, because of a dramatic increase in profitability, reorganized into the Metropolitan Mutual Assurance Company of Chicago (MMACC), a full-fledged legal reserve company. In 1953, the company once again changed its name. After a successful court battle against the giant Metropolitan Life Insurance Company of New York over MMACC's use of the term *Metropolitan*, Metropolitan Mutual became the Chicago Metropolitan Mutual Assurance Company (CMMAC).

When Robert A. Cole died in 1956, Chicago Metropolitan, which had grown into a regional life insurance company with offices in neighboring Indiana and Missouri, seemed poised to attain even greater prestige and visibility. However, Cole's successor, Thomas P. Harris, soon faced problems that would ultimately alter the company's history. During the summer of 1957, Chicago-based agents, upset over a new wage scale that allocated lower commissions than company agents in Missouri and Indiana, went out on strike. This work stoppage, among other things, unraveled the strong sense of company unity present during the Cole presidency. Moreover, besides the internal disharmony created by this work stoppage, Metropolitan soon had to face increased competition from white insurers for black policyholders.

During the 1960s, Chicago Metropolitan responded to white competition for black policyholders by seeking white clients. However, the company's attempt to desegregate its workforce and client base proved fruitless. Consequently, in lieu of becoming an interracial company, Chicago Metropolitan solidified its historic preoccupation with black community development. Chicago Metropolitan's president during the 1960s was George S. Harris. Before assuming office in 1961, Harris, no relation to his predecessor Thomas P. Harris, served in a variety of capacities within the company. George S. Harris, similar to Robert A. Cole, enjoyed interacting with personnel. Consequently, Harris's personality helped revive company morale that had been damaged during the 1957 agent strike. Moreover, George S. Harris, a longtime advocate of racial justice, made certain that Chicago Metropolitan fully participated in the black freedom struggle of that era.

Although Chicago Metropolitan experienced difficulty in attracting white personnel during the 1960s, the company compensated for this difficulty by fully utilizing the talents of African American females. Early in the decade, Chicago Met removed its historic ban against female agents. While this policy change generated early skepticism, CMMAC's new female agents rapidly won the respect of their male peers and supervisors. Anderson M. Schweich, Chicago Metropolitan's fourth president, elected in 1971, differed from his predecessors in that he possessed an extensive academic and employment background in business administration. Consequently, CMMAC, although unable to move into the mainstream of American business, began to implement more fully mainstream managerial and operational techniques. Although Schweich was an able executive, his "aloof" administrative style eventually precipitated severe employee discontent. Consequently, to raise both company morale and to reaffirm its long-time commitment to serving the African American working class, the company undertook extensive renovations of its inner-city Chicago home office complex.

The completed 1985 renovation of Chicago Metropolitan's home office at 4455 S. King Dr. represented the last high point of the company's history. Continuing pressure from white-owned companies had a devastating effect on company operations. By 1990 Metropolitan, faced with possible dissolution by the Illinois Department of Insurance, agreed to a friendly acquisition by the black-owned Atlanta Life Insurance Company.*

SELECTED BIBLIOGRAPHY: Robert A. Cole, "How I Made A Million," *Ebony* 8 (September 1954): 43–52; Robert E. Weems, Jr., *Black Business in the Black Metropolis: The Chicago Metropolitan Assurance Company 1925–1985* (Bloomington: Indiana University Press, 1996); Robert E. Weems, Jr., "The Chicago Metropolitan Mutual Assurance Company: A Profile of a Black Owned Enterprise," *Illinois Historical Review* 86 (Spring 1993).

Robert E. Weems, Jr.

CHURCH, ROBERT REED, SR. (1839–1912), Memphis, real estate, entrepreneur, philanthropist, investor, developer, speculator.

Born his father's slave, his mother (Emmeline) was also owned by his father (Charles Church), a steamboat operator. Robert Church, however, achieved success beyond that of his father. Once free, subsequently, Robert emerged as an integral player in the post–Civil War development of Memphis, Tennessee. His informal education and practical vocational training allowed his inherent entrepreneurial ability to propel him to the top of Memphis's society. While a slave, Church worked on his father's steamboats as a steward, a position responsible for the ship's entertainment operation: supervising other slaves, bookkeeping, inventorying and purchasing supplies, and overseeing gambling and saloon operations. He also saved money from his earnings.

By 1866 Church owned his first saloon. He began amassing his fortune by expanding to own more saloons in the Beale Street red-light district. These saloons offered not only alcoholic drinks but gambling and prostitution as well. He had obscure agreements with his white counterparts to allow his operation to flourish. Church continued to acquire property. During the late 1870s, Memphis was ravaged by yellow fever epidemics. Church took this opportunity to buy properties for a fraction of their value. By the time the epidemic ended, Church had expanded his vast empire of rental properties to complement his saloons. As he continued to buy property, his personal wealth soared, but he continued to manage both his saloons and his extensive rental properties. Twice his name was offered for local political offices; twice he was soundly defeated. Thereafter, he shunned the political arena, preferring to concentrate his efforts on the economic development of the black institutional community.

Church was a founder and the first president of the Solvent Savings Bank and Trust Company. It was organized with capital stock of $25,000. By 1912, the total deposits totaled over $100,000; by 1920 deposits were in excess of $1 million. The bank was successful in providing African Americans a place to save their money and to receive the opportunity for a loan without certitude of rejection. Church continued his entrepreneurial activity until his death in 1912. He was survived by both his first and second wife and four children. His daughter Mary Church Terrell was a distinguished black woman who was the first president of the National Association of Colored Women. His son Robert Church, Jr., was a politician who founded the Lincoln League. This advocacy group registered thousands of blacks in the 1910s and guaranteed Church, Jr., an influential position in the regional Republican Party. The legacy of Church and his entrepreneurial acumen remains today in Memphis.

SELECTED BIBLIOGRAPHY: Paul R. Coppock, *Memphis Sketches* (Memphis: Memphis State University Press, 1976); John N. Ingham and Lynne B. Feldman, *African-American Business Leaders: A Biographical Dictionary* (Westport, CT: Greenwood Press, 1994); Cookie Lommel, *Robert Church* (Los Angeles: Melrose Square Publishing Company, 1995); Mary Church Terrell, *A Colored Woman in a White World* (1940; reprint, New York: Arno Press, 1980).

Edward M. Apy

CHURCHES, BLACK INDEPENDENT (1890–1997), AND BUSINESS. In the early 1890s Booker T. Washington* wrote a number of articles and delivered several speeches before the annual meetings of the National Baptist Convention and African Methodist Episcopal Church. In them he criticized the African American independent church denominations both for their historical failure to use their resources to further the development of African American business ventures and for the decline in what he called "Old Time Religion," which he defined as the adherence to high moral and ethical standards. While Washington's latter criticism is still being heard today in the criticism by many younger African Americans of their religious institutions, his former critique that chastised these church movements for not participating in the economic uplifting of their race through the National Negro Business League* has had more far-reaching effects.

Of course, Washington was not alone in his critical assessments of this religious movement. Indeed, African American social, literary, and political leaders who arose during the Harlem Renaissance often publicly voiced their displeasure with the African American independent church movement's refusal to use its resources to influence the economic conditions of their race. This criticism has become a discursive ritual for each generation as it looks toward the only permanent African American independent institution to provide the impetus for the betterment of their race. And it is undergirded by the assumption that this institution has at its disposal not only tremendous human resources but also finances that could potentially be utilized to help solve some of the problems of African American communities: unemployment, inadequate housing, and the inability of businesses to acquire loans from traditional financial institutions.

While it is accurate to assume that these churches have a substantial number of members on their rolls who could better contribute to the well-being of their communities, it is problematic that African American churches generate substantial finances that can be used to create more business opportunities for their race. Indeed, in C. Eric Lincoln and Lawrence H. Mamiya's national study *The Black Church in the African American Experience*, they found the following: (1) The primary vehicles these churches use to generate income are the pledge system, offertory collections, special fund-raising drives, endowment income, and other means (church dinners, etc.); (2) individual church budgets indicate that Baptist churches with an independent or congregational polity spend 6.39 percent on missions and benevolence, 53.07 percent on the program of the local church (including the salary of the pastor and building maintenance), 3.55 percent on national programs or causes, and 2.39 percent on secular institutions.

Lincoln and Mamiya caution that since 45 to 47 percent of churches polled gave no response to these queries, it would be best to revise the aforementioned percentages into an estimate of budget allocation to the following levels: (1) 85 percent for the program of the local church, 6 to 10 percent for missions and benevolence, and 5 percent for national programs or causes and secular institutions. In addition to these estimates for all churches, the Methodists (African Methodist Episcopal [AME], AME Zion, and Colored Methodist Episcopal [CME]) and the Pentecostals (Church of God in Christ [COGIC]) who subscribe to a "connectional polity," pay $4,259.58—as an average amount per individual church—in general claims (apportionments) to the general church.

These percentages are quite significant in addressing the lack of business ventures in African American churches, since the average income of all churches is $15,000 to $24,999, with 10.8 percent having an income at $1–$4,999, 10.4 percent at $5,000–$9,999, 9.9 percent at $10,000–$14,999, 11.3 percent at $15,000–$24,999, 15.8 percent at $25,000–$49,999, and 25.3 percent at $50,000 or more (16.5 percent of churches polled did not answer the survey queries). These average income figures indicate that less than one fourth of African American churches have an average yearly income greater than $50,000, of which 85 percent is spent on the salary of the pastor and building maintenance.

Perhaps these data explain the lack of participation of these churches in business ventures, including investments, operating businesses, and income-producing property. Lincoln and Mamiya indicate that when considering investments, 15.6 percent of these churches have them, and 78.5 percent do not; when focusing on business ventures, 6.9 percent operate at least one commerical business (defined as a bookstore, religious articles store, parking lot, or service enterprises like housing projects, child care centers, etc.), and 90.5 percent do not; when taking into account income-producing property, 13.5 percent own such properties, and 83.5 percent do not.

While this information indicates that at least 70 to 80 percent of African American churches are not financially capable of sustaining business ventures, a number of large churches have become involved in economic development. Lincoln and Mamiya cite, among others, the following churches: The Concord Baptist Church in Brooklyn, New York, the nation's largest church with 15,000 members, operates a nursing home, private school from elementary to eighth grade, clothing bank, and credit union and has two full-time social workers on its staff; the 4,000-member Bethany Baptist Church, also located in Brooklyn, raised $1 million to open the Harvest Manor Restaurant that employs 44 people and serves lunch and dinner daily; the Allen A.M.E. Church in Jamaica, Queens, has a church-sponsored housing corporation that rehabilitates stores in the neighborhood, a housing development fund, a home care agency, a 300-unit, $11 million complex for senior citizens, and a 480-pupil elementary school; the St. John's Baptist Church in Miami, Florida, has the St. John's Community Development Corporation, a nonprofit agency designed to rehabilitate the neighborhood surrounding the church; the Allen Temple Baptist Church in Oakland, California, operates a 75-unit housing development for low-income and elderly citizens, a 51-unit project, a job information center, blood bank, and credit union with $1 million in assets; the Hartford Avenue Baptist Church in Detroit, Michigan, has a multipurpose social service agency, print shop, book bindery, auto shop, 460-pupil school, and a $2 million credit union.

In my own research, I have found a number of large churches in other denominations that are also involved in commerical business enterprises, although I have been unable to confirm the exact monetary value of these entrepreneurial entities. I take the liberty to cite, among others, the following: The West Angeles Church of God in Christ in Los Angeles, California, operates a bookstore, day care center, private school from elementary to eighth grade, Bible college, and credit union; the Bethel A.M.E. Church, also located in Los Angeles, operates a bookstore, day care center, and credit union; the Light of the World Christian Church in Indianapolis, Indiana, operates a day care center, bookstore, and credit union; and the Mt. Zion Baptist Church, also located in Indianapolis, operates a day care and youth center, senior citizens facility, nursing home, bookstore, burial plot, and two housing units.

The independent nature of African American churches, which are unduly reliant on pastoral leadership, combined with the lack of financial resources for the vast majority of these churches, renders the ability of these institutions to generate economic development extremely difficult. In addition, pastors, lay leadership, and congregations insist that entrepreneurial activities are not the primary mission of the church. Indeed, while many feel that commercial business ventures conflict with the spiritual mission of the church, others are downright suspicious of these activities, since to them they smack of "worldliness," which they believe is in direct opposition to the divine nature of the church as an institution.

In an attempt to move the largest African American denominations from this oppositional posture, Rev. Henry Lyons, president of the National Baptist Convention of America, Inc., founded in 1996, along with John Lowery, a white businessman, Revelation Corporation, a for-profit business entity to spur economic development within these national church movements. Begun by a $1 million contribution from Lowery, Reverend Lyons successfully enlisted his own convention, the African Methodist Episcopal Zion Church, the Progressive National Baptist Convention, and the Christian Methodist Episcopal Church as shareholders in this business venture and attempted to forge agreements with white corporations to sell consumable goods and other merchandise through the individual churches that held membership in these national bodies in return for 30 percent of the total sales being returned to the Revelation Corporation as a commission.

The Revelation Corporation would, after having amassed a considerable sum of money, develop a central economic base to support the needs of its member churches and individual members, specifically to rebuild economically depressed urban America. Ten percent of the rebate was to be used to fund a pension program for local church pastors, whereas the other 20 percent was to immediately benefit the local churches. The other 70 percent of Revelation's proceeds were to be invested in a National Housing Fund to make loans that would be too risky for regular banks. The goods that were to be sold included credit cards, health insurance, car insurance, travel business, mortgage loans, investments, coupons, and catalog sales of consumable goods. Hanover Direct, a white catalog sales company, was enlisted to head up this aspect of Revelation's sales, but the deal fell apart after initial tests showed that there was not sufficient interest either in pastors or lay leadership to guarantee the success of this endeavor.

Unfortunately, this history-making cooperative project by 1997 collapsed under its own weight. Reverend Lyons has been implicated in a number of fraudulent financial deals, including some involving Revelation Corporation (specifically the credit card distribution program), and is the subject of federal and state criminal investigations. The "United Program," the phrase Reverend Lyons used to characterize this economic program, has virtually been brought to a halt not only by the public scandal centered in Reverend Lyons but also by the reluctance of individual pastors, lay church leaders, and the general membership of member churches to support this activity through a regular monthly contribution (3 percent of the church's annual budget). Also, there was a rebellion of a large segment of Revelation's members when Reverend Lyons attempted to cut a deal with Rev. Jerry Falwell, a white conservative, to get his mailing list of 5 million potential customers. Finally, there was the suspicion that Lowery, an influential Republican, and not Reverend Lyons, was the chief negotiator for the cooperative venture.

These factors contributed to only 2 million people out of a projected 20 million even bothering to sign up for the free membership. The tremendous opportunity afforded by this cooperative venture to African American churches to utilize their combined purchasing power to gain an economic advantage for the benefit of their membership and African American communities failed, undermined by dependence on pastoral leadership for authentication, direction, and governance. It is ironic that the very criticisms leveled against the independent African American church movement by Booker T. Washington in the early 1900s also prevailed as issues in African American pastoral leadership at the end of the same century.

SELECTED BIBLIOGRAPHY: W.E.B. Du Bois, "The Negro Church," in David Levering Lewis, ed., *W.E.B. Du Bois: A Reader* (New York: Henry Holt and Company, 1995); W.E.B. Du Bois, "The Religion of the American Negro," in Dan S. Green and Edwin D. Driver, eds., *W.E.B. Du Bois, on Sociology and the Black Community* (Chicago: University of Chicago Press, 1978); C. Eric Lincoln and Lawrence H. Mamiya, *The Black Church in the African American Experience* (Durham, NC: Duke University Press, 1990); Hart M. Nelsen and Anne Kusener Nelsen, *Black Church in the Sixties* (Lexington: University Press of Kentucky, 1975); Carter G. Woodson, *The History of the Negro Church* (Washington, DC: Associate Publishers, 1921).

Chester J. Fontenot, Jr.

CIVIL RIGHTS MOVEMENT AND BLACK BUSINESS. The federal government was only one, albeit powerful, ally in blacks' struggle for more social and economic resources during this period. Civil rights legislation passed in the 1960s and 1970s designed to improve the economic position of African Americans was preceded, however, by a decade of black-white confrontations in the South and in tandem with the escalation of black activism and civil disorder in northern urban areas. Consequently, the narrow and more conservative, that is, legalistic, approach to winning racial equality, used by the National Association for the Advancement of Colored People (NAACP) during the 1940s and 1950s, gave way to direct action and confrontational strategies used by newer black organizations that reflected both the growing cohesiveness among blacks and the rise of black militancy.

In the South, changing attitudes helped in 1957 to create the Southern Christian Leadership Conference (SCLC) and, in 1960, the more militant Student Non-Violent Coordinating Committee (SNCC). Based in the North, the Congress on Racial Equality (CORE) was long known for its broad-based appeal to blacks and its bold, unorthodox, and militant methods of reform. These organizations used nonviolent and mass collective activities to disrupt the status quo and pressure white institutions they sought to change. Protest demonstrations transcended issues relevant only to the South, and as militancy increased, demands for better housing, education, and jobs spread across the entire nation. As black protest shifted from the South to the North, sit-ins, shop-ins, and other forms of demonstration highlighted the need of blacks for broader economic opportunities. The *Harvard Business Review* notes that *Fortune* 500 companies were approached by the militant minority group organizations such as CORE, SNCC, and the Welfare Rights Organization.

The use of black economic boycotts, in which black consumers withheld their patronage from white businesses as a tool to negotiate for jobs and for black economic development in the North, proliferated in the 1960s. In Chicago, Operation Breadbasket, the economic arm of the SCLC, emerged to attack the lack of jobs for blacks in firms that had heavy black patronage. Operation PUSH (People United to Save Humanity) was launched with the same purpose: to use black consumer power to increase the number of black jobs and black business procurement opportunities in white corporations. Black economic boycotts had vast impact on the southern social structure; the impact of such boycotts in the North is not precisely known. However, retail outlets and consumer goods manufacturers are particularly vulnerable to adverse sales resulting from a black boycott of products. In the early 1980s, a dozen moral (i.e., not legally binding) covenants were established with major corporations such as Coca-Cola, Seven-Up, and General Foods.

Private industry faced pressures in addition to those placed on them by federal legislation and the potential for loss of profit and bad public relations. A series of long hot summers of urban riots began in the mid-1960s and continued in each following year until the end of the decade. Between 1965 and 1970 *Fortune* 500 companies started programs "principally to help discourage boycotts, violence, and other threats to company well-being." Faced by the need to preserve an operating environment in which profit continued to be possible, U.S. businessmen responded to the riots and the shock waves generated by the Kerner Commission's report by starting black economic development programs as one solution to the urban crisis.

At the same time, these escalating social factors also contributed to the expansion of managerial job opportunities for blacks. The growth of black representation in managerial jobs during the 1960s and 1970s was linked to four vehicles that implemented federal fair employment legislation and affirmative action policies: the Equal Employment Opportunity Commission (EEOC); the Office of Federal Contract Compliance Programs (OFCCP); federal contract set-aside* programs; and federally funded social welfare expansion. The Equal Employment Opportunity Commission Title VII of the 1964 Civil Rights Act, however, was the fundamental force behind federal attempts to eradicate employment bias in America. Under it, the EEOC was established as the law's administrative agency. The EEOC required private sector firms with 100 or more employees to report the numbers of minority workers to the government commission. Federal contractors with 50 or more employees and federal contractors—or subcontractors—selling goods or services worth at least $50,000 also are covered by the law.

Initially, the EEOC was authorized to use "informal methods" to resolve complaints of job discrimination. But by 1972 the enforcement powers granted to the EEOC by Congress gave it the right to initiate civil suits in district courts. And, by 1973, the EEOC gained further leverage in the private sector by winning a consent decree from American Telephone and Telegraph (AT&T), which agreed to pay $38 million to workers who were discriminated against by the company. At the same time, the EEOC created a "track system" that focused on discrimination and "patterns and practices" charges against limited numbers of large employers. This demonstration of serious intent on the part of the EEOC was a major impetus for corporate employers to seek black labor. Federally required programs involving job quotas favoring minorities made minority hiring an explicit goal of major corporations.

Affirmative action was a government-mandated or voluntary program in employment settings designed specifically to identify, recruit, promote, and/or retain qualified members of disadvantaged minority groups. The OFCCP enforced requirements that federal contractors identify, hire, and promote minorities and women in numbers roughly proportional to their availability in the labor market. The guiding principal was that if employers acted in a nondiscriminatory fashion, their workforce would at some point reflect the composition of the populace that surrounded their establishments.

Towards this goal, the OFCCP was vested with the authority to withhold or withdraw federal funds from businesses with federal contracts or subcontracts worth at least $50,000. Loss of contract because of noncompliance was a sanction of last resort, and not well documented, yet 45 percent of all *Fortune* 500 companies reported in 1979 that they had been threatened with ineligibility on compliance issues. Comparative research during the 1970s and 1980s on the impact of contract compliance in the white private sector found that government contractors increased the employment of black males significantly more than did nongovernment contractors and positively affected employment opportunities for blacks.

New arenas for black managerial and administrative employment also emerged as public welfare services and federally funded, black-run community organizations grew. Between the early 1960s and the middle 1970s, the public sector grew and social service bureaucracies, especially, proliferated. Estimates have been made that at least two thirds of the recent growth in public employment can be attributed to social welfare programs. The federal government increased funding to social programs such as education, health, welfare, public housing, and manpower-training areas, which contributed to the growth of the public sector. Over a nineteen-year period from 1960 to 1979, the proportion of employed blacks found in government positions increased at twice the rate of white proportions. The relative chances of blacks securing employment in government rose from a point of about equal probability when compared to whites to over one-third more likely than whites in these two decades.

Federal government policies were also important to black businesses. By the late 1970s, the largest proportion of black-owned business (98 percent) remained concentrated in retail and selected services where, historically, black businesses have been forced to market their wares almost exclusively to black consumers. In the early 1980s, minority business owners made efforts to secure federal assistance in their efforts to penetrate general (i.e., white) consumer markets. Opportunities for African American business owners were supported directly by the government. Federal departments, such as the U.S. Department of Commerce, established specialized minority procurement procedures, known as the contract set-aside program.

The federal government is a vast consumer of goods and services from private enterprise, but prior to guidelines covering these transactions, government contracts were awarded almost exclusively to white-owned businesses. The federal government contract set-aside program established the percentage of government contracts that should go to minority-owned businesses. This program was an effort to assist the black-owned businesses sector that historically has been hindered by the inability to secure capital from white banks and to compete outside black communities, which constrains both the size and type of black firms. Thus, set-aside programs helped to elaborate the black business community by giving black entrepreneurs a chance to gain a foothold in the competition for sizable contracts in a protected setting.

These data indicate that black businesses were relegated to the limited growth markets in inner-city neighborhoods and tied to public aid income. In this racialized situation they were useful for meeting the service and product needs of low-income blacks in potentially volatile environments. In addition, they are indirectly linked to policy fluctuation, which adversely affects disadvantaged blacks. Even when federal policy on black business development stimulated business expansion among nontraditional service businesses during the 1970s, blacks were in racialized and functional positions related to black populations. A sizable proportion of all minority business was based either on federal procurement or on sales to the minority community.

Salaried blacks employed in the white private sector showed similar relationships in the late 1970s and early 1980s. A 1979 survey of *Fortune* 500 companies reported over 29 percent of black executives versus 3 percent of white were in personnel specialties that, typically, are responsible for affirmative action plans and implementation. In general, not only were these positions functional in dealing with the problem of blacks; they were an effective way for corporate entities to address government hiring policies while minimizing black power. Personnel and labor relations and public relations officials are not in the strategic planning or production areas that typically lead to power within the corporation. Over 22 percent of black executives in *Fortune* 500 companies in 1979 were in manufacturing, which Bureau of Labor Statistics (BLS) data showed had the second largest industrial concentration of black labor. One could project that these executives were useful in managing large numbers of blacks, while helping the company to meet affirmative action requirements. At the same time, they were concentrated in the "soft" sector of the economy in an area of jobs that experienced a steep decline in the 1980s.

SELECTED BIBLIOGRAPHY: Jack M. Bloom, *Class, Race, and the Civil Rights Movement* (Bloomington: Indiana University Press, 1987); Sharon Collins, *Black Corporate Executives: The Making and Breaking of a Black Middle Class* (Philadelphia: Temple University Press, 1997); Sharon Collins, ''The Making of the Black Middle Class,'' *Social Problems* 30 (April 1983): 369–382; Leonard Hausman et al., eds., *Equal Rights and Industrial Relations* (Madison, WI: Industrial Relations Research Association, 1977); Jonathan S. Leonard, ''The Impact of Affirmative Action on Employment,'' *Journal of Labor Economics* 2 (1984).

Sharon Collins

COFFEY SCHOOL OF AERONAUTICS—CORNELIUS ROBINSON COFFEY (1903–1994) **AND WILLA BEATRICE BROWN** (1906–1992). The Coffey School of Aeronautics, founded at Harlem Airport in Oak Lawn, Illinois, in 1937, was instrumental in securing inclusion of African Americans in the expansion of civil aviation in the years just prior to World War II. A lobbying effort led by its operators, Willa Brown and Cornelius Coffey, in 1939 helped to gain acceptance for African Americans in the federally funded Civilian Pilot Training Program (CPTP), the largest government flight training program ever established for nonmilitary pilots. The pair helped form in that year the National Negro Airmen's Association, which pressured Congress to set aside funds for instructing blacks. Their efforts were rewarded when the bill, authorizing establishment of the CPTP, included an amendment banning racial discrimination.

The majority of the students under the new program received their training on college campuses, but the Coffey School landed a contract with the Civil Aeronautics Authority in January 1940 to teach 30 students, both black and white, in a noncollege unit and in an off-campus college group. The school, with Brown as ground instructor and Coffey as one of two flight instructors, produced many pilots who later enlisted in the U.S. Army Air Forces. It operated under government and private contracts until 1945, when most of its assets were destroyed by fire.

Adamantly opposed to segregation, Brown and Coffey also entered the fray over the establishment of the segregated 99th Pursuit Squadron at Tuskegee Institute, campaigning heavily for an integrated force. Despite their inability to influence the War Department, their efforts, combined with those of the black press, the National Association for the Advancement of Colored People (NAACP), and other organizations, helped lead to the eventual decision in 1947 to integrate the U.S. military.

Willa Brown was born January 22, 1906, in Glasgow, Kentucky, the daughter of Eric and Hallie Mae (Carpenter) Brown. She received a B.A. from Indiana State Teacher's College in 1927 and an M.A. in business administration from Northwestern University in 1937. She earned a master mechanic's certificate from the Aeronautical University in Chicago in 1935 and held Department of Commerce pilot's license No. 43814. A member of Alpha Kappa Alpha sorority,

Brown served during World War II as a second lieutenant in the Illinois Civil Air Patrol and won election in 1948 as Republican Committeewoman for Chicago's Second Ward. Between 1971 to 1974 she sat on the Federal Aviation Administration's Women's Advisory Committee on Aviation. Brown first married Cornelius Coffey in 1939 and later the Rev. J. H. Chappell.

Cornelius Coffey, born September 6, 1903, in Newport, Arkansas, was the son of Henry and Ada (Wright) Coffey. He learned to fly in 1928, receiving Department of Commerce license No. 36609. Coffey earned a master mechanic's certificate from the Aeronautical University in 1932 and taught there until 1936. He served as a first lieutenant in the Illinois Civil Air Patrol during World War II.

SELECTED BIBLIOGRAPHY: Clifford J. Campbell, "They're Learning to Fly in Chicago," *Opportunity*, May 1941; Robert J. Jakeman, *The Divided Skies: Establishing Segregated Flight Training at Tuskegee, Alabama, 1934–1942* (Tuscaloosa: University of Alabama Press, 1992); Catherine Patricia Strickland, *The Putt-Putt Air Force: The Story of the Civilian Pilot Training Program and the War Training Service (1939–1944)* (Washington, DC: U.S. Federal Aviation Administration, 1970); Writer's Program of the Work Progress Administration, *Who's Who in Aviation: A Directory of Living Men and Women Who Have Contributed to the Growth of Aviation in the United States, 1942–1943* (Chicago: Ziff-Davis Publishing Company, 1942).

Jill D. Snider

COLONIAL AMERICA, BLACK BUSINESS. During the colonial period African American business had access to the total American consumer market. One is unable to determine the aggregate value of black business from the extant sources, but even if this information were available, determining the monetary value of the business would probably be meaningless because the passing years have inflicted irreparable damage upon our ability to depict accurately the real income of the seventeenth and eighteenth centuries. At the time Congress created the first national Bank of the United States in 1791, only three banks existed in the country, one each in Philadelphia, New York City, and Boston, which forced budding entrepreneurs to depend upon their own financial resources or upon loans secured from individuals, unlike today when enterprisers often turn to lending institutions and to the federal government for funds to establish businesses.

Although permeated with intense competition, the business world of the colonial period had less cutthroat competition than at later periods. Thus, African Americans who ventured into the business world found an uninhibiting, maybe even sanguine, environment. African Americans created enterprises that met the demands of the urban consumer market. Potential consumers ranged from urban slaves to prosperous merchants and from destitute free African Americans to wealthy physicians and lawyers; however, white patrons usually sustained the most successful enterprises. Since demand for food and domestic services appears to have been high, a plethora of vendors and domestic service-type enterprises sprang up among black entrepreneurs. Similarly, demands for rental property, for transporting of goods, and for a myriad of other goods and services also led to the establishment of African American proprietors.

In an age when emphasis in business ownership was upon being self-employed rather then upon capturing a segment of the colonial market, and intercolonial conglomerates were not in vogue, black entrepreneurs were competitive in certain areas of the marketplace. Anticipating Booker T. Washington's* advice to another generation of African Americans that one should do for oneself that which one would do for an employer, the typical black entrepreneur was self-employed. Although a few were fortunate enough to hire assistants and some even owned slaves, most black businesses were a one-person operation. The typical black business, moreover, was a small male-owned single proprietorship that offered its customers services, perishables, and dry goods.

It required little money to start these kinds of enterprises, a situation that doubtless encouraged people with little capital to become entrepreneurs. Most of those who provided services probably owned the tools of the trade, those who sold produce usually grew their own food, and those who sold seafood may have owned boats. None of these required a building in which to operate the business. Sometimes, however, a building was required to operate the enterprise, for instance, a barbershop or restaurant. More often than not, therefore, operating a business was merely a matter of setting up shop. One of the first blacks to establish an enterprise in the Northwest, Jean Baptiste Du Sable, came into the territory from New Orleans where his Haitian father had sent him to start a family business. After France ceded Louisiana to Spain, Du Sable moved to the Northwest and in the early 1770s opened a trading post on the site that subsequently became Chicago.

The highly skilled but poorly educated were not deterred from operating a business because little learning of the three Rs was required. If one could count money and give the correct change, the mathematics problem was frequently solved. Few of the small enterprisers kept books or records of any kind to aid them in conducting their business. Most of those persons carried their business records in their heads, relying heavily upon rote memory, a common practice of the day. Many African American enterprisers pursued diverse interests simultaneously. For instance, an owner of a chimney sweep business operated a shoemaking shop and rented property, a grocery store owner also sold furniture and operated a loan service, a funeral director also operated a catering service, and an owner of a shipping enterprise also owned a salt works. This practice transcended race because many whites also engaged in diverse economic interests.

By pursuing diverse interests, black enterprises could meet the consumer demands of African Americans and Europeans without tampering with social convention. Some black businesses, such as restaurants, hairdressers, and barbershops, were forced to discriminate against other blacks because whites would not patronize their businesses if they served blacks. Owners of these types of businesses served a black clientele in other endeavors, for instance, rental property, funerals, and lending money. Conversely, grocery stores, fish markets, and bakeries were some businesses that served both African Americans and Europeans because whites did not perceive patronizing these enterprises as commingling with African Americans.

In the early 1760s, Samuel Fraunces opened one of the finest lodging accommodations in the colonies: Fraunces Tavern. Located at Broad and Pearl Streets in New York City, this tavern was the site of both the founding of the New York Chamber of Commerce in 1768 and the banquet and reception celebrating the British evacuation of New York in 1783. Fraunces Tavern, moreover, was one of those black-owned businesses that refused to serve African Americans at the insistence of white customers. Traditionally, in the history of the United States, immigrant groups have used experiences gained as employees to their advantage by eventually starting businesses of their own, using the skills, business knowledge, and customer contacts gained while in the employ of another person.

Slave domestic servants, boatmen, and artisans, besides African Americans apprenticed in those endeavors, often started businesses once they were manumitted or served their apprenticeship—so the plethora of barbershops, hairdressers, tailor shops, seamstresses, caterers, pastry shops, pilots services, shipping enterprises, seafood vendors, and construction businesses. Duchess Quamino of Newport, Rhode Island, exemplified this practice. Starting her enterprise with a small initial outlay of capital and enjoying the patronage of some of the same persons who patronized her when she was a slave, Duchess Quamino, the most popular cake baker in Rhode Island, operated a profitable catering and pastry business from her small house.

On the other hand, African Americans in industrial jobs did not readily establish businesses. Tobacco factories, ropewalks, iron works, and shipbuilding companies did not lend themselves to small business-type operations, for they required many employees, a relatively large capital outlay, and mastery of the three Rs, with some bookkeeping knowledge being desirable. Black businesses in Colonial America were generally modest by today's standard of measuring businesses. Nevertheless, with few dollars but an abundance of determination they competed successfully in the colonial marketplace.

SELECTED BIBLIOGRAPHY: Lorenzo J. Greene, *The Negro in Colonial New England, 1620–1776* (Washington, DC: Association for the Study of Negro Life and History, 1930); Whittington B. Johnson, *The Promising Years, 1750–1830: The Emergence of Black Labor and Business* (New York: Garland Publishers, 1993); Henry Minton, *Early History of Negroes in Business in Philadelphia* (Philadelphia: Henry Minton, 1913); Juliet E. K. Walker, "Racism, Slavery, and Free Enterprise: Black Entrepreneurship in the United States before the Civil War," *Business History Review* 60 (August 1986): 343–382.

Whittington B. Johnson

COLONIAL AMERICA, SLAVE MARKET WOMEN. The nature of slavery was such that African American women were denied a free choice of economic activities, for most masters assumed that positions in household service or field labor would maximize the economic output of black females. Nonetheless, in the earliest years, African American women still tried to harmonize their labor as much as possible with the familiar patterns and rhythms of work in their former homelands. Perhaps the most interesting of the economic decisions colonial black women made in this regard was to maintain a strong interest in female entrepreneurship despite the prejudices of the white male elite who thought commerce should be clearly outside the purview of both blacks and women.

In western Europe, business was manifestly a male-dominated enterprise, but the situation was far different in West Africa, where women were ubiquitous local and regional entrepreneurs, controlling the buying and selling in most local markets. Farm surpluses from the fields, fish from nearby waters, and herbs from the surrounding forest were all brought to market by women traders. In the international trading stations of the Gambia and Senegal Rivers, large-scale female entrepreneurs called *signares* rose far beyond local market enterprise, developing commanding positions in the international trading alliances of the region.

It was probably one of these notable trading ladies who disembarked in colonial Georgia in 1772 with enough financial clout to travel freely throughout the slaveholding colony on her business despite our expectations that she might be held back by both her color and her sex. According to a remarkable story recorded in the Georgia Archives Deed Book, the African trader Fenda Lawrence arrived in July 1772 aboard the vessel *Snow New Briffania*; the ship's captain, Stephen Deaux, persuaded local officials to give her permission as a free black woman and major trader on the River Gambia on the Coast of Africa to pass and repass unmolested on her lawful and necessary occupations.

When other African women began settling in colonial North America, as a result of the slave trade, they, too, maintained an interest in local trading and market culture. Rapidly, they began to reproduce African-style markets as best they could within the limitations of North American slavery. Although whites generally disapproved of black trading and so tried to inhibit black enterprise, African American women were still often able to take advantage of gender and ethnic stereotypes to fill commercial niches as street vendors and "hucksters." In this guise, black women were able to specialize in marketing an African-style, highly spiced, pepper pot soup in the streets of Philadelphia, and African "weedwomen" similarly marketed medicinal herbs and barks (and sometimes doctoring and dentistry) door to door in the colonies from New England southward.

Unfortunately, throughout the North American colonies the powerful African American interest in outdoor marketing ran afoul of both law and custom; nonetheless, black trading could not be so easily restrained. The city fathers of Boston rationalized their attempted repression of African American Sunday markets on moral grounds, saying such Sabbath enterprises attracted too many blacks away from church while their energetic selling of corn, apples, and other produce disturbed the public peace and scandalized the Christian notion of a day of rest. In the more southern colonies, African-style markets were commonly discouraged because slaves might too easily sell their master's goods illegally along with their own merchandise. But wherever significant numbers of blacks could gather for urban exchange, such black markets (in both meanings of the word) flourished whatever the law might say.

The problem for Charleston's white businessmen was that black female traders were too competitive; as early as 1720 the colony's whites were being warned not to patronize black retailers, and in 1734 white businessmen complained about blacks trying to unfairly corner the market: Negroes, they complained, were permitted to buy and sell, and be hucksters of produce, fish, and fowls; since the blacks traded night and day on the town's wharves, they often momentarily cornered the market in necessities and raised prices to what the whites considered an exorbitant level. Over the years the same unresolved complaints kept reappearing, and in 1772 the *South Carolina Gazette* grumbled that black women continued to so successfully sell fish, fruits, dry goods, and baked items in the public markets and streets that they began to drive out their white competitors.

Threatened with an ambition and competence they could not match, white businessmen disparaged their black competitors on gender as well as economic grounds as seen in the *South Carolina Gazette* of September 24, 1772; "Near [the Lower Market], constantly resort a great number of loose, idle, disorderly negro women, who are seated there from morn 'til night, and buy and sell on their accounts, what they please in order to pay their wages, and get as much more for themselves as they can." Small-scale white merchants were becoming less and less willing to compete with the aggressive marketing strategies of newly arrived African and West Indian women who worked longer hours than whites and who made full use of their racial advantage in dealing with fellow blacks, both slave and free. White Charleston merchants complained: "These [black trading] women have such a connection with, and influence on, the country negroes who come to that market, that [these women] generally find means to obtain whatever they choose, in preference to any white person."

Particularly, the merchants denounced the market strategies of these women claiming that "thus they forestall and engross many articles, which some few hours afterwards you must buy from them at 100 or 150 percent advance." Their aggressiveness in the market in acquiring merchandise went beyond insolence, for the writer said: "I have known these black women to be so insolent as even to wrest things out of the hands of white people, pretending they had been bought before, for their masters or mistresses, yet expose the same for sale again within an hour afterwards, for their own benefit."

Here it is clear that the real complaint about black traders was the competitive ferociousness of black women as entrepreneurs. The entrepreneurial drive often noted among present-day African and West Indian immigrants to the United States was clearly not lacking among their colonial North American counterparts; in fact, it took long-term and concerted interference unfairly rigging the market by limiting both physical access as well as lending resources, using what was in effect a caste-based legal system to prevent African American entrepreneurs, and especially women, from successfully using business enterprise as a lever of social mobility—so as to diminish the entrepreneurial impulse among North American blacks.

SELECTED BIBLIOGRAPHY: Ulrich B. Phillips et al., *A Documentary History of American Industrial Society*, 4 vols. (Cleveland, OH: Arthur H. Clark Company, 1910), 2: 141–142; William D. Piersen, *Black Yankees: The Development of an Afro-American Subculture in Eighteenth Century New England* (Amherst: University of Massachusetts Press, 1988); William D. Piersen, *From Africa to America: African-American History from the Colonial Era to the Early Republic 1526–1790* (New York: Twayne Publishers, 1996); Leila Sellers, *Charleston Business on the Eve of the American Revolution* (Chapel Hill: University of North Carolina Press, 1934); Peter H. Wood, *Black Majority* (New York: Norton Library, 1974).

William D. Piersen

COLONIAL NEW ENGLAND, AFRICAN ECONOMIC SURVIVAL-ISMS. The Africans who arrived as slaves in colonial New England often fell back on skills they had learned in their former homelands to earn money when their years of active slavery had come to an end. Although as bondsmen they seldom had the economic autonomy to choose their own work roles or conditions of labor, in their free time and in what we might call retirement they were often able to acquire extra funds by developing an old talent into a part-time business or occasional moneymaker.

African-born women and their daughters, for example, sometimes turned their traditional interest in collecting wild plants to good use by selling roots, herbs, and berries door to door, the most talented of these women also prescribed and dispensed herbal medicines, and in recognition of their skills such women were given the informal title of "doctress." Women who had traded in the local markets of Africa often continued to put their entrepreneurial skills to use in New England during informal Sunday markets where they sold produce they had gathered from the countryside or hawked special treats like gingerbread they had prepared for sale.

Men and women from families who were oral historians and court musicians in western Africa often found new American employment for certain of their former professional skills. Thus, Old Caesar who had been a carpenter as a slave augmented his income in his old age by putting his highly trained memory to use as a perpetual calendar; as Boston's William Bentley noted in his diary: "Twenty years ago I gave him the age of my parents and kindred of three generations with the promise of a reward upon notice of their birthday. I have never known that he lost one or confounded it with any other.''

Many, if not most, of the colonial-era black musicians had been trained in Africa, and they quickly profited from their talents by playing and singing for black dances in America. Black musicians commonly hired their free time as fiddlers, and the African expertise in improvisational lyrics was perfectly suited to calling the figures during the local country dances at which they played. Later, when they had learned the requisite tunes, they also became, like Occramer Marycoo, musicians of choice for white dances as well. Marycoo also used his musical training to open a singing school in Newport, where he later became both a dance master and a composer.

In New England where the weather was often too cold for outdoor dances, local black social and musical gatherings were frequently held indoors during the colder months; African American businessmen helped fill this need by setting up small clubs in upstairs or waterfront rooms so as to accommodate many of the black community's social occasions. Unfortunately, as New Bedford's William Grimes discovered, when he lost his lease, white neighbors were likely to find the late hours, drinking, and noise level associated with black clubs extremely annoying, and so these businesses were riskier than most.

Since African men were usually far more proficient at hunting than their first-generation European-American counterparts, certain of New England's black men found profit in their skills by earning extra cash as deer hunters or fox exterminators. Others used their Old World expertise to build snares and small traps to capture small game they could either eat or trade. African men who had grown up along rivers often fished Yankee shores in their free time and marketed part of the catch; the boatmen among them found employment in the New England fisheries and whaling vessels, but the particular African contribution to New England's maritime industry is not easy to isolate.

A clearer example of turning an old African skill to profit came in the decision of a Middletown, Connecticut, slave to manufacture small drums that he sold as children's toys. The use of larger, more traditional African-style drums was generally discouraged by white authorities. Other African immigrants created small flutes, whistles, guitars, and an assortment of idiophones that they commonly sold and traded. Also, Africans adept at weaving grass baskets and mats put their old talents to American use in weaving and mending clothes baskets and caning chairs. Moreover, women's familiarity with cooking and washing permitted many older black women to make a small income out of skills they would have offered their families.

Most African slaves in early New England served a variety of domestic roles within their masters' households. They had the requisite cultural polish for positions in household service because of the high level of decorum and dignity expected of citizens in West Africa, and their dignified manners gave them an advantage when they were later forced into competition with Irish and other European immigrants for service employment.

Ironically, even the esoteric knowledge of Old World religious ideas could sometimes bring a profit. In New England certain specialists among the African-born men and women were paid for their expertise in divination; beyond telling the future, these black seers continued to follow an African pattern featuring both finding and recovering lost or stolen objects and the supernatural punishment of the thieves; some of the seers also won fame for their skilled performances of legerdemain. The early generations of Africans and African Americans harvested much from their Old World heritage to improve their lives as Americans. Yet, limited by slavery and racism, Africans in colonial New England could never advance to the more profitable areas of enterprise central to the Yankee economy.

SELECTED BIBLIOGRAPHY: William Bentley, *The Diary of William Bentley, D.D.*, vol. 3 (Gloucester: Essex Institute, 1962); Lorenzo Johnston Greene, *The Negro in Colonial New England* (New York: Columbia University Press, 1942); William D. Piersen, *Black Yankees: The Development of an Afro-American Subculture in Eighteenth-Century New England* (Amherst: University of Massachusetts Press, 1988).

William D. Piersen

CORPORATE AMERICA, BLACK MANAGERS. During the 1960s and 1970s, a new echelon of college-educated blacks emerged into previously closed managerial job and business-related professions. Indeed, the 1960s witnessed the reversal of the long-standing pattern of declining black-white income ratios with education, and the ratio of black-to-white income rose most rapidly for managers. Employed black men, in particular, experienced a new demand in the labor market for blacks in prestigious occupations. In 1960, only about 7 percent of nonwhite male college graduates were managers, compared to 18 percent of college-educated white men. By 1970 the proportion of black men college graduates employed as managers increased almost twofold over the 1960 level, and from 1970 and 1980 the number of black men holding executive, administrative, or managerial jobs increased each year at twice the rate of white men.

The economic advances witnessed in the black middle class, since the 1960s civil rights movement, were notable, but the emergence of African American professional and managerial workers in white corporations was politically mediated. Blacks in managerial and business-related professions filled socially useful but vulnerable functions in corporations. During the 1960s and 1970s, administrative functions and race-specific programs targeting blacks were created or expanded in white corporations, which led to an increase in the number of professional and administrative jobs available to middle-class blacks.

While a black-oriented delivery system was created in white institutions, college-educated black professionals and managers remained "functionally segregated" in the labor market. Blacks were employed in white institutions in roles tied to the appeasement of blacks, rather than to meet the demands of total (or predominantly white) constituencies. Functional segregation developed in a variety of employment domains. In the 1970s, professional and administrative jobs for blacks in the public sector were differentially concentrated in urban bureaucracies that served disproportionately large concentrations of blacks.

This pattern of segregation also appeared in Chicago's private sector among nontraditional black-owned businesses established between 1965 and 1979. The strongest customer base outside of black consumer markets for black enterprises in advertising, accounting, management consulting, personnel service, and law firms was in various "black-related" specialties sold to white corporations. The first black-owned advertising agency was founded in Chicago in the 1970s and used by white companies to reach black (but not white) consumer markets. The reorganization of work into racialized roles also ghettoized blacks' gains in management during the 1960s and 1970s. Particularly, as revealed by the U.S. census, the demand for black labor emerged disproportionately within personnel departments and labor and public relations jobs. Such positions administer corporate policies sensitive to blacks and, hence, lessen racial pressures on white corporate environments.

Evidence of segregation was evident in Chicago, based on the Collins study of the most successful black corporate executives in *Fortune* 500 companies. Conformity to corporate cultures, personal networks, and skill are key factors in individual mobility among high-ranking executives, but successful African Americans, with these capabilities, still filled racialized roles, indicating that they were not able to break racial barriers. The criteria used to identify high-ranking executives in the study were: (1) They were employed in a banking institution and held the title of comptroller, trust officer, vice president (excluding "assistant" vice president), president, or chief officer; or (2) they were employed in a nonfinancial institution and held the title of department manager, director, vice president, or chief officer. Race-based policies facilitated upward mobility for this segment of the African American population, but resilient systems of segregation remained, as seen in racialized tracks that developed in mainstream careers.

African Americans moved into management functions, such as urban affairs, affirmative action jobs, and manpower training and technical assistance programs, that interacted predominantly with black community organizations and/ or helped white companies to recruit black labor. These jobs, however, are outside the corporate mainstream career paths, the line and support jobs leading to senior executive positions that oversee the strategic planning, human resource/ personnel development, or production components of a company. As an example, racialized staff jobs, such as urban affairs managers, were a type of corporate ambassadorships. They plugged corporations into black civil rights and social service organizations and, in general, represented white companies in black-dominated settings whenever necessary. Racialized jobs in sales protected product markets. Given the volatility that prevailed among blacks at that time, retail companies in a competitive marketplace exploited and protected their existing market share by hiring black salesmen to court and keep black consumers.

The movement into racialized jobs created barriers to corporate mobility. Racialized jobs limit career advancement in that they are predominantly staff, or support, positions. In general, these support jobs are less desirable than line jobs because they lack influence and have shorter and more limited chains of career opportunities. These jobs not only impose relatively lower career ceilings; they lead to an underdevelopment of human capital that is valued by corporations and therefore marginalize the skills of the job holder. Over time racialized jobs became routine work centered on a narrow set of administrative tasks, primarily number counting, extracted from generalist personnel functions. In addition, these jobs rely on interpersonal skills and external relationships to the detriment of building administrative skills and internal networks critical for job promotion.

At the same time, these jobs require little or no investment on a company's part in terms of preparation and training. Managers in these jobs are not cross trained to add value in mainstream corporate functions. Consequently, managers in racialized jobs are cut off from the internal networks and skill building that would enable them to move into, and then move up in, the job mainstream of corporations. The result was a process that deskilled a cohort of highly educated African Americans due to the absence of on-the-job mainstream work experiences. Thus, an initial cohort of black managers entering the white private sector was eased out of the running for top executive jobs via racialized careers. Ultimately, racialized jobs are a factor in reducing competition for power in organizations along racial lines. In essence, this system of allocation led to glass ceilings.

In addition, affirmative action, urban affairs, and community relations functions in companies worked in dual ways. They were mechanisms that made social and economic resources more available to the aggregate black population. They also created a system of occupations that helped to minimize change and maintain the status quo. That is, these roles alleviated political pressures on companies by defending them and deflecting groups that attacked them on racial grounds. As a corporate tool, an executive's value was commensurate with skill in abating political pressures, in protecting profits, in not rocking the boat, rather than with consolidating black power and changing the makeup of institutions and power brokers.

In the 1980s, the Reagan administration promoted a major reversal in equal employment opportunity and affirmative action policies. And the substantive focus of racialized jobs made them vulnerable to changes in the administrative structure in white corporations. Job vulnerability in the 1980s, however, could not be viewed merely as a product of racial inequality in the job structure. It was also a feature of a heightened economic competition and globalization. Yet politically useful jobs in white companies, such as racialized jobs, became economically expendable, particularly in a context of racial quiescence, corporate buyouts, and economic reorganization. During the 1960s, racialized jobs were created when economic expansion and race-specific employment demands converged. In the 1980s these trends reversed.

Political pressure placed on employers by government and the African American public weakened. At the same time, competition for market share intensified. Racial functions, therefore, had greatly reduced value. By 1986, managers in racialized jobs were leaving or had left companies with which they had been identified. These people once filled very important functions and included vice presidents. Moreover, in the same year only 4 executives found among the 1,362 executives with a title of functional vice president or above, working in a *Fortune* 500 and *Fortune Service* 250 company, were African American. In the group of exiting managers were the highest-ranking African American managers in their respective companies. One person was cited in a major publication in 1982 in a list of the top black managers nationwide in major white corporations. Two managers were the first blacks to reach the level of director in each of their respective companies, and a third was the first African American to reach the level of full vice president in a company. One manager was one of only three African American managers to succeed to the rank of middle-level manager in a company. By 1993, 36 of the 76 executives from the Collins Chicago study left their company, collateral evidence that their attainments in racialized jobs—once useful tools for restoring peace in urban centers—are intrinsically fragile.

Managers in mixed and mainstream careers were compared with those in racialized careers. People in racialized careers left their original employer at almost twice the rate as their mainstreamed counterparts (68 percent versus 35 percent). Thus, the exodus varied among individuals according to their previous work experience. Theoretically, people in nonracialized careers in 1986 would fare relatively better over the decade vis-à-vis individuals in racialized careers because of the generalized nature of the functions they performed. African Americans with executive titles in Chicago's white corporations, however, were concentrated in support positions, such as personnel, not in the profit-driven planning and production jobs that lead to power within organizations.

Although support jobs are not racialized, neither are they in the corporate loop of power, nor are they in the mainstream work arena. They are peripheral functions with no responsibilities for profits or loss and out of the mainstream route for upward mobility. These are the jobs that white graduates from the country's top business schools (Kellogg, Wharton, Harvard, and Stanford, for example) don't take on their road to the top of major companies. Only 4 percent of 1,362 executives with an M.B.A. degree responding to a Korn/Ferry 1986 survey of senior-level executives in *Fortune* 500 Industrial companies and the *Fortune* Service 500 companies started in personnel. In the same survey, just 6 percent of the executives reported they were in personnel when the study was conducted. In comparison, 20 percent of nonracialized executives in my study with a graduate degree in business started in personnel; 30 percent of nonracialized executives were in personnel when they were interviewed.

If racialized careers were included in this profile, the disparity in the occupational outcomes of interviewees and white executives would be even larger. In sum, personnel jobs in this study, but not in studies of successful white executives, represent a sizable proportion of the opportunity structure filled by black men and women deemed to be successful managers. In 1980, African Americans employed in management-related occupations were almost twice as likely as whites to be in a personnel, training, and labor relations job (28 percent versus 15 percent). By 1990, African Americans were even more concentrated relative to whites. These functions are not viewed in the corporate culture as critical contingencies of an organization, and incumbents typically are the least prestigious team members.

The managers in the Collins study are part of a black middle class that occupied a useful but nonadversarial position in white companies. Racialized jobs were a factor in reducing competition for power in organizations along racial lines. The initial cohort of black managers, entering the white private sector, was eased out of the running for top executive jobs in Chicago via racialized careers. Ultimately, racialized jobs are a factor for reducing competition for power in organizations along racial lines, since this system of allocation led to glass ceilings, while at the same time it diminished the pool of blacks in Chicago corporations, whose careers took off in the 1960s and 1970s, who could have been in a position to manage mainstream units in the 1980s and beyond. Consequently, gains respondents made over the last three decades did not—and could not—blossom into meaningful numbers of executives heading production, planning, or support areas.

Moreover, since they were unable to succeed in policy- and decision-making positions in meaningful numbers, it is doubtful that the makeup and resource allocation of organizations will change dramatically. Even the current policy decision on whether or not to continue or dissolve affirmative action programs is contested outside any arena in which blacks exercise power. What we have, therefore, is a structure of achievement that preserved inequality while it carried out its role in reinstating social order. In addition, we have a class position with obsolete features built in. People in this study were desirable candidates for affirmative action and pubic relations jobs when there was an atmosphere of intense social upheaval. Conversely, when pressure from blacks abated, the status of many of these respondents tumbled. As racial pressures were ameliorated in Chicago, racialized jobs lost their value. By the late 1970s the rationale for appeasement functions, such as community affairs oriented to African Americans, in companies was undermined by an atmosphere in Chicago in which pressure from blacks was absent.

By the 1990s, then, with over 30 years of social and political efforts to diversify corporate manpower and management teams, the net result was more black managers but negligible gains for African Americans in the powerful decision-making jobs of white Corporate America. African Americans clearly stagnated in their climb up the managerial hierarchy, thereby failing to make inroads into key decision-making positions and in racial redistribution of corporate power.

SELECTED BIBLIOGRAPHY: Sharon Collins, *Black Corporate Executives: The Making and Breaking of a Black Middle Class* (Philadelphia: Temple University Press, 1997); Rosabeth Kanter, *Men and Women of the Corporation* (New York: Basic Books, 1977);

Korn/Ferry, *Korn/Ferry International's Executive Profile: A Survey of Corporate Leaders in the Eighties* (New York: Korn/Ferry, 1986, 1990); Farley Reynolds, *Blacks and Whites: Narrowing the Gap?* (Cambridge: Harvard University Press, 1984).

Sharon Collins

CORPORATE AMERICA'S BLACK EXECUTIVES. With the 1964 Civil Rights Act and subsequent affirmative action policies and mandates, employment opportunities expanded for blacks in white Corporate America. While an increasing number of blacks moved into middle-management positions, by the end of the twentieth century, there were few blacks who made it to the top of white Corporate America. In 1970, out of 3,000 senior-level *Fortune* 500 executives, only 3 were blacks: Clifton Wharton, Jr. at Equitable Life; Thomas Wood at Chase Manhattan; and Robert Weaver at Metropolitan Life.

Since 1970, more blacks advanced to high-level management executive positions in white Corporate America, but it was not until 1987 that an African American, Clifton Wharton, Jr., became the first and only head of a *Fortune* 500. At that time, Wharton was appointed chief executive officer (CEO) of the $70 billion TIAA-CREF (Teachers Insurance and Annuity Association–College Retirement Equities Fund). He left in 1992 but provided for the appointment of Thomas W. Jones, as president and chief operating officer. Previously, Jones had worked as senior vice president and treasurer at John Hancock Mutual Life Insurance in Boston.

Moreover, while an increasing number of blacks held top management positions, still, in the closing decade of the twentieth century, only a few were senior executives, positioned for advancement to *Fortune* 500 CEOs. Kenneth I. Chenault is the leading black in white Corporate America. In 1993 he was appointed president of American Express's Travel Related Services, U.S. Division; in 1995, vice chairman of American Express; and in 1997, an American Express president.

Other top black executives in the 1990s included Ann Fudge the highest-ranking black woman in white Corporate America. In 1996, Fudge was appointed CEO and president of Maxwell House Coffee Co., a division of General Foods USA, where she heads Maxwell's three coffee processing plants with 2,400 employees. Prior to her promotion, Fudge, a Harvard M.B.A., was executive vice president of General Foods USA, a division of the Philip Morris Companies. In the 1990s, black women comprised 3 percent of all women in corporate management and 5 percent of officers and managers in Equal Employment Opportunity Commission (EEOC) companies. At the shoe manufacturer Nine West, Brenda Lauderback is group president. In 1995, Noel Hord, with more than 20 years in the industry, was appointed president and chief operating officer at Nine West, which has a $14 billion retail shoe market.

In addition to Chenault and Fudge, Richard D. Parsons, president of Time-Warner Inc., and Xerox's executive vice president A. Barry Rand, formerly Xerox U.S. Marketing Group president, also hold high-ranking positions in white Corporate America. In addition, Roy Roberts, as general manager of the Pontiac–GMC Division, is the highest-ranked black in the automobile industry. Also slated for advancement to a CEO *Fortune* 500 position are Richard Nanula, chief financial officer (CFO) for Disney, who held previous positions as president of Disney Stores Worldwide, and Lloyd Ware, Maytag president, who held position as president, Central Division, of Frito-Lay, a subsidiary of Pepsi-Cola.

Black Enterprise has charted the rise of blacks in white Corporate America. Since it first began publication in 1973, the magazine has featured articles on individuals such as Robert Holland, who in 1995 was hired as president and CEO of Ben & Jerry's, the ice cream manufacturer. Despite improving the company's economic performance, Holland held the position for only one year. It was not until August 1997 that the significance of the accomplishments of blacks in white Corporate America were highlighted in *Fortune*, with the front cover announcing "The New Black Power."

The articles featured blacks who held high positions in white Corporate America such as Kim Green, senior vice president at Aon Risk Services; William Lewis, managing director at Morgan Stanley; and Warren C. Shaw, CEO, chancellor at LGT Asset Management. While the focus was on the leading black corporate executives, the article also included blacks who left top white Corporate America executive management positions to start their own multimillion-dollar enterprises. Investment banker John Utendahl, formerly a bond trader at Merrill Lynch, established Utendahl Capital Partners, holding 80 percent interest, with the remaining 20 percent held by Merrill Lynch.

Beginning in the 1980s, the phenomenon of blacks leaving white Corporate America, then, was a significant factor that furthered the expansion of black Corporate America in new areas of enterprise. In 1982, William Davis, downsized* from Occidental Petroleum, founded Pulsar Data Systems. With sales of $166 million, Pulsar in 1996 was the fourth-ranked firm listed on the *BE* 100. Michael Fields, formerly president of U.S. Operations of the $5 billion Oracle software company, left in 1992 and launched his Open Vision Technologies, which went public in 1996.

At the same time, blacks who left white Corporate America also took high-level positions in black Corporate America. Joyce Roché, now president of Carson Inc., a hair products manufacturing enterprise, left a high-ranking position at Avon. Marianne Spraggins, formerly at Smith Barney, in 1997 held the position of CEO at W. R. Lazard, a black investment banking house. On the other hand, Kim Greene, who left white Corporate America to start her own business, returned as senior vice president of Aon Risk Services.

Yet, in the late 1990s, with the dismantling of federal affirmative initiatives and the downsizing and restructuring of white Corporate America, what does the future hold for blacks in white Corporate America in the twenty-first century? *Fortune*'s Roy Johnson said, "With the $115 million racial discrimination settlement against Texaco still fresh in our minds, and others certain to follow, it's evident that people of color still confront high obstacles in the work place."

Moreover, as *Black Enterprise* noted in 1995, blacks made up only 2 percent of the board members of *Fortune* industrial and service corporations.

In an increasingly multicultural society and an expanding global economy, doubtless new opportunities for blacks in white Corporate America will expand in the twenty-first century. Still, with the corporate culture as it presently exists, the racially hostile environment seems particularly unfavorable for blacks, such as GMC's Roy Roberts, to attain the position of CEO in a *Fortune* 500 company by the end of the twentieth century.

SELECTED BIBLIOGRAPHY: Caroline V. Clarke, "Meeting the Challenge of Corporate Leadership," *Black Enterprise* (August 1995); "Features," *Fortune*, (August 4, 1997); Cassandra Hayes, "20 Women of Power and Influence in Corporate America," *Black Enterprise* (August 1997); Ernest Holsendolph, "More Minorities and Women in Key Jobs," *Emerge* (August 1996); Mark Lowery, "Sold on Ice Cream," *Black Enterprise* (April 1995); Lynn Norment, "Fifty Years of Progress in Corporate America," *Ebony* (April 1995); Rhonda Reynolds, "Ann M. Fudge: Brewing Success," *Black Enterprise* (August 1994); William R. Spivey, *Corporate America: Black and White* (New York: Carlton Press, 1993); Dave A. Thomas, *Breaking Through: The Making of Minority Executives in Corporate America* (Boston: Harvard Business School Press, 1999); Juliet E. K. Walker, *The History of Black Business in America* (New York: Macmillan, 1998); John W. Work, *Race, Economics, and Corporate America* (Wilmington, DE: Scholarly Resources, 1984).

Juliet E. K. Walker

COTTRELL, COMER J. (1931–), Texas, founder, chairman, and chief executive officer (CEO) of Pro-Line Corporation, hair products manufacturer.

The Pro-Line Corporation is the largest African American–owned company in the southwestern United States. In 1994, less than 25 years after Cottrell launched his business, Pro-Line reported sales of $40 million. Today, Pro-Line products are manufactured and sold in the Ivory Coast, Kenya, Nigeria, Europe, Saudi Arabia, Taiwan, and the Caribbean. In 1970, with $600, a borrowed typewriter, and warehouse space (that was obtained on a six-month moratorium on rent in exchange for repairs), he formed Pro-Line Corporation in Los Angeles, California. The company had one product—an oil-based hair spray with a strawberry fragrance. Cottrell sold strictly to barbers and beauticians, and sales resulted immediately in generating revenue. After six months, two additional products were added—Pro-Line Comb Out and Pro-Line Hold Spray.

In expanding his enterprise, Cottrell, an ex-serviceman, found an untapped market in the military. African Americans in the military and their families could not obtain hair care products. So Cottrell approached his representative in Congress, who in return contacted the Army Air Force Exchange Service (AAFES) in Dallas. Shortly afterward, Pro-Line became AAFES' first customer. By the end of Pro-Line's first year in business, sales reached $86,000. By 1973, Pro-Line sales had hit the million-dollar mark, and Cottrell and his younger brother, James, who also helped to establish the company, bought their first manufacturing plant in Gardena, California.

With each year, sales continued to double. The greatest growth in the company came between 1973 and 1976 with a product entitled "Hair Food," a gel-type hair conditioner. Other innovative products by Pro-Line include the introduction of the "Kiddie Kit," a hair treatment designed to make children's hair more manageable. In 1980, the company made extraordinary stride's first by introducing an at-home kit for the curly look called Curly Kit. The Curly Kit posted a record one-day sales gross of $1.4 million, making it the fastest, highest demand item to ever hit the marketplace. That same year Pro-Line relocated its corporate headquarters and manufacturing warehouse facility to Dallas, Texas.

Cottrell profits are reflected in his philanthropy. In 1990, he paid $1.5 million for the Oak Cliff campus of Bishop College, a then 108-year-old historically black college. He has also established the Cottrell Foundation to manage the company's charitable donations, which has provided money for employee scholarships and for the Dallas Independent School District's Adopt-a-School program. In expanding his business interests, Cottrell became a limited partner of the Texas Rangers baseball team, which made him the first African American to hold an equity stake in a major league baseball team, and he has been inducted into the Texas Business Hall of Fame.

Cottrell was born in Mobile, Alabama. He served in the United States Air Force, and was a division manager for Sears, Roebuck and Co. between 1964 and 1969.

SELECTED BIBLIOGRAPHY: Richard R. Aguirre, "Entrepreneur Rich in Advice to Blacks," *Dallas Times Herald*, October 20, 1990; "Breaking into the Majors," *Black Enterprise* (September 1989); Chip Ricketts, "Comer Cottrell Looks at Issues beyond the Bottom Line, Pro-Line's Founder Hopes His Legacy Is More Than Just Building the Southwest's Largest Black-Owned Business," *Dallas Business Journal*, April 13, 1989; Mitchell Schinurman, "An Innovator Owns a Stake in the Rangers, But Concentrates on His Hair Care Firm, Keeping Eyes on the Shelf," *Fort Worth Star Telegram*, June 11, 1989.

Nancy J. Dawson

COX, OLIVER CROMWELL (1901–1974), Missouri, Sociologist and critical theorist.

Oliver Cox was born in Port-of-Spain, Trinidad, the son of William Cox, a successful businessman, and Virginia Blake. At 18, Cox followed his two older brothers and immigrated to America to attend college, settling in Chicago. He spent the next 15 years of his life in various schools, beginning with the preparatory YMCA High School (graduating in 1923), followed by the Lewis Institute (associate degree, History and Economics, 1927), and Northwestern University (B.S. in Law, 1929).

Intending to finish his legal training at Northwestern, he suddenly contracted poliomyelitis and spent 18 months recovering, although he walked with crutches the remainder of his life. Cox decided that he would never be mobile enough to be a lawyer, so he enrolled in the prestigious Economics Department at the University of Chicago in 1930 and embarked on a career as an academic. He received his M.A. in economics in 1932 but, disillusioned by the inability of economists to predict the Great Depression, switched to sociology. He received his doctorate in sociology in 1938, writing a dissertation on factors affecting African American marital status.

Like nearly all black scholars of the era, despite excellent credentials, Cox was denied a position at the larger white institutions and began teaching at a variety of black colleges, beginning with Wiley College in 1939, moving to the Tuskegee Institute in 1944, Lincoln University in 1949, and finally Wayne State University in 1970. He was a prolific writer who published dozens of articles in the leading journals and five monographs on subjects ranging from race and class in America to scathing critiques of the capitalist system. Branded a Marxist early on, Cox spent the remainder of his career denying this label, although his works nonetheless carry a definite Marxist slant.

Evidence of this can be seen even in his first important work, *Caste, Class and Race* (1948), where he argued against the view that racism in America was the product of a presumed racial caste system in the American South, instead positing that it was based on class conflict. Cox's next three books were all critiques of capitalism, arguing that the deterioration of race relations in America was the consequence of its leadership in the capitalist system and that racism was a modern construct brought about by capitalism. His last major work, *Race Relations* (1976), argued that the economics of race relations helped explain black exploitation and discrimination in America.

Cox believed that the place of black business in America was one of the most critical issues facing the country. He argued that by creating the current state of race relations, American capitalism had excluded blacks from full participation in the system and denied them free access to entrepreneurship. Thus, the black businessperson remained outside the major forces of capitalism, especially foreign trade, international banking, money markets, and major manufacturing. In addition, he believed that despite instances of remarkable success, as a whole the record of black business in America was dismal because blacks did not have "a hospitable *cultural milieu* for the growth of business among them."

A controversial figure even among other black sociologists, Cox toiled in relative obscurity his entire career, and only recently has he received much scholarly attention. In a cold war–dominated climate, his Marxist-influenced works found few defenders or proponents, and his later career was somewhat tainted by accusations of anti-Semitism arising from a 1974 article on black nationalism that some saw as outlining a Jewish conspiracy to promote ethnicity at the expense of African Americans. Unfortunately, he died before he could answer this charge.

Cox's work shows an originality and depth of thinking not seen in many of his more widely read contemporaries; for example, Herbert Hunter has argued that Cox's critique of capitalism was a forerunner of Immanuel Wallerstein's influential world-system theory. But it is his work on furthering the dialogue on race relations that is his greatest legacy, and to this effect the American Sociological Association created the Oliver Cromwell Cox Award for Distinguished Anti-Racist Scholarship to honor a sociological work that makes a distinguished and significant contribution to the cause of antiracism. It is a fitting tribute to this neglected but undeniably brilliant scholar.

SELECTED BIBLIOGRAPHY: Oliver C. Cox, *Capitalism as a System* (New York: Monthly Review Press, 1964); Oliver C. Cox, *Caste, Class, and Race* (New York: Doubleday, 1948); Oliver C. Cox, *Race Relations: Elements and Social Dynamics* (Detroit: Wayne State University Press, 1976); Herbert M. Hunter, "The Political Economic Thought of Oliver C. Cox," in Thomas D. Boston, ed., *A Different Vision: African American Economic Thought*, vol. 1 (New York: Routledge, 1997); Herbert M. Hunter and Sameer Y. Abraham, eds., *Race, Class, and the World System: The Sociology of Oliver Cox* (New York: Monthly Review Press, 1987).

Todd E. Larson

CRAFTSMEN, MANUFACTURING, CONSTRUCTION. In preindustrial America, from the colonial era on, blacks, slave and free, worked in all areas of the craft trades. They were furniture makers, cabinetmakers, wagon and carriage makers, wheelwrights, and coopers (barrel makers). They also participated in the metalworking trades as silversmiths, coppersmiths, goldsmiths, gunsmiths, and blacksmiths. In the clothing industry, blacks worked as tailors, shoemakers, dressmakers, and tanners. In the construction trades, black craftsmen worked as bricklayers, brick molders, plasterers, brick makers, glaziers, caulkers, and carpenters. Indeed, Johann D. Schoef, who visited America from 1783 to 1784, emphasized: "There is hardly any trade or craft which has not been learned and is not carried on by negroes."

With the ending of slavery in the northern states in post-Revolutionary America, free black craftsmen, however, found it increasingly difficult to secure employment. Most white craftsmen objected to working with them and refused to take jobs where blacks were employed. Consequently, unless black craftsmen established their own enterprises, they were forced to find work in unskilled areas of employment. In Philadelphia a contemporary survey of the black male population in the 1830s showed that "less than two thirds of those who have trades follow them." In the entire state of Massachusetts in 1860, moreover, there were only 20 black carpenters, one cabinetmaker, and two chair makers. In the South, however, by the Civil War, 100,000 of the 125,000 craftsmen in that region were black. Most were slaves.

Also, in the South, the most successful free black craftsmen employed slaves. After black slave plantation holders, free black craftsmen ranked second in owning the largest number of slaves. Yet there were always a few slave craftsmen who established shops, and some even hired slaves. There were free black craftsmen who were successful. Some even established manufacturing enterprises. The slave-born William Ellison* (1790–1861) of South Carolina, who made cotton gins, was the largest black manufacturer in the South. His 14 slaves, who were skilled in all areas of gin production (carpentry for the frame and black-smithing for the production of steel saw teeth, which separated the cotton seed from the fiber), were his employees. Cotton gin prices ranged from $150 to $1,200 to as high as $2,000. Ellison's market extended west to include cotton planters in Mississippi. By 1860, Ellison owned 63 slaves, valued at $53,000, and 900 acres, valued at $8,300.

In Charleston, South Carolina, Anthony Weston,* only nominally a slave, established a millwright shop, considered one of the best in the South. Weston profited from his innovations in the design of the rice threshing machine, which doubled the output of processed rice from 500 to 1,000 bushels a day. Martin Delany explained that he "acquired an independent fortune, by his mechanical ingenuity and skillful workmanship." Through his free wife, Weston owned 13 slaves, including the 6 who worked in his millwright factory, manufacturing and repairing mills. In addition to property in slaves, Weston's real estate holdings were valued at $40,075.

One of the most successful free black furniture makers in the South was Thomas Day* of Milton, North Carolina, who made beds, chairs, and cabinets. His shop, part of his residence, also included a showroom. Day advertised in the local papers, announcing that he specialized in "Mahogony [sic], Walnut and Stained FURNITURE." Many of Day's pieces, his chifforobes and four-poster beds, which were enormous, are museum pieces. Day also crafted interior woodwork, fireplace mantles, stairways and banisters, and intricate ceiling and wall moldings. In 1847, despite submitting the highest bid to build library shelving at the University of North Carolina, the governor of the state awarded the contract to Day, who employed his own slaves in addition to a white journeyman. In 1860, Day's property was valued at $4,000.

In the North, Henry Boyd in Cincinnati, a furniture maker, doubtless, was the most successful antebellum black manufacturer. The Dun mercantile records listed his enterprise as a "Patent Bedstead Factory." While there is no patent record, the distinctiveness of Boyd's invention and its impact on the market were such that *patent* became part of the brand name for Boyd's bed, which he manufactured in addition to other kinds of furniture. Boyd established his furniture manufacturing plant in 1836. He had constructed the shop himself, which eventually expanded to four buildings. As did the sailmaker James Forten,* Boyd employed both blacks and whites, including immigrants in his workforce that ranged from 23 to 50 employees, depending on orders. Boyd had a three-state market for his beds and was worth $26,000 in 1850. By 1859, however, after being burned out three times and with continuous sabotage by his white employees in addition to being extremely liberal in granting credit, Boyd was out of business.

The most successful antebellum free black craftsmen were carpenters, and from this trade, some moved into construction as building contractors and in real estate as developers. William Goodrich, who speculated in real estate in

York County, Pennsylvania, was reported as having "built one of our finest stores here." Centre Hall, constructed by Goodrich in the 1850s, was a five-story building, then the tallest in the city. In antebellum Ohio, several blacks owned construction companies or excavating companies and even made bids on city contracts. Others used whites to front for them so they could obtain jobs.

In the South, free blacks in construction had to compete with slaves. In the seven states in the Upper South and Washington, D.C., Loren Schweninger identified 221 free black carpenters whose property holdings averaged $885. In the eight Lower South states, he found 210 carpenters whose property holdings averaged $1,300. Some free black carpenters, such as building contractor James Boon in Raleigh, North Carolina, who established his construction company in 1808, also made furniture when construction jobs were slow in coming in. Yet it was not only free black craftsmen in the trades that faced competition from white craftsmen. Unlike in the North, white craftsmen in the South were not successful in driving slaves out of the trades, especially since the leading white craftsmen either owned or hired slaves with crafts skills. There was the incident in Wilmington, North Carolina, in 1857 when white carpenters burned a building constructed by slaves, with the threat that "all buildings erected by slaves in the future would receive similar treatment."

During Reconstruction, black craftsmen were also needed in the rebuilding of the South, but, increasingly, racism and segregation, especially with the formation of organized labor unions in the crafts and trades, found blacks locked out of opportunities for skilled employment in the construction industry. By 1890, even before the South was unionized, the majority of skilled white workers in the building trades were white, with blacks representing only 25 percent of workers in the industry. The carpentry skills of blacks had provided the basis for their participation in the construction industry in preindustrial America. With industrialization, the change in building materials from lumber to structural steel and new construction techniques placed blacks at a disadvantage in the industry, as compared to the period before the Civil War, where historians Lorenzo Greene and Carter G. Woodson have emphasized that in the South slaves performed "the bulk of the building work."

Moreover, industrialization in the manufacturing of goods previously produced by black craftsmen in addition to motor transportation also made crafts skills, such as wheelwrights, wagon makers, blacksmiths, and coopers, obsolete. At the same time, with segregated unions, blacks found it difficult to secure apprenticeships in the construction industry. On the other hand, as Gunnar Myrdal notes, despite unionization, blacks did maintain a significant presence in the trowel trades as "bricklayers, masons, plasterers, and cement finishers," even after unionization in the South. Also, in 1900, three fourths of the laboring jobs in the building trades were done by blacks, although their percentage had dropped to two-thirds by 1930. Myrdal also notes that in 1930 almost half of the skilled black workers, some 80,000, worked in the building trades.

In addition to union segregation and societal racism, ultimately, blacks in the

South lost their hold in the building trades because capital requirements in the new construction industry were beyond the financial resources of most black builders. Consequently, by 1910, there were only 2,900 contractors, who comprised 1.8 percent of the industry. Yet by the early twentieth century, as the black urban population increased, the demand for black contractors did as well. The New South's creation of two worlds of race found black contractors not only building residential houses but also developing subdivisions and building housing tracts in addition to churches, office buildings, hotels, theaters, and auditoriums.

Construction of these properties was financed by black churches, black fraternal orders, and black real estate companies. The True Reformers fraternal orders had real estate holdings in 14 cities and used black contractors to build a $45,000 office building, a hotel, and other business buildings, including department stores. Black building and loan associations also provided financing for both building repairs and new construction. In the early twentieth century, blacks in construction were able to make money. In Birmingham, the Windham Brothers Construction Company was founded in 1895 by Thomas C. Windham. Subsequently his brother Benjamin joined the company. From 1903 to 1914, the company's building contracts increased from $50,000 to $300,000. The company began expansion to several states and remained in business until 1966.

By the 1920s, a large number of black contractors in construction were working on multimillion-dollar projects. Also, a few construction companies were founded by architects and engineers. In the 1920s engineer contractor Frederick Massiah did the reinforced concrete work for the $10 million, 10-story Walnut Plaza Apartment building in Philadelphia, which required 700 tons of steel, and also the foundation work for the Hospital Center of New York, including the Presbyterian and Columbia Medical Schools and Sloan Hospital. Archie Alexander, one of the nation's leading black engineers, a 1912 graduate of the University of Iowa engineering school, established his first company in 1914. Alexander built the $2.5 million central heating plant for the University of Iowa. In two subsequent companies founded by Alexander, he was in partnership with whites.

Herman Perry (1873–1928), one of the most successful black entrepreneurs in the early twentieth century, owned a conglomeration of enterprises including his Service Engineering & Construction Company. His Service Realty developed Atlanta's Westside, an area that covered "200 blocks with twenty-four residences to the block, with an average value of $4,500 per residence for a total value of $21,600,000." Service Engineering was the contractor. Construction activities slowed for blacks during the Great Depression. In 1930 there were only 2,400 blacks in the industry, comprising 1.6 percent.

The building boom during World War II helped revitalize the black construction industry, of course, not to the extent that it did for whites. It appears that black construction firms, with an established pre–World War II record of successful operations, were the ones that secured government contracts in construction, especially in the building of military installations. The Nashville-based, black-owned McKissick Brothers Construction Company, founded in 1909, won a $4 million defense contract in 1941 to build a 2,000-acre airfield and air base at Tuskegee Institute for the training of the black 99th Pursuit Squadron. They employed 1,900 workers, including some 450 black carpenters in addition to black electricians, plumbers, and masons.

After World War II, blacks in construction took advantage of a new building boom. Alexander continued to secure million-dollar engineering contracts for construction of municipal power and sewer plants, bridges, highway, and railroad relocation work. In Birmingham, Arthur Gaston,* who established his Vulcan Realty and Investment Corporation in 1952, purchased Birmingham downtown property for redevelopment. Construction of new office buildings was done under his A. G. Gaston Construction Company. Early on, Gaston had built the A. G. Gaston Home for Senior Citizens and several black housing subdivisions in addition to apartment complexes and his Gaston Motel.

Increasingly, after 1954, black businesses made attempts to capitalize on the federal government's programs to aid small businesses. Congress had strengthened the Small Business Administration (SBA), giving it authority to make construction loans to hotels and motels and other types of small business enterprises. Despite the 1954 *Brown* decision, the SBA did initially finance some business projects that tapped segregated markets. The growth of black construction companies in the post–civil rights era underscores the importance of federal mandates as a contributory factor in black business growth. The most important factor that contributed to the expansion of these companies from the 1970s to the 1980s, however, was black mayoral* politics, which also encouraged joint venture projects with white construction firms.

In 1973, the year before Atlanta's election of Maynard Jackson, who served two terms from 1974 to 1982, black contractors in Atlanta had received only $41,758 out of a $33 million in city contracts. In 1981, however, they were allocated $19.2 million out of $56 million in city contracts. Also, in the following cities with black mayors, minority and women business owners were awarded the following in municipal contract procurement dollars: Cleveland, $96 million of $247 million; Denver, $100 million of $391 million; Minneapolis, $11 million of $74 million; Rochester, New York, $3 million of $38 million.

By the late 1980s, even these modest gains made by blacks in the construction industry were under attack. In 1989 the Supreme Court with its *Richmond v. Croson* decision struck down as unconstitutional a Richmond City ordinance that required 30 percent of each construction contract to be awarded a minority business. It ruled that cities must first show a pattern of discrimination before instituting a minority set-aside program. A study undertaken by one of the nation's leading economists, Andrew Brimmer (1926–), revealed, however, that discrimination still existed in the city's construction industry. Brimmer found that 92.7 percent of total revenue received by black-owned construction firms came from the public sector. Also, contracts for blacks in construction averaged

$180,000 compared to $15,000 private sector contracts, whereas with white contractors, 80 percent of their total revenue was from the private sector.

In 1995 the *BE* 100s racked up sales of $13,092,832 billion, which included the $239 million in sales from construction. In 1995 the Atlanta-based H. J. Russell & Co., the nation's largest black construction and development company, ranked fourth on the *BE* 100s, with sales of $172.8 million and a staff of 1,197. It was founded in 1959 by Herman J. Russell.* In 1996, black construction industry sales had increased to $331.5 million, which in the industry represents the amount that one average size white construction company would have in sales. With the retrenchment in affirmative action, it appears that this sector of black business to sustain itself will have to compete for more private sector contracts. Also, in response to the *Croson* decision, joint venturing contracts can provide greater financial leverage and increased manpower. In 1995 the Atlanta-based Thatcher Engineering, Inc., which ranked nineteenth on the *BE* 100s for that year with $76.8 million in sales, formed a general partnership with the Gaston Construction Company, reflecting the direction of black Corporate America for the twenty-first century in the move toward mergers and acquisitions.

Despite advancements made by blacks in construction in the post—civil rights period black participation rates remain extremely low based on the number of black-owned firms in this industry. Based on the 1992 Survey of Minority-Owned Business Enterprises (SMOBE), there were only 43,381 black firms in the construction industry out of a total of 1,829,629 in the United States. There were 6,023 black general building contractor firms out of a total of 345,069. In heavy construction, except buildings, there were 730 black firms out of a total of 37,420. With special trade contractors, there were 36,057 black firms out of a total of 1,391,115. And, out of a total of 56,016 firms that were subdividers and developers, only 571 were owned by blacks. Racial parity in construction in 1992 would have required the participation of at least 183,000 African American firms instead of the 43,381 enterprises in the industry.

SELECTED BIBLIOGRAPHY: Catherine W. Bisher, "Black Builders in Antebellum North Carolina." *North Carolina Historical Review* 61 (October 1984); Andrew Brimmer, "A Battleplan for Fairness," *Black Enterprise* (November 1990); Martin R. Delany, *The Condition, Elevation, Emigration and Destiny of the Colored People of the United States* (Philadelphia, 1852, reprint, New York: Arno Press, 1968); William E. B. Du Bois, *The Negro Artisan* (Atlanta: Atlanta University Press, 1902); *Forbes*, February 2, 1924; John Hope Franklin, "James Boon, Free Negro Artisan," *Journal of Negro History* 30 (April 1945); Lorenzo J. Greene and Carter G. Woodson, *The Negro Wage Earner* (New York: AMS Press, 1970); John N. Ingham and Lynne B. Feldman, *African-American Business Leaders: A Biographical Dictionary* (Westport, CT: Greenwood Press, 1994); Gunnar Myrdal, *An American Dilemma* (New York: Harper, 1944); Loren Schweninger, *Black Property Holders in the South, 1790–1915* (Urbana: University of Illinois Press, 1990); SMOBE web data, http://www.census.gov/agfs/smobe/view/b__1.txt and http://www.census.gov/agfs/smobe/view/u__1.txt; Juliet E. K. Walker, *The History of Black Business in America* (New York: Macmillan, 1998).

Juliet E. K. Walker

CUFFE, PAUL (1756/9–1817), Massachusetts, entrepreneur, shipbuilder, shipping company owner, coastal trader, international merchant, philanthropist.

A visitor to New Bedford, Massachusetts, in 1806 wrote, "In the next township lives Paul Cuff [*sic*], the owner and master of a fine ship. He is a man whom I suppose to be worth 20,000 dollars, of more extensive credit & reputation than any other in the township—and has his family settled about him who are also much respected." By this time, Paul Cuffe had built at least 10 crafts along the Acoaxet River, from small sailing sloops to the 268-ton ship *Alpha*. He was approaching the peak of his American business activities and would soon launch into West African commercial ventures.

At the turn of the nineteenth century, people of color from British Canada to the southern states excelled in the seafaring trades, but nowhere were conditions more amenable for black shipping entrepreneurs than in Quaker New England. Within that environment, Cuffe's parents, ex-slave Coffe Slocum from West Africa and Ruth Moses, a Wompanoag Native American, instilled an enduring family work ethic. Beyond household chores, 10 children were taught farming, carpentry, and seafaring. By the conclusion of the Revolution, during which time he had whaled as a common ship hand and successfully run the British blockade to Nantucket Island, Cuffe welcomed seafaring risks. At that early stage he cautiously commenced implementation of a business philosophy: He would limit partnerships to members within the extended family and to people of color rather than include members of the white community.

Prominent pillars of the region's white mercantile establishment amply demonstrated the material benefits of familial entrepreneurship, typified by the Rotch and Rodman families, who simultaneously exchanged marriage bonds and mercantile contracts. The Westporter's earliest business partnership brought together Cuffe and his sister Mary's husband Michael Wainer, who, like Cuffe's wife Alice, was a Pequot Indian. This profitable union eventually netted reliable crews, captains, and investors for the family business. News of a more public copartnership, Cuffe & Howards, appeared in the press over the summer of 1809. Cuffe & Howards, later P. & A. Howards, became one of New Bedford's establishments for "W.I. [West Indies] Goods & Groceries." Cuffe's youthful partners, ex-slaves Peter and Alexander Howard, had married daughters Alice and Ruth; subsequently, upon Alexander Howard's death, his widow Ruth married Richard Johnson, who enlisted as one of William Lloyd Garrison's New Bedford agents for the *Liberator*.

Vessels built in the Cuffe yards bore the stamp of family and racial solidarity. Together, Cuffe and Wainer constructed and sailed the coastal schooners *Sunfish* and *Mary!*—the latter named for the partner's third member, Mary Cuffe Wainer. Before the turn of the century, the schooner *Ranger* inaugurated Cuffe's public American reputation as a master who sailed with an all-black crew. The sensation continued to make news years later in London when the *Times* announced Cuffe's arrival aboard the brig *Traveller*. "Perhaps the first vessel that ever reached Europe, entirely owned and operated by Negroes."

Cuffe entered into slave trading waters with seeming impunity. In 1795 he commanded the brig *Ranger* into the Chesapeake Bay and Maryland's eastern shore plantation community, his trading there vividly described in years to come by Frederick Douglass. Personal and business impediments notwithstanding, the brig twice returned home with handsome profits. A decade later in command of the ship *Alpha*, the black captain safely lay over several months in Savannah, Georgia's principal slave trading entry port, before heading for the Baltic Sea. Accounts of that venture suggest that Cuffe had less reason to fear Georgia slave traders than seizure by French patrols off the coast of England, while he sailed in European waters. All such journeys were reminders of his most valued commodity: reputation.

Paul Cuffe was a sagacious and deeply religious individual—he joined the Society of Friends in 1808—who had Quaker abolitionist allies at every turn, including Friend William Rotch, Jr., of nearby New Bedford, heir to Nantucket's wealthiest whaling family, whose connections and endorsements proved indispensable on numerous occasions, and also Friend William Allen of London. Characterized in a British publication as "An African Captain," Cuffe committed his final years to "commerce and philanthropy for the African family." In late 1810 he embarked for Sierra Leone aboard the brig *Traveller*, Thomas Wainer in command, in order to promote a complex commercial-philanthropic scheme. There he discovered that a British colonial merchant monopoly systematically obstructed business opportunities for black settlers, many of whom were former American slaves who had escaped during the Revolution. His scheme called for a supportive commercial network, promoting legitimate trade as well as settling industrious emigrants from the United States. To implement this scheme, black settler merchants formed the Friendly Society of Sierra Leone; Britishers followed with "The Society for the Purpose of Encouraging the Black Settlers at Sierra Leone, and the Natives of Africa Generally."

Upon his return to the United States, Cuffe gathered urban free blacks into branches of the organization African Institutions. Presidents of two such bodies, sailmaker James Forten* of Philadelphia and Rev. Peter Williams, Jr., of New York, joined Cuffe in advocating a black joint stock company "trading fund," just as American Anti-Slavery societies would envision 30 years hence and Marcus Garvey* a century afterward. However, individually underwriting the scheme, especially the resettlement costs for 38 passengers in 1816, proved to be a considerable burden. Paul Cuffe died on September 17, 1817, at his home in Westport, Massachusetts. He bequeathed an estate of $20,000. His dream of a transatlantic Pan-African unity remained for the generations to follow.

SELECTED BIBLIOGRAPHY: George E. Brooks, Jr., *Yankee Traders, Old Coasters, and African Middlemen* (Boston: Boston University Press, 1970); Arthur Diamond, *Paul Cuffe: Merchant and Abolitionist* (New York: Chelsea House Publishers, 1989; Lamont D. Thomas, *Paul Cuffe: Black Entrepreneur and Pan-Africanist* (Urbana: University of Illinois Press, 1986, 1988).

Lamont D. Thomas

CULLERS, VINCENT T. (1930?–), Illinois, advertising executive, social activist.

As founder of the nation's first black-owned full-service advertising agency in 1956, Vincent T. Cullers is the acknowledged "Dean" of African American agencies. Chairman and chief executive officer (CEO) of Vince Cullers Advertising, Cullers and his wife Marian have been credited with creating the $350 million a year ethnic-targeted industry and serving as mentors for many of the nation's top black advertising executives. His philosophy that "selling black" requires "thinking black" led to an entirely new and innovative approach for reaching the huge but untapped black consumer market.

A native of Chicago, Cullers attended the Chicago Art Institute and studied business at the University of Chicago. He served as a combat artist in the U.S. Marine Corps in World War II and began his career in 1953 as the promotional art director for *Ebony* magazine. After freelancing in art and advertising, he opened his own agency three years later. At that time, however, Corporate America did not consider black consumers a viable and profitable market, and Cullers spent the next 12 years struggling against the odds. In 1968 his efforts finally paid off: Vince Cullers Advertising acquired Lorillard Corporations as its first national client.

Since 1956 Vince Cullers Advertising has had a roster of big-chip clients: Sears, Roebuck & Company, Kellogg Company, Amoco, Pizza Hut, Coors Brewing, the Chicago White Sox, and the U.S. Department of the Treasury. Cullers ads are known for conveying a sense of national and racial pride. In 1996 his company earned $20 million in billings. With a staff of 21, Vince Cullers Advertising provides a full range of services including marketing and strategic planning, market research, creative development and production, media planning, promotions development, and public relations. Cullers Advertising remains a family business, with his wife Marian serving as executive vice president; his son Jeff is president; and son Terry is also involved in the business.

Cullers and his organization are acknowledged trailblazers and helped establish the tradition of mentoring found among other African American advertising agencies. Commenting on the strong philanthropic aspect of his company, Cullers says, "Just as it's important to establish goals for business, it's equally important to teach our youth about establishing positive goals for themselves. We must give something back."

SELECTED BIBLIOGRAPHY: *Black Advocate* (May–June 1995); *Chicago Defender*, September 9, 1996; Vince Cullers Advertising, Inc., Archives, Chicago.

Teresa Savage

D

DAY, THOMAS (1801–1861), North Carolina, furniture manufacturer, master carpenter, woodworker, artist.

Thomas Day was a successful furniture maker particularly renown for beds but also for furniture suites and interior design. Living near the Virginia state line in Milton, North Carolina, Day produced furniture for many North Carolina and Virginia clients including North Carolina's governor. Day's furniture, reflecting the Greek revival fashion of the period, often included distinctive variations of the "thumb" or curved Ionic style. Although no one has yet established an explicit connection, some pieces, including many newel posts Day made for the staircases of local plantations, resemble art made in West Africa.

It was in 1822 or 1823 that Day established himself in Milton with the intention of staying only long enough to refine his furniture-making skills. Although there is no record of his early business, by 1827 Day purchased his own shop on Milton's Main Street for $550. With a reputation as an upstanding, churchgoing individual, Day enjoyed steady growth in his business. The region's successful tobacco growers often had Day furnish interior trim and complete rooms of furniture. The 1830 census records Day as a black artisan with two slaves in his possession. It is also known that Day employed white apprentices. It is uncertain how Day used his slaves, but it is reasonable to conclude that they were involved with his business, particularly after 1848 when Day consolidated his family and business under one roof.

Increasing business and lack of room led Day to purchase the Yellow Tavern in 1848. Located on Main Street and built in 1815, the Tavern was well made and lasted until a fire destroyed it in 1989. Day added a two-story wing shortly after he bought the building and established his workshop, storage, showroom, and office on the first floor, while his family resided on the second floor. Day's business prospered for a number of years, and he employed 12 workers in 1850 when his estate was valued at $8,000. Uncompensated work and debt eventually caught Day in the financial Panic of 1857, and he planned to liquidate his business in 1859 until his son, Thomas Day, Jr., assumed control of the business and ran it until 1871.

Day was born in Halifax County, Virginia, to a free black woman named Morning S. Day. Day's father is unknown. Little is certain about his early life; however, it is clear that Day learned to read and write and was probably apprenticed to a carpenter. As a young man he moved to Caswell County, North Carolina, and the growing town of Milton, where there were a number of cabinetmakers for whom he might have worked. He married Acquilla Wilson, a free black five years his junior from Halifax County, in 1830 and planned to return to Halifax County, Virginia.

Day's reputation as a valuable part of the Caswell County community helped him when white residents successfully petitioned the state legislature to exempt Acquilla Wilson from an 1826 law banning the migration of free blacks into the state. A letter in support of the petition came from Romulus Saunders, the state attorney general and native of Caswell County. Day and his wife had three children, and they educated all of their children in Wilbraham, Massachusetts. Thomas Day's business philosophy was: Offer quality products at low prices with punctual service.

SELECTED BIBLIOGRAPHY: Caswell County web site, available from http://www.caswellnc.com/ent.htm#ThomasDay; John Hope Franklin, *The Free Negro in North Carolina, 1790–1860* (Chapel Hill: University of North Carolina, 1943); William S. Powell, *When the Past Refused to Die: A History of Caswell, 1777–1977* (Durham, NC: Moore Publishing, 1977); W. A. Robinson et al., "Thomas Day and His Family," *Negro History Bulletin* 8 (March 1950).

David F. Herr

DeBAPTISTE, GEORGE (c. 1814–1875), Detroit, entrepreneur, abolitionist.

George DeBaptiste rose to prominence among Detroit's black community, where he worked as both a businessman and community leader. Before arriving in Detroit, DeBaptiste worked in a variety of jobs, most often barbering. While in Ohio, DeBaptiste met William Henry Harrison and worked as his personal servant through Harrison's 1840 political campaign and then as a White House steward until Harrison's death in 1841. DeBaptiste returned to barbering and clerked with a wholesale clothier after moving to Detroit. Subsequent ventures included running a bakery, owning a steamboat piloted by white captains, operating a catering service, running an ice cream parlor, and owning two restaurants. By 1867, after the Civil War his realty holdings in Detroit were valued at $10,000 in 1867.

DeBaptiste was born free in Fredericksburg, Virginia. His father John De-Baptiste was a successful businessman, and it appears that he apprenticed his son to a barber in Richmond, Virginia. During his early adult years DeBaptiste began to help slaves escape to the North. Around 1837 DeBaptiste settled in Madison, Indiana, where he barbered and worked as a conductor on the Underground Railroad.* His reputation as a suspected abolitionist and conductor caused him to leave Indiana. In Detroit, DeBaptiste apparently belonged to a secret antislavery society known variously as the Order of the Men of Oppression, African-American Mysteries, and the Order of Emancipation. DeBaptiste was the president of the Black Union League and continued his work with the Underground Railroad in Detroit. As a community leader, DeBaptiste worked for the Freedmen's Association after the war, helped black children receive an education, and participated in numerous community events.

SELECTED BIBLIOGRAPHY: Ruth Coder Fitzgerald, *A Different Story: A Black History of Fredericksburg, Stafford, and Spotsylvania, Virginia* (Greensboro, NC: Unicorn, 1979); David M. Katzman, *Before the Ghetto: Black Detroit in the Nineteenth Century* (Urbana: University of Illinois Press, 1973); Emma Lou Thornbrough, *The Negro in Indiana* (Indianapolis: Indiana Historical Bureau, 1957).

David F. Herr

DELANY, MARTIN ROBISON (1812–1885), Pennsylvania, newspaper publisher, physician, abolitionist, black nationalist, business promoter.

Martin Delany was born in Charles Town, Virginia, to a free mother and slave father. A medical doctor, he was also publisher of the *Mystery* newspaper and the first black commissioned office in the United States Colored Troops (USCT) in the Civil War. Delany's nationalism and, at one time, his promotion of black immigration to Africa have been the focus of scholarly inquiry. Delany, however, in his 1852 book *The Condition, Elevation, Emigration and Destiny of the Colored People of the United States* also chronicled the expansion of black business in antebellum America, for the purpose, as he said, "to refute the objections urged against us, that we are not useful members of society. That we are consumers and non-producers—that we contribute nothing to the general progress of man."

Delany's book thus provides an essential starting point in the reconstruction of black business history and the entrepreneurial participation of blacks. In a chapter entitled "Practical Utility of Colored People of the Present Day as Members of Society—Business Men and Mechanics," Delany details the diversity of enterprises operated by antebellum blacks at mid-century. The black businesspeople selected by Delany for discussion in his treatise were considered among the most prominent, although not necessarily the wealthiest in antebellum America. Those were the large black slave plantation holders, primarily in Louisiana. Of the 21 antebellum blacks identified by Juliet E. K. Walker in "Racism, Slavery, Free Enterprise" whose wealth holding exceeded $100,000, only two were mentioned by Delany, James Forten* and Stephen Smith.*

Delany's purpose, however, was not to provide a comprehensive listing of the leading black wealth holders. Rather, he considered it more important to emphasize that black businesses represented an integral part of the American business community. He also wanted to stress that profits could be realized through business participation, as well as to illustrate the existence of enterprises owned by blacks, which were usually not associated with black business activity.

More than 38 black businessmen were discussed by Delany. Some of the enterprises described were: Merchant Clothiers; Pharmaceutical; Employment Agencies; Merchant Tailor House; Money Broker; Lumber Merchants; Jeweler; Construction/Real Estate; Wood Factor/Shipping; Steamboat Owners/Shipping; Resort Owner; Restaurateur/Caterers; Sail Manufactory; Merchant/RR Cars Owner; Daguerreotype Gallery; Tanner/Currier Building Contractor/Glazier; Concert Band Leader; Livery Stable/Hotelier Construction/Plastering; Bootmaker; and Wholesale Grocery/Food Processing/Ship Chandlery. Even the Charleston slave entrepreneur millwright manufacturer Anthony Weston* was included in his discussion of black businesspeople in 1850.

While Delany stressed that an expansion of business participation by blacks was an important strategy to be used in elevating the race, he was also writing for two distinct audiences. In response to vicious racist stereotypes that denigrated the competence of blacks, Delany emphasized promoting black business success as a means to vindicate the race. At the same time, he called on race pride to prompt a more aggressive pursuit of business by the black community to keep money in the black community.

Then, in a chapter entitled "Our Elevation in the United States," Delany advocated that antebellum blacks "buy black," for he emphasized that of the consumer goods purchased by blacks that "all are the products of the white man, purchased by us from the white man, consequently, our earnings and means, are all given to the white man."

Invariably, Delany's discussion of black businesspeople in his 1852 book have been ignored. Antebellum black history has focused primarily on the abolitionist activities of free blacks and the conditions of slave blacks, while literary critics in their examinations have been more concerned with analysis of black literature, form as opposed to content. Most important, there seemed to be no way to provide supportive documentation of the more expansive business holdings of the black entrepreneurs identified by Delany. The lumber merchant Stephen Smith ran his own railroad cars in making interstate deliveries of lumber.

It was not until Walker's 1986 use of the R. G. Dun mercantile credit records that business holdings described by Delany of Stephen Smith, the wealthiest antebellum black from the 1850s, were corroborated. By 1865, Dun records indicate that he was worth $500,000. Delany was also an important member of the National Negro Convention Movement,* which also promoted black business before the Civil War. Delany, however, in his 1852 book, provides an example of the record keeping of black business activity that would be expanded after the Civil War to the present, most notably in *Black Enterprise*.

SELECTED BIBLIOGRAPHY: Martin R. Delany, *The Condition, Elevation, Emigration and Destiny of the Colored People of the United States* (Philadelphia, 1852; reprint, New York: Arno Press, 1968), Nell Irvin Painter, "Martin Delany and Elitist Black Nationalism," in August Meier and Leon Litwack, eds., *Black Leaders of the Nineteenth Century* (Urbana: University of Illinois Press, 1988); Victor Ullman, *Martin R. Delany: The Beginnings of Black Nationalism* (Boston: Beacon Press, 1971); Juliet E. K. Walker, "Promoting Black Entrepreneurship and Business Enterprise in Antebellum America: The National Negro Convention, 1830–1855," in Thomas D. Boston, ed., *A Different Vision: Race and Public Policy*, vol. 2 (London: Routledge Press, 1997); Juliet E. K. Walker, "Racism, Slavery, and Free Enterprise: Black Entrepreneurship in the United States before the Civil War," *Business History Review* 60 (Autumn 1986): 343–382.

Juliet E. K. Walker

De PASSE, SUZANNE CELESTE (1947–), California, entertainment executive, record producer, and television movie producer.

Formerly a talent coordinator for Cheetah, a New York club, De Passe got a break when Cindy Birdsong (of the Supremes) introduced her to Berry Gordy* in 1968 and was soon director of the Artists and Repertoire Department. In 1980 she became president of Motown Productions, and the first major project was the eight-hour CBS miniseries *Lonesome Dove*. She purchased the rights for $50,000, although major studios rejected it, and later sold a 50 percent profit interest to Quintex Entertainment for $1 million, and $16 million investment from CBS. She has also produced a movie, Berry Gordy's *The Last Dragon*, and television specials, "Motown 25" and "Motown Return to the Apollo." Her production company, De Passe Entertainment, has produced shows *Sister Sister* and *On Our Own*.

Her many awards include Essence Awards for Business, Women in Film Crystal Award, Equitable Black Achievement Recognition Award, and Brotherhood Crusade Black Pioneer Award. She is also on the board of the Los Angeles Chamber of Commerce and the American Film Institute.

SELECTED BIBLIOGRAPHY: Berry Gordy, *To Be Loved: The Music, the Magic, the Memories of Motown* (New York: Warner Books, 1994); "Hanes Salutes the 1989 Essence Awards," *Essence*, October 1989, 62; "Motown Soars with 'Dove' " *Essence*, May 1989, 40.

Sundiata A. K. Djata

De PRIEST, OSCAR STANTON (1871–1951), Illinois, entrepreneur, realtor, U.S. congressman.

Oscar Stanton De Priest was born in a cabin in Florence, Alabama, in 1871, the fifth child of ex-slaves. Violence that attended the end of Reconstruction in Alabama prompted his parents to move to Salina, Kansas, where De Priest learned the decorating trade from his uncles and a local painter to whom he was apprenticed at 15. After two years at the Salina Normal School, he decided to run away with two white companions to Dayton, Ohio, and a year later, he set out alone for Chicago. In Chicago, his fair complexion and sandy-brown hair allowed him to pass for white in order to secure employment. While still in his early twenties De Priest set up his decorating business, which specialized in renovating run-down buildings.

It was clear early on that De Priest had a special talent for negotiation and barter, in both the economic and political arenas. While he may have viewed politics as "recreation," he moved rapidly up Republican Party ranks and at 33 was elected county commissioner. During his tenure in office, his rapidly expanding decorating business was awarded an estimated $25,000 in contracts from the Chicago Board of Education. De Priest served two terms as a Cook County commissioner but was denied a third term. He then expanded his decorating firm and acquired a fortune in Southside real estate. By the 1920s, largely as a result of black migration from the South, De Priest was reputedly a millionaire.

In 1915, however, De Priest was elected the city's first black alderman. He was a "race man," whose election to the city council in 1915 was a source of immense pride to the city's African American community, and his popularity remained undiminished by his bribery indictment just two years later. (He was acquitted with the aid of Clarence Darrow.) Also De Priest had displayed real courage during the Race Riot of 1919, and in 1928, he became the first African American from the North elected to Congress. For much of his career in local and national politics, De Priest was a hero, a symbol of black political empowerment, and ironically, a symbol of the triumph of Booker T. Washington's* gospel of entrepreneurship and self-help. But that changed with the coming of the Great Depression and the election of Franklin Roosevelt.

De Priest's election to Congress gave him genuine national standing, but he was initially opposed to New Deal legislation, especially Roosevelt's relief initiatives. De Priest feared black dependency on the government dole. At the same time, he attacked the Bankhead Cotton Control Act for reducing cotton acreage and putting thousands of black farmers out of work and the National Recovery Act for forcing employers to pay higher wages, reducing the amount of work available to blacks. After the devastating winter of 1932, De Priest did support some relief projects, but he continued to vote a generally Republican and largely anti–New Deal line and was defeated by a virtual unknown, Chicago black Arthur W. Mitchell, when he ran a fourth time in 1934.

De Priest was clearly out of step with the times. During the 1930s, the Left, most notably the Communist Party, picketed his headquarters, labeling him a blockbuster whose high rents gouged his tenants. They were at least partly right. De Priest built at least part of his fortune from "blockbusting," purchasing homes or apartment buildings in white neighborhoods and moving in blacks. When the white residents fled, he moved in more blacks and raised their rents. Given the dire housing shortage from the Great Migration era in Bronzeville, De Priest was largely viewed as a shrewd entrepreneur rather than an usurious exploiter. He was a past president of the local chapter of the National Negro Business League* and, along with *Chicago Defender*'s Robert S. Abbott,* cosmetic manufacturer and bank founder Anthony Overton,* and Jesse Binga,* also a real estate tycoon and bank founder, was one of the principal symbols of the golden era of black entrepreneurship in Bronzeville. By the 1930s he was a defeated politician, reviled by the Left, whose national stature vanished virtually overnight.

But De Priest was not finished. He made a triumphal return to Chicago politics in 1943 when he was once again elected to the Chicago City Council. He lost his bid for reelection four years later and in 1951, while crossing an intersection near his home, was knocked down by a Chicago Motor Coach. He died of his injuries several months later.

SELECTED BIBLIOGRAPHY: William L. Clay, *Just Permanent Interests: Black Americans in Congress* (New York: Amistad Press, 1992); Edward T. Clayton, *The Negro Politician: His Success and Failure* (Chicago: Johnson Publications, 1964); St. Clair Drake and Horace Cayton, *Black Metropolis: A Study of Negro Life in a Northern City*, 2 vols. (1945; reprint, New York: Harper & Row, 1962); Harold F. Gosnell, *Negro Politicians: The Rise of Negro Politics in Chicago* (Chicago: University of Chicago Press, 1935); Allan H. Spear, *Black Chicago: The Making of a Negro Ghetto, 1890–1920* (Chicago: University of Chicago Press, 1967); Dempsey J. Travis, *An Autobiography of Black Chicago* (Chicago: Urban Research Press, 1987).

Charles Branham

DISPARITY STUDIES. *Disparity studies* are research reports commissioned by state and local government agencies to determine whether or not there is sufficient evidence under constitutional standards to devise a race-conscious procurement preference program. Disparity studies grew out of the response of state and local governments to the U.S. Supreme Court's decision in *Richmond v. Croson* (1989), where the Supreme Court held that race-conscious business preference programs were subject to "strict scrutiny." This means that programs, which granted minority businesses an edge in public contracting, had to satisfy both a "compelling government interest" and be "narrowly tailored."

A *compelling government interest* meant essentially that the local government agency had to demonstrate that there was a "strong basis in the evidence" that the local agency was either an active or passive participant in discrimination against minority businesses. *Narrow tailoring* means that if a local agency decided to implement a minority business enterprise (MBE) program, the program had to be flexible, aspirational, and limited in duration and scope. A disparity study serves as this strong basis in the evidence for the program. A well-crafted ordinance with goals (instead of set-asides,* waivers of these goals, and sunset provisions) would serve as the basis for a narrowly tailored program.

One of the first studies conducted was in Hillsborough County (Tampa, Florida) by D. J. Miller & Associates (DJMA) around the time period as the release of the *Croson* decision. Dr. Edward Davis of the business school at Clark Atlanta University was instrumental in developing the methodology of the early disparity studies. The major firms involved in producing disparity studies have been the Minority Business Enterprise Legal Defense and Education Fund (MBELDEF) in Washington; DJMA in Atlanta; Andrew Brimmer and Associates in Washington; National Economic Research Associates in Cambridge, Massachusetts; Brown Boortz and Coddington in Denver; MGT of America in Tallahassee; Boston Consulting Group in Atlanta; and Mason Tillman in Oakland. Mason Tillman, DJMA, Boston Consulting Group, and Brimmer and Associates are African American–owned firms. MBELDEF is a primarily African American nonprofit organization.

It is estimated that over $60 million has been spent on disparity studies. The studies have ranged in price from around $50,000 to over $1.2 million. The main purchasers of these studies have been local governments, airports, state departments of transportation, school boards, and a few states (Florida, Massachusetts, North Carolina, Texas, to name a few). Some cities formed consortia of agencies to commission these studies (e.g., Memphis, Portland, Orlando, among others). Some of the studies have been slim reports, and some have been seven or eight volumes.

Collectively, these disparity studies constitute the compelling government interest portion for federal minority business programs. The *Adarand v. Pena* (1995) decision imposed strict scrutiny on federal race-conscious programs. The federal government at present is relying on the Washington, D.C.–based Urban Institute review of disparity studies as a basis for the factual predicate for federal race-conscious procurement programs.

Disparity studies generally had the following elements: (1) analysis of the procurement processes of the agency being studied, (2) anecdotal interviews with majority and minority contractors, (3) analysis of MBE availability, (4) an analysis of MBE contract awards and/or payments, (5) disparity ratios, (6) an evaluation of the adequacy of race-neutral programs that promote business development as an alternative to race-conscious programs, and (7) recommendations. Some studies had historical chapters as well. The availability analysis is the crucial part of the report and the most controversial. In general the courts have preferred measures of firms that are ready, willing, and able to compete for agency contracts. Typically, disparity studies used lists of certified MBEs and vendors lists in addition to the census data to estimate the availability of black businesses.

The core of the disparity study is the *disparity ratio,* which is typically defined as the ratio of the percentage of MBEs in a market area to the percentage of contract awards or contract payments made to MBEs. Generally, a confidence interval is constructed around this ratio. If the ratio was significantly different from one, then an inference of discrimination could be made. Over 130 cases have been filed across the United States as of 1997 challenging the legality of MBE programs. The Association of General Contractors (AGC) has generally taken the lead in mounting legal challenges to state and local MBE programs. In the course of litigation the AGC has generally hired George La Noue, a political science professor at the University of Maryland, as an expert witness to attack the credibility of disparity studies that serve as factual predicates for MBE programs.

MBE programs that were instituted without a disparity study have generally been struck down (see, e.g., *Milwaukee County Pavers Assn v. Fiedler*, 707 F. Supp. 1016 [WD Wis. 1989]). In early years courts were more accepting of studies that were done (see, e.g., *Cone Corp. v. Hillsborough County*, 906 F.2d 908 [11th Cir. 1990]). In recent years the courts have also been more exacting in their evaluation of disparity studies. Recently, some MBE programs have been struck down by the courts because the disparity study was considered to be flawed (see, e.g., *Engineering Contractors v. Metropolitan Dade County*, No. 94–1848-CIV-RYSKAMP [SD Fl 1996]).

SELECTED BIBLIOGRAPHY: George La Noue, "Standards for the Second Generation of *Croson*-Inspired Disparity Studies," *The Urban Lawyer* 26 (Summer 1994): 485–540; MBELDEF, Memorandum, "Litigation and On-going Investigations," February 28, 1997; Mitchell Rice, "Justifying State and Local Government Set-aside Programs through Disparity Studies in the Post-*Croson* Era," *Public Administration Review* (September–October 1992): 482–495.

J. Vincent Eagan

DOBBS, JOHN WESLEY (1882–1961), Atlanta, business and community leader.

While not himself a full-time entrepreneur, John W. Dobbs played a significant role in the development of the Sweet Auburn* business district in Atlanta, Georgia. He served on the board of directors of Citizens Trust Bank and was a founding director of Mutual Federal Savings and Loan in 1925. The underlying philosophy and call to action for which he was famous was that of the need for blacks to gain the "weapons" of the ballot, the book, and the buck: citizenship, education, and economic parity.

Dobbs was also an active Thirty-third Degree Mason, holding several offices in the Prince Hall Masonic Lodge during his 50-year membership. After financially reorganizing the Georgia Prince Hall Masons, following the Great Depression, he built the order into a force that was nationally known. His experience as insurance salesman, as the order's treasurer and financial secretary, and as manager of the Widows and Orphans Home and the Masonic Relief Association equipped him to organize the business affairs of this large statewide enterprise and to later mobilize it nationally. He was elected Grand Master of the Most Worshipful Prince Hall Grand Lodge of the Ancient Free and Accepted Masons, Jurisdiction of Georgia, in 1932 and yearly until his death. Dobbs, who worked for 32 years in the U.S. Railway Mail Service, 8 of these years as Clerk in Charge of an integrated crew, was also a founder in 1916 of a National Alliance of Postal Employees, Chattanooga, Tennessee.

Dobbs's organizational acumen and powerful oratorical abilities are legend; he distinguished himself as a humanitarian who applied a broad and practical political-historical sociology to the needs of his people. His fervent desire to "help his people get back the ballot" lost during the Jim Crow era was realized through his founding of the Atlanta Civic and Political League of 1936 and its later development into the Georgia Voters League and Statewide Registration Committee. These successful early movements resulted in the demise of the Georgia Democratic White Primary and led to a formidable bipartisan black voters alliance of 1949 known nationally as the Atlanta Negro Voters League. With the grounding of the Masonic Statewide structure, the black voting power was increased from 300 in Atlanta to 175,000 statewide in 15 years.

As a community activist, fund-raiser, and humanitarian, Dobbs was also a past vice chairman, State Central Committee, Georgia Republican Party, a life member. His desire to better his race knew no political or party boundaries, and in 1935, Dobbs executed a national speaking tour for the Franklin D. Roosevelt campaign. Dobbs, a national vice president of the National Association for the Advancement of Colored People (NAACP) and a close personal friend to Thurgood Marshall, was a significant benefactor for the NAACP Legal Defense Fund of the 1950s. He nationally organized the largest single black funding through the Prince Hall Masons in support of the *Brown v. Board of Education* effort for Marshall and received, posthumously, the Thurgood Marshall Award in 1965 for achievements in the area of civil rights and law.

Dobbs was also an informal adviser to President Dwight D. Eisenhower and a mentor to the young Dr. Martin Luther King, Jr. Dobbs's legacy took on national proportions through the affirmation action initiatives of his grandson, Maynard H. Jackson, mayor of Atlanta from 1974 to 1982 who championed the first successful model of enactment for this program.

A devout and family man and scholar of Negro and world history, literature, and the arts, Dobbs was a renown orator and community leader. Born near Marietta, Georgia, John Wesley Dobbs attended elementary school in Savannah and worked his way through Morehouse Academy, class of 1901, followed by two years at Morehouse College. He was extremely proud of Morehouse and continued his relationship throughout his life. He and wife, Irene Thompson Dobbs, raised six daughters, all of whom earned master's degrees (two earned doctorates) and were accomplished in their own rights. Dobbs felt education to be the best way for African Americans to achieve economic freedom. Dobbs's Masonic Scholarship Fund for black youth continues.

SELECTED BIBLIOGRAPHY: John Ditmer, *Black Georgia in the Progressive Era 1900–1920* (Urbana: University of Illinois Press, 1977); Alton Hornsby, "John Dobbs," in Kenneth Coleman and Charles Stephen Gurr, eds., *Dictionary of Georgia Biography* (Athens: University of Georgia Press, 1983); Benjamin E. Mayes, "He Gives Flowers to the Living: The J. W. Dobbes Are Exceptional," *Atlanta Inquirer*, 1951; Sweet Auburn Neighborhood Projects, *Sweet Auburn Chronicle* (Atlanta: Sweet Auburn Neighborhood Projects, 1978).

Juliet D. Blackburn-Beamon

DOWNING, GEORGE THOMAS (1819–1903), New York, Newport, and Providence, caterer, restaurateur, hotelier, civic leader.

George Downing was one of the most successful African American entrepreneurs in the North before the Civil War. The son of Thomas Downing, proprietor of the famous Oyster House Restaurant in New York, young Downing acquired wealth in his own right through a catering business that served some of the most elite families in New York City and Newport and Providence, Rhode Island. Besides inheriting a talent for business from his highly regarded father, he shared his commitment to securing equal rights for African Americans.

By the time he was in his midtwenties, Downing had already established a successful catering business on Broadway and had leased property in Newport, where he opened an enterprise. Before the end of the 1840s, he had made other significant purchases in that city and had opened catering establishments in Providence as well. In 1854, he built the Sea Girt Hotel, whose elegantly furnished accommodations attracted the wealthy summer migrants who flocked to Newport. Its destruction by an arsonist in 1860 represented a loss of $40,000. Undaunted by this setback, he erected Downing Block, a building whose upper floors were leased to the U.S. Naval Academy, when the midshipmen were removed from Annapolis to Newport during the Civil War. Downing's reputation as a successful restaurateur eventually earned him an invitation to manage the U.S. House of Representatives restaurant, a position he held from 1865 to 1877.

Downing's commitment to civil rights revealed itself early in his life, when at the age of 14 he helped organize a literary society, whose members pledged to abstain from observing the Fourth of July because the Declaration of Independence gave African Americans very little for which to celebrate. As an adult, he became an active participant in antislavery societies and pre-Emancipation conventions held by African Americans. An ardent critic of separation of the races, Downing led the effort to desegregate the public schools in Newport after his own children were denied equal access to education. Years later, while in Washington, D.C., he pressed for an end to discriminatory practices against African Americans traveling between the District of Columbia and Baltimore on the Baltimore and Ohio Railroad.

When the Civil War came, Downing was at the forefront of those insisting that the conflict between North and South be extended beyond preservation of the Union to that of freedom for the enslaved and equality for all people of color. He agitated for inclusion of black men in the Union military as combatants. When President Abraham Lincoln finally agreed to enlist black troops, Downing was instrumental in their recruitment and organization into regiments. After the war, Downing continued his fight for equality and fair treatment by pressing for the passage of the Civil Rights Bill introduced by Massachusetts Senator Charles Sumner. He revealed his commitment to improving the condition of the black worker by serving as vice president of the National Negro Labor Union, an organization founded in 1869.

SELECTED BIBLIOGRAPHY: Irving Bartlett, *From Slave to Citizen: The Story of the Negro in Rhode Island* (Providence RI: Urban League of Greater Providence, 1954); James Egert, *The Negro in New York* (New York: Exposition Press, 1964); Philip S. Foner and Ronald L. Lewis, eds., *The Black Worker: A Documentary History from Colonial Times to the Present* (Philadelphia: Temple University Press, 1978); S. A. Washington, *George Thomas Downing: Sketch of His Life and Times* (Newport, RI: Milne Printery, 1910).

Edna Greene Medford

DOWNSIZING, CORPORATE. The phenomenon of downsizing, a deliberate organizational decision to reduce the workforce that is intended to improve organizational performance in American organizations, corporate and otherwise, has become a pervasive practice over the last two decades in the United States, reaching what appears to be the peak in 1993, when more than 615,000 employees were laid off. Although there is no way to be certain, in the late 1990s, as to whether or not the peak has been reached, available evidence shows a downward trend of the downsizing numbers. Downsizing has been occurring in all of our major institutions—corporate, educational, military and government, and even nonprofits. Also, while downsizing may encompass the divestiture of unrelated businesses, or the sale of capital assets, it is primarily associated with the reduction of human resources, whether by layoffs, attrition, redeployment, or early retirement.

The presumed benefits of downsizing are reduced costs and increased profits for the company and faster decision making, greater flexibility, improvement in quality, and increased efficiency and productivity among the remaining workers. Research has indicated that only one fourth of firms that downsized have achieved improvement in productivity, cash flow, or shareholder return on investment and that downsizing may have unintended negative consequences for the survivors, employees who remained in the employ of the downsized organization following the downsizing process.

The downsizing phenomenon was initiated by the large corporations of America in response to global competition for the markets for their product. For several decades following World War II, the United States dominated the world markets with its manufacturing processes. During the latter part of the 1970s, however, most consumer goods and many capital goods were manufactured at higher-quality levels and lower cost by other industrialized and developing countries than that produced by American corporations. It was this phenomenon that gave rise to the downsizing phenomenon by American corporations. Once the downsizing phenomenon was set in motion by the corporate sector, like the domino effect, it spread to most of the other American organizations that are linked in various and sundry ways to corporations—that is, educational, military, and other nonprofit organizations.

By the mid-1990s, downsizing had become a pervasive phenomenon in American corporations. A report issued by the Conference Board in 1992 stated that more than 85 percent of the 406 large U.S. corporations surveyed had taken at least one of eight specific downsizing measures in the previous year. The impact on workers was and continues to be brutal. The traumatic impact upon those who lost their jobs is fairly self-evident. What is not so obvious is the trauma suffered by those who were left behind—the survivors. Most research on layoffs has focused on the underlying causes or on their effects upon the employees who lost their jobs. Overlooked was the highly practical matter of how productivity, service, and morale of the employees who did not lose their jobs were affected by the layoffs. After all, it is the reactions of the employees who remain (the survivors) that will dictate the organization's effectiveness in the future.

The emerging organizational trends and workforce reductions have resulted in negative psychological effects upon the surviving employees of the corporations. These negative effects comprise such factors as increased levels of anxiety, high levels of stress, fear, anger, guilt, depression, burnout, high levels of illnesses, and higher levels of absenteeism and attrition, all of which can undermine the organization's productivity, profitability, and stability in the long run. Downsizing has also been found to result in feelings of job insecurity, anger, decreased loyalty and organizational commitment, and increased resistance to change. These characteristics can lead to decreased levels of cooperation, motivation, and job satisfaction and decreased performance levels within these organizations. The irony is that downsizing has a similar effect upon management.

The enduring success of any organization depends upon the maintenance of and adequate level of psychological health of the employees who remain after downsizing. The paradigm shift from the era of stability to that of downsizing has caused phenomenal changes with respect to both employees and employers. Corporations, which once perceived employees as long-term assets to be nurtured and developed, now see them as cost centers to be reduced at will. Today, many corporations view employees as ''things'' or ''commodities'' to be kept or discarded, according to the fluctuations of profit, and like machines, to be cared for and maintained as long as they are needed. Under the old paradigm, work was a career rather than a job, where retirement with its benefits were expected and the work environment was predictable and generally mutually supportive.

Downsizing and restructuring of organizations in the 1980s and the concomitant reduction in force have brought pervasive anxiety into the workplace. These anxieties stemmed from shifting power bases that leave employees feeling vulnerable. Unfortunately, unlike machines, the process of discarding employees has a significant impact upon those who remain. In fact, those who remain are victims of what David Noer calls *survivor sickness*. Survivors suffer from anxiety, burnout, and stress, and they feel empty, lethargic, and guilty and no longer enjoy their jobs. According to Morin, in his book, *Silent Sabotage*, ''survivors of traumatic layoffs experience the same stages of grief, including denial, anger, and depression as employees who lose their jobs, and survivors can take even longer to recover. It, then, becomes a nightmare to manage.''

While African Americans have suffered the same fate as survivors, generally, their fate was more pronounced. One reason is the predominance of African Americans in blue-collar jobs, which are being wiped out en masse by global labor competition. Another is that "many companies are still operating under a last hired, the first fired pattern, which is enforced by powerful labor unions." Kenneth P. DeMeuse, associate professor of management at the University of Wisconsin at Eau Claire, adds, "On top of that, of course, there's discrimination." As Earl S. Washington, president of the Executive Leadership Council, a Washington, D.C.–based group of senior-level black corporate executives, said: "It didn't take a study in the *Wall Street Journal* to let me know that African Americans were disproportionately affected by emphasis on restructuring." Consequently, despite purported gains among higher-ranking African Americans, the problems remain the same. More devastating, he emphasizes: "Once you look back over the shoulders of our most senior ranking members, there are not a lot of folks moving up to take their places. And, last year, that pipeline was thinned out even more."

In a 1992 survey asking how members were being affected by restructuring, the National Black MBA Association* (NBMBAA) found that of 900 respondents, 24 percent believed their positions were being threatened by downsizing; another 17 percent had already been laid off. Furthermore, according to an analysis of the 1990–1991 Equal Employment Opportunity Commission by the *Wall Street Journal*, it was found that African Americans were the only group that suffered a net loss during that period, whereas whites, Hispanics, and Asians gained jobs, thousands of them. The study that canvassed 35,242 companies showed that black employment fell dramatically in 36 states and six of the nine major industries. Hardest hit were blue-collar job holders, service workers, and those in sales. Among the most shocking cases, at Sears, Roebuck and Company, black lost 54.3 percent of the jobs; Dial Corporation, 43.6 percent; and Coca-Cola Enterprises, the bottling arm of Coca-Cola, 42.1 percent.

It should be pointed out, however, that some of these layoffs were due to the recession of the 1990–1991 period. There is no way to determine, definitively, the precise number of layoffs of African Americans attributed to downsizing, except to state these reduction levels are higher than even the layoffs during the Great Depression, which averaged approximately 25 percent at its peak. In addition, African Americans were the only labor sector suffering these levels of layoffs during this period. "I hear a lot of alibis as to why blacks suffered more in downsizing," says H. C. Smith, whose executive recruiting firm by the same name is based in Shaker Heights, Ohio. Yet he notes that while Corporate America embraces diversity, at the same time, "an awful lot of talented African-Americans get hard hit with the reality that companies are not as concerned with keeping them once they've been wooed."

African American managers have suffered the same fate as African American employees in nonmanagerial positions in the downsizing process, according to several studies. In fact, they are the first to feel the axe. Managers in staff functions such as public affairs and human resources, where large numbers of blacks work, usually get cut first, because their units aren't income generators. Managers employed in line positions, such as finance, marketing, and sales, are usually insulated from deep cuts. "The crunch is hitting managers across the board," asserts Wendell Johnson, executive recruiter in Danbury, Connecticut, "but the areas that are hit the hardest are those departments where blacks have traditionally been employed."

Moreover, as Yvonne Shaw, a consultant specializing in affirmative action for Organization Resource Counselors, a management consulting firm in New York City, said: "Blacks are losing their jobs and some are not old enough in the corporation to really benefit from severance packages or early-retirement." The consensus among affirmative action officers and personnel administrators interviewed by *Black Enterprise* is that "the prospects for many top-ranking black corporate officials in the near future is bleak." Given that downsizing will be a fact of life in the predictable future, African American employees must change the way they think about the environment in which they work. As Wesley and Silverman state, "Once you accept the fact that there is no job security, you will protect yourself by putting your career in your own hands."

This is a new paradigm. Corporate America will never be the same. The old way of doing things is gone forever. No jobs will be permanent.

There are no permanent jobs; there is no permanent security. The key criterion for future survival will be superior skills. However, always keep the organization's goals in mind and strive to make a contribution to the achievement of those goals. This will give you more leverage to survive when the next round of downsizing occurs.

SELECTED BIBLIOGRAPHY: Caroline V. Clarke, "Downsizing Trounces Diversity." *Black Enterprise* (February 1994): 69–74; Derek Dingle, "Will Black Managers Survive Corporate Downsizing?" *Black Enterprise* (March 1987): 49–55; Roger E. Herman and Joyce L. Gioia, *Lean and Meaningful: A New Culture for Corporate America* (Greensboro, NC: Oakhill Press, 1998); Joyce C. Irons, "An Analysis of the Psychological Effect of Downsizing and Job Satisfaction of Survivors in Selected Educational Institutions and Corporations," Ph.D. diss., Clark Atlanta University, 1995; William J. Morin, *Silent Sabotage: Rescuing Our Careers, Our Companies, and Our Lives from the Creeping Paralysis of Anger and Bitterness* (New York: AMACOM, American Management Association, 1995); David M. Noer, *Healing the Wounds: Overcoming the Trauma of Layoffs and Revitalizing Downsized Organizations* (San Francisco: Jossey-Bass, 1993); Annette Williams, "When Downsizing Hits Home," *Black Enterprise* (March 1994): 52–59.

Joyce C. Irons

DUDLEY, JOE L. (1937–), North Carolina, entrepreneur, humanitarian, founder and president of Dudley Products Inc.

Dudley was born in Aurora, North Carolina. He grew up in a small three-room farmhouse with 10 brothers and sisters. Retained in first grade, Dudley was labeled mentally retarded and diagnosed as having a speech impediment. However, through the encouragement of his mother, his own hard work, and perseverance, Dudley overcame these obstacles and was a millionaire by the age of 40. In 1993, Dudley Products Inc., located in Kernersville, North Carolina, had annual sales of $35 million. In 1994, the company ranked forty-six on the *Black Enterprise* "Top 100 List of Black Businesses."

Dudley Products Inc. manufactures and distributes more than 200 professional hair care and personal care products directly to cosmetologists and barbers. His products are sold strictly through salons to help cosmetologists build their businesses. This marketing strategy has earned Dudley Products the title "the Avon of the Ethnic-Salon Business." Most companies have concentrated on retail trade, which makes up some 80 percent of the ethnic hair care and cosmetic market. Also, in 1989, the Dudley Cosmetology University was founded, and the company operates 16 beauty schools from Sumter, South Carolina, to Chicago, Illinois. Dudley Products also operates a travel agency, hotel, convention complex, cafeteria in North Carolina, and a beauty school in Zimbabwe.

Dudley launched his career in the beauty business during the late 1950s, selling Fuller Products door to door while a student in business administration at North Carolina A&T State University. Upon completion of his Bachelor of Science degree, Dudley moved to New York, where he continued to work as a Fuller Products salesman for five years. S. B. Fuller,* founder of the company, became his mentor. In 1967, Dudley and his wife Eunice, whom he met in 1960, moved to Greensboro, North Carolina, to open a Fuller Products distributorship. Today, Eunice is Dudley Products chief financial officer.

In 1969, when the Fuller Products Co. incurred financial difficulties, the Dudleys started their own company, making beauty products on their kitchen stove. By 1976, the company had grown to include a chain of beauty supply stores, beauty shops, a beauty college, a manufacturing plant, and more than 400 employees. In that same year, Fuller asked Dudley to come to Chicago and run the Fuller Products Co. Dudley ran both companies for eight years. The Fuller Products Co. sales had fallen from $10 million in 1962 to $1.5 million in 1976. Although the Fuller Co. climbed in sales under Dudley's watchful eye, it never fully recovered. In 1984, Dudley returned to Greensboro, where he opened a 37,500-square-foot headquarters and manufacturing plant. Fuller died in 1988, and Dudley acquired the rights to manufacture and distribute Fuller Products.

Dudley Products Inc. has several high-profile community service projects, for example, the Dudley Fellows and Dudley Ladies Programs, mentoring programs for high school students, and the Black Teenage World Scholarship Pageant. The company gives 32 full scholarships annually to students in business-related majors at North Carolina A&T and Bennett College in Greensboro, North Carolina. After the rioting in Los Angeles in 1992, Dudley established the "Resurrection to Beauty Fund," which aided cosmetologists whose businesses were ravaged. Dudley has been the recipient of numerous awards. He holds honorary doctorate degrees from Edward Waters College in Jacksonville, Florida, and North Carolina A&T, where he also serves on the board of trustees. In 1991, Dudley Products accepted the Direct Selling Association's coveted "Vision for Tomorrow Award" for outstanding community service. In 1995 he received the Horatio Alger Award. Dudley has been inducted into the National Black College Alumni Hall of Fame in the category of Business/Industry.

SELECTED BIBLIOGRAPHY: Duncan Maxwell Anderson, "Force of Character: The Philosophy That Built a $35 Million Company," *Success* (April 1996); J. Tol Broome, Jr., "Grooming for Success," *Nation's Business* (March 1996); Carole Boston Weatherford, "Joe Dudley, Sr., Building a Company with a Heart," *Minorities and Women in Business* (March–April 1993).

Nancy J. Dawson

DURNFORD, ANDREW (1800–1859), Louisiana, sugar planter, physician.

In 1828 Durnford, the son of Thomas Durnford, a white Englishman, and Rosaline Mercier, a free woman of color of New Orleans, purchased 10 arpents of Mississippi River frontage in Plaquemines Parish, Louisiana ($25,000) and 14 slaves ($7,000). The land and labor were purchased to build a sugar plantation out of the swamps of southern Louisiana. Durnford's father had died two years earlier, but no inheritance is recorded for the son. When Durnford moved to the country, he was accompanied by his 18-year-old wife, Marie Charlotte Remy, free woman of color and the mother of their 2-year-old son, Thomas Durnford (the son eventually took the middle name McDonogh).

Durnford built his sugar plantation at St. Rosalie bend in the Mississippi River, a slight eastward twist about 33 miles south of New Orleans—the plantation may have been named for the bend, or the bend for the plantation, or perhaps the plantation for Durnford's mother Rosaline. Financing for the venture came from the seller of the land and slaves, John McDonogh, a prosperous white merchant of New Orleans and Baltimore and a friend and business associate Durnford had first known through his father. Durnford paid 6 percent on his loans, often paying only interest while rolling over principal. Durnford's white father had paid McDonogh 10 percent for business loans.

On July 22, 1829, McDonogh financed the sale of a contiguous five arpents of Mississippi River frontage to Durnford for $22,500. The smaller tract, which cost Durnford nearly twice the price per arpent of the larger tract, was probably improved land complete with facilities. A third tract was also sold to Durnford by McDonogh. St. Rosalie was completed with the purchase, in 1832, of a contiguous nine arpents, 165 feet 4 inches along the Mississippi River north of the first addition to the property. The price was $25,000, and the terms were the same as those for the original purchase and addition. By 1832, Durnford held assets of land and slaves against a $79,500 debt. He was already producing and selling sugar: His first crop had gone to market in 1831.

Sugar planter was a prestigious title for Durnford's vexatious occupations: farmer, manufacturer, wholesale merchant, and slave owner/manager. Sugar cane cultivation was no simple undertaking in southern Louisiana, where climate made successful crops a challenge. In the frost-free Caribbean cane grows continuously, and farmers cut when they are ready to process. In Louisiana the cane

does not reach maturity but usually develops enough to produce granulated sugar if planters carefully balance the increase in sugar that growing days represent against the risk of destruction by severe weather, a risk that expands as the season extends: Cut too early and sacrifice sugar; cut too late and lose cane. Caribbean cane regenerates from the old roots for a decade or more, but the Louisiana planter could expect at best two regrowth (ratoon) crops from seed; so about a third of each crop was committed for replanting.

Sugar produced on plantations—raw, or plantation, sugar—is a light brown crystal that is sold to consumers and refiners or, in Durnford's day, to confectioners who worked it into white sugar and its by-products, brown and dark brown sugar. Molasses, which imparts the color to plantation sugar and derivatives, is a by-product of sugar cane manufacturing. Nineteenth-century molasses was sold to firms with advanced machinery for further processing or to distillers. The quality of plantation sugar, and the price it commanded, was determined by the planter's processing equipment. The better the machinery, the higher the price, but of course superior machinery was expensive. Simple horse-driven hand-fed mills were inexpensive, but they did not extract as much juice from the cane as the expensive steam-powered grinding machines driving gangs of steel rollers that repeatedly squeezed the pulpy cane. Durnford may have begun operations with a small mill, but he purchased a steam engine in 1832 for $3,745 (drawing on McDonogh for credit). The engine was probably sold complete with mill.

If properly managed by a professional sugar maker, open kettles were sufficient to produce crystallized sugar. Advanced equipment replaced the open flame of the kettles with steam heat piped from the engine boiler into steam jackets. Steam permitted better control of the boiling process by which excess water was removed from the sugar juice; burning and discoloration were reduced, and sugar quality and prices were improved. Durnford employed a steam process. Steam allowed the boiling of molasses to produce second sugar, which brought more on the market than the molasses. Steam was also used to create a partial vacuum in the kettles for boiling at temperatures below the 100° C required at atmospheric pressure. Although Durnford did not use Norbert Rillieux's advanced vacuum-pan system, the two free black men were acquainted.

Cane growing and sugar manufacturing were complicated by the usual routines of large agribusiness. Durnford had to make trade-offs between cane and food crops. The more land he put into cane, the more food he had to buy for his family, slave force, and livestock. Typically Durnford determined to be self-sufficient in food because he found it difficult and expensive to procure, but if the cane looked good in its early stages of development, he plowed under the corn and replaced it with cane. If he was fortunate and made a fine sugar crop, he found that the other sugar planters also had good crops; so sugar and molasses prices were down because of swollen supply, and food prices were up because most planters had likewise neglected food for cane.

Once the crop was harvested and manufactured, Durnford faced the market.

From his first crop in 1831 until John McDonogh died in 1850, Durnford usually relied on his friend to sell the sugar and molasses on consignment as best he could. In some years, if McDonogh or McDonogh's agent did not succeed in selling the products of St. Rosalie, Durnford assumed the responsibility himself. The results were rarely satisfactory; Durnford could not remain long in New Orleans to manage his business, and when he was in town the buyers usually got the better of the impatient, inexperienced planter.

Durnford's aggravation with the market spurred him to express his business philosophy in letters to McDonogh. "Did I not write you that there is too much selfishness about New Orleans? The nest of thieves think of nothing but money." In 1834 when he wrote, "You know my aversion for borrowing money; the world in general thinks too much of that article for my use," he was in debt to McDonogh for over $80,000. In that same year he stated, "Money is the perdition of certain people who could have died and lived happily without it." Summing up his philosophy of business and life he wrote: "Poor Mankind! How it has become degraded. . . . I think society is made up of two distinct parts. On the one hand wolves and foxes, and on the other hand lambs and chickens providing food for the former."

Part of operating a business is managing labor. Durnford worked his plantation with his own slaves, rented slaves, and hired free labor—slave owners typically employed free labor to perform work that would endanger the health of their capitalized labor force. Durnford purchased slaves from McDonogh and from the New Orleans market. Although he sold a few of his people, they were transfers to freed parents; he did not buy and sell slaves as a business. In 1835, eschewing the professional slavers, Durnford accompanied his sugar and molasses to market in Philadelphia and then went to Virginia in pursuit of bargains in slaves. His letters to McDonogh reveal the market for people and the difficulties and expenses of transporting coffles from Virginia to New Orleans.

At that time, Durnford purchased 25 men, women, and children to add to his St. Rosalie slave force, but the experience sufficiently impressed Durnford that he made no further adventures to the slave-selling states. At his death in 1859 Durnford owned 77 slaves with an estimated market value of $71,550. Although McDonogh supported plans for the private abolition of slavery, Durnford doubted enough slave owners supported such programs to permit success. On Christmas Eve day in 1843, he wrote: "The total extinction of slavery in these United States will be in future ages to come. . . . Self interest is too strongly rooted in the bosom of all that breathes the American atmosphere. Self interest is a la mode."

Durnford's medical practice was an adjunct to his slave business. In an era of primitive health care a fortune in slaves could be annihilated quickly by disease or slowly from overwork and malnutrition. One physician was as good as another and not measurably better than an informed layperson. Durnford was hailed a physician and entreated to bring his talents to neighboring plantations and farms to administer to family and slaves. Durnford also treated his family, himself, and his slaves. Returns from the medical business were reflected in the well-being of his family and labor force and the respect of the community, but not in money. Durnford treated his medical work beyond the plantation as a charitable function.

Was Durnford a successful businessman? No. He held his sugar plantation together by paying interest on a debt that McDonogh declined to foreclose. At McDonogh's death, Durnford was forced to sell a portion of St. Rosalie to satisfy long-standing debt. A year-by-year analysis of his sugar and molasses production reveals a plantation overcapitalized for its capacity. Specifications of costs and interest rates influence the outcomes of profit studies, but not even unrealistically low figures would pull the estimates of Durnford's profitability into a positive range. Profitability notwithstanding, the Durnfords lived the life of country gentry, not from entrepreneurial success but from the labor of slaves. Durnford died on his plantation. His family lost St. Rosalie to creditors during the Civil War.

SELECTED BIBLIOGRAPHY: Andrew Durnford Collection, Louisiana State Museum, New Orleans; David O. Whitten, *Andrew Durnford: A Black Sugar Planter in Antebellum Louisiana* (Natchitoches, LA: Northwestern State University Press, 1981; reprinted, with a new introduction, New Brunswick, NJ: Transaction Publishers, Rutgers University, 1995); David O. Whitten, "A Black Entrepreneur in Antebellum Louisiana," *Business History Review* 45 (Summer 1971); David O. Whitten, "Rural Life along the Mississippi: Plaquemines Parish, Louisiana, 1830–1850," *Agricultural History* 48, 3 (July 1984); David O. Whitten, "Slave Buying in 1835 Virginia as Revealed by Letters of a Louisiana Negro Sugar Planter," *Louisiana History* 11 (Summer 1970).

David O. Whitten

E

ELLISON, WILLIAM (1790–1861), South Carolina, cotton gin maker, repairer, planter.

Born in Fairfield District, South Carolina, and originally named April, by his death, William Ellison was one of the richest African Americans in the South, perhaps the richest outside Louisiana. According to the 1860 census, his assets amounted to $68,000. At that time he owned 63 slaves, some 800 acres of land, and a thriving cotton gin business. After his death Ellison's family made a considerable fortune selling provisions to the Confederate government, suggesting that the family at that point was more southern than black.

Ellison's mother was an unknown slave, and his father was either William Ellison or his son Robert, both white planters. In 1802 William Ellison apprenticed him to a master ginwright, William McCreight, with whom he worked until 1816, when he purchased his freedom from William Ellison and moved to Stateburg, in the Sumter District of South Carolina. In 1817, he purchased the freedom of his wife Matilda (d. 1850) and a daughter Eliza Ann. Ellison had four other children. His daughter Maria (b. 1815) remained a slave throughout Ellison's life, although he purchased her in 1830. Manumission was difficult, requiring special permission from the state assembly, and manumitted slaves were required to leave the state, unless special permission was obtained from the legislature. Maria, however, lived as a free black in fact if not in law.

Ellison established himself as a cotton gin repairer and manufacturer soon after his manumission and achieved great success. By 1820 he owned two male slave artisans. In 1822 he spent the exorbitant sum of $375 to purchase an acre of land on a crossroads location where he founded a cotton gin manufacturing establishment. He had a considerable professional reputation, and planters from as far away as Mississippi purchased his cotton gins. In the 1830s Ellison expanded into plantation agriculture, using his artisan slaves as collateral for an 1837 loan of $5,094.68, which he used to purchase field hands. By 1840 he owned 30 slaves, including women and children. Eleven were agricultural workers, and 12 worked in the cotton gin shop. By that time he had spent some $6,700 on 335 acres of land. In 1860 he had 44 agricultural slaves working 800 acres of land. They produced 80 bales of cotton as well as peas and corn.

William Ellison was in some ways an exceptional man. Although born a slave, he died one of the richest African Americans in the South and one of the richest men in his region. He was fortunate in being apprenticed to a man who taught him a trade that was absolutely vital to every southern cotton farmer. Also, he contributed to the design of an improved cotton gin. Ellison's business success, aside from its moral implications, would be notable even if he were not an African American, and that his success came in the antebellum South makes it all the more remarkable.

SELECTED BIBLIOGRAPHY: Michael P. Johnson and James L. Roark, *Black Masters: A Free Family of Color in the Old South* (New York: W. W. Norton & Company, 1984); Larry Koger, *Black Slaveowners: Free Black Slave Masters in South Carolina, 1790–1860* (Columbia: University of South Carolina Press, 1994); Loren Schweninger, *Black Property Owners in the South, 1790–1915* (Urbana: University of Illinois Press, 1990).

Ian Binnington

EMPLOYMENT PATTERNS, BLACK BUSINESS. Declining blue-collar employment at the nation's largest corporations and the interrelated phenomenon of shrinking employment of less-skilled workers in manufacturing generally are weakening the employment prospects of groups, such as African American males, traditionally reliant on industrial jobs. Net creation of low-skilled and blue-collar employment opportunities in recent years has been most pronounced in the small business arena. Largely unprotected by antidiscrimination safeguards, black workers compete for employment in a small business sector where institutionalized practices tend to undercut their chances of being hired. Small businesses that utilize paid employees are overwhelmingly owned by nonminorities. Among the very small firms in this sector, employees are most commonly either members of the immediate family, relatives, or friends. Employees are likely to be members of social networks that are family based; blacks are not likely to be included in the applicable networks.

Affirmative action, equal employment opportunity law, and policies, by their very nature, are not designed to assist the black worker who is seeking employment in this milieu. Consider, for example, the landmark Executive Order 11246, which established rules for nondiscrimination by federal contractors, subcontractors, and construction projects operating with federal assistance. Contractors with 50 or more employees and contracts of $50,000 or more were required to develop and submit affirmative action compliance programs with goals and timetables for the hiring and promotion of minorities. The key phrase here is "with 50 or more employees." The relevance of social networks to job access helps to explain why the racial composition of the workforce employed by black-owned businesses differs so profoundly from that employed by non-minority enterprises. These small firms largely draw employees from family-based networks, and blacks are commonly not members of these networks. For essentially the same reasons, black-owned firms employ a labor force consisting almost entirely of minority workers.

A large-scale study of 28 major metropolitan areas measured the incidence of minority employees on the payrolls of small businesses owned by whites and blacks. While over 93 percent of the black business employers rely upon minorities to fill 50 percent or more of their available jobs, nearly 60 percent of the nonminority employers have no minority employees. Among black employers, whose firms were located in nonminority sections of the applicable 28 large metropolitan areas, 86.7 percent of them had workforces that were made up of 50 percent or more minorities; most of these relied on minority employees for over 75 percent of their workforce. Among the white-owned small businesses in these same areas, most firms had no minority employees whatsoever. Prevalence of minority employees typifies large as well as small black firms, white-collar industries such as finance and insurance, and blue-collar industries such as manufacturing and construction.

Looking solely at minority communities located in these same 28 metropolitan areas, 96.2 percent of the black-owned firms but only 37.6 percent of the white-owned small businesses employed a predominantly minority labor force. Black firms located outside the minority community are clearly much more likely to hire minority employees than nonminority-owned businesses located within minority residential areas. The evidence clearly indicates that, irrespective of firm location, white-owned small businesses tend to employ whites, whereas African American firms tend not to. This pattern is consistent with the hypothesis that the network-hiring propensities of small business owners tend to limit the employment alternatives of black job seekers. Underrepresentation of African Americans in the ranks of small business ownership potentially becomes a major obstacle to black job seekers in a world where (1) new job opportunities are increasingly likely to be found in the small business sector and (2) white owners of small businesses prefer to draw their employees from networks that contain few blacks.

Black-owned firms employed fewer than 250,000 workers nationwide in 1987. If most of the jobs available in the small business sector are found in white-owned firms, and most of the white-owned firms prefer to hire relatives, family members, friends, and friends of friends—few of whom are black—then it follows that black job seekers will fare poorly in this sector. In the small business world of network hiring, black workers will tend to have greatest job access when black-owned businesses are hiring. These firms have, after all, already demonstrated their hiring priorities. In such a world, expanded black ownership of small business is an option worthy of serious consideration.

SELECTED BIBLIOGRAPHY: Timothy Bates, *Banking on Black Enterprise* (Washington, DC: Joint Center for Political and Economic Studies, 1993); Timothy Bates, "Utilization of Minority Employees in Small Business: A Comparison of Nonminority and Black-Owned Urban Enterprises," *Review of Black Political Economy* 23, 1 (Summer 1994); Daniel Fusfield, *Political Economy of the Urban Ghetto* (Carbondale: Southern Illinois University Press, 1984); Bennett Harrison and Barry Bluestone, *The Great U-Turn: Corporate Restructuring and the Polarization of America* (New York: Basic Books, 1985).

Timothy Bates

ENCLAVES, ENTREPRENEURIAL. An *enclave* is a community that has both residential houses and business enterprises. Enterprises hold the community together and provide economic stability for business owners, jobs for family members and other members of the community, role models for children, and income for the continued education of children. Although enclaves have been a component part of the research literature, it was not until recently that scholars began to give a strong consideration to the importance of enclaves.

Much of the research on enclaves is concerned with the development of business activity by racial and ethnic groups. Enclave theory takes as its major topic of interest the process by which groups capitalize and maintain enterprises as going concerns. As such it is concerned with the entire development of communities that revolve around a business axis—communities that put business enterprise at the center of the analysis. Although enclaves have been around since the inception of the country, its researchers are just beginning to understand how important they have been for ethnic or racial groups to achieve a degree of economic success in America.

Singularly important for the socioeconomic advancement of enclave residents is that these business communities have long served the function of launching children into higher education, thus allowing them to compete in the labor force for the best jobs. Research has consistently shown that children of business owners have a long tradition of attending colleges and universities. For example, Edna Bonacich and John Modell found that higher education of children was one of the most consistent outcomes of the Japanese experience in California at the turn of the century. This has also been true of black Americans. Because of the reality of racial discrimination, however, they were not able to take their education to the labor market and compete with whites and other nonblack racial groups. As early as 1938, the sociologist Charles Johnson, in *The Negro College Graduate*, emphasized that the importance of higher education was very strong.

As noted in *Entrepreneurship and Self-Help among Black Americans*, black business communities were the launching pads for the black graduates and black success. Recent research shows that as early as 1910 blacks were more likely to be self-employed than whites, thus pointing to the fact that black educational success is standing on the shoulders of black entrepreneurs. Indeed, blacks in this tradition, who can trace their roots back to a self-employed person, are more likely to be in the third or fourth generation of college matriculation. Thus, enclaves have always been important as launching pads for success. Although there have been many enclaves in the black experience, Durham, North Carolina, and Tulsa, Oklahoma, are two that have been primary subjects of research for scholars throughout the years.

Before scholars developed concepts such as dual economy and dual labor market, the American economy was a collection of small businesses, run mainly by families within communities. As ethnic groups immigrated to this country, cities developed economies that reflected names of the old country. Thus, in all major cities, especially on the eastern seaboard, one could find a "little" Italy, Poland, or Germany. These "unassimilated" turn-of-the-century America groups essentially tried to create businesses that would bring about economic stability. For those who created "successful" businesses, their lives became more "comfortable." They were able to build homes away from the old ethnic neighborhoods and send their children to universities and colleges. For Euro-American immigrant families, a class structure revolving around education and economic standing was evolving. Sociologists began to document the assimilation process, showing how economic stability accrued to second-generation ethnic groups as they learned the lessons of thrift, education, and the American economy.

Durham, North Carolina, is an excellent example of an early enclave of business activity among black Americans. At the turn of the century, it was called "The Black Wall Street* of America." Early research indicates the powerful image of Durham, a city that was held up by America as a center of enterprise. In 1923, after a research visit to that city, the sociologist E. F. Frazier noted: "We have in Durham today the outstanding group of colored capitalists who have entered the second generation of business enterprise. . . . These men have mastered the technique of modern business and acquired the spirit of modern enterprise."

Durham was indeed a special kind of enclave. In 1910, when the black business leadership was escorting Booker T. Washington* through the hinterlands of North Carolina, Washington was very impressed with "farms, truck farms, well-kept grocery stores, thriving drug stores, insurance houses, and beautiful though modest homes." He repeatedly expressed to the Negro businessmen in charge of his travels that here were excellent encouraging signs of Negro business development. And the men repeatedly kept saying that he hadn't seen anything yet—"Wait till you get to Durham."

Black Americans were excited about Durham at the turn of the century because it stood as an example of economic progress and the development of successful business enterprises. Not only did this community have service businesses; it also had enterprises dedicated to manufacturing. The beginning and success of these enterprises can be traced to the willingness of African Americans to invest in businesses and the support of the white community of Durham. Consider the analysis of Durham by the famous historian William Kenneth Boyd, who was also impressed with the Afro-American community of Durham. In his 1927 book on Durham he noted that the "progress of the whites has been accompanied by corresponding progress among the Negroes." He attributed their progress to the character of the early blacks who settled in Durham after 1865, whom he described as "industrious and thrifty citizens" who "established a tradition of industry, reliability, and integrity." Continuing with his analysis, he notes the importance of opportunity vis-à-vis the white community, emphasizing, "A second factor in the progress of the Negro has been the policy of the white people, a policy of tolerance and helpfulness."

The enclave in Durham operated a successful hosiery mill. Significant numbers of blacks within the community were hired in addition to white salespeople to carry the product nationwide. The reality of segregation within American society meant that Afro-American salespeople could not penetrate the white market. Also, in Durham, the leading manufacturer of bricks was an African American who closely operated with Payton Smith, a general contractor who had built some of the largest buildings in the city of Durham.

After black enterprises were stable, the community organized the Durham Commercial and Security Company, with the purpose of aiding and financing Negro enterprises of all sorts. Indeed, black business in the city was so stable and so promising for the future that in 1925 Durham was selected as the site for the National Negro Finance Corporation (NNFC), capitalized at $1 million. Its president was Robert R. Moton, successor to Booker T. Washington at Tuskegee, and Charles C. Spaulding* was vice president. The purpose of NNFC was to provide working capital for individuals, firms, and corporations in all parts of the United States, to point out new opportunities for investment, to market securities, and to stimulate business among Negroes. There were also successful banks and insurance companies established within the enclave in addition to a professional class of doctors, lawyers, and others. Durham stands as an excellent example of a community that dedicated itself to the importance of business enterprise and an excellence that can still be seen today.

Tulsa, Oklahoma, also provides an example of an enclave. Throughout world history, scholars have documented the relationship between the economic success of a group in an enclave and the hostility from the larger society that can be associated with that success. The Ibo in Africa, the Jews in Europe, and the East Indians in Africa have all experienced this hostility. Tulsa, Oklahoma, represents this experience in the tradition of black Americans, a story of destruction and rebirth. It is in this tradition that the Greenwood district of Tulsa was built. This district was like others within the African American tradition. Unlike immigrants of European descent who came to Tulsa, it was different for the African American businessperson to expand his interests outside the community. It is important to understand the background of this historical enclave.

The settlement of African Americans in Oklahoma dates from about 1830.

Although they were part of early expeditions, most came with the Native Americans on the "Trail of Tears." When the American government relocated the "five civilized tribes" from the Southeast so that the cotton kingdom could grow, these tribes brought their slaves with them. Emancipation brought allotments of land and new beginnings. Like African Americans in other states, legal battles over segregation and discrimination are testimony to the quality of race relations from the end of the Civil War to the turn of the century. The first bill presented to the Oklahoma Senate, after statehood was granted in 1907, provided for Jim Crow public transportation. Although African American protest groups sought to develop the state along egalitarian lines, legal systems of racial inequality triumphed. Soon Oklahoma resembled other southern states that had killed the political aspirations of black Americans.

In 1905 the oil boom made Tulsa into a center of commerce. Between 1900 and 1921 the population grew from 1,390 to 98,878, but unlike white American immigrant groups, blacks were not welcome to locate their enterprises in the business district. They also were not welcomed as customers. It was this situation that created the enclave called Greenwood. According to Scott Ellsworth, the first two blocks of Greenwood Avenue was known as "Deep Greenwood," which comprised the heart of Tulsa's black community and was known by some as "The Negro Wall Street." The avenue was lined by two- and three-story brick buildings, which housed a variety of commercial establishments, including a dry goods store, two theaters, groceries, confectioneries, restaurants, and billiard halls. In addition, there were four hotels and 11 rooming houses. Also, Tulsa's unusually large number of black lawyers, doctors, and other professionals established their offices in the "Deep Greenwood" area. In the tradition of most racial and ethnic enclaves, service enterprises were dominant.

In 1921, "Deep Greenwood," however, was destroyed by a race riot. With the initial exchange of gunfire, several people died. As shooting between the races continued, African Americans retreated to the business community of "Little Africa." At first the white community was satisfied in containing blacks to this section. But for reasons unknown, whites began to "invade" the community and destroyed black businesses. The $84,000 Mount Zion Church was burned to the ground. When the riot ended, over 50 people had died. The entire section known as Black Wall Street—over 1,000 homes and businesses—lay in ruins. Thousands of occupations were lost, producing significant unemployment, and the lives of African Americans in Tulsa were changed because of the loss of "Little Africa."

The racial climate in which the "ugly disaster" occurred is important to understand. Like other African American communities, there remained the issue of civil rights. In 1920, the year before the destruction of the Black Wall Street, W.E.B. Du Bois spoke in Tulsa, generating interest in the establishment of a branch of the National Association for the Advancement of Colored People (NAACP). A chapter of the African Blood Brothers in Tulsa, however, argued not only for business development but also for paramilitary organizations to protect the community. There were also significant numbers of World War I veterans who had fought overseas and were somewhat adamant about the development of civil rights. While African American religious leaders spoke against the possible use of violence, they did note that people should use arms when necessary to protect their homes. The years to come brought an intense period of racial inequality, the marches of the 1950s and 1960s, and the passage of the Civil Rights Bill.

There are many entrepreneurial enclaves in the history of black America. In a real sense they are as important as the political movement in which black Americans engaged during the 1950s and 1960s. They represent the hidden springboards on which the success of black Americans now rests.

SELECTED BIBLIOGRAPHY: Edna Bonacich and John Modell, *The Economic Basis of Ethnic Solidarity* (Berkeley: University of California Press, 1980); William Kenneth Boyd, *The Story of Durham* (Durham, NC: Duke University Press, 1927); John Sibley Butler, *Entrepreneurship and Self-Help among Black Americans: A Reconsideration of Race and Economics* (New York: State University of New York Press, 1991); John Sibley Butler and Kenneth L. Wilson, "Entrepreneurial Enclaves: An Exposition into the Afro-American Experience," *National Journal of Sociology* 2, 2 (Fall 1988); Scott Ellsworth, *Death in a Promised Land* (Baton Rouge: Louisiana State University Press, 1982); Jimmie Lewis Franklin, *Blacks in Oklahoma* (Norman: University of Oklahoma Press, 1980); E. Franklin Frazier, "Durham: Capital of the Black Middle Class," in Winold Reiss, ed., *The New Negro* (New York: Albert and Charles Boni, 1925); Charles S. Johnson, *The Negro College Graduate* (Chapel Hill: University of North Carolina Press, 1938).

John Sibley Butler

ENTERPRISE ZONES. In the post–civil rights era, enterprise zones were programs developed to revitalize America's most seriously distressed neighborhoods and communities. The concept originated in Britain by Professor Peter Hall of Reading University in 1977 as the "Freeport" solution to the decline of inner-city communities. He suggested that businesses and jobs could be created within these areas if the same policies that stimulated entrepreneurship and economic development in Hong Kong during the 1950s and 1960s were utilized. For businesses this would mean freedom from governmental controls and low taxation. The areas would be absent of rent, price, and wage controls. Only minimum health and safety standards would be sought.

Building on Professor Hall's Freeport solution, in 1978 Sir Geoffrey Howe, Chancellor of the Exchequer in Prime Minister Thatcher's government, put forward the enterprise zone concept. Howe proposed that enterprise zones could be used as extensive urban policy, to economically revitalize extremely deteriorated urban areas. Businesses within the zones would be exempt from property taxes; they would receive exemptions for expenses related to investment in buildings and machinery. The proposal also called for the relaxation of zoning and planning regulations within the enterprise zone.

While enterprise zones were being discussed and implemented in Britain in the late 1970s through the early 1980s, the economy in the United States was undergoing a recession. The recession of 1980 was one of the most severe downturns since the recession of 1953–1954. Average unemployment was almost 12 percent; for whites and African Americans, it was 6 and 14 percent, respectively. Ronald Reagan was campaigning for president, and a general trend of fiscal and political conservatism was taking hold in America. Public concern focused on reducing federal spending and governmental regulations as a way to reverse the economic downturn.

During the late 1970s and early 1980s, two reports were issued that were to have a significant impact on the future of enterprise zones in the United States. One of the documents was the *Sourcebook on Enterprises Zones* issued by the Sabre Foundation, a Washington, D.C.–based research, lobbyist organization and proponent of enterprise zones. The report provided detailed analysis of a wide range of programs that could be utilized to develop enterprise zones. The report also included model state enterprise zone legislation that was soon to be utilized by legislators to enact enterprise zone legislation. The Sabre Foundation and its *Sourcebook* became one of the major resources to influence enactment of enterprise zone legislation in nearly 40 states. The other influential document, *Enterprise Zones: A Solution to the Urban Crisis?*, was written in 1979 by Stuart M. Butler, a policy analyst with the Heritage Foundation, a conservative research organization. In this and another report, *Enterprise Zones: Pioneering in the Inner City*, Butler succinctly presented the argument for enterprise zones as a conservative policy for revitalization of America's most distressed inner-city neighborhoods.

The enterprise zone concept and subsequent proposals represented a different and new approach to solving America's urban problems. The Heritage Foundation reports prepared by Butler, for example, proposed suspension of minimum wage laws within zones. This would be done to stimulate employers to hire zone employees. The Heritage Foundation also suggested instituting below–minimum wage laws within the zones. The objective of this proposal would be to encourage employers to employ youth. Advocates of enterprise zones also proposed that instead of massive federal aid to inner cities for housing and employment programs the private sector could revitalize America's most deteriorated neighborhoods. Their contention was that federal spending on social programs, such as the War on Poverty programs, and federal housing and community development programs did not reverse urban blight but instead contributed to the federal deficit and were ineffective.

In 1980, Congressman Jack Kemp introduced the first enterprise legislation in Congress. In 1980, Ronald Reagan in a speech to the National Convention of the Urban League presented the enterprise zones concept as a major element for urban policy. In his 1982 State of the Union Message to Congress, President Reagan proposed enterprise zones as a federal approach for urban policy, and in March 1982, the Reagan administration's enterprise zone proposal was released. The basic tenet of the proposal was that the free market economy could solve the problems of America's urban areas. The proposal called for the creation of a free market environment by the removal of taxes and the burden of governmental regulations.

The Reagan administration's proposal further maintained that a federal enterprise zone program would require no federal appropriations to create jobs and rebuild the economy of the worst inner-city neighborhoods. The proposal encouraged providing incentives to businesses located within the zones. The intent was to provide public sector incentives that would stimulate private sector free market economic activity, thereby increasing economic investment, jobs, and revitalization within the zone. The Reagan administration's proposal also recommended tax relief at all levels of government, regulatory relief, improved delivery of neighborhood services (primarily by privatization), and lastly, the formation of for-profit neighborhood associations, referred to as *neighborhood enterprise associations.*

The federal program was based on the premise that state and local governments would design and implement programs, which would be similar to the federal program. States were to compete for designation as a federal enterprise zone. Then states would be selected to participate in the federal program based on the similarity of their program to the federal zone program and the effectiveness of their program. In anticipation of obtaining federal designation as an enterprise zone program, almost 40 states implemented enterprise zone programs without a funded federal program being enacted.

Although state and local enterprise zone programs were enacted in anticipation of a federal program, they were also implemented in order for states and localities to compete with each other to attract businesses, thereby creating jobs. Given the dramatic cutback in federal spending after Ronald Reagan assumed the presidency, there was a perceived need for the programs. Enterprise zones were viewed as one of the few alternatives available for economic development. Following the Reagan administration's free market philosophy for enterprise zones, state programs included many program components similar to those in the *Sourcebook on Enterprise Zones* and the administration's proposed legislation. For example, state programs included items such as state income tax exemption on gains from the sale of qualified zone property, sales tax exemption, a moratorium on property taxes, and regulatory relief.

Studies on the effectiveness of enterprise zones have yielded results that have not been totally consistent. Even though results of enterprise programs are debatable, the overall consensus of the research shows that the programs have not had a significant impact in creating jobs for economically disadvantaged zone residents and are at best marginal with regard to this specific objective. Creating employment opportunities was one of the major objectives of proposed federal legislation, but as a result of studies, such as that produced by the U.S. General Accounting Office, indicating the high cost of a federal program, the importance of enterprise zones as an effective program for reducing urban ills weakened.

With the 1992 election of William Clinton as president, national urban policy turned away from the conservative policy of enterprise zones as a major program for the economic revitalization of America's most distressed inner-city neighborhoods and communities. At the end of the twentieth century, the need for economic revitalization of these communities, however, persists.

SELECTED BIBLIOGRAPHY: Stuart M. Butler, *Enterprise Zones: Pioneering in the Inner City* (Washington, DC: Heritage Foundation, 1980); Mark Frazier, ed., *Sourcebook on Enterprise Zones* (Washington, DC: Sabre Foundation, 1981); Earl R. Jones. "Enterprise Zones—Promise or Product for the Black Community," *Western Journal of Black Studies* 11, 1 (Spring 1987); National Urban League, *Can Enterprise Zones Work for Us* (Washington, DC: Urban League, 1982); White House, *The Administration's Enterprise Zone Proposal* (Washington, DC: White House, 1982).

Earl R. Jones

ENTREPRENEUR MODELS, BLACK COMMUNITY ECONOMIC DEVELOPMENT.

The potential of an entrepreneurial strategy to improve the circumstances of African Americans, both historically and contemporarily, can be assessed using the following four measures of economic development:

Size (S1). Does the strategy increase the annual gross domestic product (GDP) national income of the African community?

Structure (S2). How does the strategy affect the functional distribution of income flows to land, labor, and capital? How does it impact the stock and productivity of land, labor, and capital held in the African American community?

Shape (S3). What are the strategy's distributional effects on income and wealth among households in the African American community? Does it increase/decrease the degree of income and wealth inequality in the African American community?

Share (S4). Does the strategy reduce the disparity of income and wealth between the African American community and the white community of the United States?

These indicators can be represented by the equations:

$$S1 = w_{bt} L_{bt} + i_{bt} K_{bt} + r_{bt} Ld_{bt}$$
$$S2 = w_{bt} L_{bt} / (w_{bt} L_{bt} + i_{bt} K_{bt} + r_{bt} Ld_{bt} iK_{bt}) / (w_{bt} L_{bt} + i_{bt} K_{bt} + r_{bt} Ld_{bt}) r_{bt} Ld_{bt} / (w_{bt} L_{bt} + i_{bt} K_{bt} + r_{bt} Ld_{bt})$$
$$S3 = \text{Gini coefficients for income and wealth}$$
$$S4 = [w_{bt} L_{bt} + i_{bt} K_{bt} + r_{bt} Ld_{bt} / (w_{wt} L_{wt} + i_{wt} K_{wt} + r_{wt} Ld_{wt}), \text{ as a ratio of } Pop_{wt}]$$

where

w_{gt} = average wage rate

L_{gt} = number of labor hours worked

i_{gt} = average rate of profit on capital

K_{gt} = total amount of capital

r_{gt} = average rental rate on land

Ld_{gt} = total amount of land owned

where g = b if African American group membership and w if white and t = time period of interest.

It is assumed the entrepreneur initiates the production process by bringing together land, labor, and capital and assumes the risk of success or failure based on private profit-maximizing calculations. To the extent he or she is successful, S1 increases via the increase in i_{bt}; w_{bt} and r_{bt} will increase, depending on the nature of the production function, that is, to what extent it utilizes L_{bt} and Ld_{bt} to produce the product or service. S2 will be positively affected depending on the good or service produced and whether it increases the stock of economic resources—L_{bt}, Ld_{bt}, and K_{bt}; S3 is unlikely to be affected. There are neither theoretical claims nor historical evidence that free enterprise economic systems tend toward equal distributions of income—w, i, and r—if there are unequal distributions of wealth—K, L, and Ld.

Income inequalities in the African American community will mimic those of white America. The reduction in S4 depends totally on the scale of the production function of the minority entrepreneur relative to his white counterpart. To date, there are no *Fortune* 500 African American corporations. Unless there are land and capital redistribution policies, the enormous historical inequities of land and capital can be expected to persist into the future structuring into the U.S. economy of a perpetual white land and capital advantage.

Empirical estimation of the model's parameters enables one to move from speculation to objective quantification of any development strategy but also provides a common framework and terminology to discuss and debate alternate strategies for economic development of the African American community both historically and contemporarily. Discussions, controversies, debates, and assessments of such issues in the African American community as "uplift," "progress," "development," "empowerment," and "equality" have been characterized by ambiguity acuity reflecting a lack of clarity and specificity in language. The reference model above provides a commonality of terms that will aid discussions across time/history and paradigms.

The great debates of Booker T. Washington* and W.E.B. Du Bois reflect, in the first instance, a different prioritization of the four parameters of economic development for the African American community. More specifically, Washington was committed to S1, increasing in absolute amounts the income flowing to the newly freed slaves. For him the stock of land, labor, and capital owned by the freedmen was a given and not to be changed without incurring the wrath of the former white slave owners. This is reflected in his often-quoted advice to "caste down your pockets where you stand." For him, uplift of the Negro need not be measured by S4—its relation to whites—but rather by how well they make do with what they have.

By contrast, Du Bois was focused on the S4 as the key measure of progress. Moreover, he felt the flow of income—w_{bt} i_{bt}, r_{bt}—would be negligible to the newly freed slaves in the absence of an increase in their ownership of land in the southern states and capital in the northern states. A long-term development strategy had to improve the structure, S3, of the African American community.

Abram Harris,* an academic economist and less known by the general public, weighed into the debate with an emphatic and comprehensive rejection of the ability of an entrepreneurial strategy to achieve any measure of economic progress, given both the relative size of Negro-controlled land, labor, and capital to that of whites and the dynamic of the free enterprise system to not only perpetuate the disparity but increase it over time. In Harris's own words, "The greatest limitation upon the development of Negro enterprises arises from the fact that basic industries, essential raw materials, transportation and finance are all controlled by white capital." For Harris, growth of a Negro middle class had to rely on increasing w_{bt} through the increase in the productivity and occupational composition of L_{bt}. With vigilant attention to the S2 parameter, both Du Bois and Harris rejected the individualistic philosophy of entrepreneurship.

The "militant" separatists, best exemplified by Martin Delany,* in antebellum America, and in the early twentieth century, by Marcus Garvey,* found improvements in S4 impossible, given the historical relationships between subordinate blacks and whites. In their analysis the causes of the disparity in the stock of economic resources was as important as its size. With Delany, African slaves had been the source of capital accumulation of white plantation owners and freed blacks the pool of exploitable labor to increase the profits of the industrial capitalists of the North. The African Americans were a "colonized" people analogous to their African ancestors.

Government intervention policies to alleviate the economic suffering of the Great Depression of the 1930s combined with black participation in World War II and the much heralded prosperity of the 1950s brought small increases in the national income, S1, of African Americans but increased the "gap," S4, between African Americans and whites. Spawned by the civil rights movement and the urban rebellions of the 1960s, debate over development strategies reached new levels of intensity. While some were new, most were revisions of those proposed at the turn of the century. In the 1960s, *self-determination* became the euphemism for those strategies that focused on S1 and emphasized the role of the entrepreneur. No longer protected by segregated African American markets, "buy black" campaigns were an appeal to minority consumers to support minority enterprises as a matter of race unity. The Nation of Islam* is one of the more notable advocates of this strategy.

President Richard Nixon's "Black Capitalism" offered federal subsidies to assist and integrate the African American entrepreneur into the mainstream of the U.S. economy. Unfortunately, the primary agency designated to develop minority enterprises was the Small Business Administration (SBA). But the size of such businesses had little positive impact on African American employment, wages, and resource ownership, S2. In fact, many of the subsidized enterprises claimed a competitive disadvantage if they were to employ unskilled African American labor and to locate in African American communities.

The four-S model of economic development, then, offers historians, political scientists, and policymakers a common frame of reference and nomenclature to compare across both time and disparate ideologies the varied strategies to improve the economic circumstance of the African American community. The four-S model requires the development of a strategy to reduce the disparity of income and wealth between the African American community and the white community in the United States.

The reduction in S4, then, depends totally upon the scale of the production function of the minority entrepreneur relative to his white counterpart. While small businesses, as a category, employ the largest numbers of workers, the comparatively limited numbers of small black businesses precludes them from offering full employment to black America, despite that there are *"Fortune 500"* African American corporations. Consequently, unless there are land and capital redistribution policies, as emphasized, the enormous historical inequities of land and capital can be expected to persist into the future.

SELECTED BIBLIOGRAPHY: William Darity, Jr., ed., *Race, Radicalism, and Reform: Selected Papers of Abram L. Harris* (New Brunswick, NJ: Transaction Publishers, 1991); Abram Harris, *The Negro as Capitalist: A Study of Banking and Business among American Negroes* (Philadelphia: American Academy of Political and Social Science, 1936); Earl Ofari, *The Myth of Black Capitalism* (New York: Monthly Review Press, 1970); Melvin L. Oliver and Thomas M. Shapiro, *Black Wealth, White Wealth: A New Perspective on Racial Inequality* (New York: Routledge, 1995).

Bernadette P. Chachere and Rodney D. Green

ETHICS, AFRICAN AMERICANS AND BUSINESS. Professional ethics involves the desire to do the right thing in relation to business endeavors and within interpersonal relationships. Ethics takes on numerous characteristics as it concerns African Americans. Our ethical framework requires not only a personal ethic but a communal or social ethic as well. Ethics, within this context, provides a basis to address the foundational elements of African American morality and the manner in which it affects our business endeavors. Much of our understanding of morality is either biblical or grounded in an African historical context, which also provides a basis to consider the implications of such an ethical framework and how it does or should influence African American thinking in relation to ethical behavior.

Webster's Dictionary defines *moral* as "relating to dealing with or capable of making the distinction between right and wrong in conduct." Human society, inspired by figures such as Plato, Aristotle, and Sophocles, has created literature that addresses the issue of justice and morality. Western as well as nontraditional philosophers have also addressed the issue of morality, justice, and ethical behavior. It should be noted that one's understanding of ethics and morality is, of course, based upon a person's worldview. Persons who come from a Eurocentric context have a worldview that differs from those who live in developing nations or are people of color. Business ethics and the ability to "do the right thing" are affected by this clash of cultures and perceptions of what actually represents ethical business activity.

The first written evidence of human morality appeared in an ancient Ethiopian drama during the twenty-fifth dynasty (712–633 B.C.), according to Wilton Blake. The Memphis Drama, as it was known, was chiseled in black basalt in order to preserve its teachings to future generations. The principal test of the Memphis Drama sets out the moral code of society accordingly: "And thus justice is given to one who does what is loved and punishment is given to one who does what is hated. Thus, also, is life given to the peaceful and death given to the one who violates the Law."

The Memphis Drama emphasizes that African society is based upon a religious and moral foundation. The Drama also establishes the African ethic placing the welfare of the community above that of the individual. In fact, if an individual is a threat to African society, through immoral or unethical behavior, it is better that the person is eliminated from the society. The Memphis Drama therefore seems to condone capital punishment, if it is used to eradicate immoral and unethical elements from the society. This harsh moral framework is the foundation of African American thinking with regard to ethics and morality.

In the United States, Corporate America is driven by the free market enterprise system of capitalism, where businesses take a utilitarian or bottom-line approach in the marketplace. The primary factors that generally drive American business are (1) the greatest good for the greatest number, which generally translates into doing that which benefits the most executive staff and shareholders, and (2) limiting corporate expenditures, at any cost, in order to maximize corporate profits. According to Al Y. Chen, Roby B. Sawyer, and Paul F. Williams, ethicists, then, are faced with the dilemma of challenging rigid corporate structures with innovative changes designed to change traditions and effectuate ethical decision making. Consequently, there has been a call to develop a view of business as a moral practice. In such a context, managers are concerned about the ethical consequences of their decisions. Paramount in such an ethical framework is the creation of values that enhance the welfare of communities and persons.

Some would posit that managers have the ethical obligation to fulfill the expectations of corporate shareholders. From a legal perspective, managers are agents or fiduciaries of their shareholders, as Joseph L. Badaracco, Jr., notes. Such a view assumes or discounts the necessity of shareholder ethics. Yet, oftentimes, shareholders determine the moral compass of the corporation. In order to address the culture of a corporation, then, it is important to address the attitudes of shareholders. Corporate managers and shareholders must develop a partnership that enables ethical decision making to occur in the workplace. Investors, therefore, must think ethically as they consider their profit-making strategies.

Such partnerships are not easily forged. For example, in the 1980s and 1990s, the antiapartheid movement in this country forced corporate managers and shareholders to make difficult moral decisions concerning the removal of investments in South Africa. The far-ranging goal of such a partnership was based upon the vision of a united South Africa, which would prove to be an even greater investment avenue for investors.

Helping investors to see the benefits of social responsibility and ethical behavior is one of the responsibilities of management as it relates to their fiduciary responsibilities. Corporate managers and executives are challenged to embrace a paradigm shift that affects the way in which we do business. This shift causes corporations to view the world in all of its diversity and recognize that success is ultimately tied to creating an inclusive corporate culture that maximizes the contributions of all persons.

One example of this need to change corporate culture is the way in which business is presently addressing the prevalence of sexual harassment in the workplace. For generations male-dominated corporations functioned without an awareness of, or sensitivity to, the ways in which women were either harassed or discriminated against. The change in corporate structure, reflective of a higher awareness of women's experience, speaks to the issue of ethical behavior. The lesson to be learned from corporate structure is that traditionally women are less valued employees (as is reflected in salary disparity in comparison to their male counterparts), are oftentimes exploited, and are not considered equals.

The matter of race is another area that poses an ethical dilemma for Corporate America. Derrick Bell, in *Faces at the Bottom of the Well*, describes what he calls the Permanence of Racism. Racism, Bell says, is a permanent reality on the American landscape. If racism is inescapable, it is, as Bell articulates, essential for people of color to develop and cultivate skills in order to deal with its perpetual presence. In addressing racism, it is also incumbent upon corporate leadership to assist people of color in the development of skills that will enable them to survive and flourish. One of the paradigm shifts in the corporate culture requires executives to consider the ways in which diversity enhances the value of the corporation.

Creating a corporate culture that enables people of color to make an optimum contribution, then, is an ethical consideration for managers. Moreover, the onslaught of international business competition is transforming the business environment on a global scale. Enhancing the contributions of people of color is not only ethical, but it is cost-effective and makes the most business sense as global competition requires creativity and the maximum participation of a diverse workforce.

The concept of a corporate culture is based upon a community of standards and practices. Corporate cultures are created through a form of socialization and cooperation, but, as Mark Pastin notes, the nature of such corporate cultures is conservative and centered around self-preservation. Corporate cultures are generally shaped by white males who lack sensitivity to the experience of women and people of color. In fact, there is a collision that occurs between conservative corporate cultures and the change that diversity causes. Women and people of color often experience a social schizophrenia because there is a sentient expectation that they will ''fit in'' as opposed to bringing new and innovative cultural experiences and insights to the corporate experience.

One of the ethical requirements of African Americans in such a climate is to resist the temptation to simply ''fit in.'' It is incumbent upon African Americans to educate and influence corporate cultures that oftentimes lack sensitivity to their experience. This may, in some instances, require African Americans to challenge corporate structures and cultures to become more inclusive and open to change. African Americans are called to become transformers of corporate structures in order to enhance the opportunities of others who will follow.

What is required in business ethics, then, is both personal and corporate integrity. The requirement of integrity must be juxtaposed against the reality of sin and evil in the world. Stephen Carter in his work *Integrity* points out the Christian concept of free will and the human ability to make choices and reflectively determine our actions. Christianity expresses that followers should submit to the will of God as an expression of human integrity. Through further analysis, Carter establishes that our concept of integrity is further developed through reflective and sometimes self-sacrificing judgments on right and wrong.

Ethical behavior, then, is borne out of the ability to actively reflect upon one's actions. The basis of such reflection is whether our experience, tradition, and reason tell us if the considered act is right or wrong. Personal and corporate integrity requires moral reflection that enables the individual or entity to avoid evil and will that which is good. Oftentimes we think of evil as only existing in acts such as the Holocaust, ethnic cleansing in Bosnia, or the Oklahoma City bombing, but it is much more basic. The reality of evil and moral decay begins with the incidental and unreflective acts of dishonesty that grow to the point that they dull our senses to that which is ethical. The daily acts of dishonesty cause persons to lose their moral compass and the ability to discern between right and wrong. Therefore, individuals and corporate structures must constantly reflect upon their actions to determine their efficacy.

In a culture where racism is intrinsic, African Americans must also fulfill the need to improve opportunities and raise the conditions of our people. This is not the particular burden for African Americans, but those of us who have achieved success must not forget others who are left behind. African Americans who have achieved success must impress upon corporate structures the need to provide access and opportunities for other people of color. We must resist becoming tokens within white corporate structures. We are called to be wedges to keep open the doors of corporate and social opportunities to our people. That is why for African Americans ethics are not solely personal but corporate and global.

SELECTED BIBLIOGRAPHY: Joseph L. Badaracco, Jr., *Business Ethics, Roles and Responsibilities* (Chicago: Irwin, 1995); Derrick Bell, *Faces at the Bottom of the Well: The Permanence of Racism* (New York: Basic Books, 1992); Wilton Blake II, "The African Origin of Morality," *Howard Scroll: Social Justice Review* 1, 1 (Fall 1992); Stephen Carter, *Integrity* (New York: Basic Books, 1996), 231; Al Y. Chen, Roby B. Sawyer, and Paul F. Williams, "Reinforcing Ethical Decision Making Through Corporate Culture," *Journal of Business Ethics* 16, 8 (June 1, 1997); Mark Pastin, *The Hard Problems of Management* (San Francisco: Jossey-Bass, 1986), 14.

Larry D. Pickens

ETHICS AND AMERICAN DEMOCRATIC CAPITALISM. Ethics is the branch of philosophy that is concerned with what is morally good and bad, right and wrong; a synonym for it is *moral philosophy*, the study and evaluation of human conduct in the light of moral principles. Moral principles may be viewed either as the standard of conduct that the individual has constructed for himself or as a body of obligations and duties that a particular society requires of its members. Ethics has developed as man has reflected on the intentions and consequences of his acts. From this reflection on the nature of human behavior the business corporation has evolved into a moral institution in its essence.

Business is about creating goods and services, jobs and benefits, and new wealth that did not exist before. The moral nature of business is creative and can transform the conditions of human life for the better or the worse. Those practicing it often see business as a way of giving back to society. Business has a special role to play in bringing hope and economic progress to the poor. And that is one of the noblest callings inherent in all business activities: to raise up the poor. If the huge numbers of poor in the world are ever to lift themselves out of poverty, they need those with ideas and capital to invest in creating the industries, jobs, and wealth that will give the masses a base from which to build. To that end, it could be summarized that to engage in business and create new wealth, ethically, is each citizen's moral assignment in a democratic capitalist society.

The unethical treatment of blacks and the ethical deterioration in business have been a historical problem in democratic capitalism. A democratic society has inherent weaknesses, and maintaining high moral ideals in its business institutions is one of them. For a period of nearly 250 years the institution of slavery fueled the business and economic needs of growing nations. Yet the moral rationale constructed to justify one of man's greatest inhumanities to man was both economically and theologically based. The African came to be looked upon as the source of an almost inexhaustible, cheap, and tractable labor supply. Africa also supplied the Western world not only with labor but with much of the gold that was necessary for a staple money economy in the Western European nations.

In the United States, the profits that the Atlantic slave trade* yielded to New England, for example, were an important factor in the growth of the shipping industry and, at the same time, a source of surplus wealth for American industrialism, as it developed. Preceding the Civil War and, then, Reconstruction, blacks were confined to menial work and little or no economic upward mobility. The politics of Reconstruction, moreover, reflected the initial expression of a profound economic change, the triumph of capitalistic finance and industry over agrarianism and the plantation economy.

In this country, as in western Europe, the triumph of capitalism also carried with it the ascendancy of new ethical ideals—political liberty, legal equality, and enfranchisement for all peoples. Thus the demand of the northern Republicans for equal citizenship for the Negro can be understood only in terms of these broad economic changes and their social consequences. Therefore, the enfranchisement of the Negro served their economic interests.

The Radical Republicans realized that it was only with the aid of the Negro vote that the southern farmer aristocracy, so hostile to northern business interests, could be overturned and the economic legislation that they wanted could be effected. Yet even as new legislation was passed, the federal government withdrew its support of blacks, quietly accepting their economic disfranchisement. White business owners enacted unethical deterrents to limit the growth of enterprise and wealth for blacks. From Reconstruction on, these deterrents included formulating public policies that made it difficult for blacks to obtain capital and credit; earn a living wage; achieve occupational mobility; and acquire real property that could generate wealth. Attempts to redress these inequities were limited in the face of poverty and civic and educational handicaps. Moreover, mob violence driven by racism, envy, and petty jealousies of the economic initiatives of blacks took place with impunity. Even escape to the West was made difficult in the face of racial hostility on settlement.

The New South wanted gradualism. White conservatives believed equal citizenship should be accorded the Negro upon the gradual attainment of education, business acumen, and the accumulation of property. This led to competing ethics and approaches by blacks as to how to solve the problem of Negro economic upward mobility. W.E.B. Du Bois promoted the ideology of civil libertarianism, whereas Booker T. Washington* advocated a program of conciliation, thrift, and industry. Yet from the 1880s on, despite strong unethical deterrents, the black masses, urged by their leadership, were led to place increasing faith in business and property as a means of escaping poverty and achieving economic independence.

The promotion of black business enterprise was ethically motivated primarily by the desire to profit from personal economic initiative, to better their conditions for the sake of their children, and to establish a Negro capitalist employer class for the employment of their people. Between 1888 and 1934, over 134

Negro-owned banks and savings and loans institutions were opened. This period marked an expansion of black capitalism in America. It was driven by the powerful emerging forces of the Negro church, fraternal organizations, and burial societies of such groups as the Masons, Elks, and the Knights of Pythias.

These organizations created the need for black-owned banks because blacks generally were unable to obtain credit from white banks for commercial ventures, building houses or churches. By the turn of the century, black businesses slowly expanded beyond the enterprises historically limited to them (i.e., livery services, tailoring, barbering, cooking, catering, saloon keeping, domestic services, burial services, and farming). Also, blacks gained white-collar training from newly formed Negro financial institutions. Yet their growing population and economic spending power forced many local white-owned businesses to rethink unethical and unprofitable practices. Gradually, with economic pressure from threatened boycotts, whites began to expand job opportunities and provide greater public access to goods and services.

The black struggle for equal opportunity at work and in the community on moral grounds reached its climax with the landmark passage of the 1964 Civil Rights Act, the results of the movement led by Martin Luther King, Jr.* The economic boycotts of Operation PUSH (People United to Save Humanity) led by Reverend Jesse Jackson* extracted jobs and minority purchasing and business opportunities from corporations dependent upon the black consumer. Beginning in the 1970s young white business radicals and liberals began to stress new business values to include equal opportunity, affirmative action, spirituality, protection of the environment, and increasing outreach and care for the indigent. Then, too, blacks raised business ethics to a new level when in 1977 Reverend Leon Sullivan,* a black minister and founder of the Opportunities Industrialization Corp., was the first American to promulgate successfully a Code of Conduct that set the standards for American businesses and institutions operating in South Africa. The Sullivan Principles in large part helped to cause the fall of apartheid.

By the late 1980s, the topic of business ethics began to emerge on center stage, as more and more companies were exposed and heavily fined for gross violations of ethical-based behaviors (i.e., discrimination, health and environmental damage, etc.). It was felt that everywhere Americans turned, there were signs of ethical deterioration in the conduct of business. For blacks in America the deterioration of hard-fought affirmative action laws was facilitated by the courts. There were also racial disparities in annual income for comparable professions. And subsequent studies (the glass ceiling report of 1995) confirmed charges made by blacks against white Corporate America that there was indeed restricted upward mobility in the public and private sectors. Research findings also verified the existence of continued discrimination and redlining in bank-lending policies and housing and insurance coverage. All necessitated a new, ethically based movement focused on economic development and self-help.

This rekindled economic movement in the early 1990s was now being fueled by a more educated and wealthier black population, with a solid business background and a new middle-class status, acting with civil rights protection and greater public access. Embraced by the black church and prestigious national organizations, such as the National Urban League* and the National Association for the Advancement of Colored People (NAACP), this new movement is fueled by historical spiritual beliefs, increased public rhetoric, new books, formal and informal training, and the solid values and ethics that influenced those of America's most inclusive and successful white-owned businesses.

These ethics include a series of internal and external moral business responsibilities, as defined by a variety of noted black and white businessmen, theologians, and ethicists. The internal responsibilities include, but are not limited to, satisfying customers with goods and services of real value; making a reasonable return on the funds entrusted to the business corporation by its investors; creating new wealth; creating new jobs for all willing citizens; defeating envy through generating upward mobility and putting empirical ground under the conviction that hard work and talent are fairly rewarded; promoting invention, ingenuity, and progress in the arts and useful sciences; and promoting a healthy diversity of business interests by encouraging all employees to be as entrepreneurial as possible.

The external moral responsibilities of business include establishing within the business a sense of community and respect for the dignity of all people; encouraging a free society so that businesses may grow unencumbered by political tyranny; exemplifying respect for law; promoting social justice by finding ways to contribute to the improvement of the community; keeping an open line of communication with investors, shareholders, customers, and employees; promoting self-government over big government by taking a leadership role in society; and protecting the business community against public scandal and excessive "for-profit" media depiction of negative business stereotypes. In this light, business ethics today means meeting these responsibilities whether one is a large or small business, black or white owned, and is also inclusive of the businesses established by the nation's new immigrants.

Some of these responsibilities may not seem like ethics at all. They are simply behaviors necessary to make a business succeed, so as to benefit the poor and those willing to work hard, to enable a people and country to flourish, and finally to glorify God—the latter point being a belief African Americans have championed for hundreds of years. In America's business history, the unethical treatment of blacks has slowly but surely reared its ugly head for all the world to see. This amoral treatment has been recognized for its destructive forces on capitalism and democracy. It has moved what was once an overtly racist nation to now understand that "right has Might."

Black America is now engaged in its fourth and final struggle. The first began in the seventeenth century, when blacks struggled to survive the Middle Passage and landed on America's shores alive and sane, then were made to eke out an existence within the extremes of racial oppression while their forced labor profited others. The second struggle ended in the nineteenth century with emancipation from the tyranny of slavery. The third struggle has taken place in the twentieth century with their fight for civil rights and public access to education and jobs. It has taken over 350 years, but they have won each battle on moral grounds. And now the fourth struggle comes at the start of the twenty-first century, and that is to create economic parity for themselves. This struggle will require higher education, strong discipline, expanded relationships, and a moral imperative for each black person to create new wealth for their families and community.

A new American business ethic, if truly embraced and acted upon by all, will lay the foundation for economic development for all in the foreseeable future.

SELECTED BIBLIOGRAPHY: Ken Blanchard and Norman Vincent Peale, *The Power of Ethical Management* (New York: William Morrow and Company, 1988); George C. Fraser, *Race for Success: The Ten Best Business Opportunities for Blacks in America* (New York: William Morrow and Company, 1998); Abram L. Harris, *The Negro as Capitalist: A Study of Banking and Business among American Negroes* (Chicago: Urban Research Press, 1992); John H. Johnson, *Succeeding against the Odds* (New York: Warner Books, 1989); Dennis Kimbro and Napoleon Hill, *Think and Grow Rich: A Black Choice* (New York: Warner Books, 1989); Michael Novak, *Business as a Calling: Work and the Examined Life* (New York: Free Press, 1996).

George C. Fraser

EXTRACTIVE INDUSTRIES, ENTERPRISES. African Americans, both slave and free, by establishing enterprises, participated in developing the nation's extractive industries. In colonial New England, enslaved Africans, using African mining and smithing skills, worked the iron beds and forges at the Hope Furnace and also at the Cranston Forges. Their expertise in mining, as one contemporary said, explains why it was an enslaved African and not a European who in 1710 "discovered the copper deposits of nearby New Barbados Neck, New York." The merchant shipper Paul Cuffe* held part ownership in a New England salt works. By the early nineteenth century, both free blacks and a few slave entrepreneurs* participated in the extractive industries by developing businesses in mining, lumber, and coal.

During the War of 1812, the Kentucky slave Free Frank McWorter* established a saltpeter manufactury, processing saltpeter, the principal ingredient used in making gunpowder, from the crude nitre that he mined from limestone caves. Pulaski County, where he set up his enterprise, was adjacent to Rockcastle County, where crude nitre was also mined and shipped to the gunpowder mills in Lexington. Crude nitre from Kentucky's Mammoth Cave, however, was shipped to the Du Pont gunpowder mills in Wilmington, Delaware. After he purchased his freedom from profits earned in this enterprise, Free Frank expanded his manufactory by opening a branch of this enterprise in Danville, Kentucky. Moving to Illinois in 1830, Free Frank again proceeded with mining activities. He set up an enterprise for stone to be quarried on his Pike County land. In the South, blacks as masons and fencers mined the stone and rock quarries in Fauquier County, Virginia.

The lumber industry, especially, proved profitable for blacks in both the North and South, who established logging and saw mill enterprises. In preindustrial America, the demand for building materials and firewood increased as the nation expanded. Also, until the extensive mining of coal, wood was also used to provide power for steamers, vessels, and factories. In addition, free blacks who owned lumber yards profited from the tremendous expansion of construction and manufacturing; as Martin Delany said, "In this business a very heavy capital is invested." In antebellum America, former slave Stephen Smith* was the most successful lumber merchant. He operated both logging enterprises and lumber yards in Lancaster and Philadelphia, Pennsylvania. In one year alone, the winter of 1849, Smith shipped on his own railroad line "two million two hundred and fifty thousand feet of lumber" from Philadelphia to Baltimore." In western New York, the leading lumber merchants were William Platt and Joseph Cassey.

In the North, all the lumber merchants employed fugitive slaves who as loggers, throughout the cutting and logging period, lived isolated in the forest in lumbermen's shacks, which lessened their chances for capture. In the South, the leading free black lumber and wood dealers owned slaves. Most were employed as loggers, and they also brought in wood from the countryside. In Charleston, South Carolina, the leading wood dealers who owned slaves were Robert Howard, who used slaves in his business from 1841 to 1865, as did R. H. Harney, William Rollins, and the Dereef brothers, Richard and Joseph. In addition, the leading lumber merchants, referred to as "Wood-Factors," also employed clerks and bookkeepers.

Indeed, the demand for lumber in the Charleston market was so great that over 50 percent of Charleston's free black businesspeople were wood dealers. Most carried on their business alone. In North Carolina, Lunsford Lane indicated that in Raleigh he "entered into a considerable business in firewood." He purchased trees by the acre, cut them, and used his horses and drays to haul the lumber to the city. Then he used his drays to make firewood deliveries. In both Charleston and Philadelphia, moreover, more than 50 percent of the firewood was delivered by blacks who owned draying enterprises. In eastern North Carolina, with its extensive pine forests, more than 100 free blacks established small enterprises in turpentine extraction and distillation.

On the West Coast, wealthy San Francisco merchant William Leidesdorff* was a lumber dealer, and one of his newspaper advertisements in 1847 stated: "LUMBER—William Alexander Leidesdorff has made arrangements to supply this town with LUMBER, persons wishing any kind of lumber can have their orders executed by leaving them at the Store." But for his untimely death, Leidesdorff would have been involved in gold mining. With his extensive property holdings, his estate was valued at $1.4 million and included land across from Sutter's Field where gold was discovered in June 1848. A gold mine was also discovered on Leidesdorff's property after his death in June 1848.

African Americans, both slaves and free blacks, were also caught up in the California gold rush of 1849. Early on, however, free blacks were involved in gold mining in the 1830s, as individual prospectors, mining gold in both North Carolina and Georgia. In California, some of the early black miners were slaves who purchased their freedom from the gold they obtained by placer or surface mining. Indeed, one area was known as "Negro Bar" because of the numerous black miners. Free blacks also organized mining companies. In Brown's Valley in Yuba, California, two black mining companies were established—"The Sweet Vengeance Mine Company" and the "Rare, Ripe Gold and Silver Mining Company," which was incorporated in 1868 with a capital stock of 1,200 shares at $10 per share and offices in Marysville, California. The slave-born Moses Rodgers, who was recognized as one of California's leading mining engineers and metallurgists, arrived in 1849 from Missouri and eventually owned several mines. California's first quartz mill was established by Robert Anthony, who purchased his freedom from money earned by mining.

While the production of bituminous coal increased some 163 percent after the Civil War, there was also a strong market for coal before 1861. Several antebellum African Americans owned coal yards. Stephen Smith combined the sale of coal with his lumber yard. Cincinnati coal dealer Robert Gordon, using aggressive cutthroat business tactics, was able to succeed in the competitive coal market in that city. In their attempts to drive Gordon out of business, which failed, white Cincinnati coal dealers acted in collusion, by lowering the price of their coal. Rather than attempt to compete, Gordon stockpiled his own coal. Then, using blacks who could pass for white, Gordon had them purchase coal from his competitors, which he then sold to fill his orders. The winter ended the "coal war." With the river frozen, white coal dealers were soon sold out; Gordon, who had stockpiled his coal, was able to corner the market. He also sold his coal at the highest prices the market would bear. As Carter G. Woodson said, while the white coal dealers recognized Gordon's business ability, they failed to consider "the large amounts of capital at his disposal." Gordon's coal yard was an extensive operation. He not only employed both bookkeepers and laborers; he also owned his coal wagons that made deliveries, built his own docks, and purchased coal by the barge. By 1879 Gordon's wealth was estimated at more than $200,000. The coal yard business was profitable for antebellum free blacks. In Philadelphia, William Still, who operated a retail ice and coal yard before the Civil War, had also expanded his coal yard enterprise by the 1870s. Since Still's coal was brought in by train, he moved his yard to a larger site and built railroad tracks to his yard, which cut operating costs in transportation and increased his profits.

While black-owned coal yards were part of the urban landscape in the late nineteenth century, African Americans also attempted to capitalize on the booming coal industry by establishing coal mining enterprises. In Alabama, the Birmingham Grate Coal Mining company, which leased a mine 18 miles from Birmingham, was founded in the late 1890s. It was entirely black owned and operated. President Reverend T. Walker was black, as were the mining supervisor and the miners. Their customers were white. The company began mining operations in 1898, with a capital of $10,000. Production in their initial operation was 25 to 30 tons of coal mined daily, with a goal of 250 tons. The company continued its operations into the early twentieth century.

Yet, in the late nineteenth century, there was no way blacks could compete in the coal industry with great success. The Henry Clay Frick Coke Company, for example, which supplied coal to the iron and steel industries, owned 40,000 acres of coal mine and 2,688 railway cars for shipping. Millions of dollars were invested in industries that were becoming increasingly monopolized by the "robber barons" of industrial America who emerged after the Civil War. Consequently, the attempt by Californian Moses Rodgers in 1898 to establish a natural gas company failed. Rodgers, who had been involved in several gold mining companies, was the first person in that state to successfully drill for natural gas. Lacking sufficient capital to develop this enterprise, Rodgers was unable to make the venture pay.

African Americans also continued in the lumber business after the Civil War. In South Carolina, J. J. Sulton and Sons, a sawmill enterprise, had been in operation since 1825. It was started by a white slaveowner who left it to his black son Dennis; in 1876, Dennis turned the sawmill over to his son, J. J. Sulton, who took his two sons into partnership. In 1903, as their business expanded, they moved the mill to Orangeburg, South Carolina. The lumber business was also profitable for East Saginaw, Michigan, lumber merchant W. Q. Atwood. In 1880 he was worth $100,000. In Savannah, Georgia, however, a land and lumber enterprise in which a consortium of blacks had invested $50,000 failed.

Indeed, with the rise of industrial America in the early twentieth century, black business leaders promoted increased black business participation in the extractive industries. In a keynote address given in 1912 at the thirteenth annual convention of the National Negro Business League* (NNBL) in Chicago, Booker T. Washington* said: "If the white man can secure wealth and happiness by owning and operating a coal mine, brick yard, or lime kiln, why can not more Negroes do the same thing?" By that time, however, both lack of capital and changes in American business organization, owing to the development of large corporations, constituted countervailing forces.

Consequently, while John D. Rockefeller could establish his oil refinery business with $10,000 in the 1860s, by 1882, Rockefeller's Standard Oil, worth $70 million, owned 95 percent of the oil refining business, a clear monopoly. Moreover, Standard owned virtually all of the means of transporting oil by rail, through forced rebates in shipment costs, and by pipelines. By the early twentieth century the increasing vertical integration and monopolization of America's extractive industries in coal, iron, steel, and oil represented billions of dollars of investment. Indeed, by 1904, with mergers in these industries, 300 firms holding enterprises worth $20 billion were said to own over 40 percent of America's industrial wealth. Even though there had been an expansion of black capital accumulation by blacks since the Civil War, by 1903, when Andrew Carnegie's U.S. Steel became the nation's first billion-dollar business, the entire wealth holding of black America amounted to only $700 million.

In the extractive industries, then, African Americans could only hope to develop small-scale enterprises. The discovery of oil in Oklahoma, however, provided blacks with an opportunity to get in on the ground floor in the development of the oil industry in that state. Most of the Oklahoma oil lands owned by blacks were located in the state's Indian Territory. Before the Civil War, blacks had lived in Indian Territory, and some were free, whereas others were slaves owned by the Creek nation. After 1865, these former slaves—known as Creek freedmen or "native Negroes"—and the Creeks were each allocated 160 acres of desolate land before the government opened Oklahoma to settlement. Oil, however, was discovered on what was considered wasteland. Notwithstanding that blacks owned land rich in petroleum, most sold their land, or development of their oil lands was undertaken by whites.

Moreover, few blacks invested their profits from leasing in establishing drilling enterprises or refineries. Even fewer realized the profits from leasing that accrued to Sarah Rector. In 1913, oil was discovered on her land, which she had leased to a white man who had set up two oil wells. Black newspapers reported that the two wells were producing 3,800 barrels or oil a day, from which she would make "$14,250 a month." With nine more wells scheduled for operation in 1914, it was anticipated that Rector's leases would earn her in the millions. By the 1920s, however, several black oil companies had been founded. The Black Panther Oil Company was the first black-owned petroleum company in Oklahoma, and the Ardmore Lubricating Oil Co. was established in 1920. The Jake Simmons family, descendants of Creek Negroes, however, capitalized on the oil industry with some success. They drilled on their land and expanded their holdings by purchasing land from other blacks. Also, by acting as brokers, they expanded their oil interests internationally in the 1960s.

By the 1940s, however, one of the oldest black-owned enterprises in the extractive industries was the Kerford Quarry Stone Mining Company, which was also one of the largest and most profitable black-owned businesses in the United States at that time. The three-generation black-owned Kerford Quarry Stone Mining Company was established in Atchinson, Kansas, in 1887 by George W. Kerford. Through underground mining operations in the caves he owned, Kerford produced crushed rock, limestone, ballast sand, and gravel. His two sons, Lloyd and George, inherited the business. Both blacks and whites were employed by the Kerford Company, which employed some 300 men in the 1930s and during the war years. In the mining of nonmetallic limestone, the Kerford Company was classified as a heavy industry.

During World War II, the War Food Administration (WFA) negotiated a lease with the Kerfords in 1944 for the use of the company's limestone caves for the storage of foodstuffs and experimental wool and cotton. With blast refrigeration the cave could be cooled from its normal 50 degrees to 30 degrees and provide a storage capacity, 1.4 million square feet, equivalent to 3,500 refrigerator freight cars. Construction of a storage plant equal in size to the Kerford caves would cost $15 million. The government invested $2 million to provide for the refrigeration of the cave, but the project was abandoned at the end of the war; in 1950 a proposal put before the Senate to purchase the caves was defeated.

By the World War II era, however, most blacks with enterprises in the extractive industries were distributors. The Grimes Oil Company, a petroleum distributor founded in 1940, remains one of the nation's largest black businesses. In the first listing by *Black Enterprise* of the leading 100 black businesses in 1976, five black fuel oil companies were listed. In that year, the New York–based Wallace & Wallace Chemical & Oil Corporation, which owned a fleet of 16 trucks, with 60 employees, grossed $17 million in sales. In addition, *Black Enterprise* published an article on the "First Black-Owned Refinery," predicting record sales. The company, founded in 1968 with a Small Business Administration loan of $350,000, had selected the former Tuskegee air base as the site of its refinery.

In 1997, the Connecticut-based Yancy Minerals, Inc., which specializes in industrial metals and minerals, along with coal distribution, by the 1990s remained one of the nation's leading businesses. In the post–civil rights era, however, blacks in the business of coal and oil distribution, invariably, have combined this enterprise with other ventures. Dick Griffey, whose success was made in the entertainment world through his African Development Public Investment Corp., has investments in oil trading. In 1995, Griffey ranked twenty-seventh on the *BE* 100s, with sales of $56 million, half generated by African Development and the other by Dick Griffey Productions. Percy Sutton Intercontinental, a multimillion-dollar holding company, with some 23 subsidiaries, includes investments in energy sources in oil and coal.

The participation of blacks in the extractive industries had paralleled that of the nation. Prior to the Civil War, blacks had access to land to develop natural resources. In the twentieth century, with the growth of industrialization and the billion-dollar monopolization in the development and processing of natural resources, African Americans were effectively locked out of any future opportunities in the extractive industries. The Kerford Quarrying Company survived into the mid-twentieth century because the founder had purchased the caves in the late 1880s. By the end of the twentieth century the new growth industry for African Americans was in computers and high-tech enterprises, while black business ownership in the extractive industries continues at a comparative minimal level of participation.

The following black participation rates in the nation's extractive industries in 1990 underscore their virtual exclusion from these enterprises. In forestry, there were 371 black firms out of a total of 14,423 U.S. firms, and in fishing, hunting, and trapping there were 678 black firms out of a national total of 77,928. In mining industries, there were 490 black firms out of 150,368 firms nationwide.

In addition, in metal mining there were 21 black firms out of 1,997, and in coal mining there were 14 black firms out of 2,076. There were only 424 black firms in oil and gas extraction out of a total of 141,537 U.S. firms and only 31 black firms in nonmetallic minerals out of a total of 4,758 of those firms nationwide. Consequently, the limited participation of blacks as business owners in the extractive industries reflects the limited access by blacks to the nation's vast stores of natural resources.

SELECTED BIBLIOGRAPHY: Delilah L. Beasley, *The Negro Trail Blazers of California* (Los Angeles: Delilah Beasley, 1919); Census Bureau Public Information Office at (301) 763–5726 and e-mail address pio@census.gov; Martin Robison Delany, *The Condition, Elevation, Emigration, and Destiny of the Colored People of the United States* (1852; reprint, New York: Arno Press, 1968); John Hope Franklin, ''The Free Negro in the Economic Life of North Carolina,'' *North Carolina Historical Review*, pt 1 (July 1942); pt 1 (October 1942); Jonathan Greenberg, *Staking a Claim: Jake Simmons, Jr. and the Making of an African-American Oil Dynasty* (New York: Penguin Group, 1991); Luther Porter Jackson, *Free Negro Labor and Property Holding in Virginia* (New York: Russell & Russell, 1942); U.S. Census, ''Minority- and Women-Owned Business Enterprises'' web data, http://www.census.gov/agfs/www.smobe.htlm; Juliet E. K. Walker, *The History of Black Business in America. Capitalism, Race, Entrepreneurship* (New York: Macmillan, 1998); Carter G. Woodson, ''The Negroes of Cincinnati Prior to the Civil War,'' *Journal of Negro History* 1 (January 1916): 21–22.

Juliet E. K. Walker

F

FATHER DIVINE [GEORGE BAKER] (ca. 1880–1965), New York, founder of the Peace Mission Movement.

Once a raucous religious demonstration landed George Baker before a Long Island judge. The judge fined him $500 and sentenced him to a year in the county jail. Several days later, the judge fell dead from a sudden heart attack. Legend has it that Baker, better known as Father Divine, commented from his jail cell: "I hated to do it." Accounts of this sort amused and confounded outside observers, but they only added to Divine's mystique among his followers. To them, these tales illustrated that he was not only a preacher and healer but God incarnate. However, the expensive Duesenberg car and 12-passenger Balank airplane Divine owned suggest he was also a consummate businessman.

Baker's beginnings are as enigmatic as the folklore surrounding him. Little is known about his background, except that he was the child of sharecroppers, born around 1880 on Hutchinson Island, Georgia, located on the Savannah River. As a young man, his experiences were shaped by a stint on a chain gang, work as a garden laborer, and occasional preaching. It was the latter that proved most formative. "Apprenticed" under several self-styled evangelists, Baker was anointed "God in Sonship Degree." In 1914, he migrated to Valdosta, Georgia, with a small following. However, trouble with the law led him north—first to Baltimore, then later to New York City—where he settled in Harlem under the name Major J. Divine. Proclaiming himself God, he established a church in the Afro-American district of Brooklyn and called on followers to embrace celibacy, social separation of the sexes, and renunciation of all "worldly" trappings, including money and wealth.

By 1919, he and his new wife, "Sister Penny" (a follower from Georgia), were able to purchase a home in Sayville, Long Island. By then, his congregation numbered about 20. In the late 1920s, its ranks swelled as Baker actively recruited Long Island domestic workers. A number of whites, many of them financially well-to-do and educated, joined also. Despite divergent backgrounds, all members expressed their newfound salvation by taking on descriptive baroque names: "Sing Happy," "Mother's Delight," and "The Prodigal Son" were but a few. It was in this period that Baker formally took the name Father Divine and launched his nondenominational, interracial Peace Mission Movement. Based primarily in Harlem, the movement came to encompass branches (or "heavens," as they were called) along the East Coast. Divine even made inroads in the Midwest and California and formed dispersed "kingdoms" overseas. At its height, the Peace Mission claimed some 2 million members worldwide.

Divine and his coterie wielded considerable political weight in local New York politics and often were approached for support by white politicians and Harlem grassroots activists. Yet Divine is perhaps best remembered for the Peace Mission's charitable work. During the Great Depression, when economic desperation and social dislocation alienated black workers from employment and mainstream churches, Divine sponsored elaborate "Holy Communion" banquets at Harlem's Rockland Palace. The bountiful meals, given at no cost to the unemployed, ensured Divine's rise to prominence.

Given the industrial training films screened during Mission services, speculation persists that big business interests actually funded Divine's ornate feasts, primarily to draw black Harlemites away from the radical, militant influences like the Communist Party. However, Divine's shrewd economic sense makes it just as likely that the Peace Mission drew from its own resources to sponsor these dinners. While charitable work was a major part of the Mission's program, Father Divine considered it only a temporary stopgap. The Mission's long-range goal was collective prosperity through economic activity.

Indeed, Divine was one of the biggest landlords in Harlem. Among his real estate holdings were three apartment houses, nine private houses, some 20 flats, and several meeting halls with upper-level dormitories. He also operated a lodging house and employment bureau in Long Island. In rural Ulster County, he owned a 2,000-acre estate, used by Mission members to pursue cooperative community resettlement programs. He even held properties in Sweden, Germany, Switzerland, and England.

In the area of commerce, Divine's presence was equally as formidable. In the words of biographer Robert Weisbrot, Divine stepped to the "common march of prophet and profit." The Mission's periodical *New Day* featured paid advertisements by major firms like F. W. Woolworth and Company. Between holdings in Newark, Baltimore, and Philadelphia, he operated 25 restaurants, six groceries, 10 barbershops, and 10 cleaning stores. He also owned an ice cream and bakery shop, a tailoring business, and 24 "huckster wagons" with seafood and fresh vegetables. This complemented a major Peace Mission emporium for meat, fish, fowl, and vegetables. As well, Divine maintained a thriving coal business replete with three trucks, which shuttled between Harlem and Pennsylvanian mines.

Father Divine, however, did encourage members to launch their own individual businesses, which many did. Enterprises ran the gamut between the relatively simple (selling shaved ice treats from vending carts) to the more complex (sponsoring extravagant, daylong boat cruises on the Hudson River). Still, the common denominator was that all of these entrepreneurs returned their net profits to the Mission, given their supposed renunciation of personal possessions. Others worked voluntarily for fellow Peace Mission members, receiving compensation only for transportation and other job-related costs.

By all accounts, these businesses were successful, and many of the reasons had to do with the ''Divinite'' lifestyle. Communal living arrangements and prohibitions against costly vices like cigarettes kept personal expenses to a minimum and allowed members to funnel the bulk of their earnings into the Peace Mission pool. Consequently, the Mission was able not only to supply members with their basic material needs but also to maintain immense reserves of liquid capital. This enabled Divine and his followers to purchase all properties with cash, thereby avoiding loan interests and debt. Combined, these factors provided Peace Mission businesses with low overhead prices, which in turn made it easy to undersell competitors: For $.15, one could purchase a Peace Mission chicken dinner; for $.10, a haircut; for $.05 a shave; and for $.03 a shoeshine or a can of soda. At the same time, the Mission did extend economic support to other black Harlem businesses throughout the 1930s.

As the conditions of the depression waned, so did Divine's pervasive influence. Sordid accounts of violence, fraud, and sexual impropriety involving Divine's associates in the 1940s further damaged the Mission's integrity. Divine's personal credibility suffered when he married one of his young white secretaries following his first wife's death. On September 10, 1965, he died of complications from diabetes.

Historians have sought different meanings in Father Divine's life. Some focus on the interracial character of the Peace Mission Movement as a daring prelude to battles against segregation. Others are particularly impressed by the fact that a black man claiming to be God was able to draw middle-class whites into his fold; such individuals view Divine's life as a potent statement of religious black nationalism. Still others are intrigued by the communal nature of the Mission Movement. However, one should not overstate its cooperative character, considering Divine lived a more affluent lifestyle than most of his flock. Overlooked may be Divine's legacy as a black entrepreneur. In a period before the civil rights movement opened doors for black middle-class opportunity, Divine amassed wealth in both the United States and Europe. Because he apparently filed no income tax returns, nor paid taxes, there is as of yet no way of assessing his wealth. Until this is possible, Divine's true legacy in black business history may remain as shrouded as his early life.

SELECTED BIBLIOGRAPHY: Arthur Huff Fauset, *Black Gods of the Metropolis* (Philadelphia: University of Pennsylvania Press, 1944); Jill Watts, *God, Harlem U.S.A.: The Father Divine Story* (Berkeley: University of California Press, 1992); Robert Weisbrot, *Father Divine* (Boston: Beacon Press, 1983).

Clarence Lang

FAUSTINA, GILBERT (c. 1878–1941), Mobile, Alabama, cigar maker, real estate developer, civil rights activist, community leader.

Gilbert Faustina was born in New Orleans, Louisiana, the second son of a seafaring trader of Cuban descent. His mother, Angela, was of French ancestry and died shortly after his birth. His father was last known to be in Cuba at the outbreak of the Spanish-American War and never returned to New Orleans. Gilbert and his brother Manuel, left in the care of two spinster aunts, while young, migrated to Mobile, Alabama, in search of employment. Gilbert obtained an apprentice position with a cigar manufacturer in Mobile, whereas Manuel pursued a career as a professional musician and music teacher and eventually moved on to Los Angeles, California. In Alabama, both were legally designated as "colored."

In the early 1900s the factory where Gilbert worked fell on hard times and closed. Unable to pay his workers, the owner gave each a parcel of tobacco leaf. With this severance, Gilbert began to make and sell his own line of hand-made cigars. By 1918 High Grade Union Made Cigars, commonly called Faustina's Best, was fully incorporated; housed in a two-story factory, the company employed nine full-time cigar makers and produced a line of cigars that included G. F. Tampa Smokers, Little Orco, Porto Rico Specials, and Excelsior (named for his brother's jazz band in which he occasionally sat). Undeterred by the racial restrictions on property ownership and location, Gilbert constructed his cigar factory behind his residence in one of Mobile's poorest black neighborhoods. In spite of location and limited capital, his operation was distinguished for its craftsmanship, professionalism, and creativity in marketing techniques. In addition to business cards, his promotional calendars, wrappers, and cigar boxes were flaunted by his predominantly wealthy white customers in Mobile and New Orleans for originality and artistic design. Unwilling and unable to compete with cheap machine-made cigars introduced in the 1920s, Faustina closed his business in the early 1920s.

With profits from his cigar factory, Gilbert purchased numerous dilapidated houses and rehabilitated them into affordable rental units. His status as a property owner and successful businessman made him eligible for certification as one of Mobile's first colored bail bondsmen. It is said that Faustina never took a loss on his bails because he personally knew every client, and they knew and respected him in the colored communities. Gilbert would have the occasion to post his own bail when arrested for attempting to vote without paying the "poll tax." He considered the poll tax unconstitutional and believed that it served no purpose other than to disenfranchise poor blacks.

With cunning and determination not to be constrained by Jim Crow laws, Gilbert bought a seven-acre plot of land on Mon Luis Island, situated on the Mobile Bay, 20 miles south of the city of Mobile. Whites with summer homes on the island were unaware that a Negro had purchased a prime water front parcel. (It is speculated that a white lawyer and patron of his cigars sneaked the purchase through the legal process.) Then, in 1922, Gilbert opened Faustina Beach—a five-acre picnic ground and bathing beach for Negroes, the first and only place in the entire western and eastern shoreline where Negroes could go swimming in the Mobile Bay or any other part of the Gulf of Mexico. Gilbert marketed his beach as a place for families, churches, and other nonprofit organizations.

The response was overwhelming. Groups came from as far away as Birmingham, Alabama, Pascagula, Mississippi, and Pensacola, Florida. Faustina Beach did experience moderate financial success. Still, in its 30 years of operation, the admission fee never exceeded $.10 for adults, and children were always free. Faustina Beach did not go without notice from whites on the island and in the city of Mobile. The harassment and efforts to shut it down were numerous, varied, and severe. Gilbert won all legal challenges, but physical threats to him, his family, and patrons were persistent. But so was his determination.

Faustina Beach did not close until racial integration arrived in the late 1950s, and other water accesses became available for Negroes in the Deep South. It should be noted that with the relaxation of Jim Crow laws the Negro professional elite of Mobile began to purchase property on Mon Luis Island, and ironically, they, too, took exception to the "publicness" and "riffraff" that Gilbert permitted on his property. His own formal legacy of community commitment came with the founding of the Knights of Peter Claver. Gilbert was a devout Catholic but felt the Catholic Church was not providing for its colored parishioners as it was for its whites. He made repeated requests to form a chapter of the Knights of Columbus, a lay fraternal organization of the Catholic Church, in his segregated parish. After repeated denials, responding in his typical fashion, Gilbert, with two other Negro laymen and four white priests, in 1909 incorporated Knights of Peter Claver, an all-black organization. Its purposes were to "render pecuniary aid to its members and beneficiaries of its members; mutual aid and assistance to the sick and disabled" and the "promotion of social and intellectual intercourse among its members." The Knights of Peter Claver filled a void for Catholic men of color. During Faustina's 17-year leadership, chapters were formed throughout Louisiana, Alabama, Mississippi, and Texas and as far away as Oklahoma and Missouri, to the displeasure of the Catholic Church hierarchy.

In the legal battle that ensued, Faustina's position was that he respected the role of the clergy as "spiritual advisers" but insisted that the financial conduct and other activities of the order rest with the layman. The courts found in his favor, and the autonomy of the Knights of Peter Claver was upheld. Contemporarily, the Knights of Peter Claver has a membership of 25,000 in 23 states and the District of Columbia. Its publication, initially named *The Shield* and published monthly, currently exists as *The Claverite* and is published quarterly. In spite of the ambiguous position of the Catholic Church on matters of racial, gender, and political issues, the Knights of Peter Claver expanded to the formation of women's and youth groups and retains its financial and community sponsorship of young men desiring to become priests both from the United States and the continent of Africa.

Gilbert Faustina died of a massive heart attack. An extraordinary man with no formal education, without parents or extended family and during one of the most brutal and oppressive times in American history, Faustina left to his six sons and three daughters a life of accomplishment and a philosophy of hard work and persistence. His most often quoted saying was "Lost time is never found again."

SELECTED BIBLIOGRAPHY: Albert S. Foley, *God's Men of Color: The Colored Catholic Priest of the United States, 1854–1954* (New York: Farrar, Straus & Co., 1955); Michael J. O'Neal, *Some Outstanding Colored People: Interesting Facts in the Lives of Representative Negroes* (Baltimore: Franciscan Sisters, 1943), 148–149; *The Shield & The Claverite*, Knights of Peter Claver Archives, 1825 Orleans Avenue, New Orleans, LA 90122.

Bernadette P. Chachere

FELTON, WILLIAM McDONALD (1876?–1930), New York, Pennsylvania, aeronautical and automotive entrepreneur, theater and club owner.

William "Hack" Felton, a native of Marshallville, Georgia, entered the mechanical trades as a watch repairman in Marshallville in the 1890s, then migrated northward to New York City in 1898, where he opened a bicycle, clock, and gun repair shop. Soon afterward, while the automobile industry was still in its infancy, he became a partner in 1901 in a chauffeurs' school at 240 Eighth Avenue. One year later Felton opened a garage, first located at 353 West Thirty-ninth Street and later at 309 West Forty-first Street. Expanding this business into the Auto Transportation and Sales Company, in 1910 he moved its operations to 304–306 West Forty-ninth Street.

Described by the *New York Age* as "the largest automobile business conducted by Negroes in New York," this concern was a combined auto dealership and repair shop. It commanded four floors of a seven-story building and employed 15 persons. Using profits from his automotive business, Felton also opened the Fifty-ninth Street Theatre in Harlem in the spring of 1913. In 1914 Felton moved to Steelton, Pennsylvania, and by 1919 he had opened there the Auto and Aeroplane Mechanical School, the first black-owned school known to offer airplane mechanics in its curriculum.

Drawing numerous students from young men, both black and white, who were just returning from World War I and seeking job training, Felton also opened his school to women, advertising that he was offering classes for men and women on alternate days of the week. How many women actually ever enrolled, however, is uncertain. He expanded his school in 1921, moving it to 22 North Cameron Street in nearby Harrisburg. While at this location Felton hired World War I pilot Walter Diehl to offer flying lessons at an airstrip he owned at Fourteenth and Sycamore Streets, advertising nationally in publications such as the *Chicago Defender* and *Crisis* magazine that students could, in addition to taking automotive and airplane mechanics courses, also learn chauffeuring and airplane piloting at the school. Felton's business was thus also the first documented black-owned flying school to open its doors.

Prospering, in 1923 the Auto and Aero Mechanical School dedicated a newly constructed two-story building, valued at $100,000, and Felton announced plans to expand his airfield operations, although objections from local whites prevented his doing so. In 1924, the school further expanded to offer a home study program, which allowed students to take correspondence courses in automobile and aircraft engine repair. As he had in New York, Felton also invested some of his profits in a sideline business, opening a small dance club in Harrisburg during this time. Felton closed his school after a fire destroyed the building it occupied at 44 North Cameron Street in May 1927. He died in Harrisburg three years later in November 1930.

Felton was the son of Sonnay Felton of Marshallville, Georgia. He married Josephine Souza of St. Kitt's, British West Indies, and had one son, William McDonald Felton, Jr., and a daughter, Evelyn, who died as a child.

SELECTED BIBLIOGRAPHY: "Automobile Instructions Now Given in Your Own Home," *Chicago Defender* (national ed.), December 13, 1924; "Conduct Automobile Schools in New York," *New York Age*, February 13, 1913; "New $100,000 Auto and Aero Mechanics' School in Harrisburg to Be Dedicated," *Pittsburgh Courier*, October 27, 1923; "Scenes Typical of the Automobile and Aeroplane Mechanical School," *Harrisburg Telegraph*, March 15, 1919; Telephone interview, Jill Snider with William McDonald Felton, Jr., December 6, 1995.

Jill D. Snider

FILM PRODUCTION. The role of the production company in the making of a film is to raise the capital necessary to ensure the film is completed. Because the production company controls the finance of the film, they have a great deal of control over the shaping of the project. The history of production company ownership by African Americans began with great promise, boasting high levels of participation and creative control in the early twentieth century. Yet, paradoxically, as African American participation in front of the camera has grown over the decades, their participation in formal production company ownership has conversely declined.

Race films of the late 1910s and early 1920s brought the first participation by African Americans in the production of film in America. From the beginning, African Americans had found themselves the victims of stereotypes and ridicule in films with such titles as *The Wooing and Wedding of a Coon* (1905), *The Dancing Nig* (1907), *The Pickaninnies Doing a Dance* (1904), and *How Rastus Got His Pork Chops* (1908). Although African Americans strongly complained about the manner in which they were being presented in film, little was done to effect change until the release of *Birth of a Nation* (1915).

Protest by African Americans galvanized with the release of the film, based on Thomas Dixon's novel *The Clansman*, which told the story of the post–Civil War South, focusing on the creation of the Ku Klux Klan, portraying them as heroes helping to control rampaging ex-slaves. More than any other film of the period, *Birth of a Nation* reflected the power of film to communicate negative ideology. This power did not go unnoticed by the National Association for the Advancement of Colored People (NAACP). The NAACP organized protests in a number of cities in an effort to keep the film from being shown. Their protest was unsuccessful and in some cases only helped the film reach a larger audience, as curiosity seekers wanted to see the cause for such controversy.

Prior to 1915 the only African American–owned production company of note was the Foster Photoplay Company. Its owner, William Foster, produced many of the first all-black-cast films, including *The Pullman Porter* (1910) and *The Railroad Porter* (1912). The company produced a number of films throughout the 1910s and 1920s; unfortunately, only two or three of the films exist today. The company disappeared by the end of the 1920s, but Foster continued to direct films into the 1930s. The last series for which he is given credit is *Buck and Bubbles*, an all-black comedy series of films. Moreover, while there were film production companies owned by African Americans dating to the 1890s, most historians begin documentation of the history of African American film production with the Lincoln Motion Picture Company, founded by brothers, George and Noble Johnson.

Owing to his light-skin complexion, Noble had built a career in Hollywood films playing Indians and other ethnics, whereas George had no film experience. The company had pledged to make serious film about African Americans. Their first effort was *The Realization of a Negro's Ambition* (1917), a film about a Tusksegee Institute graduate who leaves the farm and his sweetheart to seek his fortune in California. After having made his fortune, proving himself as an outstanding engineer, he is allowed to marry his sweetheart and live happily ever after. The film was successful with audience members and was key to providing funding for the company's second film, *The Trooper of Company K* (1917).

As the company produced more films, featuring Noble as a leading man, Noble was faced with making difficult choices. He could continue to work in his company's films with a limited audience and ongoing financial struggles, or he could take his newfound success and return to Hollywood. Noble chose to return to Hollywood and became one of Universal's most successful African

American contract players. He turned over the operations of the company to his brother, George, but without Noble's leadership, the company was soon dissolved.

Another important film company during the race film period was Micheaux Pictures, formed by Oscar Micheaux.* His first film was *The Homesteader* (1919), based on his own novel. The Johnson brothers had originally approached Micheaux to purchase the rights to the novel, but Micheaux refused unless he could direct the film. The Johnsons declined to purchase the novel under those conditions. Prior to his film endeavors, Micheaux achieved a great deal of success as a writer by controlling his own property. Micheaux would publish the books himself and then travel the Midwest, selling the books door to door. On many occasions, he was able to secure advances for books that were not yet written.

Micheaux garnered success in film production based on his skills as a businessman as well as the quality of his films. The Micheaux formula for success in selling his books translated well to the financing and distributing of his films. He often carried the prints by hand to theater owners, to make his distribution deals. He would also presale pictures based on ideas and use the money collected from the presale to make the films. Some of Micheaux's titles include *Within Our Gates* (1920), *The Girl from Chicago* (1933), and *Harlem after Midnight* (1934). Micheaux Pictures was one of the few companies that survived the transition into the sound film era; most were forced to close simply from the inability to raise the capital needed to convert to sound production.

Micheaux and the Johnson brothers were not the only important figures in film production by African Americans during the race film era. The Norman Film Manufacturing Company obtained success from producing primarily all-black-cast Westerns. Other successful African American companies were Dunbar Film Company, Lone Star Motion Pictures Company, Democracy Photoplay Corporation, and Monarch Productions. It should be noted that there were companies that produced all-black-cast films but were not owned by blacks, including the Colored Players Film Corporation, which produced one of the period's most widely acclaimed films, *The Scar of Shame* (1927), and Reol Motion Picture Corporation, which produced *The Burden of Race* (1921).

Many of the films produced by African Americans during the race film period have been lost or, in many cases, have simply faded away due to age, as the technologically poor film stock used then chemically decomposes. Much of the information on films of the period comes to us in the form of advertisements for the films or movie reviews that appeared in the African American press. Further complicating the historical archive is the fact that because of limited financial resources only a small number of the film prints were made. This meant that these few prints were used heavily to meet audience demands, becoming damaged after short periods of time, further limiting the archival material. It was not uncommon during the period to have a print of a film being used by more than one theater simultaneously. The theaters would stagger the film's showing times so the print could be shuttled between various locations.

As the motion picture industry moved into the 1930s many of the companies producing race films were forced out of business by a number of circumstances. Leading the list of circumstances was a market saturated with companies producing race films. Not only was the market saturated, but many of these new companies lacked the skilled personnel to produce a quality product. Some companies failed to make the transition to sound due to lack of the resources necessary. The struggle for survival was further complicated by Hollywood's discovery of the African American box office. The attendance at race films did not go unnoticed; Hollywood began to make their own all-black-cast films. MGM's *Hallelujah* (1929) was one of the first films of this type. The large Hollywood studios could provide audiences with the all-black casting to which they had become accustomed. Throughout the 1930s and 1940s all-black-cast movies appeared periodically; two of the most noteworthy are *Cabin in the Sky* (1943) and *Stormy Weather* (1943).

Although African Americans became more visible in films throughout the 1950s and 1960s, they never regained the controlling reins of production that they enjoyed in the 1920s. There were a few African American directors but none controlling production companies. The next season of production success for African Americans came in the 1970s. The change in the landscape was prompted by the release and success of *Sweet Sweetback's Baadasssss Song* (1971). This independent film was made on a low budget and released to theaters in the inner city. It was a tremendous success and is given credit for having initiated what is now referred to as the Blaxploitation film movement.

The movement was driven by films that starred African Americans, made on small budgets and marketed to inner-city audiences. In the beginning, most of these films were made by the major studios, but as actors became movie stars, they began to produce some of the films themselves. The most successful of these black producers was Fred Williamson, a football-player-turned-actor-turned-producer. His Po Boy Productions produced several films during the period and still produces films in the 1990s, with the most recent release being *Original Gangstas* (1996). Actor Max Julien, who began his career starring in one of the era's defining films, *The Mack* (1973), finished the period as a respected writer and owner of a production company. Sidney Poitier also formed a production company in the 1970s, First Artist production. The company produced two of the most successful comedies—*Uptown Saturday Night* (1974) and *Let's Do It Again* (1975), a sequel.

Blaxploitation ran its course by the end of the 1970s, primarily due to the rising costs of producing the product. The films were designed to be made quickly and inexpensively; yet as low-price actors became stars, they demanded larger salaries, better scripts, and higher production values, all of which increased the cost of the product. The Blaxploitation films also faced competition for box office dollars from other films successful with black audiences, such as Kung Fu action films, which were made at half of the Blaxploitation films' average cost. The end of the movement was also hastened by the decline of inner-city movie houses, when multiplexes in the suburbs began to open. Those who once had to produce films for the inner city could now concentrate on a newfound audience in the suburban multiplexes.

The current state of African American ownership of production companies is primarily connected to movie stardom. Giving a star his or her own production company has become one of the standard perks in Hollywood. In the 1980s both Richard Pryor and Eddie Murphy had their own production companies as part of long-term contracts with Hollywood studios. It is hard to determine if these star-owned companies function as a business. These companies do not have to function under the same type of constraints as other production companies; for example, they are usually bankrolled by the studios, working under a contract to produce a certain number of films within a certain period of time. The livelihood of the company is not tied to the marketplace; rather, it is tied to the pursestrings of the studio.

Forty Acres and a Mule, founded by filmmaker Spike Lee, operates in much the same manner as the African American film companies of the 1920s. The company raises much of its own capital to produce films in a manner that will allow the filmmaker to control his own vision. This vision has been responsible for some of the more interesting films in the 1980s. Among the films produced by the company are *She's Gotta Have It* (1986), *School Daze* (1988), and *Do the Right Thing* (1989).

In the 1990s it is difficult to track production companies owned by African Americans for two reasons. First, a company is often formed to produce a specific film, and upon completion of the project, the company is dissolved. Second, as film financing becomes even more difficult to secure, many successful African American filmmakers look for the shelter of the studios to finance their projects. Also, it is very difficult to maintain a production company without an ongoing relationship with a major studio.

The only African American company to be consistently successful at maintaining some level of autonomy has been Spike Lee's Forty Acres and a Mule production company. African American film production companies have seemingly missed the opportunity to take control of the reins of film production and have instead settled all too often for the role of employee of major film companies. In the 1920s a successful film meant that funding was available to make the next film. In the 1990s a successful film created by African Americans becomes the calling card to the big studios with larger budgets and seemingly unlimited resources.

In 1993 the Hughes brothers, Allen and Albert, wrote, directed, and coproduced *Menace II Society*. The film, produced on a budget of only $3 million, went on to gross over $30 million at the box office. Based on the success of this film, the brothers were able to sign with Disney to produce their next two films. *Menace II Society* was produced by the brothers along with Darin Scott and Tyger Williams. This group was formed to produce one film, and the partnership dissolved after the film was completed. Another example of this move to greener pastures are the Hudlin Brothers, who parlayed the success of *House Party* (1990), which was produced for $2.5 million and grossed over $27 million, into a big-budget production, *Boomerang* (1992), with a budget of over 30 million.

The increasing percentage of African Americans making up the U.S. film audience has not gone unnoticed by the Hollywood studios. African Americans currently make up almost 30 percent of the movie ticket–buying audience. In the information age, where film audiences are getting smaller, African Americans are making up an even larger portion of the audiences. The recent placement of cineplexes into African American communities, which for years had few theaters, further reflects this audience's importance. The Hollywood raid on black talent will continue as the need to give audiences what they want remains a Hollywood priority.

Due to the ever more complex and complicated structure of film financing, locating and giving credit for production have become progressively more difficult. The production company and the film's producer previously could be looked upon for the financing and overall vision of the film. Today, everyone from the star of the film to a family member of the star is given production credit. When tracking African American film production, one has to go film by film, for most of these production companies have little or no track record to examine. For example, Darin Scott has been one of the most successful producers of films for the African American film market in the 1990s. Among the films for which he has producer's credit are *Fear of a Black Hat* (1994), *Tales from the Hood* (1995), *Sprung* (1997), *Menace II Society* (1993), and *Love and a .45* (1994). Although Darin Scott has an extensive track record as an individual producer, his corporate track record is illusive.

The 1997 release and success of *Soul Food* reflect the importance of the African American audience. The film, which was produced by Edmonds Entertainment, an African American production company, was the number-two film at the box office during its initial week of release. The number-one film was the heavily promoted *The Peacemaker*, which was the first film from Hollywood's newest studio, DreamWorks. Although the film was second in the total box office, the per screen average for the film tells a different story. *The Peacemaker* had a total box office of $16,030,673, with a per screen average of $6,786, whereas *Soul Food* had a total box office of $14,327,093, with a per screen average of $10,699. Theaters showing *Soul Food*, consequently, were 25 percent more full. This trend of a high per screen average was consistent during the first three weeks of the run. It should be noted that young black writer George Tillman, Jr., and his longtime producing partner, Robert Teitel, are now receiving offers from the major studios for their next project. The raid on successful black talent by Hollywood continues.

The 1990s represent the first opportunity in over 50 years for African Americans to guide and control a strong film presence. With African Americans making up almost 30 percent of the film audience, few can challenge the monetary significance of the African American film market. The placement of theaters in African American communities acknowledges both the presence and importance of the market. Judging by Hollywood's constant hiring of African American talent, it is safe to say that individuals with the skills to best capitalize on audience interest at a specific historical moment are in demand. The key, however, is with African American production companies. They can give young filmmakers the opportunity to reach an audience and ensure that their talent will be available for subsequent projects. It is very hard for a company to establish a track record, which can translate into a greater financial base, if its talent is constantly being hired away. African American production companies are key to shaping the vision of African American images in film.

SELECTED BIBLIOGRAPHY: Donald Bogle, *Blacks in American Films and Television* (New York: Garland Publishing, 1988); Daniel J. Leab, *From Sambo to Superspade: The Black Experience in Motion Pictures* (Boston: Houghton Mifflin Company, 1975); James R. Nesteby, *Black Images in American Films, 1896–1954* (Washington, DC: University Press of America, 1982); Lindsay Patterson, *Black Films and Film-Makers* (New York: Dodd, Mead and Company, 1975).

Eric Pierson

FORD, BARNEY L. (1822–1902), Denver, barbershop owner, restaurateur, hotelier, civic leader.

One of the first African Americans to settle in Colorado, Barney Ford's entrepreneurial skills earned the attention and respect of fellow pioneers. At a time when most people of color were either enslaved or struggling to subsist as sharecroppers or wage-earning laborers, this former fugitive from bondage established and amassed wealth from a number of business ventures. Imbued with the desire to uplift his race, Ford used his position of prominence to press for citizenship rights for black Coloradans.

Ford, born into slavery in Virginia, by his midtwenties escaped and made his way to Chicago. His eventual arrival in Breckenridge, Colorado, in 1860 resulted from the lure of recently discovered gold. When his efforts as a prospector failed, Ford moved to Denver and over the next few years established a number of successful businesses, including People's Restaurant, whose two-story building also housed a barbershop and saloon. Shortly after it opened in August 1863, an advertisement in the *Rocky Mountain News* beckoned customers to come in with promises of "the most choice and delicate luxuries of Colorado and the East" and the "very finest liquors and cigars." In July 1868, Ulysses S. Grant, presidential nominee, attended a reception in his honor held at Ford's establishment.

The success of Ford's early business ventures led to the building of the elegantly appointed Inter-Ocean Hotel in 1873 and later to the construction of a second Inter-Ocean establishment in Cheyenne, Wyoming. J. H. Triggs, a contemporary, described the latter as "a first-class hotel in every respect, and one of the finest west of Chicago." The prominence Ford enjoyed from his entrepreneurship led him to be recognized as a leader of African Americans, not simply in Denver but in all of Colorado, especially in their efforts to secure equal rights and access to the ballot. When Colorado attempted to insert a discriminatory provision in its petition for statehood, Ford went to Washington, where he successfully lobbied to have it removed. For the next several years, he exercised his right to a political voice through his active participation in the local Republican Party organization.

SELECTED BIBLIOGRAPHY: "Barney Ford's People's Restaurant," *National Register of Historic Places Nomination* Washington, DC: U.S. Department of the Interior, National Park Service; Frank Hall, *A History of the State of Colorado*, vols. 1,3 (Chicago: Blakely Printing Company, 1889, 1895); J. H. Triggs, *A History of Cheyenne and Northern Wyoming* (Omaha, NE: Job Printing House, 1876).

Edna Greene Medford

FORD, CORNELIUS EVARTS (c. 1870–1950), New York, cattle broker, Urban League, promoter/leader.

Cornelius Ford was the founder in 1907 of the C. E. Ford Company, a Buffalo, New York, cattle brokerage company, with annual earnings amounting to over $1 million. Ford speculated in the high-profit-margin-based Canadian cattle market. For 25 years, his company was one of the chief buyers for Armour and Company and Cudahy and Company. For cattle shipment to the Midwest stockyards, Ford leased railroad yards from the New York Central. Highly respected for his capital-generating abilities and expertise in livestock trading, Ford was elected to the Buffalo Livestock Exchange Board of Directors in 1937 and became its president in 1945, then the fifth largest livestock exchange in the nation.

Ford was born in Jonesboro, Tennessee, and grew up on his grandparents' farm, attending school intermittently until he was 13. Then he became a farm manager, supervising some 30 farm laborers. Ford was 15 when his parents, Mark and Angeline Ford, died. Until he was 21, he divided his time between studying at the American Missionary Association Warner Institute in Jonesboro and learning the livestock brokerage trade in Addison, Michigan. By 1891, Ford was working as a cattle broker in Michigan, Illinois, and New York, where he moved in 1907. Four years earlier, he had been in partnership in a livestock and shipping business. Ford married Martha Thompson of Painted Post, New York, in 1911. They had one son, Cornelius, Jr. Ford, Sr., was active in the Buffalo Urban League. His business philosophy: Know the value of your expertise—profits can be gained by using one's expertise to make money for others.

SELECTED BIBLIOGRAPHY: Robert H. Kinzer and Edward Sagarin, *The Negro in American Business: The Conflict between Separatism and Integration* (New York: Greenberg Publisher, 1950); Vincent Suitt, "A Livestock Exchange President," *Opportunity* (Spring 1947).

Juliet E. K. Walker

FORTEN, JAMES (1766–1842), Philadelphia, sail maker/manufacturer, abolitionist, activist.

As the owner of a successful sail-making establishment and a highly respected community leader, James Forten, Sr., was also one of the leading nineteenth-century antebellum activists. Forten's early activities at sea provided him first-hand knowledge of sailing ships. In 1780, he served as a powderboy aboard the *Royal Louis*, a Pennsylvania privateer under the command of Stephen Decatur, Sr., during the Revolutionary War. In 1785, Forten was a crewman on the London-bound vessel *Commerce*. After a year in London, on returning to America, Forten worked as a sail maker, the craft of his late father, by apprenticing himself to Robert Bridges, a prominent white merchant. In 1786, at the age of 20, Forten became foreman of Bridges's sail lofts. Increasingly, Bridges relied on the good business judgment of his black foreman. In 1798, when Bridges retired, Forten purchased the business.

Forten financed the purchase of the sail loft through a loan from Thomas Willing, a wealthy white merchant. The loan was partially secured by a contractual arrangement. Forten would equip each of Willing's ships with a sail-making device that Forten had invented. Beyond the manufacture and managerial components of sail making, Forten had always maintained an interest in sail-making technology. That interest had led to his discovery of a new device for handling sails. Although he did not secure a patent for his invention, Forten marketed the device in and around Philadelphia. The invention netted him a substantial profit.

Located at 95 South Wharves and situated above the stores of Thomas Willing, the Forten sail loft establishment became a successful business venture. For over four decades, from 1800 to 1844, the Forten business employed an interracial workforce of between 30 and 40 men. He insisted upon racial equality at his business establishment, and his employees enjoyed job security. Indeed, according to Forten's daughter Sarah, one white journeyman worked with her father for over three decades. Charles Anthony, a skilled African American sail maker, was Forten's foreman for 20 years. The racial composition of Forten's employees was unique on the Philadelphia wharves. Aware that immigrants often displaced black laborers, Forten preferred an interracial, native-born workforce. His competitors typically hired only white apprentices and tradesmen.

As he expanded his business interests, Forten considered the prospects of developing trade relations on the African continent. With the end of the War of 1812, the sail-making business rebounded from its wartime slump. As prosperity returned, Forten responded favorably to a plan suggested by his friend and fellow entrepreneur, Paul Cuffe.* Since 1811, Cuffe, a black Quaker merchant, shipowner, and Pan-Africanist from New Bedford, Massachusetts, had promoted black immigration to West Africa. In a letter to Forten, Cuffe proposed that a group of African Americans finance construction of a vessel for the legitimate African trade. Forten presented the proposal to members of the Philadelphia African Institution, a group of free blacks, who endorsed Cuffe's plan for limited and voluntary immigration to Africa.

Concern over the infamous slave trade and racial prejudice in America prompted Cuffe and others to consider black colonization in the British colony of Sierra Leone. At the same time, businessmen Cuffe and Forten hoped to stimulate an African and African American trade exchange of foodstuffs, cloth, and other commodities. Moreover, an expansion of trade could lead to developing new employment opportunities for blacks. Cuffe's death in 1817 and the establishment of the American Colonization Society, with its plans of large-scale settlement of emancipated slaves and free blacks in Africa, abruptly curtailed the prospect that Cuffe's plan would come to fruition. Forten's receptivity to the idea, nonetheless, reveals his desire to explore new business ventures.

Apart from the prospect of African trade, Forten and Cuffe consummated a number of business transactions. Forten supplied the rigging for Cuffe's brig *Traveller* for the December 1815 voyage to Sierra Leone. Evidence of a joint venture is also contained in a January 18, 1817, letter to Forten from Cuffe, who wrote that his nephew Captain Paul Wainer and his crew of the sloop *Resolution* of Troy were making their way south along the Atlantic Ocean from Massachusetts to North Carolina with cargo. Cuffe promised to repay Forten for any money he might be obliged to extend to Wainer, who had embarked on the voyage without sufficient funds. Four months later, in April 1817, Forten's letter to Cuffe enthusiastically introduced a friend who planned to write to Cuffe concerning yet another business transaction.

Throughout the Philadelphia business community, James Forten enjoyed a reputation for integrity, fair business dealings, and high personal ethics. He adamantly refused to supply rigging or transact business with shipowners engaged in the infamous slave trade. Forten remarked to fellow abolitionist Lydia Maria Child that he considered a request for rigging from a slave trader to be an insult to any honest or humane man. Although during the early 1840s Forten's sons encountered some discriminatory treatment in their business dealings, there is considerable evidence that a great many persons seeking sail-making services placed James Forten's business acumen above any racial biases they may have harbored.

Judging from Forten's statements about his business activities, the fall and winter months were the busiest times for sail makers. In a letter dated July 28, 1832, to William Lloyd Garrison, Forten explained that with the onset of the summer leisure season he had more time for correspondence and to pursue his activist work. Years earlier, in 1787, Forten began his activism with membership in the Free African Society,* a religious-based beneficial organization. By the early 1790s Forten assumed a leadership role in the formation of Philadelphia's African Episcopal Church of St. Thomas.

During the 1830s, James Forten and his family participated in the various organized units of the antislavery crusade. Forten, his two oldest sons, James, Jr., and Robert, and his son-in-law Robert Purvis were members and financial supporters of the American Anti-Slavery Society and the Pennsylvania Anti-Slavery Society and spearheaded the creation of the American Moral Reform Society in 1835. Forten's wife Charlotte, their daughters Margaretta, Harriet, and Sarah, and daughter-in-law Mary Woods Forten, along with an interracial group of 17 other women, founded the Philadelphia Female Antislavery Society.

The Forten family members and Purvis participated in the interracial Phila-delphia Vigilant Committee, an essential link in the Underground* network. Also, Forten helped launch support of William Lloyd Garrison's abolitionist newspaper, *The Liberator*, with money paid for the paper's first twenty-seven subscriptions. Other abolitionists, white and black, would come to depend on the steadfast cooperation, hospitality, advice, and even financial support from Forten. Over the years, Forten effectively used his wealth, his community stand-ing, and his position of influence to champion the causes of antislavery and racial uplift.

Profits from the business permitted Forten to live in comfort, even luxury, for his time. It was reported that by 1823 Forten owned both city and country residences as well as a carriage. A two-story dwelling on Lombard served as the primary residence of the Forten family for nearly a century. On March 4, 1842, after a lingering illness, James Forten, Sr., died, leaving an estate worth $67,000 to his wife and children. At his funeral, a procession of several thou-sand persons accompanied his casket from the service held at the African Epis-copal Church of St. Thomas to the burial site. When the elder Forten died, his sons, James, Jr., and Robert, who had joined their father's company in 1837, maintained the family business for an additional two years. In 1844, they sold it to their foreman, the African American Charles Anthony, and his partner Bo-livar.

James Forten was not only a successful entrepreneur; he also initiated an activist family tradition. He was born in Philadelphia, the second child and first son of sail maker Thomas Forten and his wife Sarah. At the time of his birth, the Forten family had resided in the colony of Pennsylvania for three genera-tions. Brought to America from West Africa, as a youth, Forten's great-grandfather eventually purchased his freedom. Thomas Forten, the father of James Forten, was born free. For two generations of his family before the Civil War, the Forten name was closely associated with the fight against slavery and the promotion of civil rights.

SELECTED BIBLIOGRAPHY: Esther M. Douty, *James Forten, the Sailmaker and Pi-oneer Champion of Negro Rights* (Chicago: Rand-McNally, 1968); Charles Lydell, *Trav-els in North America, in the Years 1841–1842* (New York: Wiley and Putnam, 1845); Benjamin Quarles, *Black Abolitionists* (New York: Oxford University Press, 1969); Jan-ice L. Sumler-Lewis, "The Forten-Purvis Women of Philadelphia and the American Anti-Slavery Crusade," *Journal of Negro History* 66 (Winter 1981–1982).

Janice Sumler-Edmond

FRANCHISE UNITS. An alternative path to traditional small business ownership is to be a franchisee. Clearly the franchise path seems enticing to many entrepreneurs, for franchise sales have been growing at an annual rate of about 10 percent in recent years. Furthermore, franchising can be an especially good path for aspiring entrepreneurs who lack managerial experience or a college degree. One recent survey found that 13 percent of new franchisees have blue-collar backgrounds, and 60 percent did not finish college. Since the entry of blacks into traditional small business has been a long and relatively slow process, with only moderate gains to date, it is logical that blacks should seek to become entrepreneurs as franchisees, as well as through independent small business ownership.

Yet here, too, progress has been limited. U.S. Department of Commerce data in the 1990s show the gross sales of black-owned franchises accounting for only 0.7 percent of total franchise sales. Obstacles to black entry are both racial and financial. Certainly some franchisers have consciously limited or discouraged blacks from becoming their franchisees, but also many blacks have found it very difficult or impossible to raise the necessary start-up money to become a franchisee. A 1994 listings and rankings of those franchise organizations with the largest number of black-owned franchise units (by *Black Enterprise*) include well-known national franchise chains, such as McDonald's, Burger King, KFC (Kentucky Fried Chicken), Southland (7-Eleven), Wendy's, and Pizza Hut. Also included high in the rankings are much less known chains such as Coverall North America, O.P.E.N. Cleaning Systems, and D&K Enterprises. Coverall led the listing with 980 black-owned franchise units in 1994 (out of 2,820 total units, or 35 percent), whereas McDonald's was second with 658 units (out of 9,086, or 7.2 percent).

An alternative measure would be the *percentage* of black-owned to total units, and in 1994 the highest was Accent Hair Salons, with 9 of its 11 (82 percent) franchise units black-owned. Second was RACS International, another commercial cleaning franchiser, with 35 of 45 (78 percent) units black-owned. Giant franchisers, such as McDonald's and Burger King, require start-up investments of $400,000 and more. Obviously, such an amount is difficult for both blacks and whites to raise. But these franchisers and many other large national franchisers have developed formal programs to increase the number of their black- and other minority-owned units. These programs involve guarantees for bank loans, reduced start-up cash requirements, special training programs, and so on. Also, several investment financing organizations will provide equity and debt financing to qualified minority franchise applicants.

The small, less-known franchiser organizations have attracted black franchisees without such assistance programs via low start-up costs (often only $5,000 to $10,000), word-of-mouth reputation spread by existing black franchisees, and the nature of franchises that involve a product or service that can be sold on a part-time basis. Both measures of black-owned franchise unit success rates are valid and meaningful. McDonald's and other franchisers, with a sizable number of black-owned franchise units, each with many employees, have a *macro*impact upon our overall economy and also upon the communities in which the units are located.

Such large black-owned franchise units are a significant aspect of increased black participation in a national economy in which such black participation is still far below the population proportion. Furthermore, the typical McDonald's or similar franchise unit provides employment to many people, usually residents of the local neighborhood. The unit can also provide major income and investment opportunities for the unit's owner or owners. Some black franchisees own multiple units, and in these situations the investment performance becomes quite substantial. Thus, the local economic impact on the black community can be very meaningful.

On the other hand, the economic impact on the economy or on the community created by one black owner/operator of a small franchise cleaning service is minimal. Yet there is still an important *micro*impact on that one person. Such a small franchise unit can provide important business experience and training for blacks and other minorities who may eventually move on to more substantial entrepreneurial and business endeavors. This is supported by various research studies that have found that business failure rates are higher for minorities than for whites and are primarily due to a lack of business training and experience, youth, and a rush to start one's own business.

Studies of black franchisees' attitudes toward their success and their franchisers indicate mixed degrees of satisfaction. Certainly some black franchisees have reason to be pleased with their performance and success, yet surveys show a number of areas of concern and disappointment. Too many black-owned franchise units are located in the inner cities, where operating costs, such as security, pilferage, and employee quality and turnover, tend to be more expensive. Thus, many inner-city franchisees believe that it is more difficult to make a profit in such locations than in other franchise locations. Furthermore, these franchise unit owners feel that these extra difficulties are not recognized by the national franchisers.

Also, some black franchisees and others in the black community question the sincerity of the minority franchise development and assistance programs of the large national franchisers, seeing these programs as simply responses to general and specific pressures and the need to achieve quotas or numerical objectives. Clearly, there has been progress and success in black-owned franchise unit development, yet there is a considerable distance still to travel along this path.

SELECTED BIBLIOGRAPHY: Robert D. Hisrich and Candida Brush, "Characteristics of the Minority Entrepreneur," *Journal of Small Business Management* (October 1986); Matthew C. Sonfield, "An Attitudinal Comparison of Black and White Small Businessmen," *American Journal of Small Business* (January 1978); Matthew C. Sonfield, "Progress and Success in the Development of Black-Owned Franchise Units," *Review of Black Political Economy* (Fall 1993).

Matthew C. Sonfield

FRATERNAL ORGANIZATIONS. Until the depression, the fraternal lodge among blacks was often the single most popular community institution. The defining characteristics of a fraternal organization, generally, are as follows: an autonomous system of lodges, a democratic form of internal government, a ritual, including degrees and passwords, and the provision of mutual aid. Other common features were sickness and burial benefits and, by the end of the nineteenth century, life insurance. In 1910, sociologist Howard W. Odum estimated that "total membership of the negro societies, paying and nonpaying, is nearly equal to the church membership."

Prince Hall Freemasonry represented the oldest, and most prestigious, of all the fraternal societies. The origins of the order were traceable to 1775, when British soldiers in Boston initiated Prince Hall, a West Indian, and several other blacks. Denied recognition by their white American "brethren," these members created an entirely separate organization that still exists today. By the Civil War, Freemasonry among blacks had spread to urban areas throughout the North. In the meantime, an array of other societies had been organized. The Brown Fellowship Society of Charleston, founded in 1790, engaged in one of the first recorded efforts to encourage entrepreneurship. It offered members access to a "credit union" to finance new businesses and home improvements. The antebellum period also witnessed the establishment of the Grand United Order of Odd Fellows in 1843. By 1916, it was the largest society among blacks, with over 300,000 members and a thriving female auxiliary, the Household of Ruth, of nearly 200,000 members.

In the decades after the Civil War, the Grand Fountain of the United Order of True Reformers made an especially notable impact on business development. Founded in 1872, it grew rapidly under the leadership of William Washington Browne, an ex-slave from Georgia and Union Army veteran. He hoped that blacks could be both "united in finance" and "united in brotherhood." The Order, in addition to providing life insurance, organized the first black-owned bank in the United States with assets of over $500,000 by 1907. In addition, it established a hotel of 150 rooms, retail stores, and a newspaper. While most of these enterprises had failed by 1910, the Order gave financial and organizational experience to many future business leaders.

The economic accomplishments of another group, the Independent Order of Saint Luke, were more durable. In 1903, it opened the Penny Savings Bank of Saint Luke in Richmond. As a result, the head of the Order, Maggie L. Walker,* became the first female bank founder and president in American history. Shortly thereafter, the society established a printing plant, a newspaper, and for a brief time, a department store, the Saint Luke Emporium.

Fraternal societies of all varieties among blacks often stressed the cultivation of "good moral character," most importantly thrift and self-reliance, as a prerequisite for economic success. They closely associated these values with racial pride. According to Browne, the man who had toiled in the cotton field "can beat the plan laid by people that have been free all their lives" because "he is the best financier who can make money go the farthest." Moreover, these societies provided the initial foundation for the formation of commercial banks and legal-reserve insurance companies. The North Carolina Mutual Company,* founded in 1898, had evolved out of the Royal Knights of King David. John Merrick, the founder of the company, had once worked for the True Reformers, as had Samuel Wilson Rutherford, who organized the National Benefit Insurance Company in Washington, D.C., in 1898. Another prominent enterprise, the Atlanta Life Insurance Company,* chartered in 1905, could trace its genealogy to a small church-based mutual aid society.

By the 1930s, black fraternal societies had entered a sustained period of decline from which they never recovered. Several factors were responsible, including the rise of alternative sources for entertainment, the provision of social welfare services by government and employers, actuarial instability, restrictive insurance regulation, and competition from commercial insurance companies. Many societies suffered from the collapse of real estate values because of heavy investments during the 1920s in mortgages and rental property. More directly, the massive and long-term unemployment of the 1930s paved the way for countless lapses by the rank and file.

There were notable exceptions to this story of decline, however. Some, often state-based, societies such as the Lily White Security Benefit Association (Florida), the United Order of Friends (Arkansas), the Mississippi Jurisdiction of the International Order of Twelve Knights and Daughters of Tabor, and the United Order of Friendship (Mississippi) underwent significant expansion during and after the depression. All opened hospitals that served thousands of members. In some cases, they established credit unions, operated newspapers, built apartment houses, and founded credit unions. Nevertheless, even most of these enterprises soon declined.

Black fraternal societies have played an extensive, but little studied, historical role. Before the rise of the welfare state, they performed vital social welfare functions including health care, orphanages, and unemployment assistance. Their importance to the development of business was equally great. Fraternal societies not only were sources of start-up capital for new commercial enterprises but also were training forums for future entrepreneurs.

SELECTED BIBLIOGRAPHY: David T. Beito, "Mutual Aid, State Welfare, and Organized Charity: Fraternal Societies and the 'Deserving' and the 'Undeserving' Poor, 1900–1930," *Journal of Policy History* 5 (1993): 419–434; Elsa Barkeley Brown, "Womanist Consciousness: Maggie Lena Walker and the Independent Order of Saint Luke," *Signs* 14 (Spring 1989): 610–633; David M. Fahey, *The Black Lodge in White America: "True Reformer" Browne and His Economic Strategy* (Dayton, OH: Wright State University Press, 1994); William Muraskin, *Middle-Class Blacks in a White Society: Prince Hall Freemasonry in America* (Berkeley: University of California Press, 1975).

David T. Beito

FREE AFRICAN SOCIETY. Throughout the colonies, economic advancement for free blacks was hindered because of white discrimination, especially in hiring, creating apprenticeships, and lending money. Additionally, white businessmen exploited the racial advantages of an unequal legal system to harass and cripple black competition. Nonetheless, despite stacked odds, many colonial African Americans maintained their entrepreneurial spirit. A few tried to augment their economic opportunities by adopting a West African style of pooling investment funds in the form of rotating credit associations. Organizations or associations such as the Yoruba *esusu* society required members to make fixed payments every market day so that all associates could be given the use of the joint savings on a rotating basis. Comparable arrangements to multiply capital were in operation by social organizations along the coast from Sierra Leone to the Niger Delta, and the principles were soon carried across the Atlantic to islands such as the Bahamas, Jamaica, and Trinidad.

Since lack of capital was also a serious handicap to blacks in the North American colonies, it is not surprising that a similar form of capital formation arose here as well in the founding of the economic organization of the Free African Society, established in Philadelphia in 1787. Local members contributed both initiation fees and regular monthly payments that after one year could be used on a rotating basis by members of the society who were in need. With the death of a subscriber, his widow and children became eligible for his share. Although the insurance and charity functions of the Free African Society were like those of Euro-American benevolent societies, already in operation in Philadelphia, the Free African Society was not necessarily simply an imitation of the others.

Probably the insurance functions served by such corporate savings, which in their own right ultimately led to the development of the African American life insurance industry, were modeled after those of nearby Euro-American benevolent associations. The revolving access to credit, however, seems more African. In a similar manifestation of the communal principle, Africans in late eighteenth-century New England often pooled their small savings to purchase lottery tickets so that they might buy their own and their families' freedom. At it turned out, in Philadelphia the joint savings of the Free African Society were eventually used mostly for the purpose of financing a new African Church rather than a number of small businesses. Nonetheless, given the racist nature of early American society, an investment in black religious autonomy may have been a wiser economic decision, even if it was not explicitly capitalistic in intent.

Whatever the ultimate significance of the Philadelphia joint savings venture, the history of the Free African Society should remind us that colonial African Americans were able to develop their own Afro-American engine of capital formation, in this case, putting African communalism to work serving the needs of North American individualism.

SELECTED BIBLIOGRAPHY: Whittington B. Johnson, *The Promising Years, 1750–1830: The Emergence of Black Labor and Business* (New York: Garland Publishing,

1993); Ivan Light, *Ethnic Enterprise in America* (Berkeley: University of California Press, 1972); William D. Piersen, *From Africa to America: African-American History from the Colonial Era to the Early Republic 1526–1790* (New York: Twayne Publishers, 1996).

William D. Piersen

FREE BLACK ENTREPRENEURS. By the Civil War, 21 blacks in business had accumulated wealth in excess of $100,000. Only one person of African descent achieved millionaire status before the Civil War, however. William Leidesdorff,* a San Francisco, California, merchant and landowner, on his death in 1848 left an estate that was settled at $1.5 million. Indeed, in 1846, a pamphlet, entitled in part "Some of the Wealthy Citizens of Philadelphia with a Fair Estimate of Their Wealth," established wealth holding of $50,000 as the minimum for one to be listed. Moreover, by 1860, the national mean wealth of Americans was $2,580. There were sectional differences in wealth holding. In the South the mean wealth was $3,978; in the North, it was $2,040.

By 1860, there were several blacks with combined holdings of $500,000. In New Orleans the Soulie brothers, Albin and Bernard, who were listed in both the federal census and the R. G. Dun and Company mercantile credit records as "capitalist," "broker," and "merchant," held combined wealth of $500,000. Also in New Orleans were the Lacroix brothers—Francois, whose occupation was listed as a "tailor" was worth $300,000; and Julien, listed as a grocer, was worth $250,000. Stephen Smith,* with $250,000 in 1860, was worth $500,000 in 1865—a lumber and coal merchant in Philadelphia who was also a financier. Also, by 1860, there were nine blacks whose wealth exceeded $150,000 up to $250,000. There were four sugar planters, a cotton broker, a capitalist, a merchant, a landlord, and also the combined wealth of two brothers who were master tailors.

In addition, there were seven blacks who accumulated wealth from $100,000 to $149,999. In this group of leading antebellum black entrepreneurs were three cotton planters, one sugar planter, one commission broker (who was also an undertaker), a sail maker and a barber. Only one woman—Madame Cecee McCarty, a merchant—had accumulated $155,000 by 1848. Only four of the leading black entrepreneurs lived outside the state of Louisiana: Leidesdorff in California; the sail maker James Forten* and Stephen Smith in Pennsylvania; and Washington Spaulding, a Louisville, Kentucky, barber.

In antebellum America the leading black entrepreneurs, as did white men of wealth Stephen Giraud and John Jacob Astor, had extensive real estate holdings. Black entrepreneurs were also heavily involved in informal banking activities. As Martin Delany* said in discussing Stephen Smith: "The principal active business attended by Mr. S. in person, is that of buying good negotiable and other paper." The Soulie brothers were also actively involved in informal banking activities, so much so that one entry in the Dun records recorded their occupations as "capitalists." Also, most of the leading black entrepreneurs invested in stocks and municipal bonds and had large bank accounts, which provided them cash for their financial activities in addition to the rent they collected on their property as well as the profits made in their real estate speculation activities (Table 1).

While many of the most successful black businesspeople established service enterprises—indeed, antebellum black America's "high-status" occupations were barbering, catering,* and tailoring—the leading black businessmen in those occupations used their profits to expand their wealth through real estate speculation and informal banking activities. Francois Lacroix, worth $300,000 in 1860, owned one of the most fashionable tailoring houses in New Orleans. His advertisement in an 1853 New Orleans city directory stated: "Merchant tailor (established 1817) importer of French cloth, fancy casimere, and the best and most extensive assortment of clothing of every description, made in Paris, by the first fashionable tailors, and an elegant variety of gloves, cravats, stocks, etc." The most successful black tailors, however, were also designers, who traveled frequently to France. Before the Civil War, their designs influenced the fashion industry in both America and Paris. Ironically, it would not be until the post–Civil rights era that black tailors, such as Karl Kani, would become a significant force again in the fashion industry (ranked 28th on the *BE* 100s in 1996, with sales of $65 million, Kani's hip-hop designs closed out the twentieth century).

In antebellum America, however, Lacroix's profits from tailoring went into real estate and his informal banking activities. The most successful black barbers, caterers, and tailors had only elite wealthy whites as their clientele, which provided an entry to their activities in finance as informal bankers in money-lending and currency note exchanges. William Tiler Johnson,* a free black barber in Natchez, Mississippi, was born a slave but acquired his freedom. In working as a barber, he used his profits to establish several barbershops, a cotton plantation managed by a white overseer and worked by slaves, and several retail stores, in addition to running his horses on the Natchez racetrack. Johnson was also involved in informal banking activities. These economic activities were carried out in a state that by 1860 had 436,631 slaves and only 773 free blacks.

In preindustrial antebellum America, most blacks who generated wealth were involved in a diversity of enterprises. In Pennsylvania, the Dun credit records reported that William Goodridge "trades extensively." His mercantile business was described by them as "Fancy Goods," with an inventory that ranged from jewels to toys. Goodridge was also a printer and had an Oyster Company in addition to a construction company, besides running railroad cars on the Columbia Railroad. As the Dun entry emphasized, Goodridge had "a great many irons in the fire." He was worth over $20,000, and he owned property both in the United States and Canada. In New York City, Edward V. Clark, who owned a jewelry store, was also a caterer. In addition to using his $5,000 in silver and crystal glassware and cast silver and plate dining and tea sets in his catering

Table 1
Wealthholding of Representative Leading Black Entrepreneurs, 1820–1865

NAME	LOCATION	BUSINESS ACTIVITY	ASSESSED WEALTH
Leidesdorff, William	San Francisco	merchandising, real estate	$1,500,000
Smith, Stephen	Columbia; Philadelphia, Pa.	lumber merchant, real estate	500,000
Soulie, Albin & Bernard	New Orleans	merchant broker, capitalists	500,000
Lacroix, François	New Orleans	tailor, real estate	300,000
Lacroix, Julien	New Orleans	grocer, real estate	250,000
Ricaud, widow, & son, Pierre	Iberville Parish	sugar planters	221,500
DuBuclet, August	Iberville Parish	sugar planter	206,400
Pottier, Honore	New Orleans	commission broker, in cotton	200,000
DuPuy, Edmond	New Orleans	capitalist	171,000
Reggio, Auguste and Octave	Plaquemines Parish	sugar planter, overseer	160,000
McCarty, Mme. Cecee	New Orleans	merchandising, money broker	155,000
DeCuir, Antoine	Pointe Coupee Parish	sugar planter	151,000
Logoaster, Erasme	New Orleans	landlord	150,000
Colvis, Julien and Dumas, Joseph	New Orleans	tailors	150,000
Metoyer, Augustin	Natchitoches Parish	cotton planter	140,958
Durnford, estate of Thomas	Plaquemines Parish	sugar planter	115,000
Metoyer, Jean Baptiste	Natchitoches Parish	cotton planter	112,761
Casenave, Pierre A. D.	New Orleans	commission broker, undertaker	100,000
Donato, Martin	St. Landry Parish	cotton planter	100,000
Forten, James	Philadelphia, Pa.	sailmaker	100,000
Spraulding, Washington	Louisville, Ky.	barber, real estate	100,000

Source: Juliet E. K. Walker, ''Racism, Slavery, Free Enterprise: Black Entrepreneurship in the United States before the Civil War,'' *Business History Review* 60 (Autumn 1986).

business, Clark also loaned these articles out, according to Dun, to the "upper ten."

There were sectional and regional differences in the kinds of businesses established by blacks. In the South, the existence of slavery influenced occupational participation in craft enterprises. By 1860, 80 percent of the 125,000 craftsmen were slaves, including some 6 to 8 percent who hired out their own time,* including slave entrepreneurs who established enterprises, thus competing with both white craftsmen as well as free black craftsmen. In the South, the largest number of free black craftsmen were carpenters. Loren Schweninger found that in 1860 in the seven states in the Upper South and Washington, D.C., only 221 carpenters owned property holdings averaging $885, whereas in the eight Lower South states, 210 carpenters held property holdings averaging $1,300. In the North, however, black craftsmen seldom were able to secure employment due to the opposition of white craftsmen. In the North, antebellum blacks who pursued craft activities invariably were the few who opened their own businesses.

In both the North and South, not only racial societal constraints limited black business participation before the Civil War; states and local governments passed laws and ordinances to suppress black participation in many occupational areas in which self-employed economic activities could be developed. In New York blacks were by law excluded from working as draymen, an occupation that was profitable and required only manual strength as the basic entry-level requirement. In his analysis of black occupational participation in several cities in 1850, Leonard Curry found that less than 3.5 percent of black males were businesspeople, which also included those who established marginal enterprises as hawkers, peddlers, laundresses, and chimney sweeps and those doing odd jobs or working as jacks-of-all-trades. The largest number of blacks in business lived in New Orleans, where some 8.0 percent of free blacks had established various enterprises.

By 1860, there were 488,070 free blacks, and most were impoverished. Yet the most economically successful were those who were self-employed. Interestingly, too, the most successful black businesspeople before the Civil War were those with human capital skills in the service occupations whose clientele were primarily the white elite. Ironically, in the post–civil rights era, human capital skills continue to be important for blacks who generate wealth and high incomes—specifically, the black superstar entertainers and athletes—whereas the leading black entrepreneurs, with wealth in excess of $100,000, find their counterparts in the *Black Enterprise* listing of the leading 100 black businesspeople. Historical consideration of black business history, then, must be inclusive of these leading antebellum black entrepreneurs.

SELECTED BIBLIOGRAPHY: Ira Berlin, *Slaves without Masters: The Free Negro in the Ante-bellum South* (New York: Oxford University Press, 1981); Leonard P. Curry, *The Free Black in Urban America* (Chicago: University of Chicago Press, 1981); Loren Schweninger, "Black-Owned Businesses in the South, 1790–1880," *Business History*

Review 63 (Spring 1989): 22–60; Loren Schweninger, *Black Property Owners in the South, 1790–1915* (Urbana: University of Illinois Press, 1990); Juliet E. K. Walker, *The History of Black Business in America: Capitalism, Race, Entrepreneurship* (New York Macmillan, 1998); Juliet E. K. Walker, "Racism, Slavery, and Free Enterprise: Black Entrepreneurship in the United States before the Civil War," *Business History Review* 60 (Autumn 1986): 343–382.

Juliet E. K. Walker

FREEDMAN'S BANK. The National Freedman's Savings and Trust Company, more popularly known as the Freedman's Savings Bank, was established on March 3, 1865, when it was incorporated by a congressional act. While the bill to establish the Freedman's Bank was signed by President Abraham Lincoln, it was not a federal bank. The Freedman's Bank was a privately white-owned and -managed financial institution that, however, gave the impression that it was a government institution. The passbook carried the inscription: "The government of the United States has made this bank perfectly safe." Also, passbooks carried the pictures of Lincoln, General Ulysses S. Grant, General Howard, and the U.S. flag unfurling over an imposing public building.

The Freedman's Bank remained in existence until June 1874. Branches were established in 35 cities, all in the South except for St. Louis, Philadelphia, New York, and Washington, D.C., where the first branch bank opened in August 1865. The central office of the Freedman's Bank was the New York branch from 1865 to 1869, until 1870, when the Washington branch became the central headquarters. Only a few blacks were ever hired in the branch banks and then only as tellers, clerks, and bookkeepers. There was a black cashier in the Washington, D.C., branch, but he was considered a figurehead. Also, a few blacks were appointed to advisory positions, but whites were the principal employees and managers. Only when the bank was failing, a casualty of white misman-agement and the Panic of 1873, did whites leave their positions. Then blacks were put in management positions, including Frederick Douglass, who was named president of the Freedman's Bank in January 1874, six months before it closed.

Blacks, moreover, were never able to capitalize on their deposits for loans to invest in development of the black community. Deposits made by blacks at the branch banks were sent to the Washington branch for investment in government bonds, stocks, and treasury notes. Only when investment profits exceeded 10 percent could branch banks make real estate loans. Blacks did, initially, earn 1 percent interest on their deposits, which had increased to 6 percent by the early 1870s. After the bank's failure, two congressional committees established fraud, embezzlement, and corruption on the part of the white bank managers. Some even took out personal and business loans, sometimes without security, and even on occasion canceled their loans. The New York central bank office was con-servatively managed, unlike the Washington, D.C., branch. Its head was H. D. Cooke, president of the First National Bank in Washington and a cousin of Jay

Cooke, who at one time was granted a loan of $500,000 from the Freedman's Bank. During its existence, $57 million had been deposited by blacks. By 1900, only 62 percent of the amount on deposit—$1,638,259.49—at the time the bank failed in 1874 was repaid.

SELECTED BIBLIOGRAPHY: Walter L. Fleming, *The Freedman's Bank: A Chapter in the Economic History of the Negro Race* (Chapel Hill: University of North Carolina Press, 1927); Abram L. Harris, *The Negro as Capitalist: A Study of Banking and Business among American Negroes* (Washington, DC: American Academy of Political and Social Science, 1936); Nettie Nesbary, *Index to the Signatures of Deposits for the Freedman's Savings and Loan Bank, 1865–1869, for the State of Mississippi: Columbia, Natchez, Vicksburg* (Bowie, MD: Heritage Books, 1997); Carl Osthaus, *The Freedman's Savings Bank: Philanthropy and Fraud* (Urbana: University of Illinois Press, 1976).

Juliet E. K. Walker

FULLER, S. B. (1905–1988), Illinois, entrepreneur, manufacturer, real estate investor, newspaper publisher, department store owner, business interests also included farm and livestock enterprises.

Fuller was one of the wealthiest and most successful black entrepreneurs in mid-twentieth-century America. His Chicago-based business empire included Fuller Products, which manufactured health and beauty aids and cleaning products; a $3 million ownership in real estate, including the famous Regal Theater, comparable to Harlem's Apollo Theater; the South Center (changed to Fuller) Department Store and Office Building; a New York Real Estate Trust, the Fuller Guaranty Corporation, the *Pittsburgh Courier*, the largest black newspaper chain; and, the Fuller Philco Home Appliance Center; as well as farm and livestock operations. Post–World War II Chicago black millionaires John H. Johnson,* publisher, and George Johnson,* hair products manufacturer, acknowledged Fuller as their role model.

Fuller, a protégé of wealthy Chicago black entrepreneur Anthony Overton,* cosmetic manufacturer, banker, and newspaper publisher, started in business as a door-to-door salesman in 1935. By 1960, at the height of his business success, with sales of $10 million, there were 85 branches of his Fuller Products Company in 38 states. His employees, black and white, included 5,000 salespeople and some 600 workers in his office and factory, who produced and sold the 300 different products manufactured by Fuller. In 1947 Fuller secretly purchased Boyer International Laboratories, a white cosmetic manufactory, which opened a southern white consumer-based market. Fuller also held interest in the Patricia Stevens Cosmetic Company and J. C. McBrady and Company.

In the early 1960s Fuller's financial empire collapsed. Southern whites discovered his ownership in Boyer International Laboratories. A 100 percent white boycott of the company's products resulted in an abrupt drop of 60 percent of the Fuller Product Line. Despite a proven remarkable business success, Fuller was unable to raise professional capital to offset losses. Attempts to generate capital by selling stock in Fuller Products failed. In 1964, the Securities Exchange Commission charged Fuller with sale of unregistered securities. He was forced to pay $1.5 million to his creditors, including black salespeople who also filed claims. Fuller sold off various enterprises to meet his debts.

Fuller was born in Monroe, Louisiana. His parents, sharecroppers, moved to Memphis after World War I. Fuller moved to Chicago in 1928. With less than a sixth-grade education, he was a determined, ambitious promoter of black business, with the goal that profits remain in the black community. After bankruptcy, but with six-figure financial support in gifts and loans from leading Chicago black businesspeople, Fuller Products was reorganized in 1972 but never recovered as a major black business. Fuller continued manufacturing a line of cleaning products and cosmetics, with sales through distributorship franchises: $1,000 for Fuller products valued at $26,000. In 1975, Fuller showed sales of almost $1 million.

SELECTED BIBLIOGRAPHY: John N. Ingham and Lynne B. Feldman, *African-American Business Leaders: A Biographical Dictionary* (Westport, CT: Greenwood Press, 1994), 244–249; "A Man and His Products," *Black Enterprise* (August 1975); "S. B. Fuller, Master of Enterprise: A Great Businessman Is Remembered," *Issues & Views* 5 (Winter 1989).

Juliet E. K. Walker

FUNERAL AND MORTUARY ENTERPRISES. Historically, African American entrepreneurs have clustered in personal services, often performing tasks that involve intimate contact between provider and consumer. For the most part, this clustering has occurred because other entrepreneurs have disdained close contact with African American consumers or have lacked the knowledge to serve them effectively. Case in point: African American entrepreneurs have gravitated into cosmetology not only because outsiders have refused to provide this service to African Americans but also because these outsiders have been unfamiliar with the unique cosmetics and hairstyles of African Americans.

Undertaking has been another personal service into which African American entrepreneurs have clustered. Remarkably, M. S. Stuart observed that as of 1895 "there were few, if any, established colored undertaking concerns in existence." A handful of white undertakers, he reported, did provide funeral and mortuary services to African Americans, but they were reluctant to do so. It was less profitable for them to serve African Americans, owing to the "additional expense required to maintain equal, separate accommodations" for the corpses of African Americans and whites. Indeed, the deceased were more often segregated by race than were the living, and in both the South and the North, most white undertakers served only whites, for they found it distasteful or demeaning to handle the African American dead. Moreover, as the color line tightened in the early twentieth century, white undertakers became even more reluctant to serve African Americans.

By sheltering them from outside competition, this reluctance created opportunities for African American entrepreneurs to provide funeral and mortuary services to coethnics. Before long, these entrepreneurs monopolized these services in their own communities; and by the early twentieth century, according to Stuart, undertaking was "one of the most profitable of all the lines of business" in which African Americans were engaged. Not surprisingly, African Americans entered undertaking in growing numbers. Compilation of census data made by Robert Boyd showed that between 1890 and 1930 the number of African American undertakers increased by almost 1,200 percent, from 231 to 2,946. By the latter year, Gunnar Myrdal noted that African American undertakers constituted "nearly one-tenth of all undertakers in America." African American undertakers, he furthermore remarked, were a "real business group," unlike the majority of African American entrepreneurs who toiled in marginal enterprises.

The success of African American undertakers during the early twentieth century was also based upon the importance of the funeral ceremony in traditional African American culture. In all cultures, the disposal of the dead is a socially salient event, and among African Americans, the significance of this event has been evidenced in part by a venerable tradition of creating institutions to ensure the proper burial of the deceased. This tradition has been documented by E. Franklin Frazier. During the antebellum era, free African Americans in southern and northern cities established fraternal orders and mutual aid societies to help their members cope, emotionally and financially, with the crisis of death.

In the rural South of the postbellum era, the congregations of African American churches organized benevolent societies to provide "sickness and burial relief." The death benefits of these societies ensured that their members would be "put away right." This was a significant guarantee, according to Frazier, for a decent Christian burial was "the last consolation that life had to offer" to many poor African American southerners. As African Americans moved en masse to cities during the early twentieth century, numerous "burial associations" arose in urban African American communities. These institutions, which provided affordable funeral insurance to low-income African Americans, were especially popular in northern cities. St. Clair Drake and Horace Cayton observed that burial associations proliferated in Chicago during the Great Migration, offering their members the guarantee of an "impressive burial" in exchange for weekly or monthly dues.

Owing to the rise of segregated African American communities, undertaking became a vital entrepreneurial niche for African Americans in northern cities. Before the Great Migration of 1915–1930, there were few African American undertakers in these cities. Afterward, however, the number of African American undertakers increased precipitously, and African Americans became overrepresented in undertaking. This overrepresentation was, furthermore, positively correlated with the spatial isolation of African Americans, a finding that supports the hypothesis that residential segregation by race helped to create an exploitable coethnic consumer market for African American undertakers.

In addition to economic benefits, African American undertakers have also reaped the reward of social status. Owing to their close ties to lodges, churches, and other institutions, these undertakers have been more than entrepreneurs. They have also been important social benefactors in African American communities, and the prestige associated with this role has, no doubt, attracted African Americans into this occupation.

While undertaking is still a rewarding vocation for many African Americans, its prominence as a field of African American entrepreneurship has declined. This is evidenced by a decrease since the 1960s in the number of African American entrepreneurs in this occupation. In point of fact, my analyses of the *Survey of Minority-Owned Business Enterprises* showed that between 1972 and 1982 the number of African American–owned businesses in funeral and mortuary services declined by nearly 35 percent, from 1,880 to 1,231. This trend, I concluded, was part of a general decline of African American entrepreneurs in fields of commerce that exist because of ''protected'' consumer markets of coethnics.

Thus, like their counterparts in cosmetology, African American entrepreneurs in undertaking will continue to provide an important personal service to African Americans; yet these entrepreneurs will also continue to be a diminishing segment of the African American business world.

SELECTED BIBLIOGRAPHY: Robert L. Boyd, ''Black Business Transformation, Black Well-Being, and Public Policy,'' *Population Research and Policy Review* (May 1990); Robert L. Boyd, ''The Protected Market Hypothesis and Ethnic Residential Segregation: The Case of Black Undertakers in Northern Cities during the Great Migration'' (paper presented to the annual meeting of the American Sociological Association, Toronto, Canada, August 1997); St. Clair Drake and Horace Cayton, *Black Metropolis*, vol. 2 (1945; reprint, New York: Harcourt, Brace & World, 1970); E. Franklin Frazier, *The Negro in the United States* (New York: Macmillan, 1949); Gunnar Myrdal, *An American Dilemma*, vol. 1 (New York: Harper & Row, 1944); M. S. Stuart, *An Economic Detour: A History of Insurance in the Lives of American Negroes* (College Park, MD: McGrath Publishing, 1940).

Robert L. Boyd

FUNERAL BUSINESS FIRMS. African American funeral service developed simultaneously with American funeral service, as we know it, following the Civil War. Unlike other personal service industries, the black community has been served almost exclusively by black firms. Some experts claim that this is due to the notion that whites at once refused to handle black funeral cases. However, there is evidence that, in at least some cases, the inverse was true, and it was blacks who refused to be serviced by whites. Whatever the case, it was not until blacks began receiving the training to be undertakers that the black community began to receive funeral service on a large scale.

The years leading up to and following the Great Depression saw the establishment of the first very successful African American funeral businesses. These firms became successful during a booming industry of over $120 million annually by the early 1950s. It was during this time that black funerals were actually more expensive than the national average, owing primarily to the demands for lavish service at that time. The average black funeral home had an income of over $40,000 in 1953. The black funeral industry was referred to as—and was for the most part—free from white competition during these "fat years."

Between the 1950s and the 1970s, the number of black funeral establishments burgeoned, and although the proportion of firms kept pace with the mortality of the population (3,000 firms serving 150,000 cases in 1953 versus 4,000 firms serving 200,000 cases in 1976), inflation led to a fall in profitability, on average, among black firms. By the mid-1970s, the average black funeral cost about 90 percent of the national average, yet the average black funeral home had an income of $60,000, less than 50 percent of the national average. Large numbers of black funeral homes closed their doors because between 1953 and 1976, the cost of the average black funeral increased by only about 50 percent, or 2 percent per year, while inflation was about 9 percent per year over the same period.

By 1980, inflation had reached more than 10 percent, leading to the demise of a large number of firms going into the Reagan era. Inflation was of course coupled with the fact that the 1970s firm handled the same number of cases each year as the 1950s firm. So the profitability in the African American sector of funeral service fell due to the glut of funeral service providers that drove down funeral prices. It is more likely that the "economy" firms ran themselves out of business, since relatively few of the established firms have fallen away due to low-priced competitors. Also, it appears that the established firms are supplanted by more costly competitors, who have appeal for reasons other than low cost. This is true because the nature of the funeral profession is modularity and accommodation. The same funeral home can accommodate the very poor to the very wealthy through goods and services of different prices and quality.

In the 1990s, the landscape prospects for the average black funeral establishment have somewhat improved. The black sector of the industry now is estimated to be between $1.2 and $1.5 billion with roughly 4,000 firms servicing approximately 375,000 cases each year. The national average cost for a funeral has grown to around $4,800, whereas the black funeral averages around $3,500. Nationally, the industry collects $15 billion, whereas the average funeral home nationwide has an income of nearly $700,000 annually, with black firms averaging about $350,000. Now, however, the average black funeral home handles about 100 cases per year (around the national average, due in part to less competition but due also in part to increased mortality through AIDS and violence).

Also in the 1990s an inescapable reality is consolidation of industries. Even though 87 percent of the 22,500 funeral homes in the United States are small, family-owned operations, there are a number of conglomerate corporations that purchase, market, and manage funeral homes. Some of these firms include Service Corporation International; Morlan International; Stewart Enterprises; and the Loewen Group. Most conglomerates are not black-owned, and the largest of these in the world is the Houston-based Service Corporation International (SCI). This publicly traded organization commands $1.1 billion in revenue annually, almost as much as the entire African American sector of the industry. In four countries, SCI owns over 1,500 funeral homes, more than half of which are in the United States. Together, the conglomerates own more funeral homes than exist in the black industry and have revenues that vastly exceed that of the entire black segment of the funeral industry.

In 1990, SCI began using demographic data in its business planning, so that it now targets underserved markets for development of new facilities. In the past, SCI subsisted on purchasing established, suburban firms, yet its future plans are to build new, competing facilities in development areas. This kind of aggressive expansion coupled with relatively deep pockets and therefore sustaining power could be a threat to the African American funeral industry, should it choose to invade on a large scale. In 1996, SCI, in an unsuccessful bid, offered to buy the Loewen Group (the second-largest conglomerate) for $3.1 billion.

How many black funeral home owners might opt to sell their operations if given a similarly attractive offer? Although loyalty in the funeral industry is extremely high, substantial numbers of black firms could be eliminated due to the introduction of properly marketed, well-financed, conglomerate-controlled funeral homes into service areas. Because of this growing threat (and the intense competition among black funeral homes), a firm resolution and redeeming qualities in a funeral home are critical to its survival. A wary black population can guarantee success to a deserving firm so long as that firm remains "the people's choice."

The average figures notwithstanding, the observable trend is that in a particular locale one black funeral home will dominate while numerous others take in far fewer cases. One case in particular is seen in Cincinnati, Ohio, where around 1,500 African Americans die each year. One funeral business, Hall-Jordan, performs about 1,000 of these services, making it the largest funeral business in the Cincinnati/northern Kentucky/southeastern Indiana area. The remaining 500 cases are divided among the city's seven other black funeral homes. This massive success is due to mergers, acquisitions, and a commitment to providing nice facilities at the funeral homes. By 1998, Hall-Jordan will operate seven locations. With a payroll of 25 of Cincinnati's highest-paid funeral home employees and a fleet of service vehicles of about the same number, the success of Hall-Jordan is pinned on convenience and comfort. Numerous other similar cases exist nationwide.

Despite the observations of some critics to the contrary, funeral consumers actually have a choice when it comes to services that they receive and the price that they pay for these services. In the United States, the services of funeral homes are only mandatory in cases where the deceased is not immediately buried or cremated. Every funeral home is required to disclose this information to each client and to receive a signed form from the client family as proof that this information was disclosed. There are certainly firms that practice high-pressure selling; yet most firms derive their success from giving their customers timely information and affordable options. A funeral home must be endowed with redeeming qualities that will produce appeal to its potential customers.

Generally speaking, the black funeral consumer will patronize a firm based on expectations. Some firms rely on luxury; some on location; and others on legend. Stunning facilities and vehicles are the marks of many very successful firms. Other populations patronize the nearest funeral home. In other places the reputation of the firm and the personalities of the staff members are attractive. A few firms are notable due to their wealth of talent and exceptional merit in restorative art. If a firm becomes successful in one of these areas, then it should invest in the other areas in order to enhance its service and improve its prospects.

Success or failure in the black funeral profession has always been based on providing dignified service. The 1950s were clear proof that money is no object when it comes to the demands of bereaved black families, although less affluent families usually request fewer services and cheaper merchandise. Accolades are an asset to a funeral home more than any other business for the simple reason that everyone experiences death at one time or other. In a saturated marketplace, one's wares must be that much more outstanding to cause an attraction.

SELECTED BIBLIOGRAPHY: William M. Alpert, "Anticipating the Worst," *Barrons*, August 25, 1986; "The Business Side of Bereavement," *Black Enterprise* (November 1977): 55–57, 61; Mark Curnutte, "Life of Impossible Dreams," *Cincinnati Enquirer*, September 12, 1996; "Death Is Big Business," *Ebony*, May 1953, 17–31; *Federal Trade Commission Regulations of the Funeral Industry*, available from any funeral director; Pablo Galarza, "The Loved Ones," *Financial World*, September 12, 1995; Pablo Galarza, "Service Corporation: The Unloved One," *Financial World*, October 21, 1996; Henry McGill, "Report of Demographic Inquiries of the Cincinnati Area" (unpublished paper, Cincinnati, 1997); Gary McWilliams, "Dustup in 'Death Services,' " *Business Week*, October 7, 1996; Jessica Mitford, *The American Way of Death* (New York: Simon and Schuster, 1963), 15–38; Personal interviews by the author.

Henry Jackson McGill

FUNERAL BUSINESS HISTORY. The funeral business is vastly important as a source of wealth in the African American community. The black funeral business was shaped by the limitations placed on black participation in market transactions within the general American economy. Both discrimination and the self-help philosophy of African Americans have contributed to the pattern and the dynamism of the funeral business. Black funeral homes grew from the ugliness of segregation to become mainstays of black community and culture. Today, in many locations throughout the country, they remain the last black-owned business catering to and supported almost exclusively by African American consumers. Although only about a century old, the funeral establishment has a distinctive place in Afro-American history and culture. The classic black funeral home start-up was a one-man operation that developed into a family-managed business as the owner added spouse and offspring. Black funeral homes are today almost the singular example of the black business continuum.

Prior to the Civil War, body preparation was largely a family affair. With the home funeral, the body was buried immediately, as embalming was not available. In the South, where most black Americans lived, families washed and dressed the body, laid coins on the eyes to keep them closed, made the coffin, dug the grave, and carried the body to the cemetery in the household wagon or one borrowed from a friend or neighbor. The funeral business was born of necessity. Someone was needed to conduct funerals of those who died in the community. The black-owned funeral establishment Locks Funeral Parlor in Baltimore dates to 1831.

The first afterlife entrepreneurs were those who provided mourners' clothes and funeral decorations for houses. Undertakers made house calls preparing bodies and then delivered them to the cemetery. Families with means would contract for coffin, pay a grave digger, and hire a formal livery. Livery stable operators who had horses and wagons were called on to provide transportation for the dead to the cemeteries. Cabinetmakers and carpenters built the coffins, and in time, these artisans began to make coffins and keep them in reserve so that there would be no delay in burial service.

The Civil War ushered in the modern age in death care. The war demonstrated the efficacy of embalming as a body-preserving technique. Black man Prince Greer was hired to replace one of the assistants of W. R. Cornelius, who held contracts with the Confederates to bury their dead and also with the Union to preserve theirs. Greer reportedly enjoyed embalming so much that he became an expert and continued in the work. In 1891, James M. Wilkerson II was the first African American embalmer to be licensed in the state of Virginia. In 1874, Wilkerson's father, James M. Wilkerson, Sr., had founded a funeral establishment known as the James M. Wilkerson's Undertaking Company in Petersburg, Virginia. At his death in 1890 his eldest son and namesake inherited the family business, which he operated with his brother, Samuel C. Wilkerson. They later expanded to Washington, D.C., establishing one of the earliest funeral operations in the nation's capital.

Funeral parlors began to open in profusion in the 1880s. A report of the U.S. Census Bureau in 1890 listed 231 undertakers. As these undertaking enterprises took shape, a few impressed themselves upon the public. In 1890, George C. Jones, a black businessman, opened the first undertaking establishment in Little Rock, Arkansas. In 1895, the Ragsdale Mortuary evolved from a livery stable. In the all-black township of Muskogee, Indian Territory (later Oklahoma), William Ragsdale purchased a horse-drawn hearse that he rented to bereaved families. The enterprise grew quickly and was incorporated as the People's Undertaking Company.

In its infancy in 1900, undertaking, along with banking and insurance, contributed to the large increase in black enterprises from 1900 to 1940. Significant growth was evident by undertakers between 1890 and 1920. Their numbers increased from 231 in 1890 to 453 in 1900, to 953 in 1910, reaching 1,558 by 1920. In general, undertakers operated mainly as merchants selling goods to customers; but undertakers had also begun to develop the management aspects of the death care industry. Thus, as the century turned, the funeral business had begun to shift toward its modern form—one-stop shopping with removal, storage, preparation, and viewing facilities, all the pertinent equipment as well as a wide array of services under a single roof.

The Great Migration of the early twentieth century brought about the paradox of a dramatic rise in the number of blacks in business coupled with an increased isolation from whites. African Americans established all of their largest and most profitable businesses in the wake of the migration. Black centers of business sprang up in urban centers—North and South. In Detroit, Milwaukee, St. Louis, and Chicago, with increasing number and concomitant spatial concentration, funeral businesses flourished. In Chicago, the number of undertakers grew steadily from 1 in 1885 to nearly 70 in 1938. The greatest increase took place between 1920 and 1938. In 1920 there were 21 undertakers; by 1930, despite the depression, there were 50; and by 1938, 70 establishments existed.

The first generation of Afro-American funeral homes developed amid the self-help and solidarity efforts fostered by Booker T. Washington.* Primarily family-owned or individual proprietorships, the funeral homes were small-scaled operations that were nurtured by and thrived in a climate of enterprise based on qualities of persistence, thrift, initiative, and risk taking. In 1922, Charles C. Diggs, father of Congressman Charles Diggs, Jr., of Detroit, started an undertaking business. Two years later he owned the largest black funeral home in Michigan. In 1923, Arthur George Gaston,* who would become one of this century's leading entrepreneurs, started his first venture—a funeral business in Birmingham, Alabama. He used the revenues from that business to fund his other ventures including cemeteries, a chain of funeral homes, and motels.

The depression took a heavy toll on many black financial and business enterprises. The total number engaged in business diminished considerably, dropping from 103,881 in 1930 to 87,475 in 1940, a 16 percent decline. Overall, black undertakers increased from 2,946 in 1930 to 3,415 in 1940, roughly a 15 percent increase. In 1940 there were 112 undertakers in the nation's capital, including 53 black undertakers who provided services to the city's black population of 166,000, whereas the 59 white undertakers served approximately 500,000 individuals. In the 1940s, Gunnar Myrdal noted that nearly one tenth of all undertakers in America were African American. He described the 3,000 black undertakers as "constituting a real business group."

In 1953, on the eve of desegregation, it was estimated that 3,000 black funeral parlors grossed over $120 million annually from the burial of 150,000 people. In the 1950s, funeral establishments ranged in size from small one-man operations to very large multioperations. Marconi C. Smith in Saundersvillle, Georgia, typified the small operation. The richest man in a town of 5,000, Smith started his business in 1931. In 1953, it was still a one-man business that averaged three funerals weekly or about 150 a year. Smith had four cars, including the latest-model Cadillac, and his funeral parlor, completed in 1951, was valued at $25,000. By contrast, Angelus Funeral Home located in Los Angeles, California, was one of the largest in the country. It employed a staff of 24 and was valued at over $300,000. Angelus handled the funeral of Hattie McDonald and other entertainment notables.

In the mid-1970s, 4,000 black funeral directors grossed receipts of $390 million. By 1977, state and federal regulations, rising costs, and increased competition had forced major adjustment in operations. It was necessary for funeral operators to find innovative ways to improve service in order to increase the total number of bodies handled. In the 1950s a funeral home could meet basic expenses with about 40 bodies a year. By 1976 the average black funeral home handled about 50 bodies a year at a cost of about $1,200, according to the National Funeral Directors and Morticians Association (NFDMA). The national average in 1976, however, was 94 bodies, with about $1,348 as the average for each funeral. The largest black funeral homes—Angelus Funeral Home in Los Angeles, Baker Funeral Home in Philadelphia, Benta's in Detroit, Harris and Ross in Los Angeles, and A. R. Leak and A. A. Rayner in Chicago—each averaged about 850 bodies yearly. Despite the virtual monopoly that black funeral directors had in burying their race's dead, and the efficiency with which most ran their businesses, no black funeral home grossed sufficient profits to be included in the million-dollar club. A 1972 business census showed that 655 black funeral firms employed 2,854 persons and had average receipts of $93,000. Another 1,250 firms had no paid employees and on the average had receipts of $24,000. By the mid-1990s, there were an estimated 4,000 mostly family-owned black funeral homes located in various black communities.

Blacks in the funeral business, and undertakers in general, have been attacked as being unscrupulous and unethical by profiting from human grief and need. But, for the most part, funeral prices have been in line with the expenses necessary to operate a business and make a profit. The objective of any system of pricing is, at the very least, to pay for all expenses related to the service and for the business to make a profit. Furthermore, black funeral professionals have relied on consumer demand as a major market force to determine the prices for their products and services. An impressive funeral, or "going out in style," has been a part of the African American funeral tradition. Relatives of the deceased do not want to economize on the funeral of a loved one. Funerals were regarded as major events and in financial outlay were frequently larger and more spectacular events than weddings.

Given their resources, blacks expended a greater percentage of their resources to provide funerals. In 1927, the average cost of a funeral was $363. In the 1950s, a funeral ranged from $75 for the "pine box" to a $20,000 extravaganza with a couch. Black undertakers grossed over $120 million, for 105,000 black funerals. In 1997, the average funeral cost was $3,500. Funeral costs have traditionally been paid through burial associations and insurance plans. The intense desire to guarantee a decent funeral was one of the strongest incentives for black support of the insurance industry. Since midcentury, one third of all death premiums paid to blacks were paid to burial associations. In the mid-1990s, when it averaged $3,500 to have someone "put away right," the larger businesses, such as Strong and Jones in Tallahassee, Florida, have maintained a company tradition to bury anyone, even if the family cannot afford to pay. The larger, more established funeral homes bury people of all social levels—high and low, rich and poor. Hence, at least 10 percent of funerals for some enterprises fall significantly below the funeral cost average.

Important capital investments for the funeral business operator were the hearse and car fleet. In the 1920s, motorized hearses replaced the horse-drawn kind. Black undertakers were forced to keep pace with the times. The last journey taken has traditionally required magnificence and splendor in the transport vehicles. Costly and impressive "rolling stock" has been a staple expense of the black funeral industry. The constant modernizing of the funeral fleet has remained a major capital outlay. Black undertakers spent more annually for plush cars to drive families to cemeteries than on caskets to bury the dead. In 1952, for example, black undertakers spent $25 million for automobiles—mostly Cadillacs—but their bill for caskets was $11 million.

The funeral establishment itself is another significant expense for the business. Beginning in the 1930s, there was competition among the undertakers to have the "smartest funeral home in the country." Whereas some built only the basics—a chapel and embalming room—others, like Cleveland's House of Willis and Chicago's Metropolitan Funeral Home, had more elaborate operations. Willis's funeral business was housed in a five-story reconverted theater valued at over $250,000. The viewing rooms had cove ceilings and modern indirect lighting. In the 1970s, Metropolitan had 16 slumber rooms and a chapel that seated 1,000.

Operating expenses for a funeral home business included in excess of 40 line items. Many expenses had to be borne whether or not the funeral home had a body. The complexity of funeral operations as well as increased governmental regulations added to the standard operating expenses. Innovators made use of varied tactics to ensure some margin of profit. Business integration was a most common approach to profitability. Some morticians operated every phase of their business. Kiblah, Arkansas's John Jay Jones organized one of the most extensive independent funeral operations in the country. His holdings, in 1953, were valued at over $1.5 million. Jones grew and cut trees from his own timberland, carried them to his own mill, and fashioned caskets from his timber in his factory. The caskets were used for funerals from the Jones Funeral Home. Cleveland's House of Willis manufactured its own, Wilco Products Caskets. It also carried a line of burial garments including gowns, suits, and shoes.

Others in the funeral business, such as Gaston, owned and operated their own cemeteries and insurance companies. Cemeteries constituted a significant investment in land, which added substantially to the total value of the funeral business. In nearly every town in the South, blacks owned cemetery land. Many cemeteries operated as cooperative businesses and were maintained by associations or church committees. In other instances, both North and South, the cemetery was operated as a business by groups or individual proprietors. In addition to the cemeteries, blacks owned and operated coffin-making and casket distribution businesses as well as manufacturing facilities for embalming products. Ulysses S. Bond of Madison, Arkansas, manufactured and sold his embalming fluid to both white and black firms in 28 states. His 50-year-old business sold on the average more than 30,000 cases yearly of his products.

An undertaker's success was based on popularity as well as the quality of his service. Funeral directors have been very careful to maintain wide connections with lodges, churches, and civic and social clubs. A church affiliation was an essential for the funeral director. Some have special arrangements with ministers to have business thrown their way. One Harlem funeral home started in 1899 remained the official undertaker to seven lodge groups for over 50 years. Other funeral homes provided the exclusive work for fraternities and sororities in their communities. The church, then, was an important center of marketing and promotional efforts, designed to increase business without direct reference to the product. Advertising techniques and campaigns consisted mainly of fans distributed to churches. In addition, calendars were provided to families, organizations, and other businesses. It was estimated that in the 1950s funeral directors annually spent more on advertising than on embalming fluid. In 1953, $750,000 was spent for calendars and only $420,000 for embalming fluid.

For funeral directors, an important marketing strategy has been to play down the profit making and to stress community benefactor aspects of the business. As a solid and contributing member of the community, the undertakers performed favors for clients and friends, such as signing bonds, making loans, and providing job references. Funeral homes provided folding chairs for weddings, social gatherings, and community events. Hearses have been used as ambulances on standby for black sporting events. Cars from funeral establishments are used to ferry older church and community members. During the civil rights era, Dr. Martin Luther King, Jr., and other leaders were chauffeured from rallies in hearses by black undertakers.

By support for community projects and as active members of the community, these entrepreneurs make contacts that garner clients for their business. The largest and most consistent advertising in the African American press has been the undertaker. The press provided various promotional returns and helped to develop the mortician's social benefactor image. The opening of a new funeral establishment has always made the news. In addition, the National Funeral Directors and Morticians Association produced its own news publications.

Just before the turn of the century, almost anyone who had the money could set himself up as a mortician. Even as late as the 1940s, the nation's capital required only a letter from an undertaker already registered. There were no character requirements for certification. But by 1910 most states had established some educational standards. Most states required either an apprenticeship or a course in embalming or mortuary science. Black morticians were, for the most part, well qualified since they met the licensing standards required in their states. Some, especially blacks in the South, received training from a white mortician, Auguste Renouard. The owner of a mortuary school in New York, he traveled the country giving two-week training courses. Other blacks attended mortuary schools, notably Exter in Philadelphia, or took home-training correspondence courses. A few received training in preclinical courses at all-black schools such as Meharry Medical College and Louisville National Medical College. Still others obtained degrees from funeral or mortuary programs. By the 1990s, 75 percent of all African Americans working in the funeral industry were licensed either as funeral director, mortician, or both. Many had college degrees in business and management.

The organization of business associations went hand and hand with the growth in the funeral business. Trade associations monitored business activity and advocated for blacks within the profession. White and black undertakers rarely communicated on a professional basis before the 1960s. In 1938 the National Negro Funeral Directors and Morticians Association was founded. The ''Negro'' was dropped in 1957. In the 1970s the NFDMA had over 4,000 members in chapters throughout the United States. It published a monthly magazine and held a national as well as numerous state conventions. When claims of abuse and unethical practices led to government investigations, NFDMA members testified before and supported Federal Trade Commission (FTC) rulings for price disclosure and business reforms. By the mid-1990s, the NFDMA had subsidiaries in 26 states with a total membership of 2,500. In addition to NFDMA, black professionals founded the Epsilon Nu Delta Mortuary Fraternity and the Independent Black Funeral Directors Association. Affiliation with the National Association of Funeral Directors, the white organization, however, resulted in a drop in numbers.

Historically, the black funeral industry has had limited competition from whites. Most blacks used their own undertakers almost exclusively. Segregation policy, with respect to funerals, continued, as an unwritten agreement, well after civil rights legislation had removed public racial restrictions. In recent years, black funeral directors are under siege on the business side. By relocating to the suburbs, some blacks are located outside of the traditional black service area and use white funeral homes. Conglomerations and diversification have become the hallmarks of a trend toward national funeral service where large corporate chains challenge the supremacy of black funeral proprietors in their local markets. Whites have actively targeted the black funeral market since blacks pay for more costly funerals. The changing pattern of dominance in funeral operations within their community is highlighted by a 1996 controversy between the National Baptist Convention (NBC) and the NFDMA.

Dr. Henry Lyons, president of the NBC, encouraged the National Council of African American Churches, a coalition totaling more than 20 million members, to make the white-owned Canadian-based Loewen Group Inc. its choice in planning funerals and burials. In return, Loewen agreed to pay the NBC $100,000 and to hire members of the coalition as salesmen. The NFDMA challenged the plan and contended that under the guise of generating and fostering jobs NBC had undermined the survival of the black funeral home—"one of the few service businesses left in the community that is owned by us."

SELECTED BIBLIOGRAPHY: "Black Funeral Homes Fear a Gloomy Future as Big Chains Move In," *Wall Street Journal*, July 18, 1997; "The Business Side of Bereavement," *Black Enterprise* (November 1977); "Death Is Big Business," *Ebony*, May 1953; Michael Dolan, "Lots of Life in a Dying Business: A History of the Pope Funeral Home," Washington, D.C., *City Paper*, November 18–24, 1994; St. Clair Drake and Horace Cayton, *Black Metropolis*, 2 vols. 1945; reprint, New York: Harper & Row, 1962); Robert Habenstein and William M. Lamers, *The History of American Funeral Directing* (Milwaukee: Bulfin Printers, 1952); Albon L. Holsey, "Seventy-five Years of Negro Business," *Crisis* 45 (July 1938); Gunnar Myrdal, *American Dilemma: The Negro Problem and Modern Democracy*, vol. 1 (New York: Harper & Brothers, 1944); Vishnu V. Oak, *The Negro's Adventure in General Business* (Westport, CT: Negro University Press, 1949).

Barbara J. Flint

G

GARDNER, EDWARD G. (1925–), Illinois, hair care products manufacturer, founder of Soft Sheen Products, Inc., educator.

Soft Sheen Products, Incorporated, was the largest African American–owned hair care manufacturer and one of the nation's largest minority-owned firms. The Soft Sheen legacy begins with Gardner, a Chicago native and educator. From 1945 to 1964, Gardner used his B.A. from Chicago Teachers College and M.Ed. Degree from the University of Chicago to first teach and later serve as assistant principal in the Chicago public school system. In the evenings, he worked for a beauty supplier. Although the company went out of business, Gardner established a rapport with his customers that he wanted to continue. In 1957 Gardner formed E. G. Gardner Beauty Products Inc. The company was named Soft Sheen Products in 1964. In the early days of his business, Gardner would ask women their desires regarding hair care products. At this time, many black women, who had migrated from the South, where there was extreme humidity, were using heavy bergamots and pomades to press their hair. Gardner's customers expressed to him that they wanted something lighter. So Gardner developed the Soft Sheen Hair and Scalp Conditioner that he supplied to Chicago's black salons. This became the impetus for a series of products manufactured by Soft Sheen.

In 1983, Gardner's son, Gary, became president of Soft Sheen. Gary Gardner, with an M.B.A. and law degree from Northwestern University, used the marketing principles acquired in graduate school to increase the company's profit level. He had long worked with the Soft Sheen Company, particularly in the development and marketing of one of the company's most successful products—

the Care Free Curl. The Care Free Curl system took beauticians less time to apply than other curl products sold on the market at that time. Within a year, the Care Free Curl became the top-selling curl on the market. By the 1980s, Care Free Curl's growth tapered off, according to *Crain's Chicago Business*, which reported that the Care Free Curl accounted for 42 percent of Soft Sheen sales in 1993, compared to 90 percent in 1986. As a result, Soft Sheen Products shifted to the production of hair relaxers and baby products.

In 1995, Soft Sheen made national news when the Gardner family contemplated selling the company. Although the plan never came to fruition, this came just two years after the sale of the Chicago-based Johnson Products Co. to a white-owned corporation, the IVAX Corporation. Historically, the African American community has expressed outrage at the thought of selling African American–owned and–operated companies to nonblacks. In 1996, Gary Gardner resigned as president of the company, although he continues to serve on the board, while his sister, also a longtime company officer, was appointed chief executive officer (CEO).

Soft Sheen remains a force within the African American community in Chicago. Edward Gardner provided substantial financial support in the Harold Washington mayoral race and also helped initiate a voter registration drive that contributed to the election of the first African American woman U.S. senator, Carol Mosely-Braun of Illinois. The company has spearheaded several community service projects and provides jobs to its employees' teenage children. Until the company was sold in 1998 to Paris-based L'Oreal (the world's largest cosmetic manufacturer), Soft Sheen Products, Inc., was one of the nation's largest black businesses.

SELECTED BIBLIOGRAPHY: Paul Besson, "The Guts to Go Global: Soft Sheen Acquires a London-Based Hair-Care Distributor and Joins the Fray to Capture the International Market," *Black Enterprise* (June 1988); Judith Crown, "Gary Gardner, 38, President, Soft Sheen Products," *Crain's Chicago Business*, September 27, 1993; "Gary Gardner: A Legacy of Excellence," *Shoptalk* (Fall 1987); Mark Veverka, "Soft Sheen Heir Quits Family Firm; Gardners Seek Outside CEO after Deal Stalls," *Crain's Chicago Business*, February 5, 1996.

Nancy J. Dawson

GARVEY, MARCUS (1887–1940), New York City, nationalist, business promoter, founder of the Universal Negro Improvement Association (UNIA), businessman, publisher.

Jamaican-born Marcus Garvey was one of the most ambitious African American businessmen of all time, but his entrepreneurial ventures were motivated more by the desire for racial uplift than personal or corporate gain. Through his Universal Negro Improvement Association and African Communities League (ACL), both founded in Jamaica in 1914 and reestablished in the United States in 1917, Garvey built the Black Star Line Steamship Corporation, the *Negro World* newspaper, a Negro Factories Corporation, and considerable real estate holdings. In addition, the UNIA and ACL acted as a mutual aid society, employment agency, and bank for members.

While the largest UNIA businesses were centered at the organization's Harlem headquarters, many local branches in other states as well and some 40-plus countries ran their own businesses and purchased real estate as well. African businessmen outside the organization were often attracted to Garvey's efforts. One such, Isaiah Morter of British Honduras (now Belize), left a bequest of $100,000 to the organization for African uplift, a sentiment deemed illegal by a British judge. Garvey built the UNIA on the principles of race first, self-reliance, and nationhood. Garvey saw the organization, with membership reputed in the millions, as a vehicle to mobilize African power and to reverse the backward slide of the race into disfranchisement, loss of political power, and myriad forms of victimization.

Economic self-reliance was crucial to Garvey's program since no race, he argued, could effectively seek real emancipation while economically dependent on others. He accordingly approved of the economic emphasis of Booker T. Washington,* whom he admired. (He suggested, however, that Washington would have been forced to adopt a more aggressive political posture, had he lived beyond 1915.) During his first tour of the United States in 1916–1917, Garvey professed great admiration for the businesses forced upon African Americans by segregation. He saw a nucleus of restaurants, funeral homes, mutual aid organizations, newspapers, and the like, more developed than elsewhere in the African world. The presence of this infrastructure may have influenced his decision to cast down his bucket in the United States, where a conglomeration of businesses were established by the UNIA under Garvey's leadership.

The UNIA's Negro Factories Corporation ran a variety of smaller businesses, mostly in New York City, from about 1918. The list included restaurants, grocery stores, butcher's shop, hat factory, tailoring establishment, hotel, printing shop, trucking business, black doll factory, and more. These and other UNIA businesses employed over a thousand persons in the New York area in the early 1920s. Possibly the most successful of the UNIA businesses was the *Negro World*, organ of the UNIA. The paper boasted an array of brilliant editorial talent in T. Thomas Fortune, John Edward Bruce, Hubert H. Harrison, Eric Walrond, William H. Ferris, Amy Jacques Garvey (Marcus Garvey's wife), and others. It was the most widely circulated African publication of its time. Imperialist governments banned it in many places, but it penetrated most areas of African settlement anyway. Apart from its political content, the *Negro World* made a major contribution to the arts and helped usher in the Harlem Renaissance. It remains one of the best African American newspapers of all time.

The most spectacular of the UNIA businesses was the Black Star Line Steamship Corporation. The combination of economic and noneconomic motives was very apparent. The line would facilitate trade within the African world, transport emigrants and visitors from one country to the next, and demonstrate to a struggling race that really big business was within the realm of African possibility.

The line would also trade outside the race with whoever desired to trade with it. In addition, the line would provide a nursery for African seamen and a dignified mode of travel free of the segregation besetting Africans on international carriers at the time. The Black Star Line launched its first ship, the *Yarmouth* (renamed the *Frederick Douglass*) in October 1919. Two more followed in 1920. A fourth, to be called the *Phyllis Wheatley*, was never procured, despite money paid down for its purchase.

The combination of race uplift and economics stirred the imaginations of millions of African people like nothing else in that period. The line collected $750,000 in its first 10 months, mostly from sale of stock. By May 1920 there were Black Star Line offices in New York City, Cuba, British Guiana, Haiti, Jamaica, Panama, Costa Rica, Liberia, Sierra Leone, and 15 of the United States. On its voyages in the United States, Central America, and the Caribbean, the line's ships were greeted by scenes of great jubilation. Crowds danced and sang, showered the ships with flowers and fruit, and manually breasted the vessels ashore. Black Star Line ships carried both passengers and cargo. The company contracted to take whiskey to Cuba on the eve of Prohibition. It brought coconuts from the Caribbean to the United States. On one trip 500 passengers traveled from Panama to Santiago, Cuba. Several Jamaicans immigrated to the United States on Black Star Line ships. A Black Star Line ship once refloated a stricken Japanese vessel, which had run aground in the Caribbean.

Garvey conceived of the Black Star Line more as a cooperative racial venture than a strictly capitalistic business. "Remember," he said, "the Black Star Line Steamship Corporation is not a private company. The ships that are owned by this corporation are the property of the Negro race." There was an upper limit on individual shareholding, and only persons of African descent could buy shares. The line came under intense pressure from those opposed to African uplift. These included various agencies of the U.S. government and also the National Association for the Advancement of Colored People (NAACP), with its integrationist outlook and heavy Jewish influence.

Also, the non-African media kept up a constant barrage of scurrilous commentary. The inexperienced leadership of the company found itself precariously perched between a runaway venture successful beyond all expectation, on the one hand, and a veritable onslaught from enemies of the race, on the other. Dishonest employees and independent contractors added to the pressure. The Black Star Line suspended operations in 1922. Of the three ships, one was sold, one sank in New York's Hudson River, and one ran aground and was abandoned off the Cuban coast.

A successor company, the Black Cross Navigation and Trading Company, was organized in 1925. Garvey was jailed shortly afterward on trumped-up charges of mail fraud, and this latest ship was sold. Garvey was deported to Jamaica in 1927, from where he moved to England in 1935. He died in London in 1940.

Although Garvey's most successful businesses spanned the heyday of the

UNIA (about 1918 to the mid-1920s), his interest in business was lifelong. For Garvey, final racial emancipation was impossible without the independence that could result from economic success. He urged African people to be producers as well as consumers. A master at the rhetorical device of harsh criticism, he once told his followers that they had no right to protest Jim Crow on streetcars if they did not manufacture any. "It is indeed unfair to demand equality," Garvey wrote about 1915, before ever setting foot in the United States, "when one of himself has done nothing to establish the right to equality." The UNIA owned considerable amounts of real estate, often in prime areas in cities such as New York, Philadelphia, Toronto, Chicago, Pittsburgh, Montreal, New Orleans, Port Limon (Costa Rica), Cleveland, Kingston (Jamaica), Detroit, and elsewhere. In a few instances, as late as 1997, these buildings still belong to the UNIA organization.

SELECTED BIBLIOGRAPHY: Amy Jacques Garvey, ed., *The Philosophy and Opinions of Marcus Garvey, or, Africa for the Africans* (pub. 1923 and 1925 in 2 vols.; reprint, Dover, MA: Majority Press, 1986); Tony Martin, ed., *Marcus Garvey, Message to the People: The Course of African Philosophy* (Dover, MA: Majority Press, 1986); Tony Martin, *Race First: The Ideological and Organizational Struggles of Marcus Garvey and the Universal Negro Improvement Association* (1976; reprint, Dover, MA: Majority Press, 1986).

Tony Martin

GASTON, ARTHUR GEORGE (1892–1996) Birmingham, Alabama, Entrepreneur, insurance, banking, real estate, construction, radio, civic leader.

In 1992 Arthur Gaston on his 100th birthday was honored by *Black Enterprise* as the "Black Entrepreneur of the Century." Gaston's business activities began in the 1920s, with the founding of both a burial society, which he incorporated in 1932 as the Booker T. Washington Insurance Company, and a funeral* home. In 1939, with the proceeds from life and health insurance premium sales, Gaston established the Booker T. Washington Business College, whose graduates were hired by Gaston and other black businessmen. Also, in 1939, having secured a Joe Louis Punch franchise, Gaston established the Brown Belle Bottling Company. In 1952 Gaston expanded his enterprises with the founding of the Vulcan Realty and Investment Corporation, a real estate firm that financed the construction of office and apartment buildings, as well as the development of housing divisions. He also established the Gaston Construction Company that built the Gaston Motel, located in downtown Birmingham, which was constructed in 1954. He also built the A. G. Gaston Home for Senior Citizens and several black housing subdivisions in addition to apartment complexes.

While promoting his own enterprises, Gaston was also active in the National Negro Business League (NNBL). In 1943, he was vice president of the NNBL and also president of the Birmingham branch of the organization, which sponsored a two-day joint conference on black business, designated as a "War-Time Clinic" in conjunction with the Negro Division of the U.S. Department of

Commerce. Black and white government officials participated. Topics discussed included, "How Small Businesses May Turn Their Productions to the War" and "Financing Negro War Production Enterprises." Yet, while respected by Birmingham blacks for his business and civic contributions to their community Gaston, however, was subjected to criticism during the civil rights era for denouncing the participation of black children in protest demonstrations.

Still, Gaston's motel was made available to provide accommodations for civil rights protestors and Southern Christian Leadership Conference (SCLC) participants who held their strategy meetings at the motel, which was bombed. Also, Gaston donated money to civil rights organizations. Gaston also "put up the bail for [Martin Luther] King when King's 'letter from a Birmingham Jail' was penned." Then, too, in 1957 Gaston established the Citizens Federal Savings and Loan Association in response to difficulties blacks faced in securing mortgage loans from white institutions.

In the early 1960s, Gaston's Vulcan Realty and Investment corporation began purchasing Birmingham downtown property for redevelopment. Also, his A. G. Construction Company built new office buildings in the central business district, including the A. G. Gaston building, where he relocated Citizens Federal. After the 1960s his bank served as depositor for the city of Birmingham, its county government, and the state of Alabama. Gaston's ownership of financial institutions, construction and property development enterprises, media ventures, both a gospel and an FM rhythm and blues radio station (Booker T. Washington Broadcasting), and even a 2 percent interest in a racetrack paralleled mainstream American business activities in mid–twentieth-century America. Gaston's holdings were valued at $140 million.

Then in 1987, in an unprecedented move for a black business of that size, Gaston sold his insurance company to his 400 employees for $3.5 million. The company had $34 million in assets and $725 million of insurance in force and was the holding company for all of Gaston's enterprises, except his bank. In the late twentieth century, both remain ranking *Black Enterprise* financial institutions.

Gaston's personal wealth was over $40 million. He had only one business failure, the bottling enterprise. Gaston attributed his business success both to the models provided by black businesspeople in the segregated economy of Birmingham in the early twentieth century and to the discipline learned in the segregated U.S. Army where he served during the World War I era. He was also motivated by the self-help philosophy of Booker T. Washington,* who emphasized the importance of blacks participating in business to provide goods and services to the black community. Yet, despite the expansion of his enterprises from the 1930s on, Gaston remained completely in charge of his enterprises. Final decisions were always made by Gaston who, according to John N. Ingham and Lynne B. Feldman, pursued his business activities on the following basis: "Pay yourself first; never borrow what you could not repay upon demand; and start a business only when there is a demand for a service."

Gaston's motel did not survive the new era of equal access to public accommodations. Moreover, his conservative fiscal philosophy would be difficult to emulate by the post–civil rights era generation of black businesspeople, whose million dollar ventures would never get off the ground without access to substantial outlays of capital. Yet, in 1995 the Gaston Construction Company formed a general partnership with the Atlanta-based Thatcher Engineering, Inc., ranked nineteenth on the *BE* 100s for that year with $76.8 million in sales. The merger would provide greater financial leverage, particularly critical for black construction companies, generally with limited bonding capacity. The decision to merge arguably reflects that Gaston at 103 years of age not only recognized the economic challenges confronting black businesspeople in the late twentieth century but also that he possessed the business acumen to confront those challenges. Arthur Gaston's wife Minnie headed the Booker T. Washington Business College. They had one son and four grandchildren.

Citizens Federal and the Booker T. Washington Insurance Company have continued in the late twentieth century as ranking *Black Enterprise* financial institutions.

SELECTED BIBLIOGRAPHY: Timothy Bates and William D. Bradford, "Lending Activities of Black-Owned Controlled, Savings and Loan Associations," *Review of Black Political Economy* (Winter 1978); Arthur G. Gaston, *Green Power: The Successful War of A. G. Gaston* (Birmingham: Southern University Press, 1968); John N. Ingham and Lynne B. Feldman, *African-American Business Leaders: A Biographical Dictionary* (Westport, CT: Greenwood Press, 1994); Howell Raines, *My Soul Is Rested: The Story of the Civil Rights Movement in the Deep South* (New York: Putnam, 1977); David Stout, "A. G. Gaston, 103, a Champion of Black Economic Advances," *New York Times*, obituary January 20, 1996; Juliet E. K. Walker, *The History of Black Business in America: Capitalism, Race, Entrepreneurship* (New York: Macmillan/Prentice Hall International 1998).

Juliet E. K. Walker

GEORGIA, BLACK BUSINESS, 1890–1915. In 1891, the Georgia legislature, following the lead of other southern states, enacted legislation that segregated the races in public transportation. This discrimination soon spread to other aspects of southern life including private facilities. By 1896, the southern white position relative to race relations became dominant on the highest court of the land. In that year, the Supreme Court, in *Plessy v. Ferguson*, upheld the "separate but equal" doctrine. This law opened the path for further escalation of racial injustice in Georgia. Also, legalized and socially sanctioned discrimination spilled over to their business ventures. Thus it was that between 1890 and 1915, black entrepreneurs in Georgia found themselves going into businesses in which whites offered the least resistance or were not interested in pursuing.

From 1890 to 1910 service-oriented trades, where black Georgians were most dominant, included draymen, hackmen, caterers, teamsters, janitors, barbers, laundresses, and servants. Some of these positions generated low rates of return. In the fields of barbering, catering, and hack driving, many black business proprietors prospered due to the near monopoly they had in these trades. Also, they served both white and black customers. But by 1910, due in part to the enactment of legislation separating the races in public and private facilities, whites began to make inroads into these areas, especially barbering, while changing technology and business organization adversely impacted the others. Large white hotels and restaurants displaced the black caterers, and white taxicabs and trolleys replaced the hackman.

Consequently, black businesses began to market their services and wares primarily to the black community, concentrating in the areas of general merchandise stores, liquor stores and saloons, banks and insurance, publishing houses and newspapers, drugstores, hotels, and dry goods. Business owners exemplified a lofty entrepreneurial spirit, considering the constraints they faced in the hostile, changing socioeconomic environment prevailing at the time. In *The Negro in Business*, W.E.B. Du Bois provided the following information on black businesses in Georgia. In Americus in 1898, where most of the businesses were new, capital invested was small, and the average longevity for all businesses was 7.8 years. The average amount invested was $712, while the largest amount invested was $3,000 in a furniture store.

In Atlanta in 1898, Du Bois reported that some 61 black enterprises, including the 22 grocery stores, had a total investment of $64,260. Most of these businesses grew from small beginnings. The one drugstore began with a capital investment of $900; in 1898 its capital had grown to $1,900. A grocer whose capital investment in 1898 was $600 started with only $150. Du Bois shows that capital investment in the 21 black Atlanta grocery stores in 1898 totaled $11,925 as follows: $1,000 invested in 2 stores; $800, 4 stores; $600, 1 store; $500, 6 stores; $400, 1 store; $300, 1 store; $250, 2 stores; $200, 2 stores; $150, 1 store; $100, 1 store. Capital investments in the 39 other black enterprises were somewhat larger, amounting to $52,335. The two funeral* establishments had the largest capital investments, respectively, $7,000 and $6,000, followed by the real estate company, with $5,000 capital invested. An investment company was capitalized at $4,000. Barbershop investments ranged from $3,000 to $300. General merchandise store capital investments ranged from $500 to $3,800, whereas the drugstore had a capital investment of $1,900. The pool room and saloon investments were, respectively, $1,600 and $1,500 (Table 2).

No set pattern prevailed with reference to the relationship between longevity and capital investment. The 29-year-old general merchandise store and the 25-year-old grocery both had investments of $1,000. However, a 3-year-old grocery had the same amount of capital invested ($1,000), whereas both the 20-year-old groceries had investments of only $400 and $500. Among the larger black firms in Atlanta was a $3,800 general merchandise store in business for 15 years. A funeral home, in business 14 years, had an investment of $7,000; another operating for 10 years had an investment of $6,000. The life span of black busi-

Table 2
Capital Invested in Sundry Black Atlanta Enterprises, 1898

Business	Amounts Invested							Average amount Invested
	Store # 1	Store # 2	Store # 3	Store # 4	Store # 5	Store # 6	Store # 7	
General merchandise	$ 3,800	$ 2,000	$ 1,000	$ 500	$ 500	--	--	$ 1,560
Wood yard	500	500	400	200	150	50	--	300
Barber shop	3,000	2,500	2,000	1,800	400	300	--	1,666
Meat market	500	200	150	80	75	75	30	158
Restaurant	500	125	--	--	--	--	--	312
Undertaker	7,000	6,000	--	--	--	--	--	6,500
Blacksmith	800	600	--	--	--	--	--	700
Saloon	1,500	1,200	--	--	--	--	--	1,350
Tailor	200	--	--	--	--	--	--	200
Drug store	1,900	--	--	--	--	--	--	1,900
Creamery	300	--	--	--	--	--	--	300
Pool room	1,600	--	--	--	--	--	--	1,600
Investment Co.	4,000	--	--	--	--	--	--	4,000
Carriage builder	900	--	--	--	--	--	--	900
Real estate	5,000	--	--	--	--	--	--	5,000
Total								$52,335

Source: W.E.B. Du Bois, *The Negro in Business*, p. 69.

nesses on the average was short, with few companies falling in the category of 15 to 30 years of existence, consistent with one of the characteristics of the proprietorship form of business, the predominant business organization of blacks.

Of the proprietorship form of business, blacks were more involved on the retail rather than the wholesale level. The 1910 census showed 1,733 black retail dealers in Georgia out of a total of 19,464 but only 27 black wholesale dealers out of 818 in that state. In proportion to the total number of establishments, then, black participation remained minuscule. The prevailing assessment was that if an area comprising both blacks and whites could support one merchant, that merchant would more than likely be white, either native or foreign-born.

Interestingly, Robert Higgs discovered foreign-born white merchants to be especially prominent in Georgia during the period 1890–1910. In 1890, there were 3 black merchants for every 1,000 gainfully employed black males; for every 1,000 gainfully employed native-born whites, there were 35 white merchants; but there were 188 foreign-born white merchants for every 1,000 gainfully employed foreign-born whites. In 1910, a similar comparison revealed 5 black merchants to 37 native-born white and 221 foreign-born white merchants.

Some have postulated that a segregated society can serve to buttress black business operation due to the absence of external competition. There is an element of truth to this thesis regarding the black capitalist in a segregated market and, perhaps, best exemplified by the insurance industry. Many white-owned insurance companies were hesitant to insure blacks, so insurance companies* owned and operated by blacks emerged to fill the vacuum. These companies represent one of the most successful and long-lasting businesses operated and owned by blacks. The prosperous black-owned Atlanta Life Insurance Company* was organized in 1905 by Alonzo Herndon,* who used savings from his lucrative barbering business (before segregation, he served both white and black clientele) to buy the firm.

In the late nineteenth and early twentieth centuries the black entrepreneur faced insurmountable obstacles in the quest for a profitable business venture. Few succeeded. Previous conditions of servitude, the advent of a legalized racially stratified society, and the changing commercial structure all gave rise to an economic order that was repressive and served to stymie the growth and development of businesses owned and operated by blacks. Although small in number and facing increasing competition and discrimination as business organization and the racial atmosphere in society intensified and changed at the turn of the twentieth century, black entrepreneurs served the general public, and a few of them prospered.

In the main, however, businesses owned and operated by blacks during this period were largely in the incubatory stage, struggling for survival in a society becoming increasingly hostile to black socioeconomic life. The fact that some of these concerns thrived bodes well for the potential of black business.

SELECTED BIBLIOGRAPHY: W.E.B. Du Bois, *The Negro in Business* (New York: AMS Press, 1899); Robert Higgs, "Participation of Blacks and Immigrants in the American Merchant Class, 1890–1910: Some Demographic Relations," *Explorations in Economic History* 13 (1976); U.S. Department of Commerce, Bureau of the Census, *Negro Population in the United States, 1790–1915* (Washington; DC: Government Printing Office, 1918); U.S. Department of Commerce, Bureau of the Census, "Thirteenth Census of the United States: 1910" in *Population*, vol. 4 (Washington, DC: Government Printing Office, 1913).

Anne R. Hornsby

GORDY, BERRY, JR. (1929–), Detroit and California, entrepreneur in recording industry, television, and film.

Born in Detroit, Berry Gordy took a few hundred dollars in 1958 and created a recording empire, Motown Records, which at one time was the largest black business in profits in the United States. It consisted of seven labels; a licensing and publishing division, Jobete; Hitsville USA; and International Talent Management Incorporated. Gordy promoted his company as the "Sound of Young America" and succeeded in getting his artists to cross over to young white audiences, mainly by marketing the Supremes. Gordy expanded his interests into movies and television specials.

In 1973 he formed Motown Industries as a parent company and made E. G. Abner II, former president of Vee Jay, the president. One division, Motown Productions, handled $50 million worth of film production by 1988. In 1988 Gordy sold Motown Records to MCA Records but maintained divisions to establish the Gordy Company, worth $105 million.

SELECTED BIBLIOGRAPHY: Berry Gordy, *To Be Loved: The Music, the Magic, the Memories of Motown* (New York: Warner Books, 1994); John N. Ingham and Lynne B. Feldman, *African-American Business Leaders: A Biographical Dictionary* (Westport, CT: Greenwood Press, 1994); Richard Lingeman, "The Big Happy, Beat, Heart of the Detroit Sound: Motown's Records," *New York Times Magazine*, November 27, 1966; Martha Reeves, *Dancing in the Street: Confessions of a Motown Diva* (New York: Hyperion, 1994).

Sundiata A. K. Djata

GRAVES, EARL GILBERT (1935–), New York, publisher, editor, corporate executive, business consultant, soft-drink franchise owner.

In 1990, when Earl G. Graves and Earvin "Magic" Johnson "teamed up" to acquire controlling interest in Pepsi-Cola of Washington, D.C., they became owners of the second largest minority-controlled Pepsi-Cola franchise in the United States. Craig E. Weatherup, president and chief executive officer of Pepsi-Cola Co., lauded the new partnership: "This is a unique venture, . . . one that we have been discussing and evaluating for over two years. Earl and Earvin . . . bring more to it than just their knowledge and expertise. They bring their experience. Their stature and the unique position they occupy as role models for the black community.''

Born in Brooklyn, New York, Earl G. Graves has become one of the most successful African American businessmen in the United States. After graduating from Maryland's Morgan State University in 1958 with a bachelor's degree in economics, Graves worked in real estate and as a national commissioner of scouting for Boy Scouts of America. In the mid-1960s, he became an administrative aide to New York Senator Robert F. Kennedy. Working in Senator Kennedy's New York office Graves, who became an effective liaison for Kennedy to the African American community, played a key role in organizing the Bedford-Stuyvesant Project.

In 1968 Graves formed Earl Graves Associates, a consulting firm for social programs in urban affairs and economic development. With a $150,000 loan from Chase Manhattan Bank, Graves launched *Black Enterprise* in 1970. A slick mass market magazine about African American business, *Black Enterprise* had gross receipts of $930,000 at the end of its first year of publication. By 1990, *Black Enterprise* was reporting annual revenues of about $15 million and had a monthly circulation of 230,000. Aimed at middle-class African Americans, each issue of *Black Enterprise* carries lead editorials by Graves trumpeting little-known accomplishments of African Americans in the business world. Well-written feature articles showcase African Americans making new inroads in business and the professions.

Today, Earl G. Graves Ltd. includes Earl G. Graves Publishing Company, which publishes *Black Enterprise*, and Pepsi-Cola of Washington, D.C. In 1988 Graves sold EEG Dallas Broadcasting Company, Inc., for $14 million. Ever mindful of the economic plight of African Americans and African American business, Earl G. Graves took a dim view in 1995 of the Republican Party's ''Contract with America.'' As he said, ''The GOP's legislative agenda, as represented by its Contract with America, is not encouraging. . . . [T]he removal of barriers to minority business development is not addressed by the Contract— this from a party that preaches entrepreneurial independence as an antidote to government dependence.''

SELECTED BIBLIOGRAPHY: "The Big Three in D.C.," *Black Enterprise* (October 1990); Earl G. Graves, *How to Succeed in Business without Being White* (New York: Harper Business, 1997); Earl Graves, "Publisher's Page, Contract on America," *Black Enterprise* (January 1995); "Earl Graves Is the Publisher of Black Enterprise, and He Practices What He Preaches," *Changing Times* (November 1990); John N. Ingham and Lynne B. Feldman, *African-American Business Leaders: A Biographical Dictionary* (Westport, CT: Greenwood Press, 1994); George Plimpton, ed., *American Journey: The Times of Robert Kennedy. Interviews by Jean Stein* (New York: Harcourt Brace Jovanovich, 1970).

Donald Franklin Joyce

GRAY, SIMON (c. 1800–?), Natchez, Mississippi, slave, flatboat captain, slave entrepreneur in lumber industry.

Andrew Donnan, Gray's owner and a blacksmith and merchant, hired Gray to Andrew Brown, the senior partner of Andrew Brown and Company, a lumber company that operated on the Mississippi River. Gray rose quickly as an employee of Brown, directing a rafting crew bringing logs to a lumber mill in Natchez, some three years after first appearing in company records. In 1845, Andrew Brown, Jr., made Gray a flatboat captain and assigned him to trips between Natchez and the company's new operations in New Orleans. Serving as the chief boatman until 1863, Gray delivered lumber to New Orleans, sold lumber along the river, took new orders, quoted prices, and even extended credit to buyers. Gray commanded crews of black slaves and white hands and sometimes even paid his white crew their wages and also extended loans to them.

Little is known of Gray's early life. After serving reliably as a flatboat captain, Andrew Brown purchased part of Gray's family in 1850 for $500. Around 1856 Brown purchased Gray's son Washington for $500, money that Gray raised through independent ventures transporting sand to New Orleans, earning as much as $400. Throughout his tenure with Brown, Gray handled large sums of money, wrote reports, and kept detailed records of his business transactions. After 1853 Gray lived as a free black in all but name. Brown's business thrived in the 1850s, and he assigned Gray to the purchasing and transportation of lumber in the Yazoo River area, eventually putting him in charge of all the company's logging business in the Mississippi Delta. Gray worked for Brown until the Union Army captured Vicksburg in July 1863, after which there is no record of his subsequent life.

SELECTED BIBLIOGRAPHY: John Hebron Moore, "Simon Gray, Riverman: A Slave Who Was Almost Free," *Mississippi Valley Historical Review* 49 (December 1962): 472–484.

David F. Herr

GREAT MIGRATION, BLACK ENTREPRENEURSHIP. The mass exodus of African Americans from the South during the early twentieth century was one of the largest migrations of human history. Between 1900 and 1930, more than 1 million African Americans left the South, and during 1916–1918, the peak years of out-migration, over 500 African Americans moved from the region each day. Displaced by the demise of the South's low-wage, agricultural economy, the vast majority of migrants went to the Northeast and Midwest, where they sought the higher-paying jobs of the nation's emerging industrial cities. This Great Migration dramatically changed the African American communities of these cities, and its impact on African American entrepreneurship was profound.

Before 1900, many African Americans in northern cities lived in racially mixed neighborhoods, and while a color line did exist, the economic and social contacts between African Americans and whites in these cities were remarkably intimate and frequent. African American entrepreneurs had particularly close relationships with whites, serving them in such fields as barbering, catering,* laundering, and tailoring. As Bart Landry noted, most of these entrepreneurs belonged to a "mulatto elite," descended from the antebellum "free persons of color." But as southern African Americans moved to northern cities en masse, race relations in these cities deteriorated. The growing African American populations were seen by whites as economically and politically threatening and erected racial barriers in employment, housing, education, and public accommodations.

As the social and spatial distance between the races increased, African American entrepreneurs who had thrived during the era of racial harmony lost their white consumer base, often replaced in their businesses by European immigrants. By 1915, the entrepreneurial activities of African Americans in the urban North were largely restricted to their own racially segregated communities. Within this new environment, African American entrepreneurs at first struggled for a foothold. Many found their best opportunities for business ownership in services that others were unwilling to provide to African Americans, such as barbering, beauty culture, and undertaking.*

African American entrepreneurs monopolized these services in their own communities. Many also entered other fields—most notably, finance, insurance, real estate, and newspaper publishing—to serve the demands of the rapidly expanding coethnic consumer markets of northern cities. In such endeavors, African American entrepreneurs prospered during the 1920s as never before. The rise of thriving business enclaves, such as the one in Chicago's African American community, during these "Fat Years" even bolstered the popular belief that African Americans could create their own self-sufficient economy. Furthermore, by this time, a new class of African American entrepreneurs had supplanted the old African American petit bourgeoisie. The members of this new business elite tended to come from the masses of southern migrants rather than from the older mulatto elite.

The expansion of entrepreneurship among African Americans in the urban North was due largely to the emergence of large and segregated African American communities. St. Clair Drake and Horace R. Cayton observed in their study of Chicago, "The Great Migration created the 'Negro market,' " as African American entrepreneurs "became increasingly conscious of the purchasing power of several hundred thousand people solidly massed in one compact community." Consistent with this statement, I found that in large northern cities between 1915 and 1930 the participation of African Americans in the occupations of barbering, retailing, undertaking, and insurance was positively correlated with the spatial isolation of the African American population. Evidently, as Andrew Brimmer stated, the "wall of segregation" was also a "wall of protection" for many African American entrepreneurs.

The entrepreneurial successes of African Americans in the urban North were short-lived, however. In the wake of the Great Depression, thousands of African American businesses failed, including many large African American banks. Notable among the casualties was the famous Binga State Bank, which had been the centerpiece of the African American business enclave of Chicago. The collapse of the bank not only wiped out the life savings of thousands of depositors; it also psychologically devastated the African American community, for, as Drake and Cayton observed, the bank had been a prominent symbol of "racial advancement."

African American retailers in northern cities were especially hard hit by the depression, according to Timothy Bates. During the crisis, many tried to secure the patronage of African American consumers by appeals to racial loyalty. Yet, as Drake and Cayton found, African American consumers were unswayed by these appeals and tended to patronize immigrant retailers, who, in most cases, offered a greater variety of goods at lower prices and easier credit terms than did their African American competitors. As unemployment became widespread in the urban North during the depression, the first wave of the Great Migration ended. But when the economy recovered due to wartime mobilization in the 1940s, a new wave of in-migration began; and during the prosperous years of the 1950s and 1960s, African Americans continued to move from the South to other regions, seeking better living conditions.

Yet things were never the same in northern cities. After the business enclaves* of these cities collapsed in the 1930s, the walls of segregation that arose during the Great Migration came to be viewed by African Americans as barriers to progress rather than as walls of protection. Moreover, the faith in entrepreneurship that existed in the 1920s almost completely dissipated, according to August Meier and Elliott Rudwick, and the vision of creating a racially separate economy never regained currency among African Americans. The early years of the Great Migration, then, may well have been the heyday of the belief that business enterprise could provide African Americans with a sure path to economic success.

SELECTED BIBLIOGRAPHY: Timothy Bates, *Black Capitalism: A Quantitative Analysis* (New York: Praeger, 1973); Robert L. Boyd, "Demographic Change and Entrepreneurial Occupations: African Americans in Northern Cities," *American Journal of Economics and Sociology* (April 1996); Robert L. Boyd, "The Great Migration to the North and the Rise of Ethnic Niches for African American Women in Beauty Culture and Hairdressing, 1910–1920," *Sociological Focus* (February 1996); Robert L. Boyd, "Residential Segregation by Race and the Black Merchants of Northern Cities during the Early Twentieth Century," *Sociological Forum* (forthcoming); Brimmer, Andrew, "Desegregation and Negro Leadership," in *Eli Ginzburg, Business Leadership and the Negro Crisis* (New York: McGraw-Hill, 1968); St. Clair Drake and Horace R. Cayton, *Black Metropolis*, vol. 2 (New York: Harper & Row, 1962); Landry, Bart, *The New Black Middle Class* (Berkeley: University of California Press, 1987); Carole Marks, *Farewell—We're Good and Gone: The Great Black Migration* (Bloomington: Indiana University Press, 1989); August Meier and Elliott Rudwick, *From Plantation to Ghetto* (New York: Hill and Wang, 1976).

Robert L. Boyd

H

HAIR CARE PRODUCTS INDUSTRY. The names of products such as "The California Curl," "Isoplus," "The Care Free Curl," "Ultra Sheen," and "African Royale" are household words within the black community. The entrepreneurial geniuses responsible for these and other ethnic hair care products are people such as Madame C. J. Walker,* Annie Pope Turnbo-Malone,* S. B. Fuller,* George E. Johnson,* Edward Gardner,* and Willie Morrow.* They developed a sophisticated network and overcame tremendous odds to bring these products to the consumers. The black hair care industry is an economic gold mine and for nearly a century has been one of the few industries where black people have demonstrated considerable success.

Market researchers have found that African Americans, who account for about 12.7 percent of the population, buy 34 percent of all hair care products sold. African American women have specifically been a target of market research. On the average, black women who visit a hair salon do so every two weeks, whereas white women visit once every seven weeks. In addition, the chemical treatment process for most African American women has traditionally begun at the age of 12, but this initial age is steadily decreasing. There is even a market for hair care appliances, special curling irons and hair dryers made specifically for African American women's hair.

Overall, black people represent about 37 percent of the hair care market, spending $1.5 billion annually. Hair care manufacturer Joe Dudley,* founder of Dudley Products Co., states in a company brochure, *Dudley's Haircare Fact Book*: "The cosmetology industry represents the salvation of Black America. Without this industry, there would be very little business activity in most

African American communities. Drive, walk, or pass through any Black community and you are bound to encounter the inevitable—a beauty salon or barbershop on every block.'' Detroit is considered by some as the ''Black hair capital of the United States.'' According to the Michigan Department of Commerce, there are 16,000 licensed hairstylists and barbers in the city.

The ethnic hair care industry is composed of cosmetologists, manufacturers, distributors, and retailers. This industry is an intricate part of the African American business community. Dudley suggests that cosmetologists are the single largest group of African American business owners, operators, and managers in America.

In addition, in the 1970s, black women bought about 40 to 50 percent of all wigs sold. The Naomi Sims Collection, manufactured by former supermodel Naomi Sims, manufactured the first ''natural-looking wigs'' designed for black women. Sims's business venture made her $10 million.

Black hair care entrepreneurs have definitely made their mark in black business history. The hair care industry produced the first black self-made millionaires in this country, Turnbo-Malone, of the Poro Company, and Madame C. J. Walker of the Madame C. J. Walker Manufacturing Company. In 1971, the Johnson Products Company was the first African American company to be traded on the American Stock Exchange. In that same year, Johnson Products became the first black company to sponsor a nationally syndicated television show, *Soul Train*. Also, black entrepreneurs have used profits from the hair care industry as a springboard into other business ventures. Comer J. Cottrell,* founder of Pro-Line Corporation, became the first African American to hold equity in a major league baseball team—the Texas Rangers.

Historically, the art of hairdressing has been an economic mainstay for black people. During slavery, barbering was a service-related occupation open to African Americans. Blacks lost their monopoly on the trade toward the turn of the century. Robert Boyd's research on entrepreneurial occupations in northern cities notes that in 1870 while African Americans were only 2.8 percent of Detroit's population, they comprised 55 percent of the city's barbers. In Cleveland, African Americans were only 1.4 percent of the city's population but 43 percent of its barbers. Boyd suggests that the decline in blacks in the barbering trade was the result of increased competition by foreign-born whites, discrimination against black barbershop owners, and the tightening of the color line in barbering.

Booker T. Washington,* who advocated that blacks learn skilled trades, observed the shift in the barbering trade in his 1901 autobiography, *The Story of My Life and Work*, for he said: ''Twenty years ago every large and paying barber shop over the country was in the hands of black men, today in all the large cities you cannot find a single large or first class barber shop operated by colored men.'' Washington added, ''The black men had had a monopoly of that industry, but had gone on from day to day in the same old monotonous way, without improving anything about the industry. As a result the white man has taken it up, put brains into it, watched all the fine points, improved and progressed until his shop today was not known as a barber shop, but as a tonsorial parlor.''

Yet some of the most influential African Americans of this century—John Merrick,* one of the founders of the North Carolina Mutual Life Insurance Co.;* Alonzo F. Herndon,* founder of the Atlanta Life Insurance Company;* and Daniel H. Williams, who performed the first open heart surgery—all started their careers in the barbering business. The barbering profession gave Merrick a privileged view of business, as it did the leading black barbers with elite whites as their customers. These black men used their shops as schools and acquired ''information and business methods through such contact.'' Moreover, some three decades later, however, Henry Morgan* established a national chain of barber colleges for African Americans, starting with the Tyler Barber College in 1934. He understood the black barbering tradition and established colleges throughout the country to train blacks to meet the new standards set forth by the now-white-dominated barbering profession.

Moreover, to a great extent, the early manufacturers of black hair care products created their market. After emancipation from slavery, blacks had more time to concentrate on personal appearance and hygiene. Techniques in grooming were an intricate part of the curriculum of many normal schools established after slavery. In his autobiography, Booker T. Washington shared the lessons he was taught at Hampton regarding the importance of good grooming. ''While teaching I insisted that each pupil should come to school clean, should have his or her hands and face washed and hair combed,'' a philosophy also emphasized at Washington's Tuskegee Institute.

Annie Malone, who entered the hair care scene in 1900 in Lovejoy, Illinois, garnered support for her Poro products with a message similar to Washington's. Malone's business philosophy was that clean scalps encouraged clean bodies and that better appearance also meant greater business opportunities, higher social status, clean living, and beautiful homes. Then black people could receive recognition and self-respect through cleanliness. African Americans embraced Malone's marketing idea because cleanliness was an important value to former slaves. Madam Walker used a similar strategy to sell her products. Malone and Walker, consequently, became millionaires because they capitalized on a national trend among African Americans that associated good grooming with social, economic, and political status.

Most important, they also offered economic outlets for black women who would normally be relegated to being either domestics or washerwomen. Robert Boyd contends that hairdressing and beauty culture was an ethnic niche for African American women in northern cities. The beauty culture business combined paid work with family activities. In addition, training in the profession was easily obtained. The hierarchical structure of the trade provided upward mobility for black women. A woman could move from home shop to salon to selling and/or manufacturing cosmetics. The barbering profession offered a similar outlet for black men. Crucial to the success of the early ethnic hair care industry was what Boyd calls "close and personal contact."

In order for whites to dominate the black beauty culture profession they had to be willing to provide services directly to blacks. In contrast, African Americans could work in a mostly hassle-free racial environment. They were not subjugated to the constant humility and frustration associated with occupations such as domestic work, where blacks were providing services for a white clientele. During legal segregation, most whites desired social distance. Particularly, too, many African Americans were sensitive about disclosing their hair care concerns to whites. Traditionally, this factor has given black hairdressers a tremendous edge. Increasingly in the post–civil rights era, black women are patronizing white shops, since beauticians are required to be proficient in the care of all types of hair. Their ability to do so has been enhanced by the advancements in black hair products, especially those that straighten hair.

In the development of the black hair care products industry, attempts to capitalize on this market were not limited to Madame Walker (and a few historians mention Malone); there were other entrepreneurs such as Sarah [Sara] Spencer Washington,* founder of the Apex News & Hair Company. A cursory overview of some of the leading African American newspapers will uncover countless advertisements for hair care products. These advertisements identify a large segment of forgotten entrepreneurs who, although not as successful as Annie Malone, Madame Walker, or Sarah Washington, were able to achieve some business success. There are several other hair care entrepreneurs that have received little recognition for their business accomplishments, including E. F. Young, Jr., founder of the E. F. Young Jr. Manufacturing Company in 1933 in Mississippi. In the 1940s in Harlem, New York, Rose Morgan had the largest black-owned beauty shop in the United States—Rose Meta House of Beauty.* In Detroit in 1944, Austin W. Curtis founded Austin W. Curtis Laboratories, manufacturer of skin and hair care products. In the 1950s Bettie Esther Parham was founder and president of the National Beauty Supply Company and Esther Laboratories.

There exists within the ethnic hair care industry a long-standing tradition of networking* and mentorship. The industry has prided itself in helping to develop black businesses and business organizations. The network has been pivotal to the creation of many black millionaires in this industry. This is particularly important since for many decades the white business world was virtually closed to African Americans. Madame Walker was an agent for Malone's Poro Company. Poro stated in its literature that the company was committed to the economic empowerment of "race women." Walker is considered the queen of the beauty culture industry, and she was a shining example to many. Walker gave lectures on the "Negro Woman in Business" and addressed organizations such as the National Negro Business League.* Walker mentored Majorie Stewart Joyner,* who professionalized the beauty industry. Joyner participated in the formation of the National Beauty Culturalist League, the Alpha Chi Pi Omega

Sorority and Fraternity Inc., and the United Beauty School Owners and Teachers Association.

An informal mentoring network also developed, whereby established black entrepreneurs in the health and beauty aids business provided training for a new generation of black businesspeople. S. B. Fuller, founder of the Chicago-based Fuller Products Company and one of the wealthiest and most successful black entrepreneurs in mid–twentieth-century America, was the protégé of cosmetic manufacturer Anthony Overton.* Both George Johnson and Joe Dudley were mentored by Fuller. George Johnson, of Johnson Products, worked as a chemist for Fuller at the age of 18. In New York, Dudley sold products for Fuller Products, then managed a Greensboro, North Carolina, branch of the company.

Dudley became president of Fuller Products Co. in 1976, where he sold both Dudley and Fuller Products. Ernest Joshua,* founder of J. M. Products Co., one of the largest minority-owned aerosol manufacturing companies in the United States, received his chemistry background working for the Luster Products Company in Chicago. Nathaniel Bronner was an agent for the Apex News & Hair Co. Willie Morrow, who is considered the "Father of the Curl" (hairstyle), developed the California Curl. In the 1980s, the curl gave the ethnic hair care industry new vitality because curl and curl-related products contributed to rapid industry growth and development.

Most of the exceptional hair care entrepreneurs started with the help of their immediate families, manufacturing products from their kitchen and distributing them, often, from the back of the family automobile. In the cases of Ernest Joshua, Edward Gardner, George Johnson, Nathaniel Bronner, and Madame Walker, their children eventually took over the operations of the companies. The entrepreneurs' spouses often played a significant role in the development and stability of the company. For example, Eunice Dudley is now chief financial officer of Dudley Products Company.

Yet family ties have also been weakened by the politics of the industry. Joan Johnson, George Johnson's spouse, became chief executive and controlling shareholder of the Johnson Products Company after their divorce in 1989. Although bombarded by expressions of discontent from some black community leaders and her ex-husband, Ms. Johnson sold Johnson Products Company to the IVAX Corporation—a white-owned company. The $46 million black-owned company sold to IVAX in a one-for-one stock swap valued at $67 million.

The concern of the black community reflects what W.E.B. Du Bois argued in his 1929 essay "Business as Public Service": Social service is a large aspect of black business. As Du Bois said: "The colored business man is looked upon by his public and conceived in his own mind as a benefactor." He goes into business to "help his race!" This is certainly true for the ethnic hair care industry, whose primary customers are black. As mentioned earlier, philanthropy is synonymous with the ethnic hair care industry. Proof of Malone's good deeds are still found at 2612 Annie Malone Drive in St. Louis. The Annie Malone Children and Family Service Center was renamed for Malone, in 1946, because of her generous contributions. The home is one of the only black residential foster care facilities in America to provide continuous service for a century. Each month of May, the center sponsors a major fund-raising event known as the Annie Malone Parade.

Also, upon her death, the estate of Madame C. J. Walker listed dozens of organizations and individuals as beneficiaries. A $100,000 trust fund was established, and its proceeds were to go to "worthy charities." Incidentally, the revenue generated from the hair care industry helped to sustain black newspapers. In 1946, a story devoted to Walker's life in *Color* thanked the Walker Company for its support of black newspapers: "The 500 Negro newspapers and magazines of the United States are the heaviest moulders of public opinion in the fight for freedom of the Negro world and since these papers would vanish or be too weak to speak except for the advertising support of the Walker-born cosmetic business."

Sarah Spencer Washington of Apex gave 20 acres of her Egg Harbor, New Jersey, farm to the National Youth Administration for a campsite for black youth. Henry Morgan made regular financial contributions to Butler College and to Texas College. Comer Contrell paid $1.5 million for a campus of Bishop College to attract another black college to the deteriorating facility. Dudley Products provides 32 full scholarships annually for students in business-related majors at North Carolina A&T University and Bennett College. Also, in 1992, Dudley established the "Resurrection to Beauty Fund," to aid cosmetologists whose businesses were ravished after the rioting in Los Angeles in 1992.

Historically, the giants in the ethnic hair care industry have been philanthropists. Since the hair care industry has such a personal relationship with its customers, many of the well-established entrepreneurs feel it is their duty to contribute to the people, thus becoming "benefactors."

Since the hair care industry has assumed such social obligations, its continued success is important to the black community. Increasingly, however, large white-owned companies are hiring African Americans to operate their ethnic hair care divisions. Moreover, in a white-oriented business world, which has little sympathy for the social service aspect of black businesses, providing support to the black community imposes a dual burden on these businesses, as they struggle to sustain themselves.

Consequently, the 1993 sale of the Johnson Products Company was considered a tragedy by some in the black community. Those who control black companies are often concerned about what the black community will think. An article in *Black Enterprise* considered the sale of Johnson Products as an outgrowth of the increasing diversity and capital requirement of the nation's largest black-owned businesses. White businesses, however, are sold every day to raise capital and finance expansions and acquisitions—the essence of American free enterprise. A 1997 article in *Fortune* profiled Carson Incorporated—a company that is in the new spirit of the developing African American business world. In 1995, Carson, manufacturers of Dark & Lovely hair relaxers, was a privately held white-owned company. Understanding Carson's potential, Leroy Keith, then president of Morehouse College, assembled an investment group and bought Carson. He then organized a group of top-notch corporate executives and took Carson public. Carson now trails Soft Sheen Products in sales with $78 million in annual revenues. As black business diversifies, the Carson model will become increasingly popular.

Still, despite their success, black hair care pioneers, historically, have endured tremendous injustices in relationship to race and gender. In 1924, the Poro company was nearly destroyed after Aaron and Annie Malone's bitter divorce. Aaron demanded one-half of the Poro College fortune. Claude A. Barnett of the Associated Negro Press considered Malone's ordeal a race fight. During the divorce, a judge ordered the Poro company into receivership under a white lawyer who tried to force Annie Malone to give him her formula for her famous "Wonderful Hair Grower." Although Malone maintained the company, she lost hundreds of thousands of dollars.

In 1971 Revlon was one of the first large white-owned corporations to market products to black consumers. Alberto-Culver Co. entered the ethnic hair care market with its TCB brand in 1974. Gillette Co. came into the industry about 1986, when it brought Lustrasilk Corporation, a small white-owned company that manufactured products for black consumers. Today the three largest manufacturers of ethnic hair care products are Alberto-Culver, Gillette, and Revlon. Black-owned companies argue that their megagiant white competitors have certain advantages. In the distribution of products, they have established track records with distribution companies; consequently, their products easily receive shelf space from retailers.

Interestingly, too, in 1975, the Federal Trade Commission (FTC) ordered Johnson Products to place a warning notice of the danger of using lye on its packages. This was after major white-owned companies such as Revlon took an interest in the black hair care industry. The FTC did not require Revlon to warn its customers on packages until 22 months later, after a lawsuit filed by Johnson Products Co. In response to white competition in the industry, the American Health and Beauty Aids Institute (AHBAI) was formed in 1981. It is a national nonprofit association of black-owned companies who produce hair care and cosmetic products specifically for the black consumers. AHBAI created the "Proud Lady Logo" (a black woman in silhouette featuring three layers of hair). The logo is stamped on the back of all manufacturing members' products, printed materials, and packing and promotional materials.

The mission of the organization is to make black consumers aware of products manufactured by African American–owned companies. Unfortunately, since many black consumers are extremely bargain conscious, they often buy hair care products that are cheaper in price—despite the Proud Lady symbol. Also, since many people in African American communities have limited transportation, they buy products that are easily accessible. Most important, many black consumers just do not understand that supporting black businesses ultimately creates stronger black institutions.

At the same time, some blacks in the hair care industry are discussing what has been termed "The Asian Invasion." In an interview, published in *Crisis*, Matthew Knowles, a Houston entrepreneur, expressed his concerns about the ethnic hair care industry: "Koreans came into this country and figured out quickly how much we spend. . . . They really mastered this business and learned how to purchase so they could buy collectively and price low. They buy 100 cases and negotiate the best price and then undercut the black distributor. It's a cultural thing. They do business with each other and they pool money and resources."

In October 1986, a major controversy erupted in the ethnic hair care industry when Irving J. Bottner, president of Revlon's Professional Products Division, said, "The black-owned businesses will disappear. They'll all be sold to white companies. . . . We are accused of taking business away from black companies, but black consumers buy quality products—too often, their black brothers didn't do them any good." In response to Bottner's statement, Jesse Jackson* launched a boycott against Revlon, demanding that the company divest its South African operations, hire more black managers, and use more black-owned suppliers. Black publications such as *Essence, Ebony*, and *Jet* magazines temporarily stopped carrying Revlon advertisements. In response to the clamor, Revlon sponsored a $3 million advertising campaign, announcing that money spent with black businesses supports the black community.

In another instance of competition, Shark Products, a white-owned hair care company, in 1993 filed a trademark infringement suit against the Rasta Group, a black-owned firm, to prevent it from marketing its "African Natural" products. Part of the suit asserted that the company used the word *African* and the colors red, black, and green—the colors that were adopted by black leaders more than 70 years earlier for the African American liberation flag. Shark's move to protect its Afrocentric trademarks upset some black community leaders. The company admitted later that it made a mistake, stressing that 76 percent of the company's employees were black.

The ethnic hair care industry has been the avenue by which many black entrepreneurs have become millionaires. The ability of these individuals to network with other businesspeople has enabled them to overcome poverty, racism, and other extraordinary odds. In addition, using their immediate and extended family in the operation of these businesses has created several black family empires. The zealous philanthropic activity of blacks in the ethnic hair care industry has helped many people. Their successes have opened the doors of opportunity to barbers and beauticians, who despite minimal education could earn a respectable income and provide upward mobility for their families. The stories of many of the black entrepreneurs in the ethnic hair care industry are forgotten by history. However, the fruit of their labor lives in bottles, cans, containers, and boxes on the bedroom dressers and in the bathroom cabinets of millions of African Americans.

SELECTED BIBLIOGRAPHY: Robert Boyd, "Demographic Change and Entrepreneurial Occupations: African Americans in Northern Cities," *American Journal of Economics and Sociology* 55, 2 (April 1960); Robert Boyd, "The Great Migration to the North and the Rise of Ethnic Niches for African American Women in Beauty Culture and Hairdressing, 1910–1920," *Sociological Focus* 29, 1 (February 1996); Denise Crittendon, "Who's Minding the Store—Asians or African Americans?" *Crisis* (October 1994); W.E.B. Du Bois, "Business as Public Service," *Crisis* (November 1929); Dudley Products Co., *Dudley's Haircare Fact Book* (Greensboro, NC: Dudley Products Inc., 1993); Christine Dugas and Dreyfack Dugas, "A Gaffe at Revlon Has the Black Community Seething," *Business Week*, February 9, 1987; Alfred Edmond, Jr., "Should Black Businesses Be Sold to Whites?" *Black Enterprise* (November 1993); Josh Givens and Lou Roppolo, "The Ethnic Market 2000: A Survey of the Growing Importance of This Beauty Category," *Beauty Store Business* (August–September 1995); Betty Pulley, "A Crown Jewel: The Johnson Family Splits on What Is Best for Black-Owned Firm," *Wall Street Journal*, July 29, 1993; Shaifali Puri, "A Cut Above," *Fortune*, August 1997; "Tyler Barber College Was First of Its Kind," *Beauticians Journal & Guide* (September 1949).

Nancy J. Dawson

HARRIS, ABRAM LINCOLN, JR. (1899–1963), Virginia, economist.

Abram Harris, the first African American to achieve professional prominence in the field of economics, was born in Richmond, Virginia. A 1922 graduate of Virginia Union University, Harris went on to complete an M.A. in economics at the University of Pittsburgh, then received his Ph.D. in economics in 1930 from Columbia University. Harris's academic career encompassed teaching posts at West Virginia State (1924–1925), Howard University (1927–1945), and the University of Chicago (1945 until his death). A prolific writer and intensely critical thinker, Harris was the intellectual leader of a group of socialist-oriented scholars, including Ralph Bunche, E. Franklin Frazier, Charles Thompson, and Alain Locke. Harris was to mount one of the most powerful critiques ever advanced of "black capitalism," or business development, as the route to black improvement.

The critique was posed most comprehensively in his study of black enterprise in the United States, *The Negro as Capitalist* (1936), the eighth chapter entitled "The Future of Negro Banking." The book was written during the period in Harris's career when he espoused a radical perspective on social change in America. Harris conceived of *The Negro as Capitalist* as meeting his goals for the third phase of a tripartite research project on "the whole subject of Negro labor in the development of modern industrialism." While some of the terrain was covered in Harris's book coauthored with Sterling Spero, *The Black Worker* (1931), according to Harris, the projected "larger study . . . was to cover: (1) Africa and the Rise of Capitalism; (2) The Accumulation of Wealth among Negroes Prior to 1860; and, (3) The Economic Basis of the Negro Middle Class."

The first and second phases were sketched briefly by Harris in the first chapter of *The Negro as Capitalist*. His M.A. student Wilson Williams completed a thesis in 1938 entitled "Africa and the Rise of Capitalism," which brought greater substance to the first phase of the study, explicitly linking Africa and the British industrial revolution via the Atlantic slave trade* and plantation slavery in the Americas. But fulfillment of the first phase really came in the form of Eric Williams's *Capitalism and Slavery* (1944). Eric Williams, later to serve as the first postindependence prime minister of Trinidad and Tobago, was Harris's colleague at Howard from 1939 to the mid-1940s. A comprehensive treatment of the second phase, "The Accumulation of Wealth among Negroes Prior to 1860," was never completed by Harris or any of his associates.

The third task—the investigation of "The Economic Basis of the Negro Middle Class"—was covered in the rest of *The Negro as Capitalist*, beyond chapter 1, which, according to Harris, "although confined to a study of Negro banks, shows the struggle of the Negro to gain economic status and social respectability by erecting within the larger framework of capitalism a small world of Negro business enterprise, hoping thereby to develop his own capitalist-employer class and to create employment opportunities for an increasing number of Negroes in the white collar occupations." For Harris, this "small world of Negro business enterprise" was particularly fragile. He contended that the dream held by many, including Booker T. Washington* at the turn of the century and W.E.B. Du Bois in the 1930s, of "an independent black economy" was a mere chimera fueled by "optimistic naiveté."

Harris began chapter 8 commenting on the small size and short lifetime of banks organized by blacks. Aside from a polite comment about the continued existence of the Mechanics and Farmers Bank of Durham and Raleigh, which Harris attributed to "the skillful management of C. C. Spaulding,"* he has little positive to say about black banks or black business in general. Black banks, to the extent that their lending activities were necessarily limited to small and marginal black concerns as clients, would find their growth potential restricted "even if they had expert management." Blacks lacked any significant large-scale industrial or commercial undertakings. As a result black-owned banks had "to find . . . [outlets] for [their] funds in church and fraternal lodge loans, in the development of theaters, in amusements, . . . in real estate, [and, the greatest part of their lending] to small-salaried persons and wage-earners for consumptive purposes with the integrity of the borrower as the only security."

As Harris put it so pithily, "The Negro bank is small because Negro business is." The general vulnerability of small banks, particularly in the midst of the Great Depression, carried over to black banks because they, too, were small in scale. Harris anticipated that federal regulation was imminent for the banking system, and the result would be greater bank concentration, including the incorporation of black banks as branches of larger white-owned financial institutions. This would, of course, mean an end to "independence" for black banks, but Harris did not see this as a loss. Such vaunted independence was "only nominal'' at best, since the black-owned banks of whatever size already had relied upon large white-owned banks ''as a depository, for assistance in making investments, and for rediscounting and clearing.''

Moreover, for Harris, black-owned banks were a source of positive harm to the black working class. Not only was the black working class the most victimized by bank failures, but they also were victimized by usurious interest rates and high rates of mortgage loan foreclosures. Harris recommended that black workers rely upon more cooperative financial institutions: ''the credit union, the industrial loan society, and the building loan society.'' Consequently, Harris hardly was disturbed by the prospect of black-owned banks being absorbed by larger white banks. Patently, in the 1930s Harris had no enthusiasm for the utopianism of black capitalism hoisted on the crane of black-owned banks.

SELECTED BIBLIOGRAPHY: William A. Darity, Jr., ''Introduction'' to Abram L. Harris, Jr., *Race, Radicalism and Reform* (New Brunswick, NJ: Transaction, 1989); William A. Darity, Jr., ''Soundings and Silences: Abram Harris, Jr. in the Great Depression,'' in Thomas D. Boston, ed., *A Different Vision: African American Economic Thought*, vol. 1 (London: Routledge, 1997); Abram L. Harris, Jr., *The Negro as Capitalist: A Study of Banking and Business among American Negroes* (Philadelphia: American Academy of Political and Social Science, 1936).

William A. Darity, Jr.

I

ILLEGAL BLACK BUSINESS, ORGANIZED CRIMINAL ACTIVITIES.
Organized crime and illegal business activities are found in many inner-city African American communities, fueled by economic disadvantage and blocked legal employment and self-employment opportunities. The predominance of evidence, however, suggests that the organization of criminal activities in black communities parallels that of the organization of legal business activities: African Americans are largely workers and not owners. This was true during the 1920s and 1930s, when many criminal enterprises thrived in American cities, and is true in the post-1980s era, when black gangs and criminal trades appear to be on the rise once again.

Conventional theories of entrepreneurship suggest that blocked employment opportunities and economic disadvantage represent one of many pushes into self-employment. Self-employment offers an alternative to low-wage work and yields opportunities for accumulation of capital and social and economic mobility. When opportunities for financing entrepreneurship and legal business development are also blocked, however, the push of low wages and economic disadvantage often is into illegal activities.

Inner-city African Americans are severely underrepresented among the self-employed, even though conventional disadvantage theories of entrepreneurship—which explain, for example, Korean small business development—would suggest high rates of black self-employment and small business ownership. But the absence of traditional revolving credit institutions, such as the Susu, and discriminatory barriers in commercial and mortgage credit markets have hampered

African Americans in replacing low-wage work with individual legal enterprise. As a result, illegal income-earning activities have become more attractive and available.

Illegal business activities are found in competitive markets and in monopolistic markets. Black markets—or markets where illegal goods and services are sold or where illegal methods of conducting economic transactions are undertaken—include those where drugs, sex, food stamps, and stolen goods are bought and sold. Black markets involving gambling, production, and distribution of narcotics and large-scale sale of weapons are often organized and monopolistic. Markets dealing with such drugs as heroin and cocaine and such products as military-grade automatic weapons find tremendous economies of scale and efficiencies when organized as monopolies.

Many black markets in inner-city areas, however, are organized loosely, without the formal organization typical of single or monopolistic criminal enterprises. Unlike members of other ethnic groups that have organized syndicates and monopolistic criminal enterprises, African Americans largely have been the employees of monopolistic criminal enterprises, rather than the owners of them. The rapid deployment of law enforcement resources to combat the drug trade in inner-city areas during the 1980s and the advances to break up gangs helped thwart the development and expansion of potential monopolistic criminal enterprises among African American gangs and drug-selling families. Similarly, gang peace initiatives and efforts to shift gang-related activities to such legitimate enterprises as clothing manufacturing and entertainment companies have been met with skepticism among policymakers and community leaders, who contend that these efforts are scams.

The conventional wisdom is that illegal activities have served as a source of capital among immigrant groups, often denied initial access to bank loans and traditional lending opportunities to start businesses. Although many of these illegal operations started as small-scale criminal enterprises, with growth and expansion into legal activities, they were able to support and sustain ethnic enterprise among various white immigrant groups. This conventional wisdom, which also includes the role of the immigrant entrepreneur as a middleman between the established class and the underclass, does not describe adequately the organization and development of entrepreneurship in African American communities. One reason is that in many southern communities legal monopolies arose to provide goods and services to African American consumers. These businesses—often run and controlled by an educated professional elite—included funeral parlors, medical and dental facilities, and law offices. Ostensibly, the professional class shunned criminal activities, which were largely controlled by white criminal monopolies.

In contrast, the vast majority of legal enterprises in the black community were mom-and-pop stores, shoe-shine parlors, barbershops, and beauty parlors, often operating with low revenues, little capital, and few chances for growth and development. These enterprises sometimes served as the trading grounds for the exchange of illegal goods and services, for illegal gambling, or drug sales. But there is little evidence that the shop owners were also the owners of the larger criminal enterprises. Rather, the black shop owners were more like workers within larger white-controlled organized syndicates rather than operators of small-scale illegal enterprises.

With desegregation and the opening up of economic opportunities for the black middle class, the legal monopolies in professional services largely were displaced, and the small businesses where criminal transactions took place went out of business. The rise of legal gambling and the apparent disorganization of illegal drugs at the local level have weakened the potential of criminal activities to serve as the historic springboard to legitimate business ownership among poor and working-class African Americans. Those who do work in crime apparently earn no more than they could in low-wage legal employment. Drug dealing among blacks, for example, does not seem to follow a model of monopolistic enterprise or large-scale organization where blacks are profitable entrepreneurs. Rather, it is low-wage work. If legal wages were higher, one study found, black drug dealing would drop drastically.

However, there are many parallels between illegal activities in black communities and legitimate entrepreneurship. The "criminal job" entails considerable risk taking; it encourages and rewards managerial success; and it offers prospects for independence and self-employment. Efforts to redirect the criminal activities of inner-city youth into legitimate entrepreneurial activities represent a largely unheralded policy that some scholars believe might work to reduce crime and increase black business ownership.

SELECTED BIBLIOGRAPHY: John Sibley Butler, *Entrepreneurship and Self-Help among Black Americans: A Reconsideration of Race and Economics* (Albany: State University of New York Press, 1991); Ivan Light, *Ethnic Enterprise in America* (Berkeley: University of California Press, 1972); Ivan Light and Carolyn Rosenstein, *Race, Ethnicity, and Entrepreneurship in Urban America* (New York: Aldine De Gruyter, 1995); Samuel L. Myers, Jr., "Crime, Entrepreneurship, and Labor Force Withdrawal," *Contemporary Policy Issues* 10, 2 (April 1992); Samuel L. Myers, Jr., "Economics of Crime in the Urban Ghetto," *Review of Black Political Economy* 9 (1978).

Samuel L. Myers, Jr.

INSURANCE COMPANIES. With risk sharing in the compensation against loss and provisions for death benefits as the principal features of insurance, black insurance companies in America had their origins in the seventeenth century, with the founding of African secret burial societies. A slave's ability to accumulate funds for funeral expenses was limited. Mutual cooperation in savings reflected vestiges of African burial societies, where the dead were buried with dignity and afforded the collective respect of the community. One could not just be thrown into the ground. Doubtless, slave owners had demonstrated that they would not undertake the cost of coffins and other funeral* expenses. Moreover, they also objected to slave organizations, which meant these African burial societies were forced to operate in secrecy.

Mutual aid activities also emerged in the impoverished free black population, who organized mutual aid savings societies. The African Union Society, established in Newport, Rhode Island, in 1780 was the first, and its financial activities not only included burial funds but also benefits to widows and children. The Philadelphia Free African Society,* founded in 1787 by Richard Allen and Absalom Jones, however, has the most historic prominence. This society also paid benefits to widows and orphans. The number of mutual aid societies increased through the period of slavery and provided a cultural base for the origin of black insurance companies, as did membership in black fraternal orders, such as the Masons, Oddfellows, and Knights of Pythias, organizations that after the Civil War established insurance companies. The first black insurance company, the African Insurance Company, however, was established in Philadelphia in 1810 by the Reverend Absalom Jones. Indeed, black church* leaders, especially ministers, would play an important role in the founding of black insurance companies, many of which began as burial societies.

It was not until the late nineteenth century that the first black insurance companies were founded after the Civil War. Between 1880 and 1910, blacks founded some 500 fraternal insurance organizations, which, during that period, held the largest amounts of black insurance funds. The Richmond-based Southern Aid Society in Virginia was founded in 1893 by B. L. Jordan, who had worked with True Reformer founder Reverend William Washington Browne, founder of the fraternal Order of True Reformers in 1881. Invariably, some of the founders of insurance companies, including leaders of fraternal organizations, were also involved in establishing black banks, primarily for the deposit of insurance funds collected from their members.

Indeed, the Savings Bank of the Grand Fountain United Order of True Reformers Bank of Richmond was the first black bank, chartered on March 2, 1888 (it did not begin operations until April 3, 1889); it was founded by slave-born William Washington Browne. He established the bank to provide a depository for the insurance premiums collected from members of the True Reformers, rather than to continue placing these funds in white banks. The Independent Order of St. Luke (IOSI), under Maggie Lena Walker,* established an insurance department in 1901. In 1903, Walker founded the Saint Luke Penny Savings Bank to serve as a depository for its insurance premiums.

The takeoff in the founding of black insurance companies, however, began in the early twentieth century. The leaders were C. C. Spaulding* of North Carolina Mutual* and Alonzo Herndon* of Atlanta Life.* In this case, too, black insurance companies preceded the founding of black banks. The Mechanics and Farmers Bank of Durham and Raleigh was established by the founder/officers of North Carolina Mutual Life Insurance Company. Also, the Nickel Savings Bank was the depository of the funds of the People's Insurance Company of which Reverend Evans Payne was founder.

North Carolina Mutual Life Insurance Company was founded in 1898 by slave-born John Merrick, who had built a real estate fortune from his barbershop enterprises. The company almost failed in its first year. In 1900 Charles Clinton Spaulding, who was hired in 1900 as its general manager, was the driving force in promoting the growth and expansion of North Carolina Mutual, expanding the company's coverage beyond industrial sickness, accidents, and burial benefits until it became a full-line insurance company. In the 1990s, North Carolina Mutual was the ranking black insurance company in assets and insurance in force. Atlanta Life ranked second.

The Atlanta Life Insurance Company, founded by Alonzo Franklin Herndon, developed from a failing mutual aid association, which Herndon purchased in 1905 for $160, then renamed his new company Atlanta Mutual. Herndon expanded by purchasing other small assessment companies and also by buying out 15 other black insurance companies. Herndon, a former slave, like the founder of North Carolina, had become wealthy as a result of his success as a barber and real estate investor. At one time, his three barbershops employed 75 blacks. In 1927, he was worth more than $500,000.

The first black Old Line legal reserve company to write only ordinary business, however, and the third to qualify as a legal reserve, was Standard Life Insurance Company of Georgia, founded by Herman Perry in 1908. Mississippi Life was the first, followed by North Carolina Mutual. Perry also founded the Mechanics Savings Bank in Augusta and, in 1921, the Citizens Trust Company in Atlanta. By 1924, Standard, with its affiliates in 11 states, employed some 2,500 people.

In part, black insurance companies were founded at the turn of the century because white companies, at that time, with the exception of Metropolitan Life, were reluctant and generally refused to sell insurance policies to blacks, unless they were willing to accept benefits amounting to only one third that paid white premium holders. Indeed, a report published in 1896 said: "Because of social diseases, living conditions, and other undesirable circumstances, companies would be unwise to insure Negroes." Blacks, however, did insure blacks, and as these companies became successful, they allowed their policyholders to pay their premiums in small weekly installments; attempts were made by whites to drive them out of the business. In some cases, state laws were passed that imposed stringent requirements, which many black insurers could not meet.

The state of Virginia provides a case in point. Before the Civil War, it had the largest number of black mutual aid burial societies. Also, it had the largest number of black insurance companies after 1865. The first black insurance company, the Richmond-based Southern Aid Society in Virginia, was founded in 1893 by B. L. Jordan, who had worked with True Reformer founder Reverend W. W. Browne. In 1903, laws were passed in that state that required these companies to pay not only a $200 license fee but also 1 percent of an insurance company's gross receipts and a $10,000 deposit; this led many of these companies to go out of business, and white companies attempted to pick them up.

W.E.B. Du Bois made the following assessment of these laws, explaining that "southern legislatures only began to awaken to his need of protection when Negro societies began driving the whites out of business."

Consequently, by 1927, when the 32 largest black insurance companies held 85 percent, some $316 million worth, of policies in force on blacks, just one single, average white-owned company held $900 million worth of insurance in force on blacks. Still, black insurance industry survived the depression, even though in 1940, yet again, one large white-owned company had a greater value of policies in force on blacks than the top 40 black insurance companies combined. Moreover, by 1944, of the 46 black insurance companies that belonged to the National Negro Insurance Association (NNIA), figures obtained from 43 of the companies showed a total of 3,695,628 black policyholders; $630,156,539 worth of policies in force; $32,840,158 in premium income; and a total income of $36,091,516. Yet, in 1942, the total insurance on blacks, held by 262 black and white companies, amounted to almost $1.7 billion on 9,420,298 black policyholders with total annual premiums of $67.9 million. Consequently, while white-owned companies carried more than $1 billion worth of policies in force on blacks and had 5.7 million more black policyholders, black insurance companies had almost 40 percent of the annual premium income from black policyholders.

By 1946 there were 204 black-owned companies in the insurance business: 23 were legal reserve companies; 39 were miscellaneous (assessment, life, health, accident, and industrial); 91 were burial organizations; and 51 were fraternal benefit societies. By 1963, there were 50 legal reserve insurance companies, but the number of black burial associations and fraternal benefit societies, which carried insurance, showed a marked decline, holding only $1 million in assets. Also, while the 43 NNIA member companies in 1944 held $57.3 million in assets, by 1963 the 20 leading black companies, which held virtually all the assets of black insurance companies, had total assets of $311 million, which, however, represented only 0.23 percent of the $133 billion of total assets owned by all life insurance companies. Moreover, while the leading 20 black insurance companies sold $592.3 million of new life insurance policies, overall industry sales amounted to $79.6 billion.

Invariably, death benefits have been the primary form of payment made by black-owned insurance companies, including the Chicago Metropolitan Assurance Company,* founded in 1925 from a merger of black funeral societies, a response to black southern migrants, assuring themselves of burial benefits. Chicago Metropolitan, however, failed in 1985, since it competed with Supreme Liberty Life Insurance Company,* founded in 1929. Its founding also represented a merger of several insurance companies, managed over the years by Harry Pace,* Earl B. Dickerson, and Truman Gibson, father and son. By 1964, John H. Johnson,* however, was the largest stockholder. And, at one time, Supreme had the reputation of being "the largest black business in the North."

As chairman of the board, Johnson took an active role in the management of the company, where he once worked part-time, while attending the University of Chicago.

The insurance business for blacks is extremely competitive. By 1976 there were 41 black insurance companies out of a total of 1,800 American insurance companies. While these black insurance companies had $590 million in assets and $9.7 billion insurance in force, the industry totals were $2.139 trillion of life insurance in force and $289 billion in assets. The number of black insurance companies, however, declined from 42 to 23 in the 20-year period from 1973 to 1993. Moreover, among the 10 leading black insurance companies for 1995, 9 were founded before 1950. Simply put, black insurance companies, from their founding, have had difficulty competing on any level with white companies, except with life insurance.

With white insurance companies, unlike their black counterparts, 58 percent of the benefits are paid to living policyholders in matured endowments, disability, annuity payments, dividends, and policies surrendered for cash. Moreover, in the 1960s black insurance companies were unable to capitalize on two areas of industry expansion, group life insurance and credit life insurance. Indeed, the E. G. Bowman Co. Inc., founded in 1954 by Ernesta Bowman, was the first black-owned insurance brokerage firm on Wall Street.

With an increasingly finance-wise middle-class black population, black insurance companies need to capitalize on this market, to compete more effectively in the twenty-first century. Specifically, they need to explore the benefits of consolidation for themselves. Also, greater emphasis should be placed on providing benefits to living policyholders in the form of matured endowments, disability benefits, annuity payments, and especially, dividends and policies that can be surrendered for cash.

SELECTED BIBLIOGRAPHY: James H. Browning, ''The Beginnings of Insurance Enterprise among Negroes,'' *Journal of Negro History* 22, 4 (October 1937); Winfred Bryson, ''Insurance Companies: An Overview,'' *Black Enterprise* (June 1977); W.E.B. Du Bois, ''Economic Co-operation among the Negroes of Georgia,'' Atlanta University Publication No. 19 (Atlanta: Atlanta University Press, 1917); J. H. Harmon, A. G. Lindsay, and C. G. Woodson, *The Negro as a Business Man* (Washington, DC: Association for the Study of Negro Life and History, Inc., 1929; reprint, College Park, MD: McGrath Publishing Company, 1969); Alexa Benson Henderson, *Atlanta Life Insurance Company: Guardian of Black Dignity* (Tuscaloosa: University of Alabama Press, 1990); John N. Ingham and Lynne B. Feldman, *African-American Business Leaders: A Biographical Dictionary* (Westport, CT: Greenwood Press, 1994); M. S. Stuart, *An Economic Detour: A History of Insurance in the Lives of American Negroes* (New York: Wendell Mallett and Company, 1940); Walter B. Weare, *Black Business in the New South: A Social History of the North Carolina Mutual Life Insurance Company* (Urbana: University of Illinois Press, 1973); Juliet E. K. Walker, *The History of Black Business in America: Capitalism, Race, Entrepreneurship* (New York: Macmillan/Prentice Hall International, 1998); Robert E. Weems, Jr., *Black Business in the Black Metropolis: The Chicago*

Metropolitan Assurance Company, 1925–1985 (Bloomington: Indiana University Press, 1996), 119–124.

Juliet E. K. Walker

INTERNATIONAL TRADE ENTERPRISES. Beginning with the first century of settlement in English Colonial America in the seventeenth century, Africans in America were involved in international enterprises. Their first ventures were capital investments in ocean trading vessels. In the late 1660s, New Englander former slave Bostian Ken, who purchased his freedom, owned a one-third interest in a 14-ton ocean trading vessel, the *Hopewell*. In the early 1800s, former slave Christopher McPherson in Virginia also held investment interests in a cargo ship. Beginning in the late eighteenth century, free blacks established shipping lines.

Blacks were also involved in overseas trade. Paul Cuffe* was the leading black international shipper. By 1806 he owned a shipping line of five vessels and also held interest in a sixth. A sea captain, Cuffe's trading activities in the shipment of agricultural commodities and manufactured goods carried him to the West Indies, England, Sweden, Russia, and West Africa. The African-born Holman brothers, sons of a white slave trader and an African woman, after settling in South Carolina in the 1790s, where they established a rice plantation with the slaves brought over in their own ships, returned to Africa. By 1820, they had resumed their activities in the international African slave trade.

African Americans established overseas enterprises. New England–born Nancy Gardner Prince (1799–c. 1856), who accompanied her black American–born husband to Russia, lived in St. Petersburg from 1824 to 1833, where she established two enterprises. As Prince said, she learned Russian in "six months so as to be able to attend to my business." First, she ran a boardinghouse for children. Then, responding to a demand from the Russian nobility for children's clothes, Prince established a clothing business, writing: "The baby linen making and children's garments were in great demand. I started a business in these articles." Her clients included the empress, who purchased baby clothes that were "handsomely wrought in French and English styles." She also made women's clothes. The business was a success, and to meet demand in filling orders, Nancy employed both "a journeywoman and apprentices."

In the decades before the Civil War, most of the overseas enterprises established by African Americans were located in Liberia, reflecting an increasing interest by blacks in international trade as merchant shippers and owners of import-export trading companies. Initially, Sierra Leone and Haiti attracted the attention of black businessmen interested in either investing or participating in international trade. Indeed, Paul Cuffe made his initial African voyage to Sierra Leone in 1811, where he formed a trading and mercantile company, the Friendly Society of Sierra Leone, in partnership with African-born John Kizell. A repatriate, Kizell, a South Carolina slave, fought with the British and left with them at the end of the Revolutionary War, finally settling in Sierra Leone.

Once Liberia was established for the colonization of African Americans, it became the focal point of their international trading ventures in West Africa. The first African Americans immigrated to Liberia in 1820, and free blacks in Maryland and Virginia were the most active in establishing enterprises in Liberia. The Reverend Daniel Coker from Baltimore, briefly considered for the first bishop of the African Methodist Episcopal (AME) Church, established a shipping business on Sherbro Island as a coastal trader, even captaining one of several vessels that he owned.

In Baltimore, several trading companies were formed to establish trade relations with West Africa. In that city, Hezekiah Grice was active in founding a black mercantile company to trade with Liberia, and he said in 1829 that "there are fifteen or twenty coloured persons here who will adventure $100 each and that several others up the Susquehanna in Philad. and N. York and at Liberia will become stockholders to a similar amount; and that he believes that several societies that exist among the blacks in this city will invest a portion of their funds in such an enterprise." It was not until 1845, however, that Maryland finally granted the company, the Chesapeake and Liberia Trading Company, a charter of incorporation.

The largest antebellum black mercantile trading import-export company was Roberts, Colson, and Company established in Baltimore in 1829. One of the partners, Joseph Jenkins Roberts (1809–1876), immigrated to Liberia, where the company purchased products for export, such as an 1833 shipment that included "forty-seven tons of camwood, eight puncheons of palm oil, eighty-eight small ivories and seven large ivories." This shipment, purchased by the Philadelphia Grant and Stone store, netted the company $3,389.80. The company also owned their own ship, the schooner *Caroline*. Robert's commercial success, enhanced by his acquisition of property, town lots, and farmland, including a coffee farm, enhanced his prestige and political standing. After an appointment as governor, Roberts was elected Liberia's first president in 1847, serving two terms.

There were also African American firms based solely in Liberia. The mercantile trading firm of Colston Waring (1793–1834) and Francis Taylor, established in Monrovia in the mid-1820s, was successful from the start in the sale of "firearms, ale, and rum imported from Liverpool." In 1830 the firm had sales in the amount of $70,000. Also, several large plantations were established in Liberia by expatriate African American sugar planters, who with their own steam mills processed sugar cane for both local and export markets. "Several settlers had amassed considerable wealth by this means." Also, a shipbuilding yard was established in Monrovia. By the late 1850s, a thriving international trade in palm oil, rice, camwood, and animal skins developed with Europeans and Americans whose ships docked in Liberian ports.

Also, some black Americans who initially attempted to immigrate to Haiti and to develop businesses in that country eventually went to Liberia. George McGill, who owned an oyster cellar and messenger service, and who had purchased himself and several family members from slavery, was the leader of the

Maryland Haytian Company, organized by Baltimore blacks to charter ships for immigration to Haiti. In 1819, the group chartered the *Dromo* and sailed to Haiti, but their venture failed. McGill and his family returned to America but later immigrated to Liberia, including his daughter and her husband John Russwurm. In 1827 he was one of the founders of the first black American newspaper, *Freedom's Journal.*

In Liberia, McGill's sons acquired a fleet of shipping vessels and became successful merchant-traders. By 1859, one McGill brother was the agent for Lloyds of London in Liberia, and the other was worth $30,000. Interest in establishing international trading ventures by African Americans escalated in the decade before the Civil War. Liberia was not the only destination. In the 1850s, some wealthy Louisiana black planters immigrated to Haiti and established plantations. Omar Chevalier immigrated to Mexico and established a short-lived shipping business. In the 1850s, Barney Ford* (1821–1902), a fugitive slave who first escaped to Chicago, left for California, via the Panama route. In Nicaragua, Ford established a first-class hotel, which he constructed and managed for several years before he returned to the States.

Some expatriate African Americans before the Civil War established overseas enterprises in England and Europe. Julius Melbourne, a former North Carolina slave, inherited an estate of $20,000 from his former slave owner, which he increased to $50,000. He then immigrated to England, where he set his son up in a London mercantile business for $20,000. Louisiana free people of color, including the Soulies, Dumases, McCartys, and Lacroixs, particularly those involved in real estate, early on had acquired extensive international business connections in France, where they maintained offices in Paris. In the United States, these businessmen all had wealth in excess of $100,000.

Blacks also established businesses in Canada before the Civil War. From 1830 to 1860, some 40,000 African Americans settled in Canada, including 30,000 fugitive slaves and 10,000 free blacks. Most fled to Canada west in Ontario, living primarily in impoverished rural areas Only a few fugitive slave refugee settlements prospered. In an Elgin settlement, blacks established a general store, a hotel, a sawmill, a grist mill, and a potash factory, along with craft enterprises. Over 1,000 blacks settled in Toronto, where they established small stores; restaurants; craft enterprises in carpentry, bricklaying, and cabinetmaking; and barber- and tobacco shops—a replication of businesses established by blacks in antebellum urban America.

One of the most successful expatriate African American businesspeople in Canada was San Francisco retail merchant Mifflin W. Gibbs (1823–1915). In 1858 he immigrated to Vancouver, a response to the gold strike in British Columbia, where he established a general store that provided food and supplies for miners. Gibbs expanded his enterprise in the 1860s, when he became a railroad builder and director of the Queen Charlotte Island Coal Company. After the Civil War, more than two-thirds of the African American population in Canada returned to the United States.

By the Civil War, as the international business interests of blacks on the East Coast were focused on establishing trade relations with Africa, blacks on the West Coast also expressed an interest in establishing trade relations with Pacific Rim countries. There were people of African descent, however, who had settled in Hawaii from the early 1800s on who established business enterprises. On Oahu, Anthony D. Allen, a former slave from New York, who immigrated to Hawaii, where he married a Hawaiian woman in 1813, established several enterprises, including a boarding house and a saloon. He was also a farmer and a blacksmith.

Maritime participation in the Pacific trade as sailors and on whaling vessels was a factor that generated interest among blacks in international trade in the East. In 1865, former New Yorker Peter K. Cole (1831–1900), who had migrated to San Francisco, gave a series of lectures in that city in which he advocated that blacks purchase merchant trading ships and establish "Commercial Trade with Japan."

Still, in the Civil War era, Liberia remained the focus of African American interest in international trade and overseas enterprises. Moreover, in the 1850s, the economic plans formulated by black Americans to advance their international trading ventures, as well as those made to encourage African economic development, were also based on strategies to undermine the institution of slavery and the African slave trade.

Yet while altruistic in sentiment, at the same time these economic ventures could be construed as decidedly imperialist, particularly those of the African Civilization Society. Headed by Henry Highland Garnet, the society called for black Americans to "go to Africa, raise cotton, civilize the natives, become planters, merchants, compete with the slaves States in the Liverpool cotton market, and thus break down American slavery." Indeed, in late 1858 Martin Delany* led an expedition to West Africa; in 1859 treaties were signed with Nigeria—the purpose: to acquire land for cotton production.

Beyond undercutting slavery in the United States, African American settlement in Liberia was also seen as an effective means to combat the African supply side of the slave trade. As Alexander Crummell said in 1862: "This little nation, of only 15,000 civilized black Americans has, during some 20 or 30 years, held under control nigh a half a million of bold and warlike heathen, and completely interdicted their participation in the Slave trade." And in emphasizing the contribution of expatriate African Americans to African economic development, he noted that in addition to establishing schools and churches, Liberia was the only country in West Africa where manufacturing was taking place with sugar, saw-, and brick mills. Crummell also noted that with their 40 Liberian-made vessels African American–Liberians owned more ships than "all the sons of Africa."

Black American immigration to Liberia persisted to the late nineteenth century as blacks sought to escape the racial violence and oppression that continued after the Civil War. Paradoxically, paralleling the "white man's burden," rationale for their colonial exploitation of Africa, the economic and political agenda pursued by African Americans in Liberia, then, might also be construed as the "black man's burden."

Even while there was an insistence that black American immigration to Africa was needed to bring Christianity and "civilization" to the "heathen" indigenous population, increasingly, the emphasis was on the need for the migration of black "enterprising and moneyed men," who could provide investment capital. While advancing their own economic interests, at the same time expatriate African Americans, as in Liberia, would also expedite African development. Indeed, throughout the nineteenth century, as black Americans pursued their economic programs for African development, the rationale for exploiting African resources was their expertise as capitalists.

Still, even in the late nineteenth century, black Americans in the development of overseas markets did not limit their overseas trade ventures to Africa. The successful grocer William Hamilton Johnson in Baynesville, Virginia, who owned property in walnut forests, was also involved in international trade. He developed a market in Germany where he shipped walnut logs before his business failed in 1896. Also, in the early twentieth century African Americans expanded their international trade with Africa, beyond Liberia, and the West Indies. The Chicago-based J. H. Zedricks & Co., a mail-order house established in 1905, developed an international market by offering American-made products for sale through its 25-page catalog. By 1907, the company was exporting merchandise to Panama, Haiti, and Cuba as well as Liberia.

African Americans also established overseas enterprise. In 1913, the New York–based African Union Company leased mahogany and timber lands and oil palm plantations in West Africa. The company developed extensive markets for their exports in both America and Europe. With World War I, the Atlantic trade in consumer exports came to a virtual standstill, and the company went bankrupt.

With the war's end, African American interest in developing international trade ventures escalated, and several African American import-export companies were founded. The Thomas and Thomas Company, incorporated in New York in 1919, imported cocoa, spices, and fruits from the West Indies and exported American products to those islands. The Newport News, Virginia–based Paris Import and Export Corporation, incorporated in 1920, exported American products to Africa and imported mahogany, palm oil, coca, cocoa beans, and hides from Lagos in Nigeria.

The most ambitious attempt by blacks to expand international trade in the African diaspora was made by Marcus Garvey* with the 1919 founding of his Black Star Line Steamship Corporation. According to his second wife, Amy Jacques, its founding was a response by Garvey to West African producers who said that in the international transport of their exports a black shipping line would provide a profitable alternative to the white commodities produce brokers and shipping companies in Africa that exploited them.

Garvey's goal—"Africa for Africans"—won worldwide support among blacks, but his international trading program seemed to offer tremendous advantages primarily for the economic advancement of African Americans, since Africans would remain producers. Simply put, Garvey proposed the continued production of African resources by Africans. These products would then be shipped to the United States for processing and manufacturing, encouraging the development of an African American industrialist class, who would then sell the manufactured goods on international markets to Africa and African diasporan–populated countries.

Moreover, in his political agenda, Garvey had designated himself as the provisional governor of Africa. But from the turn of the century, the position of African Americans in their economic development plans for Africa had changed. Particularly after World War I, with a growing respect for the territorial integrity of African states, W.E.B. Du Bois said in a critique not only criticizing Garvey's political and economic agenda for Africa but also denouncing the white imperialists in their colonial scramble to exploit Africa's wealth: "Africa belongs to the Africans. They have not the slightest intention of giving it up to foreigners, white or black."

Still, Africa and the Caribbean remained important markets for international trade by African American manufacturers, and the major exports were hair care products and cosmetics for people of color. Until the 1930s, Annie Turnbo-Malone,* Madame C. J. Walker,* and Anthony Overton,* all of whom had product sales in the millions of dollars, were the leading black Americans in the international export trade, primarily through mail orders and through their overseas agents. Mrs. Turnbo-Malone, who established her company in 1898, sold her Poro hair care products and cosmetics in the West Indies, South America, Africa, and the Philippines. Her mail orders were so extensive that a branch of the St. Louis post office was established in her St. Louis manufactory.

Sarah Breedlove (Madame C. J.) Walker, who began manufacturing hair preparation products in 1905, also developed an extensive overseas mail-order distribution market in the West Indies, Cuba, Panama, and Africa, with a monthly gross sales, nationally and internationally, of $100,000. By 1916 her Indianapolis-based Walker Manufacturing Company produced a line of 100 hair and skin care preparations. By 1920, Anthony Overton's Chicago-based Overton-Hygenic Manufacturing Company was the leading producer of cosmetics for women of color, with international sales not only to Africa and the West Indies but also to Egypt, India, the Philippines, and Japan. In 1927 Dun & Bradstreet assessed Overton's Company as a million-dollar enterprise. By then, over 250 products were manufactured by him, including products for other companies.

In the 1930s and 1940s the leading exporter of black hair products were Sarah Spencer Washington,* who established her New Jersey–based Apex News and Hair Company in 1920. Unlike Poro and the Walker manufacturing company (its peak annual earnings in 1920 at $595,000 had dropped to $48,000 by 1933), Apex profited during the depression. By 1937, Washington, who built her own laboratories and manufacturing plant, was producing a line of 75 hair and beauty aids products, which were sold in the West Indies and Africa. Also, the Murray Cosmetic Company, founded in 1926 in Chicago by Charles D. Murray, Sr., and his wife Lilli, developed an extensive international market, primarily with its Murray's Hair Pomade for black men, which they sold in Honolulu, France, England, Germany, the Far East, Middle East, and South Africa.

Consequently, even during the depression, blacks persisted in developing international markets. In the 1930s black banker Major R. R. Wright* established an import-export firm that specialized in importing Haitian coffee. Moreover, as the *Pittsburgh Courier* newspaper columnist George Schuyler said in 1939 in promoting black international trade ventures: "There must be many things that the Haitians import which a Negro-owned company could supply. Soap, perfume, and cotton clothes come immediately to mind. We already have the cosmetic factories (Walker, Poro, Apex, etc.) to supply the first two."

During World War II, however, blacks focused their economic ambitions on developing business enterprises on the home front that would contribute to the victory of America and its Allies. Yet with the World War II curtailment of American international trade in consumer goods, black Americans began to reexamine their importance in the nation's economy as consumers in the domestic market. At a meeting of the Hampton University Association of New York in 1940, it was reported that the $2 billion of goods purchased by blacks in the South's 17 largest cities was "annually, two and one-half times greater than our exports to Great Britain, France, Germany, Poland and Finland, which in 1938 totaled $800,000,000."

Yet while African American international trading ventures virtually ceased during World War II, there were instances of African Americans who expanded their enterprises by providing goods or services for the nation's Allies. The Phoenix Color and Chemical Company, founded in 1922 by Jamaican-born Dr. Thomas M. Williams, who did research in high-octane gases, color pigments, and camouflage paints, as well as manufacturing gasoline bleaches and dyes, supplied these goods both before and during the war to Central and South American countries. The company also exported large orders of various chemicals for "public health work," primarily to Brazil, Mexico, and Cuba.

Also during World War II, there were African American expatriates who established overseas enterprises. On Malta, then a British possession, the Mississippi-born James Samuel Lynch Fykes, Jr., continued to operate his Floriana-based restaurant, Chez Jim, during the war. In Mexico, the expatriate Jones brothers (Chicago's policy kings) had established two dress shops in the downtown business section of Mexico City. They specialized in hand-painted skirts for women's beach wear. Their inventory was manufactured in their clothing factory that had 15 employees. Then, too, by 1944, successful black architect Paul Williams had completed contracts in several South American countries for projects that included designs for a large air terminal, a 10-story hotel, and private homes.

With the end of World War II, black Americans not only resumed their interest in international trade but also established overseas enterprises. Perhaps the most extensive were the Asian enterprises established by Dr. Dunbar McLaurin, an army lieutenant who served under General McArthur in the South Pacific. McLaurin remained in the Philippines after the war. In 1945 he began selling surplus army vehicles in Manila, expanding his firm to include the sale of spare parts, reconditioned trucks and jeeps, purchased from the United States. By 1948 his enterprises included a gold mine, sugar plantation, taxicab company, and rattan bamboo factory. His Oriental Picture Exchange produced Tagalog films. With his Far Eastern Trade Association, McLaurin established offices in Shanghai and Hong Kong. By 1950, it was reported that McLaurin's gross sales were in the "seven figures" and that in Manila alone he employed 400 Filipinos.

Significantly, McLaurin's enterprises in Asia underscore a historic pattern of black participation in international trading ventures and the establishment of overseas enterprise. From the early 1800s, even with the larger enterprises established by immigrant African Americans in Liberia, most blacks who participated in international trade or developed overseas enterprises were those who had maritime occupations, primarily as seamen, such as Paul Cuffe, or those who had served overseas in the American military. Rather than return home, expatriate African Americans, who participated in the nation's wars throughout the twentieth century, established small-scale enterprises, primarily in the food service or entertainment industry in Europe, Asia, and Australia.

Moreover, in the post–World War II era, African Americans' interest escalated, not only in developing overseas enterprises and in expanding international trade markets but also in generating overseas contracts. The nation's leading black engineer, Archie Alexander, a 1912 University of Iowa engineering school graduate, secured several international contracts. His American Caribbean Contracting Company, established in 1950, secured engineering contracts for projects in Venezuela, Puerto Rico, and Haiti, where he negotiated contracts to build a hydroelectric power, flood control, and irrigation and drainage works.

Invariably, while various import-export companies were founded in the immediate postwar era, few moved beyond the planning stage. One of the most ambitious was the International Merchandising Corporation, an import-export firm, founded in 1947. It planned to import rum from the West Indies, Scotch whiskey from Scotland, and fruits, sugar, spices, and silk from India, while also developing "a promotion campaign that will touch 37 countries of the world." The decolonization of Africa and the civil rights era were the two most important factors that provided the catalyst that positioned blacks to achieve these goals in establishing worldwide trading ventures by the end of the twentieth century.

In 1957 Ghana emerged as the first independent nation in the decolonization of Africa. The Oklahoma-based Simmons Royalty Company, headed by Jake Simmons, Jr., until his death in 1981, exemplifies the expansion of black American business activities in Africa. Beginning with Liberia in 1952, Ghana in 1965, and Nigeria and the Ivory Coast in the 1970s, Simmons brokered and negotiated multimillion-dollar oil leases for American multinational oil companies, including Philips Petroleum and Texaco. The Simmons Company, then, is symbolic in underscoring not only the increasing diversity of African American international business activities in the post–civil rights era but also the financial structuring of ventures that represented multimillion-dollar investments. The California-based African Development Public Investment Corporation, founded in 1985 by Dick Griffey, imports African commodities. By 1995 international business activities accounted for half of the company's sales of $56 million.

The black hair care products and cosmetics industries, with virtual global international trading activities in the post–civil rights era, not only expanded in developing new markets but also new products. Johnson Publishing Company's Fashion Fair Cosmetics division sold its products not only in West Africa, the Bahamas, Virgin Islands, Bermuda, and Canada but also in France, England, and Switzerland. Also, several black hair care products manufacturers established overseas enterprises.

In the early 1980s Johnson Products, with international sales in Liberia, Zaire (Congo), and the Ivory Coast, established a hair products manufacturing plant in Nigeria, and in 1988 Soft Sheen constructed a manufacturing plant in Kingston, Jamaica. This project, a joint venture with a local businessman, provided the company a basis to expand its international market, in tapping both the Caricom (Caribbean Economic Community) and also the 64 nations that make up the African-Caribbean-Pacific (ACP) group, which has strong ties with the EEC (European Economic Community).

In 1987 Soft Sheen, which exported hair care products to several African countries, including Nigeria and the Ivory Coast, expanded its international market when it acquired a 66 percent interest in the London-based Dyke and Dryden Company in 1987. Dyke and Dryden, England's largest black business, not only manufactures hair care products but also is the overseas distributor for Soft Sheen and some 40 European and American hair care and cosmetics companies. This acquisition also opened a black consumer market of 1.3 million in the United Kingdom and 3 million in western Europe for Soft Sheen products.

The Dallas-based Pro-Line hair products company also developed extensive international markets in some 43 counties, not only in sub-Saharan Africa and the Caribbean but also in Europe, Malta, the Middle East (Saudi Arabia, Yemen, the United Arab Emirates), and Australia. In the development of a Latin American market, Pro-Line participated in the Commerce Department's International Trade Development Center. It pairs American and foreign businesses and provides companies with assistance in developing markets in Jamaica and Brazil. By 1995 Pro-Line's international sales accounted for 10 percent, up 25 percent from the previous year, of the company's total $43 million in sales.

The post–civil rights era also marked an expansion in black international business activities beyond Africa and Latin America, as black Americans also established trade relations with both Asian and European countries. Throughout the 1970s and 1980s, Percy Sutton Intercontinental developed joint ventures in several Southeast Asian, African, and Latin American countries, which included investments in oil and coal and food processing plants. In Nigeria the company owns a flour mill and macaroni factory. It also imports meat and sugar from Brazil for processing and overseas sales.

The entertainment industry provided the basis for Percy Sutton's* initial international trade ventures in 1978, when his Inner City Broadcasting, founded in 1972, and a consortium of black businessmen from America and Nigeria established NATRAL (Nigerian-American Tapes and Recordings Associates, Ltd.). A multimillion-dollar enterprise, it manufactures records and tapes sold in both countries. Sutton owned the first full-time radio station in the Caribbean and serviced 18 radio stations in Africa and several western European countries. Also, Dick Griffey Productions, with licensing arrangements in 11 countries, tapped the European market in the early 1980s, when the French-based Vogue Record Company contracted to market his SOLAR Records catalog and records.

Then, in 1985, Black Entertainment Television (BET) began satellite programming in the Caribbean, and in 1993, Robert Johnson,* BET's founder and chief executive officer, established BET International (BETI), which includes "BET on Jazz," the Cable Jazz Channel, which is carried by satellite, with plans to extend BETI satellite coverage to South Africa, Botswana and Zimbabwe, Central Europe (Germany, Sweden, Austria, Belgium, Luxembourg, and the Czech Republic), North Africa and the Middle East, and the South Pacific (Australia and New Zealand).

In the post–civil rights era, black participation in the expanding telecommunications industry provided a basis for the development of overseas trade ventures. In 1984 the Waltham, Massachusetts–based Input Output Computer Service, Inc. (IOCS), a computer software, voice processing, and systems integration company, established a subsidiary, IOCS/African Informatics, in Douala, Cameroon. A joint venture, IOCS holds 70 percent ownership, with the remaining 30 percent owned by Cameroonian investors. Most of the company's contracts come from the Cameroon government. Its first project was to computerize documentation flow from the port of Douala.

Also in the 1980s, the international markets of the New Jersey–based H. F. Henderson Industries, founded in 1954, a company that manufactures control panels and engineering systems, had overseas sales to several Asian companies, including the People's Republic of China. Industries Network Solutions Inc. (INS), a global network information center service for the Internet and the Defense Data Network, developed international markets in both Central Africa and Asia, which accounted for 25 percent of its sales. Significantly, federal affirmative initiatives in 8(a) procurement contracts was an important factor for the company in its international business activities. Yet four years after leaving the program, INS, which in 1990 ranked eleventh on the BE 100s, showed a drop in sales of $48.8 million to $18.3 million. In 1995 the company was sold.

While an eight-year Small Business Administration (SBA) 8(a) federal contract set-aside program participant (1982–1990), INS, however, also had contracts to monitor the manufacturing of silicon chips in Japan. International business ventures between Japanese and African Americans have dated to the 1960s, when the Nation of Islam* negotiated with a major Japanese-based food company to supply fish for their shops and restaurants. Also, Fair Oaks Farms (formerly Brooks Sausage), a McDonald's supplier, exported a special pork sausage for Fujita's Japan McDonald's, which in 1995 comprised 35 percent of its 40 percent international market. In 1993, some $4.4 million out of its total sales of $31.5 million were to Japan. Sales in 1997 increased to $44 million, also including the Hong Kong market.

In another Japanese trading venture, black businessman Theodore A. Adams, founder of Pyrocap, who in 1994 established Saudi Pyrotech, which sells B-136 in Saudi Arabia, and Pyrocap International Bermuda Ltd., had initially contracted with the 130-year-old Japanese trading firm Cornes & Co., Ltd., for his U.S.-patented environmentally safe fire retardant, Pyrocap B-136.

African Americans have also established Japan-partnered business enterprises. International trader Eugene Matthews, who founded ASHTA International, Inc., in New York in 1988, holds a 51 percent ownership in TLA, the American subsidiary of the Japanese-based Think Laboratory Ltd., which manufactures short-run gravure printing equipment. A Harvard College and Law School graduate, Matthews also studied at Tokyo's Waseda University in 1980. He was hired by Think Laboratory in 1985. Matthews, who is based in Japan, is attempting to develop markets in Vietnam and Thailand. In its first year ASHTA International made $4.8 million in sales.

By the mid-1990s some 7,000 African American expatriates lived in Japan. Some have established small businesses. In Tokyo, Kyle Sexton's bakery has sales of U.S.$100,000, whereas E. C. Burnette, a 22-year army veteran, generates sales of U.S.$225,000 from his Edward Burnett's Casual Fashions store. Indeed, one of his suppliers is the Los Angeles black-owned Herb Sportswear, whose customers also include 19 Japanese retail stores. African American expatriate filmmaker Regge Life's Tokyo-based production company produced the documentary *Struggle and Success: The African-American Experience in Japan*.

Black Americans have also established consulting firms that provide services for both Japanese and American businesses. Atlanta-based Iris Harvey, who also has a Tokyo office, brokers information to Japanese on the American market. Her clients include Mitsubishi and Sumitomo. The publisher of *Japan Watch*, Kathryn D. Leary, who established the New York–based Leary Group, Inc., in 1991, pioneered in developing Japanese markets for American products, especially in high-demand goods such as sports equipment, home building supplies, geriatric products, and hip-hop clothing for the youth market.

Indeed, black culture has provided the basis for new Japanese-owned businesses. In Tokyo the Japanese-owned Brooklyn Hip-Hop Boutique, a clothing apparel store, has capitalized on this market. Interestingly, because the market is so hot, some Japanese-owned clothing stores place signs in their shops that the store is owned by African Americans, a marketing move to suggest that their stores carry the latest and most authentic hip-hop apparel. Even some Japanese hairdressers provide dreadlocks styles for their Japanese customers.

China has also provided opportunities for international business ventures for the post–civil rights generation of African Americans who have established both trade relations and business enterprises. The New Orleans–based Le International Imports, founded in 1993, with sales to K-Mart, Wal-Mart, and JCPenney, imports its inventory from China and other Asian countries. In 1995, the company's gross business receipts amounted to $3 million. In Hong Kong, Louisiana-born Lori Granito in 1992 opened her restaurant, "The Bayou," which specializes in African American cuisine. Moreover, black investment banks,* also a post–civil rights development, have leveraged significant international investments in Asia. Calvin Grigsby, chief executive officer (CEO) and founder of the defunct San Francisco–based Grigsby Brandford and Co., at one time negotiated multimillion-dollar investment ventures in Beijing.

In the post–civil rights era, African American management investment capital, however, has been increasingly slated for Africa. The black investment bank Pryor, McClendon Counts & Co. placed investments in several African financial institutions including, "Ghana's CAL Merchant, the National Merchant Bank of Zimbabwe and Securities Discount Co., a Ghanaian firm that has a wholly owned stock brokerage operation." In 1990 the potential for attractive investment opportunities in a postapartheid South Africa prompted the founding of New Africa Advisers, a subsidiary of the $4 billion Sloan Financial Group, which also manages the Calvert New Africa Fund recognized as "the first of its kind with a portfolio devoted primarily to African and African-related investments." Indeed, New Africa Advisers was the first American investment group to establish offices in the New South Africa.

Still, in international markets, black multinationals have not limited their markets to Africa or to the African diaspora–populated countries in the Caribbean and South America, nor have the products manufactured and traded been limited specifically to people of African descent. Indeed, the most extensive overseas enterprise in which African Americans have been involved is TLC Beatrice International, acquired by Reginald Lewis* in his 1987 $985 million leveraged buyout of the French-based Beatrice International Foods. Lewis's acquisition represented the first enterprise owned by an African American that generated multibillion-dollar sales.

With his purchase, the French-based TLC Beatrice International owned 64 companies located in 31 foreign countries, including Italy, Spain, Portugal, the Netherlands, Belgium, Germany, Denmark, 12 Latin American companies, Thailand, Australia, and Canada. In acquiring funds for the leveraged buyout, Lewis, however, sold off his Canadian and Australian assets. In 1988, Lewis sold off his Latin American subsidiaries to a Venezuelan company and his Hong Kong Winners Food to two Japanese companies, Nissin Foods and C. Itoh. Still, in 1988, TLC Beatrice food company operations, divided into food distribution and grocery products, had European sales of $1.63 billion.

For 10 years, TLC Beatrice was "the largest wholesale distributor of food and grocery products to supermarkets in the Paris metropolitan areas." It operated 418 Franprix stores (35 were owned by TLC and 383 were franchises) and the LeaderPrice stores (43 were owned and 43 were franchisees). In 1996, TLC International had sales of $2.3 billion. Its French holdings, which accounted for $1.9 billion, however, were sold in 1997. Still, in 1998, the New York–based international company in its debt restructuring continues as the major supplier for ice cream in western Europe, with manufacturing plants in Spain and the Canary Islands. It also remains the leading maker of potato chips and snacks in Ireland and continues its bottling operations in Europe and Thailand. Projected sales for 1998 are estimated at around $400 million.

Consequently, as African Americans expanded their international trading ventures in the late twentieth century, the goods they produced for export were not limited to a distinct black consumer market. In addition, African American manufacturers, beyond those in the hair products industries, following the trend of American multinationals, began to move production overseas. The Detroit-based Stone Merchant Company, which produces a signature line of hip-hop accessories, contracted the manufacturing of its signature backpack to a Seoul, South Korean, company. Also, in 1995 Karl Kani, the leading hop clothing designer, with sales that year of $59 million, began manufacturing in Turkey, Macao, the Philippines, and China, which the company claims reduced production costs by 20 percent. In expanding his designs, a couture line of apparel is planned, with manufacturing in Italy.

At the same time, African American overseas manufacturing has not been immune from criticism not only in the exporting of jobs but also in the exploitation of employees in these factories. American clothing designer Liz Claiborne and celebrity TV talk show host Kathie Lee, both of whose brand-name clothing lines are manufactured overseas, as well as black basketball superstar Michael Jordan of the Chicago Bulls, who endorses Nike and has his own line of Jordan-Nike products, have been singled out for scrutiny in response to charges of employee exploitation in the overseas manufacturing of their product lines.

Yet Black Americans in the post–civil rights era also expanded overseas business activities in areas beyond manufacturing and overseas enterprises. In another international business venture, Guyanese-born Lex Nigel Barker, a naturalized American citizen, in 1991 established his International Aircraft Trading Inc., an aircraft sales and maintenance operation. Since then, some 90 percent of its business contracts have been from China, India, eastern Europe, Africa (Ghana, Zaire, South Africa), Latin America, and various Caribbean countries, where he sells used 747s.

Also, the Chicago area–based Fuci Metals, USA, founded in 1988 by former basketball pro Demetrius "Tony" Brown, which specializes in the international trade of metals, included one venture in which the company sold four industrial steel furnaces to a Turkish dealer. As an international metal trades broker, however, Brown has a global market. His London office buys metals, primarily aluminum, from Europe and Russia. Fuci Metals not only is the agent for acquiring raw materials for Bratsk Aluminum, the largest aluminum producer in Siberia but is also the largest distributor of Russian silicon in the United States. In the United States, Fuci's domestic customers include Reynolds Aluminum, GMC, and Ford Motor Co. In its first listing on the *BE* 100s for sales in 1995, Fuci Metals USA, with a staff of four, ranked twenty-fourth, with $61 million in sales, and in 1997 ranked twenty-fourth, with $86.5 million in sales.

At the close of the twentieth century, then, in expanding their participation in the global economy, with historic origins in international trading ventures that date to the early 1800s, the post–civil rights era generation of black Americans not only had increased their international trade ventures but also had established overseas enterprises as well. Doubtless, in the twenty-first-century global economy, African Americans will play an increasingly important role in international business. Significantly, too, not only did African decolonization provide a basis for black America's expanded participation in international business activities; federal affirmative action initiatives also positioned blacks to increase their participation in partnering with Corporate America to develop and secure investment capital.

At the same time, for African Americans in the twenty-first century, their international trading ventures will be challenged in several ways, especially in Africa. For one, they will be confronted with problems internal to the politics of the nations in which they seek to develop markets. In the mid-1980s, INS withdrew its Central African business interests, claiming payment issues and time factors in closing deals. In 1985 Johnson Products closed its Nigerian manufacturing plant. While political instability and internal disorders in that country contributed to production difficulties, there was also the problem of payment issues. Moreover, international sales for Johnson Products, primarily to Liberia, Zaire (Congo), and the Ivory Coast, amounted to only 2.5 percent of the company's total sales, some $35 million.

Black multinationals with overseas enterprises can continue to expect competition from white multinationals in those same industries. While international sales of American hair products and cosmetics reached $2.4 billion in 1994, the American Health and Beauty Aids Institute (AHBAI) reported that in 1995 its 18-member black hair companies had international sales of only $70 million. Despite fierce competition, rather than retreat from this multibillion-dollar market, black American multinationals have launched aggressive international business plans. In South Africa, a cosmetic manufacturing plant is scheduled for opening in 1999 by New Yorker Diane Stevens, whereas Luster Products, a leading Chicago-based hair products manufacturer, with sales that increased from $43 million in 1996 to $57.5 million in 1997, is considering expanding its international trade to South Africa.

In the closing decade of the twentieth century, the Savannah, Georgia–based Carson Products Company, acquired in 1995 by a black investor–led group, headed by former Morehouse College president Dr. Leroy Keith, not only has developed an extensive export market with its "Dark & Lovely" hair products and cosmetics but also has established overseas manufacturing plants. In Ghana, the site of one plant, Carson brokered an agreement with the Ghanaian government that granted the company a "100% exemption from duties on products exported from the Ghana facility, and a 60% reduction in duties on products sold within Ghana." Carson, which is also listed on the New York Stock Exchange, has also obtained approval for trade of its products in Brazil in addition to establishing a manufacturing plant in South Africa.

Predominantly black-populated countries (of the 45 million South Africans, whites comprise 14 percent and Indians 3 percent) represent an important market for African American international trading ventures. In the United States, with a population of 263.8 million, the third largest in the world, African Americans, numbered some 33 million, some 13 percent. In 1995 Africa's population was 878 million, including Nigeria, the largest, with 101.2 million (projections for 2020, 215.9 million; the United States, 326.3 million). South America's population, including the Caribbean, is 481 million, compared to Europe's 509 million. Brazil, the world's fifth largest country, has a population of 160.7 million, of whom, at a minimum, 85 to 90 percent would be considered black in the United States. Consequently, not only is there a significant potential market for hair care products for people of African descent; the market for cosmetics for women of color, worldwide, is even greater, which accounts for the aggressive marketing efforts by both black and white multinationals to increase their international sales.

Not only will black Americans with international trading ventures have to compete with American multinationals; they will also encounter competition from similar businesses in those countries. In one instance, Pro-Line, which in 1983 withdrew sales in South Africa in support of antiapartheid economic sanctions, lost its market to the South African hair products company Black Like Me, founded during that era. Moreover, in the New South Africa, with a 100 percent tax on their imported products, black American health and beauty aid companies will find it difficult to compete for sales in that market, compounded by competition with white multinationals that also produce black hair care products and cosmetics.

Apartheid ended in South Africa in 1994, and that country, under the leadership of President Nelson Mandela, emerged as the new market of opportunity for African Americans with international business interests. In addition to expanding markets in international trading ventures, some black multinationals established subsidiaries in that country or initiated joint ventures with South Africans. In 1995, Johnson Publishing Company, the nation's second largest black business (with sales of $361.1 million in 1997), launched a new subsidiary—EBCO International—in a joint venture with white investors for publication of *Ebony South Africa*. Interestingly, within two years, Johnson Publishing "increased its ownership stake of *Ebony South Africa* from 51% to 85%, buying out the publication's white individual investors." Perhaps this was a marketing move to increase circulation, promoting the magazine as a wholly owned black enterprise.

At the same time, however, *Ebony South Africa* represents an enterprise in competition with South Africa's viable black journals, such as *Enterprise* and *Tribute*, which, interestingly, in their format and news coverage of South Africa, are modeled to a great extent after their African American counterparts, respectively, *Ebony, Black Enterprise, Essence*, and *Emerge*. Quite possibly, in meeting competition, a South African–printed edition of *Ebony* would be as successful in circulation, if not more so, than *Ebony South Africa*.

Consumer product preferences, as opposed to race, ethnicity, or even the politics of producers or kinds of business ownership, seem to be a major factor in the purchase of goods sold by American multinationals. In one instance, what was thought to be perhaps the most successful international black joint business venture, the Pepsi-Cola New Age Beverages venture, a $20 million investment project established in 1995, failed in 1997. Pepsi had put up $5 million, while Egoli Beverages, L.P., a consortium of both black American and South African investors, put up $15 million. Pepsi, however, could not sustain competition with Coca-Cola. Ironically, despite antiapartheid sanctions, Coca-Cola continued to sell its products in South Africa, as opposed to Pepsi, which had withdrawn sales in response to those sanctions.

Doubtless there are factors beyond race, ethnicity, and nationality that can determine the success or failure of black business ventures in sub-Saharan Africa. Moreover, in seeking to develop overseas enterprises and markets, black multinationals, increasingly, will find themselves confronted not only with competition from American multinationals but also with competition from parallel enterprises, as they develop in those countries. As the president and chief operating officer (COO) of BET Holdings said, reviewing its overseas cable ventures, while BETI returns of 20 to 30 percent are expected by the year 2001, "once a country gets cable, they want to produce their own shows." In the telecommunications industries, such as cell phones, American international trading ventures with Asian countries provide an example of this increasing phenomenon.

In 1995 Asia's 3.2 billion people comprised 56.6 percent of the world's population, including India with a population of 936 million and China with a population of 1.2 billion. With projections for 2020, 1.3 billion (India) and 1.4 billion (China), Asian countries have the capacity in the next millennium for developing the largest internal domestic markets in the global economy. Specifically, as Asia develops the manufacturing infrastructure needed to supply its domestic market, these countries will rely less and less on international trade, including American exports, to supply their domestic markets.

Yet even as Asia expands its international markets and becomes a formidable competitor to the United States in overseas trade, the one American product in which there is a large Asian consumer market demand is the one area in which black Americans have a monopoly in development: African American cultural expressions. Since the early twentieth century African American culture has sustained itself as a marketable commodity. Billions of dollars in profits have been made from the profitable production and distribution of black American cultural commodities, such as in the record industry, but not by blacks. A vertical integration in the marketing of African American cultural resources by black corporate business organizations, inclusive of investments in development, production, and distribution, offers profitable ventures for African Americans as a basis to expand international trade ventures in the global economy in the twenty-first century.

Despite the financial crisis in Asia in the late 1990s and its growing manufacturing infrastructure to supply its internal domestic markets, still in the first two decades of the millennium, 75 percent of the world's trade growth is projected to come from the big emerging markets (BEMs), not only Mexico, Argentina, and Brazil in Latin America but also China, Taiwan, Indonesia, South Korea, and India in Asia, in addition to Turkey, Poland, and South Africa. Eventually, however, international trade will reach a saturation point as the BEMs increasingly produce for their own domestic markets.

As the millennium advances, Africa will stand as the last frontier in the development not only of new international markets but also of natural resources for the economic superpowers in both the West and East. In addition to oil, timber, cocoa, and coffee, the 45 sub-Saharan African countries have tremendous natural resources—"97 percent of the world's chromium, 84 percent of its platinum, 64 percent of its manganese and 25 percent of its uranium." Yet in considering global politics, especially within the context of African nationalism and militarism, as W.E.B. Du Bois said: "Africa belongs to the Africans. They have not the slightest intention of giving it up to foreigners, white or black." Simply put, unlike the colonial exploitation of African natural resources, the development of viable consumer markets for international trade investments will require expanded employment opportunities for Africans and increases in per capita incomes.

Moreover, standing as the last continent for development, Africa, with global assistance, especially humanitarian aid, can also position itself to avoid problems of industrialization, such as in China at the turn of the century. In that nation's efforts to provide employment for its 1 billion people, industrial wastes and the use of coal for energy to fuel the new industries in just 10 years have resulted in disastrous environmental consequences in the form of the destruction of its natural resources, water, and air. In the new millennium, then, the economic superpowers, for the first time, will find it to their distinct economic and political disadvantage to attempt to carve out sub-Saharan Africa in "spheres of influence."

Rather than a continuation of neocolonial economic activities in Africa, the world's economic powers must include channeling significant financial investments to African countries, especially in a relocation of overseas manufacturing. The development of African-based enterprises, which can produce durable, semidurable, and nondurable goods, can not only provide a base to encourage

African industrialization but also lead to an expansion in the development of both domestic and interregional consumer markets. African American multinationals in copartnership with American multinationals can have a significant impact on African economic development.

In the first venture of its kind, Barden International (BI), a subsidiary of the Detroit-based Barden Companies (established in 1981), copartnered with General Motors (GM) in securing a contract to retrofit GM cars in Namibia (Southern Africa) from left-hand to right-hand drive. In 1996 Don Barden began construction of his $15 million plant located in Windhoek, the capital of Namibia. Construction of the plant was completed in 1998. In addition to its manufacturing activities, BI, headed by Detroit's former finance director from 1982 to 1993, Bella Marshall (Barden's wife), as president and COO, is also a fleet distributorship of GM cars and trucks and retail dealership for GM's Chevrolets and Cadillacs.

This tripartite business arrangement with GM, which resulted in construction of the 100 percent Barden-owned Namibian plant, was achieved because of the cooperative spirit of enterprise between the Namibian government, which agreed to purchase $31 million in GM vehicles, and Barden in assuming the risk for GM's competition in the Namibian market, which is dominated by Toyota. Also, Namibian president Sam Nujoma's and GM's confidence in Don Barden's entrepreneurial abilities and financial holdings was a factor. In 1995, Barden, who founded the Detroit-based Barden Cablevision, sold his enterprise for $100 million. In 1997, Barden Companies had sales of $110 million.

In the twenty-first century, based on the potential for expansion in black Corporate America, there can be not only an increase in overseas enterprises established by African Americans as well as international trade activities but also an expansion of copartnered multinational enterprises between black and white Corporate America. African Americans can perhaps, finally, play a significant role not only in America's international trade but also in achieving the goal of contributing to African economic development.

SELECTED BIBLIOGRAPHY: *Black Enterprise* (June 1989, 1994 and May 1994–1998); *Fortune*, August 4, 1997; Jonathan Greenberg, *Staking a Claim: Jake Simmons, Jr. and the Making of an African-American Oil Dynasty* (New York: Penguin Group, 1991); A. Doris Bank Henries, *The Life of Joseph Jenkins Roberts and His Inaugural Address* (London: Macmillan, 1964); Robert A. Hill, ed., *The Marcus Garvey and Universal Negro Improvement Association Papers*, 7 vols. (Los Angeles: University of California Press, 1983–1991); Reginald F. Lewis and Blair S. Walker, *Why Should White Guys Have All the Fun? How Reginald Lewis Created a Billion-Dollar Business Empire* (New York: John Wiley & Sons, 1995); *Newsweek*, May 4, 1998; Juliet E. K. Walker, *The History of Black Business in America: Capitalism, Race, Entrepreneurship* (New York: Macmillan/Prentice Hall International, 1998).

Juliet E. K. Walker

INTERNET, BLACK BUSINESS ONLINE, WORLD WIDE WEB. The overwhelming popularity of the World Wide Web (WWW) sometimes obscures the fact that as an entity it is only a few years old. Developed at European Laboratory for Particle Physics (CERN) in 1990–1991 and refined by the creation of Mosaic, the first graphics-based Web browser, at the National Center for Supercomputing Applications (NCSA) in 1993, the Web has become one of the great communication phenomena of the century. Starting with literally a handful of users, it has been projected that by the year 2001 there will be over 200 million people online. In the span of only five years it has developed into one of the most influential technologies in recent memory, affecting everything from government to education to business.

African Americans have been part of this information revolution from the very beginning. Unlike earlier technological innovations such as radio and television, developments that due to race relations of the time originally ignored the interests and needs of black America, African Americans tapped into the Web from the start, establishing Web sites on subjects ranging from black culture in America to Afrocentric newspapers. The proliferation of such sites included many by black-owned businesses.

African American businesses on the Web are a by-product of the growth in black ownership of advanced technology enterprises, with companies such as Resource One Computer Systems, Pulsar Data Systems, and RMS Technologies establishing a vibrant presence in the field of high technology in the 1980s and early 1990s. Thus, when the Web exploded on the scene in 1994, these black businesses and others like them were in a position to take full advantage of it. In doing so, they showed the way for other black-owned businesses and helped spur the further growth of the Web.

For example, Pulsar Data Systems, a full systems integrator that combines hardware and software with advanced technical services and is one of the top five minority firms in the nation, has a strong presence on the Web. Other important black-owned technology companies currently utilizing the Web include Maxima Corporation and Open Vision Technologies, both previously successful high-tech companies that have taken advantage of the business opportunities the Web offers.

But high-technology companies are not the only black-owned companies capitalizing on this new technology. Johnson Publishing Co. Inc., the publishers of *Ebony* and *Jet* magazines, is on the Web, and Granite Broadcasting Corp. and BET Holdings both have excellent sites. Avis Ford, Inc., one of the largest black-owned automotive dealerships, has an advanced Web site, as does Motown Records. A quick search of Internet search engines shows that of the top 10 black-owned companies in the *BE* 100 Industrial/Service category, 90 percent have information readily available on the Web, as do 70 percent of the top 10 companies on the *BE* 100 Automotive Dealership list, and every year more and more of the *BE* 100 companies are coming online.

There is also a myriad of Web pages by and about African Americans in the entertainment business, many of them innovative sites that utilize advanced technologies. The Black Entertainment Network, in partnership with Microsoft, has an extensive series of Web pages, as does the magazine *Vibe*. *Black Talent News*, an online journal dealing with African Americans in the entertainment industry, is available on the Web, and Magic Johnson Theaters has a site with information on the company, theater locations, and a list of other resources. Entering the name of individual black entertainers or athletes into a search engine will provide a long list of official and unofficial Web sites dealing with the subject.

With more and more of black America coming online, several black-owned Internet service providers have been founded with the express purpose of providing networking services to African American individuals, businesses, and organizations. United States Black On-Line (USBOL) claims to be the largest black Internet service provider in the United States, with hundreds of local access points across the nation. The USBOL home page has a variety of useful sections that provide links to pages it supports, information on how to sign up, and so on. Netnoir, a collaborative effort with America On-Line, is an example of another black-owned online service provider.

To facilitate navigation of the Web for those interested in black business, there are a number of useful "gateways," that is, sites designed as a clearinghouse of links to other sites. The Universal Black Pages, a product of the Georgia Institute of Technology Black Graduate Student Association, has links to black-owned businesses both in the United States and internationally. USBOL lists a large number of business sites that it supports on its home page. In addition, a number of directories for black-owned businesses have come online, meaning that African Americans who change communities have easy access to lists of predominantly black-owned companies and services. For example, the *Greater Pittsburgh Black Business Directory and Resource Guide* is available online. It divides its listings into about 100 different subject categories and is also searchable alphabetically, both by subject and by company name. On a national level, the Buy Black Network is a private enterprise that encourages black America's support of black-owned businesses and has a searchable national database.

There is also a proliferation of sites designed to help African American businesses utilize the Web to its fullest. For example, companies such as Blkbusiness.com seek to help black-owned companies, online and otherwise, by advertising pertinent information like services offered, job openings, and products through the creation of Web pages and a searchable database of black-owned business. *Black Enterprise*, a business service publication for African American entrepreneurs, corporate executives, professionals, and decision makers, also has an extremely useful site. Besides a digest of the magazine, the home page includes such things as an overview of the *BE* 100s, a list of resources of interest to black business, a special techwatch section, a bulletin board, and a section of classified ads.

There are a number of black business–related professional organizations online, including the National Society of Black Engineers, the National Black

MBA Association,* the National Black Media Coalition, the United Negro College Fund, and the Association of Black Psychologists, to name a few. The Web allows such organizations to diffuse information, network, and advertise on a global scale in a timely and cost-effective manner.

There are approximately 120 historically black colleges and universities (HBCUs) in the United States, and many of them have Web sites that offer information on business programs both for undergraduate and graduate students. Howard University's School of Business, for example, has an informative set of Web pages, and Florida A&M's School of Business and Industry, Morehouse College's Business Program, and North Carolina A&T's School of Business and Economics all have information on their respective business programs available on their Web sites. These are only a few examples; a search of the Web using the keywords "historically black colleges and universities" will reveal a detailed list of sites by and about these schools.

While many African American businesses are on the Web, there is still much work to be done. This is particularly true in the area of smaller black-owned businesses, which could benefit greatly by utilizing advanced technologies like the Web for marketing, advertising, and diffusing company information. There is also much room for Web development by the larger black-owned businesses. All *BE* 100 companies not currently online should work to get there, and those that already have a Web presence should constantly strive to improve and expand their existing sites.

Unprecedented growth of the World Wide Web will also demand more technical advising by African Americans for African Americans. Further creation of jobs for black Americans in the fields of computer programming, graphic design, and Web development will allow black businesses to seek skills and advice within their community. To this effect, colleges and universities—especially HBCUs—need to train all African American students, not just those in business, to be aware of the latest technologies like the Web and to show how they can be used as viable research, teaching, and business tools. Hopefully, future technical developments like a search engine designed primarily to find African American Web sites and the expansion and the creation of more black business gateway sites will greatly help those interested in expanding onto the Web.

Because the Web has grown so quickly, it has been argued that those companies that have not already used it as a business tool missed the boat and that, having lost out on the first wave, it is now too late to move in this direction. Nothing could be further from the truth. Indeed, with the World Wide Web expanding by leaps and bounds, black-owned businesses could not find a better time to go online than today. As we enter a new century, developments such as the Web will only become more important, and those businesses who most effectively use these kinds of resources will be the most successful. Black-owned businesses, having already recognized the potential of the Web, can be in a position to help lead the way.

Due to space constraints, the uniform resource locators (URLs) for the Web sites mentioned in this article could not be published. Those wishing to visit these and other sites can find them by accessing a search engine such as Webcrawler (http://www.webcrawler.com/) or Yahoo (http://www.yahoo.com/) and typing in the name of the company or subject. Generic searches such as "black business" will also yield many more sites than were mentioned in this brief overview.

SELECTED BIBLIOGRAPHY: Stafford L. Battle and Rey O. Harris, *The African American Resource Guide to the Internet and Online Services* (New York: McGraw-Hill, 1996); Phaedra Hise, *Growing Your Business Online: Small-Business Strategies for Working the World Wide Web* (New York: Holt, 1996); Robert H. Reid, *Architects of the Web: 1,000 Days That Built the Future of Business* (New York: Wiley, 1997); Juliet E. K. Walker, *The History of Black Business in America: Capitalism, Race, Entrepreneurship* (New York: Macmillan/Prentice Hall International, 1998).

Todd E. Larson

INVESTMENT BANKING. While African Americans have a long history of investing in stocks and bonds, beginning in the early nineteenth century, the establishment of black-owned investment banks, however, began in the twentieth century. In 1815, the New York African Society for Mutual Relief owned $500 in bank stock. In South Carolina the 1835 estate of South Carolina barber Thomas Inglis included $19,303 in stocks and bonds from the Mechanics Bank. In the 1830s, wealthy Pennsylvania lumber merchant Stephen Smith* was the largest stockholder in the Columbia Bank. In New Orleans in the 1830s, several blacks owned stock in the Citizens Bank of Louisiana. In 1833, two black men purchased stock. One owned $20,000, or 200 shares; the other, $15,000, or 150 shares. In 1836, wealthy Natchez, Mississippi barber William Johnson* purchased 26 shares in the Natchez Railroad for $2,000.

Wealthy black women also owned stocks and bonds before the Civil War. In 1836 Marie Louise Panis in New Orleans owned 490 shares of capital stock in the Citizens Bank of Louisiana, worth $49,000. Cotton planter Suzanne Meullion owned stock in the New Orleans, Opelousas and Great Western Railroad Company. The South Carolina free black woman rice planter Margaret Mitchell Harris purchased $25,300 in stocks and bonds just before the Civil War with money made from the sale of her slaves. During the Civil War, black commission broker John Clay owned 19 shares of the New Orleans Gas Light Company and 10 shares in the Bank of Louisiana. Also, before the Civil War, abolitionist Arthur Tappan, who was also one of the founders of Dun Mercantile Credit Company, reported that an attempt was made by an African American to deal on the New York Stock exchange, but he was refused a seat.

It was not until the twentieth century that blacks as investment bankers sold stocks and bonds. Investment banks specialize in the issue of long-term corporate, municipal, and foreign bonds, as well as common stock. A corporation, proposing to sell securities, can arrange with an investment banking firm to underwrite the new securities issues. Consequently, an investment banker is an underwriter who buys the entire issue at an agreed-upon price. The investment banker then sells the issue piecemeal. Usually, these issues are purchased by insurance companies and pension funds. Investment banks also sell municipal bonds, but competitive bidding is required by law for investment banks and brokerage houses in buying bond issues from state and local governments and public utilities. Black brokerage firms, however, preceded black investment banks.

In the early twentieth century a newspaper reported that W. Fred Trotman was the only Wall Street black investment broker, who had been in business on the Street since 1903. In 1923, Robert T. Bess founded the R. T. Bess Company, located initially on Broadway, until Bess relocated to Wall Street in 1930. By then, Bess had 15 employees, nine whites and six blacks. In 1932, it was reported that he was attempting to interest black investors in the Standard Television and Electric Company, manufacturers of television receivers and transmitters. By 1935, the Evanita Holding Company, located on Broadway, and founded by John J. Gundles, was also announced as the only black securities firm operating on Wall Street.

In the late 1940s the number of blacks in investment increased. In 1949 Lawrence Lewis, who was registered by his employer, Abraham and Co., members of the New York Stock Exchange, New York Curb Exchange, and Chicago Board of Trade and Commodities Exchange, was reported as the first black to sell stocks and bonds on Wall Street. Then, in the 1950s, several black investment firms were founded. In 1952, Norman L. McGhee established his Cleveland-based McGhee & Co. Investment Securities. McGhee, licensed as a broker-dealer, was said to be the first black to establish an investment firm authorized to deal in general securities. In the mid-1950s McGhee had offices in five states. In 1955, when Philip M. Jenkins established his investment firm, Special Markets, Inc., he was also announced as the first black to head his own brokerage firm in the Wall Street area. Jenkins's investment strategy was to tap the ethnic market in the United States and also an international market, as he said: "[W]ith the recent economic stirrings in Asia and Africa there are definite advantages in introducing a Negro brokerage house at this time."

The post–civil rights era marked an upsurge in black interest in Wall Street, although, in 1970, there were only 60 blacks among the 35,000 stockbrokers nationwide. By 1990, however, there were 15 black investment banks. In 1991, *Black Enterprise* (*BE*) began publication of its first annual listing of the top black-owned investment banks, but some 20 years earlier, there were only 2 black investment banks. Daniels and Bell, founded by Willie E. Daniels and Travers J. Bell, and First Harlem Securities, established by Russell Goings, were the first black-owned investment banking firms to be admitted to the New York Stock Exchange (NYSE). In 1975 the New Orleans–based Doley Securities became the third black investment firm to trade on the NYSE. In 1973 founder Harold Doley was the first black to own his own seat on the New York Stock Exchange.

From the 1970s to the early 1990s, black investment bankers profited from the municipal bond industry, a market developed initially by Bell, who made this lateral move when he found that black investment firms were being blocked in corporate trading. Other black investment banks followed and achieved some success, primarily because of black mayors who made sure that black investment banking firms were given a chance to bid successfully for these bonds, which were sold to provide funding for projects such as convention/civic centers, transportation projects (such as airports and rapid transit), schools and universities, hospitals, housing, and utilities.

By 1993 *BE* investment banks had "co-managed bond issues worth $162.7 billion." By 1996, muni (municipal) bond deals had dropped to $60 billion. In the 1990s, tax-exempt and taxable securities, municipal bond, and mortgage-backed securities, which since the 1970s had made up the bulk of black investment banking financial activities, had begun to dry up. Even so, by 1990, the 12 black investment banks had managed less than 1 percent of the total bond business. Also, in the mid-1990s, there was closer scrutiny of investment banking houses by the federal government. The impact was devastating on some black investment banking firms. In December 1994, Daniels and Bell were forced to close when they could no longer make payments to lease their New York Stock Exchange seat. Also, the investment banking firm Grigsby Brandford in 1996 fell. In 1995 it had ranked second on the *BE* Financial Companies.

The new generation of black investment bankers, those who established their firms in the 1990s, are staying away from bond markets as much as possible. In order to survive, black investment banks have to generate a deeper capital base, which has been the direction of new black investment banks, often securing capital from white investment banks. Utendahl Capital Partners was founded in 1992 by John Utendahl. He owns 80 percent interest, whereas Merrill Lynch, where John was once employed as a corporate bond trader, owns 20 percent. With his access to deep pockets, Utendahl is now the nation's largest black-owned investment bank.

Indeed, by 1997, according to *Forbes*, Utendahl had structured, placed, or underwritten securities "worth more than $250 billion." Moreover, with the diversity of its financial activities, Utendahl is becoming more and more of a full-service investment bank. Black investment banking firms, without backing from Wall Street, view the new development in black investment banking history in much the same way that blacks in the 1970s and 1980s viewed white-owned companies that, to secure funds from the federal government for minorities, used blacks to front for them as minority firms. As black business expands in the twenty-first century, increasingly more partnerships will be established with whites in investment banking in much the same way that whites acquire ownership interest through the stock market in black-owned companies that go public through the purchase of shares in those companies.

Black investment banks have been involved in black business expansion. Pryor, McClendon, Counts & Company Inc. (PMC), founded in 1981, has been one of the leading black investment banks. In 1992 PMC was the lead manager of the $400 million debt offering for the new Denver International Airport, the largest municipal finance deal by a black firm, but it also helped fund the establishment of the black United Bank of Philadelphia and raised $5.6 million of Maceo's Sloan purchase of a personal communications services (PCS) license. Sloan said, "Banks will not loan $100 million to a minority no matter how good the idea or deep his or her cash flow."

Also, black-owned venture capital firms have been important in raising money for black business. Edward Dugger III founded Boston-based UNC Ventures in 1974, which raises funds to finance minority businesses. Black businesses that have had UNC financial ties include Envirotest Systems Corporation and Broadcast Enterprises Network, Inc., established in 1974 by Ragan Henry. UNC Ventures also funded $45 million for the short-lived black airline, Air Atlanta. There are several organizations, such as the National Association of Securities Professionals, founded in 1985, to advance minority and women participation in investment banking.

SELECTED BIBLIOGRAPHY: Eleanor Branch, "How High Is Up?" *Black Enterprise* (October 1990); Forbes, August 4, 1997; Yolonda Gault, "Now That the Smoke Has Cleared," *Black Enterprise* (June 1997); Frank McCoy, "Investment Firms Show What They Can Do," *Black Enterprise* (June 1993); Frank McCoy, "The Nonstop from Durham," *Black Enterprise* (May 1995); "The Tough Get Going," *Black Enterprise* (June 1995); "25 Years of Blacks in Financing," *Black Enterprise* (October 1994); Juliet E. K. Walker, *The History of Black Business in America: Capitalism, Race, Entrepreneurship* (New York: Macmillan, Prentice Hall International, 1998); Terry Williams, "They've Got the Capital," *Black Enterprise* (October 1991).

Juliet E. K. Walker

J

JACKSON, JESSE LOUIS (1941–), Chicago and Washington, D.C., civil rights activist, founder of Operation PUSH.

Since the civil rights era, ask someone, Who is Reverend Jesse Jackson? and most people will immediately see visions of a civil rights leader or former candidate for president of the United States. Ask again, and others will describe him as an all-around social gadfly who moves from city to town to support "victims" of labor strikes, sexual harassment, or police brutality or economic underdogs who have lost the family farm to a bank in foreclosure. Jackson is probably the world's most well-known civil, social, and human rights activist. However, long before his move into elective politics, and before he became a "celebrity" who seems to be everywhere all the time, he established a reputation as a brilliant organizer and strategist for helping African Americans in business and industry. Jackson is credited with serving as a catalyst and engine for economic empowerment, helping African American entrepreneurs and businesses gain access to practically every sector of large corporations that traditionally had shut doors in their faces. Early in his career he was instrumental in persuading Corporate America to hire and buy not only from black-owned companies that provided building maintenance and other nonprofessional services but also from law firms, publishing companies, office supply vendors, and other professional services providers.

Jackson, who was born in Greenville, South Carolina, experienced sitting at the back of buses and "Whites Only" signs throughout his formative years. Early on he showed promise as a rising star and was elected to the honor society in high school, where he impressed fellow students and teachers with his intelligence as a star debater. He also demonstrated excellence outside the classroom on the basketball and football teams. Even then, Jackson showed signs of what his life work would become: He turned down a contract with the San Francisco Giants when he learned that another player who was white and who apparently was not as good as Jackson had been offered better terms. Instead, in 1959 Jackson accepted a football scholarship to attend the University of Illinois at Urbana. When he returned to the campus in the early 1990s to attend his son's graduation from law school, Jackson recalled that he left Illinois after one year because he said he found an equal form of discrimination against black students and athletes on that northern campus three decades earlier. It was providential that Jackson transferred from Illinois to North Carolina A&T State University in 1960; he arrived on campus the same year that four black students had been refused service at an all-white Greensboro lunch counter, which triggered the sit-in protest movement that spread rapidly across the South.

During his years in Greensboro, Jackson participated regularly in the sit-in movement. Even though he left for Chicago after graduation to attend Chicago Theological Seminary, the young minister soon found that his calling in life was to help fight racial discrimination and injustice. In a biography titled *Jesse*, Marshall Frady, who has covered Jackson since his early 1960s civil rights days for *Newsweek*, chronicled Jackson's turning point. While in Chicago he witnessed TV coverage of Dr. King's heroic Selma march. That experience inspired Jackson to make the 18-hour drive nonstop from Chicago to join the campaign. Once among King's Southern Christian Leadership Conference (SCLC) leadership, Jackson was destined for greatness on the national economic and political stage.

After the Voting Rights Act was passed in 1965 and the civil rights movement began to tackle racial discrimination in the North, the SCLC assigned Jackson to direct its economic equality project in Chicago. In two years, Operation Breadbasket, as it was called, was credited with creating 3,000 new jobs for Chicago blacks and enlarged the annual income for Chicago's South Side residents by $22 million. Through 1971, Jackson would continue his unrelenting focus on black economic power, on getting more jobs for blacks, and on patronizing black-owned businesses.

Jesse Jackson left SCLC in 1971 to found Operation PUSH (People United to Save Humanity). Although PUSH took an interest in electoral politics and endorsed candidates who supported black causes, as its president Jackson continued to seek economic justice for black workers and businesses. Early on, PUSH demonstrated clearly that it was a force to be reckoned with. The organization concluded covenants in 1972 with two corporations, General Foods and Schlitz Breweries, totaling more than $150 million, which covered employment of blacks, purchases of goods and services from blacks, and deposits in black-owned banks. Over the next decade, PUSH would build on that track record and secure economic empowerment agreements with a sterling lineup of large corporations such as Pillsbury, Burger King, and AT&T.

In 1984, after years of playing a major role in virtually every movement for empowerment, peace, civil rights, gender equality, and economic and social justice, Jesse Jackson broke new ground in U.S. politics. His 1984 campaign for president won 3.5 million votes and registered more than 1 million new voters. Four years later in 1988, his candidacy won 7 million votes and registered 2 million new voters. Through the National Rainbow Coalition, which he founded in 1986, Jackson has worked with management and labor to address employment and other economic issues. He also has continued to serve as a leader in negotiating economic opportunity for African American workers and black-owned businesses.

As African American entrepreneurs approach the twenty-first century, they are finding once again that some of the same barriers that were in place 30 years ago remain in place. Discrimination against blacks is subtler. Indeed, Jackson found himself summoned back to the table in the 1990s to resolve institutional discrimination disputes involving high-profile cases such as Denny's and Texaco. He also traveled to Asia to meet with the executives of five major automobile manufacturers to discuss the lack of fair trade with minority communities and sex and race discrimination. Specifically, he urged Mitsubishi and other Japanese corporations to set goals, targets, and timetables to integrate their management teams; settle sex harassment and racial discrimination suits; empower someone in the parent corporations to address effectively the pattern of discrimination and harassment; conduct in-depth multicultural seminars; and plan for inclusion of minority dealerships, franchises, suppliers, access to capital, and professional services. "We must remove ancient walls that divide and deny, and build bridges of economic opportunity and expanded trade and a shared commitment to an equal playing field for the workers," Jackson stated during his Japan trip.

Closer to home, Jackson also took his economic empowerment message to Hollywood in 1996. He pointed out that behind the glamor and glitz, behind the fantasy of inclusion and opportunity, so carefully nurtured by the film industry, that Hollywood itself practiced institutional racism in several ways: racial exclusion, cultural distortion, lack of employment opportunities, and lack of positions of authority for blacks and minorities. Perhaps less well known and, indeed, perhaps more damaging from the business perspective, are the cases involving corporations such as Chevy Chase Federal Savings Bank, which found new and improved ways to make loans unavailable on the basis of race. Credit Jesse Jackson for helping to bring the current trends in economic discrimination onto everyone's radar screen.

In the late twentieth century, then, Jackson pioneered the civil rights movement's shift from its traditional agenda to a focus on economic empowerment. In targeting companies that did not employ African Americans in sufficient numbers or that had a poor record of working with minority suppliers, Jackson helped to influence the culture of Corporate America. By aggressively reminding companies that it makes good business sense to draw a bigger circle to include African Americans as suppliers and partners, and not as some pet project of the human resources department to gain favorable publicity in the news media, Jackson has motivated a number of companies to take the initiative to correct their past problems and adopt a new commitment to nondiscrimination.

SELECTED BIBLIOGRAPHY: Elizabeth O. Colton, *The Jackson Phenomenon: The Man, the Power, the Message* (New York: Doubleday, 1989); Bob Faw and Nancy Skelton, *Thunder in America: The Improbable Presidential Campaign of Jesse Jackson* (Austin: Texas Monthly Press, 1986); Marshall Frady, *Jesse: The Life and Pilgrimage of Jesse Jackson* (New York: Random House, 1996); James R. Ralph, Jr., *Northern Protest: Martin Luther King, Jr., Chicago and the Civil Rights Movement* (Cambridge, MA: Harvard University Press, 1993); Barbara A. Reynolds, *Jesse Jackson: The Man, the Movement, the Myth* (Chicago: Nelson-Hall, 1975); Andrew Young, *An Easy Burden: The Civil Rights Movement and the Transformation of America* (New York: Harper-Collins, 1996); www.cais.com/rainbow/rchrome.html

William E. Berry

JAJA OF OPOBO (1821–1891), Amaigbo, Iboland, palm oil trader.

With the decline of the transatlantic slave trade in the nineteenth century, Europeans continued in their attempts to exploit the wealth in natural resources of Africa. The economic success of the African palm oil trader Jaja exemplifies in microcosm the economic motivation of Europeans to colonize Africa. At the age of 12, Jaja was sold as a slave to Chief Iganipughuma Allison of Bonny, who in turn gave him as a gift to a minor chief of the Anna Pepple (corporate trading) House of Bonny on the Niger Delta on the Atlantic Coast. Jaja worked his way up from a "pull boy" slave to a major palm oil trader. By 1861 Jaja had risen to the rank of the first-line chiefs and was offered the leadership of the Anna Pepple House. Jaja quickly paid off the 15,000 pound sterling debt of his predecessor and within a year expanded his palm oil operations to over 50,000 pounds sterling.

Competitive jealousies of rival Bonny houses forced Jaja to move his operations eastward and into the interior to develop new sources of palm oil, where he established the trading state of Opobo that by 1870 dominated the 500,000 pound sterling a year Niger River palm oil trade with England. In subsequent years British merchants along the coast made many efforts to establish direct trading links to Jaja's interior oil markets, only to be thwarted by Jaja. In 1885 England declared Eastern Nigeria a protectorate colony, increasing merchant demands for access to Jaja's markets. Jaja continued to refuse the merchants' demands, and with an army of 4,000 men, a yearly income estimated at over 100,000 pounds sterling, and agreements with African oil merchants far into the interior, he was not about to concede his sovereignty. In 1887 they invited Jaja to their ship to negotiate, where he was seized, taken to Ghana, and then deported to St. Vincent in the West Indies, where he died in 1891.

SELECTED BIBLIOGRAPHY: J. C. Anene, *Southern Nigeria in Transition 1885–1906* (Cambridge: Cambridge University Press, 1966); K. O. Dike, *Trade and Politics in the Niger Delta* (London: Clarendon, 1965).

Gary J. Hunter

JAMES, CHARLES HOWELL (1862–1929), and Edward Lawrence James (1893–1967), West Virginia, wholesale food distribution.

C. H. James & Co. is one of America's oldest black-owned businesses. The founder, Charles Howell James, was the son of Francis James, who after fighting in the Union army during the Civil War had become the first black Baptist minister in West Virginia. He was also a schoolteacher. In the early 1880s, Charles and his three brothers started a business in which they bartered a variety of dry goods and notions, including pictures of assassinated President James A. Garfield, for fresh produce that they sold in urban areas, notably Charleston, West Virginia. The business prospered as the coal mining business expanded in West Virginia during the late 1800s. Blacks accounted for a significant part of the mine labor force, and yet the business of C. H. James & Co. continued to depend almost exclusively on white customers and wholesalers. The family was not immune to racial violence; in 1894 Charles James's brother Garland was shot and killed by segregationists, and yet Charles persevered, maintaining his belief that "business is business, and race has no business in business."

In 1916, Charles persuaded his son Edward to leave Howard University and help transform the firm into a wholesale food distributor. Within two years the firm had 30 employees and seven salesmen. Charles retired in 1926, with the firm's assets worth $140,000. However, the business was forced into bankruptcy by the Great Depression, and Edward had to work on Works Progress Administration (WPA) projects to support the family. He turned down a job as postmaster and was eventually able to rebuild the family business, concentrating on selling fresh eggs and poultry. By the time Edward retired in 1961, the firm had also moved into frozen foods.

After Edward's death, Charles James II became president and chief executive officer (CEO). Educated at the Wharton School, Charles James II oversaw a period of substantial growth in the 1960s, only to be followed by stagnant growth in the 1970s and much of the 1980s. In 1988, Charles (Chuck) James III took over the firm. Also educated at Wharton, Chuck James has pursued growth aggressively, seeking national food distribution contracts. By the early 1990s, half of the company's business came from large contracts. Chuck James has described the company as a family trust in which "[e]very day when I walk into my office, I have to face my great-grandfather, and my grandfather, and my father."

SELECTED BIBLIOGRAPHY: John N. Ingham and Lynne B. Feldman, *African-American Business Leaders: A Biographical Dictionary* (Westport, CT: Greenwood Press, 1994); Charles H. James III, "A History of the James Corp. of Charleston, West Virginia, the Oldest Black Business in the United States, 1883–1984" (Honors thesis,

Wharton School of Business, University of Pennsylvania 1985); Matthew Scott, "109 Years Old and Going Strong," *Black Enterprise* (June 1992).

                                                                            Peter Botticelli

JOHNSON, GEORGE E. (1927–), Illinois, hair care products manufacturer.

George Johnson, a pioneer of the black hair care industry, founded Johnson's Products Co., the first black-owned firm traded on the American Stock Exchange. Johnson, like his contemporary Joe Dudley* of Dudley Products Co., launched his career in the black hair care industry working with the Fuller Products Co. By the early 1950s, the Mississippi native was a manager with the company. Johnson collaborated with a Chicago barber, Orville Nelson, on improving a straightening product that he used in his shop. Johnson then consulted with a Fuller Products Co. chemist, Herbert A. Martini, and together they experimented with different formulas until they perfected the product. Nelson tested the new product in his shop. The product received rave reviews from Nelson's customers. So Nelson and Johnson decided to go into business together. Each individual contributed an initial $250 investment. The new product was named the Ultra Wave Hair Culture. After three months, the partnership with Nelson ended, but Johnson retained full ownership of the Ultra Wave name.

Then, with the assistance of family, the Johnson legacy began. The product brought in thousands of dollars in sales during the first few years. Johnson incorporated Johnson Products Company in 1957. During the late 1950s most women were still straightening their hair with pressing combs. So when Johnson developed Ultra Sheen in 1958, a hair straightener, he revolutionized the hair care industry. Johnson Products Co. introduced the first no-base creme relaxer for professional use in 1965. In the same era, to accommodate the "Afro," he developed the Afro-Sheen line. In 1975, Johnson Products Co. reported $37.6 million in sales.

Johnson is considered to be a pioneer in the black hair care industry for several reasons. First of all, in 1971, Johnson Products Co. was the first African American company traded on the stock exchange and to sponsor a nationally syndicated television show, *Soul Train*. By 1981, the company reported $47 million in sales and had expanded internationally, with 40 percent ownership in Johnson Products of Nigeria.

As black-owned and -operated businesses became increasingly successful in the 1970s and 1980s, larger white-owned corporations, for example, Revlon, took a serious interest in the black hair care industry. Consequently, black sales forces were hired and products were developed and marketed to the black community. This caused a decline in sales at Johnson Products and other black-owned companies. In 1975, the Federal Trade Commission (FTC) ordered Johnson Products to warn customers on packages of the danger of using lye. The FTC did not require Revlon to do the same until 22 months later, after a lawsuit by Johnson Products. Ironically, company sales fell 14 percent in 1976. Johnson Products suffered another blow when it delayed entry into the curl market, which had given other black hair care manufacturers such as Pro-Line and Soft Sheen Products tremendous boosts. In the 1980s sales and earnings plummeted at Johnson Products.

In 1988, Johnson made his son Eric chief operating officer and president. In 1989, Johnson's wife, Joan B. Johnson, gained the controlling shares in the company after the Johnson marriage ended in divorce. Joan became the company's chairwoman, chief executive, and controlling shareholder. Under the leadership of Eric and his mother Joan, sales increased. However, in 1993, Joan sold the company for $67 million to the IVAX Corporation—a Miami-based company with interest in chemicals, pharmaceuticals, and cosmetics. The sale sparked a heated debate within the African American community, since the Johnson Products Co. was a role model for black businesses. Newspaper accounts detailed George Johnson's disapproval of the sale, since he had long vowed to keep the company within the black community. Earl Graves,* publisher of *Black Enterprise*, was quoted in the *Wall Street Journal* as saying, "This is just one phase of the continuing expansion of black owned business." In 1998, the black-owned and controlled publicly listed company, Carson, Inc., purchased Johnson Products from Ivax.

Johnson, in the philanthropic tradition of black hair care entrepreneurs, donated $1 million of his personal money for scholarships for minority students. He serves on the board of directors of many organizations and businesses. He was one of the founders of Independence Bank of Chicago, which was sold to whites. He has received numerous awards and honorary doctorates for his business success and philanthropy.

SELECTED BIBLIOGRAPHY: Tony Chapelle, "JPC Sold in Merger with Ivax Corp.," *Black Enterprise* (September 1993); Paul Delaney, "He's Good to Hair; Hair's Good to Him," *New York Times*, June 20, 1976; "Johnson Products Buoyant as 1st Quarter Profits Grow," *Cosmetics International*, February 25, 1993; Brett Pulley, "A Crown Jewel: The Johnson Family Splits on What Is Best for Black-Owned Firm," *Wall Street Journal*, July 29, 1993.

Nancy J. Dawson

JOHNSON, JOHN HAROLD (1918–), Chicago, publisher, hair care and cosmetics manufacturer, insurance—major shareholder and chairman of board; real estate—owner developer; radio station ownership.

One has to wonder whether John H. Johnson sometimes needs to remind people that once upon a time there was no *Ebony* or *Jet* magazines or a Johnson Publishing Co. His communications, cosmetics, and assorted businesses empire has triumphed for so long that his "brand" seems as enduring as Sears, Merrill Lynch, Ford, and other businesses that seem to have been around forever.

Contrary to perception, however, Johnson Publishing Co. made its debut in Chicago in 1942 when a 20-something John Johnson launched *Negro Digest* magazine. The quest began obscurely with a $500 loan that Johnson received after his mother believed enough in her son to allow him to use her furniture as collateral. Fortified with a sharp focus, a clear sense of purpose, and "can-do" confidence, he used the money to pay for his first direct mail advertising about his magazine. This netted the ambitious entrepreneur 3,000 subscriptions, but he still needed to demonstrate that his product had appeal on the newsstand. To stimulate sales, Johnson persuaded 30 of his friends to ask for *Negro Digest* at newsstands and thus create demand. The strategy worked, and circulation climbed steadily.

Johnson was born in Arkansas City, Arkansas, and in 1933 moved to Chicago, with his mother, after attending the Century Progress Exposition. Convinced that her son's chances for a better life would be greater in Chicago, his mother remained in the city. (His father had been killed in a sawmill accident when Johnson was six years old.) Growing up poor during the depression dampened Johnson's attitude toward the times, he later would recall, but it did not diminish his determination to succeed in life. He was an honor student and class president in high school, where he also received his first taste of journalism, serving as editor of the school newspaper and yearbook. After graduating, he enrolled at the University of Chicago and took a job at Supreme Life Insurance Co* to help make ends meet. At Supreme, which he later would own, Johnson experienced another foreshadow of what was in store—he was assigned to help edit the house magazine, *The Supreme Liberty Guardian.*

While working on the *Guardian* and deciding that there was a great deal of information about blacks that simply was not being publicized or communicated to the general public, Johnson came up with the idea of *Negro Digest*. Initially he tried, but failed, to win investment support for his proposed magazine from friends and coworkers. Consequently, Johnson decided to pursue his dream independently. From the *Negro Digest* venture to the present, it seemed that everything Johnson touched turned to gold. In 1945, Johnson rolled out *Ebony* magazine, which not only was celebrated immediately by African American readers but also demonstrated to skeptical advertisers that there was a significant market among black consumers.

Tan Confessions (later *Black Stars*), a monthly women's interest magazine, followed in 1950, and *Jet*, a weekly newsmagazine, was unveiled in 1951. Over the next five decades, several other magazines would appear, enjoy their season, and then be replaced, either with a new publication or some other venture. *Hue, Ebony International, Black Stars, Black World* (originally *Negro Digest*), *Ebony Jr!* (a children's magazine), and *Copper Romance* were among the Johnson titles that eventually ceased publication. At the end of 1997, *Ebony, Jet* and *EM* (*Ebony Man*, a men's magazine) survived.

Ever the entrepreneur, Johnson continuously understood his market and continuously introduced new products to satisfy the appetite of African American consumers. Affiliated businesses Johnson introduced would include a book club; Ebony-Jet Tours and Mahogany Travel Co. (both travel service units); Ebony Fashion Fair (a traveling event that featured black models wearing the most celebrated apparel from both couture collections as well as African American designers); Supreme Beauty Products Co.; and Fashion Fair Cosmetics (an upscale product line carried in exclusive department stores in the United States, Europe, and Africa). Other communications interests included a book publishing unit; radio stations in Chicago and Lansing, Illinois, and Louisville, Kentucky; syndicated television programs; and multimedia video productions, both independently and as joint ventures.

Although many of the jewels in Johnson's corporate empire are well known and highly visible, what many people do not see is the economic impact he made by creating thousands of jobs, almost exclusively for African American workers. One testament to the significance of this was offered in the late 1980s by a vice president who retired from the Johnson family of companies, after nearly four decades of service. "When I came here to work for Mr. Johnson, my wife and my brothers said I was making a mistake for giving up a good job with a 'White' company to gamble my future with this upstart Black guy," he related. "As I leave here today, I'm reminded that that White company went out of business nearly 15 years ago. But Johnson Publishing Co. still is here. And I'm glad to say that Mr. Johnson never missed a payroll in all the years I've worked for him."

Who was John H. Johnson, and what were some of the elements of his success? People who worked with him over the years point to his immense charm, an instinctive feel for what African Americans likely would spend their money on, and a wide-ranging interest in people and ideas. Moreover, an inside joke among Johnson's employees focused on what they referred to as his "elephantine memory." This was viewed as a priceless attribute of Johnson: the knack for storing names of people, places, and events in his vast mental compartment, an then retrieving them at the right moment—often it would be an opportunity to close a deal with a prospective advertiser. Indeed, Johnson's special gift was that he was more than a visionary who saw the vast potential for communications media products and other lines of business within the black economy. Part of the John Johnson legend is that he had the gift and ability of a hustling salesman who could persuade major corporations such as Zenith, Kraft, General Foods, and others to advertise in his publications. His pitch was simple: The Johnson magazines had black America's attention; if you wanted to speak with that audience, you had to appear in Johnson's pages.

With the instinctive frugality of the well-to-do, Johnson shunned high-flung trappings of success such as corporate jets, chauffeured limousines, and villas on every continent. Instead, he consistently supported black economic empowerment by supporting major organizations such as the United Negro College Fund (UNCF), the National Association for the Advancement of Colored People (NAACP), and the National Urban League.* He also was quick to support young black entrepreneurs who sought to make their dreams come true, so long as they were not aspiring to compete directly with the Johnson organization lineup. At a Chicago gathering of practically all the major players in the advertising industry in 1996, the leaders of the nation's top black-owned advertising agencies expressed publicly what only they and Johnson had known for years: John Johnson had been the invisible angel that had helped firms like Burrell Advertising, Vince Cullers Advertising, Uniworld, Inc., and Procter & Gardner succeed. The chief executive officer (CEO) of one agency shared an intimate anecdote concerning how Johnson allowed him to continue to run advertisements in *Ebony*, even though the firm had been delinquent regularly because Johnson confided that he could relate personally to the fledging entrepreneur's need to juggle funds when starting out in business.

As his companies moved into the next century, Johnson began to adapt and innovate his product line to meet today's marketplace. Given the internationalization of the economy, he expanded beyond the business involvements he already had in place with his cosmetics division and existing magazine products. In November 1995, he launched *Ebony South Africa*, a joint venture with investors in South Africa that seemed destined to mirror in that country the success *Ebony* has enjoyed in the United States. He also retrofitted the production and printing systems used to create his magazines, using both digitization and remote delivery processes to achieve cost efficiencies. Where publications once were produced and printed in Chicago, with new technologies Johnson was able to have his writers, editors, and art directors produce the magazines there and then electronically transmit them to printing facilities in the South, resulting in reduced production and distribution expenses.

In the 1990s, Johnson and his company still were standing on solid ground in the hotly competitive publishing industry, as *Ebony, Jet,* and *EM* saw their value rise in the marketplace. Several celebrity-endorsed cosmetics lines that sprung up overnight flopped embarrassingly and quickly were pulled from store shelves, whereas Fashion Fair Cosmetics found itself being added to the repertoire of an expanding network of high-quality stores not only in the United States but also overseas. Recognizing that his radio stations apparently were more for their signal and spectrum value than their potential operating revenues, Johnson sold them off and poured the profits back into his core units. The company also began shoring up its product line by investing more heavily into market research to better understand its customers and to head off competition from major communications firms that have learned from Johnson's success just how lucrative the African American economy is.

With his daughter Linda Johnson Rice firmly in place to lead the company into its next 50 years, Johnson's financial empire appeared ready to continue to enjoy its second "golden age."

SELECTED BIBLIOGRAPHY: William E. Berry, "The Popular Press as Symbolic Interactionism: A Sociocultural Analysis of Ebony Magazine, 1945–75" (Ph.D. diss., University of Illinois at Urbana, 1978); Michael Emery, Edwin Emery, and Nancy L. Roberts, *The Press and America: An Interpretive History of the Mass Media*, 8th ed. (Needham Heights, MA: Allyn & Bacon, 1996); John Johnson with Lerone Bennett, Jr., *Succeeding against the Odds* (New York: Warner Books, 1989); Theodore Peterson,

Magazines in the Twentieth Century, rev. ed. (Urbana: University of Illinois Press, 1964); Enoch P. Waters, *American Diary: A Personal History of the Black Press* (Chicago: Path Press, 1987); Roland E. Wolseley, *The Black Press, USA* (Ames: Iowa State University Press, 1971); www.ebonymag.com/jocindex.html

William E. Berry

JOHNSON, ROBERT L. (1946–), Maryland, entrepreneur in television and publishing industries.

Robert L. Johnson, chief executive officer (CEO) and chairman of BET Holdings, Inc., the parent company of Black Entertainment Television (BET), not only expanded the reach of the industry sector referred to as the "black press"— by introducing the nation's first African American–oriented network—but also revolutionized its scope through an aggressive alignment of diversified associated businesses. Johnson's major contribution to the communications business was the introduction and use of new multimedia technologies to produce and deliver news, entertainment, and community affairs programming content to cable subscribers throughout the world.

In the 1970s, most owners of "black press" companies continued to put the lion's share of their efforts and capital into newspapers, magazines, and other print media forms or in radio, broadcast television, or motion picture products. Johnson observed, anticipated, and planned for the tremendous change that was evolving in the communications industry, as cable television became less of an exotic information channel that primarily was used to transmit content to people who lived in remote rural areas and more of the vast new pathway that would be used to deliver news, entertainment, sports, interactive services, and educational programs to viewers. When the "information age" arrived in America in the 1980s and 1990s, and as personal computers and other new communications technologies became more widely available, Johnson became celebrated as a visionary businessman who had an astute and keen eye for identifying emerging economic market opportunities within the African American community.

Alert to the possibilities of technology and buoyed by the unspoken urges of the African American economic market, Johnson in 1980 launched Black Entertainment Television, Inc., an advertiser-supported, basic cable television programming service. Initially, he had to win the confidence of skeptics who wondered not only whether there would be an audience for the BET network but also whether Johnson had the necessary business and technical know-how to direct a complex enterprise that involved connecting with that audience via satellites stationed 23,000 miles from earth in space. Undeterred, Johnson pressed forward and quickly found a significant following from African American cable subscribers who both viewed the BET network and voiced their enthusiasm for it to their local cable companies to ensure that BET remained among the channel lineup. The BET Cable Network aired a variety of music video shows; originally produced and syndicated programming; news and public affairs shows; and entertainment programs that soon became a major vehicle for aspiring African American comedians and musicians to showcase their talent.

Johnson was born in East St. Louis, Illinois, in 1946 and grew up there. His interest in communications was shaped at the University of Illinois at Urbana, where he studied social sciences and began to observe the powerful impact that the mass media have in modern society. During his college years, almost everyone who knew Johnson became familiar with his oft-repeated ''dream'' that he someday would manage his own television station. Little did they anticipate that two years later he would better that vision and lead a network that would beam programming to points around the world. Johnson continued his formal education at Princeton University, earning a master's degree in public affairs from the Woodrow Wilson School of Public and International Affairs. Out of college, Johnson put his education to work, serving first as press secretary to the Honorable Walter E. Fauntroy, a congressional delegate from the District of Columbia. Prior to founding BET, Johnson served as vice president of government relations for the National Cable Television Association (NCTA), a trade association representing more than 15,000 cable television companies.

Since launching the BET Cable Network, Robert L. Johnson has continued on a bright trajectory as a significant leader not only in the communications industry but also in other business and commercial enterprises. Merely by surviving for nearly two decades in the uncharted, risky, unpredictable, extremely competitive, and highly volatile waters that characterized the fledgling cable industry since 1980, Johnson destroyed forever one nagging issue in the communications field: Can an African American business owner swim in deep waters and compete and win alongside industry giants with names such as CBS, ABC, Tribune, NBC, HBO, Cinemax, and Disney? One thing is certain: Johnson is successful because even his competitors are eager to cut deals with him. How successful is Johnson and his BET Holdings, Inc.?

By the end of 1997, his holdings, partnerships, and business triumphs included BET Cable Network, a basic cable service that airs a variety of entertainment and information programs 24 hours a day to 50 million households; BET on Jazz: The Cable Jazz Channel; BET Movies/STARZ!3, the first black movie channel; Action Pay-Per-View; BET on Jazz International; BET Direct, distributor of BET's Color Code skin care line and other direct marketing products; BET Films Productions and BET Pictures, joint ventures that produce motion pictures; and two publications, *Emerge* magazine and *BET Weekend*, a publication that is distributed monthly in major newspapers in Atlanta, Chicago, Detroit, Los Angeles, Miami, New York, Philadelphia, Washington, D.C., and seven other major cities.

In addition, as Johnson expanded his enterprises, he opened BET SoundStage, a themed restaurant. In its financial products and services division, Johnson established BET Financial Services, which marketed a BET-branded Visa card to African Americans; BET SoundStage Casino, a proposed joint venture with the Hilton Hotels Corp. in Las Vegas that would be targeted toward the more than 2 million African Americans who visit the city each year; BET-branded apparel, a retail clothing and accessory line that will be targeted to African Americans and urban consumers under a joint venture with G-III Apparel Group Ltd.; and BET Networks, a joint venture with Microsoft to provide online information and entertainment for blacks.

With Robert L. Johnson at the helm, BET Holdings, Inc., by the end of 1997, continued to make innovative and highly successful breakthroughs in business. For sure, Johnson secured his place in history in 1991 when BET became the first black-owned company on the New York Stock Exchange. Its initial public offering (IPO) raised $72.3 million. Six years later the company could boast a market capitalization profile worth $390.5 million—apparently, Johnson succeeded in converting skeptics into believers. On the dawn of the next century, BET's future looked optimistic and promising. Based on performance through July, the company appeared destined to realize more than $150 million in annual revenues in 1997. In 1998, BET went private.

SELECTED BIBLIOGRAPHY: Alton Hornsby, *Milestones in 20th Century African-American History* (Detroit: Visible Ink Press, 1993); Horace Newcomb, ed., *Encyclopedia of Television*, vol. 1, (Chicago: Fitzroy Dearborn Publishers, 1997); Tariq K. Muhammad, "The Branding of BET," *Black Enterprise* (June 1997); Allen Warren, ed., *Television & Cable Factbook*, vol. 65 (Washington, DC: Warren Publishing Inc., 1997); www. betnetworks.com

William E. Berry

JOHNSON, WILLIAM TILER (1809–1851), Mississippi, barber, landowner, slave owner, land speculator, stock investor, moneylender.

Known as the "Barber of Natchez," the slave-born William Johnson acquired freedom at the age of 11 on the basis of a petition to the state legislature made by William Johnson, the white slave owner of his mother. There were few free blacks in Mississippi, a state that by 1860 had only 1,775 free blacks and a slave population of 436,631. The Barber of Natchez kept an extensive diary, which covers the period from 1835 to 1851, when he was murdered by a white man over a land boundary dispute. The diary also includes an accounting of his expenditures and investments. In addition to owning three barbershops and a bathhouse in Natchez, with plans for establishing another shop in Jackson, before he was murdered, Johnson also owned a plantation, a general merchandise and notions store, and race horses and held part interest in the Natchez race course. Emulating the lifestyle of wealthy whites, Johnson provided music lessons for his daughter, kept an extensive library, and subscribed to New York journals.

Johnson was taught the barbering business by his brother-in-law. After working as an apprentice, William Johnson established his first barbershop in Port Gibson, which he sold when he moved to Natchez. He opened his first shop in that city in 1830, which he indicated in his cash book: "[Natchez] October 12th

1830. being The first commencement of my work after I had Bought out the interest of Wm. Miller." Johnson's employment of slave apprentice barbers in his three barbershops increased his profits. Averaging $100 per month from each of his three shops, Johnson's income could approach $3,600 annually. The significance of his diary, which includes cash books of his daily earnings, is that it provides insight on how much money could be earned by antebellum barbers. Also, information is provided on profits made from the sale of commodities produced on his slave-worked plantation, where Johnson employed a white overseer and both free black and white laborers. At the time of his death, Johnson was worth $25,000, including the $6,000 in the value of the 15 slaves he owned. After the Civil War, the Johnson plantation was worked by black sharecroppers and managed subsequently by his son and then daughter.

SELECTED BIBLIOGRAPHY: Ira Berlin, *Slaves without Masters: The Free Negro in the Antebellum South* (New York: Pantheon Books, 1974); Edwin A. Davis and William R. Hogan, *The Barber of Natchez* (Baton Rouge: Louisiana State University Press, 1954); Edwin A. Davis and William R. Hogan, eds., *William Johnson's Natchez: The Antebellum Diary of a Free Negro* (Baton Rouge, Louisiana State University Press, 1951); John N. Ingham and Lynne B. Feldman, *African-American Business Leaders: A Biographical Dictionary* (Westport, CT: Greenwood Press, 1994); Juliet E. K. Walker, *The History of Black Business in America: Capitalism, Race, Entrepreneurship* (New York: Macmillan Prentice Hall International, 1998).

Juliet E. K. Walker

JOINT VENTURING. Joint venturing is the key to black entrepreneurial success in the "new economy." As America moves into the twenty-first century, arguably, one of the most pressing issues is the distribution of wealth and economic power among its heterogeneous population. In America, history has shown that the one proven way of building wealth and attaining economic power is through the formation and nurturing of an entrepreneurial class within the community and the development of business enterprises. In the 1990s, of all the millionaires and billionaires in the nation, 75 percent of them created their wealth via the development and growing of successful businesses. Others inherited wealth from businessmen ancestors. Many businesses were started as microenterprises. In their growth, some of the successful ones also made the transition to become larger, multinational conglomerates that dominate industries on a global level.

For the African American community to be successful in the next millennium and in the new economy, it must become proficient at developing successful, thriving, and robust business enterprises. The blueprint for successfully completing this task, however, has been altered forever. Indeed, the efforts of the lone entrepreneur, successfully conceiving, building, and growing a dominant business enterprise, have been superseded by cooperative efforts of corporate-minded entrepreneurs, who reach out to external resources to build partnerships and formulate joint ventures. Developing joint ventures, while easy to suggest, is often difficult to achieve. However, there are some specific tasks and development models that can be followed by African Americans to build lasting and mutually beneficial joint ventures. Failure to successfully master the art of building joint ventures will ultimately lead to the demise of promising business ventures and the demoralization of bright, motivated, and promising young entrepreneurs.

The need for long-term business success through joint venturing is most apparent within the black community. For despite more than 30 years of "attention" given to the economic disparity between black and white Americans, the economic condition of the black community still leaves much to be desired. Specifically the condition of black businesses relative to the collective earning power of the community as a whole is disproportionately impacted. Consider for a moment that black Americans earn approximately $400 billion per year as a group. If this amount is viewed as gross national product (GNP), the black community would rank as 1 of the 20 largest nations on the face of the earth. Yet of this $400 billion of earned income, less than 6 percent is spent with African American–owned businesses. African Americans make up 12 percent of the population, yet own slightly more than 3 percent of the nation's businesses.

From the late nineteenth century until the mid-twentieth, viable black business communities existed in cities as diverse as Tulsa, Atlanta, Richmond, Philadelphia, Durham and Wilmington, North Carolina, and Chicago, to name but a few. Their demise was precipitated by many factors: racist violence directed against African American institutions, in the cases of Tulsa and Wilmington; the effects of the Great Depression; the end of legalized segregation; and misguided urban renewal policies that, as in Durham, devastated the Hayti "Black Wall Street"* district, destroying hundreds of black-owned businesses in the process.

Even before the 1990s, there was a drastic decline, almost to invisibility, of black ownership of businesses—laundromats, dry cleaners, food markets, gas stations, appliance repair shops, clothing stores—that provide the most basic services to local residents in African American inner-city neighborhoods. Now, most of those enterprises are operated by first- and second-generation immigrants who, at the end of the business day, leave for their own communities and take their profits with them. This massive outflow of capital has had a devastating impact on the inner cities. It has severely retarded the prospects for African Americans in wielding the level of economic (and political) influence and power that their numbers would seem to entitle them. The most logical vehicle for black businesses to use to overcome these many challenges is joint venturing.

There are many definitions of *joint ventures*, generally understood as the coming together of two or more independent businesses for the sole purpose of achieving a specific outcome that would not have been achievable by any one of the firms by itself. The participants in such a venture may be corporations, partnerships, limited liability corporations (LLCs), individuals, trusts, or any other form of business entity. Although the joint venture can be operated in any business form that the partners desire, most joint ventures tend to operate in a form similar to that of a general partnership. Also, any attempt to construct joint ventures must be predicated on the fact that there must be a clear definition of specific duties for each member and the business purpose must be clearly defined. The members of the joint venture must agree on a target customer base, the type of product to be sold, the services to be provided, the vendors to be used, and the prices to be charged for goods and services.

The "weakest" form of joint venturing, where the partners are "loosely coupled," is termed a *mutual service consortia*, where two similar companies in similar industries pool resources. An example may be a case where Company A is expert in the design, installation, and maintenance of computer networks. Company B, on the other hand, may provide training services for educating end users on how to use the computer network properly and efficiently. Together, these two companies can provide a complete package to the customer set and thus leverage the strengths of each to build both businesses to the next level.

Another type of joint venture might be a "moderately coupled" arrangement where the partners have an equal partnership. A third type of joint venture is one that could be described as "tightly coupled." This value chain partnership allows potential partners, who might be in different industries but possess complementary skills, to link their capabilities to create value for the customer. These type of joint ventures require tight linkage of the partner's capabilities and strong commitment from both sides. The partners often develop joint activities in many functions, operations often overlap, and the relationship thus creates substantial change within each partner's organization.

Entering into a joint venture arrangement is not a decision that should be taken lightly. It could severely impact one's business, and the fallout could be fatal. Research has shown that entrepreneurs typically enter into a joint venture agreement for one or a combination of three reasons. The first is to acquire the use of resources from Company B that Company A may not have, which could include facilities, technical expertise, managerial expertise, manpower, access to contracts, access to new markets, credit strength, licenses, patents or copyrights, or financial resources. Another reason is to acquire expertise or skills that Company A does not presently have but that Company B possesses and is willing to transfer to Company A in return for some other benefit. This type of arrangement is especially prevalent when there exists a mentor/protégé relationship between the two companies and one company has a self-serving interest in developing the skills and expertise of the smaller company.

Many of today's successful minority-owned businesses have used this form of joint venturing in working with *Fortune* 500 corporations. Some large corporations have shown a sincere interest in working with and helping to develop minority firms as long-term business partners. The minority firms learn from the larger, better financed, and older firms while allowing the large mentoring firm to expand its market coverage and capabilities without expanding its overhead and payroll.

The third and probably most important reason to consider initiating a joint venture is quite simply to minimize the risk to each party, particularly when firms are positioned to enter new and emerging markets versus old and established ones. Nowhere is this need to minimize risk in new markets more obvious than in the burgeoning Internet* infrastructure and Internet services businesses. The business opportunities embedded in this new and exciting industry are full of promise and quick riches yet interspersed with danger and financial ruin. Thus, in this type of environment, joint venturing is a popular and quite viable option for minimizing a company's risk.

Research has shown that one of the biggest stumbling blocks to developing a successful and mutually advantageous joint venture is the issue of who is in charge. One model used to construct a joint venture suggests that Company A be the primary partner and that Company B becomes the secondary partner. Who will be the primary partner and who will become the secondary partner is often determined by which partner has the closest relationship with the customer. Thus, whichever firm "owns" the customer relationship, that partner becomes the de facto primary partner. Even if the issue of who becomes the primary and secondary is resolved, the two firms need to agree on how the engagement will be managed. The options available to the partners for how the relationship is to be managed can be divided into four major options—committee based, primary based, primary and secondary based, and a hybrid of the first three.

In a committee-based management structure the partners make important decisions through the workings of a management committee. The management committee is made up of high-level representatives from each company, with each having equal voting power. This committee serves as the governing arm of the venture and can be set up to operate by either making decisions via strict majority rules voting or through consensus voting. Majority rules voting is driven by what the majority of the committee decides. Conversely, in consensus voting, all committee members have to agree on a decision before the venture endorses it. Overall, consensus voting is the most adopted version of the two because it helps the unit to operate as a team, although this approach to management may make it more difficult and time-consuming to make valuable decisions.

In a primary–based management structure the primary partner is given total authority to make all decisions for the joint venture. The assumption is that since the primary owns the customer relationship, he or she has a better gauge on what is best for the client and will make decisions accordingly. Primary-Based management is a difficult approach to use because it could put the secondary partner at risk if the primary partner is incompetent or dishonest. Unless there is a minimum level of trust between the partners, this form of management is doomed to fail. The issue of trust is especially important when the relationship built is between a minority-owned firm and a majority-owned firm. In this situation the team not only contends with the basic relationship issues that all joint venture participants deal with but with the racial and gender-based tensions that exist in the overall American society. A successful primary-based management approach hinges on how well the two parties got to know one another and were able to build a strong relationship prior to consummating the joint venture arrangement. Similar to a committee-based approach, the primary-secondary–based management approach is defined as one where each partner is given primary control over specific areas. This form of management allows Company A to make all decisions in one or more specific areas, whereas Company B is permitted to make all decisions in another area.

The options for legal forms for joint ventures include corporations, limited liability companies (LLCs), and partnerships. The corporate option has both advantages and disadvantages. The major advantage to using this option is that it provides limited liability for the participants as well as unlimited duration. That is, should the corporation become insolvent, creditors' claims are limited to the assets of the corporate entity. The corporate approach also facilitates the raising of large amounts of funds through the issue of shares by the corporation. The corporate form also makes transfer of ownership interests relatively easy, because individual shares can be sold by current owners to others without interfering with the ongoing operations of the business. However, the disadvantages are the obvious ones, such as double taxation and the fact that a corporation has limited flexibility in terms of structure, management, and the allocation and distribution of benefits and losses.

Limited liability companies, on the other hand, have the same advantages as a regular corporation. Additionally, management of profits can be set with great flexibility, absent the need for separate shareholder agreements or separate classes of stock. Similar to LLCs, partnerships (limited and general) provide the advantages of the pass-through of losses and avoidance of double taxation of profits as well as great flexibility in how profits are managed and allocated. Unfortunately for partnerships, there is partner liability for debts of the partnership, and dissolution of the entity is easier, due to specified events under state law.

Every joint venture agreement must have a plan that addresses the distribution and allocation of benefits or losses accrued from the venture. Many joint venture teams establish capital accounts that are used to hold funds resulting from a transaction until time of disbursement. Some accounts are set up in such a way that at the end of a specific time period a proportionate amount of funds is distributed to the various parties. The allocation and distribution formula could be based upon various criteria such as performance, initial capitalization, percent ownership in the venture, and the meeting of revenue/profitability targets.

Despite all the good intentions of all parties involved in a joint venture, there are times when the arrangement does not work out, and either party desires to exit early. To allow for the organized and structured exiting of one or both partners, a set of rules and guidelines need to be established. Most exit strategies require that limitations and restrictions be placed on the right of a partner to exit the arrangement. Such limitations and restrictions may include a mandatory put or call on the interest of the joint venture partner in the venture, the requirement for a specified period of time to elapse before exiting is an option, or compensatory payments to the other joint venture partner should his or her investment be put at risk as a result of the other partner's actions. These are only a few of the many nuances that must be understood before black entrepreneurs venture into the murky and unpredictable waters of joint venturing. But however cumbersome or complex, effective joint venturing will be the key to black entrepreneurial success in the new economy and into the next millennium.

SELECTED BIBLIOGRAPHY: Gerard M. D. Bean, *Fiduciary Obligations and Joint Ventures: The Collaborative Fiduciary Relationship* (New York: Clarendon Press, 1995); William H. Bergquist, *Building Strategic Relationships: How to Extend Your Organization's Reach Through Partnerships, Alliances, and Joint Ventures* (San Francisco: Jossey-Bass Publishers, 1995); Jennifer Lindsey, *Joint Ventures and Corporate Partnerships: A Step-by-Step Guide to Forming Strategic Business Alliances* (Chicago: Probus Publishing Company, 1989); Joanna Poyago-Theotoky, ed., *Competition, Cooperation, Research and Development: The Economics of Research Joint Ventures* (New York: St. Martin's Press, 1997); Robert L. Wallace, *Black Wealth through Black Entrepreneurship* (Edgewood, MD: Duncan & Duncan, Inc., 1993).

Robert L. Wallace

JONES, JOHN (1816?–1879), Chicago, tailor, clothier, abolitionist.

One of Chicago's most important nineteenth-century African American entrepreneurs and the spearhead behind the repeal of the Illinois Black Laws, John Jones was born on a plantation in Greene County, North Carolina. The son of a German named Bromfield and a "free woman of color," Jones's mother feared that his father's relatives might attempt to reduce him to slavery. He was apprenticed to a man named Sheppard, who took him to Tennessee where he was "bound over" to a tailor, Richard Clere, who taught young Jones the trade. The future leader of black Chicago pursued his trade in Memphis, where he met Mary Richardson, the daughter of a local blacksmith. When she moved to Illinois, Jones followed. They married and lived for a time in Alton, Illinois, before coming to Chicago in 1845, 12 years after the city's founding.

They rented a one-room cottage on the corner of Wells and Madison and opened a small tailoring shop a few blocks away. Gradually, Jones attracted the patronage of several prominent white families, including several outspoken abolitionists. Jones taught himself to read and write and was generally considered the wealthiest African American in the Midwest.

From the 1850s until his death in 1879, John Jones was the unquestioned leader of black Chicago. An ardent abolitionist who frequently played host to such luminaries as John Brown and Frederick Douglass, Jones became involved in antislavery activity soon after he arrived in Chicago. His first leadership role came when 300 blacks assembled at the African Methodist Church on Wells Street, later renamed Quinn Chapel, to protest the passage of the Fugitive Slave

Law of 1850. He later became a leader in the local Vigilance Committee, and his home was a terminal on the Underground Railroad.*

In 1853 he was elected vice president of the Colored National Convention in Rochester, New York, and three years later, as Illinois's most prominent black leader, he convened the state convention to launch a petition campaign for legal rights in the state. Enlisting the support of such powerful white allies as former Free Soil journalist and editor of the *Chicago Tribune* Joseph Medill and Illinois Governor Richard Yates, Jones used his contacts in the white abolitionist movement and the new state Republican Party to launch an aggressive crusade against the Black Laws. His 16-page pamphlet *The Black Laws of Illinois and a Few Reasons They Should Be Repealed* was a skillful appeal to white self-interest as well as humanitarian sentiment.

Jones was a successful entrepreneur whose cleaning and tailoring shop catered to many of the city's elite. As early as 1860 he described his Clothes Cleaning and Repairing Rooms at 119 Dearborn as the "oldest and best establishment in the city." His rise to success was the archetypical Horatio Alger story. Arriving in the city with $3.50, he opened a tailoring shop and massed a fortune, estimated at between $85,000 and $100,000, before the Great Chicago Fire. Although the 1871 fire substantially reduced his fortune, he remained among the wealthiest African Americans in the country. By every applicable standard, then, Jones was an appropriate choice for public office. He was an active Republican at a time when the party dominated city politics, he had wealthy and powerful white allies, his success reflected the expanding entrepreneurial ethos of the era, and even in his social life (duly recorded by the *Tribune*) he emulated contemporary patterns of upper-class entertaining, complete with quadrille orchestra for the "terpsichorean pleasures" of the evening.

In 1871 Jones became the state's first African American elected official. After the Great Fire, Jones was proposed by Republicans and accepted by Democrats for the county board on a bipartisan Fire Proof Ticket. After a one-year term, he was reslated and reelected for a three-year term in 1872 and defeated with his fellow Republicans in an 1875 reelection bid. Jones died four years later. His obituaries described him as an important Chicago leader, the principal force behind the successful campaign to repeal the hated Black Laws, and a successful black entrepreneur.

SELECTED BIBLIOGRAPHY: Arna Bontemps and Jack Conroy, *Anyplace But Here* (New York: Hill and Wang, 1966); Harold F. Gosnell, *Negro Politicians: The Rise of Negro Politics in Chicago* (Chicago: University of Chicago Press, 1935); June Skinner Sawyers, *Chicago Portraits* (Chicago: Loyola University Press, 1991); Allan H. Spear, *Black Chicago: The Making of a Negro Ghetto, 1890–1920* (Chicago: University of Chicago Press, 1967); Dempsey J. Travis, *An Autobiography of Black Chicago* (Chicago: Urban Research Press, 1981).

Charles Branham

JONES, WILEY (1848–1904), Arkansas, entrepreneur in real estate, public transportation, and entertainment, sportsman.

In August of 1886 Wiley Jones received a franchise from the Pine Bluff City Council to build and operate a mule-drawn street railway system. Public transportation was badly needed because of the city's growing population. Between 1880 and 1890 the city's population tripled, growing from 3,000 to 9,000. The Jones Street Railway and Equipment Company represented a personal investment of $35,000 and involved 12 railway cars, 70 head of stock, and 25 employees. Jones also had a personal interest in developing municipal transportation. The railway would provide a means to transport people from downtown Pine Bluff to the Wiley Jones Race Track. Jones owned 24 stallions. He also owned the Colored State Fair Grounds. The black state fair attracted 20,000 visitors annually to Pine Bluff, to the delight of black and white merchants alike.

The Wiley Jones Street Railway Company was the second company to receive a franchise to provide Pine Bluff with public transportation. The first was the Citizens Street Railway Company, owned by a group of white entrepreneurs, franchised in 1885. The Citizens company served downtown Pine Bluff and the white community. Jones was authorized to serve the downtown area and the black community. The two companies operated parallel tracks in the downtown area of the city. While the Jones Railway Company was never very profitable, except during the meeting of the Colored State Fair, it managed to provide year-round daily service. The same cannot be said of the Citizens company. By 1890, it was experiencing serious financial difficulties and was put up for sale.

After failing to reach an agreement on a sale price with two out-of-state investment companies, the owners of the Citizens "agreed to sell the entire properties, franchise and all appurtenances for $125,000" to Wiley Jones and two associates, Thomas S. James and Arthur Murray, who was the owner/publisher of the *Pine Bluff Press Eagle*, a local black weekly. The transaction was financed by the St. Louis Trust Company, which authorized the issuance of 90 $1,000 gold bearing bonds at 7 percent interest and a maturity date of 15 years. The name "Citizens" was retained by Jones for the consolidated Citizens Railway Company and the Jones Street Railway Company. The new Citizens Railway Company was operated by Jones and his associates for 3 years with little profit. In 1894 they sold the consolidated company back to the original owners of the Citizens Company for $90,000.

Although out of the street railway business, Jones was not out of business. In June 1885, he had entered a partnership with Edward Houston, a well-known white real estate developer, for the purpose of creating Pine Bluff's first modern suburb, the town of White Sulphur Springs. Land was purchased, plotted, and sold to noted local citizens. In 1892, the Jones-Houston partnership was expanded through incorporation of the White Sulphur Springs Land and Improvement Company, which became a fashionable summer resort and remained so well into the early twentieth century. In addition to his transportation company and real estate ventures, Jones established the Southern Mercantile Company, a wholesale supply house, in 1888. It proved to be another profitable enterprise. By the turn of the century, Wiley Jones was the wealthiest black man in Arkansas and one of the wealthiest in the South.

Born in Madison County, Georgia, on July 14, 1848, Wiley Jones was one of six children born to George Jones, a white Georgia planter, and his common-law slave wife Anna. Prior to his death in 1858 the slave owner told his wife and children that he had arranged for their freedom, but after his death, no freedom papers were ever found and the family remained slaves until 1865. During the Civil War, Jones served as the camp servant of his owner, Confederate General James Yell. When the general was killed, Wiley rejoined the Yell family in Waco, Texas, where he worked as a wagon driver, hauling cotton from Waco to San Antonio, Texas. In 1868 he returned to the Pine Bluff area and worked in agriculture and as a mule skinner.

Subsequently, he took a job as a night porter in a local Pine Bluff hotel and worked as a barber during the day. He saved and invested his earnings wisely and was able, after a few years, to purchase a profitable saloon business. Jones invested the profits from his saloon business in real estate, and by 1880, he had accumulated considerable property in Pine Bluff and throughout Arkansas. It was the profits from his saloon business and real estate sales that allowed Jones to purchase and build his own horse racing park and railway system and organize the Colored State Fair. Wiley Jones died intestate, and his estate was managed by one of his brothers, James Jones, for a few years until he was forced to sell most of the property in order to settle the estate. Commenting upon Jones's death, the *Pine Bluff Commercial* said that "although Wiley Jones has not altogether pleased everybody, yet he has accomplished much more than many who have found fault could have done."

SELECTED BIBLIOGRAPHY: Willard B. Gatewood, "Arkansas Negroes in the 1890s: Documents," *Arkansas Historical Quarterly* 33 (1974): 305–306; F. L. Gordon, *Caste & Class: The Black Experience in Arkansas, 1880–1920* (Athens: University of Georgia Press, 1995), 78–79; John W. Graves, *Town and Country: Race Relations in an Urban Rural Context, Arkansas, 1865–1905* (Fayetteville: University of Arkansas Press, 1990); J. W. Leslie, "Street Cars: Earliest Public Transportation Was Drawn by Mules, Pine Bluff (Arkansas)," *Commercial*, February 8, 1976.

C. Calvin Smith

JOSHUA, ERNEST P. (1928–), Arkansas, founder of J. M. Products Co.

One of the largest minority-owned aerosol manufacturing companies in the United States, the multimillion-dollar J. M. Products is best known as the manufacturer of the nationally recognized brand ISOPLUS, which is marketed in Canada, the Caribbean, Europe, and across the United States. The company has two manufacturing facilities, in Little Rock and North Little Rock, and affiliate operations in Jamaica, the West Indies, and Africa. Although J. M. Products now employs 100 people, when Joshua first started the business in the mid-

1970s, it was almost a one-man operation. Joshua was born in Arkansas and received his background in chemistry working at Luster's Products, located in Chicago, Illinois.

In 1969, Joshua started a small hair care company in Chicago called Ravel Products but later sold the company to his partner. In 1970 he moved his family to Los Angeles and started a company called "J. M. and Company by Ernest P. Joshua, Jr." Joshua, like many of his hair care contemporaries, sold products door to door to barbers and beauticians. His leading product, ISODINE (now ISOPLUS), was designed to eliminate thinning caused by chemical hair services such as perms. In 1976, J. M. Products was established in Los Angeles. Unfortunately, in 1977, Joshua was diagnosed with lymphatic cancer. This proved to be a long and costly battle, which prompted Joshua and his family to return to Little Rock, Arkansas, where he operated a small storefront operation—a mere $28,000 a year operation.

In 1982, the company became J. M. Products, Inc., and is continuing to grow into a major minority-owned and -operated manufacturing facility. For many years Joshua's four children have been involved in the business. Eventually, his son Michael W. Joshua became president and general manager of J. M. Products, Inc. Joshua also operates other business enterprises including a construction company and an entertainment and supper club. He has received numerous awards and was runner-up for the National Small Businessman of the Year Award in 1987. In 1987 he was honored at the White House for his achievements as a small businessman by President Ronald Reagan, and in 1994, he was invited by President Bill Clinton to participate in the first U.S. Trade Mission to South Africa.

SELECTED BIBLIOGRAPHY: "Ernest Joshua: Arkansas' Manufacturing Giant," *Shoptalk* (Winter 1987); J. M. Products, Inc., *Ernest P. Joshua, Sr., Biography* (Little Rock: J. M. Products, 1994); J. M. Products, Inc., *J. M. Products, Inc., Company History* (Little Rock: J. M. Products, 1994).

Nancy J. Dawson

JOYNER, MAJORIE STEWART (1896–1994), Illinois, hair care business pioneer, philanthropist, inventor, community leader.

Joyner has an undisputed reputation in the field of cosmetology. So outstanding were her contributions that she was the subject of an exhibit at the Smithsonian Museum of American History in Washington, D.C., in 1987. Born in Monterey, Virginia, Joyner officially launched her career in the beauty culture business in 1916, the year she met her mentor, Madame C. J. Walker.* After becoming a certified Walker agent, Joyner immediately became a major player in the Madame C. J. Walker Manufacturing Co. She was not only Walker's confidante, but she was chief spokesperson and organizer in Chicago.

The three years Joyner worked with Walker proved to significantly affect Joyner's life. Fifty years of Joyner's life was dedicated to the Walker Co. By

1919 Joyner was vice president and national supervisor for the Walker Company's beauty schools. Joyner had the responsibility of recruiting and training instructors, known as Walker agents. This included some 15,000 women who sold Walker products. Joyner established the first Walker Beauty School in Chicago. Throughout her life Joyner pioneered in the beauty culture business. In 1921, she helped to found the National Beauty Culturalist League, a national organization for black beauty professionals. She became president of the organization in 1938. In 1924, she, along with two other women, wrote the first Illinois Beauty Culture Law, which was also the first in the country. In 1928, she received a patent for a permanent hair wave machine. Joyner developed many products for the Walker Company.

Legal segregation made it almost impossible for African American beauticians to receive advance training, so Joyner organized a highly publicized study trip to Paris for 195 cosmetologists in 1954. To meet the needs of black beauticians, she founded Alpha Chi Pi Omega Sorority and Fraternity Inc. and the United Beauty School Owners and Teachers Association, both in 1945, in Washington, D.C. The purpose of Alpha Chi Pi was to raise the educational standards of beauticians. Also, the fraternal organization was established to promote civic work and to encourage support of black-owned and -operated businesses.

Alpha Chi Pi Omega was organized with Mary McLeod Bethune and Congressman William L. Dawson, of Chicago, as sponsors. Both Bethune and Dawson were Joyner's comrades for many years. She worked closely with both national leaders in civic affairs. She was a founding member of the National Council of Negro Women, organized by Bethune in 1935. Joyner and Alpha Chi Pi Omega were dedicated to raising funds for Bethune-Cookman College. In 1961, Joyner received an honorary Doctor of Humanities degree from Bethune-Cookman College, and she received her Bachelor's of Psychology from the college when she was nearly 80 years old. At the request of Eleanor Roosevelt, she became chairwoman of the Women's Division of the Democratic National Campaign Committee in 1944. In this capacity, Joyner traveled throughout the country, gathering support for President Roosevelt and Congressman Dawson.

In her later years of life, when Joyner was almost 100 years old, she was still zealous in her philanthropic work. She worked everyday at the *Chicago Defender*, which Joyner had been affiliated with since 1929. She raised funds for the *Chicago Defender* Charities, an organization where she served as the chairwoman.

SELECTED BIBLIOGRAPHY: The Majorie Stewart Joyner Papers, Vivian G. Harsh Research Collection of Afro-American History and Literature, Chicago Public Library, Carter G. Woodson Regional Branch; Adam Langer, "You Know, I'm 95 and I Know What I'm Talking About," *Reader*, September 11, 1992; Lou Ortiz, "Black Cosmetology Pioneer Is a Role Model for Success," *Chicago Sun-Times*, November 18, 1991.

Nancy J. Dawson

JULIAN, PERCY LAVON (1899–1975), Chicago, chemist, pharmaceutical entrepreneur civil rights activist.

Percy Julian was an internationally renowned scientist and researcher as well as a vocal proponent of the civil rights movement of the mid-twentieth century. The research that Julian pioneered continues to have momentous economic impact. By creating synthetic reproductions of naturally existing substances, he gave countless people the opportunity to receive medical treatments, which were formerly prohibitively expensive. Julian was born to James S. and Elizabeth L. Julian in Montgomery, Alabama. His father was a railway mail clerk, his mother, a homemaker. All five of Julian's siblings would go on to achieve advanced degrees, as did he.

Julian received his B.A. from DePauw University in 1920 and his M.A. from Harvard University in 1923. He taught chemistry at both West Virginia State College and Howard University before pursuing doctoral studies, made possible by a General Education Board Fellowship. Julian then pursued his Ph.D. at the University of Vienna, where he was awarded his doctorate in 1931. From 1932 to 1936, Julian taught at DePauw University, where he established an international reputation for his research and development of the drug physostigmine, which was used to treat glaucoma.

In 1936, Julian accepted an offer from the Glidden Paint Company for the position of director and manager of the fine chemicals research department, one of the first examples of Corporate America's recruitment of blacks. At Glidden, Julian directed their soy bean research for its uses in coating paper, cold water paints, and textile sizing and during World War II, as an ingredient for a product used as an extinguisher for gas and oil fires. He left Glidden in 1953 and established his own business, Julian Laboratories, Inc., headquartered in Chicago, with a satellite facility in Mexico City, Mexico.

While Julian was president of his company, he continued with research and development, focusing on pharmaceuticals. His research laboratories ranked first, internationally, in the development of drugs processed from yams. Julian's research was also revolutionary in that he created, for the first time, a synthetic version of cortisone, cutting the cost by over 10,000 percent. As the company grew, so too did his administrative responsibilities in managing his company, which took Julian away from his research. In 1964, Julian sold his corporation to Smith, Kline, & French for $2.4 million. He established a small research laboratory, while also acting as consultant for other labs.

Dr. Percy Julian registered over 130 patents in his name. When he retired, Julian turned his attention to the civil rights movement. Along with the president of North Carolina Mutual,* Asa Spaulding,* they served as cochairs of a group of prominent black Americans who raised $1 million to finance National Association for the Advancement of Colored People (NAACP) civil rights lawsuits. He spoke at functions and generously contributed to organizations championing the cause of equality under the law. He also was the recipient of 12 honorary degrees and other awards. His award-winning tulip garden was a great source of pride. His legacy lives on in the drugs that he pioneered. His life's goal was in "making life a little easier for the persons who come after me."

SELECTED BIBLIOGRAPHY: Louis Haber, *Black Pioneers of Science and Invention* (New York: Harcourt, Brace, & World, 1970); Edward S. Jenkins, *To Fathom More: African American Scientists and Inventors* (Lanham, MD: University Press of America, 1996); Percy L. Julian, "On Being Scientist, Humanist, and Negro," in Stanton L. Wormley and Lewis H. Fenderson, eds., *Many Shades of Black* (New York: William Morrow, 1969); Vijaya L. Melnick and Franklin D. Hamilton, eds., *Minorities in Science: The Challenge for Change in Biomedicine* (New York: Plenum, 1977); Obituary, *New York Times*, April 20, 1975.

Edward M. Apy

K

KING, DON [DONALD FERRIN] (1932–), Ohio, Las Vegas, boxing promoter.

In the post–civil rights era, Don King had achieved unparalleled success and great wealth as a boxing promoter. He was born in Cleveland, Ohio, to Clarence and Hattie King and had six siblings. His father died the day before his ninth birthday. King's mother continued to support the family, but it was a difficult time. King drifted in and out of various jobs, including working as numbers* runner for a local gambling operation. He also owned a night club. In 1967, he was charged with murder, found guilty, and sentenced to four years in the Ohio Marion Correctional Institution. After his September 1971 release (in 1983 he was pardoned by the governor of Ohio), King became a small-time sports promoter, which he used as a basis to force his way into the spotlight.

King first used his power of persuasion to convince then–World Heavyweight Champion Muhammad Ali to participate in a charity boxing event. Once King persuaded Ali's two chief advisers, manager Herbert Muhammad (son of Elijah Muhammad*) and lawyer Charles Lomax, to allow him to get Ali in his camp, his success grew rapidly. He was soon able to get the sport's top talent to seek him out to represent them. The first successful King spectacle was the $30 million "Rumble in the Jungle," in 1974 in Kinshasa, Zaire, which pitted Ali against George Foreman (who was knocked out), which placed him at the top of boxing promoters. Since then, many other championship-caliber boxers have been represented by King, including Leon Spinks, Roberto Duran, and "Sugar Ray" Leonard. Most recently, Mike Tyson has been the most prominent in the King camp.

Don King has made a flamboyant use of his wealth. He wears designer suits and gold rings and chains, and his hair, a trademark, stands a full four inches straight up from the top of his head. He is a true showman, always managing to upstage those whom he promotes in widely publicized events, which increases his vast wealth and influence in the boxing world. Yet King revolutionized boxing, which was dying out as a popular sport. Also, through his use of television, he has raised the size of boxing purses from hundreds of thousands, when he began promoting, to tens of millions of dollars. In 1976 ABC Sports, Inc., contracted with King to televise boxing championships. This deal was worth over $2 million to King.

King's net worth is nearly impossible to calculate. His boxing empire contains various entities, and he is particularly astute and shrewd in the business decisions that he makes, which also enables him to increase his wealth. Invariably, King is always certain to get his cut of the revenue before anyone else. His Don King Productions, a mammoth organization that he heads as president, chairman, and chief executive officer, provides the capital to stage huge fights between his fighters and others. Also, King scouts new talent through his King Training Camp and televises it on the Don King Sports Entertainment Network. Still, King's hands-on management style and involvement in all phases of his business are typical of many black business owners of private companies.

SELECTED BIBLIOGRAPHY: Peter Blauner, "King on the Ropes," *New York Times*, March 18, 1991; Walter L. Hawkins, *African-American Biographies* (Jefferson, NC: McFarland & Co., Inc., 1992); John Lombardi, "King's Gambit," *GQ* 63, 3 (March 1993); Jeffrey T. Sammons, *Beyond the Ring: The Role of Boxing in American Society* (Urbana: University of Illinois Press, 1988); "Street Talk: Don King Making B-School Scene with Business Advice," *South Florida Business Journal* 17 (December 1993); John Peter Sugden, *Boxing and Society: An International Analysis* (Manchester, England: Manchester University Press, 1996).

Edward M. Apy

KWANZAA, COMMERCIALISM OF. Kwanzaa, a nonreligious holiday, celebrates African American heritage, pride, community, family, and culture. Its development was inspired by the civil rights struggles of the 1960s and based on ancient African celebrations. The seven-day festival commences the day after Christmas and culminates on New Year's Day. Dr. Maulana Karenga, chairman of the Department of Black Studies at California State University at Long Beach, is credited with the conceptualization of Kwanzaa in 1966 following the Watts riots in Los Angeles. Contributing to the birth of this holiday were the observations that many in the African American community were being commercially exploited during the months of October, November, and December, had disconnected from their African heritage, and did not have a national holiday commemorating their heritage.

Kwanzaa's roots lie in African first-fruit harvest celebrations, from which it takes its name. The word *Kwanzaa* is derived from the Swahili phrase "matunda ya kwanza," which means "first fruits." Celebrants are encouraged to incorporate seven principles (Way of Life) into their daily lives:

1. Unity: to strive for and maintain in family, community, nation, and race
2. Self-Determination: for self-definition, creativity, and self-advocacy
3. Collective Responsibility: to accept responsibility to problem solve, build, and maintain collectively, the African American community
4. Cooperative Economics: to develop, support, and collectively profit from African American businesses
5. Purpose: to restore and develop the richness of African tradition
6. Creativity: to contribute to the beauty and health of communities
7. Faith: to believe in the power of the community to better itself

The Kwanzaa celebration is organized around five activities common to other African first-fruit celebrations: the gathering of family, friends, and community; reverence and respect for the creator and the environment; commemoration of ancestors and history; a recommitment to the cultural ideals and values of the African community; as well as the celebration of achievements. Feasts of mostly African dishes, songs, speeches, and prayers characterize Kwanzaa. During the holiday season, red, green, and black candles are placed in a ceremonial seven-shank candleholder (*kinara*). The kinara and an ear of corn for each child are placed on a straw mat (*mkeka*). Other items placed on the mat include, as a tribute to ancestors, a unity cup, presents for the children, *tambiko* (soil and water), and a basket of fruit. The flag of the Black Nation is hung to face East. In some families, there is a week of fasting from sunrise to sunset.

The celebration of Kwanzaa has become increasingly popular over the last decade. By the mid-1990s, more than 20 million people, primarily of African descent, celebrated the holiday not only in the United States, but also in Canada, England, the Caribbean, and Africa. In the United States, it is estimated that at least 2 percent of all African American adults celebrate Kwanzaa. Cowles Business Media reported that African Americans spend about $350 billion annually in purchasing consumer goods. According to the Bureau of Labor Statistics' *Consumer Expenditure Survey, 1994–1995*, America's 11 million black households spent a total of $2.6 billion on gifts for people in other households. In 1995 Kwanzaa generated more than $500 million in consumer spending, and even shoppers who do not celebrate Kwanzaa buy gifts for friends and relatives who do participate in the holiday.

Consequently, as increasing numbers of Americans began to include this holiday into their buying activities, retailers responded to their demand by providing goods that reflected the Kwanzaa celebration. In New York City the Kwanzaa Exposition was started in 1989 with 60 vendors and as early as 1991 many vendors were turned away for lack of space. By 1994 the New York Expo had expanded to include 450 vendors who sold goods to 40,000 shoppers during its four-day run at the huge Jacob Javits Center. Since then, other major American cities have begun to host their own Kwanzaa expositions. While most vendors sell finished consumer products made in the United States, some supply the material shoppers need to create their own handmade gifts, while others sell products imported from Africa.

Popularity for the holiday has increased the demand for African art, statues, dolls, and educational books. However, items like the kinara candlestick holder, which was once handmade and sold exclusively at African American owned stores, are now being mass produced and sold at national chain stores. In 1992, Hallmark came out with a line of Kwanzaa cards decorated by the Harlem Textile Works, a not-for-profit organization that provides job training for inner-city youth. By 1994, it had expanded its African American product line to include Kwanzaa wrapping paper. By 1998, more than 134 books on Kwanzaa were sold in book stores.

Yet some black retailers object to the increasing commercialism. Particularly, they emphasize not only that commercializing Kwanzaa detracts from the holiday's meaning but also debases and devalues the holiday's spirit. Tradition requires that *zwandi*, or gifts given as part of Kwanzaa, be handmade instead of store bought. Then, there is concern that the commercialization of Kwanzaa has led to profits being siphoned out of the black community. The emphasis is that it is the minority businesses that should be supported, especially since one of the seven Kwanzaa principles is cooperative economics, which emphasizes the development of African American businesses. Despite these objections, it is expected that the commercialism of Kwanzaa will follow that of other American holidays. Even those who hate to see the growing commercialism say the increased emphasis on the holiday can have a positive side, if black businesses, cooperatively, produce and market goods demanded by Kwanzaa celebrants.

SELECTED BIBLIOGRAPHY: Cowles Business Media, Web data, available from http://www.mediacentral.com/magazines/mid/oldarchives/1997; Dr. Maulana Karenga, founder, web data, available from http://www.officialkwanzaawebsite.org; Maulana Karenga, *Kwanzaa: A Celebration of Family, Community, and Culture* (Los Angeles: University of Sankore Press, 1998); Tibbett L. Speer, "Stretching the Holiday Season," *American Demographics* 19, 11 (November 1997); U.S. Bureau of Labor Statistics, *Consumer Expenditure Survey, 1994–1995* (Washington, DC: Government Printing Office, 1998); Judith Waldrop, "Happy Kwanzaa," *American Demographics* 12, 12 (December 1994).

Melodye Wehrung

L

LAWLESS, THEODORE KENNETH (1892–1971), Chicago, dermatologist, businessman, philanthropist.

While a medical doctor, Theodore Lawless also was involved in banking and real estate. His success in his private practice and his business activities eventually made him a millionaire and enhanced his philanthropy.* After receiving his B.A. from Talladega University in 1914, Lawless, who was born in Thibodeaux, Louisiana, left the South to further his education. He earned his M.D. from Northwestern University in 1919 and pursued extensive postdoctoral work, spending a year each at Columbia University (1920) and Harvard University (1921). Then, from 1921 to 1924, Lawless attended the University of Paris, the University of Freiburg, and the University of Vienna, where he also continued his research in dermatology.

After his international training ended, Lawless returned to Chicago in 1924, where he established his medical practice in dermatology, generally charging only $3, while his peers were charging from three to five times that sum per visit. Lawless often had dozens of patients lined up down the street outside his South Side office. Also, he would see people without appointments, and veterans of foreign wars were seen regardless of their ability to pay. His patients were from all ethnic, religious, and economic backgrounds. Lawless was on the faculty at Northwestern University from 1924 to 1941, while continuing his private practice. Yet notwithstanding his reputation as an internationally renowned researcher and physician, he was passed over for a promotion for which he felt he was deserving. He left in 1941.

From 1945 to 1953, while continuing his medical practice, Lawless was president of the 4213 South Michigan Corporation, a real estate venture dedicated to providing low-cost housing for African Americans; and from 1951 to 1953, he was president of the Service Federal Savings and Loan Association. Lawless also served as the director of the Supreme Life Insurance Company* during this era. At the same time, he was appointed to sit on several boards and served on steering committees, as well as directing youth services at the B'nai B'rith Foundation. His support of the Jewish community reflected reciprocity for its previous support of his work as a doctor and researcher. Before being accepted to study abroad, 12 letters of support were needed; 11 of those letters were from Jewish physicians. Also, Lawless donated $160,000 toward construction of a hospital in Israel. In addition, Lawless donated hundreds of thousands of dollars to southern colleges and universities that were historically black, including Dillard University.

Lawless's philanthropy and distinguished career as a physician and researcher earned him countless honors and awards. He died at the age of 79, having helped thousands of patients with skin disorders. He also pioneered in treatments for syphilis, publishing nine papers on the dermatological effects of the disease in the period from 1921 to 1941. Theodore Lawless was the son of Alfred and Harriet (Dunn). His father was a minister.

SELECTED BIBLIOGRAPHY: *Chicago Tribune*, May 2, 1971; W. Montague Cobb, "Theodore Kenneth Lawless," *Journal of the National Medical Association* 62 (July 1970); Louis Haber, *Black Pioneers of Science and Invention* (New York: Harcourt, Brace, & World, 1970); Herbert M. Morais, *The History of the Negro in Medicine* (1967; reprint, New York: Publishers Co., 1969).

Edward M. Apy

LEE, GEORGE WASHINGTON (1894–1976), Memphis, businessman, writer, civic and political leader.

George W. Lee, in 1919, joined the black-owned Mississippi Life Insurance Company, which was based in Memphis, Tennessee, as a $10-a-week salesman. In just a few weeks he was promoted to manager, and a year later he was vice president. After Mississippi Life was sold, Lee joined Atlanta Life,* another distinguished black-owned insurance company. He established a branch of the company in Memphis, and for three decades, he helped it achieve prominence as one of the country's outstanding corporations. Lee was a staunch believer in capitalist enterprise as the best route to economic independence. He supported all efforts to create and expand black-owned businesses. He was a founder of the National Negro Insurance Association, a trade organization, and a director of both Universal Life Insurance Company and the Tri-State Bank.

Lee was born in Sunflower County, Mississippi, just outside Indianola. After his father's death, the family was reduced to sharecropping and Lee helped his mother financially by finding odd jobs as well as working in the field. In spite of his duties, he managed to attend a rural elementary school until his mother moved the family to Indianola. There he worked alternately as a grocery clerk, a houseboy, and a wagon driver, before attending Alcorn Agricultural and Mechanical College. This school provided him with the equivalent of a sound high school education.

During summers, Lee traveled to Memphis, where he stayed with his older brother Abner and worked as a hotel bellhop. He was greatly impressed by the vibrant cultural life of Memphis's black community and felt pride in seeing the many businesses and stores owned by blacks. However, in 1917, World War I and the U.S. military claimed him for duty in France. Two years later, after receiving a citation for bravery, Lee was promoted to first lieutenant and honorably discharged. (He was to be known as "Lieutenant Lee" for the rest of his life.)

In 1919, he returned to Memphis and joined Mississippi Life Insurance, which he would leave for Atlanta Life and go on to become a significant presence in the business and social life of black Memphis. He was a strong advocate of self-help, which to him meant aggressive business development to produce wealth. Lee joined the protest for black civil rights but never ceased to emphasize the importance of business development. In a journal article by his biographer David Tucker, Lee is quoted as claiming that the best way to advance the cause of blacks is through "an intelligent exercise of citizenship rights, buying homes, buying farms, building businesses, and producing wealth." Lee was a lifetime Republican, shared in strategy sessions with leading Republican politicians, met with President Dwight Eisenhower in the White House several times, and participated in Republican National Conventions. He actively joined campaigns to increase voter registration among blacks.

Lee was a prolific writer of books, stories, and magazine articles. A major interest was jazz music, and his works about musician W. C. Handy, Beale Street, and the Blues are considered important for his original observations on these subjects. His book *Beale Street: Where the Blues Began* was a Book-of-the-Month Selection.

SELECTED BIBLIOGRAPHY: John N. Ingham and Lynne B. Feldman, *African-American Business Leaders: A Biographical Dictionary* (Westport, CT: Greenwood Press, 1994); The George W. Lee Collection, Memphis/Shelby County Public Library, Memphis, Tennessee; David M. Tucker, "Black Pride and Negro Business in the 1920's; George Washington Lee of Memphis," *Business History Review* 43 (Winter 1969); David M. Tucker, *Lieutenant Lee of Beale Street* (Nashville: Vanderbilt University Press, 1971).

Elizabeth Wright

LEIDESDORFF, WILLIAM ALEXANDER (1811?–1848), California, merchant, trader, rancher, major landholder, hotelier, ship captain, elected city official, diplomat, steamboat innovator.

William Leidesdorff was a central figure in the early commercial and political development of San Francisco and northern California and an activist in the efforts to annex Mexican Alta California to the United States. He is considered the first African American millionaire, although this net worth was not realized until after his death, when it was found that he was of African descent. A light-complexioned man of mixed parentage, Leidesdorff was born in St. Croix, Danish Virgin Islands, one of five children born to the slave Anna Maria Spark, a woman of African descent, and Alexander Leidesdorff, a white Danish citizen. In the United States, where he migrated in 1822, Leidesdorff passed for white. In 1834, when he applied for American citizenship, Leidesdorff declared in writing that he was a white man, a U.S. statutory requirement for citizenship. Leidesdorff became a naturalized U.S. citizen in New Orleans, where he worked for several years as a ship's captain, before he settled in California. He had been hired by diplomat John Coffin Jones to be commander of the schooner *Julia Ann*, which Leidesdorff sailed to California. He arrived in Monterey in 1841, and in 1842, Leidesdorff established himself as a merchant in Yerba Buena, which was later called San Francisco.

Between 1843 and 1848 Leidesdorff amassed one of California's most extensive and varied business enterprises, which included a wide range of goods and services. He obtained a grant in 1843 for two city lots in Yerba Buena, and on this property he built at a cost of $15,000 an edifice that eventually became the City Hotel. This building, often called "The Big Adobe," was reported to be the town's largest private residence and was the second hostelry in the city. In order to compete with the other hotel, he added a dining room, bar, and billiard room. Leidesdorff also constructed a warehouse on the waterfront in 1844 and built a 70-foot landing for rowboats on the shore of Yerba Buena Cove. In the city of Yerba Buena his trade involved a variety of merchandise, from buttons, corned salmon, and peanut butter to hides, saddles, and lumber. In addition, Captain Leidesdorff worked as a business agent, which included such duties as collecting money from gold mining pioneer John Sutter for the Hudson Bay Company and hiring workers and purchasing supplies to build the residence of U.S. Consul Thomas Larkin.

On June 1, 1844, Guillermo Leidesdorff became a Mexican citizen, which made him eligible to receive land grants, by which he acquired massive amounts of property, becoming one of California's major landholders. Leidesdorff's holdings included Rancho Acalanes in the East Bay, Rancho Rio de los Americanos, which consisted of 35,000 acres in the Sacramento Valley and including the site of the present city of Folsom, and several lots in the town of Yerba Buena. In 1847, Leidesdorff made a profit by selling his East Bay holding of Rancho Acalanes to Elam Brown of New York, who had come with several other families to settle in California. From Rancho Rio de los Americanos, he was a major vendor of supplies to the gold miners, including Sutter. On this property Leidesdorff raised livestock, including cattle and sheep. This vast Sacramento Valley property, which adjoined Sutter's New Helvetia, was run by Leidesdorff's manager, Willard Buzzed. Several years after Leidesdorff's death, Rancho Rio de los Americanos was sold for $163,360.

Leidesdorff was an enthusiastic and outspoken advocate of the Americanization of California. In 1845 he was appointed by Thomas O. Larkin, the U.S.

consul in Monterey, to be vice-consul for the Port of San Francisco, thus becoming, in spite of his Mexican citizenship, the first U.S. diplomat of African descent. One motive for Leidesdorff's pro-Americanization activities appears to have been the desire for increased wealth-producing opportunities. In a letter to Larkin, Leidesdorff stated: "As regards the hopes of a change, and the coming events, I can hardly express my pleasure. I only hope that it will take place soon, as it will be a few thousands in my pockets." Among his other commercial ventures, Leidesdorff sold groceries and other supplies to U.S. troops stationed in northern California.

Following the successful efforts to Americanize California, San Francisco's first election took place on January 30, 1847, in the building of Leidesdorff's City Hotel. He became a member of San Francisco's first city council and served as the first city treasurer. The record Leidesdorff kept of San Francisco's financial affairs from October 7, 1847, to May 12, 1848, in the *San Francisco Town Journal* includes several of his business transactions with the city, including an 1847 notation of his sale of $1,000 worth of lumber. Also, Leidesdorff was a member of the school board, when San Francisco's first public school was established in April 1848.

In January 1848 gold was discovered at Sutter's Mill. A few months later, just days after receiving word that gold had been discovered on his own Rancho Rio de los Americanos property in the Sacramento Valley, William Leidesdorff, unmarried, died intestate on May 18, 1848, reportedly of brain fever. The resulting controversy concerning the disposition of his estate was the object of lengthy and complicated legal proceedings, which led to disputes over such issues as international jurisdiction and the identification of Leidesdorff's heirs. Captain Joseph Libby Folsom traveled to St. Croix and purchased the rights to the estate from Leidesdorff's mother, described by some as a "negress," and other heirs for $75,000. Estimates of the estate's indebtedness range from $40,000 to $60,000. Since the property included a huge land grant in gold country, the Leidesdorff property was worth a fortune, even after the estate's debts were paid. The Leidesdorff estate, which was acquired by Folsom, eventually yielded $1,442,232.35.

After his death, Leidesdorff was given an elaborate public funeral. His is only one of four burial spaces within the walls of Mission Dolores. Leidesdorff's legacy includes a small street named for him in San Francisco's financial district; a school system that, ironically, became segregated less than a decade after he had helped to establish it; and the creation of California estate law that resulted from the many years of legal contention over his property. In addition, the *San Francisco Town Journal*, Leidesdorff's city treasurer report, provides important historical documentation of the city's early financial activities. It is interesting to note that Negro Bar, which was first mined by African Americans in 1849, was located on the site of Leidesdorff's Rancho Rio de Los Americanos.

SELECTED BIBLIOGRAPHY: Robert Ernest Cowan, "The Leidesdorff-Folsom Estate: A Forgotten Chapter in the Romantic History of Early San Francisco," *Quarterly Review of the California Historical Society* 5 (June 1928); Ralph Herbert Cross, *The Early Inns of California, 1844–1869* (San Francisco: Cross & Brandt, 1954); John N. Ingham and Lynne B. Feldman, *African-American Business Leaders: A Biographical Dictionary* (Westport CT: Greenwood Press, 1994); Thomas O. Larkin, *The Larkin Papers: Personal, Business, and Official Correspondence of Thomas Oliver Larkin, Merchant and United States Consul in California* (Berkeley: University of California Press, 1951); Leidesdorff Papers, Huntington Library, San Marino, California; San Francisco Room, San Francisco Public Library, San Francisco; *San Francisco Town Journal, 1847–1848* (San Francisco: H. S. Crocker Co., 1926); William Sherman Savage, "The Influence of William Alexander Leidesdorff on the History of California," *Negro History Bulletin* (July 1953).

Rosemary M. Stevenson

LEWIS, BYRON EUGENE (1931–), New Jersey, publisher, advertising executive, television producer, public relations.

As president and chief executive officer of Uniworld Group, Inc., Byron Lewis's company is one of the handful of black-owned advertising agencies responsible for bringing positive images of blacks to radio, television, and the mainstream media. With annual accounts totaling $157 million and more than 100 advertising awards, Uniworld is a full-service general market advertising company handling specialty work in the African-American, Latino, and Asian markets.

Byron Lewis was born in Newark, New Jersey, to Thomas Eugene Lewis and Myrtle Evelyn Allen. He received a bachelor of science degree in journalism from Long Island University in 1953. After college he worked as a social worker for a number of years but was determined to break into the advertising field. However, his efforts to break into the predominantly white industry proved unsuccessful. Despite these disappointments he remained committed to the communications industry. He became cofounder of *Urbanite Magazine* in 1961–1962 and worked as an assistant ad manager for Amalgamated Publishers in 1963 to 1964. From 1964 to 1968 he was vice president of *Tuesday*, a national newspaper supplement focusing on issues of concern to the black community, and in 1968 he became president and publisher of Afro Marketing Company, serving from 1968 to 1969.

In 1969, with $250,000 in seed money from venture capital groups, Lewis, with five employees in a three-room office near the Times Square quarter in New York, established his advertising agency, which later became known as Uniworld. After five years the fledgling company ran out of money, hit by a recession. Faced with the prospect of losing his business, in 1974–1975 Lewis produced the black radio soap opera *Sounds of the City*. This show brought in the agency's first million dollars in gross sales, and its success marked Uniworld's entry into the entertainment industry. In 1977 Byron Lewis created the radio show *This Far by Faith*, and in 1989, Uniworld's entertainment division began producing the syndicated news program *America's Black Forum (ABF)*. In 1997 *ABF* reached more than 1 million viewers weekly and was syndicated in 70 markets. Lewis's only child, Byron Eugene Lewis, Jr., is the program's executive producer.

When Burger King Corporation selected Uniworld to develop its national mainstream campaign in 1994, Uniworld's efforts resulted in Burger King's greatest six-month sales increase in a decade. The following year Uniworld won Mars, Inc.'s Three Musketeers candy general mainstream account. These achievements underscored the ability of ethnic-owned agencies to successfully advertise to mainstream America. By 1997 Uniworld had grown to more than 130 employees, handling major accounts for blue-chip companies including AT&T, Colgate-Palmolive, Eastman Kodak, Quaker Oats, and Ford Motors–Lincoln Mercury Divisions, Kraft Foods, and Texaco.

In 1997 Lewis created the Acapulco Black Film Festival, the first international film festival for African American filmmakers. Under Byron Lewis's leadership, Uniworld has expanded into an international organization that targets publishing, promotion, broadcast production, and entertainment projects. Uniworld has agencies in South Africa and interests in the Caribbean.

SELECTED BIBLIOGRAPHY: Biography of Byron Lewis, Uniworld's Public Relations Department, New York City; *Black Enterprise* (January 1995).

Teresa Savage

LEWIS, REGINALD FRANCIS (c. 1942–1993), Baltimore, New York, Paris, financier, business owner, entrepreneur, attorney, philanthropist.

Blessed with an unshakable belief in self, a keen intellect, and an unwavering desire to own a major business, in 1987 Lewis purchased the international arm of Beatrice Foods in a leveraged buyout worth $1 billion. The deal gave Lewis a conglomerate with 64 companies in 31 countries in what was the largest offshore leveraged buyout of its time. Lewis investigated the possibility of acquiring Paramount Pictures and Chrysler Corp. shortly before his death of brain cancer in January 1993 at the age of 50.

Born to working-class parents in Baltimore, Maryland, Lewis excelled at high school athletics and was a standout quarterback. He earned a football scholarship to Virginia State College in Petersburg, Virginia, but injured his throwing arm during his freshman year. Lewis responded by concentrating fully on his studies, which elevated him to the dean's list. After graduation, Lewis participated in a Harvard Law School summer program designed to acquaint African American students with the law. He studied everything about the law he could get his hands on and was a standout in the summer program. He used the opportunity to identify Harvard Law School faculty associated with admissions, then talked his way into Harvard Law School without ever filling out an application.

After graduation in 1968, Lewis worked briefly with Paul, Weiss, Rifkind, Wharton & Garrison, a prestigious Manhattan law firm. But dissatisfied with being a small cog in the overall scheme of things, he left after two years and set up a Wall Street practice designed to help minority businesses obtain start-up capital. Intrigued by the business world and convinced he could acquire and successfully operate companies himself, in 1984 Lewis bought the McCall Pattern Co. in a leveraged buyout valued at $22.5 million. Although unfamiliar with the sewing pattern business and lacking experience as a chief executive, Lewis did his homework, allowing him to strengthen McCall's balance sheet and guide the firm to its two most profitable years.

In the summer of 1987, Lewis sold McCall for $65 million, netting a small band of personal investors a spectacular 90-to-1 return. A 44-year-old multimillionaire at that point, Lewis was hardly ready to rest on his laurels. He began searching in earnest for a business acquisition whose size would dwarf McCall's. He found his quarry in Beatrice International, which was already being pursued by Citibank, among other suitors. Whereas Citibank had an army of financial experts devoted just to the Beatrice chase, Lewis entered the fray with just four people—himself and three associates!

Beatrice International was being sold by Kohlberg, Kravis and Roberts through an auction conducted by Morgan Stanley and Salomon Bros. Lewis's offer of $985 million was the winning bid, and he was able to get at least $400 million from junk bond king Michael Milken, an admirer of Lewis's. It took two days and 180 lawyers, accountants, and financial advisers to close the complex deal in December 1987. Lewis brilliantly sold Beatrice's Latin American, Canadian, and Australian operations in order to pare down his debt. That left him with a food distribution and grocery products empire spanning four continents but concentrated primarily in western Europe and headquartered in Paris.

Beatrice was renamed TLC Beatrice, with *TLC* standing for The Lewis Company. As had been the case with McCall, Lewis became the top manager of TLC Beatrice. He visited his far-flung operating units regularly, and a typical day might see his corporate jet shuttling between Paris, Denmark, West Germany, and Ireland. A romantic who once surprised his wife Loida by flying her on his private jet from Paris to Vienna just to hear a classical music concert, Lewis was a Francophile who spoke French fluently and maintained a Paris apartment in King Louis the XIV's historic Place Du Palais Bourbon. In Manhattan, Lewis maintained a 15-room co-op purchased for $11.5 million from John DeLlorean.

An avid philanthropist in the final five years of his life, Lewis established a foundation responsible for distributing more than $12 million in charitable gifts, including $1 million for Howard University and $3 million for Harvard Law School, which named a building after Lewis. At the time of his death in 1993, Lewis's personal fortune was estimated by *Forbes* magazine to be in excess of $400 million. More than 2,000 people attended his funeral and memorial service, and his family received words of condolence from Bill Clinton, Ronald Reagan, Colin Powell, and Bill Cosby, among others. TLC Beatrice's operations were taken over and successfully managed by Lewis's wife.

SELECTED BIBLIOGRAPHY: "Buying into the Big Time," *Time*, August 24, 1987; Reginald F. Lewis and Blair S. Walker, *Why Should White Guys Have All the Fun? How Reginald Lewis Created a Billion-Dollar Business Empire* (New York: John Wiley &

Sons, 1995; Elliott Wiley, ed., *RFL, Reginald F. Lewis, A Tribute* (New York: Bookmark Publishing Corp., 1994).

Blair S. Walker

LLEWELLYN, JAMES BRUCE (1927–), New York, Buffalo, New York City, entrepreneur, government official.

While Llewellyn was born in Harlem, New York, his parents had immigrated there from Jamaica in 1921. When Bruce was 2 years old, the family moved to White Plains, New York, in suburban Westchester County, where his father operated a bar and restaurant. As a child, Llewellyn attended schools that were racially integrated, which he later credited as a factor in his business success. His sister eventually became a New York District Supreme Court judge. In 1943, Llewellyn joined the U.S. Army. Since he was only 16 years old, the army sent him to Rutgers University to study engineering as an aviation cadet. He was made a second lieutenant after graduating from Officer Candidate School, though by this time the war had ended. In 1948, Llewellyn decided to leave the army, partly because he found his responsibilities less than challenging but also because his father had become seriously ill.

After his discharge from the military, Llewellyn opened a liquor store in Harlem. At the same time, he attended City College of New York, from which he received a B.A. degree. He then attended the School of Business at Columbia University and New York Law School, from which he received a J.D. in 1960. At this point, Llewellyn decided that his best career prospects were in government service rather than the business world. As he later said, in those days "you weren't going to get a job with some major Wall Street firm, that's for sure." After passing the bar exam, Bruce worked for a time in the New York district attorney's office and also in private practice. He was then hired by the Housing and Redevelopment Board of New York City. From there he moved on to become regional director for the Small Business Administration and later executive director for the Upper Manhattan Small Business Development Corporation. In 1968, he became deputy commissioner of the New York City Housing Commission.

In 1969, Llewellyn took advantage of an opportunity to leave government service and enter the private sector. He engineered a $3 million leveraged buyout (raising funds through the sale of securities backed by the future profits and assets of the company being acquired) of Fedco Foods Corporation, a 10-store grocery chain based in the Bronx. By 1983, Fedco had grown to 27 stores, with annual sales of $85 million. Llewellyn's hard work made the venture a notable success, especially given the economic deterioration of the Bronx in the 1970s. He sold the chain in 1984 for $20 million. The sale enabled Bruce to realize two long-held business goals: full ownership of a major soft-drink bottling franchise and a stake in a network television station.

In 1983, Llewellyn, along with Julius Erving and Bill Cosby, had acquired 36 percent of the Coca-Cola Bottling Company of New York. Two years later, the three partners bought out the Philadelphia Coca-Cola Bottling Company, making it one of the largest black-owned businesses in the United States. Also in 1985, Llewellyn led a group of investors in buying the ABC affiliate station in Buffalo, New York. In 1990, he divested his holdings in this station, then led a buyout of a cable television company in New Jersey. With these deals, Bruce Llewellyn had clearly established himself as one of the most powerful black business leaders in America.

In 1997, Philadelphia Coca-Cola Bottling Company was listed by *Black Enterprise* magazine as the nation's third largest black-owned business, worth $325 million. Throughout his successes, Llewellyn has maintained a sense of realism about the role of minorities in the business world. In his words, ''A positive attitude is critical. This is a prejudiced society. It's not going to go away. But you can still succeed.''

SELECTED BIBLIOGRAPHY: John N. Ingham and Lynne B. Feldman, *African-American Business Leaders: A Biographical Dictionary* (Westport, CT: Greenwood Press, 1994); Sandra L. Kirsch, ''Today's Leaders Look to Tomorrow . . . It Won't Be Easy, But Go Out and Do It'' (interview with J. Bruce Llewellyn), *Fortune*, March 26, 1990, 52.

Peter Botticelli

M

MARKETS, PROTECTED, AND BLACK ENTREPRENEURSHIP. Ethnic minority groups sometimes have unique, culturally based consumer demands. Immigrants, for example, often demand ''exotic'' foods. Such demands can be readily exploited by ethnic entrepreneurs, who have an insider's knowledge of the distinctive tastes of coethnics. Other entrepreneurs, ignorant of these tastes, are excluded from trading with the group in the relevant fields of commerce. Ethnic entrepreneurs in these fields are thus sheltered from external competition and have what Ivan Light calls a ''protected market.'' In several areas of commerce, protected markets developed for African American entrepreneurs not only because of the special demands of African American consumers but also because of the refusal of entrepreneurs from other ethnic groups to serve certain needs of African Americans.

African American entrepreneurs have had protected markets in barbering, hairdressing, and beauty culture. One factor in the rise of these markets has been African American entrepreneurs' insider's knowledge. Simply put, they are most familiar with the hairstyles and cosmetics demanded by other African Americans. But another factor has been the reluctance of barbers and beauticians from other groups to cater to African Americans. No doubt, this has been due in part to ignorance of the special consumer demands of African Americans. Few white barbers and beauticians know how to properly cut or style the hair of African Americans. Yet the reluctance has also been due to cultural norms regarding the ''appropriate'' social distance between the races. Many whites still will not serve African Americans in occupations that require close, personal contact.

Undertaking* is another occupation in which African American entrepreneurs have long had a protected market. This protected market arose because of social distance and special consumer demands. Historically, white undertakers, particularly those in the South, have refused to touch the corpses of African Americans, and this has allowed African American undertakers to monopolize funeral and mortuary services in African American communities. In addition, these undertakers have had the advantage of an insider's knowledge of the funeral services traditionally desired by African Americans and of the social institutions, namely, churches and lodges, that have helped ensure the deceased of a "proper" burial.

Life insurance is yet another field in which a protected market has existed for African American entrepreneurs. The social distance between the races created this market. As the color line tightened in the late nineteenth century, most white-owned insurance companies refused to insure the lives of African Americans, and the few that would serve African Americans charged them extraordinarily high premiums. These practices were based on reports that African Americans were poor insurance risks, owing to venereal diseases and unhygienic living conditions. As a result of this discrimination, African Americans sought alternatives to white insurance providers, and thus an opportunity arose for African American entrepreneurs. These entrepreneurs followed in an old tradition of self-help, as John Sibley Butler has argued.

Since colonial times, African Americans have created institutions for protection from life's uncertainties. These institutions—church beneficials, fraternal lodges, and mutual aid societies—were often forerunners of the first legal-reserve insurance companies founded by African Americans. African American entrepreneurs in the mass media have had a long-standing protected market based on special consumer demands. Early in the twentieth century, the literacy rate of the African American population increased dramatically, and this helped to create a demand for books, newspapers, and magazines dealing with social and political events of particular interest to African Americans. Within the growing African American communities of major cities, numerous black-oriented publications emerged during this time, and as Bart Landry has noted, African American publishers were well represented among the new class of African American entrepreneurs.

Historically, protected markets have provided many African Americans with opportunities for entrepreneurship. Some African American entrepreneurs have prospered by serving these markets. Notable among such entrepreneurs are Madame C. J. Walker* in hair care and cosmetics and John H. Johnson* in publishing. Yet, overall, the economic benefits of protected markets to African Americans have been limited. The cash flow generated in racially segregated and, in many cases, impoverished African American communities simply has been inadequate to foster a critical mass of successful African American entrepreneurs.

Protected markets are thus incapable of economically advancing African

Americans as a group. Furthermore, the influence of protected markets on African American entrepreneurship seems to have declined. In large part, this has resulted from the movement of African Americans into the larger national economy after the 1960s. Andrew Brimmer and Henry Terrell found that when African American consumers gained access to the business mainstream, they became less likely to patronize African American entrepreneurs. Consequently, those African American entrepreneurs who have depended on protected markets now constitute a dwindling share of the African American business population.

My analysis of the *Survey of Minority-Owned Business Enterprises*, for instance, revealed sharp declines during the 1970s in the number of African American–owned businesses in barbering, beauty culture, and funeral and crematory services. In addition, white-owned corporations have moved into some of the consumer markets formerly monopolized by African American entrepreneurs. Insurance is a case in point. After white insurance providers began serving the African American market, they made serious inroads into the consumer base of the African American insurance companies. As early as 1940, a single white-owned insurance company did more business with African Americans than did the 40 largest African American companies combined, according to Ivan Light. Hair care is another example. It was once the exclusive province of African American entrepreneurs. But in the 1980s, the giant cosmetics company Revlon, attracted by the rising disposable incomes of African Americans, developed a line of hair care products for African American consumers.

Protected markets will continue to provide entrepreneurial opportunities to many African Americans. Some African American entrepreneurs will even become wealthy by serving the special consumer demands of coethnics. In this regard, the recent proliferation of black-oriented mass media suggests that many African American entrepreneurs in the field of communications will have promising careers. But as Timothy Bates has argued, the overall future of African American entrepreneurship will depend on opportunities for African American entrepreneurs to penetrate the larger and more profitable consumer markets of the wider society.

SELECTED BIBLIOGRAPHY: Timothy Bates, *Banking on Black Enterprise* (Washington, D.C.: Joint Center for Political and Economic Studies, 1993); Robert L. Boyd, "Black Business Transformation, Black Well-Being, and Public Policy," *Population Research and Policy Review* (May 1990); Robert L. Boyd, "Demographic Change and Entrepreneurial Occupations: African Americans in Northern Cities," *American Journal of Economics and Sociology* (April 1996); Robert L. Boyd, "The Great Migration to the North and the Rise of Ethnic Niches for African American Women in Beauty Culture and Hairdressing, 1910–1920," *Sociological Focus* (February 1996); Andrew F. Brimmer and Henry S. Terrell, "The Economic Potential of Black Capitalism," *Public Policy* (Spring 1971); John Sibley Butler, *Entrepreneurship and Self-Help among African Americans: A Reconsideration of Race and Economics* (Albany: State University of New York Press, 1991); Bart Landry, *The New Black Middle Class* (Berkeley: University of California Press, 1987); Ivan H. Light, *Ethnic Enterprise in America: Business and Welfare among Chinese, Japanese, and Blacks* (Berkeley: University of California Press, 1972).

Robert L. Boyd

MARKET STRUCTURE BARRIERS, BLACK-OWNED BUSINESS. In virtually every instance, black business receipts are concentrated in highly competitive industries and sectors in which the barriers to entry are low. Such a pattern presents a fundamental challenge to both black owners and black workers. For owners, the highly competitive industries in which black receipts are concentrated are characterized by lower profit margins and higher firm turnover rates. For workers, the near absence of black-owned firms in the less competitive industries suggests that black-owned firms will provide little pressure in reducing earnings or employment discrimination that may persist in those industries. This is unfortunate as these same less competitive industries have been identified as the ones more likely to engage in racial discrimination.

In 1987 the gross receipts of black-owned businesses totaled nearly $20 billion, slightly less than 1 percent of the total receipts of all U.S. businesses. This low percentage for a minority group comprising almost 13 percent of the U.S. population suggests that potential black entrepreneurs face substantial barriers to successful entry. This suggestion is confirmed by detailed examination of the pattern of black-owned business across the major sectors and individual industries of the economy.

Economists often focus on barriers to entry when determining whether an industry is structurally competitive. The existing firms in a market will be successful in coordinating a higher price only if there are relatively few of them and their actions are protected by barriers that forestall otherwise profitable entry by new firms. These barriers may include patents, scale economies, unique knowledge, specialized production techniques, great brand loyalty (generated from advertising), and large capital requirements together with imperfect capital markets. Thus, the entry barriers to the automobile or mainframe computer industry are substantially greater than are the barriers to retail trade or much of the service industry. As a consequence, new domestic entry will be frequent in the latter industries but very rare in industries such as computers and autos. Industries with low barriers to entry will be characterized with many firms and active competition. Industries with high barriers to entry will be characterized by relatively few firms and a heightened chance of cooperative behavior that reduces the strength of competition.

This realization seems key in understanding the pattern of black-owned business. In 1987, black business was disproportionately concentrated in the service sector, in retail trade, and in transport and utilities and dramatically underrepresented in manufacturing. This largely mirrors the height of barriers to entry. Those sectors with low barriers that can be easily entered are the most competitive and the locus of black business activity. Empirical analysis by Bates shows that minority enterprises are more profitable when entrepreneur human capital (education and specialized skills) is greater. Important, those minority entrepreneurs with greater human capital are largely outside the retail and personal service industries that dominate black business activity. This suggests that the relative lack of formal schooling and specialized skills is a further barrier to entry that helps explain the pattern of black business.

Even the seeming anomaly of transport and utilities actually confirms the role of entry barriers. Of the many modes of transport and types of services in this category, certainly that with the lowest entry barriers is trucking. Here an entrepreneur can enter without specialized skills and for the modest investment of a truck. This single category, which represents about 2.0 percent of total U.S. receipts, represents 5.1 percent of all black receipts. This high black concentration in trucking largely explains the transportation category's prominence in the black distribution. The growth of black receipts in trucking also helps explain the category's relative growth since 1972. In addition to the inherently low barriers to entry in trucking, the deregulation of the trucking industry in the late 1970s helped increase the number of black owner operators. Blacks had been hurt by the limits to entry perpetuated by government regulation. Thus, the conditions of entry (both inherent and government imposed) are crucial in understanding the relative prevalence of black business in the transport and utilities sector.

The low black representation in manufacturing reflects high barriers to entry, often associated with large-scale production, development, and marketing, but hides a great deal of variation within the manufacturing industries. While black-owned manufacturing receipts are less than one half of 1 percent of total U.S. manufacturing receipts, that fraction varies dramatically from industry to industry within manufacturing. Of the 20 broad manufacturing industries identified by the census, two—printing/publishing and lumber/wood products—account for fully one third of all black manufacturing receipts. Those same two broad industries account for only 19 percent of overall U.S. receipts. On the other hand, receipts originating in the production of nonelectrical machinery account for 10.5 percent of overall U.S. receipts but only 4.5 percent of black manufacturing receipts. Even within manufacturing, black business remains concentrated in those industries with relatively low barriers to entry.

At least three studies have attempted detailed statistical analysis of the relationship between barriers to entry and the presence of black-owned firms. In 1986 Woolf collected data on 52 moderately disaggregated manufacturing industries. Regression analysis was used to explore the partial correlation between the share of industry sales produced by black firms and a variety of specific barriers to entry. His results confirmed the role of several barriers. Black shares are significantly lower when advertising expenses are higher, when average firm sizes are larger, and when the product is oriented toward other businesses rather than final consumers. Data collected by Heywood in 1988 on 43 detailed (more disaggregated) industries were used to estimate the partial correlation between the black share of sales and a composite measure of the structure of the industry.

The composite measure was the share of all industry sales accounted for by the four largest firms. This measure reflects, at least in part, the height of entry barriers. When that share is high, the black share of sales is routinely and substantially lower even after accounting for other variables that might influence the black share.

The 1985 Ando study created a panel of minority business formation rates generated across broad industries, region of the country, and minority group (Asian, Hispanic, and black). Regression analysis on the panel reveals that both capital intensity and higher concentration ratios are associated with lower minority business formation rates. In addition, it reveals that in those industries in which a particular minority group has a relatively large share of salaried managers, that same minority group also has higher business formation rates. This again highlights the role of the relevant skills required for successful entry: The skills learned as a managerial employee can be crucial as an owner.

Together these detailed studies confirm the general pattern that black-owned firms are less likely to be found in industries that are less competitive, characterized by a few firms and by high entry barriers. Theoretically this follows naturally from understanding that blacks are, on average, less well positioned to surmount high-entry barriers. They lack entrepreneurial experience, since blacks are only one-fourth as likely as the general population to be self-employed. Also, blacks often lack crucial business skills and contacts and have much lower net wealth. Estimates are as low as $.09 on the dollar compared to white families. These factors, when combined with differential access to capital and banking relationships, make black entry less likely when barriers are high.

This pattern is not, however, only of relevance for the potential black entrepreneur. Rather, it is of interest to all blacks who work, or apply for work, in those industries that are less competitive. Economists have long contended that these industries are the ones that have the latitude to engage in discriminatory hiring and pay policies. The higher profits and barriers to entry allow the firms to pass on the costs of discrimination to customers in ways that firms in competitive industries could not. This theory is nearly four decades old but finds recent confirmation from Peoples in 1994, who found that racial earnings differentials in the 1980s were greater in less competitive U.S. industries.

At the same time it is a well-ingrained part of public policy that the entry of black-owned firms can help eliminate discrimination. Profitable entry by such firms can bid up the earnings of black workers, help change the racial composition of employment, and reduce the ability of white competitors to continue discrimination. Regardless of how well such black entry would actually work to accomplish these goals, the existing pattern of black business is not encouraging. The industries most likely to engage in discrimination are those protected by entry barriers. These same entry barriers make black entry unlikely. With black business concentrated in the most competitive industries and with the least competitive industries the most likely to discriminate, the growth of black business by itself does not hold great promise for reducing employment and earnings differentials. In order for black business entry to substantially reduce such differentials, the entry must be targeted to the industries where market structures are characterized by high entry barriers but yet where such entry is inherently more difficult.

SELECTED BIBLIOGRAPHY: Faith Ando, "An Analysis of Formation and Failure Rates by Industry Groups and Regions" (Minority Business Development Agency, U.S. Department of Commerce, Washington, D.C., November 1985); Timothy Bates, "Entrepreneur Human Capital Endowments and Minority Business Viability," *Journal of Human Resources* 20, 4 (Fall 1985); John Heywood, "Market Structure and the Pattern of Black Owned Firms," *Review of Black Political Economy* 16, 4 (Spring 1988); John Heywood and James Peoples, "Deregulation and the Prevalence of Black Truck Drivers," *Journal of Law and Economics* 37, 1 (April 1994); James Peoples, "Monopolistic Market Structure, Unionization and Racial Wage Differentials," *Review of Economics and Statistics* 76, 1 (February 1994); Arthur Woolf, "Market Structure and Minority Presence: Black-Owned Firms in Manufacturing," *Review of Black Political Economy* 14, 4 (Spring 1986).

John S. Heywood

MATZELIGER, JAN EARNST (1852–1889), inventor, craftsman, artist.

Jan Matzeliger was born in Paramaribo, Surinam. His father was a native of Holland and an engineer by trade, and his mother was a native-born Surinamese woman of African descent. At age 10, he was apprenticed in the shops his father managed, which peaked Matzeliger's interest in mechanics, which would manifest itself later in life. Despite the fact that Matzeliger received no formal education, he revolutionized the shoe industry with his inventions.

In 1871 Matzeliger left Surinam, working first on the seas as a sailor for two years, until he finally settled in Philadelphia in 1873 at the end of the ship's voyage. In 1876, he moved to Lynn, Massachusetts, where he found employment at a shoe factory. As he worked, with an innate ability at problem solving and an aptitude in mechanics, Matzeliger felt impelled to improve the method by which shoes were produced. Using his spare time, he came up with an idea to last shoes, that is, attach the sole to the leather upper by a single machine. Matzeliger's first prototype was constructed of scraps of wood and cigar boxes, held together with wire. Soon thereafter, he built another model with cast iron parts.

Despite the phenomenal impact that Matzeliger's invention would have on the shoe industry, he found it difficult to secure investment capital to establish a factory for manufacturing his machine. He rebuffed his first offer from a purchaser who wanted to buy his idea for $1,500. Despite repeated attempts to secure investment capital, Matzeliger was unsuccessful until he finally received a commitment from C. H. Denlow and M. S. Nichols, who agreed to invest, but at the cost of two-thirds of Matzeliger's profits. Matzeliger was finally granted a patent for his lasting machine, and in 1885 the first factory test was performed. The machine worked without a flaw. Further refinements brought the speed of the machine up to manufacturing 700 pairs of shoes in a single day. Most important, unskilled laborers could operate the machine, replacing skilled artisans in shoemaking, who were paid more than the unskilled machine operators. As a result, the cost of shoes was cut in half within two years of the machine's introduction.

While the Consolidated Lasting Machine Company was created to produce the machinery to utilize this innovative technology, Denlow and Nichols were unable to secure additional capital for shoe manufacturing and were bought out by Sidney W. Winslow, who founded the United Shoe Machinery Corporation with $20 million. Within 12 years, the corporation earned $50 million. Matzeliger, by then, no longer had any financial interest in his invention, a result of his failure to obtain the necessary capital that would have allowed him to profit from his invention. Ultimately, his invention was responsible for doubling wages to factory workers while cutting the cost of shoes in half. In 1991, Matzeliger was honored on postage stamps, cited as the "first black inventor."

SELECTED BIBLIOGRAPHY: Louis Haber, *Black Pioneers of Science and Invention* (New York: Harcourt, Brace & World, 1970); Vivian Ovelton Sammons, ed., *Blacks in Science and Medicine* (New York: Hemisphere Publishing, 1990).

Edward M. Apy

MAYORS, BLACK, AND BLACK BUSINESS. Among the most critical of urban problems is the fragile nature of the economic base of many older central cities. Elements of this problem include industrial job loss, declining retail sales, high unemployment rates, and municipal fiscal problems. In addition, household composition, tenure patterns, and social and physical environments have also been impacted by the industrial restructuring that has been occurring for the past 30 years. The failure of traditional economic development strategies to address these problems has encouraged new reform-minded civic leaders to seek office. During the 1970s and 1980s an African American leadership emerged, which sought to restructure urban development policies to make them more sensitive to the needs of central cities. Among them were the new black mayors elected to hold office in major central cities in the United States who attempted the economic revitalization of their respective cities, particularly the black mayors in Atlanta, Georgia, since 1973. The black mayors in East St. Louis, Illinois, represent the opposite end of the spectrum of the myriad of problems faced by African American mayors during the past three decades in their attempts to develop and implement economic revitalization strategies for their respective cities.

Many of the predominantly African American cities tend to have significant economic and social problems that local governments are asked to address, including high unemployment rates, decreasing tax revenues, and a high incidence of poverty. The 10 metropolitan areas with the largest concentrations of poor accounted for almost half of all ghetto poor. New York alone accounted for more than one-third of the increase of ghetto poor, whereas New York and Chicago combined account for half; adding Philadelphia, Newark, and Detroit brings the total to two-thirds of America's ghetto poor. In addition, Atlanta and Baltimore, unlike many other cities in the South, also had large increases. Frustrated by traditional approaches to urban problems, several cities chose mayors who expressed a commitment to initiating alternative approaches to key economic development policy issues.

The mid-1980s, when African American mayors governed 4 of the 10 largest cities—Chicago (Harold Washington,* 1983–1987), Detroit (Coleman Young, 1974–1993), Los Angeles (Thomas Bradley, 1973–1993), and Philadelphia (Wilson Goode, 1983–1991)—and 19 communities with populations over 100,000, can be considered marking the era of the African American mayors. By 1997 African American mayors governed Atlanta, Detroit, Cleveland, Seattle, Baltimore, Kansas City, St. Louis, Minneapolis, Birmingham, Dallas, San Francisco, and Washington, D.C. When African American mayors began to take office in the 1960s, they faced a new era in central cities. Manufacturing firms were leaving, shutting down, moving to the suburbs or other regions, or moving out of the country altogether. For example, between 1972 and 1982 Chicago and Detroit lost 417,000 jobs in manufacturing, wholesaling, and retailing. Atlanta and Newark lost between 19,000 and 24,000 jobs. Components of additional challenges facing African American mayors included a myriad of municipal fiscal problems, high property taxes, demographic changes, shifts in property values, unfunded federal and state mandates, shifts in federal and state responsibilities and funding priorities, a volatile global economy, declining retail sales, interlocal competition, and high unemployment rates.

Suburbanization and decentralization during the 1950s and 1960s set the stage for the rapid job loss in older cities. There were two important reasons that accounted for employment decentralization. One was the availability of comparatively cheap vacant land in suburbs. Vacant land made new development and growth in suburbs easier and more inexpensive compared to new development in densely built-up older areas. Also, transportation and communications innovations such as the truck, automobile, and telephone facilitated access to suburban areas and so contributed to the surburbanization of industry and retailing.

During the 1970s and 1980s African American mayors throughout the United States were faced with a rising indifference to the fiscal problems of declining central cities by state and particularly national government bodies. Facing constant job loss, disinvestment, and the tax base deterioration, mayors in such major cities as Detroit, Gary (Richard G. Hatcher, 1967–1988), and Newark (Kenneth A. Gibson, 1970–1986) became increasingly dependent on state and federal funds. However, budget constraints, changes in federal economic development programs, and the orientation toward limited federal assistance through block grants to states and municipal governments are reducing the federal role and the contribution of federal resources to meet local needs.

Financial institutions, fearing a contraction in business activity, tightened their lending activities. Many higher-income residents responded to service cuts and tax increases by moving to suburbia. Outward migration of both residents and economic activity, combined with tight local money markets, will generate declining property values. The mobility of capital and willingness of industry to offer itself to the highest bidders unleash destructive competition among cities to attract runaway American businesses or international investment dollars. Irrational and unrestrained competition has led some municipal jurisdictions to seriously compromise their revenue base with lucrative tax abatement incentives or to make rash commitments to finance infrastructure improvements or initiate land use changes through high-risk public indebtedness or fiscally questionable bonding programs. During the 1970s, many of our once financially and economically vibrant cities were now near bankruptcy. In the spring of 1975, New York City was unable to market its debt because the bond market had discovered that New York had, for more than 10 years, been using questionable accounting and borrowing practices to eliminate its annual budget deficits. In 1978, when the state auditor in Ohio discovered the city of Cleveland had overdue accounts in excess of $36 million and a large general fund deficit, a state of emergency was declared. From 1972 to 1992 there have been a reported 103 municipal bankruptcies.

Economic growth is necessary to protect the fiscal base of a community. To achieve this end, growth policies were initiated by many of the African American mayors in partnership with state and federal governments, private organizations such as the Chamber of Commerce, independent groups of bankers and real estate developers, and quasi-governmental bodies such as industrial authorities or planning agencies. John Mollenkopf provided a cogent account of the sources and composition of pro-growth politics at the local level. The guiding principle of the pro-growth framework has been the aggregation of local interests to effect federally authorized local development projects.

Governments at all levels may play a role in promoting growth. In collaboration with private organizations and independent groups, governments may allocate money to bolster a municipality's name and image as a means of attracting industry. In some localities this responsibility may be given to an industrial agency. In this framework, mayors and other government officials are expected to be "ambassadors" to outside investors, traveling to meet them in their home cities, showing them the local community, and answering their questions when business firms come to inspect the community as a possible site for investment. African American mayors of cities over 100,000 using this approach include Atlanta under Andrew Young, Freeman Bosley, Jr., of St. Louis, Norman Rice of Seattle, Ronald Kirk of Dallas, Dennis Archer of Detroit, Michael White of Cleveland, Marc H. Morial of New Orleans, and Kurt L. Schmoke of Baltimore. From the cities listed, only Atlanta Mayor Andrew Young (1973–1982), and Mayor Ernest N. Morial of New Orleans (1978–1986) preceded the era of African American mayors.

Metropolitan Atlanta, considered the "black mecca" of the South, has emerged as the commercial, industrial, and financial center of the southeastern United States during the tenures of three African American mayors—Maynard Jackson (1982–1990), Andrew Young, and Keith "Bill" Campbell (1994–)—and predominantly African American city councils. It is the center for federal operations in this region, as well as the center of communications, transportation, and distribution. The new midfield terminal at Atlanta's Hartsfield Airport is presently the largest in the world (2.2 million square feet) and the largest employer in Georgia. In 1981, the airport employed nearly 30,000 persons and had an annual payroll of $892 million.

More than 430 of the *Fortune* 500 companies have operations in Atlanta. The presence of regional, national, and international corporate headquarters has fostered the development of a large local service sector, including law firms, accounting firms, banks, and insurance companies. Government is a big employer in Atlanta. The city is the capital of Georgia and the seat of Fulton County. Moreover, Atlanta is second only to Washington, D.C., in the number of federal government employees.

A high priority of the Mayor Maynard Jackson administration was the inclusion of minority firms in city contracting. His record on this specific issue is one that clearly points to success. For example, just over 1 percent of the city contracts (that is, $43,759 of the city's $33 million contracts) went to minority firms when Jackson first took office in 1973. By 1983, black business firms accounted for 27 percent of the city's contracts, which totaled nearly $44 million. Mayor Jackson also mandated the minority participation in the new Atlanta airport terminal when he held up more than $400 million of airport construction until contractors complied with the minority participation plan. The contractors complied, and the project was completed on time and within the allotted budget. There were seven *Black Enterprise* "Top 100" firms in the metropolitan area in 1986; the Chicago Standard Metropolitan Statistical Area (SMSA) was the only other area that did as well. In the July 1997 issue of *Governing Magazine* Maynard Jackson was cited as one of the "top five" mayors of all time among major cities.

Much of the effort to promote development in Atlanta's central business district has been undertaken by Central Atlanta Progress. This organization of downtown business interests was first established in 1941 as the Central Atlanta Improvement Association. In 1983, the "Forward Metro Atlanta" marketing campaign was initiated by the Metropolitan Atlanta Council for Economic Development, a body representing the six largest chambers of commerce in the metropolitan area. The $3 million campaign was designed to produce 90,000 jobs in the metropolitan area over a three-year period.

During Mayor Maynard Jackson's tenure, Atlanta experienced dramatic growth in downtown office and motel construction in the 1970s. However, the city's net central area employment declined by 3,500 employees between 1970 and 1978. All categories experienced growth during this period, with the exception of manufacturing jobs, which declined by 2.3 percent. Despite attempts to bolster the central-city economy, the total labor force in Atlanta declined during the 1970–1980 period. While 50 percent of the city's labor force were employed in professional, managerial, technical, clerical, and sales occupations in 1970, over 54 percent of the city's labor force were employed in these occupations in 1980. The city has been losing blue-collar jobs. The city had a net loss of more than 8,000 manufacturing jobs between 1970 and 1978. The largest decreases were in craftsmen, foremen, and operatives occupations.

Atlanta has become a major convention and trade center. It ranked third in the number of conventions hosted annually. In 1982, almost 1.3 million convention delegates visited Atlanta, boosting the city's economy by more than $500 million. Over 75,000 Atlanta blacks were employed in the convention and tourism industry in 1980, with approximately 50 percent in unskilled job categories. Atlanta's Visitor and Convention Bureau estimated that more than 8,760 new hotel rooms were constructed in 1985, with approximately one new job for each room. African American workers continue to be concentrated in the low-paying service jobs of the convention industry.

While many of Atlanta's black middle class did benefit from the city's white-collar economy, many low-income, poorly educated residents found few of their needs met during the boom that the Atlanta Metropolitan Area experienced in the 1960s and 1970s. The economic renaissance has largely been concentrated in the mostly white suburban counties that encircle the city. Many central-city residents are isolated from the employment and housing opportunities because of inadequate transportation and the outright discrimination that occurs in the suburbs. Atlanta's greatest challenge is to move the city's large underclass into the economic mainstream. The solution to this dilemma seems to be tied to the white business establishment, which holds the economic purse strings.

Paradoxically, the political unpopularity of urban revitalization programs makes it difficult for African American mayors to pursue the types of policies most apt to attract private capital to the central city. As a consequence, large sections of many central cities' downtown districts remain riddled with abandoned, crumbling, and fire-scarred buildings. The blight extends far beyond downtown, where block after block of substandard homes and vandalized projects are reminiscent of a wartime aftermath. Incompatible land uses and home-made structures are common, especially in the older areas surrounding the central business district. However, housing and land conditions comprise only one aspect of the adverse physical environment. Streets, buildings, school buildings, and recreational buildings are also seriously deteriorated.

Declining property values create a need for higher local taxes and/or cuts in services. The city economy spirals downward; local employment opportunities diminish. If local government does not cater to the interests of the business community, firms will cut back drastically on their local investment plans. Thus, even in cities where African Americans have achieved political control, they are almost forced to become hostages to the economic interests of the corporate elite. Firms that had contemplated moving job-generating activities into central cities were inclined to locate in "friendlier" environments.

The truest reality faced by African American mayors is the fact that black people in the United States function essentially as appendages to the body of the American economic system. They are not connected in any significant way with capitalism's most important objective, the creation of surplus value or wealth. The machines, the plants, the oil wells, and the stock certificates, which represent capital value and play such an important part in contributing to individual and institutional economic freedom and power, are owned and controlled entirely by whites. It is whites alone who primarily own the means of production and engage in production of goods. African Americans, on the other hand, have a labor-based economy. They have no capital, blacks own nearly no machinery, and they do not control any noticeable part of the means of production. The control of capital, particularly in corporate hands, plays such an important role in the allocation of employment and other valued positions.

If declining cities are to have a healthy economic future, they must generate and build upon new industries. This will require mayors at the local level to improve business climates and to build modern infrastructure and facilities required by businesses today. In many cases, it will require direct public assistance from state and federal government, in addition to businesses to neutralize the cost disadvantage of cities, particularly land and local tax costs. In the case of mature cities, the problems met in trying to link development policy and capital allocation are primarily financial and political. Mature cities lack funds to address even the most serious capital needs. They are seeking to finance capital renovation and maintenance at the same time they are beset by demands for increased delivery of social services. While citizens expect service levels to increase or at least be maintained, the exodus of taxpaying residents and businesses makes this increasingly difficult, creating an ever-widening gap between needs and revenues.

SELECTED BIBLIOGRAPHY: Timothy Bates and Daniel R. Fusfield, *The Political Economy of the Urban Black Ghetto* (Carbondale: Southern Illinois University Press, 1984); E. J. Kuler, "The Impact of Black Mayors on Urban Policy," *Annals of the American Academy of Political and Social Science* 439 (Spring 1978); John H. Mollenkopf, *The Contested City* (Princeton: Princeton University Press, 1983); W. R. Nelson, Jr., "Black Mayors as Urban Managers," *Annals of the American Academy of Political and Social Sciences* 439 (Spring 1978): 53–67; G. A. Persons, "Reflections on Mayoral Leadership: The Impact of Changing Issues and Changing Times," *Phylon* 46 (Spring 1985): 205–218; Ishaq Shafiq, "Economic Development in East St. Louis: The Carl Officer Administration, 1979–1991" (master's thesis, University of Illinois at Urbana, 1992).

Ishaq Shafiq

McWORTER, FREE FRANK (1777–1854), Kentucky, Illinois, slave entrepreneur, saltpeter manufactury, frontier land speculator, commercial farmer, town founder.

The life of Free Frank, a black pioneer, is very unique. He participated in the development of three successive frontiers in the period between the Revolutionary War and the Civil War. Free Frank McWorter was one of the nation's unknown entrepreneurs, and his business activities offer a new frame of reference for our understanding not only of the history of blacks in business but also of African American participation in the development of America's frontiers. Free Frank was born a slave in Union County, South Carolina. His mother was the West African-born Juda; his father was slave owner Scotch-Irish George McWhorter.

His owner-father moved to Kentucky in 1795. By 1810 Free Frank began hiring his own time.* During the War of 1812, Free Frank became a slave entrepreneur. He established an extractive mining operation and manufactory for the production of saltpeter from crude niter. Profits remaining after paying his owner for allowing him to hire his own time enabled Free Frank to purchase his wife's freedom in 1817 and then himself, two years later in 1819. After purchasing his own freedom, the pioneer entrepreneur's repertoire of business pursuits included frontier land speculator, commercial farmer, stock raiser, town founder, and town developer.

Free Frank left Pulaski County, Kentucky, in September 1830 for Illinois. He was able to settle in the state legally because he purchased land before he left. Without capital, free blacks were required by Illinois law to post a $1,000 bond to settle in the state. In 1836, Free Frank founded the town of New Philadelphia, thus becoming the first African American town founder. His purpose was clear: The money obtained from the sale of town lots would be used to buy his family from slavery, in addition to his profits from commercial farming and cattle raising.

In addition to selling town lots and encouraging town business, the most significant activity in which Free Frank was involved in promoting and developing New Philadelphia at this time was his plan to build a private school that would also serve as a church. It was to be called the Free Will Baptist Seminary. The Free Frank family remained constantly prepared to provide aid to the escaped slaves. In a span of 40 years, with money earned from his business activities on the frontier, Free Frank purchased 16 family members, including himself, from slavery with a total cost of some $15,000, which he made from his diverse business enterprises.

In 1988, Free Frank's grave site was entered into the National Register of Historic Places. In Illinois, only three graves are listed on the National Register, the other two being President Abraham Lincoln and Stephen Douglas. In 1990, the significance of Free Frank's entrepreneurial activities, especially the founding of New Philadelphia, also won recognition in the *Congressional Record* and the Illinois General Assembly. Despite those honors, few Americans, black or white, are aware of Free Frank's New Philadelphia, the black presence on the Old Northwest Frontier, or the historic tradition of black entrepreneurship/business participation in the period before the Civil War.

SELECTED BIBLIOGRAPHY: George C. Fraser, *Success Runs in Our Race: The Complete Guide to Effective Networking in the African-American Community* (New York: William Morrow and Company, Inc., 1994); Benjamin Quarles, *Black Abolitionists* (New York: Oxford University Press, 1969); Juliet E. K. Walker, *Free Frank: A Black Pioneer on the Antebellum Frontier* (Lexington: University Press of Kentucky, 1983; paper ed., 1995).

Jeffrey E. Walker

MICHAUX, LIGHTFOOT SOLOMON [ELDER], (1885–1968), Washington, D.C., businessman, Independent Church evangelist.

Whether dressed in a neat suit and tie or clothed in a black robe and skullcap, Lightfoot Solomon Michaux cut a flamboyant figure of black evangelicanism. The founder of the grassroots Church of God Movement, Michaux rose to prominence in the 1920s. Subsequently, he won national fame through a "War on the Devil" mission he waged over national radio and under traveling revival tents. He remained influential well into the 1960s, combining religious missionary zeal with a program of social welfare and shrewd business enterprise.

Michaux was born in 1885 in Buckroe Beach, Virginia. From the beginning, he was exposed to the possibilities of black self-employment. His father operated a seafood business, and while the young boy received some formal education in public school, he quit to work full-time. As an 11-year-old, Michaux peddled seafood for his father to local well-to-do whites and military personnel in nearby Petersburg. Michaux began to hone not only business skills but also the talents of personal persuasion that would serve him later. Demonstrating an uncommon acumen for his age, Michaux invested his savings at the black-owned Sons and Daughters of Peace Penny, Nickel and Dime Savings Bank. This apparently paid off in 1904, when Michaux opened his own seafood and poultry shop.

Supplementing this investment, he also opened a dance school, where he met Mary Eliza Pauline. The two wed in 1906 but never had children. Mary was to become Lightfoot's lifelong religious partner. At her insistence, they began attending Saint Timothy Church of Christ, where he became the secretary-treasurer. While Mary, an avid convert to evangelicalism, concerned herself with saving their souls, Lightfoot busily tended to business: In the midst of the World War I mobilization effort, he increased the family's fortunes through government contracts to supply provisions to U.S. vessels. He reinvested these profits in new stores in Hopewell, Virginia, where they lived.

In 1917, Mary, dissatisfied with mainstream Baptist congregations, was encouraged by Lightfoot to conduct their own services. Named "Everybody's Mission," the church was nondenominational and interracial. Initially, Michaux attended services only at his wife's entreaties. It was not until an elder in the church challenged him to take the pulpit that Michaux considered trading his lifestyle as a prosperous businessman for religious leadership. Michaux subsequently joined the black, southern-based "Holiness" movement, affiliating with the Church of Christ. From this institution, he received counsel in scriptural interpretation. In 1919, he organized a local Church of Christ assembly in Newport News, Virginia.

He seceded from the church in 1921, taking his congregation with him, and moved into a recently bought three-story structure. That same year, his Gospel Spreading Tabernacle Building Association won incorporation under Virginia law. As the church's financial vehicle, it received funds, paid debts, and accumulated property. On this economic foundation, the congregation was able to fund outreach and recruitment. Michaux proved to be as tireless an evangelist as he had been a businessman and established assemblies in Hampton, Virginia; Baltimore, Maryland; and by 1928, Washington, D.C. The average member was a young black laboring migrant, aged 19 to 30 and disoriented by the vagaries of urban life. However, membership also included black professionals and white shopkeepers and workers.

In a later period, honorary deacons included Harry Butcher, vice president of the Columbia Broadcasting Company, and U.S. President Dwight Eisenhower. Curiously, meetings in Maryland even drew avowed members of the Ku Klux Klan receptive to Michaux's messages of Victorian morality and patriotism. Indeed, a strict code of moral cleanliness governed members' behavior, particularly women's. Michaux apparently took to heart a gospel that acknowledged neither race nor class. He conducted integrated baptisms, arranged whites and blacks to room together in the church's building, and held integrated church services. In 1926, Virginia authorities arrested Michaux for violating state statutes prohibiting race mixing in places of public accommodation and assembly. However, Michaux ignored such laws and increasingly used radio, and later television, broadcasting to facilitate his message.

During the depression of the 1930s Michaux's church provided food and shelter for evicted tenants and even collected evictees' furniture from the curbsides. However, such initiatives may not have been possible without the church's business pursuits. The church published the monthly *Happy News*, which had a peak circulation of 8,000. It also operated an employment agency, farms, orphanages, schools, hotels, and an eatery named the Happy News Cafe. Michaux was an ardent supporter of the New Deal. His most ambitious project was a partnership leading to the development and ownership of the Mayfair Mansions. Federally subsidized, the complex provided some 594 apartments for middle- and working-class blacks.

While social welfare figured prominently in the church's program, Michaux's politics, however, often were questionable. In the 1960s, he not only opposed black nationalist leaders like the Nation of Islam's* Elijah Muhammad* but also criticized civil rights activists like Martin Luther King, Jr., for racial polarization. Friendly acquaintances included Federal Bureau of Investigation (FBI) director J. Edgar Hoover. When Michaux died in October 1968, 3,000 people attended his funeral services, and Hoover eulogized him in a telegram. Such relationships may tend to support contemporaries' claim that Michaux was more committed to battling the devil than fighting racism.

Yet Micheaux's legacy is perhaps more complex. While there were similarities between him and his contemporaries, including Bishop "Daddy" Grace and Father Divine,* Micheaux criticized them for milking their congregations for personal fortune. Even so, before his death, accusations arose from his congregation that Micheaux transferred church funds to personal accounts. Also, through its mixture of religious vocation and business enterprise, the Church of God was, organizationally, a forerunner to the Nation of Islam, despite the enmity that existed between Muhammad and Micheaux. However, Micheaux's group advanced a social welfare agenda that made it particularly distinct in its day and the present.

With his prominence, Micheaux was an adviser to U.S. presidents Franklin D. Roosevelt and Dwight Eisenhower. In the late 1990s, Micheaux's church survives as the Gospel Spreading Church of God. It is based on the East Coast in Newport News, Virginia; New York City; and Washington, D.C., which is the site of its major edifice.

SELECTED BIBLIOGRAPHY: Lillian Ashcraft Webb, *About My Father's Business: The Life of Elder Michaux* (Westport, CT: Greenwood Press, 1981).

Clarence Lang

MICHEAUX, OSCAR (c. 1884–1951), South Dakota, New York City, Chicago, movie producer.

Inspired by Booker T. Washington's* philosophy of economic empowerment through landownership and black business development, Oscar Micheaux began his career as a homesteader by purchasing a relinquished homestead on part of the Rosebud Reservation in South Dakota that had been opened for "settlement" by the Dawes Act of 1913. After overcoming the hardships of establishing a successful farm in spite of the attempts of his white neighbors to sell him inferior farming equipment and animals, the death of his wife during childbirth, and the hostile environment of what was known as the "great Northwest," Micheaux turned to writing novels: *The Conquest* (1913); *The Forged Note* (1915); *The Homesteader* (1917); and *The Wind from Nowhere* (1941).

He considered these novels as another business venture, since he controlled the production of them from start to finish, by submitting to the press a print-worthy original of his manuscript, paying in cash for the publication of his novels, and distributing them himself by selling door to door his texts to African Americans throughout the Midwest and South. His novels were appealing to African Americans, since Micheaux attempted in them to present a critique of black urban life, of the problems that plagued African Americans who lived in the cities, and to offer a possible solution to the predicament in which black people found themselves. His solution was that African Americans should abandon the cities and look at the Great Plains as a place where they could build an alternative to American urban society.

Micheaux's attempts to popularize his novels led him to filmmaking. In 1918, after having established the Western Book and Supply Company in Sioux City, Iowa, to produce and distribute his novels, he was contacted by George P. Johnson, general booking manager of the black-owned and -operated Lincoln Film Company of Los Angeles, California, who had read *The Homesteader*. Johnson, who also operated an office in Omaha, Nebraska, contacted Micheaux about the possibility of producing *The Homesteader* for the Lincoln Film Company. In May 1918, Micheaux traveled to Omaha to sign a contract with Johnson to go to Los Angeles and experience the filming of *The Homesteader*. But Micheaux's desire to supervise the actual filming of the production, combined with his lack of experience in directing, caused the contract to fall through.

This experience led Micheaux to form his own film company. In the latter part of 1918, he formed the Micheaux Film and Book Company with offices in Sioux City and Chicago. As he had done previously with the Western Book and Supply Co., Micheaux sold stock in the newly formed film and book company to white farmers around Sioux City. He finally raised enough money from selling shares to produce *The Homesteader* as an eight-reel film. Subsequent to the initial production of *The Homesteader*, Micheaux produced over 44 black-cast films nationally, some of which were distributed in Europe. His films were not widely distributed because he refused to propagandize them. He felt that black people did not want racial propaganda, such as that evident in many of the films produced by Hollywood and by some of the white independents, but that they wanted a good story, a film that mirrored reality and reflected the social, economic, and political conditions under which African Americans existed in America.

In an article published in the *Philadelphia Afro-American* (January 24, 1925), Micheaux stressed that film is an art that requires extraordinary "encouragement and financial backing," neither of which he received in great amounts. The black producer, Micheaux asserts, dares to "step into a world which has hitherto remained closed to him. His entrance into this unexplored field is, for him, trebly difficult. He is united in his themes, in obtaining casts that present genuine ability, and in his financial resources."

Although most of his critics have taken him to task for casting light-skinned African Americans in leading roles, for imitating the manners and sensibilities of white society, and for using his people as plastic models, Micheaux did not attempt to shield himself from criticism. In the same article cited above, he comments, "I do not wish anyone to construe this as a request for the suppression of criticism. Honest, intelligent criticism is an aid to the progress of an effort. The producer who has confidence in his ideals, politics, constructive criticism . . . also asks fairness, and fairness in criticism demands a familiarity with the aims of the producer, and a knowledge of the circumstances under which his efforts were materialized."

Nonetheless, many of his critics categorized his films as second-rate "underground" films, comparable to a Hollywood C-grade production. After Micheaux released a seven-reel feature, *The Dungeon*, in 1922, the *Chicago Defender* criticized him for using light-skinned actors and for not advertising the film as a "race" promotion. D. Ireland Thomas, commenting on this film, wrote: "The advertising matter for this production has nothing to indicate that the feature is colored, as the characters are very bright; in fact almost white." At this time, the *Defender* had a national circulation, and its critique would have an impact on black filmgoers, particularly since it also emphasized in that review that " 'The All-Star Colored Cast' that is so noticeable with nearly every race production is omitted on the cards and lithographs. Possibly Mr. Micheaux is relying on his name alone to tell the public that it is a race production or maybe he is after booking it in white theatres."

These criticisms ignore the fact that Micheaux produced films under difficult circumstances, lacking the funding necessary to achieve high technical standards and the ability to produce special effects and stage massive action scenes. He usually did all of the work in his productions, except for perfunctory tasks. He wrote scenarios, supervised filming, handled bookkeeping, and so on. His pictures took an average of 10 days to shoot and usually cost between $10,000 and $20,000. Once the production of a film was under way, Micheaux would often make a contract with a theater to supply him with money in return for the theater receiving first rights to showing the films. He would take several of the actors with him on the train to visit prospective patrons. The actors would perform a couple of scenes from the script for the theater manager as prospective donor, while Micheaux emphasized the importance and marketability of the script.

In 1920 Micheaux's brother Swan joined him as manager of Micheaux Film and Book Company. Later Swan Micheaux was promoted to secretary and treasurer and general booking manager. In 1921, the corporation had a cash dividend of 25 percent and established an office in New York City for better facilities and actors, although the distribution and financial office remained in Chicago under the supervision of Swan Micheaux and Charles Benson. Micheaux was enterprising enough to secure a number of firms to distribute his films: Tiffany Tolliver and W. R. Crowell distributed his films in the East from a branch office in Roanoke, Virginia, whereas A. Odanes, owner of the Verdun Theater in Beaumont, Texas, distributed the films in the Southwest.

Between 1918 and 1931, Micheaux produced 27 films, most of which were silent. His first all-sound feature was *The Exile* (1931), which was made from his novel *The Homesteader*. Between 1931 and 1940 he produced and directed 16 all-sound features. In 1948 he wrote the screenplay for and directed *The Betrayal* for Astor Pictures Corporation, which was adopted from his novel *Wind from Nowhere*. This was Micheaux's last known film activity. This film opened in a white movie theater in downtown New York to poor reviews. The lack of financial resources forced Micheaux to file a voluntary petition of bankruptcy in 1928. At this time, the Micheaux Film Company listed assets at $1,400 and liabilities at $7,837. Yet his perseverance, combined with the ingenuity of Alice Russell, an actress Micheaux married in 1929, allowed him to reorganize the company as a new corporation in New York State during the latter part of 1929 with new money. The officers of this newly formed corporation were Oscar Micheaux, president, Frank Scheiffman, vice president, and Leo Bracheer, treasurer.

When Micheaux died in Charlotte, North Carolina, the Micheaux Film Corporation was virtually bankrupt. In spite of this, Oscar Micheaux's entrepreneurial activities won for himself the distinction of the first independent African American film director and producer. His legacy continues today with the Micheaux Film Society in Oakland, California.

SELECTED BIBLIOGRAPHY:Donald Bogle, *Toms, Coons, Mulattoes, Mammies and Bucks* (New York: Viking, 1973); Thomas Cripps, *Slow Fade to Black* (New York: Oxford University Press, 1977); Chester J. Fontenot, Jr., "Oscar Micheaux: Black Novelist and Filmmaker," in Frederick Luebke, ed., *Vision and Refuge: Ethnic Writers on the Great Plains* (Lincoln: University of Nebraska Press, 1980); Chester J. Fontenot, Jr., "Oscar Micheaux as Mythmaker," *Journal of American Studies* (Spring 1979); Henry T. Sampson, *Blacks in Black and White: A Source Book on Black Films* (Metuchen, NJ: Scarecrow Press, 1977).

Chester J. Fontenot, Jr.

MINORITY-OWNED BUSINESSES, 1992 SURVEY. Information in the 1992 Survey of Minority-Owned Business Enterprises (SMOBE) illuminates the advances made by minorities between 1987 and 1992. The specific racial and ethnic groups designated as minorities by the U.S. Bureau of the Census include black (African Americans), Hispanics (identified by surname, can be any race), Asian and Pacific Islanders and American Indians and Alaska Natives (API/AIAN). Women of all races are considered minorities, but SMOBE assessments were gender specific. Following is information on businesses owned by minority males. Based on both the "1992 Characteristics of Business Owners" (CBO) and the 1992 SMOBE data on percentage increases in the number of firms and sales receipts, minority businesses outpaced comparable gains made in businesses owned by white (non-Hispanic) males. While gains made by African American male business owners surpassed those made by white male business owners, those made by Hispanic- and API/AIAN-owned businesses surpassed both white and black business in percentage increases in number of firms and business income of all U.S. firms.

In 1992 the total number of all U.S. firms was 17,253,143, including the 2,149,184 minority-owned firms that comprised 12.5 percent of all American firms. Black-owned firms in 1992 numbered 620,912, 3.6 percent of all U.S. firms, up from 3.1 percent (424,165) in 1987. Hispanic firms also comprised 3.1 percent of all U.S. firms in 1987, but in 1992, the 862,605 Hispanic-owned firms comprised 5.0 percent of all U.S. firms. The 705,672 API/AIAN firms comprised 4.1 percent of all U.S. firms, up from 2.8 percent of all U.S. firms in 1987. Consequently, while the total number of all the nation's firms increased 26 percent by 1992, from 13.7 million in 1987, there was a 60 percent increase in minority-owned businesses, up from 1,343,910 firms in 1987 to 2,149,184 in 1992. Yet, while black-owned firms increased 46 percent from 424,165 to 620,912 firms, the 439,271 API/AIAN firms in 1987 had increased 61 percent by 1992. Hispanic firms, however, showed the largest increase, 76 percent, up from 489,973 firms to 862,605 in that five-year period.

Also, from 1987 to 1992, while the total U.S. business sales and receipts increased 67 percent from $2 trillion to $3.2 trillion, minority-owned firms showed a 128 percent increase, up from $92.1 billion to $210.0 billion. The receipts of black-owned firms increased 63 percent from $19.8 billion to $32.2 billion. Hispanic business receipts, however, increased 134 percent from $32.8 billion to $76.8 billion, while business receipts of API/AIAN firms showed the most spectacular increase, 159 percent, from $40 billion to $104 billion. (API receipts increased 163 percent from $36.5 billion to $96.0 billion.)

Despite the percentage and dollar increases made by minority firms in 1992, the business sales of minority firms amounted to only 6.3 percent, $209,739,000, of the $3.3 trillion of all U.S. firms. Even then, it was only with African Americans that the percentage amount of business receipts of all U.S. receipts did not change. In 1987 black business receipts accounted for 1.0 of all U.S. business receipts. In 1992 black business receipts still accounted for 1.0 percent of all U.S. business receipts. Hispanic business receipts, 1.2 percent of all U.S. business receipts in 1987, however, increased to 2.3 percent in 1992, while API/AIAN business receipts increased from 1.75 percent in 1987 to 3.1 percent in 1992. Consequently, despite a substantial absolute dollar increase in sales and business receipts made by African Americans from 1987 to 1992, the percentage amount of their sales did not contribute to the percentage increase in sales from 3.95 percent in 1987 to 6.3 percent in 1992 made by minority businesses in the United States during that five-year period.

Assessing the comparative average mean income of American business provides another indicator of minority business performance. In 1992 the average mean income of all American business firms was $193,000. With non-Hispanic white male business owners, the mean income average in business receipts was $250,000 (non-Hispanic white women business owners had a mean income average of $115,000). The mean business income average for all minority firms was $98,000, but for API/AIAN firms, the mean business income was $165,000. Males in this group averaged $188,000, while API/AIAN women business owners had mean average receipts of $119,000. The mean business income for Hispanic-owned firms was $94,000. Male business owners had a mean income average of $106,000, and Hispanic women business owners had a mean average of $70,000.

The mean average of African American business owners in 1992, however, was $52,000. African American male business owners had a mean income average of $69,000, while African American women business owners had a mean income average of $31,000. Based on comparative assessments of minority business performance, growth in number of firms and percentage income increases, the advances made in business by Hispanic and API/AIAN exceeded those of African Americans.

Some economists insist, however, that the business performance rates of African Americans would have been much greater had information from all black businesses been included in the 1992 SMOBE. Certainly, this assessment has merit. Indeed, as a result of the sampling methodology, limiting the selection of firms by legal forms of business organization, the SMOBE is not inclusive. Specifically, the sampling was taken from three groups of businesses: sole proprietorships, an unincorporated business owned by an individual; partnerships, unincorporated business owned by 2 or more people; and, subchapter S corporations, incorporated businesses with up to, but no more than 35 shareholders. The SMOBE, however, did not include information from "C" corporation businesses owned by blacks. A "C" corporation is any incorporated business, other than a subchapter S corporation, and can have an unlimited number of shareholders.

The 1992 survey on women business enterprises, however, did include "C" corporations, which showed 520,000 of the 6.4 million firms owned by women were "C" corporations, which generated $932 billion of the $1.6 trillion made by women-owned businesses. In reviewing African American business activity economist Thomas D. Boston found, based on his study of black business in Atlanta, Georgia, that the fastest growing and the most successful businesses owned by black men were "C" corporations. Since the 1992 SMOBE did not include information on these enterprises, assessments of black business development in the twentieth century and especially those that focus on black business ownership since 1969 emphasize that the SMOBE does not reflect the full extent of black business activity.

Yet, these same assessments would apply to analysis of the business performance of other minorities, since data on Hispanic and API/AIAN owned "C" corporations were also excluded from the SMOBE. Moreover, based on Internal Revenue Service (IRS) tax forms, 94 percent of black businesses in 1992 were sole proprietorships, and 2 to 4 percent were partnerships and subchapter S corporations. With Hispanic businesses, 89 percent were sole proprietorships, while partnerships and subchapter S corporations comprised 4 to 7 percent. With API/AIAN firms, 83 percent were sole proprietorships, while partnership and subchapter S corporations comprised 8 to 9 percent. At the most, then, 4 percent of African American, 7 percent of Hispanic, and up to 9 percent of API/AIAN businesses could be "C" corporations.

Consequently, while the business picture of black firms would show improvement with inclusion of black-owned "C" corporation data, the relative position of black firms to other minority firms, doubtless, would show few substantial comparative changes. Indeed, based on the 1992 SMOBE, even with the inclusion of information from black-owned "C" corporations, the prospective comparative business picture for African Americans in the twenty-first century, despite anticipated growth, realistically might be much more bleak than it is now.

In 1992, for example, almost half, 46 percent or 904,226, of all minority businesses had receipts under $10,000, while only 1.2 percent, or 23,380, had sales of $1.0 million or more. With API/AIAN businesses, 12,517 firms in this group had sales of $1.0 million or more, while 212,928 or 35 percent had receipts under $10,000. Among Hispanics, 9,200 business firms had sales of $1.0 million or more, while 359,588 firms, 47 percent, had receipts under $10,000. With African American businesses, 56 percent had receipts of less than $10,000, while only 3,000 firms had sales that exceeded $1.0 million.

The majority of minority business owners in 1992 launched their enterprises with less than $5,000, including 66 percent of firms started by African Americans. API/AIAN-owned firms started with the most capital, 10 percent of these firms were launched with $100,000 or more. Also, only 64,478 of the 620,912 black businesses were firms with paid employees. There were 345,193 people employed by black firms with payrolls that totaled $4.8 billion. Of the 862,605 Hispanic firms, 115,364 had paid employees (691,056) and payrolls amounting to $10.7 billion. Of the 705,672 API/AIAN firms, 136,363 firms had 861,026 paid employees and payrolls that totaled $13.3 billion.

Analysis of African American business, then, should be informed by assessments that include information on the business performance of other minority groups. Simply put, given the present comparative minority business picture, especially within the context of changing U.S. racial demographics, to what extent will the picture of African American business show even a comparative improvement? As recently as 1975, blacks comprised 90 percent of the minority population. In 1980 African Americans comprised 12 percent of the U.S. population, Hispanics, 6 percent, API, 2 percent, and AIAN 1 percent. In 1995, African Americans numbered 33 million, 13 percent of the population, Hispanics, 26.8 million, 10 percent, API, 9.2 million or 4 percent, AIAN, 2.2 million or 1 percent, and 193.3 million, 74 percent of the U.S. population were non-Hispanic whites.

Certainly, the comparative business performance of African Americans (as much the income and wealth of blacks), is a cause for national action. And, contrary to popular assessments and conservative public policy analysis, African American business performance rates at the close of the twentieth century cannot be attributed to the absence of a historic tradition of business activity. Simply put, despite racism and slavery, black business activity dates to the 1600s in Colonial America, while in the 1990s 45 percent of Hispanic business owners and 63 percent of Asian and Pacific Islander business owners were not born in the United States.

SELECTED BIBLIOGRAPHY: Thomas D. Boston, ''Characteristics of Black Owned Corporations in Atlanta (With Comments on SMOBE Undercount),'' *Review of Black Political Economy* 23, 4 (Spring 1995); Melvin Oliver and Thomas M. Shapiro, *Black Wealth, White Wealth: A New Perspective on Racial Inequality* (New York: Routledge,

1995); U.S. Bureau of the Census: "1992 Black-Owned Business" (MB92–1); idem, "1992 Survey of Minority-Owned Business Enterprises, Hispanic" (MB92–2); idem, "1992 Minority- and Women-Owned Business Enterprises" (MB92–4); U.S. Bureau of the Census, at http://www.census.gov/agfs/www.smobe.htlm; for "Income," http://www.census.gov/hhes/www/income97.html; for "Poverty," http://www.census.gov/hhes/www/povty97.html; for "Summary of Findings Characteristic of Business Owners (CBO)," http://www.census.gov/agfs/cbo/view/sum.txt; Census Bureau Public Information Office at (301) 763–5726 and e-mail pio@census.gov

Juliet E. K. Walker

MONTGOMERY, BENJAMIN T. (1819–1878), Mississippi, entrepreneur, cotton plantation owner, merchant, inventor, mechanic, civil engineer.

As a slave Ben Montgomery was purchased by Joseph Davis, and his brother Jefferson Davis, to work on the Davis Bend plantations. He was an expert in carpentry, designing, and building his own instruments. In the late 1850s, he invented a boat propeller. Jefferson Davis was unsuccessful in gaining a patent for the propeller in Montgomery's name. At the same time, Benjamin was given a great deal of business latitude. In 1842, the slave established a merchandise store on the Davis Bend plantations. The Davis slaves traded or sold commodities produced through their independent economic activities, including wood, eggs, and vegetables in exchange for, or purchase of, dry goods and staples.

The whites on the Davis plantations also purchased goods at Montgomery's store, which was also the post office for the Davis plantations, with Montgomery acting as postmaster, notwithstanding that it was illegal for slaves to handle U.S. mail. Indeed, one riverboat captain complained to the Postmaster General, who refused to interfere with the Davis management of their slaves. In addition, because of Montgomery's business acumen, he was assigned by Joseph Davis to act as business manager of his plantation, which included responsibilities of an agent in buying supplies and arranging for the sale of the cotton crop.

After the Civil War, Montgomery in 1866 was extended long-term credit, which enabled him to purchase the Davis Bend plantations, 4,000 acres, for $300,000, at $18,000 annual interest. By 1873, Montgomery's cotton production was the third largest in Mississippi. By 1877, Benjamin's net worth was reported to be $230,000. He eventually lost the plantations, which reverted back to the Davis family.

SELECTED BIBLIOGRAPHY: Janet Sharp Hermann, *The Pursuit of a Dream* (New York: Oxford University Press, 1981); George Alexander Sewell, *Mississippi Black History Makers* (Jackson: University Press of Mississippi, 1977).

Quincy T. Mills

MORGAN, GARRETT AUGUSTUS (1877–1963), Ohio, inventor, manufacturer, newspaper publisher, civic leader.

Garrett Augustus Morgan, a prolific early twentieth-century inventor, is best known for his invention of the modern gas mask and the first automatic traffic signal. Morgan's first invention, however, was a belt fastener for sewing machines, which he developed in 1901 and later sold for $150. In 1907 he opened his own sewing machine and repair shop, and in 1909, a tailoring shop. Using designs created by his wife, the shop rapidly expanded into a clothing firm that manufactured dresses, suits, and coats. Within a year, Morgan's company employed 32 workers. Profits from this business provided venture capital for Morgan's next enterprise, a hair products manufacturing company, which also developed from one of his inventions.

Then, while looking for a more effective lubricant that would reduce the probability of scorching the materials that were being sewn by rapidly moving needles, Morgan inadvertently wiped his hands on ''a piece of coarse, wiry pony fur.'' Several hours later, he noticed that the fur was straight and quite pliable. Test on an Airedale dog produced the same result as it had on the pony fur. Morgan then applied some of the compound to his own hair, with a similar outcome. Combined with a little petroleum jelly, the new product developed by Morgan was called the G. A. Morgan Hair Refining Cream, which provided the basis for his next manufacturing enterprise, the G. A. Morgan Hair Refining Company, established in 1913. Its name was later changed to the G. A. Morgan Refining Company, which remained in business at its original location, 5204 Harlem Avenue in Cleveland, even after his death.

The clothing firm failed, however, but its profits enabled Morgan to continue with his invention activities. In 1910, he began to focus on the field of safety devices. Morgan had become concerned that firemen, sometimes required to work inside burning buildings, were often overcome by smoke and other noxious fumes. While devices were available, they were cumbersome and difficult to use. Morgan began working on what he would call a ''breathing device'' that was more reliable and less complicated to use and would not require two men to enter a building at the same time, one to help the other in case anything went wrong. On August 19, 1912, Morgan submitted a model of his invention to the U.S. Patent Office.

In his description, Morgan said, ''Its purpose was to provide a portable attachment which will enable a fireman to enter a house filled with thick suffocating gases and smoke and to breathe freely for some time therein and thereby enable him to perform his duties of saving life and valuable without danger to himself from suffocation.'' Further, he wrote, the ''device is also efficient and useful for protection to engineers, chemists and workmen who are obliged to breath noxious fumes or dust derived from the materials in which they are obliged to work.'' On October 13, 1914, Morgan was granted Patent # 1,113,675 for his safety mask, which corrected many of the difficulties of previous protective wear. Subsequently, with additional refinements he made, Morgan's breathing device became the forerunner of the modern gas mask and the basis for his fourth manufacturing company.

In 1912 Morgan, along with several prominent Cleveland businessmen, formed the National Safety Device Company, a public company whose shares were initially offered at $10. Within four months their value had increased to $100 a share. Some two months later, although shares to the company had increased to $250, they were promptly sold out. Morgan was the only black to purchase shares in his company, despite having approached the black community first to invest. Moreover, having learned much about marketing from his earlier commercial experiences, he took out advertisements in trade periodicals and traveled around the country demonstrating the Morgan National Safety Hood.

In some instances, however, Morgan employed white men to show off the product, especially in the South, or he passed himself off as ''Big Chief Mason,'' a full-blooded member of the Walpole Reservation in Canada, a response to the then-extant etiquette of race relations in the nation. Most whites were reluctant to do business with blacks in other than a personal service capacity. Eventually Morgan's race became a matter of public record, and competition cut into his sales. Still, Morgan received a contract from the U.S. Navy, and his helmet did see some use during World War I.

Safety concerns also prompted Morgan's next invention, a response to the increasing number of automobile accidents. One particular incident, the collision of an automobile and a horse and carriage at an unmarked intersection, resulted in the carriage passengers' being thrown out, the driver of the car being knocked unconscious, and the horse having to be destroyed. In response, Morgan invented the first automatic traffic signal: electric lights with different colors to signal stop and go, installed at selected intersections. On November 20, 1923 (filed on February 27, 1922), Morgan was granted Patent # 1,475,024 for a device to regulate traffic flow. Subsequently, the manufacturing rights were sold by Morgan to the General Electric Corporation for $40,000.

With profits earned from his inventions and his success as a businessman, Morgan early emerged as a leader of Cleveland's black community. In June 1908, he was one of the chartering members of the Cleveland Association of Colored Men, whose object was ''to advance the varied interests of the colored people of Cleveland.'' From 1914 until it merged with the National Association for the Advancement of Colored People (NAACP), he served as its treasurer. Then in 1920, sufficiently distressed by the way black concerns were reported in the Cleveland newspapers, while also seeking a venue to advertise and promote his line of hair care products, Morgan founded the *Cleveland Call*. It later become the *Call & Post*, which was also published in Columbus and Cincinnati. In 1931, Morgan ran for the city council as an independent candidate and in one campaign speech said that if elected, he would ''try to lead the people of the third district to EQUAL representation in the affairs of city government.'' In response to the depression, Morgan ran on a platform that promised relief for the unemployed and ''a more economic and efficient administration of public affairs.'' He also said that he would address housing conditions and push for improved city services—police, fire, lighting, and sanitation in the black community and, finally, improved accommodations in the city-owned hospital.

This brilliant black inventor and enterprising businessman had only a sixth-grade education. He was the son of Sydney and Eliza Reed Morgan, both freed slaves before the Civil War. Morgan, the seventh of their 11 children, left Kentucky when he was age 14. He lived in Cincinnati, Ohio, until June 1895, when, with only $.10 in his pocket, he moved to Cleveland, where he remained until his death at age 86. With his second wife, Mary Anne Hassek, Morgan raised a family of three sons, John Pierpont, Garrett, Jr., and Cosmo Henry.

SELECTED BIBLIOGRAPHY: Russell H. Davis, *Black Americans in Cleveland* (Washington, DC: Associated Publishers, 1972); Louis Haber, *Black Pioneers of Science and Invention* (New York: Harcourt, Brace & World, 1970), 61–72; Edward S. Jenkins, Gossie Harold Hudson, Sherman W. Jackson, and Exyie Ryder, eds., *American Black Scientists and Inventors* (Washington, DC: National Science Teachers Association, 1975), 10–14; William M. King, "Guardian of the Public Safety: Garrett A. Morgan and the Lake Erie Crib Disaster," *Journal of Negro History* 70, 1–2 (Winter–Spring 1985).

William M. King

MORGAN, HENRY M. (1893–1961), Texas, entrepreneur, millionaire, founder of the first noted national chain of barber colleges for African Americans.

After the Civil War, and well into the early days of this century, the barbering profession was dominated by African Americans. Many formerly enslaved African men were simply using the skills they had acquired during slavery. The first barbershops for slaves began as Sunday morning cutting sessions on the porch or in the yard of the slave's home, usually in preparation for church. In the early 1900s, it was not uncommon for a prominent black barber to own a business on both the black and white side of town. Some of the most influential African Americans of this century, John Merrick, one of the founders of the North Carolina Mutual Life Insurance Co.,* and Daniel H. Williams, who performed the first open heart surgery, started their careers in the barbering business.

African Americans lost the monopoly on the trade because of laws established that required training for barbers. Also, barber colleges were established exclusively for white people. Morgan, who was born in Smith County, Texas, recognized the need and founded the Tyler Barber College in Tyler, Texas, in 1934. The school began with three chairs in the back end of a barbershop. Between 1937 and 1949, Morgan established barber colleges in Houston, Texas, Dallas, Texas, Little Rock, Arkansas, Chicago, Illinois, Memphis, Tennessee, Beaumont, Texas, and New York, New York. Some of the schools had dormitories for students. In 1949, the *Beauticians Journal & Guide* noted that more than 14,000 men and women graduated from Tyler Barber Colleges. The school was equally responsible for producing 80 percent of the black barbers in America then. In addition, Morgan owned a beauty school, barber and beauty supply company, and oil holdings.

Morgan was also president and organizer of the Texas Progressive Voter's League and vice president of the National Association of Tonsorial Artists. He made financial contributions to Butler College and Texas College, Tyler, Texas, both historic black institutions. In 1961 he went to New York, at the invitation of President John F. Kennedy, to attend the National Conference on Constitutional Rights and American Freedom.

SELECTED BIBLIOGRAPHY: "History of Tyler Barber College," *Tyler Leader*, February 26, 1976; Willie L. Morrow, *The Art of Barbering: African American Hair: A Reference Book* (San Diego: Morrow's Unlimited, 1993); "Tyler Barber College Was First of Its Kind," *Beauticians Journal & Guide* (September 1949); "Tyler Negro Millionaire Dies After Heart Attack," *Dallas News*, May 10, 1961.

Nancy J. Dawson

MORROW, WILLIE L. (1939–), California, creator of the California Curl, founder of Morrow's Unlimited, inventor, author.

A respected authority on black skin and hair, Willie Morrow, like many African American barbers, developed his barber techniques while a youngster practicing on family members. As he enhanced his skills, Morrow's fascination with hair became a skill that he used to help supplement the family income. Born in Alabama, Morrow took great pride in the barbering tradition and dreamed of being accomplished in the field. After graduating from high school, he worked part-time as a barber before moving to San Diego, California, in 1959 to live with his uncle and attend barber school. It was in barbering school that Morrow realized that the school's curriculum did not include the art of cutting and styling black people's hair, which subsequently prompted Morrow to write a landmark book in the field of African American cosmetology, *The Principles of Cutting and Styling Negro Hair*, which he self-published in 1966. Morrow also wrote other books such as *400 Years without a Comb* (1973), which encompasses the struggle for black identity through hair.

Eventually, Morrow opened a successful barbershop in San Diego. In 1969, at the invitation of the Army and Air Force Exchange System in Dallas, Morrow trained military beauty salons and barbershops in the art of styling, cutting, pressing, and straightening black hair. Morrow was welcomed since many black troops were unhappy with the services provided for them. For four years, Morrow traveled to 19 foreign countries and bases throughout the United States, training barbers and beauticians in the art of black hair. Morrow continued on a quest to include information regarding the cutting and styling of black hair in barber and beauty schools across the country.

As the barbering profession became quite profitable, Morrow soon entered the manufacturing aspect of the business, with his "Morrow's Curly Hair Products." Next, Morrow experimented with perfecting a comb, like those used in traditional African societies, that was durable enough to pick an Afro hairstyle. As fast as Morrow could produce the combs, they sold. However, when large comb manufacturers caught on to the concept, Morrow was no longer able to compete, so he placed his energies into perfecting a permanent wave process for black women. Morrow is known as the "Father of the Curl." The curl was a cold wave chemical treatment used to straighten hair. Although he began researching the curl in 1967, it was not perfected until 1977. The end product was the famous "California Curl."

When he demonstrated the "California Curl" at a beauty and trade show, his product became an instant success. The "curl" hairstyle was a billion-dollar boom for the ethnic hair care industry, and Morrow was one of the leading pioneers of that movement. In 1980, Morrow constructed a new facility in the same location of his old barbershop in San Diego. In 1981 he purchased radio station XHRM FM 92.5 that would appeal to the minority community. By 1985, it was a top-rated station in San Diego.

SELECTED BIBLIOGRAPHY: "On the Hair and on the Air," *Black Enterprise* (September 1983); Ed Varley, "Willie Morrow; The Man and the Legend, Part I," *Beauty Classic* 3, 2 (1986); Ed Varley, "Willie Morrow; The Man and the Legend, Part II," *Beauty Classic* 3, 2 (1986).

Nancy J. Dawson

MUSEUMS. The survival of the African American community was due to the formation of independent and semiindependent black institutions. These institutions brought both economic, cultural, and social stability to the community. One such institution is the African American museum. All museums seek to minister to the soul, the psyche, and the intellectual prowess of the human being. They also serve the functional purpose of collecting, preserving, examining, and exhibiting material objects. Museums have thus taken on the position within American society as a dwelling place for our most treasured objects from our material past and present. In light of the fact that museums have a profound influence on American society, it is important to shed light on the major factor that influences how well a museum operates: money. A business needs capital to run efficiently and effectively, and museums are not an exception. This entry will therefore expunge on the economic needs of African American museums in addition to discussing the current state of African American museums.

The following information was compiled by the African American Museum Association, which consists of 99 institutions from the United States. The operating budgets of African American museums, on average, range from $1.3 million to $2 million. These expenditures are personal costs, costs related to housing, costs related to exhibits, and costs related to collections, as well as the other miscellaneous costs. Dr. Ramon Price, chief curator of Chicago's DuSable Museum of African American History (founded by Dr. Margaret Burroughs), elaborated on exactly what these costs entail. Personal costs include, for example, museum salaries. Housing costs range from paying the utilities to general upkeep to maintenance. Exhibit costs generally include the money needed in order to design, build, and preserve a gallery. Collection costs are monies set aside for the acquisition of artifacts. Miscellaneous costs include many costs such as the payments on loans.

The next essential question to ponder is how the museums receive their funding. The bulk of the money is received from state, federal, and local governments. Forty-seven percent of the money is received from the latter. The remaining 52 percent of funds generated are arranged in order from highest to lowest: individual gifts and donations, local businesses, membership dues, endowments, admission fees, gift shop revenue, United Way, trust funds, savings, loans, corporations, funding drives, membership drives, and grants.

A series of problems develop from the latter examples of soliciting funds, one of which involves the intricacies of fund-raising. Fund-raisers are not the most effective means of acquiring money because money must be spent in order to put on the event. In effect, the net profit is not high after the event. Also, a great number of African American museums do not qualify for the grants because many are not accredited institutions. Hence, African American museums are left to rely on receiving donations from individual persons and groups. Most museum scholars agree that to prepare for the future they must become more innovative and aggressive in their acquisition of funds to enhance the overall quality of their respective museums.

SELECTED BIBLIOGRAPHY: Ellis G. Burcaw, *Introduction to Museum Work* (Nashville, TN: American Association for State and Local History, 1983); Clayborne Carson, David J. Garrow, Gerald Gill, Vincent Harding, and Darlene Clark Hine, *The Eyes on the Prize Reader* (New York: Penguin Books, 1987); "Museum Ethics" (report from the American Association of African American Museums, Washington, DC, 1992).

Geneen Wright

MUTUAL AID/INSURANCE ENTERPRISES, SOUTH. In the context of black business history and in the development of African American financial institutions, the rich tradition of mutual assistance calls attention to the fine line between the social and the economic—the sacred and the secular. In the most general assessment, the black church can be seen as the great maternal institution, the basis of mutual benefit societies, which in turn gave rise to banks, insurance companies, and related enterprises such as credit unions and funeral parlors. In some instances, the benefit society preceded the church. The African Methodist Episcopal Church, for example, evolved out of the Free African Society,* a mutual aid association founded in 1787 by the free black citizens of Philadelphia.

As they expanded in number and location, the benefit societies took their place as primary institutions, almost as basic as the family, and an argument can be made for their African origins. Indeed, if it were possible to document the invisible world of institutions among slaves, especially among the early generations, one would likely discover a network of mutual assistance and clandestine commerce that owed a great deal to Africa. During the colonial period, both Virginia and South Carolina outlawed a vigorous subeconomy carried on by African slaves. The continued tightening of the slave system made assembly and communication—the life blood of economic organization—increasingly difficult and dangerous for slaves and free blacks alike. Perhaps only in Charleston and New Orleans could slaves engage in anything resembling the Sunday markets of the Caribbean, but even in small towns, slave women dominated the local markets.

Interestingly, however, it was chiefly in Charleston and New Orleans that free blacks organized a significant number of both small and large businesses, as well as mutual benefit societies. Most notable among these organizations was Charleston's exclusive Brown Fellowship Society, founded in 1790. Yet given the restrictions on African American life in the antebellum South, it was no accident that many of the major voluntary associations and churches began among free blacks in northern cities and that the heyday of the mutual benefit society and its economic offshoots would have to wait for Emancipation—for the liberation of 4 million slaves in need of social and economic services. According to W.E.B. Du Bois, the postbellum South witnessed such a proliferation of black mutual aid societies that it was "impractical to catalog them . . . so large is their number and so wide their ramification."

In many cases the benefit society, the fraternal lodge, and rudimentary insurance and business enterprises were scarcely distinguishable and were often linked by a common founder and a common domicile. Their mixed function, in Du Bois's estimation, was "partly social intercourse and partly insurance." For the history of black business, it was their insurance function that became all important. By the early twentieth century, black life insurance companies had become the dominant business institutions among African Americans. In part, these all-black enterprises had risen in response to the hateful challenge of Jim Crow, but it would be an enormous error simply to credit white exclusion for what came out of a complex pattern of black creativity. To illustrate the point, the historian can turn to case studies of the New South's most successful black insurance companies: North Carolina Mutual* (1898) and Atlanta Life* (1905), two companies that alternately boasted being "the world's largest Negro business."

Moreover, the founding of these two institutions, with their historic origins deeply rooted in the mutual benefit societies, then, are also important for providing a foundation for black business. The North Carolina Mutual drew its inspiration from the veritable hub of benefit societies in the Upper South— Richmond, Virginia—where in 1881, an ex-slave from Georgia, William Washington Browne, took command of the Grand Fountain of the United Order of True Reformers and parlayed it into a small empire. At its base lay a vast network of life insurance agencies, all funneling their dues (premiums) back to Richmond, where Browne financed an array of institutions ranging from a bank and a newspaper to a hotel and a funeral home.

Dozens of True Reformers agents struck out on their own, spinning off innumerable other insurance societies throughout the Upper South. One of these, the Royal Knights of King David, found its way to Durham, North Carolina, where John Merrick, another enterprising ex-slave, got his start in the Royal Knights and then went on to launch a chain of barbershops and organize the North Carolina Mutual. William G. Pearson, one of Merrick's cofounders, later recalled that "The Royal Knights of King David trained John Merrick. It pioneered the way for the North Carolina Mutual. These societies were the trail blazers of Negro business."

What William Washington Browne and the True Reformers did for the Upper South and the North Carolina Mutual the Reverend Thomas W. Walker and the Union Central Relief Association did for the Lower South and Atlanta Life. In Reverend Walker's terms, one institution "begat" another. In the 1880s Walker founded the Afro-American Benevolent Association, which evolved into the more important Union Central Relief Association of Birmingham (1894), which spawned the Union Mutual Relief Association of Atlanta (1897), which inspired the Atlanta Benevolent Protective Association (1904), which passed into the more secular hands of Alonzo F. Herndon* (a successful barber like Merrick), who founded Atlanta Life in 1905. Over the succeeding decades, both the North Carolina Mutual and Atlanta Life acted as midwives to an extended family of banks and other financial institutions that would bring enormous pride to Atlanta's "Sweet Auburn" Avenue* and earn Durham the title "the Black Wall Street* of America."

Finally, back in Richmond, there is a critical third story that shifts the focus to gender. A great many African American mutual benefit societies, perhaps the majority, were founded and supported by women. By all odds, the most important of these was the Independent Order of St. Luke, founded in 1867 by Baltimore freedwoman Mary Prout and given renewed life in Richmond under the leadership of Maggie Lena Walker.* The Order of St. Luke rivaled and outlasted the True Reformers as Richmond's leading black institution in the early twentieth century.

Walker was perhaps more reformer than entrepreneur, but the distinction would be ours rather than hers. She used her successful insurance business not only as a base to create a bank, a newspaper, and a department store but also as a platform to uplift the community through her leadership in the National Association for the Advancement of Colored People (NAACP), the National Urban League,* and the Virginia Federation of Colored Women's Clubs. Indeed, "Lifting as We Climb" (the motto of the National Association of Colored Women) might have been the motto of St. Luke and, in a larger sense, the motto of all black businesses in a world where mobility was measured up from slavery.

SELECTED BIBLIOGRAPHY: Elsa Barkley Brown, "Womanist Consciousness: Maggie Lena Walker and the Independent Order of St. Luke," *Signs: Journal of Women in Culture and Society* (Spring 1989); Alexa B. Henderson, *Atlanta Life Insurance Company: Guardian of Black Economic Dignity* (Tuscaloosa: University of Alabama Press, 1990); Walter B. Weare, *Black Business in the New South: A Social History of the North Carolina Mutual Life Insurance Company* (Urbana: University of Illinois Press, 1973).

Walter Weare

N

NAACP ECONOMIC DEVELOPMENT INITIATIVES. Formed in 1909 as a direct response to racial violence in America, the National Association for the Advancement of Colored People (NAACP) for years relied on a unique legal and legislative strategy to combat racial discrimination and achieve full equality in all sectors of American society. Through trial and appellate court action, government lobbying, and public demonstrations, the NAACP influenced positive change in school desegregation, voting rights, public accommodations, and open housing.

In recent years, NAACP increasingly has devoted its resources to economic empowerment. The organization's leadership has viewed this focus as the natural outgrowth of its successful push for social and legal equality throughout this century. With diminished enthusiasm for public support of economic development for African Americans, the NAACP Board of Directors launched a program strategy in 1981 focusing on private sector support to promote the growth and development of entrepreneurship and employment opportunities among blacks through a couple of key initiatives.

A central initiative in this regard has been the Operation Fair Share program, which was created in the early 1980s. The principal aim of Operation Fair Share is to ensure that a "fair share" of the money spent by African American consumers will be used by major corporations to benefit blacks in the areas of job development and business opportunities. Through this program, voluntary agreements are negotiated with major corporations to identify goals for each of several Fair Share objectives, which include: (1) establishment of minority vendor programs aimed at increasing the purchase of goods and services provided by black-owned concerns; (2) establishment of affirmative action programs aimed at the advancement of African Americans into senior management positions; (3) increased representation of African Americans on corporate boards; and (4) increased contributions to African American organizations.

To these ends, the NAACP identifies major corporations to participate in the program; negotiates agreements with these companies, setting specific goals; and monitors progress in meeting the objectives. Because of its organizational structure, the NAACP is able to operate on two levels in ensuring the success of its program. The national office works with companies focusing on national marketing efforts, whereas the local branches target local and regional firms. The program is coordinated by the national office through training and technical assistance. And the NAACP's Economic Development Program staff conducts numerous seminars, workshops, and conferences to advance the program's goals and objectives.

The NAACP has seen impressive results from its Fair Share initiative. Nearly 60 companies have entered agreements with the organization. According to an NAACP progress report, these agreements have yielded "over a billion dollars annually in procurement contracts to African American companies; a quarter million dollars in banks; $100 million in advertising with African American owned media; and $250 million in insurance coverage through African American professionals." Related to the Fair Share program is the NAACP's Commerce and Trade Council (CTC). The CTC membership is made up of black entrepreneurs who directly benefit from the "market opportunities created by the Fair Share Program." Members receive valuable assistance from NAACP Economic Development staff in marketing goods and services to corporations participating in the Fair Share program.

Recently, under the direction of NAACP president Kweisi Mfume, the Economic Reciprocity Initiative was launched with the support of 35 other national organizations. This program targets companies within specific industries in pushing for a wide range of economic empowerment objectives. Included among the goals are employment and promotion; procurement; increased franchise ownership; advertising and marketing; and community reinvestment. There were a couple of key reasons the hotel industry was selected as the first targeted group for the initiative. First, it was determined that blacks spend a significant amount of money in the industry. According to NAACP research, at least 71 percent of all black conventions held in 1975 were hosted by seven leading hotel chains, resulting in more than $29 million for rooms and catering and over $200 million in economic impact in host cities. Second, it was determined that the hotel industry provided significant opportunities for growth across all areas of economic development.

The NAACP plans to build on its success in the hotel industry to launch similar initiatives in other industries over the coming years as the organization considers innovative approaches to establishing and maintaining economic development and to counteracting what the NAACP considers to be the "aggressive assault on affirmative action and economic opportunity'' for African Americans.

SELECTED BIBLIOGRAPHY: Minnie Finch, *The NAACP, Its Fight for Justice* (Metuchen, NJ: Scarecrow Press, 1981); J. Jones, ''Sleeping with the Enemy [NAACP's Consumer Guide to the Hotel Industry]'' (New York: National Association for the Advancement of Colored People, n.d.); ''NAACP Calls for Boycott of 10 Hotel Chains,'' *Jet*, March 17, 1997, 7; Warren D. St. James, *NAACP: Triumphs of a Pressure Group* (Smithtown, NY: Exposition Press, 1980); www.naacp.org/programs/econ.html

Christopher D. Benson

NAIL, JOHN B. (1853–1942), **AND JOHN [JACK] E. NAIL** (1883–1947), New York, entrepreneurs in real estate sales and property management

A native of Baltimore, John Nail moved to New York City in 1863. Gradually, John and his brother Edward accumulated enough savings to purchase the building in midtown Manhattan in which they had established a restaurant, bar, billiard parlor, and hotel. They eventually sold this enterprise in 1909, choosing to concentrate instead on their growing real estate investments in Harlem. With the ongoing migration of blacks to New York, the Nails' holdings had appreciated dramatically by the early 1900s, giving John considerable wealth and financial clout, including an official credit rating by Dun & Bradstreet. In addition to his philanthropic activities, John Nail was also a founding member of the National Negro Business League* and the National Association for the Advancement of Colored People (NAACP). John was also an important collector of African American art. John formally retired in 1903, although he continued to hold a financial stake in his son's business.

Having learned the real estate business from his father, Jack Nail first started his own firm in the Bronx but then went to work for the Afro-American Realty Company in Harlem. In 1907, Jack and another salesman for Afro-American, Henry C. Parker, established their own firm, Nail & Parker. Like John Nail before them, Jack Nail and Henry Parker fought to expand the number of rental properties open to blacks in Harlem, which often required displacing white owners and tenants from whole blocks that had been designated as ''white'' areas by banks and neighborhood associations.

As the business expanded, Jack Nail became involved increasingly in property management. With its financial clout, Nail & Parker was also able to offer mortgages and make property deals worth in excess of $1 million. Jack Nail was a fervent advocate for Harlem, as the first black member of the Real Estate Board of New York and as a member of the mostly white Republican Business Men's Club of New York City. He was a key figure in the Colored Merchant Association and the New York Urban League.

SELECTED BIBLIOGRAPHY: John N. Ingham and Lynne B. Feldman, *African-American Business Leaders: A Biographical Dictionary* (Westport, CT: Greenwood

Press, 1994); Gilbert Osofsky, *Harlem: The Making of a Ghetto* (1963; New York: Harper Torchbooks, 1968).

Peter Botticelli

NATIONAL AFRO-AMERICAN LEAGUE. While it is often overlooked by scholars, the National Afro-American League, funded in January 1890, was the foremost black protest organization of its time. It represented an important bridge between the politics of accommodation and the emerging ethos of protest in the 1890s. It wed the seemingly contradictory tactics of agitation, legal action, and economic self-help in a comprehensive program of racial solidarity and resistance. The League drew the participation of many premier "race leaders" of the period, including William Monroe Trotter, Ida B. Wells, W.E.B. Du Bois, and Booker T. Washington.* Indeed, the organization became a battleground between the Tuskegee Institute strategy of moral suasion and black economic development, and the agitation-driven philosophy of Du Bois's Niagara Movement.

In its founding, the League was a response to popular demand for a national convention to address the legal and extralegal assaults on Black Reconstruction-era gains. It also represented the culminating efforts of radical black journalist Timothy Thomas Fortune (1856–1928), who initiated the League's founding. As the militant editor of the *New York Age*, Fortune penned several editorials in the late 1880s calling for the building of a fighting organization for African Americans. These writings helped spark the formation of local "protective leagues" against black disfranchisement. When 141 delegates from 23 states coalesced in Chicago for the League's founding convention, Fortune naturally became its temporary chair.

In his address, delivered in strident tones, Fortune upheld African Americans' right to protect their interests through all political avenues, including armed activity. "It is time to face the enemy and fight him inch by inch for every right he denies us," he declared. At length he asserted: "We propose to accomplish our purposes by the peaceful methods of agitation, through the ballot and the courts, but if others use the weapons of violence to combat our peaceful arguments, it is not for us to run away from violence." Fortune outlined a plan of action premised on universal manhood suffrage; the cessation of "lynch and mob law" in the South; equal distribution of school funds; the elimination of the convict-lease system and other forms of black peonage; a ban on racial discrimination in transportation and public accommodations; and fair wages for laborers.

Most important, Fortune called for the building of an "Afro-American Bank," without which, he said, the other initiatives were futile. Fortune envisioned the bank concentrating the savings of workers and professionals and using them to support a committee on legislation, a bureau of technical industrial education, and a bureau of cooperative industry. Bureaus on lynching and education were added later.

By February, the convention had elected as its first president J. C. Price, president of Livingstone College in Salisbury, North Carolina. Despite its promising platform for struggle, the League drew far fewer delegates to its second convention in 1891. By 1893, as a result of internal schisms, battles with competing organizations, economic insolvency, and local branches' inability to support themselves, the League was defunct. However, Fortune and Alexander Walters, a bishop in the African Methodist Zion Church, reconstituted the organization in 1898 as the Afro-American Council. By this time, the *New York Age* had grown financially dependent on Washington and his Tuskegee circle. Fortune, who had shown ideological inconsistency even in the 1880s, moved even closer to Washington politically.

At the turn of the century, he joined the Tuskegee leader in forming the National Negro Business League (NNBL).* Likewise, the *Age* became more consistent in praising the philosophy of business enterprise, counseling rapprochement with southern whites, and tacitly defending Washington against the "anti-Bookerites." While the revived Council upheld essentially the same platform from 1890, it moderated its tone as Washington solidified influence. Ironically, Washington, criticized by many contemporaries for his public accommodation to southern agrarian and northern industrial elites, clandestinely funded the Council's court battles against exclusionary provisions in several southern state constitutions.

As Fortune closed ranks with Washington, a disgruntled faction bitterly opposed his consecutive elections, in 1902 and 1903, as the Council's president. Others, like Wells, resigned from the Council altogether. With the founding of the Niagara Movement in 1905, Trotter and other political foes of Washington's sought to reassert militancy in the Council. By 1907, this "Niagara faction" successfully "eliminated several Tuskegee stalwarts from positions of influence," according to historian August Meier. Yet this perceived victory precipitated the organization's demise. Other delegates apparently defected, and Washington used his extensive contacts with newspaper editors to ensure the Council's 1908 convention received scant coverage. By 1909, the Council once again had dissolved.

Despite its tumultuous history, the Afro-American League/Council left a legacy from which to draw, even in contemporary times. While emphasizing economic development, Fortune's belief in "cooperative industry" suggested a vision of business development along collective, rather than privatized, lines. Further, the League demonstrated that economic self-help formed only one facet of a multilayered strategy of protest, moral suasion, armed action, and tactical involvement in electoral politics. From this vantage point, pursuing separate black community development, including economic enterprise, need not contradict making demands on government for democratic rights.

Given the dichotomy popularly made between "dependency" on the state and personal "self-help," the League's history particularly illuminates the importance of protest combined with self-help and economic development in business.

SELECTED BIBLIOGRAPHY: John H. Bracey, August Meier, and Elliott Rudwick, eds., *Black Nationalism in America* (New York: Bobbs-Merrill, 1970); Francis L. Broderick and August Meier, eds., *Negro Protest Thought in the Twentieth Century* (New York: Bobbs-Merrill, 1965); Philip S. Foner, ed., *The Voice of Black America: Major Speeches by Negroes in the United States, 1797–1971* (New York: Simon and Schuster, 1972); Paula Giddings, *When and Where I Enter: The Impact of Black Women on Race and Sex in America* (New York: Bantam Books, 1984).

Clarence Lang

NATIONAL ASSOCIATION OF BLACK AUTOMOTIVE SUPPLIERS (NABAS). The Detroit-based National Association of Black Automotive Suppliers (NABAS) was formed in July 1986. Its founders were 11 black business owners whose largest customers were automotive manufacturers. The founding companies saw a need for an organization to serve as a communication link with automotive manufacturers. The combined membership agreed that black automotive suppliers and automotive manufacturers have a common goal of expanding their market share and fortifying long-term improvements. Since NABAS members' destinies were so closely aligned with automotive manufacturers, the decision was made for NABAS to engage in a concerted effort to assist the automotive industry in "meeting the world challenge." Each member's goal is to gain the technical managerial and quality control expertise necessary to become a tier-one supplier capable of being competitive on a worldwide basis.

In its founding, clearly defined objectives and action programs were established to provide focused direction leading to achievement of this goal. By working together, each NABAS member has grown through a sharing of experience and skills. The board of directors and members of the NABAS include the leading black auto supply manufacturers, underscoring the significant presence of blacks in the auto manufacturing industry. In the mid-1990s, the officers on the board of directors were: Dave Bing/The Bing Group, president; Carlton Guthrie/Trumark, first vice president; Joseph B. Anderson, Jr./Chivas Products Ltd., second vice president; Homer W. McClarty/Mancelona Manufacturing, Inc., secretary; and Kirk Lewis/Bing Steel, treasurer.

Also, members provide positive role models for existing and future black entrepreneurs. In addition, the scholarship program established has as its purpose to ensure the continued participation of blacks in the auto manufacturing industry. The NABAS has established and funded fellowships for engineering, design, and production planning students. One of the most important activities of the NABAS is to serve as an informational and educational resource for black suppliers wanting to do business with automotive companies. Assistance is provided in several ways. For one, NABAS advances the economic viability of new and smaller black companies through NABAS members' self-imposed minority purchasing programs. In addition, managerial support is provided by NABAS to black-owned companies wanting to do business with automotive manufacturers. Also, through its members, a business network has developed that enables the organization to disseminate automotive information and strengthen members' understanding of automotive programs and concepts through cross-fertilization of shared experiences. Also, NABAS has developed and coordinated quality training programs to assist members in obtaining the highest available quality rating.

Moreover, the organization serves as a conduit in providing automotive manufacturers with feedback on concerns and marketing data from black automotive suppliers and the black business community in general. In addition, it encourages automotive manufacturers to support black suppliers in the form of increased business opportunities, long-term contracts, and technical assistance. According to Chrysler Corporation chairman, Robert J. Easton, "The Big Three [General Motors, Ford, Chrysler] spent $4.5 billion with minority-owned suppliers in 1995, a 28 percent increase over the $3/5 billion spent in 1994." Still, competition for contracts from all automotive suppliers is intense. General Motors (GM) has 30,000 suppliers. In 1997 GM awarded $1.7 billion in contracts to over 600 minority suppliers. The primary objective of the NABAS for the twenty-first century is to work with automotive companies to strengthen the overall supplier base to facilitate "meeting the world challenge" while ensuring their continued presence in the industry.

SELECTED BIBLIOGRAPHY: Chrysler Corporation Press Release, May 5, 1996, "Chrysler Chief Identifies Challenges for Strengthening Partnerships With Minority Suppliers," Chrysler Corporation, Auburn Hills, MI at, http://www.media.crysler.com/wwwpr96/237.htm and http://www.gm.com/about/info/news/speech/980511.htm; Samuel D. K. James and Richard Farmer, eds., *The Impact of Cybernation Technology on Black Automotive Workers in the U.S.* (Ann Arbor, MI: UMI Research Press, 1981); National Association of Black Automotive Suppliers, "Organization History," NABAS National Office, Archives, Detroit, Michigan.

Jeffrey E. Walker

NATIONAL ASSOCIATION OF MARKET DEVELOPERS (NAMD). In the years immediately following World War II, many large U.S. companies, seeking to attract increasingly important African American consumers, hired what were then referred to as "Negro Market" specialists. In 1953, these individuals coalesced in a mutual support organization known as the National Association of Market Developers. Despite their importance, early Negro Market specialists tended to operate at the margins of their respective companies. Among other things, these individuals were regularly excluded from meetings where new marketing techniques and strategies were discussed. Besides being professionally isolated in the companies they worked for, Negro Market specialists were socially isolated from their white colleagues as well. Nevertheless, the African American trailblazers in Corporate America circumvented this obstacle by establishing their own informal social network. For example, these individuals, while representing their employers at the annual meetings of such national African American organizations as the National Association for the Advancement of Colored People (NAACP), regularly shared ideas and offered encouragement to each other.

When the NAMD began in May 1953, it provided an institutional solution to the social and professional concerns of Negro Market specialists. The organization's subsequent annual conventions provided not only a venue for socializing but, more important, a venue for receiving additional professional training. Because of NAMD's central role in the evolution of Corporate America's interest in African American consumers, the organization's early membership represented a virtual "Who's Who" of blacks in U.S. business. Perhaps the most famous early member of the National Association of Market Developers was James A. "Billboard" Jackson. He joined Esso Standard Oil in 1937 as a special representative to the black community. Jackson quickly made his mark within both the company and the national marketing community. By the mid-1940s, Jackson was the first and only black member of the American Marketing Society.

Harvey C. Russell was another well-known figure within the early National Association of Market Developers. Russell joined Pepsi-Cola in 1950 as a Negro Market specialist and rose rapidly within the corporation. In 1961, he became vice president of special markets, and his appointment represented the first African American to be elected vice president of a multinational corporation. Significantly, the first president of the National Association of Market Developers, Moss H. Kendrix, was not an employee of a major corporation but headed his own firm, the Moss H. Kendrix Public Relations Company. His primary client during the 1950s was the Coca-Cola Company. Samuel Whiteman was another independent entrepreneur associated with the early NAMD. Whiteman, one of the organization's acknowledged founders, began his career with the Mars Contract Company, a distributor of hotel and motel furniture. However, in 1958, Whiteman formed his own company, Samuel Whiteman and Associates, which specialized in providing furniture to colleges and universities.

Besides "Billboard" Jackson and Harvey Russell, other prominent NAMD members who began their careers as Negro Market specialists for major companies included: Herbert H. Wright, who worked for Philip Morris Incorporated; Wendell P. Alston and James Avery, who worked with "Billboard" at Esso Standard (later Humble) Oil; Chuck Smith, who worked for the Royal Crown Bottling Company; Joe Black, who worked for the Greyhound Corporation; Bill Porter, who worked for Anheuser-Busch; James "Bud" Ward, who worked for the Marriott Corporation; and Louise Prothro of Pet Milk. Another important figure associated with NAMD's formative years, who neither was an independent entrepreneur nor worked for a white-controlled corporation, was LeRoy Jeffries. Jeffries, who served as the organization's president from 1959 to 1960, was vice president, Midwest Advertising Director, of the black-owned Johnson Publications (the publisher of *Ebony* and *Jet*).

Two other individuals also made invaluable contributions to the National Association of Market Developers' formation and development: Dr. Walter A. Davis, the president of Tennessee A & I (now Tennessee State University), which hosted NAMD's formation in 1953; and Dr. H. Naylor Fitzhugh, whose career included stints as a Howard University marketing professor, a vice president at Pepsi-Cola, and president of NAMD. In recent decades, the National Association of Market Developers' membership has included an increasing number of independent black entrepreneurs in the fields of marketing and public relations. Moreover, during the 1990s, NAMD, the historic intermediary between Corporate America and black consumers, has challenged its members to urge their respective companies and clients to invest more resources in African American enclaves.

SELECTED BIBLIOGRAPHY: "Monumental Achievement: NAMD," *National Black Monitor* 10 (September 1985): 4; Robert E. Weems, Jr., *Desegregating the Dollar: African American Consumerism in the Twentieth Century* (New York: New York University Press, 1998).

Robert E. Weems, Jr.

NATIONAL ASSOCIATION OF NEGRO BUSINESS AND PROFESSIONAL WOMEN'S CLUBS, INCORPORATED. The National Association of Negro Business and Professional Women's Clubs (NANBPWC) is the nation's oldest organization that focuses on the economic development of African American women and their families. It was founded in 1935 by Ollie Chinn Porter, Emma Odessa Young, and Effie Diton of New York; Bertha Perry Rhodes, Josephine B. Keen, and Adelaide Flemming of Philadelphia; and Pearl Flippen of Atlantic City. The purpose of the association has been to act as advocate for the interests of black business and professional women, to provide educational opportunities and entrepreneurial education to these women, and to provide bridges so that young women and girls are adequately prepared to enter business or the professions. The Washington-based organization is also a service organization that harnesses the unique talents of business and professional women to improve the status of the African American family and community. Much of NANBPWC's service work is organized under the acronym HEED, or health, education, employment, and economic development.

The NANBPWC is an association of clubs, an umbrella for more than 300 local clubs in 42 states, with affiliates in Accra, Ghana, and Bermuda. There are more than 5,000 members of the organization, including youth and young adult members and supportive men, known as ôthe Ombudsmenô. Headquartered in Washington, D.C., NANBPWC employs a small full-time staff, grants more than $50,000 in scholarship funds annually, and publishes a newsletter, *Re-*

sponsibility, three times a year. The organization has an annual conference and elects officers biennially. The bylaws mandate that NANBPWC hold meetings in the Washington, D.C., area every four years.

The organization's highest award, the Sojourner Truth Award, is conferred by local clubs to women whose advocacy and activism for business and professional women and the community at large have had a profound impact on the quality of life in that community. Currently, the national organization has commissioned Los Angeles–based sculptor Tina Allen to construct a statue of Sojourner Truth in Battle Creek, Michigan, the city where she was buried.

Seventeen distinguished women have served as president of the National Association of Negro Business and Professional Women's Clubs. Founder Ollie Chinn Porter was the first president (1936–1938). The ninth president, Florence Holmes (1959–1963), identified and purchased the present headquarters in Washington, D.C. Other recent leaders of the organization include eleventh president Margaret Belcher (1967–1971), of Columbus, Georgia; fifteenth president Frankie Jacobs Gillette (1983–1987), of San Francisco, California; and the immediate past president, Catherine Sykes (1991–1995), of Pontiac, Michigan. In 1995 Julianne Malveaux, an internationally known economist and syndicated columnist, was elected president.

SELECTED BIBLIOGRAPHY: Rosalind G. Bauchum, *The Business and Professional Woman: Selected References of Achievement: A Tribute to the 50th Year of the National Association of Negro Business and Professional Women's Clubs. Inc.* (Monticello, IL: Vance Bibliographies, 1985); National Association of Negro Business and Professional Women's Clubs, Inc., "Malveaux Reports, 1997," Archives, NANBPWC's National Office, Washington, D.C.

Julianne Malveaux

NATIONAL BLACK CHAMBER OF COMMERCE. The National Black Chamber of Commerce (NBCC), Inc., has as its mission "Developing the Path for Economic Empowerment." The National Black Chamber of Commerce was incorporated in Washington, D.C., in March 1993. This trade association represents 52,000 black-owned businesses and provides an advocacy that reaches all 640,000 black-owned businesses. There are 150 affiliated chapters that are locally based throughout the nation, and we have businesses as well as individuals who have chosen to be direct members with the national office.

The NBCC Board of Directors is composed of a national body of African American entrepreneurs and community leaders who are dedicated to the economic empowerment of African American communities. Some of the members are Dr. Arthur Fletcher, Reverend Dr. Dan Jones, and Martin Luther King III. The national agenda calls for strategies that will lead to enforcement of Title VI of the 1964 Civil Rights Act. Adequate compliance with this federal law would ensure a "level playing field" with business transactions in both the private and public sectors and ensure that competition will bring lower costs and greater business opportunities for small and local business. Also, the NBCC can act as the economic "think tank" and provider of analysis and review concerning business issues and how they relate to the black community. Another goal is to develop strategic alliances with major corporations that will incubate significant joint ventures, new business opportunities, and investments.

In addition, the NBCC seeks to provide economic educational vehicles for our black churches. A major goal is to set up trade missions for NBCC members and, particularly, to develop dialogue and strategies with business associations in Africa, South America, and the Caribbean. Another goal is to engage in the black entertainment industry via investment in and advocacy of black-owned movies—production, sales, and distribution. Black-owned studios, television/ radio stations, and theaters should populate our communities.

The NBCC is a 501(c)3 corporation. Since its founding it has developed activities that provide forums for educating and training black communities on the need to participate vigorously in the American capitalistic society. Their activities in various ways have been responsible for opening the doors that have led to hundreds of millions of dollars in new businesses for black and other minority-owned businesses throughout the nation. Major companies and many federal, state, and municipal entities have increased the amount of business done with minority companies because of direct dialogue and partnering with the NBCC. The National Black Chamber of Commerce is located in Washington, D.C.

SELECTED BIBLIOGRAPHY: National Black Chamber of Commerce, "History," Archives, National Office, Washington, D.C.; National Black Chamber of Commerce, available from blkcom@ad.com and web site at http://www.nbcc-net.com

Jeffrey E. Walker

NATIONAL BLACK MBA ASSOCIATION. The National Black MBA Association (NBMBAA) was formed in 1970 by a few young, newly minted African American M.B.A.s when they met to network and share ideas for professional growth. As Thelma Austin, a founding member said, "The history of the National Black MBA Association, Inc. is the history of a relay race. No one person or group can take all the credit (or blame), but each of us has a segment to run." The organization has come a long way since the early years of meeting in school corridors and whispering behind *closed* office doors. The pioneers who paved the way for African American M.B.A.s across the world are: Thelma Austin, Columbia University, 1972; Juanita Brown, Columbia University, 1971; Hurlon Dulan, Harvard University, 1971; Carl Fields, Jr., University of Chicago, 1972; Leroy Fykes, Stanford University, 1971; Earnestine Wallace, Columbia University, 1972; Karen Williamson, University of Chicago, 1972; and initiator Charles Fields, Columbia University, 1972.

The first national conference was held in 1979 at the Westin Hotel in Detroit. This was a turning point in our history. Past President Bill Brooks remembers the time well: "Everyone was focused on the need for perfection in the delivery of services during the conference. I can still hear them debating over the details, theme-money-speakers-money-menus-money-logistics-money-etc. It was an exciting time for all of us. We were successful in getting General Motors to contribute $5000 towards the event. Jesse Jackson,* Benjamin Hooks, Sybil Mobley and many other prominent African Americans were keynote speakers. Everyone agreed the Detroit conference was first class all the way, there was only one small problem. We lost $30,000. Somehow we overran the food budget, just a tad.'' It was their commitment to this organization, perseverance, and sheer determination that made it possible, however, to recoup such a loss.

The Association was initially incorporated in New York City. In 1983 an alliance was established with Smith-Jones and Associates to coordinate our conferences and run our national office operations. Then, in 1988, the organization celebrated its independence and moved the new office to Chicago, hiring Pamela Anderson as the first director of operations.

The astounding growth of the organization was, and still is, dependent on the volunteerism of members, chapter presidents, and board of directors. Angela Dowd Burton recalls, ''In 1980 I was elected Philadelphia chapter president. In 1981, I joined the Board of Directors. I can remember the atmosphere of some of those early Board meetings. The Los Angeles, Detroit, and Chicago contingents were some of the most articulate, dynamic and 'aggressive' professionals that I had ever met.'' It was those early years of ''dynamic'' and ''aggressive'' leadership that laid the groundwork for the services we provide today.

The mission of the NBMBAA is to lead in the creation of economic and intellectual wealth for the black community. Since its founding, the organization has implemented a host of programs and educational tools. Lee Nunery, who served as national president from 1985 to 1989, also credits the organization with ''positioning Black MBA's as responsible players in longer term scenarios.'' Nunery qualifies the organization's impact as being threefold: (1) to provide information to people with careers in business who, then, can become information brokers to the community; (2) to provide investment knowledge to African Americans who otherwise would be left out of the mainstream flow of investment tips and services; and (3) to provide experience in organizational management, giving members tools they can use in all facets of their professional careers. Perhaps, most important, for its members, as Nunery emphasizes, ''the Association provides a culture of success.''

Onetime national president Steve Lewis, acknowledging the benefits of participating in this organization, said: ''When I joined in 1987, I had just started as an analyst for Ford Motor Company. While Ford helped me learn to analyze key business issues, the NBMBAA gave me the opportunity to develop key programs that have become national. Also, the Detroit chapter started a scholarship program that awarded just $1000, but which established the framework used today to award more than $400,000 in scholarships annually.''

Moreover, while the NBMBAA recognizes how its members have greatly benefited from opportunities only possible through affirmative action laws, at the same time, in light of the antiaffirmative action decisions in the late twentieth century, the NBMBAA felt it necessary to take a position. Foremost, the NBMBAA believes in the strength of America, its potential to be a formidable global competitor, and the human capital that will be responsible for achieving and maintaining this position in world markets.

At the same time, the methods of gaining access to the arenas of education, employment, and business, however, are not fair and do not present equal opportunity. Unfortunately, many of these methods are riddled with discriminatory practices, and for this reason, African Americans are underrepresented—not because they are not qualified but because discrimination continues to exist. There is a need in this country for all kinds of individuals with a myriad of qualifications. We do not believe, however, that diversity of human capital in education, employment, and business will be achieved in a meaningful way if left to the natural course of attainment. It is for these reasons the NBMBAA believes in affirmative action and takes a position in support of it.

In 1991, under the leadership of a new executive director and small core staff, a legacy plan was developed to focus the organization on realizing its vision of leading in the creation of intellectual and economic wealth in the African American community. There are several tenets to the plan. The focus of our education programs is continued expansion to sustain African American talent and leadership through mentorship, scholarships, and business awareness. These programs impact the professional and leadership development of our members, they touch the lives and aspirations of our youth, and they build the pipeline of African American management and leadership talent. A second focus is to create a capability to support the development of African American–owned businesses and to assist African American entrepreneurs. The NBMBAA economic development strategy includes acquisition of funds, and it is currently working on the details to implement and fund this plan. Emerging businesses in the African American community with the potential for success will be targeted with the goal of sustaining and growing these businesses.

At each annual conference, programs and workshops are presented. Also, the NBMBAA leverages the conference, which represents a budget of approximately $4 million with $12 million in purchasing power. It also proactively directs more dollars into the African American markets where the conference is held. In addition, the dialogue fostered by the NBMBAA with corporations is one of partnership founded upon mutual respect for one another's goals and objectives. In one instance, the organization has developed products and services to meet corporate needs, and by 1997, its corporate partners numbered almost 300, up from 180 in 1991. Their contributions, commitment, and respect for the organization have increased. Consequently, while the legacy plan had not been completely implemented by the late 1990s, a foundation and framework had been established.

A direct correlation with the members' commitment is seen as the basis for the future success of the NBMBAA. The membership retention rate in the early

1990s was 20 percent, which meant the NBMBAA membership was turning over almost every year. By the late 1990s, the retention rate was 75 percent, with growth averaging approximately 18 percent per year. Also, the NBMBAA in this period expanded from 25 chapters with approximately 1,900 members to 39 chapters in 1998 with more than 4,300 members and an international affiliate. The beachhead for launching a global presence was established through the NBMBAA's relationship with the London-based African and Caribbean Finance Forum (ACFF). It is crucial for future competitiveness that African Americans compete on a global level. To this end, we have linked our youth and corporate diversity programs and are currently preparing to launch joint employment and membership programs. This significantly growing relationship will allow us together to meet the global needs of our membership and firmly position ourselves in key markets. Finally, the next phase in the organization's growth in the twenty-first century is to build the National Black MBA Association into a formidable institution that can promote the continued expansion of African American business activity.

SELECTED BIBLIOGRAPHY: NBMBAA, "History," Archives, National Office, Chicago, Illinois; NBMBAA web site, available from http://www.nbmbaa.org/history.html
Antoinette Malveaux and Tamara M. Brown

NATIONAL BLACK UNITED FUND (NBUF). Founded in 1972 and headquartered in Newark, New Jersey, this organization was established to provide financial support for black charitable causes with contributions from the African American community. Although some resources are generated at the national level from grants and donations, much of the fund-raising is conducted locally through the National Black United Fund chapter affiliates. Particularly significant is the money raised through payroll deduction, which was made possible as the result of a contentious legal battle with United Way of America. With 22 affiliates, 13 regional federations of charities, and the participation of 47 national organizations, NBUF has established a nationwide fund-raising network in the African American community.

The National Black United Fund evolved from an initiative of the Brotherhood Crusade in Los Angeles. The concept involved collective economic development and self-determination. This idea was based on the assumption that funds collected by and from African Americans could be distributed in a manner consistent with the priorities of the black community. In contrast, donations from individuals or institutions outside the African American community might carry restrictive conditions.

In 1980, a landmark federal case established the right of the National Black United Fund to participate in charitable donation campaigns in the workplace. This case challenged the authority of United Way to exclude NBUF from participation in the payroll deduction programs of federal employees. Moreover, *National Black United Fund, Inc. v. Alan K. Campbell and United Way of*

America provided a legal precedent that paved the way for other organizations, including the National Association for the Advancement of Colored People (NAACP) Legal Defense and Educational Fund, to participate in workplace charitable appeals.

The major efforts of NBUF are conducted at local or regional levels. For example, in 1990, employees at the University of Illinois at Urbana were given the option of selecting the Black United Fund as a payroll deduction choice. Faculty and staff who select this option designate an amount to be contributed to the Black United Fund of Illinois, which distributes funds to several programs, institutions, and agencies in the state, including Black Ensemble Theatre, Cabrini Connections, Chicago Vietnam Veterans and Family Assistance, Community Law Project, Clara's House Shelter, Illinois Council for College Attendance, Matthew House of Champaign, Shorebank Neighborhood Institute, and South Side Help Center.

Self-determination and cooperative economic development are ideas that have been used over the centuries by black religious, mutual aid, and fraternal groups for such purposes as protection, business creation, and education. The National Black United Fund has incorporated these principles with the opportunities offered by the modern workplace for the economic empowerment of African Americans.

SELECTED BIBLIOGRAPHY: Black United Fund of Illinois, *Annual Reports*, various years; Emmett D. Carson, "The National Black United Fund: From Movement for Social Change to Social Change Organization," *Fundraising Matters* 1 (Fall 1993); King E. Davis, "The National Black United Fund: Self-Help for Black People" (unpublished paper); *National Black United Fund, Inc. v. Alan K. Campbell and United Way of America* 49 F. Supp. 748 (1980).

Rosemary M. Stevenson

NATIONAL CENTER FOR NEIGHBORHOOD ENTERPRISE (NCNE). The National Center for Neighborhood Enterprise (NCNE) was founded in 1981, with the mission of helping indigenous community leaders of low-income neighborhoods empower residents to achieve economic self-sufficiency and upward mobility and to address societal problems through neighborhood-based initiatives. NCNE's strategies, pursuant to this mission, are based on the following premises: Low-income individuals and neighborhood-based organizations should play a central role in the design and implementation of programs to address the problems of their communities.

An effective approach to economic and societal problems must be driven by the same principles that function in the market economy, recognizing the importance of competition, entrepreneurship, cost efficiency, and an expectation of return on investment. Value-generating and faith-based, neighborhood-based initiatives are uniquely qualified to address problems of poverty that are related to behavior and life choices. The National Center, then, was formed to promote the economic revitalization of low-income communities, in that its programs are based on a recognition of the important interrelatedness of internal transformation (regarding the vision and values of residents) and external support (ensuring the availability of opportunities for education, training, employment, and entrepreneurship).

Funded primarily through private support, NCNE has offered support for effective grassroots initiatives for economic development and social revitalization in the form of training, technical assistance, vehicles for networking with other grassroots groups, and linkages to sources of funding. Funds contributed to NCNE have leveraged up to four times their amount for NCNE's grassroots affiliate organizations. A number of state and federal officials have requested NCNE's assistance in identifying effective community-based initiatives, coordinating forums through which neighborhood leaders could voice recommendations for the type of legislation that would promote their efforts and developing public/private efforts to meet the needs of their low-income neighborhoods.

The National Center's network of constituents now includes more than 700 organizations in 38 states. NCNE's assistance to these affiliates includes financial assistance: minigrants and vouchers for training and technical assistance. In 1991, supported by a grant from the Kellogg Foundation, the National Center established the Neighborhood Leadership Development Institute (NLDI), which has provided training for more than 600 grassroots leaders. Through this training, programs that began as spontaneous volunteer responses to community crises were developed into sustainable organizations that provide continuing services for the residents of low-income neighborhoods. NLDI's curriculum includes leadership development, personal revitalization, organizational development (including achieving 501(c)3 status and proposal writing), financial management (including budget development), personnel management, and public outreach.

The NCNE also conducts numerous conferences, seminars, and forums in which grassroots leaders describe "best practices," addressing issues ranging from entrepreneurship to job training and placement. In addition, NCNE has coordinated a number of task forces in a project entitled Grassroots Alternatives for Public Policy, which advised policymakers and elected and appointed officials on national, state, and local levels regarding legislation and public policy that would maximize the positive impact of local "community healers." The NCNE also produced a number of publications that feature the success of community-based initiatives in addressing a variety of issues.

A quarterly journal, *AGENDA*, has featured such topics as thriving black business districts that existed through the first half of this century, remarkable community revitalization produced by resident-management in public housing, an overview of "What Works & Why" testimony, the role of the church in community development, and effective responses to youth violence and gang activity. *Empowering Residents of Public Housing*, a resource guide for resident management, is also a publication of the National Center. In addition, NCNE, a nonprofit, tax-exempt organization, produced a series of monographs, including *Youth Enterprises: Race and Economic Opportunity, and Entrepreneurial Enclaves* in the African American Experience.*

The NCNE, then, has been in the forefront in the economic and social revitalization of low-income neighborhoods. In a number of areas, the strategies developed through the firsthand experience of grassroots leaders and promoted by NCNE have proved to be adaptable models that have had nationwide impact. In 1985, the National Center identified and supported a then-nascent effort of residents of public housing to take on management responsibilities for the properties in which they lived. As NCNE brought public awareness to the volunteer efforts of residents to improve living conditions in their housing developments, public officials were convinced of the value of establishing pilot projects of "resident management."

These projects were remarkably successful. In one public housing development in Washington, D.C., for example, residents who had firsthand experience of their neighborhood problems worked with heartfelt commitment to comprehensively address the interrelated factors that had once devastated their community. Within four years, they had reduced teenage pregnancies and welfare dependency by 50 percent, reduced crime by 75 percent, and inspired a 77 percent increase in payments of rent. This success sparked the creation of legislation that promoted a quickly growing movement of resident management and the establishment of an Office of Resident Initiatives within the U.S. Department of Housing and Urban Development. Today, throughout the country, hundreds of resident management corporations (RMCs) are effectively working to engender community revitalization and have formed a nationwide organization, the National Association of Resident Management Corporations, which now has over 1,300 members.

In the mid-1990s, NCNE identified and supported a network of effective grassroots initiatives whose efforts provide the foundation for an effective, adaptable model of youth intervention and a prototype for reclaiming Violence Free zones in crime-plagued urban areas. Within NCNE's network of affiliates, neighborhood leaders in Los Angeles, California, Hartford, Connecticut, Dallas, Texas, and Washington, D.C., have worked with youth gangs through their existing internal structures of leadership and peer influence to transform once-violent youths into productive, responsible role models for other young people. In the instance of Washington, D.C., an indigenous community organization, the Alliance of Concerned Men, also established a model partnership with the local housing department to ensure that crucial opportunities for job training, placement, education, and entrepreneurship were available to youths who had won personal victories over the lures of drug abuse and criminal activity. NCNE's nationwide network of youth intervention initiatives has the potential to expand and strengthen its effective outreach, just as the movement of resident managers in public housing did a decade earlier.

SELECTED BIBLIOGRAPHY: Robert L. Woodson, Sr., ed., *On the Road to Economic Freedom: An Agenda for Black Progress* (Washington, DC: Regnery Gateway, 1987); Robert L. Woodson, Sr., ed., *The Triumphs of Joseph: How Today's Community Leaders Are Revitalizing Our Streets and Neighborhoods* (New York: Free Press, 1998).

Robert L. Woodson, Sr.

NATIONAL NEGRO BASEBALL LEAGUE (1879–1930). The National Negro Baseball League, organized by Andrew "Rube" Foster in 1920, was the first sustaining organized professional black baseball league. He was also owner and manager of the Chicago American Giants. The National Negro Baseball League included six midwestern teams; the Kansas City Monarchs, owned by J. L. Wilkerson, was the only white-owned team. In 1923, Nat Strong, a white booking agent, organized the Eastern Colored League to compete against the National Negro League. Of the six eastern teams, four were white owned. Foster's goal was to prove that blacks had the athletic ability and business acumen to successfully build a profitable baseball league.

This goal was driven by a desire for inclusion into the larger society, including major league baseball. The profitability of the league is a questionable one, owing to its often illegal sources of supplemental income. Rube Foster was determined to manage the Negro League to financial success. As the league was establishing itself, he often contributed his own finances to needed teams, by way of transportation costs, hotel costs, and other pertinent operating expenses. Although he did not request a salary, he received 5 percent of all league game receipts.

In 1923, total receipts from league games were $197,218, while Foster received his income of $9,861. He had office expenses and assisted in other league expenses, of $36,212 so this was not necessarily take-home pay for him. Total league expenses for 1923 amounted to $172,285, including Foster's payment, with player salaries accounting for $101,000 of this total; transportation costs were $25,212. This provided a net profit of $24,933. This profit was redistributed among the existing teams at season's end. Only a few teams boasted large gate receipts, such as the American Giants with average receipts of $85,000 and the Monarchs with average receipts of $41,000. In 1926, Foster's mental illness toppled with the Great Depression, and ultimately, his death in 1930 led to the closing of the financially unstable league in 1931.

By the late 1920s, however, Cumberland Willis Posey's Washington Homestead Grays was considered "the best black baseball team in the world." Posey stayed abreast with the business trends of the Negro National (NNL) League and responded accordingly. When the Pittsburgh Keystones began to provide salaries for their players, Posey responded by offering the same payroll method to stay competitive. With his shrewd business practices, his biggest acquisition was catcher Josh Gibson "the home run king of black baseball," in 1930. As an independent club, it was more profitable than league-sponsored teams. Posey reportedly received 75 percent of the gate receipts. He would later have to compete with the influx of racketeer owners and their seemingly unlimited finances. But again, he responded by persuading Rufus Jackson to "put his money into the Grays as a cover-up for his other activities."

The only source of capital available to black baseball that was unaffected by the depression was racketeering funds. "Numbers"* kings saw professional Negro baseball as a legitimate front for their illegal activities. Therefore, the resurgence of the Negro Baseball League was due to the finances of gangsters. William August "Gus" Greenlee of the Pittsburgh Crawfords was the most successful. There were many other racketeer owners: Ed Semler, the Black Yankees; Tom Wilson, the Baltimore Elite Giants; Robert Cole, Cole's American Giants; Alex Pompez, the New York Cubans; and Abe Manley, the Newark Eagles, whose wife handled the business affairs of the team.

Gus Greenlee was a wealthy racketeer who reorganized the league as well as owned the Pittsburgh Crawfords. Greenlee's deep pockets helped him attract future hall of Famers Josh Gibson (from the Grays), Satchel Paige, Oscar Charlston, William Julius "Judy" Johnson, and James Thomas "Cool Papa" Bell. He kept $100 bills in his pockets and treated his players very well, financially. As Ted Page recalled, "He was all business. When a player requested money, no problem." As the employer of choice for players, due to this reputation, he had very little problem attracting the best players. Despite Greenlee's anticipated unprofitable beginning, he pumped several thousand dollars into his team. In 1933, he claimed he lost $50,000 in baseball; however, it is unknown if this was due to his baseball or racketeering activities.

Many gangster-owners passed their numbers income off as baseball income. Nonetheless, Greenlee's illegal activities were common knowledge but were overlooked because he was financing the baseball league and the black community as well. In 1932, he built the first black-owned baseball stadium, Greenlee Field, with approximately $100,000. It had a seating capacity of 7,500 and included "superb locker room facilities for both the home and visiting teams." As the league's popularity increased with a large fan support, other Negro teams were given the opportunity to rent out major league stadiums, when the major league team was on the road. Leasing costs averaged $4,000 annually or 10 to 20 percent of gate receipts for stadium use. Some clubs did not want black teams using their stadiums—Chicago's Wrigley Field did not want any "niggers messing up their ball park." However, black teams hoped the venue of the major league stadium would attract more fans, which it did.

Negro League teams had various strategies for increasing revenue. For economic reasons, the teams played, primarily, everyday and sometimes three to four games per day. They played in major cities where there was a large black population, such as Chicago, Indianapolis, and Kansas City. This strategy was known as the "barnstorming system." Black players viewed themselves as entertainers in order to attract fans. This method of "advertising" was a means to increase gate receipts. Satchel Paige, a pitcher, would often instruct the other eight members of the defensive team to "have a seat," as he was confident he would strike out the batter. Paige's exploits were so entertaining that his team—the Monarchs—would often loan him out to minor league teams. The Ethiopian Clowns (later called the Indianapolis Clowns) pulled tricks and joked around to provide entertainment. They even signed Toni Stone, a woman, with the intent of using her as an attention-getter.

Greenlee and Tom Wilson, of Nashville, introduced the biggest sporting event in black sports, the East-West (all-star) game. Although there existed a World Series for the league, this game did not receive as much fanfare as the East-West Classic. This annual game in Chicago's Comiskey Park attracted 30,000 to 50,000 people. Gate receipts from this game often turned net losses into net income for some teams. With the best black talent in one stadium and the huge fan support, this successful event proved to be the seed for the demise of black baseball, for this game precipitated talks of integrating major league baseball.

Black-owned teams were hoping for the integration of an entire black baseball club; however, the majors were not willing to go that far—only a couple of black players here and there. The 1947 integration of major league baseball by Jackie Robinson marked the beginning of the end for the Negro Baseball League. In 1947, Effa Manley developed contracts in negotiating the sale of her black players to the majors. This was not very successful, as with Monte Irvin, she claimed, "They paid me $5,000 lousy dollars for Irvin, if he'd have been white they'd have given me $100,000." Therefore, as the best black players went to the majors, they took their fans with them. So go the fans, so go the gate receipts. Consequently, black baseball teams gradually went bankrupt. The NNL folded in 1949. The social gains of integration led to the economic decline of a separate black enterprise, Negro baseball.

SELECTED BIBLIOGRAPHY: John Holway, *Blackball Stars: Negro League Pioneers* (Westport, CT: Meckler Books, 1988); John Ingham and Lynne B. Feldman, *A Biographical Dictionary of African American Business Leaders* (Westport, CT: Greenwood Press, 1994); James Overmyer, *Queen of the Negro Leagues: Effa Manley and the Newark Eagles* (Lanham, MD: Scarecrow Press, 1998); Robert Peterson, *Only the Ball Was White* (New York: McGraw-Hill, 1970); Donn Rogosin, *Life in Baseball's Negro Leagues* (New York: Atheneum, 1983).

Quincy T. Mills

NATIONAL NEGRO BUSINESS LEAGUE (NNBL). The National Negro Business League (NNBL) was founded by Booker T. Washington* in 1900, with the purpose to promote the "commercial, agricultural, educational, and industrial advancement" of African Americans. Yet its primary focus from the beginning, as Washington emphasized was "to encourage more of our people to go into business." The first meeting, held in Boston, was attended by 300 blacks from 34 states, who participated in all kinds of occupations. Invariably they were the leaders of the various communities in which they lived and included not only businesspeople but also professionals, physicians, attorneys, teachers, college and university professors, and the ubiquitous black minister.

Black church leaders were significantly important in encouraging their congregations to support black businesses. Booker T. Washington was elected president, a position he held until his death in 1915. The organization continued with leading blacks being elected to the position of NNBL president.

In the 15 years that Washington, one of the most powerful black Americans in the twentieth century, served as president, the NNBL's membership expanded quickly. In 1905 there were some 320 chapters, and in 1907, the NNBL had 3,000 members. By 1915 membership was estimated anywhere from 5,000 to 40,000, with more than 600 state and local chapters established in some 34 states and the Gold Coast in West Africa. The NNBL also inspired the 1901 founding of the Bantu Business League, which was established in South Africa in 1901 by the Reverend John Langalabele Dube. A fervent admirer of Washington, Dube also founded the Zulu Christian Industrial School. While Dube was called the "Booker T. Washington of South Africa," he was also one of the founders of the ANC (African National Congress), which was in the forefront in the fight against apartheid.

At each annual conference there were testimonies from successful black businessmen and women, who provided case studies of how they established their businesses and the techniques and strategies used to expand their consumer markets. On the local and state level, NNBL chapters addressed specific issues in the community not only of business but also the forces of Jim Crow segregation and discrimination.

In 1905 the Nashville, Tennessee, NNBL chapter, in response to a state law that required all municipal transportation services to be segregated, not only organized a boycott but established a bus company. The president of the NNBL Nashville chapter was Reverend Richard Boyd,* head of the National Baptist Publishing Board, who along with James Napier organized the Union Transportation Company. In 1907, the Mississippi state branch of the NNBL endorsed the proposal for the establishment of the Mound Bayou* Cotton Mill and published the prospectus of the project, which was initiated by Charles Banks.* Booker T. Washington solicited financial support from white industrialists to help.

At the same time, the NNBL was important for providing a model for new black business organizations, initially caucuses that grew out of the League, including the National Negro Insurance Association, the National Negro Bankers Association, the National Negro Bar Association, and the National Negro Undertakers Association. The league continued its activities after Washington's death and remained a national force until the post–World War II era. During the war the NNBL threw its full support behind the nation's war efforts, but at the same time, promoting the recovery and expansion of black business and capturing the black consumer market were major goals of the (NNBL)

In the post–World War II era of rising expectations and the increasing urbanization of black America, the community cohesiveness that had encouraged and supported broad-based organizations, such as the NNBL, began to fall apart.

Then, with the 1954 *Brown v. Board of Education* decision, there was a shift in focus from surviving economically in a separate world to benefiting fully in an integrated American society.

From 1954 to the 1964 Civil Rights Act the emphasis in black America was in securing civil and political rights. Then with the destruction of black business communities, hastened by the concomitant forces of urban renewal, the Black Revolution moved from the demand for civil rights to the cry for "Black Power."* Paradoxically, there was a resurgence of emphasis on self-help, the support and promotion of black businesses, and the expansion of "black capitalism," the heart of Booker T. Washington's philosophy of economic separatism, which would seem to encourage a renewed interest in the NNBL. The economic success of the Nation of Islam,* with its separatist philosophy, seemed to corroborate Washington's ideology.

Yet after the 1960s, few black Americans could accept the basis of Washington's ideology as providing the foundation for black business growth and expansion, which was expressed most clearly in Washington's last address to the NNBL in 1915 when he said: "At the bottom of education, at the bottom of politics, even at the bottom of religion itself, there must be for our race, as for all races, an economic foundation, economic prosperity, economic independence." Yet, considering their economic position, few black Americans could disagree with Washington when he said in that same address: "We believe that without a solid economic foundation it is impossible for any race of people to make much enduring, much permanent progress in any country of the world."

In the post–civil rights era, as the nation was moving from an industrial economy to a technologically driven economy, it would be difficult to find black Americans accepting Washington's mandate that economics supersedes education. Indeed, with the affirmative action guidelines, which opened the doors for black Americans to enter new professions, some of the brightest, most aggressive, and determined young blacks abandoned the liberal arts and sciences and flocked to the nation's business schools.* Moreover, their goal was white Corporate America, as opposed to black entrepreneurship. Their career paths were emphasized in a 1994 issue of *Black Enterprise*, which noted: "The financial warfare of the past 25 years has been fought with an arsenal of MBAs, law degrees, business plans and venture capital."

While Booker T. Washington founded the NNBL, the genesis for the organization originated at the 1898 Fourth Atlanta Conference, where the focus that year was on the "Negro in Business." The 1898 Conference was convened by the great advocate of the "Talented Tenth," W.E.B. Du Bois, who called for "[t]he organization in every town and hamlet where colored people dwell, of Negro Business Men's Leagues, and the gradual federation from these of state and national organizations." Also, Professor John Hope, then president of Atlanta Baptist College, and of Morehouse College from 1906 to 1931, introduced the teaching of business in 1921 by offering a course in money and banking. In 1925, accounting was offered, and beginning in 1924, a full department of business administration was established. Even before Washington's death in 1915, the need for education in business was recognized as the basis of black economic progress.

The NNBL, now the National Business League, is no longer seen as a force among African American business organizations. Yet its historic significance is in documenting the diversity and continuity of efforts made by black Americans to participate fully and successfully in the American capitalist economy. The organization is now the National Business League with national head quarters in Washington, D.C.

SELECTED BIBLIOGRAPHY: John H. Burrows, *The Necessity of Myth: A History of the National Negro Business League* (Auburn, AL: Hickory Hill Press, 1988); Kenneth Hamilton, ed., *Records of the National Negro Business League* [microform] (Bethesda, MD: University Publications of America, 1994); Louis R. Harlan, *Booker T. Washington: The Wizard of Tuskegee, 1901–1915* (New York: Oxford University Press, 1983); Albon L. Holsey, ''The National Negro Business League,'' in J. L. Nichols and William H. Crogman, eds., *Progress of a Race: Or, the Remarkable Advancement of the American Negro* (1920; reprint, New York: Arno Press, 1969); Juliet E. K. Walker, *The History of Black Business in America* (New York: Macmillan, 1998); Booker T. Washington, ''The National Negro Business League,'' *World's Work* 4 (October 1902).

Juliet E. K. Walker

NATIONAL NEGRO CONVENTION MOVEMENT. Indirectly, the founding of the National Negro Convention Movement (NNCM), which first met in 1830, was a response by African Americans to the American Colonization Society (ACS). The ACS was founded in 1817 for the purpose of encouraging free blacks to leave America and settle in Liberia. Also, the ACS promoted a program to encourage slaveowners to make relocation to Liberia a condition of manumission for their slaves. While opposition to colonization was a catalyst for blacks to organize nationally and present a united front, racial hostilities in Cincinnati, Ohio, in 1829, which resulted in more than 1,000 blacks fleeing the city to seek refuge in Canada, precipitated the first meeting of the NNCM. Moreover, as the name of the organization shows—''The American Society of Free Persons of Colour, for Improving Their Condition in the United States, for Purchasing Land, and for the Establishment of a Settlement in Canada''—Africans Americans were determined to make a stand and not be forced out of the United States. There was, of course, an element of realism. Refuge was needed for fugitive slaves and also for free blacks in times of heightened hostility.

The NNCM has significance not only because it was the first national black organization (most members were from northern states) outside the black church to represent blacks but also because it stood against slavery and promoted abolitionist activities. At the same time, the NNBL promoted the economic advancement of blacks. Most of the members were businessmen, and the agendas of the conferences reflected their economic interests.

Particularly, the NNBL encouraged savings and investment. Indeed, the

NNCM in its constitution required that funds generated by the organization be invested in U.S. securities. The NNCM also encouraged the purchase of real estate, promoted the establishment of black businesses, advocated the development of commercial farming activities, and sought international trade* relations with Africa and in the African diaspora. The NNCM also called for the establishment of a national black bank. Indeed, in 1847, the organization's newly formed "Banks and Banking Institutions Committee" called for the establishment of a national black bank, explaining: "[A] Banking Institution originating among the colored people of the U. States [is needed] because they at present contribute to their own degradation by investing capital in the hands of their 'enemies.' "

The NNBL met 11 times before the Civil War. In the interim, state conventions were held. In its goals and activities, the NNCM presaged those of black organizations founded in the twentieth century, including the National Negro Business League (NNBL),* the National Association for the Advancement of Colored People (NAACP), and the Black Urban League.* Its historic significance is that it underscores the heritage of African Americans in promoting business as a basis to advance their economic position in a society that was hostile to their advancement.

SELECTED BIBLIOGRAPHY: Howard Holman Bell, *A Survey of the National Negro Convention Movement, 1830–1864* (New York: Arno Press, 1969); Howard Holman Bell, ed., *Minutes of the Proceedings of the National Negro Conventions, 1830–1864* (New York: Arno Press and the *New York Times*, 1969); Juliet E. K. Walker, "Promoting Black Entrepreneurship and Business Enterprise in Antebellum America: The National Negro Convention, 1830–1855," in Thomas D. Boston, ed., *A Different Vision: Race and Public Policy*, vol. 2 (London: Routledge Press, 1997).

Juliet E. K. Walker

NATIONAL URBAN LEAGUE, BLACK EXECUTIVE EXCHANGE PROGRAM. Black economic empowerment has been a critical part of the National Urban League mission since the organization's founding in 1910. Program services related to education, job training, employment, and career development have been central to the effort, and the Urban League has developed critical ties among government, industry, and schools in meeting its objectives. Over the years, the League's efforts have progressed to keep pace with changing demands. In the beginning, the organization focused on the fundamental job training and critical readjustment needs of blacks moving from a largely rural, agrarian economy of the South to the urban industrial centers in the North. These days, job seekers are as likely to plug into the League's computerized job bank—connecting with potential employers on the Internet—as they are to participate in direct contact seminars and conferences sponsored by the organization.

Since 1969, the Urban League has been taking its mission to higher ground. The Black Executive Exchange Program (BEEP) is a voluntary partnership among business, government, and historically black colleges and universities (HBCUs). Among other things, this League initiative provides a pipeline between HBCUs and Corporate America through curriculum development, strengthening college faculty, and increasing student and faculty awareness of employment trends and current opportunities. Through BEEP, senior- and middle-level executives and managers from corporations, professional firms, and government agencies volunteer as visiting professors at HBCUs. The program provides semester-long courses in over 30 career-related subject areas, developed by BEEP staff with assistance from college faculty. The visiting professors lecture in the credit-bearing courses, usually in two-day rotations each semester. The participating companies and agencies absorb all costs related to providing this service.

BEEP visiting professors are able to bring subject matter to life for students, providing a real-world backdrop of case studies and problem solving for the theoretical material presented in most classes. They also provide something more: Given the fact that all BEEP visiting professors are African American executives and managers, they serve as role models for black students—living proof, as the League asserts, that "success depends more on competence than color" and that corporate and government career opportunities are wide and varied. The program also adds an effective new dimension to the faculty and course offerings for HBCUs, which often are financially disadvantaged in the competition for quality faculty. In addition to regular semester-long courses, BEEP also has sponsored a number of special seminars over the years focusing on such areas as career planning and women's opportunities. The BEEP program in encouraging the development of future black business leaders represents an important direction for the Urban League in the twenty-first century.

SELECTED BIBLIOGRAPHY: R. Ayres-Williams, "The New Rights Agenda," *Black Enterprise* (August. 1997): 85; Timothy Mason Bates and William Bradford, *Financing Black Economic Development* (New York: Academic Press, 1979); Roy S. Johnson, "There Is Opportunity and There Is Action" [A Conversation with Hugh Price of the National Urban League], *Fortune*, August 1997, 67–68; National Urban League, web site, available from http://www.nul.org/beep/prgm.htm; "Planning for Economic Power Focus of 1997 Urban League Confab," *Jet* (September 1, 1997), 4–6. National Urban League, web site, available from http://www.nul.org/beep/prgm.htm

Christopher D. Benson

NATION OF ISLAM ENTERPRISES—ELIJAH MUHAMMAD (1897–1975), Chicago, **AND LOUIS FARRAKHAN** (1933–), Chicago, leader of the Nation of Islam, entrepreneur, real estate and international imports and exports, minister, teacher, activist, economic visionary.

The Nation of Islam, considered by some to be an indigenous African American expression of Islam, was founded by W. D. Muhammad and developed by Elijah Muhammad. He was born Elijah Poole, the son of a Baptist minister, in Sandersville, Georgia, but left that state at the age of 16 to settle in Detroit.

There, in 1930, he met W. D. Fard, also known as Master Farad Muhammad, an Arab merchant who founded a Temple of Islam in Detroit. Elijah became a follower of the new sect. When Farad Muhammad disappeared in 1934, Elijah Muhammad assumed leadership of the sect, the Messenger of the Lost-Found Nation of Islam in the West, and served as its leader until his death.

Subsequently, Muhammad moved to Chicago, organizing Temple #2 to re-establish the roots of the Nation of Islam. During the 1930s and 1940s, Chicago was the commercial center for America's Heartland. Muhammad wanted the national center of the Nation of Islam located in a city with a flourishing economic community. Elijah Muhammad's message to black people was that by enslavement whites murdered black people, spiritually, morally, and emotionally. In order to counter the ongoing attack of the black psyche by a hostile, racist America, Elijah Muhammad tried to instill in his followers self-esteem and self-awareness. His purpose was to eliminate black self-hatred brought on by a history of racism and oppression in America. He advocated the building of love and respect of self among black people and emphasized the importance of high moral conduct, physical health, and well-being through diet and exercise, discipline, inculcated by rigorous standards set forth by the Nation of Islam. Elijah Muhammad also stressed the importance of economic independence and liberation of black people through entrepreneurship.

Elijah Muhammad taught followers that hard work, thrift, and accumulation of wealth are key to the success of blacks in America. His philosophy of wealth accumulation was published as *Economic Blueprint of the Nation of Islam*, which served as an organizational guide and creed for individual members of the Nation of Islam during the late 1950s and early 1960s. Recognizing the necessity for unity and group operation in activities, the steps outlined were (1) to pool resources physically as well as financially and (2) to stop wanton criticisms of everything that is black, black-owned, and black-operated. Many times he said, "Observe the operations of the white man. He is successful. He makes no excuses for his failure. He works hard in a collective manner.... [Y]ou do the same." Saving was emphasized as the means to escape poverty, and Muhammad advised his followers: "Spend out of what is necessary and according to your income." Particularly, he emphasized: "Stop begging from and seeking the acceptance from your slave masters and go and do for self. Seek to buy farmland so that you can grow your own food. Purchase real estate and timberland so that you can build homes and produce goods for your self and others at reasonable prices."

In many ways, Muhammad's economic philosophy differed little from the post–civil rights neoconservatives, for he also said: "We cannot continue to depend on the White man to care for us and build a future for us and our children. We must strike out for ourselves or be left behind helpless and without a future." Elijah Muhammad, however, was an advocate of supporting black-owned businesses, and he denounced blacks for failing to patronize black-owned businesses. E. U. Essien Udom noted that he said: "You, Black man, are the only members of the human race that walks past a business of your own to spend your dollar with your natural enemy. . . . The White Man . . . the Chinese, Japanese, Puerto Rican, Cuban . . . all spend money with their own kind and support their own kind and by doing so are able to give assistance and employment to their own when in need.''

As the organization grew in membership with temples being established across the country, members of the Nation of Islam were required to give one-tenth of their earnings toward the establishment of business enterprises for the Nation. These were not considered investments, and the members did not own stock. They were considered alms or charity for the growth of the organization. The purpose of the alms was also to foster a financial commitment to the welfare of the larger community among its members; to act as a channel of income to be utilized for collective enterprises; and to help members develop a habit of saving what they earned.

While members of the Nation of Islam were also encouraged to put aside the bulk of their income for savings, at the same time, they were still forced to depend on white-owned stores for most services because of the growing yet limited scope of production of black manufacturers during the late 1950s and early 1960s. On the other hand, due to the strict discipline required of the members of the Nation of Islam, the elimination of nonessential expenditures considered toxic to the mind, body, and spirit (tobacco, alcohol, gambling, drugs, expensive cars, clothes, and impure foods) and the strict dietary laws (one meal a day of inexpensive, wholesome foods) provided a basis for saving. Muhammad asked members to invest some of their saving into a three-year savings program so that the Nation of Islam could purchase banks, farmland, and warehouses to supply the black community with all the food and provisions they would need.

In the early 1960s the primary sources of financial support for the Nation of Islam came from contributions of money, time, and services provided by skilled members and supporters and contributions of Islamic literature and materials from foreign sources. There was also a fund set up to assist the poor and needy within the organization as well as to maintain a level of comfort for Elijah Muhammad and his family, with the Nation absorbing their expenses. The Muhammad Temple #2 Poor Fund would prove to be well endowed and a major source of concern after the death of Elijah Muhammad. The economic blueprint of the Nation of Islam established in the 1950s would be the foundation of the business empire that emerged in the mid-1960s to early 1970s.

Before he died, Elijah Muhammad put his economic vision for black America into action by establishing many businesses, which in the Chicago metropolitan area alone were reported to have generated $46 million by 1975. Businesses established by the Nation of Islam reflected its attempt at self-sufficiency, especially in food provisions and personal service enterprises. In addition, there was a chain of Salaam Restaurants; two Muslim Import stores; a Muslim Fish House for their line of imported fish and other products; a Temple #2 Clothing

Store; the National Clothing Factory; the National Fez Factory; and the National Trucking System. There was also the *Muhammad Speaks* Newspaper and Newspaper Plant in addition to a cold storage and warehouse facility. These were businesses located in the black community that served, serviced, and provided goods that met the needs of the members of the Nation of Islam as well as the larger black community locally and nationally.

The Progressive Land Development Company, the Nation's real estate company, was established by Muhammad to manage the extensive property owned by the Nation of Islam. The Nation's real estate holdings included over 200 apartment units and single-family dwellings and 5,000 acres of farmland in Michigan, Georgia, and Alabama. In addition, there were over 150 temples in North America, Jamaica, Honduras, and Bermuda, and over 46 University of Islam Educational Centers. The Nation also owned a Learjet to facilitate the national and international travels of Elijah Muhammad. A newly constructed Sales and Office Building was established as the national office for management of the diverse enterprise and properties held by the Nation. The Nation also owned the Guarantee Bank and Trust Company to provide banking services to its members as well as Chicago's black community.

Yet while Muhammad built the Nation's economic empire, its significance was lost in the public mind. Instead, national and international attention was focused on Muhammad's most visible junior minister, Malcolm X, a student of Elijah Muhammad, who emerged as the leading spokesperson of the Nation of Islam in the early 1960s. With the media focused on Malcolm X's bombastic critiques, based on the teaching of Muhammad that the religious, racial, and class constraints of American culture stifled the progress of black people, Muhammad's economic program for the economic uplift of African Americans was ignored in the media, as was Malcolm's message for black people to believe in themselves.

Still, as the Nation of Islam grew from a small sect to a multimillion-dollar organization with a huge bureaucracy, the character of the organization changed as well. The administrative hierarchy of the organization became more conservative and concerned itself with protecting its profits, becoming less patient with Malcolm's radical and vocal stances concerning politics and international affairs. Malcolm, too, became equally disenchanted with the policies of isolation, nonengagement, and conservatism of the Nation of Islam during the 1960s. Eventually he left in 1964. Moreover, despite the Nation's emphasis on the economic uplift of its members, there was also evidence that the Federal Bureau of Investigation, as early as 1959, placed people in positions of leadership with the goal of transforming the organization or destroying it.

In 1975, Elijah Muhammad died. The events that followed led to the decline of one of the most prominent black financial empires of the twentieth century. At the time of the death of Elijah Muhammad, the assets of the Nation of Islam were estimated at $46 million. By 1991, the estate of Elijah Muhammad was empty. Elijah Muhammad left no will, which meant that the dispersal of assets would be decided by the Cook County courts and the State of Illinois. Also, the legal battle that ensued centered on one question: What belonged to Elijah Muhammad personally and what belonged to the religious community of the Nation of Islam?

By 1980, five years after the death of Muhammad, the estate was said to contain $3.5 million, of which $3.25 million belonged to the Muhammad Temple #2 Poor Fund; $10 to $15 million in real estate held by Progressive Land Developers; four homes at 49th and Woodlawn in Chicago for family and aides; 11 businesses; $350,000 from the sale of the Learjet; $150,000 in cash; furnishings and furniture taken from the home after his death; and $350,000 that Muhammad loaned to a bank that later failed.

The biggest claims were for the $3.5 million and the properties. Herbert and Wallace Muhammad, two of Muhammad's sons and executors of the estate, admitted to spending between $10 and $12 million during the first five to six years after their father's death, not including rents collected from tenants, profits from the businesses, and donations from the faithful. They also acknowledged that they spent $3.25 million of the monies in the Poor Fund and $250,00 in other accounts. In addition court records show they sold 24 pieces of property worth between $7 and $9 million, including Chicago apartment houses, commercial buildings, and southern farmland.

They justified these expenditures, stating that they had to provide for their family and the larger religious community, with 176 temples needing assistance from the national organization to stay afloat. Legal wrangling throughout the 1980s ended in a court decision, which held that the remaining money in the estate belonged to the religious community but that the $12.9 million in properties belonged to the family of the late Elijah Muhammad. Unfortunately, the 16 years of protracted court proceedings, legal fees paid to many of Chicago's most prominent law firms, which were involved over the years, continuous claims made by heirs and former aides, and the loss of several properties due to delinquent taxes left the estate empty in 1991, drawing no income and holding no assets.

During the early years after Elijah Muhammad's death, his son Wallace Muhammad, named by his father to lead the Nation of Islam, began to move the community away from the teachings of his father, toward Islam as it is practiced by the larger world community of Muslims. He discontinued mandatory sales of the newspaper *Final Call* and also compulsory donations. The Fruit of Islam, the paramilitary arm of the Nation of Islam, was dismantled. In addition, Wallace closed the businesses and sold many of the properties to pay legal fees, consequently ending the economic program of the Nation of Islam developed by his father. In 1976, Wallace Muhammad broke away completely from the Nation of Islam and established the World Community of Islam in the West, which later evolved to the American Muslim Mission. He subsequently changed his name to Warith Deen Mohammad.

In 1978, Minister Louis Farrakhan, a former regional minister in the Nation of Islam and aide to Elijah Muhammad, began to reestablish the program of the Honorable Elijah Muhammad. In doing so, he emerged as the new leader of the Nation of Islam and continued to promote black economic independence, upright moral conduct and discipline, and prosperity, not just for the followers of the Nation of Islam. According to Minister Farrakhan, "Booker T. Washington,* Noble Drew Ali,* Marcus Garvey,* and W.E.B. Du Bois gave Black people the principles that would lead us to our ultimate liberation." He then emphasized that "the Honorable Elijah Muhammad was able to synthesize these teachings [for the] . . . economic liberation of Black people throughout the world through his formulation of the Nation of Islam."

Since the full-fledged reemergence of the Nation of Islam in 1984, under the leadership of Louis Farrakhan, it has been involved in many projects to promote the economic growth and development of the black community. In 1985, he reacquired the mosque, which also houses the University of Islam school at 73rd and Stoney Island in Chicago, which has become the National Headquarters of the Nation of Islam, as well as "The Palace," the original home of Elijah Muhammad on 49th and Woodlawn. The Nation also owns the *Final Call* administrative building and two bookstores on the 7900 block of the South Side of Chicago. Both stores sell clothing, foodstuffs, prayer rugs, Holy Qurtans, other Islamic reading materials, video and audio tapes that the Nation of Islam produces, and books by and about black people. Also, the Nation established a health and beauty aids manufacturing company that sells its own line of Liquid Gold bath and body products under the trademark "POWER" health supplies.

In 1991 Minister Farrakhan reimplemented the Elijah Muhammad Three-Year Economic Plan, which as late as 1996 was still collecting monies, with the goal of raising $10 million by the end of that year for opening Salaam restaurant outlets in Atlanta, Houston, Los Angeles, and Miami. In 1995, the Nation also opened the $5 million debt-free Salaam Restaurant of Islam on Chicago's South Side, financed by Nation of Islam members and supporters. The restaurant contains an on-site bakery, the Blue Seas Quick Service Dine-In/Carry-Out Restaurant, and several luxuriant dining areas. Future goals are to distribute Salaam-baked items to stores locally, regionally, and nationally as well as franchise both the bakery and Blue Seas restaurant.

The second phase in the Nation's economic program is the continuing development of the Chicago-based Salaam facility to include a 2,000-seat auditorium, performing arts center, and parking facility. Under Farrakhan, the Nation has purchased 1,600 acres of farmland in Dawson, Georgia, for $1.4 million in 1994, bringing the total number to 3,600 acres of farmland owned by the Nation of Islam in Georgia, Michigan, and Alabama, with plans to purchase 8,000 more acres by the end of 1996. The goal of purchasing farmland is to create a for-profit employment base to provide meat, produce, and dairy products for supermarkets in distressed inner-city neighborhoods. Plans also call for purchasing seven additional trucks for carrying farm products and other Nation of Islam products across the country.

The Nation publishes the *Final Call* newspaper, which had a biweekly circulation of 600,000, the largest circulating black newspaper in the world. In April 1996, the paper began its weekly circulation of the newspaper, with plans to increase circulation to 1 million papers sold weekly. Also, it has established a site on the World Wide Web so that media circulation of its activities remain current, with highlights of articles from recent issues in the *Final Call*. The newspaper is also accessible to the global community via the Internet. Future plans include expanding the Nation of Islam's media company and establishing a television studio.

It is difficult to assess the worth of the Nation of Islam, since its finances are not a matter of public record. In the late 1990s, it is clear that the Nation has not achieved or surpassed the wealth amassed under the leadership of Elijah Muhammad. Also, controversy developed when Minister Farrakhan was offered $5 million by Libya's leader Muammar Gadhafi. America's foreign policy makes it illegal for American citizens to accept funds from nations declared enemies of the state. Farrakhan's purpose was to use the money as venture capital to encourage black business development.

Still, Louis Farrakhan has made great strides in advancing the economic development of the Nation of Islam while promoting the goals of entrepreneurship, self-sufficiency, and economic independence and creating job opportunities for the black community in keeping with the mission set forth by his leader, Elijah Muhammad. Social programs for the community include ongoing work with AIDS patients to license a new treatment therapy for the disease. The Nation of Islam has also established an independent security company to help police neighborhoods and high crime areas.

Moreover, to ensure that the property of the Nation remains intact, every piece of property bought by the Nation of Islam bears this restrictive deed: "Upon the death of Minister Louis Farrakhan, all properties shall remain a part of the religious community of the Nation of Islam, separate, exclusive and never to be confused with the estate of Minister Louis Farrakhan." He did this to make sure that the Nation of Islam would never become embroiled in the legal quagmire that destroyed the economic growth of the organization after the death of its first leader, teacher, and guide, Elijah Muhammad.

SELECTED BIBLIOGRAPHY: Amy Alexander, ed., *The Farrakhan Factor: African American Writers on Leadership, Nationhood, and Minister Farrakhan* (New York: Grove Press, 1998); Tom Brune and James Ylisela, Jr., "Broken Legacy," *Chicago Magazine*, December 1991; Minister Louis Farrakhan, *The Victory*, documentary video, Chicago, AVC Record and Tape Productions, 1988, *Final Call* Archives of the Nation of Islam; "Farrakhan's Three Year Plan," *Business Week*, March 13, 1995; *Final Call*, March 13, 1995, February 14, 1996, March 20, 1996, and April 23, 1996; John Hope Franklin and August Meier, eds., *Black Leaders of the Twentieth Century* (Urbana: University of Illinois Press, 1982); *I'll Be the Winner, Living or Dead: Attack on Minister Farrakhan and the Nation of Islam* (Chicago: Final Call Inc., 1995), video; Maulana Karenga, *Introduction to Black Studies* (Los Angeles: University of Sankore Press, 1993);

Aminah Beverly McCloud, *African American Islam* (New York: Routledge, 1995); Elijah Muhammad, *Message to the Blackman in America* (Newport News, VA: United Brothers Communications Systems, 1965); Nation of Islam web site, available from http:// www.noi.org/main.html; E. U. Essien Udom, *Black Nationalism: A Search for an Identity in America* (Chicago: University of Chicago Press, 1965).

Nicole Denise Anderson

NETWORKS, BLACK BUSINESS. *Networking* in the world of business can be defined as the identification and building of relationships for the purpose of sharing information, opportunities, and resources. Having networks of affiliations that contain helpful and useful information, resources, and assets is critical to the success of any economic endeavor. The success of individuals in the business arena—be they entrepreneurs, job seekers, or persons pursuing upward mobility within the context of their current employment—is determined by the extent to which they can successfully access and operate the network of dense contacts that surrounds them. Their ability to shape the scope of their search for resources and effectively use them to recognize and actualize opportunity is the deciding factor of their fate in a business environment. They must use networking for problem solving, answering key questions, to gain useful information and access financial and/or physical resources (e.g., space, supplies, equipment). The informal personal network is the businessperson's most important resource.

An efficient network is one in which no matter where the businessperson enters the network, his or her needs are diagnosed and passed around the system until the necessary information, resources, and advice are gathered. Networking advice can be defined as providing (1) knowledge on how to best proceed, (2) knowledge on what opportunities are available, (3) reassurance that one's idea will work, (4) tips on acquiring equipment, space, and money and (5) a critique of one's idea regardless of whether the person asked is qualified or not. The size of a network is of little importance if it is not composed of diverse contacts with high social and business status who possess access to relevant and useful information. It is proposed by networking theorists that to acquire more useful information and resources "low-status" people should formulate relationships and networks rich in "high-status" contacts, considered more likely to possess superior knowledge and influence.

Some scholars argue that race structures economic opportunities for some blacks. Others suggest that blacks by virtue of their social networks are excluded from equal employment opportunities. It is believed that blacks en masse are not yet fully connected to strategically placed contacts who possess useful information and clout for impacting large-scale business upward mobility and opportunity. All entrepreneurship and employment are inherently networking initiatives. To that end, economic decisions and social activism by people rarely take place in isolation but rather are embedded in concrete social networks. These networks of relations form the basis or "social glue" for the development of entrepreneurial ideas as well. People's decisions are influenced by those with whom they have frequent contact.

Historical examples and evidence of blacks' early tendencies to build networks for social change and upward mobility were popularized by icons such as Harriett Tubman, one of the most successful "conductors" on the Underground Railroad,* leading over 300 slaves to freedom, forcing the timid ahead with a loaded revolver. Ms. Tubman's contacts and relationships with a wide variety of courageous blacks and whites within several socioeconomic strata have served to dramatically demonstrate to several generations of blacks the power of connectedness and working together.

An earlier, but nonetheless important, historical account of networking is that of Free Frank McWorter.* Although Free Frank was born a slave in 1777 in South Carolina, through hard work and business acumen he managed to buy his freedom, start a small business, founded the town of New Philadelphia in Pike County, Illinois, and ultimately purchased the freedom of 16 members of his family at a cost of nearly $14,000. His commitment to the black community was in using his home, 20 miles east of the Mississippi River, as a station on the Underground Railroad, while his sons, as "conductors," assisted fugitive slaves to Canada. Free Frank's ability to build the diverse relationships needed throughout his life to succeed at home, at work, and in a racist nation was also an early model of the power of networking not only for business success but also for social change as well.

Historical evidence is clear about how earlier networks were used by blacks in their struggle to overcome a hostile, racist, and exclusionary environment. As the black church* began to form en masse in the 1800s, those founded, built, ministered, and owned by black people began a new era of collective consciousness and power. Driven by theological charismatic leadership and pooled resources, a network of schools, small businesses, service and social clubs, and a critical mass of mentors and role models emerged. The black church spread across America quickly as Emancipation freed blacks. Soon the black church became the leading institutional network in the fight for education, jobs, civil rights, and access to financial resources to build small businesses, buy land, and build new homes and churches.

Between 1888 and 1934, over 139 black-owned banks and savings and loans institutions were opened. This period marked the actual beginning of black capitalism in America. Other fraternal organizations and burial societies of such groups as the Masons, Elks, and the Knights of Pythias also joined with the powerful network of churches to pool their resources and to start, manage, and maintain their own financial institutions. Although most of these financial institutions failed during the Great Depression, it was an important initiative that uncovered the need to seek strength in numbers and provide mutual support.

During this period, Marcus Garvey* was building a network of believers in a self-help and buy-black campaign as well as a back to Africa movement. W.E.B. Du Bois was leading a network of multiracial intellectuals who sought civil liberty and higher education. He also promoted black business and co-operative enterprises. Booker T. Washington* led a network of blacks and whites in a program of conciliation, thrift, and industry. Each approach added to the collective knowledge of the power and importance of effective networking.

It was Booker T. Washington's founding of the National Negro Business League* in 1900 that created the first true network for the express purpose of business advancement among Negroes. In 1898, W.E.B. Du Bois published a study showing only 1,900 Negro-owned enterprises; by 1930, 30 years after the formation of the Negro Business League, there were 70,000 businesses. This growth was paralleled by an increase in the number of Negroes in white-collar occupations, a large number of whom were employed in Negro enterprises.

Black civil rights groups such as the WATCH and the National Urban League,* which were formed during the early 1900s, demonstrated the same networking strengths for impacting social change in the courts of law and the courts of public opinion. Black professional organizations were also established in the early twentieth century. Needing a network to share information and opportunities, and excluded from white networks of the same profession, the movement was led by morticians, physicians, dentists, and lawyers.

The post–civil rights era marked an expansion of these organizations around every professional and technical discipline where a critical mass could be mustered. By 1997, there were an estimated 110 black professional and technical organizations in America. Several, such as the National Minority Supplier Development Council and the National Black MBA Association,* are interdisciplinary. They annually hold conferences to network, educate, motivate, and empower their membership. Also, in the late 1960s, doors began to open to blacks in historically white professional organizations, and many blacks joined. They maintained membership in both groups but utilized white groups to expand the diversity of their contacts. Several blacks have risen to the presidency of their historically white professional groups, including the American Library Association and the American Medical Association.

Following the Civil Rights Act of 1964, and with the publishing of new black magazines in the early 1970s, several of which focused on business, networking, and professional growth and development (i.e., *Black Enterprise, The Black Collegian*, and *Essence*), there began to emerge an informal but powerful system of contacts and relationships that helped to drive economic growth in the black business community. It was publisher Earl G. Graves* who helped to formalize the networking process among middle-class black professionals in the business world, with his networking events, annually staged in several major cities beginning in 1985. It was publisher/author George C. Fraser who wrote the first popular book on effective networking principles and strategies for African Americans, *Success Runs in Our Race*, and it, too, contributed to the popularization of networking as a viable business tool. In the early 1980s local versions of black business directories (i.e., *Black Yellow Pages*, a genre that dates to the late nineteenth century) identified and promoted support of black-owned businesses.

But it is generally agreed that at the core of the black business network is a cadre of entrepreneurs—Quincy Jones, Earl Graves, Percy Sutton,* Ernesta Procop, and a small group of high-ranking corporate executives, Ken Chenault, Richard Parsons, Marianne Spraggens—who together make up the black business elite. According to *Business Week*, this network includes countless other African American businesspeople and heavy hitters in politics, social activism, and religion. With much the same energy that characterized the civil rights movement, this network is focused squarely on economic development.

Largely because of decades spent agitating for legal and political rights, blacks have established powerful advocates nationwide in local, state, and federal government. In addition, strong unified voices in organizations like the National Association for the Advancement of Colored People (NAACP), the National Urban League,* and Operation PUSH (People United to Save Humanity) have extended black influence and reach in the business world. Deals are being made through these networks that were unheard of just 25 years ago. The late Reginald Lewis's* buyout of Beatrice Foods in 1987 for nearly 1 billion came as a result of this elite black business network. Many other deals have occurred since then, and many more will surely occur in future years.

For those who are successful in the world of business, it can be assumed they are effective networkers. They use the time-tested basic principles of networking to build the diversity of relationships they will need to advance through life and business. Those principles include: (1) making a commitment to build a network and making networking a way of life; (2) setting achievable goals as part of their agenda and making sure they have an agenda; (3) building rapport, making friends, bonding, not selling; (4) thinking race and culture first but not only; (5) when appropriate, asking for help and giving help when asked; and (6) giving praise and thanks to their network often.

While the principles and practice of networking are as old as the African principles of community and tribalism, networking has continued to evolve as an important personal practice needed in the array of life skills necessary for blacks to succeed in business in the twenty-first century.

SELECTED BIBLIOGRAPHY: George C. Fraser, *Success Runs in Our Race: The Complete Guide to Effective Networking in the African American Community* (New York: William Morrow and Company, 1994); Abram L. Harris, *The Negro as Capitalist: A Study of Banking and Business among American Negroes* (Philadelphia: The American Academy of Political and Social Science, 1936); Elizabeth Lesly, "Inside the Black Business Network," *Business Week*, November 12, 1993; Juliet E. K. Walker, *Free Frank: A Black Pioneer on the Antebellum Frontier* (1983; reprint, Lexington: University Press of Kentucky, 1995).

George C. Fraser

NOBLE DREW ALI [TIMOTHY DREW] (1886–1929), Newark, N.J., and Chicago, Founder of the Moorish Science Temple of America.

In both style and substance, Noble Drew Ali, founder of the Moorish Science Temple of America, represents a historical continuity between Marcus Garvey* and Elijah Muhammad.* An indirect descendant of the Universal Negro Improvement Association, and a forerunner of the Nation of Islam,* Ali's organization joined an economic-oriented black nationalism to an eclectic interpretation of Islam. Ali was born Timothy Drew in North Carolina and lived among the Cherokee nation in Simpsonbuck County in that state. While he received no formal education, he apparently read widely, including the writings of Garvey in the 1920s and also Eastern religious philosophers. This literature, in addition to his travels, convinced the young man that African Americans were neither "negroes," "Ethiopians," nor "Coloreds" but rather "Asiatics," or more specifically, Moorish Americans. The slave experience, Ali concluded, had stripped blacks not only of their labor but, more fundamentally, of their very identity.

In 1913 Drew began recruiting converts in Newark, New Jersey, to his teachings. Assuming the name Noble Drew Ali, he preached that Islam was the only true religion of the Moors and also claimed that his teachings derived from Egypt. A magnetic personality, he gathered disciples in Pittsburgh and Detroit. Moving to the South Side of Chicago in 1925, Ali established headquarters for the Moorish Temple of Science. Soon, he began publishing *The Holy Koran of the Moorish Science Temple of America*, whose first page bore his likeness. The Moors distinguished themselves by adding the suffix "el" and "bey" to their names, carrying cards designating their membership in the Temple, and sporting fezzes.

The Temple sustained itself through membership dues and collections during services. Business development, part of the Temple's activity, became an area of conflict. Much of the secondary leadership under Ali amassed personal wealth exploiting the rank and file through the sale of herbs, magical charms and potions, and literature. As the Temple's membership grew, Ali's leadership was challenged. Convicted of murder, then released on bond, Ali died soon after, on July 20, 1929.

Ali's influence soon became manifest beyond the Moorish Temple. Wallace Drew Fard Muhammad, one of Ali's followers, founded the Nation of Islam, which under Elijah Muhammad developed its own business program.

SELECTED BIBLIOGRAPHY: Arthur Huff Fauset, *Black Gods of the Metropolis: Negro Religious Cults of the Urban North* (Philadelphia: University of Pennsylvania Press, 1944); Wardell Payne, ed., *Directory of African American Religious Bodies: A Compendium by the Howard University School of Divinity* (Washington, DC: Howard University Press, 1991).

Clarence Lang

NORRIS, JAMES AUSTIN (1893–1976), Philadelphia, lawyer.

James Austin Norris was the senior partner of the stellar Philadelphia law firm of Norris, Schmidt, Green, Harris, Higginbotham, and Associates. The law firm served as the first professional business institution and professional socialization base for a number of African American legal giants, corporate lawyers, and public officials in the city. It served, for instance, as the nurturing ground for Third Circuit federal judges: A. Leon Higginbotham Jr., the second African American appointed U.S. district judge before serving as chief judge of the appeals court; Clifford Scott Green, the third African American appointed U.S. district judge; Herbert Hutton, the fifth African American appointed U.S. district judge; and William F. Hall, the first African American appointed U.S. Magistrate for the Third Circuit.

The firm also produced Doris Mae Harris, one of the first African American lawyers to serve as counsel to the Small Business Administration (SBA) in the city before serving as a Philadelphia common pleas court judge in 1971; and Harvey N. Schmidt, the first African American to serve as a member of the Registration Commission in Philadelphia before becoming a common pleas judge as well in 1971. Schmidt also served as executive head of community legal services in the city in the 1960s. The firm also acted in an important capacity to Robert Williams, who served as an African American member on the Superior Court of Pennsylvania. Other law firm members who received national and regional positions include William H. Brown III, law partner in the firm of Schnader, Harrison, Segal & Lewis, who became chair of the U.S. Equal Employment Opportunity Commission (EEOC) and is currently noted as one of the top civil rights lawyers in the United States; Mansfield Neal, division counsel for General Electric; in addition to public officials Senator Hardy Williams of Pennsylvania, State Representative Arthur Early of Delaware, and Germaine Ingram, legal counsel for the Philadelphia Board of Education.

During Norris's tenure with the firm between 1955 and 1976, the law firm represented many local as well as national church organizations, oftentimes referring to them as their corporate clients. This group included Father Divine* and the Peace Mission Movement, the national African Methodist Episcopal Church, the trustees of the General Assembly of the Church of the Lord Jesus Christ of the Apostolic Faith, and the National Baptist Convention, primarily through the litigation efforts of Higginbotham and Green. The firm also represented a host of labor organizations during periods of urban renewal in the 1960s and 1970s, black newspapers such as the National Leader Publishing Company, major city radio personalities (e.g., George Woods), and several community organizations and institutions, focusing on, for example, the building and maintenance of black health care facilities and business ventures involving the development of housing and small and regional black businesses in the Philadelphia area via assisting applicants for loans through the SBA.

The motif of the law practice is evident in its community infrastructure work. On the one hand, the law firm utilized underdeveloped and stabilized resources in the black community by helping to build institutions in areas of indigenous group needs and social inequality. On the other hand, firm members increased their professional opportunities by intersecting their interest with the development of the black community through black urban political and social organization.

Norris served as a catalyst in this venture as his fellow law firm partners and associates acquired much in terms of political and social capital. Born to working-class parents in the small, rural town of Chambersburg, Pennsylvania, before moving to the nearby steel town of Pittsburgh, Norris graduated from a Methodist college-preparatory high school and went on to attend Lincoln University, in Oxford, where he received a classical education. After graduating from Lincoln in 1912, Norris then attended and graduated from Yale Law School in 1917. His eventual arrival in Philadelphia in 1919 is where he began his public career as a politician, lawyer, and newspaper editor. Forced to operate within the racial caste social structure by being unable to participate in the white business legal and commerce community, Norris started a black newspaper, the *Philadelphia American*, and wrote abrasive pieces about the absence of black participation in the political social order in the city.

In the early 1920s, Norris served as chief counsel for black nationalist leader Marcus Garvey* through his Philadelphia branch of the United Negro Improvement Association. By 1932 he was much involved in local politics, heading up a campaign in support of President Roosevelt. Because of his success, Norris became the city's first black ward leader in the historic seventh ward, the subject of Du Bois's *Philadelphia Negro*. By 1935, Norris's astute lawyering and political abilities, via using the *Philadelphia Independent* in political campaigns, since he served as its editor, enabled him to receive political patronage appointments, first becoming one of the early deputy attorney generals for Pennsylvania. In 1937, he became the first black to be appointed to the powerful Republican-controlled Board of Revision of Taxes, where the city's political leadership was stationed. Norris held that position for 30 years, culminating in much business for himself and the law firm after his retirement from the board in 1967.

During his tenure, however, Norris used his political position and his savvy for mobilizing the black vote in the city by increasing the number of blacks in service and professional jobs. In 1955, he joined the law practice of Schmidt, Green, Harris, and Higginbotham and made it into a powerful and recognized institution throughout the city during its history. He brought political stature to the firm as well as major corporate clients and financial resources. The law firm at first practiced criminal law and personal injury matters, which was the bread-and-butter practice for most African American lawyers, before forging links and working with the "going concerns" of the black community. In this, the law firm moved toward civil rights activism in local and regional NAACP (National Association for the Advancement of Colored People) discrimination cases after the U.S. Supreme Court struck down the separate but equal doctrine in *Brown v. Board of Education*. Higginbotham, for example, filed the lead case against the Lower Gwyned Township School Board for operating an all-black school in Pennsylvania in Montgomery County. By the late 1960s, Neal worked with civil rights attorney Cecil B. Moore in his successful discrimination case against Girard College, which prohibited blacks from entry at the time.

Through the work of Green, a specialist in commercial law, the law firm contributed to the development of a black entrepreneurial class through incorporating black owners of bars in the 1950s and using the resources of churches and federal grants to create and maintain health care institutions like Better Family Planning and Mercy Douglas Hospital and job training programs. In this matter, the firm worked with national leader Reverend Leon Sullivan,* who headed up the national office of the Organization Industrial Center. The law firm also worked on commercial enterprises like the establishment of the Father Divine* Tracy Hotel in Philadelphia, along with many other cultural and community centers in the city.

A leading black lawyer in the Philadelphia bar for 56 years, Norris also became a national expert in the law of eminent domain. The law firm handled many of these kinds of cases including one of their most successful eminent domain cases in the Pennsylvania Supreme Court matter of the *Redevelopment Authority of the City of Philadelphia v. Irwin Lieberman*. Starting in 1971 and ending by 1975, Hutton, who served as the chief trial litigator, brought a constitutional challenge, asserting a violation of due process to confiscate property without adequate compensation. The case's significance is that it set a precedent, forcing the state to recognize and compensate individuals like the owner of a restaurant and liquor facility as real property and not merely a franchise.

Norris in particular and the law firm in general had a knack for consolidating power and collective influence for the public good in dealing with racial and social inequality through the political and legal processes. The firm received much attention, acquired many court-appointed cases, and became highly recognized for its reputation in the area of eminent domain law, a primary focus of the firm from 1967 until Norris's death in 1976.

SELECTED BIBLIOGRAPHY: *An Almanac of the Federal Judiciary*, vol. 2 (Chicago: Law Letters Inc., 1988); *The American Bench: Judges of the Nation*, 4th ed. (Sacramento, CA: Forster Long, Inc., 1995), 2049; Mark Bricklin, "His Decisions Are Worth Millions: Board of Revision of Taxes Secretary Phila. Powerhouse," *Philadelphia Tribune*, August 1, 1964; Orrin Evans, "Austin Norris Traces His Career: Spotting the Talented Early," *The Evening and Sunday Bulletin*, July 20, 1969.

Aaron C. Porter

NORTH CAROLINA MUTUAL LIFE INSURANCE COMPANY. In an official sense, the North Carolina Mutual Life Insurance Company began in 1898, when it received its charter as the North Carolina Mutual Life and Provident Association. In a cultural sense, the "Mutual" as it came to be called, began at least as early as the eighteenth century. Since the founding of the Free African Society* by Philadelphia's free blacks in 1787, life and sickness insurance among African Americans had existed as a profoundly social enterprise, associated with fraternal orders and mutual benefit societies. The North Carolina Mutual evolved out of the Royal Knights of King David, a Durham fraternal society, that had, in turn, arisen as an offshoot of Richmond's Grand United Order of True Reformers, the most significant of these all-black, post-Emancipation societies.

What set the Mutual apart, however, was its heralded success and long-term survival. By 1913 it had become a legal reserve life insurance company and, as its founders liked to boast, "the world's largest Negro business." Among the seven founders, John Merrick, a Durham barber, was easily the most important. By 1900 five of the other founders had dropped out, leaving Merrick and Dr. Aaron McDuffie Moore as part-time managers of the tottering organization. They hired Charles Clinton Spaulding,* Dr. Moore's ambitious nephew, as full-time general manager, and he soon reversed the company's fortunes. Spaulding surrounded himself with talented lieutenants and steadily extended operations throughout the South. The firm also strengthened its base to include banking and fire and casualty insurance, respectively, the Mechanics and Farmers Bank (1908), Bankers Fire Insurance Company (1920), Mutual Savings and Loan Association (1921), and Southern Fidelity and Surety Company (1926). By the 1920s Durham had become famous as the nation's center, with the Mutual as the centerpiece of black enterprise or, in the words of sociologist E. Franklin Frazier, "The Capital of the Black Middle Class"—"The Black Wall Street* of America."

Indeed, the symbolism of the company's success became no less important than the substance of its success. Under Spaulding's leadership, the Mutual survived the depression, expanded north as far as Pennsylvania, and prospered enormously during World War II. Prosperity would continue beyond Spaulding's death in 1952, but the larger meaning of the company would harken back to bad times, back to the darkest days of Jim Crow, when "race men," working against the odds, would forge a proud institution out of a spirit of racial solidarity and self-help—"taking advantage of the disadvantages," as the early leaders liked to say.

If the company owed part of its existence to segregation, it also acquired a positive life of its own in the black community. In addition to evoking pride, it provided benefits ranging well beyond insurance and banking. In offering employment to otherwise overqualified agents and executives who found themselves closed out of their professions in mainstream America, the Mutual accumulated a critical mass of the "talented tenth." This array of professionals included educators, preachers, social workers, journalists, attorneys, and physicians—an uncommon pool of personnel whose energy and skills spilled over into community and political life. To cite only one example, it is fair to say that without the men and women of the Mutual, the South's most effective community organization before the civil rights movement, the Durham Committee on Negro Affairs (DCNA), founded in 1935, would not have come into being and would not have survived over the past 60 years. Among other activities, the DCNA was registering voters and determining the outcome of local elections a full generation ahead of the Voting Rights Act of 1964.

As the North Carolina Mutual approached its centennial, it remained one of the nation's oldest and largest African American institutions; and since the number of its policyholders and employees, past and present, would run into the millions, it probably has touched the lives of more black Americans than any other single African American institution. Unlike the black church, however, it can no longer count on a culturally captive clientele; nor can it compete with *Fortune* 500 corporations as an exalted place of employment for black executives. Perhaps its position is closer to that of the black college as it strives to preserve its traditional identity while obeying the laws of the modern marketplace.

SELECTED BIBLIOGRAPHY: William Jesse Kennedy, Jr., *The North Carolina Mutual Story* (Durham: North Carolina Mutual Life Insurance Company, 1970); Walter B. Weare, *Black Business in the New South: A Social History of the North Carolina Mutual Life Insurance Company* (Urbana: University of Illinois Press, 1973).

Walter Weare

NSA, EYO HONESY, II (1767?–1858), Calabar Cross River State, Eastern Nigeria, palm oil plantation owner and trader, merchant, king, religious leader.

The son of Willie Honesy I of the Creektown section of Calabar, Eyo grew up when the Atlantic slave trade* was at a peak in Eastern Nigeria. During his youth he worked as a cabin boy on English ships on the triangular slave trade between Calabar, the West Indies, and England, where he learned English language and culture as well as business practices. Eyo's uncle Ekpenyong Nsa took over the prosperous Eyo Nsa trading house in 1820 at the death of Eyo's father and dissipated the family fortune to the point where all of Creektown became subordinate to the Duketown section of Calabar. Eyo established his own merchant trading house in Creektown and proceeded to build his fortune independent of his uncle. Eyo took the occasion of the death of Great Duke Ephraim of Duketown in 1834 to declare not only his independence from Duketown but also his claim (by virtue of his wealth) to the kingship of all the trading houses in Creektown, which went unchallenged. Eyo consolidated and expanded the commercial contracts of Creektown into the interior of the Cross River region as well as with the English and French traders who constantly came to Calabar for slaves and palm oil.

Significantly, Eyo signed the first treaties in the Cross River area that would end the slave trade. He also led the chiefs and kings of Calabar in 1846 to request missionaries to come to the region, not to evangelize but to teach their people to "sabby the book" or to read and write. By then Eyo was the most prosperous and powerful king in the Calabar area, with thousands of men employed on his palm oil plantations and palm oil houses and 400 giant canoes. Eyo quickly recovered from a fire that destroyed *one* of his compounds that contained 10,000 pounds worth of trade goods in 1852, a net worth accumulated by few African Americans at that time, with the exception of the leading black slave plantation holders, New Orleans merchants, and wealthy Philadelphia lumber merchant Stephen Smith.* By the time of Eyo's death in 1858, he had significantly transformed his society and had become one of the richest merchants of all West Africa.

SELECTED BIBLIOGRAPHY: Kannan Nair, *Politics and Society in Southeastern Nigeria, 1841–1906: A Study of Power, Diplomacy and Commerce in Old Calabar* (London: Frank Cass Company, 1972); Ekei Essien Oku, *The Kings and Chiefs of Old Calabar, 1785–1925* (Calabar, Nigeria: Glad Tidings Press, 1989).

Gary J. Hunter

O

OVERTON, ANTHONY (1865–1946), Illinois, entrepreneur, cosmetics manufacturer, insurance and bank founder, realtor, newspaper publisher.

Overton was born into slavery on March 21, 1865, in Monroe, Louisiana, to Anthony and Martha (Deberry) Overton. He attended Washburn College in Topeka, Kansas, and the University of Kansas, graduating with a bachelor of laws degree in 1888. Overton was admitted to the Kansas state bar and practiced law in Topeka. After serving a year as a judge of the municipal court in Shawnee County, he moved to Oklahoma and in 1892 was elected treasurer of Kingfisher County. Afterward, he moved to Kansas City, Missouri, where in 1898 Overton launched his business career, with the founding of the Overton Hygienic Manufacturing Company, which initially specialized in the production of its Hygienic Pet Baking Powder. Subsequently, that company became part of an early twentieth-century African American large, diverse conglomerate.

In 1911 Overton moved his company to Chicago, which was evolving into the hub of African American business in the North. Recognizing the potential market in cosmetics for African American women, the company soon had 52 products, including cosmetics, perfumes, shoe polish, hair preparations, baking power, toilet water, and flavoring extracts. Overton followed a policy of producing only high-quality products and avoiding demeaning products such as skin bleaches. Toilet articles, such as the High Brown Face Powder, soon became nationally known. By 1915, the company had $268,000 in capital with 32 full-time employees. In 1927, the credit rating service Bradstreet estimated the company at a value of over $1 million, and Overton's newspaper, the *Chicago*

Bee, estimated that the company employed 150 black men and women and that it manufactured 250 products.

In 1922, Overton opened the Douglass National Bank, the second black-owned bank to receive a national charter. The bank enjoyed impressive growth as its deposits expanded from $56,030 in 1922 to $1,507,336 in 1929. By 1929 the Douglass National Bank and nearby Binga State Bank held 36 percent of all resources of black banks in the nation. Overton also launched Victory Life Insurance Company, which was authorized by the state of Illinois on May 3, 1924. In 1927, it became the first Illinois insurance company to enter New York State and eventually expanded to 12 states. Victory Life grew and prospered, especially from its business in New York. In 1927, Overton became the first businessman to be awarded the NAACP (National Association for the Advancement of Colored People) Spingarn Medal, and the next year, he received the Harmon Business Award.

The Great Depression exposed weaknesses in both Douglass National and Victory Life, which marked the end of the Overton conglomerate. Primarily, Overton's bank management veered from conservative, safe banking practices. Loans are normally the major source of bank earnings, but Douglass National had proportionally fewer loans, especially commercial loans, than its peers. Moreover, the loans lacked diversification; over half were real estate loans, which profited the bank during the property boom of the 1920s but helped doom the bank after the real estate crash of 1929. The bank also sustained heavy losses on loans to churches and fraternal societies. Another problem was excessive investment into expensive and elaborate but nonearning bank buildings and fixtures. Douglass National Bank weathered three runs before closing in May 1932, although by 1930, 70 banks failed in Chicago.

The real estate market crash of 1929 also devastated Victory Life, with its entire original capital invested in the mortgages of black homes. In addition, Overton assisted Douglass National at the expense of Victory Life. For example, in 1927, he invested $130,000 of Victory Life's funds into Douglass stock. He and his daughter also borrowed from Victory Life. After the company was suspended by New Jersey and New York, the directors voted to oust Overton. Subsequently, the company was placed into receivership, after which it was reorganized under new management as Victory Mutual Life Insurance Company. Overton had built the Overton Hygienic/Douglass National Bank Building in 1922–1923, but after the loss of Victory Life and Douglass National, he had to relocate to the *Chicago Bee* building. He continued to administer the Overton Hygienic Manufacturing Company until his death and retained enough wealth to live comfortably in his later years.

Overton's empire was marked by its rapid ascendancy and its dramatic decline. Its demise can be attributable both to the Great Depression and his mismanagement. He may have sacrificed his early prudence to his ambition and rivalry with Jesse Binga,* another successful black Chicago businessman, to whom Overton offered assistance when Binga's bank was failing in 1929. Despite his ambition, he was modest in personal expenditures, never owning a personal automobile or extravagant home and using his wealth primarily for business interests. In 1915 Overton authored the book *Successful Salesmanship.* In 1916, he established the monthly publication the *Half-Century* to target the educated, black middle class. It advocated the creation of a separate black economy and society and emphasized racial pride and self-reliance. After the Chicago race riots of the summer of 1919, the *Half-Century* temporarily took a more militant tone by devoting more space to racial oppression and conflict and supporting the NAACP before eventually returning to its view that protest was futile. On April 18, 1925, the *Half-Century* was closed and replaced with the weekly newspaper the *Chicago Bee.*

Overton, a Republican, was a member of the Masonic order (32nd degree), Alpha Phi Alpha, Sigma Pi Phi, 100F, Knights of Pythias, and the Appomattox Club of Chicago. He married Clara M. Gregg on June 14, 1888, in Lawrence, Kansas. He had four children, Everett Van, Mabel Helena, Eva, and Frances Madison, all of whom he raised strictly in the Baptist Church.

SELECTED BIBLIOGRAPHY: Abram L. Harris, *The Negro as Capitalist: A Study of Banking and Business among American Negroes* (College Park, MD: McGrath Publishing Company, 1936); John N. Ingham and Lynne B. Feldman, *African-American Business Leaders: A Biographical Dictionary* (Westport, CT: Greenwood Press, 1994).

Nicholas A. Lash

OYSTERING, CHESAPEAKE BAY. In the post–Civil War period, African Americans all over the South sought ways to become economically independent of those who had formerly enslaved them. As landownership was the primary symbol of both freedom and economic status, many attempted to acquire enough acreage to earn a subsistence. In the Chesapeake Bay region of Virginia and Maryland, freedpeople found a way to purchase land and to gain a degree of independence by oystering. Late nineteenth-century oystering was carried out by one of two methods: by "tonging," or scooping up the crop manually, and by using steam-powered dredging machinery. Most African Americans were tongers. Many owned their boats and tonged under a license granted for harvesting in public waters. A few owned private oyster beds and hence had even greater opportunity for wealth and independence.

Oystering was seasonal, and diligent oystermen could earn anywhere from $200 to $500 in a season. The money earned could then be used to purchase land that was cultivated in the off-season. Critics charged, however, that such easy money generally was squandered on nonessentials, and the families of less-industrious oystermen were thrown into destitution, when the watermen failed to save for the off-season. Those who wished to see black men employed as wage earners in agriculture denigrated oystering as an occupation that fostered sloth. It was said that oystermen only worked long enough to pay for present needs and did not return to work until the lack of money forced them to do so.

Former slaveowners and other whites recognized that freedmen were drawn to oystering, not simply because of the money to be made but because the occupation allowed African Americans greater control over the terms and conditions of their labor. Generally, oystermen were restricted only by climate and the quantity of the crop. Whites who sought to deny blacks this independence attempted to lessen the profit margin by taxing the small boats used primarily by the tongers. Such tactics failed, however, to drive black oystermen out of the water and back to the fields.

SELECTED BIBLIOGRAPHY: J. E. Davis, "Oystering in Hampton Roads," *Southern Workman* 32 (March 1903); Edna Greene Medford, "Land and Labor: The Quest for Black Economic Independence on Virginia's Lower Peninsula," *Virginia Magazine of History and Biography* 100 (October 1992); William Taylor Thom, "The Negroes of Litwalton, Virginia: A Social Study of the 'Oyster Negro,' " *Bulletin of the Bureau of Labor* 37 (1901).

Edna Greene Medford

P

PACE, HARRY HERBERT (1884–1943), Memphis, New York City, Chicago, businessman, music publisher, founder of Black Swan Records, banker, insurance company cofounder, civic leader.

Harry Pace was born in Covington, Georgia, the son of Nancy Francis and Charles Pace, a blacksmith. An outstanding student, Pace graduated from Atlanta University as class valedictorian at the age of 19 and entered the print profession as shop manager for a black-owned printing company in Atlanta. While this work gave him valuable experience and connections that later proved useful, he eschewed the print trade for a career in law, taking a position as instructor at the Haines Institute in Augusta, ostensibly to save enough money for law school. After one year, however, W.E.B. Du Bois, his former instructor at Atlanta University, invited him to join the staff of his new Memphis-based *Moon Illustrated Weekly*, a black-owned and-operated newspaper. Pace agreed to become day-to-day manager, a job that put him into contact with many important black business owners in the South, even though the project lasted only eight issues and drained his life savings.

Broke and despondent, Pace accepted a teaching offer from Lincoln University in Missouri but once again left academia after one year, this time to become a partner in the Solvent Savings Bank of Memphis. After five years at Solvent, he left to join the Standard Life Insurance Company in Atlanta in 1912, the first black insurance company founded with the sole purpose of selling life insurance; but owing to differences with the owner, he resigned in 1920.

Settling in New York City, he cofounded the sheet music publishing company Pace and Handy Music with the legendary musician W. C. Handy, whom he had met in Memphis some years before. A gifted musician and songwriter, Pace's greatest success was in turning Handy's song "St. Louis Blues" into one of the most popular songs in history. But frustrated by the fact that white companies bought their songs and used white artists to record them, he dissolved Pace and Handy Music and founded Black Swan Records for the express purpose of recording black artists for a black audience.

Despite obstructions from white recording labels, who feared a loss of market share, Pace procured the necessary equipment and began selling records in early 1921. Pace's fortunes were in doubt until he discovered and recorded Ethel Waters, who sold over 500,000 copies of her debut record within six months of release. Black Swan became a success for the next couple of years as he surrounded himself with some of the great black musicians of the era, including Fletcher Henderson and William Grant Stills. However, Pace seemed much better at giving talent a start than in keeping it, and the artists that he did keep tended to reflect his more high-brow musical tastes; he rejected Bessie Smith because she was too "nitty-gritty."

Cutthroat competition and the advent of radio doomed Black Swan Records, and Pace sold his label to Paramount Records in 1924. As a result, many of the opportunities he created were discarded, and blacks were blocked from the management side of recording for over three decades. Undaunted, Pace helped form another black-owned insurance company that eventually became the Chicago-based Supreme Liberty Life Insurance* in 1929, with Pace as president and chief executive officer until his death. Pace was an energetic and active leader in the black community. A prominent opponent of Marcus Garvey,* he sat on the board of directors of the National Association for the Advancement of Colored People (NAACP) and served a number of black insurance associations, writing influential articles on African American insurance for such journals as *The Crisis* and *The Messenger*.

What happened the year before his death is somewhat of a mystery, but it appears that in 1942, after moving to a predominantly white suburb, rumors abounded that he was trying to pass as white (he was light skinned). A group of black employees of Supreme Life planned a demonstration to embarrass him, and when he heard of it, he became distant and withdrawn and died soon after. For his entire career, Pace was one of the strongest proponents of black-owned businesses in the country and introduced blacks into industries where they had no prior standing. But despite his eventful life, scholars have virtually ignored Harry Pace, an oversight made abundantly clear by the fact that over 50 years after his death he still awaits his first full biographer.

SELECTED BIBLIOGRAPHY: John N. Ingram and Lynne B. Feldman, *African-American Business Leaders: A Biographical Dictionary* (Westport, CT: Greenwood Press, 1994); Robert C. Puth, "Supreme Life: The History of a Negro Life Insurance Company," *Business History Review* 43, 1 (Spring 1969); M. S. Stuart, *An Economic Detour: A History of Insurance in the Lives of American Negroes* (New York: Wendell

Malliet and Co., 1940); Ted Vincent, "The Social Context of Black Swan Records," *Living Blues Magazine* (May–June 1989).

Todd E. Larson

PAYTON, PHILIP A. (1876–1917), New York, real estate, founder of Afro-American Realty Company.

Philip A. Payton, Jr., known as "the Father of Harlem," was one of the most successful black real estate speculators in the early twentieth century. He started in the business in 1900, with a short-lived partnership in the Brown and Payton realty company. Continuing in real estate activities on his own, Payton's break came in 1902, when he was asked by a white building owner to rent his vacant Harlem apartments to blacks. In the early twentieth century, new Harlem real estate was developed for middle-class whites. The rents were exorbitantly high, and the apartments remained vacant. Middle-class blacks, lacking an availability of good decent housing, however, were willing to pay high rents, while others expected to meet their rent by taking in roomers. After his initial success, Payton advertised that he was a specialist in renting white-owned Harlem apartment buildings to blacks. In 1904 Payton founded the Afro-American Realty Company, capitalized at $500,000, with 50,000 shares offered at $10, owned primarily by Payton's 10-man board of directors, who purchased 500 shares each.

Starting business, however, with $100,000 in capital, Payton Realty purchased 4 buildings and managed 10 others. By 1906, the realty company owned 6 buildings and was managing 20 others, while Payton continued buying property in his own name. Within four years, the company folded, as a result of the 1907 recession, which contributed to tenant unemployment and nonpayment of rent. The Afro-American Realty Company, consequently, failed to meet its mortgage payments and was also sued by its investors. In 1908, the Afro-American Realty Company closed. With the Great Migration,* New York City's black population increased from 91,709 in 1910 to 152,467 in 1920, with most of the new migrants living in Harlem, as other black realtors capitalized both on renting apartments for white building owners and on purchasing Harlem property.

Payton, however, continued his real estate activities. His big break came in 1917, when he acquired six large modern apartment buildings in Harlem, four years old and valued at $1.5 million, but Payton died shortly after the purchase. In 1918, the Payton Apartments Corporation with a capital of $250,000 was reorganized under new black ownership.

Philip Payton's father, an educated man, barber, and merchant, migrated from the South to Westfield, Massachusetts, where Philip, Jr., was born. In 1899, he graduated from Livingston College in North Carolina and moved to New York.

SELECTED BIBLIOGRAPHY: John N. Ingham and Lynne B. Feldman, *African-American Business Leaders: A Biographical Dictionary* (Westport, CT: Greenwood Press, 1994); David Levering Lewis, *When Harlem Was in Vogue* (New York: Oxford University Press, 1979); Gilbert Osofsky, *Harlem: The Making of a Ghetto: Negro New*

York, 1890–1930 (New York: Harper & Row, 1968); Juliet E. K. Walker, *The History of Black Business in America: Capitalism, Race, Entrepreneurship* (New York: Macmillan/Prentice Hall International, 1998).

Juliet E. K. Walker

PETTIFORD, WILLIAM REUBEN (1847–1914), Birmingham, banker, minister.

Even before he became president of the fledgling Alabama Penny Savings and Loan Company in 1890, an institution he successfully led for 23 years, Pettiford, as a church pastor, was committed to educating his congregants in finance and the wise use of money. In becoming head of Penny Savings, which opened as a private bank, he sought to encourage habits of thrift among ordinary working-class blacks. While he promoted self-help as the key to future progress, Pettiford taught that by cooperating blacks could become property owners and "substantial citizens." To foster unity among blacks, he made conscious use of race pride, urging them to patronize local businesses, in order to keep money circulating within their own communities.

Pettiford was born in Granville County, North Carolina, and because his labor was needed on the family farm, did not attend the local elementary school. His siblings did, however, and in the evenings they taught him to read and write. Later, he attended a normal school, and after teaching for a while, he became a school principal. Five years after his Christian conversion, he attended Baptist Normal Theological School and was ordained for the Baptist ministry. This led to his pastorate at the Sixteenth Street Baptist Church in Birmingham. Pettiford frequently expressed the belief that meaningful progress was only possible if blacks committed themselves to business development. To do this successfully, they had to control sources of capital, which they could create through their own banks. Pettiford emphasized the multiple duties of a bank. While it should strive to make profits as any other business, a bank should be a vehicle to educate those with little or no experience in handling money. It should also be an institution to train new generations in business practices, while providing employment.

In 1895, Penny Savings was officially chartered by the State of Alabama and eventually opened branches in Selma, Montgomery, and Anniston. Over the years, Penny Savings assisted scores of depositors to buy or build homes, initiate businesses, and make improvements on their farms and other properties. Booker T. Washington,* who had a close association with Pettiford, quotes the banker as saying, "The establishment of banks and other businesses among us gives promise of a variety of occupations for our people, thus stimulating them to proper preparation." Pettiford was an aggressive promoter of Penny Savings and made extensive use of newspaper advertising and pamphleteering to publicize the services of the bank. Some contemporaries credit his persistent advertising campaigns with inadvertently inspiring thrifty habits among Birmingham's poor whites, many of whom became bank depositors. Under Pettiford's leadership, Penny Savings survived the economic depression of 1893, which saw the collapse around the country of over a hundred banks.

Through a series of profitable real estate transactions for the bank, Pettiford proved his astuteness as a businessman. Under his guidance, in 1913, the bank was able to construct its own building. Penny Savings' reputation grew as a place to secure loans for home buying and small business initiation. Pettiford actively participated in the National Negro Business League,* an organization that encouraged blacks in their entrepreneurial endeavors. He played an important, perhaps indispensable, role as mentor to blacks who sought his help in establishing banks in other towns and cities. He seemed to enjoy his role as counselor and guide and lectured widely to spread his message of self-help. He also published pamphlets and newspaper articles on the subject. When he died, Penny Savings was financially solvent and considered among the country's best-managed banks.

SELECTED BIBLIOGRAPHY: John N. Ingham and Lynne B. Feldman, *African-American Business Leaders: A Biographical Dictionary* (Westport, CT: Greenwood Press, 1994); C. O. Boothe, *Cyclopedia of the Colored Baptists of Alabama* (Birmingham: Alabama Publishing Company, 1895); William R. Pettiford, "How to Help the Negro to Help Himself," *The Southern Workman* 30 (November 1901); Booker T. Washington, *The Negro in Business* (Boston: Hertel, Jenkins & Co., 1907).

Elizabeth Wright

PHILANTHROPY. Black organizations and institutions, churches, benevolent societies, and fraternal orders have been the focus of much of the study of black philanthropy. Historians have documented their efforts to establish schools and hospitals and provide relief for the poor and indigent. Individual African Americans who, for one reason or another, decided to become philanthropists have received much less attention in their acts of deliberate generosity, expressed in the monetary contributions that they make in a spirit of humanitarianism. Nevertheless, a tradition of African American philanthropy, both group and individual, exists, stretching back from successful black businesspeople in the colonial era to many current successful black businesspeople, celebrities, and athletes. Still, historically, in the black community the possession of great wealth was not always the basis of philanthropic activity. Primarily, pooled accumulated savings from blacks with limited disposable income provided a significant source of funds for philanthropic activity.

From the Revolutionary War era throughout antebellum America, blacks organized mutual aid societies, which provided many social services. Foremost among them was a guaranteed burial, but mutual aid societies and fraternal orders also offered their members' families support in the case of sickness or death. Leonard Curry notes that these societies, including Charleston's Brown Fellowship Society, founded in 1790, and the Woolman Benevolent Society, founded in Brooklyn in 1818, sometimes played a "dual role," devoting "some portion of their resources to assisting needy blacks who were not members."

Groups whose purpose was more clearly philanthropic included the Philanthropic Society of Pittsburgh, which black activist Martin Delany helped organize in 1834, and the African Dorcas Societies of New York and Philadelphia. The major activity of most benevolent societies was in establishing schools for black youth.

In addition, blacks in most cities founded benevolent organizations such as the Baltimore Society for Relief in Case of Seizure to provide support for free black families who lost income as a result of a family member who was kidnapped and sold into slavery. With limited funds, then, cooperative effort was the basis of most philanthropic activities of free blacks during slavery. Within the broadest definition of philanthropy, however, "goodwill toward one's fellowmen, especially, as expressed through active efforts to promote human welfare," the tradition of black philanthropy began in the colonial era with free blacks who used their money to purchase blacks from slavery. While few free blacks accumulated wealth that allowed them to engage in individual acts of philanthropy, those who did were primarily businessmen. Interestingly, several early black philanthropists—Paul Cuffe,* James Forten,* and Pierre Toussaint—provide examples of giving that extended to whites and their institutions.

The philanthropic activities of Paul Cuffe (1759–1817) from the late eighteenth century are most well known. While Paul inherited 116 acres of land from his father Cuffe Slocum (an enterprising African who purchased his freedom three years after his initial enslavement in America), his wealth was derived from the shipping company he established in the late eighteenth century. By 1806, Cuffe owned several ships (which were commanded by his relatives and run with all-black crews) and had trade interests in Europe and Africa. Cuffe engaged in several activities that would be considered philanthropy by current standards. The first was the construction of a school in Cuffe's home of Westport in 1797. Cuffe was determined to give his children a better education than he had but found no support among the local townspeople for an integrated school. Cuffe constructed the school on his own, on his own property, and afterward opened the school for all local children. Cuffe also donated nearly $600 to the construction of a new meeting house for Westport's Society of Friends during the War of 1812, when Cuffe's income from trade was uncertain at least. Cuffe's support of free black emigration to Africa can also be considered philanthropy. In 1815, he transported 38 African Americans to settle in Sierra Leone, becoming the first American of any color to sponsor a settlement in Africa.

The spirit of philanthropy that moved people like Cuffe can also be found in other successful black businessmen. James Forten, for example, was a well-known supporter of William Lloyd Garrison's famous antislavery publication *The Liberator*. Forten contributed heavily to abolitionist activities, also underwrote the costs of other publications that called for the end of slavery, and was a member of benevolent societies and a sponsor of several black organizations. A Revolutionary War hero from Philadelphia, Forten made a considerable amount of money as a sail maker. By 1830, his wealth was estimated at $100,000. Successful New York black hairdresser, Haitian-born Pierre Toussaint's (1766–1853) philanthropic contributions has led the Catholic Church in the early 1990s to consider him as a candidate for canonization. In the nineteenth century, Toussaint extensively supported the Catholic Church and the Catholic Orphan Asylum for white children and even helped pay the expenses of several New York white males studying for the priesthood in Rome. Toussaint's philanthropic activities also extended to blacks. He purchased freedom for his sister, his wife, and several unrelated slaves.

New Orleans' Madame Bernard Couvent's philanthropy was made posthumously, providing in her will for the establishment of a school for black youths. Couvent was born in Africa. She was a slave until she was purchased by her husband, a successful carpenter. She died in 1836, but her bequest was not carried out until 1848. Her gift was of several small houses for founding a school for indigent Catholic orphans. The school also received money from two other wealthy New Orleans free blacks, including Thomy Lafon and Aristide Mary. William Wells, a successful free African American of Baltimore, established a foundation with a large gift, which then operated the Wells School there from 1835 until after the Civil War.

Several leading antebellum black businesspeople continued their philanthropic activities after the Civil War. Stephen Smith* (1797–1873), while the wealthiest, is least known for his giving. Smith gained his wealth from a lumber business in Columbia, Pennsylvania, and later branched out into real estate. In 1842 he opened another business, selling lumber and coal, in Philadelphia. Smith was very active in his opposition to slavery, contributing money to the antislavery publications *Freedmen's Journal* and the *Emancipator*. He and his business partner, William Whipper, participated in smuggling slaves in the Underground Railroad.* With Smith's running his own railroad line, slaves were hidden in railroads cars used by Smith to transport his coal and lumber. His public philanthropy included support of Philadelphia's Institute for Colored Youth, Home for Destitute Colored Children, House of Refuge, and Olive Cemetery.

After the Civil War, he was one of the incorporators and a major contributor in establishing Philadelphia's Home for Aged and Infirm Colored Persons, which was renamed for him after his death. Smith's will left $15,000 for the Stephen Smith Home in West Philadelphia. Like Paul Cuffe, Smith gave charitable donations to the church of his choice, the African Methodist Church. Smith built buildings in Philadelphia and Chester, Pennsylvania, and Cape May, New Jersey, for the church.

Thomy Lafon's (1810–1893) philanthropy resembled Smith's in many ways. Lafon made his money as a real estate investor in New Orleans. He helped contribute to the school founded with Madame Bernard Couvent's estate in 1848, and in 1866, he helped the Louisiana Association for the Benefit of Colored Orphans with a donation of two lots as a site for the building. On his death, however, Lafon donated nearly $600,000, $500,000 of it in property, to several institutions, including the Catholic Institute for the Care of Orphans, the Louisiana Asylum, the Asylum of the Holy Family, and the Little Sisters of the Poor.

The story of Biddy Mason (1818–1891) illustrates some of the class tensions that characterize all philanthropy. Mason came to California in 1851 against her will, the slave property of a Mississippi plantation owner named Robert Smith. Apparently Smith did not realize when he moved to California that he was moving to a free state; California's constitution banned slavery after 1850. Smith became concerned about the security of Mason and his other slaves and began planning to leave for Texas, still a slave state, in 1855. Smith's plans hit a snag when two free black businessmen, each of whom had a son in love with one of Smith's slaves, convinced the Los Angeles and San Bernardino County sheriffs to take Mason and her family into custody to prevent Smith from leaving with them. Mason and her three daughters were able to stay in California, once a judge ruled in their favor.

As a free woman, Mason quickly earned a reputation as a skilled midwife and medical practitioner. Within 10 years after her freedom, she had saved enough money to purchase land and start her own homestead. Her initial investment of $250 in 1866 proved extremely worthwhile when the Los Angeles real estate market boomed in the late nineteenth century. In 1885 she helped her grandsons set up a livery stable on another part of her land, which she deeded them in 1890. Mason used her wealth to benefit other African Americans as well. In 1872 she helped organize the Los Angeles branch of the First African Methodist Episcopal Church. After the church was established, Mason paid both the church's property taxes and the minister's salary. In 1884 Mason told a grocery in her neighborhood to open accounts for needy families. One historian wrote of her giving: "Because she became known as a benefactor of the poor, 'a frequent visitor to the jail,' and a resource for settlers of all races, Giddy Mason was approached by many who wanted help."

Mason's philanthropic beliefs did not seem to take strong hold in her children and grandchildren. Among the small groups of elite black Los Angelenos, Mason's descendants were very prominent, attaining wealth far beyond her own. However, they were not nearly as generous. Mason's grandchildren put much more distance between themselves and the working class, but this social distance apparently did not come with a sense of noblesse oblige.

Wealthy blacks were censured by the black community for failing to use their money to support community advancement. But while they used their money to improve their material life, participating in activities that paralleled the white elites, including European tours, racism and Jim Crow limited their social life to the black community. Status and recognition did come to those who gave. Despite class antagonisms in the late nineteenth century, evidence abounds that the philanthropic impulse motivated these African American aristocrats as well.

Charleston, South Carolina's Dr. Alonzo C. McClennan, for example, helped found a hospital, and a connected nurse training school, that was "essentially a charity institution.'' In the famous 1896 court case *Plessy v. Ferguson*, Homere Plessy, a black man arrested for refusing to leave the white car on a railroad, was defended by the Citizens Committee of Colored Creoles. That New Orleans committee included Plessy, Aristide Mary, L. J. Joubert, James Lewis, and P.B.S. Pinchback.*

In his 1907 study *Economic Co-operation among Negro Americans*, W.E.B. Du Bois details the large numbers of cooperatively supported schools, mutual aid societies, hospitals, and churches in the late nineteenth century. He identified 75 to 100 homes for orphans and the elderly and 40 hospitals, all supported by cooperative efforts of blacks. No doubt, black elites in the respective cities under study (which ranged from Jackson, Mississippi, to New Haven to Cincinnati) were involved in administering these philanthropic facilities.

In the first two decades of the twentieth century, a new type of black elite emerged. These new elites, among them Madam C. J. Walker* (Sarah Breedlove Walker) and Jesse Binga,* owed their social position and wealth less to formal education and good breeding than to the large amounts of money they made in business. Regardless of their social pedigree, successful businesswomen like Walker did share in common with older elites a sense of duty to give something back to the community. They sometimes were criticized for their efforts by those who interpreted their philanthropic activities as attempts by ''African American robber barons'' to reinforce their superior social status. However, they nonetheless carried on the tradition of black philanthropy.

Walker first gave in support of a nationwide movement to build YMCAs in black communities, contributing $1,000 to the Indianapolis campaign. She also gave baskets of food to poor families in Indianapolis each Christmas, as well as supporting orphanages, old folks homes, and other social service organizations. She contributed extensively to black educational institutions, including Tuskegee Institute, Mary McLeod Bethune's Daytona Normal and Industrial Institute, the Haines Institute, and the Palmer Memorial Institute, interestingly, the last three of which were founded and headed by women. Madam Walker contributed much to the newly established National Association for the Advancement of Colored People (NAACP), including a $5,000 donation to their antilynching fight in the spring of 1919, shortly before she died. But what is perhaps most unique about her is the gospel of philanthropy she preached to her sales agents. At the annual convention honoring the local chapters of the Madam C. J. Walker Hair Culturists Union of America, she gave a highly coveted award for charitable work done by an individual or branch.

Jesse Binga (1865–1950) of Chicago, bank founder, was another prominent black philanthropist. Binga went into the real estate business for himself near the turn of the century and in 1908 opened his own bank. By 1926 he owned more frontage on State Street in Chicago's ''Black Belt'' than any other person. Binga cherished his reputation as a community leader, and both he and his wife put much effort into philanthropic endeavors. They gave to the local Old Folks Home and the YMCA and established scholarships for blacks at the University of Chicago, Fisk University, and the Chicago School of Music. They held Christmas parties for poor children and "neglected" seniors.

Examples abound of prominent African American businessmen using their wealth to give back to their community from World War II until today. Chicago's Carl A. and N. Louise Hansberry, parents of playwright Lorraine Hansberry, used part of the $100,000 annual income from their $250,000 in real estate to fund the Hansberry Foundation. His wife Louise established the foundation in 1936, with the expressed purpose of funding litigation in support of the state of Illinois's Civil Rights Law. Arthur G. Gaston* (1892–1995), whose business enterprises run the gamut from insurance to banking, received several honorary doctorate degrees from colleges in the United States and Africa in recognition of his success and philanthropic work. His charitable donations include a 1966 donation of $50,000 to start a Birmingham, Alabama, Boys' Club Affiliate. Gaston also sponsored Alabama law students.

John H. Johnson,* who has made a considerable fortune publishing magazines including *Ebony* and *Jet*, in addition to his cosmetic "Fashion Fair" manufacturing empire, has also devoted some of his resources to philanthropy. In 1958 he helped organize a charity fashion show for Flint-Goodridge Hospital in New Orleans, held in September of that year. The show has continued until today and travels to 190 cities a year. Johnson wrote in his autobiography that the show has raised $25 million for charity since 1958. In 1987, the Better Boys Club of Chicago named Johnson their Chicagoan of the Year in recognition of his philanthropy. Johnson's magazines devote considerable attention to the activities of a new breed of black philanthropists, particularly those who have made considerable fortunes in entertainment and professional sports.

The superstar television entertainer Bill Cosby and his wife Camille Cosby made news in 1989 when they donated an astounding $20 million to Spelman College during the inauguration of its first African American female president, Dr. Johnetta Cole. That gift was the largest ever given to any of the 112 historically black colleges and universities. In addition, the nearly $4.1 million the Cosbys have given to other black colleges, they have put 28 youths through college.

Other celebrities, including Oprah Winfrey,* Michael Jordan, and Earvin "Magic" Johnson, have also given some of their fortunes to the community via philanthropy. Jordan founded his own philanthropic foundation in 1989. The Michael Jordan Foundation holds a yearly benefit to raise money for charities, including the Special Olympics, the United Negro College Fund, and Xavier University. Nearly two thirds of the money Jordan's foundation gave to outside agencies from March 1991 to March 1992—almost $250,000—went to African American–oriented organizations.

SELECTED BIBLIOGRAPHY: Emmett Carson, *A Hand Up: Philanthropy and Self-Help in America* (Washington, DC: Joint Center for Political and Economic Studies, 1993); Leonard P. Curry, *The Free Black in Urban America, 1800–1850: The Shadow of the Dream* (Chicago: University of Chicago Press, 1981); Rodolphe Lucien Desdunes,

Our People and Our History (1911; reprint, Baton Rouge: Louisiana State University Press, 1973); W.E.B. Du Bois, *Economic Co-operation among Negro Americans* (Atlanta: Atlanta University Press, 1907); Willard B. Gatewood, *Aristocrats of Color: The Black Elite, 1880–1920* (Bloomington: Indiana University Press, 1990); Dolores Hayden, "Biddy Mason's Los Angeles, 1856–1891," *California History* 68, 3 (Fall 1989); John Ingham and Lynne B. Feldman, *African-American Business Leaders: A Biographical Dictionary* (Westport, CT: Greenwood Press, 1994).

Jonathan S. Coit

PIERCE, JOSEPH A. (1902–1969), Georgia, Texas, mathematician, college professor, university president.

One of the early scholars of black business enterprise was Joseph A. Pierce. Following in a tradition of scholars such as Henry Minton, Booker T. Washington,* and W.E.B. Du Bois, Pierce published a major study in 1947 entitled *Negro Business and Business Education*. His scholarship is timeless. Professor Joseph Alphonso Pierce was born in Waycross, Georgia. He received his A.B. degree in the social sciences from Atlanta University. In 1930 he completed the M.S. degree in mathematics from the University of Michigan and in 1938 the Ph.D. from the same school.

Professor Pierce's early career took him to Texas College in Tyler, Atlanta's Booker T. Washington High School, and Atlanta University. It was here, as head of the Department of Mathematics, that he published *Negro Business and Business Education*. The purpose of *Negro Business and Business Education* was to enhance the development of business enterprise within communities. It was written at a time when institutions of higher learning were beginning to follow the lead of Tuskegee Institute and add business schools to their liberal arts curriculum. The book addressed problems and needs of business education among blacks. These problems related to curricula, vocational guidance, teaching personnel, and cooperation between businesspeople and teachers. The book provides data on black enterprises from 12 cities in America, and it is the most detailed study of these enterprises since W.E.B. Du Bois's *Economic Co-operation among Negroes*, which was published in 1907.

In 1966 Pierce was named the third president of Texas Southern University. From 1967 to 1968 he served as a consultant to NASA (the National Aeronautics and Space Administration). Pierce was a member of Sigma Xi and Delta Kappa Chi honorary societies. Professionally, he held membership in the Institute of Mathematical Statistics, the American Statistical Association, the National Institute of Science (president, 1946–1947), and the National Educational Association.

SELECTED BIBLIOGRAPHY: John Sibley Butler, *Entrepreneurship and Self-Help among Black Americans: A Reconsideration of Race and Economics* (Albany: State University of New York Press, 1991); Joseph A. Pierce, *Negro Business and Business Education* (New York: Harper & Brothers, 1947); Vivan Ovelton Sammons, *Blacks in Science and Medicine* (New York: Hemisphere Publishing, 1990).

John Sibley Butler

PINCHBACK, PICKNEY BENTON STEWART (1837–1921), Louisiana, businessman, army officer, constitutional convention delegate, state senator, co-founder of a black college, lieutenant governor, acting governor, civic leader, lawyer.

The son of a white planter and a freed slave mulatto woman, Pinchback became a political organizer and served in public office for over a decade following the Civil War. As a delegate to two constitutional conventions, 1867–1868 and 1879, he offered resolutions that led to the passage of civil rights laws. A member of the State Board of Education, Pinchback was instrumental in the founding of Southern University, the first state institution of higher learning for African Americans in the state. Pinchback was the first and only black man to serve as the governer of a state during Reconstruction. Although his claim to a seat as U.S. senator was not recognized, he received payment of over $16,000, equal to his pay if seated.

While most noted for his political career, Pinchback was an energetic businessman. In 1869, he formed a cotton factorage commission merchant business with black state senator C. C. Antoine. On December 18, 1870, he became joint owner of a newspaper—the *New Orleans Louisianian*. Initially published on Thursdays and Saturdays, the paper was published under several titles—the *Semi-Weekly Louisianian* and the *Weekly Louisianan*. Pinchback was in partnership in publishing the two papers from 1870 until April 27, 1872, when his two partners withdrew from the proprietorship, giving Pinchback control of all the stocks. Also, in 1870, he became chief stockholder and president of the Mississippi River Packet Company, a ferry business designed primarily to afford black passengers transportation on the Mississippi River because of Jim Crow practices on the part of white transportation companies.

Pinchback acquired his early education in Cincinnati, Ohio. After his father's death, he took a job as a cabin boy on canal boats sailing the Miami, Toledo, and Fort Wayne Canals. From 1854 to 1862 he worked aboard steamboats on the Missouri, Red, and Mississippi Rivers. A diligent worker, he earned the position of steward, the best riverboat job a black could earn during the years of slavery. With the Civil War, he enlisted in the Union cause. He made his way to New Orleans and joined the 1st Louisiana Volunteer Infantry, a white regiment, serving briefly from August 18 until October 5, 1862. When General Benjamin Butler announced the organization of free men of color regiments, Pinchback obtained permission and organized Company A, 3d Regiment Louisiana Native Guards, in which he held the rank of captain from October 6, 1862, to September 17, 1863. Racism of white officers forced his resignation but with an honorable discharge. Still anxious and willing to fight for the Union cause, he applied for and received a commission from Nathaniel P. Banks to raise a cavalry company. Using his own money, Pinchback raised the company but was denied the opportunity to serve with it because of his race.

Pinchback married Nina Emily Hawthrone in 1860. Although two of their children died young, they saw three sons and a daughter grow to maturity.

Around 1883, the Pinchback family left New Orleans and went to Washington, D.C. In 1895 they moved to New York, where Pinchback was employed as a U.S. marshal. He returned to Washington, where he established a law practice in 1909. Pinchback died in Washington in 1921, but his remains were brought to New Orleans and buried in Metarie Ridge Cemetery.

SELECTED BIBLIOGRAPHY: James Haskins, *Pickney Benton Stewart Pinchback* (New York: Macmillan Publishing Co., 1973); Charles Vincent, "Louisiana's Black Governor: Aspects of His National Significance," *Negro History Bulletin* 32, 1 (April–May–June 1979); Charles Vincent, "P.B.S. Pinchback," in Joseph G. Dawson III, ed., *The Louisiana Governors: From Iberville to Edwards* (Baton Rouge: Louisiana State University Press, 1990).

Charles Vincent

PLEASANT, MARY ELLEN (c. 1814–1904), San Francisco, entrepreneur, real estate investor, philanthropist.

Mary Ellen Pleasant was an abolitionist, entrepreneur, and investor. She is best known for her civil rights and business activities in nineteenth-century San Francisco. When Pleasant landed in gold rush San Francisco, she brought a substantial amount of capital, perhaps thousands of dollars. Over the course of 50 years, Pleasant parlayed this initial investment into valuable California real estate worth hundreds of thousands of dollars, including San Francisco boardinghouses, a ranch in Sonoma County, a cottage to the south of San Francisco, and the best known, an enormous and ornate mansion on the corner of Octavia and Bush Streets near the city center. Like many nineteenth-century black entrepreneurs, Pleasant combined her financial wizardry with philanthropy and a tireless struggle against slavery, Jim Crow, and white supremacy.

Pleasant's earliest memories—and her first experience in business—hearken back to her childhood years in Nantucket. The years before that are murky: Pleasant claims she was born to free parents in Philadelphia and that her father was Louis Alexander Williams, a Hawaiian merchant. Others believe she was born a slave in the South. It is likely that she went to Nantucket as a respite from slave catchers whether she was free or slave. In the 1820s and 1830s she lived and worked with a Quaker family on the small New England island, where she quickly acquired the experience necessary for a future in finance and entrepreneurship. Working in a busy shop in Nantucket Town, Mary Ellen (who then went by the name "Williams") developed the kinds of skills that she would use for the rest of her life. "I could make change and talk to a dozen people all at once and never make a mistake!" she remembered.

In New England, in the 1840s, Mary Ellen met and married her first husband, James Smith, also the subject of much controversy. Pleasant described Smith as "a foreman, carpenter and contractor, who had a good business and possessed considerable means." He was also an abolitionist. When Smith died, he left her a sizable estate that Pleasant managed with the help of associates from Nantucket. Soon after Smith's death, Pleasant sailed for San Francisco (c. 1849–

1852), arriving at the peak of the gold rush. From her earliest days in the West, Pleasant invested her capital—perhaps as much as $30,000—wisely. She brought her money to Fred Langford and William West of West & Harper, who invested it at a rate of 10 percent. She also engaged in what she called an exchange business, trading gold for silver. Between the death of her first husband and her arrival in San Francisco, Mary Ellen met and married a man named John James Pleasants (the "s" was eventually dropped). Mary Ellen and John Pleasants were also the parents of a little girl, Elizabeth.

In San Francisco, Pleasant opened laundries and worked as a housekeeper for the city's leading merchants. But her elegant boardinghouses, where she hosted California's wealthiest citizens, became her most visible success. Guests were treated to sumptuous meals and elegant accommodations. Pleasant is rumored to have been a madam, and it is quite possible that she provided her male guests with female companions. The boardinghouse at 920 Washington Street grew to be her most stately establishment. The residents of this boardinghouse included Newton Booth, who became governor of California. Pleasant employed a black staff at her establishments, and her neighbors and associates also included prominent black leaders, businessmen, and artists. Nearby, at 917 Washington, the San Francisco Athenaeum Building, to which Pleasant contributed, housed a library and meeting place for the city's growing African American population. By 1870, Pleasant listed $15,000 in real estate and $15,000 in personal property as her assets. In addition to her exclusive boardinghouse, Pleasant purchased other property in San Francisco and Oakland in the 1870s.

During the tumultuous years of the war and Reconstruction, Pleasant diversified her entrepreneurial activities, dramatically increased her income, traveled to Canada where she also bought property, and fought Jim Crow practices in the Far West's largest city. Working in the homes of wealthy merchants and investors put Pleasant within earshot of political and financial decision making. The proximity to San Francisco's elite families enhanced Pleasant's knowledge about the volatile economy, political climate, and the culture of the elite. This knowledge provided the basis for her own entrepreneurial success.

Pleasant channeled funds into black-owned businesses, institutions, and civil rights efforts. She supported the black press, including one of the West's most successful nineteenth-century black newspapers, *The Pacific Appeal*. San Francisco's AME Zion Church also received Pleasant's support and patronage. Pleasant, like other San Francisco black leaders, spent the 1860s developing and promoting a free school for black children. But her most celebrated activity was her suit against the North Beach & Mission Railroad. In her testimony she explained that on September 27, 1866, she stood on Folsom Street waiting for the city's No. 21 streetcar to take her downtown to the city's Plaza. Pleasant hailed the streetcar, but the driver refused to stop even though there was room on the car and she had her tickets. She charged that the company was denying service to African Americans. Pleasant was initially awarded $500 in punitive damages, but on appeal in the state supreme court, her victory was overturned.

Pleasant's investments are difficult to trace. Although San Franciscans knew her to be a wealthy property owner, she was necessarily secretive about her means of acquisition and her specific investments. Pleasant benefited directly from the huge profits made during the Comstock mining boom in Nevada in the 1860s and 1870s. Her rise to prominence in financial and philanthropic circles can, in part, be attributed to this general economic trend; Pleasant was a keen manipulator of real estate and mining stock. Her fortune also became linked with Scottish banker Thomas Bell, also the owner of mines and valuable mining stock. Bell, vice president of the Bank of California—the institution that gleaned the most profits from the Comstock—became Pleasant's financial partner in the 1870s and took quarters in her newly built mansion.

The house that Pleasant built in 1877 stood on the corner of Octavia and Bush Streets just west of the business district. It was a lavishly furnished, multistoried Victorian mansion with expansive grounds, worth as much as $100,000 at the time of construction. The house had over 10 rooms, and the property encompassed two city blocks. Pleasant's mansion and her cohabitation with Thomas Bell made for intense speculation by her contemporaries. Rumors about a sexual liaison between Pleasant and Bell did not cease but did subside when he married a young protégée of Pleasant's, Teresa Clingan. After 1878, the three of them, and eventually the Bell children, all lived in the house Pleasant built on Octavia Street. Pleasant was assumed by many to be the "mammy" of the household, with Thomas and Teresa Bell serving as master and mistress. This masquerade proved to be advantageous for Pleasant, at least for a time. In 1891, Pleasant bought the 985-acre Beltane Ranch in Sonoma County's Valley of the Moon, which served as their weekend home.

Pleasant would spend the better part of the 1890s in litigation over the Bell estate and her own. Pleasant's financial and personal activities were scrutinized by the press and in the courts. Among other things, Pleasant was accused of supporting young black women with proceeds from the Bell estate. In 1899, Teresa Bell, accusing Pleasant of squandering Thomas Bell's life savings, forced Pleasant to move out of Octavia Street and the house at the ranch—the places where Pleasant spent most of her time. The control over Pleasant's mansion and the so-called eviction made front-page news on May 7, when the San Francisco newspaper *The Call* ran a full-page article titled "Angel or Arch Fiend in the House of Mystery." A combination of factors led to a slow but steady financial decline for Pleasant. By the turn of the century she was considered an insolvent debtor by the courts and her creditors. Pleasant lived the last five years of her life at Geneva Cottage, her property south of San Francisco, and in a house on Webster Street that she also owned. On January 11, 1904, at ten in the morning, Pleasant died at the home of her friends, the Sherwoods. Pleasant was buried in a cemetery in Napa Valley the following day.

It seems fair to say that by the end of her life Pleasant had lost a considerable amount of property and capital to creditors, lawyers, and competitors. Due to the tangled nature of the Bell and Pleasant finances, and the fact that much of what she owned lay hidden under other people's names, we will never know the exact amount of Pleasant's estate. But it is safe to assume that at points in her career Pleasant owned at least a million dollars worth of property. Given that Thomas Bell was worth over $30 million when he died in 1892—and they probably owned stock and property in common—we can assume Pleasant was at least a millionaire.

It was 1910, six years after Pleasant died, that her will was admitted to probate. All of Pleasant's possessions were left to the Sherwoods including a 114-acre ranch and the deeds and the securities that were left in a safe deposit box at Donohoe-Kelly Bank. Pleasant's estate, by that time, was valued at around $10,000—a far cry from the millions she once owned. Pleasant's visibility at the turn of the century was unprecedented for a black woman in the West: She was in court on a weekly basis for years, her name became synonymous with financial scandal, and every judge in the state knew her. Her stature as a financial wizard and entrepreneur had gained her the notoriety that was reserved for robber barons of that same age. Indeed, she engaged some of the same tactics: vertical integration, real estate speculation, and inside trading on Comstock and other mines.

Yet Pleasant's notoriety also stemmed from her manipulation of secrets—both financial and social. These kinds of strategies—a direct result of her boardinghouse business—are more difficult to identify and substantiate; they occurred in seemingly private places (dining rooms) but involved public institutions (bank presidents).

Pleasant will also be remembered for her commitment to abolition, most notably her efforts to support John Brown. If not sole contributor, Pleasant helped to finance Brown's infamous 1859 raid on Harpers Ferry that precipitated the Civil War. On her tombstone, per her request, the phrase "She was a friend of John Brown" appears in stone.

SELECTED BIBLIOGRAPHY: Lerone Bennett, Jr. "An Historical Detective Story: The Mystery of Mary Ellen Pleasant," *Ebony*, April–May 1979; Lynn M. Hudson, "A New Look: 'I'm Not Mammy to Everybody in California,' Mary Ellen Pleasant, a Black Entrepreneur," *Journal of the West* (July 1993): 35–40; Lynn M. Hudson, "When 'Mammy' Becomes a Millionaire: Mary Ellen Pleasant, an African-American Entrepreneur" (Ph.D. diss., Indiana University, 1996); *San Francisco Examiner*, October 13, 1895.

Lynn M. Hudson

POWELL, WILLIAM JENIFER (1898–1942), Illinois, California, garage owner, flight school operator.

Between 1919 and 1926, Powell quickly rose in the business ranks of Southside Chicago, opening there at least three filling stations by 1925 and the 150-car Auto-Electric Service Station and Garage in 1926. Only two years later, however, inspired by Charles Lindbergh's historic Atlantic crossing, he decided to risk his new status among the black business elite to pursue the still-young enterprise of aviation. He sold part of his Chicago operations and enrolled in 1928 at the Warren College of Aeronautics in Los Angeles. A visionary, Powell believed entrepreneurs could through aviation help solve the unemployment problem and challenge segregation in public transportation. Evincing a strong black business ethic and the high hopes many Americans felt toward the technology of flight, he imagined a national network of black-owned airplane manufacturing plants and distributorships, flying and mechanical schools, airlines, and airports.

Although unable to fulfill his dream, Powell's successes were notable for the depression, when scores of small aviation concerns folded overnight. Contributing $3,000 of his own money and soliciting funds from local investors, he established in 1928 the Bessie Coleman Aero Club (in honor of the first black pilot licensed by the Federation Aeronautique Internationale) in Los Angeles and purchased a plane to teach young men and women to fly. By May 1930, he had relocated to Phoenix, Arizona, where he opened a flying school and published at least one issue of the *Bessie Coleman Aero News*.

Returning to Los Angeles the following year, Powell staged a well-attended Labor Day air circus in the city, as well as two additional air shows that winter, which featured "The Five Blackbirds," a group of stunt pilots he had organized. As the depression wore on, however, investors became harder to convince, despite Powell's creative attempts to persuade them by means of a promotional play he wrote and produced; a 1934 autobiography; and a film. "Unemployment, the Negro and Aviation," he produced in 1935. Finally, supplementing private contributions with funding from the New Deal's Emergency Education Program, he established in 1935 or 1936 the nonprofit Craftsmen of Black Wings, Inc., in Los Angeles. Committed to providing aviation opportunities to both sexes, the Craftsmen provided close to 100 enrollees, many of them female, free ground-school instruction at Jefferson High School, as well as flying lessons and airplane mechanics and construction courses at a workshop located at Dycer Airport. By late 1936, the organization had a small branch in Harlem. From 1937 through 1938, the Craftsmen published the monthly *Craftsmen Aero-News*, the first black-owned aviation trade journal.

Born July 29, 1898, as William Jenifer in Henderson, Kentucky, Powell assumed his stepfather's surname and grew up in Chicago. He served as a first lieutenant in World War I and earned a B.S. in electrical engineering in 1922 from the University of Illinois at Urbana. An active Baptist layman, Powell belonged to the American Legion and Alpha Phi Alpha fraternity. Pursuing acting as a sideline, he also helped found the Negro Motion Picture Players Association in 1939. He and his wife Lucylle (briefly a parachutist) had two children, William, Jr., and Bernadyne. Powell died in Los Angeles in 1942.

SELECTED BIBLIOGRAPHY: James de T. Abajian, *Blacks and Their Contributions to the American West: A Bibliography and Union List of Holdings Through 1970* (Boston: G. K. Hall & Co., 1974); "Bessie Coleman Aero Club to Open Here," *California News*, May 21, 1931; "Colored Airplane Craftsmen Offer 100 Free Scholarships to Aviation

Students,'' Press release, Claude A. Barnett Papers, Box 261, Folder 1, Chicago Historical Society, Chicago, Illinois; "History and Future Plans of the Craftsmen of Black Wings, Inc.,'' *Craftsmen Aero-News*, January 1937; "Our National Organization," *Bessie Coleman Aero News*, May 1930; William J. Powell, *Black Wings* (Los Angeles: Ivan Deach, Jr., 1934); Emmett J. Scott, *Scott's Official History of the American Negro in the World War* (Chicago: Homewood, 1919); John Taitt, *Souvenir of Negro Progress, Chicago, 1779–1925* (Chicago: 1925).

Jill D. Snider

PROPERTY OWNERS, SOUTH, 1790–1880. Following the American Revolution, a wave of manumissions in the Upper South released thousands of slaves from bondage. Propertyless, with few skills, illiterate, and denied equal rights, most of them remained poverty-ridden. They worked as laborers, domestic servants, and farmhands. In 1798, in Frederick County, Maryland, there were only three black real estate owners out of a free black population of nearly 500. In Maryland, Virginia, and North Carolina, during the early decades of the nineteenth century, few free blacks were able to move out of poverty. With a population of 37,000 free people of color in 1820, for example, Virginia contained only a few hundred landowning black farmers.

Despite the hostile attitudes of whites, legal restrictions, prejudice, and violence, during the next generation a significant expansion in black property ownership occurred in the Upper South. Now removed from slavery by a number of years or the children of free blacks, African Americans had obtained experience in the marketplace. They also recognized the importance of acquiring land and other property to provide for their families. With limited capital, most who acquired farmland and city lots saved their earnings from low-paying jobs and purchased small amounts of real estate. They and their children then added to these holdings. They were predominantly black (compared with mulatto) and possessed small average holdings. In 1850, among the 4,361 black realty owners in the Upper South, the mean value of their land was only $585 and the median only $300; they represented about one out of nine free black families in the region.

A decade later, among the 7,321 owners, the mean stood at $782 and the median at $400; they represented about one out of six free black families. This growth was spurred only in part by economic factors—expansion of higher-paying jobs, increased skill levels among free blacks, and the demand for workers in the West. It was also the result of the determination of free people of color to gain acceptance as productive members of society. Although their holdings were small, and only a small proportion of Upper South free blacks owned property, by the eve of the Civil War a significant property-owning segment had emerged.

In the Lower South, a selective manumission process occurred during the late eighteenth and early nineteenth centuries. Free blacks in this region were often skilled, racially mixed, and sometimes literate. Sometimes they were provided land and slaves by their white fathers or other benefactors. The small free colored population in the region (1.6 percent of the black population in 1790; 1.5 percent in 1860) possessed many economic advantages over their brethren in the upper states. Indeed, even during the early years, a few emerged in various Louisiana parishes, in Mobile, Alabama, Charleston, South Carolina, and a few other locations who were prosperous land- and slave-owning farmers and merchants.

In the 1830s, various members of the Metoyer clan in Natchitoches Parish, mulatto Jean Baptiste Meullion of St. Landry Parish, and South Carolina mulatto planter John Garden could be counted among the wealthiest farmers in their areas. When the U.S. census first captures a relatively precise profile of the real estate holdings among free people of color in 1850, it reveals that among the approximately 7,000 families in the lower states, 1,821 owned an average of about $2,800 worth of real estate, or one out of four free black families; in 1860, the numbers rose to 2,319 free black realty owners, with average holdings of $3,100, or about one family in three. This did not reach the level of whites, but it represented a remarkable economic ascendancy.

In some sections of the South, slaves acquired small amounts of personal property. This was usually the result of incentives offered by masters to promote the work ethic among their charges, but blacks responded enthusiastically to such opportunities. The "rewards," however, were usually small, and most often only those with special skills or who worked in the task system or who were hired out by their owners were able to accumulate property. Still, some slaves owned livestock, personal items, and sometimes horses.

The Civil War brought dramatic changes among the black property owner class in the South. The release of 4 million slaves from bondage and the efforts of whites to maintain control over the land and the black labor force made it nearly impossible for former slaves to gain an economic foothold. In the Lower South, there was a rapid decline of the economic standing of the formerly free people of color. In rural areas, black landowners in 1870 represented 1 family in 31, with average holdings of about $544. In the upper states, there was more continuity from the antebellum period, as former slaves and formerly free blacks acquired real and personal holdings. In some areas there were fewer barriers against advancement than in the Deep South. The number of rural black realty owners rose from 5,615 to more than 31,000 between 1860 and 1870, and while still representing only 1 family in 26, the total value of property owned by freedmen and women in the upper states now surpassed the total value owned by blacks in the lower states.

The period 1790–1880 was therefore one of slow growth at the beginning, except in the lower states, and gradual expansion until 1830, when especially in the Upper South there was a rapid rise in the number and average holdings of black property owners. After the Civil War the process began again, with the vast majority denied access to the land but the beginnings of a gradual expansion.

SELECTED BIBLIOGRAPHY: Loren Schweninger, *Black Property Owners in the South, 1790–1915* (Urbana: University of Illinois Press, 1990).

Loren Schweninger

PROPERTY OWNERS, SOUTH, WOMEN, 1790–1880. The social, economic, and legal barriers confronting African American women who sought to gain economic independence were enormous. But beginning in the late eighteenth century, and continuing after the Civil War, there was a significant growth in the numbers of black female property holders. In the Deep South, these women were usually persons of mixed racial origin who lived with white men or freed slaves who were provided for by whites. In the upper states, they were most often emancipated or self-purchased slaves who had been able to work and save small amounts in order to buy a house or farmland. There are a few examples of very prosperous free women of color who owned extensive tracts of land or, as was the case for New Orleans resident Eulalie (Cecee) d'Mandeville McCarty, who established a profitable retail business. While the number of women who acquired property remained small, they represented a larger proportion of black property owners than white women represented white property owners. In the Lower South, during the 1850s, nearly one-third of the blacks who owned property were women; in the Upper South, about one-sixth were in the same category.

Both of these percentages dropped significantly after the Civil War, to 11 and 12 percent, respectively, as freedmen and -women now lived together in families in the aftermath of slavery. During the 1870s and 1880s, there is some evidence, at least as revealed in the census returns denoting farm ownership, that there was an increase in the proportion of female black landowners. The statistical evidence reveals the unique position of African American women in the economic life of free blacks before the war and freed people in its aftermath.

SELECTED BIBLIOGRAPHY: Suzanne Lebsock, *The Free Women of Petersburg: Status and Culture in a Southern Town, 1784–1860* (New York: W. W. Norton, 1984); Loren Schweninger, "Property-Owning Free African-American Women in the South, 1800–1870," *Journal of Women's History* 1 (Winter 1990).

Loren Schweninger

R

RADIO ENTERPRISES. African American ownership of broadcast radio stations has increased greatly during the last 25 years. In 1970, blacks owned fewer than 20 stations; in 1990, over 200 stations were black owned. Facing competition from other media outlets such as cable and satellite television networks, the radio industry in general has turned to the development of niche markets and consolidation in order to remain profitable. Accordingly, successful contemporary black radio owners target specific segments of the broadcast audience and seek to expand their holdings.

African Americans have made important contributions to commercial radio since its earliest days, especially as disc jockeys (DJs). Before the early 1960s, DJs determined playlists, thus giving them control of their own shows. During the 1930s and 1940s, several black DJs developed shows aimed at black audiences. Chicago's Jack L. Cooper introduced *The All Negro Hour* in 1929; Al Benson, also of Chicago, had a show aired on several stations. Cooper owned his own studio and oversaw the work of a team of DJs and writers. By 1949, he was a millionaire. During the 1940s, black DJs with their own shows appeared in several other cities. The success of Cooper and Benson did not result in the widespread appearance of black DJs until the 1950s, though. In 1947, there were only 16 black DJs among the 3,000 DJs in the industry, but by the mid-1950s, over 500 black DJs were working in commercial radio.

From a business standpoint, the early work of black DJs effectively made them the equivalent of contemporary program directors and sales managers. By choosing the music to be played on their shows, black DJs defined and maintained the ''Negro Appeal'' format. The first black DJs also secured advertising for their shows because they "hired" their own time on the air during the 1930s and throughout the 1940s. Jack L. Cooper, for example, owned his own advertising agency. By linking each DJ's pay to the commercial success of the station, white owners impelled black DJs not only to determine which products and services would most likely appeal to black listeners but also to persuade the appropriate manufacturers and providers to advertise on the station.

Furthermore, black DJs were responsible for creating a standard format for commercial radio. The success of black DJs in defining and reaching audiences did not go unnoticed. In the 1950s, many white DJs patterned their shows after the Negro Appeal format. These DJs included Allen Freed of Cleveland and Dewey Phillips of Memphis, both of whom are credited with nurturing rock and roll music. In the 1960s, five white-owned radio chains introduced the soul format, which drew heavily from the Negro Appeal format. By 1970, there were over 300 black-formatted radio stations in the United States. The use of standardized formats, however, which was an industry-wide response to the payola scandals of the early 1960s, took control of playlists out of the hands of DJs.

The first black-owned radio company was the Harlem Broadcasting Corporation, formed in 1929. In addition to maintaining its own studios, the company leased time on a New York City radio station and helped organize black radio performers. The Harlem Broadcast Corporation was influenced in part by the "New Negro" movement. For example, the corporation put together a live show in Harlem billed as "A Rise to Culture," featuring some 100 black performers. The Great Depression, however, took its toll on the corporation, and it folded.

Jesse B. Blayton, a successful Georgia banker and accountant, was the first black radio station owner, purchasing Atlanta's WERD in 1950. The second black-owned station was KCKA in Kansas City, acquired in 1952. For the next 20 years, black ownership increased at a slow rate. By 1970, only 16 stations were owned by blacks. Between 1970 and 1990, the number of black-owned stations reached 206—138 AM and 68 FM. What explains the rise in black ownership? Many black owners have started by first purchasing a single station, then expanding their holdings using the profits of the initial station. In 1972, Percy Sutton* acquired WLIB in New York. Sutton's holdings today, known as Inner City Broadcasting, include several stations in California and Texas. WLIB had its own news department producing shows and features on issues of importance to New York's black population. Dorothy E. Brunson, who worked for Inner City Broadcasting, bought WEBB in Baltimore in 1979; by 1990, she owned three more stations. Both Sutton and Brunson have branched into television, a common move among black entrepreneurs who begin in radio.

Black radio station owners have also sought out struggling or unprofitable stations and refashioned their formats in order to make them profitable. According to John Douglas, his business strategy is to "buy what other people don't want and make something of it." In 1996, Douglas owned 10 AM stations and 1 FM station in Los Angeles, San Francisco, Chicago, Boston, New York, and Houston. After struggling to break into television, Douglas began buying AM radio stations because they required modest downpayments and were readily available for purchase. Douglas Broadcasting Inc. relies on a multiethnic format to draw listeners. Some of his stations, for example, target Asian Americans, who Douglas sees as a growth audience. Douglas has also founded Personal Achievement Radio, Inc., which broadcasts self-help and motivational programs over his stations.

The 1978 FCC (Federal Communications Commission) tax break to minority owners and FCC "distress" sales have helped blacks become owners, though in 1995, the FCC rescinded tax breaks for minorities. Cathy Hughes is an example of an owner who has benefited from FCC help. Hughes bought Washington, D.C.'s WOL-AM in 1980 at a reduced price from the FCC. However, Hughes's pioneering work in black talk radio is primarily responsible for her success today as an owner. WOL was one of the first all news and talk stations aimed at black audiences. Although the station was not initially profitable, its success during the last 10 years has allowed Hughes to expand her holdings. Her company, Radio One Inc., now owns seven radio stations broadcasting in Washington and the neighboring market of Baltimore. In 1995, Radio One paid $34 million for Washington's WKYS-FM, a music station. In addition to heading Radio One, Hughes hosts her own show and prides herself on providing employment opportunities for blacks. Of the 210 broadcasters working for her in 1995, 195 were black.

The growth of Douglas's and Hughes's companies parallels a consolidation trend in the radio industry as a whole. Congress's passage of the Telecommunications Act in early 1996, which lifted ownership limits, is the precipitating cause of these mergers and acquisitions. Communication companies are now permitted to own as many as 8 stations in a single market. Between January and March 1996 alone, over 80 radio stations were sold, with sales totaling nearly $2 billion. Despite the prominent success of black radio station owners such as Sutton, Douglas, and Hughes, blacks, as well as Hispanics, remain underrepresented in commercial radio. In 1994, according to the National Telecommunications and Information Administration, although blacks and Hispanics comprised 27 percent of the U.S. population, they owned only 2.9 percent of the country's 10,244 commercial radio stations.

SELECTED BIBLIOGRAPHY: William Barlow, "Commercial and Noncommercial Radio," in Jannette L. Dates and William Barlow, eds., *Split Image: African Americans in the Mass Media*, 2nd ed. (Washington, DC: Howard University Press, 1993); John Downing, "Ethnic Minority Radio in the USA," *Howard Journal of Communication* 1, 4 (1989); Joyce Jones, "Keeping It in the Black," *Black Enterprise* (May 1995); Elizabeth A. Rathbun, "Niching His Way to Success," *Broadcasting and Cable* 126, 23 (May 27, 1996); Juliet E. K. Walker, *The History of Black Business in America: Capitalism, Race, Entrepreneurship* (New York: Macmillan/Prentice Hall International, 1998).

David F. Krugler

RECORDING INDUSTRY. Harry Pace* formed the first known black-owned company in 1921, leaving Pace and Handy (W. C. Handy) Music Company in New York to establish Pace Phonograph Corporation, with one clerk in a small basement room. He advertised that his label, Black Swan, would feature only black artists, produced by a company where all the stockholders and employees would be black. Pace reasoned that 12 million blacks in the United States formed a valuable market, and he used segmented advertisement to reach them. By the fall of 1921, he had hired Fletcher Henderson, a bandleader, as musical director and recording manager; moved to another location; and hired 15 clerks, an 8-man orchestra, and 7 district managers. Moreover, 1,000 dealers and agents represented the company, which shipped 2,500 records, even to the Philippines and the West Indies.

In 1922 Pace and his partner, John Fletcher, purchased the Olympic Disc Record Company and reissued the recordings of the white artists on Black Swan. He also introduced comic, hillbilly, and operatic acts on his Red Label Series. Paramount Records took over Black Swan in 1924 due to financial problems. Other black-owned companies had short tenures in the 1920s. For instance, Johnny and Reb Spikes, music store owners, founded the Sunshine Label in 1922 but issued only three releases. Thomas Chappelle and Juanita Stinnette, a black vaudeville act, produced six records (five featuring themselves) on C & S Records. There was advertisement for two others in 1922, but no releases have been found. W. C. Handy was to own one, and several individuals were to own Echo Records.

J. Mayo Williams was one of the earliest blacks to be a manager for the black division of a major company, when he headed Paramount's Race Artist Series in the 1920s. In addition, he left to start his own venture, Black Patti, which folded in 1927. He recorded jazz bands, choirs, and blues singers. After World War II, other blacks became owners. For example, Jack Lauderdale established the Swing Time Recording Company in Los Angeles in 1945 with an interracial staff, distributing its products in England, France, and Mexico. In 1946 Gladys Hampton, wife of Lionel Hampton, started Hampton Records, becoming the first known black woman to own a record company. She had plans to record jazz, swing, blues, classics, and spirituals. Leon Rene, a composer, owned Exclusive Records. In addition, Waverly Ivey was the only black owner of the three who founded the Imperial Music Records in 1946.

In the 1950s there were other short-lived companies. Leonard Allen and Samuel Smith formed the United Record Corporation in 1950 and had several major acts contracted by 1953. In 1958 Zell Sanders started J & S label, using $5,000 from her savings, after her daughter Johnnie was repeatedly turned down for a record contract. Dootone Recording Company was started by Dootsie Williams, a musician and composer, who coached his artists. A powerhouse emerged when Vivian Carter Bracken, James Bracken, and Calvin Carter, former record store owners, founded Vee Jay Records, based in Chicago, between 1952 and 1953. For a decade, Vee Jay was a real competitor for Chess Records, housed across the street. Like Pace, Vee Jay recorded white artists and was the first to release records by the Beatles in the United States. The company folded due to mismanagement in 1965.

While Vee Jay Records made its mark in the North, Don Robey built an empire in Houston. Since many in the industry disapproved of the successful independent label, Robey had to find people to sell the records and put up money to get airplay. Moreover, radio station managers told disc jockeys not to play Peacock cuts. A shrewd businessman, Robey insisted that musicians sign exclusive contracts. In addition, he used an alias, Deadric Malone, to share authorship of many songs, a standard practice. Robey sold Peacock to ABC/Dunhill in 1973 after a court battle with Chess Records.

By the time that Peacock was sold, the Detroit-based Motown was already the heir apparent. From then, Berry Gordy* built the largest independent record company in the world. Establishing the company in 1958, he eventually had 103 writers under contract. Motown had the edge over many contemporary independent record companies because everything was done inhouse, acting as a booking agent, manager, accountant, and financial adviser for the artists. When *Black Enterprise* (*BE*) began its Top 100 Black Business List in 1973, Motown held the number-one position until 1984. In 1988 Gordy sold Motown to MCA Records for $61 million (PolyGram acquired Motown Records for a reported $325 million in 1993).

Stax Records, based in Memphis, was a rival to Motown. Jim Stewart, the white owner, started the company in 1959 but made Al Bell, a former deejay (also owner of Saffice label), an executive vice president and part owner of the company. Bell took command of the company, signing acts for seven labels, handling production and finances, and writing songs. Stax relied on Atlantic for distribution, but when Gulf-Western Complex acquired the company in 1968, Bell became responsible for sales and advertising. Like Gordy, who purchased the real estate surrounding the Motown base, Stax owners acquired property on West Grand Street. Many of the executives were black, including Larry Shaw, advertising and creative director, who later established a black-owned national ad agency; Forest Hamilton, director of Special Market Development; and Deannie Parker, Director of Publicity. In August 1972 Stax brought together over 100,000 people in a musical extravaganza, Wattstax. Despite success, Stax Records became bankrupt in 1976.

In 1967 the award-winning writing team of Eddie Holland, Lamont Dozier, and Brian Holland left Motown to form Invictus Records with a publishing division, Gold Forever Music. Eddie Holland worked in an administrative capacity, leaving the creative work to his brother and Dozier. That same year, C. A. Warren, a songwriter, record producer, and musician from New Orleans, produced his first record without knowing anything about record promotion and distribution and lost his investment. However, he borrowed $500 and had more success with two other releases.

Leon Huff, a studio musician and writer for Mercury Records, and Kenneth

Gamble, a medical technician (later, the lead vocalist of the Romeos), created Gamble and Huff Enterprises in a closet-size space in the Shubert Building with a $700 loan. In 1969 Chess distributed their Neptune label releases, but the deal collapsed, and they formed Philadelphia International label with Thom Bell. The corporate cover for their enterprises was the Great Philadelphia Trading Company, directed by Earl Shelton, vice president and general manager.

Other black record companies emerged in the 1970s. Gene Russell laid plans for Black Jazz Records in 1971, owned, operated and staffed by blacks. He signed only black artists and only marketed to the black consumer. While he headed Sussex Records, Clarence Avant produced *Push*, a concert film of the Chicago Black Expo, in 1972. Later, Avant worked at Tabu Records for 18 years. After PolyGram purchased Motown, he was appointed the chairperson in 1993 (while sitting on the PolyGram Holding Board) and has helped restructure the label.

Curtis Mayfield (of the Impressions) and business associate Marv Stuart became active in production, publishing, and management. Their interests included the Curtom Record Company and publishing companies, Camad (ASCAP/ American Society of Composers, Authors, and Publishers), Chi-Sounds (ASCAP), and Aopa (BMI/Broadcast Music Incorporated). Ted Allan served as vice president, although he operated his own booking agency. By 1972 the companies had 10 million records to their credit. On the other side of the industry was Dick Griffey, a concert promoter. The Tennessee State graduate felt that white promoters were taking hundreds of thousands of dollars from black neighborhoods. The former night club owner formed Dick Griffey Associates and promoted his first concert in 1966. He attempted to always hire black ad agencies, put tickets in black-owned stores, and hire blacks to distribute posters. In 1975 he founded Dick Griffey Productions in Hollywood; the company immediately ranked tenth on the *Black Enterprise* "Top 100."

One of the more recent industry giants is Russell Simmons,* owner of Rush Communications in New York, the umbrella company for seven record labels, several management companies, a film and television division, and a radio production company. Carmen Ashhurst-Watson, former filmmaker and fund-raiser, is president of Rush Communications. Other important figures are Lyon Cohen, president of Rush Management, and David Harleston, president of the largest subsidiary, Rush Associated Labels. In 1992 the company captured the number 32 spot on the *Black Enterprise* listing of the Top 100.

There are others following the footsteps of the pioneers. For instance, Ruben Rodriguez, a former Motown employee, created Pendulum Records in 1991, although he sold 50 percent of it to EMI Records in 1993. Alan Haymon is considered the largest promotor of rhythm and blues concerts under his A. H. Enterprises. He has moved toward television and film projects and produced the syndicated show *Out All Night* in 1992. In addition, Andre Harrell acts as the chief executive officer (CEO) of Uptown Entertainment, a music, film, and television company that has a $50 million deal with MCA Music Entertainment

Group, Universal Pictures, and Universal Television. Harve Pierre, former national director of Promotions for Bad Boy Entertainment, became associate director of black music at RCA Records. General manager and executive vice president Scott Folkes runs LaFace Records, an Atlanta-based company, founded by Antonio Reid and Kenneth "Babyface" Edmonds and distributed by Arista Records. Quincy Jones is the founder and chair of Qwest Records. Finally, Michael Jackson is the founder of MJJ Productions, and Whitney Houston is the president and chair of Nibby Inc. in Fort Lee, New Jersey.

Others have served as presidents/CEOs of the black music division of white-owned companies, including Ernie Singleton (MCA), Sylvia Rhone (Atlantic), Ed Eckstine (Mercury), Jheryl Busby (Motown), Benny Medina (Warner Brothers), and Henry Caldwell (Epic/Sony). It is important to note a few major composers/producers and publishers who made the success of these companies possible, including award winners Johnny Bristol, Bernard Edward, Nile Rodgers, Ronald B. Greaves, Bobby Hebb, Eddie Heywood, General Johnson, Gene McDaniels, Raymond Minor, Sylvia Moy, Clyde Otis, Sylvia Robinson, and Stevie Wonder.

SELECTED BIBLIOGRAPHY: Alan Govenar, *The Early Years of Rhythm and Blues* (Houston: Rice University Press, 1990); Gerri Hirshey, *Nowhere to Run: The Story of Soul Music* (New York: Time, 1984); Patrick Salvo and Barbara Salvo, "The Memphis Sound of Music," *Sepia* 23 (December 1974): 64–66; Arnold Shaw, *Honkers and Shouters: The Golden Years of Rhythm and Blues* (New York: Macmillan, 1978); Juliet E. K. Walker, *The History of Black Business in America: Capitalism, Race, Entrepreneurship* (New York: Macmillan/Prentice Hall International, 1998).

Sundiata A. K. Djata

REPARATIONS AND AFRICAN AMERICAN BUSINESS. There is an increasing body of evidence that the idea of reparations emerging as a public policy concept has deep implications for minority business. Several observers have offered a defense of set-asides* and affirmative action on these grounds and have argued that the idea of restitution is key to coming to terms with the historical underpinnings of the shortfall in African American corporate ownership and participation and fundamental for finding public policy remedies for that deficiency. But as late as 1997, few policymakers had examined "minority" business problems in this context.

The argument made by advocates of this view is that slavery was instrumental in creating a basis for economic development from the nation's earliest days. It was used in manufacturing, mining, and services, as well as in agriculture, urban, and rural areas. Slavery, the analysis goes, freed up many whites, as a class, who would otherwise have had to do all the manual work, to gain advanced skills and experience in more desirable occupations, including investing and entrepreneurship. Slavery created much, if not most, of the infrastructure that was needed to support business development and expansion. And it produced massive benefits, directly and indirectly, actively and passively, for large numbers of people, North and South, who never came into contact with any slaves and also for large numbers of immigrants who came to this country after slavery and were able to enter a growing economy, often as business owners and managers, owing to the foundation that slavery built.

The argument is that the same also applies to discrimination after slavery. It, too, produced broad class benefits for generations of whites, as a class, who never individually discriminated against anyone in a public policy, hiring, training, housing, promotion, educational admissions, contracting, investment, or lending decision. But all the decisions were systematically made by white decision makers, private and public, federal, state, county, and local government, against blacks, in favor of whites as a class.

Slavery and discrimination produced massive benefits to whites at the expense of blacks, and those benefits were then transferred over the generations and compounded to the current benefit of whites in the top 30 percent of the income and wealth distributions, especially including business investors, managers, and owners. This accumulated wealth, in many forms—real, financial, and human— makes whites, as a class, better off relative to blacks as a class than they would otherwise have been, absent all these wrongful past transactions.

There is also an emerging idea called the Restitution Principle. It says that if a social group, a nation, or a race decides that past behavior—say, slavery and discrimination—was wrong, and has made it illegal, then it is wrong to receive and retain the benefits produced by those actions. And it is necessary to make restitution, giving back the wrongful benefits, by some redistributive action to the class that would have received the benefits, in order to put them in their rightful place.

The analysis shows that racial income, wealth and business ownership, and participation disparities have persisted for generations. It goes on to find that it is possible to measure the current consequences of past racial injustice. And with that knowledge, it could be possible to fashion policies of redistributive justice based on the Restitution Principle. Affirmative action in employment, lending, investment, and business contract set-asides have been controversial for decades. But it is believed that the Restitution Principle can be the basis for any remedial policy, whatever it is called.

Reparations would, according to this line of reasoning, emphasize investment in education and training, housing, health, and business development, because the income forcibly diverted from blacks to whites, had it been properly received, would have gone into savings, investments, equity, and education. So mere subsidies to marginal household and personal subsistence would not be properly viewed as payment on the social debt, because that is not an investment in development. Restitution would be made for the unjust enrichments that slavery and past discrimination produce for current, present-day beneficiaries, including most businesses, who enjoy them as members of a class or a group, not as individuals.

There have been rough estimates that whites owe blacks $5 to $10 trillion. Most of the debt is said to be owed to the bottom 66 percent and especially to the bottom 30 percent of the income and wealth distribution. But all blacks, including those who are successful in business and management today, can be seen to have been victimized by centuries of economic injustice in ways that benefit whites and white-owned businesses in the top 30 percent today.

The Supreme Court has moved to narrow the focus of affirmative action as it relates to business assistance, employment, and other matters. It has tried to create a rule that would apply a strict construction. It has tried to insist on proof of specific individual damages. Justice Antonin Scalia has said that there ''are no debtor or creditor races.'' But the Restitution Principle would instead propose that systemic, broad-based policies and practices are the issue, not isolated incidents. The Restitution Principle respects and shares the assumption that individual responsibility is the basis for social progress. At the same time, it asserts that group dynamics still powerfully account for much personal and corporate well-being or misfortune, as the case might be.

The idea of reparations as a basis for a public policy of redistributive justice rests on historically based measurements. Millions of discriminatory and exploitative transactions occur each year. But they are not recognized or are improperly accounted for. However, in other policy matters, there is an attempt to recognize and address such problems. For example, economists account for ''external ties'' in pollution and environmental damage from industrial and agricultural carelessness. And they account for wealth and income transfers between generations.

Those kinds of processes and those kinds of consequences occur in the social sector, as well, and produce a kind of social pollution, goes the argument. Such transactions include exclusionary discrimination and exploitative employment; lending, investing, and procurement decisions; and similar harmful practices in education and training, housing, and elsewhere. These events profoundly undermine overall performance and now can be explicitly recognized and measured. These analysts say that multiracial capitalist societies invariably tend toward maldistributed income and wealth. They tend to be stratified according to a cultural and racial hierarchy based not on fair, competitive outcomes but on unjust misuse of coercive power by dominant groups against others—as members of groups, not simply as individuals. So they believe that the concept of reparations, and the Restitution Principle, could help correct the problems and promote business investment and participation by African Americans at levels approaching their historically appropriate rate.

SELECTED BIBLIOGRAPHY: Richard F. America, *Paying the Social Debt: What White America Owes Black America* (Westport, CT: Praeger, 1993); Richard F. America, ed., *The Wealth of Races: The Present Value of the Benefits of Past Injustices* (Westport, CT: Greenwood Press, 1990); Boris Bittker, *The Case for Black Reparations* (New York: Random House, 1972).

Richard F. America

ROBEY, DON (1903–1975), Texas, entrepreneur in the record industry, restaurateur.

Born in Houston, Robey owned the Bronze Peacock Club and Restaurant, a showcase for black entertainers, performing to mixed audiences. In 1949 Robey decided to enter the recording industry. Evelyn Johnson, his assistant, gathered information about copyrighting, publishing, union scales, and musician fees. He also promoted recording artists, represented musicians independent of Peacock Records, and managed Robey's Buffalo Booking Agency from 1950 to 1967. Peacock was the only black company to record a wide range of gospel singers. Robey also recorded a few white singers. Respected as a promoter and record producer, his empire included Lion Publishing Company and the Songbird and Backbeat labels, and more than 100 artists were under contract, with 500 session musicians employed in a year. He acquired the Memphis-based Duke label from WDIA disc jockey James Mattis. In 1973 Robey sold Peacock Records to ABC/Dunhill after a court battle with Chess Records but remained a consultant until his death in 1975.

SELECTED BIBLIOGRAPHY: Robert Dixon and John Godrich, *Recording the Blues* (New York: Stein and Day, 1970); Alan Govenar, *The Early Years of Rhythm and Blues* (Houston: Rice University Press, 1990); Alan Govenar, *Meeting the Blues* (Dallas: Taylor, 1988); Arnold Shaw, *Honkers and Shouters: The Golden Years of Rhythm and Blues* (New York: Macmillan, 1978).

Sundiata A. K. Djata

ROBINSON, JOHN CHARLES (1903–1954), Illinois, air school operator.

John C. Robinson of Chicago, holder of Department of Commerce pilot's license No. 26,042, in 1931 organized the Challenger Air Pilots Association, which established its own flying field in Robbins, Illinois, in 1933. Many of the club's members learned airplane mechanics and flying from Robinson and another flyer, Cornelius Coffey, who were instructors at Chicago's Aeronautical University. Robinson and Coffey had been the school's first black students, and Robinson began teaching there in 1931. In 1935 he left this position to travel to Ethiopia, where he assumed charge of the small air fleet of Emperor Haile Selassie during the Italo-Ethiopian War (1935–1936).

Returning a hero, he used his fame to raise money through public appearances and speaking engagements to open the nonprofit John C. Robinson National Air College and School of Automotive Engineering in September 1936. Sharing the philosophy best represented by the National Urban League,* Robinson dedicated his school to offering low-cost training to young men to prepare them for the aviation industry, seeing training for industrial jobs as tantamount to economic progress.

The school was located on the spacious campus of Poro College (owned by cosmetics manufacturer Annie E. Turnbo-Malone)* at 4401 South Parkway (now Martin Luther King Drive) in Southside Chicago. A well-established institution by 1939, the Air College—financed by tuition charges, mechanical work completed by students for commercial clients, and occasional fund-raising—had by that year acquired over $25,000 worth of aeronautical equipment in its aircraft shop, as well as additional machinery in an automotive mechanics shop and a number of classroom and workroom spaces.

Conducting classes in aircraft and automobile mechanics and airplane construction, it also offered ground and flight instruction. In March 1939, 75 students (10 of whom were taking flying lessons) were enrolled in the aeronautical program. In addition, drawing on sources of government income, the school between 1938 and 1941 taught industrial arts (including airplane mechanics) to over 100 students for the Resident Training Program of the National Youth Administration (NYA). By 1941 the Illinois NYA had hired Robinson to supervise its aviation shops statewide.

Wearing two hats, he worked for the NYA and operated his school, which in 1941 was designated as one of several sites to teach aircraft mechanics under the National Defense Program. Robinson closed his school the following year to become a civilian instructor at Chanute Field in Rantoul, Illinois. With Ethiopia's liberation from Italy during World War II, he headed a group of pilots who went to Akaki, Ethiopia, in 1945 to help rebuild the country's air force. In 1947 he started Ethiopia's first airline, Sultan Airways Ltd.

Robinson was born in Carabelle, Florida, in 1903, and was raised in Gulfport, Mississippi, by his mother Celeste and his stepfather, Charles Cobb. He was a 1924 graduate of Tuskegee Institute. Robinson died on March 27, 1954, from injuries received two weeks earlier in a plane crash in Addis Ababa.

SELECTED BIBLIOGRAPHY: "Crash Injuries Fatal to Ace John Robinson," *Chicago Defender* (nat. ed.). April 3, 1954; Robert J. Jakeman, *The Divided Skies: Establishing Segregated Flight Training at Tuskegee, Alabama, 1934–1942* (Tuscaloosa: University of Alabama Press, 1992); Letter, F. H. Longeway to Senior Aeronautical Inspector, 28 March 1939, RG 237, Records of the Federal Aviation Administration, Records of the Civil Aeronautics Administration, General Records, 1926–1943, Central Files, Box 378, File No. 836.17–Negro Pilot Training, National Archives, Washington, DC; Letter, John C. Robinson to Claude A. Barnett, [1939], and John C. Robinson to G. L. Washington, 20 May 1941, Claude A. Barnett Papers, Box 171, Folder 1, Chicago Historical Society, Chicago, Illinois; National Youth Administration Division of Project Operations, *The Resident Training Program in Illinois* (Chicago: National Youth Administration of Illinois, 1939).

Jill D. Snider

ROSE META HOUSE OF BEAUTY—ROSE MORGAN (1913–), New York, hair salon chain, cosmetics manufacturer, banking.

A leading black hair care and cosmetic manufacturing business in post–World War II America, the Rose Meta House of Beauty, Inc., was established in 1947 in Harlem by Rose Morgan, beautician, and Olivia Clark, New York University M.A. graduate. The idea for their joint enterprise was conceived in 1944. Venture capital was $10,000 cash and $40,000 credit for the purchase of a vacant five-story mansion. In its first year, with 70,000 customers, earnings amounted to $180,000, with net profits of $45,000. In 1948, their business employed 68 operatives with a payroll of $90,000. In 1950, its three shops in New York City employed 300 people. In addition to hair care and the hair care products they manufactured, their cosmetic line included powder and lipstick for darker skins and facial creams for oily skins.

By 1950, the Rose Meta House of Beauty, Inc., was the largest black beauty salon in the United States, with gross business receipts of $3 million. Profits were earned from sale of Morgan's specially created cosmetics and hair care products sold in 42 American cities in black stores and several white chains, including Grants and Neisner, and from the company's international mail-order business. The House of Beauty, established in 1955 included a chain of beauty shops in major American cities and also in Monrovia, Liberia, Cayenne, British Guiana, Kingston, Jamaica, Puerto Rico, and Cuba. The Rose Meta House of Beauty business philosophy was: "Our market is women of color everywhere who are tired of trying to adapt their needs to cosmetics designed for white skins."

Rose Morgan was born in Shelby, Mississippi. She was married to the heavyweight boxing champion Joe Louis, her second husband, from 1955 until 1958. In addition to establishing one of the first black physical fitness centers, Trim-Away Figure Contouring in 1972, Morgan was one of the founders of the Freedom National Bank in New York City.

SELECTED BIBLIOGRAPHY: Robert H. Kinzer and Edward Sagarin, *The Negro in American Business: The Conflict between Separatism and Integration* (New York: Greenberg Publisher, 1950), 186; *Newsweek*, August 18, 1947, 63; Vishnu V. Oak, *The Negro's Adventure in General Business* (Yellow Springs, OH: Antioch Press, 1949), 145–148; Juliet E. K. Walker, *The History of Black Business in America: Capitalism, Race, Entrepreneurship* (New York: Macmillan/Prentice Hall International, 1998).

Juliet E. K. Walker

ROTATING CREDIT ASSOCIATIONS, CARIBBEAN AMERICAN CHAMBER OF COMMERCE AND U.S. COMMERCIAL BANKS. Throughout the United States of America, during the nineteenth and twentieth centuries, freed slaves and immigrants of many national origins organized mutual aid societies to facilitate and expand their survival repertoire for coping with the harsh economic realities of a new society. For many West Indian immigrants to America, rotating credit associations served such a function. These associations continue to be used as structural shields for immigrants and their offspring and manifest various adaptive and facilitative functions. Among them, the associations encourage savings or small capital formation. Often, these immigrants use the funds as a form of microlending, investing an almost religious devotion to capitalizing their businesses, engaging in the accumulation of housing wealth, or achieving more mundane goals such as the purchasing of household items.

Rotating credit associations, called *esusu* in Yoruba, originated in West Africa. They were transported first to the Caribbean societies during slavery and much later by immigrants from these societies to countries such as England, Canada, the United States, France, and the Netherlands. Then, as now, groups consisting of as many as 100 participants verbally agreed to make regular contributions to a fund (hand) in whole or in part to each contributor in rotation. The number of participants is contingent on the size of the hand. To illustrate, if an organizer (often called a banker) decided on a hand of $5,000 with payments spread over 20 weeks, then she (a banker is often female) would need about 20 members contributing (throwing) $250 a week. While the banker normally determines the amount of the hand, she may take into account the members' ability to make large or small contributions. Doubling or tripling (where one participant "throws" two or three hands) occurs frequently. Rotation and regularity are, therefore, the two essential criteria used to differentiate these associations from similar mutual aid societies such as lodges and mutual benefit clubs.

Andrew Beveridge, a New York sociologist, Adam Nossiter, a writer for the *New York Times*, and Joel Millman, associate editor at *Forbes* magazine, commented on the West Indian propensity for, and their influence in, transforming formerly gutted inner-city areas in Brooklyn and Queens and revitalizing middle-class ones in the borough of the Bronx, all in the city of New York. Many immigrants, both first and second generation, generally throw two or three hands to facilitate homeownership or become proprietors/entrepreneurs of bakeries, barbershops, beauty parlors, restaurants, or travel agencies. Throughout areas of East Flatbush in Brooklyn, Jamaica in Queens, and the northeastern sections of the Bronx, ethnic businesses and homes adorn the landscape. Rotating credit associations—called SUSU, Box, Pardner—provide a leveling or topping off function to augment venture capital needed for economic ventures.

In addition, while many West Indian–owned businesses have undergone some diversification since the mid-1960s, when initiatives in black capitalism and strengthening entrepreneurship were being promoted, currently owned businesses remain chiefly concentrated in the personal services sector, as they have been in the past. Most of these businesses tend to be small (characteristically employing about seven employees) and self-owned. Persistent challenges in achieving enough capital and the high failure rate of small businesses during the early years have accounted for a growing trend toward partnerships and the establishment of ethnic brokers and change agents to foster the maintenance and survival of these businesses.

West Indian migration to the United States is continuing. The largest numbers live in New York City, although metropolitan Miami has seen strong surges since the 1980s. Economist Ransford Palmer posits, and I concur, that New York City's greatest residential concentration abounds in the predominantly black neighborhoods of Brooklyn, where a common ethnic background coupled with an established network of support systems provide a measure of security.

The 1980s and especially the 1990s produced rapid consolidation of the banking industry in New York City and throughout the United States. As banks and their branches have closed steadily during the last two decades, many immigrants have had to improvise and rely more heavily on this parallel sector of low-level credit and finance. These revolving loan funds/rotating credit associations continue to flourish and are sometimes supplemented by illegal activities such as numbers and loan-sharking, as well as community credit unions insured by the U.S. government. One community-based credit union, the Central Brooklyn Federal Credit Union, opened in Brooklyn, New York, in April 1993. It now boasts assets of approximately $5 million and is subsumed under the aegis of a not-for-profit, self-help organization that builds community-owned financial cooperatives, conducts research and advocacy on behalf of community reinvestment, develops youth leadership, and promotes financial literacy among local residents. Mark Winston Griffith and Errol T. Louis, second-generation West Indian immigrants and Ivy League graduates of Brown, Harvard, and Yale, founded both organizations.

The continuing overlap between rotating credit associations and banks and other mainstreaming financial organizations must be acknowledged. This relationship must be viewed within the context of the Community Reinvestment Act,* passed by the U.S. Congress. Specifically, the goal is to ensure that banks channel money back into poor communities not only to finance neighborhood loan funds but also to encourage partnership in indigenous organizations to act as financial brokers and clearinghouses and socialize immigrant entrepreneurs to engage in practices designed to facilitate receipt of bank loans.

Chase Manhattan Bank as well as Republic Bank in New York now recognize the rotating credit associations—SUSUs—as a legitimate source of cash. Chase, which has written over 200 mortgages based partly on SUSU downpayments, also flags SUSUs in advertisements aimed at this market segment—West Indian neighborhoods. Chemical Bank, which recently opted to merge with Chase, also has a number of similar pioneering financial opportunities to help this rapidly growing West Indian market by helping members enhance their commercial growth. Indeed, Chemical Bank's Affordable Mortgage Unit parallels Chase Manhattan's efforts in this regard. Also, in 1993 the government of Ontario, Canada's largest province, provided substantial funding to a black credit union sponsored by the Jamaican Canadian Association in an attempt to increase the level of capital accumulated in the West Indian community there. Those entrepreneurs, like their American counterparts, are plagued by the unwillingness of banks and lending institutions to provide credit to West Indians, who, therefore, must rely largely on microlending associations such as rotating credit associations.

Approximately 10 years ago, Aubrey W. Bonnett and two of his colleagues, both sociologists, made a presentation to the then-head of the Ford Foundation, Franklin Thomas, to encourage the expansion of rotating credit unions. A second-generation West Indian immigrant himself, Thomas had directed the Foundation in an aggressive effort designed to achieve social justice in Third

World societies through microlending associations such as rotating credit associations. The Grameen Bank in Bangladesh is but one noted example. Franklin Thomas and his colleagues were interested in ways of augmenting the success of these revolving credit devices, as venture capital for inner-city New York entrepreneurs, some of whom are West Indian immigrants. Then, as now, the problem for many inner-city ethnic entrepreneurs was not only their limited credit but also their inability to network into mainstream organizations, as well as lack of marketing, bookkeeping, and other relevant skills. As a result, the failure rate of these businesses was extremely high.

Concomitant educational initiatives were envisaged. Community and senior colleges of the City University of New York were to initiate and offer certificate courses in marketing, retailing, bookkeeping, and so on. Ford Foundation was prepared to initiate or support microlending opportunities in these neighborhoods, provided recipients enrolled in and completed the appropriate certificate courses. Franklin Thomas was interested also in supporting the strengthening of local "broker" organizations to provide similar networking and commercial educational services. Indeed, Thomas had spearheaded such ventures when he headed the Bedford-Stuyvesant Restoration Corporation in Brooklyn, New York, prior to assuming a leadership role at the Ford Foundation.

Those activities encouraged the founding of the Caribbean American Chamber of Commerce and Industry in 1985 by Roy Hastick, Sr. Since then, it has become the primary advocate for this minority business community and has garnered over 900 members in the United States and the Caribbean. The Chamber, under the leadership of Roy Hastick, has provided economic development seminars, technical assistance, and referrals and sponsored trade missions and trade expositions to help develop the economic potential of minority entrepreneurs in the United States and the Caribbean.

Especially for immigrants, the Chamber established the Comprehensive Business Resource Center, which provides technical assistance in the areas of certified public accounting/accounting, legal services, loan packaging, and mortgage counseling. In addition, a 12-week training session funded by the New York State Urban Development Corporation provided training to 50 West Indian entrepreneurs with existing businesses or individuals considering business ventures. Training emphasized skills to prepare an effective business plan.

For these and other activities, the Chamber was described by the U.S. Department of Commerce as the most visible and viable Caribbean-American economic development organization in the United States. Conceivably, Roy Hastick's leadership contributed to his selection to the board of directors at Chemical Bank. Most recently, on October 12, 1995, the Republican mayor of New York, Rudolph Giuliani, publicly thanked the organization for all of its work to promote, develop, and expand small business development.

In a study almost two decades ago, Aubrey W. Bonnett argued that rotating credit associations played a pivotal role as a major source of capital formation for small business among West Indians. Further, he contended that their use was generational and would not survive among second-generation, American-born immigrants. Yet credit associations remain as firmly embedded in this ethnic community as Ransford Palmer and Joel Millman indicated in recent studies. In fact, their overlap and institutionalization with mainstream financial institutions have increased. Moreover, a thesis presented by neoconservatives about West Indian exceptionalism, which utilizes the cultural paradigm that highlights rotating credit associations as evidence, must be viewed as largely hyperbolic.

The salient and critical concept of class must be examined before applying these sweeping generalizations. West Indian entrepreneurship in the United States, Canada, and the United Kingdom, first, must be seen in the context of economic survival in an increasingly global concentration of wealth and capital influenced greatly by the interlocking factors of class and race. Furthermore, these theories must be viewed as systematically promoting, among these immigrants, the incentive and motivation to save, thereby opening alternate avenues of employment by tapping an extrainstitutional form of capital. As economist Andrew Brimmer once commented, it may be a cruel hoax to perpetuate on black people the hope of black capitalism as a major method of escaping the depths of poverty and economic deprivations under present, bleak austere conditions.

West Indian businesses continue to fail because of the inexorability of undercapitalization, despite government and white corporate intervention. What cannot be ignored—indeed, openly acknowledged—is the functional but limited economic role these African retention and survival associations continue to play among diasporic Africans.

SELECTED BIBLIOGRAPHY: Aubrey W. Bonnett, *Institutional Adaptations of West Indian Immigrants to America: An Analysis of Rotating Credit Associations* (Washington, DC: University Press of America, 1981); Frances Henry, *The Caribbean Diaspora in Toronto: Learning to Live with Racism* (Toronto: University of Toronto Press, 1994); Joel Millman, ''Brooklyn's Anti-Poverty Workers: Caribbean Immigrants,'' *APF Reporter* 16, 4 (1995); Ransford W. Palmer, *Pilgrims from the Sun: West Indian Migration to America* (New York: Twayne Publishers, 1995).

Aubrey W. Bonnett

RUSSELL, HERMAN JEROME (1930–), Georgia, entrepreneur in construction industry.

Herman J. Russell is founder and chief executive officer (CEO) of H. J. Russell & Company of Atlanta, Georgia, which he established in 1952, first as the H. J. Russell Plastering Company. In 1959 Russell established the H. J. Russell Construction Company, which initially specialized in building single-family homes and duplexes. Since 1969 he has been involved in large-scale private sector commercial projects, beginning with his construction of the 34-story Equitable Life Assurance Building in Atlanta. In the 1970s, with financing from the Department of Housing and Urban Development (HUD), Russell constructed 29 housing projects with 4,000 units for low- and middle-income families, while he maintained ownership of the properties. Since then, Russell Construction was involved in building the Atlanta Stadium, the Atlanta City Hall Complex, the Martin Luther King Community Center, and the Carter Presidential Center.

Russell Construction has also participated in joint venture projects with white construction companies, which included the parking deck for Atlanta's Hartsfield Airport, the Georgia Pacific 52-story office building, and the Atlanta Merchandise Mart. In joint ventures with the African American–owned construction company C. D. Moody Construction, the group was able to place the winning bid for construction of the $209 million Olympic Stadium contract in Atlanta for the 1996 games.

Financial success in construction, one of only five entrepreneurs who has made the *Black Enterprise* listing of the top 100 black businesses for the past 25 years, when the listing began, has enabled Russell to expand and diversify his enterprise. Now the H. J. Russell & Company "is the parent company of several subsidiary firms, including Williams-Russell and Johnson, an engineering, architecture, and construction management firm. In addition, the City Beverage Company and the Concessions International Corporation, which oversees food concessions in several major airports, are owned by Russell." Also, since 1972, Russell "secured the management rights to Atlanta's Omni sports-convention complex and a 10 percent ownership share of the National Basketball Association's Atlanta Hawks." At one time, Herman owned Russell-Rowe Communications, which operated WGXA-TV, an ABC affiliate in Macon, Georgia.

With sales of $163,756 for 1996, the H. J. Russell Company ranked fifth on the *BE* 100s. While Russell has groomed his children to succeed him, *Black Enterprise* reports that his son J. Jerome is now president/chief operating officer and head of the housing and property management division, whereas son Michael, vice president, is manager of the construction division. As of 1996, R. K. Seghal is now CEO, and Herman remains chairman of the board.

SELECTED BIBLIOGRAPHY: John N. Ingham and Lynne B. Feldman, *African-American Business Leaders: A Biographical Dictionary* (Westport, CT: Greenwood Press, 1994); Juliet E. K. Walker, *The History of Black Business in America: Capitalism, Race, Entrepreneurship* (New York: Macmillan/Prentice Hall International, 1998); Marjorie Whigham-Desir, "Marathon Men," *Black Enterprise* (June 1997).

Juliet E. K. Walker

S

SET-ASIDES, MINORITY BUSINESS. *Minority business set-asides* are affirmative action programs designed to assist minority business enterprises—firms that are at least 51 percent owned by well-defined minority group members—in obtaining contracts from government agencies or private organizations. Set-asides generally take one of two forms: (1) provisions that fixed percentages of the total number or total dollar value of contracts be allotted to minority-owned businesses or (2) requirements that recipients of prime contracts allot fixed percentages of the total amount awarded to minority-owned subcontractors and/or suppliers.

Arguments against minority business set-asides suggest they are inefficient and wasteful, concentrating most contracts on a few politically connected firms, often firms with little, if any, meaningful management or control by minority group members. Arguments in favor of minority business set-asides suggest that the abuses are isolated, whereas the assistance to minority firms is vital for their survival and growth. The most contentious argument relates to whether set-asides actually assist minority communities or whether they enrich an elite few, including white owners. The balance of research, however, seems to suggest that minority-owned businesses generally create jobs for minority workers and that efforts to assist minority businesses in obtaining contracts with state, local, and government bodies often help to increase minority employment.

Research on specific government set-aside programs, nevertheless, reveals that there may be other less costly means of assisting minority businesses or increasing their share of contracts. These alternative strategies include subsidization of start-up capital, bonding and insurance waivers, and preferences for and outreach to local enterprises in communities with large minority populations. Minority business enterprises historically have received disproportionately small shares of state, local, and federal government contracts and procurement awards. Although government agencies purchase billions of dollars of goods and services from private vendors and enter into billions upon billions of dollars of contracts with private businesses, minority and, in particular, African American firms historically have received few of these contracts.

The origins of federal mandates for minority business set-asides rest in language inserted by U.S. Representative Parren Mitchell (D–Maryland) into the 1977 Public Works Employment Act. This law required that 10 percent of all federal public works contracts be expended with minority business enterprises. In the year that the law was passed, less than 1 percent of all federal contracts were awarded to African American and other minority businesses. Almost immediately, large majority-owned contractor associations challenged the constitutionality of these set-asides. They contended that such set-asides inherently constituted impermissible discrimination based on racial classification, in violation of the Fourteenth Amendment to the U.S. Constitution.

The result of their challenge was the U.S. Supreme Court's ruling in *Fullilov v. Klutznick* (448 U.S. 1980). The Court ruled that set-asides are facially constitutional because they seek to remedy past discrimination, they incorporate flexible waiver and exemption procedures, and they are limited in extent and duration. Armed with substantial support for the constitutionality of minority business set-asides, other federal agencies and state and local governments enacted set-aside provisions. Set-asides were mandated for federal transportation and highway construction contracts; for national defense procurement contracts; for international development grants; for the development, construction, and operation of the superconducting super collider; and for National Aeronautics and Space Administration contracts, including those for the space station.

States also implemented minority business set-asides in a direct response to set-aside provisions in the federal highway transit legislation. The provisions required that state departments of transportation administering federal highway grants and contracts oversee the implementation of the federal set-aside provisions. More than 200 local governments, with strong support from black elected officials, sought to increase minority participation in city and county contracts by passing set-aside laws.

But set-asides were seriously threatened by a 1989 U.S. Supreme Court decision involving a program in Richmond, Virginia. In *City of Richmond v. Croson*, 109 S.Ct. 706 (1989), the Court ruled in a six-to-three decision that a city ordinance setting aside 30 percent of public works funds for minority-owned construction companies was unconstitutional. Justice Sandra Day O'Connor wrote in the majority opinion that such set-aside programs could only be justified if they served a "compelling state interest" of redressing "identified discrimination." Analysts have concluded this ruling affirms the Court's move toward a "strict scrutiny" interpretation of the equal protection clause of the Fourteenth

Amendment. This means that any governmental action that gives preference to one race over another is suspect and would require a demanding set of evidence of previous injustice against the beneficiary of the governmental action, as well as a compelling state's objective, to justify the preferential treatment based on race. Since minority business set-aside programs existed in more than 200 local governments and in 36 states, this case was viewed by some as the deathblow to governmental affirmative action programs designed to assist minority businesses.

The *Croson* mandate requires demonstrating (1) a factual predicate of identified discrimination, (2) evidence of discrimination against specified groups covered by the remedy, and (3) explicit evidence of prior discrimination. The implication of the *Croson* standard is that evidence of continuing discrimination, either in the private sector or by the government itself, would support the claims of discrimination justifying the race-based remedy. However, a finding only of general societal discrimination would be insufficient to justify a race-based remedy.

A direct result of the *Croson* ruling was the initiation of "disparity studies"* by hundreds of state and local governments, often at considerable public expense. Governments suspended their minority set-aside programs in order to conduct analyses that would meet the *Croson* standard. Disparity studies typically compare the numbers or percentages of available minority firms in particular industries or categories with the numbers or percentages of minority firms utilized and/or those awarded contracts by government procurement agencies. Disparity studies also attempt to document the legal barriers and the historical evidence of discrimination facing minority-owned businesses.

The *Croson* standard was extended in 1995 to include federal government contracting and procurement policies in *Adarand v. Pena*, a ruling that has stimulated many changes in the wording of existing set-aside rules. Either rules have been changed to emphasize the flexibility of the set-aside goals, or they have been eliminated altogether in favor of preferences for disadvantaged or small businesses or for businesses operating in inner-city areas. The retreat from minority business set-asides, however, is not complete. Many major corporations—often faced with enormous minority consumer buying power—continue to support minority businesses through set-aside programs they initiated voluntarily during the 1970s and 1980s. These efforts are untouched by the *Croson* and *Adarand* rulings and continue to thrive.

SELECTED BIBLIOGRAPHY: Timothy Bates, *Banking on Black Enterprise* (Washington, DC: Joint Center for Political and Economic Studies, 1993); Thomas Boston, *Meeting the Croson Standard: A Guide for Policy Makers* (Washington, DC: Joint Center for Political and Economic Studies, 1992); George R. LaNoue, "Split Visions: Minority Business Set-Asides," *Annals of the American Academy of Political and Social Science* 523 (September 1992): 104–116; Samuel L. Myers, Jr., and Tsze Chan, "Who Benefits from Minority Business Set-Asides?" *Journal of Policy Analysis and Management* 15, 2 (Spring 1996).

Samuel L. Myers, Jr.

SIMMONS, RUSSELL (1957–), New York, entrepreneur in record and television industries.

In 1977 Simmons met student Rick Rubin, who owned the record label Def Jam; together they formed a record company, doubling the value in two years (Simmons later parted with Rubin). Artists on his labels included some of the biggest names in rap and hip-hop. Simmons's goals were to be the most important person in black entertainment, double the value of the company in five years, and move into film and television. Carmen Ashhurst-Watson has been instrumental as president of Rush Communications, the parent company for seven record labels, several management companies, a film and television division, and a radio production company. Simmons made a label deal with CBS, which took charge of marketing and promotion. Moreover, he produced *Def Comedy Jam* and coproduced several movies in 1985. In 1994 Rush sold 50 percent of the label to Polygram in a $33 million distribution deal with Def films distributed through Polygram Films. Other business interests include the Phat Farm clothing line; Rush Philanthropic Arts; and two in developmental stages—a 24-hour syndicated hip-hop radio network, Def Net; and a cologne deal with Revlon for Flavor. In the *BE* 100s for 1997, Rush Communications and Affiliated Companies ranked fiftieth with sales of $40 million.

SELECTED BIBLIOGRAPHY: C. H. Coker, "What a Rush," *Vibe* 3 (December 1995–January 1996); Alfred Edmond, Jr., "Companies to Watch in the 1990s," *Black Enterprise* (June 1989); Christopher Vaughn, "Russell Simmons, Rush for Profits," *Black Enterprise* (December 1992).

Sundiata A. K. Djata

SIMS, NAOMI (1949–), New York City, wig and cosmetic manufacturer.

One of America's first successful black models, Naomi Sims capitalized on the black hair care product market by designing and manufacturing wigs that approximated the hair texture of black women. In 1973 she established the Naomi Sims Collection. With sales of $5 million the first year, Sims expanded distribution to include an international market. A cosmetic line, Naomi Sims Beauty Products, Limited, was introduced in 1986, and by 1988, sales from those products exceeded $5 million. Ingham and Feldman said that "by the early 1990s" Sims "stood as probably the preeminent black woman entrepreneur in America." Even then, she would be eclipsed in business and wealth accumulation by TV talk show host Oprah Winfrey.*

SELECTED BIBLIOGRAPHY: John N. Ingham and Lynne B. Feldman, *African-American Business Leaders: A Biographical Dictionary* (Westport, CT: Greenwood Press, 1994); Patricia O'Toole, "Battle of the Beauty Counter," *New York Times Magazine*, December 3, 1989; Naomi Sims, *All about Health and Beauty for the Black Woman*, rev ed. (Garden City, N.Y.: Doubleday, 1986).

Juliet E. K. Walker

SLAVE DRIVERS, PLANTATION MANAGERS, INTRAPRENEURS.
Slave drivers were agricultural field managers with diverse responsibilities in

commodity production and labor supervision. Most drivers worked on large plantations, but small commercial farms also used slaves in the position of driver. In the management hierarchy of large plantations, the slave driver ranked below the overseer, steward, and/or planter. In the slave hierarchy, the driver's status was comparable to that of slave artisans and household slaves. Moreover, depending on the size of the agricultural unit, several occupational levels could exist in the position of driver such as the head driver, also known as the over-driver; the underdriver; and the foreman, who directed field task gangs.

Most drivers were men, usually in their thirties or forties but, in some instances, sometimes younger; if they could maintain their health, they continued to work in the position of driver until their sixties. The traits that made for the most successful drivers were intelligence, forceful personalities, and physical prowess. Leadership and management skills were a prerequisite since their major responsibility was to maintain a highly disciplined, efficient, and well-coordinated productive agricultural slave labor force. But most important, they had to excel as "people managers," who knew how to set goals and, especially, to motivate the field laborers, if they wanted to keep their jobs. The position of driver required that he "drive" the field slaves to maintain efficiency and discipline. Given authority to punish field hands, the driver historically was often called "whipping man" or "whipping boss."

But the slave driver was more than a "straw boss" whipping man or foreman who supervised field hands from sunup to sundown. Drivers collected information on field production, which they analyzed, interpreted, and passed on to the overseer, steward, or planter. In the absence of an overseer and often the owners, the driver had to schedule production and to plan how to deploy limited resources. In fulfilling these diverse responsibilities, the slave driver in this management capacity thus provides an example of slave "intrapreneurship." Possessed of both practical and specialized knowledge of crop production, the slave driver could come to dominate field operations in the production of cotton, sugar, tobacco, and rice, which brought in the plantation dollars. Indeed, as one observer noted, for many plantation owners "the advice of the drivers is commonly taken in nearly all the administration [of plantation commodity production], and frequently they are, *de facto*, the managers."

Slave drivers were both generalists and specialists in the performance of their management duties, but more than anything else perhaps, they had to be. Their expertise was invaluable in contributing to the agricultural productivity of the antebellum South. Given the high rate of periodic absentee ownership, and that only 30 percent of plantations and farms had white overseers, as Eugene D. Genovese explains, "Probably, at least two-thirds of the slaves in the South worked under a black man who had direct access to the master with no white overseer between them—probably at least two-thirds, that is, experienced responsible and direct black leadership in their everyday work life."

Planter compensation for the success of slave drivers varied. Leather boots and a whip were often symbols of the driver's status and position. Also, drivers had better housing and more abundant food rations. Sometimes, planters provided drivers with extra land for their personal use and even gave the driver permission to use other slaves to cultivate the plot. Produce raised could be taken to town by the driver and sold for cash. Some drivers received money incentives in wages and bonuses, amounting in some instances to hundreds of dollars, for their efficiency in labor management and field production.

The management styles developed by drivers to maintain their position have become the source of great historical controversy. Was the driver the cruel, sadistic, and brutal slave driver portrayed by Sambo and Quimbo in Harriet Beecher Stowe's 1852 *Uncle Tom's Cabin?* Robert S. Starobin admits, "Sometimes drivers punished slaves more severely than did whites." Their ambiguous position as part of management but still one step away from field labor was sometimes expressed in a way whereby they would abuse their authority, to punish enemies as well as to obtain sexual favors. But most slave drivers attempted to use their position to protect the slaves and ease the burdens of bondage. Still, maintaining their position as drivers meant that they had to push for optimum labor productivity and efficiency to meet the production goals and profit expectations of their masters. In doing so, drivers often found it difficult to act in the best interests of the slave community. Some drivers were cruel and brutal.

SELECTED BIBLIOGRAPHY: Eugene D. Genovese, *Roll, Jordan, Roll: The World the Slaves Made* (New York: Vintage Books, 1974); Randall M. Miller, "The Man in the Middle: The Black Slave Driver," *American Heritage* 30 (1979); Leslie Howard Owens, *This Species of Property: Slave Life and Culture in the Old South* (New York: Oxford University Press, 1976); William L. Van DeBurg, *The Slave Drivers: Black Agricultural Labor Supervisors in the Antebellum South* (Westport, CT: Greenwood Press, 1979); Juliet E. K. Walker, "Drivers," in Randall M. Miller and John David Smith, eds., *Dictionary of Afro-American Slavery* (Westport, CT: Greenwood Press, 1988); Juliet E. K. Walker, *The History of Black Business in America: Capitalism, Race, Entrepreneurship* (New York: Macmillan/Prentice Hall International, 1998).

Juliet E. K. Walker

SLAVE ENTREPRENEURS AND INTRAPRENEURS. Slave entrepreneurs were slaves who established their own business enterprises. Most were slaves who hired their own time.* As independent business proprietors, they assumed the risk and responsibility for the production and/or distribution of their goods and services. Their commercial transactions, marketing, and management operations differed little from those of their free counterparts. Slave entrepreneurs also advertised, negotiated contracts, extended credit, and assumed debts. Their earnings depended as much on customer demand as on the extent of their business acumen, expertise, initiative, productivity, and propriety as businesspeople. Among the more successful antebellum slave entrepreneurs, annual profits in the hundreds of dollars were realized. There were notable exceptions. Included in their business expenses were owner's fees, payments made by those slaves to their owners who granted them permission to hire their own time.

The participation of slaves in the American business community began during the colonial period and was a well-established practice before the American revolutionary era, but the practice of self-hire slaves and slave entrepreneurship was illegal. Slave laws,* which imposed economic constraints, were in force throughout the period of slavery, either to discourage competition from self-hired slaves or to limit their "freedom" to pursue self-enriching economic activities. These laws, which made it illegal for slaves "to go at large and trade as freemen," were easily circumvented, particularly in urban areas where many self-hired slaves established businesses. Whether in urban places or rural areas, the self-hire slave system was, as Ulrich B. Phillips emphasizes, "too great a public and private convenience to suppress."

Most slave entrepreneurs were urban slaves who found jobs as paid employees. From their wages, they paid their owner for allowing them to hire their own time and saved what remained of their wages as start-up capital to establish a business. As business proprietors, slave entrepreneurs worked only for themselves. Management of their enterprises was independent of the master's direction, control, or supervision. Usually, the enterprises established by slave entrepreneurs were in occupational areas where regular work supervision was impractical and unprofitable. Or, slave entrepreneurs established enterprises in occupational areas shunned by southern whites as demeaning, especially in the food and personal services industries, which provided lucrative areas for business development for self-hired slave barbers and tailors.

There were also slave women who hired their own time and established laundry, dressmaking, millinery, hairdressing, nursing, or health care enterprises. Elizabeth Keckley, dressmaker for Mary Todd Lincoln, was a self-hired slave in St. Louis, who purchased her freedom with money earned from her designer dressmaking business in that city.

In transportation, occupations such as teamster, drayman, liveryman, and boatman, carrying cargo or passengers, also provided business opportunities for enterprising self-hired slaves. Richard Allen, founder of the African Methodist Episcopal (AME) Church, purchased his freedom with earnings from his enterprise as an independent self-hired slave teamster. Charles Ball,* a slave who hired his own time, was employed by a slave entrepreneur who had established a successful "odd jobs" enterprise, primarily as a teamster. Ball was one of seven or eight blacks hired by this enterprising slave, who not only had to pay the salaries of his black employees but also $250 annually to his owner, in monthly installments, all from the profits of his "odd jobs" enterprise.

As initiators and directors of production, a substantial number of self-hired slaves who risked establishing their own businesses were highly proficient craftsmen.* Carpentry, blacksmith, wheelwright, cabinetmaking, and coopering trades were among the crafts that allowed for self-employment and business development. The most successful slave entrepreneur was Anthony Weston* in South

Carolina, who built rice mills and improved the performance of rice-thrashing machines. By 1860 Weston's property in real estate and slaves—who worked in his shop and who were purchased in his wife's name, since she was a free black—was valued at $40,075.

Considering institutional constraints, which limited full expression of their business acumen, self-hired slaves were distinguished, however, by their ability to make unusual amounts of money using commonly available resources or highly developed skills. Accumulated profits were used primarily as venture capital by slave entrepreneurs to purchase freedom for themselves, family members, or friends. With the crude niter he mined on the Kentucky frontier, the self-hired slave Free Frank McWorter* (1777–1854) established a manufactory for the production of saltpeter during the War of 1812. With profits earned from this enterprise, the slave purchased first his wife's freedom in 1817 and then his own two years later. The total amount paid for their freedom was $1,600.

Invariably, some slaves who became entrepreneurs initially worked as intrapreneurs or managers for their owner's business. Free Frank had complete charge of his owner's farm from 1810 until he purchased his freedom. His saltpeter manufactory was Free Frank's "night job." After he purchased his freedom, Free Frank set up a branch of his saltpeter business in another town, purchased land, and developed his own commercial farm. The wealthy lumber and coal merchant Stephen Smith* was also a slave intrapreneur, who managed his owner's lumber yard before he became free and then established his own enterprise, as did the successful Cincinnati coal merchant Robert Gordon, who was also both a slave intrapreneur and slave entrepreneur before he purchased his freedom. While he managed his owner's Virginia coal yard, the owner allowed him to develop a sideline enterprise in processing coal for slack, which was much in demand by blacksmiths.

Slave intrapreneurship, where slaves were granted decision-making authority in managing their owners' business enterprises, then, could provide the basis for some slaves to develop entrepreneurial activities, which they continued after they purchased their freedom. The slave intrapreneur Horace King (1807–1885), a covered bridge builder and contractor, was an intrapreneur who worked in the capacity of a chief operating officer in his owner's bridge building construction company, since white observers commented that King was "more of a junior partner" in his owner's company "than a slave." King supervised construction with a slave assistant provided by his owner. Subsequently, King was granted freedom by two states, Alabama and Georgia, sponsored by a wealthy Alabama state senator and plantation slave owner, who went into partnership on several projects with King. After he was freed in 1846, King established his own construction company, which expanded from bridge building to contracts for housing and commercial institutions. After King's death the company was renamed the King Brothers Construction Company.

With its entrepreneurial dimension, the self-hire slave system in the United States could be compared to the *obrok* system in czarist Russia, where serfs were allowed to pay a yearly fee, also in exchange for "freedom," to develop their own enterprises. In the United States, the pattern of slave entrepreneurship also rested more on a subtle process of mutual compromise between the owner and the slave than it did on the owner's coercion or the slave's accommodation. The process by which a slave craftsman, initially hired out by his owner, became a slave who hired his own time and, subsequently, established his own business reveals the dynamics of slave entrepreneurship. In one such instance, a slave blacksmith, who worked in a county different from that where his owner lived, asked his master for authorization to open up his own shop, explaining, "I am satisfied that I can do well and that my profits will amount to a great deal more than any one would be willing to pay for my hire."

Southern judicial records, contemporary travelers' accounts, private papers, autobiographies, and family oral histories attest to the extensiveness of the self-hire slave system. And as Richard Wade has concluded: "The extent to which each town struggled to stop this practice is a good indication of how widespread it was." A large number of slave entrepreneurs and slave intrapreneurs who purchased their freedom continued business participation after manumission, emerging as prominent leaders of the antebellum black community. Their enterprise experience and leadership also helped shape the economic and social infrastructure of post-Emancipation black life.

SELECTED BIBLIOGRAPHY: Clement Eaton, "Slave-Hiring in the Upper South: A Step toward Freedom," *Mississippi Valley Historical Review* 46 (1960): 663–678; John Hope Franklin, "Slaves Virtually Free in Ante-Bellum North Carolina," *Journal of Negro History* 28 (1943); Sumner E. Matison, "Manumission by Purchase," *Journal of Negro History* 33 (1948); Edna Chappel McKenzie, "Self-Hire among Slaves, 1820–1860: Institutional Variation or Aberration?" (Ph.D. diss., University of Pittsburgh, 1973); Richard B. Morris, "The Measure of Bondage in the Slave States," *Mississippi Valley Historical Review* 41 (1954): 219–240; Richard C. Wade, *Slavery in the Cities: The South, 1820–1860* (New York: Oxford University Press, 1964); Juliet E. K. Walker, *Free Frank: A Black Pioneer on the Antebellum Frontier* (1983; reprint, Lexington: University Press of Kentucky, 1995); Juliet E. K. Walker, *The History of Black Business in America: Capitalism, Race, Entrepreneurship* (New York: Macmillan/Prentice Hall International, 1998).

Juliet E. K. Walker

SLAVE HIRING OUT OWN TIME. The practice of slaves hiring out their own time underscores the economic basis of the institution while illuminating the conflict between slave law and the constitutional protection of private property. Nowhere is the duality of the legal status of slaves as people and chattel property more revealed than in the practice of slaves hiring out their own time. As chattel property, slaves were forced to provide unpaid labor for their owners, who also had the legal right to hire them out as employees to work for others. The wages earned by the slave were paid to the slave owner, as opposed to the practice of slaves hiring out their own time. In this instance, the slave who hired his own time paid the owner from the wages he earned from his employment. The difference is that any amount earned by the slave, beyond the amount he paid the owner, was his own.

Still, according to Eugene Genovese, slaves who hired their own time comprised less than 5 percent of the slave population, whereas estimates of the percentage of slaves who were hired out ranged from 8 to 10 percent overall and as high as 30 percent in urban places. Yet while the practice of slave hiring or "renting" was legal, the practice of slaves hiring out their own time was illegal. The law was easily circumvented, however, on the part of all the parties, the slave owner as well as the consumer who hired the slave or purchased his goods and services, since many slaves who hired their own time established businesses.

Moreover, while the crafts were respected, black craftsmen* cornered the market. By 1860, there were 125,000 craftsmen in the South, 100,000 were blacks, and most were slaves. Hiring out slaves and allowing them to hire their own time were the only methods by which the South provided for elasticity in labor market demand. At the same time, certain occupations, such as personal services, including barbers and crafts, were occupations that did not require, and could not operate profitably with, the personal supervision of a slave owner. Slaves who hired their own time and participated in these occupations invariably were the ones who established business enterprises. These were slave entrepreneurs,* as opposed to those slaves who hired out their own time as employees, such as Frederick Douglass, who while a slave hired his own time and worked as a ship calker until he fled as a fugitive.

Of course, the question is, Why did slave owners, acting illegally, allow their slaves to hire out their own time, instead of hiring them out as employees? Money! The amount that the slave owner collected from the slave who hired out his own time was much greater than the amount received if the owner hired or "rented out" his slave. Usually, slave owners who hired out their slaves were paid, annually, $80 to $100. Slave owners who allowed their slaves to hire their own time required the slave to pay from $150 to as much as $250 annually for this privilege. As an example, if a slave earned $.50 a day for 365 days, his annual earnings would come to $182.50, of which the owner might require the slave to pay $150. That left only $32.50 for the slave. But if the slave made $1 a day and worked only 300 days a year, after paying the owner $150, the slave would have the same amount for himself. Indeed, most of the male slaves who purchased their freedom were those who hired their own time.

Prosecution was difficult, despite the laws. Indeed, slaves who hired their own time operated publicly, including those who established businesses and participated in the mainstream business community of the South. Obviously, the owner, on penalty of paying a fine, was not going to admit that he allowed his slave to hire his own time. The usual practice was that the owner gave the slave a note indicating that the slave was not working independently but with his permission. The employees of self-hired slaves also proceeded, accordingly, and would claim, if threatened with prosecution, that the slave was rented out by his owner.

Slaves, certainly, were not going to admit that they were hiring their own time, since the practice benefited them as well. Usually, slaves who hired their own time lived independently from their owners, using the earnings or profits to rent housing. Most important, slaves who hired their own time had a chance to secure their freedom if they earned enough to pay the purchase price. Invariably, slave owners who allowed the slave to hire his or her own time were willing to allow the slave to purchase his freedom. While there were instances of owners taking the slave's freedom money, once the agreed-upon purchase price had been paid, the practice of slaves hiring out their own time could not have survived if this was common practice since the slave had no recourse in law to recover the money. Still, the practice of slaves hiring out their own time was profitable for the slave, who had greater independence and a chance to earn money, which could be saved for freedom.

Ultimately, as Cecil Gray stated, the practice of slaves hiring out their own time was "grounded on fundamental economic necessity," specifically on sound economic principles of the supply and demand in providing for an elastic labor market in the South. By 1860, while there were 8 million whites in the South, only 384,000 owned slaves, who numbered almost 4 million in the year before the Civil War. In a culture where menial work and personal service occupations were associated with blacks as "nigger work," a market existed for these services. Ultimately, as Juliet Walker notes, slaves hiring their own time survived because it was a "profitable practice which allowed greater capitalization of the slave's labor by the owner, real money wages for the slave, and a more elastic labor supply for the community."

SELECTED BIBLIOGRAPHY: Clement Eaton, "Slave-Hiring in the Upper South: A Step toward Freedom," *Mississippi Valley Historical Review* 46 (1960); Eugene Genovese, *Roll Jordan Roll: The World the Slaves Made* (New York: Vintage Books, 1974); Cecil Gray, *History of Agriculture in the Southern United States to 1860*, 2 vols. (Washington, DC: Carnegie Institution of Washington, 1933); Richard Wade, *Slavery in the Cities: The South, 1820–1860* (New York: Oxford University Press, 1964); Juliet E. K. Walker, *The History of Black Business in America: Capitalism, Race, Entrepreneurship* (New York: Macmillan/Prentice Hall International, 1998); Juliet E. K. Walker, "Pioneer Slave Entrepreneurship—Patterns, Processes, and Perspectives: The Case of the Slave Free Frank on the Kentucky Pennyroyal, 1795–1819," *Journal of Negro History* 68, 2 (Summer 1983).

Juliet E. K. Walker

SLAVEHOLDERS, LARGE BLACK. By 1860 the black population in the United States numbered almost 4.5 million, 3,953,760 slaves and 487,000 free blacks. In the year before the Civil War, African Americans, then, comprised 14.1 percent of the total American population.

In the 19 free states, there were 18,936,579 whites. In the 15 slave states and

Washington, D.C., there were 8,097,463 whites including the 384,884 white heads of households who owned slaves. Of that number, only 46,884 whites owned more than 20 slaves, while 200,000 owned no more than 5 slaves, although 60 percent of all slaves lived on plantations holding more than 20 slaves, including 30 percent of that number who lived on plantations holding more than 50 slaves.

There were also black slaveholders, whose ownership in blacks as chattel property began in the 1600s and continued to the Civil War. The most extensive national study of black slave ownership was made by Carter G. Woodson. He identified the numbers of black slaveholders in 1830. At that time, the total free black population was 319,599, including 182,070 in the South. Among them, 3,775 owned a total of 12,760 slaves. In 1830, the total slave population in the United States was 2,009,043.

The largest number of black slave owners lived in the states of Louisiana, South Carolina, Maryland, and Virginia, the same states with the largest number of white slaveholders. Most black slaveholders owned less than 5 slaves, but both the number of black slaveholders and the numbers of slaves owned by them declined in the 30 years before the Civil War. The pattern of declining black slave owners also held for other slave states. Larry Koger's extensive study of black slave owners in South Carolina from 1790 to 1860 shows that the number of black slaveholders increased from 59 in 1790 to 230 in 1820. The high point of black slave ownership in that state was in 1840, when there were 454 blacks who owned a total of 2,357 slaves. By 1860, there were only 171 black slaveholders who owned a total of 766 slaves out of South Carolina's total slave force of 402,406 slaves.

Throughout the period of slavery, the largest number of black slave owners were businesspeople, and the largest occupational group of free black slaveholders were planters followed by craftsmen.* Also, most free black women who owned slaves were businesswomen. Some were dressmakers, whereas others owned and operated restaurants, inns, hotels, and boardinghouses. There were also self-employed black women laundresses who owned slaves, but usually their purchase was for humanitarian reasons. Yet free black skilled craftsmen did not comprise a significantly large occupational group in the total free black population.

By 1850 there were 242 blacks or persons of color classified as planters, that is, who owned more than 20 slaves. The slaves owned by these free blacks, planters, and craftsmen, however, were purchased for the specific purpose of acquiring lifetime unpaid labor, and if the slave purchased was a woman, the owner also had the right to the future labor of the slave woman's progeny.

In Louisiana, while there were 10 black planters who owned 50 or more slaves in 1830, by 1860, there were only 6, who held property in land and slaves valued at more than $100,000. The planter Antoine DuBuclet's real property was valued at $200,000. He owned 1,265 acres of land and 71 slaves. The Ricaud family, a widow and son, owned real property valued at $220,000, 4,300 acres of land, and 152 slaves. The black planter A. Reggio's real property was valued at $70,000. He owned 2,400 acres of land and 100 slaves. The planter A. DeCuir owned real property valued at $150,000. He owned 1,075 acres of land and 112 slaves. A. Metoyer's real property was valued at $80,000. He owned 4,100 acres and 119 slaves.

The real property of the Thomas Durnford estate was valued at $50,000, with the cash value of his farm at $30,000 and personal property at $65,000. The estate included 75 slaves. David Whitten's study of Durnford as a planter is the most specific in detailing the agribusiness activities of black planters. While the value of Durnford's property increased from $93,750 in 1835 to $124,938 by 1859, Whitten identifies factors other than Durnford's business skills as the basis for this increase. Also, only Metoyer was a cotton planter; the others were sugar planters, and the property values listed above are the assessed values, representing only 72 percent of the real value of the property.

A detailed inventory of the holdings of several of the above black planters shows that in the case of DuBuclet the cash value of his farm equipment was $6,000. His livestock was valued at $10,000. Also, only 635 of his 1,235 acres was improved. DuBuclet's commodity production for 1858 included 1,750 bushels of corn; in 1858–1859 he produced 409 hogsheads of sugar. His 94 slaves lived in 56 dwellings. Also, while the real and personal property of Antoine DeCuir was valued at $151,000, the cash value of his farm was only $20,500, with his farm equipment valued at $20,000 and livestock at $7,000. Only 675 of his 1,135 acres were improved. His 112 slaves who lived in 24 dwellings produced 2,250 bushels of corn, 110 pounds of wool, 25 bushels of peas and beans, 150 bushels each of Irish potatoes and sweet potatoes, 20 1,000-pound hogsheads of cane sugar, and 1,200 gallons of molasses.

The Reggio family consisted of two brothers, with August's occupation listed in the census as planter and Octave as overseer. While their real and personal property totaled $160,000, the cash value of their farm was listed as $48,000 and $4,000 for farm implements. Their livestock was valued at $15,000, and their slaves produced $5,000 in Indian corn, 175 hundred-pound hogsheads of cane sugar, and 11,000 gallons of molasses. Together, the brothers owned 100 slaves who lived in 48 dwellings. By 1860, slaves averaged in price from $720 to $900, with prime fieldhands, young men 18 to 26 years of age, selling for $1,800, which was also the cost of skilled slaves, although some prime full hands and skilled slaves sold for as much as $3,500.

Excluding Louisiana's wealthy black planters, South Carolina's William Ellison* was the South's richest free black. By 1860, he owned 1,000 acres and 63 slaves. In 1859, 35 of his slaves, on some 200 acres, produced 80 bales of cotton, which netted $3,840. Profits from his cotton gin works provided venture capital for his agribusiness.

While the ownership in land and slaves of the leading black planters was remarkable, given the racially based societal and economic constraints under which blacks lived during the age of slavery, their holdings could not compare with the leading white Louisiana slaveholders. John Burnside of Ascension Parish owned 735 slaves, who lived in 192 dwellings. His real property was valued at $1,336,000; his personal property at $800,000. The cash value of his plantation was $1,400,000, and the value of his farm implements and machinery was $200,000. He owned 23,600 acres, with 5,600 acres of improved land. Burnside produced 2,500 thousand-pound hogsheads of cane sugar and 160,000 gallons of molasses. The cash value of his livestock was $76,000.

Also, with 167 slaves living on Burnside's St. James Parish plantation, he owned a total of 940 slaves. The white planter Meredith Calhoun of Rapides Parish, who produced both sugar and cotton on his plantation, owned 709 slaves and held real and personal property valued at $1,100,000. In 1860 Louisiana, with 1,640 plantations, ranked fourth in the number of states where planters owned more than 50 slaves (48.4 percent of the 160,500 slaves in Louisiana were held by planters who owned more than 50 slaves). The other three were Alabama, Mississippi, and South Carolina, which ranked first among the states with planters who owned more than 100 slaves. South Carolina also ranked first among the slave states where planters held more than 200 slaves.

Invariably, black planters in Louisiana and South Carolina were known as free people of color. Some were born slaves, whereas others were the children of former slaves who had inherited land from their white fathers. The leading black slave-owning family, the Metoyers in Louisiana, however, were descendants of the matriarch Coincoin, or Marie Thereze, who was of unmixed African ancestry. Her children were fathered by slaves and, then, her white owner. But unlike most Louisiana free planters of color, Coincoin built, as opposed to inherited, her extensive holdings in land and slaves. In 1830 the Metoyers owned 287 slaves. Several Metoyers died in the 1830s, and their estates, in addition to Augustin Metoyer's holdings, valued at $140,958, totaled $405,044. By 1850, the combined real property owned by the family, the second and third generations, each with individual holdings, totaled 5,667 acres of improved land worked by a total of 436 slaves. By 1860, according to Gary Mills, the property of the Metoyer family "was assessed at $770,545."

The historiographical debate on the topic of free black owners of slaves has focused on whether ownership was for economic reasons or for benevolent and humanitarian reasons. The first record of black slave ownership was in Virginia in 1654, when free black Anthony Johnson went to court to maintain ownership of his slave, who claimed he was an indentured servant, had served his time, and was entitled to freedom. While Johnson's purchase of a slave was for economic reasons, the 1656 purchase of a slave in Massachusetts by free black Bostian Ken was for humanitarian reasons. Ironically, both Johnson and Bostian Ken had purchased their own freedom.

In the early nineteenth century, southern states passed laws requiring newly manumitted slaves to leave the state, unless special permission to remain was granted by state legislatures. Since many slaves were purchased by family or friends, manumission would mean separation of the purchased slave from family and a network of friends and fictive kin. This group of black slave owners, then, did not manumit the slave, who was allowed to live as a nominally free black person. Consequently, economic gain was not always the purpose for ownership of those slaves. At the same time the occupation of the black slaveholder was also a determining factor of whether or not a slave was owned for economic gain.

But what can account for blacks holding other blacks as slaves? Was there a sense of brotherhood between the black slave owner and the black slave? Were black slaveholders more lenient than white slaveholders? Were there other labor alternatives for blacks with large landholdings? Also, while Woodson argues that the majority of black slaveholders owned slaves for humanitarian purposes, as opposed to commercial gain, R. Halliburton and Koger disagree. From his research, Koger takes the position that black slaveholding was "primarily an institution based on the exploitation of slaves rather than a benevolent system centered upon kinship or humanitarianism."

Regardless of whether the owner was white or black, there were no incentives for slaves to work as unpaid laborers from before sunup to after sundown. While there were examples of black slave owners who treated their slaves kindly, such as the former slave Marie Thereze who saw that her slaves were baptized and buried in consecrated grounds, she still had a jail on her plantation for those who resisted their forced labor.

Then, too, according to northern traveler Frederick Law Olmsted, who questioned a slave about the difference in treatment of white and black slaveholders, the slave said that black masters were "very hard and cruel, and devoid of feeling. You might think master dat dey would be good to dar own nation; but dey is not . . . I'd rather be a servant to any man in de world, dan to a brack man." Yet slaves found it prudent for their survival to tell whites what they wanted to hear. In the final analysis, no black volunteered to be enslaved as a plantation field hand for either a white or black master.

Whether a slave was owned by a black master or a white master, the condition was still involuntary forced servitude. For black masters, then, profits and privileges took precedence over a common heritage of racial subordination. In South Carolina, slave entrepreneur Anthony Weston,* nominally free, established a millwright business. He was one of the wealthiest blacks, slave or free, in that state, leaving an estate of more than $40,000. Weston's wealth was acquired through his activities as a slave entrepreneur and in the increased value of his property, both real and chattel. Weston, although a slave, purchased 20 slaves from 1834 to 1845, but in his wife's name since she was free.

Still, for black planters and slaveholders, unlike their white counterparts, property ownership did not translate into power. Notwithstanding, with the beginning of the Civil War, black planters and slaveholders in Louisiana and South Carolina were among the first to volunteer their services to the Confederacy. Ironically, while they were rejected in the closing two months of the Civil War, the Confederacy passed a law allowing slaves to enlist in their military forces. With their wealth in slaves wiped out by the ending of the Civil War, the large black planter slave-owning class ended, as did the institution of slavery.

SELECTED BIBLIOGRAPHY: R. Halliburton, Jr., "Free Black Owners of Slaves: A Reappraisal of the Woodson Thesis," *South Carolina Historical Magazine* 76 (July 1976); Larry Koger, *Black Slaveowners: Free Black Slave Masters in South Carolina, 1790–1860* (Jefferson, NC: McFarland & Company, Inc., 1985); Joseph Karl Menn, *The Large Slaveholders of Louisiana–1860* (New Orleans: Pelican Publishing Company, 1964); Gary B. Mills, *The Forgotten People: Cane River's Creoles of Color* (Baton Rouge: Louisiana State University Press, 1977); Juliet E. K. Walker, *The History of Black Business in America: Capitalism, Race, Entrepreneurship* (New York: Macmillan/ Prentice Hall International, 1998); David O. Whitten, *Andrew Durnford: A Black Sugar Planter in Antebellum Louisiana* (Natchitoches, LA: Northwestern State University Press, 1981); Carter G. Woodson, *Free Negro Owners of Slaves in the United States in 1830* (Washington, DC: Association for the Study of Negro Life and History, 1924).

Juliet E. K. Walker

SLAVE LAWS, ECONOMIC CONSTRAINTS. With few exceptions, most economic activities developed by slaves that enabled them to make money were made illegal by state laws and municipal ordinances. These laws were in force throughout the period of slavery from the colonial era to the end of the Civil War. Trade and marketing of foodstuffs from provision ground production were the first economic activities undertaken by enslaved Africans and the first area of enterprise made illegal by colonial statutes. Most of these laws almost made it a crime for goods to be purchased from slaves. A Maryland law in force in the 1660s stipulated: "Noe person . . . shall trade, barter, commerce, or game [with slaves without the owner's permission]." Similar laws were enacted in all of the slave states.

In addition, laws in force from the colonial era on made it illegal for slaves to own certain kinds of property. Also, laws literally required whites to seize the property of slaves, such as a 1722 South Carolina statute that said: "[I]t shall be lawful for any person to seize hogs kept by slaves, and all boats and canoes belonging to any slaves" and "any horse or horses, or any neat cattle." The law was amended in 1740, after the 1739 Stono Slave Rebellion, where a slave could be stripped of his clothes if they were of any value, except for carriage drivers. Under the law, slave clothes had to be made from "negro cloth, duffelds, coarse kearsies."

Slave laws also made it illegal for slaves to hire their own time* or to rent property that would be used for a business. It was also illegal to teach slaves to read or write or to employ them in any occupation "as a scribe in any manner of writing whatsoever." Indeed, in South Carolina, the fine, "one hundred pounds current money," was higher than fines imposed on slave owners for allowing them to live independently and establish businesses. The greatest fear, of course, was that slaves would use their writing skills to forge tickets and permits to trade and market and also to write out free papers, which would enhance their ability to escape from slavery. This fine was even higher than that imposed on physicians or druggists who employed slaves.

By the nineteenth century, as slave property* ownership increased, slave laws became increasingly specific in listing the articles of property that slaves could not trade or market. In North Carolina the enumerated list of proscribed goods included "cotton, tobacco, wheat, rice, oats, corn, rye, pork, bacon, beef, leather, raw hides, iron castings, farming utensils, nails, meal, flour, spirituous liquors or wine, peas, salt fish, flax, flaxseed, hogs, cattle, sheep, wool, lumber, staves, tar, pitch, turpentine, fodder, shingles, hoops, white oak heading, potatoes, mutton, cotton or woolen cloth, yarn, wearing apparel, or gold or silver bullion." The existence of these laws did not stop slaves from accumulating property, so concessions were made. In Georgia, slave transactions—buying or selling goods, such as cotton or tobacco or grain crops—were limited to $1 per transaction. Georgia did allow unrestricted slave sales of slave-produced handicrafts such as "brooms, baskets, foot and bed-mats, [and] shuck collars," but valuable property owned by slaves could be seized and sold by the states.

The statutes enacted by state legislative bodies to suppress independent slave economic activities* were reinforced by municipal ordinances. The 1806 Charleston, South Carolina, municipal ordinances were typical of laws in force in southern towns and cities until slavery ended. Invariably it was illegal for slaves to participate in any crafts as independent businessmen or to clerk in or manage any store unless they were supervised by a white person. Also, tickets were required for slaves to buy or sell goods, except for meat, fruit and vegetables, milk, and grains. In addition, some cities limited the amount of money a slave could make. In New Orleans the maximum wage for day laborers was $1 a day: in Charleston, the maximum daily wage was $.815, in 1817, which was increased by ordinance to $1 in 1837.

Since many slaves worked without badges, these laws provided punishment for any owner or hirer of slaves who worked at occupations requiring the purchase of badges. Fines were quite high, ranging from $20 to $50, while slaves were punished by whipping, ranging from 20 to 50 lashings. Moreover, it was illegal for slaves to hire their own time* and also illegal for free people to patronize businesses established by these slaves. The extent to which the state attempted to either control or suppress slave marketing and trading practices, consequently, illuminates the pervasiveness and extensiveness of the independent economic activities developed by enslaved African Americans. Yet the state action through the South's criminal justice system did little to deter slave business initiative or their independent economic activities at any level, whether plantation, urban, or industrial or that which took place in the underground economy.

By 1860, while only 10 percent, some 400,000, of the slave population lived in urban places, the existence of state laws and municipal ordinances enacted from the seventeenth century on indicates the continuity, extensiveness, and diversity of slave independent economic activities. That slaves persisted, despite these economic suppression laws, often with impunity, indicates the extent to which their independent economic activities, especially in the urban South, were a necessary and integral part of the formal southern urban business community. By the time of the Civil War, within the context of these repressive economic laws, blacks, then, had more than two centuries of experience in establishing independent economic activities.

The existence of these economic constraint laws underscores the extent to which slaves attempted to improve their material life by participating in the economy. Even after the Civil War, the Black Codes passed also included laws that prohibited the freedmen from participating in certain self-employed occupations that could provide the basis for establishing viable enterprises. Still, after 1865, many former slave entrepreneurs joined antebellum free black businesspeople in establishing enterprises. Even slaves who had not developed independent businesses before the war established enterprises after.

During and after Reconstruction, the forces of black economic suppression continued, including violence that was often directed specifically at successful and prosperous black businesspeople. The violent repression of black business activities was revealed by Ida B. Wells (1862–1931) in the 1895 publication *A Red Record: Tabulated Statistics and Alleged Causes of Lynchings in the United States*. Again societal legal repression would have an impact on black business activity with the infamous *Plessy v. Ferguson* Supreme Court decision in 1896. In this instance, black businesspeople relied more on black consumers than white, as had been the case during the age of slavery.

SELECTED BIBLIOGRAPHY: Edward L. Ayers, *Vengeance and Justice: Crime and Punishment in the 19th Century American South* (New York: Oxford University Press, 1984); Claudia Goldin, *Urban Slavery in the American South, 1820–1860: A Quantitative History* (Chicago: University of Chicago Press, 1976); Kermit L. Hall, ed., *The Law of American Slavery: Major Interpretations* (New York: Garland, 1987); Mark V. Tushnet, *American Law of Slavery: Considerations of Humanity and Interest* (Princeton: Princeton University Press, 1981); Richard Wade, *Slavery in the Cities: The South, 1820–1860* (New York: Oxford University Press, 1964); Juliet E. K. Walker, *The History of Black Business in America: Capitalism, Race, Entrepreneurship* (New York: Macmillan/Prentice Hall International, 1998).

Juliet E. K. Walker

SLAVE-OWNED PROPERTY, CIVIL WAR CONFISCATIONS. Studies of the development of Union policy toward Confederate property in the Civil War often concentrate upon the genesis of the contraband slave policy, that slaves captured by Union forces or who entered Union lines were free. The Thirty-seventh Congress, on August 6, 1861, formalized this policy with the first Confiscation Act. A second, broader Confiscation Act followed on July 17, 1862. It was, of course, not merely slaves that the Union forces confiscated but other types of property as well. Less well known, however, is that slaves, too, suffered under the confiscation policy. Contrabands entering into Union lines were liable to have their meager possessions stripped from them in the name of the war effort, and when Union armies marched into the southern states, they were often indiscriminate in their foraging, taking from slave and free, black and white, without regard.

The theory behind such confiscations was that loyal Americans were eligible for compensation, whereas disloyal citizens, that is to say, Confederates, were not. So proof of loyalty was one aspect to gaining compensation. In theory, it was not hard to give credence to the loyalty of former slaves to the Union, especially after the Emancipation Proclamation of September 1862. The other aspect to gaining compensation was proof of ownership, and this was a far larger obstacle for former slaves. The difficulty was that under the letter of the law in most southern states slaves were banned from holding property.

Yet practice differed from theory, and some masters permitted their slaves to raise a small crop, to keep livestock, or to hire out a portion of their time for cash wages. In some cases, these slaves managed to amass considerable fortunes, but they were the exception, although many more managed to own a few animals or tools that made their existence more bearable. All of these were subject to Union confiscation.

The main vehicle for compensation was the Southern Claims Commission, authorized by Congress on March 3, 1871. Over the next nine years, the Commission heard 22,298 claims totaling $60,258,150. Of these, Congress upheld 7,092 (31.8 percent) claims, paying $4,636,929.69 (7.7 percent) to the claimants. Among their number were former slaves, and the details of their claims allow us to see what sorts of property they owned.

The slave claimants demonstrate a considerable range of property ownership. At one end were those like Littleton Barber of Adams County, Mississippi, the former owner of a horse. He received all of his $135 claim. Above them in the spectrum were people like Samuel Elliott of Liberty County, Georgia, who claimed the loss of seven cattle, 15 hogs, 30 ducks, 800 pounds of bacon, 210 pounds of rice, and a wagon and harness. He received $118.50 out of the $436 he claimed. And it was not just men who managed to amass property either, as Mary Jess of Chatham County, Georgia, claimed $625.50 as compensation for the seizure of a cow, 10 hogs, 20 turkeys, 60 fowl, 300 pounds of honey, 15 gallons of syrup, 50 pounds of lard, 100 pounds of coffee, one and a half sacks of flour, 75 pounds of sugar, 50 pounds of tobacco, 5 gallons of wine, and assorted furniture. She received $130. Leah Black of Shelby County, Tennessee claimed $1,434.50 for two horses, seven cows, 63 hogs, 23 geese, some 200 chickens, 250 bushels of corn, four stacks of fodder, and a pair of wagons. She received $350.

Leah Black was at the top of the spectrum of slave property ownership, along with people like Alonzo Jackson of Georgetown County, South Carolina. His testimony demonstrated that even though he was legally a slave, he had for 18 years before the Civil War bought all of his time from his master and lived as a free man. He claimed $1,925 for two mules, a gun, and 20 tierces of rice. His claim for the rice was disallowed, and he received $250.

Slaves like Leah Black and Alonzo Jackson were exceptional in their prewar property ownership. It is possible, too, that testimony before the Southern Claims Commission overrepresented slaves at the upper end of the property-owning spectrum. There were many more African Americans who lost some or all of their possessions who did not or could not file a claim. Still, the record of those that did illustrates both the variety of property types owned by slaves and the willingness of the Union forces to take it from them.

SELECTED BIBLIOGRAPHY: Ira Berlin et al., eds., *The Destruction of Slavery: Freedom: A Documentary History of Emancipation, 1861–1867, Series I*, vol. 1 (Cambridge: Cambridge University Press, 1985); Ira Berlin et al., eds., *The Wartime Genesis of Free Labor: The Lower South, Freedom: A Documentary History of Emancipation, 1861–1867, Series I*, vol. 3 (Cambridge: Cambridge University Press, 1990); Gary B. Mills, *Civil War Claims in the South* (Laguna Hills, CA: Aegean Park Press, 1980); Loren Schweninger, *Black Property Owners in the South, 1790–1915* (Urbana: University of Illinois Press, 1990).

Ian Binnington

SLAVE REVOLTS AND BLACK CRAFTSMEN. In American history, craftsmen, both black and white, have distinguished themselves as leaders of revolts. In the American Revolution, white craftsmen, including printer Benjamin Franklin and silversmith Paul Revere, with few economic or political ties to the Anglophile colonial aristocracy, according to Carl Bridenbaugh, "had leadership as well as organization. From their ranks they produced a number of clear-thinking and bold captains, who crystallized their discontents, formulated plans, and joined with other groups in precipitating the revolutionary movement." In much the same way, black craftsmen, both slave and free, with their skills and knowledge, and a confidence developed by successful competitive economic participation in white American business community, represented an occupational group that assumed leadership of many of the successful threats against slave institutions.

In the New York slave conspiracy of 1741, which had as its objective the burning of the city and the murder of its inhabitants, most of the leaders and participants were black craftsmen. In 1792 a slave revolt on the eastern shores of Virginia was composed of some 900 blacks, including many who were armed. In addition to guns and powder, the slaves also carried spears, which according to newspapers reports were made "by a negro blacksmith on the Eastern shore." In the nineteenth century, slave craftsmen continued to prove the greatest threat to the slave system. In the performance of their jobs, they had virtually unlimited mobility to make contacts and organize insurrections and rebellions. But like free craftsmen, because their economic success was dependent on white patronage, the white community found it difficult to believe that black craftsmen would compromise their livelihood by attacking the political and social system that allowed them an economic place.

Indeed, black slave craftsmen were considered "privileged," described in a South Carolina newspaper in the late 1850s as an "ebony aristocracy." Yet southerners who knew the reality of their history, such as the pro-slavery spokesman James H. Hammond, recognized the threat slave craftsmen posed for the security of the South, for he said: " 'Whenever a slave is made a mechanic, he is more than half freed, and soon becomes, as we too well know, and all history attests . . . the most corrupt and turbulent of his class.' " Significantly, leaders of three great slave conspiracies in the nineteenth century were craftsmen.

Gabriel Prosser (1775?–1800), a coachman, who was also a blacksmith, used the mobility afforded by his occupations to communicate his plans for a slave attack on Richmond. In formulating plans for an attack on Charleston, Prosser was joined by other slave artisans. While stockpiling weapons, including swords made by his wife Nancy, the strategy devised by Gabriel and his slave artisan compatriots was to secure the participation of field hands. But the planned revolt never took place. Gabriel's conspiracy was betrayed twice by fellow slaves, first, in revealing plans for the revolt to whites and, second, revealing the location where he had escaped. Prosser was captured, tried, and sentenced to death by hanging, as were his two brothers and 35 other slaves.

Denmark Vesey (c. 1767–1822), a South Carolina slave carpenter who also managed a small plantation, purchased his freedom from lottery winnings and established a carpenter shop in that city. While Vesey achieved success in his enterprise—by 1822 he owned $8,000 in property—at the same time, he found it increasingly intolerable to live as a prosperous free black while so many other blacks were enslaved. Literate and well read, with knowledge of the success not only of the American and French Revolution but also that led by blacks in Haiti, Vesey made plans for his own rebellion. His "lieutenants" were primarily skilled slaves and free black artisans. His scheduled revolt was planned for Bastille Day, July 15. More than 9,000 slaves were prepared to revolt, but Vesey was betrayed and, along with 35 of his rebel leaders, hanged, whereas 37 others were sent into exile.

Only the rebellion led by Nat Turner (1800–1831), in which some 57 whites were killed in Southampton, Virginia, which bordered North Carolina, was actually carried out. The slave Turner, a carpenter, was also literate, propelled by a messianic vision, as opposed to some religious fanaticism, to lead his people to freedom by destroying the slave power. On the day chosen by Turner for the revolt, August 22, and beginning with 5 followers, Turner swept through the countryside, eventually joined by some 60 to 70 slaves. While the revolt lasted, some 57 whites, men, women, and children, were killed. Whites taken by surprise soon launched an offensive, and more than 40 of Turner's men were killed, including 12 whose severed heads were placed on poles as a warning to other slaves. Turner managed to escape and hide out until the end of October. Apprehended on October 30, he was quickly tried, found guilty, and hanged on November 11.

The repercussions were tremendous. More repressive slave laws were enacted, and greater constraints were imposed on the free black population. On more immediate effects, it was reported that indiscriminate killings of blacks, slave and free, continued for several months after and that "[t]he brightest and best was killed in Nat's Time. The whites always suspect such ones."

SELECTED BIBLIOGRAPHY: Herbert Aptheker, *American Negro Slave Revolts* (New York: International Publishers, 1945); Carl Bridenbaugh, *The Colonial Craftsman* (New York: New York University Press, 1950); Charles B. Dew, "Black Ironworkers and the Slave Insurrection Panic of 1856," *Journal of Southern History* 30 (May 1964): 143–161; Daniel Horsemanden, *The New York Conspiracy, or a History of the Negro Plot* (New York: Southwick & Pelsue, 1810); John Lofton, *Denmark Vesey's Revolt: The Slave Plot That Lit a Fuse to Fort Sumter* (Kent, OH: Kent State University Press, 1983); Stephen B. Oates, *The Fires of Jubilee: Nat Turner's Fierce Rebellion* (New York: Harper & Row, 1975).

Juliet E. K. Walker

SLAVES, INDEPENDENT ECONOMIC PRODUCTION, LOUISIANA SUGAR PLANTATION.

By the late antebellum period, slaves on Louisiana sugar estates had organized extensive and integrated economic systems, accumulating and disposing of capital and property within internal economies they themselves administered. Such economic systems probably functioned on every plantation and not only reflected the ways in which slaves organized their efforts to earn and spend money but also influenced the character and development of slave family and community life. The slaves' economy thus shaped patterns of slave life, providing the material basis for African American culture in the region.

Agricultural endeavors were central to the slaves' independent economic production. On most estates, slaves controlled some land, where they raised livestock and grew crops for their personal consumption and sale. Slaves usually had kitchen gardens, where they raised fruits, vegetables, small livestock, and poultry, as well as more extensive allotments of land—commonly known as "Negro grounds"—elsewhere on the plantation, where they cultivated cash crops, most commonly corn. Slaves could tend their gardens at odd times through the workweek, but only on weekends could they work the less accessible Negro grounds. Sometimes, usually just before the sugar harvest, slaves secured additional time off from crops, while they also worked for themselves during any annual holidays.

The plantation was not only the source of the slaves' independent production but also their principal market. The growing and retailing of corn was the most lucrative dimension of the economy and the one that involved the most slaves. By marketing the produce on their home estate, slaves benefited not only themselves but also the planters, who needed corn meal for the rations they gave their slaves. Slaves could thus save shipping and marketing expenses, while planters were freed from agents' fees and transportation costs. Occasionally, however, slaves did market their crop off the plantation, and they also worked a number of other cash crops, such as pumpkins, potatoes, and hay. Poultry and hogs, the animals slaves most commonly raised, also found their principal market on the plantation. Raising poultry was ideally suited to the slaves' economy, since it demanded little investment of time or effort, required minimal capital outlay, and provided a steady income through marketing both eggs and the birds themselves.

The sale of crops, poultry, and livestock to the planter was but one source of revenue for slaves. On the estate, slaves could engage in various other money-making activities. Planters supplemented the sugar mill fuel supply by purchasing wood slaves cut on their own time, and they also paid slaves to dig ditches, since the amount of ditching done during the regular labor schedule usually proved insufficient. On time off from plantation work, slaves also undertook numerous jobs for pay, including sugar potting; fixing kettles; collecting fodder; forging hoops; mending shoes; counting hoop poles; making rails, baskets, bricks, shingles, staves, pickets, boards, shuck collars, barrels, and hogsheads; hauling wood; and serving as watchmen.

Skilled slaves, moreover, made money during sugar harvest: The sugar makers, engineers, kettle setters, firemen, and kettle tenders usually received cash bonuses for their work. Slave carpenters, coopers, and blacksmiths could also profit from their training, undertaking large-scale lucrative projects, such as making carts and handbarrows for sale. On some estates, slave coopers did piece-work, producing a specific number of barrels and earning cash for any extra production. Many paying jobs required stamina if not skills, and slaves lacking these had few opportunities apart from making themselves available for day labor. Other slaves chose not to work for the plantation, concentrating instead on farming, gardening, poultry and livestock raising, and domestic crafts, whereas many combined working for themselves and for the plantation.

Cash entered the internal economy from various other sources. Slaves who hunted or fished could sell or barter some of their catch to fellow slaves, traders, or planters, while at Christmas, some slaves received holiday cash bonuses. On the plantation, thus, slaves had numerous opportunities to earn money that planters' gifts could supplement. Slaves also bypassed the plantation and traded elsewhere. Some were involved in marketing at major Mississippi River ports, as well as at local town markets and in the neighborhood of the plantation. They also transacted business with the traders who plied southern Louisiana's waterways and highways. Slaves collected and dried Spanish moss, consigning the bales to St. Louis, New Orleans, and Natchez, where they dealt with city agents, exploiting the market for moss as upholstery stuffing. Slaves used the same network to sell molasses and, in both cases, paid for shipping, plus the agents' sales commission, out of the proceeds.

Slaves had other options for marketing their crops and goods. Some traded in the neighborhood of their plantation. Others who lived near towns could trade at the markets held there on Sundays, the slaves' traditional day off, where they could also spend their earnings. Market-day activities, however, were not confined to retailing and purchasing goods: At market, slaves could shake the plantation routine and restrictions, diverting some of their earnings to liquor, gaming, and other pleasures. The vastness of Louisiana's sugar region and its paucity of towns denied most slaves access to urban markets. But by transacting business with itinerant peddlers, slaves established trade networks beyond planter control. River traders, especially, dealt extensively with plantation slaves, because although inadequate roads impeded travel by land, all large sugar plantations were situated on navigable waterways. Moreover, river traders could move quietly and quickly and thus trade clandestinely in illicit goods.

Slaves found the independence the external trading network conferred extremely useful. They could divest themselves of plantation constraints and engage in an independent economic system they controlled. Planters could influence neither the form of the trade nor the goods being traded. Indeed, river trade often violated both plantation regulations and state law, providing slaves the opportunity to sell goods planters would not buy and to buy goods planters would neither sell nor order. For example, while slaveholders rarely sold slaves liquor, river traders did, despite laws banning its sale. In turn, traders purchased various commodities, including stolen goods, not exchanged between slaves and planters.

Theft was integral to the internal economy. Many slaves had no compunction about taking the planters' property, arguing that they were taking what was rightly theirs. Plantation records reveal the prevalence of slave theft and profile its most popular targets—the plantations' produce and livestock and the slaveholders' personal property. Although some stolen goods went to improving slaves' diet, clothing, and lodgings directly, others were traded or sold, thus contributing to the slaves' internal economy.

Like the plantation economy, the slaves' economy varied with the seasons. Large sums of money entered the internal economy in fall and winter, since slaves gained most of their income when they sold their cash crops and when they delivered wood before the sugar harvest. Stealing from the sugarhouse also was seasonal, while gifts from planters usually came at the end of harvest or at Christmas. But poultry provided year-round earnings, as did theft, day labor, moss collecting, and other commercial ventures. The uninterrupted harvest labor schedule denied slaves free time for their own economic interests, apart from the skilled slaves who received harvest bonuses and those able to "appropriate" some sugar and molasses. Slaves also had little time to spend their money during harvest.

The internal economy, therefore, had a curious seasonal profile. Earnings fluctuated considerably since plantation labor demands, especially during harvest, overlaid the seasonal nature of agrarian economies. Earnings potential also varied from year to year, since the slaves' crops were subject to the weather's vagaries. Moreover, not all slaves participated in the internal economy equally, and some may not have participated at all, although it was an integral part of community life on every sugar plantation in Louisiana. Considerable disparities even existed in the earnings of slaves on the same plantation.

Plantation records provide a partial reckoning of slaves' earnings, containing payments for certain commodities or work performed, but do not record income earned off the plantation. These earnings would also have been unevenly distributed, but not necessarily benefiting the same slaves. Those who derived the greatest profit dealing with river traders or through theft, for example, may not have been the same slaves who made the most money in transactions with the planter. The internal economy brought slaves material benefits. They and their families ate and dressed better and lived in more comfortable homes. Although earnings were often small and purchases modest—slaves could not, for example, expect to earn enough to purchase freedom for themselves or their families— they reflect slaves' independent actions as consumers and offer insight into how they dealt with their lives in bondage.

Slave purchases fell into six categories: food and drink, pipes and tobacco, clothing and other personal items, housewares, tools and implements, and live-stock. Within these six categories, however, slaves chose broadly. The purchasing profile changed little over time or from plantation to plantation: Slaves always placed high priority on a few commodities—specifically flour, cloth and tobacco, as well as shoes and some ready-made clothing. Slaves with limited resources bought these staple commodities, plus alcohol. Slaves with larger earnings, however, might purchase more elaborate goods—foodstuffs like meat, fish, coffee, beans, rice, potatoes, and fruit, as well as tools, housewares and furniture, finer cloths and clothing, and personal items like watches, umbrellas, pocket knives, and fiddles.

Slaves managed their own earnings, with planters cooperating by establishing accounts that credited slaves for work or goods and that functioned as depositories for off-plantation earnings and money accrued from intracommunity transactions. Slaves also made purchases through the planter, drawing on their personal accounts. Slaves were thus familiar with hard currency, albeit in small denominations, were acquainted with a barter system, and were even conversant with a credit economy, since they could charge purchases to their plantation accounts.

Debits and purchases indicate that these were family accounts designated by (the usually male) head of household. That few slave women had accounts in their own names neither reflects their lack of involvement nor suggests they benefited less: Wives accessed accounts listed in their husbands' names. Some accounts were held by sons in either male- or female-headed households, suggesting a "coming of age" pattern. Slaves did not purchase everything through the planter. Whether or not they had plantation accounts, slaves often wanted to buy elsewhere. Similar purchasing patterns would have prevailed, however, except for the alcohol procured from river traders, illicit "shebeens" and grog shops, or "moonshiners." Slaves also spent money gambling, while some cultural and religious items and slave-crafted artifacts would not have been purchased through the planter.

Participation in the internal economy offered slaves numerous less tangible benefits. Working for their own profit not only supplemented meager rations but also gave slaves the satisfaction of controlling aspects of their lives. Being responsible for choosing the manner and extent of their involvement in a private economy gave slaves degrees of control and independence at variance with servitude's basic tenets. Slaves qua slaves operated within a social and labor system that deprived them of personal rights, autonomous actions, decision making, and self-motivated work regimes. As independent economic agents, however, they organized their own efforts, controlled "their" land and its cultivation, and decided how to market produce and dispose of the accumulated profits. Indeed, the structure of the slaves' internal economy more resembled a peasant economy.

This control doubtless proved cathartic and satisfying, despite the potentially deleterious effects of overwork and physical stress. The independent economic activities, moreover, established the material foundation for slave family and community life and slave culture. They prompted enterprise, not subservience, and their diversity and ubiquity testify to slaves' creative initiative. Whereas the plantation economy followed the planters' will, the slaves' economy contradicted the very premises of chattel bondage and helped to shape patterns of African American life, culture, and economy that endured from slavery to freedom.

SELECTED BIBLIOGRAPHY: Ira Berlin and Philip D. Morgan, eds., *The Slaves' Economy: Independent Production by Slaves in the Americas* (London: Frank Cass, 1991); Larry E. Hudson, Jr., ed., *Working toward Freedom: Slave Society and Domestic Economy in the American South* (Rochester: University of Rochester Press, 1995); Roderick A. McDonald, *The Economy and Material Culture of Slaves: Goods and Chattels on the Sugar Plantations of Jamaica and Louisiana* (Baton Rouge: Louisiana State University Press, 1993).

Roderick A. McDonald

SLAVES, PLANTATION MARKET–RELATED ACTIVITIES. Despite their oppression, exploitation, and legal existence as chattel property, many African American slaves in the antebellum South participated in the marketplace by making, raising, selling, buying, and owning their own goods and property. We should be wary, however, of automatically equating the constellation of such activities with the concept of "business" or, more to the point, the business endeavors of a free society that entailed, among other things, the eager pursuit of profit. Plantation Slaves lacked considerable control over their day-to-day economic affairs, and more generally, the opportunity to exploit the potential of the expansive nineteenth-century market. Instead, the central reality of slavery for slaves—having little control over one's life and time—not only made these features of business largely nonexistent to slaves but, more important, insured that slaves' market-related experiences would be so different as to be distinctly unbusinesslike—at least in the terms of nineteenth-century free society.

Yet, however these market-related activities are defined or conceptualized, we should not ignore their impact on African Americans, both under slavery and, after 1865, in the first years of freedom when they were presumably in a better position to pursue more explicitly profit-making ventures. Any discussion of slaves' marketplace activity must start with their masters. Legally speaking, slaves did not own, buy, or sell their own property; both the logic of slavery and state laws stated that slaves entered the marketplace as proxies of their masters, and whatever they appeared to buy and sell as their own was ultimately their owners'; According to John Campbell, South Carolina law, for example, stated, "A slave may, by the consent of his master, acquire and hold *personal* property. All, thus acquired, is regarded in law as that of the master. . . . A slave cannot contract or be contracted with." Similarly, since masters were the ultimate owners of slave property, it stands to reason that they as owners of the slaves set many of the conditions and parameters within which slaves encountered the marketplace.

Indeed, slaves could not even participate without the master's permission. Masters, as a group, tolerated, encouraged, and even, in some instances, required slaves to participate in the market because they expected to benefit from slaves' market activities. Where some slave owners envisioned a financial savings by making their slaves underwrite all or a portion of their subsistence by buying food and clothing, others valued the reduction in disruptive activities that came when slaves spent their free time busily engaged in constructive, market-related endeavors. Most optimistically, a third group of masters thought that market involvement would resocialize their slaves, either by making them more respectful of the master's property by dint of having their own or by making them happier, more contented, and hence more productive workers because they were allowed the privilege of participating in the market.

Yet when reality fell short of these expectations, masters were quick to make adjustments, as in the 1840s and 1850s. The perception that such market activity made slaves grow more independent and willful, rather than more pliant and obedient, encouraged many slave owners in these late antebellum years to "reform" this constellation of activities. Numerous slave owners, for example, forced their chattel to stay on the plantation and conduct their business with them, thereby depriving slaves of the opportunity and pleasure of leaving the plantation to find their own crossroads trading partners who, not inconsequentially, might "pour," as the South Carolina planter Whitemarsh Seabrook put it, "new and pernicious ideas [into] the susceptible mind of the African." At the same time, some cotton planters, suspicious that their slaves augmented their own cotton with that stolen from the master, restricted slave production of their own marketable crops to corn. Yet whatever the concrete ways in which masters shaped slaves' income-related activities, the important point is that the opportunity to engage in such activities was never a right but always a privilege that could be altered or withdrawn by the master.

Shared concerns and interests among slave owners throughout the South helped create common market-related experiences among slaves, regardless of where they lived. Because slaves existed to provide labor, slaves everywhere spent the vast amount of time laboring for the master and not for themselves; as a result, much of the time used for producing sellable goods or earning a wage occurred at night or on Sunday, when slaves typically did not work for the master. In addition, masters generally placed limits on what slaves could purchase with their earnings; at all times guns and related weapons were off-limits, and by the last 30 years of the slavery era, so too were liquor and reading and writing materials.

Yet befitting a large and complex region, considerable variation existed by area and crop in slaves' market-related activities. Slaves living in the rice districts of coastal Georgia and South Carolina enjoyed the most free time for carrying out market-oriented work; unlike cotton, sugar, and tobacco slaves who worked from sunup to sundown in gangs, rice slaves worked in the tasking system. Within this form of labor organization, slaves were given a certain quantity of work to do in a day; once the work was finished—say, by 4 or 5 in the afternoon—the rest of the day was the slaves'. Accordingly, slaves worked hard to finish their work by late afternoon, in order to have more time to do their own productive labor; by contrast, slaves laboring within the gang system remained in the fields until sundown and could only work for themselves at night and/or on Sunday and, depending on the plantation, part of Saturday as well.

These task and gang differences in work and in the amount of free time available to slaves thus explain, in large part, why rice slaves had the highest earnings and most property of all slaves. Where slaves laboring in the gang system might earn, on average, $10 to $15 per year, rice slaves made considerably more; indeed, by the eve of the Civil War, slaves in one rice area (Liberty County, Georgia) had amassed property holdings worth over $300 on average. Although much of this "wealth" consisted of common consumer goods, it is especially noteworthy that many individuals also counted expensive items such as hogs, cows, and horses among their holdings. (Still, even among these "richest" of slaves, the ability to buy one's freedom occurred sparingly, it at all.)

By contrast, gang slaves, possessed of smaller earnings, were much less likely to own livestock and, instead, acquired and owned more modest consumer items such as tobacco, food (sugar, coffee, flour), kitchen utensils, and various yard goods and finished clothing (shirts, coats, shoes). While no match for the "richer" rice slaves, the earnings of, say, a cotton slave in the 1850s still afforded noticeable material improvements; with sugar, for example, at $.11 per pound, shoes at $1.25 a pair, and calico and flannel at $.10 and $.25 per yard, respectively, $10 or $15 could certainly have an important impact on the slave's material conditions of life.

While particular forms of moneymaking—hunting and fishing, collecting fodder, raising corn and poultry, and doing miscellaneous wage work (sewing, digging ditches)—could be found in all regions, the types of remunerative work slaves did frequently reflected the agricultural features of their particular region. It was not uncommon for slaves living on tobacco, rice, and cotton plantations to raise their own such crops for market; for example, during the 1840s and

1850s, slaves' cotton comprised a surprisingly high, 7 percent of all cotton produced (approximately 127,000 preginned pounds out of 1.7 million) on four Darlington (South Carolina) District plantations. By contrast, the notoriously brutal pace of labor on Louisiana sugar plantations and the sizable, factorylike mills used for grinding and processing sugar cane stalks into usable sugar precluded slaves in this state from raising their own cane; instead, they scoured the forests and sold wood to the masters for the mills' fuel and Spanish moss to local merchants who eventually marketed it as furniture stuffing.

Yet whatever the specific features of how slaves produced, sold, acquired, and consumed within the context of the market, it would be misleading, not to mention historically inaccurate, to describe slaves' market-related activity as business enterprise or even profit oriented. For the vast majority of slaves, the level of monetary participation was far too small to merit such descriptions. Moreover, the immediate purpose was often to just acquire basic subsistence goods for survival; but even then, the socioemotional benefits of "business" activity could easily outweigh material ones. Being able to strengthen their individual families through the joint earning of money and/or shared use of purchased consumer goods, or forging new relationships of, as one slave owner put it alarmingly, "perfect equality" with out-of-the-way white shopkeepers, might have mattered more to slaves than the actual amounts they earned or spent. Indeed, the central benefit of participating as sellers and buyers may have simply been the opportunity to act like, as the slave Charles Ball* put it, "a kind of freeman."

Nonetheless, these market-related activities have considerable relevance within a "business"- or profit-oriented perspective when applied to the lives of African Americans in the post-1865 period. While their small annual earnings as slaves and/or disruptions of the Civil War made it unlikely that recently liberated slaves had much of a material base from which to begin their lives as free people, participation in the market during slavery did impart to many freedpeople valuable knowledge about business terms, concepts, and practices. Not only had they become familiar with buying and selling—practices that humans learn rather than possess innately—but they also acquired, through their market activities, a familiarity with money, both as object and concept; at the same time, the notion of "credit" became familiar to many, since slaves were often paid with credit, especially if they sold their products to the master.

In the cotton country of South Carolina, slaves of the late antebellum years were more likely to be paid in credit—which could be spent at the plantation commissary or at specially designated local merchants—than in cash that could be spent anywhere, including with disreputable white shopkeepers who might sell them contraband such as liquor or firearms. Conversely, the notions of debt and indebtedness also became part of slaves' economic lexicon since many acquired debts, whether seasonally or from year to year. Even the idea of interest and the practice of paying interest payments were not uncommon, as some planters charged their slaves interest on debts that went unpaid too long. Perhaps most remarkably, some slaves experienced the twin practices of bequeathing and inheriting property.

As a result of encountering these central elements of business practice while enslaved, many freed African Americans entered freedom more equipped to handle the obstacles and opportunities of the nineteenth-century capitalist marketplace than laypeople and scholars have traditionally thought.

SELECTED BIBLIOGRAPHY: John Campbell, "As 'A Kind of Freeman'?: Slaves' Market-Related Activities in the South Carolina Up County, 1800–1860," in Ira Berlin and Philip D. Morgan, eds., *Cultivation and Culture: Labor and the Shaping of Slave Life in the Americas* (Charlottesville: University Press of Virginia, 1993); Roderick A. McDonald, *The Economy and Material Culture of Slaves: Goods and Chattels on the Sugar Plantations of Jamaica and Louisiana* (Baton Rouge: Louisiana State University Press, 1993); Philip D. Morgan, "Work and Culture: The Task System and the World of Lowcountry Blacks, 1700 to 1880," *William and Mary Quarterly*, 3rd ser., 39 (1982); John T. Schlotterbeck, "The Internal Economy of Slavery in Rural Piedmont Virginia," in Ira Berlin and Philip D. Morgan, eds., *The Slaves' Economy: Independent Production by Slaves in the Americas* (London: Frank Cass, 1991), 170–181; Betty Woods, *Women's Work, Men's Work: The Informal Slave Economies of Lowcountry Georgia* (Athens: University of Georgia Press, 1995).

John Campbell

SMITH, STEPHEN (1797?–1873), Columbia and Philadelphia, lumber and coal merchant, real estate speculator, currency speculator, philanthropist.

While the $1.4 million estate of William Alexander Leidesdorff* (who passed for white; he died in 1848) made him the leading wealth holder of African American descent, Stephen Smith, called "Black Steve," had accumulated $500,000 in wealth by 1865. Yet the significance of his extensive business activities has been virtually obscured in the historical record despite Martin Delany's discussion of Smith's extensive business activities as a lumber merchant. In his 1852 book *The Condition, Elevation, Emigration and Destiny of the Colored People of the United States*, Delany wrote that in addition to his lumber and coal business and his real estate activities "[t]he principal active business attended by Mr. S. in person, is that of buying good negotiable and other paper."

The extensiveness of his wealth became a matter of historical record in 1986, with Juliet Walker's article "Racism, Slavery, Free Enterprise." Consequently, while Delany wrote that in the winter of 1849 Smith shipped "two million two hundred and fifty thousand feet of lumber" from Philadelphia to Baltimore," Walker used the R. G. Dun mercantile credit reports to corroborate the profits made by Stephen Smith in this enterprise. In 1850, Dun lists his wealth at $100,000. In addition, Smith owned $18,000 worth of stock in the Columbia Railroad and $9,000 worth of stock in the Columbia Bridge. Also wealthy black entrepreneur Stephen Smith included "note shaving," as one of his fundamental activities.

Stephen Smith was born a slave in Pennsylvania and at 20 years of age purchased his freedom from his owner, a lumber merchant. The extractive industries,* consequently, also proved to be an even greater source of wealth for slave-born Stephen Smith, who was not only a Pennsylvania lumber and coal merchant but also a bank founder and an investor in real estate, bank stock, and railroad stock. In 1850, the R. G. Dun mercantile credit records list his wealth at $100,000. Even before then, Smith was so successful in his lumber business and real estate speculation activities that he was appointed to sit on the board of the Columbia Bank in the 1830s. Moreover, it was reported that Smith "was the largest stock-holder of his day in the Columbia Bank; and, according to its rules, would have been president had it not been for his complexion. Being thus barred, he was given the privilege of naming the white man who became president in his stead."

Smith was too successful for a black man, however, especially in his real estate speculation activities, and was eventually driven out of his hometown of Columbia, where a race riot took place in 1834. At that time, whites tried to drive Smith and other blacks out of town in an effort to force them to sell their property below market value. Smith did not leave, and in 1835 the following letter was sent to him: "S. Smith:—You have again assembled yourself amongst the white people to bid up property, as you have been in the habit of doing for a number of years back. You must know that your presence is not agreeable, and the less you appear in the assembly of the whites the better it will be for your black hide."

Smith moved to Philadelphia in the late 1830s, expanded his lumber and coal yard, and continued speculation in real estate and also activities as a "note shaver." Smith also took on several partners, all of whom became wealthy, including William Whipper (1804–1876). Yet, interestingly, while Smith was exceedingly wealthy, it is only Whipper's wealth that has been noted. In 1870, Whipper was shown in the federal manuscript census with property valued at $107,000. Also, while Whipper's work on the Underground Railroad* has been emphasized, Smith was even more involved, since the railroad freight cars used to help slaves escape were owned by Smith.

Yet while both men were outspoken abolitionists, and Smith was an ordained minister of the African Methodist Episcopal (AME) Church, Whipper was active in the American Moral Reform Society and, after the Civil War, a cashier in the Philadelphia branch of the Freedman's Bank* from 1870 to 1874. The only other black cashier was in Washington, D.C. Both men were known for their philanthropy before and after the war. Smith was married, but the couple had no children.

SELECTED BIBLIOGRAPHY: Martin R. Delany, *The Condition, Elevation, Emigration and Destiny of the Colored People of the United States* (Philadelphia, 1852; reprint, New York: Arno Press, 1968); John N. Ingham and Lynne B. Feldman, *African-American Business Leaders: A Biographical Dictionary* (Westport, CT: Greenwood Press, 1994);

Juliet E. K. Walker, "Racism, Slavery, Free Enterprise: Black Entrepreneurship in the United States before the Civil War," *Business History Review* 60 (Autumn 1986).

Juliet E. K. Walker

SOCIAL CAPITAL, BLACK BUSINESS OWNERS. Social capital affects black business owners. *Capital*, in its broadest terms, refers to all productive means that make possible the accomplishment of societal or individual ends. In a more limited sense, as applied to economic/business development, capital needed for starting and operating an enterprise includes four basic forms: physical, financial, human, and social. Physical capital consists of natural resources, equipment, or other physical entities. Financial capital is the debt and equity financing available to business owners. Human capital comprises individual characteristics like general educational attainment and entrepreneurial training. Social capital is defined as the social resources available from group support networks that aid the entrepreneur in various ways. Such support networks can furnish an owner with an entire range of assistance, for example, entrepreneurial role models, investment funding, sources of labor or clientele, valuable business contacts, and advice.

Throughout American history, many ethnic group members with their origins in Europe, Asia, or Latin America have entered the United States with little financial capital and limited formal education. Instead, they have used social capital generated through coethnic support networks, their own intense efforts, and a propensity to save their earnings to found successful business enterprises. These, in turn, have helped create the economic foundations that lead to group assimilation into mainstream society as well as providing socioeconomic opportunities for later generations. In each case, the group has been the locus of entrepreneurial effort, a coordination of many individual efforts instead of work by solitary persons, in supplying the functions essential to business ownership.

American entrepreneurs whose ancestors come from Africa also have a long history of utilizing social capital for business development. From antebellum times, black owners have depended on family funds and ethnic community resources for investment financing. Personal savings have been accumulated, often through frugal living habits in which immediate gratifications are sacrificed, not only by the individual owner but by the entire family, and are thus a product of family financial behavior over a long period. Ethnic community resources have been tapped through such mechanisms as the rotating credit association, an informal club of trusted coethnics who make regular contributions to a fund the whole of which is given to each contributor in rotation. Black West Indian immigrants, in particular, have used this means to raise business investment funds.

But other African Americans have found more direct methods through social capital development to give financial support to their own entrepreneurial efforts. The first black-operated banks were created in the nineteenth century as depositories for dues collected from fraternal/lodge groups that themselves had sprung from black churches. The True Reformers Bank (Richmond, Virginia), the Mutual Aid and Banking Company (New Bern, North Carolina), and the Bank of Galilean Fisherman (Hampton, Virginia) all had their origins within the fraternal orders or lodges giving them their names. The first black-owned insurance companies* evolved during the same period, also from fraternal/lodge organizations observing the practice of collecting membership benefits for deceased members' families. The Southern Aid Society and North Carolina Mutual Life Insurance Company* are pioneering examples. Many of these early black banks and insurance companies made investments in other African American enterprises.

One of the first champions of black business development, Booker T. Washington,* recognized the critical importance of social capital. In 1900, he helped found the National Negro Business League (NNBL),* intended as a national-level support organization to encourage enterprise. He and other NNBL members understood that given the segregated economy of the era, African American entrepreneurs could not enjoy the development of markets in the larger society. Rather, they had to rely on ethnic solidarity as a major impetus to successful business operation, which required every person who joined the League to pledge their support for all black enterprises. The NNBL worked over the years organizing local leagues, while serving as a national center for the exchange of business advice and opportunities. In addition to the League, other networking professional/trade organizations were established, such as the National Negro Insurance Association, the National Association of Bankers, the National Negro Press Association, and (during the 1930s) the Colored Merchants Association.

In the early twentieth century, black churches continued their historic role in African American business development. Black churches have long been the best organized and stable entities in their communities for building a strong economic base. They have functioned as the center of economic self-help among their congregants, possessing the financial capital available for investment and the human capital of able leadership. For example, George Baker founded Father Divine's* Peace Mission Movement, which bought farms so it could produce food for its members. The movement established many personal services such as dry cleaners, laundries, and restaurants. Bishop C. M. (Daddy) Grace's United House of Prayer also capitalized small firms, established its own manufacturing and distribution network, and carved out a large market in household and personal hygiene products among black consumers. The Nation of Islam* has also carried on a tradition of African American economic development through entrepreneurial initiatives.

Professional training in business arrived late at black institutions of higher education. But by the 1940s, most black colleges had a business/economics department offering undergraduate and graduate programs. There was a determined effort to secure cooperation and exchange of ideas between the departments and practitioners. As invited instructional aides, entrepreneurs regularly spoke before classes on business topics. Arrangements were made for students to obtain experience in applied methods by working in local black-owned enterprises. Technical guidance was given to owners by trained specialists on the teaching staffs, promoting economic development locally. Departmental faculty also sponsored special projects and research studies involving area firms. A mutually beneficial interchange grew in places like Durham and Atlanta, where long-standing African American business communities linked with black colleges in networking activities.

Before the mid-twentieth century, the nation's segregated economy gave rise to the growth of black business districts in many metropolitan areas. In the South, cities enacted ordinances that had the effect of placing restrictions on African American business owners, not just where they could locate but what types of firms they were allowed to operate. Their activities were confined chiefly to providing convenience goods and personal services for a nearby black consumer/residential market. In the North, a similar process occurred even without laws specifying distinct separation of the races. As a result, black sheltered markets or "enclaves"* evolved in central cities across the nation where African American entrepreneurs served their local community clientele. These enclaves became incubators in which entrepreneurial role models and training in neighborhood enterprises helped new owners learn business skills. Ironically, integration beginning in the 1960s weakened many social capital-producing business enclaves and local support networks as firms followed population dispersal.

Since then, a desegregated economy has brought access to more locations and expanded markets within the larger society. African American business continues to grow, now recording over half a million firms nationwide. A clear majority are concentrated in traditional industries, particularly personal services and retail trade, but with considerable growth in other emerging industries like finance and real estate. Black owners increasingly display greater amounts of financial capital (income) and human capital (education), most prominent in the emerging industries. However, something has come along during recent years to displace historical forms of social capital for black entrepreneurs. Government programs at all levels have slowly assumed that function.

The civil rights struggles of the 1960s produced certain changes in American society, especially the creation of many government programs intended to help overcome perceived discrimination against racial and ethnic minority groups. In the business development field, some programs have focused on supplying financial capital to minority owners, others on giving technical/management assistance for enhancing human capital, and still others on establishing local, state, and national support networks for minority entrepreneurship growth. Under the mandate of equal opportunity, government policy has attempted over the past three decades to supplement or replace social capital in the private sector, resulting in African Americans and other minorities becoming more dependent on government-generated social capital. How effective public sector programs have performed is a matter for systematic research, but there is no doubt they are well established in the policy apparatus of federal and state governments.

Some evidence exists indicating that black business owners may have greater need for public sector social capital than other groups. According to recent data, a smaller percentage of African American entrepreneurs have close relatives who own an enterprise or are self-employed than Asian Americans, Hispanic Americans, or nonminorities. Fewer blacks have undergone training in a family firm. They do not rely on relatives or friends for business start-up loans to the same extent as Asians and less than the other groups as well. Black owners compare favorably with Hispanics and nonminorities in using family funds as a source of equity capital but are considerably behind Asians. Moreover, black owners are the least likely of all groups to be married, which indicates less access to business-supporting family resources. African American entrepreneurs appear more vulnerable, relatively speaking, without government assistance for social capital development.

However, public sector assistance may be less forthcoming in the years ahead due to legal and budgetary restrictions. For example, in *City of Richmond v. J. A. Croson Co.* (1989), the Supreme Court ruled that state/local "set-aside"* programs, making minority contractors eligible to receive certain percentages of procurement dollars, are unconstitutional unless they specifically identify past discrimination in government procurement practices as determined by strict judicial scrutiny. Application of this ruling has resulted in the elimination of some state and local programs. More recently, in *Adarand Constructors, Inc. v. Pena* (1995), the Court has determined that all federal programs using racial/ethnic criteria as a basis for decision making are also subject to strict judicial scrutiny. Thus, minority business development efforts at the federal level face possible elimination or reduction through court action.

Another important factor is the strong political movement to decrease large budgetary deficits and shrink government bureaucracy, which may force the public sector to curtail some programs generating social capital for minority owners. Some observers recognize the dependence of black business owners on government-generated social capital and the possible consequences if that assistance is diminished. They advocate a return to private sector leadership through the re-creation and strengthening of black enterprise support networks.

Many organizations have been launched recently to help achieve such a goal, for example, the National Black Business Council, Association of African American Women Business Owners, National Center for Neighborhood Enterprise,* National Black Chamber of Commerce,* and others. These voluntary groups are part of a rapidly expanding societywide (even global) network with greater capacity to develop African American owners. Its possibilities are enormous for providing extensive business advice, management and technical assistance, increased professional contacts, entrepreneur role models, alternative financial arrangements, and youth business training. Perhaps as this support network evolves, it will combine with any remaining public sector programs, together becoming the future source of social capital for black business owners.

SELECTED BIBLIOGRAPHY: John Sibley Butler, *Entrepreneurship and Self-Help among Black Americans: A Reconsideration of Race and Economics* (Albany: State University of New York Press, 1991); Frank A. Fratoe, "Social Capital of Black Business Owners," *Review of Black Political Economy* (Spring 1988); Ivan Light, *Ethnic Enterprise in America: Business and Welfare among Chinese, Japanese, and Blacks* (Berkeley: University of California Press, 1972); Joseph A. Pierce, *Negro Business and Business Education* (New York: Harper & Brothers Publishers, 1947); Franklin D. Wilson, "The Ecology of a Black Business District," *Review of Black Political Economy* (Summer 1975).

Frank A. Fratoe

SOUTH, BLACK BUSINESS, 1790–1880. Following the wave of emancipations in the Upper South during the 1780s and 1790s, and immigration of free people of color from the Caribbean during the 1790s and early nineteenth century, free blacks in growing numbers were able to establish businesses. In the Upper South, they usually worked as skilled artisans, managing shops as blacksmiths, carpenters, shoemakers, butchers, and barbers or running small enterprises as draymen, laundresses, or shopkeepers. Unable to secure loans (except from family or friends), with limited capital, and confronting hostile racial attitudes, the early businesses were generally small, one-person enterprises. In the Lower South, by the second decade of the nineteenth century, however, a few free people of color, virtually always persons of mixed ancestry and often assisted by white relatives, managed larger enterprises as builders, mechanics, tradesmen, grocers, restaurateurs, tailors, and merchants or as shoemakers, wheelwrights, millwrights, bakers, confectioners, and livery keepers. In proportion to the free black population, the number of businesses in the lower states was far greater than in the Upper South. And by the 1820s, in Charleston, Savannah, and New Orleans, black-owned businesses were scattered in various sections of the cities.

Rural business activities among free blacks expanded during the early decades of the nineteenth century. In the upper states, the enterprises remained small, one-person operations, much the same as in towns and cities. In the Lower South, free persons of color who owned large farms or plantations engaged in various business activities and occasionally ran mercantile stores. They also acquired increasing numbers of slaves to work as builders, brick makers, and mechanics. Some who were especially skilled became partners with whites. Alabama bridge builder Horace King, for example, was emancipated in 1829 by Georgia slave owner John Godwin, and the two later formed a construction company.

As unlikely as it might seem, there were a few slaves who actually ran businesses. Usually they did so with the acquiescence of their masters who either took a share of the earnings or permitted their slaves "quasi-freedom." But there were others who, like South Carolina millwright Anthony Weston,* though legally slaves, lived and acted as free persons. A leading mechanic who built and repaired rice mills for low-country planters, Weston owned extensive property and controlled a slave labor force of 20 workers (owned in his wife Maria's name). Most slave businesspeople, however, ran small shops as bakers or barbers or worked as market vendors, hostlers, or madams.

During the 1840s and 1850s, there was an expansion of black-owned businesses in the Upper South. Rarely assisted by whites, often emerging from slavery themselves or the children of slaves, free blacks in the region confronted many obstacles in establishing businesses, but the expanding economy, urban growth, improved transportation, and increasing demands for skilled artisans provided a congenial environment for blacks to enter business. They still usually worked as blacksmiths, builders, and barbers, but now a few were becoming small-scale manufacturers or managing larger retail businesses. Baltimore caterer Henry Jakes; Milton, North Carolina, cabinetmaker Thomas Day*; Nashville gardener Lewis Doxey; and St. Louis cooper John Meachum—these were among a small but growing number of prosperous entrepreneurs in the upper states.

During the same period in the Lower South, there was a continued growth in the black business sector. While New Orleans remained the center for free black entrepreneurs, with some individuals, including tailor Francois Lacroix, becoming as wealthy as upper-class whites, in other towns and cities blacks managed businesses as carpenters, contractors, builders, bricklayers, brick makers, tailors, grocers, and storekeepers. In Charleston, South Carolina, the building trades continued to be dominated by free persons of color, and one of the most popular hotels was owned by Eliza Seymour Lee, a free woman of color, while in Sumter County, William Ellison* provided a striking example of wealth expansion as the owner of a cotton gin manufacturing (and repair) company, a cotton plantation, and 63 slaves.

Virtually all of these enterprises, in both the Upper and Lower South, catered to a white clientele and were accepted because they fulfilled a particular need in a community. White customers frequently remarked about how valuable these businesses were to the community and how the owners were not only hardworking and industrious but trustworthy, faithful, and loyal to whites. These comments were largely true, since to challenge white racial mores would be to court economic disaster and invite white violence.

The Civil War and its aftermath created significant changes in the profile of black entrepreneurs. As with whites, many black-owned businesses were destroyed during the war, and the economic dislocations, currency problems, credit difficulties, and political unrest following the war made it difficult for formerly free people of color to sustain their enterprises during the late 1860s and 1870s. In the Lower South, a significant shift occurred following the war, with the infusion of former slaves into the business class. Whereas before the war the vast majority of businesspeople in the section were mulattoes, now a majority were listed in the census as black.

Postwar black businesspeople in the section controlled about one-third of the average wealth as before the war ($2,500 in 1870 compared with $7,000), and now a near-majority were illiterate (46 percent in 1870 compared with 18 percent in 1860). In the upper states, despite wartime destruction in Virginia, portions of Tennessee, and North Carolina, there was a significant rise in the number of black-owned businesses in the postwar period. Some antebellum businesspeople actually expanded their operations during the war, including Lexington furniture dealer Moses Spencer and Nashville hauler-coachman William Napier. Former slaves also entered the business field, usually with operations requiring small capitalization. And by 1880, there was also the beginnings of a shift, especially among the smaller businesses, to a black clientele, a shift that would become more apparent by the late nineteenth century.

SELECTED BIBLIOGRAPHY: Robert C. Kenzer, "The Black Businessman in the Postwar South: North Carolina, 1865–1880," *Business History Review* 63 (Spring 1989): 61–87; Loren Schweninger, "Black-Owned Businesses in the South, 1790–1880," *Business History Review* 63 (Spring 1989): 22–60; Juliet E. K. Walker, "Racism, Slavery, and Free Enterprise: Black Entrepreneurship in the United States before the Civil War," *Business History Review* 60 (Autumn 1986): 343–382.

Loren Schweninger

SOUTH, BLACK BUSINESS, 1860–1880. By the eve of the Civil War, despite severe legal and social impediments, southern blacks had established significant business roots that laid the foundation for the postwar era. The nature of the free antebellum black business community can be documented through the federal manuscript census. While the census does not confirm if a black craftsman, shopkeeper, tradesman, or service provider actually owned a business, it can be surmised that many southern blacks who owned real estate probably were conducting their own firm. Loren Schweninger has calculated that in 1860 there were more than 2,000 free black entrepreneur/landowners in the South.

The level of opportunity in business varied for free blacks in the Upper and the Lower South. Given the fact that there were 224,963 free blacks in the Upper South compared to only 36,955 in the Lower South, it is not surprising that in 1860 7 out of 10 black business/landowners were residents of the Upper South. Nevertheless, despite their smaller numbers, black businessmen and -women in the Lower South conducted firms in disproportionate percentages to their total population, and they tended to own more real estate than their counterparts in the Upper South. This was especially the case for shopkeepers and tradesmen* in the Lower South.

While black barbers have been highlighted as important members of the antebellum black business community, barbers only composed about 5 percent of all landowning black entrepreneurs. Carpenters, the largest group of blacks in business, outnumbered barbers by about three to one. Black seamstresses, largely women, who owned land almost equaled the number of black carpenters. Further, barbers were not the most affluent black entrepreneurs. This distinction was held by merchants, who on average owned real estate valued at almost $9,000, and tailors, whose average real estate value stood at more than $10,000.

The demographic composition of free blacks in the Upper and Lower South largely dictated the clientele of black entrepreneurs. Given the fact that there were few free blacks in the Lower South, the vast majority of the clients and patrons of black firms in that area had to be white. While in the Upper South there was a much larger potential for a black entrepreneur to have black customers, given the much larger free black population, what evidence exists also points to the critical role of white customers in the success of that area's black business community.

Two exceptional black businessmen on the eve of the Civil War included Thomas Day* of North Carolina and William Ellison* of South Carolina. Thomas Day, a cabinetmaker in the village of Milton, owned more than $4,000 in property in 1860. Day was considered one of the top furniture makers in North Carolina and even employed a white journeyman cabinetmaker. If the level of his skill marked Day's distinction, the scale of wealth led William Ellison to stand out. A resident of Sumter County, Ellison opened a cotton gin shop as early as 1817. His cotton gins were purchased as far away as Mississippi. Investing in land and slaves, by 1860 Ellison had accumulated nearly $70,000 in property.

While their numbers surely were much smaller than free blacks, there were slave entrepreneurs.* Indeed, a number of slaves gained their freedom by purchasing it from the earnings they gained from their firms. Many of these slave entrepreneurs were allowed by their masters to hire out their own time (*see* Slaves Hiring out Own Time). For example, Alfred Hargrave, a North Carolina slave trained as a blacksmith, during the late 1850s was hired out by his master to work for the Atlantic Coast Line Railroad company. Hargrave received permission from the president of the railroad to earn extra money shoeing horses during his lunchtime. After the Civil War, Hargrave became one of the most successful blacksmiths in Wilmington. Significantly, Hargrave's heirs, who kept his blacksmith shop open until 1938, proudly advertised on the wall outside of their shop that the firm had been in continuous operation since 1859, when as a slave their ancestor began practicing his craft with some independence.

While virtually nothing is known about black business in the South during the Civil War, after the conflict it is possible to gain a fairly accurate picture of the emerging black business community. The foremost source that aids in understanding these entrepreneurs in every part of the South from the largest cities to the smallest hamlets are the credit ratings published in *The Mercantile Agency Reference Book* between 1865 and 1880. These credit ratings generally noted if an entrepreneur was black by indicating ''col.'' after his or her name. When supplemented with the federal manuscript census and published censuses, these credit ratings reveal numerous characteristics of southern black entrepreneurs.

An analysis of the 626 black credit-rated firms controlled by men in two

Upper South states (Virginia and North Carolina) and three Lower South states (Alabama, Georgia, and Mississippi) show that rather than being clustered in any one location, these businesses were scattered over 175 counties at 242 different post office designations. There was a clear relation between the counties where black firms were established and where blacks lived. Indeed, more than four-fifths of black firms were located in counties whose share of the black population stood above the state average.

One might speculate that since black entrepreneurs located their firms in communities with a high concentration of blacks, few of their customers were white. However, one indication that whites may have frequented these firms comes from advertising. An examination of city and business directories for North Carolina and Virginia from this era reveals that black businessmen who advertised never denoted their race in order to not attract a clientele solely of their race. Of course, for most black and white customers this was an insignificant issue, as they probably knew all of the black businessmen in their communities, most of which contained only a few hundred inhabitants. However, even in the largest cities of these states, whose total population reached into the tens of thousands and where race would not have been well known, there seems to have been no effort by black firms to stress their race.

Since some blacks were the only businessmen conducting certain trades in communities, whites had no choice but to patronize them, especially if their prices were reasonable and the quality of their service was high. In addition, the size of some of the black businesses indicates that they probably were frequented by whites. For example, Samuel Harris, a mulatto general storekeeper in Williamsburg, Virginia—a community whose blacks composed only one third of the population—was one of the largest merchants in that community. Harris, who did a business of more than $50,000 a year, was so wealthy that he owned his own vessel that he used to ship goods. He was not only one of the wealthiest landowners in Williamsburg, but he also owned property in Newport News, Norfolk, and Richmond. Therefore, while it appears that most of the customers of blacks were black, given the racial composition of communities with these firms, whites may have composed a significant share of their customers.

There was a substantial degree of similarity between the types of firms conducted in the Upper and Lower South. In both areas, mercantile establishments (which included general stores, groceries, etc.) were the leading type of credit-rated firm (38.5 percent in the Upper South and 36.7 percent in the Lower South), and they were followed by the skilled trades/service sector, which included such establishments as blacksmiths and carpenters (25.1 percent in the Upper South and 35.3 percent in the Lower South). As far as structure, more than four out of five black firms in both the Upper and Lower South were simple proprietorships—that is, only one businessman's name was noted as the owner of the enterprise. Interestingly, only 10 of the 626 firms in the five states were composed of two men who appear to be related either by such designations as ''brothers'' or ''sons'' in their title or the fact that the two men on the title shared the same last name. Given the relatively limited resources of individual blacks, it is particularly surprising that there were so few firms with large numbers of partners.

Even more rare than multiple member firms were firms composed of black and white businessmen. There were only three of them. Lazarus Bibb, a mulatto general storekeeper in Louisa Courthouse, Virginia, was a partner of a General J. Sumner, who apparently was white. Perhaps Sumner felt it wise to work with Bibb in Louisa, a county in which more than 60 percent of the residents were black. Further, Bibb may have had a particularly large clientele, as he was also the postmaster of the community. The sole black-white firm in North Carolina, Henry Harper, James Ransom, & Co., carriage makers in Warrenton, was formed in 1867 when Harper, a white, joined in business with James Ransom, a black. Ransom had been a 17-year-old freedman working as a coach maker in Warren at the outbreak of the Civil War and, despite his youth, probably was one of the most qualified craftsmen in this community when he and Harper became partners. Ransom was so well respected in the community that he was elected to the county commission, the local chief governing body, and he and Harper stayed in business together for at least 10 years.

The only hint that there was even a single partnership between a black and a white in the Lower South is the case of a general store in the village of Darien, located in the Sea Island area of Georgia. As early as 1873 Jacob Adams, a black, had formed a partnership with Charles Rothchild, who was Jewish. Rothchild, who appears to have owned more than one mercantile firm in the Georgia Sea Islands, may have seen some benefit in forming a partnership with Adams in Darien, a community in which four-fifths of the inhabitants were black.

By far the most significant difference between black firms in the Lower and Upper South was their rate of success. Black firms in the Upper South demonstrated an amazing level of success during the late 1860s and throughout the 1870s as four out of five black firms in 1870 continued operating until 1875, and nearly half survived until 1880. By comparison, three out of five black firms in the Lower South remained in operation from 1870 to 1875 and about one-third from 1870 to 1880. The rate of success for black firms in the Upper South was quite comparable—and in some ways exceeded—to that of southern white merchants, a group considered exceptionally successful.

The disparity between the rates of success of Upper and Lower South black firms is largely explained by antebellum demographic factors. Before the Civil War a far higher share of blacks in the Upper South were free compared to the Lower South. The combined free black population of North Carolina and Virginia (88,505) far exceeded that of Alabama, Georgia, and Mississippi (6,963). As evidence of the head start of these Upper South businessmen, before 1870 nearly one-fourth of the postwar Upper South firms had already been created, compared to less than one-tenth of Lower South firms. While many of the black businessmen in North Carolina and Virginia during the immediate postwar years clearly had been freedmen before the war, in a fundamental sense they were still liberated by the war. Having survived through the antebellum years and the war, they now were able to conduct business under far better legal and economic terms than ever before and with a vastly enlarged black clientele.

Black businessmen in the Upper South also succeeded at a remarkable rate because many of them were able to carve out a share of the market in their communities before the Panic of 1873 and the subsequent depression. By contrast, those businessmen who began firms in 1874 and 1875 entered the business arena at the worst possible time. Not only did they have to compete against those blacks who already had been in business as many as 10 years, but the recent entrants did so at a time when it was very difficult to gain credit, a necessity for any businessman to succeed. As a result of these circumstances, the total number of firms in business in both the Upper and Lower South peaked in 1874 and thereafter for the following four or five years declined as the number of firms failing each year equaled or exceeded the number of firms being created.

One particular advantage early entrance into business gave antebellum freedmen was the head start in accumulating property and diversifying. Because so many more Upper than Lower South firms were created before 1870, the businessmen who conducted firms in the Upper South owned a higher median value of property ($500 versus $410). The impact of capital accumulation and diversification on business success is seen in the case of William S. Williams, a black businessman in the small town of Warrenton, North Carolina. Starting life as a slave, Williams apparently gained his freedom before the war, began working in the shoemaking trade, and earned enough money to buy his wife Jane out of bondage. After his emancipation, he learned to read and write. Beginning with a general store in Warrenton, he diversified into butchering, transportation, and eventually a livery firm and acquired tens of thousands of dollars in assets.

Another important aspect of the black business community suggested by the example of William S. Williams was the fact that he was described as a mulatto. In fact, 58.2 percent of the businessmen in the Upper South and 48.8 percent in the Lower South were enumerated in the manuscript census as mulattoes. Both of these percentages far exceeded the state averages for the black population of these states—especially so for the Lower South states. One clear reason why mulattoes would have composed such a disproportionate share of postwar businessmen must be tied to the fact that such a disproportionate share of freedmen before the war had been mulatto. Hence, many mulattoes had a head start in business (as well as accumulating capital and carving out market share) because they had a head start in emancipation.

If mulattoes were overrepresented in the ranks of black entrepreneurship, clearly women were underrepresented. Very few women, who largely were concentrated in the service sector of the economy, were credit rated. Nevertheless, black women did play roles in the running of a number of firms. In some cases, businesses were conducted jointly by spouses. For example, Mr. B. Taylor was listed as a new hotel keeper in Floryeville, Mississippi, in 1876, but his wife Maria actually owned the establishment. Often a husband's firm was completely taken over by his wife upon his death. When Butch Mathews of Pulaski, Georgia, died in 1878, his general store was taken over by his widow Jennie.

Besides working with their husbands in providing goods and services, one very important way in which women may have played an essential role in business relates to the issue of literacy. While the majority of southern black men who conducted firms were literate (74.1 percent in the Upper South and 60.9 percent in the Lower South), many of those businessmen who could not read had wives who could. For example, this was the case for two-thirds of the illiterate businessmen in North Carolina. The literacy of their wives would have been essential for ordering supplies, paying bills by mail, and keeping company records.

Finally, one of the most visible characteristics of black businessmen in both the Upper and Lower South was their involvement in politics. Some of these businessmen included the leading black political figures in these five states. For example, John A. Hyman, who served in North Carolina's 1868 state constitutional convention and who later was elected to the U.S House of Representatives, was a merchant in Warren County. Likewise, Benjamin Turner of Dallas County, Alabama, ran an omnibus line and store in Selma before being elected to the U.S. House of Representatives. Many other of these businessmen served in their state legislatures or in county and municipal governments.

While business success often was the stepping-stone to politics, there were practical economic advantages to involvement in politics, especially at the local level. For example, it was a tremendous asset to be a postmaster, a primary award for political activity at this time. This position not only augmented a storekeeper's income but also made his establishment a social center in the community that even whites in this era before free rural delivery would have to visit to receive their mail. For example, Willis P. Moore, a black postmaster in Jamesville in Martin County, North Carolina, in 1874 founded a very successful combination hotel, bar, and grocery enterprise that survived into the 1890s.

The success of some black businessmen could be entirely dependent on politics. This was most obviously the case for those entrepreneurs who sold liquor—a substantial minority of both Upper and Lower South black firms. For example, in North Carolina liquor licenses were largely distributed by popular-elected county and town commissions until 1877 when the Democrats in the state legislature passed a new law ending the local election of county and municipal officials. Now these officials would be appointed by the Democratic-controlled legislature. Nearly half of the black firms in the entire state dealing in liquor went out of business within two years of the passage of the new government act. For example, Charles Smith, a black businessman in the village of Danbury in Stokes County, had survived the depression of the mid-1870s but could not compete under the new law. Despite starting his liquor business in 1873 and amassing a significant stock, the year after the state law was passed, Smith went out of business.

What is most striking about black businessmen in the Upper and Lower South during the decade and a half following the Civil War is their similarity. Given vastly different geographies and economies, there were only minor differences between firms in these two areas, and these differences can largely be accounted for by differing antebellum factors.

SELECTED BIBLIOGRAPHY: R. G. Dun & Co., compilers, *The Mercantile Agency Reference Book (and Key) Containing Ratings on the Merchants, Manufacturers and Traders Generally throughout the United States and Canada* (New York: R. G. Dun and Company, 1865–1880); John Hope Franklin, *The Free Negro in North Carolina 1790–1860* (Chapel Hill: University of North Carolina Press, 1943); Michael P. Johnson and James L. Roark, *Black Masters: A Free Family of Color in the Old South* (New York: W. W. Norton & Company, 1984); Robert C. Kenzer, "The Black Businessman in the Postwar South: North Carolina, 1865–1880," *Business History Review* 63 (Spring 1989): 61–87; Loren Schweninger, *Black Property Owners in the South, 1790–1915* (Urbana: University of Illinois Press, 1990).

Robert C. Kenzer

SOUTH, BLACK BUSINESS, 1880–1930. African American communities in the late nineteenth and early twentieth centuries, especially in the South, were created by white prejudice and demands for segregation. This negative pressure was reinforced as well by a certain amount of fellow feeling among blacks—a desire for congregation—to live among themselves. Several results followed from this. Foremost, the period from 1880 to 1930 was the heyday of African American business in the South. It was there, in the seedbed of segregation and racism, that black business was able to reach its fullest potential. Yet black business also suffered many of the crippling disabilities that stunted and frustrated so much else in African American life.

For the first time, segregation and congregation concentrated the black population into separate communities in southern cities. These African American communities, or ghettos, grew until they reached a critical mass—a concentration of blacks large enough to support the creation and sustenance of their own separate black business district (BBD). The South, in this regard, was somewhat different from the North. In the latter area, black ghettos emerged in areas formerly occupied by white ethnics, who often continued to control the stores and businesses in these areas. In the South, however, African American residential areas tended to develop in largely virgin territory. Therefore, in some cities, there was no existing white business structure to be displaced there.

As the African American population grew and became relatively more prosperous at the turn of the century, these business areas became larger and better articulated. Yet the nature of racism in the South always inhibited this growth and prosperity. The same laws that segregated blacks also restricted the scope of their business activities and limited the capital available to them. Blacks were prevented by law or custom from engaging in business activities that would result in their competing with white business for white and sometimes even black customers. Therefore, the limited nature of black enterprise in the South was built into it by the same kinds of laws that restricted African American voting, retarded black education, and stunted the creation of a large and prosperous class of professionals. To ignore the impact of racism and discrimination upon the development of African American business is tantamount to blaming the victims for their own shortcomings.

Yet African American business in the South during these years did grow and prosper. It went through three distinct stages, each of which marked an important phase in the development of black business enterprise. There had always been a core of businesses in southern cities run by African Americans. In the antebellum period, and even until the 1880s, most of these serviced the white community. Most of these early black businesses were owned by mulattoes, who tended to identify with whites and also to avoid contact with the black masses. Made up of barbershops, tailors, caterers, drayage concerns, and other enterprises, black businesses provided services to the white community that whites would not or could not provide, and these black businesses generally did not service African Americans.

As Reconstruction in the South ended, and as new, harsher, and more restrictive racial codes began to emerge, a profound transformation began to take place in black business development. Whites began to compete against African Americans in many occupations that had formerly been reserved to blacks. The competitive position of whites was often aided by state or local laws that made it illegal for blacks to provide these services for whites. At the same time, as African Americans were being increasingly concentrated in their own separate ghettos, they had a need for their own stores and shops. Generally, whites were reluctant to locate stores in these new black areas. This opened up business opportunities for a cadre of new small black business owners who opened shops designed to serve the needs of African American customers. This was the start of the black business district, and this period, characterized by the creation of a large infrastructure of small shops, lasted from the early 1880s to the mid-1890s.

As these new BBDs opened up, they provided opportunity for a new group of business leaders. Many of them had either been born slaves themselves or were the children of slaves. They tended also to be darker-skinned and to be able to identify more closely with the concerns of the newly freed black masses who were flocking to southern cities during these years. This new service sector was characterized by a variegated group of enterprises, nearly all quite small, most undercapitalized, and many probably not well managed. The new African American businesses, typically, were small corner grocers, meat and fish markets, beauty parlors and barbershops (for blacks only), saloons, cheap restaurants, and other ''nickel and dime'' operations. A step up from these firms were a number of companies that achieved a high level of stability but were short of being anchor businesses—funeral parlors and taxi and hack operations.

Beginning in the mid-1890s, a new stage in the development of these BBDs began emerging. At this point the still-growing service sector spawned a series of anchor businesses, a few large-scale manufacturing enterprises, particularly in the field of hair and beauty culture, newspapers, insurance companies and banks, which typically had their origins in African American fraternal societies. These groups, such as the Colored Free Masons, Knights of Pythias, Odd Fellows, and others, grew rapidly in African American communities in the late nineteenth century. One source of their appeal was the death benefit and insurance provisions provided members. As capital accumulated in these ventures, it had a ripple effect in the African American business community.

The next step, characteristically, was to convert the somewhat informal death benefit and insurance provisions of these fraternal organizations into full-scale insurance enterprises, institutionally separate from the fraternal groups. This allowed a great expansion of the insurance services and coverage they could offer and also allowed them to sell insurance to large numbers of African Americans who were not lodge members. The result was that these new insurance companies operated with large cash surpluses during the first couple of decades of their operation, since few of the policyholders died during this time. These surpluses were at first deposited in white banks, but when these banks refused to grant loans to African Americans to buy homes and start businesses, the heads of these insurance firms, along with other African American business leaders, started their own banks and financial institutions, using the insurance policy surpluses as the financial base for their operations.

At about the same time, black newspaper publishing expanded not only to supply uplifting news of African American community activities, invariably ignored by the white press, but also to provide advertising space and support for the emerging black business enterprises. As the banks and insurance companies grew and prospered in the early twentieth century, they loaned money to the masses of African Americans to buy homes and start businesses. With this sort of ripple effect, large and relatively vibrant black business districts were nurtured during this time.

The final stage of this period was from 1915 to 1930 and witnessed the greater growth and articulation of the anchor businesses and the further development of the small service sector, funded with capital provided by the black banks. These banks also provided capital for working-class blacks to purchase homes, automobiles, and other consumer items. This, in turn, formed the basis for the building of separate black communities characterized by pride, relative independence, and cohesion. In addition, there was the emergence of a couple of important new trends. The first of these new developments had a lasting impact. This was the development of a series of new intercity black business networks that were knit together by a series of trade associations. The earliest, and most important, of these was the National Negro Business League (NNBL),* established by Booker T. Washington* in 1900. The NNBL, in turn, was the generator of a number of other black business and professional organizations: National Negro Bankers Association, National Negro Insurance Association, National Association of Funeral Directors, the National Negro Retail Merchants

Association, and the National Bar Association. These organizations did much to raise the level of articulation and sophistication of black business from the local to the regional and national levels.

The clearest example of this new level of organization and increased militancy came in a series of national campaigns during the 1920s. Organized by these trade associations, especially the Negro Retail Merchants group, they urged their African American cohorts to "Buy Black" and admonished them, "Don't Shop Where You Can't Work." In their advertisements for these campaigns, these organizations stressed the multiplier effect of black money spent in their own communities and emphasized the sense of race pride and cohesion that would result. The second element was more dramatic. This involved a number of attempts, some abortive, to create African American business empires to rival those established by whites. The most charismatic of these was by Herman Perry in Atlanta. Perry organized Standard Life Insurance in that city, which he used as the basis for creating a vertically integrated business empire that included a large number of service establishments, a bank, a real estate development company, and other firms. His venture ended in failure in the early 1920s, but similar attempts by North Carolina Mutual* in Durham, North Carolina, and by Arthur C. Gaston* in Birmingham, Alabama, were more successful and long-lived.

During this period, 1880–1930, it is important to recognize that black business, North or South, was something more than an economic enterprise. It was an integral part of the African American community. These were "ethnic" businesses, just like their counterparts in the Jewish, Italian, or Oriental communities. As such, they were far more important as community institutions than as simply factors in a market nexus. Indeed, during the years under discussion, African American businesses were at least as important as the church and various social organizations to their communities, if not more so. Black businesses were a fundamental part of a series of complex intersecting networks that served as a key to survival by poor people in the past. Small ethnic businesses were critically important, since they were often the only local sources of credit that sustained people they knew during the times they lacked cash.

Furthermore, these businesses and their owners were "eyes on the street." As such, they played a strategic social role in their communities in a variety of ways. Unlike middle-class African American professionals—teachers, lawyers, and ministers—these owners of smaller black service establishments were integral parts of the "inner" black community. Although these business owners most likely lived in a black middle-class residential area, with the professionals, their businesses were located in the heart of the ghetto, and they had constant and daily interaction with a "tough" element. Thus, the proprietors of these restaurants, barbershops, pool rooms, beauty parlors, and even funeral homes provided important meeting places that helped to define the very character of the black community.

These African American businesses thus functioned as important bridges between the two cultures of the black community—that of the middle-class black professional, on one hand, and of the young men of the streets and the countryside, on the other. As such, they could often serve as social monitors, who maintained a sense of stability, who helped determine and enforce community mores and values, and who provided a moral core to the community. They interacted continually with passersby, exchanged news and gossip, and provided an informal forum wherein the actions of community members could be discussed, evaluated, and, if necessary, censured.

In recent years, a number of students of the African American community have theorized that the exodus of black-owned businesses from the black ghetto and the flight of the African American middle class to the suburbs have been principal causes for the present-day pathology of crime and violence. Simply by being there, even if they did not create large fortunes, or employ massive numbers of blacks, African American businesses served an essential community role—and that was their most important function.

Another important role for these African American business leaders was to promote racial pride and to foster racial cooperation in a number of ways. Most of them also were advocates of the "self-help" ideology of Booker T. Washington,* an ideology that, at least on the surface, seemed to advocate accommodation to the emerging system of racial segregation and discrimination in the South. Race pride and acquiescence in racial discrimination were difficult concepts to balance, yet the success of African American businesses, and the black communities upon which they depended, rested squarely on just this compromise: African Americans had to create their own "world within a world," yet they could not appear too subservient, appear to acquiesce too much to white prejudice and racism.

One way for black business leaders to balance this was to became militant leaders in defending the black community from white aggressions. As community leaders, and as relatively conservative individuals, they seldom advocated drastic changes in the white world and its pattern of segregation, but they did take steps to protect their community. They took essentially defensive stances to defend their community from a variety of outside threats, even several instances where they helped repel mobs of whites who threatened to destroy lives, homes, and businesses in the black community.

The Great Depression sorely tested African American business in the South. Many black businesses, large and small, were destroyed by the depression, and black communities and BBDs barely survived these traumatic years. But during their glory years of the first third of the twentieth century, they stood as an impressive monument to African American ambition, talent, and hard work. Just a generation before, blacks had been freed from slavery. They were given no land, had no capital, and were without education or generally useful skills. Yet within a very short period, they had created their own communities, started their own small businesses, and ultimately expanded those to a series of anchor businesses and national trade associations. Never have a people with so little accomplished so much in such a short time.

SELECTED BIBLIOGRAPHY: John Sibley Butler, *Entrepreneurship and Self-Help among Black Americans: A Reconsideration of Race and Economics* (Albany: State University of New York Press, 1991); Abram Harris, *The Negro as Capitalist: A Study of Banking and Business among American Negroes* (Philadelphia: American Academy of Political and Social Science, 1936); Alexa Benson Henderson, "Herman E. Perry and Black Enterprise in Atlanta," *Business History Review* 61 (Summer 1987): 216–242; John N. Ingham and Lynne B. Feldman, *African-American Business Leaders: A Biographical Dictionary* (Westport, CT: Greenwood Press, 1994); Franklin Wilson, "The Ecology of a Black Business District," *Review of Black Political Economy* 5 (Summer 1975): 353–375.

John N. Ingham

SPAULDING, ASA TIMOTHY (1902–1990), North Carolina, actuary, business executive, civic leader.

Asa T. Spaulding, America's first African American actuary, was also president of the North Carolina Mutual Life Insurance Company* from 1959 to 1967. His uncle Dr. A. M. Moore (1863–1923) was a founder and president of the company, and his cousin C. C. Spaulding* (1874–1952) is generally considered the key figure in managing the firm in its early years and presiding over its legendary success.

Asa, a prodigy in mathematics, worked part-time at the Mutual while attending North Carolina College (North Carolina Central University). After graduating with high honors in 1923, he returned to Columbus County for a teaching stint at his one-room school. In 1924 he attended Howard University for one semester before returning to work for the Mutual until 1927. In 1930, he earned a B.S. in accounting at New York University and an M.S. in actuarial science from the University of Michigan in 1932.

In 1933, armed with his graduate degree in actuarial science, he returned to the North Carolina Mutual as a celebrated "Negro First"—the nation's first black actuary. His technical achievements held great value for the management of the Mutual as well as for other black insurance firms, whose operations had been hobbled by the absence of scientifically derived mortality tables for African Americans. Without his skills, surviving the Great Depression would have been even more difficult for the company. He was quickly rewarded, becoming an officer of the firm in 1935, a member of the board of directors in 1938, controller in 1945, and vice president in 1952 before assuming the presidency in 1959.

As a civic leader, Spaulding tried to steer a middle course in the tumultuous years of the civil rights movement. Before his retirement in 1967, he worked largely behind the scenes; after his retirement, he engaged in direct politics. He served on the Durham Human Relations Committee from 1957 to 1964 and was chairman of North Carolina's Advisory Committee to the Kerner Commission on Civil Rights in 1967. In 1968 he won election to the first of two terms as Durham County commissioner. In 1971 he ran unsuccessfully as a candidate for mayor of Durham. Among his many affiliations and honors, he served on the board of directors of the W. T. Grant Company and the board of trustees for Howard and Shaw Universities, and he received honorary doctoral degrees from numerous universities, including Shaw, Howard, Morgan State, Duke, and the University of North Carolina at Chapel Hill. He was married to Elna Bridgeforth; they had four children, Asa, Jr., Aaron Lowery, Patricia A. Spaulding Moore, and Kenneth Bridgeforth.

SELECTED BIBLIOGRAPHY: John N. Ingham and Lynne B. Feldman, *African-American Business Leaders: A Biographical Dictionary* (Westport, CT: Greenwood Press, 1994); William Jesse Kennedy, Jr., *The North Carolina Mutual Story: A Symbol of Progress, 1898–1970* (Durham: North Carolina Mutual Life Insurance Company, 1970); Walter B. Weare, *Black Business in the New South: A Social History of the North Carolina Mutual Life Insurance Company* (Urbana: University of Illinois Press, 1973).

Walter Weare

SPAULDING, CHARLES CLINTON (1874–1952), North Carolina, entrepreneur in insurance and banking industries, civic leader, politician, race relations advocate, philanthropist.

C. C. Spaulding, as he was known, traced his African Indian ancestry to a long line of free landowners residing in Columbus County, North Carolina, since the eighteenth century. In 1894, Spaulding left the family farm for Durham, North Carolina, where he finished high school and worked at a succession of "Negro jobs"—dishwasher, waiter, bellhop, and "office boy." In 1898 he became the manager of an all-black cooperative grocery store, where his success won him an administrative position in 1900 with the North Carolina Mutual and Provident Association (North Carolina Mutual Life).* As general manager of the North Carolina Mutual, Spaulding became a key figure, along with John Merrick and Dr. Aaron McDuffie Moore (Spaulding's uncle), in building the enterprise into the nation's largest black insurance company. Indeed, by the 1920s the company was heralded as "the world's largest Negro business"; Spaulding, Merrick, and Moore as the "Triumvirate"; and Durham as "capital of the black middle class."

In 1923, Spaulding succeeded Dr. Moore as president of the North Carolina Mutual. He held this position until his death and gained an international reputation as America's leading black businessman. He directed not only the Mutual but also an extended family of financial institutions, including Mechanics and Farmers Bank, Bankers Fire Insurance Company, and Mutual Savings and Loan Association. Out of such business leadership, Spaulding emerged as the patriarch of black Durham with social and political influence extending throughout the southern region and beyond. He directed or served on the boards of countless organizations and institutions; a small sample would include the National Negro Finance Corporation, National Negro Insurance Association, National Negro Business League,* Howard University, North Carolina College, Shaw University, Oxford Colored Orphanage, National Baptist Convention, Lincoln Hospital,

John F. Slater Fund, National Recovery Administration, Commission on Interracial Cooperation, Urban League, United Negro College Fund, Southern Education Foundation, Boy Scouts of America, and American Aid for Ethiopia.

As a respected business executive, he functioned as a New South broker for philanthropy and employment. A letter from him, like one from Booker T. Washington* a generation earlier, carried decisive influence. As a staunch Democrat, he regularly lobbied the state legislature on behalf of North Carolina College, and behind the scenes he conspired against Jim Crow, sometimes holding the white fear of integration as a hostage to ransom a greater share of public funding for black institutions. As chairman of the Durham Committee on Negro Affairs, he charted the passage between two eras of southern politics and race relations. Cloaked in the context of disavowing ''social equality,'' he provided cover for his more radical colleagues to engage in direct politics and reenfranchise black Durham 20 years ahead of comparable southern cities. As a neo-Washingtonian, he represented a generation of ''race men'' whose careers coincided with that of Jim Crow and who believed that political liberation would grow out of business success. His skillful absorption of the politics to his Left is perhaps a test case for what Booker T. Washington himself might have done. He spent his final years accepting honors and giving speeches, his pioneering in black business long behind him, and his transitional role in southern politics nearly completed. His first wife, Fannie Jones Spaulding, who died in 1919, was the mother of their four children: Charles Clinton, Jr., John, Booker, and Margaret. His second wife, Charlotte Garner Spaulding, survived until 1971.

SELECTED BIBLIOGRAPHY: William Jesse Kennedy, Jr., *The North Carolina Mutual Story: A Symbol of Progress, 1898–1970* (Durham: North Carolina Mutual Life Insurance Company, 1970); Walter B. Weare, *Black Business in the New South: A Social History of the North Carolina Mutual Life Insurance Company* (Urbana: University of Illinois Press, 1973); Walter B. Weare, ''Charles Clinton Spaulding: Middle-Class Leadership in the Age of Segregation,'' in John Hope Franklin and August Meier, eds., *Black Leaders of the Twentieth Century* (Urbana: University of Illinois Press, 1982), 167–190.

Walter Weare

SPORTS, ATHLETE ENTERPRISES AND ENTREPRENEURS. Within 50 years, since Jackie Robinson's entry into white professional sports (the first black to play in major league baseball, when he was hired by the Brooklyn Dodgers in 1947), black athletes have emerged as the highest-paid sports figures in the nation. Once exploited by greedy, unethical managers and agents who expropriated virtually all of their earnings, black sports stars now capitalize financially on their tremendous athletic abilities in two ways, endorsements and shrewd business investments. Also, since player unions limit agents to only 4 percent to 5 percent of contract deals, black athletes now retain most of their earnings. In addition, some are now seeking advice from black lawyers and financial advisers.

Even before the 1990s, then, the stereotype of the exploited black professional athlete was history. Indeed, the black sports superstars, along with their counterparts in the entertainment industry, now rank among the new black capitalists in the history of African American business. Moreover, with their earnings, black super sports stars, in their business enterprises, seldom contend with the problem of access to credit and capital for investments, which historically has limited black advancement in business. Consequently, the business activities of black sports stars represent a new development and expansion of enterprise in the history of black business.

Until Tiger Woods's phenomenal success in golf, which in the late 1990s was still considered an anomaly in the racist rarefied world of golf (only 2.7 percent of the 24.7 million golf players are black), the four major professional sports in which black athletes have earned substantial amounts in the post–civil rights era are boxing, basketball, baseball, and football. Prior to the civil rights era, boxing was the only professional sport in which blacks could participate with whites. Yet until black boxing promoter Don King,* few black boxers made substantial sums that they were able to keep. Now the purses for heavyweight champions run into the millions. And the revitalization of boxing in the post–civil rights era can be attributed to King, beginning with the Ali/Frazier fight he promoted as the "Rumble in the Jungle," in Zaire, Africa. Each fighter was guaranteed a $5 million purse out of an estimated $30 million. King has emerged as a millionaire through promotion of the sport, including his King Vision, a pay-per-view sports and entertainment network, which features his fighters. But still he has been controversial with his relationship with boxing superstar Mike Tyson, who has accused King of mismanagement of his purses from his fights that earned over $100 million and has sought a legal settlement to regain lost earnings.

In the pre–civil rights era, even the world's heavyweight champion Joe Louis (1914–1981), who made millions from his prize-winning fights, also ended his career virtually broke. Louis attempted several business ventures, primarily endorsements of products by companies that bought his name, but none earned much profit for him. Eventually, all of the Joe Louis brand-name companies failed, despite their market in primarily large black urban communities.

The Brown Bomber Baking Company, established in 1939, which in two years had expanded to become the "largest Negro-owned and operated commercial bakery in the country," with a substantial market in New York and New Jersey, failed. In the mid-1940s the Joe Louis Punch Company was established, which guaranteed Louis $50,000 a year for five years for the use of his name, but failed. In 1952 Louis endorsed the white-owned Joe Louis Distilling Company, a subsidiary of Kentucky's National Distillers, where he was also a board member, owned a small share in the corporation, and was required to travel and endorse the product, which was eventually discontinued. In 1954, Joe Louis, in partnership with black Chicago businesspeople, established the Joe Louis Milk Company, the only black-owned dairy company in the nation, where Louis was president. It failed. Even the Moulin Rouge hotel, the first Las Vegas establishment where blacks could gamble legally, and where Louis was also employed as the hotel's official host, even though he owned a 2 percent interest, also failed.

Despite substantial earnings for that era, during World War II, and contributing several substantial amounts to the army and navy relief funds, Louis was unable to meet his IRS (Internal Revenue Service) payments. In 1949, Louis accepted $150,000 from the alleged gangster-controlled Norris International Boxing Club, which set up Joe Louis Enterprise. Norris owned Louis and hence the heavyweight title, which Louis was forced to defend. In 1950, at the age of 36, he lost to Ezzard Charles; then after his defeat to Rocky Marciano in 1951, a knockout in the eighth round, Louis retired. He had lost only 3 of his 66 professional fights, the first to Germany's Max Schmeling in 1936, whom he subsequently defeated in 1938, with a knockout in the first two minutes of the first round.

Louis's defeat marked an ignominious end to his career in boxing, which was unprecedented in the history of the sport, then or now. At the same time, the professional world of sports was changing and with it the beginning of the end of the financial exploitation of black athletes as they entered new arenas in professional sports and began to establish a personal independence in their careers. This new independence was symbolized by heavyweight boxing great Muhammad Ali, who began his boxing career as Cassius Clay. Ali refused to compromise his Nation of Islam's* religious pacifist principles by refusing to serve in the Vietnam conflict after he was drafted. While he was stripped of his heavyweight crown, Ali's defiance symbolized the coming of age of black athletes in taking control of their careers both in and out of the ring.

In the instance of Jackie Robinson (1919–1972), his postplaying days were significant in two ways for black sports stars. In 1957 Robinson accepted a position as vice president in the Chock Full O'Nuts Corporation, which demonstrated the benefit to white Corporate America of hiring black sports figures in management positions. At the same time, Robinson also reflected the black capitalist initiatives of the civil rights era. He was one of the founders of the first black bank in Harlem, Freedom National Bank.

In the 1960s and 1970s, the numbers of blacks in professional sports increased. During this time, while they commanded only five- to six-figure salaries, their income was still substantially greater than the masses of black Americans. Even so, their business investments were limited. From the 1940s to the early 1960s, most professional black sports stars, as had Joe Louis, invested in night clubs, liquor stores, record shops, motels and restaurants, primarily family-run sole proprietorship enterprises. With the new economic opportunities made available, as a result of civil rights legislation, the business investments of black sports stars have expanded into more profitable areas, which in some cases provided expanded employment opportunities for other blacks.

While former Green Bay Packer Willis D. Davis never made more than $47,000 a year, while playing football in the 1960s, the University of Chicago MBA by the 1980s was a millionaire. Profitable real estate investments, his All-Pro Broadcasting Company, and his Willie Davis Distributing Company are some of the enterprises he established. In 1969, former professional football player Brady Keys, Jr., who had established his All-Pro Enterprises, Inc., became one of the first black franchise owners, with his purchase of both Burger King and KFC (Kentucky Fried Chicken) franchises. By 1990 Keys owned 11 KFC franchises and 12 Burger King franchises; those he sold to purchase a 52 percent ownership in a steel fabricating manufacturing company, which built M-1 tank transmission containers and jet engine containers. The partners subsequently sold the company, earning a 300 percent profit.

Basketball great Dave Bing also catapulted his career earnings in the manufacturing sector. In 1980 he established a steel processing and metal distribution plant in the auto supply industry. In 1996, his company, the Bing Group, had $129.5 million in sales, ranking eleventh on the *BE* (*Black Enterprise*) 100s. In the international trade of aluminum and other metals, with a growing American market, Demetrius Brown, a Chicagoan, who played basketball in Europe, established his Fuci Metals, USA, company in 1987. With sales of $75 million in 1996, Brown ranked twenty-fourth on the *BE* 100s. Also, former Chicago Bears great Gale Sayers's computer hardware and software company, with $72 million in sales ranked twenty-seventh on the *BE* 100s for 1997.

By the 1990s, unlike the early post–civil rights era, black sport superstars were commanding salaries in the tens of millions, with their incomes substantially enhanced by endorsements. Herschel Walker, a Heisman Trophy winner, endorsed McDonald's Big Macs and Adidas sneakers. Crest toothpaste and Converse basketball shoes were endorsed by Julius "Dr. J" Erving, whereas baseball legend Reggie Jackson endorsed Pentax cameras, Panasonic video equipment, and Nabisco cereals. Some sports stars became synonymous with the products they endorsed, such as former football great O.J. Simpson, the advertising symbol for Hertz Rent-a-Car until 1995, when he became persona non grata despite being found not guilty of the murder of his white wife and a white male acquaintance. The trial ended any hope for Simpson to rebuild his movie career. Several black sports stars developed film careers after their playing days, including Jim Brown and Fred Williamson. In the mid-1990s, basketball superstars Michael Jordan and Shaquille O'Neal have also capitalized on their celebrity by starring in feature films. In the 1990s, two of the leading black sports figures who have earned substantial amounts from their endorsements have been basketball superstar Michael Jordan of the Chicago Bulls and golf pro Tiger Woods. In 1992 Jordan made $16 million from his endorsements of several food products—McDonald's, Quaker Oats, Gatorade, General Mills Wheaties cereal, and Ball Park hot dogs. Three years later, he made $30 million from endorsements. In 1997, his salary from the Chicago Bulls of $36 million and endorsements brought Jordan's income for 1997 to around $78 million, giving him the distinction of being the highest-paid athlete in the world. Jordan's wealth in 1996 was estimated at over $200 million.

In 1996, Tiger Woods, at the age of 20, turned pro, with an almost immediate $60 million in contract endorsements. By 1997 Woods's contract endorsements had increased to $100 million. In 1997, Woods also created controversy by his insistence that he be recognized as Cablinasian, which was somewhat startling to African Americans. Some 90 percent of blacks in this nation can also point to varying degrees of European and Asian (Native American) in their ancestry but still consider themselves black.

More so than ever, black sports participation has become political, and it appears that because of money generated by black sport superstars, white Corporate America is more cautious of their racial policies regarding black athletes than in any other area of race relations. When Tiger Woods won the 1997 Masters Championship, which included the right to select the menu for the Champions Dinner, fellow golfer Fuzzy Zoeller, referring to Woods as "that little boy," made the comment that he hoped Tiger would not request fried chicken or collard greens. The racially derogatory comment, which in the pre–civil rights era would have been dismissed as inconsequential, created a national controversy. In the post–civil rights era of political correctness, Zoeller's remarks were wholly inappropriate.

While he apologized personally to Woods, Zoeller still lost a lucrative endorsement contract with K-Mart, a decision that doubtless reflected the bottom line more than corporate ethics.* Even though blacks are only 12.8 percent of the population, they comprise an important proportion of K-Mart's national consumer base. In an age of competitive discount merchandising stores, K-Mart could not risk the loss not only of their black customers but also of whites and other ethnic groups who found Zoeller's remarks offensive.

While Zoeller's endorsements might not have been considered important to K-Mart, the drawing power of black athletes is considerable. Yet rather than relying on endorsements alone, black athletes are also seeking ownership interest in the companies that manufacture the products they advertise and endorse. While earning $12 million in endorsements, basketball great Shaquille O'Neal, at age 23, incorporated himself. He owns his Shaq logo and a multimedia conglomerate and is also acquiring ownership interest in the companies that manufacture the products he endorses.

In 1997, Michael Jordan, who made millions for Nike and himself in endorsing the Air Jordan brand name, now has franchise ownership of the new signature Jordan brand, a subbrand of Nike, Inc., in addition to his apparel company and continued endorsement of his "Michael Jordan" cologne. Michael will head the Jordan division of Nike, and he did not have to put up any investment money. Nike needs Jordan. According to Salomon Brothers's analyst Brett Barakett, as reported in USA Today, "Nike's rapidly expanding U.S. footwear operation has begun to slow considerably from a 36% growth rate in fiscal year 1997 to an estimated 2%–3% in fiscal year 1998.'' In addition, Michael has other investments, including, according to *Fortune*, interest in the personal and hair care products manufacturing company Carsons, Inc., makers of ''Dark N' Lovely'' products. Its president and chief executive officer (CEO) Dr. Leroy Keith took the company public in 1996, with stocks now traded on the New York Stock Exchange.

From the late 1980s on, black superstar sports figures have become increasingly sophisticated in management of their financial affairs. Some have partnered in joint ventures with other black businessmen. In 1990, Earvin ''Magic'' Johnson of Magic Johnson Enterprises and *Black Enterprise* publisher Earl Graves* acquired a $60 million Pepsi-Cola franchise. In 1985, basketball superstar Julius ''Dr. J'' Erving partnered with millionaire entertainer Bill Cosby to acquire the Philadelphia Coca-Cola Bottling Company, for which they paid $75 million. In 1990 Erving also was in on the $125 million deal with black entrepreneur James Bruce Llewellyn* for a New York Cable TV purchase.

Beginning in the late 1980s, black sports stars have moved to become professional sports team owners. Former Detroit Lions football running back out of Oklahoma Billy Sims has interest in the Carolina Panthers. In 1993 former Globetrotter Mannie Jackson and a group of investors purchased the Harlem Globetrotters for $6 million. In 1994 Magic Johnson acquired a 5 percent interest for $10 million in the Los Angeles Lakers. Also in 1994, former basketball great Isaiah Thomas acquired 10 percent ownership in the $125 million National Basketball Association (NBA) expansion team, the Toronto Raptors. While he was also vice president and general manager, Thomas left the team in 1997.

Leading black businesspeople have also attempted to buy into ownership of professional sports teams. In 1989 Boston black businessman Bertram Lee and Chicago developer Peter Bynoe headed a group of black investors who negotiated a reported $65 million deal for the purchase of the Denver Nuggetts, an NBA team. Had the purchase succeeded, it would have marked the first time for blacks to own a major professional sports team. Both businessmen were millionaires. Bertram Lee headed a $26 million BML Associates, Inc., while also holding partnership interest in a $400 million Boston real estate venture. According to *Business Week*, Lee's millionaire status resulted from a $10,000 investment in a Boston TV station that was sold for $22 million, netting Lee more than $10 million. Bynoe, with his Harvard law degree, headed the group, according to *Black Enterprise*, that built the $120 million new White Sox Comiskey Park stadium. The Bynoe-Lee group of investors, however, had to borrow $30 million to finalize the deal. In 1991, however, Lee was ousted from the group because of a financial shortfall, and by 1992, the deal had fallen through.

Black businesspeople also have been successful in purchasing part interest in major professional sports teams. Hair product manufacturers Comer Cottrell,* Pro-Line CEO, bought into the Texas Rangers baseball team, and Edward Gardner,* Soft Sheen founder, has ownership interest in the Bulls. Deron Cherry owns interest in the Jacksonville Jaguars. The black construction giant Herman

J. Russell,* through his membership in the Omni Group, had interest in the National Hockey League (NHL) team the Atlanta Flames before its sale. The Omni Group also owns the 17,000-seat sports convention center and the Atlanta Hawks. (Russell's ownership was $1.8 million of the $12 million package.) In 1999 businessman/entertainer Bill Cosby purchased interest in the New Jersey Jets.

By the end of the twentieth century, African American sports superstars were in control of their careers and their profit-making business investments. While their earnings enhance the phenomenon of the superrich black American, their enterprises and influence have yet to impact on the continuing expansion of the black underclass. While black athletes have yet to reach billionaire status, and their philanthropic giving is important, funding six- and-seven figure sports camps and recreational centers cannot have the impact of the foundations established by leading white capitalists, whose corporate giving in the tens of millions fund education, social services, and technical advancement.

At the same time, the tradition of giving by black sport superstars is less than 20 years in the making, since it has been less than 20 years that black athletes have profited from their phenomenal athletic ability. Moreover, black sport superstars, who number less than 50, if that many, despite their accumulated capital, cannot fund the economic advancement of the African American population, which numbered 37 million in 1990. Yet while sports in America have become more politicized, it appears that many black sport superstars are reluctant to use their prestige to challenge new issues of race in America that have emerged in the closing decade of the twentieth century.

Superstar black athletes have revitalized the sports world, but is the issue of race the basis for the criticism that black athletes are increasingly encountering in their demand for larger and larger salaries, thus driving up ticket prices? The overall earnings of black athletes, however, are limited when compared to the overall total amount made by franchise holders, whose incomes have also increased substantially not only from ticket sales but even more from TV and cable coverage, advertising, and the merchandising of team sports apparel. Franchise owners are not in business to break even, much less to lose money. They have to show some profits, as do advertisers of sports events, who have increased their product sales substantially through TV advertisements of sports events.

Moreover, professional sports must be recognized as entertainment. Michael Jordan, with his phenomenal drives to the hoop, gliding through the air between several opponents, then jamming the basketball, has thrilled crowds in every NBA arena from coast to coast. His spectacular clutch play and three-point shots during the last moments of a game justify the cost of a high-price ticket to see one of the greatest players in the history of the game.

With his salary, Jordan is an exception. For the most part, the salaries earned by superstar sports figures, for the amount of work they do, is comparatively minimal, when compared with the earnings of superstar movie entertainers, such as actors Bruce Willis, Arnold Schwarzenegger, Kevin Kostner, and Mel Reynolds. Their salaries, from $12 million to $20 million or more for just one movie, amount to more than the salaries of most of the leading black athletes, who must play an entire season for annual average salaries of $2 million to $7 million. Basketball players play 82 games a season, whereas football players play only 16 games a season, and professional baseball players have a 162-game season.

Consequently, in today's world of sports, issues of class and race are perhaps more apparent than in any other arena of American life. Black athletes, with their spectacular athletic abilities, are the new gladiators. The fans who crowd the stadiums, however, paying ticket prices that average $25 to $30 a game to as much as $200 to $400 for court-side seats, with sky boxes running in the six figures, however, are primarily white. Sports announcers have labeled them the "wine and cheese" crowd, many who see the games with tickets purchased by corporations and who sit in the stands with their pagers and cell phones, conducting business. Consequently, while the average fan buys the products endorsed by these leading sports stars, they are unable to afford the tickets to see the games in person.

Still, most spectacular in black business history in the post–civil rights era, then, was the rise of the black athlete businessman. Indeed, leading black athletes have acquired individual personal wealth and endorsement contracts that generally exceed that of the gross receipts of most of the businesses listed on the *B.E.* Industrial Service 100. While the nation's largest black business, TLC Beatrice International had sales of $344 million in 1987, in 1998, the personal wealth of Michael Jordan was estimated at $500 million.

Paradoxically, in 1997, the Chicago Bull's basketball great Michael Jordan, who ranked first among the nation's athletes in product endorsements, was said to have generated $10 billion in the American economy, according to *Fortune*. The magazine estimated that Jordan's Nike product line was worth $5.2 billion for the company, while his other endorsements have earned those companies $408 million in addition to $3.1 billion in sales of NBA-licensed sports products. Also, sales of Jordan's sports videos amounted to $80 million, while his movie *Space Jam*, earned $230 million at the box office and $209 million in video sales. Also, Jordan's agent sold his company for $100 million, half of which was the result of the "Jordan effect." Yet, even before the end of 1998, the successes of black athletes in product endorsement was changing. While basketball star center Shaquille O'Neal of the Los Angeles Lakers has made $28 million annually in endorsements for Taco Bell and Pepsi, he ended his $15 million five-year endorsement contract with Reebok Corporation. Also, Reebok dropped 50 of its 70 NBA players-endorsers, claiming a 12.2 percent drop in sales in early 1998.

Moreover, in the late twentieth century, the only black man who controlled a major sports industry was the boxing promoter Don King.* He not only revitalized the sport, but his promotion made millionaires of black boxers, including heavyweight champions Evander Holyfield, worth $65 million, and

Mike Tyson, who in six fights promoted by King made $140 million. King's wealth has been reported at the minimum of $100 million, while his boxers earn at least a $100 million annually. Through his King Media Enterprises, he has both national and international business holdings, including a crawfish boating fleet in the Caribbean and sugar cane plantations in the Philippines. In 1998, he purchased the bankrupt black newspaper the *Cleveland Call & Post*, which was founded in 1927, for $760,000.

In addition, despite a trail of legal challenges from murder to fraud and embezzlement, Don King has emerged not only as a powerful shrewd businessman but also as an important philanthropist. He has made substantial contributions to civil rights and black women's organizations, including the United Negro College Fund and the National Council of Negro Women. Also, in 1997, the Southern Christian Leadership Conference (SCLC) honored Don King with its Drum Major for Justice award for economic empowerment, and he also received the National Association for the Advancement of Colored People's (NAACP)s President Award.

Moreover, in the post-civil rights era, an increasing number of black athletes have used their celebrity not only to create wealth for themselves in developing multimillion-dollar enterprises separate and apart from the sports world. Former pro-basketball player Dave Bing's participation in the automobile industry as a manufacturer (steel processing and stamping and full seat assembly), has led his company to succeed as the fifth largest black business in the nation, as a base to build multimillion dollar enterprises. Consequently, generating employment for blacks and revitalizing the economy of black business communities have propelled the development of enterprises developed by leading black athletes. Yet, while Bing's company generated sales of $183 million in 1997, compared to the $10 billion generated in the American economy by Michael Jordan, Bing's company provides employment for almost 600 people, including a substantial number of blacks.

Also, unlike the "Jordan effect," the enterprises of Magic Johnson will play an integral role in furthering the economies of those same communities. The former basketball great NBA All-Star Magic Johnson has established several joint venture enterprises in pursuing these goals. In 1995, he entered a 50–50 partnership with his Johnson Development Group and Sony Theatres, a division of Sony Retail Entertainment, to establish a circuit of Magic Johnson multiplex theaters to be developed nationwide in urban and suburban minority communities. Since the June 1995 opening, it has consistently ranked among the top five grossing theaters in the country. In 1998, Baldwin Hills, California, the location of his first theater, stores, and restaurants in the theater's area reported a 25 percent to 50 percent increase in sales when compared to 1994. Also in 1995, Johnson entered a 50–50 joint venture with Starbucks Coffee company.

Moreover, in Los Angeles, basketball great Magic Johnson along with superstar entertainer Janet Jackson and former Motown president Jheryl Busby purchased controlling interest in the Los Angeles Founders National Bank for

$2.5 million. The bank, with five branches in the Los Angeles area, was established in 1991. In 1998 it had assets of $100 million. Unfortunately, Johnson's Fox-TV talk show, "The Magic Hour," lasted only nine weeks. While Magic Johnson has successfully capitalized on his human capital skills, a charismatic personality, and shrewd entrepreneurial acumen in the development of his business enterprises through joint ventures,* still, aptitude in entertainment is a requisite human capital skill for success in the talk-show television industry.

Significantly, as with many black sport stars, Magic Johnson is also known for his philanthropy, including his Magic Johnson Foundation (MJF). Its purpose is to raise money to fund HIV and AIDS organizations specializing in education, prevention, and care geared toward young people for which he was awarded a United Nations (UN) citation as a UN "Messenger of Peace." On the other hand, some black athletes have been criticized for their failure to take a stand on human rights issues. Michael Jordan has been criticized for his failure to comment on charges that Nike exploits its overseas workers. According to *Jet*, Jordan said, "I want to go to Southeast Asia to see the Nike plants for myself," explaining that once he retires from basketball that he "will take a bigger stand in social and political things." Jordan retired from professional basketball in January 1999 and immediately launched an educational program, the "Jordan Fundamentals." Funded at $5 million, the program will donate $1 million in grants of $2,500 to teachers at underprivileged schools. Jordan indicated that the funds will come from profits earned by him from the sale of his Nike Jordan brand productline.

Sports in America is big business. Its impact on American life and culture, ultimately, extends far beyond the playing field. Still, with the money generated in this sector of the nation's business, the salaries of black superstar athletes represent only the tip end of a pyramid of wealth generated by others in the sports industry who have capitalized on their phenomenal athletic abilities. Yet in the sports pyramid of wealth, built on advertising and sports apparel, few black advertising agencies or sports apparel manufacturers have profited.

Has there been advancement for the black athlete? At one time blacks only aspired to be coaches and managers, as much to give to the game as to dispel the racism that exists, predicated on the myth that while blacks could play the game, they lacked the intellectual ability to coach and manage. In the twenty-first century, hopefully, this stereotype will disappear, as did stereotypes that existed prior to Robinson's entry in professional baseball in 1947, that blacks were not as athletically competent as whites to play professional sports.

Then there was also the myth that in racist America whites would not pay to see blacks play professional sports. The post–civil rights era generation of white Americans, however, do not share this prejudice for blacks in baseball, basketball, and football. Whether blacks will enjoy this reception by hockey fans is another story. In the late twentieth century, hockey and swimming are two major sports that remain white.

Yet there have been advances in aspirations by blacks in the sports industry by those who play the game and those who support the athletes. Black lawyers and financial advisers can now aspire to be agents, whereas black businessmen can now buy interest in sports team franchises. The social costs paid by black youth who aspire to careers in sports, and the human capital loss to the nation, however, are incalculable in many ways. Too many black youth are trading off time needed for building excellence in academics, which could guarantee admission to college, to concentrate on developing superb athletic skills in the hope of a career in professional sports, which can open doors to only a few hundred out of millions who aspire.

In many ways, then, the incomplete civil rights era did make a difference in the sports arena on the financial side for black athletes, while also encouraging expansion in participation of black business people in the sports industry as team owners and sporting good suppliers and black professionals as members of the Black Entertainment and Sports Lawyers Association (BESLA), founded in 1979 and the Association of Black Sporting Goods Professionals (ABSGP) founded in 1990.

SELECTED BIBLIOGRAPHY: Arthur Ashe, Jr., *A Hard Road to Glory: A History of the African-American Athlete*, 3 vols. (New York: Warner Books, 1988); "Black America and Tiger's Dilemma," *Ebony*, July 1997; Black Entertainment and Sports Lawyers Association, web site available from http://www.besla.org; *Fortune*, August 4, 1997, June 22, 1998; Stanley O. Gaines, Jr., "O.J. Simpson, Mark Fuhrman, and the Moral 'Low Ground' of Ethnic/Race Relations in the United States," *Black Scholar* 25, 4 (Fall 1995); John N. Ingham and Lynne B. Feldman, *African-American Business Leaders: A Biographical Dictionary* (Westport, CT: Greenwood Press, 1994); *Jet*, April 22, 1991; Richard E. Lapchick, ed., *Sports in America: Equal Opportunity or Business as Usual* (Thousand Oaks, CA: Sage Publications, 1996); Bill Meyers, "Jordan, Inc.," *USA Today*, September 9, 1997; "The NBA Scores a First in the Front Office," *Business Week*, July 1989; Johnnie L. Roberts, "A Touch of Magic," *Newsweek*, June 15, 1998; Kenneth L. Shropshire, *In Black and White: Race and Sports in America* (New York: New York University Press, 1996); Eric L. Smith, "Catch the Flying Tiger," *Black Enterprise* (September 1997); "Sports," *Jet*, April 10, 1998; *Sports Illustrated*, July 1989; Jerry Thomas, "'Teflon' Don: The Trials of Boxing Promoter Don King," *Emerge* (August 1998); Juliet E. K. Walker, *The History of Black Business in America: Capitalism, Race Entrepreneurship* (New York: Macmillan/Prentice Hall International, 1998).

Jeffrey E. Walker

STOCK MARKET LISTINGS (Black-Controlled Publicly Traded Companies). As of 1998, only 12 black businesses were publicly listed on the various national stock exchanges: the New York Stock Exchange (NYSE); the American Stock Exchange (AMEX); and the Over-the-Counter (OTC) Market. Unlike the NYSE, "the Big Board," and AMEX, the OTC is not an exchange. It is a computerized telecommunications network linking broker-dealers for transactions in securities not listed on the exchanges. The OTC operates through NASDAQ ((National Association of Securities Dealers Automatic Quotations). While NASDAQ trades primarily in stock issued by small or new companies, shares in large companies, such as Microsoft, MCI, Northwest Airlines, and Dell Computers, are also sold through NASDAQ, with annual sales comparable in volume to the NYSE. There are also regional stock exchanges in the United States, and shares in American companies are also sold in foreign stock exchanges.

Usually, $500,000 is expended to set up an IPO (initial public offering), an equity-financing process to raise capital. There are other requirements, including minimums in net income, net tangible assets, and shareholders. James A. Anderson of *Black Enterprise* notes that NASDAQ requires a minimum $400,000 income, $4 million in assets, and 400 shareholders; Amex requires $4 million in stockholder's equity and a pretax income of $750,000; while the NYSE requires $40 million in net tangible assets and $2.5 million in pretax income and a minimum of 500 shareholders. Beginning in 1996, however, with SCOR (Small Corporate Offering Registration), which was set up by the Securities and Exchange Commission (SEC), for companies with less than $3 million in assets and less than 500 shareholders, outside capital can be raised without going public and costs only some $20,000.

A total of 16 African American owned and controlled companies have been publicly traded. In 1969, the Baltimore-based Parks Sausage went public on NASDAQ, with an IPO of $1.5 million. In 1970, the Chicago-based Johnson Products became the first black company to be listed on AMEX with a $6.5 million IPO. Also, Johnson was listed on NASDAQ. As of 1993, however, Johnson Products was no longer a black company. George Johnson* founded his black hair care products manufacturing company in 1954. Throughout the 1960s, Johnson Products had 80 percent of the market in black hair products. With increasing competition from other leading manufacturers of black hair care products, white as well as black, Johnson's market share declined. In 1989, he lost control of the company in a divorce settlement, which left his former wife with control of about 60 percent of the total shares. In 1993, majority interest in Johnson Products was sold to the white-owned IVAX Corporation, manufacturers of the black cosmetic and skin care line Flori Roberts.

While no longer a publicly traded company since 1998, in 1991 BET (Black Entertainment Television) was the third black-owned company to be traded publicly (with an IPO that raised $72.3 million) on the "Big Board," the NYSE. Also BET's IPO included up to 100,000 shares of previously restricted Class A common, which in sales could generate from $1.5 to $1.6 million. Some two years earlier, however, Reginald Lewis,* the first black to gain control of a billion-dollar company, had attempted to take TLC Beatrice International public in 1989 on the New York Stock Exchange, with an initial public offering of $180 million. While he viewed his failure as the "IPO Glass Ceiling," the SEC requires that before an IPO a company would have to show at least two years of increased earnings. Lewis purchased Beatrice International in 1987, and in the restructuring of the company, there were some losses, whereas BET, founded in 1980, by 1991 had shown sustained growth two years before its IPO.

In 1992, Granite Broadcasting, founded in 1988 by W. Don Cornwell, also went public, with a $24 million IPO on NASDAQ. The Phoenix-based Envirotest Systems Corporation, founded in 1990 and headed by Chester Davenport, also went public on NASDAQ in 1992. By 1994, their stock had increased from $16 to $27 a share. By 1995 there were 11 publicly traded black firms. In 1993, Theodore A. Adams, president and chief executive officer (CEO), took his Pyrocap company public on AMEX but in early 1996 stopped trading, which was resumed in 1997 on NASDAQ. Pyrocap International manufactures nontoxic biodegradable chemicals for fire suppression and waste water treatment. In 1996, the Savannah, Georgia–based Carson, Inc., which manufactures "Dark & Lovely" products, made its IPO on the New York Stock Exchange. Net sales of $38.7 million were reported for the six months ending September 1996. The company was acquired for $96 million by an investor group headed by Leroy Keith, formerly president of Morehouse College. Carson, Inc., is also listed on the Johannesburg Stock Exchange in South Africa.

The several other black-controlled publicly listed companies include three in the health industry: American Shared Hospital Services (AMS/AMEX), United American Health Care (UAH/NYSE), which provides comprehensive consulting services to managed cared organizations, and Caraco Pharmaceutical Labs, Ltd (CARA/NASDAQ/OTC), a company that develops, manufactures, and markets generic drugs for ethical and over-the-counter markets. In addition to Carson and Pyrocap International, there are two other black publicly controlled companies in the manufacturing industry. Ault, Inc. (AULT/NASDAQ), manufactures external power supplies, transformers, and battery charges. BAOA, Inc. (Black Americans of Achievement) (BAOA/NASDAQ), began with manufacturing a board game. The company expanded to produce PC and CD-Rom products and to provide telecommunication and financial services.

There are also two black-owned and controlled publicly listed companies that provide construction and engineering services. Myriad International (MRAD/NASDAQ) is a building systems company for multiple residential, public, and private buildings. In 1998, Advanced Engineering Design, which provides information technologies and engineering services, was qualified by the Securities and Exchange Commission as a publicly traded company. There are also two black-controlled financial institutions that are publicly traded, Carver Federal Savings (CNY/AMEX) and Broadway Financial.

Public sale of shares provides capital for sustained growth, development, and expansion of the corporation. Still, less than 0.3 percent of all American business corporations are publicly traded, that is, have shares in their companies sold on the national, regional, or foreign stock exchanges. Most large black businesses are family owned and have been built from the ground up. Also, there is a national community pride in large black businesses, especially those whose financial success can be attributed to a black consumer market. In two ways, then, many black business owners are afraid that with the public sale of shares not only will they lose the confidence of black consumers, but they will also lose ownership control and management of the enterprises they founded.

Interestingly, of the 12 black companies with shares publicly traded on the stock exchanges, only one, Carson, Inc., has a predominantly black customer base. Increasingly, as black-owned businesses expand in developing enterprises in the nation's new growth industries in computers and telecommunications, expansion and development will require an equity-financing process to raise capital, and more black companies will go public. Moreover, there is racial pride when a black majority-held company is listed on one of the various stock exchanges. The oldest stock exchange in the nation is the New York Stock Exchange (NYSE) where trading in shares of companies took place in the United States for the first time in 1792.

SELECTED BIBLIOGRAPHY: "African American Index of Publicly Traded Companies," December 1998, available from http://www.mbnglobal.com/african amricanindex.htm; "African American Publicly Traded Companies," June 1998, available from http://www.goodmoney.com/aframer.htm; James A. Anderson, "Taking Your Company Public," *Black Enterprise* (June 1997); *Forbes*, August 4, 1997; Reginald F. Lewis and Blair S. Walker, *Why Should White Guys Have All the Fun? How Reginald Lewis Created a Billion-Dollar Business Empire* (New York: John Wiley & Sons, 1995); Rhonda Reynolds, "Knowing the S.C.O.R.," *Black Enterprise* (June 1995); Juliet E. K. Walker, *The History of Black Business in America: Capitalism, Race, Entrepreneurship* (New York: Macmillan/Prentice Hall International, 1998).

Juliet E. K. Walker

SULLIVAN, LEON (1922–), Philadelphia, PA, minister, business promoter, antiapartheid activist.

During the 1950s and 1960s, the majority of America's civil rights organizations and leaders focused most of their attention on social problems in the southern United States, seeking to remove laws and practices that resulted in economic, political, and other forms of discrimination against African Americans. A key objective was to remove the barriers that prevented blacks having fair and reasonable access to parks, playgrounds, museums, railroad stations, concerts, hotels, housing, restaurants, theaters, taxicabs, buses, schools, and yes, the ballot box. America's news media spotlighted and amplified the discrimination that occurred in the South and only occasionally reminded readers, listeners, and viewers that restrictive housing covenants and other strategies were being used during this same period in the North to prevent African Americans from gaining economic advancement in employment so that they could improve their living standard. Leon H. Sullivan was one individual who recognized that economic position was basic to African Americans participating fully in the American dream, and in some respects, he can be credited with helping to expand the civil rights movement to include the North and in beating the drum to eradicate economic discrimination.

Sullivan was born in Charleston, West Virginia. He grew up in a poor neighborhood, graduated from the racially segregated Garnet High School, and received a basketball and football scholarship to West Virginia State College in

1939. Later in his career, Sullivan repeatedly would remember the event that charted the path that his lifework would follow. One day when he was 12, he tried to purchase a cola soft drink in a drugstore on Capitol Street. The proprietor refused to sell him the drink, saying, "Stand on your feet, boy. You can't sit here." Although taunted and denounced, the incident toughened the resolve of the young man from the small house on the dirt alley to improve the quality not only of his own life but also of others who faced similar discrimination. The steeling of Sullivan had begun and never would cease.

Fascinated with moral, ethical, and religious philosophy, Sullivan worked part-time as a minister during his college years. His charismatic oratory caught the attention of Reverend Adam Clayton Powell during a visit to West Virginia. Powell convinced Sullivan to attend the Union Theological Seminary in New York, where he also served as Powell's assistant minister at the Abyssinian Baptist Church. It was in 1950, after witnessing the end of World War II and observing how returning black troops and their families still were being denied full participation in the American dream, that Sullivan responded to a "call with a call"—that is, an invitation to take over the Zion Baptist Church in Philadelphia and a more personal crusade to secure economic, social, and political freedom for African Americans.

Sullivan wasted no time answering his callings. Under his leadership, Zion Baptist's congregation grew from 600 to more than 4,000 in just a decade. Moreover, he preached both a celestial gospel and a gospel of economic hope and prosperity for African Americans. Perhaps overshadowing Sullivan's success in the pulpit, however, was his extraordinary performance in the economic empowerment arena. The centerpiece of his strategy was Opportunities Industrialization Centers (OIC) of America, Inc., which he founded in 1964 and which continues to promote employment and career training on the eve of the twenty-first century. Sullivan's OIC spread across America and became a symbol for using knowledge and skills to break down economic barriers. OIC's mission mirrored the perspective of the 12-year-old boy who had been discriminated against at the drugstore in Charleston 30 years earlier—economic liberation is a necessary twin to achieve mental liberation in America.

With its basic philosophy—"Helping people to help themselves"—OIC grew into a national network of skills training centers serving the poor and unemployed in cities, counties, and rural communities throughout the nation. From Connecticut to California, OIC emerged as a premier agent for economic empowerment through employment training and alternative school programs. Men, women, and young adults participated in a vast lineup of programs that provided job training skills (offering instruction and other educational activities based on local marketplace needs, expectations, and indicators); job development (counseling and matching trainees with job openings); support services (arranging day care, health care, transportation of housing assistance to program participants); special programs (identifying and servicing the needs of ex-offenders, ex-drug abusers, people with language limitations, and others). Evidence of OIC's success is that during the first three decades of its operation it had served more than 1.9 million trainees, not only improving the quality of their lives but also benefiting the national economy because of the estimated $100 billion in taxes paid and unemployment/welfare payments saved.

Encouraged by the success of OIC at home, Sullivan decided to take the organization international. Twenty years before the end of apartheid in South Africa, he began promoting equal opportunity in that country, helping to pave the way for an end to segregationist policies, much as he had in America in the early 1960s. What came to be known as "The Sullivan Principles" provided one means of effecting change. Developed in 1977 by Sullivan, who at the time was a member of the board of directors of General Motors, the Principles established a set of guidelines that American multinational corporations were expected to follow in order to provide a system of equal rights and opportunities for all workers in their respective companies. Immediately, 12 large U.S. companies announced in the *Washington Post* their adoption of the Sullivan Principles. By 1985, the Principles had been signed by an estimated 100 U.S. corporations doing business in South Africa. Major elements of the Principles called for: nonsegregation of the races in all eating, comfort, and work facilities; equal and fair employment practices for all employees; equal pay for all employees doing equal or comparable work for the same period of time; initiation of and development of training programs that will prepare blacks and other nonwhites for supervisory, administrative, clerical, and technical jobs; increasing the number of blacks and other nonwhites in management and supervisory positions; and improving the quality of employees' lives outside the work environment in such areas as housing, schooling, and health facilities.

In the late 1990s, Sullivan continued his campaign for economic empowerment both within the United States and throughout the world, involving American companies, institutions, and individuals in education, health, and economic development programs in Africa and South America. In October 1996, he signed a formal cooperation agreement between UNESCO (United Nations Educational, Scientific, and Cultural Organization) and three organizations Sullivan founded—the International Foundation for Education and Self-Help, the African-American Summit, and Opportunities Industrialization Centers International (OICI). The agreement called for this partnership to work together in Africa and the United States in building a culture of peace through education, science, culture, and communication. As an example, the organizations will participate in UNESCO's Culture of Peace Programme in Africa by helping to provide education and training to demobilized soldiers and training local nongovernment organizations in the management and development of self-help programs. Further evidence of OIC's success was witnessed in July 1997 when, to mark the twentieth anniversary of the Sullivan Principles, Sullivan spearheaded a four-day summit in South Africa to develop initiatives among Africans and African Americans for economic empowerment.

During a speech at a recognition luncheon in Phoenix in the summer of 1996,

Sullivan summed up the key elements of his philosophy. "I'm not an academician, I'm a preacher," he said. "I don't believe in milk and honey in Heaven but in ham and eggs on Earth. I found that Blacks without jobs would have to stay at the back of the bus." Throughout his career, jobs and employment training and economic empowerment remained the light he chose to follow.

SELECTED BIBLIOGRAPHY: C. Eric Lincoln and Lawrence H. Mamiya, *The Black Church and the African American Experience* (Durham, NC: Duke University Press, 1990); "Negro on G.M. Board Ready for Challenge," *New York Times*, January 9, 1975; Leon H. Sullivan, *Build, Brother, Build* (Philadelphia: Macrae Smith, 1969); Andrew Young, *An Easy Burden: The Civil Rights Movement and the Transformation of America* (New York: HarperCollins, 1996); www.oicinternational.org.index.html

William E. Berry

SUPREME LIFE INSURANCE COMPANY. The Chicago-based Supreme Life Insurance Company, which incorporated in 1919 as the Liberty Life Insurance Company, historically represented a pillar of northern African American business development. Liberty Life's growth appeared intrinsically linked to the growth of black Chicago during the World War I "Great Migration." As southern black migrants streamed into the Windy City, local African American insurance professionals, who had worked for white-owned companies, decided to establish their own firms to cater to a burgeoning black consumer market. Frank L. Gillespie, Liberty Life's first president, had previously managed the white-owned Royal Life Insurance Company's black South Side district office. During the company's early years, Liberty Life, which operated under Illinois law as a legal reserve (stock-financed) company, focused upon serving black Chicago's middle and upper classes.

In 1929, Liberty Life, along with the black-owned Northeastern Life Insurance Company of Newark, New Jersey, and the Supreme Life and Casualty Company of Columbus, Ohio, merged their operations, creating the Supreme Liberty Life Insurance Company of Chicago. Harry H. Pace,* the former president of the Northeastern Life Insurance Company, assumed the presidency of the newly formed company. Pace, who possessed a multifaceted business background, including a stint in the embryonic black recording industry, proved to be an able chief executive. Similar to other leading African American insurers, Supreme Life, over the years, expanded its sphere of influence by taking over the operations of smaller, distressed black insurance companies. These acquisitions included the Carver Mutual Insurance Company of Detroit, Michigan, in 1949; the Friendship and Diamond Mutual Insurance Companies of Detroit, Michigan, in 1958; the Dunbar Life Insurance Company of Cleveland, Ohio, in 1959; the Federal Life Insurance Company of Washington, D.C., in 1960; and the Domestic Life Insurance Company of Louisville, Kentucky, in 1961.

By the 1960s, Supreme Life and its black cohorts faced increasing competition for African American policyholders from white insurers. Ironically, white insurance companies, which had historically discriminated against black consumers, actively sought to profit from African Americans' socioeconomic gains during this period. Supreme Life responded to this situation by entering into 1965 merger negotiations with its South Side Chicago neighbor, the Chicago Metropolitan Mutual Assurance Company.* Although both sides agreed with this maneuver in principle, this strategy ultimately failed because of an Illinois law that forbade the merger of a stock corporation (Supreme Life) and a mutual corporation (Chicago Metropolitan).

The failure of merger negotiations with Chicago Metropolitan and increased white competition subsequently had a profoundly negative impact upon Supreme Life's operations. Beginning in the early 1980s, the authoritative *Best's Insurance Reports* rated the company NA-7, or "below minimum standards." Despite the formidable presence of John H. Johnson* as Supreme Life's chairman of the board, in 1991, Supreme Life ceded its operations to the white-owned United Insurance Company of America.

SELECTED BIBLIOGRAPHY: *Best's Insurance Reports. Life-Health* (Oldwick, NJ: A. M. Best Co., annual, 1969–1993); *Best Insurance Reports. Life-Health–United States* (Oldwick, NJ: A. M. Best Co., annual, 1994–1998); Robert C. Puth, *Supreme Life: The History of a Negro Life Insurance Company* (New York: Arno Press, 1976); Merah S. Stuart, *An Economic Detour: A History of Insurance in the Lives of American Negroes* (1940; reprint, College Park, MD: McGrath, 1969).

Robert E. Weems, Jr.

SUTTON, PERCY ELLIS (1920–), New York City, entrepreneur, politician.

Born near San Antonio, Texas, Percy Sutton came from a family of educators, his father a high school principal and his mother a schoolteacher. Sutton's father, S. J., also had investments in real estate and a variety of other businesses in San Antonio. Percy's higher education included attendance at three all-black schools: Prairie View College, Hampton Institute, and Tuskegee Institute. During World War II, Sutton became the first black air intelligence officer assigned overseas, where he worked with a British intelligence unit. After the war, Sutton pursued a career in law, graduating from Brooklyn Law School in spite of having to work two jobs to pay his tuition.

In the 1950s, Sutton became active in politics in Harlem. He was finally elected state assemblyman in 1964, after a decade of losing campaigns. A few years later he became Manhattan borough president. In 1977, he made a well-publicized, if unsuccessful, campaign for mayor of New York City, losing to Ed Koch. When New York elected its first black mayor, David Dinkins, in 1989, Dinkins credited Percy Sutton with having paved the way for his victory, both as a personal mentor and as a pioneering minority candidate. After his mayoral campaign, the balance of Sutton's activities shifted from politics to business.

In 1971, Sutton and other investors had acquired the *Amsterdam News* of Harlem for $2 million. In 1975 Sutton had sold his 37 percent stake in the paper, owing to the perceived conflict of interest his ownership had with his political activities. In the same year, however, Sutton founded a company called

Inner City Broadcasting, which acquired the New York station WLIB-AM for $2 million. This station had limited growth potential, so Inner City purchased another New York station, WBLS-FM, for $1.35 million. Under Sutton's direction, WBLS changed its format to appeal to white listeners, making it New York's top-rated radio station in the early 1980s. The profits from WBLS helped Sutton expand Inner City's holdings, which came to include stations in San Francisco, Detroit, Los Angeles, and San Antonio. Inner City also remained committed to WLIB-AM in New York, which became influential in city politics by adopting a black-oriented talk radio format.

In 1983, Inner City formed a new black-owned company, Queens Inner Unity Cable Systems, which entered negotiations for a cable television franchise that would cover one-third of Queens, a market equal in size to Boston. After experiencing difficulty raising the needed funds, Queens Inner Unity entered a partnership with Cox Broadcasting, which provided sufficient capital to launch the franchise. By the 1980s, Sutton's personal wealth had grown to over $100 million, which gave him the financial clout to invest in a wide variety of businesses. In 1980, for instance, Sutton had acquired the historic but bankrupt Apollo Theatre in Harlem. He invested as much as $25 million into the theater in an attempt to restore its landmark status in the entertainment world. Sutton also became active abroad, investing in a record company and other trading ventures in Nigeria and other African and Asian countries through a firm called Percy Sutton International.

In 1990, Percy's son Pierre (called Pepe) took over as chairman of Inner City Broadcasting. He had already served as president of Percy Sutton International. Percy has continued to be active in the cause of civil rights, as a board member of the lobbying organization TransAfrica and Jesse Jackson's Operation PUSH (People United to Save Humanity). Sutton has never strayed far from his early experiences as a freedom rider and civil rights activist in the 1960s. In the late 1980s, he argued that for blacks to achieve full equality they could not afford to "be mild and meek and accepting the status quo. . . . [Y]ou have to agitate, demonstrate, sit in and vote aggressively."

SELECTED BIBLIOGRAPHY: Laura Landro, "New York's Percy Sutton Leaves Politics for Media World, and Vows to Make It Big," *Wall Street Journal*, December 22, 1981; Alfred Edmond, Jr., "It's Showtime," *Black Enterprise* (April 1989); John N. Ingham and Lynne B. Feldman, *African-American Business Leaders: A Biographical Dictionary* (Westport, CT: Greenwood Press, 1994).

Peter Botticelli

"SWEET AUBURN" AVENUE, ATLANTA, GEORGIA. From around 1910 until the 1960s, Auburn Avenue reigned as a mecca for African American entrepreneurship and financial activity. Dubbed "Sweet Auburn" by John Wesley Dobbs,* maternal grandfather of former Atlanta mayor Maynard Jackson, the area was alive and vibrant from early morning until late at night. In its heyday, budding small businesses, thriving financial enterprises, African American–owned buildings and institutions, civic and social activity, and lively entertainment were all to be found on Sweet Auburn.

Racial tension and segregationist policies in Atlanta were responsible for Auburn Avenue's development. Barred from many residential areas and public facilities, African Americans in Atlanta, like in other cities, were forced to create their own self-contained, self-sufficient community. In 1890 only 52 of Atlanta's 28,098 African American residents lived on Auburn Avenue. Wesley C. Redding, a black bank teller and former slave, broke the color barrier by becoming the first resident of color on Auburn east of Jackson when he bought a house there in 1884; but as the nineteenth century drew to an end, more and more blacks moved into the area.

In 1891, Redding, Alonzo Herndon,* and Richard R. Wright* established the Atlanta Loan and Trust Company on Auburn. Carrie Steele Logan, also a former slave, opened the Carrie Steele Logan Orphanage for Black Children on Auburn Avenue in 1892. In 1896, Moses Amos, the state's first African American pharmacist, and several local black doctors opened the Gate City Drug Store, Atlanta's first pharmacy for blacks. By 1900, 10 African American businesses and 2 African American professionals were located on Auburn including a laundry, bicycle repair shop, catering business, the Gate City Drug Store, Floyd Crumbly's Grocery, and the office of Dr. Thomas Slater. Then, fueled by racial tension, rumors, and politically inspired false newspaper reports, the riot of 1906 forced other African American businesses from the Central Business District (CBD) to relocate on Auburn Avenue. One year after the riot, 64 businesses and 7 professionals were located there. By the 1930s Auburn had become a unique black business center with 121 businesses and 39 black professionals who established offices on the avenue.

Of the many African American businessmen and -women who helped establish Auburn Avenue's fame and reputation, much is known of Alonzo Herndon, a former slave and successful barber and businessman. In addition to his founding role in the Atlanta Loan and Trust Company, Herndon also built the Atlanta Life Insurance Company* from the Atlanta Mutual Insurance Association. But it was perhaps the bold vision and leadership of Herman E. Perry that had profound and widespread influence on future business development. Perry, a native Texan, arrived in Atlanta in 1908 and by 1922 had established a conglomerate of businesses that included Standard Life Insurance (1913), the Service Company (1917), and Citizens Trust Bank (1921). The Service Company operated as a holding company for 11 subsidiaries with such diverse operations as an engineering and construction company, a pharmacy, printing company, laundry, and realty company. At their zenith, these companies were reportedly worth $11 million and employed 2,500.

Perry's business empire crumbled in 1925 when, ridden with debt, his firms were dissolved. He left Atlanta for St. Louis, where he died in 1928, leaving behind a legacy from which other Atlanta businesses emerged. Lorimer D. Milton, Clayton R. Yates, and Jesse B. Blayton, inspired by Perry's vision, reorganized Citizens Trust Bank. Milton and Yates had been two of the original clerks at Citizens Trust, and Blayton, the city's first African American certified public accountant, was a former auditor for Perry's businesses. Milton became president of Citizens Trust, and Yates and Blayton served as chairman of the board and auditor, respectively. Under their leadership, Citizens Trust became the first African American member bank of the Federal Reserve.

Yates and Milton bought out the Service Pharmacies and renamed it Yates and Milton Pharmacies, which they developed into a chain of four African American drugstores. Blayton established the Brown Boy Bottling Company, the first African American soft-drink firm, and later purchased WERD, the first African American–owned radio station in America. He also established Mid-Way Television Institute, which provided training in television and radio mechanics, and established the Blayton Business School, an offshoot from his position as a professor in the School of Business and Economics at Atlanta University. The three men also formed the BLMIYA Corporation (named after the principals), which served as a holding company for several of their businesses, including the Brown Boy companies and the Top Hat Night Club, a popular entertainment spot in the 1930s and 1940s. The *Atlanta Daily World*, founded by W. A. Scott in 1928, also grew out of Perry's defunct enterprises. All of these businesses were located on Auburn Avenue or on the surrounding streets adjacent to the Sweet Auburn district, including Cornelius King & Son Realty, which opened in 1921.

Real estate was among the earliest industries to thrive on Auburn Avenue. The Rucker Building erected at Piedmont and Auburn by Henry A. Rucker in 1904 was the first African American–owned building in the area, but in 1912 the six-story Odd Fellows Building became the tallest black-owned and built office building in the country. Under the leadership of Ben Davis, the Odd Fellows fraternal organization persuaded thousands of African American men to contribute to the building fund, and the $350,000 cost for the tower and annex was paid in cash. The tower housed the Atlanta State Saving Bank, the state's first chartered African American banking institution, and the prestigious Roof Garden ballroom, where a myriad of dances and social functions took place during the second and third decades of the century. In the building's annex were a haberdashery, Chandler's Sportmans Smokehouse, Mings Chinese Restaurant in the 1920s, and Charles Prothro's tailoring business, which operated for 50 years, from 1932 until 1982. Dr. Shaw, the city's first African American optometrist, was located next door.

A number of other real estate companies were founded on Auburn Avenue. Walter "Chief" Aiken and W. J. Faulkner established the Aiken and Faulkner Construction Company in 1922, and Aiken became the sole owner in 1939. Wendell T. Cunningham and Peyton A. Allen, an attorney, operated a real estate business in 1933, and Cunningham acquired more property than any African American before or since has managed to accumulate, 167 parcels throughout the city. Ora T. Bell and Jesse E. Arnold opened Bell and Arnold Realty. Bell later formed his own company and built an office building and hotel on Auburn Avenue.

The entertainment and hospitality business was another of Auburn Avenue's thriving industries. Excluded from downtown night clubs and theaters, African American entrepreneurs created an entertainment enclave for blacks (and whites) that was centered on Sweet Auburn. Street musicians and traveling and vaudevillelike shows were a part of the avenue's early entertainment scene. These events were housed in or sponsored by churches at such venues as the Peoples Tabernacle, a meeting house and auditorium owned by Bishop Henry McNeal Turner, and later at the Royal Theater, part of the Odd Fellows Auditorium. "Ma" Sutton's Restaurant, opened in 1918 by Mrs. Scottie B. Sutton, was once the most popular eating and meeting place on Auburn Avenue. It operated in the community for 32 years. Several hotels were established on Auburn Avenue to provide accommodations for blacks in the segregated city. The 35-room James Hotel opened in 1927; and in 1937, the Savoy Hotel, owned by Mrs. C. M. Pearson, opened to great fanfare, the first business on Auburn with a neon sign.

In 1949 "Mama" Carrie Cunningham, a pioneer businesswoman, reopened the Top Hat Club under the name of the Royal Peacock. She had taken over the Royal Hotel a year earlier, and it quickly became the inn of choice of many black entertainers of the era. The peacock motif was painted on the floor, ceiling, and walls of the Royal Peacock in striking reflection of Mama Carrie's colorful personality. With its carpeted dance floor surrounded by enough booths and tables to accommodate 350 persons, the club was the favorite stopping place for out-of-town celebrities. B. B. Beamon, a successful entertainment promoter during this time, utilized his railroad job to travel and provide access to out-of-town contacts. He was responsible for bringing many of the big-name entertainers like Cab Calloway, Duke Ellington, Billie Holiday, and Nat King Cole to the Royal Peacock and other Sweet Auburn establishments.

Other businesses that were a part of the Auburn Avenue scene were newspapers, hair care, and funeral homes. H. A. Hagler started the *People's Advocate* in 1891; Benjamin Davis, secretary of the Georgia Odd Fellows, edited the *Atlanta Independent* from 1904 until 1928 when Scott founded the *Daily World.* The Silver Moon Barber Shop opened in the 1920s. The Poro Beauty School, started by Ella Ramsey Martin, opened in 1920; and Louise W. Hollowell operated the Apex Hair Company and Beauty School from 1937 until 1942. She later started the Modelle Beauty Shop on Auburn. Charles and Allen Cox started the Cox Brothers Funeral Home in 1900, along with their mother Emily. The business moved to Auburn Avenue in 1910 and was joined by the Haugabrooks Funeral Home, founded by Geneva Haugabrooks in 1929.

If segregation was responsible for Sweet Auburn's development, its decline can be, in part, attributed to integration and urban renewal including the construction of the I-75/85 interstate expressway. Only a few of the original successful businesses remain today. The financial institutions Atlanta Life, Citizens Trust, and Mutual Federal Savings and Loan Association (1925) continue to operate and grow. The *Atlanta Daily World* is now published by founder C. A. Scott's great-niece, Alexis Scott Reeves; her cousin Portia Scott is managing editor; Nina King Anderson runs the realty company her grandfather started; Geneva Haugabrooks's great-great nephew, Marcus Wimby, took over operation of the Haugabrooks Funeral Home in 1994; the Cox Funeral Home still operates but without family involvement.

Having attained the status of a street of power, pride, and influence in the 1920s and 1930s, Auburn Avenue managed to survive the stock market crash and Great Depression as black entrepreneurs, some of whom lost their jobs at majority firms, came to start businesses that catered to the black community. These businesses flourished in the period between 1930 and 1960, but unlike the black business districts in Durham, North Carolina, and Tulsa, Oklahoma, "Sweet Auburn" was never accorded the title of Black Wall Street.* But in 1957 *Fortune* hailed Auburn Avenue as "the Richest Negro Street in the World." As the twentieth century winds to an end, the future of Sweet Auburn is far more uncertain than its illustrious past. Attempts to revitalize the area in light of the 1996 Centennial Olympics were more fanfare than fruitful. Still, the area stands as a legacy to future generations of aspiring entrepreneurs—a shining example of what the African American community can accomplish through hard work, dedication, and mutual support in spite of adverse circumstances.

SELECTED BIBLIOGRAPHY: William B. Calloway, *Sweet Auburn Business History* (Atlanta: Central Atlanta Progress, 1988); Alexa B. Henderson and Eugene Walker, *Sweet Auburn: The Thriving Hub of Black Atlanta* (Washington, DC: U.S. Department of Interior, National Parks Service, 1983); Clarissa Myrick and Dan Moore, eds., *Sweet Auburn Street of Pride* (Atlanta: Collections of Life and Heritage, 1988).

Lydia A. McKinley-Floyd and Juliet D. Blackburn-Beamon

T

TAXICAB ENTERPRISES. With the beginning of the automobile age in the early twentieth century, the most successful area of transportation enterprise for blacks in both northern and southern cities was in the taxicab industry. Within seven years after Ford put his Model-T on the road in 1908, this area of enterprise was known as the jitney taxicab businesses (*jitney* was the term used for a nickel). It developed in the age of Jim Crow, a response not only to segregated transportation but also to the geographical expansion of the industrial city, which prevented blacks from walking to places of employment outside of the increasingly concentrated urban ghettos. Moreover, as the urban black ghettos expanded, a quick means of transportation was needed for special trips to church, shopping, medical facilities, and social events within the black communities.

Since most blacks could not afford a car, and with limited funds could not pay the amount charged by white taxi drivers, who often refused to accept them as passengers, "jitney" taxis met their need for inner-city transportation. Moreover, those blacks who could afford to buy a car often used them as independent cabs, as a means to increase their income. In New York, William H. Peters and Samuel Hamilton started both a taxicab and car rental company in 1916 with "two Packard automobiles, one for rental business and one taxi cab." By 1930 it was reported that the company, which owned 250 specially built taxicabs and employed some 750 people, was worth almost a half million dollars investment.

In the South, the need for private automobile transportation was even more crucial. While blacks in the North had access to public transportation, this was not always the case in the South. Moreover, after the Civil War, the residential patterns of blacks in southern cities changed. During the age of slavery, blacks lived dispersed in southern cities. As these urban places expanded after the Civil War, first with the settlement of freedmen on the fringes of southern cities, concentrated black communities developed. Also, as Jim Crow housing restrictions developed in southern cities, often blacks were contained in limited residential areas of these cities. Moreover, as inner-city public transportation developed in southern cities, these municipalities often refused to build trolley lines or extend bus routes to black communities. The jitney cab, consequently, met the needs of black workers, who frequently had to travel some distance to get to their places of employment in white communities or business districts.

The jitney taxi, consequently, opened a new opportunity for blacks, which proved quite profitable for these enterprises until the 1960s. In Texas, Hobart T. Taylor, Sr.,* invested family money from the sale of farm property to start a cab company in 1931, which expanded during World War II. By the 1970s the company was worth $5 million. World War II resulted in increased profits for the black jitney taxicab businesses, especially those in large urban centers in both the North and South. Indeed, Joseph A. Pierce* found that by 1944 taxicab enterprises led in the number of employees in the miscellaneous black business group. Also, with continued segregation in public transportation after World War II, the number of black taxi firms increased. Many companies were started by World War II veterans, who also provided jobs for other veterans.

By 1958 black World War II veteran Herman Roberts in Chicago had emerged as a successful South Side businessman, beginning with the founding of his cab company in 1946. In the early 1950s, Roberts had a fleet of 36 radio-dispatched cabs and 125 drivers and mechanics who were employed in his own garage. Indeed, with its concentrated black population on the city's South Side, from World War I to the 1960s, Chicago was the leading center of the black jitney cab industry, despite the "taxi" wars that took place as drivers competed for passengers, on the one hand, while alienating them, on the other, with their rudeness and by limiting service to the main streets in the city's black community. Still, the jitney taxi business was profitable for blacks in both the North and South.

Yet, increasingly, white taxi companies in both the North and South objected to blacks entering the business, since they profited from having a monopoly. In Orlando, Florida, in September 1946, the mayor, city manager, police chief, and the white cab company owner opposed the petition of two black veterans seeking a permit to operate a "Negro taxi service," despite the fact that almost 50 percent of taxi passengers in that city were black. Moreover, both independent jitneys, as well as taxi companies owned by blacks, found it increasingly difficult to stay in business. Municipalities required taxicab owners to have liability insurance or to post liability bonds. In addition, cabs were required to install meters, which cost as much as $200. Pittsburgh, Pennsylvania, provides a classic case of the obstacles encountered by black cab companies in their attempts to survive in a competitive but almost monopolistic industry. In 1947, restrictive municipal regulations limited black-owned cabs to operating in only two wards of the city, whereas white cab companies had unrestricted access to the entire city. Also, black cab companies could only own a limited number of cabs. By 1957, the black-owned Owl Cab Company was forced out of business after some 25 years.

Ironically, segregation and discrimination in inner-city transportation precipitated the civil rights movement, beginning with the bus boycott in Montgomery, Alabama, in December 1955, which saw the emergence of the Reverend Dr. Martin Luther King as a civil rights leader. As southern cities desegregated their public transportation and white taxicabs began to service black passengers, jitney cab companies began to go out of business. In both the North and South, black car owners increased, so there was less demand for cabs. In northern cities, particularly, municipal regulations forced the black jitneys out of business; although, in some cities, especially New York, independent cabs continue to operate illegally. Yet, even today, black cab companies, without the resources of a Yellow Cab Company, are still generally restricted to operating within black communities. In the post–civil rights era, however, blacks in large cities—New York, Chicago, and Los Angeles—have begun to compete with whites in providing limousine service.

SELECTED BIBLIOGRAPHY: Martin Luther King, Jr., *Stride toward Freedom: The Montgomery Story* (New York: Harper, 1958); Joseph A. Pierce, *Negro Business and Business Education* (New York: Harper & Brothers, 1947); Howard N. Rabinowitz, *Race Relations in the Urban South, 1865–1890* (Urbana: University of Illinois Press, 1980); Juliet E. K. Walker, *The History of Black Business in America: Capitalism, Race, Entrepreneurship* (New York: Macmillan/Prentice Hall International, 1998).

Juliet E. K. Walker

TAYLOR, HOBART T., Sr. (1890–1972), Texas, entrepreneur, taxicab business franchise owner, inventor, real estate investor, black college fund-raiser, Democratic National Committee member, AME churchman, sportsman.

Hobart started his Houston taxicab* company in 1932, when he obtained a taxi franchise. Texas law required that black cab drivers carry only black passengers, most of whom lived primarily in neighborhoods with unpaved streets. Taylor's car engine design, made by Chrysler according to his specifications, increased air flow to the motor, whereby his cabs lasted five years, compared to the two-year average. Taylor achieved millionaire status before 1940. After 1941, he capitalized on increased railroad transport and new black population settlement in Houston.

The depression resulted in a decline in black business owners from 103,881 in 1930 to 87,475 in 1940, although entrepreneurial efforts by blacks, such as Taylor, continued while America's entry in World War II provided the basis for the growth of several black business fortunes. Taylor's cab business expanded during World War II. Joseph Pierce noted results from a 1944, 12-city study of 3,674 black businesses with 11,194 paid employees: 37.4 percent were employed in retail stores; 34.8 percent in service enterprises, averaging 3.2 employees per business; with miscellaneous businesses, including taxicab companies, averaging 29.1 employees, second to cosmetic manufacturers that averaged 37 employees per business.

Hobart T. Taylor, Sr., was one of the few black entrepreneurs whose family wealth provided the extensive venture capital for his enterprise. He was the grandson of a plantation slave businessman, Andrew Taylor, who, when freed in 1865, had saved up $600, money earned from the sale of shoes he made while a slave. Once freed, the former slave invested in land for cotton and rice farming and cattle and horse raising. Andrew died in 1895, leaving 4,500 acres of land to his son Jack, Hobart's father. On Jack's death in the mid-1920s, the Hobart farmland, worked by 40 tenant farmers, was left to his widow, Fisk-educated Millie Wright. Hobart graduated from Prairie View A&M and studied salesmanship at the Wharton School of Finance. Only once did Taylor work as an employee, for Standard Life in Atlanta. As an insurance salesman, he was one of the first in that company to reach the million-dollar sales mark.

Hobart's business philosophy, according to Louie Robinson, Jr., was derived from his family. From his father, he said, it was to acquire land: " 'The biggest thing in this capitalistic system is to hold something, to get our hands on something, to be successful. Man is born to be successful and your success will be measured by your accomplishments.' " From his mother, he said: " 'She taught us that the only thing that would unravel the white man's problems with the Negro was education. We had to learn some kind of skill, and we had to have some money to back it up.' " By 1970, Taylor's cab franchise business was worth $5 million. Hobart Taylor also increased his wealth by shrewd real estate speculation and investment in land, some with oil-producing capacity. His first wife, Charlotte Wallace, was the mother of his only son, Hobart Taylor, Jr., attorney and former director of the U.S. Import-Export Bank; his second wife, Virginia Dunlap, was from Indianapolis.

SELECTED BIBLIOGRAPHY: Alwyn Barr, *Black Texans: A History of Negroes in Texas, 1528–1971* (Austin: Pemberton Press, 1973); "A Negro Millionaire's Advice to His Race," *U.S. News & World Report*, September 4, 1967; Joseph A. Pierce, *Negro Business and Business Education: Their Present and Prospective Development* (New York: Harper & Brothers Publishers, 1947); Louie Robinson, *The Black Millionaires* (New York: Pyramid Books, 1972).

Juliet E. K. Walker

TELEVISION INDUSTRY. In the short history of television, blacks have made tremendous gains, despite the hurdles of racism, since 1948 when three major networks began regularly scheduled programming. Most of the gains have occurred since World War II, particularly after the civil rights movement of the 1960s. During the years following World War II, black entertainers appeared as guests on several variety shows, although few blacks hosted their own shows, among them Bob Howard (1948–1950), Hazel Scott (1950), Billy Daniel (1952), and Nat King Cole (1956–1957). Little local programming was produced for a black audience, like the amateur show *Spotlight on Harlem in New York* (1950s) and the *Mahalia Jackson Show* in Chicago in (1955). It was also in the 1950s that blacks in comedy emerged, beginning with *Beulah* (1950–1953) and *Amos 'n' Andy* (1951–1953).

In the 1960s, blacks were in dramatic programming as costars or supporting actors, including Bill Cosby in *I Spy* (1965–1968), Greg Morris in *Mission Impossible* (1966–1973), Gail Fisher in *Ironside* (1967–1975), Don Mitchell in *Mod Squad* (1968–1973), and Hari Rhodes Daktari (1966–1969) and Nichelle Nichols in *Star Trek* (1966–1969). Others had roles in comedies, like Ivan Dixon in *Hogan's Heroes* (1965–1971). Black actors playing leads were Diahann Carroll in *Julia* (1968–1971), Bill Cosby in the *Bill Cosby Show* (1969–1971), Lloyd Haynes in *Room 222* (1969–1974), and Scoey Mitchell and Tacey Reed in *Barefoot in the Park* (1970–1971). Others were leads in shows with a white supporting cast, like Nell Carter in *Gimme a Break* and Robert Guillaume in *Benson*. The few attempts at dramatic series include *Get Christie Love!, Shaft, Harris & Co., Palmerston, USA, A Man Called Hawk, Sonny Spoon, South Central, M.A.N.T.I.S.*, and *Gabriel's Fire*. *Roots*, the miniseries in 1977 and the sequel in 1979, was more successful than dramatic series.

Blacks in comedy excelled with shows like *The Jeffersons, That's My Mama, What's Happening, Good Times, Sanford and Son, The New Odd Couple, Baby I'm Back, Charlie & Company, Frank's Place, A Different World, 227, Amen, Fresh Prince of Bel Air, Moesha, Sparks, Malcolm & Eddie, Family Matters, In the House, Sister Sister, Goode Behavior*, and the variety show *In Living Color*. Syndication shows have included *The Arsenio Hall Show, Soul Train, The Oprah Winfrey Show, Ebony/Jet Showcase*, and *The Montel Williams Show*.

Although blacks have been in front of the camera, obtaining power positions behind the camera has been more difficult. Bill Cosby and Oprah Winfrey* have been exceptions in having influence in both respects. Winfrey's Harpo Productions is also responsible for *The Women of Brewster Place*. Thomas Carter, formerly on *White Shadow*, produced *Equal Justice*, and Russell Simmon* produced *Def Comedy Jam*. There have been several directors, including Carter, Roy Campanella II, Stan Lathan, Mary Neema Barnette, Helaine Head, Kevin Hooks, Tony Singletary, Reggie Life, Chuck Rallen Vinson, Gerren Keith, Eric Laneuville, and Debbie Allen, directing shows from the 1970s onward.

There has been some success with specials. Berry Gordy's* Motown Productions produced "T.C.B." (1968). In the 1980s, with Suzanne de Passe at the helm, "Motown 25: Yesterday, Today and Forever" and "Motown Return to the Apollo" aired. However, *Lonesome Dove* on CBS, an eight-hour miniseries, has been the most successful project. More recently, de Passe Entertainment has produced such television shows as *On Our Own* and *Sister, Sister*.

In sports, Jarobin Gilbert, Jr., was hired by the NBC president to be the chief negotiator for the 1980 Olympic Games. Because he made a deal that saved millions for NBC, he was selected to negotiate the 1988 Games. Fluent in Spanish, German, Japanese, and French, he also worked as vice president of business development, responsible for developing ancillary distribution for NBC Sports.

One way to influence the industry has been to own television stations. In 1973 the International Free and Accepted Masons, a fraternal organization, and Order of the Eastern Star founded WGPR-TV in Detroit, the first black-owned and -operated station in the country. George Matthews, the Supreme, Grand Master of the Masons, served as the first president and general manager, although he had no background in broadcasting. In 1995 WGPR was purchased by CBS. Clara McLaughlin was the first black woman to own stations when she founded KLMG in Longview, Texas, in the 1980s. Later, she acquired three other stations in Paris, Nacogdoches, and Denton. The stations are 80 percent minority controlled. N. Walter Gaines was the leader of a group who created KXLI in St. Cloud, Minnnesota, which began operations in 1982. Gaines, who served as president and general manager, began his career in broadcasting at age 14.

N. John Douglas owns National Group Television, parent company of KSTS in San Jose, California. The former Wall Street securities analyst applied for a license for his television station in 1974 but received the network affiliation only in 1980, and KSTS went on the air in 1981, grossing over $1 million in 1982. Most of the programming is business oriented. His parent company has several other holdings, including a subscription television operation, and International Televisions, which is geared to the area's Asian population. Also, in 1972 Johnson Products, Inc. (see George Johnson*) was the first black business to sponsor a television show, "Soul Train," first locally in Chicago and then nationwide. However, the first national black-owned station came with cable television when Robert Johnson* took $15,000 to start Black Entertainment Television (BET) in 1980.

Other blacks have held important positions at non-black-owned stations as presidents/general managers, including Jonathan Rodgers (WBBM, Chicago), Frank Melton (WLBT, Jackson), William H. Dilday, Jr. (WJTV, Jackson), Ronald Townsend (WUSA, D.C.), Eugene Lothery (WCBS, New York), Pluria Marshall, Jr. (WLBM, Meridian), Thursa Thomas (WJLA, D.C.), Valarie D. Navy (WCVB, Boston), and Dr. Patricia Prescott Marshall (KLCS). Dilday was the first black general manager to head WLBT and the first to be elected to the NBC Affiliates Board. Lothery was the only black vice president and station manager at a commercial station in 1986. Others holding important positions include Jennifer Lawson, vice president of national programming and promotion of PBS; Karen Barnes, vice president of children's programming at FOX; Kim Fleary, vice president of comedy development of ABC Entertainment; Kelly Goode, senior director of comedy development at CBS; Winifred White, director, Motion Pictures for Television at NBC Entertainment; Debra Langford, director of Current Programs at Warner Brothers Television; Charisse McGhee, director of Current Dramatic Television at NBC Entertainment; Judy Smith, senior vice president at NBC; Jonathan Rodgers, president at CBS Television

Stations Division; Toni Fay, vice president of Community Relations at Time Warner; and Rose Pinkney, director of Current Programs at Twentieth Television.

It has been difficult for blacks to become lead news anchors (including sports and weather); nevertheless, the following have worked as these positions: Clarice Tinsley (KDFW, Dallas), Dennis Richmond (KTVU, Oakland), Jerome Cray (KHOW, Houston), Lester Holt (WBBM, Chicago), Jim Vance (WRC, D.C.), Ken Watts (WAGA, Atlanta), Emery King (WDIV, Detroit), Ramona Logan (KXAS, Dallas), Reggie Harris (WCBC, New York), Donn Johnson (KTVI, St. Louis), Hosea Sanders (KCBS, Los Angeles), Warner Saunders (WMAG, Chicago), Dwight Lauderdale (WPLG, Miami), Brenda Teele (KTVT, Dallas), Arthur Fennell (WCAU, Philadelphia), Allison Payne and Jon Kelly (WGN, Chicago), Iola Johnson (KTVT, Dallas), and on the national level, Max Robinson (ABC), Ed Bradley (CBS), Bernard Shaw (CNN), Bryant Gumbel (NBC), Greg Gumbel (NBC), Asha Blake (ABC), and Rick Jackson (CBS).

SELECTED BIBLIOGRAPHY: "Blacks at the Top in Television," *Ebony*, April 1987, 82–86; "Black News Anchors," *Ebony Man*, March 1992, 24–25; "Black Women at the Top in Television," *Ebony*, June 1991, 68–74; Marilyn Marshall, "Texas TV Pioneer," *Ebony*, March 1987, 78–84.

Sundiata A. K. Djata

TENNIS. Due to the racial segregation policy of the United States Tennis Association, the American Tennis Association (ATA) was formed on November 30, 1916, in Washington, D.C. Blacks had been playing in their own major tournaments since 1898 when they played in Philadelphia in a tournament sponsored by the Chautauqua Tennis Club. Since Althea Gibson integrated professional tennis in the 1950s, blacks have made slow gains. For example, in the 1991 U.S. Open, the U.S. Open Committee was all white, and out of 256 players in the draw, only 11 were black (from four countries). Moreover, since Gibson's first Grand Slam (she won two Wimbledons, two U.S. Opens, and a French Open title), only two other black players have won Grand Slam titles, Arthur Ashe (U.S. Open, 1968, Australian Open, 1970, and Wimbledon, 1975), and Yannick Noah (French, 1983). Two others have made it to Grand Slam finals, Zina Garrison-Jackson (Wimbledon, 1990) and Malavai Washington (Wimbledon, 1996).

While several black players have had successful careers, they have failed to get major endorsements, although white players ranked below them have had them. Arthur Ashe was the most successful, but few have made gains as Yannick Noah of France. Garrison-Jackson had no clothing sponsor when she played in the Wimbledon final. Representatives have argued that she and Lori McNeil did not fit the image of tennis players in the minds of sports fans of the game. Moreover, blacks have not held important positions in the corporate professional organizations that have ruled professional tennis, nor have blacks sponsored major tournaments.

Some blacks realize the opportunities in professional tennis. Jack E. Robinson owns Martha's Vineyard Racquet and Fitness Club in Oak Bluffs, Massachusetts, with his son Jack Jr., and daughter Alicia. He organized it as a place for black vacationers to go. Fifteen years after laying the groundwork, he opened the $1 million complex in 1989. Jim Smith founded the Sportmen's Tennis Club in 1961, when he gave free lessons at the Carter Playground. In 1973 construction was completed on the Franklin Field Tennis Center, where his son Les Smith has served as executive director. The Junior Program is one of the major programs at the facility, where over 300 participants have gone to college as a result of their tennis skills. Henry Eustache and Bill Smith started an academy in San Diego in 1994, but the venture failed the following year. In 1997 Jinaki Wamuru-Wilson created Tennis in the Hood, Inc., in Atlanta in order to introduce tennis to inner-city youths. On the publishing end, Marcus Freeman founded *Black Tennis* (now *BT*) magazine in 1977, focusing on black amateur and professional players, and beginning in 1994, it became the official magazine for the ATA.

Other blacks have held important positions, like Cheryl Jones, who became the head women's tennis coach at the University of Southern California, the only black woman to coach an NCAA Division I tennis team. Stan Franker is the coach for the Dutch National Davis Cup Team, and Noah is the French Davis Cup captain. Ashe served as the captain of the U.S. Davis Cup team. Benny J. Simms, Jr., was the only black of four national coaches for the U.S. Tennis Association and the first black to be named head pro at the exclusive Longwood Cricket Country Club in Chestnut Hill, Massachusetts.

SELECTED BIBLIOGRAPHY: American Tennis Association, "1983–1984 National Rankings" (Philadelphia, January 1984); Geri Hamlin, "A Family Affair," *BT* (June 1995): 17; Marilyn Marshall, "Zina Garrison, Aiming for the Top in Tennis," *Ebony*, June 1986, 79–86; B. Wright O'Connor, "Creating a Racquet," *Black Enterprise* (July 1989): 54–55.

Sundiata A. K. Djata

THOMAS, JAMES (1827–1913), Tennessee, Missouri, barber, real estate owner.

Born in Nashville, Tennessee, Thomas's mother, Sally Thomas, was a self-hired slave laundress, and his father, John Catron, became a leading jurist, serving on the U.S. Supreme Court. As a youngster, Thomas worked as an apprentice barber in Nashville and eventually established his own shop in the capital, counting among his clientele many prominent whites, although never recognized by his father. In 1851, he obtained his freedom. During a slave insurrection scare in 1856, he left the city, and though returning briefly, he settled in St. Louis and found employment in Henry Clamorgan's popular barbershop, which also catered to prominent whites.

In 1868, Thomas married Antoinette Rutger, a descendant of one of the richest black families in Missouri. Although he continued to work as a barber, opening a large and luxurious shop in downtown St. Louis, he increasingly turned to real estate speculation and managing his wife's 48 apartment units (38 on Rutger Street and 10 on Jefferson Avenue). At the height of his business career, his total wealth surpassed $250,000, mostly in real estate holdings. In 1873, he took the Grand Tour of Europe, and during the 1870s he and Antoinette raised a family of six children—James, Pelagie, John, Joseph, Anthony, and Thomas. The depression of 1893, a disastrous tornado that destroyed many of his apartments (he was not insured), and the death in 1897 of Antoinette, however, resulted in rapid economic decline. Although in 1870, Thomas was among the half-dozen wealthiest blacks in the South (third, according to the U.S. census estimates), when he died in St. Louis, on December 17, 1913, virtually nothing remained of his once-great estate.

SELECTED BIBLIOGRAPHY: Loren Schweninger, "The Free Slave Phenomenon: James P. Thomas and the Black Community in Ante-Bellum Nashville," *Civil War History* 22, 46 (1976); Loren Schweninger, ed., *From Tennessee Slave to St. Louis Entrepreneur: The Autobiography of James Thomas* (Columbia: University of Missouri Press, 1984).

Loren Schweninger

TRANSPORTATION ENTERPRISES, HISTORY. Black participation in the nation's transportation industry began in Colonial America as slaves and as free owners of transportation enterprises. Indeed, some slaves not only captained their owners' vessels but even developed their own transportation enterprises in carrying both cargo and passengers. Some free blacks established small shipping lines. Also, both enslaved and free blacks developed transportation enterprises, with ownership of livery coaches, wagons, and drays, which hauled both passengers and cargo. Over time, black participation in transportation paralleled the growth and development of the transportation industry in America, including ownership of railroad lines both before and after the Civil War. Blacks through their inventions, both before and after the Civil War, contributed to the expansion of the nation's transportation industry. In the twentieth century, blacks made attempts to participate in the new airplane industry, although the automobile industry afforded blacks the opportunity to develop cab and bus companies. With the civil rights era, there was also an expansion of black participation in the auto industry as car dealers and even a short-lived black airline in the 1980s.

In the water transportation industry, black participation began in the colonial era when owners of enslaved Africans from coastal areas and river plains capitalized on their skills to man the first river trade boats, canoes, pirogues, flatboats, and ferries that carried cargo and passengers. As Washington Irving, the popular nineteenth-century writer, said in his history of New York in the mid-seventeenth century, Africans would "carry on all the foreign trade; making frequent voyages in canoes, loaded with oysters, buttermilk, and cabbages."

Slaves even acquired property in water transport. A 1740 South Carolina law made it illegal for slaves to own "boats, perriaugers, canoes, horses, mares."

Moreover, free blacks before the Civil War owned ocean, river, and lake vessels. Indeed, black investment in the nation's maritime shipping industry was undertaken whenever possible. In the seventeenth century the former slave Bostian Ken owned a "one-third share of the fourteen-ton ship *Hopewell*." In the early nineteenth century free black Christopher McPherson in Virginia, before 1810, held investment interests in a cargo ship. The New England merchant shipper Paul Cuffe,* who established the first black shipping company, also held three-quarter interest in a 268-ton ship. The Cuffe shipping line, one of the largest developed by blacks, had its origins in the late eighteenth century when Paul, at the age of 20, launched his enterprise with a schooner that he built. By 1806 Cuffe owned a small fleet, a 12-ton ship, an 18-ton ship, a-69-ton vessel, and a 109-ton brig, which he also built and half owned. It is reported that he had 10 vessels in his shipping line.

As the century progressed, antebellum free blacks increased their interests in shipping enterprises. In 1837, a shipping company was organized in New Bedford, Massachusetts, by a group of blacks. When the Erie Canal opened up shipping on the Great Lakes, Cleveland's John Malvin (1795–1880), who had obtained a sailing master's license, established a small shipping fleet, which included a canal boat, the *Auburn*, and a lake boat, the *Grampus*. Capitalizing on the developing iron industry in Cleveland, Malvin used his shipping line to transport limestone from Kelley's Island to that city. As the nation moved west, blacks made attempts, both individually and in companies, to capitalize on the Ohio and Mississippi River trade.

There were also blacks who owned steamboats and capitalized on the flourishing carrying trade in agricultural commodities and cotton on the Ohio and Mississippi Rivers. In Cincinnati, a cooperative steamboat company was founded by blacks. On the Mississippi River, two St. Louis blacks, David Desara and Barry Meachum, both skilled riverboat pilots, owned steamships. According to Martin Delany,* Meachum owned "two fine steamers plying on the Mississippi." On the West Coast, the black entrepreneur William Leidesdorff* brought the first steamboat to San Francisco in 1844, which he also sailed to Alaska. Yet, in the 1850s, while a large number of free black men worked in the fishing industry in California, only one black was reported to have a fishing sloop.

In the South Atlantic coastal states, antebellum blacks developed shipping enterprises in both the inland waterways and ocean transport. In this instance, the laws in force, which discouraged slave participation in the carrying trade on the South's extensive inland waterways, provided a window of opportunity for free blacks to participate in water transport enterprises. Still, the more successful free black boatmen owned slaves, despite laws such as in North Carolina in 1836 that made it illegal for slaves "to act as pilot over any bar or in-let waterway." Virginian boatman Richard Parsons, from 1840 to 1860, owned nine slaves, whereas free black Washington Logan owned one or two slaves.

Free blacks who owned shipping enterprises in the South included Richard Jarrett, who owned a fleet of sloops and schooners. Before the family of Liberia's first president Joseph Jenkins Roberts (1809–1876) immigrated to that country, they owned and operated boats on the James and Appomattox Rivers. In Petersburg, Virginia, free black John Updike owned not only a fleet of sloops and schooners from 1842 to 1862 but also 200 feet of Appomattox River front property, where he built his own wharf. At the same time, blacks in the extractive industries* were also involved in transportation enterprises. Wealthy Philadelphian lumber and coal merchant Stephen Smith* owned rafts, and South Carolina wood factors Dereef and Howard also owned a fleet of river boats and several trading vessels on the Atlantic Coast.

The interest of blacks and their persistence in participating in the nation's maritime industry are seen in the fact that during both the Revolutionary War and the Civil War one fourth of the American navy was black. As Martha S. Putney emphasizes in her study of the black merchant seamen of Newport, Rhode Island, from 1803 to 1865, a high percentage of black crewmen in all areas of shipping, except whalers, were blacks. Moreover, despite laws that made it illegal for slaves to work on inland water conveyances, these laws were evaded, and slaves even worked as pilots, such as the South Carolina Reconstruction congressman (1874–1886) Robert Smalls. A slave when the Civil War began, Smalls, with his expertise, was forced to pilot the Confederate ship the *Planter*. In 1862 he escaped with the ship and sailed it behind Union lines. Smalls was paid $1,500 for the war vessel. While he subsequently enlisted in the United States Colored Troops (USCT), Smalls continued as a pilot on the *Planter*, participating in 17 naval battles during the Civil War.

Throughout slavery, blacks also established urban land transport enterprises from the colonial era on, which included conveyances that carried both passengers and freight. In this industry, blacks in both the South and the North, especially, were confronted with competition from unskilled whites. Only strength, brawn, and endurance were the requisite skills for entry. Factors other than competition could prevent blacks from succeeding in urban land transportation enterprises. In Richmond, Virginia, free black Christopher McPherson until 1810 owned a prosperous carriage and dray business, which included both hauling freight and providing carriages for hire. Emerging as a leader in the Richmond black community, McPherson became increasingly aggressive in demanding better conditions for free blacks, and he lost his business. Indeed, his challenges to white supremacy had him declared insane, and he was sentenced briefly to a mental institution.

During the age of slavery, free blacks, especially in the South, who serviced whites could not succeed in developing prosperous enterprises by criticizing the slavery system or the subordinate status of free blacks. Yet, interestingly, in the North, many of the leading black businessmen, even those with white clientele, were the staunchest opponents of slavery and in the forefront of demanding equal rights for free blacks. In the South and especially after the 1820s, they were in no position to denounce the "peculiar institution" that provided the basis of their livelihood including the more prosperous draymen and livery stable owners. In Charleston, Joseph Morton, by 1810, owned four drays or carts, four horses, and two slaves in his drayage business. He employed them as teamsters, and their job was to haul "all sorts of items and merchandise through the city." Indeed, among black slaveholders, draymen and liverymen were ranked among the largest black slaveholders. As Luther Porter Jackson emphasized: "[T]he free Negro draymen and teamsters employed slaves on a scale comparable to the blacksmiths."

Moreover, many of the free black draymen and liverymen were former slaves who had hired their own time* as teamsters. That they were able to purchase their freedom from their pay underscores the competition that existed with unskilled whites. Yet, once freed, they either purchased or employed hired slaves. Some became quite successful. In Virginia the former slave Edmund Kean, who purchased his freedom in 1849, by 1851 owned three slaves, which he employed in his livery business. In Petersburg, former slave Robert Clark, however, purchased his freedom from money earned while working as a slave hotel waiter, then opened a livery stable. Before 1860 he owned both real and personal property valued at $9,000 and hired out "horses, buggies and carriages, open or close." In Virginia's Prince Edward County, former shoemaker Booker Jackson, who established a livery stable that included three vehicles and four horses, also owned two slaves.

While Issac Matthews, proprietor of the Matthews Livery Stable in Charleston, owned 10 slaves by 1860, still only a few blacks in Charleston were draymen. There was too much money to be made in this business, and in New York, municipal laws made it illegal for blacks to drive drays. Yet, interestingly, in several cities the largest livery stables were owned by blacks who rented saddle horses and carriages, including Robert Clark in Petersburg, Albert Brook in Richmond, William Wormley in Washington, D.C., and Henry Knight in Chicago. Moreover, in cities such as Philadelphia and Charleston, where black lumber merchants and wood factors had a significant presence, more than half of the deliveries were made by blacks. One observer recalled that in Philadelphia, when wood was the only fuel, "[n]early all of the horses and carts hauling these were owned by [blacks]." In North Carolina, Lunsford Lane, the tobacco manufacturer, also owned a firewood business, in addition to two horses and several drays and wagons that he used to make deliveries.

Technological innovations in the antebellum transportation industry, with first the steamboat and then the railroad, however, signaled the onset of Industrial America. Consequently, in addition to blacks capitalizing on the steamboat to develop enterprises, at least two black entrepreneurs capitalized on the railroad in developing their enterprises. In Pennsylvania, both the wealthy black lumber and coal merchant Stephen Smith and prosperous black businessman William Goodrich owned railroad lines. By 1840 Goodrich, as reported by Martin Delany, had "considerable interest in the branch of the Baltimore Railroad," in that he "owned ten first-rate merchandise cars of the road." The 1845 Dun credit reports indicated that Goodrich had "cars on R.R" and in 1852 noted that he "[r]uns a train of cars on the Columbia RR." Also, Delany said that "Smith's firm ran twenty-two of the finest merchantmen cars on the railway from Philadelphia to Baltimore" at mid-century.

These antebellum black entrepreneurs, Goodrich and Smith, then were railroad company owners before the industry consolidated for efficiency in the formation of large corporate entities. Moreover, wealthy blacks also invested in railroad stock. Stephen Smith owned $18,000 worth of stock in the Columbia Railroad, whereas William Goodrich owned stock in the Lancaster branch of the Baltimore Railroad. In the South, William Johnson,* the "Barber of Natchez," invested in railroads in Mississippi. The assets of New Orleans wealthy real estate speculator and free man of color Julien Lacroix (Dun reported he was worth $250,000 in 1854) included "stock holdings in two rail-roads." Also, Edmond DuPuy held 267 capital shares in the New Orleans City Railroad Company.

After the Civil War, some successful blacks in commercial farming who owned coal and lumber enterprises built railroad lines or spurs to their yards to expedite delivery as well as shipment. William Still expanded his antebellum coal yard by moving to a larger site and "laid the necessary railroad tracks" to provide easy access to the coal shipped to him. In Kansas, Junius G. Groves (1859–?), known as "The Negro Potato King," in one year produced 721,500 bushels of potatoes; he was also a broker, both buying and shipping potatoes purchased from other farmers and growers. As Booker T. Washington* noted: "[H]e has a private railroad trace which leads from his shipping station to the main line of the Union Pacific Railroad." In 1903 the black-owned Orangeburg, South Carolina, J. J. Sulton and Sons also built "a private railroad siding" for trains to enter their lumber yards.

In the post-Reconstruction era, however, there were also attempts by blacks to build passenger railroad transportation lines. In 1883 a consortium of blacks, headed by Rev. Joseph Pierce, began to build a railroad from Wilmington, North Carolina, to a sea coast summer resort at Wrightville Sound. The group's supervisor died, however, before more than nine miles of track had been built. Several years later, whites secured a charter to complete construction. Also, in the early twentieth century there was a black railroad construction company in Oklahoma owned by E. E. McDaniels and T. E. Currie that also built railroads as subcontractors for white railroad companies. Also, in 1914, a consortium of blacks in Arkansas floated stock for the financing of an interurban railroad from Washington to Columbus, Arkansas, but it was not completed.

With the rise of Jim Crow, blacks also began to establish intercity transportation lines. The Supreme Court decisions in the 1883 civil rights cases and the infamous Supreme Court railroad discrimination case *Plessy v. Ferguson* gave constitutional sanction to the "separate" but unequal segregation practices that existed in all areas of public life in both the North and the South. The result was a proliferation of segregation laws, both state and municipal, in all areas of public accommodation, including transportation. Consequently, the transportation enterprises developed by blacks at the turn of the century were direct protest responses to the Jim Crow era of racial separation and exclusion. In establishing intracity transportation enterprises, blacks proceeded individually, in partnership, through corporate and cooperative financing, and in one instance, through floating a municipal bond issue.

One of the first attempts made in inner-city transportation was in Pine Bluff, Arkansas, by black entrepreneur Wiley Jones* in 1894. Jones built a streetcar line and purchased trolley cars, primarily for the purpose of providing transportation for blacks to the amusement park and fair grounds that he owned. In 1901, blacks in Jacksonville, Florida, established a bus company, the North Jacksonville Street Railway, Town and Improvement Company. The city council not only granted blacks a franchise but also floated a municipal bond capitalized at $150,000 to finance construction of the railway. Whites, however, held the principal of the bond issue and forced blacks to accept the highest bid for construction; and although the line was profitable, the black bus company owners were limited in the time to pay the interest on the bond. The white bondholders foreclosed in 1908 and took control of the transportation company.

Blacks in Nashville, in response to a 1905 Tennessee state Jim Crow transportation law, which required all municipal transportation services to be segregated, established their own municipal bus company. Spearheaded by the president of the local National Negro Business League* branch, Reverend Richard Boyd,* head of the National Baptist Publishing Board, and James Napier, Nashville's leading black businessmen, they founded the Union Transportation Company. They raised $20,000 by stock subscription and purchased five steam-driven "auto buses," which subsequently were replaced by "fourteen electric buses." The company was in operation for only a year, unable to survive the attack by the city council to drive them out of business. First, the council reneged on its promise to provide electric power, but blacks set up their own dynamo in the basement of Boyd's National Baptist Publishing Company. Then the council levied special municipal taxes, which cut into operating costs. Unable to provide convenient service to the city's dispersed black population, the company was forced out of business.

With the beginning of the automobile age in the early twentieth century, however, eventually the most successful area of transportation enterprise for blacks, in both northern and southern cities, was in the jitney taxicab* industry, which flourished as an enterprise for blacks until the early 1960s. Most significantly, the Ohio-based, black-founded and -owned Patterson, Sons and Company, which made wagons and buggies, converted to a car manufacturing plant. In 1816 it introduced its first car, the Patterson-Greenfield.* Without the mass production facilities of the Detroit automakers, the company was only able to manufacture 30 cars before it ceased production of cars in 1920.

One of the most successful black transportation enterprises that developed in response to segregation was the Safe Bus Company in Winston Salem, North Carolina. It was founded in 1926 by blacks, a response to the Duke Power Company, which, from 1919, had refused to extend its trolley lines to the black communities. Safe Bus was established by the merger of 14 black jitney bus owners. Capitalized at $100,000, the company only had $22,000 in assets, including 35 jitney buses, actually trucks with straight plank boards for seats. By 1940 the company owned 54 Diamond T, Reo Dodge, Yellow Coach, and Twin Coach buses. Daily service for 21 hours was provided to 11,000 blacks. In 1941 Safe Bus expanded when it purchased Camel City Cabs; and in 1943, with 48 buses and 20 cabs, it employed 123 drivers. In 1958 it operated a $200,000, 55-vehicle fleet of both diesel- and gas-driven buses. Special routes extended service up to 75 miles in the Winston–New Salem area. Also, by providing "non-segregating seating," the company serviced 3 million passengers annually. By then, Safe Bus was headed by the widow of one of the founders, Mrs. Delphine W. Morgan, with 89 full-time employees and an annual payroll of more than $225,000.

In addition, from the early twentieth century on, blacks also capitalized on the new automobile industry by establishing car repair shops, gas stations, and car dealerships. Homer Roberts in Kansas City, Missouri, was one of the first black car dealers. In 1921 he established the Roberts Automobile Company, a new $65,000, 14,000-square-foot showroom, service center, and body shop, with 45 black employees. Roberts sold all makes of cars. His customers were black, and 75 percent of cars bought by blacks in the Kansas City area were sold by Roberts.

By the 1940s, however, most blacks in the automobile industry were service station owners, and some were quite successful. In the first six months of 1941, Cleveland black businessman Alonzo Wright, who owned a chain of eight gas stations, "grossed approximately $600,000." Moreover, from the early twentieth century, blacks moved from ownership of drays and wagons to trucks and established moving van companies. Only a few black truck owners were able to acquire Interstate Commerce Commission (ICC) licenses for interstate transport. In the post–civil rights era, however, the number of black auto dealers* expanded; by 1996, the total sales of the *BE* Auto Dealer 100 amounted to $5,925,244,000, compared to total sales of $7,399,179,000 of the *BE* Industrial/ Services 100.

The air age for blacks also had its beginnings in the early twentieth century. While black inventors also attempted to capitalize on this industry, they were not successful in securing venture capital to establish manufacturing plants. John McWorter, who held several patents for airplanes, sold his 1914 patent for a flying machine, in reality, a helicopter since it could "ascend vertically from the ground." He assigned his patent to the Autoplane Company of St. Louis. In the 1930s, Jennifer Snider found that several flying schools were opened by blacks. It was not until World War II that the first serious attempt was made by blacks to establish a commercial airline. The Washington-based Union Airlines was founded as an air cargo company in 1943 by William H. Hawkins. Its first purchase was a five-passenger WACO 285 H.P. Jacob, christened the *Mary Bethune*. After the war, several black veterans of the 332nd, 477th, and the Air Transport command in Chicago formed a consortium "dedicated to the establishment of a Negro owned and operated commercial airline." The company never got off the ground.

Several African American commercial airlines were established in the post–civil rights era. In 1969 Warren H. Wheeler established the short-lived Wheeler Airlines Flight Services based in Raleigh, North Carolina. A commuter airline, the company flew Beech 99 aircraft to cities on the East Coast, providing services to both the Baltimore-Washington International and the Washington, D.C. National airports. In 1972 the International Air Association (IAA), a charter airlines was formed by Herbert H. Jones, Jr. The company, which remained in operation until 1976, operated a DC-7, which it leased from Argosy and a Vickers Viscount. The IAA, based in Essex, Maryland, at the Martin State Airport, flew charter flights in the United States as well as to Montego Bay, Jamaica, the Bahamas, and other islands in the Caribbean.

The first black commercial airline to fly jet aircraft was Air Atlanta. It was founded in 1981 by Michael Hollis but did not began operations until 1984. The company provided service from Atlanta to Memphis and New York. It also extended service to cities within a two-hundred-mile radius of Atlanta, including Washington, D.C., at National Airport and Miami, Florida. While it was capitalized at $45 million, Air Atlanta failed not only because of a shortage of operating capital but also intensive competition from other national airlines.

Still, in the post–civil rights era, blacks in international trade transportation enterprises have achieved some success. In 1991, Guyanese American Lex Nigel Barker established his International Aircraft Trading (IAT) Inc., an aircraft sales, maintenance, operation, and management business. He also sells used 747s. His business receipts increased from $500,000 in the company's first year of operation to $2 million. The Red River Shipping Company was founded in 1983 by African American admiralty law professor John P. Morris, Sr. (1928–1993). It ranked 100th on the 1997 *BE* Industrial/Services 100. Also, two Virginia-based aviation enterprises, Navcom Systems Group any the Sentel Corporation, founded, respectively, in 1986 and 1987, made the *BE* list. These three companies have both private and government shipping contracts.

Consequently, while advancements have been made by African Americans in their continued development of transportation enterprises, participation rates remain low, especially in the very profitable areas of this industry. The Louisville, Kentucky-based Active Transportation company founded in 1987 with Charles W. Johnson as CEO (chief executive officer) ranked fourth on the *BE* 100s. The company with 1,600 employees hauls cars and trucks to dealers. In 1997 Active Transportation had sales of $250 million.

According to the 1992 *Survey of Minority-Business Enterprises* (SMOBE), there were only 25,756 black firms in trucking and warehousing out of a U.S.

total of 417,689 firms. With transportation by air firms, out of a U.S. total of 15,299 firms, 145 were black owned. There were 10,942 water transportation firms in the United States, 97 were owned by blacks. Also, nationwide there were 30 pipe lines (except natural gas) firms. None were owned by blacks, who fared much better in local and interurban passenger transportation enterprises. Blacks owned 15,974 firms out of 85,188 nationwide, reflecting the lower rate of car ownership by African Americans. There were only 4,882 black-owned firms in transportation services out of a national total of 102,134 firms.

Black business participation in all segments of the nation's transportation industries began in the late 1600s with development financed by private capital. The limited expansion of these enterprises over the past three centuries can be attributed to the continued lack of access to capital. Even in the post–civil rights era, according to the SMOBE, 60 percent of minority-owned businesses* were started with venture capital of less than $5,000, a somewhat insufficient sum for participation in transportation industries in the late twentieth century.

SELECTED BIBLIOGRAPHY: Edmund Berkeley, Jr., "Prophet without Honor: Christopher McPherson, Free Person of Color," *Virginia Magazine of History and Biography* 77 (April 1969): 180–187; Martin R. Delany, *The Condition, Elevation, Emigration and Destiny of the Colored People of the United States* (Philadelphia, 1852; reprint, New York: Arno Press, 1968); Luther Porter Jackson, "Free Negroes of Petersburg, Virginia," *Journal of Negro History* 12 (1927); Larry Koger, *Black Slaveowners: Free Black Slave Masters in South Carolina 1790–1860* (Jefferson, NC: McFarland & Co., 1985); SMOBE data available at http://www.census.gov/agfs/smobe/view/b 1.txt and http://www.census .gov/agfs/smobe/view/u 1.txt; Juliet E. K. Walker, *The History of Black Business in America: Capitalism, Race, Entrepreneurship* (New York: Macmillan/Prentice Hall International, 1998); Booker T. Washington, *The Negro in Business* (Chicago: Hertel, Jenkins & Co., 1907).

Juliet E. K. Walker

TRAVIS, DEMPSEY J. (1920–), Chicago, realtor, banker, insurance executive, author, publisher, civic leader.

While his first desk was an orange crate, his first chair, an upturned wastebasket, Dempsey J. Travis, president of Travis Realty Company and Sivart Mortgage Corporation, overcame formidable obstacles to become one of Chicago's most distinguished entrepreneurs, civic leaders, and authors. Travis attended Chicago public schools and graduated from DuSable High School in 1939, alongside such distinguished classmates as future *Ebony* publisher John H. Johnson,* future Mayor Harold Washington,* and legendary pop singer Nat "King" Cole. Like his father, Dempsey began playing piano at an early age and for a brief period came under the tutelage of the legendary DuSable bandmaster Captain Walter Dyett. But Travis's real training came in dozens of Southside nightspots, including the famous Savoy 13 ballroom, where he first demonstrated his considerable business skills and unflagging energy.

Inducted in the army in 1942, Travis became a band conductor at a USO

(United Service Organizations) center. In the army, he encountered virulent racial prejudice for the first time, culminating in an incident, never fully investigated, where a group of white soldiers, without provocation, opened fire on a group of blacks. Travis was wounded, and the man next to him was killed instantly. Travis recovered from his injuries and was quickly transferred. After several additional transfers, he finished his career as manager of the post exchange at the Aberdeen Proving Grounds in Maryland. Armed with the GI Bill, Travis applied to several area colleges but failed the entrance exams at each. At 25 years of age, a high school graduate and a veteran, Travis learned that he was illiterate.

From his father Louis and his mother Mittie, Dempsey had learned invaluable lessons: pride, persistence, and the honor of work. He took a job as a "mule" at the Armour Packing Company, he prepared tax returns for members of his church congregation, and he learned to read and write at Wilson Junior College, which did not require an entrance exam. He later got his bachelor of arts degree from Roosevelt University in 1949. While enrolled in Chicago Kent School of Law, Travis became interested in real estate and decided to switch careers. Getting a broker's license after finishing his real estate course, Travis encountered a distorted African American housing market, where even the most enterprising and stable black families with substantial savings and steady employment found it extremely difficult to secure a mortgage. In 1953 Travis founded the Sivart Mortgage Company (*Sivart* is "Travis" spelled backwards) and secured backing for mortgages for blacks moving into the rapidly changing Douglas Park area on the city's near West Side.

For the first, but certainly not the last, time in his career, Travis encountered criticism. Three thousand African Americans had been displaced from the near Southside in Chicago to make way for the new 100-acre Lake Meadows housing project. Travis supported slum clearance, "urban removal," which some dubbed "Negro Removal," and his firm became the first African American firm in Chicago to undertake an urban renewal project on the 4700 block of Calumet. Then, as now, he revealed a persistent thrust of his redoubtable entrepreneurial enterprises: the revitalization of the city's South Side for the African American middle class.

Throughout the 1960s Travis had been an outspoken critic of the policies of the city's white banks and lending institutions, white-owned insurance companies, and the "redlining" practices of white casualty and fire insurance companies. In 1961 he organized the United Mortgage Bankers of America to take advantage of President John Kennedy's executive order. Travis was also collaterally active in civic and civil rights activity. In 1960 he organized a march on the Republican National Convention meeting in Chicago. He served a term as president of the Chicago chapter of the National Association for the Advancement of Colored People (NAACP) and helped organize Dr. King's first march in the city. Meanwhile, he was building the largest black-owned realty firm in the city and becoming a multimillionaire. He was among the founders of the

Seaway National Bank, by the early 1960s the largest black-owned bank in the country. He also actively supported his close friend and ex-classmate Harold Washington's mayoral bid in 1983 and served as chairman of the Mayor's Real Estate Review Committee.

As a former president of the Dearborn Real Estate Board and founder and president of the United Mortgage Bankers, Travis has helped mentor a generation of black real estate entrepreneurs. He built housing: Lake Grove Villa at 35th and Cottage Grove and Vista Gardens at 62nd and Michigan. By the 1980s, however, he was becoming almost as well known as an autobiographical writer and historian. His *An Autobiography of Black Chicago* (1981) and *An Autobiography of Black Jazz* (1983) mixed history with personal reminiscences; his *An Autobiography of Black Politics* (1987) and *Harold: The People's Mayor* (1989) contained warm recollections of his dear friend. Travis also wrote numerous articles urging the black middle class to return, redevelop, and revitalize traditionally black areas on the city's South Side near the Loop and lakefront. Events of the last decade confirmed Travis's farsightedness.

In 1990 Travis broke ground for what has become his most impressive venture, a $12 million, four-and-a-half-acre, 52 townhouse housing development called Chatham Park Place. The townhouses on Chicago's South Side sell from upwards of $250,000 to $400,000. Designed to attract upscale middle-class blacks back from the suburbs as well as stimulate the local economy, it is the most ambitious project of its kind and a reflection of Travis's lifelong commitment to the African American community.

SELECTED BIBLIOGRAPHY: Dempsey J. Travis, "Can Black Builders and Bankers Survive?" *Black Scholar* (February 1974); Dempsey J. Travis, *An Autobiography of Black Chicago* (Chicago: Urban Research Press, 1981); Dempsey J. Travis, *An Autobiography of Black Jazz* (Chicago: Urban Research Press, 1983); Dempsey J. Travis, "Barriers to Black Power in the American Economy," *Black Scholar* (October 1971); Dempsey J. Travis, "The Black Businessman: Obstacles to His Success," *Black Scholar* (January 1973); Dempsey J. Travis, *Real Estate Is the Gold in Your Future* (Chicago: Urban Research Press, 1988).

Charles Branham

TURNBO-MALONE, ANNIE MINERVA POPE (1869–1957), St. Louis and Chicago, entrepreneur, founder of Poro System and Poro Beauty College, philanthropist.

Born 1 of 11 children into the Turnbo family, Malone was an orphan before she was old enough to attend school. As a child, growing up in Metropolis, Illinois, she enjoyed dressing the hair of her sisters and associates. Throughout her youth, Malone suffered a serious illness that confined her to bed. Those long hours spent in bed daydreaming launched her upon a path that would inspire Malone to build an international empire. At the request of older brothers and sisters, Malone moved to Peoria, Illinois, to live with a sister. In Peoria, she enrolled in high school, which at that time was a privilege for an African American woman. Malone had a fondness for chemistry, and she aspired to be a "beauty doctor." Her scientific experiments led her to the creation of the "Wonderful Hair Grower."

In 1900 Malone relocated to the all-black town of Lovejoy, Illinois (also known as Brooklyn), where she began her business in a weather-beaten building, rented for $5 a month. With the assistance of four women, including her sister Laura, the business grew, but Malone realized that St. Louis provided the fertile ground needed to expand her business. In 1902, Malone moved her enterprise to St. Louis, where she sold her product door to door. St. Louis offered Malone many opportunities; it had a large African American population and in two years would host the 1904 World's Fair. While her business grew, Malone's personal life was not as successful. She had two failed marriages, both related directly to her husbands' desire to control her business affairs. At the turn of the century, Malone, a single woman and a public figure, was pressured into having the "protection of a husband's name." In 1903 she married a janitor and became Mrs. Pope, but this marriage ended quickly in divorce because of his preoccupation with her business affairs. While Malone wanted to return to her maiden name, she feared losing business prestige; so she compromised by placing the "Pope" before the Turnbo and became Mrs. Annie M. Pope Turnbo.

In developing her business, Malone treated hundreds of scalps herself before she conceived of the concept of developing agents and a marketing business strategy, based on her philosophy that through cleanliness the "Negro race" could receive recognition and self-respect, which was extremely important to an African American population emancipated from slavery just 35 years earlier. In 1904 Malone traveled through the South advertising and demonstrating her methods and preparations that guaranteed to grow hair. She also appointed Poro agents. Becoming an agent was an exceptional opportunity for a black woman, who had few economical outlets except as domestic workers and washerwomen.

Malone claimed that while living in St. Louis the hair care giant Madame C. J. Walker* (then Sarah Breedlove McWilliams) was one of her early agents. In 1927, Malone's life was profiled in *The Light and Heebie Jeebies*, a tabloid geared toward black Chicagoans. The author alluded that Malone actually grew Walker's hair and that Walker moved to Denver, Colorado, and received notoriety because she was a Poro agent. A'Lelia Perry Bundles, Madame Walker's heir, and author of a children's book written about Walker, admits that Walker was a Poro agent, but for only a few months. Also, she argues that while Walker used the Poro Company's "Wonderful Hair Grower," it was not successful in growing her hair. There was definitely healthy business competition between Malone and Walker. Coincidentally, one of Walker's famous products was "Madame Walker's Wonderful Hair Grower." The Poro method, however, straightened hair with hair pullers, whereas the Walker method used the hot comb, which distinguished Walker's success.

As imitations sprung up, Malone copyrighted the name Poro in 1906. There are two accounts for the choice of name. One claims she chose a word used among the Mende of West Africa that generally relates to a secret society dedicated to developing spirituality. Another account claims it is an acronym derived from the first two letters of her name "Pope" and the first two letters of her sister Laura "Roberts," who worked with the business in Lovejoy. In 1914 Malone married Aaron E. Malone, an ex-schoolteacher and book agent who peddled Bibles. Aaron had known Annie Malone from Metropolis. Now that she was wealthy, he skillfully courted her. Aaron, who adopted the name "Prof," was said to be an extremely handsome and clever man, and his pursuit of Malone was questioned by some from the very beginning. Like Malone's first husband, Aaron abandoned his job soon after their honeymoon and decided to become a major player in the Poro business; however, this husband, subsequently, was much more successful.

Poro soon became a name that echoed throughout the homes of black people across America. As the business grew, Malone moved to expand her operations. In October 1917 the groundbreaking ceremony for the St. Louis–based Poro College was held. Within the next year, a million-dollar complex was erected; an annex was added and occupied in 1920. Poro College was a center for social and civic activities for African Americans. The African American newspaper the *St. Louis Argus* proclaimed in its headlines, "Poro College Opening Makes History for Race." The college was considered to be the largest and most complete building ever erected by a black person at that time. There were 175 people employed at the college. Turnbo-Malone claimed that 75,000 women from throughout the United States, Africa, the Caribbean, Canada, Central America, and Nova Scotia were Poro agents.

The Poro College included an instruction department, beauty parlor, auditorium, general office, cafeteria, dining department, sewing shop, dormitories, and guest rooms. The annex included a shipping department, manufacturing laboratories, laundry, filling and finishing department, bakery, storage space, and the publicity department. There was even a one-story brick structure to the rear of the college for parking. The aim and purpose of Poro College was to contribute to the economic betterment of "Race Women." During the aftermath of the St. Louis tornado of 1927, thousands were sheltered, clothed, and fed through Poro College, which served as a principal relief unit for the American Red Cross. Also, Malone was known to give generous benefits to her employees.

Meanwhile, Aaron became the public relations arm for Poro. He was active in the higher councils of the African Methodist Episcopal (AME) Church and appointed president of the AME laymens' organization. He was also named chairman of the colored division of the Missouri GOP party. In 1924 the relationship between Aaron and Annie was dissolved, but the two could not come to a legal settlement. So, in January 1925, with the help of a white lawyer, a divorce plea was filed along with a partition suit. Aaron asked for 50 percent of the Poro College fortune, claiming that his social prestige, management skills, and overall business experience made Poro College a national institution. The divorce received national attention, and the Poro company went into temporary receivership under a court-appointed white attorney.

Throughout the proceedings, battles were launched in the press, guided by Claude Barnett of the Associated Press, who accused Aaron Malone of turning his wife's millions over to "white folks" to be squandered and dissipated in court costs and attorney fees. Furthermore, since the largest fortunes accumulated in the country at that time by black people were the Madame C. J. Walker Manufacturing Co. and Poro College, Barnett claimed that Annie Malone's fight was a race fight. When the case was finally settled in 1927, Annie Malone lost hundreds of thousands of dollars. Although she maintained Poro, the company suffered immensely from the divorce settlement. In 1930, Malone moved to Chicago and opened a new Poro College, but the move could not save the company that was plagued by poor management, delinquent taxes, and lawsuits. Malone lost the Poro College building in St. Louis in 1937 as the result of a bank foreclosure. By the time of Malone's death in 1957, the millionaire's fortune was substantially depleted.

Malone's philanthropy was so extensive that it is worthy of a separate discussion. Proof of her giving is still found in St. Louis. The Annie Malone Children and Family Services Center is on Annie Malone Drive. Malone's generous contributions helped to construct the new facility, and it was thus renamed for her in 1946. Each May, the center sponsors a major fund-raising event known as the Annie Malone Parade. The Annie Malone Children's Home is one of the only black residential foster care facilities in America to provide continuous service for more than a century.

SELECTED BIBLIOGRAPHY: The Claude A. Barnett Papers, Chicago Historical Society, Chicago, IL; The Annie Malone Papers, The Western Historical Society, University of Missouri at Saint Louis; "Poro College Grand Opening," *St. Louis Argus*, November 29, 1918; Gladys L. Porter, *Three Negro Pioneers in Beauty Culture* (New York: Vantage, 1966); Howard B. Woods, "One Man's Journal: The St. Louis Woman," *St. Louis Argus*, May 17, 1957.

Nancy J. Dawson

U

UNDERGROUND RAILROAD AND BLACK BUSINESS. After 1831, the terminology of the railroad industry, as it developed and expanded in the United States, was used in discussions of the escape of fugitive slaves from the antebellum South to the North and Canada. *Stations* were the safe houses, barns, cellars, and attics where fugitives on the run were secreted; people who aided the fugitives in their escape were referred to as *trainmen* or *conductors*. Most notable was Harriet Tubman, known as the "Black Moses," who made 19 runs to the South, bringing out more than 300 slaves. Then there is the well-known escape of Henry Box Brown, who had himself boxed up in a crate and shipped off as cargo on an actual railroad train. Indeed, slaves on the run, using the Underground Railroad, were often referred to as *baggage*.

The number of slaves who escaped on the Underground Railroad, however, can only be estimated, with routes running north from Mississippi to Illinois and Canada and from middle southern states through Indiana and Ohio. Wilbur Siebert claims that 40,000 fugitives escaped to Ohio, whereas the records of businessman William Still, president of the Philadelphia Vigilance Committee, indicate that some 5,000 fugitives were brought into Philadelphia by the Underground Railroad in the five-year period from 1852 to 1857. Yet, for the fugitive to escape successfully, secrecy was imperative. Consequently, the actual numbers as well as more discrete means of escape have often escaped the scrutiny of historians, particularly the use of transportation vehicles owned by black businesspeople.

Invariably, these means of transportation, however, have been viewed as being owned by whites, and most conductors and trainmen assisting fugitives are thought of as white. In the historical reconstruction of the Underground Railroad, then, the focus invariably has been on whites and the effort made by them to assist slaves in their escape, such as the activities of Levi Coffin, who was regarded as the president of the Underground Railroad. On one occasion, Coffin brought out 28 slaves by having them travel as a funeral procession. Yet as one white abolitionist noted in reference to the Underground Railroad: "Such matters are almost uniformly managed by the colored people." Also, the nation's capital had the largest numbers of stations on the Underground Railroad.

Moreover, in the literal sense, fugitives were brought out of the South on railroad cars and on lines owned by free blacks, specifically lumber and coal merchant Stephen Smith* and merchant William Goodrich. Both lived in Pennsylvania, in counties adjacent to the Susquehanna River and the slave state of Maryland. Both men used their railroad cars to bring out fugitive slaves, who invariably were hidden in the false ends of boxcars. Smith's lumber yard business was in Lancaster, where in another instance Cato Johnson, also in Lancaster, who had a teamster business that hauled cars over the Susquehanna River bridge, also carried fugitives secreted in his wagons. In addition, black undertakers capitalized on their business by assisting fugitive slaves to escape by hiding them in caskets. In Philadelphia, black undertakers often hid slaves in caskets in their funeral parlors until it was safe to transport them out of the city, sometimes in caskets.

In other instances, blacks who owned livery stables, such as a Mr. Greenbrier in Cincinnati, used their horses to transport slaves to Canada. Black dray business owners used their wagons to transport fugitives, hiding them under the cargo they were delivering. In the countryside, black commercial farmers also used their wagons and drurries to assist fugitives, hiding them in false wagon bottoms or under ears of corn and other vegetables as they traveled to markets. Even in the South, there were some free black businessmen who placed both their lives and their enterprises in jeopardy by acting as trainmen on the Underground Railroad. A black painter used his enterprise when seeking white plantation owners as customers as a cover for arranging for the escape of fugitives on the Underground Railroad.

Knowledge of the identity of black participants in the Underground Railroad, especially black businesspeople, who depended on whites, was kept at a minimum. The efforts made by antebellum black businessmen in their activities as conductors and trainmen on the Underground Railroad add another dimension to understanding the commitment made by some antebellum free black business people to assist fugitives in their efforts to escape slavery.

SELECTED BIBLIOGRAPHY: Charles L. Blockson, *The Underground Railroad: First Person Narratives of Escapes to Freedom in the North* (New York: Prentice-Hall, 1987); Charles L. Blackson, *The Underground Railroad in Pennsylvania* (Jacksonville, NC: Flame International, 1981); Larry Gara, *The Liberty Line: The Legend of the Underground Railroad* (Lexington, KY: University of Kentucky Press, 1961); Wilbur H. Siebert, *The Underground Railroad from Slavery to Freedom* (New York: Macmillan, 1898); William Still, *The Underground Rail Road: A Record of Facts, Authentic Narratives, Letters* (Philadelphia: Porter & Coates, 1872); Juliet E. K. Walker, *The History of Black Business in America: Capitalism, Race, Entrepreneurship* (New York: Macmillan/Prentice Hall International, 1998).

Juliet E. K. Walker

W

WALKER, MAGGIE LENA [MITCHELL] (1867–1934), Virginia, bank president, philanthropist, entrepreneur, civic leader, feminist.

Throughout her life, Maggie Lena Walker was determined to promote valuable images of blacks, particularly of black women. Walker pursued her goals and accomplished them successfully through her perseverance in a variation of business establishments. She was born in Richmond, Virginia, to a former slave, Elizabeth (Draper), then a domestic worker for Elizabeth Van Lew. Walker's birth father, Eccles Cuthbert, was an Irish-born abolitionist and newspaper correspondent for the *New York Herald*. In 1868, Elizabeth Draper married William Mitchell, a butler in the VanLew household. Two years later, Maggie's half brother John B. (Johnnie) was born. Elizabeth Van Lew encouraged progress for all of her servants, including education.

In response, William Mitchell moved his family to a clapboard house in the downtown area of Richmond, today known as Maggie Walker Alley. While working as a headwaiter at the St. Charles Hotel, Maggie Lena's mother worked as a laundress and raised the children. In February 1876, tragedy struck the family. After being missing for five days William Mitchell's body was discovered floating in the James River. The apparent murder had been reported as a suicide by a coroner. To supplement their income, Elizabeth Mitchell increased her laundress business.

Maggie assisted her mother as a delivery person and babysitter, while continuing her education at Lancaster School. At this stage in her life, Maggie began to acquire the experience of an entrepreneur and learn the importance of female networks. In 1879, she attended Armstead Normal High School; it is here where she began her activism. As head of her 1883 black graduating class, Walker and her classmates protested against a segregated graduation. Instead of being able to graduate in the Richmond Theatre with white students, their graduation would be held at a local church. Bringing public attention to the issue, the students succeeded in having the ceremony in the school auditorium.

During her high school years, Walker became active in church and social organizations. In 1878, she was baptized during a revival and began her involvement as an assistant Sunday school teacher, which she later taught. At the age of 14, Maggie joined the Independent Order of Saint Luke; this organization was the pedestal of her many accomplishments. After high school, Maggie taught at Lancaster School for three years. In addition to teaching, she took classes in accounting and worked at the Women's Union, a female-owned insurance company. Her brief employment at the Union gave Walker a perspective on the importance of self-help among black women.

In 1886, she married an older, wealthy man, Armstead Walker, who was a construction worker in his father's prosperous bricklaying business. Armstead was also active in the Independent Order of Saint Luke until 1899. The Walkers bore three sons—Russell Eccles, 1890; Armstead Mitchell, 1893 (who died at birth); and Melvin Dewitt, 1897. The Walkers also adopted Margaret (Polly) Anderson in the 1890s. After marriage, Walker found herself devoted to the raising of children and traditional life. Although she enjoyed family life, she became quite bored after some time and found refuge in the Independent Order of Saint Luke. According to Margaret Duckworth, "[T]he Independent Order of Saint Luke, then, proved an ideal organization in which Walker could channel her energies; it brought out her beliefs in education, religion, race and sexism under the umbrella of economic enterprise."

In 1867, former slave Mary Prout founded the Independent Order of Saint Luke. The purpose of this organization was to provide service to the ill and funds for burials. The Order was established in Virginia and run by women, although men could join. As a member of the Order, Maggie held offices as National Deputy, Executive Secretary, Chief of Good Ideal Council, and Right Worthy Secretary in 1899, a position she held for 35 years. In 1890 Magdalene Council Number 125 was named in her honor.

While holding many offices, the goals she accomplished through the Order made her a successful entrepreneur. Walker's first accomplishment was the establishment of the Juvenile Department of the Order in 1895. This innovative program was a social channel that reached thousands of youth. By her appointment as Right Worthy Secretary, Walker was given a budget of $31.61, over $400 in unpaid bills, and a little over 1,000 members who paid dues of $3.40. By then, Walker was on a mission for expansion and community awareness.

Without staff, property, or funds, Walker established the weekly journal *St. Luke Herald* in 1902. As editor, Walker provided information to promote community awareness and consciousness. The paper was renowned for exposing injustice acts committed against blacks. Within 25 years, the journal served as a communicative force, reaching a membership of over 100,000, while the Order's funds increased to over $75,000. In addition, Walker formed the St. Luke Association—a joint stock group that aided in the purchase of property for the building headquarters. With fund-raising and service events, the headquarters was built in 1903, worth over $100,000 with 55 staff members and 145 agents in 24 states.

In 1903, Walker also became the first American woman bank president when she founded the Saint Luke Penny Savings Bank. The Second Street Bank and the Commercial Bank and Trust Company merged with her bank during the Great Depression to form Consolidated Bank and Trust Company. That bank, still in existence, is one of the oldest existing black banks today. Its initial purpose was to serve as a depository for the Order's insurance premiums collected from its members, as well as to increase black ownership of homes and to encourage savings, even from children. Most of the women members of the Order of St. Luke were domestic workers, including Maggie Walker's mother.

Expanding her business ventures, Walker established a department store, the Saint Luke Emporium, in 1905. The purpose of the store was to increase the participation of black women in business. The Saint Luke Emporium employed black women in the store and on its board. The failure of the department store was due to white business owners, who opposed black-owned enterprises in the elite business area. Yet, there was also a lack of support from the black community in patronizing the department store.

In addition to Walker's involvement with the Independent Order of Saint Luke, she was a member, organizer, and board member of many other organizations. She was founder and president of the Richmond Council of Colored Women, cofounder of the National Association for the Advancement of Colored People (NAACP) branch in Richmond, and founder and supporter of the Industrial School for Colored Girls; she established the Richmond Community House, was vice president of the Negro Organization Society of Virginia, sat on the board of trustees for the Frederick Douglass Home, and was a member of the Janie Porter Barnet Virginia Confederation of Colored Women, the International Council of Women of Darker Races, the Urban League, and the Virginia Interracial Committee.

Walker was honored with a master's degree from Virginia Union University in 1925 and a Harmon Award honorable mention for Distinguished Achievements in 1927. Walker also ran, unsuccessfully, as superintendent of public instruction on the Virginia-Lily Black Republican Party. In addition, many historic landmarks exist in Richmond in honor of Walker, including a high school that bears her name. Many black organizations declare October as Maggie Walker Month.

Tragedy, however, accompanied her accomplishments. In 1915, her eldest son shot her husband, mistaking him as a burglar. After a lengthy trial, however, her son was acquitted. In 1922 her mother died, followed by her son Russell in 1923. During the depression, Walker was confined to a wheelchair after a critical fall that shattered her knee. In 1934, she died from diabetic gangrene, complications from her knee injury. She was buried in the Evergreen Cemetery in Richmond. Walker's contributions were celebrated with the establishment of the Maggie Lena Walker National Historic Site in Richmond and the Maggie Lena Walker Foundation.

SELECTED BIBLIOGRAPHY: Elsa Barkley Brown, "Womanist Consciousness: Maggie Lena Walker and the Independent Order of St. Luke," *Signs: Journal of Women in Culture and Society* (Spring 1989); Margaret Duckworth, "Maggie Lena Walker," in Jessie Carney Smith, ed., *Epic Lives: One Hundred Black Women Who Made a Difference* (Detroit: Visible Ink Press, 1993); John N. Ingham and Lynne B. Feldman, *African-American Business Leaders: A Biographical Dictionary* (Westport, CT: Greenwood Press, 1994); Gertrude Marlowe, "Maggie Lena Walker," in Darlene Clark Hine, ed., *Black Women in America: An Historical Encyclopedia* (Brooklyn, NY: Carlson Publishing, 1993).

Oluwatoyin Caldwell

WALKER, SARAH BREEDLOVE [MADAM C. J.] (1867–1919), New York, entrepreneur, activist, philanthropist.

The first self-made African American female millionaire, Madam C. J. Walker started independently with door-to-door sales and advanced to employment of 20,000 agents. As a washerwoman, she earned $1.50 a day. At the height of her business in 1917, she made $100,000 a month in sales from the marketing of the hair care products she manufactured. Booker T. Washington* acknowledged her as "one of the most progressive and successful businesswomen of our race." Madam Walker launched a hair care empire in an era when African American women worked in fields or held domestic jobs. She helped lift their socioeconomic status, creating an ethnic business niche that catered to the hair care of women of African descent. Cosmetology remains one of the largest and most lucrative fields for African Americans.

Her parents, Owen and Minerva Breedlove, were field hands on a cotton plantation in Delta, Louisiana. Sarah, her brother Alex, and sister Louvenia were left to fend for themselves when their parents died of yellow fever. It is claimed that Louvenia and 6-year-old Sarah survived as washerwomen. They later moved to Vicksburg, Mississippi. In 1881, at age 14, Sarah married Moses McWilliams. Their daughter Lelia (changed to A'Lelia) was born on June 6, 1885. Two years later, McWilliams was lynched. Sarah continued to work as a washerwoman to support herself and her child. In 1888, she moved to St. Louis, preceding the Great Migration of the World War I era, when African Americans fled the South for new opportunities in the North. In St. Louis, Walker, however, continued as a laundress to support herself and child.

The years of exposure to steam heat and the chemicals as a laundress damaged her hair, causing severe hair loss. Hair preparation products on the market at that time failed to grow her hair. Discouraged, she experimented with concoctions and developed a hair grower, shampoo, pressing oil, and Tetter salve. The

Walker Method was a three-step procedure. The hair was washed, using her Vegetable Shampoo. The Wonderful Hair Grower was applied; then Glossine (pressing oil) was applied before pressing with a heated metal comb. Word spread quickly about her hair care products. The demand required that she hire agents. She called these hair care technicians "hair culturists" and taught these women the technique of washing, drying, treating, and pressing the hair.

Although she was given credit, Madam Walker did not invent the metal comb (pressing comb), but she did redesign the pressing comb's teeth and handle to accommodate the course hair texture of African American women. For the application of greater heat in pressing coarse hair, Walker also had the comb made out of steel.

There are three versions on the development of Madam Walker's hair care formula. The first version, by Madam Walker, states the formula was revealed in a dream. "A big black man appeared" and told her what to mix up. She sent to Africa for the ingredients and applied the formula to her scalp. Within weeks she had hair growth. A second version is that she appropriated the formula from Annie Turnbo-Malone,* who founded Poro College for hair and skin care. Turnbo-Malone was manufacturing a hair growth preparation in 1900. There are claims that Turnbo-Malone was the first self-made millionaire, according to John Ingham. However, Madam Walker was accorded that title. Ingham also indicates that Sarah worked briefly for Turnbo-Malone in 1905, selling Poro products door to door. She was also briefly married a second time, while she lived in St. Louis, according to her great-granddaughter, A'Lelia Bundles.

In St. Louis, she also met Charles Joseph (C. J.), a newspaperman and publicist, whom she subsequently married in Denver, Colorado, in 1906. According to her great-granddaughter, Madam Walker moved to Denver, Colorado, in mid-1905 to join her brother's widowed wife and four daughters. It is believed she left St. Louis so she would not be in direct competition with the Poro company and its agents. While in St. Louis, Madame Walker developed the idea for her business—although a third version, according to her great-granddaughter, is that while Madam Walker worked in Denver, as a cook for a pharmacist, she consulted with him on ingredients for the formula she developed and manufactured.

In Colorado, Sarah first peddled her products door to door. She also placed ads in the *Colorado Statesman*, an African American newspaper. Her husband C. J.'s knowledge in newspaper advertising and marketing helped to promote a mail-order business. Also, he encouraged her to name her line of hair care products *Madam C. J. Walker*. There have been several other famous hair culturists who have used the title "Madam" before their name: Madam Gold S. M. Young, prominent during the early 1900s; and Madam Sarah [Sara] Spencer Washington,* prominent during the 1930s and 1940s. But none has had the historic name recognition of Madam Walker.

In 1906, Madam Walker began a year-and-a-half journey that covered nine states. She traveled to parts of the Midwest, several eastern states, and to lower and upper southern states, selling her hair care products. She earned $35 a week, which was 2 times the salary for an Anglo American male laborer and 29 times that for an African American female doing domestic work. In 1908 the company income was $400 a month. Her travels led to the development of a lucrative mail-order business. A'Lelia, now grown, moved to Pittsburgh to run the mail-order operation. In 1908 Madam Walker and her daughter founded the Lelia College in Pittsburgh. It was both a hair salon and a cosmetology school for the Walker Method. The students completed the hair culturist program in six weeks. She also added a $25 correspondence course for others to learn the Walker Method. Also, in 1909, A'Lelia married John Robinson, whom she later divorced.

In 1910 Madam Walker and her husband moved to Indianapolis, Indiana. She set up a laboratory with 15 employees in the factory, while her other employees worked in the beauty school. According to Ingham, by 1910 she had trained 5,000 agents. By 1913, the company had gross earnings in excess of $100,000 a month. In September 1911, articles of incorporation were filed for the Madam C. J. Walker Manufacturing Company, which by then produced a complete line of hair care products. Walker's name and face were displayed on all of her products, unlike her competitors who used Anglo American women or images of black women with Eurocentric features and coloring. As the company expanded, Walker and her husband developed a conflict of interest. Seemingly, he wanted to stifle her business growth potential. While they divorced in 1912, he remained a Walker agent until his death. Also, that same year, A'Lelia adopted a neighborhood girl in Indianapolis, 13-year-old Mae Bryant, whom she and her mother had befriended.

As the company expanded, Walker began making plans for developing an overseas market. In 1913, she traveled to the West Indies. She visited Jamaica, Cuba, Haiti, Costa Rica, and the Panama Canal Zone, where she trained women on the Walker Method. That same year, A'Lelia moved to Harlem, New York, where she opened the second Lelia College. In 1916 Madam Walker moved to New York, where she built a mansion, complete with swimming pool, on four-and-a-half acres at Irvington-on-Hudson. She named the estate Villa Lewaro (an acronym from the letters in *Le*lia *Wa*lker *Ro*binson). By 1916, Madam Walker had 20,000 agents in the United States, Central America, and the Caribbean. In Pittsburgh, alone, she was ringing sales up at $2,000 a week. African American women hair culturists were earning $23 a week. This was at a time when African American women working as domestics in the South earned $2 a week, in the North, $10 a week.

In 1917, Madam Walker had annual earnings of $500,000. That year she formed the Madam C. J. Walker Hair Culturists Union of America for her agents. Membership dues were $.25 a month. The first convention was held in Philadelphia in 1917, where 200 Walker agents assembled. In a speech titled "Women's Duty to Women," Madam Walker urged her agents: "Hit often and hit hard . . . strike with all your might." Perseverance was her motto, and she told women to pursue their dreams, just as she had. Madam Walker lacked a formal education. Schoolteacher Alice Kelly became Madam Walker's personal secretary, confidant, and tutor. Madam Walker became a motivational speaker, lecturing and speaking to women's groups all over the country. She educated women on the importance of personal grooming, saying, "Look your best . . . you owe it to your race." Also, Madam Walker encouraged her agents not to feel ashamed of being hairdressers, as they were called. She instilled pride in her agents for working in the beauty hair culture trade—although not all were in awe of the Madam Walker hair methods, which straightened the hair of black women. Despite the criticism, Walker insisted her contribution was growing African American women's hair and facilitating easy management, rather than encouraging black women to imitate the straight-hair styles of Anglo American women's.

By January 1919, the Madam Walker Manufacturing Company had become the largest and most successful African American business venture in America. She enjoyed the best that life had to offer. She owned property in New York, Los Angeles, Chicago, Savannah, St. Louis, and Gary, Indiana, and surrounded herself with opulence and grandeur. She kept the latest of cars and had a chauffeur to travel around town and from city to city to promote her products. She socialized with the most prominent African Americans. In Indianapolis she purchased an entire city block downtown to build her new factory. Marjorie Joyner,* an employee who joined the company in 1916, became vice president of 200 Walker beauty schools, which she established nationwide. In 1927, the Walker Building, completed years after her death, housed the company operations, which included the factory, office spaces, a theater, casino, drugstore, and coffeeshop.

Her intense early life as a washerwoman for 30 years and then 13 intense years on the road, in addition to a rigorous schedule in managing her business, left Madam Walker in poor health. She had failing kidneys and suffered hypertension. In a letter to A'Lelia dated May 16, 1919, Madam Walker indicated she would take a trip around the world. France was to be the new headquarters. But she never realized the dream. Madam Walker died at age 51 on May 25, 1919, at Villa Lewaro. A'Lelia took over the helm of the company, but World War I, the Great Depression of the 1930s, back taxes, and A'Lelia's extravagant lifestyle drained the company's finances. The beauty salons were closed. Furnishings in the mansion were auctioned. The mansion, which had cost $350,000, was sold in 1930 for $50,000. A'Lelia's death in 1931 marked the end of a hair care dynasty. The company's presidency was relinquished to her adopted daughter Mae Walker (Perry) until her death in 1945. The family heir is Madam Walker's great-granddaughter (daughter of Mae Walker Perry), A'Lelia Perry (Bundles), who resides in Alexandria, Virginia.

The Walker Building became property of the city of Indianapolis. Later it was renovated and reestablished as the Madam Walker Urban Life Center in 1979, then the Madam Walker Theatre Center. The prominence that the Walker products once held began to wane. Larger, more progressive companies with state-of-the-art hair care techniques emerged. Mismanagement and lack of research development to bring the company into the 1980s brought about a steady decline. In 1985 the Walker company was purchased by Raymond L. Randolph but continues to manufacture products under the Madam Walker name and logo.

In 1996, under the auspices of the Madam Walker Theatre Center, the National Advisory Committee for the Madam Walker Spirit Awards was organized. The purpose is to honor the legacy of Madam C. J. Walker by recognizing those African American women entrepreneurs of distinction in the spirit of Madam C. J. Walker. Madam Walker advocated strongly for the support of African American businesses by African Americans and was very outspoken on racial inequality. She was involved with the formation of the International League of Darker Peoples. As a philanthropist she made the largest donation at that time to the NAACP (National Association for the Advancement of Colored People) antilynching fund. She donated hundreds of thousands of dollars to numerous civic groups, colleges, and church organizations. She bequeathed $10,000 to develop an industrial school in Africa.

SELECTED BIBLIOGRAPHY: Robert L. Boyd, ''The Great Migration to the North and the Rise of Ethnic Niches for African American Women in Beauty Culture and Hairdressing, 1910–1920,'' *Sociological Focus* 29, 1 (February 1996): 33–45; A'Lelia Perry Bundles, *Madam C. J. Walker* (New York: Chelsea House Publishers, 1991); John N. Ingham and Lynne B. Feldman, *African-American Business Leaders: A Biographical Dictionary* (Westport, CT: Greenwood Press, 1994); Charles Latham, Jr., ''Madam C. J. Walker & Company,'' *Traces of Indiana and Midwestern History* 1, 3 (Summer 1989).

M. Tambura Omoiele

WALLACE, PHYLLIS ANN (1923–1993), Boston, economist.

A distinguished economist and professor at the Massachusetts Institute of Technology (MIT) Sloan School of Business, Phyllis Wallace focused on the labor market. In her publications, she documented trends that characterized the post–civil rights era labor market—''dinks'' (i.e., double incomes, no kids), ''glass ceilings,'' and commuter marriages were all trends that she captured in the early days of compiling her data. Her academic work, then, was distinguished by her efforts to deconstruct exclusion. Her research on the AT&T case was published in *Women, Minorities, and Employment Discrimination* (1977). Among her most powerful work is her book *MBAs on the Fast Track* (1989), a longitudinal study of Sloan School graduates. It documented the differences between men's and women's pay and the salary differential between black and white M.B.A.s. While Wallace later became known for her work on race and the labor market, her early research focused on international trade. She wrote her dissertation on commodity trade relationships, focusing on international sugar agreements.

Phyllis Wallace majored in economics at New York University, graduating magna cum laude and Phi Beta Kappa in 1943. She received a master's degree in economics from Yale University in 1944 and the Ph.D. from Yale in 1948.

She had proficiency in several languages, including German, Russian, Spanish, and French. Segregation in her home state of Maryland enabled Wallace to secure an education in the North. In the age of segregation, state law prevented her from attending the all-white University of Maryland because of her race, but out-of-state educational expenses were provided black students whose chosen major was not offered at all-black Morgan State College. Wallace says she compared the Morgan catalog with that at the University of Maryland and chose economics as a major because it was available at Maryland but not Morgan.

After earning the Ph.D. at Yale, Wallace lived in New York, teaching at City College of New York, along with research at the National Bureau of Economic Research (NBER), specializing in trade and productivity issues. From 1953 to 1957, Wallace was on the economics faculty at Atlanta University. Then, from 1957 to 1965 she worked as an "economic analyst in intelligence" in a research capacity for the Central Intelligence Agency (CIA), translating documents and doing economic analysis on productivity data. During that time, she also coauthored an *American Economic Review* article, "Industrial Growth in the Soviet Union" (1959), and published her testimony before the Joint Economic Committee, "Dimensions of Soviet Economic Power" (1962).

The atmosphere of social change that infused the years before the passage of the Civil Rights Act of 1965 led Wallace to consider a shift in her research focus. In late 1965 she began working as chief of technical studies for the Equal Employment Opportunity Commission (EEOC), where she pioneered in research on the economics of discrimination, with emphasis on racial employment patterns in many industries, including the textile industry and the drug industry. Her research focused on the status of African Americans in poor, urban neighborhoods and on patterns of employment in private industry issues of discrimination and employment testing. Her group included legal scholars such as Rutgers University's Albert Blumrosen and industrial psychologists like Patricia Gurin, who developed the first EEOC guidelines on employee testing, which subsequently influenced the outcome of the *Griggs v. Duke Power Company* case.

When Wallace left the EEOC in 1968, she joined the Metropolitan Applied Research Center to work on issues affecting urban youth in labor markets and focused on the issues affecting young black women, an area that had been unexplored to that point. She participated actively in EEOC and other government advisory commissions on work issues and published extensively on race and gender discrimination in the labor market, in addition to numerous working papers about affirmative action and equal employment opportunity, including an *American Economic Review* article with Bernard Anderson (1975) on black economic progress, and an invited paper on measurement and societal values for the Employment Testing Service (1971).

In 1972, Phyllis Wallace joined MIT's faculty as a visiting professor. She was tenured as full professor in 1974 and continued her research on employment discrimination, which resulted in several publications. She also researched the career aspirations of young girls in Harlem in *Pathways to Work: Unemployment among Black Teenage Females* (1974); in addition, she edited a volume on women's work choices, *Women in the Workplace* (1982), and authored a study on black women's work, *Black Women in the Labor Force* (1980).

Wallace was also the first African American and first woman president of the Industrial Relations Research Association. She was awarded the National Economic Association's Westerfield Award in 1981. In emphasizing her concern about internal labor markets and the need to deconstruct the barriers to advancement of minorities and women in internal labor markets, Wallace said: "Employment and training programs may serve as the critical factor in helping the US economy maintain its competitive edge in many global marketplaces. The development and maintenance of human capital will be central in the emerging information technology where boundaries between blue collar and white collar jobs may gradually disappear."

During her years as professor at MIT, Wallace sat on several government boards and was involved in the Boston business community, serving as a board member of the State Street Bank and Stop and Shop Stores. She was also a trustee of the Museum of Fine Arts and a member of the Museum of Fine Arts Board of Trustees, where she worked to establish the Nubian Gallery. Phyllis Wallace was the recipient of dozens of honorary degrees and awards. These are important aspects of Wallace's life and work, but most important is the fact that Phyllis Wallace was a woman who refused to be defined by her race, gender, or occupation. Wallace did not travel along nontraditional paths simply because they were there but because she was convinced that the directions would be interesting. She was not discouraged by the notion that "blacks" or "women" or "black women" did not trek along a certain course. Further, she encouraged those in her orbit, those who she mentored and nurtured in business, economics, science, and the arts, to do the same. From her choice to major in economics at New York University to her leadership of the Museum of Fine Arts Committee for New Audiences, Wallace's chosen path was that of myth-buster, of one who shattered stereotypes and opened doors. Wallace was born in Baltimore, Maryland.

SELECTED BIBLIOGRAPHY: Julianne Malveaux, "Tilting against the Wind: Reflections on the Life and Work of Dr. Phyllis Ann Wallace," *American Economic Review* 84, 2(May 1944): 93–97; Julianne Malveaux, *Wall Street, Main Street, and the Side Street* (Los Angeles: Pines One Publications, 1999); Phyllis A. Wallace, Obituary, *Boston Globe*, January 13, 1993; Phyllis A. Wallace, *Pathways to Work: Unemployment among Black Teenage Females* (Lexington, MA: Lexington Books, 1974); Phyllis A. Wallace and Annette LaMond, *Women Minorities and Employment Discrimination* (Lexington, MA: Lexington Books, 1977); Phyllis A. Wallace, with Linda Datcher and Julianne Malveaux, *Black Women in the Labor Force* (Cambridge, MA: The MIT Press, 1980).

Julianne Malveaux

WASHINGTON, BOOKER T. (1856–1915), Alabama, educator, black business promoter.

Booker T. Washington was one of the most influential scholars and practitioners of his time period. Born a slave, he became president of Tuskegee University, created the National Negro Business League (NNBL),* developed scholarly publications to track the progress of black enterprise, and debated other intellectuals of his day about the proper program for the "advance of the Negro race."

After the Civil War, Tuskegee Institute was established as a result of a political deal between a local black businessperson, Lewis Adams, and W. F. Foster, a former Confederate colonel who was a candidate for the Alabama legislature. Foster informed Adams that if he could deliver the black vote to his candidacy, he would seek a state appropriation from the Alabama Legislature. Adams delivered the vote, and Foster kept his promise and appropriated money to create Tuskegee Institute. Looking for a president for the new school, Adams wrote to Hampton Institute in Virginia. The president of Hampton recommended one of his best young professors, Booker T. Washington. Tuskegee was established in 1881, and Booker T. Washington used it as a platform for his ideas and as a sea of instruction for future generations of black Americans.

As president of Tuskegee Institute, Washington had the challenge of building both the physical structure of the institute and an ideology that would bring about economic success. He utilized students to construct buildings, grow plants that would enhance the grounds, and engage in research that could be commercialized to enhance the state and the society. It is no surprise that Tuskegee Institute became the first research university in the entire South. George Washington Carver,* for example, did wonders with the peanut and sweet potato in his laboratory at the institute. The commercial results of his experiments are still with us today. Also, because of the influence of Booker T. Washington, Tuskegee Institute continues to produce outstanding graduates who make contributions to their families and communities.

Despite the legacy of Washington, which continues to improve the lives of black Americans, he is best known for his political ideology during a time when black Americans were making the transition from slavery to freedom. During Reconstruction, northern Republican troops occupied the South and guaranteed the basic political rights of ex-slaves. During this period, blacks had the right to vote, elected black governors, and sent blacks to the U.S. Senate and Congress. When northern troops were withdrawn from the South, the rights of blacks were taken away by a series of political events and white violence. Washington argued that the development of business enterprise, at that point in history, had to come before an emphasis on civil rights or the right to vote. He believed that civil rights would follow after the group had achieved a degree of economic stability.

Washington became a nationally known figure during a speech at the Atlanta Exposition in 1895, which focused on the industrial progress of the South. During his talk, Washington made the following comments: "Our greatest danger is that in the great leap from slavery to freedom we may overlook that fact that the masses of us are to live by the productions of our hands, and fail to keep in mind that we shall prosper in proportion as we learn to draw the line between the superficial and substantial.'' In addition, he emphasized: ''No race can prosper till it learns that there is as much dignity in tilling a field as in writing a poem.'' In efforts to reconciliate the races Washington said: ''In all things that are purely social we can be separate as the fingers, yet one as the hand in all things essential to mutual progress. . . . The wisest among my race understand that the agitation of questions of social equality is the extremist folly, and that progress in the enjoyment of all the privileges that will come to us must be the result of severe and constant struggle rather than of artificial forcing.''

Yet Washington also emphasized that ''[n]o race that has anything to contribute to the markets of the world is long in any degree ostracized. It is important and right that all privileges of law be ours, but it is vastly more important that we be prepared for the exercise of these privileges. The opportunity to earn a dollar in a factory just now is worth infinitely more than the opportunity to spend a dollar in an opera house.'' The metaphors utilized by Washington were designed to capture the debates of his day, one of which was the type of education that blacks should pursue. The image that compares tilling the soil with writing a poem captured the debate between majoring in business (or what was called a ''practical education'' at that time) or the arts (or what is called ''liberal arts'' today).

Scholar W.E.B. Du Bois argued that blacks should concentrate on a broad liberal education. Washington argued that blacks, at that point in history, should concentrate on a practical, industrial education. Thus, learning to till the soil is more important than learning to write a liberal poem. His comments relating to blacks and whites being ''separate as the fingers'' in things that are social but ''one as the hand in all things essential to mutual progress'' was designed to inform the audience that blacks and whites should work together in the business world but remain separate in the social world.

Washington's speech was called ''The Atlanta Compromise'' by many because he was seen as exchanging the right to vote and other basic civil rights for the ability of blacks to work strictly in the world of business with whites in the North and South. W.E.B. Du Bois was so disgusted with Washington's ideas that he opposed them in all public forms. A chapter in his 1903 *Souls of Black Folks* is dedicated to the systematic analysis of Washington's ideas. These ideas, along with the systematic denial of civil rights of blacks, were instrumental in the development of the National Association for the Advancement of Colored People (NAACP), an organization that took as its goal the complete restoration of civil rights for blacks through the court system of America. Washington considered Du Bois and the organization of the NAACP as nemeses to his ideas and organization.

The main organization that Washington created was the National Negro Business League in 1900. The purpose of the League was to generate high character, develop racial respect, develop economic stability, and lay the economic groundwork for future generations. In all of Washington's writings he stressed the theme "No job-hunting for those who are able to do something useful." Washington believed that if a black person succeeded in business, paid his taxes, and had high character, respect would come from whites who were also of high character. The League paid little attention to whites who did not succeed in business. Washington did not link all whites together but instead noted that only whites who had achieved economic stability and understood the importance of property should enjoy political rights. He argued that one of the problems with the economic development of the South was that poor whites without ingenuity were allowed to participate in the political process.

And the NNBL approach worked. In 1919, there were over 140 chartered Negro Business Leagues in 30 states. Successful business communities evolved in cities and communities throughout the South and North.

Booker T. Washington was a person who was clearly ahead of his time. Although the black American population as a group has moved away from placing entrepreneurial activities at the very center of community, those efforts have been embraced by immigrant groups such as Africans, Koreans, Chinese, and Arabs. If Washington returned today, he would see the experiences of immigrant entrepreneurs clearly in his tradition. Washington left a legacy of educational attainment at his Tuskegee Institute: Today many successful children and grandchildren of early entrepreneurs owe their intergenerational success to the ideas of Booker T. Washington.

SELECTED BIBLIOGRAPHY: John Sibley Butler, *Entrepreneurship and Self-Help among Black Americans: A Reconsideration of Race and Economics* (Albany: State University of New York Press, 1991); John Hope Franklin and Isidore Starr, *The Negro in Twentieth Century America* (New York: Vintage Books, 1967), 85–87; Louis R. Harlan, *Booker T. Washington: The Wizard of Tuskegee* (New York: Oxford University Press, 1967); Booker T. Washington, *The Negro in Business* (Chicago: Hertel, Jenkins & Co., 1907).

John Sibley Butler

WASHINGTON, HAROLD (1922–1987), Chicago, mayor, politician.

Harold Washington was the forty-second mayor of the city of Chicago and the first African American elected to that position. In the racially polarized and fiercely competitive context of Chicago politics, Washington won his initial election in 1983 with 50.6 percent of the vote and nearly 100 percent of a highly mobilized black vote as well as 12 percent of the white vote. Racial divisions were so stark, however, that whereas winning the Democratic primary in Democratically controlled Cook County usually guaranteed a candidate's election in the November general election, Washington actually had to contend with leaders in his own Democratic Party working for the Republican candidate—Bernard Upton. Nonetheless, Washington was a candidate and a mayor firmly dedicated to the progressive reform of the city government. He directly challenged the "business as usual" posture the Democratic machine had taken in managing the finances of the city and in distributing public resources, especially to Chicago's minority communities and minority firms.

As a native Chicagoan, he received his high school diploma from DuSable High School; his bachelor's degree from Roosevelt College; and his law degree from Northwestern University. Although he was weaned on city Democratic politics, for his father was a Democratic Party precinct captain, he developed his own reformist and independent-minded approach to serving his constituents, evidenced by his several terms in the Illinois General Assembly, one term in the State Senate, and one term in the U.S. House of Representatives. Then, once elected mayor, Washington wasted no time in displaying his reformist credentials by tackling the perennial problem of the city's budget deficit. He cut his own salary by 20 percent and fired 1,300 city workers—too many of whom had been employed through the largesse of the Democratic machine.

Due to the greatly diminished subsidies state and local governments received from the Reagan administration, however, these and other kinds of austerity measures were no different from those taken by other mayors of other large American cities. Washington further proved his reformist zeal by setting forth his ambitious "Chicago Works Together" policy agenda. It called for job creation, granting minority communities "a fair share" through an assertive affirmative action program, a balanced approach to economic growth, and the greater inclusion and participation of neighborhoods in development initiatives.

Affirmative action and minority hiring could only be initiated on the scale Washington desired if he circumvented the formidable opposition generated on the 50-member city council, as led by Cook County Democratic Party chair and Alderman Edward Vrydolyak and found within the machine-controlled Department of Purchasing. Therefore, Washington used the strong authority invested in the mayor's office and issued Executive Order 85–2. It established Chicago's first formal minority set-asides* program. The City of Chicago had awarded nearly $3 billion in public works contracts between 1981 and 1986, for an annual average of $450 million. Yet these dollars were so concentrated in the hands of the favored few in good standing with the machine that 50 percent of the city's purchasing dollars prior to Washington had gone to just 3.7 percent of the total number of vendors.

Washington demanded a much greater dispersion of these resources, particularly to firms representing underserved constituents. Executive Order 85–2 required city agencies to grant 25 percent of their contracts to minority businesses and 5 percent to firms run by women. Whereas African Americans had comprised 40 percent of the population, black companies received only 7.4 percent of the city contract dollars. Latinos faired even worse in that they only received 1.5 percent of the total contract dollars, although they were 14 percent of the city's population. By 1987, this trend was substantially reversed, and minority enterprises were awarded a combined 33 percent of the contract dollars, and women-owned firms were given 5.6 percent. The Washington administration also lobbied to ensure minority subcontractor inclusion in such lucrative, commercial works projects as the North Loop redevelopment. The administration's pressing for "good faith agreements" and an adherence to a 30 percent set-aside goal meant that minority firms were awarded $166 million in contract dollars just during the construction phase of the aforementioned project—not to mention the subsequent construction benefits.

Historic strides were also made by his administration in the hiring of African Americans, Latinos, and women in the city bureaucracy, although Washington decreased the overall number of city jobs to ensure the city lived within its fiscal means. In an effort to secure white ethnic support during the 1982 preelection year, Mayor Jane Byrne had extended 64 percent of that year's new city hires to whites, whereas 28 percent went to African Americans, 25 percent to women, and a mere 6 percent to Latinos. By 1986, Washington extended only 30 percent of all new hires to whites, while dramatically increasing the African American share of these jobs to 55 percent as well as 41 percent to women and 12 percent to Latinos. He furthermore ensured that the top positions in his administration reflected the ethnic and gender diversity of the city. Whereas 90 percent of all Byrne's mayoral staff were white, while only 6 percent were black and 4 percent were Latino, only 45 percent of Washington's mayoral staff were white, with 43 percent of it black and 11 percent Latino. Although Latinos faired much better under Washington's hiring practices than under Byrne's practices, they were still concerned that they only comprised a mere 3 percent of Washington's department heads.

Albeit, Washington took unprecedented steps to curb the usual, large-scale economic development focus, or ward-based largesse rationale, of Community Development Block Grant (CDBG) expenditures. He not only gave the neighborhood organizations and local service providers greater voice in the CDBG and city budget process, but he gave a greater share of the city and federal dollars allocated for public service or housing efforts. Because he was opposed by the "Vrydolyak 29" on the city council at every turn (until in the redistricting elections of 1985 he enjoyed an even split, with his mayoral vote as the tiebreaker), the normally calm CDBG budget process was contentious. Overall, Washington's CDBG allocations reflected a reordering of priorities in that moneys for housing rehabilitation, residential public improvements, and public service doubled, whereas administrative staffing was cut at least by half. At one point Washington allocated 36.9 percent of the CDBG to public services, the highest level ever set by a mayor, and proposed dramatic public improvements to all Chicago neighborhoods through a $185 million general obligation bond.

Harold Washington's most enduring legacy to the people of Chicago is that he challenged city government to be more accountable and responsive to the needs of all its citizens; thus, he broke the hegemony of the political machine. In doing so, however, he likewise provided vital opportunities for African American entrepreneurs, employed the black middle and working classes in the city's bureaucracy in unprecedented numbers, and provided all low- and moderate-income communities with the real hope that city hall cared about their plights and was actively working to better their condition. At the age of 65, ironically after his astounding reelection as mayor, Harold Washington succumbed to a heart attack while working at his desk.

SELECTED BIBLIOGRAPHY: P. and W. Clavel, eds., *Harold Washington and the Neighborhoods: Progressive City Government in Chicago, 1983–1987* (New Brunswick, NJ: Rutgers University Press, 1991); B. Ferman, *Challenging the Growth Machine: Neighborhood Politics in Chicago and Pittsburgh* (Lawrence: University of Kansas Press, 1996); W. Grimshaw, *Bitter Fruit: Black Politics and the Chicago Political Machine, 1931–1991* (Chicago: University of Chicago Press, 1991); G. Rivlin, *Fire on the Prairie: Harold Washington and the Politics of Race* (New York: Henry Holt & Company, 1992).

Todd C. Shaw

WASHINGTON, SARAH [SARA] SPENCER (1889–1953), New Jersey, entrepreneur in hair care industry, philanthropist.

At the time of her death, Washington's enterprise was worth more than a million dollars. She employed 500 people in such positions as officeworkers, salespersons, managers, and teachers and claimed that 45,000 people worldwide were Apex agents. The company motto "Now is the time to plan for your future by learning a depression-proof business" was the philosophy that carried Washington to monumental success.

Washington was born in Virginia. She was a graduate of Norfolk Mission College in Norfolk, Virginia. Washington also studied beauty culture in York, Pennsylvania, and did advance work in chemistry at Columbia University. In 1905, Washington began her career as a dressmaker. By 1914, a small hairdressing establishment was under way where she worked as an operator and taught her system to others while selling her products door to door in the evenings. In 1920, she founded the Apex News and Hair Company in Atlantic City, New Jersey, on, as the company boasted, "a proverbial shoestring." Eventually, Apex beauty schools were established in New York, New York; Chicago, Illinois; Washington, D.C.; Atlanta, Georgia; Richmond, Virginia; Philadelphia, Pennsylvania; Baltimore, Maryland; Newark, New Jersey; Brooklyn, New York; and several foreign countries. At one time she operated an office in the Bantu World Bank in Johannesburg, South Africa. More than 25,000 students graduated from these colleges annually.

Also, Washington built her own laboratory in Atlantic City and manufactured 75 different products. In response to the unemployment situation in Atlantic City, she established the Apex Community Drug Store, which employed 17 persons. She also owned and operated the Apex Rest and Tourist Home. Washington matched the competition presented by the Walker Company (Madame C. J. Walker)* and Poro (Annie Turnbo-Malone),* which were both firmly entrenched hair products manufacturing companies when Washington was beginning her own enterprise.

When the stock market crashed in 1929, many of Washington's investments were wiped out, but Washington was successful at rebuilding her enterprise and maintained her success throughout the depression and the World War II era. Washington's name was synonymous with philanthropy. Recognizing the need for more recreational facilities for the youth, she established the Ellen P. Hunter Home for Girls in Atlantic City. The building was named in honor of Washington's mother. She contributed regularly to the Betty Bacharach Home for Children in Longport, New Jersey, which served children from many races. She gave 20 acres of her Egg Harbor, New Jersey, farm to the National Youth Administration (NYA) for a campsite for black youth. She purchased other property and turned it over to the NYA as well. So sensitive was Washington to the needs of the poor that she gave coal to families during severe winter months.

In 1939, because of her business achievements, Washington was awarded a medallion at the New York World's Fair for her leadership in the international business arena. She was a committee woman for Atlantic County. When Washington died, some 2,000 persons attended her funeral in Atlantic City, where mourners waited in lines two blocks long.

SELECTED BIBLIOGRAPHY: John N. Ingham and Lynne B. Feldman, *African-American Business Leaders: A Biographical Dictionary* (Westport, CT: Greenwood Press, 1994); Gladys L. Porter, *Three Pioneers in Beauty Culture* (New York: Vantage Press, 1966); ''Sarah (Sara) Spencer Washington,'' in Jessie Smith Carney, ed., *Notable Black American Women* 2 vols. (Detroit: Gale Research, 1992); ''Sara Spencer Washington,'' *Chicago Defender*, April 11, 1953; *Who's Who in Colored America: A Biographical Dictionary of Notable Living Persons of African Descent in America*, 4th ed. (Brooklyn, NY: Thomas Yenser, 1933).

Nancy J. Dawson

WESTON, ANTHONY (c.1800–1876), South Carolina, millwright.

Anthony Weston (originally known as Toney), although he legally remained a slave until 1865, managed to amass a considerable fortune. His uncertain legal status meant that his wife held title to their possessions, as her claim to freedom was superior to his own. On the eve of the Civil War in 1860, Weston had an estate valued at $40,075, which included 14 slaves. Seven years later, unlike many southerners, he still possessed much of that property, valued at $20,300 in 1867.

Weston's exact origins are unclear, but his owner's will described him as a ''mulatto,'' and it is thus likely that one of his parents, probably his father, was white. Whether his owner, Charleston planter Plowden Weston, was also his father is purely speculatory. When Plowden Weston died in 1820, his will noted that he had customarily allowed Toney to work for himself as a millwright between May and November of each year. That arrangement was to continue for six years, at which point Toney was to be freed or allowed to leave the state. The difficulty with freeing any slave by 1826 was that an 1820 state law stipulated that any manumission required the endorsement of the state assembly. Such endorsements were rarely granted. Although the 1840 and 1860 censuses listed Anthony Weston as a free colored person, there is no documentary proof that his manumission was ever given the stamp of legality.

Regardless of this, he lived as a free person from 1826 until his death. At some point, he married another of Plowden Weston's slaves, a house servant named Maria, whose freedom he purchased, along with that of his brothers Samuel and Jacob. Anthony Weston was a gifted mechanic and millwright. While working for Benjamin Franklin Hunt in 1831, he rebuilt a threshing machine, doubling its efficiency in the process. This cemented his reputation, and he enjoyed considerable success, building and maintaining rice mills. To satisfy the labor demands of his business, Weston purchased slaves. Between 1834 and 1845, Maria Weston spent $8,950 on the purchase of 20 slaves, including artisans who worked in her husband's business.

On January 10, 1861, a few months prior to the outbreak of the Civil War, Weston and 22 other prominent African American Charlestonian businessmen signed a memorial to Governor Francis Pickens of South Carolina in which they attested their allegiance to the state and to the "white race." Their offer of service was of course rejected. This spontaneous outbreak of patriotism illustrates the precarious position of Charleston's free African American elite. On the one hand, they were under pressure to become jingoistic Confederates to avoid charges of disloyalty, but on the other hand, we cannot discount the possibility that their economic and social prominence led them to see the world more as southerners than as African Americans.

Anthony Weston certainly enjoyed considerable economic success within the institution of slavery.

SELECTED BIBLIOGRAPHY: Michael P. Johnson and James L. Roark, *Black Masters: A Free Family of Color in the Old South* (New York: W. W. Norton & Company, 1984); Larry Koger, *Black Slaveowners: Free Black Slave Masters in South Carolina, 1790–1860* (Jefferson, NC: McFarland & Co., 1985); Bernard E. Powers, Jr., *Black Charlestonians: A Social History, 1822–1885* (Fayetteville: University of Arkansas Press, 1994); Loren Schweninger, *Black Property Owners in the South, 1790–1915* (Urbana: University of Illinois Press, 1990).

Ian Binnington

WINFREY, OPRAH (1954–), Chicago, TV producer, actress, entrepreneur, philanthropist.

With wealth at $675 million in 1999, Oprah Winfrey has achieved the distinction of being the richest African American woman in the twentieth century and the richest African American in the 1990s at the end of the twentieth century.

Oprah Winfrey began her career in media in her high school senior year. As a participant in the March of Dimes walk-a-thon, Winfrey requested a donation from a disc jockey at WVOL. Agreeing to do so, the disc jockey requested that Winfrey make a voice tape, which was later submitted to the WVOL manager. Winfrey was hired as a part-time newscaster on weekends. After high school, Winfrey continued her education at Tennessee State University in Nashville full-time on a scholarship won from an Elks Club oratory contest. In addition, Winfrey continued to work part-time at WVOL.

In 1973, Winfrey accepted a new position at WTVF-TV, a CBS affiliate, in Nashville. She became the first female coanchor and first black coanchor in Nashville. Winfrey temporarily dropped out of school when she was promoted at WTVF from weekends to weekdays. In 1976, Winfrey became a reporter for WJZ-TV, an ABC affiliate, in Baltimore, Maryland. This new career move did not work for Winfrey, and she was moved to news inserts on *Good Morning America* and worked at the WJZ-TV Instant Eye Unit as a reporter in 1977. In this new position, Winfrey proved to be more personable through her stories, which led to her later success as a talk show host.

In 1984, Oprah was asked to host "*A.M. Chicago*," for WLS TV, at a salary of $230,000 a year. Inclusive of the four-year contract was a negotiated salary increase of $30,000 annually. The success of this program grew into the renowned *Oprah Winfrey Show* in 1985; in 1986, the show was syndicated. Airing on 200 stations in the United States and in over 117 foreign countries, the deal grossed over $125 million. In November 1986, Winfrey bought full ownership of her show and became the first black to own a television filming show and production company.

Harpo Studios (*Oprah* spelled backwards) cost Winfrey $20 million to purchase and renovate. With earnings of $30 million a year, during the first season, the show earned a revenue of $115 million. In 1994 the show grossed $196 million, and Harpo grossed over $100 million, $30 million in production. Inclusive of Winfrey's income is a $1.5 million option on King World; as of 1995, this investment was worth over $30 million. Winfrey is the recipient of 250,000 shares annually per renewal with King World Production. In 1997 the syndication earned an estimated $240 million. Winfrey, in 1996, earned more than $97 million, and over $104 million in 1997, ranking number three in the *Forbes* "Top Forty."

While the success of the program grew, Winfrey also began her debut in acting. In 1985 she played the role of Sophie in the movie *The Color Purple*. She produced and appeared in *Women of Brewster Place*. Winfrey also produced *Beloved*, based on the novel by Toni Morrison, and will be involved in the production of six films with ABC and Disney.

Winfrey's service commitments include her political involvement in the National Child Protection Act as well as the Oprah Bill. In 1994, in cooperation with the Jane Addams Hull House Association, Winfrey donated $6 million to assist 100 families to move from subsidized housing. However, in a three-year period, only six families were successfully assisted in this project.

With the completion of her degree in May 1987, Winfrey donated $750,000 for 10 full scholarships to Tennessee State. As a devoted believer in education, Winfrey makes yearly contributions of $250,000 to her alma mater. In 1996, Winfrey invested in the education of Morehouse College students, contributing

$1 million toward scholarships. The donations of these funds are due to Winfrey's desire to share her success.

Winfrey's successes include prestigious awards in the broadcasting industry. In 1988, TV and Radio honored her with the title of Broadcaster of the Year and a recent honor of Television Performer of the Year. Another success in Winfrey's career includes the opening of her restaurant, the Eccentric, in 1989. As coauthor of *Make the Connection*, with her personal trainer, Winfrey emphasizes the impact of weight loss and gain. Recently Winfrey released her autobiography, *The Uncommon Wisdom of Oprah Winfrey*. In addition, Winfrey continues to emphasize the importance of reading through the Oprah Book Club. In 1997, Winfrey renewed her contract with ABC for two more seasons of the *Oprah Winfrey Show*. In the final years of the twentieth century, the *Oprah Winfrey Show* remains the largest syndicated talk show.

SELECTED BIBLIOGRAPHY: Lois Dunn, *Epic Lives* (Detroit: Visible Ink Press, 1993); *Forbes* (Special Issue), October 16, 1995; *Forbes*, September 22, 1997; *Forbes*, October 13, 1997; Brian Lanker, *I Dream a World* (New York: Stewart, Tabori, & Chang, 1989); "Oprah between the Covers," *Life*, September 1997; Anne Saidmann, *Oprah Winfrey: Media Success Story* (Minneapolis: Lerner Publications, 1990); www.oprahshow.com

Oluwatoyin Caldwell

WOMEN BUSINESS ENTERPRISES. The business participation of black women began in Colonial America and reflected African survivalisms in gender-based domestic and craft manufacturing activities. In precolonial West and West Central Africa during the era of the transatlantic slave trade, African women participated in the economy at three levels: agricultural production; cottage industry craft manufacturing; and market commodity trading. In addition to agricultural skills in farming and food production, which made African women invaluable as slave laborers, they were also proficient in textile weaving and dyeing, in cloth making as spinners, carders, and weavers; and as seamstresses and quilt makers. Their handicraft skills included basketry, broom, mat, and pottery making. In health care, they demonstrated skills in midwifery and pharmacopeia. The tradition that existed among African women to pursue self-initiated, independent economic activities, derived from those skills, survived the transatlantic passage. From the colonial era on, while these African gender-based agricultural and domestic skills were exploited for profit by slaveholders, these same economic activities also provided the basis for the development of the black woman's tradition of independent business activities.

With their enslavement in America primarily for agricultural labor on plantations and small farms as field hands, domestic services were also extracted from slave women in both town and country, who worked as nurses, washers and ironers, cooks, house cleaners, spinners, and seamstresses. Based on the regimented activities of one group of Rhode Island slave women in 1730, who made from 12 to 24 cakes of cheese daily, black women were the nation's first female factory workers. Eventually, these gender-based skills were transformed by slave women who hired their time* into income-generating enterprises. The profits earned from their independent economic activities enabled many of these women to purchase freedom for themselves, their children, family members, and friends. Black women purchased real property, which they used not only for housing but also to establish shops. Property ownership* by black women began in the seventeenth century. In Virginia, in the mid-1600s, of the 13 property owners in a black settlement, 3 were women. In 1670, Zippora Potter, the free daughter of a slave, purchased both a lot and a house, for which she paid the purchase price in full.

Marketing food, an African commercial survivalism, was the initial economic activity of slave women. Selling farm produce, fruits, vegetables, and sometimes chickens and eggs, as well as handicrafts, baskets, roped rugs, and herbal concoctions, enabled African American women to participate in the economy. Passing on their clever, effective market skills from one generation to the next enabled black women, slave and free, from the seventeenth century on, to quickly dominate the produce retail distribution sector of the South's economy through their trade and marketing activities. Although most slave market women's earnings were minimal, some even acquired freedom. In the early nineteenth century, Aletha Turner, a produce vendor with a market stall, sold the vegetables she raised in a small garden plot in her home in Washington, D.C. In a 25-year period, from the profits made, Turner purchased not only her freedom but that of 22 other slaves.

Some women processed and prepared food, which they sold as street vendors and hawkers. They also set up stands, and eventually there were black women who opened fruit and vegetable stores and groceries. Some black women developed specializations in various food services activities, such as bakers and confectioners. These specialized food service enterprises were established in the early eighteenth century and continued throughout slavery. Catering,* however, was the most successful food service enterprise. In Providence, Rhode Island, in 1736, Mary Baroon and her husband, Emanuel Manna, former slaves who purchased their freedom, established a catering business and opened an oyster and alehouse. Venture capital for these enterprises came from the profits made by Mary from her illegal whiskey distillery enterprise.

Black women in the bakery business also achieved some success. In Newport, Rhode Island, "Dutchess" Quamino established a bakery during the Revolutionary War era, and it remained in business until the early twentieth century. In the early nineteenth century, Kathy Ferguson in New York City succeeded as a baker, specializing in wedding cakes. In the antebellum era, Nancy Lenox Remond in Newton, Massachusetts, established an enterprise as a fancy cake maker, whereas her daughter Susan in Salem continued in the business as a pastry cook, confectioner, and small restaurant owner. In Plymouth, North Carolina, Mary A. Lee established a profitable bakery.

By the nineteenth century, black women had not only expanded their food service enterprises but professionalized these businesses, especially in catering, a field that was dominated by men, particularly in the North, but there were black women who also succeeded as caterers. In Cincinnati, Mrs. Kate Jones established a successful catering business; in Charleston, Sally Seymour and Camillia Johnson were the city's leading caterers.

In antebellum America, then, black women established enterprises not only in the food services industry as vendors and hawkers but also in the bakery business, catering, food shops, and restaurants. A few established inns, but the majority in this industry were boardinghouse keepers. In addition to establishing shops as grocers and retail merchants, primarily in the sale of small notions, others owned secondhand clothing stores.

The occupations of free black women were listed in various censuses; but because only one occupation was listed for an individual in a census, the extensive kinds of self-employment activities developed by antebellum free blacks are obscured, especially since many antebellum blacks in business participated in a diversity of enterprises. In Rhode Island, Elleanor Eldridge (1785–1865) was invariably listed in the census as a domestic or as "keeping house." Yet she was involved in a diversity of enterprises including soap manufacturing, "Matrass [sic] Mak[ing]," and in partnership with her sister, "white-washing, papering, and painting"—occupations usually limited to men. Eldridge used her profits to purchase two lots, where she constructed a house for $1,700 that she used for rental property.

Dressmaking shops were especially profitable, especially those owned by black women who also specialized in fashion design. Some black women were successful owners of hair care enterprises or companies that manufactured hair care products. Health care services were also important areas of self-employment. In Petersburg, Virginia, former slave woman Amelia Gallé inherited a bathhouse in 1819, which she had managed while she was enslaved. Once freed, Gallé promoted her business through aggressive newspaper advertisements.

Yet while gender-based domestic and personal service occupations provided the foundation for the entry of most black women in the antebellum American business community, the leading black businesswomen were involved in the same enterprises that generated wealth for leading black businessmen. In the South, there were black women plantation owners. With their profits and holding wealth in the tens of thousands, these black women also engaged in finance as informal bankers, loaning their money with interest while investing in bank stock, municipal bonds, and internal improvements.

One of the most successful antebellum black woman financiers was Madame Cecee McCarty, whose business activities were launched in the late 1790s. By 1830, she was the largest slaveholder in New Orleans. Merchandising, however, provided her with the financial basis for her informal banking activities. She was the owner of an imported goods store, with a market that extended beyond

New Orleans. Using her 32 slaves as a traveling sales force, all with assigned territories, working out of the depot she owned in Plaquemines Parish, Madame McCarty by 1848 had accumulated more than $155,000. While merchandising contributed to her wealth, Madam McCarty also increased her profits by the interest she accumulated from the loans she made and by speculating in the currency market. Throughout her long business career, as indicated in the records of an 1848 court case in which she was involved, Madame Mccarty was recognized as "une femme extremement laborieuse et econome."

The Louisiana-born entrepreneur black woman planter Marie Therez Metoyer, who was born in slavery in 1742 of African-born parents, was the matriarch of the most successful black slave-owning family in antebellum America. Unlike many black slaveholders* who inherited their plantations from white fathers, lovers who were their slave masters, or their mulatto parents, Marie (her slave name was Coincoin) was manumitted by her owner (she had been his house slave mistress), but unlike other former slave mistresses, Coincoin built her plantation from the ground up, starting when she was 46 years old. Coincoin's entrepreneurial zeal was propelled by her drive to buy her children from slavery. She had 11 children; some had fathers who were black, and the others were fathered by her slave owner. As Coincoin purchased land to build a cotton plantation, and at the same time she began purchasing slaves to work her land, she was also buying her own children from slavery. She died in 1816, but by 1830, the Metoyer family had acquired almost 12,000 acres and owned 278 slaves. By the Civil War, the Metoyer dynasty, according to Gary Mills, had acquired wealth amounting to over $750,000.

In the antebellum South, Madame Cecee Mccarty and Marie Therez, as entrepreneurs, were not unique as slave owners. Indeed, the most successful black businesswomen before the Civil War—the caterers, dressmakers, restaurant, boardinghouse, inn, and hotel owners, as well as other black women planters—also owned property in slaves. Black female planters employed their slaves in the fields as well as the house, whereas the slaves of urban black businesswomen worked as employees in their owner's business or were hired out to others by their owners. Indeed, many of these urban free black female slaveholders were themselves, as Coincoin, former slaves. Some were slaves who hired their own time* and had established successful enterprises while enslaved. The profits made while slaves enabled them to purchase their freedom, invariably using the same initiative to succeed as free black businesswomen.

How does one explain the ownership of slaves by free black women? Can the triple-jeopardy status of black women—racism, sexism, and classism—be ignored as a motivating basis for the ownership of slaves by free black women? Given the alternatives, the oppression of poverty and racial degradation that confronted black women during the age of slavery, can these black women slaveholders be exonerated for putting self and family economic survival above societal ties of racial kinship? Must we accept, then, that the extent to which free black women slaveholders succeeded in the management of their enterprises reflects, just as with their male counterparts, that they also had internalized the capitalist ethos of the antebellum American free enterprise system, which in the South rested on the labor exploitation of black slaves?

At the same time, a black womanist consciousness inclusive of ties of racial kinship existed, which was much more pervasive and reflective of the activities and sentiments of antebellum black women than that of black women slave ownership. By 1860, the number of black women slaveholders had declined, including those black women who held slaves for benevolent reasons, as opposed to those who owned slaves for commercial purposes. Moreover, there were many more black women who purchased slaves to free them than those who purchased slaves to own them.

Indeed, a communal consciousness of mutual self-help distinguished the lives of antebellum black women much more so than the existence of black women slaveholders, reflected in both the mutual aid* and benevolent societies organized by black women. The first black women's mutual aid societies were founded in the late eighteenth century. They increased in number and membership from then until the Civil War. Also there were cooperative enterprises. In 1841, an organization of 100 black women in New York established a cooperative grocery store, the Female Trading Association. Black women were active in the Free Produce movement, which encouraged the consumer boycott of slave-produced goods. Newspaper publishing, as a business enterprise, provided a venue for abolitionist protest for Mary Ann Shadd Cary, who immigrated to Canada, where she earned the distinction of becoming the first black woman in the Americas to found and publish a newspaper, the *Provincial Freeman.*

Consequently, while the historical focus on black women during the age of slavery has been primarily on plantation slave women and the activities of black women reformers in the abolitionist and women's rights movement, the business activities of several black women have survived in the historical record, including the international business activities of New England–born Mary Gardner Prince (1799–c.1856), who traveled with her husband to Russia. In St. Petersburg, Mary established two enterprises, a boardinghouse for children and a garment-making business for children's clothes and dresses. She operated these enterprises in Russia from 1824 to 1833, employing a journeywoman, whereas her other employees were apprentices. Her customers were the Russian nobility. Elizabeth Keckley, known as the dressmaker for Mrs. Abraham Lincoln, was primarily a dress designer who employed some 20 seamstresses in her haute couture shop. On the other hand, Californian Mary Ellen Pleasant,* while involved in several entrepreneurial ventures, has been remembered primarily as a boardinghouse keeper.

Black participation in the hair care products manufacturing business developed before the Civil War. These products were made in the homes by black women who sold them from door to door. The more successful black women in the hair business were hairdressers and wig makers. Invariably their customers were white, both men and women, and usually they worked out of their own shops located in the downtown business districts of the cities in which they lived. In Pittsburgh, Pennsylvania, Virginia Proctor established her wig shop in the same building as her husband's barbershop. In Salem, Massachusetts, the Remond sisters, Cecilia, Maritcha, and Caroline, however, established a wig-making factory. They also manufactured hair tonic for hair loss, which they sold locally. Their largest market was through mail-order distribution, with sales primarily in New England.

After the Civil War, black women in business continued in developing the same lines of enterprises and self-employment in which they had participated during the age of slavery. Just as antebellum black women developed a diversity of businesses, at the same time, the majority of self-employed black women were laundresses, hucksters, market dealers, and seamstresses. While the Thirteenth Amendment in 1865 ended slavery, freedom did not bring immediate rewards in the economic life of blacks, most of whom continued in the same occupations as black women before the war. Indeed, according to the 1900 census, 83.8 percent of African American women worked in personal services as domestics and laundresses. Yet black women used their business skills in the establishment of not-for-profit community institutions, particularly schools and social services.

Since the economic success of black women was due to the gender-based enterprises they established, which were often marginal in profits, few encountered the racial hostilities experienced by black businessmen. Ida B. Wells (1862–1931), however, provides an exception. An activist and businesswoman who owned and published the Memphis, Tennessee, newspaper *Free Speech*, ironically, Wells was forced to give up her enterprise after she published an article in 1892 that highlighted the economic basis for the lynching of many blacks.

By the turn of the century, however, there was an increased professionalization of black women's business activities, especially in three of the four major areas in which they established enterprises: financial institutions, the black hair care industry, manufacturing activities, and as small shopkeepers. With the vast majority of black women, however, their primary goal from slavery to freedom was not only to secure employment but also to find avenues of financial protection, when they were sick or unemployed, and most of all, to provide themselves with a decent funeral.* During the age of slavery, mutual aid societies established by black women were important in helping to meet these needs. Invariably, the funds pooled allowed only for the most minimal allocations for sickness, unemployment, and funeral expenses. After the Civil War, these organizations expanded in number and membership.

The most historically significant financial organization in black women's history was the Independent Order of St. Luke (IOSL), founded by former slave Mary Prout in 1867 to provide sick and death benefits to its members. The financial success of the IOSL was assured when Maggie Lena Walker,* a member of the Order since 1883, was elected executive secretary in 1899. It was from her position as an officer that Maggie Lena Walker in 1903 established the first bank founded by an American woman. Walker, in heading the bank, then, was also the first American woman to sit as a bank president in this nation. The organization of the bank had two major purposes. In 1901 Walker had organized an insurance department, and the bank provided a depository for IOSL funds. Also, the bank was capitalized by the selling of $10.00 shares to IOSL members, and another purpose was to encourage IOSL members to open savings accounts. Recognizing the impoverished status of black women, Walker said that the St. Luke Bank would "take nickels and turn them into dollars." The Saint Luke Penny Savings Bank survived and continues in operation today as the Consolidated Bank and Trust Company.

In the early twentieth century, Mary McLeod Bethune, one of the foremost black women leaders in the first half of the twentieth century, was one of the founders of the Central Life Insurance Company of Tampa, Florida. In Mississippi, Minnie Cox (1869–1933), who is known historically as the black woman whose 1902 appointment by Theodore Roosevelt as post mistress of Indianola was defeated in 1904 in response to white racist objections, was also cofounder, with her husband, of both the Delta Penny Savings Bank and the Mississippi Life Insurance Company. She also held the positions of secretary and treasurer in the two financial institutions. The bank eventually closed, but after her husband's death, Cox served as president of the insurance company until 1917. The founding of black insurance companies,* however, was important in the employment activities of black women as insurance agents. In 1912, almost 25 percent of the agents that worked for North Carolina Mutual* were women whereas Metropolitan had only one woman agent until World War II.

In the early twentieth century, several historical forces had an impact on the enterprises of black women who owned retail sales and personal service enterprises. With the rise of Jim Crow, there was an escalation in racial tension. Changing urban racial demographics and an increase in the incomes of urban blacks, however, resulted in the development of a new consumer market for black women and encouraged new increases in their business participation. In 1914, a black newspaper reporting on the expansion of black business activity provided an example of the business activities of black women in Kansas City, explaining: "Quite a number of them are engaged actively in business, conducting such establishments as bakeries, cafes, dressmaking, millinery and floral shops." In the expanding urban ghettos of the nation's leading industrial centers, while black women owners of restaurants experienced an increase in black customers, there was also a concomitant increase in competition as the numbers of black restaurant owners increased during the Great Migration* of the World War I era.

Even in the twentieth century, food services provided opportunities for black women. In Harlem, Lillian Harris, known as "Pig Foot Mary," was a street vendor who, beginning in 1901, hawked food delicacies that appealed to southern migrants whose numbers increased during the Great Migration. By World

War I, Harris, who had invested her profits in real estate, was one of the wealthiest black women in Harlem. The business picture for black women shopkeepers, particularly milliners and dressmakers, was also influenced by new urban racial market demographics.

Throughout the nineteenth century, the most successful had a white customer base. By the early twentieth century, when they were abandoned by this clientele, black women dressmakers and milliners in the South, however, gained a new customer base. Simply by allowing black women to try on hats and dresses, which they were not allowed to do in the white stores, these black women shopkeepers were able to remain in business. Yet by the end of World War I, especially in northern cities, these small black women shopkeepers found that they were losing their customers not only to an increase in white-owned clothing stores in the black community but also to the large downtown department stores. Indeed, an article in a 1919 issue of the *Women's Wear [Daily]* noted: "[B]ecause of the great increase in the wages of the laborer, the Negro's trade must be taken into consideration," particularly since, as the article emphasized, "they do not buy cheap things, but the best and latest models."

The most phenomenal increase in black women business owners was in the number of beauty shops, which had "protected markets."* The growth in this new business area for black women was a response to the revolution in black hair care and the professionalization in the manufacturing and marketing of black hair products. In the black hair care business, Annie Turnbo-Malone* and Madame C. J. Walker,* with sales in the millions of dollars of black hair care products, facial creams, and cosmetics of black women, produced in the factories they established. Their market distribution was both national and international. Also, these two black women professionalized hair care by opening beauty schools, which trained thousands of black women who subsequently opened shops. Consequently, in the early twentieth century, when most black women in business were owners of dress and millinery shops or restaurants, Turnbo-Malone and Walker single-handedly opened a new area of self-employment for black women, either as door-to door saleswomen of these hair care products or beauty shop owners.

Still, aside from hair products, few manufacturing enterprises were established by black women. Access to credit and venture capital limited their opportunities, even when it appeared that some success could be achieved through manufacturing. In one instance, even had funds been available to New Jersey black woman inventor Alice H. Parker, who in 1918 obtained a patent for a gas "Heating-Furnace," establishing a factory for the production of furnaces would have proved an impossible venture in the rarefied world of industrial production in the 1920s. Certainly, aside from the racism that existed in the American business community, sexism would have precluded a black woman from running a factory that manufactured furnaces. On the other hand, the Berry & Ross Doll Manufacturing Company, established in 1918 by two black women, Evelyn Berry and Victoria Ross, developed into a successful enterprise. Manufacturing dolls was extremely less capital-intensive as well as less challenging in a sexist society than manufacturing furnaces. Indeed, in their advertisements, the women indicated that mail orders should be addressed to ''Messrs Berry & Ross.''

The company, which manufactured ''Berry's Famous Brown Skin Dolls,'' was capitalized at $10,000. Attuned to the business world of corporate finance, in 1919 they offered 800 shares of stock at $10 each to the public to generate capital for expansion. Their market was not limited to blacks, since large department stores in major cities on the East Coast and in the South also sold their dolls, primarily to whites. Business boomed, and the company purchased another building, changed its name to Berry & Ross Manufacturing Company, Incorporated, and by 1920, employed 30 women who produced 2,000 women's and children's dresses each week. Also, that same year, Berry & Ross purchased a three-story building in Norfolk, Virginia, to establish the first of a chain of Berry & Ross Department Stores.

With the depression, most black women who were able to stay in business continued operating their traditional lines of enterprises, primarily restaurants, laundries, dry cleaners, clothing stores, groceries, and supermarkets.

Overall, while black business expanded in the early twentieth century, comparative participation was limited. In 1930, in West Virginia, black males owned only 4.1 percent of all men-owned businesses in that state, whereas black females owned 10.5 percent of all women-owned businesses. The total number of black business owners in the state was 1,350. The leading businesses for black men were barbershops (343) and tailor shops (243), whereas the leading businesses for black women were beauty shops (109) and boardinghouses (224). Indeed, from 1890 to 1940, barber/hairdresser shops, restaurants, and retail merchants comprised the three major groups of black businesses during that period.

Moreover, during the Great Depression, there was a decline in the number of these enterprises, interesting when compared to the increase in the number of funeral* homes from 1930 to 1940. While limited incomes of blacks accounted for the decline in the hair care business, people had to eat, and there was a continuing market for specialized food products. In the late 1930s, two black women established successful bakeries. In 1937, Mrs. Minnie Lee Fellings, who established the Minnie Lee Pie Company in Chicago, was by 1939 selling 3,000 pies daily. She had three delivery trucks, which distributed her pies to some 225 stores and restaurants in that city. In Birmingham, Alabama, Mrs. Gertrude Alexander, a candy manufacturer, who established the Nanette Candy Company, had 400 wholesale customers before World War II, when wartime restrictions on sugar limited her candy production. In 1941, when her company grossed $60,000, Anderson was considered one of the nation's leading black businesswomen.

During World War II, business opportunities increased for black women, especially their participation in food and personal services enterprises. Black geographical mobility increased during the war, a response to war production in the nation's heavy industries. Black migration to industrial centers provided expanded opportunities for black women property owners. Many established boardinghouses, as they let out rooms to the newcomers. The incomes of blacks also increased. With greater disposable incomes, and because of the shortages in consumers goods, black women retail shopkeepers, and also dressmakers and milliners, experienced an increase in sales.

The increased incomes of blacks resulted in an increase in the number who could afford vacations, and after the war, with the demilitarization of American industry, the number of black car owners increased. Blacks were on the road more than ever before and with transportation could get away for vacations. While black businessmen from the early twentieth century had established resort hotels, only a few black women were in the business from the ground up. Resort owner Sally Walker, however, within 12 years, from 1942 until 1954, developed a 300-acre, $400,000 Catskill Mountain resort for blacks from her initial investment of $2,500 in a farm with only two buildings. Walker provided her guests, both national and international, with dance casinos, a lake for swimming, fishing, and rowing, and tennis and basketball courts. In 1954, she was making plans for an 18-hole miniature golf course. A year earlier Sarah Spencer Washington,* after being denied privileges to play on the Atlantic City, New Jersey, local golf courses, transformed her farmland into a 9-hole golf course and country club. Washington also established her $50,000 Apex Rest Tourist Retreat.

Sarah Spencer Washington, who founded the New Jersey–based Apex News and Hair Company in 1919, survived the depression and from the 1930s until her death in 1953 was the leading black businesswoman in America. During the 1930s Walker hair care products had almost disappeared, eclipsed by Apex hair products sales. A shrewd businesswoman, Washington was described as the "Genius with the Midas Touch," perhaps because she avoided credit, so her profits would not be swallowed up in interest. Simply put, Washington made all of her purchases in cash, including her manufacturing supplies, which she purchased in carload lots. She owned extensive business property, including her Apex Warehouse, Apex Auditorium, Apex Laboratory, Apex Publishing Company, and Apex Drug Store in a building with six apartments. Washington also owned the $100,000 Brigantine Hotel, which she paid for in cash and subsequently sold for $150,000. Her home was constructed for $85,000, and on completion, the contractors were paid in cash. Also, as part of her philanthropy she established the Ellen Memorial Center for Girls.

Ironically, while the leaders in developing the black hair care products industry in the first half of the twentieth century were women, beginning in the 1950s the leading manufacturers of black hair care products were men. Still, black women continued to play an important role in the development of the black cosmetic industry. While Overton's* "High-Brown" face powder represented the first market success in the sale of cosmetics for black women, Turnbo-Malone, Walker, and Washington also developed a line of skin care products and cosmetics for black women, along with their hair products. Still, as a 1946 market research survey showed, most of the hair and skin care products and cosmetics purchased by black women were made by white companies. Retail stores simply refused to stock these products made by black manufacturers. Mail-order distribution, in most cases, provided the only retail outlet for the sale of these products. John H. Johnson* and his wife Eunice, also secretary-treasurer of Johnson Publications, who eventually developed the most successful black cosmetic line, Fashion Fair, got in the black health and beauty aids industry in 1946 when they introduced their line of Beauty Star Cosmetics, which were sold through their mail-order firm.

In the post–World War II era, however, a new generation of black women moved into the cosmetics industry. The most successful enterprise, also founded in 1946, was Rose Meta,* Inc., which introduced a full line of cosmetics for black women, lipstick, rouges/blushes, and creams. Responses to her products were so great that they became the first line of cosmetics for black women that were sold in a major white department store. Also, the Chicago-based Marguerita Ward Cosmetics Company, Inc., founded in 1922, resumed manufacturing after World War II. In 1959 Lena Horne established the Lena Horne Cosmetic Company, with the home office in Oakland, California. During the 1960s, however, with its "Black Is Beautiful" emphasis, the natural look for black women in hair and skin depressed the black cosmetics market until the 1973 launching of Fashion Fair Cosmetics. Even then, it was not until 1978 that the company made a profit. By 1987 Fashion Fair was the largest manufacturer of black cosmetics. Also, it ranked in the top 10 among the companies whose line of cosmetics and skin care products were sold only in the up-market department stores.

The success of Fashion Fair encouraged competition in the cosmetic market for women of color from both white and black companies. Naomi Sims,* whose initial business success was wig manufacturing, founded a cosmetic company in 1985. Her sales were also limited to the up-market department stores, and within three years, Sims had sales of $5 million. Yet less than 20 percent of black women purchased cosmetics from the exclusive department stores. In response to a market demand from the majority of black women, who purchase their cosmetics and skin care products from drugstores and discount retail giants, such as Wal-Mart and K-Mart, Carol Jackson Mouyiaris launched her Black Opal skin care product line in 1993, which she developed specifically for the mass market. Sales were phenomenal. Black Opal increased from a 7 percent market share in 1993 to a 33 percent market share of skin products sold to blacks in 1994. In 1995, Mouyiaris introduced the Black Opal Color Cosmetics line and the Black Opal for Men skin care line.

The post–civil rights era, consequently, marked an expansion of black women in all areas of enterprise, including their participation in founding financial institutions. In the insurance industry, Ernesta G. Procope, who founded the E. G. Bowman Co. Inc., in 1954, the first minority-owned insurance brokerage firm on Wall Street, expanded her participation in finance by forming an investment firm, Bond, Procope Capital Management, with her husband John Procope and

Alan Bond in 1991. In the banking industry, Emma Chappell in 1992 founded the United Bank of Philadelphia, a full-service commercial bank, raising 55 percent, $3.3 million, the amount required by the State Department of Banking, from the black community, primarily through the black church, whose members contributed funds for the purchase of stock in the names of their church. The other 45 percent, $2.7 million, came from 14 institutional investors.

Also, from the post–World War II era to the post–civil rights era, black women increased their participation in the business side of the entertainment industry in records, radio, television, and movies. In the closing decades of the twentieth century, the hip-hop culture has been an important force in leading to an increase of black women in the business side of the entertainment business; for example, rap singer Queen Latifah, who also emerged as a TV star, established her own enterprise, Flavor Unit Record, her label/artist management/record company. Yet black women's participation on the business side of the industry began in the post–World War II era.

In 1946, Gladys Hampton, the wife of Lionel Hampton, became the first black woman to own a record company, when she established Hampton Records. Also, in 1953, Vivian Carter was a partner in the founding of the Chicago-based Vee-Jay Record Company. In radio and television, Dorothy E. Brunson has had a significant presence. In 1979, when she purchased Baltimore's WEBB, she became the first black female owner of a radio station. She subsequently purchased three other radio stations. These were sold to fund the purchase of Philadelphia television station WGTV, Channel 48, which she acquired in 1990. In 1980, Cathy Hughes purchased her first station, WOL-AM, in Washington, D.C. By 1995, with the $34 million purchase of another communications company, Hughes Radio One Inc. owned seven stations, staffed by 210 employees.

In television, black women, however, had made their mark on the business side of this industry before 1990—for example, Suzanne De Passe,* initially an executive in record production and also a producer of both feature and television films for Motown. The nation's leading talk show host, Oprah Winfrey,* also proved herself formidable as a businesswoman. First, in 1986, she bought out ownership in her *Oprah Winfrey Show* for $10 million. Then she established Harpo Productions, which not only produced her show but provided the venue for Oprah's production of television movies. In 1988, Winfrey acquired rights to 60 percent of all syndication revenues, which in 1993 grossed $180 million, and in 1993, a 45 percent interest in W. Don Cornwell's Granite Broadcasting, a network TV affiliate, one of the nation's leading black businesses. In 1996 *Forbes* placed her wealth at $415 million, ranking her 400 among the nation's leading wealth holders. In 1999 it had increased to $675 million.

In 1996 the Winfrey show was syndicated globally to 118 countries. By that time, black women in white Corporate America had also increased their participation in international business activities, holding executive management positions in the overseas branch offices of America's multinational companies, including AT&T, IBM, and the entertainment giant Polygram. The publisher of

Japan Watch, Kathryn D. Leary, also established the Leary Group, Inc., in 1991, which develops Japanese markets for American products, and Winifred Brown is co-owner with her husband in Fuci Internationals. Founded in 1989, the company specializes in the international sale of metals, with gross business receipts approximating $100 million.

As black women expanded their business activities, they became franchise owners. Valerie Daniels-Carter, a former financial analyst, established the Milwaukee-based V&J Foods, Inc., in 1983. By 1993, Daniels-Carter, chief executive officer (CEO), and in partnership with her brother, John Daniels, a corporate and real estate lawyer, owned 32 Burger King franchises, 15 in Milwaukee and 17 in Detroit, with total sales in 1996 of $36 million. As auto dealers,* black women have also made their mark. Honda dealer Barbara J. Wilson is CEO of her agency, which in 1995 had $38.6 million in sales, whereas Jacqueline L. Edgar, CEO of her Ford dealership, had $27.8 million in sales. In 1996, Theresa Jones, CEO of her Dodge dealership, had $41.7 million in sales.

At the same time, the black consumer market had expanded into the billions. In the post–civil rights era, white Corporate America acknowledged its dollar power. In competition for the black consumer dollar, demands were made for ads that could appeal to African Americans. Blacks in advertising capitalized on this market. In 1970, Barbara Gardner Proctor was the first black woman to found an advertising agency when she established her Chicago-based multimillion-dollar Proctor and Gardner Advertising, Inc. agency. Also, in the post–civil rights era, black women established multimillion-dollar businesses in various fields of science and technology, including the computer and telecommunications industry. In 1993, after working for 14 years in the area of nuclear power, Margie Lewis founded her own company, Parallax, a nuclear engineering firm, with venture capital of $10,000. By 1996, as president and CEO, with contracts from the federal government and leading *Fortune* 500 companies, Lewis's $13 million company, with offices in five states, employs a staff of 160 people.

In 1987, Pauline Brooks, CEO and president, founded Management Technology, Inc., with $1,000. By 1996, the $25 million company, with 600 employees, working in eight branches of her business, provides network services. Brooks had worked at IBM. Both businesses were founded in Maryland. Also, Kathryn C. Turner, who founded the Rockville, Maryland–based company Standard Technology, runs a multimillion-dollar business. The interest of black women in technology early on is reflected in their patented inventions; in addition to Parker's furnace, in 1945 Henrietta Bradley patented a submarine torpedo discharge mechanism. Few minorities and virtually no women were awarded federal government contracts before the Civil Rights Act of 1964. In the post–civil rights era, however, federal government contracts and *Fortune* 500 government subcontracts have been invaluable for black women in the expansion of their enterprises.

Federal equal employment affirmative action policies from the mid-1960s to mid-1970s also opened the doors of white Corporate America to black women. A few advanced to senior-level executive positions. The highest-ranking black woman in white Corporate America is Ann M. Fudge. In 1996, she was appointed CEO and president of Maxwell House Coffee Company, the $1.5 billion division of General Foods USA. The group president of Nine West, the largest maker of shoes sold in department stores, is a black woman. Also, black women became important players in the rarefied Wall Street financial world as investment bankers. These enterprises were not limited to New York. In Chicago, Barbara Landers Bowles established Kenwood Group, Inc., in 1990. By 1996, Bowles, with seven employees in her registered investment advisory firm, handled $200 million in investment. A Fisk University graduate in mathematics and University of Chicago M.B.A, Bowles, a former Kraft employee, started her business with $100,000 from her employee stock and stock options, which she took when she left Kraft.

By the end of the twentieth century, then, there was an increased participation of black women in business, not only as business owners but also as executives in both black and white Corporate America. Still, despite their remarkable abilities, many with M.B.A.s, J.D.s, and college degrees not only from the nation's prestigious colleges and universities but also from the historically black colleges and universities, by the 1990s few had reached CEO positions, such as Fudge. The retrenchment in affirmative action that began in the 1980s was reflected in the continuing racism in Corporate America as well as industry trends in downsizing.* After climbing the corporate ladder, these highly educated black women, who advanced to senior-level executive positions, reached a glass ceiling. Rather than stay in positions that offered only limited advancement and that failed to challenge their management abilities, increasingly, many began to leave.

Some black women opened their own businesses, whereas others took their management expertise and assumed management positions in black Corporate America. After 20 years at Avon, where she headed the company's international division, Joyce Roché' left to head the newly purchased black hair care products manufacturing company, Carson Inc., as president. While it remains a black majority–owned company, Carson went public in 1996, on both the New York Stock Exchange (NYSE) and the Johannesburg Stock Exchange. In 1996 Marianne Spraggins, formerly with Smith Barney, took the position of CEO at black investment bank W. R. Lazard. In the post–civil rights era, then, there has been significant advancement for black women in black Corporate America to senior management positions. At BET, Debra Lee in 1996 was appointed president and COO (chief operating officer). In addition, she holds positions as general counsel and vice president of strategic development of the nation's tenth largest black business, with sales of $132.7 million in 1996.

Also, black women began to assume CEO positions in their family businesses. In 1993, Jacqueline Lewis-Kemp, at 30 years old, became president and CEO of the Michigan-based Lewis Metal Stamping Company founded by her father in 1980. Profits in 1996 amounted to $3 million. At Johnson Publishing, joining her mother Eunice Johnson, treasurer, Linda Johnson Rice was appointed president by her father John H. Johnson,* who founded the nation's largest black, 100 percent family-owned business in 1942, with sales in 1996 of $325.7 million. At Soft Sheen Products, Inc., the nation's largest black hair care manufacturer, Teri L. Gardner was appointed CEO by her father Edward Gardner,* who founded the company in 1964, which in 1996 had sales of $91.4 million. The company was sold in 1998. The widow of Reginald Lewis,* and the mother of his two daughters, Loida N. Lewis is CEO of TLC Beatrice International Holdings, Inc., the only billion-dollar business in which blacks hold a majority financial interest among company shareholders. In 1996, Loida's sales amounted to $2.230 billion.

The activities of black women in business in the last half of the twentieth century have been documented by *Ebony*, since 1945, and by *Black Enterprise*, since 1976. Also, in response to the expanding careers of black women in business and the professions, the leading black woman's magazine, *Essence*, founded in 1970, owes its tremendous success in addressing the interests of the post–civil rights era generation of black women to Susan L. Taylor, who was appointed editor in 1981. In 1996, Essence Communications had sales of $92.784 million. Also, black women's business organizations have been founded to encourage networking and workshop sharing of expertise, such as the Detroit-based National Association of Black Women Entrepreneurs, the Association of Black Women Entrepreneurs in Los Angeles, and the Washington, D.C.–based National Association of Negro Business and Professional Women's Club's Incorporated.*

Still, most businesses established by women, including black women, have been relatively small enterprises, although, in 1992 African American women owned the largest share, 39 percent or 277,246, of the firms owned by minority women. Hispanic women owned 246,378 businesses, while Asian women owned 208,647. The total number of all women-owned firms in the United States in 1992 was 6.4 million. Yet, the mean average income of black women business owners was the lowest of all American business owners by race and gender as indicated in census reports of minority-owned businesses.* For white non-Hispanic males, their mean business income average was $250,000. The mean income average of Asian and Pacific Islanders (API) and American Indians and Alaskan Native (AIAN) males was $188,000. For non-Hispanic white women, the mean income average was $115,000 followed by Hispanic males, whose mean income average was $106,000 and Hispanic women, whose mean income average was $70,000. The mean business income average for African American males was $69,000 and for African American women, their mean income average was $31,000. Respectively, African American women owned 14.1 percent of all black firms. Hispanic women, 12.5 percent of Hispanic firms, and Asian and Pacific Islander women owned 10.6 percent of API firms.

The business history of black women from slavery to freedom, however, has also been distinguished by an entrepreneurial tradition of establishing enterprises that parallel mainstream American business activity. Yet, while there were African American business women in the twentieth century who owned and managed multimillion-dollar enterprises, at the same time, racial, societal, and economic, structural factors continue to impact on the income advancement of black business women. Still, in their business activities, black women have sustained a commercial cultural tradition of self-help that has distinguished the economic lives of black women in America for almost 400 years.

SELECTED BIBLIOGRAPHY: Donna Ballard, *Doing It for Ourselves: Success Stories of African American Women in Business* (New York: Berkley Books, 1997); Carolyn Brown, "They've Got the Power," *Black Enterprise* (August 1997); Elsa Barkley Brown, "Womanist Consciousness: Maggie Lena Walker and the Independent Order of St. Luke," *Signs: Journal of Women in Culture and Society* 14, 3(1989); Darlene Clark Hine, ed., *Black Women in America: An Historical Encyclopedia*, 2 vols. (Brooklyn, NY: Carlson Publishing, 1993); John N. Ingham and Lynne B. Feldman, *African-American Business Leaders: A Biographical Dictionary* (Westport, CT: Greenwood Press, 1994); Gary B. Mills, *The Forgotten People: Cane River's Creoles of Color* (Baton Rouge: Louisiana State University Press, 1997); *Nancy Prince: A Black Woman's Odyssey through Russia and Jamaica* (Boston, 1850; reprint, with introduction by Ronald G. Walters, ed., New York: Marcus Wiener Publishing, 1990); Rhonda Reynolds, "25 Black Women Who Have Made a Difference in Business," *Black Enterprise* (August 1994); "Special: A New Generation of African Americans is Seizing Real Power in the World of Business," *Fortune*, August 4, 1997; Autumn Stanley, "From Africa to America: Black Women Inventors," in Jan Zimmerman, ed., *The Technological Woman: Interfacing with Tomorrow* (New York: Praeger, 1985); Dorothy Sterling, ed., *We Are Your Sisters: Black Women in the Nineteenth Century* (New York: W. W. Norton, 1984); U.S. Census, "1992 Women Owned Businesses," (WB92-1) and "1992 "Minority- and Women-Owned Business Enterprises" (MB92–4) and http://www.census.gov/agfs/www.smobe.htlm; U.S. Census Bureau Public Information Office at (301) 763–5726; e-mail pio@census.gov; Juliet E. K. Walker, *The History of Black Business in America: Capitalism, Race, Entrepreneurship* (New York: Macmillan/Prentice Hall International, 1998).

Juliet E. K. Walker

WRIGHT, RICHARD ROBERT, Sr. [R.R.] (1853–1947), Georgia, Philadelphia, bank founder, president of National Negro Bankers Association, educator.

Richard Robert Wright spent the first 30 years of his professional life as an educator in Georgia. He served as teacher and as principal of black elementary schools and founded the first public high school for blacks in Georgia. In 1891, he was appointed president of a land grant college in Savannah, where he served until 1921. Richard Wright was born in slavery on a plantation near Dalton, Georgia. After the Civil War, his mother moved to Atlanta, where he attended a missionary elementary school and the prep school of Atlanta University, where he remained and received a B.A. degree.

Although his academic training had prepared him for teaching, Wright developed an interest in business and, while in Savannah, bought some real estate properties. He began to see that along with education a knowledge of business enterprise could play an important role in self-help efforts. His limited commercial ventures convinced him that capital was urgently needed in black communities, not only for the purchase of mortgages for homes but for the development and expansion of businesses.

At the time, Wright's son, Richard Robert, Jr., lived in Philadelphia, where he also was successfully dealing in real estate. In addition, he had acquired some banking experience in a previous position as a bank officer. The elder Wright, now in his sixties, consulted his children about his idea to establish a bank. After his daughter Lillian and son agreed to join him in the venture, Wright moved to Philadelphia. In 1920, a year before he resigned his post as college president, the three opened a private bank in a rental space in a building on South Street. Four years later, the Wrights had raised the necessary $125,000 to incorporate their bank as a joint stock venture, and the Citizens and Southern Bank and Trust Company was born. Wright now began an extraordinary second career, that of banker, to which he was committed until his death in his ninties.

As an educator, Wright was dedicated to principles of self-help. He took this dedication into the banking field. Not only did he prove his competency as president of Citizens and Southern, but he effectively led the National Negro Bankers Association, of which he was president for over 16 years. Through this trade association of the country's black bank officers, Wright was able to act as mentor and assist in the development of many black-owned banks. He became a central figure throughout the black business community.

Through his own bank, he was able to help fledgling businesses. Many small enterprises, such as groceries, bakeries, caterers, and private schools, were established or avoided insolvency, thanks to loans from Citizens and Southern. In terms of the bank's investments, Wright took almost no risks. He was known as very conservative in his banking policies, and he claimed that his major goal was to protect his depositors. He developed a reputation as a scrupulously honest businessman, who was held in high regard by those who dealt with him. Although the Great Depression of the 1930s brought business failures around the country and thousands of banks collapsed, Citizens and Southern not only survived but went on to become an even stronger financial institution.

In his position as president of the National Negro Bankers Association, Wright did his best to assist those who were attempting either to resuscitate failed banks or to start new ones. Thanks to the financially stable position of Citizens and Southern, the bank was able to benefit from, and be useful to, the World War II influx of blacks who migrated to Philadelphia in search of jobs. The bank continued to prosper, and when Wright died in 1947, it had over $3 million in deposits.

SELECTED BIBLIOGRAPHY: Clarence A. Bacote, *The Story of Atlanta University, a Century of Service, 1865–1965* (Atlanta: Atlanta University, 1969); Abram Harris, *The*

Negro as Capitalist: A Study of Banking and Business among American Negroes (1936; reprint, College Park, MD: McGrath Publishing Company, 1968); August Meier, *Negro Thought in America, 1880–1915* (Ann Arbor: University of Michigan Press, 1963); National Negro Bankers Association Papers, Peabody Collection, Hampton University; Booker T. Washington Papers, Library of Congress.

Elizabeth Wright

Chronology of Black Business History

Quincy T. Mills

1619	First Africans, who numbered 20, arrived in English Colonial America in Jamestown, Virginia. Like their English and European counterparts, who came involuntarily or as indentured servants or redemptioners, their labor was sold.
1640s	One of the first Africans in the United States, Anthony Johnson and his family secured freedom and acquired land through purchase and the headright system by paying for transportation of the indentured. The Johnsons cultivated tobacco.
1644	The Dutch granted land to the first 11 African Americans brought to their colony at New Netherlands. The land given to the black settlers included property that today lies in Brooklyn and Greenwich Village.
1665	A Maryland law stated, under which the *Calvert v. Wynne et al.* case was decided, "[N]oe person . . . shall trade, barter, commerce, or game, with slaves without the owner's permission."
1670	A chair-making enterprise was established by a free African in Massachusetts.
1686	In the Carolinas, a law prohibited African Americans from engaging in any trade or business.
1736	In New England, Emanuel Manna and wife Mary Baroon, slaves who bought their freedom, opened a catering establishment in Providence, Rhode Island, and an oyster and alehouse in Providence.
1740	A South Carolina slave code reveals that slaves had escalated their trading activities.

A South Carolina act stated, ''[N]o slave or slaves shall be permitted to rent or hire any house, room, store or plantations, on his or her own account.''

1764   Abijah Prince, a former slave and one of the founders of Sunderland, Vermont, acquired 100 acres in Guilford, Vermont.

1765   Samuel Fraunces opened his Fraunces Tavern in New York City, which is the oldest standing building in the city in 1999.

1766   Cyrus, a black craftsman, purchased his freedom by manufacturing wooden trays.

1775   Christopher McPherson, a slave in Virginia, was made chief operating officer of his owner's businesses, ironworks, mills, coal mines, and shipping concerns.

1776   Thomas, an illiterate Pennsylvania slave, established a successful cooper business.

1780   Newport Gardner established the African Union Society, provided benefits to widows and children, made loans to debt-encumbered members, provided apprenticeships for youth, and encouraged thrift.

1781   Amos Fortune established a successful tannery with markets in New Hampshire and Massachusetts, with both black and white youths as apprentices.

1783   Samuel ''Black Sam'' Fraunces, a prosperous tavern owner in New York, supplied American forces with food and money. The occasion of George Washington's farewell address to his troops was hosted at Fraunces Tavern.

1784   Paul Cuffe was the first black to sail as master of his own ship.

1787   Prince Hall, a Revolutionary War veteran, obtained a charter for a black Masonic Lodge in Boston.
         Richard Allen and Absalom Jones founded the Philadelphia Free African Society, a mutual aid society.

1790   Jean Baptiste Point DuSable, a Haitian immigrant, established a trading post on the southern shore of Lake Michigan, Chicago's first permanent settlement.
         The African Benevolent Society of Wilmington and the Brown Fellowship Society in Charleston, where only light-skinned blacks were allowed as members, were founded.

1791   Benjamin Banneker surveyed the nation's capital, Washington, D.C. He also published an almanac and sent a copy to Thomas Jefferson to demonstrate the intelligence of Africans.

1793   During the Philadelphia yellow fever epidemic, Richard Allen and Absalom Jones were partners in a nonprofit undertaking business.

1797	Stephen Smith, a lumber and coal merchant, real estate speculator, informal banker, and philanthropist, born a slave, by 1860 was worth $250,000; by 1865, he was the wealthiest black, with $500,000.
1798	John Stanley, born a slave, when freed became one of the wealthiest people in Craven County, North Carolina; he used profits from barbershops to invest in plantations and both purchased and freed slaves. James Forten, Sr., established the first major black-owned sail-making shop in Philadelphia and invented a sail-handling device.
1801	In Virginia, Elizabeth ''Madame Betsy'' Allergue of Petersburg established a store and operated as a shopkeeper.
1805	In Maryland, free blacks were forbidden to sell grains or tobacco without a license.
1806	A South Carolina law made it illegal for slaves to participate in mechanic or craft trades for personal benefit; to have apprentices; to buy, sell, or trade goods without tickets; or to be employed in shops without whites present. Paul Cuffe's shipping fleet included five vessels.
1808	The New York African Society for Mutual Relief was founded and invested in real estate. Founders and members were primarily craftsmen who owned their own shops.
1810	Absalom Jones founded the African Insurance Company in Philadelphia with capital stock of $5,000, the first black insurance company. In Virginia, the Richmond City Council passed an ordinance prohibiting blacks from obtaining licenses as draymen.
1811	Paul Cuffe formed a mercantile trading company in Sierra Leone, the Friendly Society of Sierra Leone, in partnership with repatriate African-born John Kizell.
1812	The slave Free Frank established a saltpeter manufactory, mining crude niter from limestone caves and processing it to make saltpeter. The profits were used to buy his freedom and that of his wife.
1816	Jehu Jones of South Carolina purchased the Burrons-Hall Inn for $13,000 from profits made in his tailoring enterprise.
1817	François Lacroix imported French cloth, fancy cashmere, and other clothing made in Paris. By 1860, with real estate investments, he was worth $300,000. Lurany Butler, of Petersburg, Virginia, managed a dray cargo handling business and employed a hired slave as her business expanded.
1818	Thomas Day in North Carolina was the first widely recognized black furniture maker. Eugene Baptiste established a catering business in Philadelphia.

1819	In Baltimore, George McGill headed the Maryland Haytian Company, which chartered ships for emigration to Haiti.
	In Louisiana, five black women paid $1,000 for permits to operate "taverns, cafes and billiards" that entitled them to sell liquor.
	The Charleston City directory showed that seven of the nine leading black grocers, fruit dealers, and confectioners were women.
1820	John Vashon opened the first public city bathhouse west of the Alleghenies.
1821	The earliest known patent given to an African American inventor was to Thomas L. Jennings for his invention to dry-clean clothes.
1825	In Maryland, free blacks needed a certificate from a justice of the peace, witnessed by two whites, to sell tobacco.
1826	North Carolina prohibited free blacks from selling certain articles and required them to have a special license to sell or trade in adjacent counties.
1830	William Wormley owned the largest livery stable in Washington, D.C.; he rented horses and carriages, but his business was destroyed in the 1834 "Snow Riot."
	Madame Eulalie "Cecee" de'Mandeville McCarty, the wealthiest antebellum black merchant businesswoman in New Orleans, the largest slaveholder in the state with 32 slaves, accumulated $150,000 by 1850 from her enterprises.
	First meeting was held of the National Negro Convention Movement, which promoted black business ownership and the establishment of a black National Bank and international trade.
1831	In South Carolina, blacks were prohibited by law from making or selling liquor.
	John Maslow was the first black to establish a prominent shipbuilding firm, in South Dartmouth, Massachusetts.
1833	In Kentucky, a Louisville ordinance made it illegal for free blacks to obtain a license to sell liquor.
1834	In New York, David Ruggles opened the first black-owned bookstore, which will be burned by a white mob a year later.
	Henry Blair received a patent for invention of a corn-planting machine.
	Lewis Woodson established his family in the barbering business.
	In Washington, D.C., Beverly Snow, who ran the hotel famous for its food services, was driven out of business by a riot (often called the Snow Riot).
1835	Slaves in Georgia were prohibited from working in pharmacies and drugstores, due to the accessibility of lethal substances.
1836	The first town founded by an African American was New Philadelphia, Illinois, by a former slave, Free Frank McWorter.
	Henry Blair received a second patent for his cotton-picking machine.

Washington, D.C., made it illegal for blacks to sell liquor or "keep any tavern, ordinary, shop, porter cellar, refectory, or eating house of any kind, for profit."

1837	Georgia state statute stipulated that slaves shall not hire their own time or trade for themselves and made it illegal to rent stores or plantations to slaves. A black shipping company was founded in New Bedford, Massachusetts. In Cincinnati, blacks founded a cooperative steamboat company to capitalize on the Ohio and Mississippi River trade.
1838	Dye Waring, a former South Carolina slave, loaned $1,600 to a white lawyer Abraham Moise. As reported by the Abolition Society of Philadelphia, 350 out of 997 blacks in this city worked in their trades.
1839	Louisville made it illegal for blacks, slave or free, to "keep a confectionery or victualling house or cellar, or a fruit store or cellar, or sell fruits or melons out of any store, house, or on any street or any other place." Dominique Metoyer loaned money at 10 percent interest, with $3,270.65 in nine outstanding loans uncollected.
1840	The Iron Chest Cincinnati Real Estate and Construction Company was founded to purchase property and construct buildings, which it rented to whites.
1842	Slave Benjamin Montgomery set up a general store on the Davis Plantation and maintained his own line of credit with New Orleans wholesalers.
1844	Goachland, Virginia, revoked the liquor license of successful tavern owner Jacob Sampson nine years before the state made it illegal for blacks to sell alcohol.
1845	After 20 years, Maryland granted the Chesapeake and Liberia Trading Company a charter of incorporation, referring to it as that "nigger company."
1846	Norbert Rillieux received a patent for an evaporating pan that revolutionized sugar-refining methods in the United States and in Central America.
1847	Entrepreneur William Alexander Leidesdorff, of Danish and African parentage and a successful businessman in California (opened San Francisco's first "luxury" hotel in 1846), launched the first steamboat and organized the first horse race in San Francisco Bay. A National Negro Convention banking committee report, calling for the establishment of a National Black Bank and claiming that "a Banking Institution originating among the colored people is needed because they at present contribute to their own degradation by investing capital in the hands of their 'enemies'," was voted down.

1848	Lewis Temple invented the toggle harpoon for whaling.
	William Leidesdorff, merchant, rancher, owner of San Francisco city lots, died (he passed for white). His estate probated at $1.5 million.
1849	A Philadelphia survey of black enterprises and occupations revealed that there were 52 blacks dealing in secondhand clothing.
	Madame Mary Ellen Pleasant opened a boardinghouse and immediately began to issue loans at high interest rates and speculate in real estate property.
1850	In Ohio, David Clay manufactured a plow, custom-made to any size, capable of plowing depths from 8 to 20 inches.
	The American League of Colored Laborers, founded in New York for the purpose of encouraging black craftsmen to become independent business owners, proposed plans to create a fund to provide venture capital to assist them.
	The number of free black barbers in three U.S. cities was: Charleston, 14; New York, 122 (80 blacks, 42 mulattos); and New Orleans, 41 (35 mulattos, 6 blacks).
	In California, within two years blacks who migrated to that state established businesses valued at $200,000 and acquired gold mines valued at $300,000.
	Stephen Smith, who purchased his freedom from slavery with a $50 loan, was grossing $100,000 from his lumber operations in Philadelphia and Columbia. Census returns reported that in New York blacks invested $755,000 in other black businesses.
	Seven and a half percent of the nation's free black population of 439,494 owned real property.
1851	An exhibition—Colored American Institute for the Promotion of the Mechanic Arts and Science—was held in Philadelphia for display of technological innovations and manufacturing contributions of blacks to the nation's industrialized economy.
	Edmund Kean, a former slave, established a livery business, in which he owned and employed three slaves.
1852	Suzanne Meullion held stock in the New Orleans, Opelousas, and Great Western Railroad Company.
1854	Fifty-eight blacks formed the Benezet Joint Stock Association of Philadelphia.
	James Richard Phillips opened a bathhouse and barbershop, Phillips and Company, which employed "ten barbers and had twenty bathtubs."
1855	With $600,000 invested in savings banks in and around New York, the National Negro Convention reported that blacks could support their own black bank.
	The National Negro Convention presented information on the value of urban black businesses by region: for the Midwest states of Ohio, Illinois, Michigan, $1.5 million; for the New England states of Massachusetts, Maine, Rhode Island, $2 million; in New York and Pennsylvania, $3 million.

1857	Nathan, a 37-year-old North Carolina slave, handled the business affairs for a North Carolina tannery, which included "week-long business trips to sell leather at markets, within a fifty mile radius of the company."
	In Wilmington, North Carolina, white craftsmen burned a building constructed by blacks with threats of doing the same to slave-erected structures.
1859	African Americans were granted land for settlement in Nigeria when Martin Delany negotiated treaties to expand production and exportation of cotton.
	Several hundred blacks left San Francisco and immigrated to Vancouver Island, a response to the gold strike in British Columbia.
	In Baltimore, slave owners advocated the removal of free blacks from the state, because they had a virtual monopoly in hotel, transportation, and coach services. The idea was later rejected owing to the significant impact free blacks had on the state's economy.
	In Philadelphia, there were 166 black shopkeepers, but not all were successful.
1860	Barney Ford escaped slavery en route to Colorado, where he built a Denver hotel and became a successful businessman.
	Louisiana's leading black planters and slaveholders had approximately $720,000 in real property. New Orleans free blacks owned $15 million in property.
	Margaret Mitchell Harris, a South Carolina free black woman rice planter, auctioned her slaves for $25,300 and invested the proceeds in stocks and bonds.
	Philadelphia had the largest number of antebellum free black dressmakers and specialists in the women's garment trade: 664.
	Former slave Elizabeth Keckley, known as Mrs. Abraham Lincoln's dressmaker, owned the largest custom-made dressmaking enterprise in antebellum America.
	Robert Adger operated the largest secondhand furniture store in Philadelphia. He owned four buildings to hold his inventory.
1863	Black business ownership was calculated at some 2,000.
1864	The Free Labor Bank was established in New Orleans by General N. P. Banks. Military Savings Banks were established at Beaufort, South Carolina, and Norfolk, Virginia, for black soldiers, but deposits were also accepted from free blacks.
1865	According to the census of occupations taken in the South, there were only 20,000 skilled white craftsmen and tradesmen compared to 100,000 skilled blacks, most of whom were former slaves. In 25 years, black artisans virtually disappeared. Crafts not phased out were usurped by whites.
	The Freedman's Savings and Trust (Freedman's Bank) was chartered by Congress.

Wealthy New Orleans black businessmen organized the New Orleans Freedmen's Aid Association to offset the failure of federal government to initiate any viable land policy that would provide freedmen with economic independence.

Charles Patterson established the C. R. Patterson and Sons Carriage Company in Greenfield, Ohio. He manufactured buggy wagons, school wagons, surreys, and hearses. The company was later named Patterson, Sons and Company.

1866	Biddy Mason, a former slave, was the first known black woman property owner in Los Angeles, California. The Chesapeake Marine Railway and Dry Dock Company of Baltimore, Maryland, was established, organized by Isaac Myers to provide jobs for blacks. Benjamin Montgomery, a former slave, purchased the Davis plantations, Briarfield, and Hurricane—approximately 4,000 acres for $300,000.
1867	The Independent Order of St. Luke was founded by former slave Mary Prout to provide sick and death benefits to its members.
1869	Blacks in Richmond organized a joint stock company to underwrite the financing of a cigar manufacturing company but failed to secure enough capital. In New York, the Corporation of Caterers was founded by 12 black caterers to consolidate the business interests of its members.
1871	The Washington, D.C., black-owned Wormley's Hotel, established by wealthy caterer James Wormley, was a five-story elevator hotel, with telephones in each room, an elegant first floor dining room, a basement bar, and a barbershop.
1872	Inventor Elijah McCoy was granted a patent for a steam engine lubricator for machines, trains, and ocean vessels. Inventor T. J. Byrd received four patents for improvements or new devices related to coupling horses to carriages.
1873	Peter Dutrieuille opened his catering business in Philadelphia. He also established the Caterer's Manufacturing and Supply Company. Clem Geddes, of New Orleans, started a mortuary business. Black business ownership was calculated at some 4,000.
1874	Frederick Douglass was elected president of the failing Freedman's Savings. Inventor Elijah McCoy received a patent for an ironing table.
1876	P. C. Fisher received a patent for a furniture caster.
1877	Six African American entrepreneurs in northwestern Kansas founded the American Nicodemus Town Company. In Washington, D.C., John Bennett Nails and his brother Edward Nails established the Shakespeare House, a hotel.

1878	African American inventor J. R. Winters devised a fire escape ladder. Inventor W. A. Lavalette received a patent for a variation on the printing press.
1879	The Colored Farmers' Alliance had a membership of 1.25 million.
1880	In Virginia's oyster industry, approximately half were black. The wealthiest black businessmen in Cincinnati were those who had established their enterprises prior to the Civil War.
1881	The first incandescent electric lamp with carbon filament was patented by Lewis Latimer, who also made drawings for Alexander Graham Bell's telephone and who was chief draftsman for General Electric and West-inghouse. Booker T. Washington opened Tuskegee Institute, the leading black agricultural and industrial institution.
1882	William B. Purvis patented a device for fastening paper bags. He will also receive 10 patents for the manufacturing of paper bags.
1883	Blacks headed by Rev. Joseph Pierce started building a railroad from Wilmington, North Carolina, to a sea coast summer resort at Wrightville Sound but did not finish. Jan Matzeliger received a patent for a shoe-lasting machine that manufactured an entire shoe, which would change the shoe industry. H. H. Reynolds patented an improvement for railroad-car window ventilators. Black business ownership was calculated at approximately 10,000.
1884	Christopher Perry and Eugene Rhodes, father and son-in-law, started the *Philadelphia Tribune*. Granville Woods received his first two patents for a steam boiler furnace and a telephone transmitter.
1885	Sarah Goode received a patent for a folding cabinet bed. D. Watson Onley built the first steam saw and planing mill owned and operated entirely by blacks in Jacksonville, Florida. The Colored Men's Professional and Business Directory of Chicago showed 200 enterprises.
1887	Isaiah Montgomery founded the all-black town of Mound Bayou, Mississippi. The town would become one of the most prosperous all-black towns in the country.
1888	William Browne founded the first black bank in America—The Savings Bank of the Grand Fountain United Order of True Reformers—in Richmond, Virginia. The Capital Savings Bank was founded in Washington, D.C., in response to a comment made in the U.S. Senate that "with all their boasted progress, the colored race had not a single bank official to its credit." In Philadelphia, the Bureau Building and Loan Association was founded and incorporated.

1889
The Hampton Institute organized the People's Building and Loan Association in Virginia to provide loans to black homeowners.
The Mutual Trust Company bank was founded in Chattanooga, Tennessee.
The Odd Fellows' Hall Association was incorporated.
Sidney and Mary Lyons established the East India Toilet Goods Company in Gutherie, Oklahoma.

1890
The Alabama Penny Savings and Loan Company was founded in Birmingham by B. H. Hudson, a successful grocer, and W. R. Pettiford, a Baptist minister.
In Atlanta, the Georgia Real Estate Loan and Trust Company was founded.
African Americans owned 120,738 farms.
William Purvis was granted a patent for a fountain pen.
Thomy Lafon was the first black man after the Civil War reputed to be a millionaire. He was a New Orleans real estate speculator and money-lender.
There were 31,127 blacks in business—owners and employees.

1891
On May 4, African American physician Daniel Hale Williams opened Provident Hospital in Chicago, which included a school to train black doctors and nurses.

1892
Andrew Beard was granted a patent for his rotary engine.
Langston, Oklahoma, an all-black town, had 25 black businesses and organized a Board of Trade.

1893
The Richmond-based Southern Aid Society in Virginia was founded.
E. P. McCabe took part in the Oklahoma Land Rush. He founded two all-black Oklahoma towns, Liberty and Langston.
Nancy Green, a former slave from Montgomery County, Kentucky, was the first Aunt Jemina and the world's first living trademark.
E. C. Berry established the Ohio Berry Hotel in Athens, Ohio; that had 50 rooms with baths and an elevator, grossing $35,000 annually.
Edward Elder Cooper started the *Colored American* in Washington, D.C.
Black business ownership was calculated at approximately 17,000.

1894
Wiley Jones built his own streetcar line and purchased his own trolley cars in Pine Bluff, Arkansas.
The Caterers Manufacturing and Supply Company was founded to supply equipment and material to Philadelphia black caterers.
In Jacksonville, Florida, contractor and builder J. H. Blodgett started his contracting business.

1895
Booker T. Washington mentioned in his Atlanta Compromise speech: "No race that has anything to contribute to the markets of the world is long in any degree ostracized."
The Windham Brothers Construction Company was founded in Birmingham, Alabama, by Thomas C. Windham, who was joined later by his brother Benjamin L.

The Frederick Douglass Memorial Hospital and Training School for nurses was founded in Philadelphia.

The National Steamboat Company in Washington, D.C., launched a luxury boat, the *George Leary*.

1896 A publication explaining the exclusionary policies of white insurance companies said: "Because of social diseases, living conditions, and other undesirable circumstances, companies would be unwise to insure Negroes"; this led to an increase in the founding and support of black insurance companies.

1897 Andrew J. Beard invented the "Jenny Coupler," automatic system for coupling railroad cars.

1898 John Merrick and other black investors founded the North Carolina Mutual Life and Provident Association, renamed North Carolina Mutual Life Insurance Company. It became the leading black insurance company in the United States, due largely to the astuteness of Charles Spaulding.

W.E.B. Du Bois proposed five strategies for the advancement of black business: (1) college education for black businessmen; (2) black businesspeople to encourage customer loyalty by being courteous and honest and using careful business methods; (3) blacks to patronize black business, even to their disadvantage; (4) black churches, schools, and newspapers to promote black business; and (5) encourage personal savings.

The Hampton Conference reported that there were 17 black-owned building and loan associations in Pennsylvania, New York, Maryland, D.C., Virginia, Georgia, Florida, and Arkansas.

The Birmingham Grate Coal Mining Company was organized with a capital stock of $10,000.

Anthony Overton founded the Overton Hygienic Manufacturing Company in the health and beauty aid industry in Kansas City, Missouri. He began manufacturing the Hygienic Pet Baking Powder.

1899 L. C. Bailey received a patent for a folding bed.

George F. Grant, an African American dentist in Boston, received a patent for a wooden golf tee.

1900 Booker T. Washington organized the National Negro Business League to encourage more blacks to go into business.

The Metropolitan Mercantile and Realty Company, a black building and loan association, was incorporated.

Annie Minerva Turnbo-Malone began manufacturing hair care products in the all-black Illinois town of Lovejoy. Her Poro products had sales in the millions.

There were 40,445 blacks in business—owners and employees.

The total wealth of black America was $700 million.

1901 African Americans in Jacksonville, Florida, organized their own streetcar line, the North Jacksonville Street Railway.

The Afro-American Industrial Benefit Association was founded in Jacksonville, Florida, by seven black men.

1902   The Mechanics Savings Bank in Richmond, Virginia, was founded by John Mitchell and grew to be one of the largest black banks.

1903   Maggie Lena Walker founded the Saint Luke Penny Savings Bank in Richmond, Virginia, and became the first woman U.S. bank president.
James Napier, Richard Boyd, Preston Taylor, and six other black investors organized the One Cent Savings Bank, later renamed the Citizens Savings Bank—one of the first black-owned banks in the country.
Black business ownership was calculated at approximately 25,000.

1904   Metropolitan Mercantile founded a bank in Savannah, Georgia, and established a store in Plainfield, New Jersey, and an industrial assessment benefit association.
Charles Banks established the Bank of Mound Bayou.
Philip A. Payton, Jr., founded the Afro-American Realty Company, capitalized at $500,000. He began in real estate in 1900, specializing in the management of ''colored tenement property'' for white building owners, but he also acquired property. He was known as the ''Father of Harlem.''

1905   In response to a law Tennessee passed that required all municipal transportation services to be segregated, Rev. Richard Boyd, James Napier, and other black businessmen organized the Union Transportation Bus and Trolley Company.
Alonzo F. Herndon founded the Atlanta Mutual Insurance Company, which has nearly always ranked second behind North Carolina Mutual.
John H. Zedricks established a mail-order house in Chicago with international markets in Liberia, Republic of Panama, Haiti, and Cuba.
Robert Abbott founded the *Chicago Defender* and built this newspaper into a million-dollar business from street sales and both local and national subscriptions.
Sarah Breedlove Walker, later named Madame C. J. Walker, began manufacturing hair preparation products and her improvements on the hair-straightening comb. She distributed her products by door-to-door sales.

1906   Wealthy real estate holder Robert R. Church was one of the founding members of the Solvent Savings Bank and Trust Company in Memphis, Tennessee.

1907   The Mound Bayou Cotton Mill, founded by Charles Banks—with a capital stock of $100,000—in Mound Bayou, Mississippi, was considered one of the largest manufacturing enterprises ever undertaken by blacks.

1908   Developer Allen Allensworth filed a plan for the all-black town of Allensworth in Tulare County, California, to provide blacks with the opportunity to develop enterprises and obtain a lifestyle equal to that of whites.
Herman Perry founded the Standard Life Insurance Company of Georgia after working for several New York white insurance companies.
Jesse Binga was the founder of the first black-owned bank in Chicago, Binga State Bank.

1909	Henry Parker and John Nails formed a realty company, Nail and Parker, and became one of the leading black realtors in New York. The People's Savings Bank and Trust Company was organized by Richard Henry Boyd and other black investors.
1910	Madame C. J. Walker was believed by some to be the first black woman to become a millionaire, disputed by supporters of Annie Turnbo-Malone. Both women produced hair care products for black women and were developing their businesses at the same time, but Walker worked as a salesperson for Turnbo-Malone's before starting her own business. Both became very wealthy. Walter Cohen, and other investors, established the People's Benevolent Life Insurance Company. By 1961, they had assets of $2.8 million. Robert Vann incorporated the *Pittsburgh Courier*, which influenced millions of black people with a national circulation. There were 30 black towns and 13 settlements in existence. There were 56,592 blacks in business—owners and employees.
1912	There were 64 black banks operating, doing an annual business of $20 million. All were located in the South (five in Oklahoma's all-black towns), except two in Illinois (the Enterprise and Binga Banks) and Philadelphia's People's Savings Bank. The Royal Union Improvement Company, a black resort company, operated a country club, Colored Citizens Country Club.
1913	Thomas Banks, who started the Banks Fried Chicken and Restaurant Company from a push cart and established four restaurants six years later, attempted to establish a chain of fried chicken take-out enterprises in 1919. The Atlanta State Savings Bank was the first chartered black banking institution in Georgia. Black businesses Atlanta Mutual, North Carolina Mutual, Pilgrim Health and Life, and Standard Life Insurance were among its depositors. Herman Perry organized Standard Life Insurance Company in Atlanta, using this as a catalyst for other enterprises: a bank, construction companies, laundries, and drugstores. The African Union Company, of New York, was organized and leased mahogany and timber lands and oil palm plantations in West Africa. Black business ownership was calculated at approximately 40,000.
1914	The Metropolitan Realty and Investment Company, founded in 1908, established the Ocola Textile Mill, the second largest black manufacturing company organized in this period. John Merrick, Asa Spaulding, and Aaron Moore founded the Durham Textile Mill. W. Fred Trotman was the only successful black broker on Wall Street. John McWorter was granted two patents: one for an "Aeroplane," the other for a "flying machine," actually a helicopter, since it was designed to "ascend vertically from the ground."

1915   The American Methodist Episcopal (AME) journal the *Christian Recorder* published an article emphasizing the opportunities available to blacks as taxicab drivers.

The New York Colored Business Men's Association was formed in response to the problems faced by black businessmen in the city.

Membership of the National Negroe Business League (NNBL) was estimated at 30,000, with over 600 chapters in 34 states and the Gold Coast in West Africa.

Frederick Douglass Patterson formed Patterson, Sons and Company of Ohio and was the first black to manufacture cars. He introduced his first car a year later—the Patterson-Greenfield.

1916   In New York, William H. Peters and Samuel Hamilton started a taxicab and car rental company, beginning with "two Packard automobiles."

A *New York Age* survey found that on 135th Street, from Fifth to Seventh Avenues, there were 117 businesses that employed 365 people. Blacks owned 65 businesses and employed 190 black men, 43 black women, and 3 white men.

1917   Frank L. Gillespie and other former employees of Royal Insurance Company organized the Public Life Insurance Company of Illinois.

Herman Perry organized the Service Company, a laundry business, with capital stock of $100,000.

1918   The Berry & Ross Doll Manufacturing Company, founded by Evelyn Berry and Victoria Ross, was one of the few manufacturing companies founded by black women.

Wage Earners Savings Bank was the only black bank invited to participate in the Half Billion Dollar English and French War Loan.

The black Florida Farmer's Cooperative Association was founded.

1919   Marcus Garvey, with the Universal Negro Improvement Association (UNIA), established the Black Star Steamship Line Corporation to develop trade relations among blacks in America, the West Indies, Central America, and Africa. He also established the Negro Factories Corporation, capitalized at $1 million, as part of the UNIA's economic development program to industrialize blacks.

The Washington, D.C., Whitelaw Hotel, the first luxury hotel for blacks, was built at a cost of $158,000. John Whitelaw Lewis, a black businessman, financed it by organizing a building association, the Whitelaw Apartment House Corporation, that sold stock to investors.

Homer Roberts, one of the first black car dealers, established the Roberts Automobile Company in Kansas City, Missouri, by selling cars "from the curb."

Alderman Robert Jackson, of Chicago's Bethel Church, established two grocery and meat market co-ops on 35th and 31st Streets, respectively.

In St. Louis, Missouri, Rev. B. G. Shaw, of Metropolitan AME Zion Church, organized the Cooperative Liberty Company, capitalized at $50,000.

Thomas and Thomas Company, of New York, imported cocoa, spices, and fruits from the West Indies and exported American commodities to these islands.

Liberty Life was organized in Chicago by Frank Gillespie.

The realty office of Fitzherbert Howell, from Trinidad, handled transactions of $1 million in property values.

The Citizen's Cooperative Stores were founded in Memphis, Tennessee.

Sarah [Sara] Spencer Washington established Apex News and Hair Company in New Jersey.

| 1920 | Overton Hygienic Manufacturing Company was the leading producer of cosmetics for women of color, with international sales extending to West Africa, the West Indies, Egypt, India, the Philippines, and Japan. |

1920   Overton Hygienic Manufacturing Company was the leading producer of cosmetics for women of color, with international sales extending to West Africa, the West Indies, Egypt, India, the Philippines, and Japan.

In Newport News, Virginia–based Paris Import and Export Corporation, capitalized at $200,000, exported American products and imported mahogany, palm oil, cocoa, cocoa beans, skins, and hides.

Mr. and Mrs. G. Matthews opened a hotel in Akron, Ohio, with 11 rooms. Within 35 years, they had expanded to 60 rooms with a beauty and barbershop with a logo of "A Business with a Soul."

Illinois law made private banks illegal; most black banks were private.

Maggie Lena Walker's bank reorganized as Citizens Savings Bank and Trust.

In New York, the National Design Model and Dressmakers' Association, a black organization, was founded.

A black oil company, the Ardmore Lubricating Oil Company, was founded.

There were 74,424 blacks in business—owners and employees.

1921   Harry Herbert Pace founded the first black-owned record company under the Black Swan label, recording diverse musical styles, from operatic arias to spirituals and blues.

An attempt, although not successful, was made to establish a stock exchange in Harlem for trading in securities of corporations owned and managed by blacks, with over 100 black corporations in New York.

A race riot destroyed one of the most successful black business districts in the country in Tulsa, Oklahoma, on Greenwood Avenue, known as Black Wall Street.

Herman Perry founded Citizens Trust Company in Atlanta, capitalized at $250,000.

The National Beauty Culturists League was founded in response to the growing African American hair products and skin care industry.

1922   Annie Turnbo-Malone introduced a black skin care product line, which along with her hair products, was sold in the West Indies, South America, Africa, and the Philippines. She employed nearly 75,000 black women across the world.

The Colorado Lincoln Hills Development Company, founded by a group of black investors, established Winks Panorama, a mountain resort for blacks.

The Douglass National Bank was founded in Chicago by Anthony Overton.

Thomas M. Williams founded the Phoenix Color and Chemical Company. The company tested high octane gas and other projects during World War II.

1923   Garrett A. Morgan, inventor of the gas mask, received the patent for the automatic traffic light, which he sold to General Electric for $40,000.

Robert T. Bess founded the R. T. Bess Company, the only black stock brokerage on Wall Street in 1932.

The National Builders Association, a black organization, was founded.

1924   The National Negro Finance Corporation, an offshoot of the National Negro Business League, was created with $1 million for black business investment.

Richard Wright, Sr., and Richard Wright, Jr., opened the Citizens and Southern Bank and Trust Company in Philadelphia, targeting small community depositors.

Anthony Overton founded the Victory Life Insurance Company in Chicago.

The Independent National Funeral Directors Association was founded.

The National Negro Bankers Association was organized.

1925   The Golden State Insurance Company, the first black-owned insurance company in California, was founded.

The Chicago Metropolitan Assurance Company was founded as an outgrowth of a consortium of black funeral companies to provide death benefits to blacks.

1926   The Safe Bus Company was incorporated in Winston–Salem, North Carolina, by Ralph Morgan, his brother, and 12 other black jitney bus owners.

A national stock exchange was organized in Detroit and focused on the sale of black securities. This venture was short-lived owing to a lack of financial support and the depression of 1929.

1927   The 32 largest black insurance companies held $316 million worth of insurance in force, whereas a single white-owned company had $900 million of insurance in force on blacks.

The Victory Life Insurance Company became the first black insurance company to operate in New York.

1928   A. C. Brown, of Montgomery, Alabama, founded the Colored Merchants' Association, a voluntary chain of black grocery stores.

Jesse Blayton became the first black certified public accountant in Georgia and started his own accounting firm, J. B. Blayton and Company.

1929   The New York stock market crashed and thus began the Great Depression, with blacks as "the last to be hired and the first to be fired."

The St. Lukes Bank and Trust Company, in Virginia, merged with two other black banks to become the Consolidated Bank and Trust Company, with Maggie Lena Walker as its chairman of the board until her death. Binga State Bank and the Douglass National Bank, with combined resources of $4 million, controlled 36 percent of total black bank resources.

There were 21 black banks with combined resources of $11 million.

Liberty Life and Casualty Company of Columbus, Ohio, and the Northeastern Life Insurance Company of Newark—merged to form the Supreme Life Insurance Company of Chicago.

1930 With Norris Henderson as second president, Atlanta Mutual's insurance in force increased from $25 million to $346 million in 1973.

The depression-related failure of the two African American banks severely affected the black community in Chicago.

There were 103,872 blacks in business—owners and employees.

1931 Alexander and Company General Insurance Agency of Atlanta, established by Theodore Martin Alexander, Sr., was the first black-owned and -controlled general insurance brokerage and risk management agency in the South.

Hobart T. Taylor, of Texas, started a cab company with proceeds from the sale of family farm property. The company grew to a $5 million business by the 1970s.

1932 Asa Spaulding was the first black actuary in the United States and became president of North Carolina Mutual Life Insurance Company of Durham in 1959. He was later voted to the state Business Hall of Fame.

The Booker T. Washington Insurance Company was organized by Arthur G. Gaston Life and Health Insurance. By 1989, it had assets of $36.8 million.

The Colored Merchants Association (CMA) opened a warehouse for the purpose of selling CMA brand label merchandise on canned goods, coffee, and detergents.

1933 Jesse Binga was convicted of embezzlement and sentenced to 10 years in prison.

The Citizens League adopted a "Don't Buy Where You Can't Work" campaign.

1934 James "BillBoard" Jackson, hired by Esso Standard Oil Company as a special representative, is considered the "first of the current crop" of black salesmen for white corporations.

Out of a total of 134 black banks founded since 1888 (some lasted from three to five years), in addition to credit unions, building and loan associations, and industrial loan societies, only 12 were still operating that year.

1935 The purchasing power of black consumers was $81 million. Black consumers spent $11 million on grocery items but only 5 percent, $550,000, at black groceries.

The National Association of Negro Business and Professional Women's Clubs was founded.

Aggregate retail sales for black businesses amounted to $98.6 million.

1936	The National Negro Congress was organized in Chicago to work for better business and economic opportunities for African Americans, with A. Philip Randolph as president.
1937	The Jones Brothers, Chicago policy kings, opened the Jones Brothers Ben Franklin store on 47th St. in Chicago. This was the only colored variety store in the city and was established from profits made from the numbers racket. The Minnie Lee Pie Company, of Chicago, was founded by Mrs. Minnie Lee Fellings. Within two years, the company was selling 3,000 pies daily.
1938	Tyrrell Credit Union established the Columbia, North Carolina Light, a producer, worker, consumer, and credit cooperative. John H. Johnson was the first black named as one of the country's "Ten Outstanding Young Men" by the U.S. Junior Chamber of Commerce.
1939	Black consumers spent $24 million in black grocery stores. With the U.S. black population totaling 12,808,073, this was equivalent to each black person in the country spending $2.00 of their annual food purchases at black-owned groceries. Thirty thousand black-owned retail stores and restaurants employed 43,000 workers with combined aggregate sales of only .02 percent of national sales—$71 million. The Brown Bomber Baking Company was established by Joe Louis and, within two years, was reported to be the largest black-owned bakery in the country. There were 3,000 black funeral directors and 1,258 funeral homes. Aggregate retail sales for black businesses amounted to $71.5 million.
1940	Joseph Bartholomew purchased the ailing Douglass Life Insurance Company and turned it around over the next several years. There were 87,475 blacks in business—owners and employees.
1941	The McKissick Brothers Construction Company, founded in 1909, received a $4 million defense contract to build a 2,000-acre airfield and air base at Tuskegee Institute for the training of the black 99th Pursuit Squadron.
1942	The *Booker T. Washington* is launched at Wilmington, Delaware, commanded by Hugh Mulzac, the first African American captain of a U.S. merchant ship. Johnson Publishing Company, Inc., was founded in Chicago by John H. Johnson with $500. He began by publishing the *Negro Digest*, his view of a black *Reader's Digest*. Within seven years, Johnson was a millionaire. The theme of this year's NNBL Conference in Chicago was "Gearing Negro Business to a War-Time Economy." The Los Angeles Pacific Parachute Company was one of a few black manufacturers to get a government defense contract.

There were only six black banks, whereas there were 136 black credit unions.

1943	Eta Phi Beta, a national professional sorority for businesswomen, was founded in Detroit. William H. Hawkins founded the Washington-based Union Airlines.
1944	On Oahu, Hawaii, the Smith Harlem Dispensary was the largest black business on the island.
1945	John H. Johnson established *Ebony* magazine, his flagship publication. A year later, he received ads from Chesterfield and Kimberly Clark. There were only 11 black banks, whereas there were 65 black credit unions.
1946	At the black National Beauty Culture League Convention, it was reported that black beauty operators did $40 million in business during the war. Gladys Hampton became the first black woman to own a record company with the founding of Hampton Records, also known as Hamp-Tone Records, Inc. Joseph E. Walker and Antonio M. Walker established the Tri-State Bank, in Memphis, to open financial opportunities to less fortunate blacks. Herman Roberts, of Chicago, started a cab company with 36 radio-dispatched cabs and 125 drivers and mechanics. There were 205 black-owned insurance companies in the United States. The first black taxicab company, in Seattle, was founded.
1947	S. B. Fuller, founder of Chicago-based Fuller Products in 1935, purchased a white cosmetics company, Boyer International Laboratories. By 1960, annual sales were $10 million. When white employees and consumers discovered that Fuller was black, they quite their jobs and launched a 100 percent boycott. A market survey reported that black women spend an estimated $300 million annually on cosmetics.
1948	Brandford Advertising Agency of New York was incorporated but did not gain recognition until it secured accounts from white Corporate America. Pepsi Cola launched an ad campaign featuring prominent blacks, starting with Ralph Bunche of the United Nations. Lever Brothers announced its new ad campaign in the black press.
1949	Lawrence Lewis was reportedly the first black to sell stocks and bonds on Wall Street.
1950	WERD, in Atlanta, was the first radio station purchased by an African American, Jesse B. Blayton.
1951	Johnson Publishing launched *Jet* magazine, a weekly pocketsize publication.

1952   Norman L. McGhee started McGhee and Company Investment Securi-
            ties. A licensed broker-dealer, he is the first reported black to deal in
            general securities.

1953   The Small Business Association (SBA) was established by the federal
            government to provide financing opportunities, through grants, loans,
            and federal contracts, to businesses with less than 500 employees. How-
            ever, it was not until 1957 that the SBA was inclusive of small black
            businesses.
            James Del Rio was the first black licensed mortgage banker in the United
            States. In Detroit he established one of the first black mortgage com-
            panies in the country.
            The Sivart Mortgage Company in Chicago, Illinois, was the first black
            mortgage banking firm. It was established by Dempsey J. Travis.
            Black New York hotel owners and managers organized the National
            Hotel Association.

1954   The Washington Shirt Manufacturing Company, founded by George J.
            Washington, was the only black shirt manufacturer in the United States.
            Ernesta G. Procope founded the E. G. Bowman Company, a commercial
            insurance brokerage.
            Henry F. Henderson, Jr., started H. F. Henderson Industries, a small
            electrical company, originally operating out of his basement. The com-
            pany ranked among *Black Enterprise*'s top 20 black businesses.
            Chicago black businessman Jesse Thornton and boxer Joe Louis estab-
            lished the Joe Louis Milk Company; the only black-owned dairy com-
            pany in the nation.
            The motel founded by A. G. Gaston was considered one of the finest
            black motels in the country.
            George Ellis Johnson founded Johnson Products with $250. His first
            success was with the Ultra Wave and Ultra Sheen hair relaxer product
            line.

1955   Philip M. Jenkins founded Special Markets, Inc., an investment firm with
            the intent to target the ethnic market of the country.
            Melvin C. Hutt opened the 23-unit desegregated Franklin Hotel in Salis-
            bury, Maryland, and targeted both black and white consumers.

1956   Vince Cullers Advertising, Inc., was the first black advertising agency.

1957   The 14 African American banks have total assets of $46,789,607.
            Cirilo A. McSween was the first black to represent a major white-owned
            insurance company, New York Life Insurance Company, and the first
            black to sell a million dollars worth of life insurance for any company
            in one year.
            Jackie Robinson was appointed vice president of Chock Full O'Nuts
            Corporation, to be among the few blacks entering white Corporate Amer-
            ica. Allen University, in South Carolina, was the first black college to
            invest funds with a black brokerage company.

1958	The Small Business Investment Company (SBIC) Act was passed to encourage the establishment of small business investment firms. Arthur B. Knight, vice president of Unity Mutual Life Insurance Company and Unity Funeral Parlor, and Roi Ottley, author and journalist, were appointed to the board of directors of white-owned Drexel National Bank of Chicago.
1959	In the United States, there were 272,541 African American farm owners, compared with 926,000 in 1920. Cotton and tobacco were the most significant crops. Herman J. Russell of Atlanta started a construction company, which became the nation's largest black construction and development company. Berry Gordy founded Motown Records, which grew to $100 million in sales by 1983.
1960	A $42 million lawsuit was brought against white cosmetic firm Helene Curtis Industries by Summit Laboratories, also a white firm, for allegedly copying a formula for a black hair care product, "Hair-Strate Permanent." Charles F. Harris, as editor at Doubleday, established Zenith Books, the first series to present minority histories for the general and educational markets.
1962	Harvey Clarence Russell, Jr., of PepsiCo, became the first African American to be appointed to a vice president position in a major U.S. corporation.
1963	James Phillip McQuay was the first and only black in wholesale-retail fur manufacturing. McQuay, who operated his fur business in New York City, won fur designer awards in 1970, 1975, and 1976. There were 13 black banks with combined assets of $77 million out of $364 billion in assets held by 14,079 banks in the country.
1964	President Lyndon Johnson's Economic Opportunity Act established the Office of Economic Opportunity Program to provide loans and assistance to inner-city poverty area residents, targeting blacks, who sought to establish businesses. Clifton W. Gates, along with M. Leo Bohanon and James Hurt of the Urban League, Howard Woods of the *St. Louis Argus*, and other blacks, organized Gateway National Bank, the first black-owned bank in Missouri. Edward Gardner established Soft Sheen, Inc., and challenged Johnson Products in the black hair care market. The Independence Bank of Chicago was founded by Alvin Boutte and George E. Johnson. The bank secured deposits from CBS, Chrysler, General Motors, Johnson & Johnson baby products, Delta Airlines, and Johnson Publishing.
1965	Seaway National Bank of Chicago was founded by a consortium of South Side black businessmen. Harold Washington, the first black mayor of Chicago, deposited municipal funds in Seaway.

The Freedom National Bank was the first black-chartered and black-operated bank in Harlem.

1966   The Minority Enterprise Small Business Investment Company, an SBA venture capital program, was established.

1967   Jesse Jackson was appointed national director of Operation Breadbasket with an objective to increase black employment and promote black business.

Albert William Johnson was the first black to be awarded an Oldsmobile dealership, which was in a predominantly black area of Chicago.

1968   According to *Fortune* magazine, the African American consumer market in the United States amounted to $30 billion a year.

The Ford Foundation, led by McGeorge Bundy, granted money to two black business development agencies: the Negro Industrial and Economic Union of Cleveland, $520,000; and the Bedford-Stuyvesant Development and Services Corporation in Brooklyn, $400,000.

Leon Howard Sullivan developed the first major black-sponsored shopping center, Progress Plaza, in Philadelphia.

Rev. Jesse Jackson, through his Operation PUSH (People United to Save Humanity) activities, promoted black business by holding business seminars and trade expositions.

The National Negro Business League reported that there were over 50,000 black-owned or black-controlled businesses.

1969   President Richard Nixon enacted Executive Order 11458, the Office of Minority Business Enterprise, as part of the Department of Commerce.

James Bruce Llewellyn headed a leverage buyout of Fedco Foods, a white grocery store chain of 10 stores in the South Bronx, for $3 million. He expanded to 27 stores with sales of $85 million.

Brady Keys, former National Football League (NFL) player, and his All-Pro Enterprises purchased Burger King and KFC franchises. He was one of the first black franchisee owners in the fast-food industry.

Henry Green Parks, Jr., founded Parks Sausage Company of Baltimore, the first black-owned public company listed for trading on the over-the-counter market.

Byron Lewis founded UniWorld Group Inc., a New York–based ad agency, after being turned down for jobs at 50 white ad agencies. His clients include Burger King, AT&T, Kodak, and Ford.

Johnson Products Company, the largest maker of African American hair care products, was incorporated.

The National Association of Black Accountants (NABA) was founded by nine New York black accountants.

1970   Earl Graves founded *Black Enterprise* magazine to encourage black economic development in the U.S. economy.

Of the 3,000 senior-level *Fortune* 500 executives, only 3 were black: Clifton Wharton, Jr., then at Equitable; Thomas Wood at Chase Manhattan; and Robert Weaver at Metropolitan Life.

Barbara Proctor established her ad agency in Chicago, Proctor and Gardner Advertising Inc. She was the first black woman to start an ad agency. She had accounts from Sears, Roebuck and E. J. Gallo Winery.

There were only 60 blacks among the 35,000 stock brokers in the country.

The National Black MBA Association was founded to help African Americans enter and progress in the business world.

1971   Johnson Products was the first black-owned company listed on the American Stock Exchange.

The firm of Daniels and Bell was the first black company to become a member of the New York Stock Exchange, founded by Willie L. Daniels and Travers Bell, Jr.

In Chicago, "Black Expo," a four-day exhibition headed by Jesse Jackson and designed primarily to stimulate interest and investment in African American enterprises, was attended by over 800,000 people.

Burrell Advertising of Chicago, founded by Thomas Burrell, was the leader in the black advertising industry through the mid-1990s. He had accounts from Crest, Ford, Quaker Oats, Jack Daniels, Coca-Cola, and McDonald's.

Melvin R. Wade purchased the Eastern Rubber Reclaiming Company, Chester, Pennsylvania. He became the first and only black to own a rubber recycling plant.

Leon Sullivan was the first black to be appointed to the board of directors of General Motors in the automobile industry.

James O. Plinton, Jr., of Eastern Airlines, was the first black to head a major U.S. airline.

1972   The new headquarters of Johnson Publishing Company was the first building built by blacks in downtown Chicago.

Albert William Johnson, who owned an Oldsmobile and Cadillac dealership, headed the nation's largest black-owned auto dealership with sales of $14.5 million.

Robert Gidron was the first black to own a Cadillac dealership in the Bronx.

One of the largest black-owned radio stations was New York's WLIB-AM, owned by Percy Sutton, which expanded as Inner City Broadcasting.

Jerome H. Holland was the first black appointed to the board of directors of the New York Stock Exchange.

1973   *Black Enterprise* (*BE*) began reporting the nation's top 100 black businesses. This initial listing of companies had annual sales of $473.4 million. Motown Industries ranked first with sales of $40 million and held the position as the ranking black business until 1983. This report was named the "*BE* 100s" a year later.

Baltimore's Park Sausage Company and Chicago's Johnson Products were the first black-owned companies to be publicly traded—NASDAQ and AMSE, respectively.

Comer Cottrell founded Pro-Line Corporation, a hair products manufacturing company and the largest black-owned business in the Southwest.
The National Black Network was the first black-owned and -operated radio news network.
Atlanta's black construction companies received only $41,758 out of $33 million in city contracts.
Naomi Sims, the first black supermodel, introduced the Naomi Sims Collection, a wig company, and grossed $5 million her first year.

1974   Chicago's Independence ranked as the nation's leading black bank.
Conyers Ford, of Detroit, became the largest black-owned car dealership in the country and would be the only car dealership to make the *BE* 100 list every year.
Don King, a major boxing promoter, promoted the Ali/Frazier fight, the "Rumble in the Jungle" in Zaire, Africa. Each fighter was guaranteed $5 million of an estimated $30 million purse.
The *BE* 100 reported annual sales of $600 million.

1975   Harvard University contracted $47 million in group life insurance with the two largest black-owned life insurance companies: North Carolina Mutual Life and Atlanta Life.
Doley Securities, based in New Orleans, became the third black investment firm to trade on the NYSE.
The National Association of Urban Bankers, an organization of minority financial institutions and bankers, was founded.
William V. Banks purchased WGPR-TV, in Detroit, for $750,000, to become the first black-owned and -operated TV station.
Wallace "Wally" Amos, Jr., launched Famous Amos Chocolate Chip Cookies.

1976   The Federal Trade Commission forced Johnson Products, ignoring white hair care companies, to produce a warning that the product contained lye that could be caustic with improper use.
There were 41 black insurance companies out of a total of 1,800 American insurance companies.
The *BE* 100 reported a decrease in annual sales, to $623.9 million. Pro-Line Corp. and H. F. Henderson Industries debuted on this list.

1977   The E. G. Bowman Company was the first major American black-owned commercial insurance brokerage firm on Wall Street.
Harambee House, Washington, D.C., was the first large hotel designed and built by blacks. It was designed by Sulton-Campbell and Associates and owned by the People's Involvement Corporation, a local citizens' group, subsequently purchased by Howard University.
Kenwood Commercial Furniture was the first black-owned company to sign a million-dollar contract with Consolidated Edison. It furnished and installed carpet in all the utility company's offices in New York City and Westchester County.

The *BE* 100 reported annual sales of $787.4 million as of December and employed 11,897 people.

1978   Joshua I. Smith founded Maxima Corporation, a computer systems and management firm, one of the largest founded by an African American. The *BE* 100 reported annual sales of $886.7 million as of December 1977. Forty-two of the *BE* 100 were car dealerships, as the Big Three (Chrysler, Ford, and General Motors) provided more dealership opportunities.

1979   The Small Business Administration published a study revealing that one out of every five recipients of federal aid for minority-owned businesses was, in fact, a front for a white-owned business. Small white businesses believed they would receive greater consideration for federal aid as a black business.
The *BE* 100 reported annual sales of $1.053 billion, reaching the billion-dollar mark for the first time.
The Kent-Barry-Eaton Connection Railway Company was the first minority-owned company to operate a railroad. The line ran 42 miles between Grand Rapids and Vermontville, Michigan.
Franklin Thomas, president of the Ford Foundation, was the first black to be appointed chief executive officer (CEO) of a major charity foundation.
Dorothy E. Brunson purchased WEBB in Baltimore to become the first black woman to own a radio station. She eventually acquired three other stations and purchased a TV station, WGTV, in Philadelphia in 1990.

1980   Black Entertainment Television Holdings, Inc. (BET) was founded by Robert Johnson, the first black-owned cable television station and the only black cable satellite network.
Wally "Famous" Amos, the creator of a $250 million cookie business, was asked to donate his trademark Panama hat to the American Collection in the National Museum of American History. It is the first exhibit requested from an African American businessperson.
Black-owned oil companies emerged with the increase in oil prices. Grimes Oil Company in Boston reported $30 million in revenues.

1981   The National Association for the Advancement of Colored People (NAACP) launched "Operation Fair Share" to increase minority participation in franchising in management, purchasing, professional services, and ownership.
Albert Johnson was the first black to own a Saab dealership.
Atlanta's black construction companies received $19.2 million out of $56 million in city contracts.
The *BE* 100 reported annual sales of $1.53 billion. The nation's black auto dealerships suffered from a financial crisis in the overall auto industry.

1982   Mildred Glenn was the first black woman bank president in Pennsylvania at New World National Bank, the only minority bank in the state.

Black sole proprietorships accounted for more than 95 percent of all black businesses, whereas black corporations accounted for 1.8 percent. The *BE* 100 reported annual sales of $1.9 billion. Motown was still number one, with $91.7 million in sales. The largest segment of black businesses was composed of "miscellaneous retail businessess" with 53,981 firms and gross sales of $993 million.

Gross sales of 3,448 auto dealerships and service stations amounted to $1.3 billion.

1983   Twenty-five percent of all American college undergraduates, including blacks, were majoring in business.

The black hair care industry was one of the fastest-growing industries among black businesses, due to the wet hairstyle, the Jheri curl. Revenues of the *BE* 100 exceed the $2 billion mark, with only three companies exceeding $100 million in sales: Motown, $104.3 million; H. J. Russell Construction, $103.85 million; Johnson Publishing, $102.65 million.

1984   Revenues for the *BE* 100 continued to increase, to $2.329 billion.

Black oil companies suffered from decreasing oil prices.

According to the Census Bureau, the number of black-owned businesses in the United States increased to 350,000.

Julius Erving, former basketball great, and Bruce Llewellyn purchased Philadelphia's Coca-Cola Bottling Company, which becomes the fourth largest black-owned business in the United States.

Drew Pearson established Drew Pearson Companies, the largest black licensed head wear dealer in the country, with four major sports leagues.

The National Association of Securities Professionals, an organization of minorities and women in the securities industry, was founded.

1986   Oprah Winfrey bought out ownership of her show *The Oprah Winfrey Show* for $10 million and established Harpo Productions.

William R. Harvey was the first black to be the sole owner of a major soft-drink bottling franchise, a Pepsi plant in Houghton, Michigan.

Spike Lee made his first film, *She's Gotta Have It*, for $175,000 and grossed $8 million. *Malcolm X*, produced for $34 million, grossed $48.1 million.

The *BE* 100 reported sales of $2.9 billion.

1987   Soft Sheen acquired 66 percent interest in the London-based Dyke and Dryden Company, England's largest black business.

Dick Gregory founded Correction Connection, Inc., a health and nutrition business to assist in weight loss and to market his "Bahamian Diet."

Publisher John H. Johnson named "Businessman of the Decade" by *Black Enterprise*.

A. G. Gaston sold his Booker T. Washington Insurance Company to his 400 employees for $3.5 million.

Clifton Wharton, Jr., appointed CEO of the $70 billion Teachers Insurance and Annuity Association–College Retirement, was the first black to head a *Fortune* 500.

Revenues for the *BE* 100 cracked the $3 billion mark and employed over 18,000 people. Approximately half of the *BE* 100 were car dealerships—53 dealers with gross sales of $1.35 billion.

Entrepreneur Reginald F. Lewis orchestrated a leveraged buyout of the multinational food company Beatrice International for $985 million. He only put up $15 million of his own money and acquired 51 percent equity in the company. TLC Beatrice International Holdings, Inc., became the largest black-owned business in the world, with sales of $1.8 billion.

1988   The MCA purchase of Motown Records, for $61 million, was a symbolic loss for black America in its economic advancement.

Demetrius Brown founded the Chicago-based Fuci Metals, USA, an international metals trader firm, trading aluminum from Europe, Chicago, and Russia.

Don Cornwell founded Granite Broadcasting and became the largest black holder of TV stations.

White manufacturers of black hair care products had 50 percent market share of the black hair care product industry.

Herman Cain purchased Godfather's Pizza in a leveraged buyout from Pillsbury.

There were approximately 340,000 black-owned companies in the United States, and only 1 percent were manufacturers.

Black Enterprise renames their report the *BE* 100s, the *BE* Industrial/Service 100 and the *BE* Auto Dealer 100, due to the increasing number of black auto dealers. Revenues for the *BE* 100s were $6.1 billion; the industrial/service companies accounted for $4.1 billion of this total.

1989   There were 37 black-owned banking institutions currently operating in the United States. The largest in terms of assets was IndeCorp Bank in Chicago.

The U.S. Supreme Court in *Richmond v. Croson* rules "unconstitutional" a Richmond, Virginia, program requiring contractors for the city to give at least 30 percent of construction jobs to companies that are predominantly owned by minorities. The Court calls the program "an unlawful form of reverse discrimination."

Roland Laird started Postro Inc., publishing a comic book, *MC Squared*, and a comic strip, the "Griots," the first to integrate hip-hop music with comic books.

Reginald Lewis was unsuccessful in his attempt to take TLC Beatrice public on the New York Stock Exchange and viewed this failure as the "IPO [initial public offering] Glass Ceiling."

North Carolina Mutual Insurance Company, the largest black-owned insurance company in the world, had insurance in force of $7.9 billion.

Bertram M. Lee and Peter Bynoe negotiated to purchase the Denver Nuggets, a franchise of the National Basketball Association, for $65 million.

K-Mart, Chrysler, and Philip Morris committed approximately $2 million to advertising in black newspapers.

Kenneth Chenault became one of the highest-ranking blacks in a *Fortune* 500 company, appointed as president of the American Express Consumer Card and Financial Services Group.

Total sales for the *BE* 100s were $6.8 billion.

1990 The Consolidated Bank and Trust Company of Richmond, the oldest surviving black bank founded as the St. Luke's Penny Savings Bank in 1903, reopened two failed black-owned S&Ls.

PUSH launched a boycott against Nike, claiming that 30 percent of its products are purchased by blacks ($669 million of its $2.23 billion annual sales) and that "blacks should receive 30% of Nike's corporate business."

In Harlem, the Freedom National Bank, with assets of over $120 million, was forced to close due to an alleged failure to meet federal regulation standards.

Black Expo, an annual national networking and recruiting convention of black entrepreneurs, businesspeople, and major corporations, was held in Chicago.

Russell Simmons established Rush Communications and became the leading black-owned record company in the 1990s.

Carl Jones established his Threads 4 Life (Cross Colours) clothing manufactory to target the urban hip-hop market.

Richard Parsons, with appointment as CEO of Dime Savings Bank, was the first black to head a major U.S. savings association.

Ninety-five to 97 percent of senior management in *Fortune* 500s and the top 1,000 industrial firms were white males; only 0.6 percent were black.

There were 206 black-owned radio stations—138 AM stations and 68 FM stations.

Total sales for the *BE* 100s leveled off at $6.8 million. Black businesses faced difficult times due to attacks on minority set-aside programs.

1991 BET was the third black-owned company to be traded publicly, with an IPO of $72.3 million.

Kathryn Leary established the Leary Group, Inc., to develop Japanese markets especially for African American products.

The top 10 black businesses: TLC Beatrice International Holdings Inc. of New York, distribution of food products, $1.54 billion; Johnson Publishing Company of Chicago, publishing, broadcasting, skin and hair care, $261.4 million; Philadelphia Coca-Cola Bottling Co., Inc., of Philadelphia, soft-drink bottling, $256 million; H. J. Russell & Co., of Atlanta, construction and food services, $143.6 million; Barden Communication, Inc., of Detroit, communications and real estate, $91.2 million; Garden State Cable TV, of New York, cable television, $88 million; Soft Sheen Products, Inc., of Chicago, hair care products, $87.9 million; RMS Technologies, of New Jersey, computer services, $79.9 million; Stop Shop and Save, of Baltimore, supermarkets, $66 million; The Bing Group, of Detroit, metal stamping and processing, $64.9 million.

Total sales for the *BE* 100s increased to $7.169 billion.

1992	U.S. Census Bureau reports blacks own only 3 percent of the nation's businesses.

A presidential commission issued a two-year report calling for a major revamp of the $4 billion Federal Minority Business Plan; it claims the plan crowds African Americans in unprofitable businesses, denying them sufficient capital to succeed.

Michael S. Fields established Open-Vision Technologies, to provide computer management services and software; its clients are Wells Fargo, Mercedes Benz, Ford.

Michael Jordan made $16 million from advertising as spokesman for McDonald's, Quaker Oats, Gatorade, General Mills Wheaties Cereal, and Ball Park hot dogs. He negotiated $30 million in endorsements in 1995.

The James Produce Company, wholesaler and food distributors in the small black population of West Virginia, was reported by *BE* as the oldest black business in the country; it was founded in 1883 and run by four generations of the James family.

Thompson Hospitality L.P., founded by Warren M. Thompson, acquired 31 Bob Big Boy restaurants for $13 million from Marriott Corporation.

Larry Lundy, of Lundy Enterprises in New Orleans, purchased 31 Pizza Hut restaurants for $15.5 million.

Granite Broadcasting went public, with an IPO of $24 million on NAS-DAQ.

Total sales for the *BE* 100s increased to $7.9 billion, with the auto dealers accounting for $3 billion of this total.

Black Enterprise honored A. G. Gaston as the "Black Entrepreneur of the Century." Gaston stated, "Money has no color. If you can build a better mousetrap, it won't matter whether you're black or white; people will buy it."

1993	Johnson Products, Inc., sold for $67 million to the IVAX Corporation, a white company that manufactures the Flori Roberts black cosmetic and skin care line.

MCA sold Motown Records to PolyGram for $325 million.

By acquisition, the black-owned United Bank of Philadelphia increased its deposits from $18 million in 1992 to $87 million.

NDI Video, Inc., of Atlanta, became the only black BlockBuster franchise with the purchase of 23 outlets in the Northeast.

V&J Foods Inc. in Milwaukee, owned by Valerie Daniels-Carter, purchased 17 Burger King franchises, increasing her ownership to 32 units.

Former Globetrotter Mannie Jackson and other investors purchased the basketball team for $6 million to become the first professional sports team owned by blacks.

Of 9,086 McDonald's franchisees, only 658 were owned by blacks.

Total sales for the *BE* 100s were $9 billion, with 12 companies reporting sales over $100 million. The combined assets of black financial institutions were $4.2 billion.

1994   Karl Kani founded his Karl Kani Infinity Company and grossed $43 million his first year. His jeans accounted for 45 percent of annual sales, with international sales in England, Germany, France, the Czech Republic, Japan, and Australia.

Six *BE* 100s and four black media firms organized a limited partnership—Urban Communications—to bid for some of the 5,628 narrowband and broad-band Personal Communication Services licenses being auctioned off by the Federal Communications Commission.

Fourteen percent of Burger King's franchisees were minority owned but only 3.5 percent by blacks. Burger King also established a $100 million set-aside fund for developing both minority franchisees and suppliers.

Isaiah Thomas claimed 10 percent ownership of the $125 million Toronto Raptors, an NBA basketball team.

"Magic" Johnson bought a 5 percent interest in the Los Angeles Lakers for $10 million.

There were only 7 black-owned movie theaters of 23,000 in the country. Revenues for the *BE* 100s reached the $10 billion mark. The top 10 black businesses each employed over 1,000 people.

1995   The top 100 black businesses combined with the top 100 black car dealerships had sales of $13 billion; health and beauty aids, $239 million; construction, $407 million; manufacturing, $789 million; technological, $877 million; media, $1.073 billion; food and beverage, $3.168 billion; other enterprises, $846 million; total sales, $7.3 billion. The top 100 black car dealerships grossed $5.7 billion in sales.

Leaders of black Corporate America organized a political action committee (PAC) to challenge the dismantling of affirmative action. Among the organizers were: Earl Graves, *Black Enterprise*; Robert Johnson of BET; Don Cornwell, Granite Broadcasting; Emma Chappell, United Bank of Philadelphia; and Calvin Grigsby, then at Grigsby, Branford & Co. Inc., a black investment bank.

NetNoire, which digitizes and archives Internet Afrocentric cultural information globally, launched a joint venture with America Online (AOL).

Johnson Publishing, the second largest black business and the largest black-oriented consumer corporation, had $316.2 million in sales and 2,000 employees.

Dan Barden, founder of Barden Cablevision of Detroit, sold his company to whites for $100 million.

Robert Holland, appointed president and CEO of Ben & Jerry's Ice Cream, was out a year later despite the company's increasing financial performance.

Kenneth Chenault became vice chairman of American Express.

Richard Parsons became the highest-ranked African American at a *Fortune* 500 company as president of Time Warner Inc.

Dennis F. Hightower was named president of Walt Disney Television and Telecommunications Department.

There were 11 publicly traded black firms.

Nearly 56 percent of black businesses had receipts of less than $10,000, whereas only 15 black businesses had over 500 employees.

1996

According to the National Association of Black Owned Broadcasters (NABOB), there were 189 black-owned stations.

The highest-ranking black in the automobile industry was Roy Roberts, general manager of Pontiac–GMC Division, the company's second largest division.

Ann M. Fudge, president and CEO of Maxwell House Coffee Company (a $1.5 billion division of General Foods), was the highest-ranking black woman in white Corporate America.

Johnson Publishing expanded publication to Africa with *Ebony South Africa*.

Tiger Woods, golf's sensation, obtained the largest endorsement totals with $60 million in contracts.

Among the 447 superrich, with $1 billion or more, not one was of acknowledged sub-Saharan African descent.

Herman Cain, CEO and president of Godfather's Pizza, expanded to 525 franchise units and is the leading black franchisor.

Total sales for the *BE* 100s increased to $13 billion, with 25 companies posting sales over $100 million.

1997

Only five companies and their CEOs have appeared on every *BE* 100 list since its beginning in 1973: John H. Johnson of Johnson Publishing Co., $325.7 million in sales and 2,702 employees; Herman J. Russell of H. J. Russell & Co., $163.8 million in sales and 1,416 employees; Edward Lewis, CEO, and Clarence Smith, president, of Essence Communications Inc., $92.8 million in sales and 130 employees; Nathan Conyers of Conyers Riverside Ford Inc., $49.1 million in sales and 92 employees; and Earl Graves of Earl Graves Ltd, $30.1 million in sales and 74 employees. *Black Enterprise* would coin them the "Marathon Men." Sales figures and employees, as of December, 1996.

Total sales for the *BE* 100s are in excess of $14 billion, with over 55,000 employees. TLC Beatrice remains the largest, with $2.23 billion in sales.

Jesse Jackson and the Rainbow/PUSH Coalition launched the Wall Street Project to encourage Corporate America's investment in impoverished inner-city and rural communities. Building space was donated by billionaire real estate entrepreneur Donald Trump.

TLC Beatrice International sold its French-based food distribution division for $573 million (the division accounted for $1.9 billion of its $2.2 billion gross sales in 1996). Projected gross sales in 1998, according to *Black Enterprise*, will be $344 million.

Investment banker Leslie Corley sold his majority interest in Convenience Corporation of America. It was established in 1995, when Corley acquired 146 midwestern 7-Eleven stores. In 1996 it was the *B.E.* 100s' 8th ranked company with sales of $138 million.

Sales figures and employees, as of December, 1996.

Black Enterprise celebrates six African American "Captains of Industry," entrepreneurs, "Marathon Men," who have made the *B.E.* 100 list every year since its inception in 1973. They are John H. Johnson (publishing, *Ebony* and *Jet*, broadcasting, TV production, cosmetics and hair care), Herman J. Russell (construction, property management, airport concessions, real estate development), Clarence Smith and Edward Lewis (publishing, *Essence*), and Earl G. Graves (publishing, *Black Enterprise*, and soft drink distribution) and Nathan Conyers (auto dealer). As of December 31, 1997, the ranking ten black businesses listed by *Black Enterprise* in its "*B.E.* Industrial/Service 100," their chief operating officers (CEOs), and sales were TLC Beatrice International, Loida N. Lewis, $1.4 billion; Johnson Publishing Co., Inc., John H. Johnson, $361.1 million; Philadelphia Coca-Cola Bottling Co., Inc., J. Bruce Llwellyn, $357 million; Active Transportation, Charlie W. Johnson, $250 million; The Bing Group, Dave Bing, $183 million; Granite Broadcasting Corp., W. Don Cornwell, $181 million; BET Holdings Inc., Robert L. Johnson, $170 million; H. J. Russell & Co., $155.3 million; Pulsar Data Systems, Inc., William W. Davis, Sr., $151 million; and, Anderson-DuBose Co., Warren E. Anderson, $138.7 million.

Only three black-owned hair care products manufacturing companies were listed by *Black Enterprise* in its "*B.E.* Industrial/Service 100," 29th ranked Dallas-based Pro-Line Corp., CEO, Comer J. Cottrell, with sales of $68 million, 36th ranked Chicago-based Luster Products, CEO, Jory Luster, with $57.5 million in sales; and, 64th ranked Kernersville, North Carolina–based Dudley Products Inc., CEO Joe L. Dudley, Sr., with $33 million in sales.

With gross sales in 1997 of $573.1 million, the nation's second largest black business was the Mel Farr Automotive Group.

| 1998 | First Wall Street Project Conference, the "Trillion Dollar Roundtable," co-hosted by Jesse Jackson and the Rainbow/PUSH Coalition with Travelers Group Chairman and CEO Sanford Weil. Attended by leading business, government, and labor leaders. |

Baltimore-based Chapman Holdings, Inc., founded by Nathan A. Chapman, became the first black-owned securities brokerage firm to become a publicly traded company. Its initial public offering (IPO), 1 million shares of stock at $9 a share, was on the NASDAQ Small Cap Market, under the symbol "CMAN."

Soft Sheen, established in 1964 by Edward Gardner, was sold to Paris-based L'Oreal, the world's largest cosmetic company.

Black-controlled publicly listed Carson, Inc., purchased the black founded Johnson Products Company from IVAX for approximately $85 million.

BET Holdings, Inc., the first black-owned company traded on the New York Stock Exchange (NYSE) in 1991, reverted to a privately held company, with BET Holdings II, Inc., holding 65 percent ownership and Liberty Media Group (a TeleCommunications, Inc. subsidiary) holding 35 percent.

BET's founder Robert Johnson launched BETMovies, the first black movie channel. Johnson has committed $100 million to produce low-budget theatrical films and made-for-cable movies.

Maxima Corporation, one of the first successful black technology companies, a systems engineering firm that provided computers and facilities management, filed for reorganization in bankruptcy court when sales dropped to $5 million. Maxima, founded in 1978 by Joshua Smith, was a leading *B.E.* 100s company, with sales as high as $60 million. In 1997 it was ranked 67th in the *B.E* 100s with sales of $31 million.

Former Motown president Jheryl Busby, Magic Johnson, and entertainer Janet Jackson purchased controlling interest in the Los Angeles Founders National Bank for $2.5 million. The bank, with assets of $100 million in 1998, was established in 1991.

Kenneth J. Chenault, Harvard J.D., appointed president and chief operating officer at American Express, becoming its second ranked executive and the highest ranked black in Corporate America.

1999   Reverend Jesse Jackson convened the second annual Rainbow/PUSH Wall Street Project conference. Keynote speaker, President William J. Clinton announced he would propose legislation to Congress to grant tax credits to corporations investing in underserved areas and to expand loan opportunities to small disadvantaged businesses.

Reverend Al Sharpton convenes his first Invitational Summit on Multicultural Markets and Media for ''Achieving fairness in the way advertising dollars are allocated to minority-owned media.''

Entertainer businessman Bill Cosby purchases interest in the New Jersey Nets basketball team.

BIBLIOGRAPHY: *Black Enterprise* (1973–1997); ''Business,'' *Jet*, February 8, 1999; Alfred A. Edmond, Jr., ''Milestones of the *B.E.* 100s: 25 years of Black Economic Empowerment,'' *Black Enterprise* (June 1997); John Hope Franklin and Alfred A. Moss, Jr., *From Slavery to Freedom: A History of African Americans*, 7th ed. (New York: Alfred A. Knopf, 1994); John N. Ingham and Lynne B. Feldman, *African-American Business Leaders: A Biographical Dictionary* (Westport, CT: Greenwood Press, 1994); Juliet E. K. Walker, *The History of Black Business in America: Capitalism, Race, Entrepreneurship* (New York: Macmillan/Prentice Hall International, 1998); also related entries in this *Encyclopedia*.

Select Bibliography

GENERAL STUDIES

History, Economics, Biography, References

Allen, Robert L. *Black Awakening in Capitalist America*. Garden City, NY: Doubleday, 1970.

Bailey, Ronald W., ed. *Black Business Enterprise: Historical and Contemporary Perspectives*. New York: Basic Books, 1973.

Bates, Timothy M. *Black Capitalism: A Quantitative Analysis*. New York: Praeger, 1973.

Bell, Derrick A. *Faces at the Bottom of the Well: The Permanence of Racism*. New York: Basic Books, 1992.

Boston, Thomas D., ed. *A Different Vision: African American Economic Thought*. Vol. 1. London: Routledge, 1997.

———. *A Different Vision: Race and Public Policy*. Vol. 2. London: Routledge, 1997.

Brimmer, Andrew F. "The Negro in the American Economy." In John P. Davis, ed., *The American Negro Reference Book*. Englewood Cliffs, NJ: Prentice Hall, 1966.

Butler, John Sibley. *Entrepreneurship and Self-Help among Black Americans*. Albany: State University of New York Press, 1991.

Du Bois, William E. B. *Economic Cooperation among Negro Americans*. Atlanta: Atlanta University Press, 1907.

———. *The Negro Artisan*. Atlanta: Atlanta University Press, 1902.

———. *The Negro in Business*. Atlanta: Atlanta University Press, 1898.

Franklin, John Hope, and Alfred Moss. *From Slavery to Freedom: A History of African-Americans*. 7th ed. New York: McGraw-Hill, 1994.

Frazier, E. Franklin. *Black Bourgeoisie*. Glencoe, IL: The Free Press, 1957.

Gatewood, Willard. *Aristocrats of Color: The Black Elite, 1880–1920*. Bloomington: Indiana University Press, 1990.

Hamilton, Kenneth. *Black Towns and Profit: Promotion and Development in the Trans-Appalachian West.* Urbana: University of Illinois Press, 1991.

Harmon, J. H., Jr., Arnett G. Lindsay, and Carter G. Woodson. *The Negro as a Business Man.* 1929; reprint, College Park, MD: McGrath Publishing Company, 1969.

Harris, Abram L. *The Negro as Capitalist: A Study of Banking and Business among American Negroes.* 1936; reprint, New York: Negro Universities Press, 1969.

Higgs, Robert. *Competition and Coercion: Blacks in the American Economy, 1865–1914.* Cambridge: Cambridge University Press, 1976.

Hill, George H. *Black Business and Economics: A Selected Bibliography.* New York: Garland Publishing, Inc., 1985.

Hine, Darlene Clark, Elsa Barkley-Brown, and Rosalyn Terborg-Penn, eds. *Black Women in America: An Historical Encyclopedia.* Brooklyn, NY: Carlson, 1993.

Ingham, John N., and Lynne B. Feldman. *African American Business Leaders: A Biographical Dictionary.* Westport, CT: Greenwood Press, 1994.

James, Portia P. *The Real McCoy: African-American Invention and Innovation, 1619–1930.* Washington, DC: Smithsonian Institution Press, 1989.

Jaynes, Gerald David, and Robin M. Williams, eds. *A Common Destiny: Blacks and American Society.* Washington, DC: National Academy Press, 1989.

Johnson, Whittington B. *The Promising Years, 1750–1830: The Emergence of Black Labor and Business.* New York: Garland Publishing, 1993.

Kenzer, Robert C. *Enterprising Southerners: Black Economic Success in North Carolina, 1865–1915.* Charlottesville: University Press of Virginia, 1997.

Kern-Foxworth, Marilyn. *Aunt Jemima, Uncle Ben, and Rastus: Blacks in Advertising, Yesterday, Today, and Tomorrow.* Westport, CT: Greenwood Press, 1994.

Kinzer, Robert H., and Edward Sagarin. *The Negro in American Business: The Conflict Between Separatism and Integration.* New York: Greenberg, 1950.

Koger, Larry. *Black Slaveowners: Free Black Slave Masters in South Carolina.* Jefferson, NC: McFarland & Company, 1985.

Oak, Vishnu. *The Negro's Adventure in General Business.* Yellow Springs, OH: Antioch, 1949.

Pierce, Joseph A. *Negro Business and Business Education.* New York: Harper & Brothers Publishers, 1947.

Saltzman, Jack, David Lionel Smith, and Cornel West. *Encyclopedia of African-American Culture and History.* New York: Macmillan/Simon Schuster, 1996.

Schweninger, Loren. *Black Property Owners in the South, 1790–1915.* Urbana: University of Illinois Press, 1990.

Sterling, Dorothy. *We Are Your Sisters: Black Women in the Nineteenth Century.* New York: W. W. Norton, 1984.

Stuart, M. S. *An Economic Detour: A History of Insurance in the Lives of American Negroes.* New York: Wendell Malliett and Company, 1940.

Walker, Juliet E. K. *African American Business and Entrepreneurship: Critical Historiographical Assessments in the Economic and Cultural Life of Blacks and Capitalism.* Westport, CT: Greenwood Press, forthcoming.

———. *The History of Black Business in America: Capitalism, Race, Entrepreneurship.* New York: Macmillan/Prentice Hall International, 1998.

Washington, Booker T. *The Negro in Business.* Boston: Hertel, Jenkins & Co., 1907.

Weems, Robert E., Jr. *Desegregating the Dollar: African American Consumerism in the Twentieth Century.* New York: University of New York Press, 1998.

Wilson, William J. *The Declining Significance of Race: Blacks and Changing American Institutions.* Chicago: University of Chicago Press, 1978.

Work, Monroe N. *Negro Year Book: An Annual Encyclopedia of the Negro, 1912–1937/38.* Tuskegee, AL: Negro Year Book Publishing Co., 1912–1938.

POST–CIVIL RIGHTS ERA

Black Business and Entrepreneurship

Bates, Timothy M. *Banking on Black Enterprise: The Potential of Emerging Firms for Revitalizing Urban Economies.* Washington, DC: Joint Center for Political and Economic Studies, 1993.

Bates, Timothy M., and William D. Bradford. *Financing Black Economic Development.* New York: Academic Press, 1985.

Battle, Stafford L., and Rey O. Harris. *The African American Resource Guide to the Internet and Online Services.* New York: McGraw-Hill, 1996.

Bell, Janet Cheatham, comp. *The Soul of Success: Great Business Quotations for African Americans.* New York: John Wiley and Sons, 1997.

Beech, Wendy. *The Black Enterprise Guide to Starting Your Own Business.* New York: John Wiley & Sons, 1999.

Biddle, Stanton F., ed. *The African-American Yellow Pages: A Comprehensive Resource Guide and Directory.* New York: Henry Holt, 1996.

Black Enterprise, magazine, 1970–.

Boston, Thomas D. *Affirmative Action and Black Entrepreneurship.* New York: Routledge, 1999.

———. *Meeting the Croson Standard: A Guide For Policy Makers.* Washington, DC: Joint Center for Political and Economic Studies, 1993.

Burrell, Berkeley, G., and John Seder. *Getting It Together: Black Businessmen in America.* New York: Harcourt, Brace, Jovanovich, 1971.

Cross, Theodore. *Black Capitalism: Strategies for Business in the Ghetto.* New York: Atheneum, 1969.

Curry, George E. *The Affirmative Action Debate.* Reading, MA: Addison Wesley, 1996.

Dingle, Derek. *Black Enterprise Titans of the B.E. 100s: Black CEOs Who Redefined and Conquered American Business.* New York: John Wiley and Sons, 1999.

Drake, W. Avon, and Robert D. Holsworth. *Affirmative Action and the Stalled Quest for Black Progress.* Urbana: University of Illinois Press, 1996.

Edley, Christopher F. *Not All Black and White: Affirmative Action, Race and American Values.* New York: Hill and Wang, 1996.

Fairley, Juliette. *Money Talks: Black Finance Experts Talk to You about Money.* New York: John Wiley & Sons, 1998.

Fraser, George C. *Race for Success: The Ten Best Business Opportunities for Blacks in America.* New York: W. Morrow and Co., 1998.

———. *Success Runs in Our Race: The Complete Guide to Effective Networking in the African-American Community.* New York: W. Morrow, 1994.

Gravely, Melvin J., and Apryl Motley, ed. *The Black Entrepreneur's Guide to Success.* Edgewood, MD: Duncan & Duncan, 1995.

Green, Shelley, and Paul Pryde. *Black Entrepreneurship in America.* New Brunswick, NJ: Transaction Publishers, 1989.

Handy, John. *An Analysis of Black Business Enterprises*. New York: Garland Publishing, 1989.

Herbert, James I. *Black Male Entrepreneurs and Adult Development*. Westport, CT: Greenwood Press, 1989.

Kijakazi, Kilolo. *African American Economic Development and Small Business Ownership*. New York: Garland Publishing, 1997.

Kimbro, Dennis Paul, and Napoleon Hill. *Think and Grow Rich: A Black Choice*. New York: Fawcett Crest, 1992.

Kunjufu, Jawanza. *Black Economics: Solutions for Economic and Community Empowerment*. Chicago: African American Images, 1991.

Loury, Glenn C. *One by One: From the Inside Out: Essays and Reviews on Race and Responsibility*. New York: Free Press, 1995.

Malveaux, Julianne. *Wall Street, Mainstreet, and the Side Street: A Mad Economist Takes a Stroll*. Los Angeles: Pine One Publications, 1999.

Marable, Manning. *How Capitalism Underdeveloped Black America*. Boston: South End Press, 1983.

Mosley, Walter, ed. *Black Genius: African American Solutions to African American Problems*. New York: W. W. Norton, 1999.

Ofari, Earl. *The Myth of Black Capitalism*. New York: Monthly Review Press, 1970.

Oliver, Melvin, and Thomas M. Shapiro. *Black Wealth, White Wealth: A New Perspective on Racial Inequality*. New York: Routledge, 1995.

Pryor, T. M. *Wealth Building Lessons of Booker T. Washington for a New Black America*. Edgewood, MD: Duncan & Duncan, 1995.

Simms, Margaret, ed. *Economic Perspectives on Affirmative Action*. Washington, DC: Joint Center for Political and Economic Studies, 1995.

Todd, Gwendolyn Powell. *Innovation and Growth in an African American Owned Business*. New York: Garland Publishing, 1996.

Trower-Subira, George. *Black Folks' Guide to Business Success*. Newark, NJ: Very Serious Business Enterprises, 1986.

———. *Black Folks' Guide to Making Big Money in America*. Newark, NJ: Very Serious Business Enterprises, 1980.

United States. Congress. Senate. Office of the Secretary. *Memorial Tributes Delivered in Congress: Ronald H. Brown, 1941–1996, Secretary of Commerce*. Washington, DC: Government Printing Office, 1997.

Wallace, Robert L. *Black Wealth Through Black Entrepreneurship*. Edgewood, MD: Duncan & Duncan, 1993.

Watkins, Ron. *Doing Business in Africa: Myths and Realities*. Chicago: Heritage Productions, 1994.

Watkins, S. Craig. *Representing: Hip Hop Culture and the Production of Black Cinema*. Chicago: University of Chicago Press, 1998.

Woodward, Michael D. *Black Entrepreneurs in America: Stories of Struggle and Success*. New Brunswick, NJ: Rutgers University Press, 1997.

Yancy, Robert. *Federal Government Policy and Black Business*. Cambridge, MA: Ballinger Press, 1974.

BLACK AND WHITE CORPORATE AMERICA

America, Richard, and Bernard Anderson. *Soul in Management: How African-American Managers Thrive in the Competitive Corporate Environment.* Secaucus, NJ: Carol Publishing Group, 1996.

Collins, Sharon M. *Black Corporate Executives: The Making and Breaking of a Black Middle Class.* Philadelphia: Temple University Press, 1997.

Dates, Jannette L., and William Barlow, eds. *Split Images: African Americans in the Mass Media.* Washington, DC: Howard University Press, 1990.

Davis, George, and Glegg Watson. *Black Life in Corporate America: Swimming in the Mainstream.* Garden City, NY: Anchor Press, 1982.

Dickens, Floyd, and Jacqueline Dickins. *The Black Manager: Making It in the Corporate Culture.* New York: AMACOM American Management Association, 1982.

Franey, Eric. *Black America: An Economic Powerhouse in the Dark.* Commack, NY: Nova Science Publishers, 1996.

Irons, Edward D., and Gilbert W. Moore. *Black Managers: The Case of the Banking Industry.* New York: Praeger, 1985.

Jett, Joseph, and Sabra Chartrand. *Black and White on Wall Street: The Untold Story of the Man Wrongly Accused of Bringing Down Kidder Peabody.* New York: William Morrow, 1999.

Kofsky, Frank. *Black Music, White Business.* New York: Pathfinder, 1997.

Lapchick, Richard E., ed. *Sports in America: Equal Opportunity or Business as Usual.* Thousand Oaks, CA: Sage Publications, 1996.

Lathan, E. LeMay. *The Black Man's Guide to Working in a White Man's World.* Santa Monica, CA: General Publishing Group, 1997.

Pierre, Ulwyn L. *The Myth of Black Corporate Mobility.* New York: Garland Publishing, 1998.

Roberts, Bari-Ellen, and Jack E. White. *Roberts vs Texaco: A True Story of Race and Corporate America.* New York: Avon Books, 1998.

Saunders, James R. *Tightrope Walk: Identity, Survival and the Corporate World in African-American Literature.* Jefferson, NC: McFarland and Company, 1997.

Simmons, Wilson. *Inside Corporate America: A Guide for African-Americans.* New York: Berkley, 1996.

Simms, Darrell D. *Black Experience, Strategies and Tactics in the Business World: A Corporate Perspective, A Handbook for Professionals.* Beaverton, OR: Management Aspects, Inc., 1991.

Spivey, William R. *Corporate America: Black and White.* New York: Carlton Press, 1993.

Toliver, Susan. *Black Families in Corporate America.* Thousand Oaks, CA: Sage Publications, 1998.

United States. Congress. House. Committee on Government Operations. Employment and Housing Subcommittee. *Racial Discrimination in Awarding Toyota Dealerships.* Washington, DC: Government Printing Office, 1993.

Watkins, Ron. *Doing Business in Africa: Myths and Realities.* Chicago: Heritage Productions, 1994.

Watkins, Steve. *The Black O: Racism and Redemption in an American Corporate Shoney's Inc. Empire.* Athens: University of Georgia Press, 1997.

Work, John W. *Race, Economics, and Corporate America.* Wilmington, DE: Scholarly Resources, 1984.

BLACK WOMEN AND BUSINESS

Ballard, Donna. *Doing It for Ourselves: Success Stories of African American Women in Business.* New York: Berkley Books, 1997.

Brossard, Cheryl D. *Sister CEO: The Black Woman's Guide to Starting Her Own Business.* New York: Viking, 1997.

Ehrhart-Morrison, Dorothy. *No Mountain High Enough: Secrets of Successful African American Women.* Berkeley, CA: Conari, 1997.

Etter-Lewis, Gwendolyn. *My Soul Is My Own: Oral Narratives of African Women in the Professions.* New York: Routledge, 1993.

Harris, Fran. *About My Sister's Business: The Black Woman's Road Map to Successful Entrepreneurship.* New York: Fireside, 1996.

Harris, Lois. *Stressors, Beliefs and Coping Behaviors of Black Women Entrepreneurs.* New York: Garland Publishing, 1994.

Hine, Darlene Clark, and Kathleen Thompson, eds. *Facts on File Encyclopedia of Black Women in America: Business and Professions.* Vol. 4. New York: Facts on File, Inc., 1997.

Kimbrough, Majorie L. *Accept No Limitations: A Black Woman Encounters Corporate America.* Nashville: Abingdon Press, 1991.

Latifah, Queen, with Karen Hunter. *Ladies First: Revelations from a Strong Woman.* New York: William Morrow, 1999.

Manning, M. M. *Slaves in a Box: The Strange Career of Aunt Jemima.* Lanham, MD: University Press of America, 1998.

Nelson, Jill. *Volunteer Slavery: My Authentic Negro Experience.* Chicago: Noble Press, 1993.

Reid-Merritt, Patricia. *Sister Power: How Phenomenal Black Women Are Rising to the Top.* New York: John Wiley & Sons, 1996.

Shields, Cydney, and Leslie C. Shields. *Work, Sister, Work: How Black Women Can Get Ahead in Today's Business Environment.* New York: Simon and Schuster, 1994.

Slevin, Kathleen F., and C. Ray Wingrove. *From Stumbling Blocks to Stepping Stones: The Life Experiences of Fifty Professional African American Women.* New York: New York University Press, 1998.

Smith, Jessie Carney, ed. *Epic Lives: 100 Black Women Who Made a Difference.* Detroit: Visible Ink Press, 1933.

Talley-Ross, Nancy C. *Jagged Edges: Black Professional Women in White Male Worlds.* New York: P. Long, 1995.

COMPANY HISTORIES

Henderson, Alexa Benson. *Atlanta Life Insurance Company: Guardian of Black Economic Dignity.* Tuscaloosa: University of Alabama Press, 1990.

Kennedy, William J. *The North Carolina Mutual Story: A Symbol of Progress, 1898–1970.* Durham: North Carolina Mutual Life Insurance Company, 1970.

Puth, Robert C. *Supreme Life: The History of a Negro Life Insurance Company*. New York: Arno, 1976.

Todd, Gwendolyn Powell. *Innovation and Growth in an African American Owned Business*. New York: Garland Publishing, 1996.

Weare, Walter. *Black Business in the New South: A Social History of the North Carolina Mutual Life Insurance Company*. Urbana: University of Illinois Press, 1973.

Weems, Robert E. *Black Business in the Black Metropolis: The Chicago Metropolitan Assurance Company, 1925–1985*. Bloomington: Indiana University Press, 1996.

BIOGRAPHIES AND AUTOBIOGRAPHIES

From Slavery to Freedom

Davis, Edwin A., and William R. Hogan. *The Barber of Natchez*. 1954; reprint, Port Washington, NY: Kennikat Press, 1969.

Hermann, Janet Sharp. *The Pursuit of a Dream*. New York: Random House, 1983.

Johnson, Michael, and James L. Roark. *Black Masters: A Free Family of Color in the Old South*. New York: W. W. Norton, 1984.

Keckley, Elizabeth. *Behind the Scenes, or, Thirty Years a Slave, and Four Years in the White House*. 1868; reprint, New York: Oxford University Press, 1988.

Mills, Gary B. *The Forgotten People: Cane River's Creoles of Color*. Baton Rouge: Louisiana State University Press, 1977.

Thomas, James. *From Tennessee Slave to St. Louis Entrepreneur: The Autobiography of James Thomas*. Edited by Loren Schweninger. Columbia: University of Missouri Press, 1984.

Thomas, Lamont D. *Paul Cuffe: Black Entrepreneur and Pan-Africanist*. Urbana: University of Illinois Press, 1988.

Walker, Juliet E. K. *Free Frank: A Black Pioneer on the Antebellum Frontier*. 1983; reprint, Lexington: University Press of Kentucky, 1995.

Whitten, David O. *Andrew Durnford: A Black Sugar Planter in Antebellum Louisiana*. 1981; reprint, New Brunswick, NJ: Transaction Publishers, Rutgers University Press, 1995.

Twentieth Century

Bundles, A'Lelia Perry. *Madam C. J. Walker*. New York: Chelsea House Publishers, 1991.

Buni, Andrew. *Robert L. Vann of the Pittsburgh Courier: Politics and Black Journalism*. Pittsburgh, PA: University of Pittsburgh Press, 1974.

Carroll, John M. *Fritz Pollard: Pioneer in Racial Advancement*. Urbana: University of Illinois Press, 1992.

Chavers-Wright, Madrue. *The Guarantee: P. W. Chavers, Banker, Entrepreneur, Philanthropist in Chicago's Black Belt of the Twenties*. New York: The Wright Armstead Associates, 1985.

Fahey, David M. *The Black Lodge in White America: "True Reformer" Browne [William Washington] and His Economic Strategy*. Dayton, OH: Wright State University Press, 1994.

Gaston, Arthur G. *Green Power: The Successful War of A. G. Gaston*. Birmingham, AL: Southern University Press, 1968.

Gordy, Berry. *To Be Loved: The Music, the Magic, the Memories of Motown, An Autobiography*. New York: Warner Books, 1994.

Graves, Earl G. *How to Succeed in Business Without Being White*. New York: HarperBusiness, 1997.

Greenberg, Jonathan D. *Staking a Claim: Jake Simmons and the Making of an African American Oil Dynasty*. New York: Atheneum, 1990.

Gregory, Shelia T. *A Legacy of Dreams: The Life and Contributions of Dr. William Venoid Banks*. Lanham, MD: University Press of America, 1998.

Johnson, Frank J. *Who's Who of Black Millionaires*. Fresno, CA: Who's Who of Black Millionaires, 1984.

Johnson, John H., with Lerone Bennett, Jr. *Succeeding Against the Odds: The Inspiring Autobiography of One of America's Wealthiest Entrepreneurs, John H. Johnson*. New York: Warner Books, Inc., 1989.

Landrum, Gene N. *Profiles of Black Success: Thirteen Creative Geniuses Who Changed the World*. New York: Galahad Books, 1982.

Lewis, Reginald F., and Blair S. Walker. *"Why Should White Guys Have All the Fun?'': How Reginald Lewis Created a Billion-Dollar Business Empire*. New York: John Wiley and Sons, 1994.

Lovett, Bobby L. *A Black Man's Dream, The First 100 Years: Richard Henry Boyd and the National Baptist Publishing Board*. Jacksonville, FL: Mega Corp., 1993.

Ottley, Roi. *The Lonely Warrior: The Life and Times of Robert S. Abbott*. Chicago: Henry Regnery Co., 1955.

Overmyer, James. *Queen of the Negro Leagues: Effa Manley and the Newark Eagles*. Lanham, MD: Scarecrow Press, 1998.

Plater, Michael A. *African American Entrepreneurship in Richmond, 1890–1940: The Story of R. C. Scott*. New York: Garland Publishing, 1996.

Rediger, Pat. *Great Americans in Business*. New York: Crabtree Publishing Company, 1996.

Sullivan, Leon Howard. *Moving Mountains: The Principles and Purposes of Leon Sullivan*. Valley Forge, PA: Judson Press, 1998.

Wier, Sadye H. *A Black Businessman in White Mississippi, 1886–1974*. Jackson: University Press of Mississippi, 1977.

Wilson, Sunnie, with John Cohassey. *Toast of the Town: The Life and Times of Sunnie Wilson*. Detroit: Wayne State University Press, 1998.

Wright, Richard Robert. *Eighty Seven Years Behind the Black Curtain: An Autobiography*. Philadelphia: Rare Book Company, 1965.

MINORITIES AND WOMEN

Barkan, Elliott. *A Nation of People: A Sourcebook on America's Multicultural Heritage*. Westport, CT: Greenwood Press, 1999.

Bird, Caroline. *Enterprising Women*. New York: W. W. Norton, 1976.

Cameron, Randolph W. *Minority Executives' Handbook: Your Essential Map and Guide to Success up the Corporate Ladder*. New York: Warner Books, 1989.

Caplan, Suzanne. *How Women and Minorities Can Launch Their Own Business*. New York: AMACOM, American Management Association, 1994.

Cummings, Scott. *Self-Help in Urban America: Patterns of Minority Business Enterprise.* New York: National University Publications, 1980.

Davidson, Marilyn J. *The Black and Ethnic Minority Woman Manager: Cracking the Concrete Ceiling.* London: Paul Chapman, Publishing, Ltd., 1997.

Failde, Augusto A., and William S. Doyle. *Latino Success: Insight From 100 of America's Most Powerful Latin Business Professionals.* New York: Simon and Schuster, 1996.

Fairlie, Robert W. *Ethnic and Racial Entrepreneurship: A Study of Historical and Contemporary Differences.* New York: Garland Publishing, 1996.

Halter, Marilyn, ed. *New Migrants in the Marketplace.* Amherst: University of Massachusetts Press, 1995.

Light, Ivan. *Ethnic Enterprise in America: Business and Welfare among Chinese, Japanese, and Blacks.* Berkeley: University of California Press, 1972.

——, and Parminder Bhachu. *Immigration and Entrepreneurship: Culture, Capital, and Ethnic Networks.* New Brunswick, NJ: Transaction Publishers, 1993.

——, and Carolyn Rosenstein. *Race, Ethnicity, and Entrepreneurship in Urban America.* New York: Aldine de Gruyter, 1995.

Mason, Patrick L., and Rhonda Williams, eds. *Race, Markets, Social Outcomes.* Boston: Kluwer Academic Publishers, 1997.

Moore, Dorothy P., and E. Holly Buttner. *Women Entrepreneurs: Moving Beyond the Glass Ceiling.* Thousand Oaks, CA: Sage Publications, 1997.

Morrison, Ann. *The New Leaders: Leadership Diversity in America.* San Francisco: Jossey-Bass, 1996.

Ng, Franklin, ed. *Asian American Issues Relating to Labor, Economics and Socioeconomic Status.* New York: Garland Publishing, 1998.

Reynolds, Paul D., and Sammis B. White. *The Entrepreneurial Process: Economic Growth, Men, Women, and Minorities.* Westport, CT: Quorum Books, 1997.

Rich-McCoy, Lois. *Millionairess: Self-Made Women of America.* New York: Harper & Row, 1978.

Sokoloff, Natalie. *Black Women and White Women in the Professions: Occupational Segregation by Race and Gender, 1960–1980.* New York: Routledge, 1994.

Sowell, Thomas. *Markets and Minorities.* New York: Basic Books, 1981.

——. *Race and Economics.* New York: Longman, Inc., 1975.

Takaki, Ronald, ed. *From Different Shores: Perspectives on Race and Ethnicity in America.* Oxford: Oxford University Press, 1987.

Thomas, Dave A. *Breaking Through: The Making of Minority Executives in Corporate America.* Boston: Harvard Business School Press, 1999.

Thomas, R. Roosevelt, Jr. *Beyond Race and Gender: Unleashing the Power of Your Total Work Force by Managing Diversity.* New York: AMACOM, American Management Association, 1991.

——. *Redefining Diversity.* New York: AMACOM, American Management Association, 1996.

Ward, Robin, and Richard Jenkins, *Ethnic Communities in Business: Strategies for Economic Survival.* Cambridge: Cambridge University Press, 1984.

Yon, In-Jin. *On My Own: Korean Business and Race Relations in America.* Chicago: University of Chicago Press, 1997.

Zimmerman, Jan, ed. *The Technological Woman: Interfacing with Tomorrow.* New York: Praeger, 1985.

GENERAL STUDIES IN AMERICAN AND INTERNATIONAL BUSINESS

Birley, Sue, and Ian C. MacMillan, eds. *International Entrepreneurship*. New York: Routledge, 1995.

Bygrave, William D. *The Portable MBA in Entrepreneurship*. 2d ed. New York: John Wiley & Sons, 1997.

Cash, James I. et al. *Building the Information Age Organization: Structure, Control and Information Technologies*. 3d ed. Burr Ridge, IL: Irwin, 1994.

Cash, James I., F. Warren McFarlan, and James L. McKenney. *Corporate Information Systems Management: The Issues Facing Senior Executives*. 3d ed. Homewood, IL: Dow Jones–Irwin, 1992.

Cassis, Youssef. *Big Business: The European Experience in the 20th Century*. New York: Oxford University Press, 1997.

Chandler, Alfred D., Jr., Franco Amatori, and Takashi Hikino, eds. *Global Enterprise: Big Business and the Wealth of Nations*. New York: Cambridge University Press, 1997.

Dannen, Fredric, and Erroll McDonald, eds. *Hit Men: Power Brokers and Fast Money Inside the Music Business*. New York: Vintage Books, 1991.

Davenport, Thomas H., with Laurence Prusak. *Information Ecology: Mastering the Information and Knowledge Environment*. New York: Oxford University Press, 1997.

Dell, Michael, with Catherine Fredman. *Direct From Dell: Strategies that Revolutionized an Industry*. New York: Harper Business, 1999.

Dyer, W. Gibb, Jr. *The Entrepreneurial Experience: Confronting Career Dilemmas of the Start-up Executive*. San Francisco: Jossey-Bass Publishers, 1992.

Geisst, Charles R. *Investment Banking in the Financial System*. Englewood Cliffs, NJ: Prentice Hall, 1995.

Gentile, Mary C., ed. *Differences That Work: Organizational Excellence Through Diversity*. Boston: Harvard Business School Press, 1996.

Godley, Andrew, and Oliver M. Westall, eds. *Business History and Business Culture*. New York: St. Martin's Press, 1997.

Gourvish, Terry, and Francis Goodall, eds. *The International Bibliography of Business History*. London: Routledge, 1997.

Gross, Daniel, and the Editors of *Forbes* Magazine. *Forbes Greatest Business Stories of All Time*. New York: John Wiley & Sons, 1996.

Hallett, Anthony, and Diane Hallett. *The Entrepreneur Magazine Encyclopedia of Entrepreneurs*. New York: John Wiley & Sons, 1997.

Haring, Bruce. *Off the Charts: Ruthless Days and Reckless Nights Inside the Music Industry*. New York: Carol Publishing Group, 1995.

Herman, Roger E., and Joyce L. Gioia. *Lean and Meaningful: A New Culture for Corporate America*. Greensboro, NC: Oakhill Press, 1998.

Heylin, Clinton. *Bootleg: The Secret History of the Other Recording Industry*. New York: St. Martin's Press, 1996.

Hill, Linda A. *Becoming A Manager: Mastery of a New Identity*. Boston: Harvard Business School Press, 1992.

Hill, Sam, and Glenn Rifkin. *Radical Marketing: From Harvard to Harley, Lesson from Ten That Broke the Rules and Made It Big.* New York: Harper Business, 1999.

Hisrich, Robert D., and Michael Peters. *Entrepreneurship: Starting, Developing, and Managing a New Enterprise.* 3d ed. Chicago: Irwin, 1995.

Hope, Jeremy, and Tony Hope. *Competing in the Third Wave: The Ten Key Management Issues of the Information Age.* Boston: Harvard Business School Press, 1997.

Ingham, John N. *Biographical Dictionary of American Business Leaders* 4 vols. Westport, CT: Greenwood Press, 1983.

———, and Lynne B. Feldman. *Contemporary American Business Leaders: A Biographical Dictionary.* New York: Greenwood Press, 1990.

Jennings, Reg, Charles Cox, and Cary L. Cooper. *Business Elites: The Psychology of Entrepreneurs and Intrapreneurs.* New York: Routledge, 1994.

Jones, Geoffrey, ed. *The Making of Global Enterprise.* Portland, OR: F. Cass, 1994.

Judson, Bruce, with Kate Kelley. *Hyperwars: Eleven Rules for Survival and Profit in the Era of Online Business.* New York: Simon and Schuster, 1999.

Kahaner, Larry. *Competitive Intelligence: From Black Ops to Boardrooms: How Businesses Gather, Analyze, and Use Information to Succeed in the Global Marketplace.* New York: John Wiley and Sons, 1998.

Kawasaki, Guy, with Michele Moreno. *Rules for Revolutionaries: The Capitalist Manifesto for Creating and Marketing New Products.* New York: Harper Business, 1999.

Kleiner, Art. *The Age of Heretics: Heroes, Outlaws, and the Forerunners of Corporate Change.* New York: Currency/Doubleday, 1996.

Kotkin, Joel. *Tribes: How Race, Religion, and Identity Determine Success in the New Global Economy.* New York: Random House, 1993.

Kuratko, Donald F., and Harold P. Welsch. *Entrepreneurial Strategy: Text and Cases.* Fort Worth, TX: Dryden Press, 1994.

Kwestel, Mendy, Michael Preston, and Gary Plaster. *The Grant Thorton LLP Guide for Entrepreneurs: The Road to Success: How to Manage Growth.* New York: John Wiley and Sons, 1998.

McCall, Morgan W. *High Flyers: Developing the Next Generation of Leaders.* Boston: Harvard Business School Press, 1997.

McCraw, Thomas K., ed. *The Essential Alfred Chandler: Essays toward a Historical Theory of Big Business.* Boston, Mass.: Harvard Business School Press, 1988.

McFate, Katherine, Roger Lawson, and William J. Wilson, eds. *Poverty, Inequality and the Future of Social Policy: Western States and the New World Order.* New York: Russell Sage Foundation, 1995.

Reuvid, Jonathan, and Ian Priestner. *Doing Business with South Africa.* London: Nichols Publishing, 1999.

Roy, William G. *Socializing Capital: The Rise of the Large Industrial Corporation in America.* Princeton, NJ: Princeton University Press, 1997.

Sexton, Donald L., and John D. Kasarda, eds. *The State of the Art of Entrepreneurship.* Boston: PWS-Kent Pub. Co., 1992.

Shropshire, Kenneth L. *In Black and White: Race and Sports in America.* New York: New York University Press, 1996.

Smilor, Raymond W., and Donald L. Sexton, eds. *Leadership and Entrepreneurship: Personal and Organizational Development in Entrepreneurial Ventures.* Westport, CT: Quorum, 1996.

Sobel, Robert. *The Age of Giant Corporations: A Microeconomic History of American Business, 1914–1992*. 3d ed. Westport, CT: Greenwood Press, 1993.

Stevenson, Howard H., Michael J. Roberts, and H. Irving Grousbeck. *New Business Ventures and the Entrepreneur*. 4th ed. Burr Ridge, IL: Irwin, 1994.

Timmons, Jeffry A. *New Venture Creation: Entrepreneurship for the 21st Century*. 4th ed. Burr Ridge, IL: Irwin, 1994.

Whitten, David O., ed. *Extractives, Manufacturing, and Services: A Historiographical and Bibliographical Guide*. Westport, CT: Greenwood, 1997.

Whitten, David O, ed., and Bessie E. Whitten, assistant editor. *Manufacturing: A Historiographical and Bibliographical Guide*. New York: Greenwood Press, 1990.

Williams, Edward E. *Entrepreneurship and Productivity*. Lanham, MD: University Press of America, 1998.

Wilson, John F. *British Business History, 1720–1994*. Manchester, UK: Manchester University Press, 1995.

Young, Jeffrey S. *Forbes Greatest Technology Stories: Inspiring Tales of the Entrepreneurs and Inventors Who Revolutionized Modern Business*. New York: John Wiley & Sons, 1998.

Index

Neighborhood Enterprise Associations, 207

Neighborhood Institute, 57

Neighborhood Leadership Development Institute (NLDI), 412

Neiman-Marcus, 19

Neisner, 474

Nelson, Orville, 330

Neoconservatives and Black Business, 422, 478

Netherlands, 311

Netnoir, 319, 644

Networks, Black Business, 285–86, **428–31**, 526. *See* Rotating Credit Associations; Social Capital

New Africa Advisers, 311

Newark Eagles, 415; Newspapers, black, 1–3

New Black Middle Class, 218, 430

New Day, 227

New Deal, 183, 380, 459

New Jersey, 19

New Jersey Jets, 536

New Negro Alliance boycott, 93

New Orleans, 88

New Orleans City Railroad Company, 565

New Orleans Freedmen's Aid Association, 622

New Orleans Gas Light Company, 321

New Orleans Louisianian, 454

New Orleans, Opelousas and Great Western Railroad, 321

New Philadelphia, IL, 78. *See also* McWorter, Free Frank

Newport News, Virginia, Black Business in, 304

New South, 216

New South Africa, 311

Newspapers, black, 1–3, 427. *See also* Black Press

New World National Bank, 639

New York African Society for Mutual Relief, 321

New York Age, 231, 400, 401

New York Amsterdam News, 2

New York, Black Business, xxii–xxiii, 48, 553, 628. *See also* Harlem

New York Black Real Estate Enterprises. *See* Payton, Philip; Nail, John B.

New York Central Railroad, 239

New York Colored Business Men's Association, 628

New York City, 7, 48

New York Cubans, 415

New York Curb Exchange, 322

New York Life Insurance, 634

New York Slave Conspiracy (1741), 499

New York State Urban Development Corporation, 477

New York Stock Exchange, 321, 322, 337, 535, 637. *See also* Stock Market Listings

New York Times, 473

New York University, 473

New York West Indian Businesses. *See* Rotating Credit Associations, Caribbean American Chamber of Conference

NFDMA. *See* National Funeral Directors and Morticians Association

Nibby, Inc., 469

Niagara Movement, 40, 400

Nicaragua, 302

Nickel Savings Bank, 296

Nicodemus, KN, 78

Niger Delta, 247

Niger River Palm Oil Trade, 328

Nigeria, 166, 303, 304, 307, 308, 313

Nigerian-American Tapes and Recordings Associates (NATRAL), 309

Nine West, 164, 610

"Nigger Company," 619

"Nigger Work," 490

Nike, Inc., 312, 534, 539, 642

99th Pursuit Squadron, 151, 173

Nissin Foods, 311

Nixon, E. D., 93

Nixon, Richard (President), 65, 77, 139, 210

Nkrumah, Kwame, 88

NNBL "War-Time Clinic," 269

Noble Drew Ali (Timothy Drew) **431–32**

Noer, David M., 190

Nonmetallic Minerals Firms 1992, 225

Nonminority (White) Employers, 200

Nonminority Markets, 102

Non-Segregating Seating, 567

Norfolk State University, 115

Norman Film Manufacturing Company, 234

Norris International Boxing Club, 532

Norris, James Austin, **432–35**

Norris, Schmidt, Green, Harris, Higginbotham, and Associates, 432

North Beach & Mission Railroad Law Suit, 456

North Carolina A&T University, 115, 193, 287, 326

North Carolina Central University, 115

North Carolina College, 528, 529. *See also* North Carolina Central University

Pace Phonograph Corporation, 466
Pacific Appeal, 456
Pacific Rim, 110, 303
Pacifist, 532
Pagers, 537
Paige, Satchel, 415
Palmer Institute, 451
Palm Oil Trade (West Africa), 437
Palmer, Ransford, 478
Panama, 100, 303, 304, 305
Panic of 1857, 130, 135, 179
Panic of 1873, 252, 521
Panic of 1893, 447, 561
Panis, Marie Louis, 321
Parachutes, 632
Parallax, 609
Paramount Race Artist Series, 466
Paramount Records, 444, 466
Parham, Bettie Esther, 285
Paris, 302
Paris Import and Export Corporation, 304, 629
Parker, Alice H., 604
Parker, Deannie, 467
Parker House Sausage Company, 138, 139, 140
Parks, Henry, 4, 636
Parks Sausage Company, 3, 541, 636, 637. *See also* Parks, Henry
Parkway Ballroom (Chicago), 141
Parsons, Richard D., 431, 642, 644
Partnerships, 386
"Passing" and Black Businesspeople, 182, 358–59, 390, 444, 509
Pastin, Mark, 214
"Patent Bedstead Factory," 170
Patent Holders. *See* Black Patentholders
Path Press, 84
Patricia Stevens Cosmetic Company, 253
Patterson, Charles and Frederick. *See* Automobile, Patterson-Greenfield
Patterson, Sons and Company, 566
Patton, Boggs and Blow, 96
Paul, Weiss, Rifkind, Wharton & Garrison, 361
Pavageau, Adele, 29
Payne, Daniel Alexander, 25
Payne, Evans (Rev.), 296
Payola Scandals, 464
Payton Apartment Corporation, 445
Payton, Philip A., **445–46**
Peabody Education Fund, 70, 73
Peabody, George, 70, 73
Peace Mission Enterprises, 227–228
Peace Mission Movement. *See* Father Divine

Peace Mission Real Estate Holdings, 227
Peace Movement, 327
Peacock (Records), 467, 472
Peanut Manufacturers. *See* George Washington Carver
Pearson, Mrs. C. M., 551
Pendulum Records, 468
Penny Savings Bank of St. Luke, 245
Pentecostals, 144
People United to Save Humanity. *See* PUSH
People's Insurance Company, 296
Peoples Involvement Corporation, 638
People's Republic of China, 96, 309
People's Restaurant, 238
People's Tabernacle, 551
Peoples, James, 370
Pepsi Cola, 165, 404, 405, 633
Pepsi Cola New Age Beverages, 315
Pepsi Cola of Washington, DC, 277, 535
Pequot Indians, 175
Percy Sutton Intercontinental, 308
Percy Sutton International, 224, 548
Perry, Christopher James, Sr., 1, 623
Perry, Herman, 172, 297, 526, 549
Perry, Mae (Bryant) Walker, 584
Personal Achievement Radio, 465
Personal Communications Services (PCS), xxv, 324, 644. *See also* Black Telecommunications Enterprises
Personal Services Enterprises, 36, 105, 106, 217, 254, 273–74, 294
Pet Milk, 404
Peters, William H., 553
Petersburg, VA, 260
Pettiford, William Reuben, **446–47**
Pettus, Theodore, 6
Phat Farm (Clothing), 483
Philadelphi American, 434
Philadelphia Afro-American, 382
Philadelphia, Black Lawyers, 17. *See also* Norris, James Austin
Philadelphia Common Pleas Court Judge, 433
Philadelphia Coca Cola Bottling Company, 363, 535
Philadelphia Female Antislavery Society, 242
Philadelphian Independent, 434
Philadelphia Institute For Colored Youth, 449
The Philadelphia Negro, 434. *See also* DuBois, William E. B.
Philadelphia Registration Commission, 433
Philadelphia Tribune, 1, 623
Philadelphia's Caterers Association, 132
Philander Smith College, 115
Philanthropic Society of Pittsburgh, 448

About the Editor and Contributors

JULIET E. K. WALKER, Ph.D., an award-winning historian, is a Professor of History at the University of Illinois at Urbana-Champaign. She has research fellowships from the National Endowment for the Humanities, the Rockefeller Foundation, the Radcliffe Bunting Institute, and the Princeton University Davis Center and a Senior Fulbright in South Africa. She is the author or editor of four books including *The History of Black Business in America*, and *Free Frank: A Black Pioneer on the Antebellum Frontier*, with articles in the *Business History Review, Journal of Negro History, New York Law School Journal of Human Rights*, and other scholarly journals and books.

SOL AHIARAH is a Professor in the Department of Business, Buffalo State College.

RICHARD F. AMERICA, M.B.A., is a Lecturer, School of Business Administration, Georgetown University.

NICOLE DENISE ANDERSON is a Ph.D. student in History at the University of Illinois at Urbana-Champaign.

EDWARD M. APY is a University of Illinois at Urbana-Champaign graduate.

TIMOTHY BATES is a Professor of Economics and Dean of Urban, Labor, and Metropolitan Affairs, Wayne State University.

DAVID T. BEITO is a Professor in the Department of History, University of Alabama.

CHRISTOPHER D. BENSON, J.D., former Professor in Journalism, University of Illinois, Urbana-Champaign, and media attorney.

WILLIAM E. BERRY is a Professor in the College of Communications and Associate Director of the Institute of Communications Research, University of Illinois at Urbana-Champaign.

IAN BINNINGTON is a Ph.D. candidate in the Department of History, University of Illinois at Urbana-Champaign.

JULIET D. BLACKBURN-BEAMON is a Professor in Humanities, Morris Brown College.

AUBREY W. BONNETT is a Professor in American Studies, State University of New York, College at Old Westbury, and Vice President for Academic Affairs.

PETER BOTTICELLI is a Postdoctoral Fellow in the Harvard University School of Business.

ROBERT L. BOYD is a Professor in the Department of Sociology, Mississippi State University.

CHARLES BRANHAM, Ph.D., is Senior Historian at the DuSable Museum of African American History.

TAMARA M. BROWN is an Administrative Assistant at the National Black MBA Association.

JOHN SIBLEY BUTLER is the Dallas TACA Centennial Professor of Sociology and the Douglass Centennial Professor in Entrepreneurship and Small Business Management.

OLUWATOYIN CALDWELL is a University of Illinois at Urbana-Champaign graduate in history and currently a University of Chicago graduate student in the Divinity School.

JOHN CAMPBELL is a Professor of History at Winona State University in Minnesota.

BERNADETTE P. CHACHERE is a Professor in Business Studies/Economics at Delgado Community College, New Orleans.

JONATHAN S. COIT is a Ph.D. student in the Department of History, University of Illinois at Urbana-Champaign.

SHARON COLLINS is a Professor of Sociology, University of Illinois, Chicago.

DIONNE DANNS is a Ph.D. student in the School of Education, University of Illinois at Urbana-Champaign.

WILLIAM A. DARITY, JR., is the Cary C. Boshamer Professor of Economics, University of North Carolina at Chapel Hill.

NANCY J. DAWSON is a Professor of Black American Studies, Southern Illinois University at Carbondale.

SUNDIATA A. K. DJATA is a Professor of History, Northern Illinois University.

J. VINCENT EAGAN is a Professor of Economics and Business Law at Morehouse College and Consultant at D. J. Miller & Associates.

BARBARA J. FLINT, Ph.D., is founder of Independent Education Enterprises, Washington, D.C.

CHESTER J. FONTENOT, JR., is a Professor in the Department of English, University of Illinois at Urbana-Champaign.

GEORGE C. FRASER, Minority Business Executive Program, Amos Tuck School of Business, Dartmouth College, is President of SuccessSource Unlimited and a publisher.

FRANK A. FRATOE, Ph.D., is a Sociologist and Program Analyst, Minority Business Development Agency, U.S. Department of Commerce, Washington, D.C.

BETTYE J. GARDNER is a Professor in the Department of History, Coppin State College.

CHARLES GIBSON is a University of Illinois at Urbana-Champaign graduate and currently a J.D. student, Miami University Law School.

BRADFORD C. GRANT is Professor and Chair, Department of Architecture, Hampton University.

RODNEY D. GREEN is a Professor in the Department of Economics and Director of the Center for Urban Progress, Howard University.

JOHN W. HANDY is a Professor in Economics in the Department of Economics and Business Administration, Morehouse College.

ROBERT L. HARRIS, JR., is a Professor of History, African-American and African Studies Research Center, Cornell University.

ALEXA BENSON HENDERSON is a Professor in the Department of History, Clark Atlanta University.

DAVID F. HERR is a Ph.D. candidate in the Department of History, University of Illinois, Urbana-Champaign.

JOHN S. HEYWOOD is a Professor in the Department of Economics, University of Wisconsin at Milwaukee.

JO ANN S. HICKEY is a Professor in the Department of Sociology, Western Carolina University.

ANNE R. HORNSBY is a Professor in the Department of Economics, Spelman College.

LYNN M. HUDSON is a Professor in the Department of History, California Polytechnic State University.

GARY J. HUNTER is a Professor in the Department of History, Rowan College, New Jersey.

JOHN N. INGHAM is a Professor in the Department of History, University of Toronto.

EDWARD D. IRONS is a Professor in Finance and Dean Emeritus, Clark Atlanta University School of Business.

JOYCE C. IRONS is a Professor in the Department of Psychology, Clark Atlanta University.

MARLO R. JENKINS, an M.B.A. from Michigan State, is manager of the Small Business Sector of the Urban Business Institute at Central Michigan University.

WHITTINGTON B. JOHNSON is a Professor in the Department of History, University of Miami.

EARL R. JONES is a Professor in Regional Planning and Chair, Department of Minority Studies, Indiana University Northwest.

DONALD FRANKLIN JOYCE, Ph.D., is Dean of Library and Media Services at Felix G. Woodward Library, Austin Peay State University.

ROBERT C. KENZER is a Professor in the Department of History at the University of Richmond.

WILLIAM M. KING is a Professor in History and Afro-American Studies, University of Colorado at Boulder.

DAVID F. KRUGLER is a Professor in the Department of History, University of Wisconsin at Platteville.

CLARENCE LANG is a Ph.D. student in the Department of History, University of Illinois at Urbana-Champaign.

TODD E. LARSON is a Ph.D. candidate in the Department of History, University of Illinois at Urbana-Champaign.

NICHOLAS A. LASH is a Professor in the Department of Finance, Graduate School of Business, Loyola University, Chicago.

ANTOINETTE MALVEAUX is Executive Director, National Black MBA Association.

JULIANNE MALVEAUX, Ph.D., is an Economist, Public Policy Analyst, Newspaper Columnist, and TV Commentator, National Public Television, *To the Contrary*.

TONY MARTIN is a Professor of African-American History, Africana Studies, Wellesley College.

JOHN MUKUM MBAKU is a Professor in the Department of Economics, Weber State University.

JOHN T. McCARTNEY is a Professor in the Department of Government and Law, Lafayette College, Easton, Pennsylvania.

RODERICK A. McDONALD is a Professor in the Department of History, Rider University.

HENRY JACKSON McGILL, M.S., Biophysics and Computational Biology, Funeral Services, and Director of Jackson and McGill Funeral Home, a third-generation family business in Cincinnati, Ohio.

LYDIA A. McKINLEY-FLOYD is a Professor and Chair of Marketing in the School of Business, Clark Atlanta University.

LINDA O. McMURRY is a Professor in the Department of History, North Carolina State University.

EDNA GREENE MEDFORD is a Professor in the Department of History, Howard University.

QUINCY T. MILLS is a University of Illinois at Urbana-Champaign graduate and M.A. graduate in Social Sciences, University of Chicago.

SYBIL COLLINS MOBLEY is Dean of the School of Business and Industry, Florida A&M University.

SAMUEL L. MYERS, JR., is Professor in Human Relations and Social Justice, Humphrey Institute, University of Minnesota.

M. TAMBURA OMOIELE is a Professor in Social Sciences at Edgewood College.

WILLIAM F. PICKARD, Ph.D., is Adjunct Professor, Entrepreneurship, University of Michigan, and Founder and CEO, Regal Plastics.

LARRY D. PICKENS, D.D., J.D., is Pastor of the Maple Park United Methodist Church in Chicago.

WILLIAM D. PIERSEN is a Professor in the Department of History, Fisk University.

ERIC PIERSON is a Ph.D. student, Institute for Communications Research, University of Illinois at Urbana-Champaign.

AARON C. PORTER is a Professor in the Department of Sociology, University of Illinois at Urbana-Champaign.

GREGORY N. PRICE is a Professor in the Department of Economics at North Carolina A&T State University.

CHRISTOPHER R. REED is a Professor in the Department of History at Roosevelt University and Director of African American Studies.

RONALD RIVERS, M.B.A., is an Urban Business Institute Researcher.

JAMES A. ROBINSON is a Professor of Entrepreneurship and Director of the Central Michigan University College of Extended Learning Detroit Center.

TERESA SAVAGE is Assistant Dean and Lecturer in Journalism, College of Communications, University of Illinois at Urbana-Champaign.

LOREN SCHWENINGER is a Professor in History at the University of North Carolina at Greensboro.

ISHAQ SHAFIQ has an M.A. in Urban Studies from the University of Illinois at Urbana-Champaign and is an assistant to the mayor of East St. Louis.

TODD C. SHAW is a Professor in the Department of Political Science, University of Illinois at Urbana-Champaign.

WILLIS B. SHEFTALL, JR., is Merril Professor and Chairman, Department of Economics and Business Administration, Morehouse College.

ALCARCILUS SHELTON-BOODRAM is a graduate of the University of Illinois at Urbana-Champaign.

C. CALVIN SMITH is a Professor in the Department of History, Arkansas State University.

JILL D. SNIDER, Ph.D., teaches U.S. History at the University of North Carolina at Chapel Hill.

MATTHEW C. SONFIELD is a Professor in Business at Hofstra University.

CHRISTOPHER M. SPAN is a graduate student in the College of Education at the University of Illinois at Urbana.

ROSEMARY M. STEVENSON, M.L.S., is the Afro-American Bibliographer and Professor in Library Administration at the University of Illinois at Urbana.

JANICE SUMLER-EDMOND is a Professor in the Department of History at Clark Atlanta University.

LAMONT D. THOMAS is a Senior Lecturer in the Department of History, University of Bridgeport.

PATRICIA M. TUCKER is a Graduate Assistant, Clark Atlanta University School of Business.

CHARLES VINCENT is a Professor in the Department of History, Southern University.

BLAIR S. WALKER is a book author, freelance writer, and financial news columnist for *USA Today*.

JEFFREY E. WALKER is a Loyola University Chicago graduate, history freelance writer, and works at the Southeastern University, Office of Finance.

ROBERT L. WALLACE, M.B.A., is an author, entrepreneur, and business consultant.

WALTER WEARE is a Professor in the Department of History, University of Wisconsin at Milwaukee.

ROBERT E. WEEMS, JR., is a Professor in the Department of History at the University of Missouri at Columbia.

MELODYE WEHRUNG, Ph.D., is Director of Equal Opportunity Programs and Compliance, Office of the Assistant to the President, Harvard University.

DAVID O. WHITTEN is a Professor in the Department of Economics, Auburn University.

SCOTT C. WOODS is a graduate of the University of Illinois at Urbana-Champaign and a Rotary International Ambassadorial Scholar.

ROBERT L. WOODSON, SR., M.S.W., is President and Founder of the National Center for Neighborhood Enterprise, Washington, D.C.

ELIZABETH WRIGHT is Editor and Publisher of *Issues and Views*.

GENEEN WRIGHT is a University of Illinois at Urbana-Champaign graduate.

ISBN 0-313-29549-2

90000>

EAN

9 780313 295492

HARDCOVER BAR CODE